THE OXFORD HANDBOOK OF

ISLAMIC THEOLOGY

THE OXFORD HANDBOOK OF

ISLAMIC THEOLOGY

Edited by

SABINE SCHMIDTKE

OXFORD
UNIVERSITY PRESS

OXFORD
UNIVERSITY PRESS

Great Clarendon Street, Oxford, OX2 6DP,
United Kingdom

Oxford University Press is a department of the University of Oxford.
It furthers the University's objective of excellence in research, scholarship,
and education by publishing worldwide. Oxford is a registered trade mark of
Oxford University Press in the UK and in certain other countries

First published in 2016

Published in the United States of America by Oxford University Press
198 Madison Avenue, New York, NY 10016, United States of America

British Library Cataloguing in Publication Data
Data available

Library of Congress Control Number: 2016935488

ISBN 978-0-19-969670-3

Cover illustration: © fulya atalay/shutterstock.com

THE OXFORD HANDBOOK OF

ISLAMIC THEOLOGY

Edited by

SABINE SCHMIDTKE

OXFORD
UNIVERSITY PRESS

OXFORD
UNIVERSITY PRESS

Great Clarendon Street, Oxford, OX2 6DP,
United Kingdom

Oxford University Press is a department of the University of Oxford.
It furthers the University's objective of excellence in research, scholarship,
and education by publishing worldwide. Oxford is a registered trade mark of
Oxford University Press in the UK and in certain other countries

First published in 2016

Published in the United States of America by Oxford University Press
198 Madison Avenue, New York, NY 10016, United States of America

British Library Cataloguing in Publication Data
Data available

Library of Congress Control Number: 2016935488

ISBN 978-0-19-969670-3

Table of Contents

PART II INTELLECTUAL INTERACTIONS OF ISLAMIC THEOLOGY(IES)—FOUR CASE STUDIES

PART III ISLAMIC THEOLOGY(IES) DURING THE LATER MIDDLE AND EARLY MODERN PERIOD

PART IV POLITICAL AND SOCIAL HISTORY AND ITS IMPACT ON THEOLOGY— FOUR CASE STUDIES

PART V ISLAMIC THEOLOGICAL THOUGHT FROM THE END OF THE EARLY MODERN PERIOD TO THE MODERN PERIOD

List of Contributors

Binyamin Abrahamov is Professor Emeritus of Islamic Theology and Mysticism, and Qur'anic Studies at Bar Ilan University, Israel.

Peter Adamson is Professor of Late Ancient and Arabic Philosophy at the Ludwig Maximilian University of Munich.

Asad Q. Ahmed is Associate Professor of Arabic and Islamic Studies at the University of California, Berkeley.

Mohammad Ali Amir-Moezzi is Professor of Classical Islamic Theology at the École Pratique des Hautes Études, Sorbonne University, Paris.

Hassan Ansari is Member of the School of Historical Studies at the Institute for Advanced Study, Princeton, NJ.

David Bennett is a Postdoctoral Fellow in the Representation and Reality research programme at the University of Gothenburg.

Lutz Berger is Professor of Middle Eastern Studies at the University of Kiel, Germany.

Harith Bin Ramli is research fellow at The Cambridge Muslim College.

Patricia Crone was Professor Emerita of Islamic History at the Institute for Advanced Study, Princeton, NJ.

Heidrun Eichner is Professor of Islamic Studies at Eberhard Karls University, Tübingen, Germany.

Maribel Fierro is Research Professor at the Consejo Superior de Investigaciones Científicas, Madrid.

Frank Griffel is Professor of Islamic Studies at Yale University in New Haven, Connecticut.

Sidney H. Griffith is Professor of Arabic Christianity at the Catholic University of America, Washington, DC.

Livnat Holtzman is Senior Lecturer and Chair of the Department of Arabic at Bar-Ilan University, Ramat Gan.

Jon Hoover is Associate Professor of Islamic Studies at the University of Nottingham.

Nimrod Hurvitz is Senior Lecturer at the Department of Middle East Studies, Ben-Gurion University of the Negev.

Steven C. Judd is Professor of Middle East History at Southern Connecticut State University in New Haven, Connecticut.

Wilferd Madelung is Laudian Professor Emeritus of Arabic at the University of Oxford.

Martin Nguyen is Associate Professor of Islamic Religious Traditions in the Religious Studies Department at Fairfield University in Fairfield, Connecticut.

Racha el-Omari is Associate Professor of Religious Studies at the University of California Santa Barbara.

M. Sait Özervarlı is Professor of Ottoman Intellectual History at Yildiz Technical University, Istanbul.

Johanna Pink is Heisenberg Professor of Islamic Studies and Islamic History at the University of Freiburg, Germany.

Reza Pourjavady is Hafis Visiting Lecturer for Religion and Culture of Iran at Goethe Universität, Frankfurt.

Khaled El-Rouayheb is Professor of Islamic Intellectual History at Harvard University.

Ulrich Rudolph is Professor of Islamic Studies at the University of Zurich.

Sabine Schmidtke is Professor of Islamic Intellectual History at the Institute for Advanced Study, Princeton, NJ.

Cornelia Schöck is Professor of Islamic Studies at the Department of Philology of Ruhr-Universität Bochum, Germany.

Gregor Schwarb is an independent scholar based in London.

Delfina Serrano Ruano is Tenured Researcher at the Institute for Languages of Cultures of the Mediterranean and the Near East of the Spanish National Council for Scientific Research in Madrid, Spain.

Ayman Shihadeh is Senior Lecturer in Islamic Studies at SOAS, University of London.

Daniel De Smet is Research Director at the French National Centre for Scientific Research and responsible for the research unit 'Canons and heterodoxies' of the Laboratory of Studies about the Monotheist Religions.

Nathan Spannaus is postdoctoral researcher at the University of Oxford.

Aaron Spevack is Assistant Professor of Islamic Studies at Colgate University.

Jan Thiele is Marie Curie Fellow at the Spanish National Research Council (CSIC), Madrid.

Alexander Treiger is Associate Professor of Religious Studies at Dalhousie University in Halifax, Nova Scotia.

Rotraud Wielandt is Professor Emerita of Islamic Studies and Arabic Literature at the University of Bamberg, Germany.

Aron Zysow is an independent scholar based in Boston, MA.

INTRODUCTION

SABINE SCHMIDTKE

THE present volume provides a comprehensive overview of theological thought within Islam, from the earliest manifestations that have come down to us up until the present.[1] Given the numerous desiderata in the study of Islamic theology, the overall picture that evolves is inevitably incomplete, and in many ways the volume is intended to serve as an encouragement and a guide for scholars who wish to engage with this field of study. The approach in the preparation of this volume has been an inclusive one—rather than defining 'theology' in a narrow way or preferring one interpretation of what 'orthodox' belief consists of over another, an attempt has been made to cover the doctrinal thought of all the various intellectual strands of Islam that were engaged with theological concerns—including groups such as the philosophers and Ismāʿīlīs, whom theologians of different shades condemned as heretics. Moreover, this volume also acknowledges the significance of inter-communal exchanges between Muslim and Christian as well as Jewish thinkers over the course of the centuries. The theological thought of Jews and Christians not only mirrored at times that of Muslims, Christian methodologies of speculative reasoning and, at times, doctrinal notions contributed to its shaping. While the Jewish reception of *kalām* methods and the doctrines of the Muʿtazilite school in particular are touched upon in Chapter 9, the interplay between Muslim and Christian doctrinal thought at various points in time is discussed in detail in Chapters 1, 5, and 31.

The overall arrangement of the chapters is primarily diachronic. The unevenness of the three parts reflects, on the one hand, the robust scholarship that has developed in the study of Islamic intellectual history from early Islam to the classical period, contrasted with, on the other hand, the deplorable paucity of scholarship on the post-classical period. Part I, by far the most detailed, comprises chapters discussing forms of Islamic theology during the formative and the early middle period; Part III focuses on the later middle and early modern periods; and Part V addresses Islamic theological thought from the end of the early modern period to the modern period. Wedged between the

[1] I thank my colleagues C. Adang, H. Ansari, S. Stroumsa, and J. Thiele for valuable comments and suggestions on an earlier draft of this introduction.

three diachronic blocs are two parts that address thematic issues. Part II comprises four case studies that explore intellectual interactions of Islamic theology(ies), while Part IV, also comprising four case studies, focuses on the impact of political and social history on Islamic theology.

I The Foundations of Islamic Theology

The thematic range of theology is, to a large extent, in the eye of the beholder. Over the centuries, Muslim theologians were preoccupied in their deliberations with two principal concerns: first, God, His existence, and nature, and, secondly, God's actions vis-à-vis His creation, specifically humankind. Both thematic concerns touch upon numerous related issues, such as anthropomorphism and the conceptualization of the divine attributes and their ontological foundation; and the thorny related questions of theodicy and human freedom versus determination. In their attempts to systematize doctrinal thinking, the various theological schools in Islam have provided an abundance of often contradictory answers to those questions. Moreover, in terms of methodology, Muslim theologians championed two different, contradictory approaches—while rationally minded theologians employed the methods and techniques of speculative theology, '*kalām*' or '*ʿilm al-kalām*', as it is typically called, traditionists categorically rejected the use of reason and instead restricted themselves to collecting the relevant doctrinal statements they found in the Qurʾān and the prophetic tradition (*sunna*). These statements are in their view the 'principles of religion' (*uṣūl al-dīn*), the second term used among Muslims for theology, alongside the above-mentioned term '*kalām*', which came to mean 'theology' for the rational theologians. Those who engaged in *kalām*, the *mutakallimūn*, went beyond the two basic doctrinal concerns, namely God's nature and His actions, by adding to the thematic spectrum of theology other concerns such as natural philosophy—encompassing the created universe, which comprises everything other than God.

The factors that have contributed to how Islamic theology has been shaped and developed in its variegated forms over the course of history are multiple and various. Although the Qurʾān, the founding text of Islam, is not a theological disquisition, it is still the most hallowed authoritative source for Muslims engaged with doctrinal concerns. It lays down some of the fundamental doctrinal conceptions that characterize Islamic theological thought and have been shared in one way or another by most if not all Muslim thinkers throughout the centuries. Beyond the revelatory text, there is the larger historical, religious, and theological context in which doctrinal thought in Islam evolved and developed over time. This doctrinal development is apparent in the treatment of issues on which the Qurʾān either remains silent or mentions, but with largely ambiguous statements, issues which Muslim theologians considered—and continue to consider—controversial. These include topics such as man's freedom to act versus determinism, which was hotly debated during the first and second centuries of Islam, as well as complex topics such as anthropology, ontology, epistemology, and cosmology, discussion of which was largely inspired by the wider intellectual-cultural environment of early Islam. These influences include religious notions that were prevalent in pre-Islamic Arabia, concepts originating in other local traditions, and the religio-philosophical heritage of late antiquity, pre-Islamic Iran, and, to some extent, India. Moreover, the political schisms in the early Islamic community following the death of the Prophet Muḥammad made questions such as the validity of the imamate, the nature of faith (*īmān*), and the conditions for salvation relevant for consideration among theologians.

The central tenet in the Qurʾānic revelation is the belief in God, and it is the notion of God as the creator and sovereign ruler of the world that is the dominant motif throughout the revealed text. He is described as 'the master of the worlds' (*rabb al-ʿālamīn*), as being 'mighty and glorious' (*dhū l-jalāl wa-l-ikrām*) (Qurʾān 55: 78), 'the sovereign Lord' (*al-malik al-quddūs*) (Qurʾān 59: 23), and 'owner of sovereignty' (*mālik al-mulk*) (Qurʾān 3: 26). He is said to be 'the high and the great' (*al-ʿalīy al-kabīr*) (Qurʾān 22: 62), and that 'in His hand is the dominion over all things' (*alladhī bi-yadihi malakūt kull shayʾ*) (Qurʾān 36: 83). God is 'the creator and the one who shapes' (*al-khāliq al-bāriʾ al-muṣawwir*) (Qurʾān 59: 24) and 'He who created the heavens and the earth' (*alladhī khalaqa l-samawāt wa-l-arḍ*) (Qurʾān 36: 81). In accordance with the idea of God as a sovereign ruler, readers of the Qurʾān are constantly reminded of God's oneness and admonished to refrain from any kind of polytheism (*shirk*)—'God, there is no God but He' (*Allāhu lā ilāha illā huwa*) (Qurʾān 2: 255 etc.). The *locus classicus* is *sūra* 112 (entitled 'Sincere Religion', *al-ikhlāṣ*), which, in the translation of A. Arberry, reads 'Say: 'He is God, One. God, the Everlasting Refuge, who has not begotten, and has not been begotten, and equal to Him is not any one'. While initially intended apparently as a refutation of pre-Islamic polytheism in Arabia, the text was later interpreted as primarily directed against the Christians. The (post-Qurʾānic) Arabic term for monotheism is *tawḥīd*. The frequent use of the root *w-ḥ-d* in the self-appellation of numerous Islamic groups throughout history up until the modern period indicates the central position the concept occupies in the self-perception of Muslim believers. Monotheism is thus one of the central doctrines of Islam, although the interpretations and conceptualizations of *tawḥīd* are manifold.

God's sovereignty sharply contrasts with the way humans—who are invariably described as His servants—are depicted in the Qurʾān. As to the question of whether man's actions and destiny are ordained by God's decree, deterministic and non-deterministic sayings stand side by side in the Qurʾān. The Qurʾānic concept of the last judgement, when God will demand individual reckoning from each human being, presupposes that human beings exercise individual liberty with respect to what they do in this world and thus are responsible for their destiny in the hereafter. Free choice is also expressly stated in those passages where God is said not to lead the human being astray, unless he or she chooses to disobey. Other passages of the Qurʾān emphasize God's omnipotence and omniscience, to an extent that human responsibility appears completely eclipsed. Here, human destiny is said to depend on the will of God. He is the originator of belief and unbelief and He guides or leads astray as He pleases. 'Whomsoever

God desires to guide, He opens his heart to Islam; whomsoever He desires to lead astray, he hardens his heart, narrow, tight, as if forced to climb to heaven unaided. So God lays abomination upon those who believe not' (Qurʾān 6: 125).

The Qurʾān contains numerous descriptions of God, which later gave rise to the conceptualization, in a variety of ways, of the divine attributes, their ontological foundation, and how they compare with the attributes of human beings. He is described as being 'alive' (*ḥayy*), 'eternal' (*qayyūm*) (Qurʾān 2: 255), 'self-sufficient' (*ghanī*) (Qurʾān 2: 263), 'all-embracing' (*wāsiʿ*), 'knowing' (*ʿalīm*) (Qurʾān 2: 247), and 'wise' (*ḥakīm*) (Qurʾān 2: 32), as the one who 'hears and sees' (*al-samīʿ al-baṣīr*) (Qurʾān 17: 1), is 'able to do all things' (*ʿalā kull shayʾ qadīr*) (Qurʾān 2: 20), and He is 'the strong and the mighty' (*al-qawī al-ʿazīz*) (Qurʾān 11: 66). At the same time, God is said to have 'knowledge' (*al-ʿilm ʿinda Llāh*) (Qurʾān 67: 26) and to possess 'might' (*al-qūwa*) (Qurʾān 51: 58). Moreover, the Qurʾān contains passages that stress God's transcendence (Qurʾān 19: 65; 42: 11) as against those which emphasize His immanence (Qurʾān 50: 16), two contrasting notions that are also expressed in Qurʾān 57: 3, 'He is the Outward and the Inward' (*huwa l-ẓāhir wa-l-bāṭin*). Also disputed were references in the Qurʾān that suggest that God has a human form. God's 'countenance' (*wajh*) is mentioned (Qurʾān 2: 115 and *passim*), as are His 'eyes' (*aʿyān*) (Qurʾān 11: 37; 23: 27; 52: 48; 54: 14), His 'hand/hands' (Qurʾān 3: 72f.; 5: 64; 38: 75f.; 48: 10; 57: 29), and His 'leg' (*sāq*) (Qurʾān 68: 42), and He is said to be seated on a 'throne' (*ʿarsh*) (Qurʾān 7: 54 and *passim*). Descriptions which may suggest deficiencies in God also gave rise to speculative thinking, such as God being 'the best of schemers' (*wa-Llāh khayr al-mākirīn*) (Qurʾān 3: 54), that He mocks (*yastahziʾ*) (Qurʾān 2: 15), derides (*sakhira*) (Qurʾān 9: 79), or forgets (Qurʾān 9: 67). Moreover, the attributes and qualifications ascribed to God that have equivalents in humans prompted speculation about the ontological foundations of God's attributes as against those of human beings, for the Qurʾān also states that 'like Him there is naught' (*laysa ka-mithlihi shayʾ*) (Qurʾān 42: 11).

The amalgam of the Qurʾānic data, doctrinal concepts, and concerns originating in the wider cultural environment of early Islam, as well as the political controversies and schisms of the early Islamic community, gave rise to a highly variegated spectrum of Muslim theological thought, with respect to both doctrinal positions and methodological approaches. Religious dissension was and is considered to be a deplorable departure from the initial ideal of unity; and what would constitute the right, 'orthodox' belief, as opposed to heresy, was typically decided by the winning power, post factum. Controversy and diversity as characteristics of Islamic theology are reflected in some of the characteristic literary genres of Islamic theology, namely professions of faith (*ʿaqīda*), the preferred genre among the traditionalists, which served to encapsulate the faith of the community and to refute 'heterodox' doctrines; heresiographies, compiled on the basis of the prophetic *ḥadīth* according to which the Muslim community will be divided into seventy-three groups, only one of which will merit paradise (*al-firqa al-nājiya*); works that display the dialectical technique of *kalām*, which was the prevalent genre among representatives of rational theology, be it in the form of refutations or, as was increasingly the case during the scholastic phase, in the form of theological summae. The variegations in doctrine and methodology notwithstanding, the historical development of Islamic theological thought is characterized by complex interdependence among the various strands.

II The State of the Art

Between 1842 and 1846, W. Cureton published his edition of the heresiographical *Kitāb al-Milal wa-l-niḥal*, by the sixth/twelfth-century Ashʿarite author Muḥammad b. ʿAbd al-Karīm al-Shahrastānī (d. 548/1153).[2] For a long time, this text was the single available source for modern scholars on the history of Islamic theology. Since then, over the course of the last century and a half, there has been a steady flow of discoveries of new textual sources. Nevertheless, contemporary scholarship on Islamic theology is still in an age of discovery, and the production of critical editions of key texts, many of which up until recently were believed to be lost, remains a major occupation for any scholar engaged in this field of research. One of the reasons for the relatively slow progress in the study of Islamic theology is that the place of reflection on doctrinal issues within the intellectual life of Muslim thinkers has for a long time been (and often continues to be) underestimated. Theology can rightly be described as one of the most neglected subdisciplines within Islamic studies, a subdiscipline which up to today attracts far fewer scholars than, for example, Islamic law, *ḥadīth*, or Qurʾānic studies. A telling indication that the discipline is still in an early stage is the numerous recent discoveries and first-time publications of works that were long believed to be lost. Surprisingly many among them date from the very first centuries of Islam, thus contradicting the commonly held assumption that the earliest literary sources of Islam are by now all well known and taken into account in scholarship. Many of these discoveries are bound to bring about revisions of long-held views about the history of Islamic theology. By way of example, mention should be made of several doctrinal texts by second/eighth and third/ninth-century Ibāḍī authors—the Ibāḍiyya being one of the earliest opposition movements under the Umayyads, with a distinct *kalām* tradition and with close interaction with the Muʿtazila, the other early religio-political opposition movement during that time. The new finds comprise six *kalām* treatises, or fragments thereof, by the second/eighth-century Kufan scholar ʿAbd Allāh b. Yazīd al-Fazārī, discovered in two twelfth/eighteenth-century manuscripts in Mzāb, in Algeria.[3] If we can assume their authenticity, Fazārī is thus the earliest *kalām* theologian whose doctrines can be studied on the basis of his own extant works. His sophisticated treatment of the divine attributes suggests that this was an issue discussed among Muslim theologians much earlier than has so far been

[2] Cureton's *editio princeps* was followed by a translation into German by Th. Haarbrücker, published in 1850–1.

[3] *Early Ibāḍī Theology: Six kalām texts by ʿAbd Allāh b. Yazīd al-Fazārī*. Ed. W. Madelung and A. al-Salimi, Leiden: Brill, 2014.

assumed (Madelung in press; Chapter 14). Several doctrinal texts by the ʿUmānī Ibāḍī scholar Abū l-Mundhir Bashīr b. Muḥammad b. Maḥbūb (d. *c.*290/908) were recently found in some of the private libraries in Oman and are now available in critical edition.[4] Other important discoveries in recent years include the *Kitāb al-Taḥrīsh* of Ḍirār b. ʿAmr, who had started out as a Muʿtazilī (Ansari 2004–5; Ansari 2007: 23–4; van Ess 2011: i. 132–40; see also Chapter 3),[5] and a substantial fragment of the *Kitāb al-Maqālāt* by Abū ʿAlī al-Jubbāʾī (d. 303/915), the earliest representative of the Basran school of the Muʿtazila during the scholastic era (Ansari 2007; van Ess 2011, i. 156–61).[6] Mention should also be made of the ever-growing number of quotations from the important early doxographical work *Kitāb al-Ārāʾ wa-l-diyānāt*, by the Twelver Shīʿī author al-Ḥasan b. Mūsā al-Nawbakhtī, who flourished at the turn of the fourth/tenth century (van Ess 2011: 219–60, esp. 224–30; Madelung 2013).[7]

Focusing on research done since the beginning of the twenty-first century, significant progress has been made in the scholarly exploration of virtually all strands of Islamic theology. These achievements go hand in hand with an ever-growing awareness of the enormous amount of unexplored sources and glaring lacunae.

The study of Muʿtazilism—arguably the most influential early theological movement in Islam—has particularly thrived over the past fifteen years. As a result of the adoption of Muʿtazilite notions by Shīʿī Muslims (both Zaydīs and Twelver Shīʿīs) as well as by Jewish thinkers, large corpora of Muʿtazilite sources are preserved among the manuscript holdings of the numerous private and public libraries of Yemen and in the various Genizah collections around the world, most importantly the Abraham Firkovitch collections in the National Library of Russia, St Petersburg. Accessibility of these materials has improved considerably over the past two decades, thanks to the enhanced technical possibilities of digitization, joint efforts of Yemeni and international scholars (in the case of the manuscript holdings in Yemen), and the fortunes of international politics (in the case of the Abraham Firkovitch collections, the dissolution of the Soviet Union, which has resulted in easier access to materials for international scholars). Recent efforts to catalogue some of the collections of manuscripts of Yemeni provenance in European and North American libraries (Sobieroj 2007; Löfgren and Traini 1975–2011), as well as their partial digitization and open-access availability,[8] have also prompted a growing

[4] *Early Ibāḍī Literature. Abū l-Mundhir Bashīr b. Muḥammad b. Maḥbūb: Kitāb al-Raṣf fī l-Tawḥīd, Kitāb al-Muḥāraba and Sīra.* Ed. W. Madelung and A. al-Salimi, Wiesbaden: Harrassowitz, 2011.

[5] The recently published edition by Ḥusayn Khasānṣū [H. Hansu] and Muḥammad Kaskīn [M. Keskin] (Istanbul: Sharikat Dār al-Irshād, 2014) is unsatisfactory and it is hoped that H. Ansari will bring his announced edition of the text to completion (Ansari 2007: 23–4).

[6] H. Ansari and W. Madelung are currently preparing a critical edition of the *Maqālāt*.

[7] See also *Al-Hasan ibn Musa al-Nawbakhti, Commentary on Aristotle 'De generatione et corruptione'*, Edition, Translation and Commentary, by M. Rashed, Berlin: de Gruyter, 2015.

[8] For manuscripts of the Bavarian State Library, Munich, see <http://daten.digitale-sammlungen.de/~db/ausgaben/gesamt_ausgabe.html?projekt=1237542282&recherche=ja&ordnung=sig&l=de&l=de>. For manuscripts of the State Library of Berlin, see <http://digital.staatsbibliothek-berlin.de/suche/?DC=au%C3%9Fereurop%C3%A4ische.handschriften>. For digitized manuscripts of Yemeni provenance at the Firestone Library, Princeton University, Princeton NJ, see <http://pudl.princeton.edu/results.php?f1=kw&v1=Yemen&collection_f=Yemeni%20Manuscript%20Digitization%20Initiative>.

awareness among scholars of the numerous Muʿtazilite (Zaydī and non-Zaydī) works in Western libraries. Over the course of the past fifteen years, a considerable number of works by Muʿtazilite authors of the fifth/eleventh and sixth/twelfth centuries have been made available, among them many works that were previously believed to be lost. One of the earliest preserved theological summae by a Muʿtazilite author is the *Kitāb al-Uṣūl* of Abū ʿAlī Muḥammad b. Khallād al-Baṣrī, the distinguished disciple of the Muʿtazilite theologian and founder of the Bahshamiyya, Abū Hāshim al-Jubbāʾī (d. 321/933), which is preserved embedded in several later supercommentaries on the work, which have partly been made available in edition[9] (cf. also Ansari and Schmidtke 2010b). D. Gimaret published an edition of the *Kitāb al-Tadhkira fī aḥkām al-jawāhir wa-l-aʿrāḍ* by the fifth/eleventh-century representative of the Basran Muʿtazila, al-Ḥasan b. Aḥmad Ibn Mattawayh, by far the most detailed extant exposition of natural philosophy[10] (cf. also Zysow 2014). In 2006 a facsimile publication of a paraphrastic commentary on the work, possibly by Ibn Mattawayh's student Abū Jaʿfar Muḥammad b. ʿAlī [b.] Mazdak, a Zaydī scholar of the late fifth/eleventh century who was active in Rayy, was published[11] (cf. also Gimaret 2008b; Schmidtke 2008). Numerous fragments of writings by ʿAbd al-Jabbār al-Hamadānī (d. 415/1025), Ibn Mattawayh's teacher and the head of the Basran Muʿtazila during his time, were found in some of the Genizah collections—apparently none of them had ever reached Yemen. Apart from some additional volumes of his theological summa, *Kitāb al-Mughnī fī abwāb al-tawḥīd wa-l-ʿadl*,[12] these comprise his *Kitāb al-Manʿ wa-l-tamānuʿ* (Schmidtke 2006: 444f. nos 26, 27) as well as his *al-Kitāb al-Muḥīṭ* which is otherwise known only on the basis of Ibn Mattawayh's paraphrastic commentary, *Kitāb al-Majmūʿ fī l-muḥīṭ bi-l-taklīf*.[13] The *Tathbīt dalāʾil al-nubuwwa*, which is attributed in the single extant manuscript to ʿAbd al-Jabbār, has attracted scholars' attention over the past years. G. S. Reynolds devoted a monograph to the work (Reynolds 2004), followed by a new edition and translation, which he produced in collaboration with S. Kh. Samir.[14] H. Ansari has recently questioned the authenticity of the

9 *Baṣran Muʿtazilite Theology: Abū ʿAlī Muḥammad b. Khallād's Kitāb al-Uṣūl and its Reception. A Critical Edition of the Ziyādāt Sharḥ al-uṣūl by the Zaydī Imām al-Nāṭiq bi-l-ḥaqq Abū Ṭālib Yaḥyā b. al-Ḥusayn b. Hārūn al-Buṭḥānī (d. 424/1033).* Ed. C. Adang, W. Madelung, and S. Schmidtke, Leiden: Brill, 2011. *The Zaydī Reception of Bahshamite Muʿtazilism: Facsimile edition of Abū Ṭāhir b. ʿAlī al-Ṣaffār's (fl. 5th/11th century) taʿlīq on Ibn Khallād's Kitāb al-Uṣūl, MS Library of the Faculty of Medicine at the University of Shiraz (ʿAllāma Ṭabāṭabāʾī Library).* Ed. H. Ansari and S. Schmidtke, Tehran: Mīrāth-i maktūb [in press].

10 *Al-Tadkira fī aḥkām al-ǧawāhir wa-l-aʿrāḍ par Abū Muḥammad al-Ḥasan b. Aḥmad ibn Mattawayh, 5e/XIe siècle.* Ed. D. Gimaret, 2 vols, Cairo: Institut français d'archéologie orientale, 2009.

11 *An Anonymous Commentary on Kitāb al-Tadhkira by Ibn Mattawayh. Facsimile Edition of Mahdavi Codex 514 (6th/12th Century).* Ed. S. Schmidtke, Tehran: Iranian Institute of Philosophy, 2006.

12 See e.g. *Nukat al-Kitāb al-Mughnī.* A Recension of ʿAbd al-Jabbār al-Hamadhānī's (d. 415/1025) *al-Mughnī fī abwāb al-tawḥīd wa-l-ʿadl: Al-Kalām fī l-tawlīd. Al-Kalām fī l-istiṭāʿa. Al-Kalām fī l-taklīf. Al-Kalām fī l-naẓar wa-l-maʿārif.* The extant parts introduced and edited by O. Hamdan and S. Schmidtke, Beirut: Deutsches Orient Institut [in Kommission bei 'Klaus Schwarz Verlag', Berlin], 1433/2012.

13 A critical edition of the *Kitāb al-Muḥīṭ* is currently being prepared by O. Hamdan and G. Schwarb. Volume iv of Ibn Mattawayh's *Kitāb al-Majmūʿ* is currently being prepared by Margaretha T. Heemskerk.

14 *Critique of Christian Origins.* A parallel English–Arabic text, edited, translated, and annotated by G. S. Reynolds and S. Kh. Samir, Provo, UT: Brigham Young University Press, 2010.

work as a text by ʿAbd al-Jabbār (Ansari 2014a, 2014b). On the basis of Jewish copies, extensive fragments of a comprehensive work on natural philosophy by the Būyid vizier al-Ṣāḥib b. ʿAbbād (d. 385/995) could be restored, together with a commentary by ʿAbd al-Jabbār, as well as large portions of what seems to be his otherwise lost theological summa, *Nahj al-sabīl fī l-uṣūl*.[15] The holdings of the Firkovitch collections also allow for a partial reconstruction of a work on natural philosophy by the *qāḍī* ʿAbd Allāh b. Saʿīd al-Labbād, another student of ʿAbd al-Jabbār.[16] In the library of the Great Mosque of Ṣanʿāʾ, a copy of the *Kitāb Masāʾil al-khilāf fī l-uṣūl* by ʿAbd al-Jabbār's foremost pupil, Abū Rashīd al-Nīsābūrī, has been identified (Ansari and Schmidtke 2010a), and D. Gimaret has laid the foundation for a new critical edition of Abū Rashīd's second major work on *kalām*, the *Kitāb Masāʾil al-khilāf bayn al-Baṣriyyīn wa-l-Baghdādiyyīn*, which is preserved in a unique manuscript in Berlin (Gimaret 2011). Kh. M. Nabhā has collected the extant fragments of exegtical works by Muʿtazilite authors that have been published since 2007, in the series *Mawsūʿat tafāsīr al-Muʿtazila*.[17]

Fragments of the magnum opus in theology of Abū l-Ḥusayn al-Baṣrī (d. 436/1045), a former student of ʿAbd al-Jabbār and the founder of what seems to have been the last innovative school within the Muʿtazila, were discovered among the manuscripts of the Firkovitch collections.[18] These are complemented by several texts by Jewish authors that testify to the impact Abū l-Ḥusayn's thought had on Jewish thinkers of his time (Madelung and Schmidtke 2006). Moreover, the doctrinal writings of his later follower Rukn al-Dīn Maḥmūd b. Muḥammad al-Malāḥimī (d. 536/1141) were retrieved from various private and public libraries in Yemen, India, and Iran, and are now also available in reliable editions.[19] The renewed engagement with Muʿtazilism in modern times (often labelled 'Neo-Muʿtazilism') has been the focus of several studies over the past years (Hildebrandt 2007; Schwarb 2012).

Among the numerous lacunae that remain for future research are critical editions of the doctrinal works by Abū Saʿd al-Bayhaqī 'al-Ḥākim al-Jishumī' (d. 493/1101), particularly his encyclopedic *ʿUyūn al-masāʾil* with his autocommentary, *Sharḥ ʿUyūn al-masāʾil*, as well as editions of the various above-mentioned doctrinal works by ʿAbd

15 *Al-Ṣāḥib Ibn ʿAbbād Promoter of Rational Theology: Two Muʿtazilī kalām texts from the Cairo Geniza*. Edited and introduced by W. Madelung and S. Schmidtke, Leiden: Brill, forthcoming.

16 A critical edition is currently being prepared by O. Hamdan and S. Schmidtke.

17 The series, published by Dār al-kutub al-ʿilmiyya in Beirut, comprises the following titles: *Tafsīr Abī Bakr al-Aṣamm ʿAbd al-Raḥmān b. Kaysān* (2007); *Tafsīr Abī ʿAlī al-Jubbāʾī* (2007); *Tafsīr Abī l-Qāsim al-Kaʿbī al-Balkhī* (2007); *Tafsīr Abī l-Ḥasan al-Rummānī wa-huwa l-tafsīr al-musammā al-Jāmiʿ li-ʿilm al-Qurʾān* (2009); *Tafsīr al-qāḍī ʿAbd al-Jabbār al-Muʿtazilī wa-huwa al-tafsīr al-musammā al-Tafsīr al-kabīr, aw, 'al-Muḥīṭ'; wa-yalīhi Farāʾid al-Qurʾān wa-adillatuh* (2009).

18 *Taṣaffuḥ al-adilla*. The extant parts introduced and edited by W. Madelung and S. Schmidtke, Wiesbaden: Harrassowitz, 2006.

19 *K. al-Fāʾiq fī uṣūl al-dīn*. Ed. W. Madelung and M. McDermott, Tehran: Iranian Institute of Philosophy, 2007; ed. Fayṣal Badīr ʿAwn, Cairo: Maṭbaʿat Dār al-kutub wa-l-wathāʾiq al-qawmiyya, 1431/2010; *K. al-Muʿtamad fī uṣūl al-dīn*, revised and enlarged edition by W. Madelung, Tehran: Mīrāth-i maktūb, 2013; *Tuḥfat al-Mutakallimīn fī l-Radd ʿalā l-Falāsifa*. Ed. H. Ansari and W. Madelung, Tehran: Iranian Institute of Philosophy, 2008.

al-Jabbār as preserved in the Firkovitch collections. Moreover, although scholarly investigation of Muʿtazilism has significantly advanced over the past decades and a fairly accurate picture of its development can by now be given (editors' introduction to Adang, Schmidtke, and Sklare 2007; Schwarb 2006a, 2011; see also Chapters 7–11 in this volume), it should be kept in mind that the extant literary sources represent only a select number of Muʿtazilite schools. For other strands within the movement, such as the School of Baghdad, whose last prominent representative was Abū l-Qāsim al-Kaʿbī al-Balkhī (d. 319/931) (el-Omari 2006), or the Ikhshīdiyya, named after the prominent theologian, jurist, and transmitter of *ḥadīth* Abū Bakr Aḥmad Ibn al-Ikhshīd (d. 326/938) (Mourad 2006; Kulinich 2012), to name only two examples, we have to rely on the scant and often biased accounts provided by their opponents, with next to no possibility of controlling this information by checking it against primary sources and next to no possibility of reconstructing their respective doctrinal systems in their entirety.[20]

The intensive scholarship that has been devoted to Muʿtazilism over the past fifteen years, which is significantly indebted to the Zaydī reception of the school's doctrine, its transmission, and the eventual preservation of its literary legacy in the libraries of Yemen, has gone hand in hand with an increase in the scholarly investigation of theology among the Zaydī communities of Iran and Yemen. Numerous doctrinal works by Zaydī authors have been made available in critical or semi-critical editions by Yemeni and other international scholars, and a number of substantial analyses on the history of theology among the Zaydī communities of Iran and Yemen have been published over the past years (with Madelung 1965 still serving as the main point of departure for contemporary scholarship), in addition to a considerable increase in Zaydī (and Yemeni) studies in general (see the editors' introductions to Schmidtke 2012b; and Hollenberg, Rauch, and Schmidtke 2015; Ansari and Schmidtke 2016). Among the rather unexpected recent findings is a fragment of a theological tract by the fifth/eleventh-century Jewish Karaite theologian Yūsuf al-Baṣīr. The fragment was transferred from Iran to Yemen, together with a large corpus of other literary texts, in the aftermath of the political unification of the two Zaydī communities of Northern Iran and Yemen, beginning in the sixth/twelfth century. Given its fragmentary state, the tract's Yemeni readers were clearly unaware of its author being a Jew (Ansari, Madelung, and Schmidtke 2015). Again, despite much progress, many lacunae remain, especially with respect to the history of Zaydī theology since the seventh/thirteenth century and the doctrinal teachings of marginal strands within Zaydism, which disintegrated at some point. An example of such a strand is the Muṭarrifiyya, against whose followers Imam al-Manṣūr bi-Llāh

[20] Two works by Abū l-Qāsim al-Kaʿbī are extant, neither of them immediately relevant for the study of his doctrine: *K. Qabūl al-akhbār wa-maʿrifat al-rijāl*, on *ḥadīth* transmitters (ed. Abū ʿUmar and al-Ḥusayn b. ʿUmar b. Abd al-Raḥīm, Beirut: Dār al-kutub al-ʿilmiyya, 1420/2000); and *Kitāb Maqālāt firaq ahl al-qibla*, which still needs to be edited in its entirety; see van Ess 2011, i. 328–75—Hüseyin Hansu mentions on his website (<http://ilahiyat.istanbul.edu.tr/?p=6342>) his critical edition (2014) of al-Kaʿbī's *al-Masāʾil wa-l-jawābāt*. The edition is, as it seems, still forthcoming.

ʿAbd Allāh b. Ḥamza (d. 614/1217) led a merciless war, which eventually resulted in the extinction of the sect (see Chapter 27).

Over the past fifteen years there has been a steady flow of new publications on Twelver Shīʿī theology (see also Chapters 11 and 26). Moreover, Twelver Shīʿī studies in general have profited immensely over the past years from the increased accessibility of manuscript collections in Iraq. Mention should be made, by way of example, of the recent edition of the *Risāla al-Mūḍiḥa*—a theological work concerned with the notion of the imamate—by the fourth/tenth-century author al-Muẓaffar b. Jaʿfar al-Ḥusaynī, which is based on a manuscript from the Āl Kāshif al-Ghiṭā collection.[21] With respect to theology during the time of the Imams, until recently scholarship had evaluated the Imami turn towards Muʿtazilism, dating from the beginning of the twelfth Imam's occultation, as a rupture with the earlier doctrinal tradition of the Imams. But W. Madelung's recent groundbreaking study of Muḥammad b. Yaʿqūb al-Kulaynī's (d. 329/941) *Kitāb al-Uṣūl min al-Kāfī* (Madelung 2014b) significantly revises this view, showing that it was already the Imams who 'progressively came to endorse Muʿtazilite perspectives' (Madelung 2014b: 468), thus preparing the groundwork for the later reception of Muʿtazilite thought during the occultation period and thereafter. For the early stages of Shīʿī theology, H. Ansari's in-depth analysis of the notion of the imamate and the evolution of the doctrine deserves to be mentioned (Ansari in press). In view of the intimate connection between *ḥadīth* and doctrinal thought, a feature characteristic of Shīʿism, especially during its early period (cf. Kohlberg 2014), the recent edition of the *Kitāb al-Qirāʾāt* by the third/ninth-century author Aḥmad b. Muḥammad al-Sayyārī, an important text for the study of early Shīʿī theology, also merits mention.[22] The renewed significance of *ḥadīth* for Twelver Shīʿī doctrine during the Safavid and, more importantly, during the Qajar period still needs to be investigated in detail (Pourjavady and Schmidtke 2015: 255ff.). Progress has also been made in the scholarly exploration of the doctrinal thought of al-Sharīf al-Murtaḍā (d. 436/1044). In 2001, M. R. Anṣārī Qummī published an edition of the single extant (partial) manuscript of al-Murtaḍā's most comprehensive theological summa, *al-Mulakhkhaṣ fī uṣūl al-dīn*,[23] and in 2003 Anṣārī Qummī published an edition of his *Kitāb al-Ṣarfa*.[24] A recent doctoral dissertation was devoted to al-Murtaḍā's life and thought (Abdulsater 2013; cf. also Abdulsater 2014). The next generation of Shīʿī thinkers was the subject of a detailed study of al-Murtaḍā's prominent student, the *Shaykh al-ṭāʾifa* Muḥammad b. al-Ḥasan al-Ṭūsī (d. 460/1067), which was published together with a facsimile edition of a commentary by ʿAbd al-Raḥmān b. ʿAlī b. Muḥammad al-Ḥusaynī (d. 582/

[21] Qum: Maktabat Āyat Allāh al-ʿUẓmā al-Marʿashī al-Najafī al-kubrā, al-Khizāna al-ʿālamiyya li-l-makhṭūṭāt al-islāmiyya, 2011.

[22] *Revelation and Falsification: The Kitāb al-qirāʾāt of Aḥmad b. Muḥammad al-Sayyārī*. Ed. E. Kohlberg and M. A. Amir-Moezzi, Leiden: Brill, 2009.

[23] Tehran: Markaz-i nashr-i dānishgāhī, 1381[/2002].

[24] *Al-Mūḍiḥ ʿan jihat iʿjāz al-Qurʾān (al-Ṣarfa)*. Ed. Muḥammad Riḍā Anṣārī Qummī, Mashhad 1424/1382[/2003].

1186) on the former's *Muqaddima*, which is preserved in a unique manuscript[25] (cf. also Ansari and Schmidtke 2014). Increasing evidence has surfaced that shows the extent to which the writings of Imami thinkers, especially al-Sharīf al-Murtaḍā and some of his students, were received by Jewish readers (Schwarb 2006b; Schwarb 2014a; Schmidtke 2012c; Schmidtke 2014; Madelung 2014a). A major lacuna in the study of Imami theology concerns the period between the generation of al-Sharīf al-Murtaḍā's students and the time of Sadīd al-Dīn Maḥmūd b. ʿAlī b. al-Ḥasan al-Ḥimmaṣī al-Rāzī (d. after 600/1204), the author of *al-Munqidh min al-taqlīd*, i.e. mid-fifth/eleventh to the end of the sixth/twelfth century. During this period, Twelver Shīʿī theologians were engrossed with the controversial rival doctrinal systems of the Bahshamiyya and of Abū l-Ḥusayn al-Baṣrī. While al-Murtaḍā and most of his students by and large endorsed the doctrines of the Bahshamiyya, al-Ḥimmaṣī al-Rāzī preferred the views of Abū l-Ḥusayn al-Baṣrī whenever the latter disagreed with the Bahshamites. The evolution of this process, which may already have started with al-Shaykh al-Ṭūsī, still needs to be reconstructed (Ansari and Schmidtke 2014; Ansari and Schmidtke forthcoming a). Scholarly interest over the past years in the doctrinal developments among the Twelver Shīʿīs up to the time of Naṣīr al-Dīn al-Ṭūsī (d. 672/1274) has been limited, but the latter's literary output, thought, and reception, as well as the later development of Imami thought, attracts considerable attention in international scholarship (e.g. Ṣadrāyī Khūyī 2003; Pourjavady 2011). Mention should be made, by way of example, of the numerous publications over the past years on Ibn Abī Jumhūr al-Aḥsāʾī (d. after 906/1501). A first monograph, in German, devoted to his life and thought, published in 2000 (Schmidtke 2000), resulted in discoveries of some of his texts that were believed to be lost, and critical editions of most of his writings have been published in recent years, as well as a detailed inventory of his writings (al-Ghufrānī 2013, with further references).

In the study of Ashʿarism, scholars have also brought to light important new sources over the past fifteen years. For the thought of the movement's eponymous founder and its early history, the numerous studies of scholars such as R. M. Frank (collected in Frank 2007; Frank 2008) and D. Gimaret still remain authoritative, with Abū Bakr Muḥammad b. al-Ḥasan Ibn Fūrak's (406/1115) *Mujarrad maqālāt al-Shaykh Abī l-Ḥasan al-Ashʿarī* being the single most important secondary source on the doctrinal thought of Abū l-Ḥasan al-Ashʿarī (d. 324/946).[26] The work also served as a basis for a still unsurpassed study on his doctrinal thought by D. Gimaret (Gimaret 1990). More recently, Gimaret published a new edition of Ibn Fūrak's *Kitāb Mushkil al-ḥadīth*, another text of central importance for the study of the history of Ashʿarite *kalām*,[27] and

25 *The Reception of al-Shaykh al-Ṭūsī's Theological Writings in 6th/12th Century Syria. Facsimile Edition of ʿAbd al-Raḥmān b. ʿAlī b. Muḥammad al-Ḥusaynī's Commentary on al-Ṭūsī's Muqaddama* (MS Atıf Efendi 1338/1). Ed. H. Ansari and S. Schmidtke, Tehran: Mīrāth-i maktūb, 2013.

26 *Mujarrad Maqālāt al-Shaykh Abī l-Ḥasan al-Ashʿarī. Min imlāʾ Abī Bakr Muḥammad b. al-Ḥasan b. Fūrak*. Ed. D. Gimaret, Beirut: Dār al-Mashriq, 1987.

27 *Kitāb Mushkil al-ḥadīth aw Taʾwīl al-akhbār al-mutashābiha li-Abī Bakr Muḥammad b. al-Ḥusayn b. Fūrak al-Iṣbahānī al-Ashʿarī*. Ed. D. Gimaret, Damascus: al-Maʿhad al-Faransī li-l-dirāsāt al-ʿarabiyya bi-Dimashq, 2003.

in 2008 his *Sharḥ al-ʿĀlim wa-l-mutaʿallim* appeared in print.[28] Substantial portions of Abū Bakr al-Bāqillānī's (d. 403/1013) magnum opus, the *Hidāyat al-mustarshidīn*, have been discovered and partly edited (Gimaret 2008a; Schmidtke 2011), and a number of works by other representatives of the Ashʿariyya during its classical period have recently been published, among them *al-Bayān ʿan uṣūl al-īmān* by Abū Jaʿfar al-Simnānī (d. 444/1052), a student of al-Bāqillānī,[29] as well as the section devoted to metaphysics from the *Kitāb al-Ghunya* by al-Juwaynī's student Abū l-Qāsim al-Anṣārī (d. 521/1118).[30] The recently discovered *Nihāyat al-marām fī dirāyat al-kalām* by Ḍiyāʾ al-Dīn al-Makkī (d. 559/1163–4), the father of Fakhr al-Dīn al-Rāzī, which is now available in facsimile publication, is a paraphrase of al-Anṣārī's *Ghunya*.[31] Over the past decade, North African scholars have been active in retrieving relevant primary sources in the libraries of the Maghrib (e.g. Zahrī and Būkārī 2011) and in studying the development of Ashʿarism in the Islamic West (e.g. al-Bakhtī 2005).[32] The retrieval of these works is an ever-growing concern, shared by scholars based in Spain and the United States (Schmidtke 2012a; Spevack 2014; Casasas Canals and Serrano Ruano forthcoming; Thiele forthcoming; El-Rouayheb forthcoming; see also Chapters 13 and 29). Recently published critical editions include works by ʿAbd al-Ḥaqq b. Muḥammad b. Hārūn al-Ṣiqillī (d. 466/1073–4),[33] Muḥammad b. al-Ḥasan al-Murādī (d. 489/1096),[34] Abū Bakr Muḥammad b. Sābiq al-Ṣiqillī (d. 493/1099–1100),[35] Abū Bakr ʿAbd Allāh Ibn Ṭalḥa al-Yāburī (d. 523/1124–5),[36] ʿAbd al-Salām b. ʿAbd al-Raḥmān b. Muḥammad 'Ibn Barrajān' al-Lakhmī al-Ishbīlī (d.

[28] Ed. A. ʿAbd al-Raḥīm al-Sāyiq, Cairo: Maktabat al-thaqāfa al-dīniyya, 2008 (2nd edn 1434/2013).

[29] *Al-Bayān ʿan uṣūl al-īmān wa-l-kashf ʿan tamwīhāt ahl al-ṭughyān*. Ed. ʿAbd al-ʿAzīz b. R. al-Ayyūb, Kuwait: Dār al-Ḍiyāʾ li-l-nashr wa-l-tawzīʿ, 2014.

[30] *Al-Ghunya fī l-kalām. Qism al-ilāhiyyāt*. Ed. M. Ḥ. ʿAbd al-Hādī, 2 vols, Cairo: Dār al-Salām, 1431/2010.

[31] Ḍiyāʾ al-Dīn al-Makkī, *Nihāyat al-marām fī dirāyat al-kalām*, MS Hyderabad, Andhra Pradesh Oriental Manuscript Library, *Kalām* 13; published as Fakhr al-Dīn al-Rāzī's Father, Ḍiyāʾ al-Dīn al-Makkī, *Nihāyat al-marām fī dirāyat al-kalām: Facsimile of the Autograph Manuscript of Vol. II*, introd. A. Shihadeh, Persian preface by H. Ansari. Tehran: Mīrāth-i Maktūb, 2013. J. Thiele has systematically compared the two works, *Nihāyat al-marām* and *Ghunya*.

[32] Special mention should be made of the Markaz Abī l-Ḥasan al-Ashʿarī li-l-dirāsāt wa-l-buḥūth al-ʿaqadiyya, based in Tetouan, Morocco; see <http://www.achaari.ma>. Noteworthy among their recent publications is a proceedings volume entitled *Juhūd al-Maghāriba fī khidmat al-madhhab al-Ashʿarī: Buḥūth al-nadwa al-ʿilmiyya allatī naẓẓamahā Markaz Abī l-Ḥasan al-Ashʿarī li-l-dirāsāt wa-l-buḥūth al-ʿaqadiyya bi-l-Rābiṭa al-Muḥammadiyya li-l-ʿulamāʾ bi-Kulliyyat uṣūl al-dīn bi-Tiṭwān, yawm al-Arbaʿa 21 Jumādā II 1432 H al-muwāfiq li-25 Māy 2011 M*. Tetouan: Markaz Abī al-Ḥasan al-Ashʿarī li-l-dirāsāt wa-l-buḥūth al-ʿaqadiyya; al-Mamlaka al-Maghribiyya: al-Rābiṭa al-Muḥammadiyya li-l-ʿUlamāʾ, 2012.

[33] *Ajwibat Imām al-Ḥaramayn al-Juwaynī ʿan asʾilat al-Imām ʿAbd al-Ḥaqq al-Ṣiqillī*. Ed. J. ʿA. al-Jihānī and S. Fawda, Amman: Dār al-Rāzī, 1428/2007.

[34] *ʿAqīdat Abī Bakr al-Murādī al-Ḥaḍramī*. Ed. J. ʿA. al-Bakhtī, Tetuan: Markaz Abī l-Ḥasan al-Ashʿarī, 2012.

[35] *Kitāb al-Ḥudūd al-kalāmiyya wa-l-fiqhiyya ʿalā raʾy ahl al-Sunna al-Ashʿariyya; wa-maʿahu Masʾalat al-shāriʿ fī l-Qurʾān*. Ed. M. al-Ṭabarānī, Tunis: Dār al-Gharb al-islāmī, 2008.

[36] *Ibn Ṭalḥa al-Yāburī (t. 523H) wa-mukhtaṣarahu fī uṣūl al-dīn*. Ed. M. al-Ṭabarānī, Tetouan: al-Rābiṭa al-muḥammadiyya li-l-ʿulamāʾ.

536/1141),[37] Abū Bakr Muḥammad b. Maymūn al-ʿAbdarī al-Qurṭubī (d. 567/1171),[38] Abū ʿUmar ʿUthmān al-Salālujī (d. 594/1198), Muẓaffar b. ʿAbd Allāh al-Muqtaraḥ (d. 612/1215–6),[39] ʿAlī b. Aḥmad b. Khumayr al-Umawī al-Sibtī (d. 614/1217),[40] Muḥammad b. Muḥammad Ibn ʿArafa (d. 803/1401),[41] Saʿīd b. Muḥammad b. Muḥammad al-ʿUqbānī (d. 811/1408–9),[42] and ʿĪsā b. ʿAbd al-Raḥmān al-Saktānī (d. 1062/1652).[43]

Despite this progress, the textual basis for the study of classical Ashʿarism remains deplorably limited, and numerous important works by representatives of the movement remain unpublished, such as the *Kitāb Taʾwīl al-aḥādīth al-mushkilāt al-wārida fī l-ṣifāt* by al-Ashʿarī's student ʿAlī b. Muhammad b. Mahdī al-Ṭabarī (d. *c.*375/985–6), one of the principal sources for Ibn Fūrak's *Mushkil al-ḥadīth* (cf. the editor's introduction to *Mushkil al-ḥadīth*, ed. D. Gimaret, Damascus, 2003, 23–5),[44] the *Kitāb al-Niẓāmī* by Aḥmad b. Muḥammad Ibn Fūrak (d. 478/1085), and the *Tafsīr al-asmāʾ wa-l-ṣifāt* by ʿAbd al-Qāhir b. Ṭāhir al-Baghdādī (d. 429/1037), who was a student of the prominent Ashʿarite theologian Abū Isḥāq al-Isfarāʾīnī (d. 411/1020), most of whose writings are lost. The majority of extant commentaries, paraphrases, and summaries of al-Juwaynī's *Kitāb al-Irshād* (Ḥibshī 2006, 1/166–8) also still lack critical edition, let alone scientific analysis. Among the exceptions are Ibn al-Amīr al-Ḥājj's (d. 735/1335) *al-Kāmil fī ikhtiṣār al-Shāmil*, a summary of al-Juwaynī's magnum opus, the *Shāmil fī uṣūl al-dīn*,[45] the commentary on the *Irshād* by the above-mentioned Muẓaffar b. ʿAbd Allāh al-Muqtaraḥ,[46] and the *Sharḥ al-Irshād* by Abū Bakr Ibn Maymūn.[47]

[37] *Sharḥ Asmāʾ Allāh al-ḥusnā*. Ed. Aḥmad Farīd al-Mizyadī, 2 vols, Beirut: Dār al-kutub al-ʿilmiyya, 2010. An earlier edition of this work was published in Madrid: Consejo Superior de Investigaciones Científicas. Agencia Española de Cooperación Internacional, 2000.

[38] *Sharḥ Kitāb al-ʿilm (Aʿazz mā yuṭlab)*. Ed. M. ʿAbd al-Salām al-Mahmāh, 2 vols, Tangier: Dār Sulaykī Ikhwān li-l-nashr wa-l-ṭibāʿa, 2006–8, being a commentary on Ibn Tūmart's (d. 544/1149) doctrinal work, *Aʿazz mā yuṭlab*.

[39] *Al-Asrār al-ʿaqliyya fī l-kalimāt al-nabawiyya*. Ed. N. Ḥammādī, Beirut: Maktabat al-maʿārif, 1430/2009. *Sharḥ al-ʿAqīda al-burhāniyya wa-l-fuṣūl al-īmāniyya*. Ed. N. Ḥammādī, Beirut: Dār Maktabat al-maʿārif, 2010. *Sharḥ al-Irshād fī uṣūl al-iʿtiqād*. Ed. Nazīha Maʿārij, 2 vols, Tetuan: Markaz Abī l-Ḥasan al-Ashʿarī, in press.

[40] *Muqaddimāt al-marāshid ilā ʿilm al-ʿaqāʾid*. Ed. J. A. al-Bakhtī, Rabat: Maṭbaʿat al-Khalīj al-ʿarabī, 1425/2004.

[41] *Al-Mukhtaṣar al-kalāmī*. Ed. N. Ḥammādī, Tūnis: Dār al-Imām Ibn ʿArafa, 1435/2014.

[42] *Sharḥ al-ʿAqīda al-burhāniyya wa-l-fuṣūl al-īmāniyya*, being a commentary on the *ʿAqīda al-burhāniyya* of ʿUthmān al-Salālujī (d. 594/1198). Ed. N. Ḥammādī, Beirut: Muʾassasat al-maʿārif, 1429/2008; *Kitāb al-Waṣīla bi-dhāt Allāh wa-ṣifātihi*. Ed. N. Ḥammādī, Beirut: Muʾassasat al-maʿārif, 1429/2008.

[43] *Al-Tuḥfa al-mufīda fī sharḥ al-ʿAqīda al-ḥafīda*. Ed. N. Ḥammādī, Kuwait: Dār al-Ḍiyāʾ, 1433/2012.

[44] Ibn Mahdī entertained sympathies towards Shīʿism as is suggested by his *Kitāb Nuzhat al-abṣār wa-maḥāsin al-āthār*, a collection of ʿAlī b. Abī Ṭālib's sermons (ed. M. B. al-Maḥmūdī, Tehran: al-Majmaʿ al-ʿālamī li-l-taqrīb bayna l-madhāhib al-islāmiyya, 2009).

[45] Ibn al-Amīr al-Ḥājj, *al-Kāmil fī uṣūl al-dīn li-Ibn al-Amīr fī ikhtiṣār al-Shāmil fī uṣūl al-dīn li-Imām al-Ḥaramayn al-Juwaynī*. 2 vols. Ed. J. ʿAbd al-Nāṣir ʿAbd al-Munʿim, Cairo: Dār al-salām li-l-ṭibaʿa wa-l-nashr wa-l-tawzīʿ wa-l-tarjama, 2010.

[46] See n. 39.

[47] Ed. Aḥmad Ḥijāzī Aḥmad al-Saqqā, Cairo: Maktabat al-Anjilū al-Miṣriyya, 1987.

The post-classical era of Ashʿarism has been very much at the forefront of international scholarship over the past fifteen years. Apart from publications devoted to the thought of Abū Ḥāmid al-Ghazālī (d. 555/1111) (Griffel 2009; Treiger 2012; Tamer 2015; Griffel 2015), the works and thought of Fakhr al-Dīn al-Rāzī (d. 606/1209) have been the subject of numerous studies (e.g. Shihadeh 2006; Eichner 2009, *passim*; Türker and Demir 2011; Jaffer 2015; Shihadeh in press). Moreover, his comprehensive theological work, *Kitāb Nihāyat al-ʿuqūl fī dirāyat al-uṣūl*, is now available in print,[48] as is his doxography, *al-Riyāḍ al-mūniqa fī ārāʾ ahl al-ʿilm*.[49] Increased attention is also being paid to his otherwise still little-explored reception, both among the generation of his immediate students and beyond (introduction to Pourjavady and Schmidtke 2007; Shihadeh 2005; Shihadeh 2013; Schwarb 2014b; Swanson 2014; Takahashi 2014). With the *Kitāb Abkār al-afkār*, which has recently been edited twice,[50] the theological oeuvre of Sayf al-Dīn ʿAlī b. Abī ʿAlī al-Āmidī (d. 631/1233), a younger contemporary of Fakhr al-Dīn, is now also available in print. Another milestone is the recent edition of Part One of ʿAlāʾ al-Dīn ʿAlī b. Muḥammad al-Qūshjī's (d. 879/1474–5) commentary on Naṣīr al-Dīn al-Ṭūsī's *Tajrīd al-ʿaqāʾid*, which served as the basis for numerous commentaries and glosses among later Ashʿarite and non-Ashʿarite scholars,[51] among them the two prominent thinkers and antagonists of Shiraz, Jalāl al-Dīn al-Dawānī (d. 909/1504) and Ṣadr al-Dīn al-Dashtakī (d. 903/1498), both of whom in theology represented Ashʿarism and whose thought is very much at the forefront of contemporary scholarship (Pourjavady 2011; Bdaiwi 2014).

Following the publication in 1997 of U. Rudolph's groundbreaking monograph on the doctrinal thought of Abū Manṣūr al-Māturīdī (d. 333/944), the eponymous founder of the Māturidiyya (Rudolph 1997), there has been a rise in the number of publications on Māturīdī and his thought (e.g. Daccache 2008; Jalālī 2008; Matsuyama 2009; Matsuyama 2013; Kutlu 2012; Brodersen 2013; and the contributions to *Büyük Türk Bilgini İmâm Mâtürîdî ve Mâtürîdîlik*). For the subsequent development of the school and its reception among later Ottoman scholars, the textual sources collected by E. Badeen should be mentioned (Badeen 2008), as well as the studies by A. Brodersen on views on divine attributes held by the representatives of the school (Brodersen 2014) and on the *Kitāb al-Tamhīd fī bayān al-tawḥīd* by the fifth/eleventh-century representative of the Māturidiyya, Abū Shakūr al-Sālimī. Numerous works by later followers of the school have been published over the past decade or so, among them Abū Muʿīn Maymūn b. Muḥammad al-Nasafī's (d. 508/1114) *al-Tamhīd li-qawāʿid al-tawḥīd*,[52]

48 Ed. M. Baktır and A. Demir, Sivas (Turkey), 2013; ed. Saʿīd ʿAbd al-Laṭīf Fawda, Beirut: Dār al-Dhakhāʾir, 2015 [<https://archive.org/details/ahbab_1_20150627>].

49 Ed. A. Jumʿa, Kairaouan: Kulliyyat al-ādāb wa-l-ʿulūm al-insāniyya bi-l-Qayrawān wa-Markaz al-nashr al-jāmiʿī, 2004.

50 Ed. A. M. Mahdī, Cairo: Maṭbaʿat Dār al-kutub wa-l-wathāʾiq, 1424/2002; ed. A. F. al-Mazīdī, Beirut: Dār al-kutub al-ʿilmiyya, 1424/2003.

51 *Sharḥ Tajrīd al-ʿaqāʾid al-mashhūr bi-l-Sharḥ al-jadīd. Al-Juzʾ al-awwal yashtamilu ʿalā l-maqṣad al-awwal fī l-umūr al-ʿāmma*. Ed. M. Ḥ. al-Zāriʿī al-Riḍāʾī, Qum: Intishārāt-i Rāʾid, 1393[/2014].

52 Ed. A. F. al-Mazyadī, Beirut: Dār al-kutub al-ʿilmiyya, 2007.

Aḥmad b. Maḥmūd b. Abī Bakr al-Ṣābūnī's (d. 580/1184) *al-Muntaqā min ʿIṣmat al-anbiyāʾ*[53] and his *al-Kifāya fī l-hidāya*,[54] Abū l-Barakāt al-Nasafī's (d. 710/1310) *al-Iʿtimād fī l-iʿtiqād*,[55] and Ḥasan b. Abī Bakr al-Maqdisī's (d. 836/1432) commentary on Abū Muʿīn al-Nasafī's *Baḥr al-kalām*,[56] as well as Abū Isḥāq Ibrāhīm b. Ismāʿīl Zāhid al-Ṣaffār al-Bukhārī's (d. 534/1139) *Talkhīṣ al-adilla li-qawāʿid al-tawḥīd*[57]—a work that was the focus of a recent doctoral dissertation (Demir 2014). What has otherwise been achieved over the past fifteen years primarily serves to consolidate research. Rudolph's monograph of 1997 has, since its initial publication in German, been translated into Russian (Almaty 1999), Uzbek (Tashkent 2001 and 2002), and English (Leiden 2012), and is thus being made available to a wide range of international scholars. Turkish scholars have been actively engaged in producing well-documented editions of Māturīdī's extant writings. In 2003, a new edition of his *Kitāb al-Tawḥīd* was published by Muhammad Aruçi and Bekir Topaloğlu, and the latter also supervised a collaborative critical edition of Māturīdī's exegesis, *Taʾwīlāt al-Qurʾān*, published between 2005 and 2011, in eighteen volumes. The remaining lacunae primarily concern the later development of the school, including editions of numerous works by its main representatives, which are preserved in manuscript (Rudolph 2012: 15ff.; see also Chapters 17, 32, 33, 39).

Ḥanbalite theology has likewise been in the forefront of research in recent years. Several scholars have critically examined the creeds traditionally attributed to the eponymous founder of the school, Aḥmad b. Ḥanbal (d. 241/855). These, as has been shown by S. al-Sarhan, in what is so far the most comprehensive study on Aḥmad b. Ḥanbal's literary oeuvre, in fact did not originate with Ibn Ḥanbal but were attributed to him only at a later stage (al-Sarhan 2011). M. Fierro has edited and analysed a version of one of the creeds attributed to Ibn Ḥanbal that circulated in al-Andalus (Fierro 2015). Studies such as these are complemented by analyses devoted to specific aspects of Ibn Ḥanbal's theological thought (Picken 2008; Williams 2002) as well as publications focusing on his biography (Melchert 2006). Several theological summae by later representatives of the Ḥanbaliyya have been edited in recent years, such as the *Kitāb al-Īḍāḥ fī uṣūl al-dīn* of Abū l-Ḥasan ʿAlī b. ʿAbd Allāh b. al-Zāghūnī (d. 527/1132),[58] though none surpasses

53 Ed. M. Būlūṭ, Beirut/Istanbul: Dār Ibn Ḥazm/Markaz al-buḥūth al-islāmiyya, 2013.

54 Ed. M. Ārūtashī, Beirut/Istanbul: Dār Ibn Ḥazm/Markaz al-buḥūth al-islāmiyya, 2013.

55 A. M. Ismail, *Die maturiditische Glaubenslehre des Abū l-Barakāt an-Nasafī (gest. 710/1310): Edition und Analyse seines* Kitāb al-Iʿtimād fī l-iʿtiqād. 2 vols. Frankfurt: Ph. D. dissertation, 2003.

56 *Kitāb Ghāyat al-marām fī sharḥ Baḥr al-kalām*. Ed. ʿAbd Allāh Muḥammad ʿAbd Allāh Ismāʿīl and Muḥammad al-Sayyid Aḥmad Shiḥāta, Cairo: al-Maktaba al-Azhariyya li-l-turāth, 1432/2012.

57 *Kompendium der Beweise für die Grundlagen des Ein-Gott-Glaubens, oder Talḫīṣ al-adilla li-qawāʿid at-tauḥīd*. Ed. A. Brodersen, Beirut/Berlin: Deutsches Orient Institut/Klaus Schwarz in Kommission, 2011.

58 Ed. ʿI. al-Sayyid Maḥmūd, Riyadh: Markaz al-Malik Fayṣal li-l-buḥūth wa-l-dirāsāt al-islāmiyya, 1424/2003. Another edition of the *Īḍāḥ* was published by M. S. ʿAbd al-Wahhāb (Cairo: Dār al-ḥadīth, 1431/2010), although the editor erroneously attributed the work to Muḥammad b. ʿAlī b. Muḥammad al-Ṭabarī.

in significance the *Kitāb al-Muʿtamad fī uṣūl al-dīn* by Abū Yaʿlā Muḥammad b. al-Ḥusayn b. Farrā (d. 458/1066) (since 1974 available in the edition by W. Z. Ḥaddād), the first Ḥanbalite author to adopt elements of speculative reasoning (*kalām*) in his deliberations on theology and legal theory (Vishanoff 2011: 190ff.). Another focus of recent scholarship is the doctrinal history of the school in its later phase, with special attention being paid to Najm al-Dīn Sulaymān b. ʿAbd al-Qawī al-Ṭūfī (d. 716/1316),[59] and the 'Neo-Hanbalites' Ibn Taymiyya (d. 728/1328) and Ibn Qayyim al-Jawziyya (d. 751/1350) (Hoover 2007; Rapoport and Ahmed 2010; Bori and Holtzman 2010; Adem 2015; Krawietz and Tamer 2013; Vasalou 2015; cf. also Chapter 35).

There is now a growing awareness of other religio-theological strands that had for a long time been completely neglected, partly as a result of their seeming marginality and at times due to a complete loss of relevant sources. Some of these have received increasing scholarly attention over the past fifteen years. Among the groups that had been considered to be of only marginal significance up until recently is the Ibāḍiyya. Its literary legacy has come to the forefront of research in recent years, partly thanks to funding by the government of Oman, resulting in numerous conference proceedings (e.g. Francesca 2015), historical studies (Wilkinson 2010), and bio- and bibliographical reference works (Nāṣir 2000–6; Custers 2006). Specifically relevant for the history of Ibāḍī theology are the above-mentioned critical text editions by A. Salimi and W. Madelung (see notes 3 and 4), as well as a recent annotated translation of two theological primers by Ibāḍī theologians of the late thirteenth/nineteenth century, namely the *ʿAqīda al-wahbiyya* by Nāṣir b. Sālim b. ʿUdayyam al-Rawahī and the *Kitāb Maʿālim al-dīn* by ʿAbd al-ʿAzīz al-Thamīmī (d. 1223/1808), with an introduction to the history of Ibāḍī doctrinal thought (Hoffman 2012). Given the growing interest of international scholars in Ibāḍī studies, Ibāḍī theology will certainly play a prominent role in future scholarship.

Another strand that has received increased attention over the past years, especially among Iranian scholars, is the Karrāmiyya, an influential theological and legal movement active from the fourth/tenth to the seventh/thirteenth century in the Islamic East. The Karrāmiyya's ideas can be only partly reconstructed and this nearly exclusively on the basis of data provided by the trend's opponents, who considered its eponymous founder, Abū ʿAbd Allāh Muḥammad Ibn Karrām (d. 255/869) and his followers to be unbelievers. Next to none of the Karrāmī literary output has been preserved, with the exception of a substantial number of exegetical works (cf. Gilliot 2000; Ansari 2001; Ansari 2002a; Ansari 2002b; Zysow 2011; as well as numerous studies by Muḥammad Riḍā Shafīʿī Kadkanī, references given in Zysow 2011; cf. also Chapter 15). Some of those

[59] Mention should be made of recent critical editions of some of his works: *Darʾ al-qawl al-qabīḥ bi-l-taḥsīn wa-l-taqbīḥ*, ed. A. M. Shiḥāda (Ayman Shihadeh), Riyadh: Markaz al-Malik Fayṣal li-l-buḥūth wa-l-dirāsāt al-islāmiyya, 1426/2005; *al-Taʿlīq ʿalā l-Anājīl al-arbaʿa wa-l-taʿlīq ʿalā l-Tawrāh wa-ʿalā ghayrihā min kutub al-anbiyāʾ = Muslim Exegesis of the Bible in Medieval Cairo: Najm al-Dīn al-Ṭūfī's (d. 716/1316) Commentary on the Christian Scriptures.* A Critical Edition and Annotated Translation with an Introduction, by L. Demiri, Leiden: Brill, 2013.

texts have been published in recent years, among them the *Tafsīr* of Abū Bakr ʿAṭīq b. Muḥammad Nīsābūrī 'Sūrābādī' (late fifth/eleventh century);[60] the *Qiṣaṣ al-anbiyāʾ* by the fifth/eleventh-century author al-Hayṣam b. Muḥammad b. al-Hayṣam;[61] and *Zayn al-fatā fī sharḥ Sūrat Hal atā* which, according to the editor of the text, was authored by Aḥmad b. Muḥammad al-ʿĀṣimī.[62] H. Ansari questioned this attribution and suggested that the work was instead written by Abū Muḥammad Ḥāmid b. Aḥmad b. Bisṭām (Ansari 2002a).

Other strands of thought that were important at some time in history have until today mostly escaped scholars' attention, as is the case, by way of example, with the Sālimiyya, named as such after the group's eponymous founders, Muḥammad b. Aḥmad b. Sālim (d. 297/909) and his son Aḥmad b. Muḥammad b. Aḥmad b. Sālim (d. 356/967) (Ohlander 2008), or the Ṣufriyya, another off shoot of the Khārijite movement (Madelung and Lewinstein 1997).

References

Abdulsater, H. A. (2013). *The Climax of Speculative Theology in Buyid Shiʿism: The Contribution of al-Sharif al-Murtada*. Ph. D. dissertation, Yale University.

Abdulsater, H. A. (2014). 'To Rehabilitate a Theological Treatise. Inqādh al-Bashar min al-Jabr wa-l-Qadar'. *Asiatische Studien—Études Asiatiques* 68: 519–47.

Adang, C., S. Schmidtke, and D. Sklare (eds.) (2007). *A Common Rationality: Muʿtazilism in Islam and Judaism*. Würzburg: Ergon.

Adem, R. (2015). *The Intellectual Genealogy of Ibn Taymiyya*. Ph. D. dissertation, University of Chicago.

Ansari, H. (2001). 'Karrāmiyya dar majālis-i Bayhaq wa čand manbaʿ-i digar'. *Kitāb-i māh-i dīn* 43: 78–81.

Ansari, H. (2002a). 'Mulāḥaẓāt-i čand dar bāra-yi mīrāth-i bar jā mānda-yi Karrāmiyya'. *Kitāb-i māh-i dīn* 56–7: 69–80.

Ansari, H. (2002b). 'Taḥqīq-i dar bāra-yi tafsīr-i riwāyi az muʾallif-i karrāmī'. *Nashr-i dānish* 19/2: 25–7.

Ansari, H. (2004–5). 'Kitābī kalāmī az Ḍirār b. ʿAmr'. *Kitāb-i māh-i dīn* 89–90: 4–13.

Ansari, H. (2007). 'Abū ʿAlī al-Jubbāʾī et son livre *al-Maqālāt*'. In C. Adang, S. Schmidtke, and D. Sklare (eds.), *A Common Rationality: Muʿtazilism in Islam and Judaism*. Würzburg: Ergon, 21–35.

Ansari, H. (2014a). 'Yek porsish-i muhimm dar bāra-yi yek kitāb mashhūr: Tathbīt-i dalāʾil al-nubuwwa'. [<http://ansari.kateban.com/post/2226> (consulted 4 September 2015)].

[60] *Tafsīr al-tafāsīr*. Ed. S. Sīrjānī, 5 vols, Tehran: Farhang-i nashr-i Naw, 1381/2002. On this work, see also Zadeh 2012: 504ff.

[61] *Tarjuma-yi Muḥammad b. Asʿad b. ʿAbd Allāh al-Ḥanafī al-Tustarī*. Ed. ʿA. Muḥammadzādah, Mashhad: Dānishgāh-i Firdawsī-i Mashhad, 1384[/2005].

[62] *Al-ʿAsal al-muṣaffā min tahdhīb Zayn al-fatā fī sharḥ Sūrat Hal atā*, taʾlīf Aḥmad b. Muḥammad b. ʿAlī b. Aḥmad al-ʿĀṣimī. Ed. M. B. al-Maḥmūdī, 2 vols, Qum: Majmaʿ iḥyāʾ al-thaqāfa al-islāmiyya, 1418[/1997–8].

Ansari, H. (2014b). 'Nawīsanda-yi Tathbīt-i dalāʾil al-nubuwwa'. [<http://ansari.kateban.com/post/2236> (consulted 4 September 2015)].

Ansari, H. (in press). *L'imamat et l'Occultation selon l'imamisme: Étude bibliographique et histoire des textes*. Leiden: Brill.

Ansari, H., W. Madelung, and S. Schmidtke (2015). 'Yūsuf al-Baṣīr's Refutation (*Naqḍ*) of Abū l-Ḥusayn al-Baṣrī's Theology in a Yemeni Zaydi Manuscript of the 7th/13th Century'. In D. Hollenberg, Ch. Rauch, and S. Schmidtke (eds.), *The Yemeni Manuscript Tradition*. Leiden: Brill, 28–65.

Ansari, H., and S. Schmidtke (2010a). 'Muʿtazilism after ʿAbd al-Jabbār: Abū Rashīd al-Nīsābūrī's *Kitāb Masāʾil al-khilāf fī l-uṣūl*'. *Studia Iranica* 39: 227–78.

Ansari, H., and S. Schmidtke (2010b). 'The Zaydī Reception of Ibn Khallād's Kitāb al-Uṣūl: The taʿlīq of Abū Ṭāhir b. ʿAlī al-Ṣaffār'. *Journal asiatique* 298: 275–302.

Ansari, H., and S. Schmidtke (2014). 'Al-Shaykh al-Ṭūsī: His Writings on Theology and their Reception'. In F. Daftary and G. Miskinzoda (eds.), *The Study of Shiʿi Islam: History, Theology and Law*. London: I. B. Tauris, in association with The Institute of Ismaili Studies, 475–97.

Ansari, H., and S. Schmidtke (2016). 'The Cultural Transfer of Zaydī and Non-Zaydī Religious Literature from Northern Iran to Yemen, 12th through 14th Century'. In S. Brentjes and J. Renn (eds.), *Thabit ibn Qurra and the 40 Mercenaries: Globalization of Knowledge in Post-Antiquity*. Aldershot: Ashgate.

Ansari, H., and S. Schmidtke (forthcoming). *Philosophical Theology among 6th/12th Century Twelver Shīʿites: From Naṣīr al-Dīn al-Ṭūsī (Alive in 573/1177) to Naṣīr al-Dīn al-Ṭūsī (d. 672/1274)*.

Badeen, E. (2008). *Sunnitische Theologie in osmanischer Zeit*. Würzburg: Ergon.

al-Bakhtī, J. ʿA. (2005). *ʿUthmān al-Salālujī wa-madhhabiyyatuhu al-Ashʿariyya: Dirāsa li-jānib min al-fikr al-kalāmī bi-l-Maghrib min khilāl al-Burhāniyya wa-shurūḥihā*. Rabat: al-Mamlaka al-Maghribiyya, Wizārat al-awqāf wa-l-shuʾūn al-islāmiyya.

Bdaiwi, A. (2014). *Shīʿī Defenders of Avicenna: An Intellectual History of the Dashtakī Philosophers of Shiraz*. Ph. D. dissertation, University of Exeter.

Bori, C., and L. Holtzman (eds.) (2010). *A Scholar in the Shadow: Essays in the Legal and Theological Thought of Ibn Qayyim al-Gawziyyah = Oriente Moderno* 90 i.

Brodersen, A. (2013). 'Göttliches und menschliches Handeln im māturīditischen kalām'. *Jahrbuch für Islamische Theologie und Religionspädagogik* 2: 117–39.

Brodersen, A. (2014). *Der unbekannte kalam: Theologische Positionen der frühen Maturidiya am Beispiel der Attributenlehre*. Berlin: Lit Verlag.

Büyük Türk Bilgini İmâm Mâtürîdî ve Mâtürîdîlik: Milletlerarası tartişmalı ilmî toplantı: 22–24 Mayis 2009 İstanbul. Istanbul: IFAU 2012.

Casasas Canals, X., and D. O. Serrano Ruano (forthcoming). 'Putting Criticisms against al-Ghazālī in Place: New Materials on the Interface among Law, Rational Theology and Mysticism in Almoravid and Almohad al-Andalus (Ibn Rushd al-Jadd and al-Qurṭubī)'. In A. Shihadeh and J. Thiele (eds.), *Philosophical Theology in Medieval Islam: The Later Ashʿarite Tradition*. Leiden: Brill.

Custers, M. H. (2006). *Al-Ibāḍiyya: A Bibliography. Vol. 1: Ibāḍīs of the Mashriq. Vol. 2: Ibāḍīs of the Maghrib (incl. Egypt). Vol. 3: Secondary Literature*. Maastricht: Datawyse / Universitaire Pers Maastricht.

Daccache, S. (2008). *Le Problème de la création du monde et son contexte rationnel et historique dans la doctrine d'Abū Manṣūr al-Māturīdī (333/944)*. Beirut: Dār al-Mashriq.

Demir, A. (2014). *Ebû İshâk Zâhid es-Saffâr'ın Kelâm Yöntemi*. Ph. D. dissertation, Cumhuriyet Üniversitesi Sosyal Bilimler Enstitüsü, Sivas.

Eichner, H. (2009). *The Post-Avicennian Philosophical Tradition and Islamic Orthodoxy: Philosophical and Theological Summae in Context*. Habilitationsschrift, Martin-Luther-Universität Halle-Wittenberg.

van Ess, J. (2011). *Der Eine und das Andere: Betrachtungen an islamischen häresiographischen Texten*. 2 vols. Berlin: de Gruyter.

Fierro, M. (2015). 'Un Credo de Ibn Ḥanbal en al-Andalus (Época Omeya)'. In M. R. Boudchar and A. Saidy (eds.), *Homenaje al Dr. Jaafar Ben El haj Soulami: Semblanzas y estudios*. Tetouan: Asociación Tetuán Asmir, 91–9.

Francesca, E. (ed.) (2015). *Ibadi Theology: Rereading Sources and Scholarly Works*. Hildesheim: Georg Olms.

Frank, R. M. (2007). *Early Islamic Theology: The Muʿtazilites and al-Ashʿarī*. Ed. D. Gutas. Aldershot: Ashgate.

Frank, R. M. (2008). *Classical Islamic Theology: The Ashʿarites*. Ed. D. Gutas. Aldershot: Ashgate.

al-Ghufrānī, ʿAbd Allāh (2013). *Fihris muṣannafāt al-Shaykh Muḥammad b. ʿAlī b. Abī Jumhūr al-Aḥsāʾī: Kashshāf biblīyūghrāfī li-muṣannafāt Ibn Abī Jumhūr al-makhṭūṭa wa-l-maṭbūʿa wa-ijāzātihi fī l-riwāya wa-ṭuruqihi fī l-ḥadīth*. Beirut: Jamʿiyyat Ibn Abī Jumhūr al-Aḥsāʾī.

Gilliot, C. (2000). 'Les Sciences coraniques chez les Karrāmites du Khorasan: Le Livre des fondations'. *Journal asiatique* 288: 15–81.

Gimaret, D. (1990). *La Doctrine d'al-Ashʿarī*. Paris: Les Éditions du Cerf.

Gimaret, D. (2008a). 'Un extrait de la "Hidāya" d'Abū Bakr al-Bāqillānī: Le "Kitāb at-tawallud", réfutation de la thèse muʿtazilite de la génération des actes'. *Bulletin d'études orientales* 58: 259–313.

Gimaret, D. (2008b). 'Le Commentaire récemment publié de la Taḏkira d'Ibn Mattawayh'. *Journal asiatique* 296: 203–28.

Gimaret, D. (2011). 'Pour servir à la lecture des Masāʾil d'Abū Rašīd al-Nīsābūrī'. *Bulletin d'études orientales* 60: 11–38.

Griffel, F. (2009). *Al-Ghazālī's Philosophical Theology*. Oxford: Oxford University Press.

Griffel, F. (ed.) (2015). *Islam and Rationality: The Impact of al-Ghazālī. Papers collected on his 900th Anniversary*. Vol. ii. Leiden: Brill.

al-Ḥibshī, ʿAbd Allāh M. (2006). *Jāmiʿ al-shurūḥ wa-l-ḥawāshī*. 3 vols. 2nd edn. Abu Dhabi: Abu Dhabi Authority for Culture and Heritage, 1427.

Hildebrandt, T. (2007). *Neo-Muʿtazilismus? Intention und Kontext im modernen arabischen Umgang mit dem rationalistischen Erbe des Islam*. Leiden: Brill.

Hoffman, V. J. (2012). *The Essentials of Ibāḍī Islam*. New York: Syracuse University Press.

Hollenberg, D., Ch. Rauch, and S. Schmidtke (eds.) (2015). *The Yemeni Manuscript Tradition*. Leiden: Brill.

Hoover, J. (2007). *Ibn Taymiyya's Theodicy of Perpetual Optimism*. Leiden: Brill.

Jaffer, T. (2015). *Razi: Master of Qurʾanic Interpretation and Theological Reasoning*. New York: Oxford University Press.

Jalālī, Sayyid Luṭf Allāh (2008). *Tārīkh wa ʿaqāʾid-i Māturīdiyya*. Qum: Markaz-i muṭālaʿāt va taḥqīqāt-i adyān va madhāhib, 1376.

Kohlberg, E. (2014). 'Shiʿi *Ḥadīth*: Introduction'. In F. Daftary and G. Miskinzoda (eds.), *The Study of Shiʿi Islam: History, Theology and Law*. London: I. B. Tauris, in association with The Institute of Ismaili Studies, 165–79.

Krawietz, B., and G. Tamer (eds., in collaboration with A. Kokoschka) (2013). *Islamic Theology, Philosophy and Law: Debating Ibn Taymiyya and Ibn Qayyim al-Jawziyya*. Berlin: de Gruyter.

Kulinich, A. (2012). *Representing 'a Blameworthy Tafsīr': Muʿtazilite Exegetical Tradition in al-Jāmiʿ fī tafsīr al-Qurʾān of ʿAlī ibn ʿĪsā al-Rummānī (d. 384/994)*. Ph. D. dissertation, School of Oriental and African Studies, London.

Kutlu, S. (ed.) (2012). *İmam Mâturîdî ve Maturidilik: Tarihî Arka Plan, Hayatı, Eserleri, Fikirleri ve Maturidilik Mezhebi*. 4th edn. Ankara: Otto.

Löfgren, O., and R. Traini (1975–2011). *Catalogue of the Arabic Manuscripts in the Biblioteca Ambrosiana*. Vols. i–iii. Vicenza: N. Pozza, 1975–95. Vol. iv, Milan: Silvana Editoriale, 2011.

Madelung, W. (1965). *Der Imam al-Qāsim ibn Ibrāhīm und die Glaubenslehre der Zaiditen*. Berlin: de Gruyter.

Madelung, W. (2013). 'Al-Ḥasan b. Mūsā al-Nawbakhtī on the Views of the Astronomers and Astrologers'. In M. Cook, N. Haider, I. Rabb, and A. Sayeed (eds.), *Law and Tradition in Classical Islamic Thought*. New York: Palgrave, 269–78.

Madelung, W. (2014a). 'Muʿtazilī Theology in Levi ben Yefet's *Kitāb al-Niʿma*'. In S. Schmidtke and G. Schwarb (eds.), *Jewish and Christian Reception(s) of Muslim Theology = Intellectual History of the Islamicate World* 2: 9–17 [Leiden: Brill].

Madelung, W. (2014b). 'Theology: Introduction'. In F. Daftary and G. Miskinzoda (eds.), *The Study of Shiʿi Islam: History, Theology and Law*. London: I. B. Tauris, in association with The Institute of Ismaili Studies, 455–63.

Madelung, W. (in press). 'ʿAbd Allāh b. Yazīd al-Fazārī's Rebuttal of the Teaching of Ibn ʿUmayr'. In L. Muehlethaler, S. Schmidtke, and G. Schwarb (eds.), *Theological Rationalism in Medieval Islam: New Texts and Perspectives*. Leuven: Peeters.

Madelung, W., and K. Lewinstein (1997). 'Ṣufriyya'. In *The Encyclopaedia of Islam. 2nd edn.*, ix. 766–9.

Madelung, W., and S. Schmidtke (2006). *Rational Theology in Interfaith Communication: Abū l-Ḥusayn al-Baṣrī's Muʿtazilī Theology among the Karaites in the Fatimid Age*. Leiden: Brill.

Matsuyama, Y. (2009). 'Assurance of Salvation in Islam' [in Japanese]. *Journal of Religious Studies* 83: 47–70.

Matsuyama, Y. (2013). 'Notes on Diverse Aspects of Studies on Maturidism' [in Japanese]. *Annals of Japan Association for Middle East Studies* 29: 145–59.

Melchert, Ch. (2006). *Ahmad ibn Hanbal*. Oxford: Oneworld.

Mourad, S. (2006). 'Ibn al-Khallāl al-Baṣrī (d. after 377/988) and his Œuvre on the Problematic Verses of the Qurʾān *Kitāb al-Radd ʿalā l-jabriyya wa-l-qadariyya* (Refutation of the Predestinarian Compulsionists)'. In C. Adang, S. Schmidtke, and D. Sklare (eds.), *A Common Rationality: Muʿtazilism in Islam and Judaism*. Würzburg: Ergon, 81–99.

Nāṣir, M. Ṣ. et al. (2000–6). *Muʿjam aʿlām al-Ibāḍiyya*. 3 vols. Beirut: Dār al-Gharb al-islāmī.

Ohlander, E. S. (2008). 'Aḥmad b. Muḥammad b. Sālim'. In *The Encyclopaedia of Islam, THREE*. Leiden: Brill, 2008–11, 84–5.

el-Omari, R. M. (2006). *The Theology of Abū l-Qāsim al-Balḫī/al-Kaʿbī (d. 319/931): A Study of its Sources and Reception*. Ph. D. dissertation, Yale University.

Picken, G. (2008). 'Ibn Ḥanbal and al-Muḥāsibī: A Study of Early Conflicting Scholarly Methodologies'. *Arabica* 55: 337–61.

Pourjavady, R. (2011). *Philosophy in Early Safavid Iran: Najm al-Dīn Maḥmūd al-Nayrīzī and his Writings*. Leiden: Brill.

Pourjavady, R., and S. Schmidtke (eds.) (2007). *Critical Remarks by Najm al-Dīn al-Kātibī on the Kitāb al-Maʿālim by Fakhr al-Dīn al-Rāzī, together with the Commentaries by ʿIzz al-Dawla Ibn Kammūna*. Tehran: Iranian Institute of Philosophy.

Pourjavady, R., and S. Schmidtke (2015). 'An Eastern Renaissance? Greek Philosophy under the Safavids (16th–18th centuries AD)'. In D. Gutas, S. Schmidtke, and A. Treiger (eds.), *New Horizons in Graeco-Arabic Studies = Intellectual History of the Islamicate World* 2: 248–90.

Rapoport, Y., and Sh. Ahmed (eds.) (2010). *Ibn Taymiyya and his Times*. Karachi: Oxford University Press.

Reynolds, G. S. (2004). *A Muslim Theologian in the Sectarian Milieu: 'Abd al-Jabbār and the Critique of Christian Origins*. Leiden: Brill.

El-Rouayheb, Kh. (forthcoming). *Muhammad b. Yusuf al-Sanusi and Radical Ashʿarism*. Oxford: Oneworld.

Rudolph, U. (1997). *Al-Māturīdī und die sunnitische Theologie in Samarkand*. Leiden: Brill.

Rudolph, U. (2012). *Al-Māturīdī and the Development of Sunnī Theology in Samarqand*. Leiden: Brill.

Ṣadrāyī Khūyī, ʿA. (2003). *Kitābshināsī-i Tajrīd al-iʿtiqād*. Qum: Kitābkhāna-yi Marʿashī.

al-Sarhan, S. S. (2011). *Early Muslim Traditionalism: A Critical Study of the Works and Political Theology of Ahmad Ibn Hanbal*. Ph. D. dissertation, University of Exeter.

Schmidtke, S. (2000). *Theologie, Philosophie und Mystik im zwölferschiitischen Islam des 9./15. Jahrhunderts: Die Gedankenwelten des Ibn Abī Ǧumhūr al-Aḥsāʾī (um 838/1434–35–nach 905/1501)*. Leiden: Brill.

Schmidtke, S. (2006). 'Muʿtazilite Manuscripts in the Abraham Firkovitch Collection, St. Petersburg. A Descriptive Catalogue'. In C. Adang, S. Schmidtke, and D. Sklare (eds.), *A Common Rationality: Muʿtazilism in Islam and Judaism*. Würzburg: Ergon, 377–462.

Schmidtke, S. (2008). 'MS Mahdawi 514. An Anonymous Commentary on Ibn Mattawayh's *Kitāb al-Tadhkira*'. In A. Akasoy and W. Raven (eds.), *Islamic Thought in the Middle Ages. Studies in Text, Transmission and Translation in Honour of Hans Daiber*. Leiden: Brill, 139–62.

Schmidtke, S. (2011). 'Early Ašʿarite Theology: Abū Bakr al-Bāqillānī (d. 403/1013) and his Hidāyat al-mustaršidīn'. *Bulletin d'études orientales* 60: 39–72.

Schmidtke, S. (2012a). 'Ibn Ḥazm on Ashʿarism and Muʿtazilism'. In C. Adang, M. Fierro, and S. Schmidtke (eds.), *Ibn Hazm of Cordoba: The Life and Works of a Controversial Thinker*. Leiden: Brill, 375–402.

Schmidtke, S. (ed.) (2012b). *The Neglected Šīʿites: Studies in the Legal and Intellectual History of the Zaydīs = Arabica. Journal of Arabic and Islamic Studies* 59 iii–iv [Leiden: Brill].

Schmidtke, S. (2012c). 'Two Commentaries on Najm al-Dīn al-Kātibī's *al-Shamsiyya*, Copied in the Hand of David b. Joshua Maimonides' (fl. ca. 1335–1410 CE)'. In M. Cook, N. Haider, I. Rabb, and A. Sayeed (eds.), *Law and Tradition in Classical Islamic Thought*. New York: Palgrave, 173–91.

Schmidtke, S. (2014). 'Jewish Reception of Twelver Shīʿī *kalām*: A Copy of al-Sharīf al-Murtaḍā's *Kitāb al-Dhakhīra* in the Abraham Firkovitch Collection, St. Petersburg'. In S. Schmidtke and G. Schwarb (eds.), *Jewish and Christian Reception(s) of Muslim Theology = Intellectual History of the Islamicate World* 2: 50–74 [Leiden: Brill].

Schwarb, G. (2006a). 'Un projet international: Le Manuel des œuvres et manuscrits muʿtazilites'. *Chronique du manuscrit au Yémen* 2 (June 2006) [<http://cy.revues.org/document198.html>].

Schwarb, G. (2006b). 'Sahl b. al-Faḍl al-Tustarī's K. al-ʾĪmāʾ'. *Ginzei Qedem* 2: 61*–105*.

Schwarb, G. (2011). 'Muʿtazilism in the Age of Averroes'. In P. Adamson (ed.), *In the Age of Averroes: Arabic Philosophy in the Sixth/Twelfth Century*. London: The Warburg Institute, 251–82.

Schwarb, G. (2012). 'Muʿtazilism in a 20th Century Zaydī Qurʾān Commentary'. *Arabica* 59: 371–402.

Schwarb, G. (2014a). 'Short Communication: A Newly Discovered Fragment of al-Sharīf al-Murtaḍā's *K. al-Mulakhkhaṣ fī uṣūl al-dīn* in Hebrew Script'. In S. Schmidtke and G. Schwarb (eds.), *Jewish and Christian Reception(s) of Muslim Theology = Intellectual History of the Islamicate World* 2: 75–9 [Leiden: Brill].
Schwarb, G. (2014b). 'The 13th Century Copto-Arabic Reception of Fakhr al-Dīn al-Rāzī: Al-Rashīd Abū l-Khayr Ibn al-Ṭayyib's *Risālat al-Bayān al-aẓhar fī l-radd ʿalā man yaqūlu bi-l-qaḍāʾ wa-l-qadar*'. In S. Schmidtke and G. Schwarb (eds.), *Jewish and Christian Reception(s) of Muslim Theology = Intellectual History of the Islamicate World* 2: 143–69 [Leiden: Brill].
Shihadeh, A. (2005). 'From al-Ghazālī to al-Rāzī: 6th/12th Century Developments in Muslim Philosophical Theology'. *Arabic Sciences and Philosophy* 15: 141–79.
Shihadeh, A. (2006). *The Teleological Ethics of Fakhr al-Dīn al-Rāzī*. Leiden: Brill.
Shihadeh, A. (2013). 'A Post-Ghazālian Critic of Avicenna: Ibn Ghaylān al-Balkhī on the Materia Medica of the Canon of Medicine'. *Journal of Islamic Studies* 24: 135–74.
Shihadeh, A. (in press). 'Al-Rāzī's Earliest *Kalām* Work'. In L. Muehlethaler, S. Schmidtke, and G. Schwarb (eds.), *Theological Rationalism in Medieval Islam: New Sources and Perspectives*. Leuven: Peeters.
Sobieroj, F. (2007). *Arabische Handschriften der bayerischen Staatsbibliothek zu München unter Einschluss einiger türkischer und persischer Handschriften*. Band 1. Stuttgart: Steiner.
Spevack, A. (2014). *The Archetypal Sunnī Scholar: Law, Theology, and Mysticism in the Synthesis of al-Bājūrī*. Albany: SUNY Press.
Swanson, M. N. (2014). 'Christian Engagement with Islamic *kalām* in Late 14th-Century Egypt: The Case of *al-Ḥāwī* by al-Makīn Jirjis Ibn al-ʿAmīd "the Younger"'. In S. Schmidtke and G. Schwarb (eds.), *Jewish and Christian Reception(s) of Muslim Theology = Intellectual History of the Islamicate World* 2: 214–26 [Leiden: Brill].
Takahashi, H. (2014). 'Reception of Islamic Theology among Syriac Christians in the Thirteenth Century: The Use of Fakhr al-Dīn al-Rāzī in Barhebraeus' *Candelabrum of the Sanctuary*'. In S. Schmidtke and G. Schwarb (eds.), *Jewish and Christian Reception(s) of Muslim Theology = Intellectual History of the Islamicate World* 2: 170–92 [Leiden: Brill].
Tamer, G. (ed.) (2015). *Islam and Rationality: The Impact of al-Ghazālī. Papers Collected on his 900th Anniversary*. Vol. i. Leiden: Brill.
Thiele, J. (forthcoming). 'Ashʿarite Theology under the Ḥafṣīd Dynasty'. In A. Shihadeh and J. Thiele (eds.), *Philosophical Theology in Medieval Islam: The Later Ashʿarite Tradition*. Leiden: Brill.
Treiger, A. (2012). *Inspired Knowledge in Islamic Thought: Al-Ghazālī's Theory of Mystical Cognition and its Avicennian Foundation*. London: Routledge.
Türker, Ö., and O. Demir (eds.) (2011). *İslâm düşüncesinin dönüşüm çağında: Fahreddin er-Râzî*. Istanbul: ISAM Yayınları.
Vasalou, S. (2015). *Ibn Taymiyya's Theological Ethics*. Oxford: Oxford University Press.
Vishanoff, D. R. (2011). *The Formation of Islamic Hermeneutics: How Sunni Legal Theorists Imagined a Revealed Law*. New Haven: American Oriental Society.
Wilkinson, J. C. (2010). *Ibadism: Origins and Early Development in Oman*. Oxford: Oxford University Press.
Williams, W. (2002). 'Aspects of the Creed of Imam Ahmad ibn Hanbal: A Study of Anthropomorphism in Early Islamic Discourse'. *International Journal of Middle East Studies* 34: 441–63.
Zadeh, T. (2012). *The Vernacular Qur'an: Translation and the Rise of Persian Exegesis*. Oxford: Oxford University Press, in association with The Institute of Ismaili Studies London.

Zahrī, Kh., and ʿAbd al-Majīd Būkārī (2011). *Fihris al-kutub al-makhṣūṣa fī l-ʿaqīda al-ashʿariyya*. 2 parts. Rabat: Dār Abī Raqrāq.

Zysow, A. (2011). 'Karrāmiyya'. In *Encyclopaedia iranica*, xv. 590–601.

Zysow, A. (2014). [Review of Ibn Mattawayh, *al-Tadhkira fī aḥkām al-jawāhir wa-l-aʿrāḍ*. Ed. D. Gimaret. Cairo: IFAO, 2009. *Kausalitat in der muʿtazilitischen Kosmologie: Das Kitāb al-Muʾaṯṯirāt wa-miftāḥ al-muškilāt des Zayditen al-Ḥasan ar-Raṣṣāṣ (st. 584/1188)*. By Jan Thiele. Leiden: Brill, 2011]. *Journal of the American Oriental Society* 134: 721–5.

PART I

ISLAMIC THEOLOG(IES) DURING THE FORMATIVE AND THE EARLY MIDDLE PERIOD

CHAPTER 1

ORIGINS OF *KALĀM*

ALEXANDER TREIGER

Islamic theology emerged in a multi-religious environment in which a Muslim ruling minority was struggling to assert itself, politically as well as religiously, amidst the indigenous populations of the Middle East. These populations spoke a variety of languages—Aramaic/Syriac, Greek, Middle Persian, Coptic, Armenian, and Arabic, among others—and followed a variety of religions.[1] Christians formed the majority or a significant minority in Syria, Palestine, Iraq, Iran, Egypt, and North Africa, Zoroastrians were prominent in Iraq and Iran, Mandeans were well represented in Iraq, Buddhists were influential in Afghanistan and Central Asia, and Jewish, Manichean, and Pagan communities maintained a significant presence throughout the Middle East (for Iraq see Morony 1984). All these communities had, to varying extents, assimilated and carried forth the Hellenic philosophical and scientific legacy and were engaged in centuries-long inter-religious and intra-religious debates (Lim 1995; Walker 2006: 164–205).[2] It was only natural that Muslim settlers came in close contact with these populations and that their nascent religious beliefs were being articulated and took shape in an atmosphere of debate and polemic with them.

Unravelling the sources of Islamic theology has proved to be an intricate task, complicated by the fact that we have diverse, yet far from complete information on the indigenous populations' religious beliefs and social life, imperfect understanding of the interactions between non-Muslims and Muslims in the early Islamic period, no established history of conversions to Islam, and fairly sketchy information, often of questionable reliability, on the earliest (first/seventh-century) development of Islamic theology itself. Disciplinary divisions within the modern academia between

[1] At the time of the Muslim conquests, Aramaic, with its most widely used dialect, Syriac, was the *lingua franca* of the Middle East. Arabic was widely used outside the Arabian Peninsula, by both urbanized Arabs (e.g. in al-Ḥīra on the Euphrates) and Arab tribal populations—many of them Christian—in Syria, Palestine, Transjordan, and Iraq.

[2] I am grateful to the late Professor Patricia Crone for referring me to Lim's book and for other helpful suggestions. It was a rare privilege to get to meet her during my last visit to Princeton in May 2015.

Islamicists in the strict sense on the one hand and scholars of late antiquity, Hellenic philosophy, Greek, Syriac, and Arab Christianity, Sasanian Iran, Rabbinic Judaism, and Manicheism (with their differing linguistic expertise) on the other have exacerbated the problem, making it difficult to arrive at a holistic account of the early development of Muslim doctrine.

The present account of the origins of Islamic theology must begin with its foremost researcher Josef van Ess, who stated his view, back in the 1970s, succinctly as follows:

> Theology in Islam did not start as polemics against unbelievers. Even the *kalām* style was not developed or taken over in order to refute non-Muslims, especially the Manicheans, as one tended to believe when one saw the origin of *kalām* in the missionary activities of the Muʿtazila. Theology started as an inner-Islamic discussion when, mainly through political development, the self-confident naïvité of the early days was gradually eroded. (van Ess 1975a: 101)

Especially in his early publications, van Ess's view can thus be characterized as 'internalist' (but see van Ess 1970: 24). While certainly conscious of the non-Muslim context and referencing it when appropriate, van Ess's treatment of it nevertheless remains minimal: Islamic theology is presented as having developed more or less independently of foreign influences and as addressing concerns internal to the early Muslim community itself. In a series of publications from the 1970s and 1980s, van Ess embarked on a quest for the 'beginnings' ('Anfänge') of Islamic theology, i.e. the earliest theological documents from the first Islamic century. As part of his search, he unravelled and published two anti-Qadarite texts (directed against the doctrine of *qadar*, human free will) that he considered to be documents of pre-Muʿtazilite *Kalām* (van Ess 1977). These texts are attributed to ʿAlī b. Abī Ṭālib's grandson Ḥasan b. Muḥammad b. al-Ḥanafiyya (d. between 99/718 and 101/720) and the Umayyad caliph ʿUmar II b. ʿAbd al-ʿAzīz (r. 99/717–101/720). In addition, van Ess drew on another supposedly very early source, the *Qadarite Epistle to Caliph ʿAbd al-Malik b. Marwān* attributed to the famous early Muslim traditionist al-Ḥasan al-Baṣrī (d. 110/728) and written *in support of* human free will. If these texts are authentic and were indeed written in the first Islamic century, as van Ess initially argued, this would make them the earliest Muslim theological texts extant; however, his argumentation was subsequently subjected to harsh criticism (Cook 1981: 107–58; Zimmermann 1984), causing van Ess to modify his original position and admit that these texts are possibly inauthentic or at least that their authenticity cannot be proven (van Ess 1991–7: i. 47, 134–5; ii. 47). As will be discussed herein, these three texts are now generally considered to be pseudepigrapha, compiled later than their claimed date.

The term *kalām* (literally, 'speech'), mentioned several times above, has two distinct meanings which ought to be clearly differentiated. First, it is a particular style of theological argumentation which, to quote van Ess once again, 'talks (*kallama*) with the opponent by asking questions and reducing his position to meaningless alternatives' (van Ess 1975a: 89; cf. van Ess 1976; van Ess 1982: 109; Frank 1992). Second (capitalized as

'*Kalām*' in what follows), it is the kind of Islamic theology—in Arabic: *ʿilm al-Kalām*—that habitually employs this style of argumentation, or at least is within the tradition that does so. (It is a major task of the present volume to trace the historical development of this tradition.) Though the term is often used generically for 'Islamic theology' *tout court*, this usage might be misleading, because there are Islamic theologies (discourses about the divine) distinct from, and in some cases critical of, *Kalām* (e.g. Ḥanbalite theology, Ismāʿīlī theology, Ṣūfī theology, Philosophical theology—i.e. the theological part of metaphysics, often called 'the divine science', *al-ʿilm al-ilāhī*—and so on) and, moreover, because *Kalām* covers both theological and non-theological areas of inquiry (e.g. epistemology and physics).

The question of 'origins', discussed in this chapter, is, therefore, to a large extent the question of the provenance of this particular type of argumentation, its extra-Islamic models (if any), and its emergence and early use in an Islamic context. Secondly, it is also the question of the origins of *ʿilm al-Kalām*, i.e. the particular type of Islamic theology that habitually employs *kalām* in the first sense, and of its most prominent themes (e.g. human free will, *qadar*, vs. divine determinism, *jabr*).

The present chapter will accordingly contain three sections. The first section will discuss the origins of *kalām*-style argumentation and of the term *kalām*. The second will touch on the vexed question of the possible origins of *Kalām* theology (this time from the point of view of its *content*, rather than argumentative technique), focusing on the origins of the *qadar* debate (on which see also the next chapter). Finally, the third section will briefly review the three texts, attributed to first/seventh and early eighth-century authorities and used, as mentioned above, in van Ess's reconstruction of the beginnings of *Kalām* in the 1970s and 1980s, yet now generally believed to be later fabrications.

I The Origins of *Kalām*-Style Argumentation and of the Term *Kalām*

It is undeniable that *kalām*-style argumentation has its deep roots in the religious debate culture of the Middle East in the period prior to and shortly after the Muslim conquests. The Middle East's extraordinary religious diversity—with members of all religions vying for ideological space and with the Christians divided, following the Councils of Ephesus (431), Chalcedon (451), and Constantinople (681), into a number of rival factions (Griffith 2008: 129–40)—fomented debate as a primary means of gaining ideological influence, vindicating one's own beliefs, and refuting those of one's rivals.

Muslims were drawn into these debates shortly after the conquests (Bertaina 2011), while the Muslim tradition itself knows of even earlier examples, such as the religious discussion reportedly held by a group of émigré Muslims with the Abyssinian emperor (the Negus) or the disputation of the Prophet Muḥammad with a delegation of the

Christians of Najrān (Mourad 2009: 63–6; Bertaina 2011: 115–20). Van Ess's contention that until the end of the Umayyad period 'Muslims were still living among a Christian majority, but in spite of this the religious contacts seem to have been weak' (van Ess 1975a: 100) neglects the evidence for such interactions, surviving especially in Syriac (Cook 1980: 41–2; Tannous 2008: 710–12; and more generally Hoyland 1997; Thomas and Roggema 2009).

Though debate culture was ubiquitous in the Middle East in the period under discussion (the Manicheans, for instance, were feared as formidable debaters; Lim 1995: 70–108; Pedersen 2004), it seems possible to define the avenues by which it was assimilated by early Muslim theologians somewhat more precisely. This requires focusing on some specific features of the *kalām* style of argumentation and then tracing these features in the Syriac disputation literature of the time. Much of this groundwork has been undertaken by Michael Cook and Jack Tannous (Cook 1980; Tannous 2008), yielding interesting results.

Cook pointed out that characteristic features of *kalām* argumentation are present in seventh-century Syriac Christological disputations, notably in a Monothelete ('Maronite') document (MS British Library, Add. 7192), containing two sets of Christological queries, addressed to Dyothelete ('Melkite') opponents and dating to the second half of the seventh century, thus excluding the possibility that these Syriac texts were themselves influenced by Muslim *Kalām*.[3]

These Christological queries, which, as Cook shows, have some parallels in anti-Chalcedonian Syriac material as well, invariably begin with a disjunctive question ('Do you believe X, yes or no?' or 'Do you believe X or Y'?) and then proceed methodically to discuss each of the possibilities ('If they say X, they should be asked …; if they say Y, they should be asked … '), either refuting the opponent's response or showing that it in fact agrees with the questioner's own position. As Cook shows, all this is strikingly similar to the kind of argumentation characteristic of early *Kalām* texts, where patterns of the same type (e.g. *in qāla… fa-yuqāl lahu…*, 'If he says X, it should be replied… ') are standard.

In view of these striking structural parallels, Cook concluded that '[the *kalām*] *genre* has the look of a product of the period of Christological schism.… [I]t presupposes in general a situation in which almost everything is agreed and schism turns on the energetic exploitation of doctrinal diacritics [as in Christological controversies]. … What is more, the *genre* could well be a rather late and specialized product of the continuing process of Christological schism that characterizes sixth- and seventh-century Syria' (Cook 1980: 40).[4] Cook further suggested that these patterns could have been adopted by the

[3] The Chalcedonian camp split into Monotheletes/Maronites and Dyotheletes/Melkites in the seventh century, after the monothelete compromise, initially promoted by the Byzantine emperors with the aim of reconciling the Chalcedonian and the anti-Chalcedonian camps, failed, and the Council of Constantinople in 681, mentioned above, ruled in favour of the Dyothelete position.

[4] For a much older example of the *kalām*-style technique (in the second-century CE Marcionite author Apelles) see Pedersen 2004: 222. I am grateful to Patricia Crone for bringing this passage to my attention. The roots of this technique are thus considerably older than the Christological schism.

Muslim community either as a result of Muslims participating in debates with Christians and learning these disputation techniques from them or as a result of Christians, skilled in these disputation techniques, converting to Islam—the two options being, in fact, compatible rather than mutually exclusive (Cook 1980: 40–1).[5]

In an important recent article, Tannous has refined Cook's findings by focusing on the figure of George, the anti-Chalcedonian ('Jacobite') bishop of the Arab tribes (d. 105/724). George's first three Syriac letters, analysed by Tannous, are examples of Jacobite polemic against the Chalcedonians. George's letters similarly challenge Chalcedonian positions with series of disjunctive questions ('if you say X then ...; but if not, then ... '), presenting the opponent with choices each of which is then shown to be either unsatisfactory or identical to the questioner's own view. Tannous also shows how George's arguments are modelled on, and in several cases repeat verbatim, Syriac versions of Greek Christological *aporiai* (the so-called *epaporēmata*) from the sixth and seventh centuries (Tannous 2008: 685–707). Thus, while Cook identified only a handful of Syriac documents featuring '*kalām*-style' argumentation, Tannous (drawing on Uthemann 1981 and Grillmeier 1987: 82–7) was able to contextualize them further as representative examples of a genre of intra-Christian disputation characteristic of sixth- and seventh-century Syria, which moreover is well attested not only in Syriac, but also in Greek.

Tannous's findings are significant for yet another reason. George was bishop over Arab Christian tribes. The tribes in question were, in Syriac terminology, the ʿAqōlāyē (i.e. Arab Christians originally from ʿAqōlā, the region of Kūfa in Iraq, but present in Syria), the Ṭūʿāyē (a confederacy of pastoral Arabs, which, according to Morony, probably included the tribes of Bakr, ʿIjl, Namir, and Taghlib), and the Tanūḵāyē (the Arabic Banū Tanūkh), all converted to Christianity by the Jacobite bishop Aḥūḏemmeh in the sixth century (Morony 1984: 374, 379; Tannous 2008: 709–12). As Tannous notes, it is precisely these three Arab Christian tribes that are said to have attended one of the earliest Christian–Muslim debates on record: the debate between the Jacobite Patriarch John Sedra and the Hagarene (i.e. Muslim) emir in Syria (probably the governor of Homs ʿUmayr ibn Saʿd al-Anṣārī), which reportedly took place on Sunday, 9 May 644 (Hoyland 1997: 459–65; Penn 2008; Roggema 2009; Bertaina 2011: 87–94; the text of the debate was probably written in the early second/eighth century, see Griffith 2008: 36, 77). Moreover, it is significant that even though the *Disputation of Patriarch John and the Emir* does not use *kalām*-style argumentation, the author calls it a 'conversation' (*mamllā*), a Syriac term exactly equivalent to the Arabic term *kalām*.

Tannous therefore puts forward what may be termed an 'Arab Christian hypothesis'. He argues that the Arab Christian (more specifically, it seems, Jacobite) milieu in Syria and Iraq is the most plausible conduit for the transmission of the *kalām*-style

[5] Conversion would seem to be the more likely route (cf. van Ess 1970: 24). This is because no *actual* debate would have proceeded according to the pattern 'If X, then...; if not, then ... ' (as in any *actual* debate the opponent would have chosen only one of the two alternative responses), and hence opportunities to learn the disjunctive argumentation technique merely from attending debates would have been limited.

disputation technique to the Muslim community, and more generally 'for the assimilation of Christian traditions, such as they were, into early Islam' (Tannous 2008: 715). Just as in George of the Arab Tribes one can observe *kalām*-style disputational patterns 'moving' from Greek Christological *aporiai* into Syriac, so also these same patterns could have been easily transferred, via the Arab Christian tribes under George's (and his predecessors') ecclesiastical authority, from Syriac into Christian Arabic and then Muslim Arabic dialectical arsenal, gaining new prominence in what was soon to emerge as Muslim *Kalām*. Tannous's argument thus partially resolves the problem that Michael Morony identified with Cook's article, namely that while providing Christian parallels for *kalām* techniques, it 'does not explain the circumstances that led some Muslims to use such methods also' (Morony 1984: 646). Studying the origins of *kalām* would thus be coextensive with studying the history of Arab Christianity in the first/seventh century—an area of research still insufficiently investigated by scholars, yet no doubt germane to the study of early Islam.

The term *kalām* corresponds, originally, to the Syriac *mamllā*, meaning 'speech', and more specifically 'conversation' or 'disputation' (as in the heading of the *Disputation of Patriarch John and the Emir*) and ultimately to the Greek terms *dialexis*, *dialektos*, or *dialektikē*, all meaning 'disputation' (van Ess 1966: 57–9; Cook 1980: 42; van Ess 1991–7: i. 53; but cf. Pietruschka 2003: 198–9).

It is a moot question how the term came to be identified with theological inquiry as a field, i.e. *ʿilm al-Kalām*, or, to put it another way, how theological inquiry in Islam received a name that originally means 'speech' or 'disputation'. It is clear that though etymologically related, the Greek terms *dialexis* and *theologia* are quite distinct. The situation is different in Syriac, where the Greek stem *leg-/log-* (meaning 'to speak') was habitually translated using forms of the equivalent Syriac root *m-l-l*. Hence 'logic', for instance, was always translated as *mᵉlīlūṯā*, and the compound noun *theologia* had to be translated periphrastically as *mᵉmallᵉlūṯ alāhūṯā* ('speech [regarding] divinity') or, less commonly, *mamllā alāhāyā* ('divine speech') (for the latter expression see Cook 1980: 42 n. 82; another example in Payne Smith 1879–1901: 197). Similarly, *theologos* was translated as *mᵉmallēl alāhāyāṯā*, *mᵉmallēl ʿal alāhā*, or *mᵉmallēl alāhāʾīṯ* ('one who speaks divine things', 'one who speaks about God', or 'one who speaks divinely').[6] Thus in Syriac (as opposed to Greek) *dialexis* and *theologia* already look quite similar: the former is translated as *mamllā*, the latter (at least occasionally) as *mamllā alāhāyā* (the same noun, with the adjective 'divine' added as a qualifier). Still, the fact is that we have no evidence that the term *mamllā*, in and of itself, without the qualifier *alāhāyā*, was ever used in Syriac in the sense of 'theology'; nor was the participle *mᵉmallēl* (or the corresponding agent noun *mᵉmallᵉlānā*), *on its own*, used in the sense of 'theologian'. Thus for the Syriac mind, a translation of the Greek *theologia* would seem to have always required a complement, corresponding to the Greek *theo-*. Consequently, we have no evidence that

6 All these expressions are particularly common as an honorary epithet of Gregory of Nazianzus, the 'Theologian'.

dialexis and *theologia* were conflated in Syriac. So, if not in Syriac, how and where did this conflation, evident in the Muslim term *kalām*, take place?

Building on Tannous's Arab Christian hypothesis, one might propose the following. It seems plausible that the simplification of terminology and the resulting conflation of *dialexis* and *theologia* could have initially occurred in first/seventh-century Christian Arabic discourse. Indeed, from the perspective of Arab Christian onlookers—the ʿAqōlāyē, Ṭūʿāyē, and Tanūḵāyē, attending inter-religious debates with Muslims such as the *mamllā* (disputation) between the Jacobite Patriarch and the Hagarene emir—theology was done primarily by 'spokesmen' (to put it in Arabic, *mutakallimūn*; cf. van Ess 1991–7: i. 50) of the disputing parties. These spokesmen (Christian bishops and monks on the one hand and Muslim officials on the other) acted as both disputants and theologians, these two functions being inextricably linked. Here, for the first time, we have a plausible milieu where the Arabic term *kalām* could have been used simultaneously for disputation and theology, i.e. as a calque for the Syriac *mamllā* both with and without the qualifier *alāhāyā*. This terminology would presumably have been used during the debates themselves by *all* Arabic-speakers in attendance, both Christians and Muslims. Such debates therefore provide the perfect environment where the term *kalām*, with its newly acquired dual meaning, could have been assimilated into Muslim discourse—ultimately to stay there for good.[7]

Despite its heuristic value and intrinsic verisimilitude, Tannous's Arab Christian hypothesis is in need of further testing and corroboration, given that the evidence presently supporting it is mostly circumstantial and comes from somewhat later (early second/eighth-century rather than first/seventh-century) sources—George of the Arab Tribes and the *Disputation of Patriarch John and the Emir*. Though highly suggestive, the philological considerations outlined above are also ultimately inconclusive. Our knowledge of the Arabic idiom of the Arab Christian tribes in first/seventh-century Syria and Iraq is scarce, and so it is impossible to ascertain whether, as suggested here, they were the ones who began using the term *kalām* (without a qualifier) in the dual sense of disputation and theology.[8] Unfortunately, we cannot even be sure that debates of the kind described in the *Disputation of Patriarch John and the Emir* were actually taking place as early as the first Islamic century, and if they were, that Arab Christians would have regularly been in attendance. Given that the actual text of the *Disputation* was probably

[7] If the argument here put forward is sound, it would lend support to Shlomo Pines's suggestion that the term *mutakallimūn* originally referred to professional disputants, charged with the task of defending Islam from arguments of non-Muslims, as well as heretical interpretations of Islam itself (Pines 1971; but cf. van Ess 1975a: 104 n. 64; van Ess 1991–7: i. 49–50).

[8] *Later* Christian Arabic sources are of little help, because when they use the terms *kalām* and *mutakallim* (without a qualifier) for 'theology' and 'theologian' they do so under Muslim influence, and moreover usually refer specifically to *Muslim* theologians (Pietruschka 2003). For Christian theologians, a qualifier is typically used: thus, Gregory of Nazianzus is called in Christian Arabic sources *al-mutakallim ʿalā l-lāhūt* (cf. Syr. *mᵉmallēl ʿal alāhā*), *al-nāṭiq bi-l-ilāhiyyāt*, or *nāṭiq al-ilāhiyyāt* (cf. Syr. *mᵉmallēl alāhāyāṯā*), etc. Some Muslim sources also use *al-mutakallim ʿalā l-lāhūt* as an epithet of Gregory of Nazianzus: see, e.g., the relevant chapters of Mubashshir ibn Fātik's *Mukhtār al-ḥikam* and al-Shahrazūrī's *Nuzhat al-arwāḥ*, dependent on the latter.

written in the early second/eighth century, it is far from obvious that it can be trusted to accurately reflect first/seventh-century social situation (Penn 2008; but see Tannous 2008: 711–12).

This section must therefore end on an inconclusive note. Further research is needed to verify or disprove the Arab Christian hypothesis. Regardless of the actual outcome of this research for the specific question of the origins of *kalām*, the role of Arabic-speaking Christians in Christian–Muslim interactions in the first Islamic century (as well as later) deserves careful consideration, and may produce important results for the study of early Islam.

II Origins of the *Qadar* Debate

The question of the origins of *Kalām* as a discipline—from the perspective of its content rather than disputational form—is even more vexed than the question of the origins of *kalām*-style argumentation. Here much of the older scholarship (beginning with von Kremer 1873: 7–9) argued in favour of the Christian origin of the earliest controversy in the history of *Kalām*: the *qadar* debate. (Other issues, such as the origins of *Kalām* atomism, would have to be left outside the scope of this chapter.)

This argument is based on a number of considerations. First, free will is a fundamental tenet of Christianity (e.g. John of Damascus, *Exposition of the Orthodox Faith*, ch. 44), while the predestinarian Muslims, it is assumed, inherited the fatalistic outlook of pre-Islamic Pagan Arabs (on which see Ringgren 1955). Second, Muslim biographical sources allege that Qadarī leaders (Maʿbad al-Juhanī and Ghaylān al-Dimashqī, on whom see the next chapter) had ties to Christianity (van Ess 1974: 61–7; Rubin 1999: 177–80). Thus, the eminent legal scholar (and a persecutor of the Qadarīs) al-Awzāʿī (d. 157/774) claimed that Maʿbad learned the Qadarī creed from a Christian named Sawsar or Sūsan, who converted to Islam and then reverted to Christianity (Ibn ʿAsākir, *Tārīkh*, 48: 192 and 49: 319).[9] In yet another report, going back to Muslim ibn Yasār (d. 101/719) and his students, Maʿbad was said to 'follow Christian teachings' (*yaqūlu bi-qawl al-naṣārā*, Ibn ʿAsākir, *Tārīkh*, 59: 322). Ghaylān al-Dimashqī is occasionally given the *nisba*

[9] Instead of Sūsan, other sources mention a certain Sasnōye (or Sastōye) ibn Yūnus (or Abū Yūnus) al-Uswārī from Baṣra, who is *not* said to be a former Christian. See al-Firyābī, *Qadar*, 205 [No. 347] and 226 [No. 408]); Ibn Saʿd, *Ṭabaqat*, 9: 264, who adds that this Sasnōye / Sastōye was the husband of Umm Mūsā (cf. van Ess 1978: 371b); and Ibn ʿAsākir, *Tārīkh*, 59: 318–19, who adds that he was a greengrocer (*baqqāl*). The *nisba* al-Uswārī indicates that he was one the *asvārān* / *asāwira*, who were Sasanian cavalrymen and their descendants in the Islamic period; see van Ess 1991–7: ii. 78–84; Zakeri 1995. On this Sasnōye / Sastōye see further van Ess 1974: 61–4; Zakeri 1995: 325–6. As Kevin van Bladel informs me, Sūsan is probably the Middle Persian name Sōšan(s), derived from the Avestan Saošyant (Justi 1895: 284a), the name of the future Zoroastrian saviour. It is therefore somewhat unexpected to find a Christian bearing this name. On the name Sasnōye see Justi 1895: 291b. It is perhaps not altogether impossible that Sasnōye and Sūsan are one and the same individual.

al-Qibṭī, which indicates that he was a *mawlā* (a non-Arab affiliate of an Arab tribe) of Coptic Christian origin. Some anti-Qadarite *ḥadīth*s also allege that Qadarī ideas are of Christian provenance (e.g. Becker 1912: 186).[10] Third, the *Disputation between a Saracen and a Christian*, written in Greek and attributed to the famous Christian theologian John of Damascus, a contemporary of Ghaylān and a fellow Damascene, discusses the issue of human free will versus divine predestination (Sahas 1972: 103–12, 142–9).[11] The 'Saracen' (Muslim) disputant in the dialogue argues for complete divine predestination, including of human sins. Since the predestinarian position is identified as being characteristic of Islam, it follows that the anti-predestinarian (Qadarī) view must have been imported from an outside source, i.e. presumably from the Christian tradition. It is also assumed that the *Disputation* is a testimony to Christian–Muslim disputations in the Umayyad period on the subject of free will and predestination, and moreover that these disputations (which might have pre-dated John of Damascus) influenced the Qadarī position and triggered the *qadar* controversy within Islam (Becker 1912: 183–6).

Several problems with this argument have been identified. Similarities between Christian and Qadarī positions on free will and related subjects (e.g. that God is not the cause of evil) do not, of course, prove dependence of the latter upon the former. The isolated reports tying Maʿbad and Ghaylān to Christianity are unverifiable and perhaps too anecdotal in nature to prove anything. Moreover, they display an obvious agenda of discrediting the Qadarī position by portraying it as alien to Islam and may thus be untrustworthy.[12] Finally, it is unlikely that the *Disputation between a Saracen and a Christian* is a work of John of Damascus. It was probably authored by (or at least reflects the ideas of) the early third/ninth-century Arabic-writing Christian theologian Theodore Abū Qurra, who is known to have criticized Muslim (and Manichean) predestinarian views in his other works (Griffith 1987a). Rather than triggering the *qadar* controversy within Islam, the *Disputation* already reflects an advanced stage of that controversy. Moreover, its author seems to have consciously appropriated Qadarī arguments and terminology to refute Muslim predestinarian beliefs. Thus, any similarities between the *Disputation* and the Qadariyya are due to Qadarī influence on the *Disputation* rather than the other way round (Griffith 1987a: 82–91). It is, moreover, striking that the subject of free will is relatively infrequently attested in Christian–Muslim disputations and Christian polemical treatises in Syriac and Arabic directed against Islam (for some exceptions see

[10] But cf. the famous *ḥadīth* which compares the Qadariyya to the 'Magians of this community' (van Ess 1975b: 137–48; cf. Stroumsa and Stroumsa 1988: 54–5).

[11] The Greek term for free will, *to autexousion*, is better translated as 'sovereignty over oneself', i.e. the power to determine one's own actions. In Syriac, this term is sometimes rendered as *m^eshall^eṭūṯ* (or *shallīṭūṯ*) *b-yāṯā* (thus in Jacob of Edessa, see Cook 1981: 149 and 217 n. 49). Cf. al-Ghazālī's expression *lā ḥukm lahu fī nafsihi* (al-Ghazālī, *Iḥyā'*, Book 35, *shaṭr* 1, *bayān* 2, 4: 345), which is used precisely in the sense of 'having no sovereignty over oneself,' i.e. having no free will.

[12] On the other hand, the biased nature of these reports does not necessarily make them factually untrue. See also Tannous 2010: 555 n. 1344, who points out that it is, in fact, quite unusual for Islamic heresiographers to characterize a teaching as being Christian in origin; Tannous thus tends to regard these reports as credible.

Griffith 1987a; Griffith 1987b; Griffith 1990). Thus, while it still remains a possibility that Christian ideas could have influenced the Qadariyya (possibly, through Christian converts to Islam 'naively solving the theological problem posed by the ambiguity of the [Qurʾān] with [Christian] categories familiar to themselves'—van Ess 1978: 371b), this cannot at present be positively proven.

Finally, something needs to be said regarding Cook's intriguing suggestion that Muslim predestinarianism 'may represent a doctrinal fixation of... a thoroughly determinist mood', characteristic of the Late Antique and early Islamic Middle East (Cook 1981: 150–2, 156; cf. Morony 1984: 392–3, 424–9, 633–4; Tannous 2008: 713–15).[13] This observation raises the possibility that the *qadar* debate within Islam is, essentially, an Islamization of older debates between champions of free will (Christians, Jews, and Zoroastrians) and proponents of various forms of determinism—e.g. astral fatalism, characteristic of Sasanian Iraq and hence often called 'Chaldeanism' (Syr. *kaldāyūṯā*), the alleged Manichean determinism (Stroumsa and Stroumsa 1988; Pedersen 2004: 171–6), or the widespread belief, found in Christian circles, that every individual's lifespan and moment of death are predetermined by God (Cook 1981: 145–7; Munitiz 2001). The Manichean challenge to early Islam may have been especially significant in both triggering and shaping the 'structure' of the *qadar* debate (Stroumsa and Stroumsa 1988: 51–8).

The Qurʾānic emphasis on God's all-pervasive determinative power provides a theistic antidote to the non-theistic fatalism of pre-Islamic Pagan Arabs, which might itself have been influenced by Sasanian 'Chaldeanism' (Morony 1984: 393, 427, 481, 483). In providing this antidote, however, the Qurʾān effectively replaces one type of determinism by another, thus inviting the same kind of anti-predestinarian reaction in an Islamic milieu. Similarly, by insisting that God is the creator of all things, the Qurʾān implicitly raises the perennial monotheistic problem of whether God is also responsible for evil (on the Christian response, heavily influenced by the Platonic tradition and forged, in part, in the course of anti-Manichean polemic, see e.g. John of Damascus, *Exposition of the Orthodox Faith*, ch. 92, 'On that God is not the cause of evils'). It is precisely this question that was the bone of contention in the polemic between the Qadarīs and the predestinarians: the former refused to acknowledge God's responsibility for evil (particularly human sinful actions), while the latter insisted that God is responsible for all things, evil included.

If Cook's theory is correct, one can expect that both Muslim Qadarīs and Muslim predestinarians would have used arguments originally employed in the older polemic over determinism. There are some indications that this might indeed be the case. For example, as Cook shows, the anti-Chalcedonian ('Jacobite') theologian Jacob of Edessa (d. 89/

[13] Tannous cites evidence that George of the Arab Tribes engaged in a debate with Pagan Arabs who were adherents of astral determinism. He calls these Arabs *ḥanpē* (Pagans), a term used by Syriac Christian authors from the first/seventh century on also for the Muslims. The Syriac practice of referring to Muslims as *ḥanpē* is not fully accounted for by the Muslim self-designation *ḥanīf*; after all, one also needs to explain *why* Syriac-speakers associated Muslims with Pagans. Could it be that from the Syriac Christian perspective, Muslims were *ḥanpē* (Pagans), among other things, on account of their predestinarian views?

708), writing in Syriac, cites a number of verses, employed by his (presumably Christian) determinist adversaries in support of their position. One of these verses is Psalm 58: 3, 'The wicked are estranged from the womb (Syr. *men karsā*); they go astray from the womb (Syr. *men marbᶜᵉā*), speaking lies.' Jacob's opponents presumably interpreted this verse as meaning that one's destiny in the afterlife is fixed (predetermined) already in the mother's womb (Cook 1981: 146).[14] Similarly, in the *Qadarite Epistle to Caliph ʿAbd al-Malik b. Marwān* (discussed in Section III below), (Pseudo)-Ḥasan al-Baṣrī accuses his predestinarian adversaries of misinterpreting the Qurʾānic verse 'Among them there are the damned and the felicitous' (*fa-minhum shaqī wa-saʿīd*, Qurʾān 11: 105) as teaching that one's destiny in the afterlife is fixed in the mother's womb (*fī buṭūn ummahātihim*, ed. Mourad 2006: 291 / trans. Rippin and Knappert 1986: 120–1; cf. Ibn Masʿūd's saying 'Damned is he who was damned in his mother's womb,' on which see van Ess 1975b: 20–30). Significantly, however, unlike the biblical prooftext, the Qurʾānic verse does not mention womb at all, and the context patently speaks about the Day of Judgement rather than the development of a foetus. The predestinarian exegesis of the Qurʾānic verse is therefore forced, and this, in Cook's view, betrays the influence of the biblical context, originally employed by Christian predestinarians and subsequently rather mechanically transferred onto the Qurʾānic verse in question (Cook 1981: 148).

Then there is the well-known predestinarian *ḥadīth*, also transmitted on the authority of Ibn Masʿūd but distinct from the saying cited above. According to this *ḥadīth*, while the foetus is in the womb, an angel records its future source of livelihood (*rizq*), lifespan (*ajal*), activity (*ʿamal*), and whether the person will be 'damned or felicitous' (*shaqī aw saʿīd*) in the afterlife (van Ess 1977b: 1–20). As shown by Goldziher (1878: 353–4 n. 6) and Ringgren (1955: 119–20), this *ḥadīth* has a fairly close Talmudic parallel (Niddāh 16b), where Laylāh, 'the angel in charge of conception,' takes a drop (i.e. of semen; cf. the Qurʾānic *nuṭfa*) and places it before God, and God declares its future, specifically whether the person will be 'mighty or weak, wise or foolish, rich or poor.' The Talmudic story emphasizes, however, that God does not predetermine whether the person will be righteous or unrighteous, for as Rabbi Ḥanīnā bar Ḥammā (early third century CE) put it, 'everything is in the power of Heaven [i.e. predetermined by God] except fear of Heaven' (van Ess 1977b: 16; Cook 1981: 148). Here we have an example where the Muslim predestinarian camp draws on an earlier tradition, attested in a Jewish source, which however specifically rejects predestination of human actions.

To conclude: while there seems to be little evidence that Christian polemic against Islam directly influenced the *qadar* controversy, as was suggested by older scholarship (e.g. Becker 1912), the *qadar* controversy can be plausibly linked to (and seen as a continuation of) older debates over various forms of determinism, current in the Late Antique and early Islamic Middle East and often crossing religious boundaries, with Christians and Manicheans being the most significant players. A comprehensive analysis of all

[14] Interestingly, the same verse is cited in the *Disputation between a Saracen and a Christian*, yet its author (Theodore Abū Qurra?) takes the predestinarian sting out by claiming that the 'womb' is the womb of baptism (Sahas 1972: 146–7)!

types of polemic over determinism in the Late Antique and early Islamic Middle East in comparison to the *qadar* controversy is still an important desideratum, which may shed light on the emergence of this controversy within Islam.

III Three 'Early' Texts on *Qadar*, Attributed to Ḥasan b. Muḥammad b. al-Ḥanafiyya, ʿUmar b. ʿAbd al-ʿAzīz, and al-Ḥasan al-Baṣrī

Finally, we need to consider the three documents drawn upon extensively by van Ess in his reconstruction of the 'beginnings' of Islamic theology. Two of the three—(Pseudo)-Ḥasan b. Muḥammad b. al-Ḥanafiyya's *Questions against the Qadarites* (to use the convenient title proposed by Cook 1980: 32) and (Pseudo)-ʿUmar b. al-ʿAzīz's *Epistle*—are rare examples of predestinarian *Kalām* (cf. Cook 1981: 141–3), though only the former uses the characteristic *kalām* disputation technique ('Tell us about ...; if they say X, say to them ...; if they say Y, say to them ... '). These two documents are preserved in later compilations—a refutation by the Zaydī imam al-Hādī ilā l-ḥaqq (d. 298/911) and Abū Nuʿaym al-Iṣfahānī's (d. 430/1038) *Ḥilyat al-awliyāʾ* respectively—and are edited, translated, and commented upon by van Ess (1977).

Van Ess considered both documents to be authentic and mounted arguments in favour of their authenticity. He dated the *Questions against the Qadarites* to between 72/691 and 80/699, based on his analysis of Ḥasan b. Muḥammad b. al-Ḥanafiyya's life and the assumption that the *Questions* must pre-date the third document under discussion—the *Qadarite Epistle* attributed to al-Ḥasan al-Baṣrī—since the author of the *Questions* appears to be 'not yet familiar' with the latter's ideas (van Ess 1977: 17–18). For (Pseudo-)ʿUmar's *Epistle*, van Ess dismisses as 'rather unlikely' the possibility that it might have been composed before ʿUmar's accession to the caliphal throne. This leaves him with the two and a half years of ʿUmar's reign (99/717–101/720). The most plausible date, according to van Ess, is 101/720, because of the possibility that a 'vague recollection' of the *Epistle* survives in the legendary reports indicating that after interrogating Ghaylān al-Dimashqī and shortly before his own death, ʿUmar dictated a letter on *qadar* to the military provinces (*ajnād*), which, because of his death, was never sent out (van Ess 1977: 131–2, 188, 199; cf. van Ess 1971–2). Van Ess's arguments for the early dating and authenticity of both documents were criticized and largely discredited by Cook and Zimmermann (Cook 1981: 124–44; Zimmermann 1984). Cook concedes that though inauthentic, the *Questions* is still an archaic text (no later than the mid-second/eighth century—Cook 1980: 32–3), possibly originating from the Murjiʾite milieu in Kūfa (Cook 1981: 144). (Pseudo)-ʿUmar's *Epistle*, likewise inauthentic and containing interpolations of secondary material (Cook 1981: 124–9, 136), probably also originated in the second/eighth century and might likewise 'at one time have been in Murjiʾite hands' (Cook 1981: 129–30, 144). By contrast, Zimmermann suggests 'late second-century Baṣra' as the place where the search for the real author and addressees of the two texts should begin (because of the concept of *nafādh*, 'inescapable implementation' of God's foreknowledge, common to both—Zimmermann 1984: 441). Thus, though both Cook and Zimmermann reject van Ess's arguments for the two documents' authenticity, they disagree on the likely milieu where they might have been produced. The question therefore is in need of further study.

From the perspective of their content, both documents seek to discredit the Qadarite worldview. The *Questions* does this by setting up a series of challenges to the Qadarite opponents. These challenges are typically based on specific Qurʾānic verses that speak about God determining human actions, leading some people to guidance and others to perdition (as well as to Hell and Paradise), inspiring faith in some and hardening the hearts of others, foretelling (and consequently determining) future events, and so on (cf. 'Verzeichnis der Koranverse' in van Ess 1977: 259–63). (Pseudo)-ʿUmar's *Epistle* presents the Qadarites as putting forward the claim that in virtue of their free will human beings are able to act contrary to what God foreknows to be the case, thus 'falsifying' (*radd*, following the translation in Cook 1981: 126) and 'going beyond' (*khurūj*) God's knowledge. By refuting this claim, the author of the *Epistle* seeks to discredit his opponents' initial thesis that human beings have free will.

Let us now move on to the third document under consideration, the *Qadarite Epistle to Caliph ʿAbd al-Malik b. Marwān*, attributed to the famous early Muslim traditionist al-Ḥasan al-Baṣrī (d. 110/728). Unlike the two texts just discussed, it is written in support of human free will and, were it authentic, would be the only surviving Qadarite document. It is preserved in three seventh/fourteenth–eighth/fifteenth-century manuscripts, two of them in Istanbul and one in Tehran,[15] and in excerpts in ʿAbd al-Jabbār's (d. 415/1024) *Faḍl al-iʿtizāl wa-ṭabaqāt al-muʿtazila* and some later sources dependent on the latter. As shown by Mourad (2006: 186–7, 238–9), none of these sources represents the original version of the *Qadarite Epistle*, which must have been longer than any of the surviving witnesses. Significantly, the excerpts in ʿAbd al-Jabbār only partially overlap with the manuscripts and include material not preserved in any of them. Of the three manuscripts, the Tehran copy, conveniently edited by Mourad along with ʿAbd al-Jabbār's excerpts (Mourad 2006: 284–302), seems to stand closest to the original version. It therefore merits special attention.

Van Ess argued for the *Qadarite Epistle*'s authenticity and attempted to date it to between 75/694 (when al-Ḥajjāj b. Yūsuf, at whose request it was allegedly written, became governor of Iraq) and 80/699 (the date of Ibn al-Ashʿath's revolt) (van Ess 1977: 18, 27–9). This early dating was discredited by Cook and Zimmermann, both of whom also offered arguments against the document's authenticity (Cook 1981: 117–23; Zimmermann 1984). Notably, van

[15] Sabine Schmidtke kindly informs me that a fourth manuscript of the *Qadarite Epistle* has now been discovered in a private library in Yemen.

Ess's contention that the *Qadarite Epistle* must be early and authentic because it does not quote predestinarian *ḥadīth* and hence pre-dates the period of genesis of such *ḥadīth* is refuted by Cook, who points out that the *Qadarite Epistle* deliberately refrains from relying on *ḥadīth* rather than pre-dates its genesis and that, moreover, one of the excerpts preserved by ʿAbd al-Jabbār does in fact quote a predestinarian *ḥadīth* and identifies it as such (Cook 1981: 121; cf. Mourad 2006: 200–1, 300–1).[16] It should also be noted that the Tehran manuscript (unavailable to both van Ess and Cook) includes an important polemical passage against the 'innovators' who have introduced new teachings and perverted the religion (ed. Mourad 2006: 284–5). It seems likely that these 'innovators' (*muḥdithūn*)—one of the many terms used for the author's opponents—are the predestinarian *ḥadīth* transmitters (*muḥaddithūn*), and that the author might be deliberately exploiting the fact that the two words are indistinguishable in the unvocalized Arabic script.

While accepting that al-Ḥasan was a firm believer in free will throughout his life, Mourad argues conclusively that the *Qadarite Epistle* is a later forgery (Mourad 2006: 172, 175, 194–239). It includes several obvious anachronisms, such as the use of the term *al-salaf* ('predecessors'), developed in the late second/eighth and third/ninth centuries as a collective designation of the first three generations of Muslims. Given the remarkable similarities between the *Qadarite Epistle* and the third/ninth-century Zaydī theology pointed out by Mourad (especially al-Qāsim b. Ibrāhīm's *Refutation of the Predestinarians*), it seems unavoidable that there is a connection between the two. Mourad argues plausibly that it is the *Qadarite Epistle* that is influenced by Zaydī theology rather than the other way round. He suggests that the *Qadarite Epistle* was forged by a Muʿtazilī theologian in the late fourth/tenth century, influenced by Zaydī theology and possibly a member of ʿAbd al-Jabbār's circle (Mourad 2006: 236–8).

Mourad's late dating has the distinct advantage of explaining why there is no trace of references to the *Qadarite Epistle* before the late fourth/tenth century. Nonetheless, an earlier, third/ninth-century date contemporary with, or slightly later than, al-Qāsim b. Ibrāhīm would also seem consistent with the evidence at hand and perhaps, in other respects, more plausible than the late fourth/tenth-century one. In his review of Mourad's book, Madelung argued that the *Qadarite Epistle* reflects the 'asymmetrical view' on *qadar*, attributed to al-Ḥasan al-Baṣrī (and the Qadariyya in general) by early authorities—namely the position that only human sins, but not their praiseworthy actions, are excluded from divine predestination. This view, Madelung claims, must have become obsolete by the time when Mourad claims the *Qadarite Epistle* was forged (Madelung 2007: 159–60; cf. van Ess 1977: 28). Nevertheless, al-Qāsim b. Ibrāhīm's *Refutation* also reflects this 'asymmetrical view', as duly noted by Mourad (2006: 232), and so does (Theodore Abū Qurra's?) *Disputation between a Saracen and a Christian*, discussed in Section II above (Sahas 1972: 103–4, 142–3). This implies that this asymmetrical view had not yet become obsolete, at least in some circles, in the third/ninth

[16] Another possible allusion to a *ḥadīth* is the phrase *jarat* (or *jaffat*) *al-aqlām bi-mā anā lāq*^{in} (ed. Mourad 2006: 291); cf. the *ḥadīth* recorded in al-Bukhārī's *Ṣaḥīḥ*, *Kitāb al-nikāḥ*: *yā Abā Hurayra, jaffa l-qalam bi-mā anta lāq*^{in}.

century, and hence that this is a plausible date for when the *Qadarite Epistle* was forged. The considerable parallelism between this document and the *Disputation between a Saracen and a Christian* (Griffith 1987a: 90) is another argument in favour of an earlier, third/ninth-century dating of the *Qadarite Epistle*.[17] This issue is not taken up in Mourad's book and deserves to be explored further.

If all three texts are later forgeries, as seems highly probable, the unavoidable conclusion is that we simply do not have *Kalām* documents from the first Islamic century. The ever so elusive 'Anfänge' of Islamic theology recede into the 'darkness of unknowing' from which they once seemed to have emerged.

Bibliography

Becker, C. H. (1912). 'Christliche Polemik und islamische Dogmenbildung'. *Zeitschrift für Assyriologie und verwandte Gebiete* 26: 175–95 [reprinted in C. H. Becker (1924–32). *Islamstudien: Vom Werden und Wesen der islamischen Welt*. 2 vols. Leipzig: Quelle & Meyer, i. 432–49; English trans.: C. H. Becker (2004). 'Christian Polemic and the Formation of Islamic Dogma'. In R. Hoyland (ed.), *Muslims and Others in Early Islamic Society*. Aldershot: Variorum, 241–57].

Bertaina, D. (2011). *Christian and Muslim Dialogues: The Religious Uses of a Literary Form in the Early Islamic Middle East*. Piscataway, NJ: Gorgias.

Cook, M. A. (1980). 'The Origins of Kalām'. *Bulletin of the School of Oriental and African Studies* 43: 32–43 [reprinted in M. Cook (2004). *Studies in the Origins of Early Islamic Culture and Tradition*. Ashgate: Variorum].

Cook, M. A. (1981). *Early Muslim Dogma: A Source-Critical Study*. Cambridge and New York: Cambridge University Press.

van Ess, J. (1966). *Die Erkenntnislehre des ʿAḍudaddīn al-Īcī: Übersetzung und Kommentar des 1. Buches seiner Mawāqif*. Wiesbaden: Steiner.

van Ess, J. (1970). 'The Logical Structure of Islamic Theology'. In G. E. von Grunebaum (ed.), *Logic in Classical Islamic Culture*. Wiesbaden: Harrassowitz, 21–50.

van Ess, J. (1971–2). 'Umar II and his Epistle against the Qadarīya'. *Abr Nahrain* 12: 19–26.

van Ess, J. (1974). 'Maʿbad al-Ǧuhanī'. In R. Gramlich (ed.), *Islamwissenschaftliche Abhandlungen: Fritz Meier zum 60. Geburtstag*. Wiesbaden: Steiner, 49–77.

van Ess, J. (1975a). 'The Beginnings of Islamic Theology'. In J. E. Murdoch and E. D. Sylla (eds.), *The Cultural Context of Medieval Learning*. Dordrecht and Boston: Reidel, 87–111.

van Ess, J. (1975b). *Zwischen Ḥadīṯ und Theologie: Studien zum Entstehen prädestinatianischer Überlieferung*. Berlin and New York: Walter de Gruyter.

van Ess, J. (1976). 'Disputationspraxis in der islamischen Theologie: Eine vorläufige Skizze'. *Revue des études islamiques* 44: 23–60.

van Ess, J. (1977). *Anfänge muslimischer Theologie: Zwei antiqadaritische Traktate aus dem ersten Jahrhundert der Hiǧra*. Beirut and Wiesbaden: Franz Steiner.

van Ess, J. (1978) [originally published in an encyclopedia fascicle in 1974]. art. 'Ḳadariyya'. *Encyclopaedia of Islam*². Leiden: Brill. Vol. iv, 368a–372a.

[17] Compare the way both texts treat the issue of the child of adultery (Mourad 2006: 234–5 and Sahas 1972: 144–5).

van Ess, J. (1982). 'The Early Development of Kalām'. In G. H. A. Juynboll (ed.), *Studies on the First Century of Islamic Society*. Carbondale and Edwardsville: Southern Illinois University Press, 109–23, 230–41.

van Ess, J. (1991–7). *Theologie und Gesellschaft im 2. und 3. Jahrhundert Hidschra: Eine Geschichte des religiösen Denkens im frühen Islam*. 6 vols. Berlin: de Gruyter.

al-Firyābī (*Qadar*). *Kitāb al-Qadar*, ed. ʿAbd Allāh b. Ḥamad al-Manṣūr. al-Riyāḍ: Aḍwāʾ al-salaf, 1997.

Frank, R. M. (1992). 'The Science of Kalām'. *Arabic Sciences and Philosophy* 2: 7–37.

al-Ghazālī, Abū Ḥāmid (*Iḥyāʾ*). *Iḥyāʾ ʿulūm al-dīn*. 5 vols. Cairo: al-Maktaba al-tawfīqiyya, n.d.

Goldziher, I. (1887). 'Ueber muhammedanische Polemik gegen Ahl al-Kitâb'. *Zeitschrift der deutschen morgenländischen Gesellschaft* 32: 341–87.

Griffith, S. H. (1987a). 'Free Will in Christian *kalām*: The Doctrine of Theodore Abū Qurrah'. *Parole de l'Orient* 14: 79–107 [reprinted in S. H. Griffith (1992). *Arabic Christianity in the Monasteries of Ninth-Century Palestine*. Aldershot: Variorum].

Griffith, S. H. (1987b). 'Free Will in Christian *kalām*: Moshe bar Kepha against the Teachings of the Muslims'. *Le Muséon* 100: 143–59.

Griffith, S. H. (1990). 'Free Will in Christian *kalām*: Chapter XVIII of the *Summa Theologiae Arabica*'. In R. Schulz and M. Görg (eds.), *Lingua restituta orientalis: Festgabe für Julius Assfalg*. Wiesbaden: Harrassowitz, 129–34.

Griffith, S. H. (2008). *The Church in the Shadow of the Mosque: Christians and Muslims in the World of Islam*. Princeton: Princeton University Press.

Grillmeier, A. (1987). *Christ in Christian Tradition*. Vol. ii/1. English translation by P. Allen and J. Cawte. London and Oxford: Mowbray.

Hoyland, R. G. (1997). *Seeing Islam as Others Saw It: A Survey and Evaluation of Christian, Jewish and Zoroastrian Writings on Early Islam*. Princeton: Darwin Press.

Ibn ʿAsākir (*Tārīkh*). *Tārīkh madīnat Dimashq*. 80 vols. Beirut: Dār al-fikr, 1995–2001.

Ibn Saʿd (*Ṭabaqāt*). *Kitāb al-Ṭabaqāt al-kabīr*, ed. ʿAlī Muḥammad ʿUmar. 10 vols. Cairo: Maktabat al-Khānjī, 2001.

Justi, F. (1895). *Iranisches Namenbuch*. Marburg: N. G. Elwert.

Lim, R. (1995). *Public Disputation, Power and Social Order in Late Antiquity*. Berkeley: University of California Press.

Madelung, W. (2007). [Review of Mourad 2006]. *Bulletin of the School of Oriental and African Studies* 70: 157–60.

Morony, M. (1984). *Iraq after the Muslim Conquest*. Princeton: Princeton University Press [reprint: Piscataway, NJ: Gorgias, 2005].

Mourad, S. A. (2006). *Early Islam between Myth and History: Al-Ḥasan al-Baṣrī (d. 110H/728CE) and the Formation of His Legacy in Classical Islamic Scholarship*. Leiden: Brill.

Mourad, S. A. (2009). 'Christians and Christianity in the *Sīra* of Muḥammad'. In Thomas and Roggema 2009: 57–71.

Munitiz, J. A. (2001). 'The Predetermination of Death: The Contribution of Anastasios of Sinai and Nikephoros Blemmydes to a Perennial Byzantine Problem'. *Dumbarton Oaks Papers* 55: 9–20.

Payne Smith, R. (1879–1901). *Thesaurus Syriacus*. 2 vols. Oxford: Clarendon Press.

Pedersen, N. A. (2004). *Demonstrative Proof in Defence of God: A Study of Titus of Bostra's Contra Manichaeos: The Work's Sources, Aims and Relation to its Contemporary Theology*. Leiden: Brill.

Penn, M. P. (2008). '*John and the Emir*: A New Introduction, Edition and Translation'. *Le Muséon* 121/1–2: 65–91.
Pietruschka, U. (2003). 'Zu den Begriffen *kalām* und *mutakallim* in christlichem Kontext'. In W. Beltz, U. Pietruschka, and J. Tubach (eds.), *Sprache und Geist: Peter Nagel zum 65. Geburtstag*. Halle (Saale): Martin-Luther-Universität Halle-Wittenberg, 185–99.
Pines, S. (1971). 'A Note on an Early Meaning of the Term *mutakallim*'. *Israel Oriental Studies* 1: 224–40 [reprinted in S. Pines (1996). *Studies in the History of Arabic Philosophy (The Collected Works of Shlomo Pines*, vol. iii), ed. S. Stroumsa. Jerusalem: Magnes].
Ringgren, H. (1955). *Studies in Arabian Fatalism*. Uppsala: Lundequistska bokhandeln.
Rippin, A., and J. Knappert (1986). *Textual Sources for the Study of Islam*. Chicago: University of Chicago Press.
Roggema, B. (2009). '*The Disputation of John and the Emir*'. In Thomas and Roggema 2009: 782–5.
Rubin, U. (1999). *Between Bible and Qur'ān: The Children of Israel and the Islamic Self-Image*. Princeton: Darwin Press.
Sahas, D. J. (1972). *John of Damascus on Islam: The 'Heresy of the Ishmaelites'*. Leiden: Brill.
Stroumsa, S., and G. G. Stroumsa (1988). 'Aspects of Anti-Manichaean Polemics in Late Antiquity and under Early Islam'. *Harvard Theological Review* 81: 37–58.
Tannous, J. (2008). 'Between Christology and Kalām? The Life and Letters of George, Bishop of the Arab Tribes'. In G. Kiraz (ed.), *Malphono w-Rabo d-Malphone: Studies in Honor of Sebastian P. Brock*. Piscataway, NJ: Gorgias, 671–716.
Tannous, J. (2010). *Syria between Byzantium and Islam: Making Incommensurables Speak*. Ph. D. dissertation, Princeton University.
Thomas, D., and B. Roggema (eds.) (2009). *Christian-Muslim Relations: A Bibliographical History*, vol. i (600–900). Leiden: Brill.
Uthemann, K.-H. (1981). 'Syllogistik im Dienst der Orthodoxie: Zwei unedierte Texte byzantinischer Kontroverstheologie des 6. Jahrhunderts'. *Jahrbuch der Österreichischen Byzantinistik* 30: 103–12.
von Kremer, A. (1873). *Culturgeschichtliche Streifzüge auf dem Gebiete des Islams*. Leipzig: F. A. Brockhaus.
Walker, J. T. (2006). *The Legend of Mar Qardagh: Narrative and Christian Heroism in Late Antique Iraq*. Berkeley, Los Angeles, and London: University of California Press.
Zakeri, M. (1995). *Sāsānid Soldiers in Early Muslim Society: The Origins of 'Ayyārān and Futuwwa*. Wiesbaden: Harrassowitz.
Zimmermann, F. W. (1984). [Review of van Ess 1977]. *International Journal of Middle East Studies* 16/3: 437–41.

CHAPTER 2

THE EARLY QADARIYYA

STEVEN C. JUDD

THE Qadariyya were one of the earliest identifiable theological movements in Islam. The movement was short-lived and most of those identified with it lived during the Marwānid period (64/684–132/750). At times, Umayyad authorities tolerated (and possibly embraced) Qadarī views, while at other times they viewed the Qadariyya as heretics and even as a threat to the regime itself. Eventually, the movement's theological views became entangled with attitudes of political dissent, inspiring more intense persecution from the Umayyads and causing the Qadariyya to adopt a more militant stance. Their direct involvement in the third *fitna* (126/744–130/747) inextricably linked the movement to a particular political faction, led by Yazīd b. al-Walīd (d. 126/744). The defeat of Yazīd's successors ultimately led to the decline of the Qadariyya. However, many of their views re-emerged as tenets of the Muʿtazilites, who thrived during the early ʿAbbāsid era.

Sources for reconstructing both the theological views of the Qadariyya and the political and scholarly activities of principal Qadarī leaders are sparse and at times problematic. With the exception, perhaps, of the documents discussed in the previous chapter (Chapter 1), there are no extant Qadarī sources. There are no known Qadarī creeds or theological treatises, and none of the letters ascribed to Qadarī authorities has survived either.

Consequently, it is necessary to rely on anti-Qadarī sources to glean the doctrines of the movement. Several sources are useful in this regard, though their biases must be acknowledged. The *Kitāb al-Qadar* by al-Firyābī (d. 301/913) describes Qadarī views extensively in order to refute them. In addition, many of the standard *ḥadīth* collections have sections on *qadar*, which mostly contain *ḥadīth* undermining Qadarī views. The heresiographical literature also preserves descriptions of Qadarī beliefs, though again in a context devoted to their condemnation. Finally, biographical sources include discussions of notable Qadarī leaders and often include descriptions of their views. These sources are somewhat problematic, however, because of their late provenance and because, as will be demonstrated, the biographical record was sometimes manipulated to sanitize particular scholars who may have been associated with the movement.

Keeping in mind the limitations imposed by the available sources, the remainder of this chapter will provide a description of Qadarī theological doctrines, followed by a discussion of the views and activities of several prominent Qadarī leaders, along with an explanation of the changing nature of the Qadarī movement and of the reasons for its prompt disappearance from the theological stage.

While Qadarī leaders produced no clear expositions of their views, the core tenets of the movement are relatively straightforward. The Qadarīs held that humans are responsible for their actions, that God does not predetermine all human choices, and that humans have some form of free will. The term Qadariyya reflects this, deriving from the movement's assertion that humans possess *qadar*, the ability to decide or determine their actions. The application of the term *qadar* is itself potentially confusing, since Qurʾānic and other references suggest that *qadar* rested with God rather than with humans, implying a predestinarian doctrine instead. Despite the potential ambiguity about who possesses *qadar*, it is clear that the Qadariyya advocated for human volition, at least in regard to sinful behaviour.

The impetus for the Qadarī position that humans have free will was their determination that evil could not come from God. Consequently, humans' evil deeds must derive from some other source, namely their own volition. While later Muʿtazilite thinkers argued in increasingly sophisticated ways about whether human responsibility for sin implied that humans actually created their acts, potentially compromising the exclusivity of God's creative power, the Qadarīs' discussion was generally more rudimentary, emphasizing simply that humans were responsible for their sins. There was some disagreement about whether human volition also produced meritorious deeds, or whether such deeds came from God. However, this discussion appears rarely and may have been a later accretion, complicating the simpler doctrinal position the Qadariyya advocated. There is no evidence that the Qadariyya engaged in a thorough contemplation of the implications of human free will for divine power. Given the paucity of available sources, it is possible that such discussions took place in now lost sources. Extant sources, however, focus more on the moral demand for accountability for sin.

Aside from their assertion of human volition, there appears to be no other unifying doctrine shared by those labelled as Qadariyya. Practically nothing is preserved about Qadarī views on issues such as the divine attributes, the nature of the afterlife, or even about how God will judge humans for the sins for which the Qadarīs declare them responsible. The Qadariyya category itself does not appear as a major heading in the heresiographical sources. Instead, Qadarīs are subsumed under other categories, based on their views on issues such as *irjāʾ*, the deferment of judgement of sinners (al-Ashʿarī, *Maqalāt*, 132–41, 154; al-Baghdādī, *Farq*, 202–30). The marginality of the Qadariyya in these sources raises a number of questions, some of which will be addressed in this chapter. In particular, one must ask how significant the Qadarīs were if they did not merit the same attention as other early theological movements such as the Khawārij, ʿAlids, and Murjiʾa. Theologically, were they a distinct sectarian movement or were views on *qadar* minor variations within other sects? Also, why do the Qadarīs appear more prominently in the historical and biographical sources than in theological texts? Were they merely a political movement clothed in theological garb?

One of the difficulties in assessing the Qadariyya stems from the lack of clear leadership or coherent organization in the movement. As the discussion herein will illustrate, a number of Qadarī leaders were later subsumed by other movements, especially the Muʿtazilites. Other Qadarī leaders were condemned and isolated in both the historical and theological sources after their association with the events of the third *fitna*. Religious movements that lack compelling, charismatic leadership and whose legacy is tainted by failure do not fare well in later sources. As a result, details of Qadarī doctrine and the extent of its following are elusive in the extant sources.

The debate over human free will in early Islam has attracted modern scholarly attention. Much of this attention has focused on the question of origins. Some modern works emphasize the contrast between Qadarī views and traditional Arab fatalism or ancient Iranian notions of time, which were more cyclical (Watt 1973: 88–9). More often, modern scholars, to some extent following medieval Arabic sources, have emphasized the influence Christian theological debates, particularly within the Syrian church, wielded over early Islamic thought.

While the question of origins and influences is interesting, it ultimately distracts from the basic doctrinal problem the Qadarīs tried to address. Early Muslims faced the same theological dilemma that confronts all monotheistic faiths, namely the need to reconcile divine omnipotence with the reality of human sinfulness and evil. Answers to this dilemma are elusive, since they generally require that either God's goodness or omnipotence be compromised. In this regard, the struggle over human free will was neither unique to Islam nor derived from earlier faiths. It was a struggle inherent to monotheism. As the following discussion of individual Qadarī thinkers will demonstrate, efforts by Muslim scholars to ascribe Christian origins to the Qadariyya were more polemical than theological.

The purported originator of the Qadarī movement was Maʿbad b. ʿAbd Allāh b. ʿUkaym al-Juhanī (Ibn Abī Ḥātim, *Jarḥ*, 8: 280; Ibn ʿAsākir, *Tārīkh*, 59: 312–26; al-Mizzī, *Tahdhīb*, 28: 244–9). Maʿbad was a well-reputed Baṣran *muḥaddith* whose father was a Companion of the Prophet who resided in Kufa. The sources offer no explanation for Maʿbad's migration from Kufa to Baṣra. Perhaps his father's advocacy for ʿUthmān made Kufa untenable during and after the first *fitna*. The sources do not, however, explicitly describe any flight from Kufa by Maʿbad's father (al-Mizzi, *Tahdhīb*, 15: 218).

In Baṣra, Maʿbad became a respected member of the Umayyad elite. He served the regime in a variety of trusted capacities. Some reports indicate that Maʿbad played a small role in the negotiations during the arbitration after Ṣiffīn, suggesting that he was not entirely anathematized by the Kufans. He also served as an ambassador to the Byzantine emperor and tutored the caliph ʿAbd al-Malik's son Saʿīd (Ibn ʿAsākir, *Tārīkh*, 59: 312–16). His fortunes eventually waned and sometime around 80/699 he was executed, most likely by al-Ḥajjāj b. Yūsuf, the governor of the East, but possibly by ʿAbd al-Malik himself (Judd 2011: 6).

The reason for Maʿbad's fall from grace has been the subject of scholarly debate. The historical sources include a variety of condemnations of his Qadarī beliefs, but also include at least one report suggesting that he participated in Ibn al-Ashʿath's failed revolt. Josef van Ess has argued that Maʿbad's involvement in the revolt was the reason for his execution (van Ess 1974: 75–7). However, the majority of the evidence suggests that Maʿbad's real offence was doctrinal rather than revolutionary (Judd 2011: 5–6).

Information on Maʿbad's doctrinal positions is relatively sparse. The sources universally agree that he was a Qadarī and that he actively preached the doctrine. Further details about his beliefs are not reported. Instead, he is typically described as 'the first to speak about *qadar* in Baṣra' (*awwal man takallama fī l-qadar bi-l-Baṣra*) (Ibn Abī Ḥātim, *Jarḥ*, 8: 280). The sources offer no further nuance about his views, nor do they even explain what Maʿbad actually said about *qadar*. One report does offer a small but significant detail. Al-Balādhurī (d. 297/892) reports that Maʿbad defended his Qadarī views by arguing that God did not will ʿUthmān's death, implying that those who killed ʿUthmān had disobeyed God, or at least acted with independence from God's decree (al-Balādhurī, *Ansāb*, 2: 256). While this application of Qadarī doctrine is not widely reported, it does illustrate one avenue the Qadarīs could use to insulate themselves from accusations of political disloyalty.

The biographical sources offer considerably more detail about the alleged origin of Qadarī doctrine. A number of sources emphasize that, while Maʿbad was the first to speak of *qadar* in Baṣra, he did not invent the doctrine. Instead, he learned it from a Christian, sometimes named as Sūsan or possibly Susnoya. This otherwise unknown figure may or may not have converted to Islam. Some sources claim that he converted but later apostatized. All of the reports to this effect ultimately originate with al-Awzāʿī (d. 157/774), who was one of the chief persecutors of the Qadarīs. Hence, the report's possible polemical nature must be acknowledged. Al-Awzāʿī's apparent determination to marginalize Qadarī doctrine by asserting its Christian origin stands in contrast to other reports emphasizing his ecumenical attitude later in life. This is a topic that merits further investigation.

Reports about the origins of the Qadariyya are especially important for understanding their treatment in historiographical sources. The fact that these reports are more prevalent than descriptions of Maʿbad's actual beliefs reflects the focus of later scholars on the question of origins. Reports describing Maʿbad as the first to speak of *qadar* in Baṣra must be considered in the context of biographies of other Baṣran religious leaders. In particular, al-Ḥasan al-Baṣrī (d. 110/728) was accused of being a Qadarī and his *risāla*, discussed in the previous chapter (Chapter 1), has been treated in some circumstances as a Qadarī text. By labelling Maʿbad as the 'first' to speak of *qadar* in Baṣra, the biographical sources not only explain who originated the doctrine, but also emphasize that al-Ḥasan did not. This widely cited detail in Maʿbad's biography is an element of the efforts to cleanse al-Ḥasan from association with the Qadarīs. Reports in which al-Ḥasan accused Maʿbad of some unspecified error and disassociated himself from Maʿbad serve a similar function (Judd 2011: 5).

The emphasis placed on the alleged Christian origin of the doctrine is also polemically important. The reports of Sūsan teaching Maʿbad his heretical views suggest that those doctrines were Christian, thus placing them outside Islam. Some reports explicitly state that Maʿbad taught Christian ideas (*yaqūlu bi-qawl al-naṣārā*) (Ibn ʿAsākir, *Tārīkh*, 59: 322). This emphasis on Christian origins is particularly important in the context of ʿAbd al-Malik's reign. It was during this period that basic Islamic beliefs began to coalesce and to distinguish themselves from other monotheistic traditions (Donner 2010: 195ff.). Labelling Qadarī views as Christian in origin served to separate them from Islam and to solidify the association between Islam and predestinarian doctrines. It is also significant that many of these reports originate with al-Awzāʿī, who was one of the Qadarīs' fiercest opponents. Other reports were circulated by Muslim b. Yasār, who was a foster brother to ʿAbd al-Malik (al-Mizzī, *Tahdhīb*, 27: 555). Historiographically, then, the sources suggest that staunch predestinarians and supporters of ʿAbd al-Malik's religious reforms attempted to isolate Maʿbad and his Qadarī views from the mainstream of Islamic thought by associating the Qadariyya with Christianity.

The isolation of Maʿbad is also a crucial element in the isolation of his most famous pupil, Ghaylān al-Dimashqī. Although it is not clear when and where they encountered each other, al-Awzāʿī describes Maʿbad as Ghaylān's teacher, an assertion that later sources universally accept (Ibn ʿAsākir, *Tārīkh*, 48: 192). The cryptic data on Maʿbad's views make it difficult to determine the extent of his influence over Ghaylān's doctrines. However, the connection between Maʿbad and Ghaylān was an important element of later Muslim interpretations of the Qadariyya.

Details of Ghaylān's biography are scarce. Unlike Maʿbad, neither his parents nor even his ethnic background can be confidently identified. He was likely a non-Arab *mawlā*, perhaps the son of a freed slave of ʿUthmān b. ʿAffān, though his place of birth is unknown. Some sources identify him as al-Qibṭī, implying Coptic origins. However, no further exploration of this possibility survives in the sources. Details of his youth are non-existent.

As an adult, Ghaylān enjoyed both respect and position in the Umayyad bureaucracy. Several reports indicate that he served as the director of the mint at Damascus for ʿUmar b. ʿAbd al-ʿAzīz (r. 99/717–101/720). This was obviously not an entry-level position. Ghaylān's employment in this capacity suggests that he had both managerial and technical expertise. It is even possible, depending on how long he worked in the mint before becoming its director, that Ghaylān was one of the unnamed mint workers who implemented ʿAbd al-Malik's ambitious currency reforms decades earlier. At the very least, his service in such a sensitive and important position illustrates that he had gained ʿUmar's trust. Ghaylān apparently lost that trust when he began to preach his Qadarī beliefs openly. Several reports describe ʿUmar confronting him, correcting him, and threatening punishment if he fell into error again (van Ess 1977: 190 ff). It is possible that later sources exaggerate this rift in order to disassociate ʿUmar from the Qadariyya (Judd 1999: 169–70).

Later in life, Ghaylān served in the army in Armenia, under the command of Marwān b. Muḥammad. The nature and length of his service there are not clear. Nor do the sources offer a clear explanation for his transfer to the frontier. It is possible that he went there to fulfil his religious duty of *jihād*, but it is also possible that his rupture with ʿUmar b. ʿAbd al-ʿAzīz was sufficiently severe that he sought geographical distance from Damascus. Eventually, he alienated Marwān as well and returned to Damascus where he was prosecuted and executed for his Qadarī beliefs. Details of Ghaylān's trial and execution vary in the sources. There is even some disagreement regarding which caliph ordered Ghaylān's interrogation. Some sources place his execution in the context of the rift between him and ʿUmar b. ʿAbd al-ʿAzīz, a few suggest he was tried by Yazīd b. ʿAbd al-Malik, but the most credible accounts place his demise during the long reign of Hishām b. ʿAbd al-Malik (r. 105/724–125/743) (Judd 1999: 170–2).

Like Maʿbad, Ghaylān was executed for his Qadarī beliefs. Both the biographical and heresiographical sources offer more details regarding Ghaylān's views. This may be a product of his more extensive scholarly output. He was rumoured to have written hundreds of *risālas*, though none of them has survived and their size and content are unknown (Ibn al-Nadīm, *Fihrist*, 171). The mere assertion that Ghaylān wrote so much about his beliefs is significant. It suggests that he was intent on both propagating and explicating Qadarī views and that his writings had an audience of followers or potential followers. The historical sources do indicate that Ghaylān had a cadre of loyal followers. For instance, al-Ṭabarī (d. 310/923) reports that Hishām exiled a group of the Qadariyya to Dahlak, presumably after Ghaylān's execution (al-Ṭabarī, *Tārīkh*, 2: 1777).

Accounts describing Ghaylān's beliefs do not appear to draw explicitly from his alleged written record. There is no evidence of any effort to refute Ghaylān's writings either. This omission, of course, raises some doubt about the extent and circulation of Ghaylān's written works. Instead, most of what is known about Ghaylān's views is derived from simple assertions about his beliefs in the heresiographical sources and from accounts of his trial and execution.

Heresiographical sources present Ghaylān's Qadarī doctrines as elements of a more sophisticated and complete set of beliefs. They generally classify Ghaylān under the broad category of the Murjiʾites, whose principal belief was that judgement of sinners' fate must be deferred to God. Some sources add that Ghaylān believed that faith was a secondary rather than innate knowledge of God and that he held that a non-Qurayshī could be the Imām. The inclusion of these additional facets of his beliefs suggests that Ghaylān had devised a more comprehensive creed, in contrast to his teacher Maʿbad. However, details of the Qadarī aspects of his beliefs are still quite limited. The heresiographical sources provide details about Ghaylān's other beliefs, but at best simply point out that he considered sin to derive from human volition and good deeds to be willed by God. The heresiographers' lack of attention to Ghaylān's Qadarī views is striking, given the efforts they devoted to explaining distinctions between later Muʿtazilite thinkers on the subject of human free will. In these sources, Ghaylān's Qadarī beliefs are clearly less consequential than his views on other topics. This stands in stark contrast to the historical and biographical sources, which focus instead on Ghaylān as a Qadarī while ignoring his affiliation with the Murjiʾa.

Historical and biographical sources pay more attention to Ghaylān's Qadarī beliefs, but still offer frustratingly few details. The most informative reports describe Ghaylān's interrogation just before his execution. Unfortunately, the questioning does not lead to careful explications of the minutiae of Qadarī doctrines. Instead, most reports of his interrogation focus on basic doctrinal issues, sometimes resorting to tropes in lieu of more thorough analysis. For instance, several reports include questions about whether God willed that Adam eat the forbidden fruit. While this example captures the difficulty of reconciling divine omnipotence with human sin, it lacks theological sophistication and offers little insight into the nuances of Ghaylān's beliefs.

These sources focus more on the origins of Ghaylān's Qadarī views than on the doctrines themselves. Ghaylān's link to his teacher Maʿbad implicitly connects his views with Maʿbad's Christian/apostate mentor Sūsan. Labelling Ghaylān as 'al-Qibṭī' accomplishes the same objective by suggesting that Ghaylān as well as his ideas had Christian origins. Other reports assert a Christian provenance for Ghaylān's views more explicitly. For instance, Ibn ʿAsākir's (d. 571/1175) biography of Ghaylān includes a prophetic *ḥadīth* referring to the Qadarīs as the 'Christians and Magians of the community' (Ibn ʿAsākir, *Tārīkh*, 48: 203). Historians and biographers typically treated Qadarī views as outside influences that seeped into Islam, usually from Christian sources.

Modern scholarship has, to some extent, followed this trend. For instance, early Western discussions of Ghaylān by A. Guillaume, A. von Kremer, and others suggested that he and the Qadariyya were influenced by their Christian contemporaries, especially John of Damascus (Guillaume 1924: 47–50; von Kremer 1873: 7). Later scholars, especially J. van Ess, have been sceptical about any direct influence John and others may have exercised over the Qadariyya or early Islamic doctrine in general. It is, however, still important to note the efforts evident in the biographical literature to connect Ghaylān and the Qadariyya to Christianity. It is also important to ponder why the heresiographical sources do not treat the Qadariyya as a prominent movement or explicate their beliefs with any thoroughness at all.

Both of these peculiarities in the treatment of the Qadariyya were in part products of the politicization of the Qadariyya that occurred under the leadership of Ghaylān. Whether the Qadarīs were politically disruptive from the beginning is difficult to determine. It does, however, appear that by the time of Ghaylān the Qadarīs had become entangled in politics. During his time in Armenia, Ghaylān and his followers seem to have begun more active dissent against the Umayyads. While details of their activities are sparse and there is no evidence of any efforts to foment open rebellion, Ghaylān and his followers were described as passing like a wave through the army (Ibn ʿAsākir, *Tārīkh*, 48: 204). Their activities in Armenia may explain in part the extreme enmity that Marwān b. Muḥammad displayed toward them in some reports (Judd 2005: 220–2). The fact that Hishām exiled Ghaylān's followers after his execution suggests that they, unlike earlier Qadarī disciples, were seen as a potential threat to the regime. Whether these reports are accurate, or whether they were devised to show that Hishām and Marwān foresaw the political threat the Qadarīs would pose is perhaps impossible to determine.

It is, however, quite clear that the Qadarīs became inextricably entangled in politics shortly after Ghaylān's execution. Yazīd b. al-Walīd, who led the uprising that began the third *fitna* and precipitated the demise of the Umayyad dynasty, embraced Qadarī doctrine as a key part of his public platform. While he does not appear to have been a prominent leader of the Qadarī movement prior to the turmoil surrounding the brief reign of his predecessor al-Walīd b. Yazīd, many of the members of his inner circle were well-known Qadarīs. Their triumph was, however, short-lived. Even before their defeat at the hands of Marwān b. Muḥammad, Yazīd had apparently begun to renege on aspects of the Qadarī agenda.

It is not surprising that the Qadariyya became a political movement. The core tenet of their beliefs, namely their insistence on human responsibility for sin, has obvious political implications. It is unclear whether Umayyad recognition of these implications contributed to their earlier persecution of leaders like Maʿbad and Ghaylān. By the time of the third *fitna*, the demand that political leaders take responsibility for their sins had become a rallying cry for the Qadarīs and others who were distressed by the debauchery of the Umayyad inner circle.

Umayyad state doctrine held, at least implicitly, that the caliph's actions were God's will and that the caliph, as God's chosen representative, should expect absolute obedience. This position was explicated in the *khalīfat Allāh* doctrine, which Umayyad rulers worked to propagate (Crone and Hinds 1986: 24–42). In its most extreme interpretation, the *khalīfat Allāh* doctrine permitted no dissent whatsoever, since even the most apparently heinous deeds committed by the caliph were God's will. By contrast, Qadarī doctrine separated evil deeds from God, placing responsibility for these deeds on human actors. The Qadarī position made dissent against sinful rulers possible and even, perhaps, mandatory for pious Muslims. The political ramifications of this doctrine are obvious.

The transition to open dissent against the Umayyads also had doctrinal implications for the Qadariyya. Specifically, their association with the Murjiʾite doctrine of deferring judgement of sinners to God was incompatible with accusations of sinful behaviour toward the Umayyad rulers. Murjiʾite thinkers did debate about what constituted a grave sin, an offence severe enough to cast doubt on one's status as a Muslim. They were quite hesitant, however, to condemn individuals for specific sinful actions, preferring instead to defer such judgement to God.

The Qadarīs involved in Yazīd's movement showed no such hesitation. Instead, they openly condemned unjust political rulers and called for their removal from power. Their actions in the third *fitna* appear to be more akin to the Khawārij, who combined their insistence on human responsibility for sin with a harshly judgemental attitude toward those who committed major sins. Perhaps this distinction explains in part why those involved in Yazīd's revolt are labelled as Qadarīs, while the Murjiʾites are invisible in the historical sources for the period.

These more activist Qadarīs did, however, play a crucial role in the fall of al-Walīd b. Yazīd. Al-Walīd had taken the Umayyad doctrine of predestination to its extreme, arguing that, as God's chosen ruler, he had absolute licence to act as he pleased. His actions, no matter how apparently depraved, were God's will for him and for the community (Judd 2008: 443ff.). Qadarī doctrine had tremendous utility for challenging this position. The Qadarīs argued that al-Walīd was responsible for his acts and accountable to God and to the community for them.

Portions of Yazīd's public speeches make clear that he embraced the Qadarī position and also sought to use Qadarī demands for accountability as a rallying point for opposition to al-Walīd. Upon attaining power, however, Yazīd appears to have softened his position and began to act in a more autocratic fashion. Whether Yazīd was sincere in his affirmation of Qadarī doctrine or whether he joined with them as an act of cynical expedience is impossible to know. The historical sources offer vague evidence to support either possibility.

For the Qadarī movement itself, however, this foray into caliphal politics was transformational. Their vaguely defined belief in human responsibility for sin evolved into a call for accountability in government and for a radically different religious foundation for the caliphate. Ultimately, their doctrine was used to justify political violence against the sitting ruler, who claimed divinely mandated authority. This embrace of political activism ultimately led to the demise of the Qadariyya. Those Qadarī figures who survived the ʿAbbāsid revolution, scholars like Thawr b. Yazīd (d. *c.*150/767), were ostracized and marginalized as a consequence of their association with the Qadariyya. The ideas espoused by the Qadarīs had more resilience and resurfaced as part of more comprehensive and sophisticated Muʿtazilite doctrines. However, the Qadarī origins of these ideas were obscured.

Historiographically, the Qadarī association with Yazīd and the third *fitna* also had an impact on how earlier Qadarīs were remembered. While it would be easy simply to assume that the persecution of the Qadarīs by earlier Umayyad caliphs, namely ʿAbd al-Malik and Hishām, reflected their recognition of the political threat the Qadarīs could pose, it is important to consider whether that political threat has been projected backward by later writers whose images of the Qadarīs were shaped by the historical memory of their involvement in the third *fitna*. While the evidence is insufficient to draw definitive conclusions, it is worth asking whether Qadarī leaders like Maʿbad, whose followers largely disappeared after his execution, really presented any sort of political threat to the Umayyad caliph. Similarly, Ghaylān's followers do not appear to have revolted before or after his execution and, by all indications, accepted their exile to Dahlak without resistance. This is not the reaction one would expect from a truly revolutionary political movement. It is important, therefore, not to dismiss entirely the possibility that the early Qadarīs were properly labelled as quietist Murjiʾites and that allusions to their political resistance could be later accretions.

The connection between the Qadarīs and the third *fitna* also has significant implications for later historiographical treatments of the Muʿtazilites. While some Muʿtazilite *ṭabaqāt* works do include references to Ghaylān and other Umayyad-era Qadarīs, for the most part links between the Qadarīs and the early Muʿtazilites are minimized in the sources (ʿAbd al-Jabbār, *Faḍl*, 231). Despite their similar beliefs about human free will, connections between the two movements are rare in the historical and biographical sources. This may stem in part from the extensive historiographical effort made to cleanse al-Ḥasan al-Baṣrī, whose pupils originated the Muʿtazilites, from any association with Maʿbad and other Qadarī figures (Judd 1999: 164–6). It may also stem from the simple fact that later Muʿtazilite scholars did not want to associate their movement with failed Umayyad-era dissenters. As in other aspects of ʿAbbāsid-era historiography, the sources on the Muʿtazilites tried to avoid signs of continuity between Umayyad and ʿAbbāsid times, especially in terms of religious doctrine. One cannot dismiss the possibility that the Muʿtazilites really were simply a continuation of the Qadarīs.

Their political involvement during the third *fitna* had a significant impact on how the Qadarīs were remembered. Their militancy may have been projected back to earlier times in an effort to illustrate their continuity. Their influence on later movements was likely downplayed in an effort by later leaders to distance themselves from the failure of the Qadarī attempt to take control of the political realm and to reform the Umayyads.

The Qadariyya were a short-lived theological phenomenon. They endured only a few decades, from the initial preaching of Maʿbad in the late 70s/690s to the failure of the Qadarī caliph Yazīd b. al-Walīd in the 120s/740s. During this fifty-year history, the Qadariyya produced little to explain their doctrines and do not appear to have been major theological actors. Their political activities are better documented and overshadow their other accomplishments. At the same time, there appears to have been a concerted effort to distance the Qadarīs from mainstream Islam by emphasizing the alleged Christian origins of their views. Unfortunately, their association with particular political actors has tainted their image in the historical record, making it difficult to ascertain the extent of their following or the influence of their doctrines on later Muslim theology.

Bibliography

ʿAbd al-Jabbār al-Hamadānī (*Faḍl*). *Faḍl al-iʿtizāl wa-ṭabaqāt al-muʿtazila*. Ed. F. Sayyid. Tunis: Dār al-Tūnisiyya li-l-nashr, 1974.

al-Ashʿarī, Abū l-Ḥasan (*Maqālāt*). *Maqālāt al-Islāmiyyīn wa-ikhtilāf al-muṣallīn*. Ed. H. Ritter. Wiesbaden: Franz Steiner, 1963.

al-Baghdādī, ʿAbd al-Qāhir (*Farq*). *Al-Farq bayn al-firaq*. Ed. Muḥammad Muḥayyā al-Dīn ʿAbd al-Ḥamīd. Beirut: al-Maktaba al-ʿaṣriyya, 1990.

al-Balādhurī, Aḥmad b. Yaḥyā (*Ansāb*). *Ansāb al-ashrāf*. MS Istanbul, Süleimaniye, Reisulküttap 598.

Crone, P., and M. Hinds (1986). *God's Caliph: Religious Authority in the First Centuries of Islam*. Cambridge: Cambridge University Press.

Donner, F. (2010). *Muhammad and the Believers: At the Origins of Islam*. Cambridge, MA: Harvard University Press.

van Ess, J. (1970). 'Les Qadarites et la Ġaylāniya de Yazīd III'. *Studia Islamica* 31: 269–86.

van Ess, J. (1974). 'Maʿbad al-Ĝuhanī'. In R. Gramlich (ed.), *Islamwissenschaftliche Abhandlungen: Fritz Meier zum sechzigsten Geburtstag*. Wiesbaden: Franz Steiner, 49ff.

van Ess, J. (1977). *Anfänge muslimischer Theologie*. Beirut: Steiner.

van Ess, J. (1991–7). *Theologie und Gesellschaft im 2. und 3. Jahrhundert Hidschra: Eine Geschichte des religiösen Denkens im frühen Islam*. 6 vols. Berlin: de Gruyter.

al-Firyābī, Jaʿfar b. Muḥammad (*Qadar*). *Kitāb al-qadar*. Ed. ʿAbd Allāh b. Ḥamid al-Manṣūr. Riyādh: Aḍwāʾ al-Salaf, 1997.

Guillaume, A. (1924). 'Some Remarks on Free Will and Predestination in Islam, Together with a Translation of the Kitabu-l Qadar from the Sahih of al-Bukhari'. *Journal of the Royal Asiatic Society* 1: 43–63.

Ibn Abī Ḥātim al-Rāzī (*Jarḥ*). *Kitāb al-Jarḥ wa-l-taʿdīl*. Beirut: n.p., 1973.

Ibn ʿAsākir, ʿAlī b. al-Ḥasan (*Tārīkh*). *Tārīkh madīnat Dimashq*. Ed. U. al-ʿUmrawī. Beirut: Dār al-fikr, 1995–8.

Ibn al-Nadīm, Muḥammad (*Fihrist*). *Kitāb al-Fihrist*. Ed. G. Flügel. Leipzig: Brockhaus, 1862.

Ibn Saʿd, Muḥammad (*Ṭabaqāt*). *Kitāb al-Ṭabaqāt al-kubrā*. Ed. I. ʿAbbās. Beirut: Dār Ṣādir, 1957.

Judd, S. (1999). 'Ghaylan al-Dimashqi: The Isolation of a Heretic in Islamic Historiography'. *International Journal of Middle East Studies* 31: 161–84.

Judd, S. (2005). 'Narratives and Character Development: Al-Ṭabarī and al-Balādhurī on Late Umayyad History'. In S. Günther (ed.), *Ideas, Images, and Methods of Portrayal: Insights into Classical Arabic Literature and Islam*. Leiden: Brill, 209–26.

Judd, S. (2008). 'Reinterpreting al-Walīd b. Yazīd'. *Journal of the American Oriental Society* 128: 439–58.

Judd, S. (2011). 'Muslim Persecution of Heretics during the Marwānid Period (64–132/684–750)'. *Al-Masāq* 23: 1–14.

al-Mizzī, Yūsuf b. al-Zakī (*Tahdhīb*). *Tahdhīb al-kamāl fī asmāʾ al-rijāl*. Ed. B. Maʿrūf. Beirut: Muʾassasat al-risāla, 1992.

al-Ṭabarī, Abū Jaʿfar (*Tārīkh*). *Tārīkh al-rusul wa-l-mulūk*. Ed. M. J. de Goeje. Leiden: Brill, 1879–1901.

von Kremer, A. (1873). *Culturgeschichtliche Streifzüge auf dem Gebiete des Islams*. Leipzig: Brockhaus.

Watt, W. M. (1973). *The Formative Period of Islamic Thought*. Edinburgh: Edinburgh University Press.

CHAPTER 3

JAHM b. ṢAFWĀN (D. 128/745–6) AND THE 'JAHMIYYA' AND ḌIRĀR b. ʿAMR (D. 200/815)

CORNELIA SCHÖCK

JAHM b. ṢAFWĀN and Ḍirār b. ʿAmr rank among the first Muslim scholars to deal with issues pertaining to philosophy of nature, ontology, and epistemology. Jahm lived and taught in North-Eastern Iran, and it may well be that he never left the territory of Khurāsān (Ibn Ḥanbal, *Radd*, 19.6; Qāḍī 1426/2005: i. 70–5; van Ess 1991–7: ii. 494). Ḍirār b. ʿAmr was of Kūfan origin. In his youth he belonged to the circle of the second generation of the Muʿtazilites of Baṣra, at the age of about 50 to those of Baghdād. Some of his adversaries, however, saw in him a 'Jahmite', despite the fact that Ḍirār never met Jahm and attacked Jahm's doctrine in one of his writings (van Ess 1979: 28; 1991–7: iii. 32f., 35; v. 229, no. 19). This chapter focuses on main issues and key concepts of Jahm's and Ḍirār's doctrines and on similarities in respect of which an adversary like al-Naẓẓām (d. before 232/847) saw an intellectual kinship between them.

With the exception of a *K. al-Taḥrīsh* (Ḍirār b. ʿAmr, *Taḥrīsh*) roughly outlined by Ḥasan Anṣārī and attributed by him to Ḍirār b. ʿAmr (Anṣārī 2004–5; 2007: 23–4; van Ess 2010: 132–40; Schöck forthcoming), no writings of Jahm or Ḍirār are extant. The doxographical accounts we rely on condense their doctrines into a few sentences which expose physical, epistemological, and theological theories. The accounts revolve around origination and corruption of the corporeal, changes observed in sensible objects, the question of causal efficacy and the distinction between the perception, description, and knowledge of composite, generated things and the intuition of the incomposite, ingenerate God. In the following, the doctrines of Jahm and Ḍirār will be treated in two separate sections on the basis of a choice of representative passages from doxographical accounts on their theses. A third section summarizes the theses and draws conclusions regarding the origins and goals of Jahm's and Ḍirār's theories.

I Jahm b. Ṣafwān and the 'Jahmiyya'

Jahm b. Ṣafwān is the first Muslim 'theologian' in the full and proper sense. His theology is part of his empiricism grounded in Aristotle's theory of knowledge (*'ilm*) explained in the *Posterior Analytics* (see ss. I(d)–(f)). With him starts the conflict between Muslim natural theology and a literalistic reading of the Qurʾānic predicates and attributes of God. In Muslim sources Jahm and later religious scholars who were associated with his theses and labelled by adversaries as 'Jahmiyya' are opposed to both extremes of the spectrum of medieval Muslim religious parties. On one side of the spectrum are a notoriously subliterate and aggressive mob (Ḥashwiyya) and anthropomorphists, i.e. those maintaining that God is like other things (Mushabbiha), who both advocated an ignorant non-reflective reading of the Qurʾān, as well as Ḥanbalites and neo-Ḥanbalites who refuse natural theology and have been advocating from the earliest time until today a literalistic reading (Halkin 1934: 12–28). Ḥanbalites and neo-Ḥanbalites react extremely hostilely to Jahm's doctrines, and call him an enemy of God who led astray or at least negatively and dangerously influenced many of the Ḥanafites, Muʿtazilīs, Zaydīs, Shiʿis, Ashʿarites, and Māturīdites, seeing in all who share Jahm's views heretics and unbelievers who must be battled (e.g. Ibn Ḥanbal, *Radd*, 19.6; 20.8–9; Qāḍī 1426/2005: i. 9f.). On the opposite side of the spectrum of Muslim theology the so-called Jahmiyya is confronted with arguments of the Muʿtazilites, the strongest party of philosophically educated early Muslims.

Despite their opposition to each other, all Muslim parties agree that Jahm is the first or among the first who introduced the principle of intellect (*'aql*) and the method of reasoning to derive opinions from propositions (*ra'y*) in Islam. Ḥanbalites and neo-Ḥanbalites say that he drew on the principles of pagan Greek philosophy which he borrowed from Hellenistic philosophers (*al-falāsifa*), Christian heretics, and Jews (e.g. Qāḍī 1426/2005: i. 9f., 141f.). However, they are not precise and do not specify from which persons, schools, or strands of thinking Jahm and the Jahmites borrowed their theses and arguments.

Richard Frank argued that Jahm's 'system manifests itself ... as clearly and unambiguously neoplatonic in structure and content' (Frank 1965: 396) and based his argument on parallels between Jahm's theses and Plotinus's *Enneades*, in particular on Jahm's distinction between God and 'things' (*ashyāʾ*) (Frank 1965: 398, *passim*). It can hardly be denied that Jahm drew on ancient and late-ancient discussions between Platonists, Peripatetics, Stoics, and Epicureans on the relationship between the incorporeal and the corporeal, the active and the passive (cf. Kupreeva 2003). Jahm's physics and ontology are grounded on his basic distinction between the existent corporeal (*al-jism al-mawjūd*) and the incorporeal which is either other than the body (*ghayr al-jism*) or non-existent (*ma'dūm, mā laysa bi-mawjūdin*). The existent corporeal hence is opposed to both, the [existent] incorporeal, i.e. God, and the non-existent non-corporeal. Causal efficacy can be assigned to the incorporeal existent only. Hence, patiency belongs to the corporeal, agency to the incorporeal. Knowledge is grounded on the existent corporeal only, because only this can be an object of perception, knowledge, or estimation. These aspects only to some extent are in line with the Middle Platonic and Neoplatonic tradition. They contain an anti-Platonic element which is crucial for Jahm's epistemology, ontology, and theology. In the Jahmite system there are no immaterial existents and causes except God. The Jahmites refused the existence of incorporeal composite things and maintained that only one incorporeal incomposite and active principle can be proven to exist, namely God who is cause of all things which is itself uncaused and necessarily exists, given that the corporeal things which come to be and pass away and change their states of being are real existent things. The epistemology of the Jahmites, including their theory that the certainty that there is a cause correlated to every alteration happens by intuition, is empiricist, based on the distinction between concept formation by characteristics (*ṣifāt*) abstracted from sensible things on the one hand and by the intuition that there must be a cause of their existence on the other hand (cf. ss. I(a), (d)–(e)). They refuse incorporeal objects of God's knowledge, which entails the refusal of the interpretation of the Platonic ideas as thoughts of God.

Some years before Frank wrote his article on Jahm's dependence on Neoplatonism Harry Wolfson had published a series of articles on the Middle Platonic, Neoplatonic, Patristic, and Muslim theories on divine attributes (Wolfson 1952; 1956; 1957; 1959). According to Wolfson the problem of the divine attributes in Muslim dialectical theology (*kalām*) 'originated under the influence of the Christian doctrine of the Trinity', and it 'has a twofold aspect, an ontological and a semantic'. Wolfson claims that 'a third aspect, a logical, was introduced later by those who are called philosophers as distinguished from those known as *Mutakallimūn*' (Wolfson 1959: 73). Wolfson then quotes a selection of doxographic accounts on Jahm's doctrine and concludes: 'Jahm was thus the first to introduce into Arabic philosophy the semantic aspect of the problem and to offer the active interpretation, already established by Philo, Albinus,[1] Plotinus, and the Church Fathers' (Wolfson 1959: 75).

The present chapter argues that these claims are untenable. The arguments of Jahm and the Jahmites are at odds with the Church Fathers and there are clear indications that they have their origin in Christian Trinitarian *debates* in which the Arian party argued on a logical basis against the godhead of the Son. The issue in question in the inter-Muslim debates on the attributes (*ṣifāt*) of God is not 'whether terms predicated of God in the Koran, such as living and knowing and powerful, imply the existence in God of life and knowledge and power as real incorporeal beings ... ' (*pace* Wolfson 1959: 73b), nor is it the question whether the attributes (*ṣifāt*) are 'real' things in God. The contentious point rather is *whether* the Qurʾānic attributes indicate that something is logically predicated of God, and if they do, *how*. Jahm and the Jahmites do not argue that the attributes are not things, but that God is not a thing, which does not mean that He is not real, but that *nothing can be logically predicated of Him* and that *He cannot be*

[1] Meant is the author of the *Didaskalikos*, i.e. Alcinous whose authorship meanwhile is almost generally accepted. See Whittaker 1990.

described by reference to properties (*ṣifāt*). Hence according to Jahm and the Jahmites the Qurʾānic attributes of God do not indicate predication (see ss. I(a), (d)–(f)). The question whether something can be logically predicated of the absolutely One or not and whether the One can be described by reference to properties is a logical and an ontological issue; the question whether the Qurʾānic attributes and verbs signify logical predications is a semantic issue. Arius, Aetius, and in particular the neo-Arian Eunomius of Cyzikus made the point that regarding God no predication is possible and that anything said of God signifies identity in sense and reference (Schöck 2012; 2014). This point disagrees with the Church Fathers Wolfson referred to and it is found in the theories of Jahm and the Jahmites (cf. s. I(f)).

Josef van Ess has collected doxographical accounts on Jahm's doctrine and has provided us with a synopsis of the Jahmite theses (van Ess 1991–7: ii. 493–508; v. 212–23). What follows in the present chapter is an analysis of a selection of doxographical accounts on the doctrine of Jahm and the Jahmites segmented according to its focal theses. These are mainly transmitted by hostile sources apart from their original context. The aim here is to reconstruct their systematical coherence.

(a) Knowledge and Ignorance Refer to Corporeal, Real Existent Things Only

> Jahm said: 'God's knowledge is temporally originated (*muḥdath*). He has brought it into temporal existence (*aḥdathahu*) with the result that he knew by it. It is something other than God (*ghayru Llāh*).' According to him it is possible that God knows all [particular] things (*ashyāʾ*) prior to their existence by a knowledge which he brings into existence prior to them.
>
> But someone reports of him the opposite of this. He claims that he has been told that Jahm used to say: 'God knows a thing in the state of its origination (*fī ḥāli ḥudūthihi*). It is absurd that a thing is object of knowledge (*maʿlūm*) and non existent (*maʿdūm*)', because 'thing' (*al-shayʾ*) according to him is the existent body (*al-jism al-mawjūd*). And that which is not existent (*mā laysa bi-mawjūdin*) is not a thing so that knowledge or ignorance of it would be possible (*fa-yuʿlama aw yujhala*). Then Jahm's opponents forced him to acknowledge [as a consequence of his aforementioned premises] that God has a temporally originated knowledge (*ʿilm muḥdath*), because he claimed that God [first] had not been knowing and then knew (*kāna ghayra ʿālimin thumma ʿalima*). Given his premise (*ʿalā aṣlihi*) [that only the existent body can be object of knowledge (*maʿlūm*)] he necessarily must say that which he says with regard to knowledge with regard to power and life as well [viz. that God's power and life also are temporally originated (*muḥdath*)]. (al-Ashʿarī, *Maqālāt*, 494.10–495.2)

In contrast to hostile Ḥanbalī sources al-Ashʿarī tries to do justice to Jahm's theses and to reconstruct his theses from a neutral point of view. He reports an alleged *reductio ad absurdum* (*ilzām* [*al-ḥujja*]) of three of Jahm's assumptions by adversaries. The external form of the narrative does not unambiguously distinguish between Jahm's suppositions and the consequences Jahm's adversaries drew from them. However, by comparison with further accounts of Jahm's doctrines it becomes evident that the first paragraph of the report refers to the consequence Jahm's opponents drew from the theses assigned to Jahm in the second paragraph, not to Jahm's actual doctrine. Other sources unambiguously report that Jahm did *not* hold that God's knowledge is something other than God (*ghayru Llāh*), but just the opposite (see s. I(d)). The report explains that adversaries of Jahm argued that his following suppositions are untenable:

(1) God knows a thing in the state of its origination (*fī ḥāli ḥudūthihi*).
(2) 'Thing' (*al-shayʾ*) is the existent body (*al-jism al-mawjūd*).
(3) What is non-existent is not a thing and not knowable (*maʿlūm*).

Jahm's opponents argue that from these premises follows:

(4) God's knowledge is temporally originated (*muḥdath*).
(5) God [first] had not been knowing and then knew.

These consequences are inconsistent with the logical postulate that God does not undergo substantial or qualitative change (cf. s. I(b)).

The point in dispute here is whether and how God knows the world. Does God know corporeal, particular things, or intelligible, universal things, or both? Jahm's opponents argued that on condition that he refused that God's knowledge refers to immaterial objects prior to the existence of material objects, as a consequence he had to admit that God's knowledge depends on material objects like our knowledge. They claimed that Jahm had to admit that God's knowledge is empirical, based on induction. Since material objects are generated (*muḥdath*), because every composite thing is generated, God's knowledge, creative power, and activity would also be generated. This would imply that God's state of being changes. Before the generation of the generated He would be unknowing and then, at the time of the generation of the generated, His knowledge would originate.

According to Jahm and his adversaries knowledge and ignorance need an object to which they refer. Knowledge is always knowledge of a thing (*shayʾ*), i.e. the correlative of knowledge which must exist together with it (cf. Aristotle, *Cat.* 7, 6b 4–5; Porphyry, *In Cat.* 112.27; Bodéüs 2008: 358). There is no knowledge of that which does not exist (*mā laysa bi-mawjūdin*).

According to Jahm's second supposition, 'existent body' (*al-jism al-mawjūd*) is the description of 'thing'. He maintains that besides corporeal things there are no knowables (*maʿlūmāt*). What does not exist at some particular time, at some particular place and is without particular qualities, i.e. what is either non-existent (*maʿdūm*) or God, is indescribable and therefore cannot be object of knowledge and ignorance (cf. ss. I(d)–(f)).

The question is how Jahm's two further suppositions have to be understood. Jahm's opponents obviously took the first supposition in the sense of 'God knows a thing *at the time* of its origination' (*fī ḥāl ḥudūthihi*) and the third supposition in the sense of 'what is *yet* non-existent is not a thing and not knowable' (*maʿlūm*). Their approach is temporal, and only from this aspect Jahm's three suppositions lead to the conclusions of the opponents in the dispute reported above. Probably they were people who affirmed the eternity of the things together with their Creator (*yuthbitu qidam al-ashyāʾ maʿa bāriʾihā*) and held that God is knowing [the things] from eternity (*lam yazal ʿāliman*) (al-Ashʿarī, *Maqālāt*, 489.2–3; cf. 158.5). They argued on the basis of the contradiction between being knowing from eternity and being knowing by origination that Jahm maintained that God's knowledge is temporally generated (*muḥdath*). But Jahm neither maintained that God is knowing from eternity, nor by origination (see ss. I(d) and (f)). And he probably understood the first supposition of the above-quoted report in the sense of 'God knows a thing *in the condition* of its origination' (*fī ḥāli ḥudūthihi*), i.e. *what* it is and *how* it is *when* it exists, namely which properties belong to it *at the time when* it exists, without reference to past, present, or future. Further, Jahm probably understood the third supposition in the sense of 'what never exists—i.e. what did not exist, does not exist, and will not exist in extramental reality—is not knowable (*maʿlūm*) and not a thing'. Under these conditions Jahm held that God knows all particular things of all times without relation to the time of their temporal origination.

Muʿtazilite opponents of Jahm's doctrine made use of the term 'thing' not only for corporeals, but also for immaterial 'things', namely substances (*jawāhir*), accidents (*aʿrāḍ*), activities (*afʿāl*) and their classes (*ajnās*), like the classes of colours, movements, tastes, etc. ʿAbbād b. Sulaymān (d. after 260/874) affirmed that these 'things' are objects of God's knowledge (*maʿlūmāt*) and objects of God's power (*maqdūrāt*) prior to the creation of particular composite bodies (e.g. al-Ashʿarī, *Maqālāt*, 158.16–159.13, 495.9–496.2). In contrast, Jahm refused the reality of universal substances (*jawāhir*), accidents (*aʿrāḍ*), and activities (*afʿāl*) and considered them as mere thoughts and concepts and epistemologically posterior to the sensible qualities and activities of corporeals. Thought and reality in his system are opposed.

(b) 'Thing' is the Genus of All Entities to which Belongs the Property 'to Be Like or Unlike'

Ever since Muslim religious scholars have disputed about the unity and simplicity of God arguing that God is incorporeal, incomposite, having neither extensional nor intensional parts, being inoriginate, without place and dimension, they have referred to Qurʾān 42: 11: *laysa ka-mithlihi shayʾun, lit.* 'no thing is like something like him [viz. God]'. The problem of this phrase is that, taken literally, it affirms that there is 'something like' (*mithlun*) God and negates that there is 'a thing' (*shayʾ*) which is alike to that which is like God. Most Muslim scholars took the 'like something like' (*ka-mithl*) as an intensifying pleonasm (*tawkīd*) and understood the verse in the sense of the 'hyper'-general negation 'no thing at all is like him' refusing any degree of 'likeness to God' (ὁμοίωσις θεῷ) (cf. al-Rāzī, *Tafsīr*, xxvii. 129.25–6; 132.7–11 and 19; al-Ṭabarī, *Jāmiʿ*, xxv. 12f.). Jahm's explanation is different. His emphasis lies on the conclusion that the term 'thing' does not refer to God:

> Because every thing is alike to something like it (*li-anna kulla shayʾin fa-innahu mithlun li-mithli nafsihi*), the meaning of [Qurʾan 42: 11:] 'no thing is like something like him [viz. God]' is: 'no thing is alike to something like him' (*laysa mithla mithlihi shayʾun*), and this [logically] requires that he is not named by the name 'thing'. (al-Rāzī, *Tafsīr*, xxvii. 132.17f.)

That is to say, to be a thing is to share the property 'likeness', i.e. to be in each particular state of being (*ḥāl*) in relation to another thing one of the two contraries 'being like' (ταυτόν) and 'being unlike' (ἕτερον), e.g. to be dead like another dead thing and unlike a living thing. The property 'likeness' then is an inseparable accident concomitant with 'thing' (cf. s. II(b)), and the term 'thing' (*shayʾ*) signifies the most general class of compounds of properties. 'Thing' (*al-shayʾ*) is that which can be object of division (διαίρεσις) and 'a thing' (*shayʾun*) is that which can be object of induction (ἐπαγωγή). These are the logical procedures on the basis of which the Arians argued against the thesis that 'God' can be understood as the common property (κοινοποιεῖν) of 'God-Father' and 'God-Son' (Schöck 2012: 22f.).

Further, according to Jahm's ontology each thing exists when it exists as an existent body (*jism mawjūd*) (cf. s. I(a)). This said, the terms 'existent' and 'body' or 'corporeal' are two different descriptions (cf. s. I(d): *waṣfayn mukhtalifayn*), in other words 'predications' of 'thing' which, in Ḍirār's words, when composed and combined (see s. II(a)–(b)) are coextensive with the term 'thing'. This said, 'existent' and 'corporeal' are also inseparable accidents and concomitant with 'thing'. God, according to the Jahmites, exists outside the realm of all things which share the property to be like and unlike other things. God therefore is denoted by terms which in the Aristotelian tradition are called 'infinite names' (ὄνομα ἀόριστον; arab. *ghayr muḥaṣṣal* or *ghayr maḥdūd*) (*De int.* 2, 16a 32; cf. Wolfson 1947; Schöck 2006: 120f.), namely 'non-body' (*ghayr al-jism*) (al-Ashʿarī, *Maqālāt*, 346.7; cf. s. I(c)) and 'a thing unlike all things' (*shayʾ lā ka-l-ashyāʾ*) (e.g. Ibn Ḥanbal, *Radd*, 20.19).

The Jahmites then distinguish three opposites of thing:

(a) the non-existent (*al-maʿdūm*) which does not exist (*laysa bi-mawjūdin*) (cf. s. I(a)),
(b) the non-thing, which is 'a thing unlike all things' (*shayʾ lā ka-l-ashyāʾ*), i.e. the existent without the property of being like and unlike something else, and
(c) the non-body (*ghayr al-jism*), i.e. the incomposite.

The opposition of 'thing' in the sense of 'existent body' on one hand and 'non-thing' and 'non-body' on the other hand is the key element of the doctrine because of which Ḥanbalites and neo-Ḥanbalites accuse the Jahmites of heresy (*zandaqa*) and infidelity (*kufr*), namely the doctrine that it is impossible to describe God by attributes (*ṣifāt*) (cf. ss. I(d)–(f)).

(c) Any Existent Thing is Corporeal

> He [i.e. Jahm] maintained that movement is a body and that it is impossible that it is something other than a body (*an takūna ghayr al-jism*), because that which is other than the body (*ghayr al-jism*) is God, … and there is no thing resembling him (*lā yakūnu shay'un yushbihuhu*).[2] (al-Ashʿarī, *Maqālāt*, 346.6–8)

The fact that according to Jahm properties are corporeal could be an indication of Stoic influence inasmuch as the Stoics deemed qualities to be corporeal (Kupreeva 2003). However, the Stoics did not negate immaterial beings besides God, and the term 'something' (τί) which signifies in their ontology the highest genus encompasses the corporeal and the incorporeal (Long/Sedley 1987: 163–5). In Jahm's system the opposition of corporeal 'thing' (*shay'*) and incorporeal non-thing, i.e. non-body (*ghayr al-jism*), is due to the overall distinctions between existent composites and non-existent mental composites on the one hand and existent composites and the existent incomposite on the other hand, distinctions which are incongruent with the Stoic ontological distinctions.

(d) God is Non-thing, Incomposite, Indivisible in Parts and Therefore not Intellectually Perceptible, not Describable, not Intelligible

> When people ask them [i.e. the Jahmites] about [the meaning of] 'no thing at all is like Him' (Qur'ān 42: 11), they say: 'No thing of all things is alike to something like Him' (*laysa ka-mithlihi shay' min al-ashyā'*) … He cannot be described nor be known by a characteristic, nor by an action (*bi-ṣifatin wa-lā bi-fiʿlin*[3]), does not have a boundary (*ghāya*) nor a limit (*muntahā*) and cannot be perceived by the intellect (*lā yudraku bi-l-ʿaql*). He is fully face, fully knowledge, fully hearing, fully seeing, fully light, fully power (*huwa wajhun kulluhu* …). Neither are two things in Him, nor is He described by two different descriptions (*lā yakūnu fīhi shay'ān wa-lā yūṣafu bi-waṣfayn mukhtalifayn*) … He does not have colour, nor body, and He is neither acted upon (*maʿmūl*) nor intelligible (*maʿqūl*). (Ibn Ḥanbal, *Radd*, 20.9–17)

[2] Or: comparable to him (*yushabbahuhu*).
[3] Reading: *bi-fiʿlin* instead of *yufʿalu*.

This explication, handed down by Ibn Ḥanbal (d. 241/855), combines ontology with epistemology. The premise that God is incorporeal and incomposite leads to the conclusion that He is non-describable, non-perceivable by the intellect, and therefore non-intelligible. What is outside the realm of things which are circumscribed by being like or unlike is infinite, i.e. without boundary and limit. The ontological oneness of God is analogous to the coextensiveness of the term 'God' with every single further term applied to God. 'Face', 'knowledge', 'hearing', etc. are not combined, but uncombined coextensive with 'God'. Hence, statements like 'He is fully knowledge' (*huwa ʿilmun kulluhu*), 'He is fully power' (*huwa qudratun kulluhu*), etc. are not predications describing the subject by something which belongs to it either *per se* or *per accidens*, but identity statements, providing no meaning of what God is. Perception by the intellect here is abstraction of a characteristic or action from a thing. Perception therefore presupposes two things referred to in language by two terms different in meaning, the thing from which the characteristic or action is abstracted, i.e. the body, and the thing which is abstracted, i.e. the characteristic or action signified in language by an attribute (*ṣifa*) or a verb (*fiʿl*). Given this, God is unperceptible by the intellect.

(e) God cannot be Described by Characteristics (*ṣifāt*); Therefore it is Impossible to Describe what He is; However it is known by Intuition that He is

> Among them (viz. the Jahmites) are people who deny God all attributes (*ṣinf min al-Muʿaṭṭila*). They say: 'God is not a thing' (*lā shayʾa*), nor is He [something] 'of' a thing (*mā min shayʾin*), nor is He [something which is] 'in' a thing (*mā fī shayʾin*). Nor does the attribute (*ṣifa*) of a thing apply to Him, nor the knowledge (*maʿrifa*) of a thing, nor the estimation (*tawahhum*) of a thing. They argue that they know God only by intuition (*bi-l-takhmīn*). They apply to Him the name 'godhead' (*ism al-ulūhiyya*), but do not describe Him by an attribute (*ṣifa*) which pertains to the godhead.[4]
> (al-Malaṭī, *Tanbīh*, 96.2–5)

The Jahmites quoted by the traditionalist (*muḥaddith*) Abū l-Ḥusayn al-Malaṭī (d. 377/987) argue on the basis of Aristotle's theory of knowledge. They distinguish between knowing 'what' something is and 'that' something is (cf. *Anal. post.* II, 7). Their argument can be summarized as follows. To answer the 'what' question and to acquire knowledge (*maʿrifa*) of *what* a thing is, at least two terms which are the same in reference but different in meaning are needed. The meanings which provide this knowledge of a thing are acquired by a kind or degree of abstraction of properties or characteristics (*ṣifāt*) from sensible things, one of which is estimation (*tawahhum*) (Gutas 2012: 426f., n. 87). The knowledge (*maʿrifa*) of *what* a thing is happens when enough properties or

[4] Reading: *wa-lā yaṣifūnahu bi-ṣifatin taqaʿu ʿalā l-ulūhiyya* instead of *wa-lā yaṣifūnahu bi-ṣifatin yaqaʿu ʿalayhi l-ulūhiyya* (ed. al-Kawtharī 1388/1968: 96.4f.).

characteristics which are peculiar to the thing in question are abstracted and constitute in the mind 'what' the thing is. The abstraction of the property or characteristic presupposes that at least two things or two states of a thing are like or unlike each other with regard to this property or characteristic, since otherwise the property or characteristic is not intellectually perceived as a property or characteristic. Being peculiar to a thing presupposes that the peculiarity does not belong to some other thing which is with regard to this peculiarity unlike the first thing. The Jahmites quoted by al-Malaṭī deny that this is the case with regard to God, arguing that He neither is a thing so that 'thing' can be predicated of Him, nor does He belong to a thing so that He can be said to be something 'of' a thing, nor is He a property or characteristic inherent in a thing so that He can be said to be 'in' a thing. Since God lacks every property or characteristic which can be said to belong or not to belong to a thing God is not object of the knowledge of what a thing is. In reply to the question 'what is God' and 'to what does the name "God" refer and what does it mean' God's 'whatness' (*māhiyya*) can only be explained by '[God is] the-being-God' (*al-ulūhiyya*), and the name refers to and means 'godhead'. Given this, the Jahmites maintained that there is no concept formation with regard to God.

However, according to them there is demonstrative knowledge *that* God is. This knowledge happens 'by intuition' (*bi-l-takhmīn*), i.e. spontaneously. 'By intuition' is usually signified in Arabic by *bi-l-ḥads*, but *bi-l-takhmīn* is also attested.[5] In Avicenna's theory of knowledge intuitive things (*ḥadsiyyāt*) are 'data provided by finding the middle term of a syllogism ... based on experience' (Gutas 2012: 396). In other words, intuition is finding the cause why something is the case based on experience. In the Jahmite theory of knowledge 'God' is the 'real' agent (*fāʿil*) of any activity (*fiʿl*) which is perceived in corporeal things (cf. s. I(g)). The knowledge *that* God is according to the Jahmite theory is knowing by intuition that every coming-to-be and passing-away and every alteration is caused by a first cause.

(f) All Attributes and Verbs Applied to God are Identical in Meaning and Reference

> They [i.e. the Jahmites] do not affirm [with regard to God] a face, nor a [property of] hearing (*lā samʿan*), nor a [property of] seeing (*lā baṣaran*), nor a [property of] knowing (*lā ʿilman*), nor a [property of] speaking (*lā kalāman*), nor any property (*ṣifa*) ... And they use the terms 'His hearing' (*samʿuhu*), 'His seeing' (*baṣaruhu*), 'His knowing' (*ʿilmuhu*), 'His speaking' (*kalāmuhu*) with one and the same meaning (*bi-maʿnā wāḥid*) ... (al-Dārimī, *Radd*, 95.19–21)

The phrase 'nor any property' at the end of the enumeration of things which are not affirmed with regard to God is used in the sense of 'et cetera'. This indicates that the

5 Regarding the term *bi-l-takhmīn* used in the sense of *bi-l-ḥads* see *Lisān al-ʿarab* s.v. ḫ-m-n.

preceding terms 'hearing', 'seeing', 'knowing', 'speaking' refer to properties or characteristics (*ṣifāt*) rather than to the activities (*afʿāl*) 'to hear', 'to see', 'to know', 'to speak', etc. which signify actualized states of being (*aḥwāl*). Further, the term *ṣifa* may either refer to 'attribute' in the sense of a morphologically defined class of words which signify that a property and characteristic (*ṣifa*) belongs to a thing, or to the property and characteristic itself, indicated by verbal nouns. In the present context it refers to the property itself abstracted from sensible activities. The Jahmites argue that it is impossible that to God belong properties, inasmuch as He is not a thing to which belongs the property of being like or unlike. Therefore they argue that terms signifying properties, when used with regard to God, are not only coextensive, i.e. identical in reference, but also cointensive, i.e. identical in meaning, affirming of God nothing except godhead (cf. s. I(e)). According to this theory of meaning, no predication of God is possible. Any affirmation regarding God indicates the identity of the terms in sense and reference (cf. s. I(d)). This also holds for the infinite term 'non-body' (*ghayr al-jism*) (cf. s. I(b)).

The theory of sense and reference reported from those Jahmites agrees with that of the neo-Arian Eunomius of Cyzikus (Schöck 2012: 26f.), and it disagrees with that of the Church Fathers, according to which with regard to God privative affirmations of properties can be taken in the sense of negative predications (Wolfson 1957: 155).

On first sight it may seem that the account that Jahm accepted descriptions (*awṣāf*) of God by which no thing can be described (Baghdādī, *Farq*, 199.10–13; van Ess 1991–7: ii. 501; v. 215) means that he accepted them as predications regarding God. But *awṣāf* means 'descriptions' in the sense of 'actions of describing', not in the sense of attributes (*ṣifāt*) which refer to properties abstracted from something. Given this, the accounts report that Jahm allowed that God is described in language by terms which refer to non-thing, i.e. that which is outside the realm of like and unlike (cf. ss. I(b) and (d)), and this reference is not a predication (*pace* Wolfson 1959: 75a).

(g) God is the Only Cause of All Things

> [Jahm said:] In reality (*fī l-ḥaqīqa*) no activity (*fiʿl*) belongs to something except God alone. He is the agent (*fāʿil*), whereas the activities (*afʿāl*) of humans only in tropical speech (*ʿalā l-majāz*) are correlated to them, in the way in which someone says: 'the tree moves', 'the celestial body moves in a circle', 'the sun goes down', but [in reality] it is God who exercises that effect upon the tree, the celestial body and the sun. However, God creates for man a particular potency by which the activity (*fiʿl*) happens, and He creates for him in each individual case a particular act of will and a particular act of choice to exercise the particular activity by that in the same way in which He creates for him a particular length by which he is long and a particular colour by which he is coloured. (al-Ashʿarī, *Maqālāt*, 279.3–9)

The account does not explain which kind of tropical speech is meant, but it seems that a metonymic inversion of agency and patiency is meant. In tropical speech agency is attributed to the patient, but in reality the sensible compound whose movement is perceived is the effect of God's agency, namely of his creation of the movement in the corporeal compound described by 'the tree moves'. What holds for movements, acts of will and choice, length and shortness, colours, etc. also holds for the Qur'ān:

> Jahm used to say that the Qur'ān is a body and the effect (*fiʿl*) of God. And he used to say that movements also are bodies. There is no agent except God. (al-Ashʿarī, *Maqālāt*, 589.3–5)

According to Jahm's theory of creation every perceivable property of the corporeal is caused anew in every instant of time. This theory is reported more elaborately from Ḍirār b. ʿAmr.

II Ḍirār b. ʿAmr

The doxographical accounts on Ḍirār's doctrine mainly focus on two issues, a bundle theory of body together with the denial of latent intrinsic powers and potencies of bodies causing change in corporeal substances. His doctrine is in line with Gregory of Nyssa's theory of the origination of the corporeal, material from the incorporeal, immaterial by an act of the divine will. Gregory developed this theory within the framework of his Christian physics of creation. According to Gregory, all material being is an assemblage (συνδρομή) and combination (σύνθεσις) of qualities (ποιότητες) or properties (ἰδιώματα, ποίαι ἰδιότητες) originating from God. By themselves they are immaterial, non-sensible concepts and thoughts (καθ' ἑαυτὰ ἔννοια ... καὶ νοήματα). When they combine with each other, they become matter (*In Hex.* 7, PG 44, 69C–D; Dobner 2009: 16.8–11; cf. s. II(c)). Gregory argues that this is evident by the fact that matter can only be conceived by these intelligible qualities and properties (*De hom. opific.* XXIV, PG 44, 212D–213B; cf. Wolfson 1970: 57–9; Sorabji 2006: 290–6; 2004: ii. 159–61). This theory of creation and epistemology is grounded in the Middle Platonic interpretation of the Platonic ideas as thoughts (νοήσεις; νοήματα) of God (Alcinoos, *Didaskalikos* IX, Whittaker 1990: 21, 31, and 33), which Gregory replaced by immaterial, intelligible qualities or properties (cf. Stead 1976: 110f.), and it is linked to discussions among Peripatetics, Platonists, and Stoics on the question of whether qualities are corporeal or not (cf. Kupreeva 2003; Köckert 2009: 422f.).

Like Gregory, Ḍirār draws an analogy between the origination of the corporeal world, its material and parts on the one hand and the intelligibility of the parts of sensible compounds on the other hand. The cosmos is intelligible by the decomposition of the parts put together by God's act of creation. Ḍirār calls the intelligible qualities or properties which materialize by being combined and assembled 'accidents' (*aʿrāḍ*) thereby making use of Alexander of Aphrodisias' and Porphyry's distinction between inseparable and separable accidents, and his theory of qualitative and substantial change evidently is based on Aristotle. But despite Ḍirār's apparent dependence on the Aristotelian tradition of philosophy of nature there is a significant difference which distinguishes Ḍirār not only from Aristotle's commentators as well as from Plotinus and Philoponus. According to Ḍirār's theory of physical creation perceptible substance is neither a conglomeration of qualities *and* matter, nor is there a form *in* matter. According to Ḍirār there is neither any prime matter whatsoever nor any material elements besides the compounds of accidents which make up the sensible world. Nor is there a form (εἶδος/*ṣūra*) or essence (οὐσία/*jawhar, dhāt*) corresponding to matter (see s. II(i)). In Ḍirār's physical theory the intelligible qualities and the sensible qualities correspond to each other one-to-one. For humans 'reality' is the sensible world without another reality behind or between man and the absolutely incomposite God.

The reason for Ḍirār's refusal of material elements and of forms and essences is that Ḍirār's analysis of the material world draws on Aristotle's methodology of natural science in which Aristotle gave up the definition of the form-*eidos* by *genus* and *differentia specifica* in favour of the definition of classes of animals by a manifoldness of coordinate, not subordinate, differences (Aristotle, *De part. an.* I 3, 643b13–644a11; Tugendhat 1958: 152; Kullmann 1974: 68–72; Liatsi 2003: 212; Cho 2003: 181–4; Kullmann 2007: 337–40). Ḍirār took the definitional 'parts' of the animals and of all sensible bodies as the intelligible things in the mind ('accidents': *aʿrāḍ*; in the terminology of his fellow Muʿtazilite Muʿammar *maʿānī*; Wolfson 1965: 677) corresponding to sensible things outside the mind ('accidents': *aʿrāḍ*; in the terminology of Muʿammar also *maʿānī, ʿilal*; Wolfson 1965: 678f.) and signified by the characterizing signs of language in the form of appellations (*simāt*; sing. *sima*; see s. II(f)). Ḍirār wrote a treatise against Aristotle's theory of substance and accidents (cf. s. II(i)) in which he presumably denied essentialism. This, of course, is not to say that Ḍirār had direct access to Aristotle's works. Probably Ḍirār's theory of God's synthesis of the cosmos and the corresponding analysis of the corporeal sensible world goes back to the Porphyrian tradition (cf. s. II(a)) mediated by Christian sources. The degree of probability of this thesis can only be assessed after the reconstruction of his thought by a detailed and meticulous analysis of the doctrines transmitted in his name, paying particular attention to terminology and phrasing.

The most systematic and comprehensive account on Ḍirār's doctrine of the physical world is extant in al-Ashʿarī, *Maqālāt*, 305.5–306.11 (cf. van Ess 1991–7: v. 231–3). What follows will comment on this account section by section and use further sources to elucidate its meaning and philosophical background. The difficulties in understanding the text result from its extreme brevity and terseness. But it becomes comprehensible in light of the framework of the ancient and late-ancient philosophical and Patristic tradition.

(a) Body is a Compound and Substrate of Accidents

> Ḍirār b. ʿAmr said: 'The body is [an aggregate of] accidents (*al-jism aʿrāḍ*), which are composed and combined (*ullifat wa-jumiʿat*)[6] and thus subsist and exist [in extramental reality] (*fa-qāmat wa-thabatat*) and become a body (*fa-ṣārat jisman*) which bears (*yaḥtamilu*) the accidents, whenever it [i.e. the body] is the substrate of inherence (*idhā ḥulla*), and [which bears] change (*taghayyur*) from one condition (*ḥāl*) to another.' (al-Ashʿarī, *Maqālāt*, 305.5–7)

This sentence, together with the following paragraph of the account on Ḍirār's doctrine (see s. II(b)), has been interpreted in the sense that 'body' is described as an aggregate of 'basic' accidents, and that the aggregate, once constituted by its basic accidents, can become the bearer of further, additional accidents inhering in the basic aggregate (Pretzl 1930: 119; van Ess 1967: 262; 1991–7: iii. 39, iv. 471, v. 232f.). The 'basic' accidents then would be temporally prior to the inhering accidents. However, Ḍirār's criterion for the distinction between the two kinds of accidents are the notions of inseparability and separability (see s. II(b)), and these notions do not entail the notions of priority and posteriority, but rather the notions of persistence (*baqāʾ*) and non-persistence (cf. ss. II(e)–(f)) and of indispensability and non-indispensability (cf. van Ess 1979: 30).

The *locus classicus* on which Ḍirār's aggregate-theory is grounded is Porphyry, *Isag.* II, 19–27 where Porphyry says that each individual is 'combined out of characteristics' (ἐξ ἰδιοτήτων συνέστηκεν) which make up an 'aggregate', in other words a 'collection', 'sum', or 'total' (ἄθροισμα) which will be found in no other thing. In his commentary on Aristotle's *Categories* Porphyry uses the term 'assemblage of qualities' (συνδρομὴ ποιοτήτων) (*In Cat.* 129.10; Bodéüs 2008: 426), i.e. the term used by Gregory of Nyssa (see above). Porphyry's example for the individual is Socrates, and his examples for Socrates's characteristics are 'white', 'approaching man', 'son of Sophroniscus'. On condition that Socrates is the only son of Sophroniscus (and, to be precise, that there is no other man named 'Sophroniscus' with a son named 'Socrates'), the name 'Socrates' and the total of 'white', 'approaching man', and 'son of Sophroniscus' are coextensive in reference. Further, Porphyry distinguishes the characteristics which are peculiar to the individual Socrates from the common characteristics of all humans inasmuch as they

[6] Van Ess supposes that the terms *taʾlīf* and *ijtimāʿ* go back to Greek ἄθροισμα (van Ess 1991–7: iii. 224), but this means 'collection, aggregate, bundle, total, sum', which has been translated by Abū ʿUthmān al-Dimashqī in his translation of the *Isagoge* by the term *jumla*; cf. e.g. also Ibn Sīnā, *al-Ilāhiyyāt* 5.4, i. 226.7 and 15). Whereas the term *ijtimāʿ* in the present context indeed is used synonymously with the term *jumla*, it is more likely that the term *taʾlīf* already in early *kalām* is an equivalent of συμπλοκή and σύνθεσις, the terms which have been translated by *taʾlīf* by Isḥāq b. Ḥunayn. The term *taʾlīf* throughout Arabic logic and philosophy can refer to the physical, logical, and linguistic composition and combination of simple items. The overall point in question is the kind of equivalence between physical and linguistic composition and logical decomposition and analysis. This ambiguity of the term *taʾlīf* which often, but not always, is used equivalent to *tarkīb* matches Aristotle's use of the terms συμπλοκή and σύνθεσις. For the present context see e.g. Aristotle, *Phys.* I, 5, 188b8–21.

are humans (*Isag.* II, 19–27). The latter are those characteristics which are peculiar to human in distinction to those characteristics which are common to the proximate genus of human.

When Ḍirār says 'the body is [an aggregate of] accidents' (*al-jism aʿrāḍ*) he refers to the common accidents of all bodies as long as they exist as bodies. 'Body' is the highest genus of all corporeal things. From the epistemological aspect the term *al-jism* ('the body', determined by the article) refers to the universal, intelligible body, from the logical aspect to the genus 'body', and from the ontological aspect to the common, persistent matter underlying all material things. The statement 'the body is accidents' (*al-jism aʿrāḍ*) signifies the coextensiveness of subject term and predicate term.[7] That is to say, the universal, intelligible body and the genus 'body' are constituted by coordinative accidents whose sum and total is coextensive with what 'body' is *simpliciter*, considered in itself, qua body (cf. Porphyry, *Isag.* I, 1.18–23). The intelligible body is, in Gregory of Nyssa's words, only in thought (κατ' ἐπίνοιαν) (*De hom. opific.* XXIV, PG 44, 212D–213A). The genus 'body' encompasses all possible individual compositions of body, but it does not have extramental reality besides or precedent to the concrete, particular combinations of particular accidents which constitute the genus in the sense of a whole and total of all things signified by the term 'body'. The common matter 'body' is by itself imperceptible, since it is neither alive nor dead, neither red nor of any particular colour, nor is it heavy or light, etc. It is rather all specifications of its properties *in potentia*, capable of bearing any of the contraries that fall under its properties. It is logically prior to individual natural bodies, but neither prior to them in generation and time nor epistemologically prior. In Ḍirār's theory the name 'body' does not signify an essence, but either the genus 'body' as a whole which is the sum of its accidents or an individual body which is the sum of its accidents.

The sources do not explicitly mention Ḍirār's views on the relation of body and spirit (*rūḥ*). But his statements that body is a compound of accidents and that man is a compound of accidents (see s. II(i)) imply that spirit is accidental to body. Ibn al-Rāwandī (third/ninth cent.) followed this theory. Like Ḍirār he holds that 'man is a compound of accidents' (*al-insān huwa aʿrāḍ mujtamiʿa*) and further 'the spirit is an accident' (Maqdisī, *Badʿ*, ii. 121.9–10; 123.1), in other words a property or characteristic belonging to the sum of 'accidents' which constitute man.

The phrase 'the body (*al-jism*) … whenever it is the substrate of inherence (*idhā ḥulla*)' does not indicate that the body as the substrate (*maḥall*; cf. e.g. al-Ashʿarī, *Maqālāt*, 193.2) of particular and individual accidents is prior to the generation of the particular and individual bodies, but rather the coincidence between the existence of corporeality as substrate and the existence of inhering accidents which determine the particular and individual bodies which make up the total of the general body as long as it exists as body, that is to say as long as the physical world is brought into being by God.

7 An analogous phrasing is found in another account on Ḍirār's doctrine (see s. II(i)).

Ḍirār's concept of body as permanent substrate of non-permanent inhering accidents goes back to Alexander of Aphrodisias. It is what Alexander, Porphyry (Simplicius, *In Cat.* 48.6–11; cf. Köckert 2009: 348), and Philoponus have called 'second substrate' (δεύτερον ὑποκείμενον). According to Alexander's commentary on *De caelo* the second substrate is the three-dimensional in the sense of the matter from which *individual* natural bodies are composed when they come to be and into which they decompose when they pass away. It is the eternal substrate of change, but considered in itself without the changing qualities of individual bodies which always coexist with three-dimensionality (Moraux 2001: 230f., 241). Also, according to Philoponus the second substrate is the unqualified body (τὸ ἄποιον σῶμα) signified by the appellative 'the three-dimensional' (τὸ τριχῇ διαστατόν) that is considered in itself indeterminate which is why it admits of an always different magnitude and shape (*In Phys.* 520.18–26; Wildberg 1988: 209). It is the generated unchanging subject of all physical change (*In Phys.* 156.10–17; Wildberg 1988: 210f.). Three-dimensionality is defined as indeterminate quantity, and since quantity is an inseparable accident (ἀχώριστον εἶναι συμβεβηκός) of body, three-dimensionality is also an inseparable accident of body (*In Phys.* 561.3–12; Wildberg 1988: 212). Basil of Caesarea and Gregory of Nyssa draw on this concept of material corporeality as the substrate of generation, corruption, and alteration of individual bodies, which in their theory of creation logically, but neither ontologically nor temporally, precedes them (e.g. Gregory of Nyssa, *In Hex.* 7, PG 44, 69C; Dobner 2009: 16.6–8; Köckert 2009: 348, 432, 437).

The third part of the sentence quoted above draws on the Aristotelian doctrine that substances can undergo change because they are receptive of contraries whereas qualities are not (cf. Aristotle, *Cat.* 5, 3b24–33; 4a10–22; Alcinoos, *Didaskalikos* XI, Whittaker 1990: 26.108; Dillon 1993: 19f.). The accidents which determine the unity of a particular body are replaceable, whereby either qualitative or substantial alteration happens (cf. ss. II(e)–(f)). Corporeality is the persistent, continuous constant through all kinds of material change as long as the composition and combination of accidents constituting a body is generated.

The term 'accident' (*ʿaraḍ*) in contrast to 'substance' (*jawhar*) is used by Ḍirār in the usual technical sense of the distinction of being in a substrate (ἐν ὑποκειμένῳ) and substrate (ὑποκειμένον) (*Cat.* 2, 1a20–1b9; cf. s. II(d)). This description of 'accident' also holds for Ḍirār's understanding of the inseparable accidents of body, inasmuch as he signifies them as 'parts' of the body (see s. II(b)). And also Alexander of Aphrodisias' definition of the inseparable 'accident' as an epiphenomenon of that from which it is inseparable (*In Top.* 50.31–51.5) matches Ḍirār's use of the term 'accident'.

(b) The Distinction between Inseparable per se Accidents and Mere, Separable Accidents

> [Ḍirār b. ʿAmr said:] Those accidents [which are coextensive with body] are those of which or of whose contrary (*ḍidd*) no body can be free, like no

> body can be free (*lā yakhlū l-jism*) of one of the two [contraries] 'life' and 'death', and like the body is inseparable (*lā yanfakku*) from one colour of the genus (*jins*) of colours and of one taste of the genus of tastes. The same holds for [the accidents which belong to the genus of] weight like heaviness and lightness, and for [the contraries] roughness and softness, heat and cold, humidity and dryness, and likewise [body is inseparable from the accident] solidity (*ṣamd*).[8] Hence, according to Ḍirār, that of which and of whose contrary it [i.e. the body] is separable (*mā yanfakku minhu*), does not belong to it [i.e. the body] as a part (*baʿḍ*), like [active] power (*qudra*) and [passive] suffering (*alam*), knowledge (*ʿilm*) and ignorance (*jahl*). (al-Ashʿarī, *Maqālāt*, 305.7–12)

In *De gen. et corr.* II, 1, 329a10–12 Aristotle insists that no existent body can be without contrariety, it must be either light or heavy and cold or hot, etc. In Ḍirār's words, as long as a body exists, it 'is inseparable' from the genus of weight, under which falls heaviness and lightness, and it is inseparable from the genus under which falls heat and cold, etc. Ḍirār here makes use of the terminology of the Aristotelian school tradition which distinguishes between 'inseparable accident' (συμβεβηκὸς … ἀχώριστον) and 'separable accident' (συμβεβηκὸς … χωριστόν) (Porphyry, *Isag.* V, 12.25–13.3; cf. Barnes 2006: 224–9; cf. also Alexander of Aphrodisias, *In Top.* 50.31–51.5), translated by Abū ʿUthmān al-Dimashqī as *ʿaraḍ ghayr mufāriq* and *ʿaraḍ mufāriq* (Badawī 1980: iii. 1086). For example, Socrates is inseparable from place, but separable from this particular place, because Socrates is always in some place, but after having left the previous place he is at another place (Porphyry, *In Cat.* 79.17–22; Bodéüs 2008: 190f.). The distinction had been introduced by Aristotle in *Analytica posteriora* I 4 and applied in *De partibus animalium* I by the contrast between per se accidents (συμβεβηκότα καθ' αὑτά) and mere accidents (συμβεβηκότα) or properties by which bodies are in passive states (πάθη). Per se accidents follow necessarily from that which a thing is by itself, are concomitant with their subject, and are predicated of a subject qua being that subject without being definitional properties (cf. Kullmann 1974: 181–3; 2007: 165; Liatsi 2003; Cho 2003: 236). In contrast, mere accidents are specializing or individualizing their substrates which are subject to

[8] Three of the manuscripts used by Ritter for his edition of the *Maqālāt* have *al-ṣamd*, one *al-ṣiḥḥa*. Zimmermann read *al-ṣamd* and translated the term for Sorabji as 'compactness' (Sorabji 2006: 295), which is correct, both on the basis of the manuscripts and regarding the grammatical context which is an enumeration of verbal nouns. Further, *al-ṣamd* is not only witnessed in three manuscripts, but also the *lectio difficilior*. Van Ess read *al-ṣamad* (one of the names of God mentioned in the Qurʾān) in Ritter's edition, which does not make any sense in the present context, and therefore he decided for the reading *al-ṣiḥḥa*, which he translated as 'Funktionieren' (van Ess 1991–7: v. 232f., iii. 39). To my mind there is no need to mistrust the reading *al-ṣamd*. The term probably translates ἀντιτυπία ('solidity, resistance'), the notion which, together with three-dimensionality (or magnitude, τὸ μέγεθος), in Stoic and Epicurean natural philosophy usually is part of the definition of sensible body (Brisson 2010: 41f., 45). See Ps. Galen, *de qualit. incorporeis* 18; Sextus Empiricus, *Adv. mathem.* 10.240 and 257, 11.226; Blank 1998: 96; Sorabji 2004: 269. Cf. Plotinus who says that ἀντιτυπία distinguishes physical body from mathematical figure (*Ennéades* VI, 1 [42], 26, 17–22). Also Gregory lists ἀντιτυπία consistently among the qualities (ποιότητες) or properties (ἰδιώματα, ποίαι ἰδιότητες) which are concomitant with body (see s. II(b)).

change when alteration from a quality to its contrary or something in between happens while the substrate persists (cf. e.g. *De gen. et corr.* I, 4, 319b8–14). Active power (*qudra*) and passive suffering (*alam*), knowledge (*ʿilm*) and ignorance (*jahl*) do not belong to all bodies, but only to particular kinds of bodies, namely power and suffering to animals and knowledge and ignorance to humans. Therefore they are separable from body qua body. But insofar as they belong to particular bodies they can be replaced by their contraries, whereby qualitative alteration of those particular bodies from one state (*ḥāl*) to another happens (cf. s. II(e)).

The concomitance of body with its inseparable properties is also found in Gregory of Nyssa. Like Ḍirār, Gregory refers to the genus of contrary properties:

> For a thing is not a body if it lacks colour, shape, resistance, extension, weight and the other properties (ἰδιώματα), and each of these properties is not body, but is found to be something else, when taken separately. Conversely, then, when these properties combine they produce material reality (*De hom. opific.* XXIV, PG 44, 213B–C; trans. Sorabji 2006: 291).

(c) The Impossibility that Sensible Accidents Come from Non-sensible Thoughts and the Material from the Immaterial

> According to him [i.e. Ḍirār] it is impossible that these accidents [i.e. the accidents of body] combine and become bodies after they have [already] existed [separately] (*baʿda wujūdihā*), and it is absurd that this effect is exerted on them except at the moment of their initial coming to be (*fī ḥāl ibtidāʾihā*), because they only emerge into existence in combination (*mujtamiʿatan*). (al-Ashʿarī, *Maqālāt* 305.12–14)

That is to say, accidents become determined by combination (*ijtimāʿ*) whereby individual bodies are generated. These are subject to qualitative and substantial change (cf. ss. II(e)–(f)). Ḍirār argues that it is impossible and absurd that the accidents of body exist without combination; in themselves they do not have 'real', extramental existence (cf. van Ess 1979: 30). This is because all existing accidents are determined and belong to an individual body. To claim the existence of undetermined accidents is absurd, i.e. self-contradictory, because by existence the accidents are determined. Probably the argument found in Gregory of Nyssa is the background of Ḍirār's teaching:

> How can quantity come from non-quantity, the visible from the invisible, some thing with limited bulk and size from what lacks magnitude and limits? And so also for the other characteristics seen in matter ... By His wise and powerful will, being capable of everything, He established for the creation of things all the things through which

matter is constituted: light, heavy, dense, rare, soft, resistant, fluid, dry, cold, hot, colour, shape, outline, extension. All of these are in themselves thoughts (ἔννοια) and bare concepts (νοήματα); none is matter on its own. But when they combine, they turn into matter. (*In Hex.* 7, PG 44, 69C–D; Dobner 2009: 15.11–16.11; trans. Sorabji 2006: 290; cf. Sorabji 2004: 159).

(d) The Impossibility of Separate Existence of Accidents

> According to him [i.e. Ḍirār] it is possible that all of them [i.e. of the accidents of body] combine and exist [as determined bodies], but it is absurd that all of them are separated and exist, since if they were separated and existed simultaneously, colour would exist without belonging to that which is coloured and life would exist without belonging to that which is alive. When you said to him: 'According to this inference (*qiyās*) separation is impossible to them', he once said: 'Their separation is their passing away (*fanāʾ*)', and another time he said: 'Separation is possible for two bodies. But it is not possible for the parts of bodies at the time of their existence.' (al-Ashʿarī, *Maqālāt*, 305.14–306.3)

This argument is grounded in the 'rule' that qualities in contrast to substances exist in a substrate (ἐν ὑποκειμένῳ) (Aristotle, *Cat.* 2, 1a20–1b9; cf. Thiel 2004: 90–3).

(e) Qualitative Change through the Replacement of Accidents by Contrary Accidents

> According to him [i.e. Ḍirār] it is possible that a part of the body passes away while the body exists on condition that it is replaced by its contrary. If, however, the difference [between the first state and the second] is not due to two contrary accidents [so that the part which passes away is not replaced by a contrary accident], the body passes away together with the part [which passes away]. (al-Ashʿarī, *Maqālāt*, 306.3–5)

(f) Substantial Change through the Passing Away of Half or More than Half of the Accidents of a Body

> According to him [i.e. Ḍirār] on that condition it is not possible that the major part or half [of the accidents] pass away, because he maintained that the judgement (*ḥukm*) [on what kind of body it is] refers to the greater part [of the accidents of a body]. So, when the major part persists, the characteristic sign (*sima*) of the body persists, and when the major part is removed, the characteristic sign does not persist with regard to the minor part. (al-Ashʿarī, *Maqālāt*, 306.5–8)

(g) Movement and Rest of a Body Persist during Qualitative and Substantial Change

> According to him [i.e. Ḍirār] it is possible that God lets pass away a part of it [i.e. of the body] and lets originate its contrary while it is moving. Then the whole to which belongs the originating part is moving by that movement at the presence (*ḥāl*) of the existence of the movement. The same holds if it were at rest. (al-Ashʿarī, *Maqālāt*, 306.8–10)

Sections II(e)–(g) refer to the distinction between coming-to-be and qualitative change explained by Aristotle, *De gen. et corr.* I, 4. Qualitative change (s. II(e)) is alteration of quality (κατὰ τὸ ποιόν) or state (κατὰ παθος), that is in Ḍirār's terminology change of a separable accident, namely when the perceptible substrate persists while one or several of its separable accidents change from one contrary to the other or to something intermediate between the two contraries. Aristotle's example is the body which, while persisting as the same body, changes from being healthy to being ill and the other way round, or bronze which persists while changing its shape (*De gen. et corr.* I, 4, 319b8–14; cf. *Phys.* VI, 10, 241a30–3).

In contrast, passing-away of one substance and coming-to-be of another substance (s. II(f)) happens when the perceptible substance does not persist and the substrate changes its identity (*De gen. et corr.* I, 4, 319b14–320a7), that is in Ḍirār's words, when the perceptible, characteristic mark or sign (*sima*) of the body does not persist, so that the body is no longer recognized as the body which had existed before. The term *sima* may stand for the perceptible characteristic and distinguishing mark and sign or for the linguistic characterizing and distinguishing sign, that is the characteristic distinguishing property and differentia which can function as predicate in a judgement about the thing in question or the corresponding appellation (*tasmiya*) by which the thing is signified. This use of the term *sima* is close to Gregory of Nyssa's use of the term ὑποδιαστολή in *ep.* 35 *Ad Petrum* (Basil of Caesarea, *ep.* 38, 2.10, in *Saint Basile: Lettres* I, ed. Courtonne, 81f.).

On these conditions it is obvious that movement and rest of a body can persist during qualitative and substantial change (s. II(g)), namely when one or several properties of a body change while the body is moving, or when a body passes away and a different body comes to be in its place while the body is moving. This indeed constantly happens in the course of the rotation of the earth.

(h) Movement does not Occur to Accidents but to Corporeal Entities Only

> According to him [i.e. Ḍirār] it is absurd that movement occurs to an accident. It only occurs to the body; and body is accidents in combination (*aʿrāḍ mujtamiʿa*). (al-Ashʿarī, *Maqālāt*, 306.10–12).

The last point is evident from what has been said in ss. II(c)–(d). According to Ḍirār, accidents are not corporeal by themselves and therefore cannot be affected by movement and rest. The same holds for all qualities of the corporeal. The doctrine that qualities are in themselves immaterial is in accordance with the Platonic and Peripatetic tradition and distinguishes Ḍirār from Jahm b. Ṣafwān (see s. I(c)).

Al-Ashʿarī's detailed report on Ḍirār's physical theory ends here. Two further short doxographical accounts should be added.

(i) There is no Prime Matter, nor Material Elements, nor Immanent Form or Essence

> Ḍirār b. ʿAmr said: 'Man' is [a unity] of many things (*al-insān min ashyāʾ kathīra*): colour, [sense of] taste, [sense of] smell, [active] potency (*quwwa*) and similar things. These [things] are man (*innahā l-insān*) when (*idhā*) they are combined. There is no other substance (*jawhar*) besides them. (al-Ashʿarī, *Maqālāt*, 330.3–5)

The statement 'these [things] are man when they are combined' again signifies the coextensiveness of the intelligible referent of the name 'man' and its accidents at the time when these accidents combine (cf. s. II(a)). This said, and given that Ḍirār like Gregory of Nyssa held that qualities in themselves are bare thoughts and concepts (cf. s. II(c)), Ḍirār refused Aristotle's and Plotinus's doctrine that sensible substance is a conglomeration of qualities *and* matter (συμφόρησίς τις ποιοτήτων καὶ ὕλης; Plotinus, *Ennéades*, VI, 3 [44], 8, 20; cf. Sorabji 1988: 51f.) as well as the concept of immanent form or essence as counterpart of prime matter. This refusal presumably is the topic of Ḍirār's unfortunately lost treatise against Aristotle's theory of substances and accidents (*K. al-Radd ʿalā Arisṭālīs fī l-jawāhir wa-l-aʿrāḍ*) (van Ess 1991–7: v. 229).

(j) Both God and Man are in Reality Agents

> Ḍirār b. ʿAmr dissociated himself from the Muʿtazila by his doctrine that the deeds (*aʿmāl*) of human beings are created and that one and the same action has two agents, one of them creates it, and this is God, and the other acquires it, and this is man. God is in reality (*fī l-ḥaqīqa*) an agent (*fāʿil*) regarding the actions of human beings, and they are in reality (*fī l-ḥaqīqa*) agents (*fāʿilūn*) regarding them. He maintained that the capacity to act (*istiṭāʿa*) exists before and after the activity (*fiʿl*) and that it is part of the one who is capable (*mustaṭīʿ*). (al-Ashʿarī, *Maqālāt*, 281.2–6)

This doctrine dissociates Ḍirār on one side from the Muʿtazila and on the other from Jahm b. Ṣafwān (see s. I(g)). In contrast to Jahm, Ḍirār distinguished between a two-sided, active capacity to act on the one hand and the fact that the effect happens in the thing acted upon on the other hand. Man's capacity to act does not only exist together with the particular activity he performs by this capacity as Jahm maintained, but also before the particular act performed later by this capacity. Active potency (*quwwa*), or capacity to act (*istiṭāʿa*), according to Ḍirār, is an inseparable accident of man (see s. II(i)), that is to say it persists in a human being as long as the human being persists. This distinguishes Ḍirār from Jahm. However, he shares with Jahm the view that there is no one-sided passive potency in corporeal things to be something or to become something else or to change its state of being, since according to Ḍirār substantial alteration is created by God through the passing away of half or more than half of the accidents of a body (see s. II(f)) and qualitative alteration happens through God's replacement of accidents of a body by contrary accidents (see s. II(e)). In contrast to the Muʿtazila, according to Ḍirār there is no passive capacity and no nature (*ṭabīʿa*) in non-rational things. Ḍirār's position is a compromise between the Muʿtazilite position which depends on the Aristotelian distinction between intrinsic active and passive potencies of things and Jahm's position which negates activity regarding the corporeal. While Ḍirār is close to al-Māturīdī's later theory of action, Jahm is closer to that of al-Ashʿarī (Schöck 2004: 109–15).

III Summary and Conclusions

Jahm's and Ḍirār's basic distinction between the composite, generate and the incomposite, ingenerate is a commonplace in later Muslim theology. It ultimately goes back to the issue of being and becoming in pre-Socratic philosophy which had been associated with the problem of the One in Plato's *Parmenides* and which attained particular importance in the Christian Trinitarian debates. The overall goal of Jahm's refusal of attributes (*ṣifāt*) of God is to preserve God's simplicity by ruling out any kind of predication regarding God and to explain the names and attributes by which God is appellated in the Qurʾān and according to reason in a way that excludes composition because the latter entails becoming and generateness. It is therefore likely that Jahm drew on arguments developed in Christian Trinitarian debates rather than immediately on pagan Neoplatonism and that he took up arguments which served in the Trinitarian debates to refute a unity of the divine essence and its hypostases. In particular Arians argued against Christian defenders of the divine 'hypostases' who interpreted the hypostases as distinct properties (ἴδια), proper features (ἰδιότητες), peculiarities (ἰδιάζοντα), specific properties (ἰδίωματα), or characteristics (χαρακτῆραι) which function as 'circumscription' (περιγραφή) of the divine essence and describe the essence in language by attaching descriptions (arab. *awṣāf*) or attributes (arab. *ṣifāt*) to the name (arab. *ism*) of the essence, saying God-Father, God-Son, God-Holy Spirit (Wolfson 1956: 6f., 15; Schöck 2012: 9, 32–4; Schöck 2014).

Jahm and Ḍirār did not follow the Aristotelian division of things into essences and accidents and into essential and non-essential parts, but applied a division into the material, mutable, passive on one hand and the immaterial, imutable, active on the other hand, assigning composition and materiality to created things and incomposition and immateriality to God. They did in no sense admit a plurality of intelligible ideas in God or between God and universe. Their theories entail the refusal of atomic material elements of the corporeal, of natural faculties inherent in things, and in particular of Aristotle's theory of prime matter and form and of nature comprehended as causal, productive power which effects generation, corruption, and change in sensible things. Jahm and Ḍirār replaced the efficacy of natural powers in the sense of principles and causes of being and becoming, of effecting and undergoing change and being at rest by God's immediate intentional creative power which generates the natural world as a sequence of contingent events of coming-to-be and passing-away. The common element of their theses is the understanding of the corporeal as the substrate of non-persistent affections and activities, and the interpretation that generation and corruption and the alteration of the states of natural bodies is due to those non-persistent properties generated *ex nihilo* by God's act of volition.

This is why the Muʿtazilite al-Naẓẓām, himself a prominent exponent of those who adhered to the theory of natures inherent in material things (*aṣḥāb al-ṭabāʾiʿ*), attacked Jahm and Ḍirār in the same breath because of their 'denial of the hiddenness' (*inkār al-kumūn*) of natures and properties in things (al-Jāḥiẓ, *Ḥayawān*, v. 10–14) and appellated them as 'the adherents of the accidents' (*aṣḥāb al-aʿrāḍ*) (al-Jāḥiẓ, *Ḥayawān*, v. 15.2; cf. van Ess 1967: 245f.; 1991–7: v. 31, no. 50).

References

Alexander of Aphrodisias (*In Top.*). *Alexandri Aphrodisiensis In Aristoteles Topicorum libros octo commentaria*. Ed. M. Wallies. Berlin: Reimer.

Alkinoos (Didaskalikos). Didaskalikos: Lehrbuch der Grundsätze Platons. Einleitung, Text, Übersetzung und Anmerkungen O. F. Summerell. Berlin/New York: de Gruyter, 2007.

Ansari, H. (1383–4sh/2004–5). 'Kitābi kalāmi az Ḍirār b. ʿAmr'. *Kitāb-i māh-i dīn* 89–90: 4–13.

Ansari, H. (2007). 'Abū ʿAlī al-Jubbāʾī et son livre *al-Maqālāt*'. In C. Adang et al. (eds.), *A Common Rationality: Muʿtazilism in Islam and Judaism*. Würzburg: Ergon, 21–37.

Aristotle (*Anal. post.*). *Aristotelis Analytica priora et posteriora*. Ed. W. D. Ross. Oxford: Clarendon, 1964.

Aristotle (*Cat.*). *Aristotelis Categoriae et Liber de interpretatione*. Ed. L. Minio-Paluello. Oxford: Clarendon, 1949.

Aristotle (*De gen. et corr.*). *Aristotelis De coelo et De generatione et corruptione*. Rec. C. Prantl. Leipzig: Teubner, 1881.

Aristotle (*De part. an.*). *Aristotelis De partibus animalium libri quattuor*. Ex recognitione B. Langkavel. Leipzig: Teubner, 1868.

Aristotle (Phys.). *Physica*. Ed. W. D. Ross. Oxford: Clarendon, 1966.

al-Ashʿarī, Abū l-Ḥasan ʿAlī b. Ismāʿīl (*Maqālāt*). *Maqālāt al-islāmiyyīn. Die dogmatischen Lehren der Anhänger des Islam*. Ed. H. Ritter. Wiesbaden, 1963.

Badawī, ʿA. (ed.) *Manṭiq Arisṭū*. 3 vols. Cairo: Dār al-Kutub al-Miṣriyya, 1948–52.

Baghdādī, ʿAbd al-Qāhir b. Ṭāhir (*Farq*). *Al-Farq bayna l-firaq*. Ed. M. Badr. Cairo, 1328/1910.

Barnes, J. (2006). *Porphyry: Introduction*. Oxford: Clarendon.

Basil of Caesarea. *Saint Basile: Lettres*. Ed. and French trans. Y. Courtonne. 3 vols. Paris: Société d'édition Les Belles Lettres, 1957–66.

Blank, D. L. (1998). *Sextus Empiricus: Against the Grammarians*. Oxford: Oxford University Press.

Bodéüs, R. (2008). *Commentaire aux* Catégories *d'Aristote*. Édition critique, traduction française, introduction et notes. Paris: Vrin.

Boeri, M. D. (2001). 'The Stoics on Bodies and Incorporeals'. *Review of Metaphysics* 54: 723–52.

Brisson, L. (2010). 'Between Matter and Body: Mass (ὄγκος) in the Sentences of Porphyry'. *International Journal of the Platonic Tradition* 4: 36–53.

Cho, D.-H. (2003). *Ousia und Eidos in der Metaphysik und Biologie des Aristoteles*. Stuttgart: Steiner Verlag.

al-Dārimī, Abū Saʿīd ʿUthmān b. Saʿīd (*Radd*). *K. ar-radd ʿalā l-ǧahmīya*. Einleitung und Kommentar G. Vitestam. Lund: Gleerup/Leiden: Brill, 1960.

Dillon, J. M. (1993). *Alcinous: The Handbook of Platonism*. Oxford: Clarendon.

Ḍirār b. ʿAmr al-Ghatafānī (*Taḥrīsh*). *K. al-Taḥrīsh*. Ed. Ḥusayn Khasānsū and Muḥammad Kaskūn. Istanbul: Sharikat Dār al-Irshād, 2014.

Dobner, H. R. (ed.) (2009). *Gregorii Nysseni In Hexaemeron: Opera exegetica in Genesim*, Pars 1. Leiden: Brill.

van Ess, J. (1967). 'Ḍirār b. ʿAmr und die "Cahmīya": Biographie einer vergessenen Schule'. *Der Islam* 43: 241–79.

van Ess, J. (1968). 'Ḍirār b. ʿAmr und die "Cahmīya": Biographie einer vergessenen Schule (Fortsetzung und Schluß)'. *Der Islam* 44: 1–70.

van Ess, J. (1979). 'Une lecture a rebours de l'histoire du Muʿtazilisme'. *Revue des études islamiques* 47: 19–69.

van Ess, J. (1991–7). *Theologie und Gesellschaft im 2. und 3. Jahrhundert Hidschra: Eine Geschichte des religiösen Denkens im frühen Islam*. 6 vols. Berlin: de Gruyter.

van Ess, J. (2010). *Der Eine und das Andere: Beobachtungen an islamischen häresiographischen Texten*. 2 vols. Berlin: de Gruyter.

Frank, R. M. (1965). 'The Neoplatonism of Jahm b. Ṣafwān'. *Le Muséon* 78: 135–424.

Gregory of Nyssa (*De hom. opific.*, PG 44). *De hominis opificio*. Patrologia Graeca, vol. 44, ed. J. P. Migne. Paris: Garnier, 1863.

Gregory of Nyssa (*In Hex.*, PG 44). *In Hexaemeron*. Patrologia Graeca, vol. 44, ed. J. P. Migne. Paris: Garnier, 1863.

Gutas, D. (2012). 'The Empiricism of Avicenna'. *Oriens* 40: 391–436.

Halkin, A. S. (1934). 'The Ḥashwiyya'. *Journal of the American Oriental Society* 54: 1–28.

Ibn Ḥanbal (*Radd*). *Al-Radd ʿalā l-Zanādiqa wa-l-Jahmiyya*. Cairo: al-Maṭbaʿa al-Salafiyya 1393/[1973].

Ibn Sīnā (*al-Ilāhiyyāt*). *Al-Shifāʾ: Al-Ilāhiyyāt*. Ed. G. C. Anawati et al. 2 vols. Cairo: al-Hayʾa al-ʿĀmma li-Shuʾūn al-Maṭābiʿ al-Amīriyya, 1380/1960.

al-Jāḥiẓ, Abū ʿUthmān ʿAmr b. Baḥr (*Ḥayawān*). *K. al-Ḥayawān*. Ed. ʿAbd al-Salām Hārūn. 2nd edn., 8 vols. Cairo: Maṭbaʿat al-Muṣṭafā al-Bābī al-Ḥalabī wa-Awlādihī, 1384/1965–1389/1969.

Köckert, C. (2009). *Christliche Kosmologie und kaiserzeitliche Philosophie: Die Auslegung des Schöpfungsberichtes bei Origenes, Basilius und Gregor von Nyssa vor dem Hintergrund kaiserzeitlicher Timaeus-Interpretationen*. Tübingen: Mohr Siebeck.

Kullmann, W. (1974). *Wissenschaft und Methode: Interpretationen zur aristotelischen Theorie der Naturwissenschaft*. Berlin: de Gruyter.

Kullmann, W. (2007). *Aristoteles: Über die Teile der Lebewesen*. Übersetzt und erläutert von W. Kullmann. Berlin: Akademie Verlag.

Kupreeva, I. (2003). 'Qualities and Bodies: Alexander against the Stoics'. *Oxford Studies in Ancient Philosophy* 25: 297–344.

Liatsi, M. (2003). '"Akzidens" (συμβεβηκός) bei Aristoteles: Der Begriff des SYMBEBÊKOS im philosophischen und naturwissenschaftlichen Sprachgebrauch des Aristoteles'. *Zeitschrift für philosophische Forschung* 57: 211–32.

Long, A. A., and D. N. Sedley (1987). *The Hellenistic Philosophers*. Vol. 1. Cambridge: Cambridge University Press.

al-Malaṭī, Abū l-Ḥusayn Muḥammad b. Aḥmad b. ʿAbd al-Raḥmān. *Al-Tanbīh wa-l-radd ʿalā ahl al-ahwāʾ wa-l-bidaʿ*. Ed. Muḥammad Aḥmad al-Ḥasan al-Kawtharī. Baghdad: Maktabat al-Muthnā/Beirut: Maktabat al-Maʿārif, 1388/1968.

al-Maqdisī, Muṭahhar b. Ṭāhir (*Badʾ*). *K. al-Badʾ wa-l-taʾrīkh. Le Livre de la création et de l'histoire d'Abou-Zéid Aḥmed ben Sahl el-Ballhi*. Publié et traduit par M. Cl. Huart. 6 vols. Paris: Ernest Leroux, 1901.

Moraux, P. (2001). *Der Aristotelismus bei den Griechen: Von Andronikos bis Alexander von Aphrodisias*. Bd. III: *Alexander von Aphrodisias*. Berlin: de Gruyter.

Philoponus (*In Phys.*). *Ioannis Philoponi in Aristotelis physicorum libros*. Ed. G. Vitelli. 2 vols. Berlin: Reimer, 1887–8.

Plotinus (*Enneads*). *Ennéades* VI. Ed. Emile Bréhier. Paris: Les Belles Lettres, 1936.

Porphyry (*Isag.*). *Porhyrii Isagoge et in Aristotelis categorias commentarium*. Ed. A. Busse. Berlin: Reimer, 1887.

Porphyry (*In Cat.*). *Porhyrii Isagoge et in Aristotelis categorias commentarium*. Ed. A. Busse. Berlin: Reimer, 1887.

Prezl, O. (1930). 'Die frühislamische Atomenlehre'. *Der Islam* 19: 117–30.

Ps.-Galen (*de qualit incorporeis*). *Galeno qui fertur de qualitatibus incorporeis libellus*. Ed. J. Westenberger. Marburg: Elwert, 1906.

Qāḍī, Y. (1426/2005). *Maqālāt al-Jahm b. Ṣafwān*. 2 vols. Riyāḍ: Dār Aḍwā al-Salaf.

al-Rāzī, Fakhr al-Dīn (*Tafsīr*). *Al-Tafsīr al-kabīr aw Mafātīḥ al-ghayb*. 32 vols. Cairo, 1354/1935.

Schöck, C. (2004). 'Möglichkeit und Wirklichkeit menschlichen Handelns: "Dynamis" (*qūwa/qudra/istiṭāʿa*) in der islamischen Theologie'. *Traditio* 59: 79–128.

Schöck, C. (2006). *Koranexegese, Grammatik und Logik*. Leiden: Brill.

Schöck, C. (2012). 'The Controversy between al-Kindī and Yaḥyā b. ʿAdī on the Trinity, Part One: A Revival of the Controversy between Eunomius and the Cappadocian Fathers'. *Oriens* 40: 1–50.

Schöck, C. (2014). 'The Controversy between al-Kindī and Yaḥyā b. ʿAdī on the Trinity, Part Two: Gregory of Nyssa's and Ibn ʿAdī's Refutations of Eunomius and al-Kindī's "Error"'. *Oriens* 42: 220–53.

Schöck, C. (forthcoming). 'Ḍirār b. ʿAmr'. In *Encyclopaedia of Islam*. THREE. Leiden: Brill.

Sextus Empiricus (*Adv. mathem.*). *Sexti Empirici Opera*. Vol. ii: *Adversos Dogmaticos libros quinque* (*Adv. mathem.* VII–XI). Rec. H. Mutschmann. Leipzig: 6, 1914.

Simplicius (*In Cat.*). *Simplicii in Aristotelis categorias commentarium*. Ed. C. Kalbfleisch. Berlin: Reimer, 1907.

Sorabji, R. (1988). *Matter, Space and Motion: Theories in Antiquity and their Sequel*. Ithaca, NY: Cornell University Press.

Sorabji, R. (2004). *The Philosophy of the Commentators, 2006–600 AD: A Sourcebook*. Vol. ii: *Physics*. London: Duckworth.

Sorabji, R. (2006). *Time, Creation and the Continuum: Theories in Antiquity and the Early Middle Ages*. Chicago: University of Chicago Press.

Stead, C. G. (1976). 'Ontologie und Terminologie bei Gregor von Nyssa'. In H. Dörrie et al. (eds.), *Gregor von Nyssa und die Philosophie*. Leiden: Brill, 107–27.

al-Ṭabarī, Abū Jaʿfar Muḥammad b. Jarīr (*Jāmiʿ*). *Jāmiʿ al-bayān ʿan taʾwīl āy al-Qurʾān*. 30 vols., 3rd edn. Cairo: Maṭbaʿat al-Muṣṭafā al-Bābī al-Ḥalabī wa-Awlādihī, 1388/1968.

Thiel, R. (2004). *Aristoteles' Kategorienschrift in ihrer antiken Kommentierung*. Tübingen: Mohr Siebeck.

Tugendhat, E. (1958). *TI KATA TINOΣ: Eine Untersuchung zu Struktur und Ursprung aristotelischer Grundbegriffe*. Freiburg/München: Verlag Karl Alber.

Westenberger (1906). See Ps.-Galen (*de qualit. incorporeis*).

Wildberg, C. (1988). *John Philoponus' Criticism of Aristotle's Theory of Aether*. Berlin/New York: de Gruyter.

Whittaker, J. (1990). *Alcinoos, Enseignement des doctrines de Platon*. Introduction, texte établi et commenté par J. Whittaker, et traduit par P. Louis. Paris: Les Belles Lettres.

Wolfson, H. A. (1947). 'Infinite and Privative Judgments in Aristotle, Averroes, and Kant'. *Philosophy and Phenomenological Research* 8: 173–87.

Wolfson, H. A. (1952). 'Albinus and Plotinus on Divine Attributes'. *Harvard Theological Review* 2: 115–30.

Wolfson, H. A. (1956). 'The Muslim Attributes and the Christian Trinity'. *Harvard Theological Review* 49: 1–18.

Wolfson, H. A. (1957). 'Negative Attributes in the Church Fathers and the Gnostic Basilides'. *Harvard Theological Review* 50: 145–56.

Wolfson, H. A. (1959). 'Philosophical Implications of the Problem of Divine Attributes in the Kalam'. *Journal of the American Oriental Society* 79: 73–80.

Wolfson, H. A. (1965). 'Muʿammar's Theory of *MAʿNĀ*'. In George Makdisi (ed.), *Arabic and Islamic Studies in Honour of Hamilton A. R. Gibb*. Leiden: Brill.

Wolfson, H. A. (1970). 'The Identification of Ex Nihilo with Emanation in Gregory of Nyssa'. *Harvard Theological Review* 63: 53–60.

CHAPTER 4

EARLY SHĪʿĪ THEOLOGY

MOHAMMAD ALI AMIR-MOEZZI

SHĪʿISM never constituted a single, monolithic phenomenon and speaking about it in the singular, especially during the early period of Islam, is problematic, as has been brilliantly shown by J. van Ess (van Ess 1991–7: i. 233–403). The heresiographical/doxographical works of the third/ninth and fourth/tenth centuries, such as the *K. al-Maqālāt* of Abū l-Ḥasan al-Ashʿarī (d. 324/936) or the *Firaq al-shīʿa* of al-Ḥasan b. Mūsā al-Nawbakhtī (d. between 300/912 and 310/922), to mention only the oldest extant sources, list dozens of Shīʿī branches during the first/seventh to fourth/tenth centuries. While the majority of branches were soon to disappear, a few gradually emerged that continued into the present times: the Zaydīs, the Ismāʿīlīs, and the Twelver Shīʿīs. This chapter is primarily concerned with the (proto-)Imāmī Shīʿīs during the pre-Būyid period, i.e. from the beginnings of Shīʿism in the first/seventh century up until the first half of the fourth/tenth century, a period that is historically as well as doctrinally of utmost significance. The end of this period coincides with the beginning of the so-called 'Major Occultation' (Kohlberg 1976). According to the Imami tradition, the twelfth and last imam entered into 'Minor Occultation' in 260/874, followed by a Major Occultation in 329/940, hence the appellation Twelver Shīʿism for this branch of Shīʿism. Moreover, the following, fourth/tenth century is generally termed the 'Shīʿite century' of Islam, to use a phrase coined by F. Gabrieli (Gabrieli 1970). Some of the central regions of the Islamic lands came under Shīʿī domination during this period: the Būyids, originally Zaydīs as it seems who then converted to imamism, controlled Baghdad and extensive parts of the Abbasid empire; the Fatimid Ismāʿīlīs ruled over North Africa and parts of Syria; the Imami dynasty of the Ḥamdanites held Syria and parts of Iraq, while the Zaydīs had the upper hand in Yemen and the Qarmatians ruled over Arabia, the Persian Gulf region, and southern Iran. This situation profoundly changed the relationship between politics and religion, especially among the Imamis who had mostly refrained from any political engagement up to this point and practised dissimulation (*taqiyya*). Moreover, this was the era that was characterized by the triumph of rationalism. For over a century, Muslim intellectuals had had time to absorb Hellenistic thought through the translation of hundreds of Greek and Alexandrian writings (Gutas 1998). Fascinated by the dialectic tradition and Aristotelian logic, these intellectuals turned *ʿaql* (which now takes the meaning of 'logical reason') into the key term for the entire period (Amir-Moezzi and Jambet 2004: 181–94). These events mark, as is becoming increasingly clear, the distinction between two opposite traditions in imamism: the ancient 'nonrational esoteric tradition' which had originated in Kufa and found its continuation in Rayy and Qum, and the most recent 'rationalist tradition' of the School of Baghdad, visible primarily in the fields of theology, law, and legal theory. The first tradition, marked by gnostic, initiatory, and mystical doctrines, seems to have dominated imamism at least since the time of Imam Muḥammad al-Bāqir (d. *c.*119/737) and his son Jaʿfar al-Ṣādiq (d. 148/765) up until the beginnings of the Būyid period. This tradition is most significantly nurtured by the *ḥadīth* collections, the oldest extant of which date from third/ninth and the first half of fourth/tenth century (Amir-Moezzi 1992: introduction). The corpus which has come down to us is monumental—it comprises the *K. al-Tanzīl wa-l-taḥrīf* [*K. al-Qirāʾāt*] of Aḥmad b. Muḥammad al-Sayyārī (*fl.* third/ninth century), the *Baṣāʾir al-darajāt* of al-Ṣaffār al-Qummī (d. 290/902–3), the *Kāfī* of Muḥammad b. Yaʿqūb al-Kulaynī (d. 329/941), and eventually the works of Muḥammad b. ʿAlī b. Bābūya (Bābawayh) al-Qummī (d. 381/991) and of Muḥammad b. Ibrāhīm b. Jaʿfar al-Nuʿmānī ('Ibn Abī Zaynab al-Nuʿmānī', d. 360/971), as well as the exegetical works of Furāt b. Furāt b. Ibrāhīm al-Kūfī (*fl.* third/ninth and fourth/tenth century), Abū Naḍr Muḥammad b. Masʿūd b. ʿAyyāsh al-Samarqandī ('al-ʿAyyāshī', d. 329/941), and ʿAlī b. Ibrāhīm al-Qummī (d. after 307/919) (Amir-Moezzi 1992: 48–54; Bar-Asher 1999: *passim*).

The beginnings of the rationalist tradition can be traced back to some of the thinkers of the pre-Būyid period, such as Ibn Abī ʿAqīl al-Nuʿmānī (*fl.* first half of the fourth/tenth century), Ibn al-Junayd al-Iskāfī (*fl.* first half of the fourth/tenth century), and Abū Jaʿfar Muḥammad b. ʿAbd al-Raḥmān b. Qiba al-Rāzī (*fl.* second half of the third/ninth century), as well as representatives of the Banū Nawbakht in Baghdad, whose doctrinal thought shows affinities with the theology of the Muʿtazila (Modarressi 1993: *passim*). This tradition gained majority status among the Imamis during the fourth/tenth and fifth/eleventh centuries with prominent figures such as al-Shaykh al-Mufīd (d. 413/1022), his two most important disciples al-Sharīf al-Raḍī (d. 406/1016) and al-Sharīf al-Murtaḍā (d. 436/1044) and, later on, the *Shaykh al-ṭāʾifa* Abū Jaʿfar al-Ṭūsī (d. 460/1067) (Amir-Moezzi 1992: 33–58; Kohlberg and Amir-Moezzi 2009: introduction; see also Chapter 11).

In the following, only those theological doctrines that are peculiar to Shīʿism will be discussed (for the reception of Muʿtazilite notions among the Imamis, see Madelung 1970, and Chapter 11). These are shared by most Shīʿī groups of the early Islamic period.

It is customary to consider Shīʿī theology to be based on five concepts, the first three of which are labelled 'principles of religion' (*uṣūl al-dīn*) while the remaining two are considered to be 'principles that are specific to imamism' (*uṣūl al-madhhab*), namely divine unicity (*tawḥīd*), prophecy (*nubuwwa*), resurrection and promise and threat (*maʿād/al-waʿd wa-l-waʿīd*), divine justice (*ʿadl*), and the imamate (*imāma*). However, this presentation, probably inspired by 'five principles' (*al-uṣul al-khamsa*) of the

Muʿtazila, seems late and reductive. The first to propose them was apparently al-Shaykh al-Mufīd (d. 413/1022) in his *al-Nukat al-iʿtiqādiyya* and the list has been repeated ever since, e.g. by Fakhr al-Muḥaqqiqīn Muḥammad b. al-ʿAllāma al-Ḥillī (d. 771/1369) in his *Uṣūl al-dīn* up until Muḥammad Khʷājagī al-Shīrāzī (*fl.* tenth/sixteenth century) in his *al-Niẓāmiyya fī madhhab al-Imāmiyya*. By contrast, the texts that pre-date the fourth/tenth century contain a different list of tenets. An example dating from the third/ninth century, cited by Iʿjāz Ḥusayn al-Nīsābūrī al-Kantūrī in his *Kashf al-ḥujub wa-l-astār*, is a treatise entitled *Uṣūl al-dīn* that is attributed to the eighth Imam ʿAlī b. Mūsā al-Riḍā (Kantūrī, *Kashf*, 49f.). Here, a different list of theological principles is given, with doctrinal and legal issues being closely interwoven: divine unity, the science of the licit and the illicit (*ʿilm al-ḥalāl*/*ʿilm al-ḥarām*), as well as compulsory and recommendable works (*wājibāt*/*mustaḥabbāt*). Other lists emerge over time: in a Persian work, titled *Risāla-yi Uṣūl-i dīn*, attributed to the ninth/fifteenth-century author Ḍiyāʾ al-Dīn al-Jurjānī, eschatology is removed from the list of doctrinal tenets while the text displays three additional concepts: love for the imams (*tawallī* or *walāya*), dissociation from the opponents of the Family of the Prophet (*tabarrī* or *barāʾa*), and commanding good and forbidding evil (*amr-i maʿrūf wa nahy-i munkar*) (al-Jurjānī, *Rasāʾil*, 225–40; on this work, see also Chapter 11, section IV). Al-Muqaddas al-Ardabīlī (d. 993/1585–6) presents a different list in his Persian theological tract, *Uṣūl-i dīn*, in which divine justice is omitted, while al-Fayḍ al-Kāshānī (d. 1091/1680) adds in his *Nawādir al-akhbār* 'reason' (*ʿaql*; meaning both spiritual intelligence and dialectical reason) and 'knowledge' (*ʿilm*; meaning both initiatory knowledge and knowledge of the religious disciplines). The concepts of *walāya*/*tawallī* and *barāʾa*/*tabarrī* (on these see below), which are peculiar to Shīʿism and highly controversial from the outsiders' point of view, took centre stage in the polemical exchanges between Shīʿīs and non-Shīʿīs (Rubin 1984; Kohlberg 1986).

Indeed, we find all these concepts being discussed among the early Shīʿī rational theologians (*mutakallimūn*). These were invariably supporters and followers of the imams and they formulated their doctrines on the basis of the teachings of the imams as reflected in the *ḥadīth*. None of their writings have come down to us directly, except for quotations from their books in the works of later authors as well as the data provided by biographical dictionaries. Among these early theologians mention should be made of Zurāra b. Aʿyan, Muḥammad b. ʿAlī b. Nuʿmān 'Ṣāḥib al-Ṭāq', Hishām b. al-Ḥakam, Hishām b. Sālim al-Jawālīqī, Ḍaḥḥāk Abū Mālik al-Ḥaḍramī in the second/eighth century (Modarressi 2003); al-Faḍl b. Shādhān, al-Ḥakam b. Hishām b. al-Ḥakam, Muḥammad b. ʿAbd Allāh al-Iṣfahānī, Ismāʿīl al-Makhzūmī in the third/ninth century; and Ibn Abī ʿAqīl, Muḥammad b. Bishr al-Ḥamdūnī al-Sūsanjirdī, Ibn Qiba al-Rāzī as well as some members of the influential family of the Banū Nawbakht, especially Abū Isḥāq Ibrāhīm, in the fourth/tenth century (see also Chapter 11).

The central themes that were discussed in the context of *uṣūl al-dīn* are thus the classic themes of the so-called rational theology, the *kalām*: the oneness of God and its implications: the unity of essence (*tawḥīd al-dhāt*) and of acts (*tawḥīd al-afʿāl*), attributes (*ṣifāt*) of essence and attributes of acts, the divine versatility (*badāʾ*), the possibility or impossibility of the beatific vision, and the ethical values of good and evil; prophecy and related issues, such as the prophet being immaculate, the capacity to perform miracles, and modes of revelation; eschatology; divine justice, including discussions on divine grace (*luṭf*), moral obligation (*taklīf*), and human actions, the notions of belief and disbelief, and the imamate with discussions relating to the status, nature, and function of the imam. None of these themes are specifically Shīʿite and the extant textual sources informing about the doctrines of the early Shīʿī *mutakallimūn* are attested both in Shīʿī and in non-Shīʿī sources. Moreover, the themes themselves are shared by Shīʿīs and non-Shīʿīs during that period—in other words, these concepts can be found, with slight variations, among the adherents of other schools, such as the Qadariyya, the Jahmiyya, the Jabriyya, the Zaydiyya, the Muʿtazila, the Murjiʾa, and others (Madelung 1979; van Ess 1991–7: index, *s.n.*).

Shīʿism, in almost all its components and especially during its early period, is a religion in which the contrast between the obvious as against the hidden, the exoteric as against the esoteric (*ẓāhir/bāṭin*), is ubiquitous. Rational theology, i.e. *kalām*, represents the exoteric branch of Shīʿī theology, which its representatives share in one way or another with their counterparts from other Muslim denominations. Its importance seems thus secondary when compared to another characteristically Shīʿī type of theology, i.e. esoteric theology. Moreover, in ancient Shīʿī *ḥadīth* collections, rational speculation about things relating to the Divine is presented as a necessary evil: *necessary* because indispensible in controversies with the adversaries and yet *evil* because of *kalām's* inadequacy to grasp the secrets of the Divine (Amir-Moezzi 1992: 35–40). Exoteric speculative theology, often labelled *kalām*, has thus only a relative value in the teachings attributed to the Imams. Ancient *ḥadīth* collections regularly contain a chapter in which the faithful are warned against the 'dangers' of speculative theology (*al-nahy ʿan al-kalām*) and its tools such as reasoning by analogy (*qiyās*), personal opinion (*raʾy*), independent reasoning (*ijtihād*), or argumentation (*naẓar*). As for 'real' theology, labelled *ʿilm al-tawḥīd*, the essential science of secret religious realities, it is essentially based on faith (*īmān*) in the teaching of the Imams and absolute submission to their teachings (*taslīm*—as against *islām* which signifies submission to the esoteric dimension of the revealed religion) (Amir-Moezzi 2011a). Let us now address the doctrinal basis of this esoteric theology as contained in the corpus of pre-Buwayhid *ḥadīth* collections, from al-Sayyārī to al-Nuʿmānī and especially al-Ṣaffār al-Qummī, al-Kulaynī, and the extant pre-Buwayhid works of exegesis.

The true axis around which the Shīʿī religion turns is the imam. One might even say that Shīʿism, as it appears in the earliest systematic books that have reached us, is an imamology. This 'imam's religion' has developed revolving two worldviews.

First, a 'dual vision': any religious reality has at least two levels, an external, apparent, exoteric level and a secret, esoteric level which remains hidden under the apparent level. This dialectic is a fundamental credo that can be encountered in virtually all domains of the faith. In theology, God Himself has two ontological levels. First, that of the Essence, which is forever inconceivable, unimaginable, beyond all thought. It can only be described by God Himself through His revelations and can be conceived merely as a negative apophatic theology. It is the Unknowable which is the hidden level, the esoteric dimension of God. Al-Kulaynī in his *al-Kāfī* or Ibn Bābawayh in his *Kitāb al-Tawḥīd* devote entire chapters to this subject (Amir-Moezzi 2011a: 110–12). But if things were to stop here, no relation would be possible between God and His creation. God thus brought forth in His own being another level, the level of 'names and attributes' (*al-asmāʾ wa-l-ṣifāt*) through which He is revealed and made known, for He is not the Unknowable but the Unknown who aspires to be known. This is the level of the revealed, exoteric dimension of God and of what can be known about Him. These names and attributes act in the created world through divine 'organs' (*aʿḍāʾ*) which are manifestations of the Divine (*maẓhar, majlā*), theophanies. The theophany par excellence is the Imam (with capital 'I') in the cosmic, archetypical, metaphysical sense; he represents the highest revelation of the divine names and attributes as their locus of manifestation, a metaphysical being who grasps God in His entirety, in His outer as well as hidden dimensions. This is the Imam in the ontological, archetypal, universal sense. Knowledge of the archetypal Imam is equivalent to knowledge of God since the Imam is the metaphysically revealed 'face' (*wajh*) of God—a topos that is elaborated in virtually all pre-Būyid *ḥadīth* compilations, such as al-Ṣaffār al-Qummī's *Baṣāʾir al-darajāt*, al-Kulaynī's *Kitāb al-Kāfī* (esp. the *Kitāb al-Ḥujja*), or Furāt al-Kūfī's *Tafsīr* (Amir-Moezzi 2011a: chapter 3).

The cosmic Imam likewise possesses two dimensions, a hidden one and a manifest one. The esoteric dimension corresponds to the metaphysical, cosmic dimension of the Imam. The cosmic Imam's exoteric dimension, his locus of manifestation, are the historical imams (with a lower case 'i') in the various cycles of history. This leads us to the level of prophetology. According to Shīʿī doctrine, all prophets who brought a new legislation were accompanied in their mission by one or more imams whose task was to unveil the hidden (*bāṭin*) meaning of the Word of God: from Adam, the first man and first prophet, to Muḥammad, with Noah, Abraham, Joseph, Moses, and Jesus in between, as is again elaborated in the early *ḥadīth* collections, such as the *Baṣāʾir al-darajāt* of al-Ṣaffār al-Qummī or al-Kulaynī's *al-Kāfī* (Rubin 1979; Amir-Moezzi 1992: 96–112). Moreover, the messengers and their imams are connected through an unbroken chain of 'minor' prophets, imams, saints, and sages which together form the sublime family of 'Friends of God' (*awliyāʾ*, sg. *walī*) who carry and transmit the divine friendship (*walāya*), a term central to Shīʿī theology to which we shall return shortly. This notion is dealt with, for example, in the *Ithbāt al-waṣiyya li-ʿAlī b. Abī Ṭālib*, a monograph attributed to ʿAlī b. al-Ḥusayn al-Masʿūdī (d. 345/955–6 or 346/956–7) (Amir-Moezzi 2011a: 266). In Twelver Shīʿism, the *awliyāʾ* par excellence, i.e. loci of manifestation of the Imam, are the 'Fourteen Immaculates' (*maʿṣūm*), namely Muḥammad, his daughter Fāṭima, and the twelve imams. Thus, in a theology of successive theophanies, the knowledge of what can be known about God, the ultimate mystery of being, begins with the knowledge of God's manifestation, the Imam.

The principal function of the 'Friends of God' is to convey and explain God's word to mankind which has otherwise repeatedly been revealed. Revelation has again two meanings, an apparent one and a hidden one. The messenger grasps both levels of meaning but his mission is to only communicate the revealed 'letter', the exoteric level of revelation, to the community of the faithful. As has been mentioned, every messenger was accompanied in his mission by one or several imams. The sources do not always agree on the names of the imams of the past but the most recurrent lists mention Seth as the imam of Adam, Ishmael as the imam of Abraham, Aaron or Joshua for Moses, Simon-Peter or all of the apostles for Jesus, ʿAlī and the imams for Muḥammad (Rubin 1975; 1979). The invariable mission of the imams is to initiate a select elite among the community into the 'spirit' of the scripture in its esoteric level by way of hermeneutical interpretation (*ta'wīl*). This elite are accordingly the 'Shīʿīs' of each religion. Thus, the prophet is said to be the messenger of the 'exoteric religion'—*islām* in the terminology of Shīʿism. At the same time, the imam or *walī* is the messenger of the esoteric religion, the initiator of the secret spiritual religion, *īmān*. The historical Shīʿīs recognize themselves as the last link of a long chain of initiation that runs throughout history, dating back to Adam and the 'Shīʿīs' of his imam Seth (Kohlberg 1980). This dual vision of the world can be outlined in a schema consisting of complementary pairs that characterize the dialectic of the manifest and the hidden in Shīʿism (Table 4.1).

Second, 'the dualistic view': the history of creation consists of a cosmic battle between forces of good and of evil, between beings of light and knowledge versus beings of darkness and ignorance. Given the central role of initiation and knowledge (see above), Shīʿīs conceive knowledge as good and ignorance as evil. The struggle between these two antagonistic powers is enshrined in the universal framework of existence. According to a large body of cosmogonic traditions—adduced for example by al-Barqī (d. 274/887–8 or 280/893–4) in his *Kitāb al-Maḥāsin* (al-Barqī, *Maḥāsin*, 1/96–8), al-Kulaynī in his *al-Kāfī* (al-Kulaynī, *Kāfī*, 1/23–6), or Ibn Shuʿba al-Ḥarrānī (*fl.* mid fourth/tenth

Table 4.1 The dialectic of the manifest and the hidden in Shīʿism

Apparent	Hidden
exoteric (*ẓāhir*)	esoteric (*bāṭin*)
God's names and attributes	God's essence
prophet-messenger (*nabī/rasūl*)	imam/friend of God (*imām/walī*)
prophecy (*nubuwwa*)	imamate/friendship with God (*imāma/walāya*)
letter of revelation (*tanzīl*)	spiritual hermeneutics (*ta'wīl*)
submission to revealed religion (*islām*)	initiation into the esoteric religion (*īmān*)
the majority/the mass	the minority/the elite

century) in his *Tuḥaf al-ʿuqūl* (Ibn Shuʿba, *Tuḥaf*, 423–5)—creation is from the outset divided into two opposing groups: it is a struggle between the armies of supreme intelligence (*al-ʿaql*) and ignorance (*jahl*)—supreme intelligence being a symbol and archetype of the Imam and his followers, ignorance symbolizing the Imam's adversary and his armies on the other (Amir-Moezzi 1993: 320). This battle of the forces of good and evil is a primordial one and it continues to be a perpetual struggle between the friends of God and their followers, the initiates, and the armies of the imams of darkness and ignorance. Using Qurʾānic expressions, it is described in the Shīʿī sources as an ongoing struggle between 'the people of the right / of the benediction' (*aṣḥāb al-yamīn/al-maymana*), characterized by their obedience to God, and 'the people of the left / of the malediction' (*aṣḥāb al-shimāl/al-mashʾama*), who refused to obey the divine order. According to complex and at times confusing theories of cycles, the world is ruled, since its creation, by two types of 'government': that of God's prophets and imams, 'the guides of light and justice,' who openly teach the hidden truths, and that of Satan. Since the world is influenced by 'the guides of darkness and injustice' these truths can only be transmitted and taught secretly. Satan was the enemy of Adam, and the history of adamic humanity is marked by adversity and violence of the demonic forces of ignorance which, throughout the adamic cycle, will remain the dominant majority, pushing the persecuted minority of initiates into the margins (Kohlberg 1980: 45ff.). This will continue until the end of time and the advent of the Mahdi, the eschatological saviour, who will eventually overcome the powers of evil and prepare the world for the final resurrection.

At the advent of each religion, the reigning 'guides of injustice' have a majority formed within the community which refuses to believe in the existence of a spirit hidden under the revealed letter of the religion and thus rejects the existence of the Imam as the master of hermeneutics. This majority, manipulated by Satan's 'guides of ignorance,' isolates the religion from its deeper level, thus condemning it to decadence and violence. The adversaries (*aḍdād*, sg. *ḍidd*), the 'Enemy of God' and his supporters, are not necessarily pagans, unbelievers, or adherents of other religions (as was the case, for example, with Nimrod facing Abraham or Pharaoh facing Moses). The Israelites who betrayed Moses by pledging faith in the Golden Calf, and Muḥammad's companions who rejected ʿAlī are not 'non-Jews' and 'non-Muslims' but people who reject the esoteric dimension of their respective religions, the notion of *walāya*, i.e. the authority of the 'Guide' who teaches the inner secrets of the religion. These are those whom the Shīʿīs call the 'people of the exoteric level' (*ahl al-ẓāhir*, according to the different senses of the word) who are submitted to the letter of the revelation only, 'the Muslims gone astray' (*muslim ḍāll*).

In the historical context of a violent struggle between Shīʿīs and their opponents, when the latter become increasingly identified with the Sunnīs, two factors affecting theological thought become essential within the dualistic view. First the discretion: to protect his own life and safety, as well as the life and safety of his Imam and his co-religionists, and the integrity of its doctrine, the Shīʿī believer is obliged to 'protect the secret' (*taqiyya, kitmān, khabʾ*). Under the 'government of Satan,' a characteristic of current humanity, the unveiling of secrets does not only arouse derision or disbelief but also misunderstanding, violence, and anathema (Kohlberg 1995; Amir-Moezzi 2014). This is followed by a mystical notion, the religious necessity of which is again and again repeated in the sources: the Shīʿī believer constantly owes his imam unfailing love, faith, and submission (*walāya/tawallī*). At the same time, the believer is urged to detach himself from the imam's opponents, i.e. to perform the duty of *barā'a/tabarrī*. In a universe governed by war and its constraints, the sacred alliance, the *walāya* with the divine Guide and the knowledge he provides cannot be complete unless it is accompanied by dissociation (*barā'a*) from his enemies, even hostility towards those who seek to destroy the true knowledge and those who possess it (Amir-Moezzi 2011a: chapter 7; Amir-Moezzi 2011b: chapter 1).

Here, too, we can map the dualistic view in schematic form based on the dialectic of good and evil (Table 4.2).

Shīʿī religion and theology seem specifically characterized by these two worldviews. The dual conception of religious reality—illustrated by two complementary poles of exoteric and esoteric, visible (*ẓāhir*) and hidden (*bāṭin*), prophet (*nabī*) and imam (*walī*), literal revelation (*tanzīl*) and spiritual hermeneutics (*ta'wīl*), submission to the revealed religion (*islām*) and initiation into its esoteric aspects (*īmān*)—can be articulated along the vertical axis of initiation which belongs to the spiritual world, because passage from the exoteric to the esoteric is defined as a progressive approach to the divine and even greater secrets of the universe, and this as a result of the teaching of the imams, who are closer to the Divine and the understanding of the secrets of the universe. The horizontal axis, which in turn belongs to the world of senses and history, likewise articulates the fight between two dualistic views of the world—illustrated by two opposing poles, imam and enemy, intelligence and ignorance, people of the right and people of the left, imams of justice and imams of violence—and it thus encapsulates the universal and perpetual struggle between the armies of supreme intelligence and of ignorance. It is noteworthy that the notion of *walāya* ('sacred love for the imams') is the only one found in both diagrams, illustrating its central importance in the structure of Shīʿī doctrine. Covering

Table 4.2 The dialectic of good and evil in Shīʿism

Good/knowledge	Evil/ignorance
cosmic Intelligence	cosmic Ignorance
imam and his initiates	enemy of the imam and his followers
Guides of the light/justice/guidance (*a'immat al-nūr/al-ʿadl/al-hudā*)	Guides of darkness/injustice (*a'immat al-ẓalām/al-ẓulm/al-ḍalāl*)
people of the right (*aṣḥāb al-yamīn*)	people of the left (*aṣḥāb al-shimāl*)
love towards the imam (*walāya/tawallī/muwālāt*)	dissociation from his adversary (*barā'a/tabarrī/muʿādāt*)

both the nature, status, and function of the imam and the attitude of the faithful towards the latter, *walāya* is real backbone of Shīʿī theology (Amir-Moezzi 2011a: chapter 7; Dakake 2007: *passim*) and the imam the ultimate reason for the creation.

References

Amir-Moezzi, M. A. (1992). *Le Guide divin dans le shî'isme originel: Aux sources de l'ésorérisme en Islam*. Paris: Lagrasse (English translation: *The Divine Guide in Early Shiʿism: The Sources of Esotericism in Islam*, New York: SUNY Press, 1994).

Amir-Moezzi, M. A. (1993). 'Cosmogony and Cosmology: v. in Twelver Shiʿism'. In *Encyclopaedia Iranica*, vi.317–22.

Amir-Moezzi, M. A. (2011a). *The Spirituality of Shiʿi Islam: Beliefs and Practices*. London: I. B. Tauris.

Amir-Moezzi, M. A. (2011b). *Le Coran silencieux et le Coran parlant: Sources scripturaires de l'islam entre histoire et ferveur*. Paris: CNRS Éditions (English translation: *The Silent Qur'an and the Speaking Qur'an: Scriptural Sources of Islam Between History and Fervor*. New York: Columbia University Press, 2015).

Amir-Moezzi, M. A. (2014). 'Dissimulation tactique (*taqiyya*) et scellement de la prophétie (*khatm al-nubuwwa*) (Aspects de l'imamologie duodécimaine XII)'. *Journal asiatique* 302: 411–38.

Amir-Moezzi, M. A., and C. Jambet (2004). *Qu'est-ce que le shiʿisme?* Paris: Fayard.

Bar-Asher, M. M. (1999). *Scripture and Exegesis in Early Imāmī Shiʿism*. Leiden/Jerusalem: Brill/Magnes.

al-Barqī, Aḥmad b. Muḥammad (*Maḥāsin*). *Kitāb al-Maḥāsin*. Ed. al-Ḥusaynī al-Muḥaddith. Tehran: Dānishgāh-i Tihrān, 1370/1950.

Dakake, M. M. (2007). *The Charismatic Community: Shīʿite Identity in Early Islam*. New York: SUNY Press.

van Ess, J. (1991–97). *Theologie und Gesellschaft im 2. und 3. Jahrhundert Hidschra. Eine Geschichte des religiösen Denkens im frühen Islam*. 6 vols. Berlin: de Gruyter.

Fakhr al-Muḥaqqiqīn Muḥammad b. al-ʿAllāma al-Ḥillī (*Uṣūl*). *Uṣūl al-dīn*. MSS Mashhad, Āstān-i quds, 349 and 350.

al-Fayḍ al-Kāshānī (*Nawādir*). *Nawādir al-akhbār*. Ed. M. al-Anṣārī al-Qummī. Tehran: Pažūhishgāh-i ʿulūm-i insānī, 1374/1996.

Gabrieli, F. (1970). 'Imamisme et littérature sous les Bouyides'. In *Le shîʿisme imâmite*. Actes du colloque de Strasbourg, 6–9 mai 1968. Ed. T. Fahd. Paris: Presses universitaires de France, 105–13.

Gutas, D. (1998). *Greek Thought, Arabic Culture: The Graeco-Arabic Translation Movement in Baghdad and Early 'Abbāsid Society (2nd–4th/8th–10th Centuries)*. New York: Routledge.

Ibn Shuʿba (*Tuḥaf*). *Tuḥaf al-ʿuqūl*. Ed. ʿA. A. Ghaffārī. Qum: Islāmiyya, 1404/1984.

Jurjānī, Ḍiyāʾ al-Dīn b. Sadīd al-Dīn (*Rasāʾil*). *Rasāʾil-i kalāmī-i taʾlīf-i ḥudūd-i qarn-i nuhum-i Hijrī*. Ed. Maʿṣūme Nūr Muḥammadī. Tehran: Mīrāth-i Maktūb/Ahl-i Qalam, 1375[/1997].

Kantūrī, Iʿjāz Ḥusayn (*Kashf*). *Kashf al-ḥujūb wa-l-astār ʿan asmāʾ al-kutub wa-l-asfār*. Ed. Ḥ. Ḥusayn. Calcutta, 1935.

Khwājagī al-Shīrāzī (*Niẓāmiyya*). *al-Niẓāmiyya fī l-madhhab al-Imāmiyya*. Ed. ʿA. Awjabī. Tehran: Mīrāth-i maktūb, 1997.

Kohlberg, E. (1976). 'From Imāmiyya to Ithnā ʿashariyya'. *Bulletin of the School of Oriental and African Studies* 39: 521–34.

Kohlberg, E. (1980). 'Some Shīʿī Views on the Antediluvian World'. *Studia Islamica* 52: 41–66.

Kohlberg, E. (1986). 'Barāʾa in Shīʿī Doctrine'. *Jerusalem Studies in Arabic and Islam* 7: 139–75.

Kohlberg, E. (1995). '*Taqiyya* in Shīʿī Theology and Religion'. In H. G. Kippenberg and G. G. Stroumsa (eds.), *Secrecy and Concealment: Studies in the History of Mediterranean and Near Eastern Religions*. Leiden: Brill, 345–80.

Kohlberg, E., and M. A. Amir-Moezzi (2009). *Revelation and Falsification: The Kitāb al-Qirāʾāt of Aḥmad b. Muḥammad al-Sayyārī*. Leiden: Brill.

al-Kulaynī (*Kāfī*). *Kitāb al-Kāfī*. Ed. ʿA. A. Ghaffārī. Tehran: Islāmiyya, 1375–7/1955–7.

Madelung, W. (1970). 'Imāmism and Muʿtazilite Theology'. In T. Fahd (ed.), *Le shīʿisme imāmite*. Paris, 13–29.

Madelung, W. (1979). 'The Shiite and Khārijite Contribution to Pre-Ashʿarite *Kalām*'. In P. Morewedge (ed.), *Islamic Philosophical Theology*. Albany: SUNY Press, 120–30.

Modarressi, H. (1993). *Crisis and Consolidation in the Formative Period of Shīʿite Islam: Abū Jaʿfar ibn Qiba al-Rāzī and his Contribution to Imāmite Shīʿite Thought*. Princeton: Darwin Press.

Modarressi, H. (2003). *Tradition and Survival: A Bibliographical Survey of Early Shīʿite Literature*. Oxford: Oneworld.

al-Muqaddas al-Ardabīlī (*Uṣūl-i dīn*). *Uṣūl-i dīn*. MSS Mashhad, Āstān-i quds, 39 and 351.

Rubin, U. (1975). 'Pre-existence and Light: Aspects of the Concept of Nūr Muḥammad'. *Israel Oriental Studies* 5: 62–119.

Rubin, U. (1979). 'Prophets and Progenitors in Early Shīʿa Tradition'. *Jerusalem Studies in Arabic and Islam* 1: 41–65.

Rubin, U. (1984). 'Barāʾa: A Study of Some Qurʾānic Passages'. *Jerusalem Studies in Arabic and Islam* 5: 76–92.

al-Shaykh al-Mufīd (*Nukat*). 'al-Nukat al-iʿtiqādiyya'. In *Silsilat muʾallafāt al-Shaykh al-Mufīd*. Qum: Dār al-Mufīd, 1413/1993, 10/16–47.

CHAPTER 5

EXCURSUS I

Christian Theological Thought during the First ʿAbbāsid Century

SIDNEY H. GRIFFITH

THE earliest notices of emergent Islam recorded by Christians living in the conquered territories of the Levant occur in Greek and Syriac texts written in the late seventh century CE. By the early years of the eighth century written notices of formal conversations between representative Muslims and Christians were already circulating in Syriac, along with accounts of apocalyptic visions of the future import of the hegemony of the Arabs for the fortunes of the subject Christian communities (Hoyland 1997). And it was also in the eighth century that theological treatises first appeared, written by Christians under the influence of the then developing, religious challenge of Islam, first in Greek and then in Arabic and Syriac. It was the beginning of a somewhat co-dependent, intellectual and cultural, albeit often antagonistic, relationship between Christian and Muslim thinkers that would hold them in tension with one another throughout the first ʿAbbāsid century (Khoury 1989–9; Rissanen 1993; Griffith 2008a; Thomas and Roggema 2009).

John of Damascus (d. *c.*750), living in the milieu of Jerusalem in the first third of the eighth century and writing in Greek (Louth 2002), is the earliest Christian theologian on record whose theological agenda was determined in large part by the challenge of Islam. While he directly addressed the topic of Islam only in the final entry in the 'On Heresies' section of his master work, *The Fount of Knowledge*, and in the report of a dialogue attributed to him between a Christian and a Muslim (Le Coz 1992), it is nevertheless clear that the comprehensive Muslim challenge to core Christian doctrines, such as the Incarnation, the Trinity, and the freedom of human moral choice, lay behind John's project to compose a summary presentation of traditional Christian thought, the first in the genre. This same Islamic milieu also determined the framework within which John addressed other challenges to his Byzantine Orthodox faith and practice, coming from both Christian and non-Christian adversaries of the time, writing in Greek, Syriac, and newly in Arabic. To put the accent on this hermeneutical approach to his works, one considers not only *The Fount of Knowledge*, but his three orations against the calumniators of the icons, and several treatises written against contemporary Christian and Manichean adversaries (Griffith 2002; 2008a).

John of Damascus composed *The Fount of Knowledge* very much within the local context of the Christian denominational controversies of the eighth century being conducted in Greek and Syriac in territories now firmly under Muslim Arab control. His principal adversaries were Nestorians, particularly Jacobites, Monotheletes, and even the Manichean views of some intellectuals of the time who had got a new lease on life in the early Islamic period (Griffith 2002). In the orations against the calumniators of the icons, John addressed a pastoral problem that first arose among Christians in his world in response to the Umayyad programme to claim the public space in the caliphate for the display of Islam; it involved the removal of Christian crosses and icons as well as polemics against their veneration on the part of Muslims and others as an act of idolatry and as proclamations of Christian beliefs contrary to the Qurʾān (Griffith 2007a; 2009; 2011). As for John's independent polemical works against Nestorians, Jacobites, and Manicheans, they directly addressed issues that divided the Christian communities in the caliphate in the first half of the eighth century. The Islamic presence conditioned everything he wrote in these treatises, for they concerned intellectual and theological issues that were, so to speak, 'in the air' and they were addressed not only by Christians but by Muslims as well (Griffith 2002).

The first half of the eighth century, the period in which the Arabophone but Greek-writing John of Damascus was composing his well-known works, also witnessed a notable development in Islamic religious discourse in two places in particular, Damascus in Syria and Baṣra in Iraq, as the very mention of the names of Ghaylān ad-Dimashqī (d. 749 CE), Jahm b. Ṣafwān (d. 745), al-Ḥasan al-Baṣrī (b. 642, d. 728), and Wāṣil b. ʿAṭāʾ (d. 748), among others, immediately brings to mind. The debates among Muslim intellectuals associated with these names about such issues as the range of authority of human willing and what to think about God and God's attributes, among other topics, formed the backdrop for the development in due course of the wide-ranging Muʿtazilī school of thought (van Ess 1991–7). It would not be stretching matters too far to suppose that the socially well-connected, Arabic-speaking John of Damascus would have been aware of these developments among contemporary Muslim thinkers. Scholars have even noted that the compositional pattern of the early Muʿtazilī *kalām* works match the order of topics as they are presented in the *De Fide Orthodoxa* section of John's master work, *The Fount of Knowledge* (Pines 1976). So too have students of the early *kalām* texts in Arabic called attention to the same coincidence of topical outline and mode of discourse in the texts they study and earlier Christian theological and exegetical texts in Syriac (Cook 1981; Rudolph 1997).

Christian theology in Arabic appears first in the second half of the eighth century CE, concomitant with the beginnings of the Graeco-Arabic translation movement in Baghdad, an enterprise largely in Christian hands, and the contemporary programme within the parameters of which the Christian communities themselves adopted the Arabic language, both to translate the Bible and other traditional ecclesiastical literature into Arabic and to compose original works in the newly dominant language of daily life

(Graf 1944–53; Gutas 1998; Griffith 1988; Griffith 1997a). The so far earliest Christian theological tract written in Arabic appeared in the third quarter of the eighth century and in it the now unknown author was already engaging Islamic thought and Qurʾānic expression. The Arabic diction of the *Treatise on the Triune Nature of God*, to give the text the name proposed by its first editor and translator (Gibson 1899), is suffused with echoes of the Qurʾān's distinctive idiom (Samir 1994). The author alludes to and quotes passages from the scripture of the Muslims in tandem with passages quoted from the Old and New Testaments in the effort to commend the credibility of the very Christian doctrines that on the face of it the Qurʾān critiques, the Trinity and the Incarnation. It is an exercise in what one might call inter-scriptural reasoning, or perhaps better, inter-scriptural proof-texting (Swanson 1998), an apologetic stratagem that would find a continuous vein in Christian theology in Arabic, reaching its apogee in the thirteenth century with Paul of Antioch's *Letter to a Muslim Friend* (Khoury 1964) and the responses it elicited in its revised and expanded form from Muslim scholars of the stature of Ibn Taymiyya in the fourteenth century (Ebied and Thomas 2005).

In the late eighth century in Iraq, in the very milieu of Baṣra and Baghdad in early ʿAbbāsid times in which the Arabic *ʿilm al-kalām* was coming into its own and the Muʿtazilī movement was burgeoning among Muslim religious thinkers, two Christians who wrote in Syriac took notice of these developments and took steps to respond to the theological challenge posed by Islam. Just as in his major work, *The Fount of Knowledge*, John of Damascus in the Jerusalem milieu had met the challenge in a comprehensive way in the early eighth century by composing a systematic and summary presentation of Christian doctrine in response to the multiple challenges of both Christian and non-Christian adversaries of the day, including a specific response to Islam, so too did Theodore Bar Kônî (*fl. c.*792), a theologian of the Church of the East, the so-called 'Nestorians', compose just such a summary at the end of the eighth century (Griffith 1982a). Theodore's *Scholion* is a systematic presentation of the distinctive doctrinal profile of his church's creed presented, in 'Nestorian' style, in the guise of a commentary on the difficult passages of the Old and New Testaments, complete with philosophical and logical prolegomena, dogmatic exposition in response to both Christian and non-Christian adversaries, along with a heresiographical supplement that includes a specific response to Islam (Griffith 1981). It was in the wake of Theodore's *Scholion* that the 'Nestorian' patriarch, Timothy I (727/8, r. 780–823) in his Syriac letters explicitly addressed Muslim challenges to Christian faith. He did so not just in the account of his famous debate with Muslim scholars in the *majlis* of the caliph, al-Mahdī (r. 775–85), soon translated into Arabic, in which the patriarch, who was now resident in Baghdad, parried Muslim objections to Christian doctrines and argued in support of their credibility (Heimgartner 2011; Putman 1975), but perhaps even more significantly in other letters. In one understudied letter, Timothy tells of his conversation with a Muslim 'Aristotelian' at the caliph's court; the conversation unfolds along lines that feature the topical agenda and mode of discourse comparable to that of the contemporary Muslim *mutakallimūn*. In another letter he answers questions from a Christian clergyman in the environs of Baṣra who has been in conversation with Muslims (Griffith 2007b). In these letters we find the blooming of a truly theological, Christian discourse articulated within the intellectual horizon of Islamic *kalām*, that came into full flower in Arabic in the second half of the first ʿAbbāsid century. Patriarch Timothy is also on record as having commissioned a translation of Aristotle's *Topics* at the behest of Caliph al-Mahdī, another marker of his participation in the intellectual life of Baghdad (Gutas 1998: 61, n. 1; Brock 1999).

The first Christian theologian regularly to write in Arabic whose name we know is the Melkite, Theodore Abū Qurra (b. *c*.755, d. *c*.830), a native of Edessa in Syria, probably a monk of Mar Saba monastery in the Judean desert, and sometime bishop of Ḥarrān. A theologian very much indebted to John of Damascus, Abū Qurra wrote in both Greek and Arabic, and by his own testimony he also composed a number of treatises on Christology in his native Syriac (Griffith 1993; Lamoreaux 2002). In his Arabic works, Abū Qurra addressed both the largely Christological issues that divided the Christian churches in his day and the defence of the credibility of Christian doctrinal claims against challenges launched by Muslims (Lamoreaux 2005). Like John of Damascus before him he also wrote in defence of the Christian practice of venerating icons of Christ and the saints, but in Abū Qurra's instance Muslims as well as Christian iconophobes were his adversaries and his treatise contains perhaps the earliest written record of the Islamic tradition against image making (Griffith 1997b). Abū Qurra was also the author of a remarkable Arabic treatise in Christian *kalām* that follows the topical outline and mode of dialectical discourse typical of the Muslim *mutakallimūn* of the first ʿAbbāsid century. In it he advances the claim of Christianity to be the true religion according to which the one God wishes to be worshipped, and he devises a rational scheme for comparing the claims to truth made by contemporary religious communities on the basis of a Neoplatonic theory of knowledge that was current in the intellectual circuits of Baṣra and Baghdad at the time (Griffith 1994). Perhaps this was the very reason why the Muʿtazilī *mutakallim*, Abū Mūsā ʿĪsā b. Ṣubayḥ al-Murdār (d. *c*.840), is on record as having written a tract, *Against Abū Qurra, the Christian* (Dodge 1970: i. 388). Abū Qurra was also involved in the Graeco-Arabic translation movement in his day; he is credited with having translated the *Prior Analytics* and the pseudo-Aristotelian treatise, *De virtutibus animae* into Arabic (Griffith 1999a). Finally, Abū Qurra was reputedly an able debater in his day; in a dispute text composed in Arabic not long after his death he is credited with having defended Christianity against the objections of prominent Muslim *mutakallimūn* in the *majlis* of the caliph al-Maʾmūn (r. 813–33) when the latter sojourned in Ḥarrān in the year 829 CE (Nasry 2008).

Following in the wake of Theodore Abū Qurra, other 'Melkite' writers of the ninth century composed summaries of Christian faith in Arabic, which were addressed to the pressing challenge of Islam. One in particular, sometimes mistakenly attributed to Abū Qurra, is the still unedited *Summary of the Ways of Faith*, the full title of which is: *The Summary of the ways of faith in affirming the Trinity of the oneness of God, and the Incarnation of God the Word from the pure virgin Mary* (Griffith 1986; Griffith 1990; Samir 1986). In introducing this work of twenty-five chapters, the author makes it clear in the introduction that the intended audience is Arabic-speaking Christians who would be in conversation with Muslims. While it is clear that the author is a 'Melkite', and in chapter 14 of the work he considers and rejects the Christological formulae of his community's Christian adversaries, nowhere else do the intra-Christian controversies preoccupy him. Throughout he is concerned with Christians whom he represents as seeking some doctrinal accommodation with Islam, including acceptance of the first phrase of the Islamic *shahāda*. In response to this proposal, the author points out, quoting the Qurʾān, that Muslims 'mean a God other than the Father, the Son, and the Holy Spirit. According to their own statement, God is neither a begetter, nor is He begotten (Q 112: 3). Their statement, "There is no god but God" and our statement are one in words but different in meaning' (Griffith 1986: 138). And again borrowing a Qurʾānic term, the author accuses such accommodating churchmen as being Christian 'hypocrites' (*munāfiqūn*), 'in flight from testifying to the doctrine of the Trinity of the oneness of God and His Incarnation, because of what strangers say in reproach to them' (Griffith 1986: 139). He goes on to say of them, 'They are neither Christians, nor are they *ḥanīfs* (*ḥunafāʾ*), Muslims, but in the meantime they are waverers (*mudhabdhabūn*)' (Griffith 1986: 140). The latter characterization borrows the term 'waverers' from a Muslim prophetic tradition, preserved in the collection of Aḥmad b. Ḥanbal (b. 780, d. 855), according to which the prophet remarked to a Muslim celibate, 'You should marry, lest you come to be among the waverers' (Griffith 1986: 140). The latter example, along with quotations of Qurʾānic words and phrases throughout the *Summary of the Ways of Faith*, shows the author's ready acquaintance with Islamic idiom—none more pointedly than his constant description of Christ throughout the work as 'Lord of the worlds', a phrase predicated of God alone in the Qurʾān. The succeeding chapters address the major Christian doctrines, discuss the proper interpretation of passages from the Old and New Testaments, and give accounts of Christian liturgical practices and canonical procedures, all in response to well-known Muslim challenges. Another text of the ninth century written in a similar vein by a 'Melkite' author, but without the high quotient of Islamic language and Qurʾānic idiom evident in the *Summary of the Ways of Faith*, is the presentation of Christian beliefs and practices in an Arabic treatise its author entitled *Book of Proof* (*Kitāb al-Burhān*). At the time of its publication, this work was wrongly attributed to the 'Melkite' patriarch, Eutychius of Alexandria (877–940) (Cachia and Watt 1960–1), but it is more likely that the author was in fact the late ninth-century 'Melkite' bishop, Peter of Bayt Ra's (Capitolias) in Trans-Jordan (Swanson 1995). The author's main preoccupation, in contrast to that of the author of the *Summary of the Ways of Faith*, was to commend the veracity of Chalcedonian orthodoxy against Christian adversaries such as the 'Jacobites' and the 'Nestorians'.

In Iraq in the early ninth century, Theodore Abū Qurra's 'Jacobite' adversary, Ḥabīb b. Khidma Abū Rāʾiṭa (d. *c*.851), while principally concerned with advancing the truth claims of his community's Christological confessional formulae against the polemics of contemporary, Arabic-speaking Melkites and Nestorians, also addressed several *rasāʾil* to his fellow Christians in which he defended Christianity as the true religion and offered arguments in support of Christian doctrines criticized by Muslims (Graf 1951; Keating 2006). Abū Rāʾiṭa's treatise on the Trinity seeks to demonstrate that the affirmation of the three hypostases of the one God (*tathlīth*) does not involve any contradiction to the affirmation of God's unity (*tawḥīd*). The treatise on the incarnation seeks to explain that Jesus, God's Word and a Spirit from Him as the Qur'ān would have it (Q 4: 171), is the incarnate Son of God, without positing any change or alteration in the divine being. Abū Rā'iṭa's purpose was to offer a proof (*burhān*) for the veracity of Christian doctrines of the sort that the Qur'ān demands of the People of the Book, 'Produce your proof (*burhān*) if you speak truly' (Q 2: 111).

At the beginning of his apology for the doctrine of the Trinity, Abū Rā'iṭa makes an explicit appeal for a discussion of the matter according to the conventions of the *'ilm al-kalām* as it was currently conducted among the Muslim *mutakallimūn*. He instructs his Christian readers to say to their Muslim interlocutors, 'The hope is that you will treat us fairly in the discussion (*kalām*) and that you will bargain with us as brothers who share in the goods they inherit from their father. All of them share in them. Nothing belongs to one rather than to another. So we and you are on a par in this discussion' (Graf 1951: i. 3–4). Like many another Arab Christian writer, Abū Rā'iṭa writes in Arabic phrases that are replete with words and expressions from the Qur'ān and he consciously reflects the style and the idiom of the Arab *mutakallimūn*. He appropriates their modes of expression for the purpose of giving a new voice, or at least a new defence, to traditional Christian doctrines. In addition to defending the doctrines of the Trinity and the Incarnation, he argues on behalf of Christianity's claim to be the true religion, employing in the process a distinctive line of reasoning shared by a number of Arab Christian writers of the first 'Abbāsid century, according to which that religion is the true one in which none of six or seven negative features can be found that should disqualify a religion for the allegiance of intelligent people (Griffith 1979).

A centrepiece of Arab Christian theology in the first 'Abbāsid century was the undertaking to demonstrate the credibility of the doctrine of the Trinity in Arabic terms that figured in the burgeoning systematic theology of the contemporary Muslim *mutakallimūn* about the ontological status of the divine attributes. In the wake of the development of theoretical Arabic grammar as exemplified in works like 'Amr b. 'Uthmān Sībawayhi's (d. 793) well-known *al-Kitāb*, some Muslim religious scholars already in the second half of the first 'Abbāsid century were seeking ways systematically to articulate how the affirmation of the Qur'ān's 'beautiful names of God' (*al-asmā' al-ḥusnā*), the divine attributes (*ṣifāt Allāh*), could bespeak truths about the one God without in any way even theoretically compromising the confession of God's absolute one-ness (*tawḥīd*) (Frank 1978; Gimaret 1988). While this undertaking and numerous other issues engaged the attention of Muslim scholars in the ninth century and thereafter, contemporary Arab Christian apologists were not slow to perceive in these developments in Arabic systematic thought about the divine attributes an opportunity to argue in the same idiom on behalf of the credibility of the doctrine of the three 'hypostases' (*aqānīm*) in the one God. They proposed that of all the attributes, three are logically and ontologically prior to all the others, namely those that bespeak the real subsistence of acts of existence, life, and rationality in the divine nature. Each apologist in his own way then articulated this perception in Arabic terms reminiscent of the vocabulary of the

Islamic discourse about divine attributes to parse the talk of God's existence, life, and rationality into an expression of the Christian affirmation of the one God as Father, Son, and Holy Spirit (Haddad 1985). Arguably this borrowed discourse in Christian apologetics in turn posed a challenge for Muslim *mutakallimūn* who wished to avoid conclusions in their own thought that would seem to favour Christian claims that this line of reasoning potentially supported the reasonableness of the doctrine of the Trinity.

Both Theodore Abū Qurra and Ḥabīb b. Khidma Abū Rā'iṭa argued on behalf of the credibility of the doctrine of the Trinity in this Arabic idiom reminiscent of the current Islamic discussions of how rightly to understand and to articulate the significance of the affirmation of the truth of the divine attributes. So too did a number of other more popularizing Christian writers in Arabic of the ninth and tenth centuries (Griffith 2008b: 75–105). But the Christian Arab writer whose reasoning in this vein was the most obviously intertwined with the discourse of the Muslim *mutakallimūn* was the 'Nestorian', ʿAmmār al-Baṣrī (*fl.* *c.*850). This is not surprising given his Baṣrian origins and the fact that ʿAmmār's surviving Arabic works fit programmatically and formally, in terms of their topical outlines and mode of discourse, the pattern typical of the *kalām* texts of his day (Hayek 1977; Griffith 1983). What is more, in his discussion of the divine attributes and his use of the systematic construction put upon their significance according to the logic of the theoretical Arabic grammar that lay behind the discussion of the *ṣifāt Allāh* in his intellectual milieu, ʿAmmār took issue specifically with the views of the Muʿtazilī writer, Abū Hudhayl al-ʿAllāf (d. *c.*840), about the ontological status of what the divine attributes affirm of God, arguing that Abū Hudhayl's position logically reduces God and His attributes to accidents (Griffith 1982c). So it is no surprise to find in Ibn al-Nadīm's *Fihrist* a notice to the effect that Abū Hudhayl had written a treatise entitled, *Against ʿAmmār the Christian, in Refutation of the Christians* (Dodge 1970: i. 394).

Other Muslim thinkers of the period also took notice of developments in Christian theology in Arabic, most notably and most comprehensively the alleged free-thinker, Abū ʿĪsā al-Warrāq (d. *c.*860), who wrote extensively and knowingly not only about the several Christian denominations in the Arabic-speaking world but also specifically in critique of the doctrines of the Trinity and the Incarnation (Thomas 1992; 2002), as they were proposed and defended in Arabic by the systematic Christian apologists of the first ʿAbbāsid century. Later Muslim writers, such as the Muʿtazilī summarist ʿAbd al-Jabbār al-Hamdhānī (d. 1025), took pains to describe and discuss Christian history and thought at some length (Reynolds 2004; Reynolds and Samir 2010), while other *mutakallimūn* regularly included refutations of Christian doctrines in their treatises (Thomas 2008).

In addition to essays and treatises in systematic and apologetic theology, Arab Christian controversialists in the first ʿAbbāsid century also composed numerous more popular, polemical works, intended for a Christian audience, in which the emphasis was on both the defence of Christian doctrines and polemical attacks on Islamic thought and practice (Gaudeul 2000; Thomas and Roggema 2009). A particularly ingenious composition in this vein, in both Syriac and Arabic recensions of the ninth century, is the anonymous *Legend of the Monk Baḥīrā*. In this work the Christian author takes his cue from the story in the biographical traditions of Muḥammad about the future prophet's meeting as a teenager with a monk who recognized him as a prophet foretold. Incorporating earlier apocalyptic themes, the author of the legend builds on this story to develop a scenario according to which a renegade monk, having met the prophet in his youth, instructed Muḥammad in basic Christian thought with a view to catechizing the Arabs in Christianity, including a ruse whereby Muḥammad would bolster his message with records of divine revelation that would in due course become the Qurʾān. According to the story, the Christian message therein originally expressed was subsequently distorted by hostile Jewish scribes among Muḥammad's early followers (Roggema 2009).

A number of Arab Christian writers of the ninth century CE wrote popular works featuring debates between Christian and Muslim spokespersons, quite often presenting a scenario in which a monk appeared in an emir's or caliph's *majlis*, modelling how a Christian might defend the credibility of his faith in the face of challenges posed by Muslims. These texts are markedly polemical in tone and seem to have been composed in an effort to support the faith of wavering Christians (Griffith 1999a; Newman 1993). By far the most vigorous and most popular of Christian polemical tracts against Islam written in Arabic in this period is the anonymous work presented in a fictitious epistolary exchange between a Muslim, ʿAbd Allāh b. Ismāʿīl al-Hāshimī, and a Christian, ʿAbd al-Masīḥ b. Isḥāq al-Kindī, whose very names indicate their respective confessional allegiances. The unknown Christian writer has ʿAbd Allāh write a letter to ʿAbd al-Masīḥ, in which the former invites the latter to embrace Islam, laying out the principal features of Muslim faith in a clear and straightforward fashion. In his much longer reply, ʿAbd al-Masīḥ then puts forward a withering critique of Muḥammad's claims to prophecy, of the Qurʾān's status as a divinely inspired scripture, and of Islam's bid to be considered the true religion. The unknown author's knowledge of contemporary Islamic traditions and religious thought is impressive and the text includes accounts of such events as the collection of the Qurʾān that in some respects pre-date the surviving Muslim records of the undertaking. The text is by far the most hostile Christian polemic against Islam written in Arabic. Some Muslim scholars, such as Abū Ḥayyān at-Tawḥīdī (d. 1023) and Abū Rayḥān al-Bīrūnī (d. 1048) mentioned al-Kindī's name in their works as if he were a well-known Christian author, but they say nothing of the al-Hāshimī/al-Kindī correspondence (Haddad 1985: 41). Not surprisingly, it circulated widely among Arabophone Christians, having been recopied many times; it was even translated into Latin in the twelfth century (Bottini 1998; 2008).

Already in the ninth century, Christian intellectuals writing in Arabic took a step away from the *kalām* style of the earliest systematic theologians among them toward the more philosophical and logical approach that would characterize the works of the important Christian thinkers of the tenth and eleventh centuries in the environs of Baghdad, such as the Jacobites, Yaḥyā b. ʿAdī (b. 893, d. 974) and ʿĪsā b. Zurʿa (b. 943, d. 1108). The way was paved for them by the earlier translators and transmitters of the Greek sciences such as the Nestorian Ḥunayn b. Isḥāq (b. 808, d. 875), who in addition to his role as professional translator was also the one who laid the groundwork for the future 'Christian

Aristotelians' of Baghdad. He had put a premium on the philosophical life itself, on the primacy of reason in religious thought and the pursuit of happiness not only personally and individually but socially and politically as well (Griffith 2008c). And by the time a generation later the Christian logician, Abū Bishr Mattā b. Yūnus (d. 940) was tutoring the Muslim Abū Naṣr al-Fārābī (b. *c.*870, d. 950) and the latter's Christian pupil and successor in logic and philosophy, Yaḥyā b. ʿAdī, Christian theological thought in Arabic had already taken a turn in the new direction of envisioning the 'perfect man' (*al-insān al-kāmil*) and the virtuous polity in which he might safely live the good life and practise right religion (Ibn ʿAdī 2002). Even in their apologies for the doctrine of the Trinity, Yaḥyā b. ʿAdī and his more philosophically minded followers were turning away from the methods employed by the earlier generation of Christian *mutakallimūn* in the first ʿAbbāsid century toward the logically more sophisticated models of the one and the many they found in the works of Greek philosophers (Platti 1980).

References

Bottini, L. (1998). *Al-Kindī: Apologia del Cristianesimo; traduzione dall'arabo, introduzione.* Milan: Jaca Book.

Bottini, L. (2008). 'The Apology of al-Kindī'. In Thomas and Roggema (2009: 585–94).

Brock, S. (1999). 'Two Letters of the Patriarch Timothy from the Late Eighth Century on Translations from Greek'. *Arabic Sciences and Philosophy* 9: 233–46.

Cachia, P., and W. M. Watt (eds. and trans.) (1960–1). *Eutychius of Alexandria, the Book of the Demonstration*. 4 vols. Louvain: Peeters.

Cook, M. (1981). *Early Muslim Dogma*. Cambridge: Cambridge University Press.

Dodge, B. (ed. and trans.) (1970). *The Fihrist of al-Nadīm: A Tenth-Century Survey of Muslim Culture*. 2 vols. New York: Columbia University Press.

Ebied, R., and D. Thomas (eds.) (2005). Muslim–*Christian Polemic during the Crusades: The Letter from the People of Cyprus and Ibn Abī Ṭālib al-Dimashqī's Response*. Leiden: Brill.

van Ess, J. (1991–7). *Theologie und Gesellschaft im 2. und 3. Jahrhundert Hidschra: Eine Geschichte des religiösen Denkens im frühen Islam*. 6 vols. Berlin: de Gruyter.

Frank, R. (1978). *Beings and their Attributes: The Teaching of the Basrian School of the Muʿtazila in the Classical Period*. Albany, NY: State University of New York Press.

Gaudeul, J. M. (2000). *Encounters and Clashes: Islam and Christianity in History*. 2 vols. Rome: Pontificio Istituto di Studi Arabi e d'Islamistica.

Gibson, M. (1899). *An Arabic Version of the Acts of the Apostles and the Seven Catholic Epistles, with a Treatise on the Triune Nature of God*. London: C. J. Clay & Sons.

Gimaret, D. (1988). *Les Noms divins en Islam: exégèse lexicographique et théologique*. Paris: Cerf.

Graf, G. (1944–53). *Geschichte der christlichen arabischen Literatur*. 5 vols. Vatican City: Biblioteca Apostolica Vaticana.

Graf, G. (1951). *Die Schriften des Jacobiten Ḥabīb ibn Ḫidma Abū Rāʾiṭa*. 2 vols. Louvain: Peeters.

Griffith, S. (1979). 'Comparative Religion in the Apologetics of the First Christian Arabic Theologians'. In *Proceedings of the PMR Conference: Annual Publication of the Patristic, Medieval and Renaissance Conference, Villanova University*. Philadelphia, 63–87.

Griffith, S. (1981). 'Chapter Ten of the Scholion: Theodore bar Kônî's Apology for Christianity'. *Orientalia Christiana Periodica* 47: 158–88.

Griffith, S. (1982a). 'Theodore bar Kônî's *Scholion*: A Nestorian Summa contra Gentiles from the First Abbasid Century'. In N. Garsoïan, T. Mathews, and R. Thomson (eds.), *East of Byzantium: Syria and Armenia in the Formative Period*. Washington, DC: Dumbarton Oaks, 53–72.

Griffith, S. (1982b). 'Chapter Ten of the Scholion: Theodore bar Kônî's Apology for Christianity'. *Orientalia Christiana Analecta* 218: 169–91.

Griffith, S. (1982c). 'The Concept of al-uqnūm in ʿAmmār al-Baṣrī's Apology for the Doctrine of the Trinity'. In S. Kh. Samir (ed.), *Actes du premier Congrès International d'Études Arabes Chrétiennes (Goslar, septembre 1980)*. Rome: Pontificium Institutum Studiorum Orientalium, 169–91.

Griffith, S. (1983). "ʿAmmār al-Baṣrī's *Kitāb al-burhān*: Christian *Kalām* in the First Abbasid Century'. *Le Muséon* 96: 145–81.

Griffith, S. (1986). 'A Ninth Century Summa Theologiae Arabica'. In S. Kh. Samir (ed.), *Actes du Deuxième Congrès International d'Études Arabes Chrétiennes*. Rome: Pontificio Istituto degli Studii Orientali, 123–41.

Griffith, S. (1988). 'The Monks of Palestine and the Growth of Christian Literature in Arabic'. *Muslim World* 78: 1–28.

Griffith, S. (1990). 'Islam and the Summa Theologiae Arabica; *Rabīʿ* I, 264 A.H.' *Jerusalem Studies in Arabic and Islam* 13: 225–64.

Griffith, S. (1993). 'Reflections on the Biography of Theodore Abū Qurrah'. *Parole de l'Orient* 18: 143–70.

Griffith, S. (1994). 'Faith and Reason in Christian Kalām: Theodore Abū Qurrah on Discerning the True Religion'. In S. K. Samir and J. S Nielsen (eds.), *Christian Arabic Apologetics during the Abbasid Period (750–1258)*. Leiden: Brill, 1–43.

Griffith, S. (1997a). 'From Aramaic to Arabic: The Languages of the Monasteries of Palestine in the Byzantine and Early Islamic Periods'. *Dumbarton Oaks Papers* 51: 11–31.

Griffith, S. (trans.) (1997b). *Theodore Abū Qurrah: A Treatise on the Veneration of the Holy Icons*. Louvain: Peeters.

Griffith, S. (1999a). 'Arab Christian Culture in the Early Abbasid Period'. *Bulletin of the Royal Institute for Inter-Faith Studies* 1: 25–44.

Griffith, S. (1999b). 'The Monk in the Emir's Majlis: Reflections on a Popular Genre of Christian Literary Apologetics in Arabic in the Early Islamic Period'. In H. Lazarus-Yafeh et al. (eds.), *The Majlis: Interreligious Encounters in Medieval Islam*. Wiesbaden: Harrassowitz, 13–65.

Griffith, S. (2002). 'Melkites, Jacobites, and the Christological Controversies in Arabic in Third/Ninth-Century Syria'. In D. Thomas (ed.), *Syrian Christians under Islam: The First Thousand Years*. Leiden: Brill, 9–55.

Griffith, S. (2007a). 'Christians, Muslims and the Image of the One God: Iconophilia and Iconophobia in the World of Islam in Umayyad and Early Abbasid Times'. In B. Groneberg and H. Spieckermann (eds.), *Die Welt der Götterbilder*. Berlin: de Gruyter, 347–80.

Griffith, S. (2007b). 'The Syriac Letters of Patriarch I and the Birth of Christian Kalām in the Muʿtazilite Milieu of Baghdad and Baṣrah in Early Islamic Times'. In W. van Bekkum, J. Drijvers, and A. Klugkist (eds.), *Syriac Polemics: Studies in Honour of Gerrit Jan Reinink*. Leuven: Peeters, 103–32.

Griffith, S. (2008a). 'John of Damascus and the Church in Syria in the Umayyad Era: The Intellectual and Cultural Milieu of Orthodox Christians in the World of Islam'. *Hugoye* 11 ii <[http://syrcom.cua.edu/Hugoye/Vol11No2/HV11N2Griffith.html]>.

Griffith, S. (2008b). *The Church in the Shadow of the Mosque: Christians and Muslims in the World of Islam*. Princeton: Princeton University Press.

Griffith, S. (2008c). 'Ḥunayn ibn Isḥāq and the Kitāb Ādab al-falāsifah: The Pursuit of Wisdom and a Humane Polity in Early Abbasid Baghdad'. In G. Kiraz (ed.), *Malphono w-Rabo d-Malphone: Studies in Honor of Sebastian P. Brock*. Piscataway, NJ: Gorgias Press, 135–60.

Griffith, S. (2009). 'Crosses, Icons and the Image of Christ in Edessa: The Place of Iconophobia in the Christian-Muslim Controversies of Early Islamic Times'. In P. Rousseau and M. Papoutsakis (eds.), *Transformations of Late Antiquity: Essays for Peter Brown*. Farnham: Ashgate, 63–84.

Griffith, S. (2011). 'Images, Icons, and the Public Space in Early Islamic Times: Arab Christians and the Program to Claim the Land for Islam'. In K. Holum and H. Lapin (eds.), *Shaping the Middle East: Jews, Christians, and Muslims in an Age of Transition 400–800 CE*. Bethesda, MD: University Press of Maryland, 197–210.

Gutas, D. (1998). *Greek Thought, Arabic Culture: The Graeco-Arabic Translation Movement in Baghdad and Early 'Abbāsid Society (2nd–4th/8th–10th Centuries)*. London/ New York: Routledge.

Haddad, R. (1985). *La Trinité divine chez les théologiens arabes (750–1050)*. Paris: Beauchesne.

Hayek, M. (1977). *'Ammār al-Baṣrī: apologie et controverses*. Beirut: Dar el-Machreq.

Heimgartner, M. (2011). *Timotheos I, Ostsyrischer Patriarch: Disputation mit dem Kalifen al-Mahdī*. Louvain: Peeters.

Hoyland, R. (1997). *Seeing Islam as Others Saw It: A Survey and Evaluation of Christian, Jewish, and Zoroastrian Writings on Early Islam*. Princeton: Darwin.

Ibn ʿAdī, Yaḥyā. (2002). *The Reformation of Morals*. Trans. S. Griffith. Provo, UT: Brigham Young University Press.

Keating, S. (2006). *Defending the 'People of Truth' in the Early Islamic Period: The Christian Apologies of Abū Rā'iṭah*. Leiden: Brill.

Khoury, P. (1964). *Paul d'Antioche: Évêque melkite de Sidon (XIIe.s.)*. Beirut: Imprimerie Catholique.

Khoury, P. (1989–9). *Matériaux pour servir à l'étude de la controverse théologique islamo-chrétienne de langue arabe du VIIIe au XII siècle*. 4 vols. Würzburg/Albenberge: Echter & Oros Verlag.

Lamoreaux, J. (2002). 'The Biography of Theodore Abū Qurrah Revisited'. *Dumbarton Oaks Papers* 56: 25–40.

Lamoreaux, J. (2005). *Theodore Abū Qurrah*. Provo, UT: Brigham Young University Press.

Le Coz, R. (1992). *Jean Damascène: Écrits sur l'Islam*. Paris: Les Éditions du Cerf.

Louth, A. (2002). *St John Damascene: Tradition and Originality in Byzantine Theology*. Oxford: Oxford University Press.

Nasry, W. (2008). *The Caliph and the Bishop: A 9th Century Muslim–Christian Debate: Al-Ma'mūn and Abū Qurrah*. Beirut: CEDRAC-Université Saint Joseph.

Newman, N. (ed.) (1993). *The Early Christian–Muslim Dialogue: A Collection of Documents from the First Three Islamic Centuries (632–900 A.D.). Translations with Commentary*. Hatfield, PA: Interdisciplinary Biblical Research Institute.

Pines, S. (1976). 'Some Traits of Christian Theological Writing in Relation to Moslem Kalām and to Jewish Thought'. *Proceedings of the Israel Academy of the Sciences and the Humanities* 5: 105–25.

Platti, E. (1980). 'Yahyā b. 'Adi, philosophe et théologien'. *Mélanges de l'Institut Dominicain d'Études Orientales du Caire* 14: 167–84.

Putman, H. (1975). *L'Église et l'islam sous Timothée I (780–823): étude sur l'église nestorienne au temps des premiers 'Abbāsides avec nouvelle edition et traduction du dialogue entre Timothée et al-Mahdī*. Beirut: Dar el-Machreq.

Reynolds, G. (2004). *A Muslim Theologian in the Sectarian Milieu: 'Abd al-Jabbār and the Critique of Christian Origins*. Leiden: Brill.

Reynolds, G., and S. Samir (eds. and trans.) (2010). *'Abd al-Jabbār: Critique of Christian Origins*. Provo, UT: Brigham Young University Press.

Rissanen, S. (1993). *Theological Encounter of Oriental Christians with Islam during Early Abbasid Rule*. Åbo: Åbo Adademis Förlag.

Roggema, B. (2009). *The Legend of Sergius Baḥīrā: Eastern Christian Apologetics and Apocalyptic in Response to Islam*. Leiden: Brill.

Rudolph, U. (1997). *Al-Māturīdī und die sunnitische Theologie in Samarkand*. Leiden: Brill.

Samir, S. Kh. (1986). 'La "Somme des aspects de la foi": œuvre d'Abū Qurrah?' In S. Kh. Samir (ed.), *Actes du Deuxième Congrès International d'Études Arabes Chrétiennes*. Rome: Pontificio Istituto degli Studii Orientali, 93–121.

Samir, S. Kh. (1994). 'The Earliest Arab Apology for Christianity (*c*.750)'. In S. Kh. Samir and J. S Nielsen (eds.), *Christian Arabic Apologetics during the Abbasid Period (750–1258)*. Leiden: Brill, 57–114.

Swanson, M. (1995). 'Ibn Taymiyya and the *Kitāb al-burhān*: A Muslim Controversialist Responds to a Ninth-Century Arabic Christian Apology'. In Y. and W. Haddad (eds.), Christian-*Muslim Encounters*. Gainesville, FL: University Press of Florida, 94–107.

Swanson, M. (1998). 'Beyond Prooftexting: Approaches to the Qur'ān in Some Early Arabic Christian Apologies'. *Muslim World* 88: 297–319.

Thomas, D. (ed. and trans.) (1992). *Anti-Christian Polemic in Early Islam: Abū 'Īsā al-Warrāq's 'Against the Trinity'*. Cambridge: Cambridge University Press.

Thomas, D. (2002). *Early Muslim Polemic against Christianity: Abū 'Īsā al-Warrāq's 'Against the Incarnation'*. Cambridge: Cambridge University Press.

Thomas, D. (2008). *Christian Doctrines in Islamic Theology*. Leiden: Brill.

Thomas, D., and B. Roggema (eds.) (2009). *Christian–Muslim Relations: A Bibliographical History. i: 600–900*. Leiden: Brill.

CHAPTER 6

EXCURSUS II

Ungodly Cosmologies

PATRICIA CRONE

THE reader may wonder both what the title means and why a subject of this nature should be included in a volume on Islamic theology.[1] The answer is that a number of cosmologies of late antique origin which left little or no room for God in the creation and management of the world played a major role in the development of Muslim *kalām*, a field normally translated as (dialectical) theology. In fact, *kalām* covered much the same range of topics as Greek physics, if in a very different way: the principles (in the sense of the ultimate constituents of the universe), the origin and end of the material world, the nature of man, God and his relationship with us. To Greek philosophers, physics was a key to the nature of the gods; to Muslim theologians, it was God who was a key to physics. This was a well-known source of tension between reason as the sole basis of the search for the truth and reason as the handmaid of revelation. Al-Jāḥiẓ (d. 255/869), who distinguished between *kalām al-falsafa*, dialectical philosophy (covering natural science), and *kalām al-dīn*, dialectical theology (covering God and his relationship with us), readily admitted that philosophy was dangerous, but nonetheless insisted that a good practitioner of *kalām* had to master both fields (Crone 2010–11: 75f).

When the curtain opens on Muslim *kalām* in the mid-second/eighth century, the field of *kalām al-falsafa* was dominated by thinkers whom Muslims called Zindīqs and Dahrīs and bracketed as *mulḥids*, a term sometimes translated as 'atheists' but better rendered as 'godless' or 'ungodly people'. All *mulḥids* denied that God had created the world from nothing, and some denied his creation, government, and ultimate judgement of the world altogether along with any form of afterlife. The Muslims had to develop their own cosmology to counter the ungodly systems, and they did so by assimilating and gradually transforming those of their rivals. The ungodly cosmologies thus show us a bridge between late antique and Islamic thought.

[1] I am indebted to Michael Cook for reading and commenting on a draft of this article.

Cosmology had acquired great religious importance in late antiquity, for Zoroastrians, Gnostics, and Platonists (Christian, pagan, and other) had all come to share the conviction that the key to our troubled human condition was to be found in primordial events leading to the creation of this world, rather than in early human history. All offered detailed accounts of these events, and most drew on Greek philosophy for their formulation. Thinkers such as Basilides (*fl.* 120–40), Valentinus (d. *c.*160), Marcion (d. *c.*160), Bardesanes/Bar Dayṣān (d. 222), and Origen (d. *c.*254), who had a huge impact on Near Eastern thought on both sides of the Euphrates, all drew their main philosophical inspiration from Middle Platonism and Stoicism. So too did the immensely influential physician Galen (d. *c.*200). The Platonic-Stoic legacy is still discernible in the thought of the Zindīqs and Dahrīs, and in *kalām* influenced by them, along with occasional input from the rival Sceptical and Epicurean schools and intriguing suggestions of a strong interest in the Presocratics. Also discernible, however, is the magnetic pull exercised from perhaps the sixth century onwards by Aristotle's *Categories*, treated as a guide to ontology, not just to logic. But by the fourth/tenth century the irresistible force was Neoplatonism, carried by Ismailis and philosophers (*falāsifa*) of a new type who owed their ideas to Arabic translations of Plato, Aristotle, and the Neoplatonist commentators. Henceforth it was the emanatory scheme of the Neoplatonists that dominated cosmological debates; the old-style *mulḥid*s no longer played a major role in them, though they still attracted attention, especially for their denial of the creator and of the afterlife (Dhanani 1994: 4f., 182–7; *Encyclopaedia of Islam*,² s.v. 'Dahriyya'; *Encyclopaedia Iranica*, s.v. 'Dahrī'; *Encyclopaedia of Islam*,³ s.v. 'Dahrites').

I The Actors

The *mulḥid*s had complicated backgrounds. Some were Marcionites, Bardesanites, or Manicheans by origin, that is to say they came from Christian communities of a type proscribed by the victorious Christian churches. (Even the Manicheans counted themselves as Christians.) But by early Islamic times the Marcionites and Bardesanites had become so heavily Iranianized that they were barely recognizable as Christians, and the Muslims classified all three sects as dualist, deeming them ineligible for protected status. The communities nonetheless survived, but many of their members appear to have been forced to convert, or to have found it prudent to do so. It was nominal converts from these three religions and others attracted to their beliefs who were called Zindīqs. The term is derived from the Aramaic *ṣaddīq* by which the Manichean 'elect' were known,[2] and the Muslims sometimes used it of real Manichaeans too. Just as the Zindīqs were not true Muslims, however, so they were not true adherents of the religions they had left

[2] Cf. *Encyclopaedia of Islam*², s.v. 'zindīḳ' (de Blois), decisively eliminating the derivation of the word from *zand*.

behind. A Zindīq in the period *c.*750–900 was usually a man who had lost faith in any positive religion, or even in any God.

The Dahrīs mostly seem to have their intellectual roots in the older belief systems dismissed by Christians as 'pagan'. When the emperor Justinian (r. 527–65) set out to eradicate paganism from the Roman empire, he took the precaution of also persecuting those pagans who had 'decided to espouse in word the name of Christians' (Procopius, *Anecdota*, 11: 32), and it was probably as nominal Christians that most of them survived. Those persecuted by the Sasanians, who imposed Zoroastrianism as understood in Pārs (Ar. Fārs) on their Iranian and occasionally also non-Iranian subjects, seem likewise to have included pagans in the sense of people who were not Zoroastrians, Jews, or Christians,[3] but mostly they were bearers of local, non-Persian forms of Zoroastrianism (cf. Crone 2012a: chs. 15–16). The *Baga Nask*, an Avestan book preserved only in a Pahlavi summary, tells of 'apostates' (*yašarmogān*) who had been defeated and kept their apostasy concealed, reluctantly calling themselves Zoroastrian priests and teaching the good religion despite their heretical inclinations (*Dēnkard*, book IX, 52: 3). These 'apostates' would hardly have been forced to officiate on behalf of official Zoroastrianism if they had not been priests of what the Sasanians took to be deviant forms of their own faith.

Whatever their origin, Dahrīs shared with Zindīqs the feature of having lost belief in their ancestral religion without having acquired belief in another. A disillusioned attitude is attested even among pagans who had not been forced into any religious community. In the Jewish-Christian Pseudo-Clementines, probably composed in Antioch or Edessa *c.*300–60, one of the heroes is a well-born pagan who believes in astrology and denies the existence of both God and providence on the grounds that everything is governed by chance and fate, meaning the conjunctions under which one happens to have been born, and who resists conversion because he simply cannot believe that souls are immortal and subject to punishment for sins. Nemesius of Emesa (*c.*390) also mentions deniers of providence and the afterlife (Nemesius, *Nature*, 213f., 217). So too does Theodoret of Cyrrhus (d. *c.*460), but now they were nominal Christians to whom it was still physics that provided a key to God rather than the other way round: it is by appeals to nature and the ancient Greeks that Theodoret tries to persuade them (Theodoret, *Providence*, 9: 23f.). Saint Simeon the Younger (d. 592) found Antioch to be teeming with impious mockers whose errors included denial of the resurrection, astrological beliefs to the effect that natural disasters and human misbehaviour were caused by the position of the stars, 'automatism' (presumably meaning the view that the world had arisen on its own), and the claim, here characterized as Manichean, that the creation was due to fate or chance (van den Ven 1962: §§157, 161). On the Sasanian side there is evidence for denial of the resurrection already in the third century. The first attestations could concern belief in reincarnation, widespread in the Jibāl and elsewhere, but by the sixth century the denial is coupled with loss of faith in God/the gods, the creation, and afterlife

[3] Cf. Theodore Bar Koni, *Liber*, mimrā 1: 29f.; Moses Bar Kepha, *Hexaemeronkommentar*, I.13.1–15; Muqammiṣ, *ʿIshrūn*, 7: 6, where they are *ṣābiʿa*, clearly in the sense of pagans, not Sabians of Harran; compare Yaʿqūbī, *Tārīkh*, 1: 166, 179 (Greek, Roman, and Iranian kings as Sabians); Balīnūs, *Sirr*, 1: 2.3.6, p. 35.

of any kind. When the famous physician Burzoē, active under Khusraw I (r. 531–70), lost faith in his ancestral religion, he *tried* not to 'deny the awakening and resurrection, reward and punishment'. A Pahlavi advice work informs us that man becomes wicked on account of five things, one of which is lack of belief 'in the (imperishableness of) the soul', i.e. denial of afterlife of any kind; and several other works stress that one should be free of doubts concerning the existence of the gods, paradise, hell, and the resurrection (Crone 2012a: 373ff.). Burzoē remained an unhappy sceptic who held the truth to be beyond us, but others turned into assertive materialists, that is to say Dahrīs.

In short, the *mulḥids* had their roots in proscribed communities whose members had been directly or indirectly forced into Christianity or Persian Zoroastrianism, and thereafter into Islam. Dahrīs were insincere Muslims who professed Islam out of fear of the sword, as al-Qummī remarks (*Tafsīr*, 2: 270, *ad* Q 45: 24).[4] There can hardly be much doubt that the massive use of coercion on behalf of God in late antiquity and early Islam had played a role in eroding their faith in anything except their own reason, but other factors were also at work. One was the sheer diversity of rival religions. When religions compete in a free market situation, as in modern America, the competition can apparently increase religiosity (Stark and Finke 2000, and other works by the same authors; Kraus 1934: 15ff.), but it certainly did not do so in the past, when religion was not a freely purchased commodity and when the competition between rival forms was often felt to undermine the truth of all of them. In the sixth century the sheer diversity of beliefs troubled Burzoē and Paul the Persian; by the tenth century it troubled Muslims too (Crone 2006: 21f.). The only way to evaluate the competing claims was by use of reason.

One way in which reason came to sit in judgement over religious claims was by disputation, a competitive sport of enormous popularity on both sides of the Euphrates both before and after the rise of Islam (Lim 1995; Cook 1980; Cook 2007). The rules required the disputers to base their arguments on shared premisses, meaning that appeals to scripture and tradition were only allowed in disputation with co-religionists, and even then it was reason which had to sit in judgement over the different interpretations. Debaters thus learned to translate their beliefs into claims that could stand on their own and be defended by Aristotelian logic. The *Categories* was the disputer's Bible. Already the third-century Apelles, a deviant Marcionite, had used dialectical syllogisms to discredit the Pentateuch, and the Manicheans soon learned to set aside their extravagant mythology to become fearsome disputers (Grant 1993, ch. 6; Lim 1995, ch. 3). There is no trace of mythology in the debate staged by Justinian at Constantinople between a (chained) Manichean and a certain Paul the Persian representing the Christian side,[5] nor is there in the cosmologies of Manichean, Marcionite, Bardesanite, and Zoroastrian origin that the Zindīqs and Dahrīs fielded in disputation with the Muslims. Inevitably, many disputers came to regard reason rather than scripture and tradition as the ultimate authority at all times, not just for purposes of disputation. Al-Jāḥiẓ complains that

[4] For the Dahrīs as interlopers, see also Jāḥiẓ, *Ḥujaj*, 118.

[5] Photinus, *Disputationes*. On the several persons called 'Paul the Persian', see Gutas 1982: 239 n.

young men would foolishly rush into disputations with *mulḥids*, convinced of their own dialectical skills, only to be seduced by them, and roundly declares that 'countless' people had apostatized as Zindīqs and Dahrīs over complicated questions of *kalām* (Crone 2010–11: 72). It was in their relentless refusal of claims based on scripture and tradition that both the godlessness and the seductiveness of the Zindīqs and Dahrīs lay.

Zindīqs and Dahrīs are first mentioned in the 120s/740s and receive particular attention in the third/ninth century, though they continue to be attested down to the Mongol invasions. They formed loose clusters of individuals, not sects. Dahrīs seem mostly to have been doctors, astrologers, and others interested in the workings of nature; Zindīqs were predominantly secretaries, courtiers, poets, and other members of the elegant set. How far similar convictions flourished among uneducated urbanites and villagers is unknown.[6] In learned gatherings Zindīqs and Dahrīs would pick out inconsistencies in the Qurʾān and *ḥadīth*, scoff at accounts of claims running counter to normal experience, and sometimes mock Islamic ritual. But they lived like everyone else, observing the normal rules of propriety and formalities of the law (Masʿūdī, *Murūj*, 5: 84 [3, §1846]; Ṭabarī, *Tārīkh*, 3: 422f.; van Ess 1991–7: ii. 17; al-Rāzī, *Tafsīr*, 23: 18, *ad* Q 22: 17f.), and relations between them and Muʿtazilite *mutakallims* appear to have been friendly. Al-Naẓẓām (d. *c*.220–30/835–45), who wrote against both Dahrīs and *mulḥids*, had a brother-in-law who attributed everything to natural causes and the stars (Jāḥiẓ, *Ḥayawān*, 1: 148). Zindīqs were particularly close to the Shīʿites. Shīʿite sources abhor them and invariably depict the imams as refuting them in Medina (Vajda 1938: esp. 222f.; Chokr 1993: esp. 109, 111–13), but it is clear from the doctrines of the Shīʿite *mutakallim* Hishām b. al-Ḥakam (d. *c*.179/795) that the interaction was in Iraq and involved Muslim appropriation and reshaping of the rival doctrines, not just refutation of them.

Dahrīs seem rarely to have been persecuted,[7] but Zindīqs came in for a purge under the caliph al-Mahdī (r. 775–85), to whom a Zindīq seems to have been anything from a genuine Manichean to an irreverent courtier. There is no mention of Dahrīs in this connection, perhaps because the two terms were sometimes used synonymously, but more probably because the Zindīqs flourished at the court, where they sometimes inclined to Manicheism in a religious sense and where the poets would shamelessly jockey for position by denouncing their rivals as Zindīqs. *Mutakallims*, by contrast, would close ranks against outsiders (Jāḥiẓ, *Ḥayawān*, 4: 450; 6: 37). Al-Mahdī is reported to have ordered the *mutakallims* to write refutations of the *mulḥids* (Masʿūdī, *Murūj*, 8: 293 [5, §3447]; Yaʿqūbī, *Mushākala*, 24), and whatever he may have meant by that term (if he used it), the *mutakallims* did not limit their refutations to Zindīqs. Books against dualists, Manicheans, Dahrīs, and *mulḥids* in general were composed by theologians active under and after al-Mahdī. But only their titles survive, and we have no statements by the Zindīqs or Dahrīs themselves. We do, however, have works presenting cosmologies

6 For a suggestion that the *ʿāmmī* might be a Dahrī, see Maqdisī, *Badʾ*, 1: 121.2; cf. also Maimonides on the multitudes (below, n. 73 and the text thereto).

7 For an exception, see Rashīd b. al-Zubayr, *Dhakhāʾir*, 140.

closely related to theirs in the *Book of Treasures* by the Christian doctor Job of Edessa (writing *c.*817), the *Sirr al-khalīqa* attributed to Apollonius of Tyana (Balīnūs, Balīnas) (*c.*205/820?), and the mostly fourth/tenth-century alchemical corpus attributed to the Shīʿite Jābir (heavily Neoplatonized). We hear of books by Zindīqs, including a *Kitāb al-shukūk* by a Zindīq espousing Sceptical views, but not of books by Dahrīs (Ibn al-Nadīm, *Fihrist*, 204, 401; trans. Dodge, i. 387; ii. 804).[8] Whether they wrote or not, all *mulḥids* aired their views in disputations, the main vehicle of religious and philosophical discussion at the time.

II Epistemology

(a) Scepticism

The *mulḥids* included both doubters and deniers (Jāḥiẓ, *Ḥayawān*, 6: 35f.). Some doubters were people suffering from religious uncertainty and loss of faith, like Burzoē, but those who fielded doubts in disputations were Sceptics in the technical sense of adherents of an epistemology to the effect that we can never know the true nature of things. Such Sceptics were known as *shākkūn, juhhāl, mutajāhilūn, ḥisbāniyya, muʿānida, lā adriyya*, and the like, and also, for reasons that remain obscure, as Sūfisṭāʾiyya, 'sophists' (van Ess 1966: index s.v. 'Skepsis'; van Ess 1968).

Scepticism is attested both as dogmatic assertion of our inability to know and as suspension of judgement. Al-Jāḥiẓ mentions a Sceptic who held that one could only know things by preponderance (*bi-l-aghlab*). This was the position of Academic Sceptics, and Galen had expounded both their views and those of their Pyrrhonic rivals in his *De optimo docendi*; perhaps al-Jāḥiẓ's Sceptic had found inspiration in this work (Jāḥiẓ, *Ḥayawān*, 6: 37; Floridi 2002: 17). More commonly, however, it is Pyrrhonic Scepticism with its suspension of judgement that is reflected in the sources. Pyrrhonic Scepticism had gone into empiricist medicine (Hankinson 1995: ch. 13), and also into disputation practice. As Gregory of Nazianzus (d. 389) remarked, Pyrrho, Sextus, and the practice of 'arguing to opposites' had infected the churches (Floridi 2002: 12); the sixth-century disputer Uranius is reported by Agathias to have been a Sceptic in Sextus's tradition, and Manichean missionaries would apparently field Sceptical arguments in order to undermine the beliefs of potential proselytes and convert them (Agathias, *Histories*, 2: 29.1, 7; Pedersen 2004: 207).

According to Sceptical *mulḥids*, all claims about reality had to be based on sense impressions, preferably or exclusively autopsy (*ʿiyān*, what one had seen for oneself) (Jāḥiẓ, *Ḥayawān*, 4: 449; *Ḥujaj*, 247; Muqammiṣ, *ʿIshrūn*, 14: 1; Ibn Qutayba, *Taʾwīl*, 133;

[8] Cf. van Ess 1991–7: ii. 17 and n. 20. This Zindīq, Ṣāliḥ b. ʿAbd al-Quddūs, is also credited with dogmatist views.

trans. 149 [§170]). Bashshār b. Burd (d. 163/783), a poet variously classified as a Zindīq, Dahrī, and *mutaḥayyir* (somebody perplexed or sceptical),[9] is said to have believed only in what he had seen for himself and what was similar to it (*mā ʿāyantuhu aw ʿāyantu mithlahu*) (Abū l-Faraj, *Aghānī*, 3: 227). The meaning of 'similar' is unclear. Perhaps he was referring to the principle of 'transition to the similar' current in empiricist medicine (if you had personal experience of a disease affecting the upper arm, you could apply it to the upper leg);[10] but he could also have meant unanimous transmission from others. In any case, as this and other passages show, Scepticism was based on empiricist premisses.

The premisses were meant for rejection, however, for even sense impressions were unreliable, the Sceptics said. They would trot out the better-known tropes of their Greek predecessors (honey tastes bitter to a jaundiced patient; buildings appear small at a distance; poles appear bent under water, and so on); and as in antiquity their exasperated opponents would react by wanting to slap or beat them in order to demonstrate the reality of the sense impressions they were dismissing (van Ess 1966: 172f.; van Ess 1968: 1f. Māturīdī, *Tawḥīd*, 153.18). As Sextus said, this rested on lack of familiarity with Sceptical doctrine: Sceptics did not reject the sense impressions that induced assent involuntarily, but merely refused to dogmatize about the reality behind them; they granted that honey *appeared* to be sweet, but whether it was sweet in *essence* only a dogmatist would claim to know (Sextus Empiricus, *Outlines*, 1.13.19f.). This was the position of the Sūfisṭāʾīs too. Unlike their Greek predecessors, however, they are often presented as doubting the very existence of such a truth or essence (*ḥaqīqa*), not just its knowability (this could reflect Buddhist influence, cf. Crone 2012b: 31f).

A Sceptic who asserted that we cannot know the truth laid himself open to the charge of self-contradiction, since his assertion was a truth-claim. The prudent Sceptic would suspend judgement. Though both positions are reflected in the arguments against Sceptics in the Muslim material, there is no term for suspension of judgement there: the prudent Sceptic merely says, 'I don't know' (e.g. Baghdādī, *Uṣūl*, 319). Two terms for it turn up among the believers, however. One is *irjāʾ*, coined around 100/720 by Murjiʾites on the basis of Q 9: 107. The Murjiʾites subscribed to the Sceptical claim that one could only judge things on the basis of autopsy and unanimous information from others; since neither was available in the case of the caliph ʿUthmān (killed in 35/656), one had to suspend judgement on the divisive question whether he had been rightly guided or a sinner (Cook 1981: chs. 5, 7). The scope of their scepticism was narrow and the term *irjāʾ* remained tied to their doctrines. The other term is *wuqūf* or *tawaqquf*. Al-Jāḥiẓ, for example, observes that the common people are less prone to doubt than members of the elite because they do not 'hold back' (*yatawaqqafūna*), but rashly declare things to be true or false (Jāḥiẓ, *Ḥayawān*, 6: 36f.). The term appears in later texts too, but it is less prominent than *takāfuʾ al-adilla*, the expression for the equal weight (*isostheneia*)

9 Ibn Durayd, *Ishtiqāq*, 299; Abū l-Faraj, *Aghānī*, 3: 147 (*mutaḥayyir mukhallaṭ*); Chokr 1993: 285.

10 Hankinson 1995: 229. Ḥunayn was later to translate 'transition to the similar' as *al-intiqāl min al-shayʾ ilā nāẓirihi* (Strohmaier 1981: 188).

of competing proofs that made suspension of judgement necessary. We first hear of belief in the equipollence of proofs in the mid-third/ninth century; a century later the philosopher Abū Sulaymān al-Manṭiqī (d. *c*.375/985) depicted it as a characteristic of *mutakallims* in general, including their leading men, saying that he would give their names if he did not prefer to leave them alive (Tawḥīdī, *Muqābasāt*, 227 [no. 54]).[11] The proofs that were so often found to be of equal weight, and thus to cancel each other out, were those tried and tested in disputations about *kalām al-dīn*. Some adherents of *takāfu' al-adilla* would suspend judgement on inner-Islamic disagreements alone, but others found it impossible to affirm anything apart from the existence of the creator; and still others would suspend judgement even on him (Ibn Ḥazm, *Faṣl*, 5: 119f.).[12] There were also Sceptics who declared all religious tenets to be sound, the truth being relative to those who asserted it (Baghdādī, *Uṣūl*, 319.10; Ibn al-Jawzī, *Talbīs*, 41, citing Nawbakhtī); the judge al-ʿAnbarī (d. 168/784) upheld this principle in inner-Islamic disagreements (Goldziher 1920: 178f.). Scepticism affected Christians and Jews no less than Muslims (Jāḥiẓ, *Radd*, 315; Saadia, *Amānāt*, 13, 65ff.; trans. 17, 78ff.), and it had its uses for believers too. The tropes against the reliability of sense impressions were apparently adduced in support of Ashʿarite atomism (Macdonald 1927: 336; van Ess 1966: 178), and all arguments against the ability of humans to reach the truth could be used in a fideist vein.

(b) Dogmatism

Most *mulḥid*s were dogmatists. They agreed with the Sceptics that all claims about the realities of things had to be based on sense impressions, preferably or only on autopsy,[13] but unlike the Sceptics they deemed sense impressions to be reliable and admitted a modest amount of inference from them. One could make deductions (*istidlāl*) from perceptions to the reality of things, provided that they were perceptions of regularities (*al-ʿādāt*) (Jāḥiẓ, *Ḥayawān*, 6: 269). Anything regularly observed in large or common objects could be postulated for small or rare ones too, since quantity did not affect their epistemological status (*ḥukm qalīl al-shay' ka-ḥukm kathīrihi*). The nature of invisible or absent things could similarly be observed from those observed (*mā ghāba ʿanhum mithl alladhī shūhida*), but only as long as they were of the same type: 'they assign everything to its likes (*ashkāl*) and oblige it to follow the rules of the genus (*jins*)' (Abū ʿĪsā al-Warrāq in Ibn al-Malāḥimī, *Muʿtamad*, 550f./597f.). They would reject all postulates about the invisible world (*al-ghā'ib ʿanhum*) that ran counter to what they themselves could observe (*al-ḥāḍir ʿindahum*); they applied 'criteria for corporeal things to spiritual entities', as Ibn Qutayba said in defence of *ḥadīth* that the *mulḥid*s deemed ridiculous

[11] Cf. van Ess 1966: 221ff.; van Ess 1991–7: index, s.v. 'takāfu' al-adilla'.

[12] Typically, he does not name any Muslims, only two Jewish doctors.

[13] E.g. Jāḥiẓ, *Ḥayawān*, 4: 89f., 449.4; 6: 269.5; Ibn Qutayba, *Taʾwīl*, 133; trans. 149 (§170); Māturīdī, *Tawḥīd*, 111.-2; Saadia, *Amānāt*, 63; trans. 75; Ibn al-Jawzī, *Talbīs*, 41.

(Ibn Qutayba, *Taʾwīl*, 127.1; trans. 142f. [§164f.]). Information from others (*akhbār, samʿ*) they admitted only if it conformed to these rules. Accordingly, they rejected the Qurʾānic account of sinners who were transformed into monkeys and pigs, or accepted it only in a naturalist interpretation. They scoffed at the Qurʾānic story of the *jinn* who tried to listen in to conversations in heaven only to have balls of fire thrown at them (Q 72: 8f.; cf. 15: 17f.; 37: 7f.), objecting that creatures supposedly endowed with superior intelligence would have learned better from the Qurʾān (which they had supposedly heard), from their long experience, from plain seeing for themselves, and from information passed around among themselves. They also found fault with the Qurʾānic story of Solomon and the Queen of Sheba, deeming it to be 'evidence of the corrupt nature of your historical tradition' (*dalīl ʿalā fasād akhbārikum*) (Jāḥiẓ, *Ḥayawān*, 4: 70ff., 85f.; 6: 265ff.; cf. Cook 1999: 60). That the *jinn* should have learned from the Qurʾān is an argument based on the opponents' premisses; the rest tells us what counted as legitimate sources of knowledge to the Dahrī: experience, seeing for oneself, and information from others (*empeiria, autopsia,* and *historia* in the terminology of Greek empiricist doctors) (Hankinson 1995: 227f.).

Both al-Aṣamm (d. *c.*200/815) and al-Naẓẓām were empiricists in some respects (Ashʿarī, *Maqālāt*, 331.7, 335.13; van Ess 1991–7: ii. 399; iii. 334f.). For the rest the believers refuted the *mulḥid*s on the latter's own premisses by means of the argument from design: one could see with one's own eyes that the world had been created by a wise and provident maker; it simply was not credible that so intricate and well-designed a construction should have come about on its own (Jāḥiẓ, *Ḥayawān*, 7: 12f.; Eutychius, *Burhān*, §4).[14] These points are developed at length in a work falsely attributed to al-Jāḥiẓ and in the Imāmī Shīʿite works *Kitāb al-Tawḥīd* and *Kitāb al-Iḥlīlija* (Jāḥiẓ, *Dalāʾil*; Chokr 1993: 97ff.).

III Cosmology

All the godless people denied creation *ex nihilo*. Some believed God to have created the world out of pre-existing material, others held it to have originated on its own, and still others held that it had always existed. We may start with the Zindīqs.

(a) Zindīqs

Zindīqs believed the pre-eternal principles to be two, light and darkness, and explained the world as the outcome of their mixture. Those who retained belief in God typically held the highest God to have sent a figure, variously identified as Jesus, the holy

[14] Other arguments include the need for someone to hold the conflicting 'natures' (cf. below) together.

spirit, or the apostle of light, to impose order on the chaos resulting from the mixture; the Marcionites diverged by crediting this task to the devil. Other Zindīqs explained the formation of the world in terms of natural processes that are not further identified. Both the creationists and the automatists often saw the mixture as having come about by accident.[15]

The synthesis of Middle Platonism and Stoicism was attractive to dualists because the Platonists shared their negative view of matter, sometimes deeming it positively evil (Dunderberg 2008: 125f.), while the Stoics also explained the world as a mixture of two pre-eternal principles, one active, that is God/*logos*/*pneuma*, and the other passive, that is matter or 'unqualified substance'. The concept of a divine *logos* (reason, word) or *pneuma* (spirit) that shapes and regulates pre-existing matter, now as a demiurge sent by the highest God and now as an impersonal principle, appears in several Platonizing and Gnosticizing systems in late antiquity, including that of Bardesanes. The latter is said also to have shared the Stoic view that everything which exists is a body (Syriac *gushmā*, Arabic *jism*) (Furlani 1937: 350), even a line or a sound (Ephrem, *Prose Refutations*, 2: 20, 29f.; trans. ix, xiii; cf. Ramelli 2009: 19). This implies that he also held that bodies could completely interpenetrate and blend with one another without losing their separate substance, a doctrine developed by the Stoics to explain how *pneuma* could be present throughout matter;[16] instead, however, Bardesanes is reported to have been an atomist. According to Ephrem, he held that the pure elements (light, air, water, and fire), suspended in the vacuum between God and darkness (inert matter), were composed of atoms (*perdē*, seeds) and that the same was true of darkness;[17] some Bardesanites held reason (*hawnā*), power (*ḥaylā*), and thought (*tarʿīthā*) likewise to be composed of atoms (Ephrem, *Prose Refutations*, 2: 220; trans. civ; Possekel 1999: 119f.). Both the Stoic concept of interpenetration, based on the premiss that bodies are infinitely divisible, and the Epicurean concept of atoms, directed against infinite divisibility, allow two ingredients to blend completely without losing their identity, a crucial point to those who saw the world as composed of ultimately separable light and darkness. (The Zoroastrians, to whom the world was composed out of Ohrmazd's own substance, saw darkness as mixed in by juxtaposition.[18]) And whatever Bardesanes himself

[15] Cf. *Encyclopaedia Iranica*, s.v. 'Bardesanes'; *Encyclopaedia of Islam*³, s.v. 'Dayṣanīs'; Crone 2012a: ch. 10. The beginning was *bi-ihmāl lā ṣanʿa fīhi wa-lā taqdīr wa-lā ṣāniʿ wa-lā mudabbir*, as Ibn Abī l-ʿAwjāʾ says in Jaʿfar al-Ṣādiq (attrib.), *Tawḥīd*, 9.

[16] Cf. Long and Sedley 1987: no. 48: the soul pervaded the whole body while preserving its own substance in mixture with it, as did fire and glowing iron, and a drop of wine in the ocean (contrary to what Aristotle said). Long and Sedley adopt 'blending' for complete interpenetration without destruction of the bodies involved (fire and red-hot iron; a drop of wine in the ocean), and use 'fusion' for the mixture of the type in which the bodies are destroyed and another generated (as in drugs); but there seems to be no consistent terminology in the Greek material: the qualification *di' holou/holōn* is used in connection with both blending and fusion, and both are called *krasis* and *mixis* too.

[17] Ephrem, *Refutations*, 1: 53 (vacuum); 2: 214ff.; trans. lv; II, ciff. (darkness at 215; trans. cii); *Encyclopaedia Iranica*, s.v. 'Bardesanes'; Possekel 1999: 116ff. Ephrem is the only source for Bardesanite atomism.

[18] Cf. de Ménasce 1973: no. 403: light and darkness do not mix absolutely, as proved by fire; light has merely adjoined smoke.

may have said, both doctrines seem to have been current in his and other schools. All things commingled were capable of being separated again, as third-century Sethians of apparently Mesopotamian origin declared, encouraging their disciples to study the doctrine of *krasis* and *mixis* (Hippolytus, *Refutatio*, 5: 21.1f., 4f.).[19] Interpenetration is reported under the name of *mudākhala* in Muslim sources on the Manicheans (Ashʿarī, *Maqālāt*, 327.15),[20] and it appears without a name of its own in the Melkite Christian Eutychius (d. 940) in explanation of the mixture of the divine and human nature in Christ.[21] The idea that all things are bodies interpenetrating one another went into early Muslim cosmology in the physics of Hishām b. al-Ḥakam, al-Aṣamm (at least partially), and al-Naẓẓām.[22] Other *mutakallims* rejected infinite divisibility and interpenetration in favour of atomism.

Muslim sources report atomism for some Manicheans/dualists, including one al-Nuʿmān al-Thanawī (executed by al-Mahdī), Isḥāq b. Ṭālūt, and Ibn Akhī Abī Shākir (al-Dayṣānī) (Ibn al-Malāḥimī, *Muʿtamad*, 566f., 590/611, 631; ʿAbd al-Jabbār, *Mughnī*, 5: 20; trans. 173). But more mainstream Christians also seem to have included atomists, for Epicurus, normally denounced by Christians as an atheist and hedonist, is praised as one of the great philosophers by the West-Syrian David Bar Paulos (Brock 1982: 25);[23] and the mid-third/ninth-century Muʿtazilite Ibn Mānūsh, a pupil of al-Naẓẓām of Origenist/Evagrian background, envisaged humans in pre-existence as atoms (Baghdādī, *Farq*, 258, trans. van Ess 1991–7: vi. 220; cf. Crone forthcoming). The idea of disembodied humans as atoms was probably due to Plato, who had defined the soul as 'uncompounded, indissoluble, and indivisible', according to Albinus's handbook, or, as Israel of Kashkar (d. 877) put it, as a *jawhar wāḥid ghayr munqasam ajsāman*, 'one substance/an atom, not divisible into bodies'.[24] The idea of man as an atom was also espoused by the Muʿtazilites Muʿammar (d. 215/830) and Hishām al-Fuwaṭī (d. 220s/840s?), both atomists in cosmological terms as well (Ashʿarī, *Maqālāt*, 331.13; ʿAbd al-Jabbār, *Mughnī*, 11: 311). In short, atomism probably reached the Muslims from both Christians and dualists.

Muslim *mutakallims* seem to have accepted the existence of atoms as a matter of course, reserving their ire for the infinite divisibility of bodies because there could not in their view be infinity in the created world. Atoms and accidents were all there was to it in their view. Some third/ninth-century *mutakallims* held atoms to have sides, explained as accidents, while others denied that they had either sides or magnitude (Ashʿarī, *Maqālāt*, 316.1, 10, cf. also 8; trans. with comments in Dhanani 1994: 99, nos. 1, 3, cf.

19 For these Sethians, cf. Crone 2012a: 200f. Note also the Valentinian idea that Jesus, the Church, and Wisdom formed a complete blending of bodies (*di' holōn krasis tōn sōmatōn*) in Casey 1934: 17.1.

20 Cf. Ashʿarī, *Maqālāt*, 349.11 on the Dayṣānīs, where the term is *imtizāj*.

21 Eutychius, *Burhān*, nos. 122f., with the soul and body, fire and glowing iron as examples. The use of Stoic mixture theory in this context goes back to Gregory of Nazianzus (cf. Stewart 1991: 182, 186).

22 Cf. van Ess 1991–7: i. 362, 365f.; ii. 398ff; iii. 335ff.; van Ess 1967: 250ff. The doctrine of *mudākhala* is not mentioned in the exiguous material on Ḍirār.

23 Democritus is also lauded, but he had come to stand for many things.

24 Albinus, *Didaskalikos*, 59 (cf. Plato, *Phaedo*, 80b); Israel of Kashkar, *Unity*, no. 49. The date of the work is not certain.

also 2). Both groups seem to have conceived of the atom as an Epicurean minimal part: several such minimal parts (*elachista, minima*) made up an atom according to Epicurus, though it could not in practice be divided. To Epicurus, however, the minimal parts had magnitude. To the *mutakallims*, by contrast, magnitude was either added as accidents which could not in practice be separated from it, or else it was generated by the combination of several atoms. On their own, the minimal parts had lost their dimensions. The first known Muʿtazilite propounder of the atom without dimensions is Abū l-Hudhayl (d. 226/841), according to whom bodies had length, breadth, and depth, whereas atoms did not.[25] It has long been suspected that he and others were indebted to dualists such as Bardesanites or Manicheans for their atomism (Pretzl 1931: 127ff.; Dhanani 1994: 4f., 182ff.), and he must be refuting dualists when he denies that atoms have life, power, or knowledge, the characteristics of light. He also denied that they possessed colour, taste, or smell, the properties possessed by Bar Dayṣān's elements and, presumably, the atoms of which they were composed (Ashʿarī, *Maqālāt*, 315.5). But only corporeal atoms are attested for the dualists. Bar Dayṣān's elements varied from light to heavy and fine to coarse;[26] and the atoms of al-Nuʿmān al-Thanawī, a Manichean who disputed with Abū l-Hudhayl (van Ess 1991–7: i. 443), certainly had three dimensions (Ibn al-Malāḥimī, *Muʿtamad*, 590/631; ʿAbd al-Jabbār, *Mughnī*, 5: 20; trans. 173). By contrast, humans in pre-existence are unlikely to have possessed corporeal dimensions, since they were with God; and some Christians or dualists do in fact seem to have envisaged the lightest atoms as mere points, for the sixth-century Barḥadbeshabbā envisages Epicurus and Democritus as believing in fine bodies which were 'incorporeal atoms' (*perdē delā geshūm*).[27]

It was probably from Christians of some kind that atoms passed to the author of the *Sirr al-khalīqa* (*c.*210/825?). He operates with a prime substance (*al-jawhar al-awwal*) which is present in everything (*Sirr*, 1: 1.1.3, p. 3.9), which was clearly pre-eternal in the work he was adapting (*Sirr*, 2: 4.1, pp. 104f.; 2: 5.1, pp. 109ff.),[28] and which must be the source of the atoms (*ajzāʾ lā tatajazzaʾu*) of which he says that the world was built and the whole macrocosmos made (*Sirr*, 2: 18, p. 197.9; 2: 19.1, p. 203.ult.). As to how this happened, all we are told is that the substance was uniform until the accidents arose in it, whereupon its particles or atoms (*ajzāʾ*) diversified (*Sirr*, 1: 1.1.3, p. 3.10). Mostly the author writes as one of the *aṣḥāb al-ṭabāʾiʿ* (discussed in Section III [b]) to whom 'everything is from the four natures, which are heat, cold, moisture, and dryness' or 'which are fire, air, water, and earth' (*Sirr*, 1: 1.1.3, p. 3.4; 3: 20, p. 307.5), and the only atoms that interest him are those of light and subtle things such as fire, the subtlest of all bodies, composed of heat and atoms, or 'resting air', composed of warmth, moisture, and atoms, or the air between the spheres, which is full of atoms (*Sirr*, 2: 18, p. 197.9, cf. 2: 17.2, p. 192;

25 Ashʿarī, *Maqālāt*, 307.10, where Muʿammar and al-Jubbāʾī agree. Abū l-Hudhayl died after Muʿammar, but at the age of around a hundred.

26 Ephrem, *Refutations*, 1: 52f.; trans. livf.; 2: 159; trans. lxxiv; cf. Ehlers 1970: 346f.

27 Barḥadbeshabbā, *Cause*, 365. He locates them in Alexandria.

28 Cf. Weisser 1980: 174f.

2: 16.3, p. 190.1; 2: 19.1, p. 203.11). The different types of spiritual beings (*rūḥāniyyāt*) or angels were created out of the subtle (particles) of the prime substance (*laṭīf al-jawhar al-awwal*), more precisely from the heat of the wind, the light of fire, and the flow of water. Like the prime substance before the onset of accidents, they were *jawhar wāḥid* (lit. 'one substance'), here in the sense of uncompounded, and they were so subtle that they had no corporeal matter (*lā ajrāma lahā*) and did not take up space; 'everything which is not a body with six sides (*jirm musaddas*) does not take up space (*makān*)' (*Sirr*, 2: 15.1, p. 149; 2: 15.3, pp. 153f.). In short, spiritual beings formed part of the created, material world, but not that of gross, tangible matter (*jirm, ajrām*). They had spiritual bodies, as one might say. Like everything else, they must have been made of atoms, but apparently these atoms lacked dimensions. Abū l-Hudhayl called an atom a *jawhar wāḥid* and he too distinguished them from bodies with six sides, meaning top, bottom, front, back, left, and right, an archaic definition of bodies which appears four times in the *Sirr* (Ashʿarī, *Maqālāt*, 302f.; *Sirr*, 1: 3.5.2, p. 64; 1: 3.9.4, p. 94; 6: 28.7, p. 510), but which is replaced by the standard three dimensions in later summaries of Abū l-Hudhayl's doctrine.[29] The evidence of the *Sirr* suggests that it was the desire to identify the atomic structure of intelligibilia below the level of God himself (angels, humans in pre-existence and in spiritual afterlife, numbers, and ideal geometric figures) that had generated the concept of incorporeal atoms.[30]

It was clearly atoms of Greek rather than Indian origin that the dualists transmitted (Dhanani 1994: 97ff.), though the Muslim recipients are unlikely to have been aware of their ultimate cultural origin. The *Mīzān al-ṣaghīr* attributed to Jābir, which expounds a cosmology related to that of the *Sirr*, tells us that the prime substance is dust which becomes visible when the sun shines on it (Haq 1994: 55). According to Lactantius (d. *c*.325), who wrote against Epicureans, Leucippus had compared the atoms to 'little particles of dust in the sun when it has introduced its rays and light through a window'.[31] This comparison could also have reached the Muslims via Platonist Christians and/or dualists, whose formative period lay in the second and third centuries; back then the Epicurean school tradition was still alive.

(b) Dahrīs: *Aṣḥāb al-ṭabāʾiʿ*

Dahrīs were either *aṣḥāb al-ṭabāʾiʿ* or *aṣḥāb al-hayūlā*. The former, whom I shall henceforth call physicists, owed their name to their belief that everything in this world is

[29] Thus already Ashʿarī, *Maqālāt*, 307.11, 314.14; two further examples in van Ess 1991–7: v. 37.

[30] Cf. Dhanani 1994: 185, who points to the role of geometry. Sextus Empiricus's *Against the Mathematicians* and the late antique development of Aristotle's concept of noetic matter might repay a study from this point of view. Both Epicureans and Pyrrhonic Sceptics rejected Euclidean geometry (Dhanani 1994: 103). Cf. also Langermann 2009, suggesting that Galen played a role.

[31] Lactantius, *De ira Dei*, 10: 9. Lactantius quotes him as calling the atoms seeds (*semina*, 10: 3), cf. Syriac *perdē*. For the dust as partless (*habāʾ lā juzʾ lahu*), see Kraus 1942: 154 n.; Fakhr al-Dīn al-Rāzī in Pines 1997: 157, on the atomic theories of the ancients (who could be Greeks or Muslims).

composed by four 'natures' (Greek *physeis*, Syriac *kyānē*, Arabic *ṭabāʾiʿ*), that is the four elementary qualities, hot, cold, dry, and wet, which combined to form the four elements, fire, water, air, and earth. Each element had two qualities according to Aristotelians (fire was hot and dry), but only one according to the Stoics (fire was hot). Since the Stoics identified both the elements and their qualities as bodies, they did not distinguish sharply between the two, as Plutarch (d. 120), Galen (d. *c.*200), and Alexander of Aphrodisias (*fl. c.*200) complained (Lammert 1953: 489f.); and assisted by the medical humour theory, the qualities came to acquire ontological, as opposed to purely analytical, priority. When late antique authors speak of the elements, they often mean the qualities,[32] and the term 'natures' was used of both.[33] In Arabic the 'natures' are usually the qualities, but sometimes the elements, otherwise known as *usṭuqussāt, ʿanāṣir*, and *ummahāt* (mothers).[34]

Some physicists refused to affirm the existence of anything other than the four elementary qualities, whereas others added a fifth (Abū ʿĪsā in Ibn al-Malāḥimī, *Muʿtamad*, 547.13/594.17; Ashʿarī, *Maqālāt*, 348.5f.). Just as the diverse colours produced by dyers were all mixtures of white, red, black, and green, so all things in this world were really mixtures of hot, cold, moisture, and dryness, the former said, using a comparison strikingly similar to that of Empedocles, the ultimate author of the four-elements theory (Māturīdī, *Tawḥīd*, 112, 141).[35] The fifth nature added by others was often identified as spirit (*rūḥ*), which pervaded and regulated everything and was also life: this was presumably another Stoic legacy (Abū ʿĪsā in Ibn al-Malāḥimī, *Muʿtamad*, 547/594; Ashʿarī, *Maqālāt*, 335.4, 11).[36] Others held the fifth nature to be a wind different from moving air, perhaps related to the breath or breeze (*nasīm*) that some held to be life (Baghdādī, *Uṣūl*, 53.10; cf. Abū ʿĪsā in Ibn al-Malāḥimī, *Muʿtamad*, 549.9/596.3), or else it was space (*al-faḍāʾ*), identified as the place of things (*makān al-ashyāʾ*) (Abū ʿĪsā in Ibn al-Malāḥimī, *Muʿtamad*, 549.2/596.10), or knowledge (Yaʿqūbī, *Tārīkh*, 1: 170.14, of Greek and Roman Dahrīs). Still others opted for the heavenly sphere (Maqdisī, *Badʾ*, 1: 132.-2; Baghdādī, *Uṣūl*, 320.12),[37] which acted on the four qualities and so caused generation and corruption, or which was the source of the four natures and everything else in the world.[38]

[32] The elements are identified as the qualities in, for example, Philastrius, *Diversarum*, XIX: 5 (47, 5f.), citing the mid-second-century Apelles; Athanasius, *Contra Gentes*, par. 27; Job of Edessa, *Treasures*, 1: 1 (p. 78; trans. 5).

[33] Cf. Kraus 1942: 45, 165 n. 7; Ephrem, *Commentary*, 75 and n. 24 *ad* Gen. 1: 1; Jacob of Sarug, *Sermons*, 2: 177, cf. 4: 319f.; Jacob of Edessa in Teixidor 1997: 125.

[34] For the mothers, see Yaʿqūbī, *Tārīkh*, 1: 170.11; *Sirr*, 2: 16.2, p. 187.ult, 3: 20, p. 308.2; *mulḥaq* 1, pp. 532f.; Weisser 1980: 176, citing *K. Isṭamāṭīs*; Abū Ḥātim al-Rāzī, *Iṣlāḥ*, 166.15; Māturīdī, *Tawḥīd*, 60.17, where they are coupled with 'fathers', i.e. the spheres and the stars or the lords in charge of their motion, cf. Walker 1993: 103 (al-Sijistānī); Madelung 2005: 159.

[35] Cf. Empedocles, fr. 23, on painters who mix pigments to make pictures of everything.

[36] Cf. al-Naẓẓām in Jāḥiẓ, *Ḥayawān*, 5: 47; Baghādī, *Uṣūl*, 53.12; Daiber 1999: 40.

[37] This view is ascribed to Aristotle (e.g. Maqdisī, *Badʾ*, 2: 9) and to Hermes and Ptolemy (Israel of Kashkar, *Unity*, no. 34).

[38] Jāḥiẓ, *Ḥayawān*, 7: 12f.; Māturīdī, *Tawḥīd*, 60.16; Maqdisī, *Badʾ*, 1: 126.12; Asadī, *Garshāspnāma*, 139; trans. 2: 30; al-Rāzī, *Tafsīr*, 27: 269f., *ad* Q 45: 24. cf. Balīnūs, *Sirr*, 2: 19.8, p. 212, where their motion generates the *mawālīd*; cf. also Saadia, *Amānāt*, 58; trans. 70.

Al-Māturīdī had heard an astronomer compare the universe to a giant weaving machine, with the heavenly bodies producing the variegated textile that is life down here (Māturīdī, *Tawḥīd*, 143). Those who identified the heavenly spheres as the source of everything else often credited their science to Hermes and associated figures,[39] but devotees of Hermes believed in spiritual realities and credited themselves with both inner and external senses,[40] whereas Dahrīs had no inner eye (Asadī, *Garshāspnāma*, 140.11; trans. 2: 31).

The Christian physician and philosopher Job of Edessa (writing *c.*817) held God to have created the 'simple elements' (i.e. the qualities) and put them together as 'compound elements', meaning the fire, water, air, and earth of which everything was composed (Job of Edessa, *Treasures*, 1: 4; 1: 6). Several Muslim *mutakallims*, al-Jāḥiẓ, Thumāma b. Ashras, and al-Māturīdī among them, also operated with 'natures' created by God, without being Dahrīs, as al-Juwaynī noted (disapproving of their view that the natures had causative power).[41] But the author of the *Sirr* is a creationist only in the sense that his God sets the formation of the elements in motion with his creative command; for the rest the process unfolds on its own. Other Dahrīs agreed that the world had originated in time, but not that it had a creator: it had been born of the four eternal 'uncompounded simples' (*al-afrād al-sawādhij*), i.e. the elementary qualities, which made things grow on their own without intent, wish, or will.[42] Still other physicists held the natures to be pre-eternal, but put together by God; and one Ibn Qays apparently held God to have joined them since pre-eternity, so that the world was pre-eternal too (Baghdādī, *Uṣūl*, 70, 320). This aligned him with the common physicist view that the four or five natures had always existed in a state of combination or mixture (both mechanical and chemical terms are used), so that the world as we know it had always been and always would be.[43] The universe had neither beginning nor end, be it in terms of time or extent (*misāḥa*), and apparently not in terms of number (*kathra*) either;[44] the several worlds implied were presumably successive rather than concurrent, and separated by Stoic-type conflagrations, for at least some Dahrīs saw time as cyclical.[45]

[39] For a (perhaps) ninth-century summary of Hermetic doctrine, see Israel of Kashkar, *Unity*, nos. 28–35; cf. also van Bladel 2009.

[40] Balīnūs, *Sirr*, 1: 1.1.1, p. 2, and index s.v. 'al-ḥawāss al-bāṭina/ẓāhira'.

[41] Juwaynī, *Shāmil*, 237f.; Frank 1974 (where the *ṭabāʾiʿ* are not properly distinguished from *ṭabʿ*); cf. Ashʿarī, *Maqālāt*, 517.2, where we hear of physicists with views on God's speech.

[42] Balīnūs, *Sirr*, 1: 3, p. 103; Yaʿqūbī, *Tārīkh*, 1: 170.7, of Greek and Roman Dahrīs (*sawādhij* is an Arabic plural of the Middle Persian form of Persian *sādha*, simple); compare Saadia, *Amānāt*, 61; trans. 73, where those who hold heaven and earth to have originated by chance explain the process along the same lines as the *Sirr*, without God's creative command to set the process going.

[43] Abū ʿĪsā in Ibn al-Malāḥimī, *Muʿtamad*, 547.12, 549.18/594.18, 596.19; Māturīdī, *Tawḥīd*, 143.12. But Saadia, *Amānāt*, 55; trans. 66, and Juwaynī, *Shāmil*, 239.5, present them as claiming that the four originally existed in isolation.

[44] Abū ʿĪsā in Ibn al-Malāḥimī, *Muʿtamad*, 549.19, 552.9/596.20, 598.21; *Sirr*, 1: 3.9.3, p. 93.10.

[45] Yaʿqūbī, *Tārīkh*, 1: 168.6 (*inna l-dahr dāʾir*), of Greek and Roman Dahrīs; Maimonides, *Guide*, 2: 13 (28b); Ibn Kathīr, *Tafsīr*, 4: 150, *ad* Q 45: 24 (cycles of 36,000 years); cf. the cycles in the thought of the communities from which Dahrīs seem often to have been drawn (Crone 2012a: 209f., 235f., 239, 245f., cf. also 481).

In agreement with the Stoics the *aṣḥāb al-ṭabāʾiʿ* identified the four or five natures as bodies rather than incorporeal characteristics (al-Naẓẓām in Jāḥiẓ, *Ḥayawān*, 5: 40; Ashʿarī, *Maqālāt*, 348.4). Space (*al-faḍāʾ*), defined as the place of things (*makān al-ashyāʾ*), is explicitly said not to have been a body, suggesting that it is the Stoic *topos* or place, identified as 'that which is able to be occupied by what is' and counted as one of the four incorporeals (Abū ʿĪsā in Ibn al-Malāḥimī, *Muʿtamad*, 549.2/596.3; cf. Long and Sedley 1987: nos. 27, 49). According to the pneumatic physicists, the four bodies had always been in motion, either because movement was natural to them or because the spirit was moving them, and their movements caused them to come together. This sounds Epicurean, but they interpenetrated in the Stoic style (*yaghullu baʿḍuhā fī baʿḍin*) instead of simply combining. By mixing in different ways they became sounds, smells, minerals, plants, and so on (Abū ʿĪsā in Ibn al-Malāḥimī, *Muʿtamad*, 547.16; 548.4; 551.12/594.21,[46] 595.9, 598.4). The matter (*mādda*) formed by their mixture was composed of particles (*ajzāʾ*), presumably infinitely divisible, and things were strengthened and weakened by conjunction with similar and contrasting forms (*ashkāl* and *aḍdād*). When a living being died, the particles dispersed to join the concordant forms closest to it, and the same particles might accidentally come together to form a living being of the same kind, or of a different kind, or just a plant, or the particles might simply be dispersed in water or the earth.[47] In short, the physicists allowed for the possibility of what others called reincarnation, but explained it in materialist terms. If their roots went back to the third century, they could have picked up this explanation from the Epicurean school tradition (cf. Lucretius, *On the Nature of Things*, 3: 845–60). But whether they did so or not, it is not the only evidence to suggest that they hailed from communities in which belief in reincarnation was widespread. In fact, while some members of these communities were making godless science out of their ancestral beliefs, to be dismissed as Dahrīs, others were reformulating them as Muslim doctrine, to be dismissed as Khurramīs and Ghulāt (Crone 2012a: 248f.).

Neither the dualists nor the *aṣḥāb al-ṭabāʾiʿ* needed a material substratum to carry their corporeal qualities, for even qualities were bodies, so they did not accept the Aristotelian concept of prime matter,[48] nor the Aristotelian distinction between substance (*jawhar*) and accidents (*aʿrāḍ*). Some had come round to accepting one accident, however, namely motion, a key concept in that it was coterminous with action and change.[49] But there were also some who claimed that there was no such thing as motion or any other accident.[50] The Muʿtazilite al-Aṣamm shared this view (Ashʿarī, *Maqālāt*, 343.12; Baghdādī, *Uṣūl*, 7.14; cf. van Ess 1991–7: ii. 398f.; v. 194f.). Motion was a

46 Wrongly *yuqillu* for *yaghullu* in the new edition.

47 Abū ʿĪsā in Ibn al-Malāḥimī, *Muʿtamad*, 548.1, 9/595.6, 13; cf. *Sirr*, 1.1.1.3 (p. 4.4); Ashʿarī, *Maqālāt*, 329.6; Maqdisī, *Badʾ*, 1: 127.11.

48 It is rejected as nonsense in Job of Edessa, *Treasures*, 1: 2. Jābir, who does operate with a substrate, mentions those who do not (Kraus 1942: 169f.).

49 Abū ʿĪsā in Ibn al-Malāḥimī, *Muʿtamad*, 548.17, 566.13/595.20, 611.8; Ashʿarī, *Maqālāt*, 348.7, 12; 349.12; Ibn Shabīb in Māturīdī, *Tawḥīd*, 141.15, 143.21.

50 Ibn al-Malāḥimī, *Muʿtamad*, 549.15/596; Muqammiṣ, *ʿIshrūn*, 3:11; Ashʿarī, *Maqālāt*, 348.11; 349.6, 15; Baghdādī, *Uṣūl*, 52.16.

body, i.e. the body moving, as some put it, which is also what a Stoic would have said.[51] As a certain Plato the Copt from Ḥulwān is reported to have declared, we do not see motion or any other action, only the person or thing moving or acting.[52] The *Sirr* refutes him as if he were a Sceptic, assimilating him to a different set of people who denied the reality of change as an illusion, claiming that the created word was all one and the same, and who seem to have invoked Parmenides ('Munīs').[53] It is those who dismiss diversity (*ikhtilāf*) as an illusion generated by the senses who trot out Sceptical tropes in al-Yaʿqūbī's account of Greek and Roman Dahrīs (Yaʿqūbī, *Tārīkh*, 1: 168f.).

Many Dahrīs had succumbed to the advancing tide of Aristotelianism, however. They defined the elements as substance and the elementary qualities as accidents (al-Naẓẓām in Jāḥiẓ, *Ḥayawān*, 5: 40), and postulated a substrate in the form of prime matter (*hayūlā, ṭīna*).

(c) *Aṣḥāb al-hayūlā*

Some people held the world to have been created from nothing while others held it to be drawn from matter (*hylē*), Paul the Persian observed (Land 1862–75: 4, fo. 56ʳ; trans. 2). Two centuries later the adherents of the latter view were known as *aṣḥāb al-hayūlā* and singled out for refutation by al-Naẓẓām (van Ess 1991–7: vi. 1 [no. 3]). Some *aṣḥāb al-hayūlā* were creationists who held God to have created the world out of pre-existing matter (Greek *hylē*) by means of movement and rest, which caused accidents to arise. The author of the *Sirr*, who tacitly operates with prime matter, is an example.[54] Al-Maqdisī, who deemed them guilty of dualism, informs us that they also held that the creator had always created (a Platonist view rooted in the *Timaeus*), so they were eternalists too.[55] Judging from the frequency with which the emergence of the world is described in impersonal terms, other *aṣḥāb al-hayūlā* were automatists. Their Platonism notwithstanding, the adherents of prime matter are mostly envisaged as Aristotelians,[56] with some justice in that their *hayūlā* (also called *ṭīna*) was clearly Aristotle's *protē hylē*, a material substrate devoid of extension, dimensions, or any other properties, endowed with the potential to be anything. (They do not seem to have known about Simplicius's and Philoponus's modifications of Aristotle on this point. Māturīdī, *Tawḥīd*, 147.5; Sorabji 1988: ch. 2.) *Hayūlā* was empty of accidents, as the sources will say (Maqdisī, *Badʾ*, 1: 47.8; Baghdādī, *Uṣūl*, 57.5), thinking in terms of substance and accidents (as in

[51] Ibn al-Malāḥimī, *Muʿtamad*, 566.-5/611.13 (Manichean majority); Ashʿarī, *Maqālāt*, 349.2; cf. 346.6, on Jahm b. Ṣafwān (on different grounds); Sedley in Algra et al. 1999: 399.

[52] *Sirr*, 1: 2.2.11, p. 28.

[53] *Sirr*, 1: 2.2.10, pp. 26f.; cf. Rudolph 1995: 133f.

[54] Theodore Bar Koni, *Liber*, mimrā 1: 30; Maqdisī, *Badʾ*, 1: 92; compare the *Sirr*, 2: 3ff, pp. 103ff.

[55] Maqdisī, *Badʾ*, 1: 92; Māturīdī, *Tawḥīd*, 86.13; Pines 1997: 41, 48, on the tenth-century Īrānshahrī, one of the *aṣḥāb al-hayūlā*; Goodman 1993: 148; Plato, *Timaeus*, 29e.

[56] Job of Edessa, *Treasures*, 1: 2; Yaʿqūbī, *Tārīkh*, 1: 170.14 (*aṣḥāb al-jawhar*); Māturīdī, *Tawḥīd*, 147; cf. Bar Koni, *Liber*, mimrā 11: 9, and Zurqān in Maqdisī, *Badʾ*, 1: 140, on Aristotle himself.

the *Categories*) rather than matter and form.[57] Thanks to its potentiality (*quwwa*), which often seems to be envisaged as a separate entity, accidents arose in it, and the appearance of accidents transformed the *hayūlā* into substance (*jawhar*) (Māturīdī, *Tawḥīd*, 147; cf. also 30.17). Some called prime matter 'substance' or 'simple substance' or 'first substance' (*jawhar basīṭ /awwal*) from the start. The term *ʿunṣur* also came to be used. Some held every species of being to have its own prime matter (Baghdādī, *Uṣūl*, 53.5).

The *aṣḥāb al-hayūlā*, then, held that matter/substance was pre-eternal (*qadīm*), but accepted that accidents originated in time (*ḥadītha*), with or without divine intervention. They held that the bodies preceded the accidents, as al-Baghdādī puts it (*Uṣūl*, 55.8). He held this to distinguish them from other Dahrīs, for most of the Dahrīs who operated with accidents were eternalists in respect of them too, in three different ways. Some, labelled Azaliyya Dahrīs by al-Baghdādī, did agree that the accidents originated in time, but they added that before every origination there had always been another: the process had no beginning; the world had always existed as we see it now with its stars, animals, procreation, and so on.[58] Others held that the accidents had always existed in potentiality (*bi-l-quwwa*). According to them, and also to (some?) Manicheans, the accidents or the world or the phenomena (? *maʿānī*) were in the prime matter/substance in potentiality and emerged from there into actuality (*ẓaharat bi-l-fiʿl*); in support of this they would adduce the presence of the man in the sperm, of the animal in the sperm or egg, of the tree in the kernel, and so on.[59] This doctrine was also known to the Zaydī al-Qāsim b. Ibrāhīm (d. 246/860), whose *mulḥid* opponent adduces the date palm in the pit (Pines 1997: 165f.). Finally, some Dahrīs held that the accidents had always existed in the bodies, apparently in actuality. Colours, tastes, and smells were hiding in the earth, water, and fire and became manifest in fruit by transfer (*intiqāl*) and the conjunction of likes (*ashkāl*) (Ashʿarī, *Maqālāt*, 329.4; cf. Maqdisī, *Badʾ*, 1: 47, 134.6). The adherents of this view were the *aṣḥāb al-kumūn wa-l-ẓuhūr*, 'those who believed in latency and manifestation', and al-Baghdādī may have conflated them with the defenders of the second position (Baghdādī, *Uṣūl*, 55.12 [where the second position is omitted]; Maqdisī, *Badʾ*, 1: 47.4). They too seem to have adduced the chicken and the egg, the wheat in the grain, and so on by way of confounding those who believed the world to have a beginning and an end, or perhaps all Dahrīs did so.[60] At all events, they said that when one accident was manifest, its opposite disappeared from view and was hidden in the body until the

[57] All things are either substance (*ousia*) or accident, as Job of Edessa remarks (*Treasures*, 1: 3, p. 81; trans. 10). The terminology was to be revised in the light of the translations, cf. matter versus form (*ṣūra*) and the elementary qualities as *kayfiyyāt* in Shahrastānī, *Nihāya*, 163ff.; Shahrastānī, *Milal*, 257.ult.; trans. 2: 187.

[58] Baghdādī, *Uṣūl*, 55, 59; Muqammiṣ, *ʿIshrūn*, 5: 36, 42; Ibn al-Malāḥimī, *Muʿtamad*, 566.14/611.9 (of some dualists, apparently Manicheans); Maqdisī, *Badʾ*, 1: 123.4.

[59] Māturīdī, *Tawḥīd*, 63.9, cf. 30.16; Muqammiṣ, *ʿIshrūn*, 5: 8, 10, 14 (claiming to know nobody adhering to this view, but associating it with Dahrīs and Manicheans); Guidi, *Lotta*, 46.9; trans. 107.

[60] Jāḥiẓ, *Tarbīʿ*, no. 46; Kraus 1935: *Rasāʾil Jābir b. Ḥayyān*, 299f. (where the doctrine is primarily Manichean); Maqdisī, *Badʾ*, 1: 118f., 133; 2: 134; Baghdādī, *Uṣūl*, 319.14; Juwaynī, *Shāmil*, 224.1; Ibn al-Malāḥimī, *Muʿtamad*, 160/152.

roles were reversed, as for example in the case of motion and rest, and so it would go on forever.[61] There was no origination (*ḥudūth*).[62]

Wolfson thought that the Dahrīs were Aristotelians, with reference to their doctrines of potentiality and *kumūn* (Wolfson 1976: 504ff.); Horovitz related these views to the Stoic concept of 'seminal reasons' (*logoi spermatikoi*), according to which the creative fire or reason was 'like a seed' containing the causes of all things past, present, and future (Horovitz 1903: 186); and Nyberg thought that al-Naẓẓām's *kumūn* theory (cf. below) must be rooted in the concept of Plato's ideas as thought (and thus potentiality) in the mind of God.[63] But whatever philosophical language the Dahrīs may have used, what they, and sometimes also Zindīqs, really wished to express was a deep-seated Near Eastern conviction, namely that everything is endless recurrence. This is what shaped their understanding of Greek philosophy, and also what gave them an affinity with the Presocratics. Whether the chicken or the egg was originated or pre-eternal, hidden in the body, in Aristotelian potentiality, in Stoic 'seminal reasons', or in the mind of God, the point was that there was nothing new under the sun. The chicken produced eggs which produced chickens which produced eggs; so it had always been and so it always would be. Denial of origination and destruction coupled with belief in eternal recurrence and pantheism also appears in the Hermetic corpus (Copenhaver 1992: xii. 15–17). Simon Magus is credited with the view that fire, the principle of all things, possessed hidden and manifest parts corresponding to the potentiality and actuality of Aristotle, the intelligible and sensible of Plato (Hippolytus, *Refutatio*, 6.9.5f., adduced by Wolfson 1976: 510). The Gnostic Basilides, who believed in a 'not-being God' (*ouk ōn theos*) utterly beyond us, held this deity to have caused a seed to exist in which all things were contained just as the entire plant is contained in the mustard seed and the multicoloured peacock and other birds in the egg (Hippolytus, *Refutatio*, 7: 21).[64] Basilides's system, or something similar to it, was known to al-Yaʿqūbī, according to whom one of the Dahrite groups among the pagan Greeks and Romans believed the origin (*aṣl*) of things in pre-eternity (*al-azaliyya*) to be a seed (*ḥabba*) which split open, whereupon the world with all the diversity of colours and other sense impressions appeared from it (Yaʿqūbī, *Tārīkh*, 1: 168.16): here as elsewhere, al-Yaʿqūbī's ancient Dahrīs are actually late antique and/or Islamic. Al-Maqdisī also knew them.[65]

Al-Naẓẓām, who shared the view of everything as interpenetrating bodies, also held that motion was the only accident and subscribed to the theory of *kumūn*: God created everything in one go, hiding future things in the bodies; and fire was not originated, but hidden in the stone.[66] His view that God created the world all at once aligns him

61 Muqammiṣ, *ʿIshrūn*, 5:12; Baghdādī, *Uṣūl*, 55; Baghdādī, *Farq*, 139.

62 Yaʿqūbī, *Tārīkh*, 1: 168.3; Guidi, *Lotta*, 45.6; trans. 105.

63 Nyberg 1919: 52, adding that al-Naẓẓām linked it with Anaxagoras's homoiomery theory, which must be a slip for Anaxagoras's opposite theory that 'there is a portion of everything in everything'.

64 Hippolytus saw him as a follower of Aristotle.

65 Maqdisī, *Badʾ*, 1: 141.11, on *aṣḥāb al-juththa* (read *aṣḥāb al-ḥabba*? For *inqalaʿat*, read *infalaqat*).

66 Cf. van Ess 1991–7: iii. 339ff., 360ff., 367ff. (where it is noted that he is also credited with the opposite doctrine that God creates everything new in every moment).

with Origen, but almost all his other views on physics align him with the Dahrīs. His affinities were with the physicists, as al-Shahrastānī said.[67] The same was true of other early Muʿtazilites.[68] The *aṣḥāb al-hayūlā* also had an afterlife as *falāsifa*, represented by Īrānshahrī and Abū Bakr al-Rāzī (the latter an atomist) (Pines 1997: 41f., 47, 48).

IV Godless Religion

Dahrīs are often said not to have believed in God,[69] and some must indeed have denied his existence. But others clearly believed in him,[70] and in any case the key issue between Dahrīs and 'monotheists' (*muwaḥḥidūn*) was not whether God existed or not, but rather what significance he had for humans. To monotheists he had created the world and administered it, sent prophets to mankind to make his wishes known, and would eventually call everyone to account. To 'pure Dahrīs' all this was nonsense: whether there was a deity or not, there was no creator, providential ruler (*mudabbir*), or lord (*rabb*) of the world, nor any angels, spirits, prophets, religious laws, veridical dreams, or afterlife of any kind.[71] The alleged miracles of prophets could be explained rationally, and demons (*shayāṭīn*), spirits (*jinn*), paradise, and hell had been invented to deceive people and make them obey.[72] Like the Zindīqs, the Dahrīs saw the world as simply too full of inequality, injustice, illness, violence, hostility, pain, and death to have a creator or providential overseer.[73] Some, however, accepted that the world had a creator (*muḥdith*), but held that he had ceased to exist. 'We see people fall into water without being able to swim, or into fire, and call upon the provident maker (*al-ṣāniʿ al-mudabbir*), but he does not rescue them, so we know the creator is non-existent (*maʿdūm*)', unidentified philosophers observed. After completing the world and finding it good the creator had destroyed himself so as not to add or detract from his handiwork, leaving behind the laws (*aḥkām*) current among the living beings and things he had made. Alternatively his

[67] Shahrastānī, *Milal*, 1: 39; trans. 208; cf. Baghdādī, *Farq*, 113f., 127, 139; Baghdādī, *Uṣūl*, 48 (with much polemical exaggeration); cf. van Ess 1991–7: iii. 307, 332.

[68] Shahrastānī, *Milal*, 1: 44, 52, 53; trans. 228, 257, 260, on Bishr b. al-Muʿtamir and Jāḥiẓ; Baghdādī, *Uṣūl*, 36.ult., on al-Aṣamm; cf. also van Ess 1991–7: iii. 333.

[69] E.g. Abū l-Faraj, *Aghānī*, 13: 280; al-Māturīdī, *Taʾwīlāt*, 4: 94, ad Q 4: 150; cf. Kulaynī, *Kāfī*, 1: 76.9, on a Zindīq.

[70] Cf. Ibn Qays and his likes (above, note 43 and the text thereto).

[71] Jāḥiẓ, *Hayawān*, 7: 12ff.; Abū ʿĪsā in Ibn al-Malāḥimī, *Muʿtamad*, 587.13; Khushaysh in al-Malaṭī, *Tanbīh*, 72; Yaʿqūbī, *Tārīkh*, 1: 168.1; Maqdisī, *Badʾ*, 1: 119.3. For the 'pure Dahrī', see Jāḥiẓ, *Ḥayawān*, 4: 90.1. For *tadbīr* (and *siyāsa*) as a translation of Syriac *purnāsā*, rendering Greek *pronoia*, see Daiber 1980: 12.

[72] Jāḥiẓ, *Ḥujaj*, 3: 263f. (cf. also 278, 281); Māturīdī, *Taʾwīlāt*, 17: 400.ult., *ad* Q 114: 4–6; Maqdisī, *Badʾ*, 5: 25; Asadī, *Garshāspnāma*, 139; trans. 30 (ch. 44); Pretzl 1933: *23; trans. 46.

[73] Kaʿbī on Dahrīs in Maqdisī, *Badʾ*, 1: 116; Ṣāliḥ b. ʿAbd al-Quddūs in van Ess 1991–7: ii. 18; another Zindīq (Ibn al-Muqaffaʿ?) in Guidi, *Lotta*, 22.23, 24.3; trans. 52, 54; cf. Maimonides, *Guide*, 3: 2 (18a) on Abū Bakr al-Rāzī, noting that the multitudes often shared this view. Sextus had also shared it, showing us yet another affinity between Sceptics and Manicheans (cf. Hankinson 1995: 238).

particles had dispersed in the world so that every force in it was of the divine essence. Or a defect (? *tawalwul*) had appeared in the essence of the creator so that all his power and light had been sucked out of him and into this world; all that remained of him was a cat (! *sinnawr*), which would suck the light out of this world again so that eventually he would be restored; meanwhile he was too weak to attend to his created beings; their affairs were left unattended with the result that injustice had spread.[74] The *sinnawr* could be a misreading for something to do with *nūr*, but the members of the Hāshimite movement in Khurāsān were accused of worshipping cats, so maybe we should take it as it stands; al-Māturīdī confirms that there were *mulḥid*s who held God to suffer defects and illnesses (*āfāt*) (*Akhbār*, 282; Māturīdī, *Taʾwīlāt*, 15: 283, *ad* Q 67: 1). All these explanations accounted for the orderly design of the world, the key argument against Dahrism, while also explaining its unjust nature. There was nobody up there to look after us any more. The heavens were no longer inhabited, as Zindīqs reportedly said (Kulaynī, *Kāfī*, 1: 75 [*kharāb laysa fīhā aḥad*]; cf. Māturīdī, *Taʾwīlāt*, 16: 309, *ad* Q 75: 36).

Opponents occasionally accused Dahrīs of making the elements or the heavenly sphere divine, but rarely of actually worshipping them. Though natural scientists often had a strong occult side to them, as they do in the *Sirr al-khalīqa* and the Jābir corpus, the 'pure Dahrīs' and their Zindīq counterparts come across as reductionists singularly lacking in religious feelings. Their ethics were rationalist. People were obliged to know and avoid naturally evil things such as anger, killing, and theft, nothing else, as Bashshār b. Burd said (Ibn al-Malāḥimī, *Muʿtamad*, 590/631f.; ʿAbd al-Jabbār, *Mughnī*, 5: 20; trans. 173); Dahrīs determined right and wrong (*ḥasan, qabīḥ*) on the basis of their own fancy, as al-Jāḥiẓ caricatured them (Jāḥiẓ, *Ḥayawān*, 7: 13). Like atheists everywhere, they were often envisaged as utterly immoral and depraved.

V The Persistence of Godlessness

Muʿtazilite and Shīʿite *mutakallim*s who interacted with Zindīqs and Dahrīs sometimes became unhinged (*khulliṭa*), as their colleagues said. They include the third/ninth-century Abū Saʿīd al-Ḥadrī/Ḥuṣrī, the fourth/tenth-century Abū Isḥāq al-Naṣībī,[75] and Abū Ḥafṣ al-Ḥaddād (van Ess 1991–7: iv. 89–91), as well as the notorious Ibn al-Rāwandī (d. mid or late fourth/tenth century).[76] The latter is said to have written a book on the eternity of the world and another on its evil, but he is more famous for his view that prophets were tricksters whose alleged miracles were open to rational explanation. This was a theme of considerable prominence in fourth/tenth- and fifth/eleventh-century

74 Yaḥyā b. Bishr b. ʿUmayr al-Nihāwandī (writing before 377/987f.) in Ibn al-Jawzī, *Talbīs*, 46 (ch. against the *falāsifa*).

75 Tawḥīdī, *al-Imtāʿ*, 1: 141; cf. id., *Akhlāq al-wazīrayn*, 202, 211f., 297.

76 Cf. *Encyclopaedia of Islam*², s.v. 'Ibn al-Rāwandī'; Stroumsa 1999: ch. 2; van Ess 1991–7: iv. 295ff.

theology and philosophy (another famous exponent was Abū Bakr al-Rāzī); so too was the denial of the afterlife, but covering these developments would require another chapter. Dahrī cosmology, on the other hand, went into a phase of *kumūn*,[77] to make a *ẓuhūr* in post-Mongol Iran. It was now Sufis who said that 'there is nobody here except us', that the world has always existed, that God does not look after it, that he does not send messengers to it, that there is no afterlife, and that time is endless recurrence, while Dahrī materialism reappeared in the Nuqṭavī heresy of Maḥmūd Pasīkhānī (d. 831/1427f.). But the tone was no longer scoffing, nor was the materialism irreligious. Maḥmūd claimed that the four elements were all that existed, but what he meant was that God was those elements, not that he did not exist, and though his explanation of reincarnation was materialist (humans had no soul), it was merit which determined how one was reborn.[78] Such cosmologies were still heterodox, but they were no longer ungodly.

References

ʿAbd al-Jabbār (*Mughnī*). *al-Mughnī*. Vol. 5. Ed. M. M. al-Khuḍayrī. Cairo: Wizārat al-Thaqāfa wa-l-Irshād al-Qawmī, 1965 [partially trans. G. Monnot, *Penseurs musulmans et religions iraniennes*, Paris: J. Vrin, 1974]. Vol. 9. Ed. M. ʿA. al-Najjār and ʿA.-Ḥ. al-Najjār. Cairo: Wizārat al-Thaqāfa wa-l-Irshād al-Qawmī, 1965.

Abū Ḥātim al-Rāzī (*Iṣlāḥ*). *Kitāb al-Iṣlāḥ*. Ed. Ḥ. Ḥasan Mīnūchihr and M. Muḥaqqiq. Tehran: Muʾassasa-yi Muṭālaʿāt-i Islāmī, Dānishgāh-i Tihrān, McGill University, 1998.

Abū l-Faraj al-Iṣfahānī (*Aghānī*). *Kitāb al-Aghānī*. Cairo: Dār al-Kutub al-Miṣriyya/al-Hayʾa al-Miṣriyya al-ʿĀmma li-l-Kitāb, 1927–74.

Agathias (*Histories*). The Histories [= *De imperio et rebus gestis Iustiniani*]. Trans. J. D. Frendo. Berlin: de Gruyter, 1975.

Akhbār al-dawla al-ʿAbbāsiyya wa-fīhi akhbār al-ʿAbbās wa-waladuhu li-muʾallif min al-qarn al-thālith al-Hijrī. Ed. ʿA.-ʿA. al-Dūrī and ʿA.-J. al-Muṭṭalibī, Beirut: Dār al-Ṭalīʿa li-l-Ṭibāʿa wa-l-Nashr, 1971.

Albinus (*Didaskalikos*). *The Platonic Doctrines of Albinus* [= *Didaskalikos*]. Trans. J. Reedy. Grand Rapids, MI: Phanes Press, 1991.

Algra, K., et al. (eds.) (1999). *The Cambridge History of Hellenistic Philosophy*. Cambridge: Cambridge University Press.

Asadī Ṭūsī, Aḥmad b. ʿAlī (*Garshāspnāma*). *Garshāspnāma*. Ed. Ḥ. Yaghmāʾī. Tehran: Būrūkhīm, 1317/1938 [trans. C. Huart and H. Massé, *Le Livre de Gerchasp: Poème persan*. 2 vols. Paris: P. Geuthner, 1926].

al-Ashʿarī (*Maqālāt*). *Die dogmatischen Lehren der Anhänger des Islam* [= *Maqālāt al-islāmiyyīn wa-ikhtilāf al-muṣallīn*]. 2 vols. Ed. H. Ritter. Istanbul: Devlet Matbaasi, 1929–33.

Athanasius (*Contra Gentes*). *Contra Gentes*. Ed. and trans. R. W. Thomson. Oxford: Clarendon Press, 1971.

[77] The last presentation in which it is alive, as opposed to an object of routinized refutation, is Asadīs *Garshāspnāma* (ch. 44), completed in 458/1065f.

[78] See the eighth/fourteenth- or ninth/fifteenth-century heresiography *Haftād u sih millat*, nos. 5, 19, 26, 33–5, 71; Crone 2012a: 481ff.

al-Baghdādī, ʿAbd al-Qāhir (*Farq*). *al-Farq bayna l-firaq*. Ed. M. Badr. Cairo: Maṭbaʿat al-Maʿārif, 1328/1910.

al-Baghdādī, ʿAbd al-Qāhir (*Uṣūl*). *Uṣūl al-dīn*. Istanbul: Devlet Matbaasi, 1928.

Balīnūs al-Ḥakīm (attrib.) (*Sirr*). *Buch über das Geheimnis der Schöpfung und die Darstellung der Natur, [oder], Buch der Ursachen = Sirr al-khalīqa wa-ṣanʿat al-ṭabīʿa, [aw], Kitāb al-ʿilal*. Ed. U. Weisser. Aleppo: Maʿhad al-Turāth al-ʿIlmī al-ʿArabī, Jāmiʿat Ḥalab, 1979.

Barḥadbeshabbā (*Cause*). *Cause de la fondation des écoles*. Texte syriaque publié et traduit par A. Scher. Paris: Firmin-Didot, 1908.

van Bladel, K. (2009). *The Arabic Hermes: From Pagan Sage to Prophet of Science*. Oxford: Oxford University Press.

Brock, S. (1982). 'From Antagonism to Assimilation: Syriac Attitudes to Greek Learning'. In N. Garsoian et al. (eds.), *East of Byzantium: Syria and Armenia in the Formative Period*. Washington, DC: Dumbarton Oaks, Center for Byzantine Studies, Trustees for Harvard University, 17–34.

Casey, R. P. (ed. and trans.) (1934). *The Excerpta ex Theodoto of Clement of Alexandria*. London: Christophers.

Chokr, M. (1993). *Zandaqa et zindīqs en Islam au second siècle de l'hégire*. Damascus: Institut français de Damas.

Cook, M. (1980). 'The Origins of Kalām'. *Bulletin of the School of Oriental and African Studies* 43: 32–43.

Cook, M. (1981). *Early Muslim Dogma*. Cambridge: Cambridge University Press.

Cook, M. (1999). 'Ibn Qutayba and the Monkeys'. *Studia Islamica* 89: 43–74.

Cook, M. (2007). 'Ibn Saʿdī on Truth-Blindness'. *Jerusalem Studies in Arabic and Islam* 33: 169–78.

Copenhaver, B. P. (1992). *Hermetica: The Greek Corpus Hermeticum and the Latin Asclepius in a New English Translation, with Notes and Introduction*. Cambridge: Cambridge University Press.

Crone, P. (2006). 'Post-colonialism in Tenth-Century Islam'. *Der Islam* 83: 2–38.

Crone, P. (2010–11). 'The Dahrīs According to al-Jāḥiẓ'. *Mélanges de l'Université Saint-Joseph* 63: 63–82.

Crone, P. (2012a). *The Nativist Prophets of Early Islamic Iran: Rural Revolt and Local Zoroastrianism*. Cambridge: Cambridge University Press.

Crone, P. (2012b). 'Al-Jāḥiẓ on *aṣḥāb al-jahālāt* and the Jahmiyya'. In R. Hansberger et al. (eds.), *Medieval Arabic Thought: Essays in Honour of Fritz Zimmermann*. London: The Warburg Institute, 27–40.

Crone, P. (forthcoming). 'Pre-existence in Iran: Zoroastrians, Ex-Christian Muʿtazilites, and Jews on the Human Acquisition of Bodies'. *Aram* 26: 1–27.

Daiber, H. (ed. and trans.) (1980). *Aetius Arabus: Vorsokratiker in arabischer Überlieferung*. Wiesbaden: Steiner.

Daiber, H. (1999). 'Rebellion gegen Gott: Formen atheistischen Denkens im frühen Islam'. In F. Niewöhner and O. Pluta (eds.), *Atheismus im Mittelalter und in der Renaissance*. Wiesbaden: Harrassowitz, 23–44.

Dēnkard. *The Dinkard: The Original Péhlwi Text*, the same transliterated in Zend characters, translations of the text in the Gujrati and English languages, a commentary and a glossary of select terms by P. D. B. Sanjana. 19 vols. Bombay: Duftur Ashkara Press, 1874–1928.

Dhanani, A. (1994). *The Physical Theory of Kalām: Atoms, Space, and Void in Basrian Muʿtazilī Cosmology*. Leiden: Brill.

Dunderberg, I. (2008). *Beyond Gnosticism: Myth, Lifestyle, and Society in the School of Valentinus*. New York: Columbia University Press.

Ehlers, B. (1970). 'Bardesanes von Edessa, ein syrischer Gnostiker'. *Zeitschrift für Kirchengeschichte* 81: 334–51.

Ephrem (*Commentary*). 'Commentary on Genesis'. In E. G. Matthews and J. P. Amar (trans.), *St Ephrem the Syrian: Selected Prose Works*. Washington, DC: Catholic University of America Press, 1994, 59–213.

Ephrem (*Refutations*). *Ephraim's Prose Refutations of Mani, Marcion, and Bardaisan: Transcribed from the palimpsest BM Add. 14623*. 2 vols. Ed. and trans. C. W. Mitchell. London: Williams and Norgate, 1912 [repr. Piscataway, NJ: Gorgias Press, 2008].

van Ess, J. (1966). *Die Erkenntnislehre des Aḍudaddīn al-Īcī: Übersetzung und Kommentar des 1. Buches seiner Mawāqif*. Wiesbaden: Steiner.

van Ess, J. (1967). 'Ḍirār b. ʿAmr und die "Cahmiya", I'. *Der Islam* 43: 241–79.

van Ess, J. (1968). 'Skepticism in Islamic Religious Thought'. *al-Abḥāth* 21: 1–18.

van Ess, J. (1991–7). *Theologie und Gesellschaft im 2. und 3. Jahrhundert Hidschra: Eine Geschichte des religiösen Denkens im frühen Islam*. Berlin: de Gruyter.

Eutychius (Saʿīd b. Biṭrīq) (*Burhān*). *Kitāb al-Burhān*. Ed. and trans. P. Cachia and W. M. Watt. Louvain: Secrétariat du Corpus Scriptorum Christianorum Orientalium, 1960–1.

Floridi, L. (2002). *Sextus Empiricus: The Transmission and Recovery of Pyrrhonism*. Oxford: Oxford University Press.

Frank, R. M. (1974). 'Notes and Remarks on the *ṭabâʾiʿ* in the Teaching of al-Māturīdī'. In P. Salmon (ed.), *Mélanges d'islamologie: volume dédié à la mémoire de Armand Abel par ses collègues, ses élèves et ses amis*. Leiden: Brill, 137–49.

Furlani, G. (1937). 'Sur le Stoicisme de Bardesane d'Édesse'. *Archiv Orientální* 9: 347–52.

Goldziher, I. (1920). *Die Richtungen der islamischen Koranauslegung*. Leiden: Brill.

Goodman, L. E. (1993). 'Time in Islam'. In A. N. Balslev and J. N. Mohanty, *Religion and Time*. Leiden: Brill, 138–62.

Grant, R. M. (1993). *Heresy and Criticism: The Search for Authenticity in Early Christian Literature*. Louisville, KY: Westminster/J. Knox Press.

Guidi, M. (ed. and trans.) (1927). *La lotta tra l'Islam e il manicheismo: un libro di Ibn al-Muqaffaʿ contro il Corano confutato da al-Qāsim b. Ibrāhīm*. Rome: R. Accademia Nazionale dei Lincei.

Gutas, D. (1982). 'Paul the Persian on the Classification of the Parts of Aristotle's Philosophy'. *Der Islam* 59: 231–67.

Haftād u sih millat, yā iʿtiqādāt-i madhāhib, risāla-yi dar farq-i Islām az āthār-i qarn-i hashtum-i Hijrī. Ed. M. J. Mashkūr. Tehran: Muʾassasa-yi Maṭbūʿātī-yi ʿAṭāʾī, 1341/1962.

Hankinson, R. J. (1995). *The Sceptics*. London: Routledge.

Haq, S. N. (1994). *Names, Natures and Things: The Alchemist Jābir ibn Ḥayyān and his Kitāb al-Aḥjār (Book of Stones)*. Dordrecht: Kluwer.

Hippolytus (*Refutatio*). *Refutatio omnium haeresium*. Ed. M. Marcovich. Berlin: de Gruyter, 1986 [trans. J. H. MacMahon, *The Refutation of all Heresies*. Edinburgh: T. & T. Clark, 1868 (the chapter divisions are those of the edition)].

Horovitz, S. (1903). 'Über den Einfluss des Stoicismus auf die Entwickelung der Philosophie bei den Arabern'. *Zeitschrift der Deutschen Morgenländischen Gesellschaft* 57: 177–96.

Ibn Durayd (*Ishtiqāq*). *al-Ishtiqāq*. Ed. ʿA.-S. M. Hārūn. Cairo: al-Maṭbaʿa al-Sunniyya al-Muḥammadiyya, 1958 [references are to the marginal pagination].

Ibn Ḥazm (*Faṣl*). *al-Faṣl fī l-milal wa-l-ahwāʾ wa-l-niḥal*. Cairo: n.p., 1899–1903.

Ibn al-Jawzī (*Talbīs*). *Talbīs Iblīs*. Ed. M. M. al-Dimashqī. Cairo: Idārat al-Ṭibāʿa al-Munīriyya, 1928.

Ibn Kathīr (*Tafsīr*). *Tafsīr*. Cairo, n.d., n.p.

Ibn al-Malāḥimī (*Muʿtamad*). *al-Muʿtamad fī uṣūl al-dīn*. Ed. M. McDermott and W. Madelung. London: Al-Hoda, 1991 [revised and enlarged edition by W. Madelung, Tehran: Institute of Philosophy, 2012 (cited in that order, separated by a slash)].

Ibn al-Nadīm (*Fihrist*). *al-Fihrist*. Ed. R. Tajaddud. Tehran: Ibn-i Sīnā, 1971 [trans. B. Dodge, *The Fihrist of al-Nadīm: A Tenth-Century Survey of Muslim Culture*. 2 vols. New York: Columbia University Press, 1970].

Ibn Qutayba (*Taʾwīl*). *Taʾwīl mukhtalif al-ḥadīth*. Ed. M. Z. al-Najjār. Cairo: Maktabat al-Kulliyyāt al-Azhariyya, 1966 [trans. G. Lecomte, *Le Traité des divergences du hadīṯ d'Ibn Qutayba (mort en 276/889)*. Damascus: Institut français, de Damas 1962].

Ibn al-Zubayr, Aḥmad b. al-Rashīd (*Dhakhāʾir*). *Kitāb al-Dhakhāʾir wa-l-tuḥaf*. Kuwait: Dāʾirat al-Maṭbūʿāt wa-l-Nashr, 1959.

Israel of Kashkar (*Unity*). *A Treatise on the Unity and Trinity of God by Israel of Kashkar (d. 872)*: Introduction, edition, and word index by B. Holmberg. Lund: Plus Ultra, 1989.

Jacob of Sarug (*Sermons*). *Quatre homélies métriques sur la creation*. Ed. and trans. K. Alwan. Louvain: Peeters, 1989.

Jaʿfar al-Ṣādiq (attrib.) (*Tawḥīd*). *Kitāb al-Tawḥīd*. Ed. M. ʿA.-R. Ḥamza. N.p.: Dār al-Salām, 1329/1911.

al-Jāḥiẓ (*Ḥayawān*). *Kitāb al-Ḥayawān*. Ed. ʿA.-S. M. Hārūn. Cairo: Maktabat Muṣṭafā al-Bābī al-Ḥalabī, 1938–58.

al-Jāḥiẓ (*Ḥujaj*). *Ḥujaj al-nubuwwa*, in al-Jāḥiẓ, *Rasāʾil*. Ed. ʿA.-S. M. Hārūn. Cairo: Maktabat al-Khānjī bi-Miṣr, 1979, 3: 222–81.

al-Jāḥiẓ (*Radd*). *al-Radd ʿalā al-naṣārā*, in al-Jāḥiẓ, *Rasāʾil*. Ed. ʿA.-S. M. Hārūn. Cairo: Maktabat al-Khānjī bi-Miṣr, 1979, 3: 302–51.

al-Jāḥiẓ (*Tarbīʿ*). *Kitāb al-Tarbīʿ wa-l-tadwīr*. Ed. C. Pellat. Damascus: Institut français de Damas, 1955.

al-Jāḥiẓ (attrib.) (*Dalāʾil*). *Kitāb al-Dalāʾil wa-l-iʿtibār ʿalā l-khalq wa-l-tadbīr*. Cairo: Maktabat al-Kulliyyāt al-Azhariyya, 1987 [trans. M. A. S. Abdel Haleem, *Chance or Creation? God's Design in the Universe*. Reading: Garnet, 1995].

Job of Edessa (*Treasures*). *Encyclopædia of Philosophical and Natural Sciences as Taught in Baghdad about A.D. 817, or, Book of Treasures, by Job of Edessa*. Ed. and trans. A. Mingana. Cambridge: W. Heffer, 1935.

al-Juwaynī (*Shāmil*). *al-Shāmil fī uṣūl al-dīn*. Ed. ʿA. S. al-Nashshār et al. Alexandria: Munshaʾāt al-Maʿārif, 1969.

al-Khayyāṭ (*Intiṣār*). *Kitāb al-Intiṣār wa-l-radd ʿalā Ibn al-Rāwandī al-mulḥid*. Ed. A. N. Nader. Beirut: al-Maṭbaʿa al-Kāthūlīkiyya, 1957.

Kraus, P. (1934). 'Zu Ibn al-Muqaffaʿ'. *Rivista degli Studi Orientali* 14: 1–20.

Kraus, P. (ed.) (1935). *Mukhtār Rasāʾil Jābir b. Ḥayyān*. Cairo: Maktabat al-Khānjī wa-Maṭbaʿatihā.

Kraus, P. (1942). *Jābir b. Ḥayyān. Contribution à l'histoire des idées scientifiques dans l'Islam*. Vol. ii: *Jābir et la science grecque*. Cairo: Impr. de l'Institut français d'archéologie orientale.

al-Kulaynī (*al-Kāfī*). *Al-Uṣūl min al-Kāfī*. 8 vols. Ed. ʿA. A. al-Ghaffārī. Tehran: Dār al-Kutub al-Islāmiyya, 1377–81/1957–61.

Lactantius (*De ira Dei*). *De ira dei. Vom Zorne Gottes*. Ed. and trans. H. Kraft and A. Wlosok. Darmstadt: Gentner, 1971.

Lammert, H. (1953). 'Zur Lehre von Grundeigenschaften bei Nemesios'. *Hermes* 81: 488–91.

Land, J. P. N. (1862–75). *Anecdota syriaca*. Collegit, edidit, explicavit. 4 vols. Leiden: Brill.

Langermann, Y. T. (2009). 'Atomism and the Galenic Tradition'. *History of Science* 47: 277–95.

Lim, E. (1995). *Public Disputation, Power and Social Order in Late Antiquity.* Berkeley: University of California Press.

Long, A. A., and D. N. Sedley (1987). *The Hellenistic Philosophers.* 2 vols. Cambridge: Cambridge University Press.

Lucretius (*De rerum natura*). *De rerum natura = On the Nature of Things.* Ed. and trans. W. H. D. Rouse, rev. M. Ferguson Smith. Cambridge, MA: Harvard University Press, 1982.

Macdonald, D. B. (1927). 'Continuous Re-creation and Atomic Time in Muslim Scholastic Theology'. *Isis* 9: 326–44.

Madelung, W. (2005). 'An Ismaili Interpretation of Ibn Sīnā's *Qaṣīdat al-Nafs*'. In T. Lawson (ed.), *Reason and Inspiration in Islam: Theology, Philosophy and Mysticism in Muslim Thought. Essays in Honour of Hermann Landolt.* London: I. B. Tauris, 157–68.

Maimonides (*Guide*). *The Guide of the Perplexed.* Trans. S. Pines. Chicago: University of Chicago Press, 1963.

al-Malaṭī (*Tanbīh*). *Kitāb al-Tanbīh wa-l-radd ʿalā ahl al-ahwāʾ wa-l-bidaʿ.* Ed. S. Dedering. Istanbul: Maṭbaʿat al-Dawla, 1936.

al-Maqdisī (*Badʾ*). *Kitāb al-Badʾ wa-l-tārīkh = Livre de la création et de l'histoire.* Ed. and trans. C. Huart. Paris, 1899–1919 [references are to the Arabic text].

al-Masʿūdī (*Murūj*). *Murūj al-dhahab.* 7 vols. Paris, 1861–1917 [ed. C. Pellat. Beirut: al-Jāmiʿa al-Lubnāniyya, 1966–79 (cited in that order, by page and paragraph respectively; the volumes are identical)].

al-Māturīdī (*Tawḥīd*). *Kitāb al-Tawḥīd.* Ed. F. Kholeif. Beirut: Dar el-Machreq, 1970.

al-Māturīdī (*Taʾwīlāt*). *Taʾwīlāt al-Qurʾān.* Ed. B. Topaloğlu et al. Istanbul: Dār al-Mīzān, 2005–10.

de Ménasce, J. (trans.) (1973). *Le Troisième Livre du Dēnkart.* Paris: C. Klincksieck.

Moses Bar Kepha (*Hexaemeronkommentar*). *Der Hexaemeronkommentar des Moses bar Kepha.* Einleitung, Übersetzung und Untersuchungen von L. Schlimme. Wiesbaden: Harrassowitz, 1977.

al-Muqammiṣ (*ʿIshrūn*). *Dāwūd ibn Marwān al-Muqammiṣ's Twenty Chapters* (*ʿIshrūn Maqāla*). Ed. and trans. S. Stroumsa. Leiden: Brill, 1989.

Nemesius of Emesa (*Nature*). *On the Nature of Man.* Trans. R. W. Sharpless and P. J. van der Eijk. Liverpool: Liverpool University Press, 2008.

Nyberg, H. S. (1919). *Kleinere Schriften des Ibn al-ʿArabī.* Leiden: Brill.

Pedersen, N. A. (2004). *Demonstrative Proof in Defence of God: A Study of Titus of Bostra's Contra Manichaeos. The Work's Sources, Aims, and Relation to its Contemporary Theology.* Leiden: Brill.

Philastrius (*Diversarum*). *Diversarum Hereseon Liber.* Ed. F. Marx. Vienna: F. Tempsky, 1898.

Photinus (*Disputationes*). 'Disputationes Photini Manichaei cum Paulo Christiano'. *Patrologia Graeca* 88, 1864: 529–78.

Pines, S. (1997). *Studies in Islamic Atomism.* Trans. M. Schwarz. Jerusalem: Magnes Press, 1997.

Possekel, U. (1999). *Evidence of Greek Philosophical Concepts in the Writings of Ephrem the Syrian.* Louvain: Peeters.

Pretzl, O. (1931). 'Die frühislamische Atomenlehre'. *Der Islam* 19: 117–30.

Pretzl, O. (1933). *Die Streitschrift des Ġazālī gegen die Ibāḥīja, im persischen Text hrsg. und übersetzt.* Munich: Verlag der Bayerischen Akademie der Wissenschaften, 1933.

Procopius (*Anecdota*). *Anecdota.* Trans. H. B. Dewing. London/Cambridge, MA, 1969.

al-Qummī (*Tafsīr*). *Tafsīr.* 2 vols. Ed. Ṭ. al-Mūsawī al-Jazāʾirī. Beirut: Dār al-Surūr, 1991.

Ramelli, I. (2009). *Bardaisan of Edessa: A Reassessment of the Evidence and a New Interpretation.* Piscataway, NJ: Gorgias Press.

al-Rāzī, Fakhr al-Dīn (*Tafsīr*). *al-Tafsīr al-kabīr* [*Mafātīḥ al-ghayb*]. Tehran: Intishārāt-i Asāṭīr, 1413/1992–3.
Rudolph, U. (1995). 'Kalām im antiken Gewand: Das theologische Konzept des *Kitāb Sirr al-Ḫalīqa*'. In A. Fodor (ed.), *Proceedings of the 14th Congress of the Union Européenne des Arabisants et Islamisants. Budapest... 1988. Part 1*. Budapest: Eötvös Loránd University Chair for Arabic Studies & Csoma de Kőrös Society, Section of Islamic Studies, 123–36.
Saadia Gaon (*Amānāt*). *Kitāb al-Amānāt wa-l-iʿtiqādāt*. Ed. S. Landauer. Leiden: Brill, 1880 [trans. S. Rosenblatt, *The Book of Beliefs and Opinions*. New Haven, CT: Yale University Press, 1948].
Sextus Empiricus (*Outlines*). *Outlines of Pyrrhonism*. Ed. and trans. R. G. Bury. Cambridge, MA: Harvard University Press, 1933.
al-Shahrastānī (*Milal*). *Kitāb al-Milal wa-l-niḥal*. Ed. W. Cureton. London: Printed for the Society for the Publication of Oriental Texts, 1842–6 [trans. D. Gimaret and G. Monnot, *Livre des religions et des sectes*. Paris: Peeters, 1986].
al-Shahrastānī (*Nihāya*). *The summa philosophiae of al-Shahrastānī = Nihāyat al-aqdām fī ʿilm al-kalām*. Ed. with a summary translation A. Guillaume. Oxford: Oxford University Press, 1934.
Sorabji, R. (1988). *Matter, Space, and Motion: Theories in Antiquity and their Sequel*. Ithaca, NY: Cornell University Press.
Stark, R., and R. Finke (2000). *Acts of Faith: Explaining the Human Side of Religion*. Berkeley: University of California Press.
Stewart, C. (1991). *'Working the Earth of the Heart': The Messalian Controversy in History, Texts, and Language to AD 431*. Oxford: Oxford University Press.
Strohmaier, G. (1981). 'Galen in Arabic'. In V. Nutton (ed.), *Galen: Problems and Prospects*. London: Wellcome Institute for the History of Medicine, 197–212.
Stroumsa, S. (1999). *Freethinkers of Medieval Islam: Ibn al-Rāwandī, Abū Bakr al-Rāzī and their Impact on Islamic Thought*. Leiden: Brill.
al-Ṭabarī (*Tārīkh*). *Tārīkh al-rusul wa-l-mulūk*. Ed. M. J. de Goeje et al. Leiden: Brill, 1879–1901.
al-Tawḥīdī (*Akhlāq*). *Akhlāq al-wazīrayn*. Ed. M. al-Ṭanjī. Beirut: Dār Ṣādir, 1992.
al-Tawḥīdī (*Imtāʾ*). *Kitāb al-Imtāʾ waʾl-muʾānasa*. Ed. A. Amīn and A. al-Zayn. Cairo: Lajnat al-Taʾlīf wa-l-Tarjama wa-l-Nashr, 1939–44.
al-Tawḥīdī (*Muqābasāt*). *al-Muqābasāt*. Ed. M. T. Ḥusayn. Baghdad: Maktabat al-Irshād, 1970.
Teixidor, J. (1997). 'Les Textes syriaques de logique de Paul le Perse'. *Semitica* 47: 117–37.
Theodore Bar Koni (*Liber*). *Liber scholiorum (Seert version)*. Ed. A. Scher. Paris: E Typographeo Reipublicae, 1910, 1912 [trans. R. Hespel and R. Draguet. Louvain: Peeters, 1981–2].
Theodoret (*Providentia*). *On Divine Providence* [= *De providentia*]. Trans. T. Halton. New York: Newman Press, 1988.
Vajda, G. (1938). 'Les Zindīqs en pays d'Islam au début de la période abbaside'. *Rivista degli Studi Orientali* 17: 173–229.
van den Ven, P. (ed. and trans.) (1962). *La Vie ancienne de S. Syméon Stylite le Jeune (521–92)*. 2 vols. Brussels: Société des bollandistes.
Walker, P. E. (1993). *Early Philosophical Shiism: The Ismaili Neoplatonism of Abū Yaʿqūb al-Sijistānī*. Cambridge: Cambridge University Press.
Weisser, U. (1980). *Das 'Buch über das Geheimnis der Schöpfung' von Pseudo-Apollonios von Tyana*. Berlin: de Gruyter.
Wolfson, H. A. (1976). *The Philosophy of the Kalam*. Cambridge, MA: Harvard University Press.
al-Yaʿqūbī (*Mushākala*). *Mushākalat al-nās li-zamānihim wa-mā yaghlibu ʿalayhim fī kull ʿaṣr*. Beirut: Dār al-Kitāb al-Jadīd, 1962.
al-Yaʿqūbī (*Tārīkh*). *Tārīkh*. 2 vols. Ed. M. T. Houtsma. Leiden: Brill, 1883.

CHAPTER 7

THE MUʿTAZILITE MOVEMENT (I)

The Origins of the Muʿtazila

RACHA EL-OMARI

I Introduction

Scholarship on the origins of the Muʿtazila in the early to mid-eighth century CE remains highly speculative and inconclusive.* After this initial obscure period, the Muʿtazila flourished as a theological group well into the sixth/twelfth century, passing through both an early phase (see Chapter 8) and a scholastic phase (see Chapter 9). Although the Muʿtazila saw its decline in the Sunnī world in the sixth/twelfth century, it survived in various forms in Zaydism and Twelver Shiʿism until later centuries (see Chapters 10, 11, 26, and 27).

We must preface any introduction to the questions addressed here with a brief account of the doctrines of the Muʿtazila. Once established as a theological school the adherents of the Muʿtazila distinguished themselves from prior experiments in theology in general and *kalām* in particular (see Chapters 1 through 4) by their steadfast commitment to reason as the basis for theological inquiry; indeed the Muʿtazila were the strongest exponents of 'rationalism' in Islamic theology. This is not the rationalism of the free-thinkers of the Enlightenment, as early nineteenth-century scholars of Muʿtazilism mistook it to be (e.g. Steiner 1865; cf. Schmidtke 1998: 386–7). Ignaz Goldziher's inquiry cleared up this misunderstanding of Muʿtazilī doctrine (Goldziher 1910: 117–19; cf. Schmidtke 1998: 387). Aside from inquiries into physics and cosmology (*daqīq al-kalām*) that had minimal dealings with scripture (Pines 1936), the aims of Muʿtazilī rationalism were theological, and thus could never be fully independent of the dictates of scripture. The Muʿtazila sought to ascertain and explain God through rational axioms. This included, chiefly, making sense of His attributes as presented in the Qurʾān, and His actions, mainly understanding what it means for Him to be just. The result of the Muʿtazilī discussion of

* I thank Sabine Schmidtke for her feedback on an early draft of this chapter. All errors are mine.

these two topics—unity (*tawḥīd*) and justice (*ʿadl*)—amounted to two of the five principles upon which the Muʿtazila built their theology. In later writings these two principles were presented as the first two principles that summarize the Muʿtazilī doctrine. In earlier writings they were presented in a different order: the principle of unity (*tawḥīd*) was the fifth principle, and the principle of justice (*ʿadl*) was the first. The other three principles were as follows in their original order: the second was the principle of 'punishment and threat' (*al-waʿd wa-l-waʿīd*). Because of the Muʿtazila's espousal of free will and God's justice, they held that God does not forgive the grave sinner except through his repentance and that God is obligated to reward the believer. The third principle was that of 'the intermediate rank' (*al-manzila bayn al-manzilatayn*), by which they deemed that someone who commits a grave sin does not merit the legal category of a believer (*muʾmin*) or an unbeliever (*kāfir*); rather he should be labelled a 'grave sinner' (*fāsiq*). The fourth principle was the obligation 'to command right and forbid wrong' (*al-amr bi-l-maʿrūf wa-l-nahy ʿan al-munkar*) in any way that one is capable.[1]

The subject of the origins of the Muʿtazila Movement has been approached from three angles. One concerns the origin of the name Muʿtazila, what the word means, why it was given to this group, and in what circumstances. A second focus has been on the history of the movement, the early figures of Wāṣil b. ʿAṭāʾ (d. 131/748–9) and ʿAmr b. ʿUbayd (d. 144/761), as well as their relationships to one another and to their disciples. A third angle concerns the extent of intellectual continuity between the doctrines of the period of origin and later Muʿtazilī doctrines, as attested in the five principles. What follows is chiefly a summary of these approaches in the order outlined here, as it reflects—to a significant extent—the development of scholarship on the subject. These angles were never mutually exclusive and shifted over time, partially in response to the available sources.

The principal limitation has to do with the sources. They are scarce, late, and conflict with one another. The earliest sources date from at least a century after the period of origins, and the evidence they relate ranges widely in its scope and relevance.[2] Furthermore the material in these sources in the form of reports and opinions expresses the differing standpoints of their authors, and cannot be free of their doctrinal biases. The sources can be divided into two main groups: Muʿtazilī and proto-Sunnī and Sunnī.[3] This division influences, for example, the accounts about the founders of the school: early Muʿtazilī sources favour Wāṣil as the founder while the proto-Sunnī sources favour ʿAmr.[4] Later Muʿtazilī sources regard Wāṣil and ʿAmr as equally responsible for establishing the

[1] The early ordering of the principles is attested in the work of al-Kaʿbī/al-Balkhī (d. 319/931) (*Maqālāt*, 63–4). For the late ordering of the principles see the example of al-Masʿūdī's (d. 346/956) listing of the five principles (*Murūj*, 4: 50–60).

[2] Examples of early sources and their divergent scopes are the heresiographical work of the Muʿtazilī Jaʿfar b. Ḥarb (d. 236/850), *Uṣul*, 54, and the literary work of al-Jāḥiẓ (d. 255/868–9), *Bayān*, 1: 14–16, 20–3, 3: 169.

[3] The earliest proto-Sunnī source is Ibn Qutayba's (d. 276/889) *Maʿarif*. Two other late Sunnī sources are al-Baghdādī (d. 429/1037), *Farq*, 92, and al-Shahrastanī's (d. 548/1153) *Milal*, 31–4. The earliest Muʿtazilī source to speak about Wāṣil and his contribution is al-Kaʿbī's *Maqālāt*, 64–9.

[4] Cf. the discussion of Wāṣil and ʿAmr in the earlist proto-Sunnī source, viz. Ibn Qutayba's *Maʿārif*, 482–3, 625, to that of al-Kaʿbī's 'Dhikr al-Muʿtazila' in *Maqālāt*, 64–9.

school.[5] On other points, conflicting reports cannot be decoded by an account of the doctrinal constraints of the sources. This is especially the case regarding the reports of the origin of the name Muʿtazila, where some Muʿtazilī sources speak of how little they know of the initial meaning of the term and recount quite different interpretations of it.[6] A summary of the difficulty of the sources would not be complete if we do not also note the fundamental fact that no single work attributed to figures of this period is preserved. All that we have are the mention of titles, and few and scattered mentions of their doctrines that cannot be verified as direct citations or quotations by the professed founding figures.[7] In short, any evidence about the doctrines of the Muʿtazila from this period remains twice removed in terms of time and genre.

II The Name Muʿtazila

The earliest studies of the origin of the Muʿtazila focus on identifying the origin of the lexical use of the term 'Muʿtazila', the infinitive '*iʿtizāl*' and the verb '*iʿtazala*', in writings from the first/seventh and early second/eighth centuries. Ignaz Goldziher suggested that the original meaning of the movement related to the ascetic and pious tendencies of the founders (Goldziher 1910: 100). He reached this conclusion by first mapping out the various extant uses of the word Muʿtazila (Goldziher 1887: 196),[8] and then favoured the use of the word Muʿtazila to describe groups who 'retire' or 'withdraw', and the noun '*iʿtizāl*' in the expression *kāna madhhabuhu l-iʿtizāl* to refer to a path of asceticism (Goldziher 1918: 207–8). He preferred this meaning for the origins of the Muʿtazila based on his consideration of the biographical evidence about the ascetic practices of both Wāṣil and ʿAmr (Goldziher 1910: 101). He considered *kalām* tendencies as later developments to the Muʿtazila, as notions that did not exist at its genesis. Louis Massignon supported an ascetic meaning for the doctrine of the intermediate rank, although he provided little by way of textual evidence to advance Goldziher's theory.[9] Other than that, Goldziher's theory of its ascetic origins was not taken up again until Sara Stroumsa's work, examined below.

[5] See e.g. al-Sharīf al-Murtaḍā (d. 436/1044), *Amālī*, 1: 165–7, Ibn al-Murtaḍā (d. 840/1437), *Ṭabaqāt*, 36–40.

[6] al-Kaʿbī, *Maqālāt*, 115; al-Maqdisī, *Badʾ*, 5: 142; Ibn al-Nadīm (d. 385/995 or 388/998), *Fihrist*, 201; ʿAbd al-Jabbār (d. 415/1025), *Faḍl*, 165–6; al-Jishumī (d. 494/1101), *Sharḥ*, 28b–29a.

[7] See e.g. al-Khayyāṭ's (d. *c.*300/913) discussion of Wāṣil's doctrines (*Intiṣār*, 73–4).

[8] In Goldziher's earliest mention of the question of the origin of the name Muʿtazila, he also cites a political meaning of the term 'Muʿtazila' as referring to 'political dissidents' (Goldziher 1887: 196).

[9] Massignon labelled the term Muʿtazila as a 'voluntary solitude of the heart', but offered no foundation for this interpretation based on attested semantic usage, and did not explain how his argument is derived from the Muʿtazilī doctrine of the intermediate rank (Massignon 1975: iii. 189). He did document the connection between the follower of one disciple of ʿAmr and Basran ascetic circles (Massignon 1954: 168).

Goldziher's approach of mapping out the meaning of the word Muʿtazila was followed by Carlo Nallino, who expanded on it, but was led to a very different understanding of the origin of the name. For Nallino the genesis of the Muʿtazila is rooted in what he called the 'political Muʿtazila' who 'abstained from the internal struggles of the first century' (Nallino 1916: 447). A group was called 'Muʿtazila' because they abstained (*iʿtizāl*) from giving the oath of allegiance to ʿAlī (r. 656–61 CE) after the death of ʿUthmān (r. 644–55 CE) (Nallino 1916: 442). Nallino recognized another instance in which a group was called Muʿtazila, namely when they abstained from giving allegiance to either party; that is, they neither supported the party of ʿAlī nor the supporters of ʿUthmān (Nallino 1916: 446; al-Ṭabarī, 1:3342). Indeed Nallino explained that during the first part of the second/eighth century, when *'iʿtazala'* was used as a transitive verb, it implied abstaining from taking part in public life and in war; when used in relation to two parties in dispute it meant abstaining from joining either party (Nallino 1916: 444).

H. S. Nyberg also located the origins of the Muʿtazila in a response to the political strife between ʿAlī and his opponents when arguing that the political Muʿtazila were those who 'separated from ʿAlī' (*iʿtazalū ʿAlī*) and 'took up a neutral attitude in the quarrels between ʿAlī and his adversaries' (Nyberg 1913–36: 787–8). Nyberg's translation of the verb '*iʿtazala*' as 'to separate' reflected the wording of Abū Muḥammad Ḥasan b. Mūsā al-Nawbakhtī (d. betw. 300/912 and 310/922) in his *Firaq al-shīʿa*, who is the only primary source to trace the origin of the Muʿtazila to the political Muʿtazila of the first civil war (Madelung 1965: 30). But Nyberg's theory about the political origins of the Muʿtazila differed greatly from Nallino's initial hypothesis, as Nyberg argued that the official theology of the ʿAbbāsid movement was Muʿtazilī. This claim was largely facilitated by Nyberg's interpretation of the doctrine of the intermediate rank as a political response to the strife that plagued the community after the murder of ʿUthmān (Nyberg 1913–36: 788).

Nallino and Nyberg's stance that the origin of the name Muʿtazila lies in political neutrality was revisited by Montgomery Watt, who based it on Wāṣil's doctrine of abstaining from taking a position on ʿAlī and his opponents, namely the doctrine of *liʿān*. Watt saw the Muʿtazila as advocates of political neutrality; however, he did not adopt Nallino and Nyberg's methods for deriving their conclusion nor did he trace the Muʿtazila back to the political Muʿtazila of the first civil war. Indeed, Watt believed that the Muʿtazila only became a distinct group around the beginning of the third/ninth century (see Section III).

One shared thrust of Nallino and Nyberg's hypotheses regarding the Muʿtazila's political genesis seems to have survived in the works of Wilferd Madelung and Josef van Ess (van Ess 1992: 339). Although in different ways, both reached the same conclusion that the movement had a political genesis. More importantly, they broke with Nallino and Nyberg's approach to the history of origins by shifting their focus from a semantic treatment of the term Muʿtazila toward a critical documentation of the history of the movement and its doctrines.

Sections III and IV mainly focus on this approach; Madelung's and van Ess's contributions, which employ the material available for the history of the movement, as tentative as it is, confirm that initial speculation based solely on the semantic uses of the term is no longer tenable.

We must mention one last example of this semantic approach, namely Stroumsa's argument in support of Goldziher's theory of an ascetic meaning, for which she expanded his initial examination of the semantic use of the term Muʿtazila (Stroumsa 1990). She argues that a flexible use of the verb '*iʿtazala*' and the noun '*muʿtazila*' is attested in the literature of the period prior to the Muʿtazila, and this includes the meaning of asceticism. But, she adds, it was only with Wāṣil and ʿAmr that the word '*muʿtazila*' became the proper name of the movement. She describes a process of 'diversification' of the word *muʿtazila*, even as other words became technical terms for asceticism (Stroumsa 1990: 273). Underlying Stroumsa's critique of the scholarship on the origins of the Muʿtazila is her vision of a larger role for asceticism in the emergence of the early Islamic period, which she believes has been sidelined in favour of political frameworks (Stroumsa 1990: 292–3). While there is much work to be done on the origins of asceticism in order to test Stroumsa's line of inquiry, we must keep in mind her argument, as it resolves one of van Ess's hypotheses about the intellectual-political triggers of the movement, as discussed in Section III.

III The Movement

Watt maintained that the Muʿtazila started with the figure of Abū l-Hudhayl al-ʿAllāf (d. 227/842); it was only in the mid-third/ninth century, he states, that Wāṣil and ʿAmr were presented as the founders of the Muʿtazila (Watt 1948: 61; Watt 1963: 52–4). With the exception of Watt, however, even when scholars disagreed on the nature of the contributions of Wāṣil b. ʿAṭāʾ and ʿAmr b. ʿUbayd, they at least recognized that both had a hand in its genesis. But determining the contributions of these two figures presents difficulties: each one had an independent intellectual profile, and the material available on them is not only scarce but anecdotal. Indeed, this material requires verification and a critical anchoring to the wider picture of historical events of the time. Van Ess undertook this task over the course of several decades (van Ess 1967, 1971, 1975, 1987, 1992). Nyberg had already charted a path into the origin of the movement, especially highlighting the distinct intellectual characteristics of ʿAmr and Wāṣil, but his presentation of their biographies was marred by his theory that they had supported the ʿAbbāsid movement (Nyberg 1913–36: 788–9; Nyberg 1957: 125–31). This is a misconception that Madelung corrected, for Nyberg's theory had distorted the biographies of the two men (Madelung 1965: 24–30).

Wāṣil moved to Basra, but remained an outsider (van Ess 1992: 244) and his discipleship under al-Ḥasan al-Baṣrī (d. 110/728) most likely did not occur there (van Ess 1992: 257–8). His early ties to Medina do not necessarily mean that he was a student of Abū

Hāshim, the son of Muḥammad b. al-Ḥanafiyya (d. 81/700–1) (Nyberg 1913–36: 788; Madelung 1965: 31; van Ess 1992: 236, 251–2). Yet his early Medinese connections must have played a part in his pro-ʿAlīd stances and his espousal of the doctrine of the *imāma* of the less excellent (*imāmat al-mafḍūl*), by which he deemed the *imāma* of Abū Bakr (r. 632–4 CE), ʿUmar b. al-Khaṭṭāb (r. 634–44 CE), and ʿUthmān b. ʿAffān (with the exception of his last six years) to be valid although these three were not the most excellent, since Wāṣil deemed ʿAlī b. Abī Ṭālib to be the most excellent for that position (van Ess 1992: 259, 270–1, 273).

Wāṣil's asceticism was a defining feature of his personality, but it was his outstanding performance in theological debates where he showed his mastery of *kalām* and rhetorical skills (van Ess 1992: 241–3) that attracted attention and followers (van Ess 1992: 253, 254, 259). His lexical talent allowed him to find synonyms for words to compensate for his inability to pronounce the letter R correctly. There is no reason to reject the report that he gave a memorable sermon as a member of the Basran delegation before the Umayyad governor ʿAbd Allāh b. ʿUmar b. ʿAbd al-ʿAzīz (van Ess 1992: 241–2) but its two published versions cannot be considered authentic (Hārūn 1951; Daiber 1988; Radtke 1990; Gilliot 1990; van Ess 1992: 246–8). Wāṣil sent his followers as missionaries (*duʿāt*) around the Muslim world; it is likely that he modelled this on the practices of the Ibāḍīs with whom he had debated in his youth (van Ess 1992: 255). The aim of these missionaries was the dissemination of religion through *kalām*; they relied on their commercial activities to survive, and combined their teacher's asceticism and rhetorical mastery (van Ess 1992: 310–11). We must recall that Wāṣil was a proponent of free will, a characteristic that he shared with ʿAmr and which, van Ess suggests, allowed him to win followers in a city to which he was an outsider (van Ess 1992: 340–1).

While free will was one component of Wāṣil's intellectual characteristics, it was at the centre of ʿAmr's thought (Nyberg 1957; van Ess 1967: 39–45; van Ess 1992: 308). ʿAmr's contribution to the Qadariyya movement was not as a *mutakallim* but as a traditionist (van Ess 1992: 308) which prompted the traditionists to censor ʿAmr and his students (van Ess 1992: 342). Aside from his contributions as a traditionist and the attention, albeit negative, that his position on free will earned, ʿAmr was not an original thinker or a prolific author; rather it was his asceticism that seems to have left the strongest impression (van Ess 1992: 280, 305), so much so that most of his opponents among the *ahl al-ḥadīth* conceded that he was a pious individual (van Ess 1992: 280–1, 296). Although ʿAmr was not al-Ḥasan al-Baṣrī's favourite student, his ties to him were significant enough, including his transmission of *ḥadīth* from him, to prompt the *ahl al-ḥadīth* to distance al-Ḥasan from him (van Ess 1992: 297, 302–4). It is important to note that, like al-Ḥasan al-Baṣrī and the Basrans, ʿAmr was sympathetic to ʿUthmān and upheld the *imāma* of the most excellent (*imāmat al-fāḍil*) (van Ess 1992: 308). Above all, unlike Wāṣil whose success was defined by his excellence in *kalām*, there is no evidence that ʿAmr was interested in *kalām* (van Ess 1992: 305).

Clearly Wāṣil and ʿAmr both advocated the doctrine of free will and both led ascetic lives. But it was in their shared politics—not their political theology (that is, their views on the *imāma*)—that van Ess saw the initial coherence of the Muʿtazila movement (van

Ess 1992: 339–40). Both ʿAmr and Wāṣil thought that one of the parties involved in the battle of the camel was culpable, although it cannot be known which party. Their verdict was modelled on the legal verdict of *liʿān*, in which it is declared that either the man or wife is culpable for adultery but that identifying the culpable one is impossible. Applying this legal model allows one to safeguard the reputation of the companions of the Prophet (van Ess 1992: 272). Furthermore, van Ess goes to great lengths to show that the political neutrality of Wāṣil and ʿAmr was not confined to their judgement about the past, but can also be seen in their attitude to contemporary political upheavals. Thus, Wāṣil and the majority of his followers practised political neutrality in a world of competing political claims (van Ess 1992: 339). ʿAmr's political neutrality was tied to his sense of social justice and distrust of the ruling elite—by which he distanced himself from those in power (van Ess 1992: 295–6). Van Ess expanded Madelung's clarification of the reported encounter between ʿAmr and the second ʿAbbāsid caliph al-Manṣūr (r. 754–75 CE), an encounter that had been misunderstood by Nyberg, and implied a close connection between the two in which ʿAmr acted as a mentor to al-Manṣūr and showed support for the ʿAbbāsids (van Ess 1992: 287–8). Van Ess explains that their encounter rather expresses al-Manṣūr's apprehension of ʿAmr's authority as a leader of the Qadariyya in Basra during a time when al-Manṣūr was concerned about the Qadariyya's participation in the revolt of Muḥammad b. ʿAbd Allāh al-Nafs al-Zakiyya (d. 145/762–3) and his brother Ibrāhīm. He argues that these reports show instead that al-Manṣūr was keen to persuade ʿAmr to maintain the political neutrality that he had shown during the turmoil at the end of the Umayyad caliphate (van Ess 1992: 287–94).

For van Ess, political neutrality was the one element that ties Wāṣil to ʿAmr while allowing them to disagree on theological matters and to have different doctrinal priorities (van Ess 1992: 341). Yet van Ess's view that it is political neutrality that defined the beginning of the Muʿtazila is complicated by the evidence he notes about the opposing political orientation of the group first labelled Muʿtazila who participated in the revolt of al-Nafs al-Zakiyya after the death of ʿAmr; it is this group that is said to have formed the kernel of the army that led the revolt (van Ess 1992: 327–8). Additionally, aside from their view on justice (*qālū bi-l-ʿadl*), almost nothing is known about the doctrines of these Muʿtazilites of the revolt (van Ess 1992: 328). But if indeed we must accept this group as Muʿtazila, then we must also ask: why would the first group (in these sources) to be recognized as Muʿtazila take a political stance so contrary to the ideals of both ʿAmr and Wāṣil? Clearly much remains unknown, and is needed to explain this contradiction in the very first decades of the movement.

There is one key difficulty in the narrative van Ess weaves of the movement: the issue of the encounter between Wāṣil and ʿAmr, its manner and context. There is ample evidence that they knew each other: Wāṣil was married to ʿAmr's sister, and they were both weavers. More importantly they both attended the circle of al-Ḥasan al-Baṣrī. Van Ess seems inclined to accept the evidence in the poetry of Ṣafwān al-Anṣarī, that speaks of ʿAmr as a student of Wāṣil (van Ess 1992: 259). Van Ess, however, is reluctant to accept that there was a turning point at the start of the movement, in which ʿAmr converted to Wāṣil's doctrine after a debate the two held on the doctrine of the intermediate rank (van Ess 1992: 256–7). Based on his analysis of the content of the arguments of Wāṣil and ʿAmr, van Ess argues that the latter's views on the grave sinner match those of the Bakriyya, a group of followers of al-Ḥasan that flourished in the second part of the second/eighth century, and were projected back to Wāṣil and ʿAmr (van Ess 1992: 257). Van Ess rejects Madelung's defence of the validity of this story based on a work entitled 'About what occurred between him [Wāṣil] and ʿAmr b. Ubayd' (*Kitāb mā jarā baynahu wa-bayna ʿAmr b. ʿUbayd*); he believed the work to have circulated around the same time as the report (van Ess 1992: 256; Madelung 1965: 12).

Van Ess thought that it was Wāṣil's intellectual leadership, especially his mastery of *kalām* and his formulation of the doctrine of the intermediate rank (discussed in Section IV), that ushered in the new movement. While ʿAmr's contribution was in opening up the Basran community to Wāṣil, who was an outsider (van Ess 1992: 254), doctrinally and intellectually, van Ess argues, he did not contribute to the movement in any innovative manner.

Wāṣil and ʿAmr's students held intellectual profiles as divergent as those of their teachers (van Ess 1992: 310). ʿAmr's students were mainly traditionists, while the majority of Wāṣil's students were jurists, whose aims focused on religious disputations (van Ess 1992: 302). After the death of their master, Basra was no longer a friendly environment for them, and many left for North Africa (van Ess 1992: 310–12). ʿAmr's followers split with the revolt of al-Nafs al-Zakiyya, but we have very little information about the moderate followers who did not participate (van Ess 1992: 321). All this leaves yet another gap in the narrative of the movement's origin, this time between the immediate students and the first generation after the early Muʿtazila of the second half of the second/eighth century. The reports that the early Muʿtazilī Abū l-Hudhayl al-ʿAllāf received the teachings of Wāṣil through ʿUthmān al-Ṭawīl (d. 150/767) cannot be taken at face value (van Ess 1992: 313–14).

Among the threads van Ess pursues in tracing the history of the movement, the one he is most certain about is Wāṣil's contribution as a preacher and his mastery of *kalām*. In reaching this conclusion, van Ess was influenced by early Muʿtazilī accounts of Wāṣil. Later Muʿtazilī accounts incorporated those of the early *ahl al-ḥadīth* that favoured ʿAmr as the father of the school in order to distance al-Ḥasan al-Baṣrī from any Qadarī connection (van Ess 1992: 260–307).

IV The Doctrines

Van Ess's work on the history of the movement, as outlined above, disproved earlier less sceptical stances that date the five principles to this period. Nyberg traced the five principles to this period and considered them part of ʿAmr and Wāṣil's propaganda (Nyberg 1913–36: 791–2). Madelung also believed that all five principles go that far back, and even traced their roots, with the exception of the principle of unity, to the thought of al-Ḥasan al-Baṣrī (Madelung 1965: 18). Goldziher believed that it was impossible to trace the five principles of the Muʿtazila back to this period of their origins because he maintained that neither Wāṣil nor ʿAmr practised *kalām* (Goldziher 1910: 101–2). Nallino also denied the dating of the five principles to this period, but he made an exception for the doctrine of the intermediate rank—although he misunderstood its genesis and its content—(Nallino 1916: 448). Despite Watt's overall sceptical stance about the historicity of a period of origins, he did, however, acknowledge the attribution of the doctrine of the intermediate rank to Wāṣil (1963: 53–4). For different reasons and in different contexts than presented by Nallino, van Ess also accepted that the doctrine of intermediate rank dated to this period (van Ess 1992: 273–4).

Although van Ess's work on the history of the movement proved Madelung's positive stance about the early dating of the five principles untenable, he agreed with Madelung's analysis of the content of the doctrines of the five principles and their contextualization in earlier theological trends (Madelung 1965: 8–23). Madelung's analysis includes his correction of Nyberg's misconception about the derivation of the doctrine of the intermediate rank as a statement regarding the battling parties at the first civil war (Madelung 1965: 24–30).

According to Madelung's explanation, Wāṣil agreed with his predecessors, the Khārijites, the Murjiʾites, and al-Ḥasan in deeming the 'name' (*ism*) of someone who commits a grave sin to be a 'grave sinner' (*fāsiq*), but unlike them he did not see a 'juridical regulation' (*ḥukm*) suitable for application to them. He thus disagreed with the 'judicial regulations' (*aḥkām*) of his predecessors with regard to grave sinners. The Murjiʾites upheld the view that despite his grave sin, a sinner remains a believer. The Khārijites believed that a grave sin made a servant an unbeliever. Al-Ḥasan understood the status of the grave sinner to lie between that of a believer and an unbeliever, but in legal terms (*aḥkām*) he considered him equal to a hypocrite. For Wāṣil the regulations of his predecessors had no justification in the Qurʾān, as the characteristics of the unbeliever, believer, and hypocrite do not apply to the grave sinner. Wāṣil believed that the grave sinner, although he is a Muslim, will be punished in hell for eternity (Madelung 1965: 10–11).

Wāṣil's rejection of al-Ḥasan's legal ruling of the hypocrite as an interpretation of the status of the grave sinner indicates the degree of their differing epistemologies. Wāṣil's asceticism, unlike that of al-Ḥasan, carried no suspicion of the world. A suspicion which, in part, led to al-Ḥasan's preoccupation with the Qurʾānic category of the hypocrite that shaped his understanding of the grave sinner (van Ess 1992: 45). Al-Ḥasan's asceticism meant that access to God and belief in God had to do with fear of God (Madelung 1965: 12–13). Thus knowledge of God, because it implied fear of God, could not coexist with grave sin. He thus deemed the grave sinner as a hypocrite, someone who does not know God, who is not a Muslim. For Wāṣil, sinful behaviour could coexist with knowledge of God, because knowledge is based on reason (Madelung 1965: 13); someone who commits a grave sin remains a Muslim, since he knows God through reason, but because of his grave sin he will be punished in hell for eternity.

Moreover, although van Ess dated the doctrine of intermediate rank to Wāṣil, he remained sceptical about the presentation of this doctrine in the sources: at least a century after Wāṣil, the content of the argument became more stylized and later authors may have granted Wāṣil more originality than he deserved (van Ess 1992: 264, 266). Indeed, van Ess maintains his scepticism about other material on Wāṣil, even when he accepts the material attributed to Wāṣil's epistemology from later projections (van Ess 1992: 261, 276).

V Conclusion

Of the three angles through which the origins of the movement have been approached, the angle focusing on its history yields the most evidence, though it also remains inconclusive. Van Ess, who led the research focused on this angle, was least sceptical about the following conclusions: the beginning of the movement was tied to Wāṣil b. ʿAṭāʾ's work as a preacher and theologian; it was Wāṣil who developed the doctrine of the intermediate rank; the spread of his movement was facilitated by the local support of ʿAmr in Basra; and the doctrine of political neutrality that they shared gave identity and unity to the movement. These conclusions, as restrained as they are, however, still give rise to two issues. They do not account for the change in the political orientation of the Muʿtazila during the revolt of al-Nafs al-Zakiyya. And, given the central role of ʿAmr's asceticism, and even that of Wāṣil, van Ess's conclusions do not adequately explain its role in the beginning of the movement. These two issues invite a reconsideration of elements in Stroumsa's argument that it was asceticism rather than political neutrality that bound Wāṣil and ʿAmr together (Stroumsa 1990: 280–7). But revisiting her argument is only useful if we redefine asceticism as tolerant of different political choices, and not tied to what Stroumsa describes as an apolitical stance. If the historical material allows us to redefine the Muʿtazila's asceticism in this manner, then it can account for the political neutrality of both ʿAmr and Wāṣil and the opposite stance of their followers who fought in the revolt of al-Nafs al-Zakiyya. Such a reconsideration of the role of asceticism in the origin of the Muʿtazila awaits a wider work on the history of asceticism at the time and cannot be undertaken with a re-evaluation of the sources available on the origins of the Muʿtazila only, though a re-evaluation of these sources would be an important component of such a project. One potentially useful source that merits re-examination in this context is Abū l-Ḥusayn Muḥammad b. Aḥmad al-Malaṭī (d. 377/987), who describes a group that 'separated' (*iʿtazalū*) from al-Ḥasan b. ʿAlī (d. 49/669–70) in the aftermath of his abdication of the leadership of the community in favour of Muʿāwiya. This group declared that 'we shall occupy ourselves with learning (*ʿilm*) and worship (*ʿibāda*)'. This is the reason, al-Malaṭī adds, that they were called the 'Muʿtazila'.[10] Of

[10] See al-Malaṭī, *Tanbīh*, 29. Stroumsa notes this passage as additional evidence to corroborate Goldziher's claims about the ascetic origin of the Muʿtazila, whose orientation, especially that of ʿAmr, she describes as 'apolitical' (Stroumsa 1990: 272 n. 46). An apolitical stance does not, however, necessarily follow from the description of the group called Muʿtazila in al-Malaṭī's passage.

course the historical group spoken of here cannot be taken to be the beginning of the Muʿtazila movement. But al-Malaṭī's use of the word *'iʿtazalū'* documents two—by now established—key characteristics of the Muʿtazila movement, namely learning and worship, and it ties them to a quietist asceticism orientation that is not a principled commitment to political neutrality. If we accept the evidence of al-Malaṭī as a precedent for the political meaning of the Muʿtazila, we may be able to resolve the apparent contradiction in the political orientation between Wāṣil and ʿAmr on the one hand and the supporters of al-Nafs al-Zakiyya on the other.

References

ʿAbd al-Jabbār al-Hamadānī (*Faḍl*). *Faḍl al-iʿtizāl wa-ṭabaqāt al-Muʿtazila*. Ed. Fuʾād Sayyid. Tunis: al-Dār al-Tunisiyya li-l-Nashr, 1974.

al-Baghdādī, ʿAbd al-Qādir (*Farq*). *Al-Farq bayn al-firaq*. Ed. Muḥammad Muḥyī al-Dīn ʿAbd al-Ḥamīd. Cairo: Dār al-ṭalāʾiʿ, 2005.

Daiber, H. (1988). *Wāṣil ibn ʿAṭāʾ als Prediger und Theologe: Ein neuer Text aus dem 8. Jahrhundert n. Chr.* Leiden: Brill.

van Ess, J. (1967). *Traditionistische Polemik gegen ʿAmr b. Ubaid*. Beirut: Franz Steiner.

van Ess, J. (1971). *Frühe muʿtazilitische Häresiographie: Zwei Werke des Našiʾ al-Akbar (gest. 293 H.)*. Beirut: Franz Steiner.

van Ess, J. (1975). *Zwischen Ḥadīṯ und Theologie: Studien zum Entstehen prädestinatianischer Überlieferung*. Berlin: de Gruyter.

van Ess, J. (1987). *Une lecture à rebours de l'histoire du Muʿtazilisme*. Paris: Paul Geuthner.

van Ess, J. (1992). *Theologie und Gesellschaft im 2. und 3. Jahrhundert Hidschra: Eine Geschichte des religiösen Denkens im frühen Islam* (vol. ii). Berlin: de Gruyter.

Gilliot, C. (1990). 'Review'. *Studia Islamica* 71: 187–8.

Goldziher, I. (1887). 'Materialien zur Kenntnis der Almohadenbewegung in Nord-Afrika'. *Zeitschrift der Deutschen Morgenländischen Gesellschaft* 41: 30–140.

Goldziher, I. (1910). *Vorlesungen über den Islam*. Heidelberg: Carl Winters Universitätsbuchhandlung.

Goldziher, I. (1918). 'Arabische Synonymik der Askese'. *Der Islam* 8: 204–13.

Hārūn, ʿAbd al-Salām (1951). *Nawādir al-Makhṭūṭāṭ*, vol. 2. Cairo: Maṭbaʿat al-Saʿāda.

Ibn al-Nadīm (*Fihrist*). *Al-Fihrist*. Ed. Riḍā Tajaddud. Beirut: Dār al-Masīra, 1987.

Ibn Qutayba (*Maʿārif*). *Kitāb al-Maʿārif*. Ed. Tharwat ʿUkāsha. Cairo: Dār al-Maʿārif, 1969.

al-Jāḥiẓ (*Bayān*). *Al-Bayān wa-l-tabyīn*. 4 vols. Ed. ʿAbd al-Salām Hārūn. Cairo: Maṭbaʿat Lajnat al-taʾlīf wa-l-tarjama wa-l-nashr, 1948.

al-Jishumī (*Sharḥ*). *Sharḥ ʿuyūn al-masāʾil*. vol. 1. Ms. Ṣanʿāʾ, al-Jāmiʿ al-Kabīr, al-Maktaba al-Gharbiyya, *ʿilm al-kalām* 99.

al-Kaʿbī/al-Balkhī (*Maqālāt*). 'Maqālāt al-Islāmiyyin'. In *Faḍl al-iʿtizāl wa-ṭabaqāt al-muʿtazila*. Ed. Fuʾād Sayyid. Tunis: al-Dār al-Tunisiyya li-l-Nashr, 1974.

al-Khayyāṭ (*Intiṣār*). *Kitāb al-Intiṣār wa-l-radd ʿalā Ibn al-Rāwandī al-mulḥid*. Ed. A. Nader and H. S. Nyberg. Beirut: al-Maṭbaʿa al-Kāthulikiyya, 1957.

Madelung, W. (1965). *Der Imām al-Qāsim ibn Ibrāhīm und die Glaubenslehre der Zaiditen*. Berlin: de Gruyter.

al-Malaṭī (*Tanbīh*). *al-Tanbīh wa-l-radd ʿalā ahl al-ahwāʾ wa-l-bidaʿ*. Ed. H. Ritter. Istanbul: Maṭbaʿat al-Dawla, 1936.

al-Maqdisī (*Badʾ*). *Kitāb al-Badʾ wa-l-taʾrīkh*. Vol. 5. Ed. C. Huart. Paris: Leroux, 1916.

Massignon, L. (1954). *Essai sur les origines du lexique technique de la mystique musulmane*. Paris: J. Vrin.

Massignon, L. (1975). *La Passion de Husayn Ibn Mansûr Hallâj: martyre mystique de l'Islam exécuté à Baghdad le 26 mars 922*. Paris: Gallimard.

al-Masʿūdī (*Murūj*). *Murūj al-dhahab*. 7 vols. Ed. Ch. Pellat. Beirut: Manshūrāt al-jāmiʿa al-lubnāniyya, 1974.

Nallino, C. A. (1916). 'Sull'origine del nome dei Muʿtaziliti'. *Rivista degli Studi Orientali* 14: 429–54.

Nyberg, H. S. (1913–36). 'Al-Muʿtazila'. *Encyclopaedia of Islam*, 1st edn. Leiden: Brill, vi. 787–93.

Nyberg, H. S. (1957). 'ʿAmr Ibn ʿUbaid et Ibn al-Rawendi, deux réprouvés'. In *Classicisme et déclin culturel dans l'histoire de l'Islam*. Paris: Librairie G. P. Maisonneuve, 125–39.

Pines, S. (1936). *Beiträge zur islamischen Atomenlehre*. Berlin: A. Hein.

Radtke, B. (1990). '*Subḥānallāh!* Von der Anwendung des Münchhausen-Prinzips in der Philologie'. *Der Islam* 67: 322–59.

Schmidtke, S. (1998). 'Neuere Forschungen zur Muʿtazila unter besonderer Berücksichtigung der späteren Muʿtazila ab dem 4./10. Jahrhundert'. *Arabica* 45: 379–408.

al-Shahrastānī (*Milal*). *Kitāb al-Milal wa-l-niḥal*. Ed. W. Cureton. Leipzig: Harassowitz, 1923.

al-Sharīf al-Murtaḍā (*Amālī*). *Amālī al-Murtaḍā: Ghurar al-Fawāʾid wa-durar al-qalāʾid*. 2 vols. Ed. Muḥammad Abū l-Faḍl Ibrāhīm. Cairo: Dār iḥyāʾ al-kutub al-ʿarabiyya, 1954.

Steiner, H. (1865). *Die Muʿtaziliten oder die Freidenker im Islām*. Leipzig: S. Hirzel.

Stroumsa, S. (1990). 'The Beginnings of the Muʿtazila Reconsidered'. *Jerusalem Studies in Arabic and Islam* 13: 265–93.

Watt, W. M. (1948). *Free Will and Predestination in Early Islam*. London: Luzac & Company.

Watt, W. M. (1963). 'The Political Attitudes of the Muʿtazilah'. *Journal of the Royal Asiatic Society of Great Britain and Ireland* 1/2: 38–57.

CHAPTER 8

THE MUʿTAZILITE MOVEMENT (II)

The Early Muʿtazilites

DAVID BENNETT

I Introduction

However elusive the origins of the discipline of *kalām* may be (see Chapter 1), there is no doubt that by the end of the second/eighth century a vivacious scholastic environment had emerged which could comprise diverse and dogmatic positions on all manner of theological and philosophical questions, presented by colourful and polemical figures in public disputation or at the courts of the caliphs, in (occasionally virulent) confrontation with traditionists and jurists. Although these thinkers tended to be grouped in the centres of ʿAbbasid learning, Basra and Baghdad, their influence proved decisive for the systematization of Islamic theology as it spread throughout the world. Their disputational categories determined the nature and scope of the mature *kalām* of the great classical Ashʿarites, their conceptual concerns informed the nascent Graeco-Arabic translation movement and its philosophical progeny, and their notorious encounter with political power provided the template for the humanist outlook of countless Islamicate regimes. These were the Muʿtazilites. And yet, not a single work of speculative theology attributed to the Muʿtazilites of the formative generations (to *c.*850 CE) remains intact.[1]

[1] Large fragments which amount to truncated works have been preserved: see e.g. the work on juridical authority reconstructed as al-Naẓẓām's *K. al-Nakth* in van Ess 1972 and 2014. Most of the figures discussed in this chapter were credited with dozens of 'works' by Ibn al-Nadīm and other bio-bibliographical sources. Although titles usually began with '*kitāb*' or '*risāla*', i.e. 'book' or 'treatise', this was no indication of their substantiality: they may have been polemic pamphlets or intra-school memos at best.

II The Sources

This lack of original sources makes for some strenuous reconstruction on the part of the student of early Muʿtazilism. Muʿtazilite positions were preserved for the most part in doxographical texts, of which one of the earliest and most influential, Abū l-Ḥasan al-Ashʿarī's (260–324/873–936) *Maqālāt al-islāmiyyīn*, dates from the early fourth/tenth century. Many later reporters depended on such compilations as sourcebooks and, as Ashʿarism came to dominate the theological scene, adopted an increasingly hostile attitude to the speculative excesses of the Muʿtazilites. Whereas al-Ashʿarī presented doctrines clustered by subject (e.g. 'They disagreed about man's capacity to act', followed by numerous viewpoints) while largely eschewing editorial or doctrinal criticism, later Ashʿarites were liberal in their condemnation of the doctrines they preserved. Thus al-Baghdādī (d. 429/1037), in whose *al-Farq bayn al-firaq* the Muʿtazilites are treated successively as heretical sects whose 'abominations' are painstakingly tabulated, albeit not always carefully refuted. Throughout the medieval period, doxographical and heresiographical works were the staple genre of *kalām*, culminating in such productions as al-Shahrastānī's (d. 548/1153) famous *K. al-Milal wa-l-niḥal*.[2]

Muʿtazilites themselves preserved the doctrines of their forefathers in *ṭabaqāt* ('generations') literature, best exemplified by the *qāḍī* ʿAbd al-Jabbār al-Hamadānī's (*c.*325–415/937–1024) *Faḍl al-iʿtizāl* and Ibn al-Murtaḍā's (d. 840/1437) *Ṭabaqāt al-Muʿtazila*. Such generic works were designed to illustrate the doctrinal continuity of the movement back to the archetypes of ʿAlī b. Abī Ṭālib and the Prophet.

Some contemporary sources offer snapshots of the development of Muʿtazilite theology. The great litterateur al-Jāḥiẓ (d. 255/868), for example, devoted a substantial portion of his *K. al-Ḥayawān* to the exposition of al-Naẓẓām's physical theory; the Syriac Christian Job of Edessa likewise noted the efforts of his early third/ninth-century contemporaries in Baghdād. Fossilized remains of third/ninth-century disputational topics may be lifted from al-Khayyāṭ's (*c.*220–300/835–913) *K. al-Intiṣār*, a refutation of Ibn al-Rāwandī's refutation of al-Jāḥiẓ's epitome of Muʿtazilite theory (the latter two texts are lost, but Ibn al-Rāwandī's arguments are quoted before being subjected to detailed criticism).

In short, the hermeneutical situation can be vexing. The shrillness of the invective applied by a detractor does not necessarily indicate an unfaithful reading; nor does school-affinity guarantee reliability. The fragments can be gnomic, as it is doctrines, not arguments, which are preserved. Ossified and out of context, the questions discussed in the doxographies do not always make sense to a modern reader, as when, for example, between questions about how the earth is not always plummeting and whether there is fire latent in wood, al-Ashʿarī slips the following:

> They disagreed about whether motion was at rest or not. Most theorists said: That is impossible. Some said: When a body comes to be in a place and remains there for two moments, its motion becomes a resting. (*Maqālāt*, 327)

[2] The historiography of Islamic heresiography is now conveniently analysed in van Ess 2011. In Bennett 2013, I have attempted to show how careful navigation of the source material can produce new readings of the original positions and their reception.

III Representative Scholarship

Although many of these sources are inaccessible for non-specialists, the twentieth century saw a succession of Western scholars' elucidation of early Islamic theology generally, and the earliest exponents of *kalām* in particular, some of which remain seminal texts in the field (Wolfson 1976, Pines 1936, Watt 1973). A few scholars have attempted detailed assessments of individual figures (for Abū l-Hudhayl, see Frank 1966 and 1969; for Muʿammar, see Daiber 1975). Appended to this chapter is a selective list of such treatments, but special mention must be made here of J. van Ess's *Theologie und Gesellschaft im 2. und 3. Jahrhundert Hidschra* (1991–7; referred to as *TG* hereafter), which is the authoritative account of the period. Not only has van Ess translated hundreds of pages of fragments collected from hundreds of sources and conveniently arranged according to individual thinkers, thereby providing the raw material for any assessment of the philosophical and theological positions discussed below, but he has also provided an exhaustive account of the bibliographical and biographical evidence for every named figure engaged in theology in the eighth to ninth centuries CE. The inquisitive reader will begin (and quite possibly end) every investigation with these volumes.

IV The Individuals

Traditionally, the foundation of the Muʿtazilite movement is attributed to two figures, Wāṣil b. ʿAṭāʾ (d. 131/748) and ʿAmr b. ʿUbayd (80–144/699–761), both of whom were Basrans associated with al-Ḥasan al-Baṣrī (see Chapter 7). ʿAmr seems to have come on board only after the death of al-Ḥasan. The appellation 'Muʿtazila' was regarded as having something to do with their 'withdrawal' (*iʿtizāl*) from the latter's circle, but Goldziher's argument that it had to do rather with the founders' asceticism has been convincingly resurrected.[3] The association with al-Ḥasan in doxology and biography highlighted the perceived importance of free will (Qadarism) to the Muʿtazilite project.

The generation of Wāṣil and ʿAmr's immediate students has not fared well in the doxographical tradition,[4] but by the end of the eighth century CE, several extraordinary figures represented the movement in Basra; Muʿtazilite theorists were beginning to make a foothold in Baghdad at the court of Hārūn al-Rashīd, and would come to prominence under al-Maʾmūn when the latter established court at Baghdad (see below). The most important were Ḍirār b. ʿAmr (*c.*110–200/728–815), who was old enough to have studied directly under Wāṣil and ʿAmr, and who established himself in Baghdad after 170/786; al-Aṣamm (d. *c.*200/816), who succeeded Ḍirār as a head of the 'school' in Basra;

[3] By Stroumsa 1990, who also provides the sources for the 'withdrawal' thesis and for Goldziher's evidence; see also Gimaret's article on 'Muʿtazila' in the *Encyclopaedia of Islam*, 2nd edn., for a handy summary of explanations of the name.

[4] On the decades following the two 'founders' death, see *TG* ii. 310–81.

Abū l-Hudhayl (*c.*135–227/752–841), not as famous as his contemporaries at the time, but now considered the formative figure of early Muʿtazilism; Muʿammar b. ʿAbbād (d. 215/830); Bishr b. Muʿtamir (d. 210/825), who studied under Muʿammar and other students of Wāṣil and ʿAmr before returning to Baghdād where he was essentially the head of the local Muʿtazilites; and al-Naẓẓām (*c.*148–230/763–845, with much variation), the nephew of Abū l-Hudhayl. The influence of this generation alone was sufficient to cement the reputation of Muʿtazilism in the history of Islamic theology; Gimaret may have been a tad cute in referring to it as the 'heroic' period,[5] but his comparison to the notable Pre-Socratics is apt insofar as the memory of these theologians is preserved almost exclusively in testimonia.

Al-Naẓẓām and Abū l-Hudhayl achieved some notoriety in the court of al-Maʾmūn in Baghdād (i.e. after 204/819), and Bishr had been with the caliph-to-be in Marw during the civil war. But even before al-Maʾmūn's reign, Muʿtazilites were bound up in the lore concerning the ʿAbbasid court. Although he would occasionally imprison theologians with troublesome doctrines, Hārūn al-Rashīd was a sympathetic caliph: the so-called literary and philosophical salons of the Barmakids hummed with Muʿtazilite theory.[6] Although Wāṣil and ʿAmr had been known for their asceticism, in Baghdad the Muʿtazilites typified the cosmopolitan and sophisticated environment at court; al-Naẓẓām in particular was an avid consort of the libertine poet Abū Nuwās and a master to al-Jāḥiẓ. Many of the early Muʿtazilites were accomplished poets, and their ideas permeated the ʿAbbasid literary landscape.

In rewriting their own history, later Muʿtazilites contrived to excise suspicious characters such as Ḍirār from their genealogy. Other figures who stood on the edges of the Muʿtazilite tradition include the Rāfiḍī Hishām b. al-Ḥakam (d. *c.*179/795), who was a frequent polemical opponent of Abū l-Hudhayl,[7] the suspected *zindīq* Abū ʿĪsā al-Warrāq, and Ibn al-Rāwandī. Nevertheless, it is evident that they were involved in the theological discourse of the Muʿtazilites, as many of their ideas are clearly cognate: in the *Maqālāt*, for instance, Hishām and Ḍirār appear regularly in the discussion of *daqīq* issues, although al-Ashʿarī does not include them among mainstream Muʿtazilites.[8]

V The *Miḥna*

The Muʿtazilites have come to be known as 'rationalizing' theologians, employing the methods of Christian disputation in order to argue in defence of the Muslim faith. In what follows, we will present the outstanding features of their theology in order to demonstrate that their aims were more comprehensive than apologetics. The overwhelming

5 In 'Muʿtazila' (see n. 3).

6 For an illuminating study of al-Masʿūdī's account of such salons, which he uses as a setting for a great panel discussion on the nature of love, see Meisami 1989.

7 On Hishām's role as polemical foil, and his relation to the early Muʿtazilites generally, see Madelung 1979. Cf. also Madelung 2014.

8 Various figures—Murjiʾites, Khārijites, and others—featured in the Muʿtazilite *Umfeld* (as van Ess calls it) who would not make it into the traditional *ṭabaqāt* literature (*TG* iv. 123–77).

bulk of evidence for Muʿtazilite doctrine as preserved in hostile or friendly doxographers concerns natural philosophy, divine attributes, and human action.[9] It will be seen that the interrelation of these topics amounted to a system of philosophy in its own right, even if it admitted interpretive agility on the part of its practitioners. After this early period, Muʿtazilism experienced a protracted scholastic phase, with distinct schools emerging (those of Baghdad and Basra), which will be the subject of a subsequent chapter (see Chapter 9): the later development was characterized by an increasing receptivity to immaterial modes of being in the explanation of motion, action, etc. It should be mentioned, however, that the early Muʿtazilites are most famous among historians of thought for their involvement in al-Maʾmūn's *miḥna* (trial, or 'persecution' to its victims), in which their position on divine attribution was taken up as state ideology to combat the growing influence of the Ḥanbalites. Their position was crystallized in the insistence that the Qurʾān be considered created, as opposed to co-eternal with God. The context of this doctrine will be considered below (Section IX) in our discussion of the divine attributes, but readers interested in its history specifically can still do no better than consult Madelung 1974.

VI The Five Principles

In encyclopedias of religion, the Muʿtazilites are credited with a pedagogically satisfying five-point programme: the so-called 'five principles'[10] by which Muʿtazilites were known by later adherents and detractors alike. They are as follows:

- *tawḥīd*, the unicity of God
- *ʿadl*, the justice of God
- *al-waʿd wa-l-waʿīd*, the 'promise and the threat', i.e. of eternal punishment or reward
- *al-manzila bayn al-manzilatayn*, the 'state in between', i.e. regarding the status of the Muslim sinner
- *al-amr bi-l-maʿrūf wa-l-nahy ʿan al-munkar*, the command to do right and prohibition of its contrary.[11]

But of course, these were not the sort of principles which would sufficiently distinguish Muʿtazilites from Murjiʾites[12] or, for that matter, any Muslim: these were not the sort of

9 When heresiographers like al-Baghdādī and al-Shahrastānī collected the doctrines of the early Muʿtazilites, the majority of the testimony had to do with natural philosophy: it was their physical doctrines which roused the censure of their critics.

10 These 'five principles' are said to go back to Abū l-Hudhayl.

11 This was used to justify individuals' policing of each other's morality.

12 The principle of the 'intermediate position', *al-manzila* …, was specifically an elaboration and refinement of Murjiʾism, and as such could be considered a distinguishing claim.

principles one would need to nail to a church-door. Rather they functioned as categories for theological dispute: under *ʿadl*, for example, came the typically Muʿtazilite theodicy, insisting upon the responsibility of man for his own actions. Moreover, they could not be construed to form a creed: on crucial religious issues, such as the nature and duration of heaven and hell, disagreements were the norm.

However pleasing these five principles may be to the taxonomist, the elaboration of Muʿtazilite doctrine fluctuated as it developed. Many of their positions on the natural, human, and divine spheres of reality became significant problems in the development of Islamic theology and came to demand the attention of the burgeoning philosophical movement. Although it has long been accepted by specialists, it is worth emphasizing that the 'classical' period of Islamic philosophy (al-Fārābī, Ibn Sīnā, et al.) owes as much of its conceptual foundations to the Muʿtazilites as it does to the Graeco-Arabic translation movement. As R. M. Frank put it, the '*logos* of the system of Avicenna ... can only be understood from within the Islamic tradition which preceded it, not that of classical antiquity'.[13] As Muʿtazilite thought became more sophisticated, however, certain peculiar aspects of their cosmology became entrenched in an increasingly baroque terminology and a difficult, not to say counter-intuitive, set of physical principles. For one thing, they were atomists.

VII The Atom

But they were a queer sort of atomists.[14] Not only did they not agree on any single typology of the atom, but some denied it outright: al-Naẓẓām is remembered as upholding the infinite divisibility of bodies against his contemporaries. Indeed, there was a bewildering array of Muʿtazilite conceptions of the 'particle which cannot be subdivided' (*al-juzʾ alladhī lā yatajazzaʾ*), i.e. the atom, insofar as it related to the composite body and was (or was not) capable of bearing accidents.

The term used for particle (*juzʾ*) was, for some Muʿtazilites, replaced with *jawhar*—a term which would become the typical philosophical term for substance in the hylomorphic analysis. This is not entirely surprising: the *jawhar* in both systems was the primary entity which could bear physical properties and change. Similarly, the term for the individual property inhering in the atom, *ʿaraḍ*, accident, was shared with the philosophers.

[13] Frank 1966: 9 n. 19; for a case study, see Adamson 2003. The influence of Muʿtazilism was not limited to Muslim audiences: for its reception in medieval Jewish thought (especially the Karaites), for example, see Vajda 1973.

[14] Pines 1936 remains the outstanding study of the subject; cf. van Ess 2002 for its continuing relevance. Dhanani 1994 and Sabra 2006 devote considerable attention to the Muʿtazilite contributions on the topic. Langermann 2009 proposes that atomism was received mainly through translations from Galen, who had criticized the theory; it may have been adopted by early theologians on the principle that the enemy of my enemy is my friend. Another recent analysis of the role of atomism in Islamic theology is to be found in Daiber 2012: 14f.

By the time of the great *kalām* systematic theologians, atoms and accidents were by definition the exclusive constituents of the universe (that is, of everything that exists besides God);[15] the underlying physical theory which produced *kalām* atomism and laid the seeds of occasionalism in Islamic thought was developed by the early Muʿtazilites. To be sure, such a system could vary immensely depending on the precise sense in which its concepts were explicated. The cosmological point remained, however: the contents of the universe were discrete, contingent, and admitting of two primary categories of being (that which inheres, and that in which stuff inheres). By discrete, we mean that they can be distinguished from one another. By contingent, we mean that their existence can be related to divine causality. We will see below (Section X) how various Muʿtazilites experimented with this model, but we should notice first of all that it is an exhaustive model: there could be nothing in the temporal universe which did not belong to the category of either atom or accident. Problems immediately arose (as Aristotle had foreseen) when it came to composite natures (or even the nature of composition itself—*taʾlīf*: should it inhere in two distinct atoms yielding a body, or supervene in the already constituted body?), states of being, psychological attributes, and so on. Indeed, the Muʿtazilite insistence on some form of atomism or another had serious implications on their philosophy of action and sense perception, as we will see at the end of this chapter.

The basic objections to atomism were acknowledged: for example, if one atom touches two others (as would be necessitated in the case of atoms with extension), surely it must have two sides, and therefore be further divisible. Mathematical and kinematic objections, such as those raised by al-Naẓẓām, did not seem to hinder the early Muʿtazilites, however.[16] If the number of constituent particles required to form a body, for instance, varied from two, six, eight, and thirty-six to an innumerable quantity, or if the mode of inherence of accidents (in particles or bodies as a whole) was a matter of debate, the principal dichotomy between primary entities and their accidents remained.

Abū l-Hudhayl had posited a minimum of six particles (corresponding to the directions in which another particle might be encountered) making up the body, with individual particles bearing only the properties of 'existing' (*kawn*)[17] and 'touching' (*mumāssa*); the accidents proper, colours, tastes, scents, etc., inhere in the body once it is so constituted (*Maqālāt*, 302f.). Aware of the geometrical objections to indivisible particles, he denied that they had spatial extension (*Maqālāt*, 314).[18] Hishām b. al-Ḥakam had defined the body as that which is 'existent, a thing, and self-subsistent' (*Maqālāt*,

[15] See e.g. al-Baghdād, *Uṣūl*, 33. The introduction of the void would have to wait until later Muʿtazilites and Abū Bakr al-Rāzī.

[16] Dhanani 1994 provides an exhaustive account of arguments for and against atomism in later *kalām*.

[17] *Kawn* became an important technical term for later Muʿtazilites, referring to a 'state of being'. It is clear that Abū l-Hudhayl was involved in this terminological evolution, for he allowed 'motion, rest, and isolation to apply to the indivisible particle' (*Maqālāt*, 315), although he apparently did not specify these properties as *akwān*; indeed, he denied it (355).

[18] He seems to have denied that extension is a property even for composite bodies (*Maqālāt*, 315). The problem of spatial extension led to some strange atomist claims: for example, that the indivisible particle only has one side (*Maqālāt*, 316).

304).[19] Al-Naẓẓām regarded all accidents as bodies in themselves, reserving the category of accident for motion alone (*Maqālāt*, 347). Indeed, his theory of interpenetrating property-bodies, organized as classes of *jawhar*s, included a material spirit-quality (*rūḥ*) and seems to have done away with any notion of substrate whatsoever.[20] Ḍirār considered accidents to be the constituent parts (*abʿāḍ*) of bodies (*Maqālāt*, 345).[21] 'Body is location', said ʿAbbād ibn Sulaymān (d. *c.*250/864) (*Maqālāt*, 305).

This welter of positions reflected broad disagreement about the most elemental conditions of nature. Looking at a specific quince, for example, Abū l-Hudhayl would affirm a constituted body with real parts, in the whole of which certain properties of sweetness, wetness, etc. inhered. Al-Naẓẓām would affirm the manifest (*ẓāhir*) presence of a set of primary entities (sweetness, wetness, quince-colour, etc.) together with their latent, suppressed opposites, currently invisible but ready to emerge under foreordained circumstances. Ḍirār would affirm an indefinite collection of constituent parts arranged adjacently, presumably in such a fashion that all the wetness wouldn't suddenly leak out.

Once the properties of bodies (or atoms) were distinguished, they had to be correlated to a system of causality which would serve to explain change in the natural world. There were three general approaches that could be considered: (1) accidents were caused directly (and continuously) by God; (2) some accidents could proceed naturally from their substrate, thereby obviating the need for divine intervention in natural processes; or (3) certain accidents could be related to the causal efficacy of the human agent. We will discuss the third possibility, and its problematic relationship to the first, later in this chapter (Section X), when we arrive at human action. It is in regard to the caused or created nature of things that the peculiar accidents of 'being created', 'remaining', and 'perishing' come to the fore, for if an accident is to persist, it should persist by virtue of some further accident.[22]

Muʿammar had claimed that physical properties emerge from the body by virtue of the body's natural disposition: 'When the particles are combined, the accidents are necessitated. [The particles] perform them according to what their nature necessitates; each particle performs in itself the accidents which inhere in it' (*Maqālāt*, 304; see also 405). Causality in al-Naẓẓām's system of latency and manifestation seems also to have been somewhat obscure, resting on the natural proclivity of certain properties to arise. A typical case study for the explanation of causality was the case of the conflagration of cotton. In al-Naẓẓām's system, the heat and light of fire would have to overpower the predominating non-combustible qualities of the cotton.[23]

19 As we will see below, Hishām also said that God is a body in this sense.

20 On al-Naẓẓām's theory of interpenetration and latent properties, its implications, and its reception, see Bennett 2013.

21 He apparently even considered motions and rest to be *abʿāḍ*; he may have had similar ideas about psychological qualities, such as the capacity to act—the sources offer conflicting accounts.

22 It was in this context that the term *maʿnā* was employed as a causal impetus for some state or accident.

23 The cotton test-case (for al-Naẓẓām's explanation, see al-Jāḥiẓ, *Ḥayawān*, 5.20f.) became a canonical problem: see the 17th Discussion of al-Ghazālī's *Tahāfut*.

Accidents were taken to be momentary by their nature as inhering attributes: should they endure or perish, something must provoke them. The 'remaining' of accidents, *baqā'*, became a tricky consideration, being an attribute applied to accidents. On the question of whether the remaining thing remains by virtue a remaining, as scholastic a point as can be imagined, al-Ashʿarī isolates no fewer than eight *kalām* positions (most of them attributed to specific Muʿtazilites). Just as he had claimed that the existence of a thing is precisely God's saying 'be!' to it, Abū l-Hudhayl made remaining and perishing functions of God's direct command to remain or to perish respectively. Muʿammar insisted on an infinite chain of 'remainings' and 'perishings', adding, curiously, that it is impossible for God to annihilate all things. But most of the Muʿtazilites seemed uncomfortable with adding layers of existential accidents (*Maqālāt*, 366f.).[24] It was the continuous need for re-creation of each atom which led to the doctrine now known as 'Occasionalism'.[25]

In their haste to make all accidents concrete (if not actually bodies themselves, as with al-Naẓẓām), some Muʿtazilites made the very 'createdness' of things, their *khalq*, a super-added quality. Abū l-Hudhayl solved this by making accidents part of the created structure of the thing they qualified: thus, a thing's extension, colour, etc. were simply the thing created as such: extended, coloured, etc. God's creation or reiteration (*iʿāda*) of some accident or other is not identical to the accident itself: *khalq* is simply a function of God's creative (or sustaining) causality (*Maqālāt*, 363f.). Many modal properties could be reduced thereby, just as Hishām had called motions and other acts 'attributes' (*ṣifāt*), but not in the sense of accidents, which, for him, were bodies; he used this strategy to deal with the divine attributes (*Maqālāt*, 344). The analysis of motion as a discrete accident, instantaneous and, as it were, atomic, left open (as always with the Muʿtazilites) the possibility of asserting the exact opposite: sure enough, al-Ashʿarī preserves a position going back to Jahm b. Ṣafwān (see Chapter 3) that motions are in fact bodies, since 'whatever is not body is God, and there is nothing like Him' (*Maqālāt*, 346).

VIII Dualism, Greek, Indian and Iranian Influences

Jahm, of course, was no Muʿtazilite, and his introduction in this context is jarring. Less so, however, is the presence of Dualist groups: on questions of motion, sensible properties, and mixture, their positions are intermingled with those of the Muʿtazilites. It was no accident

24 Al-Naẓẓām avoided the problem: qualities, for him, were 'bodies which persist over time' (al-Khayyāṭ, *Intiṣār*, 36).

25 Much more might be said about the mechanics of accidents remaining. A classic case study was that of the stone suspended in air, just before its (inevitable) descent. At one point, its accident of upward motion is removed and replaced by one of downward plummeting. This moment provoked considerable speculation: see *Maqālāt*, 310ff.

that al-Ashʿarī includes reports of doctrines of the Dualists when listing Muʿtazilite physical doctrines. When discussing the classes of primary entity, for example, he gives the general Muʿtazilite position (in this case, attributed to al-Jubbāʾī, that there is only one type of primary entity, and, it is implied, primary entities only differ by virtue of the accidents which inhere in them), but proceeds to mention those who believe in a multiplicity of classes of primary entity: the Dualists (here, *ahl al-tathniyya*) with two, light and dark classes; the Marcionites (*al-Marqūniyya*) with three, for (although al-Ashʿarī does not elaborate on this) they posited a third principle between Light and Darkness;[26] the 'proponents of the elemental natures' (*aṣḥāb al-ṭabāʾiʿ*)[27] with four, for the elemental natures themselves (hot, cold, wet, dry); and another unnamed group who added *rūḥ*, spirit (*Maqālāt*, 308f.).

The inclusion of Dualist and Dahrī (generally, 'materialist') positions is a regular feature in most of our sources: al-Khayyāṭ is usually defending some Muʿtazilite or other against Ibn al-Rāwandī's accusations of Dualist or Dahrī tendencies, and specific Dualist doctrines are often cognate with those of the Muʿtazilites.[28] Certainly no Muʿtazilite would posit dual principles of light and darkness directing the fate of the cosmos, but the general Dualist approach to nature and the mixture of properties bore an unmistakable resemblance to that of the Muʿtazilites. Such accusations as those levelled by Ibn al-Rāwandī thus had some justification; moreover, the popular association of *zindīq* behaviour with the poets and literati of the ʿAbbasid court could not have helped matters. There were even more concrete connections: Hishām, for one, was associated with one Abū Shākir al-Dayṣānī, so-named because he represented a school of thought which went back to Bardesanes, the third-century CE heresiarch; latter-day proponents of Bardesanes's philosophy were called Dayṣāniyya. Although Hishām wrote extensively *against* Dualists, it cannot be denied that his physical theory resembled theirs.[29] The Dayṣāniyya espoused interpenetration like Hishām and al-Naẓẓām, denied incorporeal creatures, and called colours bodies. Curiously conflating Naẓẓāmian metaphysics with Hudhaylian reluctance to concretize modes of being, they said that colours *are* tastes, and tastes *are* scents,[30] but they only differ in the mode of their perception.[31]

The 'proponents of the elemental natures' mentioned above, that is, the Dahriyya,[32] the Dualists, and the early Muʿtazilites, were participants in a broad materialistic trend,

[26] See ʿAbd al-Jabbār, *Mughnī*, 5: 17 among other sources for a fuller account of the Marcionites; they were always listed along with the Dualists.

[27] See Crone 2010 for the case that Dahriyya and *aṣḥāb al-ṭabāʾiʿ* are equivalent labels.

[28] The taxonomy of Dualist heresies was appropriated from Syriac sources, notably Ephrem (306–73 CE), and survived long after Dualism could realistically be considered a doctrinal threat.

[29] On Hishām's relationship with Abū Shakir, see *TG* i. 354f.

[30] Hishām's assertion that God's colour *is* His taste and His taste *is* His scent, etc., is unmistakeably Dayṣānī.

[31] Gutas 1998 made a rather strong case for Dualist involvement in the development of *kalām*; see also now Ali 2012.

[32] As before, I refer the reader to Crone 2010, where it is claimed that 'not only were the Dahrīs real, they clearly played a major role in the formulation of Muʿtazilite doctrine' (81); Crone 2012 is now the authoritative study of the historical Dahrī movement.

syncretic and trans-confessional, breaching the temporal limits of late antiquity. It has long been realized that Muʿtazilite atomism was not simply a recasting of Greek antecedents; Iranian intermediaries and Indian influences have been explored, and the field remains open for deeper comparative assessments.[33]

IX God and Attributes

The Muʿtazilite struggle to qualify precisely the accident–body relationship reflects their concern with the divine attributes. 'All of the Muʿtazilites agree', writes al-Ashʿarī, 'that God is one, and that there is nothing like Him.' On behalf of 'all Muʿtazilites', al-Ashʿarī affirms God's seeing and hearing, but denies any physical properties, be they appropriate to extended bodies or simply attributes of some quality or other. The quintessential Islamic attributes of God are all affirmed: 'He is always knowing, powerful and living' (*Maqālāt*, 155f.). This passage has been called the '*credo* of Muʿtazilism ... and a declaration of negative theology' (Alami 2001: 27f.). Indeed it was their reluctance to admit *tashbīh*, anthropomorphism, which distinguished them from their Ḥanbalite rivals in the third/ninth century. At one level, they refused to admit any distinct attribute as co-eternal with God, for fear of *shirk*: thus, the Qurʾān must be either indistinct from God or created. But this required a new technique of attribution, which affirmed the Qurʾānic account of the divine reality without insisting on the corporeality of His hands, for example.

Oddly, this new technique entered the Muʿtazilite repertoire by way of Hishām b. al-Ḥakam, who was also known for positing that God is a body: a giant, spherical body, a 'radiant light ... a pure ingot shining like a pearl in every direction'. He is a 'body not like other bodies' (*Maqālāt*, 32f.). As strange as the descriptions provided by Hishām may seem, they came with a crucial caveat regarding attribution. For Hishām, attribution was neither identical to the thing described nor *not* so: God's attributes (*ṣifāt*) belong to God, but without any inherence as one would expect in the case of accidents (*Maqālāt*, 37f).[34]

With respect to God being knowing (*ʿālim*), a number of problems had to be resolved. Is God knowing in the same way that a human is knowing? If God is knowing, is there an object of His knowledge? Since the nature and condition of existents is necessarily changing and even inevitably ceasing, should it be said that God's knowledge of them is susceptible of change or non-existence? And if God knows something regardless of its current existence, does that not lead by some argumentation to a position of absolute predestination? The Muʿtazilite encounter with these questions was provocative, and ran afoul of the literalism of the Ḥanbalites.

[33] On the suggestion of Indian (Buddhist) sources, see Pines 1936 and van Ess 2002: 24f.

[34] Hishām's reasoning was made easier by his denial of accidents generally.

Sorting the meaning of the proposition 'God is knowing' was evidently a scholastic endeavour: no Muʿtazilite could avoid it. Wāṣil had apparently denied the separate reality of the divine attributes (see Wolfson 1976: 112, 125), but as with Jahm, there was a danger of retreating to a Neoplatonic God, removed from all His objects of knowledge and power. This would soon be taken up by the 'Necessary Being' of the philosophers, and the Muʿtazilites seemed wary of that route. It was taken up, however, by Ḍirār (as always, an outlier, and doomed to be removed from the Muʿtazilite roster), who had reformulated the proposition as a negative attribution: 'the meaning of "God is knowing" is that He is not unknowing; the meaning of "God is powerful" is that He is not powerless; the meaning of "God is living" is that He is not lifeless' (*Maqālāt*, 166).[35]

Hishām b. ʿAmr al-Fuwaṭī (d. *c.*218/833), a marginal figure among the Muʿtazila, nevertheless offered the clearest account of the problem: 'I do not say that God is always knowing with respect to things; rather, He is always knowing that He is One and does not have a second. If I were to say He is always knowing with respect to things, I would be positing that they were always with God' (*Maqālāt*, 158). When ʿAbbād took the plunge, asserting God's unceasing knowledge of all primary entities and their accidents, he was obliged to admit that primary entities and accidents are what they are prior to their existence: yet he took pains to deny that bodies, 'created things', and effects, are what they are prior to their existence. When asked whether a particular existent thing was what it was before it was, if you will, he denied it; when asked if it was not what it was before it was, he said: 'no, I do not say that either' (*Maqālāt*, 159).

By far the most elegant case was made by Abū l-Hudhayl, whose doctrine 'was to become the predominant and most influential among all the branches of the Muʿtazila' (Frank 1969: 452). God was taken to be knowing, powerful, and living 'by virtue of a knowledge [or power or life, respectively] which *is He Himself*' (*Maqālāt*, 165).[36] Effectively Abū l-Hudhayl had removed the prospect of a discrete accident inhering in God, marrying Hishām b. al-Ḥakam's attribution technique to Ḍirār's negative assertion: 'When I assert that God is knowing, I affirm knowledge for him, and I deny ignorance with respect to Him, regardless of whether the object of knowledge exists' (*Maqālāt*, 165). R. M. Frank's study of Abū l-Hudhayl's doctrine remains a masterpiece in the field; his thesis that whereas Christians and philosophers approached the notion of God through the mind, through how one knows of Him, Abū l-Hudhayl approached it through 'the nature of the createdness of the material world', an observation that epitomizes the Muʿtazilite inclination generally. The human subject's knowledge *of* God was not the issue—nor even knowledge of one's self, for, as Frank put it, in the Muʿtazilite

[35] These three attributes exerted a peculiar hold on early *kalām*, rather like the transcendentals on the Latin scholastics. In an influential 1956 article (revised as part of Wolfson 1976: 112ff.), Wolfson argued that, given the lack of insistence upon the 'reality' of the divine attributes in the Qurʾān, Neoplatonic and Christian antecedents must have been an influence.

[36] The novelty of this approach seems to have impressed even Ibn al-Rāwandī: see al-Khayyāṭ, *Intiṣār*, 59. Frank discusses the possibility of an Aristotelian influence, 1969: 455 n.7. Ashʿarite heresiographers like al-Baghdādī were quick to derive the absurd conclusion that God would then be identical to a specific object of His knowledge: see *Farq*, 127.

'framework there is no central and essential reality such as the "soul" which is the principle of life' (Frank 1969: 462, 464).

X Acts and Man

If the distinction between God and His attributes informed Muʿtazilite cosmology down to the lowly atom, the tools they developed in its service proved equally productive when it came to philosophical anthropology.

By virtue of their theodicy resting on divine justice (*ʿadl*), the Muʿtazilites became known as *Qadariyya*, proponents of human free will—but their position on the precise operation of the will, the power (*qudra*) to act, was not without nuance. Once the cosmology had been reduced to a simple dichotomy of bodies and accidents, the *metaphysical* phenomena of human experience had to be explained. Human agency, although guaranteed by divine justice, had to be squared with the absolute power of God, to be sure, but the nature and reality of the human act itself required special analysis if it were to be to coordinated with an atomistic outlook, regardless of God's causal stature. Moreover, the attribution approach to concrete atomic theory threatened the very category of 'human': for Ḍirār, for example, the human is resolved into a composition of 'colour, taste, scent, capacity-to-act (*quwwa*), and the like; they are "man" when they are combined, and there is no *jawhar* besides these things' (*Maqālāt*, 330). For al-Naẓẓām, the category 'man' was likewise empty: man is rather the *rūḥ*, spirit, 'interpenetrating and intertwined' with those *other* property-bodies manifest in the place of the human body (*Maqālāt*, 331).[37] The spirit upon which Muʿtazilites based their anthropology was decidedly material, a subtle body (in al-Naẓẓām's expression) which could not benefit from the super-sensible or immaterial status of the philosophers' *nafs* ('soul'). There were exceptions: al-Muʿammar's man is 'not in a place in reality, and it does not touch anything—nor does anything touch it. It cannot have motion or rest or colours or taste, but it can have knowledge, capacity-to-act, life, volitions, and aversions. It moves this body by volition and disposes of it freely, but does not touch it' (*Maqālāt*, 331f.). Crucially, he describes the 'visible human body' as man's *āla*, 'tool', employing precisely the same term used to translate *organikon* in the *De anima*.[38]

Al-Naẓẓām described the supervening human qualities—having power, living, knowing—as belonging to man by virtue of his essence (*dhāt*) (*Mughnī*, 11: 310), just as Hishām and others had negotiated the divine attributes: they are qualities just as 'burning' qualifies the heat of fire. Sense perception, then, could not be resolved along

[37] The expression 'intertwined' in the context of a subtle material spirit suggests a Lucretian pedigree. An extensive discussion on the Muʿtazilite definitions of man is preserved in ʿAbd al-Jabbār, *Mughnī*, 11: 310ff.

[38] That is, Aristotle's famous definition of the soul as the first *entelecheia* of *sômatos phusikoû organikoû*.

hylomorphic lines: there could be no immaterial faculties for the reception and representation of forms. Instead, al-Naẓẓām proposed that 'the perceiving agent does not perceive a thing by means of vision: rather vision leaps into the perceiving agent, interpenetrating it'.[39] Perception, for the material spirit, is a matter of mixture.[40] Since *qudra*, whether taken as the power to perform a specific act, or as the capacity to act in general, cannot be resolved into this materialistic scheme, there is no prior awareness or volition regarding particular acts: 'every act proceeds from man suddenly (*ʿalā l-mufājiʾa*); he has no will for it beforehand, nor any mental representation (*tamthīl*)—indeed, it is out of a natural impulse (*gharīza*)'.[41] Admittedly, this is an isolated report, but it does not sound like a ringing endorsement of intelligent, willed human action.

Yet all Muʿtazilites were supposed to adhere to a strict acknowledgement of human free will: man is 'the creative, originating, generating agent in reality—not metaphorically speaking' (*Maqālāt*, 539). Only Ḍirār explicitly said otherwise, claiming that both man and God are the agents of man's acts: 'acts are created, and the single act belongs to two agents: one of them creates it, and that is God; the other acquires it, and that is man. God is the agent of the acts of men in reality, and men are their agents in reality' (*Maqālāt*, 281). Ḍirār introduced the concept of acquisition, *iktisāb*, which was to become so important for Ashʿarite analyses of action. If al-Naẓẓām's physical theory and Ḍirār's anticipation of Ashʿarite equivocation on free will were exceptional, the resolution of human action according to an atomist scheme introduced a new set of problems. Acts and instances of knowledge had to be considered as concrete accidents or bodies or relinquished into the semi-real ocean of attributes with no predicative substance.

Muʿtazilite theory of human action (and, by extension, human knowledge) came to rest on the manipulation and application of a few key concepts. First of all, objects of knowledge (*maʿlūmāt*) were not considered as forms to be abstracted: rather the epistemology would deal with distinct instances of knowledge about objects (*ʿilm*). These could be coordinated with the atomic make-up of man, whether as interpenetrating property-bodies or superadded constituents of the perceiver. Second, the act itself had to be analysed according to its concrete presence: thus the first discussions of the notorious doctrine of *tawallud*, the secondary generation of effects, had to do with the production of real *asbāb* (causes, sing. *sabab*) outside of man's immediate domain. Each *sabab* acted as an engine generating effects, such that (in the famous example) an archer shooting an arrow generated a series of causes impelling the arrow in its flight: should the archer be killed before his arrow reached its target, the causal chain would preserve his agency. Thus, a human could be said to perform the pain inflicted upon another—an effect that otherwise would have to be relegated to God's causal

[39] *Maqālāt*, 384: note the terminology of the 'leap', *yaṭrifu*, to leap, n. *ṭafra*, which is largely remembered by scholars only insofar as it was employed in his critique of atomism.

[40] Perception by mixture was also advocated by Hishām, whose God perceived sublunar objects by means of blending 'rays contiguous with him proceeding into the depths of the earth' (*Maqālāt*, 33). On Hishām as al-Naẓẓām's source for perception by interpenetration, see *TG* i. 365ff.

[41] al-Maqdisī, *Badʾ*, 2: 126.

authority. As an added twist, the corresponding theory of non-action (*tark*: omission of some act) became equally atomized: individual instances of *tark* were considered, and the question was raised as to whether it was possible to simultaneously abstain from more than one act. It may be said that Muʿtazilites pursued theodicy, too, to the atomic level.

The early Muʿtazilites were altogether a stimulating bunch. Their programme was not monolithic, nor merely apologetic. Ensconced in the philosophical and theological traditions bequeathed to them by diverse antecedents, they were creative elaborators of the Qurʾānic revelation. Although their assays into physical and psychological speculation met with opprobrium, the notes they sounded resonated across sectarian, cultural, and confessional borders: considering even a few of their doctrines as we have done here, we must excavate thought buried in layers of interpretation. They allowed that one may know 'that God created the colours of arsenic, even if one does not know that God created the colours and sweetness of the melon' (*Maqālāt*, 395).

References

ʿAbd al-Jabbār al-Hamadānī (*Faḍl*). *Faḍl al-iʿtizāl*. Ed. F. Sayyid. Tunis: al-Dār al-Tūnisiyya li-l-Nashr, 1974.

ʿAbd al-Jabbār al-Hamadānī (*Mughnī*). *Al-Mughnī fī abwāb al-tawḥīd wa-l-ʿadl*. General editor Ṭāhā Ḥusayn. Vols. 4–9, 11–17, 20. Cairo: Wizārat al-thaqāfa wa-l-irshād al-qawmī, al-Idāra al-ʿāmma li-l-thaqāfa, n.d.

Adamson, P. (2003). 'Al-Kindī and the Muʿtazila: Divine Attributes, Creation and Freedom'. *Arabic Sciences and Philosophy* 13: 45–77.

Alami, A. (2001). *L'Ontologie modale: étude de la théorie des modes d'Abū Hāšim al-Ǧubbāʾī*. Paris: J. Vrin.

Ali, Gh. (2012). 'Substance and Things: Dualism and Unity in the Early Islamic Cultural Field'. Ph.D. dissertation, University of Exeter.

al-Ashʿarī (*Maqālāt*). *Kitāb Maqālāt al-islāmiyyīn*. Ed. H. Ritter. 4th edn. Berlin: Klaus Schwarz, 2005.

al-Baghdādī (*Farq*). *Al-Farq bayna l-firaq*. Ed. M. ʿAbd al-Ḥamīd. Cairo: Muḥammad ʿAlī Subayḥ, 1964. (English translation: K. C. Seelye, *Moslem Schisms and Sects*, New York, 1920.)

al-Baghdādī (*Uṣūl*). *Uṣūl al-dīn*. Istanbul: Madrasat al-Ilāhīyāt bi-Dār al-Funūn al-Tūrkiyya, 1928.

Bennett, D. (2013). 'Abū Isḥāq al-Naẓẓām: The Ultimate Constituents of Nature are Simple Properties and *Rūḥ*'. In M. Bernards (ed.), *Abbasid Studies IV: Proceedings of the 2010 Meeting of the School of Abbasid Studies*. Exeter: Gibb Memorial Trust, 207–17.

Crone, P. (2010). 'The Dahrīs According to al-Jāḥiẓ'. *Mélanges de l'Université Saint-Joseph* 63: 63–82.

Crone, P. (2012). *The Nativist Prophets of Early Islamic Iran*. Cambridge: Cambridge University Press.

Daiber, H. (1975). *Das theologisch-philosophische System des Muʿammar ibn ʿAbbād as-Sulamī*. Beirut: Franz Steiner.

Daiber, H. (2012). *Islamic Thought in the Dialogue of Cultures: A Historical and Bibliographical Survey*. Leiden: Brill.

Dhanani, A. (1994). *The Physical Theory of Kalām: Atoms, Space, and Void in Basrian Muʿtazilī Cosmology*. Leiden: Brill.

van Ess, J. (1972). *Das Kitāb an-Nakt des Naẓẓām und seine Rezeption im Kitāb al-Futyā des Ǧāḥiẓ: Eine Sammlung der Fragmente mit Übersetzung und Kommentar.* Göttingen: Vandenhoeck & Ruprecht.

van Ess, J. (1991–7). *Theologie und Gesellschaft im 2. und 3. Jahrhundert Hidschra: Eine Geschichte des religiösen Denkens im frühen Islam*. 6 vols. Berlin: De Gruyter. (*TG*)

van Ess, J. (2002). 'Sixty Years after: Shlomo Pines's *Beiträge* and Half a Century of Research on Atomism in Islamic Theology'. *Proceedings of the Israel Academy of Sciences and Humanities* 7: 19–41.

van Ess, J. (2011). *Der Eine und das Andere: Beobachtungen an islamischen häresiographischen Texten*. 2 vols. Berlin: de Gruyter.

van Ess, J. (2014). 'Neue Fragmente aus dem *K. an-Nakt* des Naẓẓām'. *Oriens* 42: 20–94.

Frank, R. M. (1966). *The Metaphysics of Created Being According to Abū l-Hudhayl al-ʿAllāf: A Physical Study of the Earliest Kalām.* Istanbul. (Reprinted in D. Gutas (ed.), *Philosophy, Theology and Mysticism in Medieval Islam.* Aldershot: Ashgate Variorum, 2005.)

Frank, R. M. (1969). 'The Divine Attributes According to the Teaching of Abū l-Hudhayl al-ʿAllāf'. *Le Muséon* 82: 451–506. (Reprinted in D. Gutas (ed.), *Philosophy, Theology and Mysticism in Medieval Islam*. Aldershot: Ashgate Variorum, 2005.)

Gutas, D. (1998). *Greek Thought, Arabic Culture*. London: Routledge.

Ibn al-Murtaḍā (*Ṭabaqāt*). *Ṭabaqāt al-Muʿtazila*. Ed. S. Diwald-Wilzer. Wiesbaden: Harrassowitz, 1961.

al-Jāḥiẓ (*Ḥayawān*). *Kitāb al-Ḥayawān*. Ed. A. M. Hārūn. 7 vols. Cairo: Muṣṭafā al-Bābī al-Ḥalabī, 1938–45.

al-Khayyāṭ (*Intiṣār*). *Kitāb al-Intiṣār*. Ed. A. N. Nader (with French translation). Beirut: al-Maṭbaʿa al-Kāthūlīkiyya, 1957.

Langermann, Y. T. (2009). 'Islamic Atomism and the Galenic Tradition'. *History of Science* 47: 277–95.

Madelung, W. (1974). 'The Origins of the Controversy Concerning the Creation of the Koran'. In J. M. Barral (ed.), *Orientalia Hispanica* [Festschrift Pareja]. Leiden: Brill. (Reprinted in *Religious Schools and Sects in Medieval Islam*, 1985.)

Madelung, W. (1979). 'The Shiite and Khārijite Contribution to Pre-Ashʿarite Kalām'. In P. Morewedge (ed.), *Islamic Philosophical Thought*. Albany, NY: SUNY Press, 120–39.

Madelung, W. (2014). 'Early Imāmī Theology as Reflected in the Kitāb al-Kāfī of al-Kulaynī'. In F. Daftary and G. Miskinzoda (eds.), *The Study of Shīʿī Islam*. London: I. B. Tauris, 465–74.

al-Maqdisī (*Badʾ*). *Kitāb al-Badʾ wa-l-taʾrīkh*. Ed. C. Huart. 6 vols. Paris: E. Leroux, 1899–1919.

Meisami, J. S. (1989). 'Masʿūdī on Love and the Fall of the Barmakids'. *Journal of the Royal Asiatic Society* 2: 252–77.

Pines, S. (1936). *Beiträge zur islamischen Atomenlehre*. Berlin: Hein.

Sabra, A. I. (2006). 'Kalām Atomism as an Alternative Philosophy to Hellenizing Falsafa'. In J. E. Montgomery (ed.), *Arabic Theology, Arabic Philosophy: From the Many to the One. Essays in Celebration of Richard M. Frank*. Leuven: Peeters, 191–272.

al-Shahrastānī (*Milal*). *Kitāb al-Milal wa-l-niḥal*. Ed. W. Cureton. London: Society for the Publication of Oriental Texts, 1964. Ed. M. Badrān. 2 vols. Cairo: Maṭbaʿat al-Azhar, 1951–5. (French translation: D. Gimaret, G. Monnot, and J. Jolivet, *Livre des religions et des sects*. 2 vols. Louvain: UNESCO, 1986–73.)

Stroumsa, S. (1990). 'The Beginnings of the Muʿtazila Reconsidered'. *Jerusalem Studies in Arabic and Islam* 13: 265–93.

Vajda, G. (1973). 'Le "Kalām" dans la pensée religieuse juive du Moyen Âge'. *Revue de l'histoire des religions* 183: 143–60.

Watt, W. M. (1973). *The Formative Period of Islamic Thought*. Edinburgh: Edinburgh University Press.

Wolfson, H. A. (1976). *The Philosophy of the Kalam*. Cambridge, MA: Harvard University Press.

CHAPTER 9

THE MUʿTAZILITE MOVEMENT (III)

The Scholastic Phase

SABINE SCHMIDTKE

THE early phase of the Muʿtazila was characterized by individual thinkers some of whom were primarily concerned with a select number of theological issues rather than attempting to formulate a comprehensive doctrinal system. Around the turn of the fourth/tenth century the movement entered a new 'scholastic' phase. Two principal school traditions evolved at this stage, the so-called 'School of Basra' and the 'School of Baghdad'. The beginnings of this phase coincide with the lives of Abū ʿAlī al-Jubbāʾī (d. 303/915–16) as the leader of the School of Basra and Abū l-Qāsim al-Kaʿbī al-Balkhī (d. 319/931) as the head of the School of Baghdad. The scholastic phase was characterized by coherent doctrinal systems addressing the whole range of the Muʿtazilite tenets, viz. divine unicity (*tawḥīd*) and justice (*ʿadl*), which include discussions about God's nature, His essence, and His attributes, God's relation to the created world, the ontological status of ethical values (objectivism versus subjectivism) and related epistemological questions, the nature of created beings, man's autonomy to act and his accountability for his actions, and the question of the origin of evil; eschatological issues such as promise and threat (*al-waʿd wa-l-waʿīd*) and the intermediate position of the grave sinner (*al-manzila bayn al-manzilatayn*); themes such as prophecy and the imamate; and the notion of commanding good and prohibiting what is reprehensible (*al-amr bi-l-maʿrūf wa-l-nahy ʿan al-munkar*) which by now had lost much of its earlier prominence among the Muʿtazilite tenets (Cook 2000). At the same time, ontology, cosmology, natural philosophy, and biology constituted important parts of the various doctrinal systems. Issues belonging to these fields were typically discussed under the rubric of 'subtleties of *kalām*' (*laṭāʾif al-kalām*) (Dhanani 1994). Apart from purely doctrinal issues, the majority of Muʿtazilites of this period were also engaged in exegesis (*tafsīr*) and legal theory (*uṣūl al-fiqh*) and, at times, *ḥadīth* transmission, and their works in these domains had often a far longer-lasting impact than was the case with their writings in *kalām*.[1]

I The Early Generation

Abū ʿAlī Muḥammad b. ʿAbd al-Wahhāb al-Jubbāʾī hailed from Jubbāʾ in Khūzistān (for a detailed biography, see Gwynne 1982). As a youth he came to Basra where he studied with Abū Yaʿqūb Yūsuf b. ʿAbd Allāh al-Shaḥḥām who is singled out as his most significant teacher. Al-Shaḥḥām is stated to have been 'the youngest and most perfect' of the students of Abū l-Hudhayl al-ʿAllāf (van Ess 1991–7: iii. 291, iv. 45–54). Abū ʿAlī left Basra sometime between 257/871 and 259/873 for Baghdad where he spent the next two decades. Sometime before 277/890, or possibly before 279/892, Abū ʿAlī left Baghdad and took up residence in ʿAskar Mukram in Khūzistān, where he remained until his death in 303/915–16. Since none of Abū ʿAlī's numerous writings is extant (Gimaret 1976; 1984a; 1984b)[2] his doctrine can only be reconstructed through the scattered references in later works, particularly those by Muʿtazilite authors as well as the *Maqālāt al-islāmiyyīn* of Abū ʿAlī's former student Abū l-Ḥasan al-Ashʿarī (d. 324/935–6), the eponymous founder of the Ashʿariyya who around the year 300/912–13 repented from Muʿtazilite doctrines. Abū ʿAlī saw himself in the tradition of the thought of Abū l-Hudhayl whose doctrines he set out to revive and to refine, thereby formulating a comprehensive theological system (Frank 1978, 1982; Gimaret 1980: 3ff., 39ff.; Perler and Rudolph 2000: 41ff.), yet not without disagreeing with Abū l-Hudhayl's view regarding a number of issues; he is known to have composed a treatise entitled *Masāʾil al-khilāf ʿalā Abī l-Hudhayl* in which he presumably treated the issues with regard to which he disagreed with Abū l-Hudhayl (on Abū l-Hudhayl's thought, see Frank 1966; 1969; van Ess 1991–7: iii. 209–96).

Among Abū ʿAlī's students was his son, Abū Hāshim ʿAbd al-Salām b. Muḥammad b. ʿAbd al-Wahhāb al-Jubbāʾī (b. 247/861 or, more likely, 277/890; d. 321/933). He disagreed with his father on a number of doctrinal issues and when, following the death of his father and despite his young age,[3] Abū Hāshim claimed succession of the latter

[1] The extant fragments of exegetical works by Muʿtazilite authors have been collected and edited by Khiḍr Muḥammad Nabhā in the series *Mawsūʿat tafāsīr al-Muʿtazila* (Beirut: Dār al-kutub al-ʿilmiyya, 2007–). For legal theory, Ibn Khaldūn (d. 808/1406) lists four books that he considers to be 'the basic works and pillars of this discipline'—among them two by Muʿtazilite authors, viz. ʿAbd al-Jabbār al-Hamadānī's (d. 415/1025) *K. al-ʿUmad* and Abū l-Ḥusayn al-Baṣrī's (d. 436/1044) *Kitāb al-Muʿtamad* (Ibn Khaldūn, *Muqaddima*, 3/28f.). For examples of *ḥadīth* transmission among Muʿtazilites, see Ansari 2012.

[2] With the exception, however, of his *Kitāb al-Maqālāt*. See Ansari 2007. H. Ansari and W. Madelung are currently preparing a critical edition of the text.

[3] ʿAbd al-Jabbār apologizes for mentioning Abū Hashim as the first of the generation of Abū ʿAlī's disciples. Considering his age, ʿAbd al-Jabbār admits, he should be dealt with later as he was younger than many of the persons mentioned in this generation (ʿAbd al-Jabbār, *Faḍl*, 304).

as the leader of the Basran Muʿtazila, he was opposed by fellow-students of his father. Muḥammad b. ʿUmar al-Ṣaymarī (d. 315/927) apparently led the group of adversaries of Abū Hāshim, a group which became later known as the Ikhshīdiyya, being named so after al-Ṣaymarī's student, Abū Bakr Aḥmad b. ʿAlī b. Maʿjūr al-Ikhshīd (or: al-Ikhshād) (d. 320/932 or 326/937).[4] This would explain Ibn al-Nadīm's statement that 'after the death of Abū ʿAlī, the leadership culminated with him [al-Ṣaymarī]' (Dodge 1970: i. 427). Yet despite significant differences of opinion between Abū Hāshim and his father Abū ʿAlī which were systematically described by later authors, such as ʿAbd al-Jabbār al-Hamadānī (on him, see Section III) in his lost work *al-Khilāf bayn al-shaykhayn* (ʿUthmān 1968: 62;[5] Heemskerk 2000: 22 n. 32), both shaykhs were of utmost significance to the later followers of the Basran Muʿtazila and are constantly referred to—much more frequently than is the case with other later representatives of the School.

Abū Hāshim seems to have spent most of his life in ʿAskar Mukram and in Basra. In 314/926–7 or 317/928–9, he took up residence in Baghdad where he died in 321/933. He is known to have authored numerous works, none of which have survived. As is the case with his father, the most detailed information about his writings is provided by the numerous scattered references in later Muʿtazilite works. These also testify to a significant development of his thought throughout his lifetime, especially concerning issues belonging to the subtleties of *kalām*. Among his independent works, the principal ones were *al-Abwāb* (or: *Naqḍ al-abwāb*), *al-Jāmiʿ* (or: *al-Jāmiʿ al-kabīr*), and *al-Jāmiʿ al-ṣaghīr*. He further authored numerous tracts that were concerned with specific doctrinal issues, and he composed responsa as well as refutations that were partly directed against opponents in theology as well as against philosophers, such as *al-Naqḍ ʿalā Arisṭūṭālīs fī l-kawn wa-l-fasād* (Gimaret 1976; 1984a).

Abū l-Qāsim al-Kaʿbī al-Balkhī hailed from Balkh in Khurāsān in the north-east of Iran (on him, see van Ess 1985; el Omari 2006). His teacher in *kalām* was Abū l-Ḥusayn al-Khayyāṭ (d. *c*.300/913), author of the *Kitāb al-Intiṣār*, with whom he studied in Baghdad and whose doctrinal views he continued to develop following his return to Khurāsān. Although he was highly regarded in his homeland as the leading theologian, there is no indication that al-Kaʿbī's school played any significant role after his lifetime. The most renowned Muʿtazilī theologian to have been raised in the tradition of al-Kaʿbī's doctrines was Abū Rashīd al-Nīsābūrī, who moved at some stage of his life to Rayy, where he became the most prominent student and follower of ʿAbd al-Jabbār. Abū Rashīd's work on the differences between the views of the Basrans and the Baghdadians, *Kitāb al-Masāʾil fī l-khilāf bayn al-Baṣriyyīn wa-l-Baghdādiyyīn* (see Section III), constituted a major source for the reconstruction of al-Kaʿbī's thought. Beyond (Sunnī) Muʿtazilism, al-Kaʿbī's views had a major impact on Transoxanian

[4] Next to nothing is known about the doctrinal views of al-Ṣaymarī and Ibn al-Ikhshīd; see Mourad 2007; Thomas 2010. Another follower of Ibn al-Ikhshīd was ʿAlī b. ʿĪsā al-Rummānī (d. 384/994) who composed a Qurʾān commentary as well as several tracts on the miraculous character of the Qurʾān (all extant); cf. Kulinich 2012.

[5] ʿUthmān's identification of Ms. Vatican ar. 1100 as containing a manuscript of the text is erroneous.

Ḥanafism and specifically on Abū Manṣūr al-Māturīdī (d. 333/944) who considered al-Kaʿbī's Muʿtazilite teachings as an important challenge and at the same time a source of inspiration (Rudolph 2015; see also Chapter 17). Moreover, al-Kaʿbī's doctrines also significantly influenced Imami and Zaydi theologians, such as al-Shaykh al-Mufīd (d. 413/1022) and al-Hādī ilā l-ḥaqq Yaḥyā b. al-Ḥusayn (d. 298/911) (see Chapters 11 and 27). Their writings constitute another important source for the reconstruction of al-Kaʿbī's doctrines, whose works, with the exception of his *Kitāb al-Maqālāt* (van Ess 2011: i. 328–75), have not come down to us.

II The Teachings of the Bahshamiyya

Abū Hāshim is primarily known for his notion of 'states' (*aḥwāl*) which he developed in an attempt to formulate a conceptual framework for analysing the ontology of God and created beings within the established Muʿtazilite view of divine attributes (Gimaret 1970; Frank 1971a, 1971b, 1978, 1980; Alami 2001; Thiele 2013). For the Muʿtazilites, God's attributes cannot be entities distinct from Him without violating the idea of His oneness. On the other hand, they considered that God can neither be identical with His attributes without undermining His absolute transcendence. For this purpose, Abū Hāshim adapted the concept of 'state' (*ḥāl*, pl. *aḥwāl*) employed by the grammarians for a complement in the case of the accusative occurring in a sentence which consists of a subject and a form of *kāna* (to be) as a complete verb. In this case, the accusative cannot simply be taken as a predicate to *kāna* as it would be if *kāna* were incomplete and transitive; it must rather be understood as a *ḥāl*. On this foundation, Abū Hāshim elaborated a system of five different categories of 'states'. These categories are distinguished by the respective ontological basis which brings forth their actuality. According to Abū Hāshim, a 'state' is not an entity or a thing (*dhāt, shayʾ*) and can thus neither be said to be 'existent' (*mawjūd*) nor 'non-existent' (*maʿdūm*). Not being entities themselves, the 'states' can likewise not be known in isolation. Rather, things are known by virtue of their being qualified by a state. Thus, Abū Hāshim speaks of the 'actuality' (*ḥuṣūl*) of the 'states' and their 'initiation' (*tajaddud*) while he refrains from asserting for them a 'coming to be' (*ḥudūth*) which would imply their coming into existence. The first category is the attribute of essence (*ṣifa dhātiyya*/ *ṣifat al-dhāt*/ *ṣifat al-nafs*) through which things (*dhawāt*) differ from each other. The atom (*jawhar*), for instance, is described as an atom by virtue of its very being; predicating that an atom is an atom consequently defines it as it is in itself. The same applies to God, who is described by His attribute of essence as what He really is, and who differs from other entities that are not described as such. The second category of 'states' are the essential attributes (*ṣifāt muqtaḍāt ʿan ṣifat al-dhāt*) which are by necessity entailed by the attribute of essence as soon as things become existent. The attribute of essence of being an atom, which is attached to an essence, entails the occupying of space (*taḥayyuz*) of the atom whenever it exists. Thus, occupying a space is an essential attribute of an atom. With regard to God, the specific divine attribute of essence entails His essential attributes. These are His being powerful, knowing, living, and existing. Thus, God must necessarily and eternally be described by these attributes which cannot cease as long as His eternal attribute of essence lasts. Man's attributes of being powerful, knowing, and living differ in their quality from the corresponding attributes in God. They belong to the third category of 'states' which gain actuality by virtue of an 'entitative determinant' (*maʿnā*) or 'cause' (*ʿilla*) in the subject. Since man's 'states' are caused by entitative determinants, which are by definition created, he cannot be described as permanently or necessarily powerful, knowing, etc. Moreover, since these determinants inhere in parts of man's body, he needs his limbs as tools for his actions and his heart in order to know. The determinant itself is therefore not sufficient to actualize man's being capable and knowing. Further conditions like the health of heart and limbs have to be fulfilled for them to serve as tools in carrying out actions or to acquire knowledge. Thus, the realms of man's capability and knowledge are limited by the natural deficiencies of his body. God, by contrast, is unconditionally powerful and knowing since His attributes of being powerful and knowing are essential attributes which do not inhere in any locus and, thus, do not require any limbs. Yet, Abū Hāshim applied this category to God when he reportedly asserted that God is willing or disapproving by virtue of a determinant which is His will or His disapproval. Since it is impossible that a determinant may inhere in God, he maintained that God's will and aversion do not inhere in a substrate (*lā fī maḥall*). The fourth category of 'states' are those which are actualized by the action of an agent (*bi-l-fāʿil*), in particular the existence of a temporal thing which is founded in its producer's capability. This category is inadmissible in God. While the existence of all created beings is considered as belonging to this category, God's existence is counted as an essential attribute entailed by His attribute of essence. The fifth category are 'states' which gain actuality neither by virtue of the essence nor by an entitative determinant (*lā li-l-dhāt wa-lā li-maʿnā*). To this category belongs the attribute of 'being perceiving' (*kawnuhu mudrikan*) which is entailed by the perceiver's being living. In regard to God, it gains actuality when the condition (*sharṭ*) of the presence of the perceptible is fulfilled. Man, in order to perceive, must possess healthy senses in addition to the existence of the perceptible. This is not required for God, whose being alive is an essential attribute. Thus, He perceives without senses.

Abū Hāshim reportedly further differed from Abū ʿAlī on the issue of how God knows things in their state of non-existence and existence. Abū ʿAlī taught that things are not things prior to their being existent since 'existence' (*kawn*) means 'being found' (*wujūd*). However, a thing may be called a thing and may be known prior to its existence insofar as it is possible to make a statement about it (Ashʿarī, *Maqālāt*, 161f.). Owing to his notion of 'states', Abū Hāshim was not confronted with the issue of whether a thing may be known prior to its existence. The attribute of essence through which it is what it is is always attached to it, regardless of whether the thing exists or not.

Abū Hāshim is further reported to have disagreed with his father who had maintained that God may inflict pain upon man for the sake of mere compensation. For Abū Hāshim and his followers, the pain itself must result in a facilitating favour (*luṭf*) either for the sufferer himself or for a morally obliged person (*mukallaf*), in addition to compensation (ʿAbd al-Jabbār, *Mughnī*, 13/390).

In regard to whether God may inflict illnesses or other calamities upon men because they are deserved, Abū ʿAlī held that illnesses inflicted upon infidels and sinners may serve either as a punishment or a trial. This punishment could, in his view, be appropriate insofar as God would render to man there and then some of the punishment he deserves in the hereafter. Abū Hāshim, by contrast, maintained that every illness inflicted by God on men, regardless of whether they are morally obliged or not, can only have the purpose of a trial and never of a deserved punishment. He supported this view by pointing to the principal difference between undeserved pains and deserved punishment: men must be content with their illnesses and bear them patiently and they are not allowed to be distressed about them just as in regard to favours which God bestows on them. This is, however, not necessary in regard to pains which are a deserved punishment. Owing to these different characteristics, man would therefore be unable to recognize whether a specific illness or calamity is inflicted upon him as a trial or as a deserved punishment. Thus, Abū Hāshim concluded, illnesses can be inflicted by God only for the purpose of trial (*Mughnī*, 13/431ff.).

Abū ʿAlī is further reported to have maintained that God may inflict pain upon man for the sake of mere compensation. In arguing against his father's position, Abū Hāshim had reportedly admitted that pain ceases to be unjust when it is compensated. Even with compensation, however, it would by itself still be futile (*ʿabath*) and thus evil and inadmissible for God. Pain inflicted by God thus must result in some kind of benefit (*maṣlaḥa*) in addition to compensation (*Mughnī*, 13/390–2; Mānkdīm, *Taʿlīq*, 493).

On the issue of the nature of passing away and restoration (*fanāʾ wa-iʿāda*) Abū Hāshim had to assert the possibility of passing away without infringing two other vital notions of his teachings. One of these was that all atoms (*jawāhir*) and most accidents (*aʿrāḍ*) endure by themselves. The second notion which he had to take into consideration was that an agent may effect only production (*ījād*) but not annihilation (*iʿdām*). This also applies to God. Thus, He can undo something only through the creation of its opposite. The solution of Abū Hāshim, therefore, was that God causes the passing away of the atoms through the creation of a single accident of passing away (*fanāʾ*). This accident is the opposite of all atoms and, thus, is capable of annihilating any atom. It must itself be existent (*mawjūd*), but it cannot inhere in a substrate (*lā fī maḥall*). Furthermore it does not endure. Most of the points of this concept had been introduced already by Abū ʿAlī. However, Abū Hāshim disagreed with his father on a number of details. In his earlier works, Abī ʿAlī is reported to have maintained that there are different types of passing away, each of which causes the annihilation of only the corresponding type of atoms. In a later version of his *Naqḍ al-tāj*, he is reported to have revised his position, stating that only one passing away is required for all atoms. Abū ʿAlī further maintained that it is reason which indicates that the atoms will in fact pass away. Abū Hāshim and his followers disagreed. If it were not for scriptural evidence, there would be no indication that the passing away will actually occur. Abū ʿAlī further rejected on principle that anything which does not subsist in a substrate may be defined as an accident. Thus he refrained from classifying passing away as an accident. Abū Hāshim and his school admitted a category of accidents which do not inhere in a substrate (Ibn Mattawayh, *Tadhkira*, 212ff.; ʿAbd al-Jabbār, *Mughnī*, 11/441ff.).

On the issue of mutual cancellation (*taḥābut*) of man's acts of obedience and disobedience upon which a person's fate in the hereafter is founded, Abū Hāshim disagreed with Abū ʿAlī about how this cancellation works. While the latter maintained that the smaller amount of reward or punishment will simply be cancelled by the larger amount, Abū Hāshim adhered to the principle of *muwāzana* which means that the smaller amount will be deducted from the larger (Mānkdīm, *Taʿlīq*, 627ff.).

Abū Hāshim furthermore disagreed with his father whether, and on what grounds, repentance is incumbent upon man for all his sins. Abū ʿAlī reportedly held that a sinner is always, by virtue of reason and scriptural evidence, obliged to repent for major and minor sins (Mānkdīm, *Taʿlīq*, 789; ʿAbd al-Jabbār, *Mughnī*, 14/393). Abū Hāshim, on the other hand, considered repentance as obligatory only for the grave sinner (*ṣāḥib al-kabīra*). In respect to minor sins, he denied that repentance is rationally obligatory and held that scriptural authority also does not definitely indicate this obligation (ʿAbd al-Jabbār, *Mughnī*, 14/394). He compared repentance for a minor sin with a supererogatory act (*nāfila*) which is not obligatory in itself. It is, however, good to perform it since it helps man to perform his duties or, in this case, to repent for his major sins.

Abū Hāshim is further reported to have held that it is impossible to repent of some sins while still carrying on with others when the penitent is aware of the evil nature of the acts he is persisting in. He reportedly argued that man repents because of the evil nature of the major sin in question. Since the characteristic of evil is shared by all major sins it would be inadmissible that one repents only of some major sins because of their evil while carrying on with others which are of the same gravity. With this position, Abū Hāshim disagreed with Abū ʿAlī, who admitted the possibility of repenting of some sins while carrying on with others. The only condition Abū ʿAlī made was that the sin repented and that which was continued must not be of the same kind (*jins*). It would, therefore, be impossible to repent of drinking wine from one pot while continuing to drink from another, whereas it would be possible to repent of drinking wine while at the same time carrying on with adultery (Mānkdīm, *Taʿlīq*, 794f.).

On the issue of *al-amr bi-l-maʿrūf wa-l-nahy ʿan al-munkar*, Abū Hāshim disagreed with his father regarding the sources of the obligation. While Abū ʿAlī maintained it to be both reason and revelation, Abū Hāshim held it to be revelation only, the only exception being that the mental anguish (*maḍaḍ wa-ḥarad*) of the spectator provides a reason for him to act in his own interest (Cook 2000: 199–201).

III The Later Bahshamiyya

The most renowned students of Abū Hāshim were Abū ʿAlī Muḥammad b. Khallād (d. 350/961?), Abū ʿAbd Allāh al-Ḥusayn b. ʿAlī al-Baṣrī (d. 369/980) (Anvari 2008; Schwarb 2011b), and Abū Isḥāq Ibrāhīm b. ʿAyyāsh al-Baṣrī. While the latter two did not apparently compose any substantial works, Ibn Khallād wrote a *Kitāb al-Uṣūl*, to which he added a commentary, *Sharḥ al-Uṣūl*. The *Kitāb al-Uṣūl/Sharḥ al-Uṣūl* have reached us embedded in two works by later Muʿtazilī authors, viz. the *Kitāb Ziyādāt Sharḥ al-uṣūl* by the Zaydī Imam al-Nāṭiq bi-l-ḥaqq Abū Ṭālib Yaḥyā b. al-Ḥusayn al-Buṭḥānī (d. 424/1033) in the recension of Abū l-Qāsim Muḥammad b. Aḥmad b. Mahdī al-Ḥasanī, which is completely preserved (Adang, Madelung, and Schmidtke 2011), and a second supercommentary or *taʿlīq* on Ibn Khallād's work by the Zaydī author ʿAlī b. al-Ḥusayn b. Muḥammad Siyāh [Shāh] Sarījān [Sarbījān] which is only partially extant (Ansari and Schmidtke 2010b). Both commentaries convey an impression of the original structure of Ibn Khallād's work, the earliest systematic Muʿtazilite *summa* that has come down to us albeit indirectly.

It is not entirely clear who succeeded Abū Hāshim as leader of the Basran school. ʿAbd al-Jabbār states that a group of well-advanced disciples (*mutaqaddimūn*) transmitted Muʿtazilite knowledge received from Abū Hāshim, mentioning only two persons by name, namely Ibn Khallād and Abū ʿAbd Allāh al-Baṣrī (ʿAbd al-Jabbār, *Faḍl*, 164). Others, such as Abū Saʿd al-Muḥassin b. Muḥammad b. Karrāma (or: Kirāma) al-Bayhaqī al-Barawqanī ('al-Ḥākim al-Jishumī', d. 494/1101) (Ms. Leiden OR 2584A, fols 119bf.) and Muḥammad b. Aḥmad al-Farrazādhī (cf. Mānkdīm, *Taʿlīq*, 24 n. 1; ʿImāra 1988: i. 87) mention Ibn Khallād as his successor. Be that as it may, Abū ʿAbd Allāh eventually became the leader of the Bahshamiyya and he was succeeded by ʿAbd al-Jabbār al-Hamadānī (d. 415/1025), the author of the comprehensive theological summa *Kitāb al-Mughnī fī abwāb al-tawḥīd wa-l-ʿadl* which is for the most part preserved, as well as other comprehensive doctrinal works (ʿUthmān 1968; Peters 1976). Originally an Ashʿarite theologian (he remained a Shāfiʿī throughout his life while the majority of his fellow Muʿtazilites of the fourth/tenth and fifth/eleventh centuries were Ḥanafīs), ʿAbd al-Jabbār had joined the Muʿtazila as a young man and eventually become a pupil of Abū ʿAbd Allāh al-Baṣrī in Baghdad. After the latter's death in 369/980, ʿAbd al-Jabbār soon came to be recognized as the new head of the Bahshamiyya. It was during his lifetime that the Muʿtazilite movement blossomed in an unprecedented manner. The Būyid vizier Abū l-Qāsim Ismāʿīl b. ʿAbbād ('al-Ṣāḥib b. ʿAbbād', b. 326/938, d. 385/995), a former student of Abū ʿAbd Allāh al-Baṣrī and an important representative of the Muʿtazila in his own right,[6] was instrumental in promoting the teachings of the Muʿtazila throughout Būyid territories and beyond, with Rayy as its intellectual centre. Especially since Muḥarram 367/August–September 977 when Ibn ʿAbbād appointed ʿAbd al-Jabbār chief judge in Būyid territories, the latter attracted a large number of students and followers, Muʿtazilites as well as Zaydīs, to Rayy, turning it into the leading intellectual centre of the movement (Reynolds 2004, 2005; Pomerantz 2010: 74ff.).[7]

[6] For an edition of the extant fragments of his comprehensive summa *Kitāb Nahj al-sabīl fī l-uṣūl*, see Madelung and Schmidtke forthcoming.

[7] Apart from works on theology, ʿAbd al-Jabbār also wrote on legal matters (e.g. his *Risāla fī dhanb al-ghība*) (see Ansari 2012: 268 n. 3) and he transmitted *ḥadīth*. His *Amālī* is preserved in manuscript; cf. Ansari 2012: 270.

ʿAbd al-Jabbār's successor as head of the Bahshamiyya was Abū Rashīd al-Nīsābūrī, who in turn was followed by Ibn Mattawayh, one of the younger students of ʿAbd al-Jabbār. Originally a follower of the doctrines of the School of Baghdad, Abū Rashīd turned towards the doctrines of the Bahshamiyya under ʿAbd al-Jabbār's influence. Among his extant works, mention should be made of his *Kitāb al-Masāʾil fī l-khilāf bayn al-Baṣriyyīn wa-l-Baghdādiyyīn*, a systematic comparison between the doctrines of the Basrans and the Baghdadis (Gimaret 2011), as well as his *Kitāb Masāʾil al-khilāf fī l-uṣūl*, a systematic theological summa which is heavily based on ʿAbd al-Jabbār's *Kitāb al-Mughnī* (Ansari and Schmidtke 2010a).[8] Abū Muḥammad al-Ḥasan b. Aḥmad Ibn Mattawayh (Matūya) joined ʿAbd al-Jabbār as a student when the latter was already advanced in age and his discipleship with the *qāḍī l-quḍāt* may have been short. This seems to be corroborated by chains of transmission in which Ibn Mattawayh is depicted as a student of Abū Rashīd, with whom Ibn Mattawayh apparently continued his studies after ʿAbd al-Jabbār's death. Ibn Mattawayh's most influential independent work is a book on natural philosophy, *al-Tadhkira fī aḥkām al-jawāhir wa-l-aʿrāḍ*, the most comprehensive of its kind among the preserved Muʿtazilite literature. The book contains a detailed chapter on atoms (*jawāhir*), followed by sections devoted to physics (*al-juzʾ wa-furūʿihi*) and detailed discussions of the various accidents. A paraphrastic commentary on the *Tadhkira* was apparently written by Ibn Mattawayh's student Abū Jaʿfar Muḥammad b. ʿAlī [b.] Mazdak (Gimaret 2008; Schmidtke 2008). Ibn Mattawayh also wrote an explicative, independent, and at times critical commentary on ʿAbd al-Jabbār's *al-Muḥīṭ bi-l-taklīf*, titled *al-Majmūʿ fī l-Muḥīṭ bi-l-taklīf*. The exact relation between ʿAbd al-Jabbār's *al-Muḥīṭ* and Ibn Mattawayh's *al-Majmūʿ* which was disputed (cf. Gimaret's introduction to vol. 2 of *al-Majmūʿ*) can be established on the basis of the numerous fragments of the *Muḥīṭ* that are preserved in the various Genizah collections which need to be critically edited (Ben-Shammai 1974).[9] Ibn Mattawayh also composed paraphrastic commentaries (*taʿlīq*) on ʿAbd al-Jabbār's *al-Jumal wa-l-ʿuqūd* and his *al-ʿUmad fī uṣūl al-fiqh* which are lost (Schmidtke 2012; Thiele 2014).

One of the last prominent representatives of the Bahshamite school was Abū Saʿd al-Muḥassin b. Muḥammad b. Karrāma al-Bayhaqī al-Barawqanī ('al-Ḥākim al-Jishumī', b. 413/1022, d. 494/1101), a Ḥanafī in law and Muʿtazilī in theology who embraced Zaydism towards the end of his life (van Ess 2011: ii. 761–75; Thiele 2012), a student of Abū Ḥāmid al-Najjār al-Nīsābūrī (d. 433/1042) who in turn had studied with ʿAbd al-Jabbār (al-Ḥākim al-Jishumī, *Ṭabaqāt*, 367). Among his numerous voluminous writings, his *Sharḥ ʿUyūn al-masāʾil*, an autocommentary on his *ʿUyūn al-masāʾil*, is of particular significance.[10] Arranged in ten parts (*aqsām*, sing. *qism*), the work is an encyclopedia of

[8] A critical edition of Abū Rashīd al-Nīsābūrī's *Kitāb Masāʾil al-khilāf fī l-uṣūl* is currently being prepared by H. Ansari and S. Schmidtke.

[9] A critical edition of ʿAbd al-Jabbār's *al-Muḥīṭ* is currently being prepared by O. Hamdan and G. Schwarb.

[10] A critical edition of *ʿUyūn al-masāʾil* and *Sharḥ ʿUyūn al-masāʾil* is currently being prepared by H. Ansari and S. Schmidtke.

Muʿtazilite theology replete with information on and quotations from earlier Muʿtazilite writings, many of which are otherwise lost, and it contains extensive parts devoted to the history of the various theological schools, especially the Muʿtazila, as well as a part dealing with legal theory.[11]

The doctrines of the Bahshamiyya proved very influential among a number of groups outside Sunnite Islam, namely the Zaydiyya, the Imāmiyya, and the Karaites. Numerous Zaydī scholars were students of representatives of the Bahshamiyya, such as the Buṭḥānī brothers al-Muʾayyad bi-llāh (d. 411/1020) and al-Nāṭiq bi-l-ḥaqq (d. c.424/1033), who studied with Abū ʿAbd Allāh al-Baṣrī and, in the case of al-Muʾayyad bi-llāh, also with ʿAbd al-Jabbār, as well as Abū l-Ḥusayn Aḥmad b. Abū Hāshim Muḥammad al-Ḥusaynī al-Qazwīnī, known as Mānkdīm Shashdīw (d. c.425/1034), who was a student of al-Muʾayyad bi-llāh, and possibly also of ʿAbd al-Jabbār (see also Chapter 10). During the sixth/twelfth century, the literary heritage of the Caspian Zaydis, including numerous Muʿtazilite works by ʿAbd al-Jabbār and his students, reached the Zaydis in Yemen. In addition to the many private libraries of Yemen, particular mention should be made of the library of the Great Mosque in Ṣanʿāʾ which originated with Imam al-Manṣūr bi-llāh ʿAbd Allāh b. Ḥamza (d. 614/1217), who founded a library in Ẓafār for which he had numerous Zaydī and non-Zaydī works from Northern Iran copied, including many Muʿtazilite works. It was from this library that the Egyptian scientific expedition, headed by Khalīl Yaḥyā Nāmī, in 1951 procured microfilms of numerous theological texts of adherents of the Bahshamiyya such as fourteen out of twenty volumes of ʿAbd al-Jabbār's *Mughnī*, Mānkdīm's critical paraphrase (*taʿlīq*) of ʿAbd al-Jabbār's *Sharḥ al-Uṣūl al-khamsa*, several works by Abū Rashīd al-Nīsābūrī, Ibn Mattawayh's critical paraphrase of ʿAbd al-Jabbār's *al-Muḥīṭ bi-l-taklīf*, *al-Majmūʿ fī l-Muḥīṭ bi-l-taklīf*, and his *Kitāb al-Tadhkira*, many of which were published in Egypt during the 1960s, thus initiating an upsurge in scholarship on the Muʿtazila (Sayyid 1974: 417–77).

Specifically Muʿtazilite Islamic ideas, such as theodicy and human free will, as well as the stress on God's oneness (*tawḥīd*) also resonated among Jewish thinkers, many of whom eventually adopted the entire doctrinal system of the Muʿtazila. The earliest attested Jewish compendium of Muʿtazilite thought is the *Kitāb al-Niʿma, The Book of Blessing*, of the Karaite Levi ben Yefet, in Arabic Abū Saʿīd Lāwī b. Ḥasan al-Baṣrī (late fourth/tenth to early fifth/eleventh century), the son of the prominent Karaite Bible exegete and legal scholar Yefet ben Eli ha-Levi (whose Arabic name was Abū ʿAlī Ḥasan b. ʿAlī al-Lāwī al-Baṣrī) (d. after 396/1006). Levi wrote the book at the request of his father as a vindication of Judaism on the basis of Muʿtazilite rational theology, but unlike his father, who disapproved of *Islamic* Muʿtazilite theology, Levi adopted the doctrines of the Muʿtazila and implicitly recognized Muḥammad as a friend of God endowed with

[11] The structure of the work is as follows: Part 1: *fī dhikr al-firaq al-khārija ʿan al-islām*; Part 2: *fī firaq ahl al-qibla wa-kayfa hādhā l-khilāf fīhā*; Part 3: *al-kalām fī dhikr al-Muʿtazila wa-rijālihim*; Part 4: *al-kalām fī l-tawḥīd*; Part 5: *al-kalām fī l-ʿadl*; Part 6: *al-kalām fī l-nubuwwāt*; Part 7: *al-kalām fī adillat al-sharʿ*; Part 8: *al-kalām fī l-waʿīd wa-l-manzila bayn al-manzilatayn wa-l-asmāʾ wa-l-aḥkām*; Part 9: *al-kalām fī l-imāma*; Part 10: *al-kalām fī l-laṭīf*.

prophethood, though ranking below Moses (Sklare 2007; Madelung 2014a). Further evidence as to when (and why) Jewish thinkers began to adopt Muʿtazilite thinking can be gleaned from the extant Jewish copies of Muʿtazilite works of Muslim representatives of the movement, as preserved in the various Genizah collections, most specifically the Abraham Firkovitch Collection of literary texts of Near Eastern Jewish communities in the National Library of Russia in St Petersburg, a collection of manuscripts of Jewish provenance most of which originally belonged to the library of the Karaite Rav Simḥa Synagogue in Cairo. Although a full inventory of the relevant collections and its Muʿtazilite materials is still a major desideratum, it seems that the writings of the Būyid vizier and patron of the Muʿtazila, al-Ṣāḥib b. ʿAbbād, constitute the earliest Muslim Muʿtazilite works, copies of which can be traced in the various Jewish collections. This suggests that the major turn towards Muʿtazilism occurred during the later decades of the tenth century (Madelung and Schmidtke forthcoming). Levi ben Yefet's *summa* was soon eclipsed by the theological writings of the Rabbanite Samuel ben Ḥofni Gaon (d. 1013 CE) (Sklare 1996) and his Karaite opponent and younger contemporary Abū Yaʿqūb Yūsuf al-Baṣīr (d. between 1037 and 1039 CE), whose *kalām* works gained an almost canonical status among the Karaites (Vajda 1985; Sklare 1995; Schwarb 2010a, 2010b, 2011a). Literary evidence suggests that Muʿtazilite ideas constituted the central doctrinal foundation of the Rabbanite community until the middle of the twelfth century. For the Karaites Muʿtazilism continued to provide a significant doctrinal framework at least through the seventeenth century, an observation that also applies to the Byzantine Karaite milieu where many of the works originally composed in Arabic were transmitted in Hebrew translation.

IV Abū l-Ḥusayn al-Baṣrī and his School

A major revision of some of the central Bahshamite notions was initiated by Abū l-Ḥusayn al-Baṣrī (d. 436/1044), one of the disciples of ʿAbd al-Jabbār who is reported to have challenged some of the views of his teacher during his lectures and eventually founded his own school (on him, Madelung 2007; Ansari and Schmidtke forthcoming).

Abū l-Ḥusayn Muḥammad b. ʿAlī b. al-Ṭayyib al-Baṣrī was born around the year 370/980 and raised as a Ḥanafī in law and a Muʿtazilī in doctrine. As is suggested by his *nisba*, he hailed from Basra. To pursue an education in medicine, Abū l-Ḥusayn had moved at some point to Baghdad, and it was in the course of his formation as a physician that he also embarked on the study of philosophy: he is known to have studied medicine and physics with Abū ʿAlī b. al-Samḥ (d. 418/1027) and Abū l-Faraj Ibn al-Ṭayyib (d. 435/1043), the leading representatives of the Baghdad School of Aristotelian philosophers.

In addition to his formation in medicine and philosophy, Abū l-Ḥusayn al-Baṣrī embarked at some point on studying dialectic theology (*kalām*) with ʿAbd al-Jabbār al-Hamadānī. Although there is no indication that Abū l-Ḥusayn had ever spent a considerable length of time outside Baghdad, he may temporarily have moved to Rayy for this purpose where ʿAbd al-Jabbār was based since 367/977. Following his return to Baghdad Abū l-Ḥusayn had revised central positions of Bahshamite *kalām* that were problematic in his view. He set these forth in his theological writings, none of which survived in Muslim circles: his *opus magnum* in this discipline is the *K. Taṣaffuḥ al-adilla*, a comprehensive work of two volumes in its final stage which he had evidently repeatedly revised over his lifetime and which had never reached completion—Abū l-Ḥusayn did not go beyond the chapter on beatific vision. The *Taṣaffuḥ* was apparently the first theological work Abū l-Ḥusayn had started to compose, critically reviewing the proofs and arguments employed in *kalām* theology. Parts of his book were published before its completion and aroused charges of heresy and even unbelief (*kufr*) as Abū l-Ḥusayn's views seemed to undermine the standard Muʿtazilite proof for the existence of God. Rather than completing the *Taṣaffuḥ*, the author now wrote a book on what he considered as the best proofs, *Ghurar al-adilla*, as evidence that he upheld the basic tenets of the Muʿtazilite creed. The work, a complete theological *summa*, eventually became his most popular work in this discipline, as is indicated by lengthy quotations from the work in a large variety of later sources (Adang 2007; Schmidtke 2013; Ansari and Schmidtke forthcoming). Abū l-Ḥusayn also composed a commentary on the *Uṣūl al-khamsa* (or *Sharḥ al-Uṣūl al-khamsa*) of his teacher ʿAbd al-Jabbār. In contrast to the *Ghurar* and the *Taṣaffuḥ*, which are regularly cited by later authors, the *Sharḥ* is rarely mentioned and no later author is known to have quoted from the work. This may suggest that the *Sharḥ*, possibly a rather succinct book, was primarily intended as a teaching manual. An extract from the work containing the section on the imamate has been preserved in a manuscript of Yemeni provenance. His most popular book was a work on legal theory, *al-Muʿtamad fī uṣūl al-fiqh* (Ansari and Schmidtke 2013).

Abū l-Ḥusayn denied the Bahshamite doctrine that accidents (*aʿrāḍ*) were entitative beings (*maʿānī* or *dhawāt*) inhering in the bodies and producing their qualities. For him, accidents constitute mere descriptive attributes (*ṣifāt*), characteristics (*aḥkām*), or 'states' (*aḥwāl*) of the body, a position that was clearly influenced by his earlier study of Aristotelian philosophy. This led him to negate the well-known Bahshamite notion of 'states', a conceptual framework to rationalize the ontological foundations of the attributes of the Divine and of created beings, as well as the related doctrine that essences (*dhawāt*, sing. *dhāt*) are 'real' or 'actual' (*thābit*) in the state of non-existence, that the 'non-existent' (*maʿdūm*) therefore is a 'thing' (*shayʾ*). In his view, the existence of a thing is rather identical with its essence, both with respect to God and created beings. Abū l-Ḥusayn also rejected the Bahshamites' position that accidents may exist without a substrate, as is the case, for example, with the divine act of will, an accident according to Bahshamite doctrine that does not inhere in God. For Abū l-Ḥusayn God's being willing is rather to be reduced to His motive (*dāʿī*) that is based on His knowledge. He also negated the Bahshamite proof for the oneness of God that is based on the argument of an assumed mutual prevention (*tamānuʿ*) of two gods. Abū l-Ḥusayn maintained that two assumed gods would have the same motives and would thus act jointly rather than preventing each other.

The notion of the reality of accidents was central for the Bahshamites' proof for the existence of God: they reasoned that knowledge of the temporality of bodies—which implied an eternal Creator—was based on the temporality of accidents. Abū l-Ḥusayn's denial of the reality of accidents led him to reject the traditional Muʿtazilite proof for the existence of God and to formulate a revised proof for the temporality of the world. It was evidently Abū l-Ḥusayn's rejection of the traditional *kalām* proof for the existence of God that scandalized his Bahshamite fellow-students of ʿAbd al-Jabbār and evoked their sharp rejection of his theological thought, rather than any of the other points of conflict between Abū l-Ḥusayn al-Baṣrī and the Bahshamites (Madelung 2006; Madelung and Schmidtke 2006, 2007; Ansari, Madelung, and Schmidtke 2015).

Abū l-Ḥusayn disagreed with the Bahshamiyya on other doctrinal questions as well. He maintained that the knowledge of man being the author of his actions is compulsory (*ḍarūrī*) rather than acquired (*muktasab*). For men know compulsorily that it is good to blame and to praise others for their actions. This, however, has as premiss the knowledge that they are the producers of their actions which is therefore likewise known compulsorily. The Bahshamites had argued that it is known compulsorily that man acts in accordance with his intention and motives. As a result of this it is known through derived knowledge that if an action were not to occur on the part of the agent whose intention the act reflects, it would have no connection with him.

This difference of opinion was rooted in Abū l-Ḥusayn's divergence from the Bahshamite notion of actions. According to his understanding, an action cannot occur but for a motive (*dāʿī*) conjoined by power. Abū l-Ḥusayn and his followers distinguish therefore between two meanings of efficacy (*ṣiḥḥa*) for capacity. Power without a motive attached to it is potentially efficacious either to produce or not to produce an act. As such, it is defined as the mere denial of the impossibility either to produce or not to produce. The actuality of the efficacy to produce a specific act requires the motive attached to it as a further condition (*sharṭ*). The function of the motive is described as that of a preponderator (*murajjiḥ*)—because of this motive a certain act preponderates over another. Abū l-Ḥusayn regarded this principle as valid with regard to both man and God. The Bahshamiyya maintained with respect to man's actions that power is the efficacy to act and that it is sufficient as such to produce an act even without a motive. Examples for this are the category of unconscious acts, such as the movement of the sleeper or the action of an inattentive agent (*sāhī*) who acts without apparent motive. Abū l-Ḥusayn is reported to have argued that even in such cases there is a motive even if the agent fails to realize it. Although they asserted that motives have an effect upon man's actions, the Bahshamites denied any causal relation between motive and the occurrence of actions. Having a motive for an action rather means that man has a better reason to perform it rather than its opposite. There is no need for a motive in their view, and contrary to what was maintained by Abū l-Ḥusayn, to turn power from potential into actual efficacy to produce a specific action (Madelung 1991).

Although Abū l-Ḥusayn was virtually ostracized by his Muslim fellow-students and later Bahshamite Muʿtazilīs because of his criticism of ʿAbd al-Jabbār, his thought left a major impact on the later development of Muslim *kalām*, well beyond the confines of the Muʿtazila.[12] Despite the increasing repression of Muʿtazilite thought during the late Būyid period and even more so under the Saljuqs, Abū l-Ḥusayn had actively engaged in teaching *kalām* during his lifetime. Ibn ʿImād al-Ḥanbalī (d. 1089/1679) reports in his *Shadharāt al-dhahab* that Abū l-Ḥusayn regularly taught Muʿtazilite doctrine in Baghdad and that he had a large circle of regular students (Ibn ʿImād, *Shadharāt*, 5: 172). The biographical sources mention numerous scholars to have studied with Abū l-Ḥusayn, including the following (for further details, see Ansari and Schmidtke forthcoming):

- Abū ʿAlī Muḥammad b. Aḥmad b. ʿAbd Allāh b. Aḥmad b. al-Walīd al-Karkhī *al-mutakallim* al-Muʿtazilī ('Ibn al-Walīd', b. 396/1005–6, d. 478/1086) (Makdisi 1963: 4, 18, 19, 20, 50, 407–9). He was Abū l-Ḥusayn's foremost pupil in *kalām* who later taught the prolific Ḥanbalī jurist and theologian Abū l-Wafāʾ ʿAlī b. ʿAqīl (d. 477/1119). Following his teacher's death, Ibn al-Walīd became the leading figure of the Muʿtazilite movement in Baghdad. His home was located in Karkh which he hardly left over the last five decades of his life and where he is reported to have secretly taught Muʿtazilite doctrine, logic, and philosophy. Only twice, in 456/1063 and 460/1067, is he reported to have publicly taught Muʿtazilite doctrines, and on both occasions he was persecuted (Makdisi 1963: 332ff., 337ff., 408).
- Abū l-Qāsim Ibn Tabbān al-Muʿtazilī (*fl.* 461/1068), possibly the son of Abū ʿAbd Allāh b. al-Tabbān al-Mutakallim (d. 419/1028) (Makdisi 1963: 409).
- Abū l-Qāsim ʿAbd al-Wāḥid b. ʿAlī b. Barhān al-ʿUkbarī al-Asadī ('Ibn Barhān', d. 456/1064), a literate and renowned grammarian who came to Baghdad, where he studied theology with Abū l-Ḥusayn (Makdisi 1963: 331, 392–4). Following Abū l-Ḥusayn's death he is reported to have continued studying *kalām* with his younger contemporary Ibn al-Walīd. Ibn Barhān is said to have been inclined towards the '*Murjiʾat al-Muʿtazila*' as he maintained, against the majority view among the Muʿtazila, that the grave sinners are not exposed to eternal punishment.
- al-Qāḍī Abū ʿAbd Allāh al-Ṣaymarī (d. 436/1045), a Ḥanafī scholar of Baghdad, who led the prayer for Abū l-Ḥusayn when the latter had died and who had also studied with him (Makdisi 1963: 170–1).

Abū l-Ḥusayn's influence continued in Baghdad into the seventh/thirteenth century, when the man of letters Ibn Abī l-Ḥadīd (b. 586/1190, d. 656/1258) mentioned both the *Ghurar* and the *Taṣaffuḥ* in his commentary on the *Nahj al-balāgha*, and he composed a commentary on the *Ghurar* that is lost. Ibn Abī l-Ḥadīd, who died either immediately before or immediately after the capture of Baghdad by the Mongols (20 Muḥarram 656/

[12] The reception of his doctrinal thought among the Zaydis and Imamis is discussed in detail in Chapters 11, 26, and 27.

28 January 1258), was a contemporary of al-Mukhtār b. Muḥammad, another follower of Abū l-Ḥusayn's doctrines in Khʷārazm.

It was apparently the grammarian, physician, and man of letters Abū Muḍar Maḥmūd b. Jarīr al-Ḍabbī al-Iṣfahānī (d. 508/1115) who had introduced the doctrine of Abū l-Ḥusayn to Khʷārazm, where it was accepted and spread by Rukn al-Dīn Maḥmūd b. Muḥammad al-Malāḥimī al-Khʷārazmī (d. 536/1141), a Ḥanafī and leading Muʿtazilī scholar of his time. Abū Muḍar may well have been Ibn al-Malāḥimī's teacher in *kalām*—other than that, the names of the latter's teachers are not attested in the available sources. The principal source for the spread of Muʿtazilism in Khʷārazm during the sixth/twelfth century can be gleaned from an incompletely preserved and still unedited biographical dictionary by the Khʷārazmī author Abū l-Karam ʿAbd al-Salām al-Andarasbānī (d. second half of the sixth/twelfth century), himself a follower of the Muʿtazila, that the author began to compile after 569/1173 (Khalidov 1974; Prozorov 1999; Prozorov 2007).

Ibn al-Malāḥimī had summarized Abū l-Ḥusayn's *Taṣaffuḥ al-adilla* in his voluminous *K. al-Muʿtamad fī uṣūl al-dīn*. In the introduction Ibn al-Malāḥimī states that he intends to complete his own work in the spirit of Abū l-Ḥusayn, but his *Muʿtamad* is only partly preserved. Following the request of his students and friends, Ibn al-Malāḥimī composed an abridgement of the *Muʿtamad*, entitled *al-Fāʾiq fī uṣūl al-dīn* (completed in 532/1137), which is completely preserved. He further wrote a refutation of philosophical doctrines, entitled *Tuḥfat al-mutakallimīn fī l-radd ʿalā l-falāsifa*, completed between 532/1137 and 536/1141, which contains numerous references to Abū l-Ḥusayn and his *Taṣaffuḥ* (Madelung 2007b; Madelung 2012). In the field of legal theory, Ibn al-Malāḥimī wrote the *K. Tajrīd al-Muʿtamad*, a work that can aptly be described as a summary of Abū l-Ḥusayn's *Muʿtamad fī uṣūl al-fiqh*, with occasional critical remarks (Ansari and Schmidtke 2013). There is no doubt that the popularity of Ibn al-Malāḥimī's theological works made Abū l-Ḥusayn's writings in this domain appear to be redundant, this certainly being the main reason why they were no longer transmitted in the Islamic world.

Ibn al-Malāḥimī in turn taught *kalām* to his colleague Jār Allāh al-Zamakhsharī (d. 538/1144) (Madelung 1986; Lane 2006, 2012; Ullah 2013; Zamakhsharī, *Minhāj*), as well as most probably to a certain Abū l-Maʿālī Ṣāʿid b. Aḥmad al-Uṣūlī, author of a *K. al-Kāmil fī uṣūl al-dīn* in which the doctrines of Abū l-Ḥusayn are systematically compared with those of the Bahshamiyya.[13] Ṣāʿid hailed most likely from Khurāsān where one of the two extant manuscripts of his *K. al-Kāmil* had originated. During the fourth/tenth to sixth/twelfth centuries, the famous Āl Ṣāʿid, a Ḥanafī family, resided in Nīshābūr, and it is possible that Ṣāʿid b. Aḥmad originated within this family, many of whose members were called Ṣāʿid. Ṣāʿid b. Aḥmad's *K. al-Kāmil* circulated among later Imami

[13] The work has been partly edited on the basis of Ms. Leiden OR 487, by E. Elshahed (al-Shahīd) (Elshahed 1983). Cf. the critical review by W. Madelung (Madelung 1985). Al-Shahīd has meanwhile published a full edition of the text ('Najrānī', *Kāmil*), again on the basis of the Leiden manuscript only. As is the case with Elshahed 1983, his introduction and edition is marred by glaring errors and misidentifications, including the author's *nisba* 'al-Najrānī'.

theologians and it was later on extensively quoted in the *K. al-Mujtabā fī uṣūl al-dīn* of the Ḥanafī scholar Najm al-Dīn Mukhtār b. Maḥmūd al-Zāhidī al-Ghazmīnī (d. 658/1260), a later follower and supporter of the doctrines of Abū l-Ḥusayn in Khʷārazm (Ibn al-Malāḥimī, *Muʿtamad*, editor's introduction; Madelung 1985). Mukhtār b. Maḥmūd had studied Muʿtazilite *kalām* with Yūsuf b. Abī Bakr al-Sakkākī (d. 626/1229), who is otherwise mostly renowned for his *K. Miftāḥ al-ʿulūm*, a work covering all linguistic disciplines.

Abū l-Ḥusayn's thought also left a major impact on Ashʿarite theologians. It was due to his influence that Imam al-Ḥaramayn Abū l-Maʿālī al-Juwaynī (d. 479/1085) formulated a proof for the existence of God that relied on the philosophical notion of contingency (Madelung 2006). By the turn of the seventh/thirteenth century, Fakhr al-Dīn al-Rāzī (d. 606/1209) states that in his time the school of Abū l-Ḥusayn al-Baṣrī and the Bahshamiyya are the last active of the Muʿtazilite schools—Fakhr al-Dīn had visited Khʷārazm, *c.*560/1164–570/1174, where he had debated with some of the local Muʿtazilī scholars. These were most probably followers of the doctrines of Abū l-Ḥusayn al-Baṣrī. Moreover, it is in view of the theological thought of Abū l-Ḥusayn that Fakhr al-Dīn thoroughly revised the Ashʿarite doctrines (Schmidtke 1991: *passim*). In doing so, he served as a model for later Ashʿarite theologians. Another telling indication of Abū l-Ḥusayn's lasting influence on Sunnī thinkers is Ibn Taymiyya (d. 728/1328). In several of his writings, most importantly his *Darʾ taʿāruḍ al-ʿaql wa-l-naql*, Ibn Taymiyya repeatedly refers to Abū l-Ḥusayn and his writings and he quotes extensively from the latter's *Ghurar al-adilla* (cf. Michot 2003: 162 and *passim*). Among later neo-Ḥanbalite theologians references to Abū l-Ḥusayn al-Baṣrī and his notions are likewise common.

It was still during his lifetime that Abū l-Ḥusayn al-Baṣrī's doctrines also came to the attention of Karaite Jews, among whom they soon found many followers. The earliest indication for this is the refutation of Abū l-Ḥusayn's innovative proof for the existence of the Creator by the leading Karaite theologian of his time, Abū Yaʿqūb Yūsuf al-Baṣīr. In this text, Yūsuf al-Baṣīr shows himself to be a staunch supporter of the Bahshamite school of ʿAbd al-Jabbār and his circle. Yūsuf al-Baṣīr also related critically to the doctrine of Abū l-Ḥusayn in another work of his that is incompletely preserved and may perhaps be identified with his *Aḥwāl al-fāʿil* (Madelung and Schmidtke 2006, 2007; Ansari, Madelung, and Schmidtke 2015).

Moreover, during the latter third of the fifth/eleventh century the authoritative Karaite theologian in Egypt, Sahl b. al-Faḍl (Yāshār b. Ḥesed) al-Tustarī, fully endorsed Abū l-Ḥusayn's criticism of the principles of the school of ʿAbd al-Jabbār and encouraged the study of his theology in the Karaite community of Egypt. Three large fragments of Abū l-Ḥusayn's most extensive work on rational theology, *Taṣaffuḥ al-adilla*, are preserved in the Firkovitch collection, presumably coming from the *genizah* of the library of the Karaite Dār Ibn Sumayḥ synagogue in Cairo. One of the fragments contains a dedication to a pious endowment to Yāshār, the son of the nobleman Ḥesed (al-Faḍl) al-Tustarī (on him, cf. Madelung and Schmidtke 2006; Schwarb 2006) and to his descendants. It is likely that the manuscript was copied during Sahl b. al-Faḍl al-Tustarī's lifetime. The copyist of another *Taṣaffuḥ* manuscript among the three is to be identified as the renowned Karaite theologian of the fifth/eleventh century, Abū l-Ḥasan ʿAlī b. Sulaymān al-Muqaddasī, who hailed from Jerusalem. Later on he became closely associated with Sahl b. al-Faḍl al-Tustarī, whom he adopted as his teacher (Madelung and Schmidtke 2006).

Although Yūsuf al-Baṣīr refers on one occasion to Abū l-Ḥusayn's other major book on theology, *K. Ghurar al-adilla*, no fragment of this work has so far surfaced in any of the Jewish *genizah* repositories. The work is known to have contained a detailed polemical section directed against the Jews on the question of the abrogation of the Pentateuch and the Hebrew Bible (Schmidtke 2008), which may explain why it was less popular among Jewish readers than his *Taṣaffuḥ*.

References

ʿAbd al-Jabbār al-Hamadānī (*Mughnī*). *Al-Mughnī fī abwāb al-tawḥīd wa-l-ʿadl*. General editor Ṭāhā Ḥusayn. Vols. 4–9, 11–17, 20. Cairo: Wizārat al-thaqāfa wa-l-irshād al-qawmī, al-Idāra al-ʿāmma li-l-thaqāfa, n.d.

ʿAbd al-Jabbār al-Hamadānī (*Faḍl*). *Faḍl al-iʿtizāl wa-ṭabaqāt al-Muʿtazila*. Ed. Fuʾād Sayyid. Tunis: al-Dār al-tūnisiyya li-l-nashr, 1393/1974.

Abū l-Ḥusayn al-Baṣrī (*Muʿtamad*). *Kitāb al-Muʿtamad fī uṣūl al-fiqh*. Ed. M. Hamidullah. Damascus: al-Maʿhad al-ʿilmī al-faransī li-l-dirāsāt al-ʿarabiyya bi-Dimashq, 1965.

Abū l-Ḥusayn al-Baṣrī (*Taṣaffuḥ*). *Taṣaffuḥ al-adilla*. The extant parts introduced and edited by W. Madelung and S. Schmidtke. Wiesbaden: Harrassowitz, 2006.

Adang, C. (2007). 'A Rare Case of Biblical "Testimonies" to the Prophet Muḥammad in Muʿtazilī Literature: Quotations from Ibn Rabban al-Ṭabarī's Kitāb al-Dīn wa-l-Dawla in Abu l-Ḥusayn al-Baṣrī's Ghurar al-adilla, as Preserved in a Work by al-Ḥimmaṣī al-Rāzī'. In C. Adang, S. Schmidtke, and D. Sklare (eds.), *A Common Rationality: Muʿtazilism in Islam and Judaism*. Würzburg: Ergon, 297–330.

Adang, C., W. Madelung, and S. Schmidtke (eds.) (2011). *Baṣran Muʿtazilite Theology: Abū ʿAlī Muḥammad b. Khallād's Kitāb al-Uṣūl and its Reception. A critical edition of the Ziyādāt Sharḥ al-uṣūl by the Zaydī Imām al-Nāṭiq bi-l-ḥaqq Abū Ṭālib Yaḥyā b. al-Ḥusayn b. Hārūn al-Buṭḥānī*. Leiden: Brill.

Alami, A. (2001). *L'Ontologie modale: étude de la théorie des modes d'Abū Hāšim al-Ǧubbāʾī*. Paris: J. Vrin.

Ansari, H. (2007). 'Abū Alī al-Jubbā'ī et son livre al-Maqālāt'. In C. Adang, D. Sklare, and S. Schmidtke (eds.), *A Common Rationality: Muʿtazilism in Islam and Judaism*. Würzburg: Ergon, 21–35.

Ansari, H. (2012). 'Un muḥaddiṯ muʿtazilite zaydite: Abū Saʿd al-Sammān al-Rāzī et ses *Amālī*'. *Arabica* 59: 267–90.

Ansari, H., and S. Schmidtke (2010a). 'Muʿtazilism after ʿAbd al-Jabbār: Abū Rashīd al-Nīsābūrī's *Kitāb Masāʾil al-khilāf fī l-uṣūl*'. *Studia Iranica* 39: 227–78.

Ansari, H., and S. Schmidtke (2010b). 'The Zaydī Reception of Ibn Khallād's *Kitāb al-Uṣūl:* The *taʿlīq* of Abū Ṭāhir b. ʿAlī al-Ṣaffār'. *Journal asiatique* 298: 275–302.

Ansari, H., and S. Schmidtke (2013). 'The Muʿtazilī and Zaydī Reception of Abū l-Ḥusayn al-Baṣrī's *Kitāb al-Muʿtamad fī uṣūl al-fiqh*: A Bibliographical Note'. *Islamic Law and Society* 20: 90–109.

Ansari, H., and S. Schmidtke (forthcoming). *The Transmission of Abū l-Ḥusayn al-Baṣrī's (d. 436/1044) Thought and Writings.*

Ansari, H., W. Madelung, and S. Schmidtke (2015). 'Yūsuf al-Baṣīr's Refutation (*Naqḍ*) of Abū l-Ḥusayn al-Baṣrī's Theology in a Yemeni Zaydi Manuscript of the 7th/13th Century'. In D. Hollenberg, Ch. Rauch, and S. Schmidtke (eds.), *The Yemeni Manuscript Tradition*. Leiden: Brill, 28–65.

Anvari, M. J. (2008). 'Abū ʿAbd Allāh al-Baṣrī'. *Encyclopaedia Islamica*. Leiden: Brill, i. 417–23.

al-Ashʿarī, Abū l-Ḥasan (*Maqālāt*). *Kitāb maqālāt al-islāmiyyīn (Die dogmatischen Lehren der Anhänger des Islam)*. Ed. H. Ritter. Beirut: Steiner, 2005.

Ben-Shammai, H. (1974). 'A Note on Some Karaite Copies of Muʿtazilite Writings'. *Bulletin of the School of Oriental and African Studies* 37: 295–304.

Cook, M. (2000). *Commanding Right and Forbidding Wrong in Islamic Thought*. Cambridge: Cambridge University Press.

Dhanani, A. (1994). *The Physical Theory of Kalām: Atoms, Space, and Void in Basrian Muʿtazilī Cosmology*. Leiden: Brill.

Dodge, B. (ed. and trans.) (1970). *The Fihrist of al-Nadīm: A Tenth-Century Survey of Muslim Culture*. New York/London: Columbia University Press.

El Omari, R. (2006). 'The Theology of Abu l-Qāsim al-Balḫī/al-Kaʿbī (d. 319/931): A Study of Its Sources and Reception'. Ph.D. dissertation, Yale University.

Elshahed, E. (1983). *Das Problem der transzendenten sinnlichen Wahrnehmung in der spätmuʿtazilitischen Erkenntnistheorie nach der Darstellung des Taqiaddin an-Nağrānī*. Berlin: Klaus Schwarz.

van Ess, J. (1985). 'Abu'l-Qāsem al-Kaʿbī'. *Encyclopaedia Iranica*. Vol. i. 359–62.

van Ess, J. (1991–7). *Theologie und Gesellschaft im 2. und 3. Jahrhundert Hidschra: Eine Geschichte des religiösen Denkens im frühen Islam*. 6 vols. Berlin: de Gruyter.

van Ess, J. (2011). *Der Eine und das Andere: Beobachtungen an islamischen häresiographischen Texten*. 2 vols. Berlin: de Gruyter.

Frank, R. M. (1966). *The Metaphysics of Created Being According to Abū l-Hudhayl al-ʿAllāf: A Philosphical Study of the Earliest Kalām*. Istanbul: Nederlands Historisch-Archaeologisch Instituut.

Frank, R. M. (1969). 'The Divine Attributes According to the Teaching of Abū l-Hudhayl al-ʿAllāf'. *Le Muséon* 82: 451–506.

Frank, R. M. (1971a). 'Abū Hāshim's Theory of "States": Its Structure and Function'. In *Actas do IV Congresso de Estudos Arabes e Islāmicos. Coimbra-Lisboa 1 a 8 septembro de 1968*. Leiden: Brill, 85–100.

Frank, R. M. (1971b). 'Several Fundamental Assumptions of the Baṣra School of the Muʿtazila'. *Studia Islamica* 33: 5–18.

Frank, R. M. (1978). *Beings and their Attributes: The Teaching of the Baṣrian School of the Muʿtazila in the Classical Period*. Albany, NY: SUNY Press.

Frank, R. M. (1980). '*Al-maʿdūm wa-l-mawjūd*. The Non-Existent, the Existent, and the Possible in the Teaching of Abū Hāshim and his Followers'. *Mélanges de l'Institut dominicain d'études orientales du Caire* 14: 185–210.

Frank, R. M. (1982). 'Attribute, Attribution, and Being: Three Islamic Views'. In P. Morewedge (ed.), *Philosophies of Existence Ancient and Medieval*. New York: Fordham University Press, 258–78.

Gimaret, D. (1970). 'La Théorie des *aḥwāl* d'Abū Hāšim al-Ǧubbāʾī d'après des sources ašʿarites'. *Journal asiatique* 258: 47–86.

Gimaret, D. (1976). 'Matériaux pour une bibliographie des Jubbāʾīs'. *Journal asiatique* 264: 277–332.

Gimaret, D. (1980). *Théories de l'acte humain en théologie musulmane*. Paris: Vrin.

Gimaret, D. (1984a). 'Matériaux pour une bibliographie des Jubbāʾī: Note complémentaire'. In M. E. Marmura (ed.), *Islamic Theology and Philosophy: Studies in Honor of George F. Hourani*. Albany, NY: SUNY Press, 31–8.

Gimaret, D. (1984b). *Une lecture Muʿtazilite du Coran: le Tafsīr d'Abū ʿAlī al-Djubbāʾī (m. 303/915) partiellement reconstitué à partir de ses citateurs*. Louvain/Paris.

Gimaret, D. (2008). 'Le Commentaire récemment publié de la *Tadkira* d'Ibn Mattawayh'. *Journal asiatique* 296: 203–28.

Gimaret, D. (2011). 'Pour servir à la lecture des *Masāʾil* d'Abou Rašīd al-Nīsābūrī'. *Bulletin d'études orientale* 60: 11–38.

Gwynne, R. W. (1982). 'The *Tafsīr* of Abū ʿAlī al-Jubbāʾī. First Steps Toward a Reconstruction with Texts, Translation, Biographical Introduction and Analytical Essay'. Ph.D. dissertation, University of Washington.

al-Ḥākim al-Jishumī (*Ṭabaqāt*). 'al-Ṭabaqāt al-ḥādiya ʿashara wa-l-thāniya ʿashara min Kitāb Sharḥ al-ʿuyūn'. In Fuʾād Sayyid (ed.), *ʿAbd al-Jabbār al-Hamadānī, Faḍl al-iʿtizāl wa-ṭabaqāt al-Muʿtazila*. Tunis: al-Dār al-tūnisiyya li-l-nashr, 1393/1974, 365–393.

Heemskerk, M. T. (2000). *Suffering in Muʿtazilite Theology: ʿAbd al-Ǧabbār's Teaching on Pain and Divine Justice*. Leiden: Brill.

Ibn ʿImād, ʿAbd al-Ḥayy b. Aḥmad (*Shadharāt*). *Shadharāt al-dhahab fī akhbār min dhahab*. 11 vols. Ed. Maḥmūd Arnaʿūṭ. Beirut: Dār Ibn Kathīr, 1986–95.

Ibn Khaldūn (*Muqaddima*). *The Muqaddimah: An Introduction to History*. Translated from the Arabic by Franz Rosenthal. 3 vols. New York: Pantheon Books, 1958.

Ibn al-Malāḥimī al-Khwārazmī, Rukn al-Dīn Maḥmūd (*Fāʾiq*). *K. al-Fāʾiq fī uṣūl al-dīn*. Ed. W. Madelung and M. McDermott. Tehran: Iranian Institute of Philosophy, 2007.

Ibn al-Malāḥimī al-Khwārazmī, Rukn al-Dīn Maḥmūd (*Muʿtamad*). *K. al-Muʿtamad fī uṣūl al-dīn*. Revised and enlarged edition by W. Madelung. Tehran: Mīrāth-i maktūb, 2013.

Ibn al-Malāḥimī al-Khwārazmī, Rukn al-Dīn Maḥmūd (*Tuḥfa*). *Tuḥfat al-Mutakallimīn fī l-Radd ʿalā l-Falāsifa*. Ed. H. Ansari and W. Madelung. Tehran: Iranian Institute of Philosophy, 2008.

Ibn Mattawayh (*Tadhkira*). *al-Tadhkira fī aḥkām al-jawāhir wa-l-aʿrāḍ*. 2 vols. Ed. D. Gimaret. Cairo: Institut français d'archéologie orientale, 2009.

Ibn Mattawayh (*Majmūʿ*). *al-Majmūʿ fī l-muḥīṭ bi-l-taklīf*. Vol. 1. Ed. J. J. Houben. Beirut, 1965. Vol. 2. Ed. J. J. Houben and D. Gimaret. Beirut, 1981. Vol. 3. Ed. J. R. T. M. Peters. Beirut: al-Maṭbaʿa al-Kāthūlīkiyya, 1999.

Ibn al-Nadīm (*Fihrist*). *al-Fihrist*. 2 vols. in 4. Ed. Ayman Fuʾād Sayyid. London: Furqān Foundation, 2009.

ʿImāra, M. (ed.) (1988). *Rasāʾil al-adl wa-l-tawḥīd*. Cairo: Dār al-Hilāl.

Khalidov, A. B. (1974). 'Биографический словарь ал-Андарасбани *[The Biographical Dictionary of al-Andarasbani],' Письменные памятники Востока. Историко-филологические исследования [The Written Monuments of the Orient. Historical and Philological Researches]*. Ed. L. N. Menshikov, S. B. Pevzner, A. S. Tveritinova, and A. B. Khalidov. Annual issue 1971. Moscow, 143–61.

Kulinich, A. (2012). 'Representing "a Blameworthy *Tafsīr*": Muʿtazilite Exegetical Tradition in *al-Jāmiʿ fī tafsīr al-Qurʾān of* ʿAlī b. ʿĪsā al-Rummānī (d. 384/994)'. Ph.D. dissertation, University of London.

Lane, A. J. (2006). *A Traditional Muʿtazilite Qurʾān Commentary: The* Kashshāf *of Jār Allāh al-Zamakhsharī (d. 538/1144)*. Leiden: Brill.

Lane, A. J. (2012). 'You Can't Tell a Book by its Author: A Study of Muʿtazilite Theology in al-Zamakhsharī's (d. 538/1144) *Kashshāf*'. *Bulletin of the School of Oriental and African Studies* 75: 47–86.

Madelung, W. (1985). '[Review of] Elsayed Elshahed: *Das Problem der transzendenten sinnlichen Wahrnehmung in der spätmuʿtazilitischen Erkenntnistheorie nach der Darstellung des Taqīaddīn an-Naǧrānī*. Berlin: Klaus Schwarz Verlag, 1983'. *Bulletin of the School of Oriental and African Studies* 48: 128–9.

Madelung, W. (1986). 'The Theology of al-Zamakhsharī'. In *Actas del XII Congreso de la U.E.A.I. (Union Européenne des Arabisants et Islamisants) (Malaga, 1984)*. Madrid: [s.n.], 485–95.

Madelung, W. (1991). 'The Late Muʿtazila and Determinism: The Philosophers' Trap'. In B. Scarcia Amoretti and L. Rostagno (eds.), *Yād-nāma in memoria di Alessandro Bausani*. Vol. i: *Islamistica*. Rome: Bardi, 245–57.

Madelung, W. (2006). 'Abū l-Ḥusayn al-Baṣrī's proof for the existence of God'. In J. E. Montgomery (ed.), *Arabic Theology, Arabic Philosophy. From the Many to the One. Essays in Celebration of Richard M. Frank*. Leuven: Peeters, 273–80.

Madelung, W. (2007a). 'Abu l-Ḥusayn al-Baṣrī'. *The Encyclopaedia of Islam. Three*. Leiden: Brill, fasc. 2007-1, 16–19.

Madelung, W. (2007b). 'Ibn al-Malāḥimī's Refutation of the Philosophers'. In C. Adang, S. Schmidtke, and D. Sklare (eds.), *A Common Rationality: Muʿtazilism in Islam and Judaism*. Würzburg: Ergon, 331–6.

Madelung, W. (2012). 'Ibn al-Malāḥimī on the Human Soul'. *Muslim World* 102: 426–32.

Madelung, W. (2014). 'Muʿtazilī Theology in Levi ben Yefet's *Kitāb al-Niʿma*'. *Intellectual History of the Islamicate World* 2: 9–17.

Madelung, W., and S. Schmidtke (2006). *Rational Theology in Interfaith Communication: Abu l-Ḥusayn al-Baṣrī's Muʿtazilī Theology among the Karaites in the Fāṭimid Age*. Leiden: Brill.

Madelung, W., and S. Schmidtke (2007). 'Yūsuf al-Baṣīr's First Refutation (*Naqḍ*) of Abu l-Ḥusayn al-Baṣrī's Theology'. In C. Adang, S. Schmidtke, and D. Sklare (eds.), *A Common Rationality: Muʿtazilism in Islam and Judaism*. Würzburg: Ergon, 229–96.

Madelung, W., and S. Schmidtke (eds.) (forthcoming). *al-Ṣāḥib Ibn ʿAbbād Promoter of Rational Theology: Two Muʿtazilī* Kalām *Texts from the Cairo Genizah*. Leiden: Brill.

Makdisi, G. (1963). *Ibn ʿAqīl et la résurgence de l'Islam traditionaliste au xi*[e] *siècle (v*[e] *siècle de l'Hégire)*. Damascus: Institut Français de Damas.

Mānkdīm Shashdīw, Aḥmad b. Abū Hāshim Muḥammad al-Ḥusaynī al-Qazwīnī (*Taʿlīq*). *[Taʿlīq] Sharḥ al-uṣūl al-khamsa*. Ed. ʿAbd al-Karīm ʿUthmān [as a work by ʿAbd al-Jabbār]. Cairo: Maktabat Wahba, 1384/1965.

Michot, Y. J. (2003). 'A Mamlūk Theologian's Commentary on Avicenna's Risāla Aḍḥawiyya, Being a Translation of a Part of the Darʾ al-taʿāruḍ of Ibn Taymiyya, with Introduction, Annotation, and Appendices'. *Journal of Islamic Studies* 14: 149–203, 309–63.

Mourad, S. A. (2007). 'Ibn al-Khallāl al-Baṣrī (d. after 377/988) and his Œuvre on the Problematic Verses of the Qurʾān Kitāb al-Radd ʿalā l-jabriyya al-qadariyya (Refutation of Predestinarian Compulsionists)'. In C. Adang, S. Schmidtke, and D. Sklare (eds.), *A Common Rationality: Muʿtazilism in Islam and Judaism*. Würzburg: Ergon: 81–99.

'al-Najrānī, Taqī al-Dīn' (*Kāmil*). *Al-Kāmil fī l-istiqṣāʾ fīmā balaghanā min kalām al-qudamāʾ*. Ed. al-Sayyid al-Shahīd. Cairo: Wizārat al-awqāf, 1999.

Perler, D., and U. Rudolph (2000). *Occasionalismus: Theorien der Kausalität im arabisch-islamischen und im europäischen Denken*. Göttingen: Vandenhoeck & Ruprecht.

Peters, J. R. T. M. (1976). *God's Created Speech: A Study in the Speculative Theology of the Muʿtazilī Qāḍī al-Quḍāt Abū l-Ḥasan ʿAbd al-Jabbār b. Aḥmad al-Hamaḏānī*. Leiden: Brill.

Pomerantz, M. A. (2010). 'Licit Magic and Divine Grace: The Life and Letters of al-Ṣāḥib Ibn ʿAbbād (d. 385/995)'. Ph.D. dissertation, University of Chicago.

Prozorov, S. M. (1999). 'A Unique Manuscript of a Biographical Dictionary by a Khorezmian Author'. *Manuscripta Orientalia* 5: 9–17.

Prozorov, S. M. (2007). 'Intellectual Elite of Mawarannahr and Khurasan on the Eve of the Mongolian Invasion (Based on al-Andarasbani's Biographical Dictionary)'. International Conference on Islamic Civilization in Central Asia, 4–7 September 2007, Astana, Kazakhstan, 2007. <[http://www.orientalstudies.ru/eng/index.php?option=com_publications&Itemid=75&pub=1210]>.

Reynolds, G. S. (2004). *A Muslim Theologian in the Sectarian Milieu: ʿAbd al-Jabbār and the* CRITIQUE OF CHRISTIAN ORIGINS. Leiden: Brill.

Reynolds, G. S. (2005). 'The Rise and Fall of Qāḍī ʿAbd al-Jabbār'. *International Journal of Middle East Studies* 37: 3–18.

Rudolph, U. (2015). *Al-Māturīdī and the Development of Sunnī Theology in Samarqand*. Leiden: Brill.

Sayyid, A. F. (1974). *Sources de l'histoire du Yémen à l'époque musulmane = Maṣādir tārīkh al-Yaman fī l-ʿaṣr al-islāmī*. Cairo: Institut Français d'Archéologie Orientale.

Schmidtke, S. (1991). *The Theology of al-ʿAllāma al-Ḥillī (d. 726/1325)*. Berlin: Schwarz.

Schmidtke, S. (2008). 'MS Mahdawi 514. An Anonymous Commentary on Ibn Mattawayh's *Kitāb al-Tadhkira*'. In A. Akasoy and W. Raven (eds.), *Islamic Thought in the Middle Ages. Studies in Text, Transmission and Translation in Honour of Hans Daiber*. Leiden: Brill, 139–162.

Schmidtke, S. (2012). 'Ibn Mattawayh'. *The Encyclopaedia of Islam. Three*. Leiden: Brill. Fascicle 1: 147–9.

Schmidtke, S. (2013). 'Biblical Predictions of the Prophet Muḥammad among the Zaydīs of Yemen (6th/12th and 7th/13th Centuries)'. *Orientalia Christiana Analecta* 293: 221–40.

Schwarb, G. (2006). 'Sahl b. Faḍl al-Tustarī's Kitāb al-Īmā'. *Ginzei Qedem* 2: 61*–105*.

Schwarb, G. (2010a). 'Kalām'. *Encyclopaedia of the Jews of the Islamic World*. Leiden: Brill, iii. 91–8.

Schwarb, G. (2010b). 'Yūsuf al-Baṣīr'. *Encyclopaedia of the Jews of the Islamic World*. Leiden: Brill, iv. 651–5.

Schwarb, G. (2011a). 'Muʿtazilism in the Age of Averroes'. In P. Adamson (ed.), *In the Age of Averroes: Arabic Philosophy in the Sixth/Twelfth Century*. London: The Warburg Institute, 251–82.

Schwarb, G. (2011b). 'Abū ʿAbdallāh al-Baṣrī'. *The Encyclopaedia of Islam. Three*. Leiden: Brill, fasc. 2011-3: 3–5.

Sklare, D. (1995). 'Yūsuf al-Baṣīr: Theological Aspects of His Halakhic Works'. In D. Frank (ed.), *The Jews of Medieval Islam: Community, Society, and Identity*. Leiden: Brill, 249–70.

Sklare, D. (1996). *Samuel Ben Ḥofni and his Cultural World: Texts and Studies*. Leiden: Brill.

Sklare. D. (2007). 'Levi ben Yefet and his Kitāb al-Niʿma: Selected Texts'. In C. Adang, S. Schmidtke, and D. Sklare (eds.), *A Common Rationality: Muʿtazilism in Islam and Judaism*. Würzburg: Ergon, 156–216.

Thiele, J. (2012). 'La Causalité selon al-Ḥākim al-Ǧišumī'. *Arabica* 59: 291–318.
Thiele, J. (2013). *Theologie in der jemenitischen Zaydiyya: Die naturphilosophischen Überlegungen des al-Ḥasan ar-Raṣṣāṣ*. Leiden: Brill.
Thiele, J. (2014). 'The Jewish and Muslim Reception of ʿAbd al-Jabbār's *Kitāb al-Jumal wa-l-ʿuqūd*: A Survey of Relevant Sources'. *Intellectual History of the Islamicate World* 2: 101–21.
Thomas, D. (2010). 'Ibn al-Ikhshīd'. In D. Thomas and A. Mallett (eds.), *Christian–Muslim Relations: A Bibliographical History*. Vol. ii (900–1050). Leiden: Brill, 221–3.
Ullah, K. (2013). '*Al-Kashshāf*: Al-Zamakhsharī's (d. 538/1144) Muʿtazilite Exegesis of the Qurʾān'. Ph.D. dissertation, Georgetown University, Washington, DC.
ʿUthmān, ʿAbd al-Karīm (1968). *Qāḍī l-quḍāt ʿAbd al-Jabbār b. Aḥmad al-Hamadhānī*. Beirut: Dār al-ʿArabiyya.
Vajda, G. (ed. and trans.) (1985). *Al-Kitāb al-Muḥtawī de Yūsuf al-Baṣīr*. Texte, Traduction et Commentaire. Ed. D. R. Blumenthal. Leiden: Brill.
al-Zamakhsharī, Jār Allāh (*Minhāj*). *Kitāb al-Minhāj fī uṣūl al-dīn*. Ed. S. Schmidtke. Beirut: Arab Scientific Publishers, 1428/2007.

CHAPTER 10

THE SHĪʿĪ RECEPTION OF MUʿTAZILISM (I)

Zaydīs

HASSAN ANSARI

I The Muʿtazilization of Iranian Zaydism

By the end of the third/ninth century, so it is reported by the Twelver Shīʿī author Abū Jaʿfar Muḥammad Ibn Qiba al-Rāzī (d. after 319/931) in his *Naqḍ al-Ishhād*, a refutation of the *Kitāb Ishhād* by Abū Zayd ʿĪsā b. Muḥammad b. Aḥmad al-ʿAlawī (d. 326/937–8), there were two trends among the Zaydīs—those who were close to the *ḥadīth* folk and thus opposed to Muʿtazilism and those who had adopted Muʿtazilite doctrines. Ibn Qiba's description seems to reflect the situation of Zaydism in Rayy, his hometown in Northern Iran. Abū Zayd al-ʿAlawī, the author of the *Kitāb al-Ishhād*, was a Zaydī *mutakallim* and a *muḥaddith* (Ansari forthcoming a). He spent most of his life in Rayy fulfilling the function as the *shaykh* of the ʿAlawīs and it was here that he died. His family hailed from Iraq, where Abū Zayd had studied for some time. Among his teachers were the Zaydī *muḥaddith* al-Ḥusayn b. al-Ḥakam al-Ḥibarī (d. 286/899) whom Abū Zayd met in Kūfa, the Zaydī *muḥaddith* Muḥammad b. Mansūr al-Murādī (d. *c*.290/903) with whom he studied law and *ḥadīth*, and Abū ʿAbd Allāh al-Ḥusayn b. ʿAlī al-Miṣrī (d. 312/924–5), the brother of the Zaydī Imam al-Nāṣir al-Kabīr al-Ḥasan b. ʿAlī al-Uṭrūsh (d. 304/917). Among al-ʿAlawī's pupils was Abū l-ʿAbbās Aḥmad b. Ibrāhīm al-Ḥasanī (d. *c*.352/963) who in 322/934 came to Rayy to study *kalām* and law with him and later on became one of the most prominent Zaydī scholars of Iran and Iraq. He in turn was the teacher of the two Buṭḥānī brothers, Imam al-Muʾayyad bi-llāh Abū l-Ḥusayn Aḥmad b. al-Ḥusayn (d. 411/1020) and Imam al-Nāṭiq bi-l-ḥaqq Abū Ṭālib Yaḥyā (d. 424/1033). The significance of Abū Zayd al-ʿAlawī for the transmission of the

Zaydī legacy, even as far as Yemen, can hardly be overestimated. Abū Zayd al-ʿAlawī transmitted numerous prophetic traditions many of which are included in Abū l-ʿAbbās al-Ḥasanī's *Sharḥ al-Aḥkām* (Ansari 2005). Abū Zayd al-ʿAlawī's above-mentioned *Kitāb al-Ishhād* is a refutation of the Twelver Shīʿīs' notion of the imamate, addressing specifically their belief in the occultation (*ghayba*) of the 'hidden imam'. While the work itself is lost, quotations from it were included in Ibn Qiba's above-mentioned refutation of the book, the *Naqḍ al-Ishhād*, which in turn is fully quoted (with the exception of the introduction, the *khuṭba*), in the *Kitāb Kamāl al-dīn* by Ibn Bābawayh al-Ṣadūq (d. 381/991–2) (Modarressi 1993: 117ff.; Ansari 2000b). While the later Zaydī literature has not preserved any quotations from the *Kitāb al-Ishhād*, its impact on the literary genre of Zaydī refutations of Twelver Shīʿism is evident. The *Kitāb al-Ishhād* also provides some glimpses into the doctrinal beliefs of the Zaydīs of Iran during that period, most specifically of Abū Zayd al-ʿAlawī himself. In contrast to some scholars among the Zaydīs of his time, Abū Zayd al-ʿAlawī maintained that the Prophet had appointed ʿAlī b. Abī Ṭālib to the imamate by rule of investiture (*naṣṣ*) according to the tradition of Ghadīr Khumm. Moreover, his doctrinal beliefs were close to those of the Muʿtazilites as he refuted notions such as determinism (*jabr*) and anthropomorphism (*tashbīh*). Contrary to some of his Zaydī contemporaries, he also propagated analogy (*qiyās*) and personal reasoning (*ijtihād*) in legal theory. As for Abū Zayd al-ʿAlawī's student Abū l-ʿAbbās al-Ḥasanī, it is noteworthy that he may have also studied with one of the representatives of the Muʿtazilite School of Baghdad in Rayy, although we do not know of any work of his that would reflect his theology—Abū l-ʿAbbās was primarily a jurist (Madelung 2004). It was during the reign of the Būyids and, indeed, in Baghdad that Zaydīs began to study Muʿtazilī thought with Muʿtazilī scholars as part of their curriculum. During the second half of the fourth/tenth century, a number of Zaydīs studied with Abū ʿAbd Allāh al-Baṣrī (d. 369/980), the prominent Bahshamite theologian in Baghdad, among them Imam al-Mahdī li-Dīn Allāh Abū ʿAbd Allāh b. al-Dāʿī (d. 360/970–1) as well as the two above-mentioned Buṭḥānī brothers, Abū Ṭālib and Abū l-Ḥusayn. Ibn al-Dāʿī was the son of al-Dāʿī al-Ṣaghīr al-Ḥasan b. al-Qāsim (d. 316/928–9), and a Zaydī Imam in northern Iran who by studying with Abū ʿAbd Allāh al-Baṣrī played an important role in pushing the Zaydīs towards Muʿtazilism. None of Ibn al-Dāʿī's writings are extant (al-Ḥākim al-Jishumī, *Sharḥ*, 371–5; Madelung 1988: 89–90). Prior to this, there are indications that some Zaydī Imams and scholars showed interest in Muʿtazilism following al-Hādī ilā l-ḥaqq Yaḥyā b. al-Ḥusayn's (d. 298/911) inclination towards Muʿtazilī *kalām* (see Chapter 27). Al-Hādī is reported to have studied in Iran with Abū l-Qāsim al-Kaʿbī al-Balkhī (d. 319/931), the head of the School of Baghdad (Zaryāb 1994: 151). While during the late third/ninth century only a fraction of Zaydīs sided with the Muʿtazilīs, by the middle of the fourth/tenth century the majority of Zaydīs in Iraq (especially in Baghdad) and Iran identified themselves as Muʿtazilīs and studied with Muʿtazilī scholars. When *qāḍī* ʿAbd al-Jabbār b. Aḥmad al-Hamadānī (d. 415/1025) came to Rayy, following the invitation of the Būyid vizier Abū l-Qāsim Ismāʿīl b. ʿAbbād ('al-Ṣāḥib b. ʿAbbād', d. 385/925), Rayy became a centre of Muʿtazilism. Ibn ʿAbbād, a former student of Abū ʿAbd Allāh al-Baṣrī and an important representative of the Muʿtazila in his own right with inclinations towards Zaydism, actively promoted the study of Muʿtazilī *kalām* in Rayy. During this time, the Buṭḥānī brothers also moved to Rayy—Abū l-Ḥusayn had studied with Abū ʿAbd Allāh al-Baṣrī in Baghdad and now continued his studies with *qāḍī* ʿAbd al-Jabbār in Iran. He hailed from the area of Āmul, in Ṭabaristān, a northern region of Iran on the shores of the Caspian Sea. His father was a Twelver Shīʿī scholar and both Abū l-Ḥusayn and his brother Abū Ṭālib were raised as Twelvers (al-Murshad bi-llāh al-Jurjānī, *Sīrat al-Muʾayyad bi-llāh*; Madelung 1987: 123–7, 143, 262–315, 353, 354). According to a report by al-Shaykh al-Ṭūsī (d. 460/1067) which is confirmed by al-Ḥākim al-Jishumī (d. 494/1101), the brothers converted to Zaydism in view of differences in opinion among the Imami traditionists (al-Ṭūsī, *Tahdhīb*, 1/2; Madelung 1987: 127). Initially, Abū l-Ḥusayn had studied *fiqh* and Muʿtazilite *kalām*, specifically the doctrines of the School of Baghdad, with his maternal uncle, the above-mentioned Abū l-ʿAbbās al-Ḥasanī, in Baghdad. As a result of the variegated affiliations of his teachers, Abū l-Ḥusayn was well versed with the different school traditions, including that of Imam al-Qāsim b. Ibrāhīm al-Rassī (d. 246/860), the founder of the Qāsimī legal tradition among the Zaydīs, which Abū l-Ḥusayn got acquainted with by studying the doctrines of al-Qāsim's grandson, al-Hādī ilā l-Ḥaqq, the founder of the Zaydī state in Yemen who espoused the teachings of his grandfather with some adjustments. At the same time, Abū l-Ḥusayn got acquainted with the legal doctrines of Imam al-Nāsir al-Uṭrūsh. When attending the lessons of *qāḍī* ʿAbd al-Jabbār in Isfahan, Abū l-Ḥusayn studied the latter's *K. Sharḥ al-Uṣūl*, 'adding' (*ʿallaqa*) the explanations and comments (*ziyādāt*) of his teacher to his own copy of the text. Abū l-Ḥusayn also studied *ḥadith* and law with some other Zaydī and Sunnī scholars. As a result, Abū l-Ḥusayn had a precise understanding of the sciences of his time, including *kalām*, legal theory, Shīʿī as well as Sunnī law, and *ḥadīth*. This is reflected in his oeuvre where he shows himself deeply influenced by the surrounding strands of thought which allowed him to formulate innovative views in a variety of ways and disciplines. His innovative approach to the Zaydī legacy is one of the reasons that made him acceptable for Zaydīs of Northern Iran and Yemen alike (Ansari 2000c; Ansari forthcoming b). Abū l-Ḥusayn is the author of several works on law, *ḥadīth*, and *kalām*. His *Tajrīd*, together with his auto-commentary *Sharḥ al-Tajrīd*, on the Hādawī legal tradition, are among the most influential books on Zaydī law in Iran and Yemen (Ansari and Schmidtke 2015: 139 n. 125). In theology, Abū l-Ḥusayn composed a concise systematic summa, titled *Kitāb al-Tabṣira fī ʿilm al-kalām*, which later on became part of the Zaydī canon both in Iran and Yemen, as well as *Ithbāt nubuwwat al-Nabī*, on the prophecy of Muḥammad and the miraculous character of the Qurʾān (Madelung 1965: 177f.; 1988: 90; van Ess 1981: 151–4; Ansari 2010a; Ansari 2015, 196–200; Schmidtke 2012).

Abū l-Ḥusayn's brother, Abū Ṭālib, was a traditionist, jurist, and an expert in legal theory as well as theology. He likewise hailed, as it seems, from Āmul where he also began his education, in addition to studying in some nearby cities, like Jurjān. He studied *ḥadīth* with his father while his uncle Abū l-ʿAbbās al-Ḥasanī was his teacher in Zaydī jurisprudence as it seems. He studied Sunnī *ḥadīth* with scholars such as Ibn ʿAdī al-Jurjānī (d. 365/976) and ʿAlī b. Mahdī al-Ṭabarī (Ansari 2001b), while another teacher of his in Imami *ḥadīth* was the renowned Imami traditionist Ibn Ḥamza al-Marʿashī (d. 358/968–9). As was the case with his brother, Abū Ṭālib was well versed in the different Zaydī legal traditions, viz. the Qāsimī, the Hādawī, and the Nāṣirī traditions, and he also spent some time in Baghdad, where he studied *kalām* and legal theory with Abū ʿAbd Allāh al-Baṣrī. Still during the lifetime of his teacher, Abū Ṭālib began to write about *kalām* and legal theory, and upon his return to Iran, he was considered a Muʿtazilī theologian and now also engaged in teaching *kalām*. Abū Ṭālib probably also studied *kalām* with his *shaykh* in *ḥadīth*, Abū Aḥmad Ibn ʿAbdak al-Jurjānī (d. after 360/970–1), one of the students of Abū Hāshim al-Jubbāʾī (d. 321/933), and Abū l-Qāsim al-Kaʿbī (Ansari 1998: 198f.), as well as *fiqh* with Abū l-Ḥusayn Yaḥyā b. Muḥammad al-Murtaḍā, a grandson of al-Hādī ilā l-Ḥaqq who came to Daylam and with whom he read the latter's *Kitāb al-Aḥkām*.

Being considered as one of the Zaydī Imams in Iran, his writings, which were transferred to Yemen at the very latest by the early sixth/twelfth century, became very influential here. His books, as well as those of his brother Abū l-Ḥusayn, were specifically used by the Bahshamite Zaydīs of Yemen in their doctrinal battle against the Muṭarrifiyya, a faction among the Zaydīs of Yemen which had dominated Zaydī intellectual circles there for approximately two centuries (see Chapter 27). Like his brother, Abū Ṭālib developed good relations with the vizier Ibn ʿAbbād and he taught in different cities in Iran, including Jurjān and Daylam. Following the death of his brother Abū l-Ḥusayn, Abū Ṭālib claimed the imamate for himself in northern Iran (Madelung 1965: 177ff.; 1987: 125–7, 213, 317–21; 1988: 90; Ansari 2000a). Abū Ṭālib is a leading authority of the Hādawī legal tradition with numerous innovative impulses to his credit. His most important work in jurisprudence is the *Kitāb al-Taḥrīr*, together with his autocommentary, *Sharḥ al-Taḥrīr* (Ansari forthcoming c; Ansari and Schmidtke 2015: 137 n. 117; 140 n. 129). He also wrote two works on legal theory which are based on Muʿtazilī thought. In his *Jawāmiʿ al-adilla fī uṣūl al-fiqh*, written still during the lifetime of Abū ʿAbd Allāh al-Baṣrī, Abū Ṭālib primarily presents the views of his teacher. His *Kitāb al-Mujzī fī uṣūl al-fiqh* is a more comprehensive work and in fact one of the most influential books on Muʿtazilī legal theory among the Zaydīs (Madelung 1986; Ansari and Schmidtke 2013: 94f.). Abū Ṭālib also composed several titles on theology. Leiden University Library owns a unique manuscript of Yemeni provenance of a work attributed to Abū Ṭālib, entitled *Kitāb Ziyādāt Sharḥ al-Usūl mimmā ʿulliqa ʿan al-Sayyid al-Imām al-Nāṭiq bi-l-ḥaqq Yaḥyā b. al-Ḥusayn al-Hārūnī raḍī Allāh ʿanhu*. The work is a supercommentary on an originally Muʿtazilī text, viz. the *Sharḥ al-Uṣūl* by Abū ʿAlī Muḥammad b. Khallād (d. first half of fourth/tenth century), an autocommentary on his *K. al-Uṣūl* (Adang, Madelung, and Schmidtke 2011; Ansari and Schmidtke 2010a). The full title of the supercommentary provides some insights into the genesis of the work. It took the form of a critical paraphrastic commentary (*ziyādāt*) that was transcribed by one of Abū Ṭālib's students, Abū l-Qāsim Muḥammad b. Aḥmad b. al-Mahdī al-Ḥasanī (d. 465/1072–3). The latter penned Abū Ṭālib's comments down in a composition of his own, in the form of a *taʿlīq*, thus preparing a new paraphrase of Ibn Khallād's *Sharḥ al-Uṣūl*. However, there is reason to believe that the Leiden manuscript cannot be attributed to Abū l-Qāsim directly. It seems that an unidentified student of Abū l-Qāsim rather composed this *taʿlīq* and added some additions of his own to the text. The manuscript may in fact be a copy of a *Vorlage* in which the transmitter cites a notebook of Abū l-Qāsim that contained his transcribed notes of the *Ziyādāt* of Abū Ṭālib. The Leiden manuscript was moreover transcribed from a copy in the possession of a Zaydī scholar from Khurasan, Zayd b. al-Ḥasan b. ʿAlī al-Bayhaqī (d. *c.*545/1150–1), who acquired it from this unidentified student before visiting Yemen and making it available there (on him, see Chapter 27, Section I; cf. also below). When commenting upon Ibn Khallād's text, Abū Ṭālib probably did not use the supercommentary which *qāḍī* ʿAbd al-Jabbār had written on Ibn Khallād's *Kitāb al-Uṣūl*, but rather the latter's autocommentary. As we have seen, Abū Ṭālib and his brother Abū l-Ḥusayn studied with Abū ʿAbd Allāh al-Baṣrī in Baghdad, who in turn was also the teacher of ʿAbd al-Jabbār. When the latter came to Rayy, Abū l-Ḥusayn continued his studies with ʿAbd al-Jabbār once he had moved to Iran. Unlike his brother and although he was the younger among the two, Abū Ṭālib did not continue studying with ʿAbd al-Jabbār and therefore had no reason to base his own book on the latter's *Sharḥ al-Uṣūl*. However, he may have used ʿAbd al-Jabbār's supplement (*takmila*) to Ibn Khallād's *Sharḥ* since the latter had never finished his commentary—this being the reason that *qāḍī* ʿAbd al-Jabbār completed it in his *Takmilat al-Sharḥ*. Rather, Abū Ṭālib based his *Ziyādāt* on Ibn Khallād's autocommentary, reproducing it through critical paraphrase and citing the teachings of Abū ʿAbd Allāh al-Baṣrī as well. Since the latter was a student of Ibn Khallād, it can be assumed that he had taught the work to Abū Ṭālib, who in turn wished to teach it to his own students. Abū l-Qāsim b. al-Mahdī al-Ḥasanī, who penned down Abū Ṭālib's *Ziyādāt* in the form of a *taʿlīq*, also contributed some of his own thoughts to the book. Abū Ṭālib, as we have seen, probably did not cite *qāḍī* ʿAbd al-Jabbār's *Sharḥ* although there may have been a few exceptions. The citations of ʿAbd al-Jabbār most likely originated with Abū l-Qāsim, who perused ʿAbd al-Jabbār's supercommentary (Ansari 2012a: 381–402). Abū Ṭālib is also reported to have composed a book on philosophical theology (*laṭīf al-kalām*) (Ansari and Schmidtke 2011a: 198, n. 66), as well as a *K. al-Mabādī fī ʿilm al-kalām*. W. Madelung tentatively identified an incomplete manuscript, copied in Rabīʿ I 499/December 1105 in Ṣaʿda (MS Milan, Ambrosiana ar. X 96 Sup., ff. 1–67), as probably being a copy of this work. The manuscript contains a Bahshamite theological summa, and throughout the text the author regularly mentions the teachings of Abū ʿAbd Allāh al-Baṣrī (Madelung 1986; see also Ansari 2012a: 301–12). Abū Ṭālib also wrote a book titled *al-Muṣʿabī*, a heresiographical work, as well as a commentary on *al-Bāligh al-mudrik* by al-Hādī ilā l-Ḥaqq. Abū Ṭālib also composed a book on the imamate, entitled *Kitāb al-Diʿāma fī tathbīt al-imāma*, which he dedicated to Ibn ʿAbbād. This book has been published repeatedly under various titles, such as *Nuṣrat madhāhib al-Zaydiyya* or *Kitāb al-Zaydiyya* and has erroneously been attributed to al-Ṣāḥib b. ʿAbbād (Madelung 1986; see also Ansari 2015, 185f.).

Among the students of *qāḍī* ʿAbd al-Jabbār in Rayy were a number of Zaydī scholars, some of whom also studied with the Buṭḥānī brothers. Mention should be made of Abū l-Qāsim Ismāʿīl b. Aḥmad al-Jīlī al-Bustī (*fl.* early fifth/eleventh) who is reported to have participated in a debate (*munāẓara*) with the Ashʿarite theologian, Abū Bakr al-Bāqillānī (d. 403/1013), in Baghdad. He is the author of several theological texts, the most famous being his *Kitāb al-Baḥth ʿan adillat al-takfīr wa-l-tafsīq* in which he critically discusses the practical legal aspects of charging Muslims with unbelief (*kufr*) or grave sin (*fisq*). The work by and large reflects the teachings of ʿAbd al-Jabbār on this issue (al-Bustī, *Baḥth*). Al-Bustī is also the author of another work on the imamate, entitled *al-Muʿtamad fī l-imāma*, in which he elucidates the Zaydī views on the subject by utilizing the Muʿtazilī approach. The way he refers to his teacher ʿAbd al-Jabbār throughout the text suggests that the work was written still during the latter's lifetime. The work is preserved in at least one incomplete manuscript (Ansari 2001c; 2012a: 613–18; 2015, 187–92; Ansari and Schmidtke 2015: 131 n. 91, 135 n. 103).

Another Zaydī student of ʿAbd al-Jabbār in Rayy was Abū Saʿd Ismāʿīl b. ʿAlī b. al-Ḥusayn al-Sammān al-Rāzī al-Ḥāfiẓ (d. 445/1053), who composed a *K. al-Amālī*, a compilation of *ḥadīth*. He also wrote on *kalām*, although none of his theological writings appear to be extant. Abū Saʿd, who had studied with numerous Sunnī scholars across various regions, played an important role in transmitting Sunnī *ḥadīth* among the Zaydīs. He is also the author of *Kitāb al-Muwāfaqa bayna ahl al-bayt wa-l-ṣaḥāba*, one of the earliest Zaydī works in which the Rightly Guided Caliphs are being praised (Ansari 2012c).

Another Zaydī student of ʿAbd al-Jabbār whose writings later on became popular among the Zaydīs of Yemen was Abū l-Faḍl al-ʿAbbās b. Sharwīn. He hailed from Astarābād, had studied with ʿAbd al-Jabbār in Rayy, and later on returned to his home town. Ibn Sharwīn was also a companion of al-Muʾayyad bi-llāh Abū l-Ḥusayn, he taught Bahshamite theology, and was the author of several theological texts. Ibn Sharwīn's most comprehensive work on *kalām* is *Yāqūtat al-īmān wa-wāsiṭat al-burhān fī uṣūl al-dīn* which is only preserved in the recension of al-Ḥasan b. Muḥammad al-Raṣṣāṣ (d. 584/1188), a prominent Zaydī theologian of sixth/twelfth-century Yemen. Al-Raṣṣāṣ's paraphrastic, and at times critical, commentary is entitled *al-Tibyān li-Yāqūtat al-īmān wa-wāsiṭat al-burhān*. Ibn Sharwīn is also the author of a *kalām* treatise which is preserved in a unique manuscript, entitled *Ḥaqāʾiq al-ashyāʾ*. As the title suggests, it belongs to the literary genre of definitions and contains explanations of 122 terms. Ibn Sharwīn is also known to have written a *Kitāb al-Madkhal fī ʿilm al-kalām* which was among the books studied in a later period in Yemen. Moreover, he also composed a treatise on moral obligation (*taklīf*), titled *al-Wujūh allatī taʿẓum ʿalayhā al-ṭāʿāt*, which is extant (Ansari and Schmidtke 2012; Ansari 2015, 201–7).

Another Zaydī theologian who apparently started out as a pupil of ʿAbd al-Jabbār and later continued studying Muʿtazilī *kalām* with the Buṭḥānī brothers is Abū ʿAbd Allāh al-Ḥusayn b. Ismāʿīl al-Shajarī al-Ḥasanī al-Jurjānī, the later Imam al-Muwaffaq bi-llāh, author of a comprehensive theological summa entitled *al-Iḥāta fī ʿilm al-kalām*, which is only partially extant. A later Zaydī scholar in Iran produced a paraphrastic commentary on the work, *Taʿlīq al-Iḥāta*, which is incompletely preserved in a unique manuscript (Madelung 1988: 90; Ansari 2012a: 293–300; 2013a, *sīn-ʿayn*; Schmidtke 2012).

Aḥmad b. al-Ḥusayn b. Abī Hāshim al-Ḥusaynī al-Qazwīnī, known as Mānkdīm Shashdīw (d. *c.*425/1034), is another important Zaydī theologian who also probably began his studies with ʿAbd al-Jabbār and later continued as a pupil of Abū l-Ḥusayn al-Hārūnī. He is the author of a paraphrastic commentary on ʿAbd al-Jabbār's *Sharḥ al-Uṣūl al-khamsa, Taʿlīq Sharḥ al-Uṣūl al-khamsa* (Mānkdīm, *Taʿlīq*), which was one of the most popular Bahshamite works among the Zaydīs of Yemen, as is suggested by the numerous manuscripts preserved in the libraries of Yemen as well as the various super-commentaries written on it (Gimaret 1979).

The Zaydīs of the 'school of Rayy' who had studied with Abū ʿAbd Allāh al-Baṣrī and/or ʿAbd al-Jabbār all adhered to the Bahshamite strand whose doctrines they endorsed. This also applied to those Zaydīs in northern Iran, viz. in Ṭabaristān, Daylamān, and Jīlān, who belonged to the Hādawī tradition—they now became Bahshamites in theology due to the influence of the Buṭḥānī brothers who were prominent representatives of Hādawī tradition. By contrast, al-Nāṣir li-l-ḥaqq al-Uṭrūsh, the founder of the Nāṣirī legal tradition that prevailed in Northern Iran, had not considered himself a Muʿtazilī. In his theological writings he agreed only in some issues with the Muʿtazilites (Nāṣir, *al-Bisāṭ*; Sergeant 1953; Madelung 1965: 189f; 1988: 88f.). As a result, the adherents of the Nāṣirī tradition did not immediately follow the two Buṭḥānī brothers in their Bahshamite tendencies. However, in view of the fact that the Buṭḥānī brothers nevertheless considered al-Nāṣir al-Uṭrūsh as a respected authority, that they cited and incorporated elements of his doctrine in their works, and in view of the increasingly close relationship between the adherents of the Hādawī and the Nāṣirī traditions, Bahshamite doctrine eventually also spread among the followers of the Nāṣirī tradition of northern Iran (Ansari and Schmidtke 2011b; Ansari 2012a: 583–96).

A Zaydī scholar of late fifth/eleventh-century northern Iran, ʿAlī b. al-Ḥusayn b. Muḥammad al-Daylamī Siyāh [Shāh] Sarījān [Sarbījān], had composed, as it seems, a supercommentary or *taʿlīq* on Ibn Khallād's above-mentioned *Kitāb al-Uṣūl*. Unlike Abū Ṭālib, Shāh Sarbījān also used the supercommentary (*Kitāb Ziyādāt al-Sharḥ*) of Abū Rashīd al-Nisābūrī, the prominent student of ʿAbd al-Jabbār, when writing his own *taʿlīq* (Ansari and Schmidtke 2010a; 2011a: 183 and 201 n. 91).

During the fifth/eleventh and sixth/twelfth centuries there was a sizeable community of Zaydīs in Khurasan, especially in Nishapur and in Bayhaq. They were also significantly influenced by the teachings of the two Buṭḥānī brothers (some of the direct or indirect students of the Buṭḥānī brothers lived in Khurasan) and as a result adopted Muʿtazilism (Ansari 2013b). The most prominent representative of the Muʿtazila during the late fifth/eleventh century in this region was Abū Saʿd al-Muḥassin b. Muḥammad b. Karāma al-Bayhaqī al-Barawqanī ('al-Ḥākim al-Jishumī', d. 494/1101) who was active in Bayhaq. His numerous comprehensive writings were available to Zaydīs of both Khurasan and Rayy and played an important role in propagating Bahshamite theology. Al-Jishumī was a Hanafi scholar who had studied Bahshamite theology in Khurasan with some of the students of ʿAbd al-Jabbār and of Abū Ṭālib al-Hārūnī. Apart from being an important *mutakallim*, he was also an exegete and a historian. From his pen, we have several comprehensive theological summae as well as treatises on selected doctrinal issues, addressing specifically the differences between the positions of the Bahshamiyya as against those of the School of Baghdad. Al-Jishumī also composed numerous refutations directed against Ismāʿīlis, Twelver Shīʿīs, and, most importantly, Ashʿarites. According to later Zaydī Yemeni sources al-Jishumī converted to Zaydism towards the end of his life. This is not corroborated by other sources. Although his writings display his sympathies for Zaydism, expressed by his praises for the Zaydī Imams up until the time of the two Buṭḥānī brothers, al-Jishumī rejects in his extant writings the Zaydī doctrine on the imamate. In his *Tanbīh al-ghāfilīn ʿan faḍāʾil al-ṭālibiyyin*, in which al-Ḥākim al-Jishumī discusses Qurʾānic passages that were taken to support ʿAlī b. Abī Ṭālib and the *ahl al-bayt*, as well as in some of his other works, he consistently argued that all the Imams of the *ahl al-bayt* or descendants of the Prophet were in fact Muʿtazilites (Ansari 2012a: 313–28, 477–82, 507–22, 553–64; Thiele 2012; Ansari and Schmidtke 2015: 140 n. 133). Al-Jishumī's writings proved particularly influential among the Zaydīs in Yemen. His comprehensive theological encyclopedia, *ʿUyūn al-masāʾil*, together with his autocommentary, *Sharḥ ʿUyūn al-masāʾil*, were influential theological texts that served as models during the sixth/twelfth century for the works of *qāḍi* Jaʿfar b. Aḥmad b. ʿAbd al-Salām al-Buhlūlī (d. 573/1177–8) and the latter's students in Yemen (see Chapter 27). Al-Jishumī's section on legal theory in the *Sharḥ ʿUyūn al-masāʾil* served as a model for the writings of the Zaydīs of Yemen on this discipline (Ansari and Schmidtke 2013; Ansari 2015, 173–9). His exegetical work, *al-Tahdhīb fi-l tafsīr*, along with Jār Allāh al-Zamakhsharī's (d. 538/1144) *al-Kashshāf ʿan ḥaqāʾiq al-tanzīl*, were the two most widely read Qurʾān commentaries among the Zaydīs of Iran and Yemen (Zarzūr 1971; Mourad 2012; 2013). Although he did not write as a Zaydī scholar, his books were exclusively preserved amongst the Zaydīs of Iran and Yemen.

During the late fifth/eleventh and early sixth/twelfth centuries, Rayy was home to several Zaydī families who played an important role in studying and expounding Bahshamite theology among the Zaydīs of Iran. One of the most important families during this period was the Farrazādī family (Ansari 2006; 2009a; 2011; 2013a, *nūn-ʿayn*; see also Ansari 2014). Prominent members of this family transmitted Zaydī Bahshamite thought across multiple generations. Abū Muḥammad Ismāʿīl b. ʿAlī b. Ismāʿīl al-Farrazādī studied Bahshamite theology with Abū Jaʿfar Muḥammad b. ʿAlī Mazdak (or: Mardak), a Zaydī student of Abū Muḥammad al-Ḥasan b. Aḥmad Ibn Mattawayh (Matūya), who in turn had studied with Abū Rashīd al-Nisābūrī and probably with ʿAbd al-Jabbār (see Chapter 9, Section III). Ibn Mazdak descended from a Zaydī family in Rayy. One text that was studied during this period in Rayy was Ibn Mattawayh's *al-Tadhkira fī aḥkām al-jawāhir wa-l-aʿrāḍ* on natural philosophy. A paraphrastic commentary (*taʿlīq*) on Ibn Mattawayh's *al-Tadhkira*, that had possibly been dictated by Ibn Mazdak, is preserved in a unique manuscript. The commentary resulted from his teachings (*taʿlīq*) of the text and it was probably written down by his student Ismāʿīl b. ʿAlī al-Farrazādī (Ansari 2006; Schmidtke 2008; Gimaret 2008). Another text which was widely read among the Zaydīs of the time is the *Sharḥ al-Uṣūl al-khamsa* of ʿAbd al-Jabbār, which was considered to be an authoritative textbook of Muʿtazilite thought at the time. It was again Ismāʿīl b. ʿAlī al-Farrazādī who composed a commentary (*taʿlīq*) on this work. He also wrote a *taʿlīq* on the *Kitāb al-Tabṣira* by Abū l-Ḥusayn al-Hārūnī on theological issues. Both *taʿālīq* are preserved in manuscript form (Gimaret 1979: 60f.; Ansari 2015, 206f.).

At the time of Ismāʿīl b. ʿAlī al-Farrazādī, the Muʿtazilīs of Rayy invariably endorsed the doctrines of the Bahshamiyya while rejecting the teachings of Abū l-Ḥusayn al-Baṣrī (d. 436/1044), one of the disciples of ʿAbd al-Jabbār who is reported to have challenged some of the views of his teacher during his lectures and eventually founded his own school (see Chapter 9, Section IV). Ismāʿīl disagreed with Abū l-Ḥusayn and it seems that he was in contact with Rukn al-Dīn Maḥmūd b. Muḥammad al-Malāḥimī al-Khʷārazmī (d. 536/1141), the renowned representative of the school of Abū l-Ḥusayn al-Baṣrī at the time. According to what Ibn al-Malāḥimī states in his *Kitāb al-Muʿtamad*, he exchanged some correspondences with Ismāʿīl al-Farrazādī (Ibn al-Malāḥimī, *Muʿtamad*, 371, 376, 378; Ansari 2012b). This suggests that the Bahshamites of Rayy were in contact with the Muʿtazilites of Khʷārazm. During the same period, Ibn al-Malāḥimī's Khʷārazmian contemporary al-Zamakhsharī travelled to Rayy where he studied with some Zaydī scholars (Ansari 2011). Later on, the above-mentioned Zaydī scholar, Zayd b. al-Ḥasan b. ʿAlī al-Bayhaqī al-Barawqanī, who was a student of al-Ḥākim al-Jishumī and of ʿAlī b. al-Ḥusayn al-Daylamī Siyāh [Shāh] Sarījān [Sarbījān], spent some time in Rayy (on his way to Yemen where he arrived in 541/1146) where the local Zaydīs studied with him the Zaydī and Muʿtazilī writings, including of al-Ḥākim al-Jishumī. Another member of the Farrazādī family is Abū ʿAlī al-Ḥasan b. ʿAlī b. Abī Ṭālib Isḥāq al-Farrazādī, known as *Khāmūsh*. He played an important role as transmitter of Zaydī *ḥadīth* literature in Rayy (Ansari 2006; 2009a; 2011). During the sixth/twelfth century, another family involved in these scholarly activities was the family of al-Kanī (Madelung 1988: 91). The leader of the Zaydī community in Rayy by the middle of the sixth/twelfth century was ʿImād al-Dīn Abū l-ʿAbbās Aḥmad b. Abī l-Ḥasan b. ʿAlī al-Kanī, who was a *muḥaddith* and a theologian. Aḥmad had studied with at least two members of the Farrazādī family as well as with Zayd b. al-Ḥasan al-Bayhaqī (when he arrived in Rayy before continuing on his way to Yemen), and he played an important role as transmitter of numerous Zaydī writings on *ḥadīth* and *kalām* (Ansari 2006; 2009a). When Zayd b. al-Ḥasan al-Bayhaqī arrived in Yemen and taught in Ṣaʿda, *qāḍī* Jaʿfar b. Aḥmad b. ʿAbd al-Salām, the above-mentioned Zaydī scholar from Yemen, was among his students. Having spent some three years in Yemen, al-Bayhaqī decided to return home, in the company of *qāḍī* Jaʿfar who intended to visit Rayy and Kūfa. Soon after their departure, Bayhaqī died, while *qāḍī* Jaʿfar continued his trip. The latter spent some time in Rayy where he studied with Aḥmad b. Abī l-Ḥasan al-Kanī as well as with one of the members of the Farrazādī family. While in Rayy, *qāḍī* Jaʿfar obtained manuscripts of numerous Zaydī and Muʿtazilī works and was granted several *ijāzāt* for transmitting Muʿtazilī as well as Zaydī writings. Upon his return to Yemen, he brought along numerous books, and his role in their transmission is indicated in the chains of transmission cited in the beginnings of the respective manuscripts as well as in the *ijāzāt*. On the basis of what he studied in Rayy and the books he brought to Yemen, *qāḍī* Jaʿfar is known to have propagated Bahshamite Muʿtazilī thought in Yemen and thus contributed to its spread among the local Zaydī community. It seems that while all the Bahshamite works that originated with Iranian authors are by now mostly lost in Iran, some of the original Iranian codices apparently still exist in the libraries of Yemen. Moreover, it seems that both prior to al-Bayhaqī's trip to Yemen and *qāḍī* Jaʿfar's journey to Iran as well as after it, scholars travelled between the two communities (Ansari 2013a; Zayd 1986; Schwarb 2011; Ansari and Schmidtke 2010b; Ansari and Schmidtke in press). Zaydīs from Iran not only went to Yemen but also regularly met Zaydīs in Mecca where they exchanged books and issued *ijāzas* to each other. Yaḥyā, the son of Aḥmad b. Abī l-Ḥasan al-Kanī, for example, undertook a trip to Mecca where he met some Zaydīs of Yemen (Ansari 2009a).

During the seventh/thirteenth century, Rayy had largely lost its significance as an intellectual centre for the Zaydīs, while northern Iran, Ṭabaristān and Jīlān, was now an important centre for the Hādawī and Nāṣirī legal traditions as well as the leading centre of Iranian Zaydī *kalām*—a position the region held up until the early Safavid period. Here, the study of Muʿtazilite *kalām* continued throughout the following generations, although only a few texts have been preserved that testify to this. However, compared to the lively intellectual scene of the Zaydīs in Yemen (see Chapter 27), the Zaydīs of Iran had by now mostly lost their place as intellectual stimulators in the field of theology (Madelung 1987: introduction and 137f.; 1988: 91f.; Dānishpazhūh 1971; Ansari and Schmidtke 2011b; Ansari 2012a: 339–56, 361–72; 2015: 140–4, 151–66).

II Different Literary Traditions among the Zaydīs in Iran

Among Zaydīs in Iran the practice of narrating Shīʿī *ḥadīth* was limited. While the early Zaydīs of Kūfa and Yemen had their own respective *ḥadīth* traditions, during the fourth/tenth and fifth/eleventh centuries the Zaydīs of Iran, most of whom were Bahshamites, predominantly cited Sunnī traditions which supported Zaydī doctrine as well. In contrast to the Twelver Shīʿīs, the Zaydīs of Iran were mostly interested in referring to Sunnī *ḥadīth* to substantiate their own views. Abū l-Ḥusayn al-Hārūnī in his *Sharḥ al-Tajrīd*, for example, extensively cites Sunnī *ḥadīth* to support the Hādawī legal tradition (Ansari 2005). *Ḥadīth* was thus one of the preferred genres of literature among the Zaydīs of Rayy, Khurasan, and northern Iran that was employed to teach and to transmit Zaydī doctrine. In contrast to the majority of Sunnī Muʿtazilites who showed little interest in *ḥadīth*, the genre played a significant role for the Zaydīs, and this alongside *kalām*. The Buṭḥānī brothers composed *ḥadīth* collections, and copies of their respective *Amālī* works figure among the more important Zaydī *ḥadīth* collections both in

Iran and Yemen. The above-mentioned Abū Saʿd al-Sammān also composed a *Kitāb al-Amālī*. Later on, al-Murshad bi-llāh Yaḥyā b. al-Ḥusayn al-Shajarī al-Jurjānī acted as an important transmitter of *ḥadīth*. He composed at least two *Amālī* works of *ḥadīth* which were penned down by his students, and he was one of the most influential Zaydī scholars to cite Sunnī *ḥadīth* in support of Zaydism. His father, Imam al-Muwaffaq bi-llāh, had composed a book on *ḥadīth*, titled *al-Iʿtibār wa-salwat al-ʿārifīn*. These works soon figured among the popular *ḥadīth* books among the Zaydīs (Ansari 2001d; 2009a; 2010b; 2011).

While composing exegetical works was an established literary genre among the Zaydīs in Yemen, the early Zaydīs of Iran refrained from composing similar works. The only exception among the early Imams in Iran is al-Nāṣir al-Uṭrūsh whose *Tafsīr* is lost. Other than this, the Zaydīs of Iran mostly relied, as it seems, on the exegeses of al-Jishumī and al-Zamakhsharī (Ansari 2012a: 339–56; Ansari and Schmidtke 2011b; see also Ansari 2009b).

In contents and style, the Zaydī authors of *kalām* works during this period very much followed the model of other Muʿtazilite books of their time, with the exception of the sections on the imamate, which they regularly adapted to the specifically Zaydī notions of *imāma*. Obviously, the manner in which early Zaydīs such as al-Qāsim b. Ibrāhīm, al-Hādī ilā l-Ḥaqq, and others discussed the imamate differed considerably from the discussions of the later Muʿtazilī Zaydīs. Abū Ṭālib al-Hārūnī treats the topic in his *al-Diʿāma fī tathbīt al-imāma*, employing a distinctly Muʿtazilī approach, and he is the first to choose this approach to defend the Zaydī notion of the imamate; it is on this topic that Zaydī authors regularly criticized their Muʿtazilī (non-Zaydī) co-religionists. A prominent example is Mānkdīm's *Taʿlīq Sharḥ al-uṣūl al-khamsa* in which the latter completely replaced ʿAbd al-Jabbār's discussion of the topic, now lost, with his own view of the imamate. At times, Zaydī copyists of Muʿtazilī works simply replaced the original chapters on the imamate with their own contributions. Even in cases when the original work would not have a chapter on the imamate, Zaydī copyists would add such a section to mark their Zaydī identity (Schmidtke 1997; Ansari 2012a: 385f.).

Another characteristic of the literary activities of the Zaydīs in Iran is their engagement in refuting the doctrines of the Twelver Shīʿīs and the Ismāʿīlīs (or Bāṭinīs). Abū l-Ḥusayn al-Hārūnī, for example, devoted much space to refuting the Bāṭinīs in his writings and his *fatāwā*. In his *Kitāb Ithbāt nubuwwat al-Nabī* he refutes the doctrines of the Ismāʿīlīs and in doing so he employs a Muʿtazilite approach (Schmidtke 2012). It is also reported that he judged the Ismāʿīlīs to be unbelievers. He also composed a treatise mostly devoted to their refutation. This in turn provoked his contemporary, the Ismāʿīlī preacher (*dāʿī*) Ḥamīd al-Dīn al-Kirmānī (d. 412/1020), who was well known in Iran at the time, to respond (Ansari 2010a). Abū l-Ḥusayn is also known to have written a refutation of the Imami scholar Ibn Qiba al-Rāzī. The Zaydī tradition of refuting Twelver Shīʿī doctrine goes back to the time of al-Qāsim b. Ibrāhīm al-Rassī, and it was continued thereafter by al-Hādī and his circle. The first Zaydī scholar of Iran to compose such a refutation was Abū Zayd al-ʿAlawī, mentioned at the beginning of this chapter. The

Zaydīs particularly attacked the recently developed Imami notions of the 'occultation' (*ghayba*) of the last Imam which was unacceptable in their eyes. This is evident from al-ʿAlawī's argumentation in his *al-Ishhād* which in turn prompted Ibn Qiba to respond. It is to be assumed that both the *Ishhād* and Ibn Qiba's response, *Naqḍ al-Ishhād*, were composed towards the end of the eighth decade of the third century/beginning of the ninth decade of the ninth century, or the beginning of the ninth decade of the third century/the first decade of the tenth century. Abū Zayd al-ʿAlawī is also known to have been among the first Zaydīs to compose a work—or a chapter—refuting the doctrine of Ismāʿīlīs (Modarressi 1993; Ansari 2000b; forthcoming a). During the early fourth/tenth century, Rayy was a place with strong Ismāʿīlī, Twelver Shīʿī, and Zaydī presence so that they were well aware of each other (Amir-Moezzi and Ansari 2009: 197f.). The principal opponent according to Abū Ṭālib al-Hārūnī's *al-Diʿāma* are the Twelvers. The criticisms Abū Ṭālib directs towards them largely echo those formulated by Abū Zayd al-ʿAlawī and those transmitted by Abū l-ʿAbbās al-Ḥasanī to Abū Ṭālib al-Hārūni. ʿAlī b. al-Ḥusayn al-Daylamī Siyāh (Shāh) Sarījān [Sarbījān] composed a commentary on Abū Ṭālib al-Hārūnī's *Diʿāma*, entitled *al-Muḥīṭ bi-uṣūl al-imāma ʿalā madhāhib al-Zaydiyya*, in which he regularly responds to *al-Shāfī fi l-imāma* by the Imami al-Sharīf al-Murtaḍā Abū l-Qāsim ʿAlī b. al-Ḥusayn al-Mūsawī ("Alam al-Hudā", d. 436/1044) (on him, see Chapter 11, Section III) (Ansari 2001a; 2015, 180–4; Ansari and Schmidtke 2011a: 199f. n. 75). Abū Ṭālib's student, the above-mentioned Abū l-Qāsim al-Ḥasanī, wrote also a refutation of another book by the Sharīf al-Murtaḍā, *al-Muqniʿ fī l-ghayba (al-Naqḍ al-muktafī ʿalā man yaqūlu bi-l imām al-mukhtafī*; cf. Ansari and Schmidtke 2015: 132f. n. 97; Ansari 2013b). Writing against the Ismāʿīlis was an established tradition among the Zaydīs of Rayy and other places of northern Iran. Abū l-Qāsim al-Bustī had not only composed a book against Ismāʿīlis (Stern 1961), he also wrote, as has been mentioned before, the *Kitāb al-Muʿtamad*, a book on the imamate in which he criticized the doctrine of the Twelvers (Ansari 2001c). When the Zaydīs of Iran confronted the Nizārī Ismāʿīlis of Alamūt during the time of Ḥasan al-Ṣabbāḥ and his followers due to political tensions, they endeavoured to compose a number of works against Ismāʿīlīs (Madelung 1987: 137f., 165f.).

References

Abū l-Qāsim al-Bustī (*Baḥth*). *Kitāb al-Baḥth ʿan adillat al-takfīr wa l-tafsīq (Investigation of the Evidence for Charging with Kufr and Fisq)*. Ed. W. Madelung and S. Schmidtke. Tehran: Iran University Press, 1382/2004.

Adang, C., W. Madelung, and S. Schmidtke (eds.) (2011). *Baṣran Muʿtazilite Theology: Abū ʿAlī Muḥammad b. Khallād's Kitāb al-Uṣūl and its Reception. A critical edition of the Ziyādāt Sharḥ al-uṣūl by the Zaydī Imām al-Nāṭiq bi-l-ḥaqq Abū Ṭālib Yaḥyā b. al-Ḥusayn b. Hārūn al-Buṭḥānī*. Leiden: Brill.

Amir-Moezzi, M. A., and H. Ansari (2009). 'Muḥammad b. Yaʿqūb al-Kulaynī (m. 328 ou 329/939–40 ou 940–1) et son Kitāb al-Kāfī: une introduction'. *Studia Iranica* 38: 191–247.

Ansari, H. (1998). 'Ibn-i ʿAbdak'. *Dāʾirat al-maʿārif-i buzurg-i islāmī*, iv. 198f.

Ansari, H. (2000a). 'Kitābī arzishmand dar tārīkh-i imāmān-i zaydiyya az muʾallifī Ṭabarī'. *Kitāb-i māh-i dīn* 33 (1379): 12–16.

Ansari, H. (2000b). 'Abū Zayd ʿAlawī va kitāb-i ū dar radd-i Imāmiyya'. *Maʿārif* 49: 125–9.

Ansari, H. (2000c). 'Waṣiyyat-i Junayd-i Baghdādī va yāddāshtī darbāra-yi Siyāsat al-murīdīn'. *Maʿārif* 50: 141–7.

Ansari, H. (2001a). 'Zaydiyya wa-manābiʿ-i maktūb-i Imāmiyya'. *Majalla-yi ʿulūm-i ḥadīth* 20: 149–61.

Ansari, H. (2001b). 'Nahj al-balāgha pīsh az Nahj al-Balāgha'. *Nashr-i dānesh* 19/1: 63–7.

Ansari, H. (2001c). 'Abū l-Qāsim-i Bustī wa Kitāb al-Marātib'. *Kitāb-i māh-i dīn* 39: 3–9.

Ansari, H. (2001d). 'Kitāb-hā-yi ṣūfiyāne-yi zaydiyān-i irānī wa yamanī'. *Ayene-yi mīrāth* 15: 24–9.

Ansari, H. (2005). 'Kitābī ḥadīthī az muʾallifī zaydī va īrānī'. *Kitāb-i māh-i dīn* 99: 34–7.

Ansari, H. (2006). 'Kitābī az maktab-i mutakallimān-i muʿtazilī-i Rayy'. *Kitāb-i māh dīn* 104/105/106: 68–75.

Ansari, H. (2009a). 'Nāgofte hāʾī az jāmiʿi-yi Rayy dar sada–ha-yi panjum u shishum-i qamarī'. <http://ansari.kateban.com/entry1567.html> (consulted 7 May 2015).

Ansari, H. (2009b). 'Abū Yūsuf al-Qazwīnī'. *Encyclopaedia Islamica* ii. 760–2.

Ansari, H. (2010a). 'Al-Imām al-Muʾayyad bi-llāh al-Hārūnī: fatāwā wa-ajwibat al-masāʾil wa istiftāʾāt wujjihat ilayh fī l-radd ʿalā al-Bāṭiniyya wa-ghayrihā min al-masāʾil'. *al-Masār* 33: 57–72.

Ansari, H. (2010b). 'Sunnat-i *Amālī* nawīsī dar miyān-i Zaydiyya'. <http://ansari.kateban.com/entry1701.html> (consulted 7 May 2015).

Ansari, H. (2011). 'Chand khāndān-i zaydī madhhab dar Rayy-i sada-hā-yi panjum u shishum-e qamarī u riwāyat-i *Amālī*-e Sammān'. <http://ansari.kateban.com/entry1827.html> (consulted 7 May 2015).

Ansari, H. (2012a). *Barrasīhāyi tārīkhī dar ḥawza-yi islām wa ṭashayyuʿ: Majmūʿa-yi nawad maqāla wa yāddāsht* [*Historical Studies on Islam and Shīʿism*]. Tehran: Kitābkhāna, mūze wa markaz-i asnād-i Majlis i shūrā-yi islāmī, 1390.

Ansari, H. (2012b). 'Pishguftār: al-Malāḥimī u Kitāb al-Muʿtamade-u'. Rukn al-Dīn Ibn al-Malāḥimī al-Khwārazmī, *al-Muʿtamad fī uṣūl al-dīn*. Ed. W. Madelung. Tehran: Mīrāth-i maktūb.

Ansari, H. (2012c). 'Un *muḥaddiṯ* muʿtazilite zaydite: Abū Saʿd al-Sammān et ses *Amālī*'. *Arabica* 59: 267–90.

Ansari, H. (2013a). 'Persian Introduction'. Sulaymān b. ʿAbd Allāh al-Khurāshī, *Kitāb al-Tafṣīl li-jumal al-Taḥṣīl*. Facsimile edn. of Ms Berlin, Glaser 51. With Introductions and Indexes by H. Ansari and J. Thiele. Tehran: Mīrāth-e maktūb.

Ansari, H. (2013b). 'Yek raddiyya-yi kuhansāli zaydī az Nīshābūr-i sadayi panjum bar Kitāb al-Muqniʿ-yi Sharīf-i Murtaḍā dar bāra-yi masʾalat-i ghaybat-imām (2)'. <http://ansari.kateban.com/entry1984.html> (consulted 7 May 2015).

Ansari, H. (2014). 'Yek mutakallim-i muʿtazilī-yi zaydī az Astarābād dar nīma-yi āghāzīn-i sada-yi shishum'. <http://ansari.kateban.com/entry2182.html> (consulted 7 May 2015).

Ansari, H. (2015). *Az ganjīna-hā-yi nusakh-i khattī: muʿarrifī-yi dast-niwishta-hā yī arzeshmand az kitābkhāne-hā-yi bozorg-i jahān dar Ḥowze ye ʿulūm e islāmī*. Vol. i. Isfahan: Daftar-i tablīghāt-i ialāmī, 1394.

Ansari, H. (forthcoming a). 'Abū Zayd al-ʿAlawī'. *The Encyclopaedia of Islam*. Three. Leiden: Brill.

Ansari, H. (forthcoming b). 'al-Muʾyyad bi-llāh al-Hārūnī'. *The Encyclopaedia of Islam*. Three. Leiden: Brill.

Ansari, H. (forthcoming c). 'Abū Ṭālib al-Hārūnī'. *The Encyclopaedia of Islam*. Three. Leiden: Brill.

Ansari, H., and S. Schmidtke (2010a). 'The Zaydī Reception of Ibn Khallād's *Kitāb al-Uṣūl:* The *taʿlīq* of Abū Ṭāhir b. ʿAlī al-Ṣaffār'. *Journal asiatique* 298: 275–302.

Ansari, H., and S. Schmidtke (2010b). 'Muʿtazilism after ʿAbd al-Jabbār: The *Kitāb Masāʾil al-khilāf fī l-uṣūl*'. *Studia Iranica* 39: 227–78.

Ansari, H., and S. Schmidtke (2011a). 'The Literary-Religious Tradition among 7th/13th Century Yemenī Zaydīs: The Formation of the Imām al-Mahdī li-Dīn Allāh Aḥmad b. al-Ḥusayn b. al-Qāsim (d. 656/1258)'. *Journal of Islamic Manuscripts* 2: 165–222.

Ansari, H., and S. Schmidtke (2011b). 'Iranian Zaydism during the 7th/13th Century: Abū l-Faḍl b. Shahrdawīr al-Daylamī al-Jīlānī and his Commentary on the Qurʾān'. *Journal asiatique* 299: 205–11.

Ansari, H., and S. Schmidtke (2012). 'Muʿtazilism in Rayy and Astarābād: Abū l-Faḍl al-ʿAbbās b. Sharwīn'. *Studia Iranica* 41: 57–100.

Ansari, H., and S. Schmidtke (2013). 'The Muʿtazilī and Zaydī Reception of Abū l-Ḥusayn al-Baṣrī's *Kitāb al-Muʿtamad fī uṣūl al-fiqh*: A Bibliographical Note'. *Islamic Law and Society* 20: 90–109.

Ansari, H., and S. Schmidtke (2015). 'The Literary-Religious Tradition among 7th/13th Century Yemenī Zaydīs (II): The Case of ʿAbd Allāh b. Zayd al-ʿAnsī (d. 667/1269)'. In D. Hollenberg, C. Rauch, and S. Schmidtke (eds.), *The Yemeni Manuscript Tradition*. Leiden: Brill, 101–54.

Ansari, H., and S. Schmidtke (in press). 'The Cultural Transfer of Zaydī and non-Zaydī Religious Literature from Northern Iran to Yemen, 12th through 14th Century'. In S. Brentjes and J. Renn (eds.), *Thabit ibn Qurra and the 40 Mercenaries: Globalization of Knowledge in Post-Antiquity*. Aldershot: Ashgate.

Dānishpazhūh, M. T. (1971). 'Du mashīkha-yi Zaydī'. *Nāma-yi Mīnuvī: Majmūʿa-yi sī va hasht guftār dar adab u farhang-i Īrānī bih pās-i panjāh sāl taḥqīqāt u muṭāliʿāt-i Mujtabā Mīnūvi*. Ed. Īraj Afshār. Tehran: Chāpkhāna-yi Kāvīyānī, 1350, 179–88.

van Ess, J. (1981). 'Some Fragments of the Muʿāraḍat al-Qurʾān Attributed to Ibn al-Muqaffaʿ'. In Wadad al-Qadi (ed.), *Studies Arabica et Islamica: Festschrift for Ihsan Abbas on his Sixtieth Birthday*. Beirut, 151–63.

Gimaret, D. (1979). 'Les *Uṣūl al-ḫamsa* du Qāḍī ʿAbd al-Ǧabbār et leurs commentaires'. *Annales islamologiques* 15: 47–96.

Gimaret, D. (2008). 'Le Commentaire récemment publié de la *Taḏkira* d'Ibn Mattawayh'. *Journal asiatique* 296: 203–28.

al-Ḥākim al-Jishumī (*Sharḥ*). 'Sharḥ ʿuyūn al-masāʾil'. *Faḍl al-iʿtizāl wa ṭabaqāt al-Muʿtazila*. Ed. Fuʾād al-Sayyid. Tunis, 1974.

Ibn al-Malāḥimī al-Khʷārazmī, Rukn al-Dīn Maḥmūd (*Muʿtamad*). *K. al-Muʿtamad fī uṣūl al-dīn*. Revised and enlarged edn. by W. Madelung. Tehran: Mīrāth-i maktūb, 2013.

Madelung, W. (1965). *Der Imām al-Qasim ibn Ibrahim und die Glaubenslehre der Zaiditen*. Berlin: de Gruyter.

Madelung, W. (1986). 'Zu einigen Werken des Imams Abū Ṭālib an-Nāṭiq bi l-Ḥaqq'. *Der Islam* 63: 5–10.

Madelung, W. (ed.) (1987). *Arabic Texts Concerning the History of the Zaydī Imāms of Ṭabaristān, Daylamān and Gīlān*. Wiesbaden: Steiner.

Madelung, W. (1988). *Religious Trends in Early Islamic Iran*. New York: Columbia University Press.

Madelung, W. (2004). 'Ḥasanī, Abu 'l-ʿAbbās Aḥmad b. Ebrāhīm'. *Encyclopaedia Iranica* 12/41.

Mānkdīm Shashdīw (*Taʿlīq*). *Taʿlīq Sharḥ al-Uṣūl al-khamsa*. Published as *Sharḥ al-Uṣūl al-khamsa* [erroneously attributed to ʿAbd al-Jabbār]. Ed. ʿAbd al-Karīm ʿUthmān. Cairo: Wahba, 1384/1965.

Modarressi, H. (1993). *Crisis and Consolidation in the Formative Period of Shiʿite Islam*. Princeton: The Darwin Press.

Mourad, S. (2012). 'The Revealed Text and the Intended Subtext: Notes on the Hermeneutics of the Qurʾān in Muʿtazila Discourse as Reflected in the Tahdhīb of al-Ḥākim al-Jishumī (d. 494/1101)'. In F. Opwis and D. Reisman (eds.), *Islamic Philosophy, Science, Culture, and Religion: Festschrift in Honor of Dimitri Gutas on his 65th Birthday*. Leiden: Brill, 367–97.

Mourad, S. (2013). 'Towards a Reconstruction of the Muʿtazilī Tradition of Qurʾanic Exegesis: Reading the Introduction to the Tahdhīb of al-Ḥākim al-Jishumī (d. 494/1101) and its Application'. In K. Bauer (ed.), *Aims, Methods and Contexts of Qurʾanic Exegesis (2nd/8th–9th/15th Centuries)*. Oxford: Oxford University Press, 101–37.

al-Murshad bi-llāh Abū l-Ḥusayn Yaḥyā b. al-Ḥusayn b. Ismāʿīl al-Shajarī al-Jurjānī (*Sīra*). *Sīrat al-Imām al-Muʾayyad bi-llāh Aḥmad b. al-Ḥusayn al-Hārūnī*. Ed. Ṣāliḥ ʿAbd Allāh Qurbān. Ṣanʿāʾ: Muʾassasat al-Imām Zayd b. ʿAlī al-thaqafiyya, 1424/2003.

Nāṣir al-Uṭrūsh al-Kabīr (*Bisāṭ*). *al-Bisāṭ*. Ed. ʿA. A. Jadbān. Saʿda, 1997.

Schmidtke, S. (ed. and trans.) (1997). *A Muʿtazilite Creed of az-Zamaḫšarī (d. 538/1144) (al-Minhāǧ fī uṣūl ad-dīn)*. Stuttgart: Steiner.

Schmidtke, S. (2008). 'MS Mahdawi 514: An Anonymous Commentary on Ibn Mattawayh's Kitāb al-Tadhkira'. In A. Akasoy and W. Raven (eds.), *Islamic Thought in the Middle Ages: Studies in Text, Transmission and Translation in Honour of Hans Daiber*. Leiden: Brill, 139–62.

Schmidtke, S. (2012). 'Biblical Predictions of the Prophet Muḥammad among the Zaydīs of Iran'. *Arabica* 59: 218–66.

Schwarb, G. (2011). 'Muʿtazilism in the Age of Averroes'. In P. Adamson (ed.), *In the Age of Averroes: Arabic Philosophy in the Sixth/Twelfth Century*. London: Warburg Institute, 251–82.

Sergeant, R. B. (1953). 'A Zaidī Manual of Ḥisbah of the 3rd Century'. *Rivista degli studi orientali* 28: 1–34.

al-Shaykh al-Ṭūsī, Muḥammad b. al-Ḥasan (*Tahdhīb*). *Tahdhīb al-aḥkām*. Ed. Ḥasan Mūsawī Kharsān. Tehran, 1971.

Stern, S. M. (1961). 'Abū l-Qasim al-Busti and his Refutation of Ismaʿilism'. *Journal of the Royal Asiatic Society* 14–35.

Thiele, J. (2012). 'La Causalité selon al-Ḥākim al-Ǧišumī'. *Arabica* 59: 291–318.

Zaryāb, ʿA. (1994). 'Abū l-Qāsim Balkhī'. *Dāʾirat al-maʿārif-i buzurg-i islāmī*. Tehran, vi. 150–7.

Zarzūr, ʿA. M. (1971). *al-Ḥākim al-Jishumī wa-manhajuhu fī tafsīr al-Qurʾān*. Beirut: Muʾassasat al-Risāla.

Zayd, M. ʿA. (1986). *Les Tendences de la pensée muʿtazilite au Yemen au 4ème/12ème siècle*. Ph.D. dissertation, Université de Paris III (Arabic trans. Sanaa 1997).

CHAPTER 11

THE SHĪʿĪ RECEPTION OF MUʿTAZILISM (II)

Twelver Shīʿīs

HASSAN ANSARI AND SABINE SCHMIDTKE

I Shīʿī Theology during the Lifetime of the Imams

The history of rational theology among the Twelver Shīʿites between the mid-third/ninth and seventh/thirteenth centuries passed through a series of phases, each one characterized by distinct doctrinal features.[1] Shīʿī (proto-Imami) theology began to evolve still during the lifetime of the Imams (*ʿaṣr al-ḥuḍūr*) (see also Chapter 4). It was particularly since the time of Imam Jaʿfar al-Ṣādiq (d. 148/765) that the extant biographical and doxographical literature testifies of a lively scene of *mutakallimūn* among the companions of the Imams (Modarressi 1984: 24ff; 1993: 109ff; Kohlberg 1986; 1988; van Ess 1991–7: i. 272–403). The attitude of the Imams towards their followers' engagement in *kalām* was ambiguous. Numerous accounts are preserved that report that they condemned manifestations of speculative reasoning in doctrinal questions, while other reports attest to disputations on theological issues between the Imams and their companions (Kohlberg 1988; Modarressi 1993: 110ff.; Abrahamov 2006; Madelung 2014). There is also evidence that the *mutakallimūn* enjoyed the encouragement and explicit support of the Imams, who appreciated their ability to aptly defend Shīʿī doctrines in disputations with non-Shīʿī opponents, Muslim and other (Modarressi 1984: 25–32; 1993: 115; Madelung 2014: 468). Moreover, the Imams unambiguously affirmed the primacy of reason over revelation (Madelung 2014: 466f.). The *mutakallimūn*'s engagement in defence of Shīʿī notions

[1] Hassan Ansari wishes to thank the Institute for Advanced Study at Princeton NJ, which hosted him as a member during the preparation of this chapter.

is reflected by the many titles of works preserved in the biographical and bibliographical literature that are concerned with the *imāma* and related Shīʿī doctrines.[2] These also demonstrate that the early Shīʿī *mutakallimūn* were at the same time concerned with other theological issues that went beyond the narrow thematic confines of the notion of the *imāma* and were hotly debated.[3] Moreover, they testify to the wide intellectual spectrum the early Shīʿī *mutakallimūn* had mastered—they were not only extremely well versed in *kalām* and took an active part in the theological discussions of their times, they also engaged in other disciplines such as philosophy. Additional information on the doctrinal views of the early Shīʿī *mutakallimūn* can be gleaned from the early heresiographical and doxographical literature, most importantly the *Kitāb al-Intiṣār* of al-Khayyāṭ (d. *c*.300/913) and the *Kitāb al-Maqālāt* of al-Ashʿarī (d. 324/936). These, however, need to be used with some caution, given the agenda of their authors. More reliable information about their theological views, as well as the doctrines of the Imams themselves, can be gleaned from the Imami literature of later centuries (Madelung 2014).

As a result of the ambiguous attitude of the Imams towards their engagement in speculative theology, the early Shīʿī *mutakallimūn* were constantly challenged by the overwhelming majority of their co-religionists who defined their role as unquestioningly receiving and transmitting what they had learned from the Imams alone and thus refraining from engaging in theological debates (Modarressi 1984: 110ff., 114ff.). The traditionists blamed the *mutakallimūn* for challenging the authority of the Imams when expressing independent views. This being said, it is important to note that in contrast to Sunnism, where *mutakallimūn* and *muḥaddithūn* as a rule opposed each other in the evaluation of the *aḥādīth*, this was not the case with early Shīʿism. The Shīʿī *mutakallimūn* were at the same time disciples and companions of the Imams as well as their faithful transmitters (Modarressi 2003), and they derived their doctrinal notions by and large from the teachings of the Imams, whom they considered as the ultimate source of knowledge, while relegating reason to the role of a means in dialectic and to delve into the so-called subtleties of *kalām* (*laṭīf al-kalām*) (Modarressi 1993: 112f.; see also the relevant in-depth studies by Madelung 1970; 1979; 2014; van Ess 1991–7: i. 272–403; also Bayhom-Daou 2001). Doctrinally, the *mutakallimūn* were thus in basic agreement with their opponents among the traditionists.

The teachings of the Imams can be gleaned from the Imami *ḥadīth* literature. In his analysis of Muḥammad b. Yaʿqūb al-Kulaynī's (d. 329/941) *Kitāb al-Uṣūl min al-Kāfī*, W. Madelung has shown that the Imams 'progressively came to endorse Muʿtazilite perspectives' (Madelung 2014: 468) thus paving the way for the later reception of Muʿtazilite

[2] The earliest extant Shīʿī biographical literature comprises the *Kitāb al-Rijāl* attributed to al-Barqī (d. 274/887–8 or 280/893), the *Kitāb al-Rijāl* of al-Kashshī (*fl.* early fourth/tenth century), the *Kitāb al-Rijāl* of Ibn al-Ghaḍāʾirī (*fl.* early fifth/eleventh century), the *Kitāb al-Rijāl* of al-Najāshī (d. 450/1058), and the *Kitāb al-Rijāl* of al-Shaykh al-Ṭūsī (d. 460/1067) as well as his *Kitāb al-Fihrist*.

[3] For the first two centuries, see Modarressi 2003; for the Shīʿī *kalām* literature until the end of the third/ninth century, see van Ess 1991–7: v. 66–103. Bio-bibliographical reference works for Shīʿī *mutakallimūn* and their writings from the third/ninth century onwards are MTK, MṬM, as well as, more generally, Āghā Buzurg al-Ṭihrānī 1983.

thought among the Imamis during the occultation (see Section II). They not only affirmed the primacy of reason over prophetic tradition, their notions of the reality of God as a transcendent immaterial being, His unicity as well as their distinction between God's essential and originated attributes were also very much in line with the doctrines of the Muʿtazila (Madelung 2014: 468–72). With respect to man's actions, the Imams upheld an intermediary position between the opposing views of constraint (*jabr*) and empowerment (*tafwīḍ*), a position that is expressed in the famous saying of Jaʿfar al-Ṣādiq, *lā jabr wa-lā tafwīḍ wa-lakinna amr bayn al-amrayn*—essentially an attempt to combine the notions of God who creates and controls everything and of Him being a just judge who rewards and punishes human beings on the basis of their actions. This was, it seems, also the Imams' motivation in formulating the doctrine of *badāʾ*, which implies the notion that God can suspend or change His decision when circumstances change (Madelung 2014: 473f.).

This general tendency notwithstanding, various circles of theologians evolved among the Shīʿīs during this period with numerous differences in the minutiae of their argumentations and in their doctrinal conclusions, although a comprehensive picture is still a desideratum. Arguably the most renowned theologian was Abū Muḥammad Hishām b. al-Ḥakam (d. 179/795–6). Unlike most Shīʿī *mutakallimūn* of his time, Hishām had converted to Shīʿism later in his life, apparently under the influence of Imām Jaʿfar al-Ṣādiq. Prior to this, he had apparently been introduced to dualist notions by the *zindīq* Abū Shākir al-Dayṣānī and he leaned towards the thought of Jahm b. Ṣafwān (on him see Chapter 3). This explains some of the disputes on doctrinal matters that specifically occurred between Hishām b. al-Ḥakam and Imam Jaʿfar al-Ṣādiq—this also being the reason for doctrinal disagreements between Hishām and some of the other Shīʿī *mutakallimūn* of the time (Madelung 2014; see also al-Ḥusaynī 1989–90; van Ess 1991–7: i. 349–82; Bayhom-Daou 2003). Among his pupils, Abū Muḥammad Yūnus b. ʿAbd al-Raḥmān al-Qummī was the most prominent representative of his circle (van Ess 1991–7: i. 387–92). Yūnus in turn was succeeded by Abū Jaʿfar Muḥammad b. Khalīl al-Sakkāk, another student of Hishām b. al-Ḥakam. The next in line to continue this tradition was Abū Muḥammad Faḍl b. Shādhān al-Nīshābūrī (d. 260/873) (Najāshī, *Rijāl* 306–8, no. 840). Ibn Shādhān is one of the earliest among the Shīʿī *mutakallimūn* a work of whom has been preserved, viz. his *Kitāb al-Īḍāḥ* (authenticity still disputed; cf. Modarressi 2003: xvii; Ansari 2012: 685–91). Moreover, it is noteworthy that he is the earliest author to have written a refutation of Muḥammad Ibn Karrām (or: Kirām) (d. 255/869), the eponymous founder of the Karrāmiyya (see Chapter 15), most likely still during the latter's life (editor's introduction to Faḍl b. Shādhān, *Īḍāḥ*; Bayhom-Daou 2001; Pākatčī 1998b).

II Shīʿī Theology during the Minor Occultation

During the brief interim period of the so-called 'Minor Occultation' (*al-ghayba al-ṣughrā*) (260/874–329/941) (for a general characterization, see Modarressi 1993;

Hayes 2015; Ansari in press), Twelver Shīʿism experienced an increased turn towards Muʿtazilism, with major consequences not only for the *mutakallimūn* among the Imamis but also for the traditionists. With the Imam no longer being immediately available as the ultimate source of knowledge, the *mutakallimūn* now attributed an even larger role to reason as a source of knowledge and they employed Muʿtazilite notions—most importantly the concept of divine justice—to bolster the doctrine of the *imāma* conceptually (Modarressi 1993: 115ff; Ansari in press). Earlier characteristic Shīʿī doctrinal notions, such as the intermediate position with respect to man's actions, were now replaced by the Muʿtazilite notion of man's autonomy to act. When discussing the ontology of God and His attributes, Imami theologians increasingly adopted Muʿtazilite terminology and notions. This new trend was initiated by a number of theologians from within Shīʿism and it was further supported by others who had formerly been associated with the Muʿtazilites and now joined the ranks of the Imamis. Among the first group mention should be made of two early fourth/tenth-century scholars Abū l-Ḥusayn Muḥammad b. Bishr al-Sūsanjirdī and Abū Muḥammad ʿAbd al-Raḥmān b. Aḥmad b. Jabrawayh al-ʿAskarī (Modarressi 1993: 116, 118f.). Among the most prominent Shīʿī theologians during the 'Minor Occultation' were two members of the Nawbakht family of Baghdad, the socio-political centre of Shīʿism where rational sciences including *kalām* thrived, viz. Abū Sahl Ismāʿīl b. ʿAlī (b. 237/851, d. 311/924) and his nephew Abū Muḥammad Ḥasan b. Mūsā (d. betw. 300/912 and 310/922). They were not only engaged in the doctrinal conceptualization of the doctrine of the *imāma* and the notion of occultation (*ghayba*) employing Muʿtazilite notions but also played an active role in the socio-political sphere, following a long family tradition (Iqbāl 1966; Anthony 2013). Together with Ḥusayn Ibn al-Rawḥ al-Nawbakhtī (d. 326/938) (Klemm 1984), the third *wakīl* of the Hidden Imam, Abū Sahl al-Nawbakhtī was arguably the most outstanding representative of the family during the 'Minor Occultation'. He was renowned both as a *mutakallim* and as a poet and patron of literature, and he seems to have held a secretarial position during most of his life. The titles of Abū Sahl's works as transmitted in the biographical literature indicate the wide scope of his intellectual pursuits. These covered a broad range of themes: the imamate; critique of non-Shīʿī sects, including the Muʿtazila; legal theory; refutations against the Jews and others who rejected the Prophet's call; specific themes of theology; critiques of other theological matters (Najāshī, *Rijāl*, 31f. no. 68; Ibn al-Nadīm, *Fihrist*, 1 ii/634f.; Madelung 1985a; Ansari 2009a). Ḥasan b. Mūsā in turn was most renowned for his *Kitāb Firaq al-shīʿa*, our most important source for the early sects of the Shīʿa. As was the case with Abū Sahl, he accepted numerous Muʿtazilite positions while at the same time rejecting those that were not in line with the general views of the Shīʿa, in the domains of the imamate and the notion of the divine threat of eternal punishment of the unrepentent grave sinner (*al-waʿīd*) and his intermediate position (*al-manzila bayn al-manzilatayn*). In addition, he was intimately familiar with Aristotelian philosophy as is evident from his lost *Kitāb al-Ārāʾ wa-l-diyānāt*, numerous quotations of which are preserved in the works of later authors (Madelung 2013; cf. also Rashed 2015). While none of their theological writings are extant, extensive excerpts are preserved in the writings of al-Shaykh al-Ṣadūq (on him see Section III) and others (Ansari 2009a), and the doctrinal positions of the Banū Nawbakht are regularly referred to by later Shīʿite and non-Shīʿite authors, such as al-Shaykh al-Mufīd (on him, see Section III) who regularly mentions the doctrinal positions of the Banū Nawbakht in his doxographical work *Awāʾil al-maqālāt fī l-madhāhib al-mukhtārāt* (McDermott 1978: 22–5), while the Muʿtazilite author Rukn al-Dīn Maḥmūd b. Muḥammad Ibn al-Malāḥimī al-Khʷārazmī (d. 536/1141) relies heavily on Ḥasan b. Mūsā's *Kitāb al-Ārāʾ wa-l-diyānāt* in his *Kitāb al-Muʿtamad fī uṣūl al-dīn* (Madelung 2013).

Prominent Muʿtazilite converts to Twelver Shīʿism during the Minor Occultation were Abū ʿAbd Allāh Muḥammad b. ʿAbd Allāh b. Mumlak (or: Mamalak) al-Iṣbahānī (Modarressi 1993: 116f.), Abū Aḥmad Muḥammad b. ʿAlī al-ʿAbdakī ('Ibn ʿAbdak') who apparently remained between Shīʿism and Muʿtazilism (Ṭūsī, *Fihrist*, 229 no. 906; Ansari 1998a) and, most prominently, Abū Jaʿfar Muḥammad b. ʿAbd al-Raḥmān b. Qiba al-Rāzī (Modarressi 1993: 117ff.). Ibn Qiba, who lived during the second half of the third/ninth century in Rayy, alongside Baghdad one of the leading intellectual centres of Twelver Shīʿism during this period, is renowned as author of 'books on theology' (*lahu kutub fī l-kalām*), including some titles devoted to the *imāma*. He was a contemporary of Abū l-Qāsim al-Balkhī (d. 319/931) with whom he engaged in a written disputation on the issue of the imamate, and he is credited with a refutation (*radd*) of Abū ʿAlī al-Jubbāʾī (d. 303/916). His engagement with al-Balkhī and al-Jubbāʾī indicates his influence beyond Rayy, as does his correspondence with Ḥasan b. Mūsā al-Nawbakhtī as well as the impact his writings left on al-Sharīf al-Murtaḍā (on him, see Section III). In addition to Ibn Qiba, the biographical sources mention the following scholars during the period of the 'Minor Occultation' and beyond: Abū ʿAbd Allāḥ Jaʿfar b. Aḥmad b. Wandak al-Rāzī (Najāshī, *Rijāl*, 122 no. 316), Abū Bakr Muḥammad b. Khalaf al-Rāzī (Najāshī, *Rijāl*, 381 no. 1034), Abū Ṭayyib al-Rāzī (Ṭūsī, *Fihrist*, 225 no. 874), Abū Manṣūr al-Ṣarrām who was active in Nishapur (Ṭūsī, *Fihrist*, 225 no. 873), as well as the following three scholars all of whom acted as teachers of al-Shaykh al-Mufīd: Abū l-Jaysh al-Balkhī (d. 367/978) (Ansari 2009a), Ṭāhir Ghulām Abī l-Jaysh (Ansari 2009b: 181), and Ibn Abī ʿAqīl al-ʿUmānī (Modarressi 1984: 35–7).

III Shīʿī Theology during the Major Occultation

The first centuries of the so-called 'Major Occultation' (*al-ghayba al-kubrā*) (since 329/941) may aptly be characterized as a period of consolidation. It witnessed the heyday of 'muʿtazilization' among the Imāmiyya, heralded by the work of Abū ʿAbd Allāh Muḥammad b. Muḥammad b. al-Nuʿmān al-Ḥārithī al-ʿUkbarī ('al-Shaykh al-Mufīd', b. 336/948, d. 413/1022) (Sourdel 1972; 1973; McDermott 1978; 1989; Sander 1994; al-Jaʿfarī 1992–3a; Ṭabāṭabāʾī 1992–3; Bayhom-Daou 2005; Ansari in press) and culminating in the work of his student, the Sharīf al-Murtaḍā Abū l-Qāsim ʿAlī b. al-Ḥusayn al-Mūsawī ('ʿAlam al-Hudā', b. 355/967, d. 436/1044) (on his life, see Muḥyī al-Dīn 1957; Maʿtūq

2008), brother of the renowned al-Sharīf al-Raḍī (d. 406/1016), the compiler of *Nahj al-balāgha*.

However, Muʿtazilism had left its mark on the Imami traditionists during this period, as is evident in the work of Abū Jaʿfar Muḥammad b. ʿAlī b. Bābūya (Bābawayh) al-Qummī ('al-Shaykh al-Ṣadūq', d. 381/991). Ibn Bābūya was the most prominent representative of Imami traditionalism of his generation and at the same time he was well aware of the doctrinal developments among the *mutakallimūn* both within Imamism and beyond. He hailed from Qum but spent most of his life in Rayy—the intellectual centre of Muʿtazilism during the vizierate of Abū l-Qāsim Ismāʿīl b. ʿAbbād ('al-Ṣāḥib b. ʿAbbād', b. 326/938, d. 385/925)—where he also died (for his biography, see Ansari in press). Although categorically opposed to *kalām*, he nevertheless rejected any notion of assimilating God to created beings (*tashbīh*). In the course of the introduction to his *Kitāb al-Tawḥīd*, a traditionist theological summa which Ibn Bābūya compiled while residing in Rayy, he explains his motivation in composing the work—Twelver Shīʿīs had been accused of accepting anthropomorphism and determination (some of the Imami *muḥaddithūn* of his time did in fact believe in this). His intention in this work is to defend the Imāmiyya against this reproach and to show its compatibility with the Muʿtazilite notions of *tanzīh* and divine justice. Though based primarily on *ḥadīth* rather than reason, he treats in his book some of the topics that were typically discussed by the Muʿtazilites and the structure of the work echoes that of contemporary *kalām* works (cf. McDermott 1978: 13, 315–69; Sander 1994: *passim*). He displays a similar approach in his brief credal work, *Iʿtiqādāt al-Imāmiyya* (Fyzee 2014).

Departing from the traditionist outlook of Ibn Bābūya, his *shaykh* in *ḥadīth*, whose metholodogy he refuted in his critical commentary on Ibn Bābūya's *Kitāb Iʿtiqādāt al-Imāmiyya*, titled *Taṣḥīḥ* ('Rectification') *Iʿtiqādāt al-Imāmiyya*, al-Mufīd had formulated a new type of theological thought for the Twelver Shīʿites, this work thus being a refutation of the Imami *aṣḥāb al-ḥadīth* (McDermott 1978: 313–69; Sander 1994: 82–122).[4] For this purpose, he drew in particular on the doctrinal system of the School of Baghdad and Abū l-Qāsim al-Kaʿbī al-Balkhī (d. 319/931). However, al-Mufīd refrained from identifying himself with the School stressing rather the distinctive character of the Imāmiyya as against the Muʿtazila. In his *Awāʾil al-maqālāt* he lists the differences between the Imāmiyya and other groups, especially the Muʿtazilites, and a work of his that was published under the title of *al-Ḥikāyāt fī mukhālafāt al-Muʿtazila min al-ʿadliyya wa-l-farq baynahum wa-bayn al-Shīʿa al-imāmiyya* is devoted, as its title indicates, to the differences between the Muʿtazilites and the Imamis. Al-Mufīd's criticism is primarily aimed at Abū Hāshim al-Jubbāʾī (d. 321/933) and his followers (McDermott 1978: 47–311). Among the particularly objectionable doctrines of the Bahshamiyya, al-Mufīd singles out the following: the notion of the 'states' (*aḥwāl*) as a conceptual framework for the ontological foundation of the attributes of God and created beings

[4] All extant works of al-Shaykh al-Mufīd were republished in 1413/1993 to celebrate his millenary; al-Mufīd, *Muṣannafāt*.

(*Ḥikāyāt*, 49ff.; *Awāʾil*, 52, 56), the related issue of the thingness of the non-existent (*shayʾiyyat al-maʿdūm*), and the doctrine that God's attribute of willing is an originated attribute (*ṣifa ḥāditha*) that is subject to change and that His will subsists in no substrate (*lā fī maḥall*) (*Awāʾil*, 53). In many issues he identifies the views of the Baghdādīs and of Abū l-Qāsim al-Balkhī with those of the Imams. The Imāmiyya and the Muʿtazila (Baṣrans and Baghdādīs alike) further disagree in his view on the issue of the imamate and related questions, such as the definition of belief (*īmān*), which leads him to reject the Muʿtazilite notions of promise and threat (*al-waʿd wa-l-waʿīd*) and of the intermediary position of the grave sinner (*al-manzila bayn al-manzilatayn*) (*Ḥikāyāt*, 63–5).

Al-Murtaḍā departed from the theological views of his teacher al-Mufīd in favour of those of the Bahshamiyya, the only exceptions being again the notion of the *imāma* and related issues (esp. the definition of belief and promise and threat) with respect to which al-Murtaḍā maintains the characteristic Imami positions (for al-Murtaḍā's doctrinal thought, see Madelung 1970: 25ff.; McDermott 1978: 373ff.; al-Jaʿfarī 1992–3b; Abdulsater 2013; 2014).[5] Quṭb al-Dīn Saʿīd b. Hibat Allāh al-Rāwandī (d. 573/1177–8) enumerates more than ninety doctrinal differences between al-Mufīd and al-Murtaḍā in his lost work *al-Khilāf alladhī tajaddada bayna l-Shaykh al-Mufīd wa-l-Murtaḍā* (Kohlberg 1992: 217 no. 264). Al-Murtaḍā's predilection for the doctrines of the Bahshamiyya reflects the predominance of this school within the Muʿtazila during his lifetime. It was mostly during the vizierate of al-Ṣāḥib b. ʿAbbād that the teaching of Muʿtazilī theology, and primarily its Bahshamite brand, were promoted throughout Būyid territories and beyond.

The intellectual centre for *kalām* among the Imamis during the late fourth/tenth century until the Saljuq invasion of the city in 447/1056 was Baghdad, marked by the presence of prominent scholars such as al-Mufīd, al-Murtaḍā, and their most prominent student Abū Jaʿfar Muḥammad b. al-Ḥasan al-Ṭūsī ('al-Shaykh al-Ṭūsī', b. 385/995, d. 460/1067) (Ansari and Schmidtke 2013; 2014). As was the case with the Shaykh al-Ṭūsī, virtually all leading Twelver Shīʿī scholars who flourished during the first half of the fifth/eleventh century had studied either with al-Mufīd, with al-Murtaḍā, or both (Ansari and Schmidtke 2014: 476–80). These include Abū l-Ḥasan Muḥammad b. Muḥammad b. Aḥmad al-Buṣrawī (d. 443/1051), author of *al-Mufīd fī l-taklīf*, a work that presumably dealt with theology and legal issues (lost); Abū l-Ṣalāḥ Taqī b. Najm b. ʿUbayd Allāh al-Ḥalabī (d. 447/1055), author of *al-Kāfī fī l-taklīf* on theology and legal issues and *Taqrīb al-maʿārif* on theology; Abū Yaʿlā Sallār [Sālār] b. ʿAbd al-ʿAzīz al-Daylamī (d. 448/1057?), who composed *al-Tadhkira fī ḥaqīqat al-jawhar wa-l-ʿaraḍ* and apparently a work entitled *Tatmīm al-Mulakhkhaṣ*, completing al-Murtaḍā's *al-Mulakhkhaṣ* (both

[5] Al-Ḥākim al-Jishumī reports (in his *Sharḥ ʿUyūn al-masāʾil*) that al-Murtaḍā had studied with ʿAbd al-Jabbār. This is not confirmed by any Imami source. See al-Ḥākim al-Jishumī, *Ṭabaqāt*, 383. It was only in recent years that al-Murtaḍā's most comprehensive works on *kalām* were made available through publication, viz. *Rasāʾil, Dhakhīra, Mulakhkhaṣ*. The year 1436/2014–15 marking the millenary of al-Murtaḍā's year of death, various events will be devoted to him which will undoubtedly instigate further scholarship on his oeuvre over the coming years.

are lost); Abū l-Fatḥ Muḥammad b. ʿAlī b. ʿUthmān al-Khaymī al-Karājikī (d. 449/1057), who wrote extensively on theology, including a commentary on al-Murtaḍā's *Jumal al-ʿilm*; Abū Yaʿlā Muḥammad b. Ḥasan b. Ḥamza al-Jaʿfarī (d. 463/1070?); and *qāḍī* ʿAbd al-ʿAzīz b. Niḥrīr b. ʿAbd al-ʿAzīz b. al-Barrāj al-Ṭarābulusī (b. *c*.400/1009, d. 481/1088–9). Mention should also be made of Abū ʿAlī al-Ḥasan b. Aḥmad b. ʿAlī b. al-Muʿallim al-Ḥalabī (d. after 453/1061), who was a student of Abū l-Ṣalāḥ al-Ḥalabī and wrote a commentary on al-Murtaḍā's *Mulakhkhaṣ*. While al-Karājikī, Abū Yaʿlā al-Jaʿfarī and possibly Abū l-Ḥasan al-Buṣrawī remained faithful to al-Mufīd, maintaining as a rule the Baghdādī positions, all other theologians of this generation apparently followed al-Murtaḍā in their preference for the doctrines of the Bahshamiyya.

Some of these theologians were also familiar with at least some aspects of Abū l-Ḥusayn al-Baṣrī's (d. 436/1044) theological thought—a former student of *qāḍī l-quḍāt* ʿAbd al-Jabbār al-Hamadānī, who disagreed with most of the specifically Bahshamite teachings of his teacher (see Chapter 9)—albeit in a negative manner. It was mostly the latter's criticism of the Twelver Shīʿite notion of the imamate, expressed for example in his refutation (*naqḍ*) of al-Murtaḍā's *Kitāb al-Shāfī*, that was known to and refuted by Sallār [Sālār] b. ʿAbd al-ʿAzīz (*al-Radd ʿalā Abī l-Ḥusayn al-Baṣrī fī Naqḍihi Kitāb al-Shāfī*; cf. MTK 3/366 no. 6477) and by al-Karājikī (*Risālat al-Tanbīh ʿalā aghlāṭ Abī l-Ḥusayn al-Baṣrī fī faṣlin fī dhikr al-imāma*; MTK 2/333f. no. 4022). None of these refutations is extant.

The later Imami literature contains some few glimpses that seem to suggest that in some of his lost writings al-Shaykh al-Ṭūsī departed from the doctrines of the Bahshamites, presumably due to the influence of the doctrinal views of Abū l-Ḥusayn al-Baṣrī. Our knowledge of al-Ṭūsī's doctrinal views is based only on his commentary on al-Murtaḍā's *Jumal al-ʿilm* and on his briefer writings in this discipline, in which al-Ṭūsī shared al-Murtaḍā's preference for the doctrines of the Bahshamiyya. By contrast, all of al-Ṭūsī's more comprehensive works on theology are lost and it is unclear to what extent he maintained Bahshamite positions in them, particularly in those works that he composed at a more advanced stage of his life (Ansari and Schmidtke 2014). In a *fatwā* by Sharaf al-Dīn Abū ʿAbd Allāh al-Ḥusayn b. Abī l-Qāsim al-ʿAwdī al-Asadī al-Ḥillī (*fl.* first half of the eighth/fourteenth century) concerning the status of one who upholds the doctrine that the 'non-existent' (*maʿdūm*) is 'stable' (*thābit*), the latter rejected the Bahshamite position that the 'non-existent' (*maʿdūm*) is 'stable', is a 'thing' (*shayʾ*) (Schmidtke 2009). To support his argument, Sharaf al-Dīn refers to al-Ṭūsī who, Sharaf al-Dīn claims, had maintained the same view in his *Riyāḍat al-ʿuqūl*. This would imply that al-Ṭūsī had criticized or even rejected the Bahshamite notion of states in their entirety in this (lost) work, doubtless due to the influence of Abū l-Ḥusayn al-Baṣrī.

During the early sixth/twelfth century Bilād al-Shām (Tripoli and Aleppo) had emerged as a significant centre of Twelver Shīʿite learning, alongside Rayy and Khurāsān in Iran as well as Iraq. Mention should be made of Abū l-Faḍl Asʿad b. Aḥmad al-Ṭarābulusī (d. early sixth/twelfth century) who had composed a number of works on theology, among them *ʿUyūn al-adilla fī maʿrifat Allāh* and *al-Bayān fī ḥaqīqat al-insān*

(Ansari 1998b). The Imami theologian Rashīd al-Dīn Abū Jaʿfar Muḥammad b. ʿAlī Ibn Shahrāshūb al-Māzandarānī, who hailed from Sārī in Māzandarān (b. 489/1096) and had been educated in Rayy and Khurāsān, later on went to Aleppo where he died on 16 Shaʿbān 588/27 August 1192. Among his writings, his *Kitāb Aʿlām al-ṭarāʾiq fī l-ḥudūd wa-l-ḥaqāʾiq* is partly concerned with theology (Pākatčī 1998a; Ansari 2001). One of the most prominent members of the Banū Zuhra, the leading family of the Imami community in Aleppo (Salati 1992; 2010; Eddé 1999: 438ff.), was Abū l-Makārim ʿIzz al-Dīn Ḥamza b. ʿAlī b. Zuhra al-Ḥusaynī al-Ḥalabī (b. Ramaḍān 511/1117, d. 585/1189–90), author of *Ghunyat al-nuzūʿ ilā ʿilmay al-uṣūl wa-l-furūʿ*. In the first part of his *Ghunya*, which is devoted to theology, he adheres to the doctrinal views of al-Murtaḍā. Abū l-Makārim's brother, Jamāl al-Dīn Abū l-Qāsim ʿAbd Allāh b. ʿAlī b. Zuhra al-Ḥusaynī al-Ḥalabī (b. 531/962–3, d. after 597/1200), is known to have composed several works on doctrinal questions, viz. *Jawāb suʾāl warada min Miṣr fī l-nubuwwa, Kitāb al-Tabyīn li-masʾalatay al-shafāʿa wa-ʿuṣāt al-muslimīn, Tabyīn al-maḥajja fī kawn ijmāʿ al-Imāmiyya ḥujja, Masʾala fī nafy al-taḥābuṭ* (or: *Masʾala fī nafy al-takhlīṭ*), *Jawāb suʾāl warada ʿan al-Ismāʿīliyya*, and *Jawāb sāʾil saʾala ʿan al-ʿaql* (MṬF 6/162f.; Salati 1992: 130 no. 4). Among Abū l-Makārim's students, we know of Muʿīn al-Dīn Abū l-Ḥasan Sālim b. Badrān al-Māzinī al-Miṣrī (alive in 629/1232) (MṬM 2/381f. no. 263), who later became a teacher of Naṣīr al-Dīn al-Ṭūsī (d. 672/1274) to whom he issued an *ijāza* for Abū l-Makārim's *Ghunya* (dated 18 Jumādā II 629/April 1232) (Mudarris Raḍawī 1991: 161–7). In Aleppo, another Imami theologian, Najīb al-Dīn Abū l-Qāsim ʿAbd al-Raḥmān b. ʿAlī b. Muḥammad al-Ḥusaynī (d. 582/1186), commented on the *Muqaddima* of al-Shaykh al-Ṭūsī (Ansari and Schmidtke 2013; 2014).

IV Shīʿī Theology since the Sixth/Twelfth Century

Over the course of the first half of the sixth/twelfth century and increasingly during its second half, a growing reservation against the controversial doctrines of the Bahshamiyya can be observed among the Imami *mutakallimūn* that went hand in hand with a slow—real or imagined—'return' towards the early doctrines of the Imams. While the beginnings of this 'imamization' of Muʿtazilite theology are still unclear, the most prominent (though not the earliest) representative of this new trend was Sadīd al-Dīn Maḥmūd b. ʿAlī b. al-Ḥasan al-Ḥimmaṣī al-Rāzī, who flourished during the second half of the sixth/twelfth century and who had completed his comprehensive theological *summa, al-Munqidh min al-taqlīd*, on 9 Jumādā I 581/8 August 1185 in al-Ḥilla. In this work, al-Ḥimmaṣī departed from the doctrinal views of al-Murtaḍā and his followers by adopting the teachings of Abū l-Ḥusayn al-Baṣrī which he apparently considered to be closer to those of the Imams than the Bahshamite teachings. Although historically inaccurate, al-Ḥimmaṣī held the doctrines of Abū l-Ḥusayn and his followers to be essentially in agreement with those of the School of Baghdad. This identification, which pre-dates al-Ḥimmaṣī (Ansari, Madelung, and Schmidtke 2015: 35f.) and can also be observed among Zaydī theologians (see Chapter 27), may be interpreted as an attempt to re-establish the theological system of al-Mufīd, who had argued that his doctrine was in basic agreement with the teachings of the Imams. Later Imami theologians shared the perception of al-Mufīd's doctrines having been in agreement with the teachings of the Imams, and this against al-Murtaḍā, who had diverged from them when adopting Bahshamite concepts. Raḍī al-Dīn ʿAlī b. Mūsā Ibn Ṭāwūs (d. 664/1266), for example, who rejected *kalām* and was particularly critical towards the Muʿtazila, harshly criticized al-Murtaḍā while he praised al-Ḥimmaṣī and his theological thought (Ibn Ṭāwūs, *Faraj*, 146).

Abū l-Ḥusayn al-Baṣrī's theological notions were known to and had apparently been controversially discussed among the Imami theologians of Rayy (and, to a lesser extent, in Khurasan) over most of the late fifth/eleventh and early sixth/twelfth centuries. During the Saljuq period, 434/1042–600/1203, Imami *kalām* seems to have significantly flourished in Rayy, unlike Baghdad, whose most prominent theologian of the time, al-Ṭūsī, had fled to Najaf after his home and library had been looted and burned during the Saljuq invasion of the city in 447/1056 and where scholarly and other activities of Twelver Shīʿites were significantly restricted (Van Renterghem 2015). This renewed flourishing of Imami theological thinking in Rayy came to an end as a result of the civil war between Ḥanafīs, Shāfiʿites, and Shīʿīs in Rayy at the turn of the seventh/thirteenth century. The final blow for the city came with the Mongol occupation of the city (Ansari 2013a). This led to the virtual destruction of the literary legacy of Shīʿī *kalām* in the city, and it is exclusively the bio-bibliographical literature that provides us with some information on the protagonists and their respective doctrinal views. The following Imami theologians are mentioned in the sources as having been active in Khurasan (Nishapur and Bayhaq) and in Rayy during the Saljuq period (434/1042–600/1203):

- **al-Faqīh Abū l-Ḥasan Amīrkā b. Abī l-Lujaym b. Amīra al-Maṣdarī al-ʿIjlī al-Qazwīnī** (d. 514/1120) (Muntajab al-Dīn, *Fihrist*, 35 no. 15; ʿAbd al-Jalīl Rāzī, *Naqḍ*, 46, 226; Capezzone 2006: no. 23), the author of several works on theology (and/or legal theory) ('*wa-lahu taṣānīf fī l-uṣūl minhā al-Taʿlīq al-kabīr, al-Taʿlīq al-ṣaghīr, al-Ḥudūd, masāʾil shattā*').
- **al-Shaykh Zayn al-Dīn ʿAlī b. ʿAbd al-Jalīl al-Bayāḍī *al-mutakallim*** (Muntajab al-Dīn, *Fihrist*, 114 no. 236; Capezzone 2006: no. 71; Āghā Buzurg 2009: 2-ii. 193, 302f.) was another supporter of the Bahshamite doctrine, as is suggested by the work title mentioned by his student Muntajab al-Dīn, entitled *Masāʾil fī l-maʿdūm wa-l-aḥwāl* (lost). At the beginning of Rajab 544/November 1149, al-Shaykh Masʿūd b. Muḥammad b. Abī l-Faḍl al-Rāzī transmitted from him.
- **Quṭb al-Dīn Abū Jaʿfar Muḥammad b. ʿAlī b. al-Ḥasan al-Muqriʾ al-Nīsābūrī** (d. mid-sixth/twelfth century) was another Imami *mutakallim* in Khurāsān. He is the author of the *Taʿlīq fī ʿilm al-kalām*, a partly preserved work that was intended as a paraphrase of al-Murtaḍā's *Mulakhkhaṣ* as well as his *Dhakhīra* as it seems (see the editor's

introduction to al-Muqriʾ, *Taʿlīq*; the beginning of the text is missing). Al-Muqriʾ also composed a work of definitions, *al-Ḥudūd* (al-Muqriʾ, *Ḥudūd*). Throughout both works, the author endorses the doctrines of the Bahshamiyya and he refrains, as a rule, from even mentioning alternative views of Abū l-Ḥusayn al-Baṣrī and his followers. However, when discussing whether God is distinct from other essences by virtue of His essence (*dhāt*) or an additional attribute of essence (*ṣifat al-dhāt*), al-Muqriʾ states that both positions are compatible although the majority of Imami scholars tend to affirm an additional attribute of essence (al-Muqriʾ, *Taʿlīq*, 49). Al-Muqriʾ was in turn the teacher of Quṭb al-Dīn al-Rāwandī (d. 573/1177) (on him see below) in *kalām*.

- **Zayn al-Dīn Abū Saʿīd ʿAbd al-Jalīl b. ʿĪsā b. ʿAbd al-Wahhāb al-Rāzī**, a *mutakallim* who has several unspecified doctrinal writings to his credit (*lahu taṣānīf uṣūliyya*) (Muntajab al-Dīn, *Fihrist*, 77 no. 227). While otherwise nothing is known about him, he was the teacher of Abū l-Makārim Saʿd b. Abī Ṭālib b. ʿĪsā *al-mutakallim* al-Rāzī (see below).
- **Rashīd al-Dīn Abū Saʿīd ʿAbd al-Jalīl b. Abī l-Fatḥ Masʿūd b. ʿĪsā *al-mutakallim* al-Rāzī** (d. mid-sixth/twelfth century) (Āghā Buzurg 2009: 2-ii. 155) was a pupil of Amīrkā al-Qazwīnī and the author of a *Naqḍ Kitāb al-Taṣaffuḥ li-Abī l-Ḥusayn*, a (lost) refutation of Abū l-Ḥusayn's doctrinal views as laid down in his *Taṣaffuḥ al-adilla* as it seems. According to Muntajab al-Dīn (*Fihrist*, 110 no. 226), he also has a *Masʾala fī l-maʿdūm* (lost). The title suggests that he dealt in this work with the Bahshamite notion of *shayʾiyyat al-maʿdūm*, possibly defending it against Abū l-Ḥusayn, who negated that the non-existent can be real. Rashīd al-Dīn also wrote refutations directed against the Ashʿarites and the Zaydīs.
- **Muʿīn al-Dīn Abū l-Makārim Saʿd b. Abī Ṭālib b. ʿĪsā *al-mutakallim* al-Rāzī** ('al-Najīb', d. mid-sixth/twelfth century) (Āghā Buzurg 2009: 2-ii. 121; Muntajab al-Dīn, *Fihrist*, 68 no. 185; Capezzone 2006: no. 62) is the author of a *Kitāb al-Mūjaz fī l-uṣūl* and *Kitāb ʿUlūm al-ʿaql*. He also composed a *Masʾala fī l-aḥwāl* and *Safīnat al-najāt fī takhṭiʾat al-nufāt* (all lost). The latter two titles suggest that the author was an adherent of the Bahshamite notion of the 'states' (*aḥwāl*). This is corroborated by the fact that al-Ḥimmaṣī al-Rāzī, a follower of Abū l-Ḥusayn al-Baṣrī's doctrines, wrote a refutation of the *Kitāb al-Mūjaz*, *Naqḍ al-Mūjaz* (see below). Abū l-Makārim also composed a book directed against the Ashʿarites, viz. *Naqḍ Masʾalat al-ruʾya li-Abī l-Faḍāʾil al-Mashshāṭ*. Abū l-Makārim was a student and nephew of Zayn al-Dīn Abū Saʿīd ʿAbd al-Jalīl b. ʿĪsā b. ʿAbd al-Wahhāb al-Rāzī who was also a *mutakallim* (on him, see above).
- **Abū l-Futūḥ al-Ḥusayn b. ʿAlī al-Rāzī** (b. *c.*480/1087, d. after 552/1157) (Gleave 2007; Āghā Buzurg 2009: 2-ii. 79f.; Muntajab al-Dīn, *Fihrist*, 48 no. 78) is the author of a Persian commentary on the Qurʾān, entitled *Rawḍ al-jinān wa-rawḥ al-janān*. Throughout the commentary he regularly discusses theological questions, opting as a rule for the Bahshamite position (Ansari 2013b). His pupils included well-known Shīʿī authors such as Ibn Shahrāshūb (see Section III) and the bio-bibliographer Muntajab al-Dīn ʿAlī b. ʿUbayd Allāh al-Rāzī (b. 504/1110–11, d. after 600/1203), author of *Fihrist asmāʾ ʿulamāʾ al-Shīʿa wa-muṣannafihim*.

- **Saʿīd b. Hibat Allāh 'Quṭb al-Dīn al-Rāwandī'** (d. 573/1177), the author of *al-Khilāf alladhī tajaddada bayna l-Mufīd wa-l-Murtaḍā* (see Section III) and a commentary on the *Muqaddima* by al-Ṭūsī, *Jawāhir al-kalām fī sharḥ Muqaddimat al-kalām* (likewise lost). He hailed from Rāwand in the vicinity of Kāshān and had spent an extended period of time in Rayy (cf. the editor's introduction to Quṭb al-Dīn al-Rāwandī, *Lubb*, 1/8f.). Muḥammad b. ʿAlī b. al-Ḥasan al-Muqriʾ (see above) was one of his teachers in *kalām*. Quṭb al-Dīn al-Rāwandī in turn was the teacher of Ibn Shahrāshūb and Muntajab al-Dīn, the author of the *Fihrist*. Quṭb al-Dīn was familiar with some of the writings of a later follower of Abū l-Ḥusayn al-Baṣrī, Rukn al-Dīn Ibn al-Malāḥimī, as is evident from his *al-Farq bayn al-ḥiyal wa-l-muʿjizāt*, which is based heavily on a work by Ibn al-Malāḥimī, most probably his *Kitāb al-Fāʾiq*.
- **Naṣīr al-Dīn ʿAbd al-Jalīl b. Abī l-Ḥusayn b. Abī l-Faḍl al-Qazwīnī al-Rāzī** (d. mid-sixth/twelfth century), whose family hailed from Qazwīn, spent most of his life in Rayy (Madelung 1985b) where he authored the *Kitāb al-Naqḍ*. The full title of the work, *Baʿḍ maṭālib al-nawāṣib fī naqḍ baʿḍ faḍāʾiḥ al-rawāfiḍ*, reflects its origin as a refutation of a polemical attack on Imamism composed by an anonymous author who claims to have converted from Imamism to Sunnism. H. Ansari has suggested that this anonymous opponent was in fact Ḍiyāʾ al-Dīn, the father of Fakhr al-Dīn al-Rāzī (d. 606/1210) (Ansari 2013a). Throughout the work, the author regularly sides with the moderate rationalists repudiating the traditionists, which indicates ʿAbd al-Jalīl's predilection for *kalām* in general.[6]
- **Naṣīr al-Dīn Abū Ṭālib ʿAbd Allāh b. Ḥamza b. ʿAbd Allāh b. Ḥamza b. al-Ḥasan b. ʿAlī al-Shāriḥī al-Mashhadī ('Naṣīr al-Dīn al-Ṭūsī')** hailed from Khurasan. He was a pupil of Abū l-Futūḥ al-Rāzī (on him see above). Ibn Ḥamza is the author of *Kitāb al-Wāfī bi-kalām al-muthbit wa-l-nāfī*. In this tract, Naṣīr al-Dīn critically discusses the Bahshamite notion that the non-existent is a thing (*shayʾiyyat al-maʿdūm*) and the arguments of its protagonists (*aṣḥāb al-ithbāt*) and he sides with the *aṣḥāb al-nafy*. He is one of the earliest Imami theologians to endorse the views of Abū l-Ḥusayn al-Baṣrī while rejecting the Bahshamite notion of 'states' and the related doctrine that the non-existent is a thing (Ansari and Schmidtke forthcoming).
- **Sadīd al-Dīn Maḥmūd b. ʿAlī b. al-Ḥasan al-Ḥimmaṣī al-Rāzī** (b. *c.*500/1106–17, d. after 600/1204) (Muntajab al-Dīn, *Fihrist*, 164; ʿAbd al-Jalīl Rāzī Qazwīnī, *Naqḍ*, 227; Capezzone 2006: n. 68), the author of the *Kitāb al-Munqidh min al-taqlīd wa-l-murshid ilā l-tawḥīd al-musammā bi-l-Taʿlīq al-ʿirāqī*, completed in 581/1185 in al-Ḥilla, a work in which al-Ḥimmaṣī fully endorsed the doctrine of Abū l-Ḥusayn al-Baṣrī and his school. Al-Ḥimmaṣī's support for the latter's doctrines is corroborated by the title of his (lost) *Naqḍ al-Mūjaz*, a refutation of the *Kitāb al-Mūjaz fī l-uṣūl* of Abū l-Makārim, a follower of the Bahshamite doctrine (on him, see above).

[6] With his usage of the term *uṣūlī* (as against *akhbārī* tendency) he is the earliest Imami author to employ the term, although its meaning later changed during the Safavid period.

> In the introduction to the *Munqidh*, al-Ḥimmaṣī relates that after returning from the Ḥajj, he passed through Iraq where some Imami scholars of al-Ḥilla invited him to stay with them for several months. Al-Ḥimmaṣī accepted the invitation and engaged during his sojourn in the city in scholarly discussions and teaching. He was also asked to dictate summaries of his lessons in theology, a request he eventually accepted, aiming at first at a rather slim volume. However, when touching upon the central theological issues he felt the need to expand, so that the various sections of the eventual book, he explains, are not entirely harmonized with respect to their length. Moreover, since he only saw the work after it had been completed, repetitions and redundancies were unavoidable. He apparently used al-Murtaḍā's *al-Dhakhīra* and *al-Mulakhkhaṣ*, with some variations, to structure the *Munqidh* (al-Ḥimmaṣī, *Munqidh*, 1/17f.).

Further details about al-Ḥimmaṣī are given in the extant fragments of *Kitāb al-Ḥawī fī rijāl al-imāmiyya* of Ibn Abī Ṭayy al-Ḥalabī (d. 630/1232–3), who quotes Muntajab al-Dīn—probably from his lost *Tārīkh al-Rayy*. According to this source, it was not before the age of 50 that al-Ḥimmaṣī turned to scholarship while up to this time he earned his living as a seller of chick-peas (*ḥimmiṣ/ḥimmaṣ*), which is the reason for his *nisba* 'al-Ḥimmaṣī' (Ibn Ḥajar, *Līsān*, 5/317). Since in 560 AH he was already an accomplished scholar, he must have been born around 500 AH. He must therefore have been around 80 when he sojourned in al-Ḥilla and dictated his *Munqidh*.

Al-Ḥimmaṣī is credited with other works in the two disciplines of *kalām* and legal theory, neither of which is extant: (1) *al-Taʿlīq al-kabīr*. The genre of *taʿlīq* was a typical one during his lifetime for the disciplines of *kalām* and legal theory. (2) *al-Taʿlīq al-ṣaghīr*. (3) *al-Maṣādir fī uṣūl al-fiqh*, an important book on legal theory. Numerous quotations are preserved in the *Kitāb al-Baḥr al-muḥīṭ fī uṣūl al-fiqh* of the Shāfiʿī scholar Badr al-Dīn Muḥammad b. Bahādur b. ʿAbd Allāh al-Shāfiʿī al-Zarkashī (d. 794/1392) (al-Wāthiqī n.d.). For the development of legal theory among the Imamis the work apparently constituted an important incentive for the subsequent development of the discipline of *uṣūl al-fiqh* among the scholars of al-Ḥilla. (4) *al-Tabyīn wa-l-tanqīḥ fī l-taḥsīn wa-l-taqbīḥ*. The title suggests that it was concerned with ethical objectivism. (5) *Bidāyat al-hidāya*. Nothing is known about this work, although the title suggests that is was concerned with *kalām*.[7] It is likely that al-Ḥimmaṣī's theological works, with the exception of the *Munqidh*, the only work of his that was available in al-Ḥilla as it seems, fell prey to the virtual destruction of Rayy around the turn of the seventh/thirteenth century.

This brief overview of Imami *kalām* in Rayy and Khurāsān during the Saljuq period suggests that the doctrinal writings of Abū l-Ḥusayn al-Baṣrī were available in Rayy and

[7] A brief extant theological text, entitled by the editor as *al-Muʿtamad min madhhab al-shīʿa al-imāmiyya*, is also ascribed to al-Ḥimmaṣī (*Mīrāth-i islāmī-yi Īrān*, 6/16–34; MTK 5/180 no. 11094). In fact, however, this is a text written by a later anonymous author.

Khurasan. This was clearly the case for the *Taṣaffuḥ*, his most comprehensive theological work which remained incomplete. Moreover, al-Ḥimmaṣī's *Munqidh* has numerous extensive quotations from Abū l-Ḥusayn's *Ghurar al-adilla* which must likewise have been available in Rayy (Adang 2007). This contrasts strikingly with the pre-Saljuq period during which, to judge from the evidence of the Muʿtazilī and Zaydī sources, his works were unavailable (and perhaps not welcome) in Rayy and in Bayhaq. In addition to this, al-Ḥimmaṣī frequently refers to the *Kitāb al-Fāʾiq* of Ibn al-Malāḥimī, while Quṭb al-Dīn al-Rāwandī seems to have had his *Tuḥfat al-mutakallimīn fī l-radd ʿalā l-falāsifa* and/or his *Kitāb al-Fāʾiq* at his disposal. There is no indication that Ibn al-Malāḥimī's comprehensive *Kitāb al-Muʿtamad fī uṣūl al-dīn* was available to the Imami scholars discussed in this section.

For the period following al-Ḥimmaṣī al-Rāzī until the time of Naṣīr al-Dīn al-Ṭūsī (d. 672/1274), who had 'modernized' Twelver Shīʿī theology (see Chapter 26), very little is known about Imami theology—most theologians are again known by name only. During the lifetime of al-Ḥimmaṣī, al-Ḥilla had emerged as an important centre of Twelver Shīʿism, along with Baḥrayn (see Chapter 26) and Ḥalab (see Section III). Al-Ḥimmaṣī's teaching activities in al-Ḥilla were clearly instrumental in setting the tone for the subsequent doctrinal developments in the city. The generally positive attitude towards *kalām* in al-Ḥilla is indicated by a number of prominent figures who also engaged in *kalām*, such as Najm al-Dīn Abū l-Qāsim Jaʿfar b. al-Ḥasan b. Saʿīd ('al-Muḥaqqiq al-Ḥillī') (d. 676/1277) (Ustādī 2004), author of *al-Maslak fī uṣūl al-dīn*, a concise theological book in which he endorses the doctrines of Abū l-Ḥusayn al-Baṣrī. The Muḥaqqiq is also the author of a *fatwā* regarding the status of one who upholds the Bahshamite doctrine that the non-existent (*maʿdūm*) is stable (*thābit*), a doctrine he rejects. However, he maintains that the holder of this view is not to be charged with unbelief (*kufr*) or grave sin (*fisq*) (Schmidtke 2009: 388f.).

A number of additional texts of unclear authorship are known to have been written during this interim period. A comprehensive Imami work on *kalām* and *fiqh*, written in Persian, has been ascribed by the editor of the first part of the book, on *kalām*, to a certain Ḍiyāʾ al-Dīn b. Sadīd al-Dīn al-Jurjānī, a ninth/fifteenth-century author (Jurjānī, *Rasāʾil*, 45–132). This attribution is evidently erroneous—the anonymous author of the book invariably endorses Bahshamite doctrines and is clearly unaware of competing theological views such as those formulated by Abū l-Ḥusayn al-Baṣrī. The book was most likely composed towards the end of the fifth/eleventh century, possibly in Rayy. *Khulāṣat al-naẓar*, a work by an anonymous author and preserved in a single manuscript, was evidently composed during the late sixth/twelfth or early seventh/thirteenth century, as the anonymous author also endorses in this work the doctrinal positions of Abū l-Ḥusayn al-Baṣrī and explicitly refers to al-Ḥimmaṣī al-Rāzī (Ansari and Schmidtke 2006). A work entitled *Kitāb al-Yāqūt* was composed by a certain Abū Isḥāq Ibrāhīm b. Nawbakhtī. While ʿA. Iqbāl had argued that it was composed during the fourth/tenth century, it has meanwhile been established that the work should rather be dated to the early seventh/thirteenth century. As was the case with the ʿAllāma al-Ḥillī (d. 726/1325), who commented on the book in his *Anwār al-malakūt fī sharḥ al-Yāqūt*,

Abū Isḥāq fully endorsed the teachings of Abū l-Ḥusayn al-Baṣrī and was also intimately familiar with some of the writings of Fakhr al-Dīn al-Rāzī (Schmidtke 1991: 48; Ansari 2012: 797–804).

References

ʿAbd al-Jalīl Rāzī Qazwīnī (*Naqḍ*). *Naqḍ*. Ed. Jalāl al-Dīn Muḥaddith Urmawī. Tehran: Dār al-ḥadīth, 1391[/2011].

Abdulsater, H. A. (2013). *The Climax of Speculative Theology in Buyid Shiʿism: The Contribution of al-Sharif al-Murtada*. Ph.D. dissertation, Yale University.

Abdulsater, H. A. (2014). 'To Rehabilitate a Theological Treatise: Inqādh al-Bashar min al-Jabr wa-l-Qadar'. *Asiatische Studien—Études Asiatiques* 68: 519–47.

Abrahamov, B. (2006). 'The Attitude of Jaʿfar al-Ṣādiq and ʿAlī al-Riḍā toward *kalām* and Rational Reasoning'. *Jerusalem Studies in Arabic and Islam* 21: 196–208.

Adang, C. (2007). 'A Rare Case of Biblical "Testimonies" to the Prophet Muḥammad in Muʿtazilite literature: Quotations from Ibn Rabban al-Ṭabarī's *Kitāb al-dīn wa-al-dawla* in Abu l-Ḥusayn al-Baṣrī's *Ghurar al-adilla*, as Preserved in a Work by al-Ḥimmaṣī al-Rāzī'. In C. Adang, S. Schmidtke, and D. Sklare (eds.), *A Common Rationality: Muʿtazilism in Islam and Judaism*. Würzburg: Ergon, 297–330.

Āghā Buzurg al-Ṭihrānī (1983). *Al-Dharīʿa ilā taṣānīf al-shīʿa*. Beirut: Dār Iḥyāʾ al-turāth al-ʿarabī li-l-ṭibāʿa wa-l-nashr wa-l-tawzīʿ.

Āghā Buzurg al-Ṭihrānī (2009). *Ṭabaqāt aʿlām al-shīʿa*. Beirut: Dār Iḥyāʾ al-turāth al-ʿarabī li-l-ṭibāʿa wa-l-nashr wa-l-tawzīʿ.

Ansari, H. (1998a). 'Ibn ʿAbdak'. *Dāʾirat al-maʿārif-i buzurg-i islāmī*, Tehran, iv. 198f.

Ansari, H. (1998b). 'Asʿad b. Aḥmad al-Ṭarābulusī'. *Dāʾirat al-maʿārif-i buzurg-i islāmī*, Tehran, viii. 310f.

Ansari, H. (2001). 'Aʿlām al-ṭarāʾiq'. *Nashr-i dānish* 18/4 (1380): 29–30.

Ansari, H. (2009a). 'Abū Sahl al-Nawbakhtī'. *Encyclopaedia Islamica*, Leiden: Brill, *ii*. 481–8.

Ansari, H. (2009b). 'Abū al-Jaysh al-Balkhī'. *Encyclopaedia Islamica*, Leiden: Brill, *ii*. 180–2.

Ansari, H. (2012). *Barrasī-hā-yi tārīkhī dar ḥawza-yi islām wa tashayyuʿ: Majmūʿa-yi nawad maqāla wa yāddāsht*. Tehran: Kitābkhāna, mūze wa markaz-i asnād-i majlis-i shūrā-yi islāmī, 1390.

Ansari, H. (2013a). 'Zamīna-hā-yi tārīkhī-yi taʾlīf-i kitāb-i Nihāyat al-marām'. In Ḍiyāʾ al-Dīn al-Makkī, *Nihāyat al-marām fī dirāyat al-kalām*. Facsimile Publication with Introduction and Indices by A. Shihadeh. Tehran: Mīrāth-e maktūb.

Ansari, H. (2013b). 'Čand pāra-i matn dar dānish-i kalām az Abū l-Futūḥ Rāzī'. <http://ansari.kateban.com/post/2043> [accessed 3 June 2015].

Ansari, H. (in press). *L'Imamat et l'occultation selon l'imamisme: étude bibliographique et histoire des textes*. Leiden: Brill.

Ansari, H., W. Madelung, and S. Schmidtke (2015). 'Yūsuf al-Baṣīr's Refutation (*Naqḍ*) of Abū l-Ḥusayn al-Baṣrī's Theology in a Yemeni Zaydi Manuscript of the 7th/13th Century'. In D. Hollenberg, C. Rauch, and S. Schmidtke (eds.), *The Yemeni Manuscript Tradition*. Leiden: Brill, 28–65.

Ansari, H., and S. Schmidtke (eds.) (2006). *Khulāṣat al-naẓar: An Anonymous Imāmī-Muʿtazilī Treatise (late 6th/12th or early 7th/13th century)*. Tehran: Iranian Institute of Philosophy.

Ansari, H., and S. Schmidtke (2013). *The Reception of al-Shaykh al-Ṭūsī's Theological Writings in 6th/12th century Syria: Facsimile Edition of ʿAbd al-Raḥmān b. ʿAlī b. Muḥammad al-Ḥusaynī's Commentary on al-Ṭūsī's* Muqaddama (MS Atıf Efendi 1338/1). Tehran: Mīrāth-i maktūb.

Ansari, H., and S. Schmidtke (2014). 'Al-Shaykh al-Ṭūsī: His Writings on Theology and Their Reception'. In F. Daftary and G. Miskinzoda (eds.), *The Study of Shiʿi Islam: History, Theology and Law*. London: I. B. Tauris, 475–97.

Ansari, H., and S. Schmidtke (forthcoming). *Philosophical Theology among 6th/12th Century Twelver Shīʿites: From Naṣīr al-Dīn al-Ṭūsī (d. after 600/1203–4) to Naṣīr al-Dīn al-Ṭūsī (d. 672/1274)*.

Anthony, S. W. (2013). 'Nawbakti Family'. *Encyclopaedia Iranica*, online edition, 2013, available at <http://www.iranicaonline.org/articles/nawbakti-family> [accessed 30 March 2015].

Bayhom-Daou, T. (2001). 'The Imam's Knowledge and the Quran According to al-Faḍl b. Shādhān al-Nīsābūrī (d. 260 A.H./874 A.D.)'. *Bulletin of the School of Oriental and African Studies* 64: 188–207.

Bayhom-Daou, T. (2003). 'Hishām b. al-Ḥakam (d. 179/795) and his Doctrine of the Imām's Knowledge'. *Journal of Semitic Studies* 48: 71–108.

Bayhom-Daou, T. (2005). *Shaykh Mufid*. Oxford: Oneworld.

Capezzone, L. (2006). 'Maestri e testi nei centri imamiti nell'Iran selgiuchide secondo il Kitab al-naqd'. *Rivista degli Studi Orientali* 79: 9–29.

Eddé, A.-M. (1999). *La Principauté ayyoubide d'Alep (579/1183–658/1260)*. Stuttgart: Franz Steiner.

van Ess, J. (1991–7). *Theologie und Gesellschaft im 2. und 3. Jahrhundert Hidschra: Eine Geschichte des religiösen Denkens im frühen Islam*. 6 vols. Berlin: de Gruyter.

al-Faḍl b. Shādhān al-Azdī al-Nīsābūrī, *Kitāb al.-Īḍāḥ*. Ed. Jalāl al-Dīn al-Ḥusaynī al-Urmawī al-Muḥaddith. Tehran: Muʾassasa-yi Intishārāt va-Čāp-i Dānishgāh-i Tihrān, 1363/1984.

Fyzee, A. A. A. (2014). *A Shiite Creed: A Translation of Iʿtiqadatu 'l-Imamiyyah (The Beliefs of the Imamiyya) of Abu Jaʿfar, Muhammad ibn ʿAli ibn al-Husayn, Ibn Babawayh al-Qummi known as ash-Shaykh as-Saduq*. Lexington, KY: Ahlulbayt.

Gleave, R. (2007). 'Abū l-Futūḥ al-Rāzī'. *The Encyclopaedia of Islam*. Three. Leiden: Brill, Fasc. 2007–3: 55f.

al-Ḥākim al-Jishumī (*Ṭabaqāt*). 'Ṭabaqāt al-Muʿtazila'. In ʿAbd al-Jabbār al-Hamadānī, *Faḍl al-iʿtizāl wa-ṭabaqāt al-Muʿtazila*. Ed. Fuʾād Sayyid. Tunis: al-Dār al-tūnisiyya li-l-nashr, 1393/1974.

Ḥamza b. ʿAlī b. Zuhra al-Ḥalabī (*Ghunya*). *Ghunyat al-nuzūʿ ilā ʿilmay al-uṣūl wa-l-furūʿ*. Ed. Ibrāhīm al-Bahādurī. Qum: Muʾassasat al-Imām al-Ṣādiq, 1417[/1996].

Hayes, E. (2015). *The Envoys of the Hidden Imam: Religious Institutions and the Politics of the Twelver Shiʿi Occultation*. Ph.D. dissertation, University of Chicago.

al-Ḥimmaṣī al-Rāzī, *al-Munqidh min al-taqlīd*. 2 vols. Ed. Muḥammad Hādī al-Yūsufī al-Gharawī. Qum: al-Muʾassasa, 1412[/1991].

al-Ḥusaynī, M. R. (1989–90). 'Maqūlat "jism lā ka-l-ajsām" bayna mawqif Hishām b. al-Ḥakam wa-mawāqif sāʾir ahl al-kalām'. *Turāthunā* 19 (1410): 7–13.

Ibn Ḥajar al-ʿAsqalānī (*Lisān*). *Līsān al-mīzān*. Beirut: Muʾassasat al-Aʿlamī, 1390/1971.

Ibn Ṭāwūs, ʿAlī b. Mūsā (*Faraj*). *Faraj al-mahmūm fī tārīkh ʿulamāʾ al-nujūm*. Najaf: Manshūrāt al-Maṭbaʿa al-Ḥaydariyya, 1368[/1948–9].

Iqbāl, ʿA. (1966). *Khānadān-i Nawbakhtī*. 3rd edn. Tehran: Kitābkhāna-yi Ṭahūrī, 1345.

al-Jaʿfarī, M. R. (1992–3a). ʻal-Kalām ʿindā l-Imāmiyya: Nashʾatuhu, taṭawwuruhu wa-mawqiʿ al-Shaykh al-Mufīd minhu'. *Turāthunā* 8: 144–299.

al-Jaʿfarī, M. R. (1992–3b). ʻal-Kalām ʿindā l-Imāmiyya, nashʾatuhu, taṭawwuruhu wa-mawqiʿ al-Shaykh al-Mufīd minhu II'. *Turāthunā* 8: 77–114.

Jurjānī, Ḍiyāʾ al-Dīn b. Sadīd al-Dīn (*Rasāʾil*). *Rasāʾil-i kalāmī-i taʾlīf-i ḥudūd-i qarn-i nuhum-i Hijrī*. Ed. Maʿṣūma Nūr Muḥammadī. Tehran: Mīrāth-i Maktūb/Ahl-i Qalam, 1375[/1997].

Klemm, V. (1984). 'Die vier sufarāʾ des Zwölften Imām: Zur formativen Periode der Zwölfersschiʿa'. *Die Welt des Orients* 15: 126–43.

Kohlberg, E. (1986). '*Barāʾa* in Shīʿī doctrine'. *Jerusalem Studies in Arabic and Islam* 7: 139–74.

Kohlberg, E. (1988). 'Imām and Community in the Pre-Ghayba Period'. In S. A. Arjomand (ed.), *Authority and Political Culture in Shīʿism*. Albany, NY: SUNY Press, 25–53.

Kohlberg, E. (1992). *A Medieval Muslim Scholar at Work: Ibn Ṭāwūs and His Library*. Leiden: Brill.

McDermott, M. J. (1978). *The Theology of al-Shaikh al-Mufīd (d. 413/1022)*. Beirut: Dar el-Machreq Éditeurs.

McDermott, M. J. (1989). 'Awāʾel al-maqālāt'. *Encyclopaedia Iranica*, London/Boston: Routledge & Kegan Paul, *iii*. 112f.

Madelung, W. (1970). 'Imamism and Muʿtazilite Theology'. In T. Fahd (ed.), *Shīʿisme imāmite*. Paris, 13–29 [repr. in W. Madelung, *Religious Schools and Sects in Medieval Islam*, London: Ashgate, 1985, Part VII].

Madelung, W. (1979). 'The Shiite and Khārijite Contribution to Pre-Ashʿarite Kalām'. In P. Morewedge, *Islamic Philosophical Thought*. Albany: SUNY Press, 120–39 [repr. in *Religious Schools and Sects*, Part VIII].

Madelung, W. (1985a). 'Abū Sahl Nawbaktī'. *Encyclopaedia Iranica*, London/Boston: Routledge & Kegan Paul, *i*. 372f.

Madelung, W. (1985b). 'ʿAbd al-Jalīl Rāzī'. *Encyclopaedia Iranica*, London/Boston: Routledge & Kegan Paul, *i*. 120.

Madelung, W. (2013). 'Al-Ḥasan b. Mūsā al-Nawbakhtī on the Views of the Astronomers and Astrologers'. In M. Cook, N. Haider, I. Rabb, and A. Sayeed (eds.), *Law and Tradition in Classical Islamic Thought*. New York: Palgrave, 269–78.

Madelung, W. (2014). 'Early Imāmī Theology as Reflected in the Kitāb al-Kāfī of al-Kulaynī'. In F. Daftary and G. Miskinzoda (eds.), *The Study of Shiʿi Islam: History, Theology and Law*. London: I. B. Tauris, 465–74.

Maʿtūq, A. M. (2008). *Al-Sharīf al-Murtaḍā, ḥayātuhu, thaqāfatuhu, adabuhu wa-naqduhu*. Beirut: al-Mu'assasa al-ʻarabiyya li-l-dirāsāt wa-l-nashr.

Modarressi, H. (1984). *An Introduction to Shīʿī law: A Bibliographical Study*. London: Ithaca Press.

Modarressi, H. (1993). *Crisis and Consolidation in the Formative Period of Shiʿite Islam: Abū Jaʿfar ibn Qiba al-Rāzī and his Contribution to Imāmite Shīʿite Thought*. Princeton: Princeton University Press.

Modarressi, H. (2003). *Tradition and Survival: A Bibliographical Survey of Early Shīʿite Literature*. Vol. i. Oxford: Oneworld.

Mudarris Raḍawī, M. T. (1991). *Aḥwāl u āthār-i Khʷāja Naṣīr al-Dīn Ṭūsī*. Tehran: Muʾassasa-yi muṭālaʿāt u taḥqīqāt-i farhangī, 1370.

al-Mufīd, Muḥammad b. Muḥammad (*Awāʾil*). 'Awāʾil al-maqālāt'. al-Mufid, *Muṣannafāt*, vol. iv.

al-Mufīd, Muḥammad b. Muḥammad (*Ḥikāyāt*). Ḥikāyāt'. al-Mufid, *Muṣannafāt*, vol. x.

al-Mufīd, Muḥammad b. Muḥammad (*Muṣannafāt*). *Muṣannafāt al-Shaykh al-Mufīd Abī ʿAbd Allāh Muḥammad b. Muḥammad b. al-Nuʿmān b. al-Muʿallim al-ʿUkbarī al-Baghdādī.* 14 vols. Qum: al-Muʾtamar al-ʿĀlamī li-Alfiyyat al-Shaykh al-Mufīd, 1413[/1993].

al-Muḥaqqiq al-Ḥillī (*Maslak*). *Al-Maslak fī uṣūl al-dīn*. Ed. R. al-Ustādī. Mashhad: Majmaʿ al-buḥūth al-islāmiyya, 1414/1373[/1994].

Muḥyī al-Dīn, ʿA. (1957). *Adab al-Murtaḍā min sīratihi wa-āthārihi*. Baghdad: Maṭbaʿat al-maʿārif.

MṬF = *Mawsūʿat ṭabaqāt al-fuqahāʾ*, taʾlīf al-Lajna al-ʿIlmiyya fī Muʾassasat al-Imām al-Ṣādiq, ishrāf Jaʿfar al-Subḥānī. Beirut: Muʾassasat al-Imām al-Ṣādiq, 1999–2001.

MTK = *Muʿjam al-turāth al-kalāmī*, taʾlīf al-Lajna al-ʿilmiyya fī Muʾassasat al-Imām al-Ṣādiq, taqdīm wa-ishrāf Jaʿfar al-Subḥānī. Qum: Muʾassasat al-Imām al-Ṣādiq, 1424[/2003–4].

MṬM = Muʿjam ṭabaqāt al-mutakallimīn, taʾlīf al-Lajna al-ʿilmiyya fī Muʾassasat al-Imām al-Ṣādiq, taqdīm wa-ishrāf Jaʿfar al-Subḥānī. Qum: Muʾassasat al-Imām al-Ṣādiq, 1424[/2003–4].

Muntajab al-Dīn (*Fihrist*). *Al-Fihrist*. Ed. Sayyid Jalāl al-Dīn Muḥaddith Urmawī. Qum, 1366[/1981].

al-Muqriʾ al-Nīsābūrī, Muḥammad b. ʿAlī b. al-Ḥasan (*Ḥudūd*). *Al-Ḥudūd: al-Muʿjam al-mawḍūʿī li-l-muṣṭalaḥāt al-kalāmiyya*. Ed. Maḥmūd Yazdī Muṭlaq (Fāḍil). Qum: Muʾassasat al-Imām al-Ṣādiq ʿalayhi l-salām li-l-taḥqīq wa-l-taʾlīf, 1414[/1993–4].

al-Muqriʾ al-Nīsābūrī, Muḥammad b. ʿAlī b. al-Ḥasan (*Taʿlīq*). *Al-Taʿlīq fī ʿilm al-kalām*. Ed. Maḥmūd Yazdī Muṭlaq (al-Fāḍil). Mashhad: Qism al-dirāsāt al-falsafiyya wa-l-kalāmiyya al-islāmiyya li-l-Jāmiʿa al-raḍawiyya li-l-ʿulūm al-islāmiyya, 1385/1427[/2006].

Pākatčī, A. (1998a). 'Ibn Shahrāshūb'. *Dāʾirat al-maʿārif-i buzurg-i islāmī*, Tehran, *iv.* 90–2.

Pākatčī, A. (1998b). 'Ibn Shādhān'. *Dāʾirat al-maʿārif-i buzurg-i islāmī*, Tehran, *iv.* 50–2.

Quṭb al-Dīn al-Rāwandī (*Lubb*). *Lubb al-lubāb*. Ed. al-Sayyid Ḥusayn al-Jaʿfarī al-Zanjānī. 2 vols. Qum: Āl ʿAbā, 1431[/2009].

Rashed, M. (2015). *Al-Ḥasan Ibn Mūsā al-Nawbaḫtī, Commentary on Aristotle 'De Generatione et Corruptione'. Edition, Translation and Commentary*. Berlin: de Gruyter.

Van Renterghem, V. (2015). 'Baghdad: A View from the Edge on the Seljuq Empire'. In E. Herzig and S. Stewart (eds.), *The Age of the Seljuqs*. London: I. B. Tauris, 74–93.

Salati, M. (1992). *Ascesa e caduta di una famiglia di Asraf Sciiti di Aleppo: I Zuhrawi o Zuhra-Zada (1600–1700)*. Rome: Istituto per l'Oriente C.A. Nallino.

Salati, M. (2010). 'Note in margine ai Banū Zuhrā / al-Zuhrāwī / Zuhrā zāda di Aleppo: alcuni documenti dai tribunali sciaraitici della fine del xvii e l'inizio del xviii secolo (1684–1701)'. *Annali di Ca' Foscari* 49: 23–42.

Sander, P. (1994). *Zwischen Charisma und Ratio: Entwicklungen in der frühen imāmitischen Theologie*. Berlin: Klaus Schwarz.

Schmidtke, S. (1991). *The Theology of al-ʿAllāma al-Ḥillī (d. 726/1325)*. Berlin: Klaus Schwarz.

Schmidtke, S. (2009). 'The Doctrinal Views of the Banu l-ʿAwd (Early 8th/14th Century): An Analysis of MS Arab. f. 64 (Bodleian Library, Oxford)'. In M. A. Amir-Moezzi, M. Bar-Asher, and S. Hopkins (eds.), *Le Shiʿisme imamite quarante ans après: Hommage à Etan Kohlberg*. Turnhout: Brepols, 357–382.

al-Sharīf al-Murtaḍā (*Dhakhīra*). *al-Dhakhīra ilā ʿilm al-kalām*. Ed. Aḥmad al-Ḥusaynī. Qum: Dānishgāh-i Tihrān, 1411[/1990–1].

al-Sharīf al-Murtaḍā (*Mulakhkhaṣ*). *al-Mulakhkhaṣ fī uṣūl al-dīn*. Ed. Muḥammad Riḍā Anṣārī Qummī. Tehran: Dānishgāh-i Tihrān, 1381/2002.

al-Sharīf al-Murtaḍā (*Rasāʾil*). *Rasāʾil al-Sharīf al-Murtaḍā*. Introd. Aḥmad al-Ḥusaynī. Ed. Mahdī Rajāʾī. 4 vols. Qum: Dār al-Qurʾān al-karīm, 1405[/1984–5].

Sourdel, D. (1972). 'L'Imamisme vu par le Cheikh al-Mufīd'. *Revue des études islamiques* 40: 217–96.

Sourdel, D. (1973). 'Les Conceptions imamites au debut du XIe siècle d'après le Shaykh al-Mufīd'. In D. S. Richards (ed.), *Islamic Civilization 950–1150*. London: Cassirer, 187–200.

Ṭabāṭabāʾī, ʿAbd al-ʿAzīz (1992–3). *Al-Shaykh al-Mufīd wa ʿaṭāʾuhu l-fikrī al-khālid*. Qum, 1413.

al-Ṭūsī, Muḥammad b. al-Ḥasan (*Fihrist*). *Fihrist*. Ed. Muḥammad Ṣādiq Āl Baḥr al-ʿulūm. Najaf: al-Maṭbaʿa al-Ḥaydariyya, 1960.

Ustādī, R. (2004). *Aḥwāl wa āthār-i Muḥaqqiq-i Ḥillī*. Tehran: Quds, 1383.

al-Wāthiqī, Ḥ. (n.d.). Al-Mutabaqqī min Kitāb al-Maṣādir'. *Majalla-yi fiqh-i ahl al-bayt*. Qum, no. 25.

CHAPTER 12

THE PREDECESSORS OF ASHʿARISM

Ibn Kullāb, al-Muḥāsibī and al-Qalānisī

HARITH BIN RAMLI

THE doctrine of the created Qurʾān, promoted by the instigators of the third/ninth century *miḥna* initiated by the ʿAbbāsid Caliph al-Maʾmūn, was not only opposed by *aṣḥāb al-ḥadīth* traditionalists, but also by a number of *kalām* theologians who shared core theological beliefs with the latter. They upheld and championed the broader doctrines of the 'Attributionists' (*ṣifātiyya*/*ahl al-ithbāt*): belief in the uncreated Qurʾān, the reality of eternal divine attributes, and God's predetermination of human destiny and actions. In later centuries, the dominant Sunnī schools of *kalām*, in particular the Ashʿariyya, would often recognize the pioneering efforts of theologians such as Ibn Kullāb (d. *c.*240/854–5), al-Muḥāsibī (d. 243/857), and al-Qalānisī (*fl. c.* 2nd half of third/ninth century) by referring to them as the '*kalām* theologians among the pious forbears' (*mutakallimūn min al-salaf*) or as the 'ancient theologians of the Sunnīs' (Gimaret 1989: 233; van Ess 1990: 180–1). Up until the late fourth/tenth century, it appears that there were Kullābite theologians alongside Ashʿarite ones, although, as the geographer-traveller al-Maqdisī (d. 380/990) points out, by this period the Kullābite tradition was already being absorbed into the Ashʿarite tradition. In later centuries, Ḥanbalite critics such as Ibn Taymiyya (d. 728/1328) would sometimes use the label 'Kullābiyya' as a pejorative label for all those seen as responsible for mingling the authentic creed of the Sunnī traditionalists with the taint of *kalām* theology.

While the pioneering efforts of such theologians did have a particularly significant influence on the development of Ashʿarism, we should not dismiss the possibility that they had an impact on other theological streams as well. The available information on these figures comes from a wide variety of sources—Ashʿarite, Ḥanbalite, and Muʿtazilite. Nevertheless, by the fifth/eleventh century, it seems that their relevance for Islamic theology had mainly become confined to their historical status as the earlier pioneers of Sunnī *kalām*. No works attributed to Ibn Kullāb or al-Qalānisī appear to have survived after this point of time, and while many of al-Muḥāsibī's books are still widely available today, forming an important part of the classical Sufi textual tradition, most of them are focused on questions of ethics and religious piety rather than theology (or at least have been seen in this light). Over the past century, a small but significant number of studies by scholars such as J. van Ess and D. Gimaret have attempted to reconstruct the history of early Islamic theology, and in the process provided a clearer picture of these theologians and their doctrines based on the medieval sources. Such information can be supplemented by scholarship in other fields within Islamic Studies (for example, the development of Islamic jurisprudence and mysticism, or more generally, the rise of Sunnī traditionalism), revealing the wider social context behind theological issues and doctrinal positions.

I Ibn Kullāb

The Baṣran Abū Muḥammad ʿAbd Allāh b. Muḥammad b. Saʿīd most likely earned his nickname 'Ibn Kullāb' due to a reputation for overwhelming his intellectual opponents (*kullāb* literally means 'grappling hook'). His family name, 'al-Qaṭṭān', hints at a connection with the cotton trade. Although there is no evidence that he engaged in it himself, perhaps it provided him the means to pursue a scholar's life. He died in 240/855 (only two years before his associate al-Muḥāsibī), most probably in his home town of Baṣra, although he probably spent some part of his life in Baghdad. A report tells us that he lost in a debate with the Muʿtazila at al-Maʾmūn's court at Baghdad, whereas another conflicting anecdote recounts that he refused a request inviting him to the Caliphal court, due to the Caliph's notoriety as a sinner (van Ess 1997: 180).

Generally, his theological approach could be characterized as the application of classical Baṣran *kalām* methodology to the defence and articulation of doctrinal positions that were mostly in line with the traditionalist creed. It is hard to establish which earlier theologians influenced Ibn Kullāb, or who his teachers were, although he is often associated with the name of al-Najjār (d. *c.*220/835), from whom he derived his theory that human actions were created by God but 'acquired' by their human agents. In addition, some of his theological formulations regarding the divine attributes bear similarity to the teachings of earlier Shīʿite theologians such as Hishām b. al-Ḥakam and Sulaymān b. Jarīr. It seems clear that most of his efforts were at odds with the Muʿtazilite ascendancy. A refutation of the Muʿtazila is attributed to him, and he authored two other works that also appear to be refutations of Muʿtazilite doctrine: a book on the divine attributes (*Kitāb al-Ṣifāt*), and another on God's creation of human actions (*Kitāb Afʿāl al-ʿibād*). He is reported to have been involved in many debates with the Muʿtazilite ʿAbbād b. Sulaymān (d. 250/864), who claimed that the doctrine of the uncreatedness of divine speech championed by Ibn Kullāb was suspiciously similar to the Christian idea of the Trinity. Stories circulating around Muʿtazilite circles incriminated Ibn Kullāb as a crypto-Christian secretly intending to undermine the Muslim faith (van Ess 1997: 188).

However, considering his negative profile in later Muʿtazilite sources, it is surprising that there are no reports of him (or like-minded associates such as al-Muḥāsibī) facing the persecution under the *miḥna*. Van Ess (1997: 180) suggests that Ibn Kullāb's fame might have been posthumous, and for this reason he did not attract the attention of the inquisition. The attempt to forge a synthesis between traditionalist doctrine and *kalām* methods probably attracted few followers in his lifetime, only gathering pace in the following generation. The post-*miḥna* period following the reversal of ʿAbbāsid policy under al-Mutawakkil has often been characterized as a reactionary age, one which left little room for *kalām*'s proponents. But recent research has shown that the religious policies of the Caliphs after al-Mutawakkil favoured what Christopher Melchert (1996: 316–42) has described as 'semi-rationalism', a tendency among a rather loose grouping of scholars situated halfway between the form of rationalism usually associated with the Muʿtazila and the traditionalism of Aḥmad b. Ḥanbal. These scholars were usually inclined towards Shāfiʿism in jurisprudence in one form or other, and like Ibn Kullāb, favoured some degree of application of *kalām* in the articulation and defence of doctrine.

The distinguishing feature of Ibn Kullāb's theology, which has often been described as the 'Kullābite formula', aimed at explaining the relationship between the divine essence and its attributes. Developed against the background of the *miḥna* controversy over the nature of the Qurʾān, the formula described the attributes of God as 'neither identical to God nor other than Him'. Ibn Kullāb sided with the traditionalists in resisting attempts to use metaphor or negative theology to explain Qurʾānic descriptions of God which attributed to Him seemingly human characteristics such as 'seeing' and 'speaking' or possessing a 'face' and 'speech'. But while many traditionalists were content to simply 'affirm' the truth of such statements and the reality of such divine attributes without further qualification (*bi-lā kayfiyya*), others like Ibn Kullāb believed one could demonstrate the validity of such a position through reasoning, which in his case meant applying the tools and language of Baṣran *kalām*.

Thus, Ibn Kullāb's theology shared certain basic presuppositions and ontological features with other contemporary Baṣran theologians such as Abū l-Hudhayl. But while the latter interpreted Qurʾānic descriptions of God 'seeing' or 'knowing' as particular, momentary 'acts', Ibn Kullāb saw such descriptions as representing eternal aspects of the divine, determinant entities (*maʿānī*) which subsided through the divine essence (van Ess 1997: 186–7). Like other Baṣran theologians, he formulated his position through an occasionalist ontological structure, the idea of the 'givenness' of language (*waḍʿ al-lugha*) and assuming a certain correspondence between language and reality, and between the divine and the phenomenal world (Frank 1978: 9–14). One arrived at an understanding of the divine attributes through the use of reason and the analysis of Qurʾānic Arabic. Each object in existence could be described as a 'thing' (*shayʾ*), including God and His attributes. Just as one could speak linguistically of objects and qualities predicated of them, each thing in existence is, ontologically speaking, either a quality (*ṣifa*) or object of qualification (*mawṣūf*). Just as the phenomenal world consists of substances (*jawāhir*) qualified by accidents (*aʿrāḍ*) subsisting through (*qāʾim bi-*) them, the Creator is also qualified by 'attributes' (*ṣifāt*) subsiding through the divine essence (*dhāt*). In the same way that the accidents of a substance are intrinsic to a created substance yet not entirely identical to it, God's attributes are also neither identical nor other than the divine essence. Likewise, in the same way the accidents of a created substance cannot not subsist through one another, divine attributes are eternal not due to an additional attribute of 'eternity', but due to the inherent eternity of the divine essence itself.

Beyond the broad schema of the Kullābite formula, it is hard to reconstruct, based on the scant evidence, many details of Ibn Kullāb's theology. He allowed for certain things to be said about God based on independent reasoning (even if they were not expressed explicitly in scripture) by distinguishing between attribute (*ṣifa*) and description (*waṣf*). Unlike the former, the latter is merely a report (*khabar*) which does not reflect the existence of a determinant entity (Gimaret 1989: 236). Thus, although there is no clear scriptural basis qualifying God with 'existence' (*wujūd*) or 'thingness' (*shayʾiyya*), we know from reason that God is an existing thing, not due to an attribute of existence, but the divine essence itself (Gimaret 1989: 239). However, it is not always clear what does or does not have a basis in revelation. One could argue, based on Qurʾān 42: 11, that there is some basis for affirming an attribute of 'thingness' in relation to God. It is understandable that although he accepted that God was 'ancient' or 'pre-eternal' (*qadīm*) he was hesitant to affirm 'pre-eternity' (*qidam*) as a real attribute, but it is less clear why he had difficulty accepting the reality of attributes such as persistence (*baqāʾ*, which, arguably, could be justified based on Qurʾān 55: 27) or divinity (*ilāhiyya*, the word *ilāh* occurs more than fifty times in the Qurʾān).

On most issues, he was inclined to side with the claims of the *aṣḥāb al-ḥadīth* traditionalists, affirming all the scriptural anthropomorphic descriptions of God without resorting to metaphorical interpretation, the reality of the vision of God given to believers in the Hereafter, and the scriptural description of God's seating (*istiwāʾ*) upon the Throne as a divine attribute (van Ess 1997: 191–3; Gimaret 1989: 253–4). Nonetheless, his interpretation of the doctrine of divine speech would have raised alarm bells among many traditionalists. On this issue, Ibn Kullāb's solution appears to have been aimed at a compromise which would allow people to hold to the doctrine of the uncreated Qurʾān without coming under the scrutiny of the *miḥna* (van Ess 1997: 183). According to him, one should distinguish between the essential aspect (*maʿnā*) of divine speech and its manifest expression (*ʿibāra*) in the phenomenal world. Unlike human speech, divine speech in essence was composed neither of sound nor letters, nor did it contain particular modalities associated with speech such as command, prohibition, or statement. Man 'acquires' this expression, and thus one must distinguish between the recitation (*qirāʾa*) and the transcendent object of recitation (*maqrūʾ*), in the same way one distinguishes between the remembrance (*dhikr*) and the object of that remembrance (*madhkūr*). By distinguishing between *maʿnā* and expression, Ibn Kullāb, like his contemporary

Ḥusayn b. ʿAlī al-Karābīsī (d. 245/859–60), who argued that the 'utterance' (*lafẓ*) of the Qurʾān was created, wanted to avoid making the statement that 'the Qurʾān was created' while absolving himself of the charge of attributing divinity to the human recitation of it. Furthermore, he tried to avoid using the word 'Qurʾān' as much as possible in his discourse, preferring instead to speak of 'God's speech'. Ibn Kullāb was willing to make one singular exception in the case of the prophet Moses, who the Qurʾān describes as hearing God's speech directly (van Ess 1997: 184–7).

Another interesting departure from the common traditionalist position was his definition of faith, which excluded works. His theory of human action was, for the most part, influenced by the Baṣran theologian al-Najjār, who stated that the power to act, created by God, came at the very moment of the action and was 'acquired' by Man. Man as a whole, and the body as a whole bears responsibility for actions, even though they are only committed by particular limbs. Ultimately, however, these choices were rooted in the twin poles of divine favour or disfavour (*al-tawfīq wa-l-khidhlān*), and the predestination of a person's final destination as an inhabitant of Paradise or the Hellfire (van Ess 1997: 181–2, 193–4).

II al-Muḥāsibī

Like his contemporary Ibn Kullāb, Abū ʿAbd Allāh al-Ḥārith b. Asad (d. 243/857) was also Baṣran in origin. He became known as 'al-Muḥāsibī' due to the concept of *muḥāsaba* (meditation on one's actions and inner motivations, literally, 'taking one's self to account'), frequently discussed in the many works on piety he authored. These writings, as well as his association with leading figures of the early Sufi tradition in Baghdad, are the reason he is considered one of the major precursors of Sufism. The available biographical details about his life are also few and mainly hagiographic. If anecdotes regarding his open hostility to his own father (who was either a Shīʿite or Qadarite) can be believed, he became attracted to the traditionalists at some point in his life, rejecting an earlier upbringing in a different theological tradition, although, like Ibn Kullāb, he does not seem to have completely abandoned his interest in *kalām*. While he managed to avoid being persecuted during the *miḥna*, he did not entirely succeed in ridding himself of suspicion from conservative traditionalists such as Ibn Ḥanbal and his followers, who found al-Muḥāsibī's teachings and writings in both the fields of theology and piety too 'innovatory' for their liking. Ibn Ḥanbal is said to have led a severe boycott of al-Muḥāsibī that resulted in temporary exile from Baghdad and the attendance of only four people at the latter's funeral service (van Ess 1997: 199–200). Some reports claim that this eventually resulted in al-Muḥāsibī renouncing his earlier writings and wholeheartedly adopting Ḥanbalism, although, as in the case of similar reports about Abū l-Ḥasan al-Ashʿarī (d. 324/936), such last-minute conversion reports are quite common and cannot always be taken at face value.

Al-Muḥāsibī is described by some of the historical sources as a disciple of Ibn Kullāb, although it is not clear to what degree this was really the case (van Ess 1997: 196). Like Ibn Kullāb, he engaged in *kalām* theology while adhering for the most part to the creed of the *aṣḥāb al-ḥadīth*. However, he did not adopt the Kullābite formula on the question of divine attributes. Basing himself on a variant etymological explanation for the word 'name' (*ism*), he rejected the linchpin at the very heart of the Kullābite formula, the idea that the name was neither identical nor other to the named. For al-Muḥāsibī, names were identical to the named, and thus the divine attributes were identical to the divine essence, while being distinct from one another (van Ess 1997: 200–1). In addition, he rejected Ibn Kullāb's distinction between the transcendent divine attribute of speech and its external expression in the phenomenal world, and even went so far as to characterize divine speech as 'sound and letters'. It is unclear how exactly he conceived the sound and letters of divine speech, although a fourth/tenth-century Sufi work hints that this doctrine might have been related to some mystical teaching on divine cosmogony (although there is no evidence from his writings which are available to us). One could say that by rejecting Ibn Kullāb's abstract notion of divine speech, al-Muḥāsibī was adopting a more uncompromisingly traditionalist position (van Ess 1997: 202). Ibn Kullāb's idea that God's speech was not qualified by different modalities (such as command, prohibition, statement) until it was expressed in the phenomenal world was also refuted in al-Muḥāsibī's work on Qurʾānic exegesis, *Fahm al-Qurʾān*. The main aim of this book, written before the end of the *miḥna*, was to defend the idea of Qurʾānic abrogation against its exploitation by the Muʿtazilites and Jahmites, who used it to promote their doctrine of the created Qurʾān. According to al-Muḥāsibī, abrogation repeals only the command, not the speech itself, and does not reflect a change in the mind of God, but that He had from eternity intended this abrogation to occur at some point in time (van Ess 1997: 203–5).

Compared with Ibn Kullāb's theology, al-Muḥāsibī's seems to have been closer to the traditionalist creed of Ibn Ḥanbal and his followers. Like the Ḥanbalites, and in contrast with Ibn Kullāb, he considered works part of the definition of faith, alongside affirmation of the heart and verbal testimony (van Ess 1961: 577). However, at the same time his theological methodology differed from the Ḥanbalites in its comprehensive attempt to articulate the combined role of reason and revelation (Picken 2008). He was one of the first theologians to fully outline a definition of reason (*ʿaql*), and his *Risāla fī Maʾiyyat al-ʿaql* is one of the earliest known works on this subject. Van Ess argues that while for the Muʿtazila the role of reason was self-evident, it was more crucial for theologians inclined to traditionalism like al-Muḥāsibī to demonstrate exactly how reason corresponded with revelation (van Ess 1997: 207). An earlier treatise on reason is also ascribed to the traditionist Dāwūd al-Muḥabbar (d. 205/821) and Ibn Kullāb is said to have authored a work on this very subject in relation to the idea of divine transcendence. For al-Muḥāsibī, reason is innate natural faculty (*gharīza*) placed by God in humans, distinguishing us from angels and animals. It provides us with the ability to distinguish benefit from harm, and thereby makes us bear responsibility for our actions. However, once reason was defined as 'common sense', the problem lay in explaining why not everyone who possessed reason accepted the truth of the prophetic message. Al-Muḥāsibī derived his explanation from his pietist sensibilities (in a manner that anticipates later Sufi thought), arguing that a person driven by his baser self (*nafs*) only applied reason to see what was beneficial in this world, and was blinded to what was beneficial in the Hereafter. Conversely, once a person overcomes the lower urges of the body or temptations of the devil, reason attains, through the light of revelation, 'intellection of God' (*ʿaql ʿan Allāh*) (van Ess 1997: 205–6; de Crussol 2002: 47–78). Therefore, for al-Muḥāsibī, common human reason plays a basic central role, but ultimately one subordinate to revelation, through which it attains its full potential as illuminated intellect. While he was willing to acknowledge that reason was sufficient for practical utility and establishing the existence of a Creator, the general aim of his definition was to refute Muʿtazilite and Jahmite teachings, which for him left little value to the role of revelation in the realm of ethics and theology (de Crussol 2002: 369–71).

III al-Qalānisī

There is even less biographical information on Abū l-ʿAbbās Aḥmad b. Ibrāhīm al-Qalānisī than that available for Ibn Kullāb and al-Muḥāsibī. He lived sometime in the second half of the third/ninth century, in the generation preceding al-Ashʿarī's. This would have meant that there is a possibility that he encountered members of Ibn Kullāb's circle, although this is not necessarily the case, even if the two shared certain theological positions (Gimaret 1989: 233–4). We only have an indication, based on his given toponym (*nisba*) 'al-Rāzī' that he was originally from the Iranian city of Rayy (modern-day Tehran). There is some evidence that his teachings were adopted by four leading members of the traditionalist Ibn Khuzayma circle in another Iranian city, Nīshāpūr. Upon discovering this fact, Ibn Khuzayma severely rebuked the four, and led a boycott aimed at forcing them to recant their views (Gimaret 1989: 232).

Al-Qalānisī's relationship with the Ashʿarite tradition is an interesting one. The main source we have on his theological positions is the doxographical work *Uṣūl al-dīn* by the fifth/eleventh-century Ashʿarite ʿAbd al-Qāhir al-Baghdādī. Al-Baghdādī lists al-Qalānisī together with Ibn Kullāb and al-Muḥāsibī as being among the ancient (*mutaqaddimūn*) forerunners of Sunnī *kalām* (Gimaret 1989: 233) and, interestingly, at times even favours al-Qalānisī's positions over those attributed to al-Ashʿarī himself. Nonetheless, he differed with al-Ashʿarī and the Ashʿarites on many substantial issues, and in some ways his theology bears more similarities with the Ḥanafī-Māturīdī theological school.

In line with the traditionalist creed, al-Qalānisī affirmed all scriptural descriptions of God possessing a face, hand, or His seating upon the Throne as real attributes, like divine knowledge or divine power. He also affirmed the vision of God by believers in the Hereafter, arguing that they would do so through the gift of enhanced sight, as the only thing preventing people from seeing Him in this world is the intrinsic weakness of their sight (Gimaret 1989: 251–3). One interesting aspect of al-Qalānisī's theology is his definition of divine unity, which he apparently shared with the Muʿtazilite ʿAbbād b. Sulaymān. God is 'the One' (*al-wāḥid*) not in the sense of being the first unit in a series of numbers (which would make Him part of a plurality), but as the unifying factor upon which all things depend for their existence. Generally, he adopted the Kullābite formula on the question of divine attributes, describing them as neither identical nor other than the divine essence (Gimaret 1989: 248–9). Like Ibn Kullāb, he argued that divine attributes are eternal (*azaliyya*) but not due to additional attributes of 'primordiality' (*qadīm*) or 'persistence' (*baqāʾ*), as attributes cannot subsist in one another (Gimaret 1989: 239). Similarly, he described the attribute of divine speech as free from any modalities such as command, prohibition, or statement (Gimaret 1989: 251). Less clear is how al-Qalānisī understood human speech, and whether he followed Ibn Kullāb in distinguishing between the abstract 'meaning' of speech and its physical expression (Gimaret 1989: 245–6). Like Ibn Kullāb, and in contrast to al-Ashʿarī, al-Qalānisī held that a composite whole can be qualified by qualities subsisting only in its parts (Gimaret 1989: 247–8). Likewise, he denied the possibility that accidents can be seen or sensed in any way (for al-Ashʿarī, all things that exist can be seen or heard). God, according to both Ibn Kullāb and al-Qalānisī, does not see His own attributes. However, al-Qalānisī makes an exception to this rule in the case of speech and sound (Gimaret 1989: 244–5). One clearly substantial departure al-Qalānisī makes from the position of Ibn Kullāb, and also al-Muḥāsibī (who argues strongly against this idea in his *Fahm al-Qurʾ*ān), is his division of the divine attributes into eternal attributes of essence and time-specific attributes of act. According to the Ashʿarite al-Baghdādī, al-Qalānisī saw qualities such as God's wisdom and God's love as attributes of act (Gimaret 1989: 251).

Compared with what is known about the teachings of Ibn Kullāb and al-Muḥāsibī, there is more information on the structural details of al-Qalānisī's occasionalist ontology. Bodies, by his definition, must be characterized by the dimensions of height, length, and width, and, hence, consist of at least three atoms. Against the Jubbāʾite Muʿtazila and al-Ashʿarī, he held the position that a thing is light or heavy due to entitative determinants (*maʿnā*) of lightness or heaviness, not due to the decrease or increase in the quantity of atoms (Gimaret 1989: 243–4). Similarly, he argued that a thing ceased to exist due to a quality of 'annihilation' (*fanāʾ*), and not because, as al-Ashʿarī claimed, the duration of its existence set by God had ended. Likewise, a thing which has ceased to exist comes back into existence due to a qualifying entity of 'returning' (*iʿāda*). Against al-Ashʿarī, who saw rest and motion as distinct qualifying entities, al-Qalānisī viewed them as the recurrence, in two successive basic moments of time, of the same determinant entity of 'being' (*kawn*) in either the same location or two different locations (Gimaret 1989: 240–1).

Al-Qalānisī was also concerned with formulating a description which explained how substances and accidents behave at the basic level without the intermediary of a cause (which would require another cause, *ad infinitum*) and without breaking the rule that attributes cannot subsist through one another, but only through a substance or essence. Together with two types of quality already present in Ibn Kullāb's ontology, viz. (a) qualities caused by a determinant entity, and (b) qualities arising from the thing itself (*li-nafsihi*), he suggested the existence of a third category of quality present in created things, building on Ibn Kullāb's distinction between attribute (*ṣifa*) and description (*waṣf*). Like category (b), qualities of the third category arose intrinsically out of the thing itself and not due to a determinant entity, but since the former could, properly speaking, only be applicable to the divine, it seems al-Qalānisī felt the need to explain how qualities such as colour or 'being originated' (*muḥdath*) could be predicated of a created thing. Such qualities existed, according to him, quite simply because those things were made in such a way, 'by virtue of being set by one who set them with such a description' (*li-ajl jāʿilin jaʿalahu ʿalā dhālika l-waṣf*) (Gimaret 1989: 238–9). Based on this, he went against the position of most theologians of his time by stating that two substances could be said to be the same due to their both being made 'originated' (*muḥdathān*) even though they had completely different accidents (Gimaret 1989: 241–2).

On questions of human action and responsibility, al-Qalānisī held positions which were largely in line with other 'ancient' Sunnī *mutakallimūn* such as Ibn Kullāb, applying the Najjārite formula (Gimaret 1989: 257–8). Those who believe out of conformism (*taqlīd*) are still considered believers. God's mercy extends to believing grave sinners, as well as the children of disbelievers, who will go straight to Paradise (Gimaret 1989: 254–5). In some respects, his position comes closer to those of al-Muḥāsibī and the *aṣḥāb al-ḥadīth* in general, such as his definition of faith, which includes works. Like al-Muḥāsibī, he adopts a midway point between the Muʿtazila and the Ashʿarites, by holding the view that ethical knowledge of right and wrong (*al-taḥsīn wa-l-taqbīḥ*) is attainable through reason, and not exclusively through revelation. This position seems to be echoed in the Māturīdite tradition, although, as Gimaret argues, there is little evidence that they were necessarily influenced by al-Qalānisī. He seems slightly more assertive compared to al-Muḥāsibī in arguing for the significance of reason. According to him, reason provides us with the necessary knowledge that God will send prophets with guidance for humanity, and also can allow us to understand the motives and wisdom behind divine actions (Gimaret 1989: 257).

IV Conclusion

Prior to the rise of Ashʿarism, which inherited many of the trajectories set into motion by Iraqi scholars such as Ibn Kullāb, scholars associated with the semi-rationalist tendency could have often, in the context of theology, been described as 'Kullābites', even if no such Kullābite school existed in any distinct, organized sense. Al-Qalānisī does not seem to have had such a widespread influence, although it is clear that his teachings were still being taken seriously by Ashʿarites in the fourth/tenth century. Al-Muḥāsibī, on the other hand, does not seem to have had a significant enough impact in the realm of theology to have given rise to a theological tradition named after him (or at least one that was recognized). However, his continued significance in the Sufi tradition has more than outlived the historical memory of Ibn Kullāb and al-Qalānisī. While it is hard to establish in detail how exactly the three influenced the rise of Sunnī *kalām* theology, it is clear that they played a significant role alongside other semi-rationalist scholars in creating the right conditions for it to develop and establishing foundations that al-Ashʿarī and his successors could build upon. Among these was the formulation of an elaborate ontological framework that supported the idea of the eternity of the divine attributes, an elaboration of the mechanics behind divine predestination of human action, and a definition of human reason that did not clash with the traditionalist approach to revelation. The passing of time and the build-up of newer, different layers in the *kalām* of later periods have obscured these contributions to some degree, although they have not gone completely unrecognized, by admirers and detractors alike. However, interest in their significance for the later development of Sunnī *kalām* tends to overlook their significance for their own time, and the uphill battle they faced in their attempts to bring together the concerns of the traditionalists and *kalām* theologians. Ibn Kullāb and his colleagues were not merely precursors laying the path for the rise of al-Ashʿarī and his followers, but also theologians in their own right, addressing the theological questions and challenges of their era.

Bibliography

De Crussol, Y. (2002). *Le Role de la raison dans la reflexion ethique d'al-Muhasibi: Aql et conversion chez al-Muhasibi (165–243/782–857)*. Paris: Consep.

van Ess, J. (1961). *Die Gedankenwelt des Hārit al-Muhāsibi anhand von Übersetzungen aus seinen Schriften dargestellt und erläutert*. Bonn: Selbstverlag des Orientalischen Seminars der Universität Bonn.

van Ess, J. (1990). 'Ibn Kullāb et la "miḥna"'. *Arabica* 37: 173–233.

van Ess, J. (1991–7). *Theologie und Gesellschaft im 2. und 3. Jahrhundert Hidschra: Eine Geschichte des religiösen Denkens im frühen Islam*. 6 vols. Berlin: de Gruyter.

Frank, R. (1978). *Beings and Their Attributes: The Teaching of the Basrian School of the Muʿtazila in the Classical Period*. New York: SUNY.

Gimaret, D. (1989). 'Cet autre théologien sunnite: Abū l-ʿAbbās al-Qalānisī'. *Journal asiatique* 277: 227–62.

Melchert, C. (1996). 'Religious Policies of the Caliphs from al-Mutawakkil to al-Muqtadir, A H 232–295/A D 847–908'. *Islamic Law and Society* 3: 316–42.

Melchert, C. (1997). *The Formation of the Sunni Schools of Law, 9th–10th Centuries C.E.* Leiden: Brill.

Melchert, C. (2002). 'Qurʾānic Abrogation across the Ninth Century: Shāfiʿī, Abū ʿUbayd, Muḥāsibī and Ibn Qutayba'. In B. Weiss (ed.), *Studies in Islamic Legal Theory*. Leiden: Brill, 75–98.

Picken, G. (2008). 'Ibn Ḥanbal and al-Muḥāsibī: A Study of Early Conflicting Scholarly Methodologies'. *Arabica* 55: 337–61.

Picken, G. (2011). *Spiritual Purification in Islam: The Life and Works of al-Muḥāsibī*. London/New York: Routledge.

CHAPTER 13

BETWEEN CORDOBA AND NĪSĀBŪR

The Emergence and Consolidation of Ashʿarism (Fourth–Fifth/Tenth–Eleventh Century)

JAN THIELE

ASHʿARISM was, besides Māturīdism, the most important school of Sunni *kalām*. After the decline of Muʿtazilism, it became the predominant theological school, primarily among the adherents of the Shāfiʿite and the Mālikite school of law. The influence of Ashʿarite teaching can still be felt in modern thought. This chapter intends to give an outline of approximately the first two centuries of the school's history. There is a wide scholarly consensus that during the next, that is the sixth/twelfth century, Ashʿarism entered a new phase that was marked by an increasing influence of Avicennan philosophy. The transition to this new phase is generally associated with the prominent thinker Abū Ḥāmid al-Ghazālī (d. 505/1111). This periodization of the development of Ashʿarism has also a long tradition in Muslim historiography: it was the famous North African scholar Ibn Khaldūn (d. 808/1406) who referred to the pre- and post-Ghazālian theologians as 'the earlier ones' (*al-mutaqaddimūn*) and 'the later ones' (*al-muta'akhkhirūn*). It is roughly with Ibn Khaldūn's 'earlier' representatives of Ashʿarism that we are concerned in this chapter. A number of modern scholars have referred to this period as that of 'classical Ashʿarism' (e.g. Frank 1989a; Frank 1992: 18; Frank 2000; Frank 2004; Shihadeh 2012). Yet the representatives of this period did not propagate a homogeneous set of doctrines: a number of case studies have shown that Ashʿarite teachings were subject to constant developments and revisions, and that the introduction of philosophical ideas, a shift generally identified with al-Ghazālī, even started with earlier theologians.

1 The Rise of Ashʿarism

If we can trust historical reports, the history of Ashʿarism began with a memorable symbolic act. Abū l-Ḥasan al-Ashʿarī (d. 324/935–6), a Muʿtazilite theologian with high renown, is said to have publicly broken with the doctrines of his school on a Friday in the Great Mosque of Basra. It is hardly possible to authenticate the vivid reports about al-Ashʿarī's 'conversion' and to answer the question whether they reliably reflect the historical details. The little we know about the biography of the founder of Ashʿarism widely relies on accounts with a strong hagiographical flavour.[1]

Al-Ashʿarī was born *c.*260/874 in Basra. The city was one of the oldest centres of *kalām* and, more particularly, of Muʿtazilite teaching. Muʿtazilism was the dominant doctrine during al-Ashʿarī's lifetime. He became a talented student of one of the leading Muʿtazilite theologians of that era, Abū ʿAlī al-Jubbāʾī (d. 303/915). With Abū ʿAlī as his master, al-Ashʿarī experienced a crucial phase in the evolution of the discipline of *kalām*. Down to the third/ninth century, Muʿtazilite teaching was merely an intellectual endeavour of individual thinkers. With Abū ʿAlī and his counterpart Abū l-Qāsim al-Kaʿbī al-Balkhī (d. 319/931), however, two representatives of a new generation of theologians formulated systematic doctrinal frameworks and thereby laid the foundation for the emergence of the Basran and the Baghdadi schools of the Muʿtazila. Al-Ashʿarī was consequently still highly familiar with the earlier phase of *kalām* and its theological discussions. His doxography on the 'Doctrines of the Muslims' (*Maqālāt al-islāmiyyīn*) is therefore the most comprehensive and reliable source on this era that has come down to us (al-Ashʿarī, *Maqālāt*).

When al-Ashʿarī broke with Muʿtazilite teaching, he was about 40 years old. Despite the expectable hostilities from his former fellows, he went on living in Basra, before he eventually settled in Baghdad, where he remained for the rest of his life (Allard 1965: 25–47; Gimaret 1997b; van Ess 2011: i. 454–501).

After his rupture with Muʿtazilism, al-Ashʿarī adopted the major tenets of the opposing doctrinal camp, the Sunni Traditionalists. However, despite many doctrinal overlaps, they divided over a very central issue. Essentially, they irreconcilably disagreed over the question of whether human reason is a means of knowing theological truths: whereas the Traditionalists completely rejected rational speculation, al-Ashʿarī distinguished between two major fields of knowledge and claimed that each of them requires its own epistemological method.

On the one hand, he approved of the Traditionalists' rejection of the Muʿtazilites' ethical objectivism. In other words, he agreed that man has no intellectual capacity to

[1] The most important historical accounts of Ashʿarism and its theologians are Ibn ʿAsākir's (d. 571/1176) *Tabyīn kadhib al-muftarī* (Ibn ʿAsākir, *Tabyīn*) and al-Subkī's (d. 771/1370) *Ṭabaqāt al-shāfiʿiyya al-kubrā* (al-Subkī, *Ṭabaqāt*); both authors lived in Damascus. The Andalusī Aḥmad b. Yūsuf al-Lablī also compiled a collection of bibliographies of Ashʿarite theologians (al-Lablī, *Fihrist*).

distinguish between good and evil. As a proponent of ethical subjectivism, he posited that the morally good is whatever God commands and that the evil is whatever He forbids. The upshot of this theory was that since morality is not based on rationalized principles, man depends on divine instruction by way of revelation in order to know God's obligations and prohibitions and to act in a morally good way (Frank 1983a: 207–10; Gimaret 1990: 444–5).

Beyond the question of knowing man's obligations, however, al-Ashʿarī approved of dialectical reasoning on theological questions: he affirmed that knowledge of God can only be gained by rational reflection. In this respect, he agreed with Muʿtazilite teaching. This legitimation of the methodology of *kalām* was in fundamental contradiction to the principles of the Sunni Traditionalists. Al-Ashʿarī even posited that individual reflection about God is man's first religious obligation. However, it is crucially important to understand how al-Ashʿarī defended this theory: he argued that man's duty to reflect about God is made known by revelation, just as is the case with all divine commandments. In this sense, al-Ashʿarī still maintained the primacy of revelation over rational reflection (Frank 1989a: 44–6; Gimaret 1990: 211–18; Rudolph 1992: 73–8).[2]

Despite al-Ashʿarī's agreement with the Sunni Traditionalists on many doctrines, they consequently strongly disapproved of his method. Now since the Muʿtazilites severely criticized his theological positions, al-Ashʿarī came under attack from two diametrically opposed sides. This is aptly illustrated by al-Ashʿarī's understanding of God's attributes: on the one hand, he strove to interpret the Qurʾān as literally and faithfully as possible. This also had significant implications for his interpretation of predications made about God: if the revelation speaks of God's knowledge, power, etc., al-Ashʿarī infers that God really *has* knowledge, power etc. Accordingly, he conceives of these attributes as co-eternal entities that subsist in God.

This was in line with the position of the Traditionalists, but raised much objection amongst the Muʿtazilites. They criticized that his teaching was tantamount to claiming the existence of eternal beings apart from God; in their eyes, this undermined the very

[2] The question whether al-Ashʿarī remained after his 'conversion' a real *mutakallim* was subject to some discussion in modern scholarship. G. Makdisi (1962; 1963) argued that the doctrinal traditionalism expressed in al-Ashʿarī's *al-Ibāna ʿan uṣūl al-diyāna* is in no way consistent with the manifesto for the practice of *kalām* as found in *al-Ḥathth ʿalā l-baḥth* (alternatively entitled *Istiḥsān al-khawḍ fī ʿilm al-kalām*; see Frank 1988), which is equally attributed to al-Ashʿarī. He concluded that the image of al-Ashʿarī as the founder of a new school of *kalām* is anachronistic and merely the product of the school's later narrative. Consequently, such works as Ibn ʿAsākir's *Tabyīn al-muftarī* and al-Subkī's *Ṭabaqāt al-shāfiʿiyya al-kubrā*—which both present al-Ashʿarī as a defender of traditionalist doctrines via rational argumentation—should be read as attempts to advocate the practice of *kalām* and to seek legitimization within the Sunni mainstream, primarily among the adherents of the Shāfiʿite school of law. Makdisi therefore doubted the authenticity of *al-Ḥathth* and suggested that the text cannot be earlier than al-Subkī. Against Makdisi, R. M. Frank (1991) claimed that *al-Ḥathth* is authentic. He argues that the difference between *al-Ibāna* and *al-Ḥathth* is one of form rather than of incoherent doctrinal positions. Consequently, the two texts are not in conflict with each other, nor with al-Ashʿarī's other texts—most importantly his *Lumaʿ*, an undisputedly authentic *kalām* work. Today, Frank's position represents the wide scholarly consensus. More recently, Zahrī (2013) argued that it is in fact the *Ibāna* that cannot be authentic.

principle of monotheism. As a *mutakallim*, al-Ashʿarī did not, however, refrain from providing a rational explanation to resolve such logical problems. After all, he was convinced that God's revelation can be explained by human reason. In other words, he rejected the Traditionalists' so-called *bi-lā kayf*-approach, that is their dismissal of any attempt to rationalize why their doctrinal claims should be true. Al-Ashʿarī's solution to the Muʿtazilites' objection was to claim that God's eternal attributes are neither identical to, nor other than Him (Gimaret 1990: 276–81). In order to prove that God actually has eternal entitative attributes, he went on arguing that predications like 'x knows' or 'x is powerful' always refer to the same reality or truth (*ḥaqīqa*): if human beings described as knowing or powerful merit such descriptions by virtue of an entity (*maʿnā*) of knowledge or power, the same must be true for God (Frank 1982a: 270).

Another well-known example of al-Ashʿarī's controversial approach was his theory of human acts. Again, his reflections departed from a supposition he shared with the Traditionalists: both claimed that God's omnipotence cannot be restricted in any way, and so whatever happens in the world depends on Him. Consequently, human actions—which belong to these worldly events—must be created and controlled by God (Gimaret 1990: 378–9; Perler and Rudolph 2000: 51–6). For the Muʿtazilites, this line of reasoning makes nonsense of the fundamental idea that man is individually responsible for his acts. Yet al-Ashʿarī countered this objection by developing an alternative conception of human self-determination that does not depend on the veracity of freedom of action.

A central element of al-Ashʿarī's solution to the problem consisted in his distinction between two types of human acts. We have a clear awareness, he says, of the fact that we cannot refrain from performing such motions as trembling: consequently, we all know that specific acts occur necessarily (*iḍṭirāran*). He then goes on to argue that we intuitively distinguish other motions, like, for example, our walking. Since necessary acts imply our weakness (*ʿajz*), all other acts must involve our 'power' (*quwwa* or *qudra*). Al-Ashʿarī labelled these non-necessary acts with the term 'acquisition' (*kasb/iktisāb*), a notion that had already been used by some earlier theologians. According to al-Ashʿarī, it is precisely for these 'acquired' acts that we are accountable, even if we have no power to act otherwise than we do. It would seem that al-Ashʿarī justified man's moral responsibility in the absence of freedom by the claim that we act according to our willing and wanting whenever we perform an 'acquired' act (Gimaret 1980: 80–1; Gimaret 1990: 131, 387–96; Thiele in press).

Only a handful of al-Ashʿarī's writings have survived while most of the more than 100 titles he wrote are missing (Gimaret 1985a).[3] Therefore, modern research on al-Ashʿarī's theology largely depends on second-hand information from later sources, the most important being Abū Bakr Ibn Fūrak's (d. 406/1015) *Mujarrad maqālāt al-Ashʿarī*

[3] The most important surviving *kalām* treatise composed by al-Ashʿarī himself is his *Kitāb al-Lumaʿ*; a critical edition and English translation of this text is found in McCarthy (1953).

('Excerpts (?) from al-Ashʿarī's doctrines') (Gimaret 1985b). Consequently, some caution is required when interpreting al-Ashʿarī's original thought and a number of questions cannot be satisfactorily answered.

II Dissemination and Consolidation

According to present knowledge, the generation after the school's eponym did not bring forth any prominent scholar who significantly advanced the school's teachings. Yet its transmission eastwards began as early as with a number of al-Ashʿarī's own students: since many of them hailed from Nīsābūr, the economic and intellectual centre of Khurāsān, they returned back home after their teacher's death and laid the foundation for the city's Ashʿarite community (Allard 1965: 314).

During the following generation, however, three towering theologians of the later fourth/tenth century made outstanding contributions to the elaboration and broader dissemination of the school's teachings: their names were Abū Bakr Ibn Fūrak, Abū Isḥāq al-Isfarāʾīnī (d. 411/1020), and Abū Bakr al-Bāqillānī (d. 403/1013). All three theologians studied *kalām* with al-Ashʿarī's former student Abū l-Ḥasan al-Bāhilī (d. *c*.370/980) and became instrumental in the scholastic consolidation of Ashʿarite thought. Since each one of them developed his own approach, partly under the influence of regional traditions, their teachings laid the foundations for an increasing diversity within Ashʿarism.

At the beginning of his scholarly career Ibn Fūrak lived in Iraq and studied in Baghdad. Then, after having spent some time in Rayy, the Samanid governor Nāṣir al-Dawla (d. 357–8/968–9) established a *madrasa* for Ibn Fūrak in Nīsābūr. We know a number of works he wrote in the field of theology, and some of them have even survived to the present day: Ibn Fūrak composed a commentary upon al-Ashʿarī's *al-Lumaʿ* (lost), a collection of definitions of technical terms in *kalām* and legal methodology, entitled *al-Ḥudūd fī l-uṣūl* (Abdel-Haleem 1991; Ibn Fūrak, *Ḥudūd*), the above-mentioned account of al-Ashʿarī's doctrines (Ibn Fūrak, *Mujarrad*), and some additional works that are still in manuscript form. Yet, Ibn Fūrak is particularly known for a book entitled *Kitāb (Taʾwīl) Mushkil al-ḥadīth* (Ibn Fūrak, *Mushkil*). In this text, Ibn Fūrak discusses anthropomorphic expressions found in prophetic traditions and attempts to interpret these texts allegorically. It would seem that Ibn Fūrak wrote this work in the context of his polemical encounters with the Karrāmiyya, a sect with some influence in Nīsābūr. They considered God as a substrate (*maḥall*) of accidents and therefore claimed that He is a 'substance' (*jawhar*) or body (*jism*). As a result, they were widely blamed as anthropomorphists (see Chapter 15). Hence, Ibn Fūrak's *Mushkil al-ḥadīth* may be read in the light of this specific conflict (Allard 1965: 326–9). The treatise opens with some chapters that are related to the more narrow topics of *kalām*, including God's oneness and singularity, or the meaning of His names and attributes (Allard 1965: 314–15; Montgomery Watt 1978; Brown 2007: 190–1).

Ibn Fūrak's contemporary Abū Isḥāq al-Isfarāʾīnī hailed from Isfarāʾīn. He spent many years studying in Baghdad, before he returned to his home city, where he taught for some time. Like Ibn Fūrak, he eventually received an invitation from scholars of Nīsābūr to teach at a *madrasa* specifically built for him. Reportedly, al-Isfarāʾīnī's teachings were sometimes fairly close to Muʿtazilite positions: in this context, secondary sources refer to such topics as his theory of knowledge, prophethood, the nature of the Qurʾān or human acts. Yet our sources about his theology are very limited: apart from a short creed (*ʿaqīda*) al-Isfarāʾīnī's legal and theological writings are no longer extant (Frank 1989b). However, his teachings are often quoted in the later Ashʿarite literature—a number of his works are even known by title, including *al-Jāmiʿ fī uṣūl al-dīn wa-l-radd ʿalā l-mulḥidīn* ('A compendium of the principles of religion and a refutation of the atheists'), *Kitāb al-Asmāʾ wa-l-ṣifāt* ('Book of the (divine) names and attributes'), *and Mukhtaṣar fī l-radd ʿalā ahl al-iʿtizāl wa-l-qadar* ('Brief refutation of the Muʿtazila and the proponents of human free will'). These frequent quotations are an indication of al-Isfarāʾīnī's popularity and his lasting influence among later generations of theologians (Madelung 1978; Frank 1989b; Brown 2007: 189–90; Brodersen 2008).

In later sources, al-Isfarāʾīnī's positions were often contrasted with those of al-Bāqillānī. Usually, the latter is presented as rather inclined towards the traditionalism of the school's founding father. As an intellectual, al-Bāqillānī must have been appreciated beyond the mere Sunni mainstream: he was even invited to join the court of the Būyids in Baghdad, who were Shīʿites. His patron, ʿAḍud al-Dawla appointed him judge and even sent him on a diplomatic mission to the Byzantine court (Allard 1965: 290–5; Ibish 1965).

Among the three theologians of his generation, al-Bāqillānī's theological teaching is the best known. Comparatively much of his work has survived to the present date. These texts include a comprehensive manual of theological polemics, entitled *Kitāb al-Tamhīd fī l-radd ʿalā l-mulḥida al-muʿaṭṭila wa-l-rāfiḍa wa-l-khawārij wa-l-muʿtazila*.[4] It bears witness to al-Bāqillānī's attempt to systematically compile and coherently organize the teachings of his predecessors (Eichner 2009: 160–4). It has been convincingly argued that this book was in fact one of al-Bāqillānī's early works, possibly written around 360/970 (Gimaret 1970: 76–7; Gimaret 1980: 94–5; Gimaret 2009: 259). A shorter theological treatise that focuses on disputed questions between Ashʿarism and the Muʿtazila circulated under two titles, *al-Risālā al-Ḥurra* and *al-Inṣāf fī mā yajibu ʿtiqāduhu wa-lā yajūzu l-jahl bihi* (al-Bāqillānī, *Inṣāf*). Much more important and comprehensive in length is his main work in theology entitled *Hidāyat al-mustarshidīn*. Originally, the *Hidāya* must have been a monumental work, comprising at least sixteen volumes, but only four have as yet been

[4] Al-Bāqillānī's *Tamhīd* was first published in 1947 (al-Bāqillāni, *Tamhīd*[1]); this edition is based on only one manuscript that happens to be incomplete. Later, R. J. McCarthy critically edited the text on the basis of additional manuscripts (al-Bāqillāni, *Tamhīd*[2]), but he omitted almost the whole section on the imamate. On the basis of these two editions, ʿI. D. A. Ḥaydar published the complete work (al-Bāqillāni, *Tamhīd*[3]). Nonetheless, the earlier incomplete editions remain the standard references in modern scholarship.

rediscovered. It is in this text that al-Bāqillānī expounded his original teachings and sometimes revised or further developed a number of al-Ashʿarī's positions, including some he had still defended in earlier works (Gimaret 2009; Schmidtke 2011).

Since the beginnings of Ashʿarite studies, modern scholars have highlighted al-Bāqillānī's central role in the consolidation of the school. This perception was significantly shaped by Ibn Khaldūn's account of the history of Ashʿarism in his *Muqaddima*. Although Ibn Khaldūn's report includes some imprecisions, it is beyond any doubt that al-Bāqillānī significantly contributed to the evolution of the school's teachings by broadening its conceptual framework and by further developing ideas of the school's founder. In the *Hidāya*, for example, al-Bāqillāni applies to God the term of the 'necessarily existent' (*wājib al-wujūd*).[5] The phrase is primarily known as a central notion in Avicenna's metaphysics—as the counterpart of *mumkin al-wujūd*, which refers to the contingent world—but the term already appeared in the philosophical milieu of fourth/tenth-century Baghdad, where al-Bāqillānī might possibly have become familiar with it.

A famous example for how al-Bāqillānī further developed Ashʿarite teaching by borrowing concepts from other, including rival, schools is his adaption of the Muʿtazilite theory of 'state' (*ḥāl*). Al-Bāqillānī's opinion with regard to the notion of *ḥāl* was not consistent. In his *Kitāb al-Tamhīd*, he still refutes the concept. Yet in his later *magnum opus* in theology, the *Hidāya*, he revised his earlier position. The reason behind this was that he apparently felt that the traditional Ashʿarite teaching on attributes was, in some respect, incoherent.

It would seem that al-Bāqillānī was concerned with what he identified as a weakness in al-Ashʿarī's proof for God's entitative attributes, such as knowledge, power, etc. As mentioned before, al-Ashʿarī's argument was based on the claim that such expressions as 'he is knowing' always express the same meaning or truth (*ḥaqīqa*): if man is knowing by virtue of an entity (*maʿnā*) of knowledge, the same must be true for God. Al-Bāqillānī drew on this line of reasoning and went on arguing that there must be a correlation (*taʿalluq*) between that which is expressed by our predicating 'x is knowing' and the entity of knowledge. Against al-Ashʿarī, however, al-Bāqillānī came to the conclusion that the predication 'being knowing' (*kawnuhu ʿāliman*) cannot refer to the same as the noun 'knowledge' (*ʿilm*). For if 'being knowing' referred to an entity of knowledge and not to a reality distinct from this entity, one would attempt to prove the existence of entitative knowledge by itself. Al-Bāqillānī therefore concludes that such predications as 'being knowing' refer to a *ḥāl*. According to his understanding, this *ḥāl* is grounded in, and, at the same time, evidence for, the existence of an entity of knowledge. Al-Bāqillānī consequently relied on the concept to prove the existence of entitative attributes in God that, like Him, are eternal. Furthermore, al-Bāqillānī's adoption of the notion of *ḥāl* had

[5] See Ms. St Petersburg, The Institute of Oriental Manuscripts of the Russian Academy of Sciences, C329, fos. 32b–33a, where al-Bāqillānī describes God's existence as 'His being eternal [and] necessarily existent, for ever and always' (*kawnuhu qadīman wājib al-wujūd abadan wa-dāʾiman*); and Ms. Tashkent, al-Biruni Institute of Oriental Studies, Academy of Sciences of the Republic of Uzbekistan, 3296, fo. 20b: 'the Eternal's existence is necessary under all circumstances' (*al-qadīm wajib wujūdihi fī kull ḥāl*).

also implications for his metaphysical conception of the created world, since he also applied it to predications we make about created beings (see Chapter 22).

Al-Bāqillānī furthermore attempted to achieve greater coherency with regard to the Ashʿarite teaching on human acts, the framework of which was laid down by al-Ashʿarī's theory of 'acquisition' (*kasb*). Al-Bāqillānī revised some aspects of the theory by addressing, primarily in the *Hidāya*, a number of questions that seem to have been unresolved by the school's founder. However, he stuck to al-Ashʿarī's central claim: man's moral accountability does not depend on freedom of action being true. Yet against al-Ashʿarī, al-Bāqillānī explicitly rejects the assumption that our acting intentionally, that is our 'acquiring' specific acts, depends in any way on our will being involved. For him, this claim is established by the fact that we sometimes fail to exercise our will—which is always the case with 'compelled acts'. As a logical corollary, he goes on to argue that our incapacity to do what we want reveals a lack of power. Consequently, the opposite must be true for all other acts: they occur by virtue of man's power.

Beyond al-Ashʿarī's reasoning, al-Bāqillānī asked, however, about the precise function of man's power in our performing 'acquired' acts. While al-Ashʿarī contented himself to affirm that 'acquired' acts are merely conjoined by an accident of power in the agent's body, al-Bāqillānī formulated the theory that man's power really *has* an effect (*taʾthīr*). He actually proposes different approaches to explain how our power affects our acting. His first explanation as to the effectiveness of human power is in line with his conception of the reality that underlies our predications about beings: as mentioned above, he believed that they reflect a *ḥāl*—in the case of agents of 'acquired' acts the feature of 'being powerful' (*kawnuhu qādiran*). The *ḥāl* is, according to al-Bāqillānī, caused by the agent's power, and it is precisely this feature that distinguishes him from compelled agents, who have no power and are consequently not responsible for their doing.

The mere distinction between powerful agents and others who are not did not, by itself, sufficiently explain why acts created by God should be considered as ours. Al-Bāqillānī addressed this issue by claiming that it is by virtue of their power that agents are related (*yataʿallaqu*) to their 'acquired' acts. Drawing a parallel to the relation between sensual perception and objects perceived, he argued that acts do not have to be created by man himself in order to suppose a relation between his power and his acts. Finally, al-Bāqillānī adds a further explanation as to how man's power affects his acting. In this approach, he specifically addresses the question of man's individual accountability. He appears to be aware of the logical problem that man can hardly be held responsible for the *existence* of acts if he does not create them himself. Al-Bāqillānī therefore proposes an alternative solution as to what is subject to moral assessment in our acting. He suggests that man determines an attribute of his 'acquired' acts by virtue of his power, and that it is to this very attribute that God's command, prohibition, reward, and punishment relate (Thiele in press).

While al-Bāqillānī was primarily active in Baghdad, the centre of the Abbasid caliphate, Ashʿarite doctrines were simultaneously promoted in the eastern lands by his two towering contemporaries: with Ibn Fūrak and al-Isfarāʾīnī, Khurāsān, and specifically the city of Nīsābūr, became an important centre of Ashʿarite teaching. Yet al-Bāqillānī significantly contributed to the transmission of Ashʿarism towards the Islamic west, at least indirectly. In the Maghrib, the first local tradition of Ashʿarite teaching arose in Kairouan, one of the earliest and most important intellectual hubs in the region. It would seem that one of the major reasons behind the wider approval of Ashʿarism was al-Bāqillānī's adherence to Mālikism, the predominant school of law in the western Islamic lands. His writings were transmitted by his own students, including Abū ʿAbd Allāh al-Azdī and Abū ʿImrān al-Fāsī, who settled in the North African city. Alongside al-Bāqillānī's theological works, Ibn Fūrak's *Mushkil al-ḥadīth* is known to have been transmitted to Kairouan by representatives of this generation (Idris 1953; Idris 1954; Zahrī 2011).

While the dissemination of Ashʿarite doctrines was very successful, none of the school's representatives of this generation achieved the same reputation as al-Bāqillānī, Ibn Fūrak, or al-Isfarāʾīnī. However, two comprehensive theological compendia composed at that time have come down to us and provide some insight into Ashʿarite teaching in this historical phase. The first work was written by Abū Isḥāq al-Isfarāʾīnī's student ʿAbd al-Qāhir al-Baghdādī (429/1037)—the later teacher of the famous mystic Abū l-Qāsim al-Qushayrī (d. 465/1074)—who hailed from Nīsābūr: al-Baghdādī's *Kitāb Uṣūl al-dīn* (al-Baghdādī, *Uṣūl*) appears to be rather conservative in the sense that he primarily relies on such early authorities as al-Ashʿarī himself, or even the pre-Ashʿarite Ibn Kullāb (d. *c.*240/854) (Allard 1965: 316; Madelung 1987: 331).

The author of the second work is Abū Jaʿfar al-Simnānī (d. 444/1052). He was al-Bāqillānī's disciple and, incidentally, a Ḥanafite. This is quite unusual, since Ḥanafites rather tended to be critical of Ashʿarism. Al-Simnānī completed his studies in Baghdad before he was appointed Qāḍī of Aleppo and later of Mosul. The above-mentioned theological *summa* from his pen is entitled *al-Bayān ʿan uṣūl al-īmān wa-l-kashf ʿan tamwīhāt ahl al-ṭughyān* (al-Simnānī, *Bayān*; see also Gimaret 1997a). It is the only work by al-Simnānī that is known to have survived. The famous Andalusī Ẓāhirī scholar Ibn Ḥazm (d. 456/1064) extensively quotes from another, apparently comprehensive, theological work, that he only calls 'al-Simnānī's book' (*Kitāb al-Simnānī*). The book is lost, but it would seem from Ibn Ḥazm's quotation that it was not identical with the *Bayān* (Schmidtke 2013: 384). Al-Simnānī's theological teaching is regarded as being close to that of his teacher al-Bāqillānī.

A number of al-Simnānī's students are known by name. The most prominent was Abū l-Walīd al-Bājī (d. 474/1081), who hailed from al-Andalus. Al-Bājī received his early education in the city of Cordoba. Most of his teachers in this city were trained in Kairouan and some of them even had a background in Ashʿarite theology. At the age of about 21, al-Bājī left his homeland to seek further instruction in the Islamic east. He spent several years in the Ḥijāz and Baghdad, studying with Ibn Fūrak's disciple Abū Bakr al-Muṭṭawaʿī and the prominent specialist in Shāfiʿite legal methodology, Abū Isḥāq Ibrāhīm b. ʿAlī al-Shīrāzī (d. 476/1083), who had also studied with al-Bāqillānī. Al-Bājī spent one year in Mosul attending al-Simnānī's study circle, where he was trained in Ashʿarite theology, before he continued travelling to Aleppo. There he was appointed judge, an office he exercised for a period of one year, before he eventually returned to al-Andalus (Turki 1973: 59–70; Fierro 2004).

Our extant sources do not allow us to draw a detailed picture of al-Bājī's theological teaching. Yet he must have played a central role in the dissemination of Ashʿarism in Islamic Spain. Indeed, Ashʿarite works already circulated before al-Bājī, but he appears to have significantly increased the amount of available texts. In addition, he contributed to the establishment of *kalām*, which was by his time a rather insignificant discipline in al-Andalus (Fórneas Besteiro 1977; Fórneas Besteiro 1978; Aʿrāb 1987: 192–3; Lagardère 1994).

III Ashʿarism under the Patronage of Niẓām al-Mulk

A younger contemporary of al-Bājī was the famous theologian Abū l-Maʿālī al-Juwaynī (d. 478/1085). He was born 419/1028 in the region of Nīsābūr. His father had already played a role in Khurāsānian Ashʿarism. After his father's death, al-Juwaynī followed him as teacher in Nīsābūr. Yet with the Seljuq conquest of the city in 428/1037, the Ashʿarites faced growing hostility: the vizier Tughril Beg (d. 455/1063) implemented an anti-Shāfiʿite policy and denounced Ashʿarite doctrines as an illegitimate innovation (Madelung 1971: 124–30). Together with other scholars inclined towards Ashʿarism—like the famous mystic Abū l-Qāsim al-Qushayrī (Frank 1982b; Frank 1983b; Nguyen 2012)—al-Juwaynī fled from Nīsābūr to Baghdad. Later, in 450/1058, he travelled to the Ḥijāz and taught at Mecca and Medina—wherefore he earned his honorific title of 'the Imam of the two sacred cities' (*imām al-ḥaramayn*). The Seljuqs' attitude towards Ashʿarism radically changed with the vizier Niẓām al-Mulk (d. 485/1092): he became a patron of Ashʿarism and founded a series of colleges in Iraq, the Arabian Peninsula, and Persia—specifically Khurāsān—to promote their teachings. He also invited al-Juwaynī to return to Nīsābūr and to teach at a *madrasa* that was built specifically for him. Niẓām al-Mulk also promoted other prominent Ashʿarite scholars like, for example, Abū Bakr Aḥmad b. Muḥammad al-Fūrakī (d. 478/1085), a grandson of Ibn Fūrak, who taught at the Niẓāmiyya college in Baghdad and wrote an exposition of Ashʿarite theology entitled *al-Niẓāmī fī uṣūl al-dīn* (Nguyen 2013).

Among al-Juwaynī's theological writings, two works are of particular significance. He wrote a supercommentary on al-Ashʿarī's *Lumaʿ*, which is based on al-Bāqillānī's lost commentary. This work, entitled *al-Shāmil fī uṣūl al-dīn*, has not survived in its entirety and its largest parts have not been rediscovered.[6] The second text, *al-Irshād ilā qawāṭiʿ*

[6] The portions of al-Juwaynī's *al-Shāmil* that have as yet been discovered have been published in three partial critical editions: the first was prepared in 1959 by H. Klopfer (Juwaynī, *Shāmil*[1]) and incompletely reproduces the text contained in a manuscript that was eventually published in its entirety by ʿA. S. al-Nashshār in 1969 (Juwaynī, *Shāmil*[2]). Additional portions were critically edited by R. M. Frank in 1981

al-adilla fī uṣūl al-iʿtiqād, is much shorter than the *Shāmil* but complete (al-Juwaynī, *Irshād*). Allard (1965: 380) argued that the length of al-Juwaynī's works most likely decreased over the course of their relative chronology. The *Shāmil* and the *Irshād* would then have been followed by *Lumaʿ al-adilla fī qawāʿid ahl al-summa* (Allard 1968) and finally *al-ʿAqīda al-Niẓāmiyya* (al-Juwaynī, *ʿAqīda*).

As was the case with al-Bāqillānī, al-Juwaynī did not follow a consistent teaching throughout his life. His works and the accounts of later Ashʿarite theologians bear witness to a number of revisions and changes in al-Juwaynī's doctrinal positions and argumentations. At some point in his career, for example, he followed al-Bāqillānī in adopting the concept of *aḥwāl* and applied it to his ontological understanding of predications about God and created beings. His two longer works, the *Irshād* and the *Shāmil*, contain sections with his approval of the notion of *ḥāl*. In contrast, al-Juwaynī's *Lumaʿ* and his *al-ʿAqīda al-Niẓāmiyya* no longer appeal to the theory (Allard 1965: 389–91; Gimaret 1970: 77–9; Frank 2004: 770–7).

Further contradictory positions were formulated by al-Juwaynī with regard to the function of man's 'power' (*qudra*) in the framework of the theory of human acts. Just like other school representatives before him, he struggled with the question of whether the power that accompanies man's acts has any effect or not. While in the *Irshād* al-Juwaynī completely rejects any such effectiveness, he develops in *al-ʿAqīda al-Niẓāmiyya* an original theory of human acts that departs from the assumption that man's power *must* be effective. Al-Juwaynī's central argument is that otherwise God's imposing duties and obligations (that is the notion of *taklīf*) were no longer a tenable idea. In order to resolve this theological dilemma, he affirmed that man's acting is caused by his power. He could consequently argue that whatever we do is controlled by our very own selves. By this line of reasoning, he provided an explanation why we are rightly rewarded or punished for our acts. Nonetheless, al-Juwaynī did not give up the central Ashʿarite idea that all happenings in the world originate in God: he maintained the claim of God being the all-encompassing Creator by reasoning that man's power is only an intermediate cause, which in turn is created by God (Gimaret 1980: 120–3).

On the surface, al-Juwaynī's theory has some similarity with two non-Ashʿarite concepts; however, there is no clear evidence that his reasoning really depends on them. On the one hand, Muʿtazilite theologians posited a form of acting that produces an effect outside the agent by way of an intermediate cause. The question whether or not this pattern also applies to God was subject to inner-Muʿtazilite debate. On the other hand, al-Juwaynī's theory also recalls to some extent the notion of emanation supported by hellenizing philosophers—that is the idea of God being the first cause from which all other causal relations proceed. It was precisely this alleged influence for which al-Juwaynī was blamed by the later Ashʿarite al-Shahrastānī (d. 548/1153) (Gimaret 1980: 127). Irrespective of whether or not al-Juwaynī was really inspired by the idea of emanation,

(Juwaynī, *Shāmil*[3]) on the basis of another manuscript from Tehran; this manuscript partly overlaps with the text in al-Nashshār's edition and so Frank decided to omit from his edition the parallel sections found in the two surviving manuscripts.

we know that he was actually acquainted with, and even adopted, ideas developed by the *falāsifa*—as in the case of his proof for God's existence. While several modern studies have suggested a direct Avicennan influence (Davidson 1987; Rudolph 1997), Madelung has recently found significant parallels with Abū l-Ḥusayn al-Baṣrī's (d. 426/1044) argumentation (Madelung 2006). Abū l-Ḥusayn was a Muʿtazilite theologian from Baghdad, who had lived too early for there to be a possible influence of Avicenna's theories on his thought. He was, however, trained by Christian philosophers in Baghdad and therefore familiar with their teachings (see Chapter 9).

Al-Juwaynī's starting point in revising the proof for God's existence concerned its central premiss: the traditional argument built on the assumption that the world is created. In order to prove this assumption, it was claimed that bodies, which make up the world, necessarily carry accidents that have a temporal existence. It was then reasoned that bodies must also have temporal existence. For long, however, theologians did not provide any rational proof against the possibility of an infinite series of created accidents: however, the upshot of this assumption would have been that an eternal body could be conjoined by an infinite number of accidents, an idea that would have completely undermined the argument for creation. This deficiency of the traditional proof was already identified by Abū l-Ḥusayn al-Baṣrī. Al-Juwaynī took these reflections into consideration and therefore demonstrated that whatever is created has 'a first'; he thereby neutralized the argument of an infinite series of accidents inhering in an eternal body (Davidson 1987: 144–6; Madelung 2006: 277).

The second part of al-Juwaynī's revision concerned the more narrow part of the proof for God's existence. Traditionally, it was argued that the createdness of bodies requires a creator (*muḥdith*), who must be God. This conclusion was drawn by way of analogy with our worldly experience that any such works as manufacture, writing, etc. need a manufacturer, writer, etc. Yet al-Juwaynī considered in his proof the creation of the world as a whole: he claimed that the world, instead of being existent, could also be non-existent or come into existence at different times. This, he went on to argue, implies its being possibly existent, which, as he says, self-evidently implies that there must be an agent by virtue of whose arbitrary choice the world comes into existence at a given time instead of continuing in a state of non-existence or of coming into existence at some other time. The agent, he concludes, cannot be other than God. Al-Juwaynī denotes God's choosing by the verb 'to particularize' (*ikhtaṣṣa*), and, therefore, the proof is also known as the 'particularization argument'. The central assumption that underlies the argument is an idea formulated by Avicenna, namely that the existence of the world is contingent (*mumkin al-wujūd*) and that God is necessarily existent (*wājib al-wujūd*). Referring to the world, al-Juwaynī in turn uses the formulations *jāʾiz al-wujūd* or *wujūd mumkin*. Yet the core of al-Juwaynī's line of reasoning is already found in Abū l-Ḥusayn al-Baṣrī's teaching, who uses, however, another (less Avicennan) terminology (Davidson 1987: 161–2; Rudolph 1997: 344–6; Madelung 2006: 275, 279).

From al-Juwaynī's time, we also possess a short *kalām* compendium written by his contemporary Abū Saʿd ʿAbd al-Raḥmān b. Maʾmūn al-Mutawallī (d. 478/1086). Al-Mutawallī was born in Nīsābūr in 426 or 427/1035 or 1036 and studied *fiqh* in Marw,

Bukhāra, and Marw al-Rūdh. He eventually moved to Baghdad. On the death of the Shāfiʿite master Abū Isḥāq al-Shīrāzī, al-Mutawallī succeeded him as teacher at the city's Niẓāmiyya. His theological treatise was first edited under the title *al-Mughnī* and only a little later under that of *al-Ghunya*. The work heavily depends on al-Juwaynī's *Irshād* (al-Mutawallī, *Mughnī*; Bernand 1984; Gimaret 1993).

Al-Juwaynī is considered as the last important representative of Ashʿarism before the methodological shift of Ashʿarism during the sixth/twelfth century. Yet the teaching of some later theologians remained largely unaffected by these developments: these scholars include al-Kiyāʾ al-Ḥarrāsī (d. 504/1010–11), Abū l-Qāsim al-Anṣārī (d. 512/1118), and Ḍiyāʾ al-Dīn al-Makkī (d. 559/1163–4) (Shihadeh 2012: 434). It was in particular the works of al-Juwaynī and al-Bāqillānī that continued to be studied for several centuries. An important number of commentaries on such works as the *Irshād* and to a lesser extent the *Tamhīd* provide clear evidence for the ongoing impact of these two thinkers. These works include the *Sharḥ al-Irshād* by al-Juwaynī's own student Abū l-Qāsim al-Anṣārī, a most valuable source for the study of Ashʿarism (Gilliot 2009). Many other commentaries on al-Juwaynī's *Irshād* were composed by theologians from the Maghrib and al-Andalus, such as Abū ʿAbd Allāh Muḥammad b. Muslim al-Māzarī (d. 530/1136), ʿAlī b. Muḥammad al-Fazārī (d. 552/1157 or 557/1162), and Ibrāhīm b. Yūsuf Ibn Marʾa (611/1214–15) (Shihadeh 2012: 476–7).

Acknowledgements

The preparation of this chapter has received funding from the People Programme (Marie Curie Actions) of the European Union's Seventh Framework Programme (FP7/2007–2013) under REA grant agreement no. 624808. I wish to thank Sabine Schmidtke for offering helpful suggestions.

References

Abdel-Haleem, M. A. S. (1991). 'Early Islamic Theological and Juristic Terminology: *Kitāb al-ḥudūd fī 'l-uṣūl*, by Ibn Fūrak'. *Bulletin of the School of Oriental and African Studies* 54/1: 5–41.

Allard, M. (1965). *Le problème des attributs divins dans la doctrine d'al-Ašʿarī et de ses premiers grands disciples*. Beirut: Imprimerie Catholique.

Allard, M. (1968). *Textes apologétiques de Ǧuwaynī (m. 478/1085)*. Beirut: Dar el-Mashreq.

Aʿrāb, Saʿīd (1987). *Maʿ al-Qāḍī Abī Bakr b. al-ʿArabī*. Beirut: Dār al-Gharb al-Islāmī.

al-Ashʿarī, Abū l-Ḥasan ʿAlī b. Ismāʿīl (*Maqālāt*). *Kitāb Maqālāt al-islāmiyyīn wa-khtilāf al-muṣallīn*. 4th edn. Ed. H. Ritter. Beirut: Orient Institut Beirut, 2005 (1st edn 1929–33).

al-Baghdādī, Abū l-Manṣūr ʿAbd al-Qāhir (*Uṣūl*). *Kitāb Uṣūl al-Dīn*. Istanbul: Madrasat al-Ilāhiyyāt bi-Dār al-Funūn al-Turkiyya, 1928.

al-Bāqillānī, Abū Bakr Muḥammad b. Tayyib (*Inṣāf*). *al-Inṣāf fī-mā yajibu ʿtiqāduhu wa-lā yajūzu l-jahl bihi*. 5th edn. Ed. M. Z. b. H. al-Kawtharī. Cairo: al-Khanjī, 2010 (1st edn. 1950).

al-Bāqillānī, Abū Bakr Muḥammad b. Tayyib (*Tamhīd*[1]). *al-Tamhīd fī l-radd ʿalā l-mulḥida al-muʿaṭṭila wa-r-rāfiḍa wa-l-khawārij wa-l-muʿtazila*. Ed. M. M. al-Khuḍayrī and M. ʿA. H. Abū Rīda. Cairo: Dār al-Fikr al-ʿArabī, 1947 (various reprints).
al-Bāqillānī, Abū Bakr Muḥammad b. Tayyib (*Tamhīd*[2]). *Kitāb al-Tamhīd*. Ed. R. J. McCarthy. Beirut: Librairie Orientale, 1957.
al-Bāqillānī, Abū Bakr Muḥammad b. Tayyib (*Tamhīd*[3]). *Kitāb Tamhīd al-awāʾil wa-talkhīṣ al-dalāʾil*. Ed. ʿI. D. A. Ḥaydar. Beirut: Muʾassasat al-Kutub al-Thaqāfiyya, 1987.
Bernand, M. (1984). 'Un ouvrage de kalam ashʿarite attribué à un contemporain d'al-Juwaynī'. In M. E. Marmura (ed.), *Islamic Theology and Philosophy: Studies in Honor of George F. Hourani*. Albany, NY: State University of New York Press, 54–62.
Brodersen, A. (2008). 'Abū Isḥāq al-Isfarāyīnī'. *Encyclopaedia of Islam*. Three. Leiden: Brill.
Brown, J. (2007). *The Canonization of al-Bukhārī and Muslim: The Formation and Function of the Sunnī Ḥadīth Canon*. Leiden: Brill.
Davidson, H. A. (1987). *Proofs for Eternity, Creation and the Existence of God in Medieval Islamic and Jewish Philosophy*. New York/Oxford: Oxford University Press.
Eichner, H. (2009). 'The Post-Avicennian Philosophical Tradition and Islamic Orthodoxy: Philosophical and Theological Summae in Context'. Unpublished 'Habilitation'-Thesis, Martin-Luther-Universität Halle-Wittenberg.
van Ess, J. (2011). *Der Eine und das Andere: Beobachtungen an islamischen häresiographischen Texten*. 2 vols. Berlin/New York: De Gruyter.
Fierro, M. (2004). 'al-Bāŷī, Abū l-Walīd'. In J. Lirola Delgado and J. M. Puerta Vílchez (eds.), *Biblioteca de al-Andalus*. Almería: Fundación Ibn Tufayl de Estudios Árabes, i. 233–43.
Fórneas Besteiro, J. M. (1977). '*Al-Tamhīd* de al-Bāqillānī y su transmisión en al-Andalus'. *Miscelanea de Estudios Árabes y Hebraicos* 26–8/2: 433–40.
Fórneas Besteiro, J. M. (1978). 'De la transmisión de algunas obras de tendencia ašʿarī en al-Andalus'. *Awrāq* 1: 4–11.
Frank, R. M. (1982a). 'Attribute, Attribution, and Being: Three Islamic Views'. In P. Morewedge (ed.), *Philosophies of Existence: Ancient and Medieval*. New York: Fordham University Press, 258–78.
Frank, R. M. (1982b). 'Two Short Dogmatic Works of Abū l-Qāsim al-Qushayrī. First Part: Edition and Translation of "Lumaʿ fī l-iʿtiqād"'. *Mélanges de l'Institut Dominicain d'Études Orientales* 15: 53–74.
Frank, R. M. (1983a). 'Moral Obligation in Classical Muslim Theology'. *Journal of Religious Ethics* 11/2: 204–23.
Frank, R. M. (1983b). 'Two Short Dogmatic Works of Abū l-Qāsim al-Qushayrī. Second Part: Edition and Translation of "al-Fuṣūl fī l-uṣūl"'. *Mélanges de l'Institut Dominicain d'Études Orientales* 16: 59–94.
Frank, R. M. (1988). 'Al-Ashʿarī's "Kitāb al-Ḥathth ʿalā l-baḥth"'. *Mélanges de l'Institut Dominicain d'Études Orientales* 18: 83–152.
Frank, R. M. (1989a). 'Knowledge and *Taqlîd*: The Foundations of Religious Belief in Classical Ashʿarism'. *Journal of the American Oriental Society* 109/1: 37–62.
Frank, R. M. (1989b). 'Al-Ustādh Abū Isḥāḳ: An *ʿaqīda* Together with Selected Fragments'. *Mélanges de l'Institut Dominicain d'Études Orientales* 19: 129–202.
Frank, R. M. (1991). 'Elements in the Development of the Teaching of al-Ashʿarī'. *Le Muséon* 104/1–2: 141–90.

Frank, R. M. (1992). 'The Science of *Kalām*'. *Arabic Sciences and Philosophy* 2/1: 7–37.

Frank, R. M. (2000). 'The Non-Existent and the Possible in Classical Ashʿarite Teaching'. *Mélanges de l'Institut Dominicain d'Études Orientales* 24: 1–37.

Frank, R. M. (2004). '*Al-Aḥkām* in Classical Ašʿarite Teaching'. In R. Morelon and A. Hasnawi (eds.), *De Zénon d'Élée à Poincaré: receuil d'études en hommage à Roshdi Rashed*. Leuven: Peeters, 753–77.

Frank, R. M. (2005–2008). *Texts and Studies in the Development and History of Kalām*. Ed. Dimitri Gutas. 3 vols. Variorum Collected Studies Series. Aldershot: Ashgate.

Gilliot, C. (2009). 'al-Anṣarī, Abū l-Qāsim'. *Encyclopaedia of Islam*. Three. Leiden: Brill.

Gimaret, D. (1970). 'La théorie des *aḥwâl* d'Abû Hâšim al-Ǧubbâʾî d'après des sources ašʿarites'. *Journal asiatique* 258: 47–86.

Gimaret, D. (1980). *Théories de l'acte humain en théologie musulmane*. Paris: J. Vrin.

Gimaret, D. (1985a). 'Bibliographie d'Ašʿarī: un réexamen'. *Journal asiatique* 273/3–4: 223–92.

Gimaret, D. (1985b). 'Un document majeur pour l'histoire du kalām: le *Muǧarrad Maqālāt al-Ašʿarī* d'Ibn Fūrak'. *Arabica* 32/2: 185–218.

Gimaret, D. (1990). *La doctrine d'al-Ashʿarī*. Paris: Cerf.

Gimaret, D. (1993). 'al-Mutawallī'. *Encyclopaedia of Islam*. 2nd edn. Leiden: Brill.

Gimaret, D. (1997a). 'al-Simnānī'. *Encyclopaedia of Islam*. 2nd edn. Leiden: Brill.

Gimaret, D. (1997b). 'Sur la conversion: l'exemple du théologien musulman Abū l-Ḥasan al-Ašʿarī (m. 324h./935 AD)'. In J.-C. Attias (ed.), *De la conversion*. Paris: Cerf, 107–18.

Gimaret, D. (2009). 'Un extrait de la *Hidāya* d'Abū Bakr al-Bāqillānī: le *Kitāb at-tawallud*, réfutation de la thèse muʿtazilite de la génération des actes'. *Bulletin d'études orientales* 58: 259–313.

Ibish, Y. (1965). 'Life and Works of al-Bāqillānī'. *Islamic Studies* 4/3: 225–36.

Ibn ʿAsākir, Abū l-Qāsim ʿAlī b. al-Ḥasan b. Hibat Allāh (*Tabyīn*). *Tabyīn kadhib al-muftarī*. Damascus: Maṭbaʿat al-Ṭawfīq, 1928–9.

Ibn Fūrak, Abū Bakr Muḥammad b. al-Ḥasan (*Ḥudūd*). *Kitāb al-Ḥudūd fī l-uṣūl*. Ed. M. al-Sulaymānī. Beirut: Dār al-Gharb al-Islāmī, 1999.

Ibn Fūrak, Abū Bakr Muḥammad b. al-Ḥasan (*Mujarrad*). *Mujarrad maqālāt al-shaykh Abī l-Ḥasan al-Ashʿarī*. Ed. D. Gimaret. Beirut: Dar el-Mashreq, 1987.

Ibn Fūrak, Abū Bakr Muḥammad b. al-Ḥasan (*Mushkil*). *Kitāb Mushkil al-ḥadīth aw Taʾwīl al-akhbār al-mutashābiha*. Ed. D. Gimaret. Damascus: Institut Français d'Études Arabes de Damas, 2003.

Idris, H. R. (1953). 'Essai sur la diffusion de l'ašʿarisme en Ifrîqiya'. *Les Cahiers de Tunisie* 1: 126–40.

Idris, H. R. (1954). 'Deux juristes kairouanais de l'époque zīrīde: Ibn Abī Zaid et al-Qābisī (X[e]–XIe siècle)'. *Annales de l'Institut d'Études Orientales* 12: 122–98.

al-Juwaynī, Imām al-Ḥaramayn Abū l-Maʿālī (*ʿAqīda*). *al-ʿAqīda al-Niẓāmiyya*. Ed. M. al-Zubaydī. Beirut: Dār Sabīl al-Rashād/Dār al-Nafāʾis, 2003.

al-Juwaynī, Imām al-Ḥaramayn Abū l-Maʿālī (*Irshād*). *al-Irshād ilā qawāṭiʿ al-adilla fī uṣūl al-iʿtiqād*. Ed. M. Y. Mūsā and A. ʿAbd al-Munʿim ʿAbd al-Ḥamīd. Cairo: Maktabat al-Khanjī, 1950.

al-Juwaynī, Imām al-Ḥaramayn Abū l-Maʿālī (*Shāmil*[1]). *al-Shāmil fī uṣūl al-dīn*. Ed. H. Klopfer. Cairo: Dār al-ʿArab, 1959.

al-Juwaynī, Imām al-Ḥaramayn Abū l-Maʿālī (*Shāmil*[2]). *al-Shāmil fī uṣūl al-dīn*. Ed. ʿA. S. al-Nashshār. Alexandria: Munshaʾāt al-Maʿārif, 1969.

al-Juwaynī, Imām al-Ḥaramayn Abū l-Maʿālī (*Shāmil*[3]). *al-Kitāb al-Shāmil fī uṣūl al-dīn*. The Exposition of al-Bāqillānī's Commentary on the *Kitāb al-Lumaʿ*: Some Additional Portions of the Text. Ed. R. M. Frank. Tehran: McGill University/Tehran University, 1981.
al-Lablī, Aḥmad b. Yūsuf b. Yaʿqūb b. ʿAlī al-Fahrī (*Fihrist*). *Fihrist al-Lablī*. Ed. Y. Y. ʿAyyāsh and ʿA. ʿA. R. Abū Zayna. Beirut: Dār al-Gharb al-Islāmī, 1988.
Lagardère, V. (1994). 'Une théologie dogmatique de la frontière en al-Andalus aux XIe et XIIe siècles: l'ašʿarisme'. *Anaquel de Estudios Árabes* 5: 71–98.
McCarthy, R. J. (1953). *The Theology of al-Ashʿarī*. The Arabic text of al-Ashʿarī's *Kitāb al-Lumaʿ* and *Risālat Istiḥsān al-Khawḍ fī ʿIlm al-Kalām*, with brief annotated translations, and Appendices containing material pertinent to the study of al-Ashʿarī. Beirut: Imprimerie Catholique.
Madelung, W. (1971). 'The Spread of Māturīdism and the Turks'. *Actas do IV Congresso de estudos árabes e islâmicos Coimbra—Lisboa 1968*. Leiden: Brill, 109–68.
Madelung, W. (1978). 'al-Isfarāyīnī'. *Encyclopaedia of Islam*. 2nd edn. Leiden: Brill.
Madelung, W. (1987). 'Der Kalām'. In H. Gätje (ed.), *Grundriß der Arabischen Philologie. Band II: Literaturwissenschaft*. Wiesbaden: Ludwig Reichert, 326–37.
Madelung, W. (2006). 'Abū l-Ḥusayn al-Baṣrī's Proof for the Existence of God'. In J. E. Montgomery (ed.), *Arabic Theology, Arabic Philosophy: From the Many to the One. Essays in Celebration of Richard M. Frank*. Leuven: Peeters, 273–80.
Makdisi, G. (1962 and 1963). 'Ashʿarī and the Ashʿarites in Islamic Religious History'. *Studia Islamica* 17: 37–80, *Studia Islamica* 18: 19–39.
al-Mutawallī, Abū Saʿd ʿAbd al-Raḥmān b. Maʾmūn (*Mughnī*). *Kitāb al-Mughnī*. Ed. M. Bernand. Cairo: Institut Français d'Archéologie Orientale, 1986.
Nguyen, M. (2012). *Sufi Master and Qurʾan Scholar: Abūʾl-Qāsim al-Qushayrī and the Laṭāʾif al-Ishārāt*. Oxford: Oxford Univeristy Press.
Nguyen, M. (2013). 'al-Fūrakī, Abū Bakr'. *Encyclopaedia of Islam*. Three. Leiden: Brill.
Perler, D., and U. Rudolph (2000). *Occasionalismus: Theorien der Kausalität im arabisch-islamischen und im europäischen Denken*. Göttingen: Vandenhoeck & Ruprecht.
Rudolph, U. (1992). 'Ratio und Überlieferung in der Erkenntnislehre al-Ašʿarī's und al-Māturīdī's'. *Zeitschrift der Deutschen Morgenländischen Gesellschaft* 142: 72–89.
Rudolph, U. (1997). 'La preuve de l'existence de Dieu chez Avicenne et dans la théologie musulmane'. In A. d. Libera, A. Elamrani-Jamal, and A. Galonnier (eds.), *Langage et philosophie: hommage à Jean Jolivet*. Paris: Vrin, 339–46.
Schmidtke, S. (2011). 'Early Ašʿarite Theology: Abū Bakr al-Bāqillānī (d. 403/1013) and his *Hidāyat al-mustaršidīn*'. *Bulletin d'études orientales* 60: 39–71.
Schmidtke, S. (2013). 'Ibn Ḥazm's Sources on Ashʿarism and Muʿtazilism'. In M. Fierro, C. Adang, and S. Schmidtke (eds.), *Ibn Ḥazm of Cordoba: The Life and Works of a Controversial Thinker*. Leiden: Brill, 373–401.
Shihadeh, A. (2012). 'Classical Ashʿarī Anthropology: Body, Life and Spirit'. *Muslim World* 102/3–4: 433–77.
al-Simnānī, Abū Jaʿfar Muḥammad b. Aḥmad b. Muḥammad (*Bayān*). *al-Bayān ʿan uṣūl al-īmān wa-l-kashf ʿan tamwīhāt ahl al-ṭughyān*. Ed. ʿA. ʿA. b. R. al-Ayyūb. Kuwait: Dār al-Ḍayāʾ, 2014.
al-Subkī, Tāj al-Dīn (*Ṭabqāt*). *Ṭabaqāt al-shāfiʿiyya al-kubrā*. 6 vols. Ed. M. M. al-Ṭanāḥī and ʿA. F. al-Ḥilw. Cairo: Maṭbaʿat ʿIsā al-Bābī al-Ḥalabī, 1964–76.

Thiele, J. (in press). 'Conceptions of Self-Determination in Fourth/Tenth-Century Muslim Theology: al-Bāqillānī's Theory of Human Acts in its Historical Context'. *Arabic Sciences and Philosophy* 26/2.

Turki, A. M. (1973). *Polémiques entre Ibn Ḥazm et Bāǧī sur les principes de la loi musulmane: essai sur le littéralisme ẓāhirite et la finalité malikite*. Algier: Études et documents.

Watt, W. M. (1978). 'Ibn Fūrak'. *Encyclopaedia of Islam*. 2nd edn. Leiden: Brill.

Zahrī, K. (2011). *al-Fiqh al-Mālikī wa-l-kalām al-Ashʿarī: muḥāwala li-ibrāz baʿḍ al-malāmiḥ al-ibdāʿ al-kalāmī wa-l-ṣūfī ʿind fuqahāʾ al-gharb*. Casablanca: al-Maktaba al-ʿAṣriyya.

Zahrī, K. (2013). '*Kitāb ʿal-Ibāna ʿan uṣūl al-diyāna*': taḥqīq fī nisbatihi ilā Abī l-Ḥasan al-Ashʿarī'. *al-Ibāna* 1: 116–31.

CHAPTER 14

EARLY IBĀḌĪ THEOLOGY

WILFERD MADELUNG

THE Ibāḍiyya arose as the moderate wing of the Khārijite schismatic movement that had emerged during the first *fitna*, the internal Muslim conflict beginning with the uprising against the caliph ʿUthmān in the year 35/656 and ending with the slaying of ʿAlī b. Abī Tālib by a Khārijite and the surrender of ʿAlī's son al-Ḥasan to the Umayyad Muʿāwiya in 41/661. The proto-Khārijites had participated in the violent overthrow of ʿUthmān and vigorously supported ʿAlī before his arbitration agreement with Muʿāwiya after the battle of Ṣiffīn which they viewed as a violation of the Qurʾānic commandment to fight rebels until their submission. After the surrender of al-Ḥasan to Muʿāwiya, the Khārijites continued to oppose the Umayyad caliphate. They held that any infringement of Qurʾānic law without repentance excluded caliphs and their supporters from the community of faithful Muslims. Concentrated in Baṣra, the early Khārijites mostly practised passive resistance and disobedience to the Umayyad authorities rather than armed revolt until the outbreak of the second *fitna* after the death of Muʿāwiya in 61/680. The Baṣran Khārijites at first offered their armed backing to the counter-caliph ʿAbd Allāh b. al-Zubayr in Mecca against the Umayyad regime, but soon withdrew when Ibn al-Zubayr refused to condemn the conduct of the slain caliph ʿUthmān. After their return to Baṣra, the unity of the Khārijite movement split as the militant radicals revolted and left the town in order to set up territorial states under caliphs of their choice and denounced all other Muslims, including moderate Khārijites who would not join them, as polytheists (*mushrikūn*) to be eradicated. The moderates who did not wish to join their emigration (*hijra*) distanced themselves from them and in turn declared them *mushrikūn*. The most moderate group became known as the Ibāḍiyya. They were named after Ibāḍ b. ʿAmr al-Tamīmī and his son ʿAbd Allāh b. Ibāḍ. Ibāḍ seems to have been the leader and spokesman of the moderates at the time of the split with the radical seceders. ʿAbd Allāh succeeded him as the military chief of a large section of the movement and died in ʿAbbāsid prison in *c*.142/759. Two apologetic letters by him are extant.

The Ibāḍiyya at the time of the split were looking to the prominent scholar Jābir b. Zayd al-Azdī (d. *c*.93/713) from Oman as their teacher in religion. Jābir b. Zayd personally was not a Khārijite, but readily engaged with them and taught them secretly.

His main teacher had been ʿAbd Allāh b. al-ʿAbbās, cousin of the Prophet and ʿAlī, whose religious learning was highly regarded even by the radical Khārijites since he had not participated in the battle of al-Nahrawān in which many of the early Khārijites were killed by ʿAlī's Kūfan army. He was recognized by the moderate Khārijites as their authoritative teacher in religion not only in Baṣra and Oman but also by Sālim b. Dhakwān, their leader in Sijistān, whose admonitory epistle (*sīra*) to his followers dating from *c.*82/701 is extant. Jābir advised the Ibāḍiyya to disobey the government in any action they viewed as being in violation of the religious law, but not to fight Muslims except in self-defence. The Ibāḍiyya came to consider other Muslims as merely hypocrites (*munāfiqūn*) and neglecters of the true faith (*kuffār*), not as *mushrikūn*. As such they allowed social intercourse, intermarriage, and mutual inheritance, but not religious association (*walāya, tawallī*) with them. They mostly abstained from armed revolt against the Umayyad government until the ʿAbbāsid revolution in 127/746.

By this time Abū ʿUbayda Muslim b. Abī Karīma was recognized by the great majority of the Ibāḍiyya as their spiritual leader. Abū ʿUbayda saw himself as the main disciple and successor of Jābir b. Zayd, although he probably was taught mostly by Jābir's pupils. He was in Baṣra a contemporary of the founders of the Muʿtazila, Wāṣil b. ʿAṭāʾ and ʿAmr b. ʿUbayd, and elaborated his Ibāḍī theological teaching in rivalry with their rationalist *kalām* teaching. He also sent Ibāḍī missionaries to many regions of the Muslim world to compete with the Muʿtazilī missionaries of Wāṣil in attracting and instructing converts. The major theological issue that was controversially debated in Baṣra at this time was the question of *qadar*, divine predestination versus human free will. Probably following Jābir b. Zayd, Abū ʿUbayda firmly upheld the thesis of predestination officially backed by the Umayyad government against the Muʿtazilī doctrine of free will. The Muʿtazila argued that God had sent His message, the Qurʾān, in order to offer guidance to all mankind, and in His universal justice (*ʿadl*) would determine everybody's status of faithful believer or infidel only after they made their free choice to accept or reject its guidance. Abū ʿUbayda affirmed that God's predetermination and foreknowledge of anybody's status preceded God's message from eternity and that no one was able to grasp and accept its guidance without His specific favour and aid.

There was, however, a significant minority of Ibāḍīs, among them ʿAbd Allāh b. Ibāḍ, who adopted the Qadarī doctrine of human free will. They were probably more influenced by the teaching of the famous preacher al-Ḥasan al-Baṣrī than by the Muʿtazila, but they were later commonly described as inclining to the Muʿtazila. When Ibn Ibāḍ died in ʿAbbāsid prison in *c.*142/759, his followers, who are described as Qadariyya, recognized al-Ḥārith b. Mazyad al-Ibāḍī as their Imam in succession to him. After al-Ḥārith al-Ibāḍī the sect seems to have disintegrated and joined the main body of the Ibāḍiyya. After the death of Abū ʿUbayda, most likely between 150/767 and 158/775, al-Rabīʿ b. Ḥabīb al-Farāhīdī succeeded to his position of leadership among the Ibāḍiyya in Baṣra. His authority was also widely accepted by Abū ʿUbayda's followers outside Baṣra but did not remain undisputed. Al-Rabīʿ b. Ḥabīb was primarily a traditionist and scholar of the religious law, renowned as the author of a *Musnad* of Ibāḍī *hadīth*. He displayed little interest in theology and did not participate in the discussions of questions of *kalām* which became popular and widespread during his age. In legal matters his teaching was challenged by three dissident Ibāḍī scholars, ʿAbd Allāh b. ʿAbd al-ʿAzīz, Abū l-Muʾarrij al-Sadūsī, and Shuʿayb b. Maʿrūf. In theology the Kūfan Ibāḍī scholar Abū Muḥammad ʿAbd Allāh b. Yazīd al-Fazārī began to attract students from afar and soon was widely recognized as the main spokesman of the Ibāḍiyya in *kalām* theology. He became a prominent participant in the *kalām* debates sponsored by the Barmakid courtier Yaḥyā b. Khālid in Baghdad during the caliphate of Hārūn al-Rashīd. Dissent turned into schism after the death of the Ibāḍī Imam in the Maghrib, ʿAbd al-Raḥmān b. Rustam, in 168/785, when the Nukkār, led by Yazīd b. Fandīn, opposed the succession of Ibn Rustam's son ʿAbd al-Wahhāb b. ʿAbd al-Raḥmān, who had the backing of al-Rabīʿ b. Ḥabīb. The Nukkār followed in law the teaching of the three dissident scholars, and in theology the doctrine of ʿAbd Allāh b. Yazīd al-Fazārī. They became a strong minority sect among the Ibāḍiyya in the Maghrib and have survived to the present. The majority who followed the teaching of al-Rabīʿ b. Ḥabīb and backed the Rustamid imamate became known as the Wahbiyya. In Baṣra and the east the followers of the dissident scholars rather came to be known as the Shuʿaybiyya after Shuʿayb b. Maʿrūf. They remained a significant minority in Baṣra, Oman, and Ḥaḍramawt in the first half of the third/ninth century and disintegrated soon thereafter. ʿAbd Allāh b. Yazīd after 179/795 fled from Baghdad and sought refuge among the Khārijite community in the Yemen, where he became known with the *nisba* al-Baghdādī and taught and composed books. Through his influence the Ibāḍiyya in the Yemen, in contrast to the other regions of South Arabia, became solidly Shuʿaybiyya. The community survived there until the sixth/twelfth century.

ʿAbd Allāh b. Yazīd al-Fazārī is the earliest *kalām* theologian whose teaching can be comprehensively examined on the basis of his own extant works. Six theological texts or fragments of texts have recently been discovered in two twelfth/eighteenth-century Maghribī manuscripts. Three of them are treatises composed by him in Iraq and sent to his Ibāḍī followers in the Maghrib, and the other three contain his answers to queries put to him by Maghribī questioners. A polemical refutation of the Qadariyya he wrote in the Yemen is also extant, contained in its rebuttal by the Zaydī Imam Aḥmad al-Nāṣir li-Dīn Allāh (d. 322/934). The broad range of questions discussed by him and the sophistication of his concepts and terminology indicate that *kalām* theology had developed by the middle of the second/eighth century to a much more advanced level than has often been assumed on the basis of the heresiographical sources.

Al-Fazārī's primary opponents in theology were the rationalist Muʿtazila and the radical Shīʿa (Rāfiḍa), whom he also describes as rationalists in association with the Muʿtazila. His theology is fundamentally revelationist, scripturalist, and traditionalist. He states categorically that nothing in religion can be known except by revelation and denounces rationalists as *mufakkirūn*, thinkers, who hold that the fundamental truths of religion can and must be known by reason. This applies to both theology and the religious law. Like Abū ʿUbayda, he affirms that guidance, aid, and success are given by God to the faithful and withheld from the infidels. The truthfulness of the Qurʾān thus did not need to be confirmed by miracles as the Muʿtazila claimed, and continuous broad transmission (*tawātur*) of *Ḥadīth* does not establish Sunna. The true Sunna rather is what has been transmitted by faithful Muslims mostly by single *isnād*. While al-Fazārī in general fully upheld the teaching and religious practice of Abū ʿUbayda, he expressly deviated in his definition of true Islam and the practice of religious association and dissociation. The early Ibāḍiyya had considered it obligatory to declare association with every Muslim acting in strict obedience to all Qurʾānic commandments and dissociation from all those who disobeyed them and who 'do not rule in accordance with what God has sent down' (Qurʾān 5: 44). Those from whom Muslims must dissociate thus included individual unrepentant offenders as well as caliphs who had violated Qurʾānic law and their supporters. They must declare association with all those of whom no breach of Qurʾānic law is known and who profess faith in the truth of the Qurʾān and the whole message and all rulings the Prophet has brought from God. Originally, al-Fazārī explains, the mere profession of this faith was considered sufficient for recognition as a true Muslim. Later, however, an additional affirmation was required that everyone who considers licit what God has forbidden is an unbeliever. This was necessary because ever since the first *fitna*, offences were innovated and committed by those who had initially professed faith in Islam.

Al-Fazārī refined and sharpened these rules. Muslims, he argued, are legally obliged neither to dissociate from any Muslim nor to associate with any unbeliever. After the uprising against ʿUthmān, however, the territory of Islam has become an abode in which profession of monotheism and hypocrisy are mixed (*dār tawḥīd wa-nifāq*). The status of faith of its inhabitants can no longer easily be recognized, especially since under the rule of illegitimate tyrants, precautionary dissimulation (*taqiyya*) is permitted by the Qurʾān (3: 28). The Muslims are therefore obliged to abstain from judgement (*wuqūf*) in respect to anyone about whose status of faith they cannot be certain. At the same time al-Fazārī extended the concept of heretical innovation which required dissociation by the true Muslims to include false belief as well as reprehensible acts. So far only acts had been considered sufficient cause for exclusion from the community of the truly faithful. Abū 'Ubayda had sharply censured the Qadarīs among the Ibāḍiyya, but had not been able to excommunicate them. Al-Fazārī evidently wished to excommunicate ideological dissidents, in particular the Qadariyya and radical Khārijites. He affirms that the true Muslim must uphold the divine ordainment (*qadar*) of all events and deny independent human capacity (*istiṭāʿa*), and he must acknowledge that anyone holding false beliefs based on either revelation (*tanzīl*) or interpretation (*taʾwīl*) is in error. The radical Khārijites, who view other Muslims as polytheists, are most severely condemned by al-Fazārī and themselves classified as *mushrikūn*, not only as *kuffār*. In spite of his emphatic scripturalism, al-Fazārī espouses an abstract, immaterial, and anti-anthropomorphist concept of God close to the rationalist concept of the Muʿtazila. In a fragmentarily preserved tract he refutes both corporalists (*mujassima*) and anthropomorphists (*mushabbiha*). By corporalists he means primarily Imāmī Shīʿī theologians such as his contemporary Hishām b. al-Ḥakam who argue on rational grounds that God, to be something at all, must have size and location. Some of them describe Him in size like a mustard seed (*khardala*). They hold that any action of God, including His knowledge and His will act, requires

His motion (*ḥaraka*). By *mushabbiha* al-Fazārī distinctly means the Sunnī traditionalists who cling to the literal meaning of the anthropomorphic expressions with which God is described in the Qurʾān and *Ḥadīth*. The opponents falsely accuse us, al-Fazārī notes, that we fail to describe God and do not think about Him, but we describe God as He described Himself in His Book. The Qurʾānic description of God he quotes consists of *Sūrat al-Ikhlāṣ* (112), 'there is nothing like unto Him' (42: 11), 'Vision cannot grasp Him but He grasps all vision' (6: 103), and similar passages stressing His incomparable uniqueness. Al-Fazārī, however, also quotes traditions of Companions which support his immaterial concept of God and elaborates a rational proof based on 'irrefutable analogy (*qiyās*) that cannot be rejected by anyone' establishing that everything in the world is produced in time (*muḥdath*) and must have a single eternal producer who is entirely unlike all temporal things. Al-Fazārī affirms that God is single and incorporeal, He has neither partners nor parts. From eternity He has no location in space, yet His presence is everywhere. Motion and rest cannot be predicated of Him. He cannot be perceived by senses and is invisible; there can be no beatific vision by the faithful in the Hereafter as asserted by the Sunnī traditionalists. Al-Fazārī discusses God's attributes and names at length. He explains the distinction between divine attributes of essence (*ṣifāt dhāt*) and attributes of act (*ṣifāt fiʿl*) similar to Muʿtazilī *tawḥīd* doctrine. The conceptual intricacy of his discussion strongly suggests that the Muʿtazilī theory of divine attributes including the distinction between attributes of essence and act goes back to the time of the founder of the Muʿtazila Wāṣil b. ʿAṭāʾ. Like the Muʿtazila, al-Fazārī defines divine attributes of essence as eternally applying to God. God is knowing from eternity whatever will be before it is. His being knowing does not affirm anything besides Himself. Divine attributes of act affirm something besides Himself. His being a creator affirms the existence of something created. Attributes of act cannot be eternal as this would imply the eternity of creation. Attributes of act, moreover, may apply and not apply at the same time. God may create something at a time while not creating another, or forgive someone while not forgiving another. Attributes of essence apply always and exclude their opposite. God is forever omniscient and cannot be ignorant of anything at any time. Man can implore God to activate His attributes of act and pray: 'Have mercy on me,' or: 'Provide sustenance for me.' He cannot ask for anything in relation to God's attributes of essence, praying: 'Know', or: 'be powerful'. Attributes of essence, in contrast to attributes of act, are not subject to the divine attribute of omnipotence. It is not proper to state: 'He has power to know', or: 'He has power to see.' All attributes of act are subject to God's omnipotence. It is proper to say: 'He has power to create', and: 'He has power to give sustenance.' Al-Fazārī notes that there are also combined attributes (*ṣifāt mushtaraka*) applying to both God's essence and acts in different respects. The attribute wise (*ḥakīm*) in respect to His essence implies that He knows affairs. In respect to His acts it implies their perfection and accuracy. Some of God's attributes of essence may also be predicated of humans and other creatures. In all creatures, however, such attributes entail an entitative existent (*maʿnā*), while in God they entail only the negation of the opposite. The attribute of being alive thus implies the existence of an entity of life in man, while in God it implies the negation of death. Al-Fazārī presents long lists of divine attributes of essence and of act, but mostly discusses only the attributes also discussed by the Muʿtazila as the prime attributes of essence, God's being knowing, powerful, living, seeing, hearing, and eternal. He reduces the meaning of God's attributes of hearing and seeing to that of knowing, explaining that this is necessary since otherwise a part of God would be seeing, another hearing, and yet another knowing. Against Muʿtazilī doctrine, he counts God's being willing (*murīd*) as an attribute of essence: God has from eternity been willing to create whatever He knew will exist before it exists. This formulation reflects al-Fazārī's position affirming divine determinism and predetermination and anticipates the doctrine on the attribute of will embraced by the Sunnī al-Ashʿarī. Like the Muʿtazila and unlike al-Ashʿarī, al-Fazārī treats the divine attribute of speaking (*mutakallim*) as an attribute of act.

The Qurʾān, al-Fazārī maintains, is the speech (*kalām*) of God. It does not consist of sound or letters written with ink, though it may be conveyed by them. It is what is heard and understood by humans. What is heard now is the same as what the Prophet recited. It is in pure Arabic language. God speaks with it, but not with a tongue and lips, nor does He move in speaking. He creates His speech and locates it wherever He wants. He causes His speech to be heard by anyone He wants in any language He wants on the tongue of His angels and His messengers. His speech is originated in time (*muḥdath*) and created (*makhlūq*) by God after it did not exist. Whoever denies that the Qurʾān is not created and means that it is not originated in time is a polytheist. If he affirms that it is originated in time, but does not want to say that it is created, he is an unbeliever and hypocrite (*kāfir munāfiq*), like someone who says that the acts of humans are not created by God.

Defence of the early Islamic dogma of *qadar*, divine ordainment and predestination of everything in the world, against Muʿtazilī criticism was a primary concern of al-Fazārī. A *Kitāb al-Qadar* detailing his position in the controversy was sent by him early to the Maghrib and is fully extant. It was evidently meant to guide the Maghribī Ibāḍiyya in their debates with the Wāṣiliyya on the subject. In a chapter added later to the text, al-Fazārī specifically answers questions of the Maghribīs on how to counter arguments of their Muʿtazilī opponents. He reacts apologetically to the Muʿtazilī contention that it would be incompatible with the justice (*ʿadl*) of God for Him to reward and punish humans for acts ordained and created by Himself. Al-Fazārī claims the self-designation as *ʿAdliyya* used by the Muʿtazila for his own school of thought. He maintains that God is entirely free to prefer some of His creatures over others in their shape, span of life, sustenance, and all other conditions, and that no one has a valid argument against God that He has not made all of them alike. God thus may favour some humans by granting them faith (*īmān*) while withholding it from others. In an evident concession to the Muʿtazilī thesis, he stresses that God does not punish anyone for anything He in fact created in him, such as short stature and ugliness. He does not punish the unbeliever for his lack of faith that he has not been granted, but only for the evil acts of unbelief the unbeliever commits by his own choice and volition.

While holding on to the traditional formula that God ordains and creates everything in the world, both good and evil, al-Fazārī qualifies its meaning significantly so as to absolve God from actually producing evil. He insists that the creation of faith and of unbelief are other than actual faith and unbelief, just as the creation of the heavens and earth are other than the heavens and earth. Moreover, God's creation of human acts like faith and unbelief differs from His creation of the heavens which are directly made (*ṣunʿ*) by Him. God creates faith and unbelief merely in the sense of determining (*taqdīr*), designing them, and naming (*tasmiya*) them good and evil. Al-Fazārī expressly distances himself from the more radical determinists who fail to distinguish between the direct creation of the sun, the moon, and mankind, and creation by designing and naming like God's creation of human acts. He thus distinctly sought to vindicate the justice of God by restricting His absolute arbitrariness later upheld by Ashʿarī Sunnī doctrine.

In other respects al-Fazārī espouses traditional determinist views. God guides to faith whomever he favours by His aid, incentive (*luṭf*), and granting of success (*tawfīq*). The imposition (*taklīf*) of religious duties on mankind by God and their capacity to perform them occur at the same moment upon their reaching maturity. God does not impose what is rationally impossible (*muḥāl*), but He may give people orders they are unable to carry out. Capacity to act (*istiṭāʿa*) does not precede the act as claimed by the Muʿtazila. God alone provides all sustenance, even if it is stolen, and determines the life span of all humans, even if they are wrongfully killed.

In agreement with earlier Ibāḍī theory, al-Fazārī holds that mankind in legal status is divided into only three categories, *muʾminūn*, *kuffār*, and *mushrikūn*, and sharply denounces the Muʿtazilī doctrine of an intermediate position of *fussāq*, reprobates, between the faithful and unbelievers as an innovation. The first category are the true Muslims; al-Fazārī only exceptionally uses the name Ibāḍiyya. The category of the *kuffār* includes hypocrites who conceal their unbelief as well as unrepentant grave offenders against the law. The category of the *mushrikūn* includes those who associate others with God, those who worship another than God, and those who deny God altogether. It also includes anyone who expressly repudiates any part of the Qurʾān or anything conveyed by the Prophet from God. Al-Fazārī concedes that the latter may conceptionally be considered monotheists, but legally they must be counted as polytheists since they openly defy God and His Prophet and wage war against them.

Al-Fazārī affirms that the office of Imam as the supreme chief of the Muslim community is required by the religious law since there are obligatory functions under it only the Imam is entitled and obliged to perform, such as the Qurʾānic *Ḥadd* punishments. The Imam must protect the weak from the powerful. All Muslims are obliged to recognize and obey the legitimate Imam in whatever he orders. The Imam, however, loses his legitimacy if he violates the law or fails to carry out his particular duties under it. Al-Fazārī praises the caliphs Abū Bakr and ʿUmar as exemplary Imams of the Muslims, but does not name any legitimate Imam after them.

In his teaching effort among the Ibāḍiyya in the Maghrib al-Fazārī was in active competition with a contemporary Kufan scholar, Abū ʿUmar ʿĪsā b. ʿUmayr al-Hamdānī. Ibn ʿUmayr was an expert in Qurʾān reading who transmitted the text of the Holy Book according to the codex of the early Companion ʿAbd Allāh b. Masʿūd. In theology he was also commonly regarded as belonging to the school of religious thought of Ibn Masʿūd which in the second/eighth century was still influential in Kufa. Among the Maghribī

Ibāḍiyya he professed to be adhering to the teaching of Jābir b. Zayd and Abū ʿUbayda. Like al-Fazārī, he does not seem to have ever visited the Maghrib, but he addressed letters to his followers there in which he set forth his theological views and criticized some of al-Fazārī's teaching. Al-Fazārī countered these letters with letters of his own, one of which has largely been preserved. In it al-Fazārī accuses him of heretical innovation espousing rationalist doctrine of the Muʿtazila and the Rāfiḍa. He urges his followers to sever their relations with the heretic.

Ibn ʿUmayr's teaching reflects an awareness of Christian theological concerns that must have appealed to converts with a Donatist Christian background in the Maghrib. Against al-Fazārī's view, he maintained that the fundamental truths of religion can and must be recognized by sole reason and that debates of Muslims with non-Muslims should be based on rational argument rather than the Qurʾān. The universal justice of God requires that He send further guidance to all mankind. It is man's choice to accept or reject God's guidance. Ibn ʿUmayr repudiates al-Fazārī's claim that God favours some of His creatures by His aid while withholding it from others. Divine justice also requires that God confirm the veracity of all his prophets by miraculous signs like those of Moses and Jesus or by the testimony of a recognized prophet. While upholding predestination, Ibn ʿUmayr describes it in concepts familiar in Christian theological thought, avoiding al-Fazārī's Islamic formulation that God creates all events and human acts, good and evil. He affirms that God initially created all material things and determined (*qaddara*) their natural traits and circumstances. Everything then develops, acts, and perishes in accordance with its innate nature, rather than continuous creation and recreation by God as commonly envisaged in Islamic theological thought.

Ibn ʿUmayr held that human reason is essentially capable of recognizing good and evil as well as most human obligations under the religious law. He admitted, however, that God imposes some specific obligations that can be known only by revelation and instruction by prophets. His views here accorded well with Christian theories about a natural law recognizable by human reason that had largely replaced the validity of the Mosaic law of Judaism.

Unlike al-Fazārī, Ibn ʿUmayr upheld that the People of the Book, Christians and Jews, must be acknowledged to be monotheists (*muwaḥḥidūn*) so long as they sincerely profess that God is one. Only someone who dishonestly affirms that God is one while meaning an idol or Jesus is to be treated as a polytheist. Ibn ʿUmayr denounces al-Fazārī for classifying monotheists as polytheists if they repudiate any part of the Qurʾān or of the message conveyed from God by Muḥammad. Matching Donatist anti-government sentiment, Ibn ʿUmayr maintained that the Muslims, so long as they are strong in their faith and fully obedient to God, do not need an Imam. He observed that he never had found a Muslim ruling Muslims according to religion (*dīn*); rather they all ruled on the basis of their personal judgement and discretion (*raʾy*). He evidently did not even exclude the caliphs Abū Bakr and ʿUmar from this charge.

The followers of ʿĪsā b. ʿUmayr were called the ʿUmayriyya. In the late second/eighth century they prevailed among the Ibāḍiyya in the regions east of Jabal Nafūsa in Libya. In the first half of the third/ninth century their spiritual leader was Abū Ziyād al-Ḥusayn

b. Aḥmad al-Aṭrābulusī, a local scholar from Tripoli, who adhered to the teaching of Ibn ʿUmayr in theology and to the teaching of Ibrāhīm b. ʿUlayya (d. 218/833) in jurisprudence. Ibn ʿUlayya was a pupil of the Muʿtazilī Abū Bakr al-Aṣamm, who is known to have been close to the Basran Ibāḍiyya and, like Ibn ʿUmayr, affirmed that there is no need in Islam for a supreme Imam if the faithful live fully in compliance with the religious law. In his legal methodology Ibn ʿUlayya was renowned for his extensive use of analogy (*qiyās*) on the sole basis of the Qurʾān, while disregarding the Sunna of the Prophet and the Companions. The sect is known to have survived until the sixth/twelfth century.

The main body of the Ibāḍiyya, the Wahbiyya in the Maghrib and the followers of al-Rabīʿ b. Ḥabīb in the east, maintained their conservative traditionalist attitude in theology and opposition to speculative *kalām*. In Oman *kalām* terminology and concepts were first used by Abū l-Mundhir Bashīr b. Muḥammad b. Maḥbūb b. al-Ruḥayl in his writings in the second half of the third/ninth century. Bashīr evidently was familiar with the theological thought of the Basran Muʿtazilī Abū ʿAlī al-Jubbāʾī, but in substance his views were Ibāḍī. Ibāḍī traditionalist thought did not follow the development of Sunnī traditionalism in espousing a concrete anthropomorphic concept of God and upheld God's immaterial abstract transcendence. Ibāḍī theology thus has always rejected the Sunnī dogma of the beatific vision of God by the faithful in the hereafter. It also generally denied the Sunnī tenet of the uncreated nature of the Qurʾān. Some scholars in Oman, however, upheld the Sunnī doctrine. An Ibāḍī creed officially adopted in Oman in the third/ninth century avoided the issue by merely affirming that the Qurʾān is the speech of God.

Bibliography

Cook, M. (1981). *Early Muslim Dogma: A Source-Critical Study*. Cambridge: Cambridge University Press.

Crone, P., and F. Zimmermann (2001). *The Epistle of Sālim Ibn Dhakwān*. Oxford: Oxford University Press.

Cuperly, P. (1984). *Introduction à l'étude de l'Ibāḍisme et de sa théologie*. Algier: Office des Publications Universitaires.

van Ess, J. (1991–7). *Theologie und Gesellschaft im 2. und 3. Jahrhundert Hidschra: Eine Geschichte des religiösen Denkens im frühen Islam*. 6 vols. Berlin: de Gruyter.

Gaiser, A. R. (2010). *Muslims, Scholars, Soldiers: The Origin and Elaboration of the Ibāḍī Imāmate Traditions*. Oxford: Oxford University Press.

Lewicki, T. (1958). 'Les Subdivisions de l'Ibāḍiyya'. *Studia Islamica* 9: 71–82.

Madelung, W. (2006). "Abd Allāh Ibn Ibāḍ and the Origins of the Ibāḍiyya'. In B. Michalak-Pikulska and A. Pikulski (eds.), *Authority, Privacy and Public Order in Islam: Proceedings of the 22nd Congress of L'Union Européenne des Arabisants et Islamisants*. Leuven: Peeters, 51–7.

Madelung, W. (2011). "Abd Allāh ibn Ibāḍ's Second Letter to ʿAbd al-Malik'. In *Community, State, History and Changes: Festschrift for Ridwan Al-Sayyid on His Sixtieth Birthday*. Beirut: al-Shabaka al-ʿarabiyya li-l-abḥāth wa-l-nashr, 7–17.

Madelung, W. (2012a). "Īsā Ibn ʿUmayr's Ibāḍī Theology and Donatist Christian Thought'. In R. Hansberger, M. Afifi al-Akiti, and C. Burnett (eds.), *Medieval Arabic Thought: Essays in Honour of Fritz Zimmermann*. London: The Warburg Institute, 99–104.
Madelung, W. (2012b). 'The Authenticity of the Letter of ʿAbd Allāh b. Ibāḍ to ʿAbd al-Malik'. *Revue du monde musulman et de la Méditerranée* 132, 37–43.
Madelung, W. (forthcoming). "Abd Allāh b. Yazīd al-Fazārī's Rebuttal of the Teaching of Ibn ʿUmayr'. In L. Muehlethaler, S. Schmidtke, and G. Schwarb (eds.), *Theological Rationalism in Medieval Islam: New Texts and Perspectives*. Leuven: Peeters.
van Ess, J. (1991–7). *Theologie und Gesellschaft im 2. und 3. Jahrhundert Hidschra: Eine Geschichte des religiösen Denkens im frühen Islam*. 6 vols. Berlin: de Gruyter.
Wilkinson, J. C. (2010). *Ibâḍism: Origins and Early Development in Oman*. Oxford: Oxford University Press.

CHAPTER 15

KARRĀMIYYA

ARON ZYSOW

From the third/ninth to the seventh/thirteenth century the Karrāmiyya were a major force in the competitive world of Islamic theology. They constituted not only a theological sect with distinctive teachings across a wide range of issues but also a school of Islamic law. Just as significantly they formed a community distinguished by its impressive dedication to an ascetic lifestyle. The Karrāmiyya owe their name to Abū ʿAbd Allāh Muḥammad ibn Karrām (d. 255/869), who originated in the far Eastern region of Sijistan but gained his most significant following elsewhere, notably in Gharjistan and Khurasan. Ibn Karrām's career was punctuated by a series of expulsions and several extended periods of imprisonment. These adverse events undoubtedly reflect the agitation unwelcome to the authorities that his itinerant preaching occasioned, particularly among the rural population. After a final expulsion from Nishapur, he spent the last years of his life in Jerusalem, where his tomb remained a focal point for Karrāmī visitors from the East for centuries. Despite their conversionary ambitions the Karrāmiyya never gained a significant following outside present-day Iran and Afghanistan. For most of their history their intellectual centre was Nishapur, and it was in Nishapur under the early Ghaznavids (late fourth/tenth century) that the Karrāmiyya gained their greatest social acceptance and political influence. Upon the decline of their standing in Nishapur, the Karrāmiyya survived as a strong movement only in the mountainous region of Ghur and in the vicinity of Ghazna until the Mongol invasion, after which they vanished from the scene (Zysow 2011).

Such biographical information as we have makes it clear that Ibn Karrām came from a milieu that was both fiercely attached to Ḥanafism and actively engaged in the transmission of *ḥadīth*. The combination of adherence to *ḥadīth* and commitment to rational argument that characterizes Karrāmī law is also evident in Karrāmī theology. Here too we find a bold appeal to reason in the critical service of theological data drawn from the Qur'ān and *ḥadīth*. From Ibn Karrām subsequent Karrāmī leaders inherited the practice of popular preaching and instruction through apophthegms and myth-like tales alongside their activity as theologians (Zadeh 2012: 510–18).

Any study of the theology of the Karrāmiyya faces an immediate and inescapable obstacle. So far not a single complete theological treatise of Karrāmī origin has come to light. The surviving Karrāmī works now available are virtually all devoted to Qur'ānic studies not theology, although in almost every case valuable theological information can be gleaned by a careful reading. Our understanding of the theology of the Karrāmiyya must therefore be based largely on accounts provided by their opponents, who are frequently scornful of a theological tradition that they regarded as the creation of semi-literate bumpkins professing a farrago of outlandish opinions. Obviously information from these sources must be controlled by recourse to what is known from such Karrāmī writings as are available, but there is no reason to assume that the bias of these hostile writers led them to a complete misrepresentation of what they reported.

It is most unlikely that more than a small portion of Karrāmī theological activity will ever be retrievable. Ibn Karrām was already the author of theological writings, and engagement with theology remained highly esteemed among his followers. By the sixth/twelfth century we are informed of some dozen or so Karrāmī subsects (van Ess 1980: 19–30). Even if the named subsects do not in all cases represent truly distinct theological traditions, it is safe to assume that they reflect extensive writing on theological subjects. Theological differences among the Karrāmiyya, and there were many, seem never to have threatened the unity of the community, as even their opponents acknowledged. But such an absence of bitter internal debate is not necessarily advantageous to intellectual historians. Scholarship, it seems, will have to content itself with uncovering the general development of the theology of the Karrāmiyya, with somewhat greater detail available for the revisions introduced by the last major Karrāmī theologian, Muḥammad b. al-Hayṣam (d. 409/1019), whose talents were such as to win grudging respect even from his opponents.

The immediate background for the development of Karrāmī theology is the challenge to traditional Muslim beliefs posed by the Jahmiyya, named after the theologian Jahm b. Ṣafwān, executed in 128/746 for revolutionary activity against the Umayyad regime. While the theological roots of Jahm's teachings are far from entirely clear, it has been plausibly suggested that they bear distinct traces of the influence of Neoplatonic philosophy (Frank 1965), although this has not gone unchallenged (Crone 2012).

Several objectionable features of Jahmī doctrine loom particularly large in the early anti-Jahmī literature. The God of the Jahmiyya is both excessively transcendent and excessively immanent. For the Jahmiyya the divinity is absolutely simple without real attributes and even beyond being itself. At the same time the Jahmiyya profess that God is to be found everywhere, in all things. These panentheistic teachings recall the paradoxical formulation of the Neoplatonic philosopher and student of Plotinus Porphyry (d. *c.*305): 'the divinity is nowhere and everywhere'. Along with these heretical opinions on the nature of God, the Jahmiyya placed undue reliance on reason. They rejected a number of well-known traditional teachings as opposed to reason, and they construed religious faith (*īmān*), what makes someone a Muslim, along entirely intellectualist lines as identical with knowledge (*ma'rifa*), without need for works or any public profession of belief.

The anti-Jahmī authors held that God was not the absolutely simple divinity without distinct attributes posited by the Jahmiyya. God in fact has real attributes as taught in both the Qur'ān and *Sunna*. Against the Jahmī teaching that God was everywhere, in all things, their opponents countered that far from being found everywhere, God was in fact situated above his throne (*ʿarsh*), as both the Qur'ān and *Sunna* report. The Jahmiyya, they further urged, were making abusive recourse to reason. A doctrine such as the punishment of the dead in their graves was solidly based on texts that there were no good arguments for rejecting.

Early opposition to the Jahmiyya was led above all by traditionists (*ahl al-ḥadīth*) who saw in the threat posed by the Jahmiyya a clear warning of the dangers that lurked in theological speculation. Their response to the heretical Jahmī teachings largely consisted in marshalling textual evidence from the Qur'ān and *ḥadīth* with limited recourse to inferences from these texts. These anti-Jahmī traditionists did not regard themselves as theologians and were not concerned to propound theological systems to displace those of the heretics. The Karrāmiyya exemplify a strikingly different branch of the anti-Jahmī opposition, one that unapologetically embraced full-blown theological argument to expose the errors of the Jahmiyya and the other misguided theological movements that subsequently appeared and that to one degree or another perpetuated Jahmī elements. The Karrāmiyya were not entirely alone in offering so bold a response, but no other such intellectually aggressive version of anti-Jahmism gained so wide a following or produced so extensive a theological literature.

Undoubtedly the Karrāmī teaching that is most frequently mentioned in the Islamic sources, if not always accurately presented, is their identification of faith with 'the profession of the tongue' (*al-iqrār bi-l-lisān*) alone. This minimalist teaching was already defended by Ibn Karrām, and it early gained notoriety. The marked frequency with which exegetical questions concerning references to faith in the Qur'ān appear in the commentary of Sūrābādī (d. 494/1101), a relatively late work, suggests that their doctrine of faith long remained at the very forefront of Karrāmī self-definition.

The label Murji'ism, widely used in theological literature, is perhaps not very helpful for academic analysis, but for present purposes it can be defined as the view that faith does not have a component of works (*ʿamal*). The anti-Murji'ite position, that works are integral to faith, was notably championed by the traditionists. The Karrāmī doctrine on faith represented not only a rejection of the teaching of the traditionists, and was so presented by Ibn Karrām, but it marked in a certain sense the outer limit of Murji'ism, in that it not only dispensed with works but also with any inner conviction, leaving only the profession of the tongue. The novelty of the Karrāmī doctrine lay not in its rejection of works as a constituent of faith, but rather in its complete rejection of any cognitive element. The early traditionist critic of the Karrāmiyya, Muḥammad b. Aslam al-Ṭūsī (d. 242/856), regarded Ibn Karrām's teaching that 'knowledge is not part of faith' as one of the three most vile doctrines ever espoused, on a par with that of the createdness of the Qur'ān (al-Jūraqānī, *Abāṭīl*, 1/455). The definitive theological break between the traditionists and the Karrāmiyya that persisted in the face of continued active Karrāmī participation in the transmission of *ḥadīth* is to be located precisely in this matter of faith, rather than in more arcane metaphysical questions which interested the traditionists far less.

For the Karrāmiyya faith, as completely verbal, is a matter of public affiliation. There is no need for the faith of a professed Muslim to be subjected to inquiry by others nor is there room for the Muslim to be unsure about his own faith. But what is critical to the Karrāmī position, although sometimes misunderstood by others, is that the faith that is constituted by the profession of the tongue is not sufficient for salvation. Salvation requires inner conviction, for only this renders the declaration of faith sincere. What external faith does is provide secure membership in the Muslim community with its attendant obligations, rights, and privileges.

The essential elements of the Karrāmī doctrine of faith, including some details not currently available elsewhere, can already be found in the early Karrāmī heresiography of Abū Muṭīʿ Makḥūl al-Nasafī (d. 318/930). With the passing of the Prophet, according to al-Nasafī, there is no longer any place for attending to the sincerity of professed believers as there might be while he was alive. Sincerity and hypocrisy are hidden (*bāṭin*) matters to which there is no longer the sort of access available to a prophet in communication with God, and even the Prophet was prohibited from undertaking on his own initiative an inquiry into what people believed in their hearts. Speech on the other hand is a public (*ẓāhir*) matter. The people of the *qibla* are to be regarded as believers in accordance with what God directed in the Qurʾān and the Prophet in *ḥadīth* (al-Nasafī, *Radd*, 69f.)

The Karrāmī identification of faith with a verbal profession underwent an interesting development in the period after Ibn Karrām. The roots of this development can already be found in the text of al-Nasafī, who explains that minors are to be regarded as believers on the basis of the primordial acknowledgement of God's lordship on the part of all humans as reported in Qurʾān 7: 172. This primeval covenant (*mīthāq*) constituted a declaration of faith, and hence faith is the natural condition of all humans upon birth (*fiṭra*) (al-Nasafī, *Radd*, 71). Subsequently this first confession (*al-iqrār al-awwal*) was understood as constituting faith in the literal sense as opposed to any further declarations (Ibn Fūrak, *Sharḥ*, 186). These merely confirmed one's original confession. The extent to which the Karrāmiyya were able to elaborate these notions in a fashion that was internally coherent and consistent with Islamic law is not clear.

In works of classical Islamic theology the Karrāmiyya are frequently, although inaccurately, stated to be unique among the Muslim theological sects in putting God within space and time. But while the Karrāmiyya were far from alone in their basic positions on the nature and actions of God, they did develop these positions in distinctive ways, and most importantly they did so while attempting to salvage, at least to their own satisfaction, critical elements of classical theism, including the immutability of God.

For the Karrāmiyya as for others both before and after them God to be real must have features that we may term corporeal. In ancient philosophy this was the well-known view of the Stoics, and under Stoic influence the doctrine of God's corporeality was held by influential early Christian theologians, notably Tertullian (d. *c.*230) (Jantzen 1984: 21–35). The Karrāmiyya are the best-known theological sect in Islam to have defended God's corporeality, and a Stoic influence, however remote, is very likely to lie behind their teachings. The Karrāmī writers conveyed God's corporeality through a variety of terms that were in turn variously defined and understood. The most important and the best known of these terms is *jism* (body). But we also find Ibn Karrām using the term *jawhar* (substance), while other early Karrāmīs such as al-Nasafī preferred the more acceptable Qurʾānic term *shayʾ* (thing). God is thus a body, a substance, a thing.

In asserting God's corporeality the Karrāmiyya took themselves to be upholding His existence, and as in the case of other opponents of the Jahmiyya, this assertion is directly tied to the doctrine of God's throne (*ʿarsh*). Because the panentheistic Jahmiyya held God to be everywhere, they were compelled to treat the statements in the Qurʾān and *ḥadīth* that put God on a throne as non-literal. The Jahmī approach to God's throne was inherited by the dominant theological groups that subsequently came upon the scene: the Muʿtazilīs, Ashʿarites, and Māturīdīs. All had to find ways to avert any spatialization of God that God's special relation to his throne appeared to support. The controversial topic of God's throne came to be the subject of an entire body of literature, some of which survives. But no other group appears to have pursued the theological ramifications of the throne with the tenacity of the Karrāmiyya as they grappled with the objections posed by their opponents.

Ibn Karrām put God into direct contact with his throne. God's body, he held, touched the upper surface of the throne (*mumāss liʾl-ṣafḥa al-ʿulyā min al-ʿarsh*). This physical interpretation of the Qurʾānic language *istawā ʿalā l-ʿarsh* was supported by appeal to the explanation attributed to the famous exegete Ibn al-ʿAbbās (d. 68/687–8) that the verb *istawā* here meant the same as *istaqarra*: God, 'settled' on his throne (al-Shahrastānī, *Milal*, 1/181; al-Nasafī, *Radd*, 107). One might assume that Ibn Karrām was providing a naïvely literal reading of the Qurʾānic text, but this is hardly likely given the clear evidence of an already elaborate theological vocabulary in his writings. Behind his teaching on God's contact with the throne there lay a cosmology, scattered references to which still survive in Islamic theological literature. Precisely how much of this cosmology was already explicitly presented by Ibn Karrām himself is not known, but it quite obviously formed the starting point for later developments among his followers.

Not surprisingly the cosmology of the early Karrāmiyya bears a striking similarity to that of the Stoics. Like the Stoics, the Karrāmiyya understood the cosmos to be a *plenum*. There was no empty space, no void within the created cosmos of the Karrāmiyya but only bodies in direct contact with other bodies (al-Juwaynī, *Shāmil*, 508). Unlike the Stoics, however, the Karrāmiyya had no occasion to posit a limitless void surrounding the cosmos. In place of a limitless extracosmic void they put a limitless God. The God of the Karrāmī theists is not, of course, the God of the pantheistic Stoics who, in penetrating the entire cosmos, is in the closest possible relation with it, but for the early Karrāmiyya God is in the most intimate relation to His creation that His nature as a body allows and indeed requires: He is in physical contact with it.

The logic of this early Karrāmī cosmology requires that once God, a body, has created another body, God must be in contact with that body. There can be no void to separate bodies, which these Karrāmiyya defined precisely in terms of their mutual contact (al-Juwayni, *Shāmil*, 401). God and His throne are thus connected in the closest possible fashion. For the majority of the Karrāmiyya who adhered to this cosmology God's contact with the throne is from below (*min jihat taḥt*). Such contact from one side did not prevent the label 'infinite' from being applicable to God (al-Baghdādī, *Milal*, 150).

The opponents of the Karrāmiyya deployed an array of arguments against this spatialization of God. The most important of the anti-Karrāmī arguments rested on God's independent existence, His aseity, and the most influential of these arguments was the objection that God's contact with the throne amounted to an admission that God's body was not simple but divisible into parts. God was not independent for the Karrāmiyya, it was urged, but dependent on His parts, and such dependence was the mark of things that came into being after not existing (al-Isfarāyīnī, *Tabṣīr*, 312). The Karrāmiyya had two basic strategies to cope with this objection. The first consisted of a rather unenlightening appeal to God's 'immensity' (*ʿaẓama*), which enabled God to come into contact with more than one thing while remaining indivisible (al-Nīsābūrī, *Ghunya*, 1/388). The second Karrāmī strategy involved more drastic measures than this obscure appeal to God's nature. It called for a radical revision of Karrāmī cosmology.

The second far-reaching strategy of the Karrāmiyya to address the objection from God's parts was to remove God from contact with His throne (or for that matter any other created body). But in order to achieve this, the Karrāmiyya had to give up their opposition to the void. This critical step was achieved by the adoption of atomism, for atomism brought with it the void. Tellingly, in the earliest reports of this doctrinal development the atom (*jawhar*) consistently figures as the unit of measurement for the distance between God and His throne. The Karrāmī atomists differed in the degree to which they removed God from contact with His throne. Some placed God a long but finite distance from the throne. Ibn al-Hayṣam, however, took the final step in this direction by putting God at an infinite distance from the throne. Having made this ultimate move, Ibn al-Hayṣam was in a position to jettison virtually all of the spatial vocabulary in use among his Karrāmī predecessors. All that can now be said is merely that God is in the direction 'above' (*fawq*), and God's removal from the created cosmos is guaranteed by His eternal attribute of 'separateness' (*mubāyana*) (al-Nīsābūrī, *Ghunya*, 1/381, 384).

The abandonment by leading Karrāmī theologians of the cosmology of the *plenum* in favour of atoms and the void introduced an entirely new relation between God and His throne and at the same time established a new distinction between God and His creation. Once the intimacy of direct contact between God and His throne was rejected, the exalted position of the throne in the cosmos could be called into question. It was no longer inevitable that it stand at the pinnacle of creation. Karrāmī theologians could now entertain the possibility that God's footstool, His *kursī*, was actually above His throne (al-Hayṣam, *Qiṣaṣ*, 62). It was, moreover, not merely a matter of spatial position. The Qurʾānic wording that Ibn Karrām and his followers relied upon to put God in contact with the throne now called for some alternative interpretation, and it was by no means clear what that might be. If God is not seated on the throne, what is the nature of His special relation to it? This was a problem that had already confronted the opponents of the Karrāmiyya when they defended the incorporeality of God. Now it faced the Karrāmiyya. For Ibn al-Hayṣam, whose teaching marks the last word in distancing God from his throne, and for his followers, the relation of God to His throne was simply unknown and, they had to admit, utterly beyond the scope of reason (Sūrābādī, *Tafsīr*, 2/ 754, 998f.). The atomistic cosmology also gave a new meaning to the formula that the Karrāmiyya were fond of using: 'God is a body not like other bodies' (*jism lā ka-l-ajsām*). For the older cosmology God was a body, but one with distinctive attributes and powers alongside other sorts of bodies with their distinctive attributes and powers (cf. Tertullian). For the new cosmology God differs from His creation in that He is the only body in existence not constituted of atoms.

With the introduction into Karrāmī cosmology of the void, the term 'body' was no longer fittingly characterized by its necessary contact with other bodies. Among the Karrāmī definitions for body discussed by their opponents the best known held that body is what is self-subsistent (*qā'im bi-nafs*). By the beginning of the sixth/twelfth century it had apparently been adopted by the majority of the Karrāmiyya (al-Nīsābūrī, *Ghunya*, 1/407). Since there was no ground for denying that God is self-subsistent, criticism of this usage typically turned on the inappropriateness of the term 'body' to convey the sense intended. But for the Karrāmiyya, it must be stressed, the new definition of body did not signal a departure from corporealism. Their argument was now that what is truly self-subsistent must be spatial (al-Juwaynī, *Shāmil*, 525).

The third area of Karrāmī doctrine that attracted the most mention and critical comment is their view that God is a 'substrate for things that come to exist' (*maḥall li-l-ḥawādith*), that is, for accidents. The Karrāmī teaching on this point was objectionable to their opponents because it undermined the immutability of God and in so doing made the God beyond time temporal. Because the Karrāmī doctrine here was complex, unfamiliar, and couched in a special technical terminology, it tended to receive more straightforward and detailed exposition than any other area of Karrāmī theology.

Whereas for the Karrāmiyya the assertion that God is a body with spatial relations to other bodies was integral to upholding God's real existence, the assertion that God is a substrate for things that come to exist was for them critical to acknowledging God's agency as creator. As against the Muslim philosophers (*falāsifa*) and the Muʿtazilīs, the Karrāmiyya, like the Ashʿarites and the Māturīdīs, held that God has a number of real attributes such as His eternal knowledge and power. To this extent God is not simple but complex. The Karrāmiyya, in fact, went beyond the Ashʿarites and Māturīdīs in the boldness of their assertion of such discrete attributes, which they did not shy away from regarding as 'other (*ghayr*) than God' and which they were prepared to speak of as inhering in God as a substrate in the way of accidents (*aʿrāḍ*) (Abū l-Muʿīn al-Nasafī, *Tabṣira*, 1/110, 241). In so doing they eschewed the subtle and cautious formulations of their opponents. But the real dividing line between the Karrāmiyya and their theological rivals lay in their account of how God acts.

For the Muʿtazilīs and Ashʿarites God's act of creating is not to be located in God but in what He creates. His status as creator lies in the relation between creator and created, which is simply the dependence of God's temporal creations upon God, who exists timelessly. It does not lie in any distinct creative acts within God as agent. The widely used formula to capture this analysis was that the 'bringing into existence is identical with what is brought into existence' (*al-takwīn ʿayn al-mukawwan*). On this analysis God can be eternally as He is with His unchanging attributes of knowledge, power, and (for the Ashʿarites) will and yet serve to explain the appearance within time of the created world. This picture of a static God appeared to some to be missing the heart of the matter: God's activity. The characteristic Māturīdī doctrine of a distinct attribute of 'bringing into existence' (*takwīn*) was meant to remedy this lack, and the Māturīdīs tirelessly argued on behalf of its necessity against their theological rivals. Their formula for the relation of God to his creation was that 'bringing into existence is not identical with what is brought into existence' (*al-takwīn ghayr al-mukawwan*). The problem with the Māturīdī solution from a Karrāmī point of view was that the additional attribute of *takwīn* was eternal and thus static, unable to account for the constant flux of the world. The necessary element of divine activity was still missing. In place of these unsatisfactory solutions to the problem of God's creative action the Karrāmiyya sought to provide a more adequate account of creation as a process within God. What makes their account particularly interesting is that they were unwilling to accept the criticism of their opponents that this process within God amounted to change and that it took God from eternity into time.

The creative process that according to the Karrāmiyya takes place within God is rooted in his eternal attributes. More specifically it can be regarded as an 'activation' of His eternal attribute of power (*qudra*). Behind the creation of each body (later atom) and of each accident in the world there lies the occurrence within God both of an intention (*irāda*) for the coming into existence of that body or accident as well as an utterance of the imperative *kun* ('be'). The Karrāmiyya sharply distinguished between the events of this inner process, the occurrence of the requisite intention and utterance, and the products of this process in the world. For the former they employed the Arabic verb *ḥadatha* in the first form. For the product of the process, the body or accident that is brought into being outside God, they used the same verb *ḥadatha* in the fourth form (*muḥdath*). Because for the Karrāmiyya all bodies and accidents are inherently enduring (*bāqī*), it requires God's intervention to bring them to an end. The process of bringing to an end (*iʿdām*) corresponds closely to that for bringing into existence and requires in each case an appropriate intention and an utterance, for example the command *ifna* ('cease to be'). The term *iḥdāth* (literally 'bringing into existence') was used in a broad sense to cover the inner process as a whole in its two aspects, both bringing into existence (*ījād*) and bringing to an end. Because there were multiple occurrences within God for each body and each accident that came into being or came to an end, it is readily apparent that the God of the Karrāmiyya is at an extreme remove from the static God of their theological rivals. The complexity of God's inner life was compounded for many Karrāmiyya by the additional occurrence within God of aural and visual perceptions of the created world that they termed *tasammuʿ* and *tabaṣṣur* respectively.

Of God's eternal attributes His will, for which the Karrāmiyya used the term *mashīʾa*, and his power (*qudra*) each play a critical although quite distinct role. The eternal attribute of will encompasses the occurrences within God and their product, the bodies and accidents created outside God, but it attaches to the latter in only a general way, giving them a sort of blanket approval. It is God's eternal attribute of power that is the source of His creative agency. Thus both the specific intentions (*irādāt*) and utterances involved in the process of bringing into existence occur within God by virtue of His power. In their theological language the Karrāmiyya made every effort to bring out this essential role of the eternal attribute of power. The basis for calling God a speaker (*qāʾil*) is not the specific utterances that occur within Him but His eternal power over such utterances. Similarly God has intention, hears, and sees not by virtue of the specific intentions or aural or visual perceptions that occur in Him but by virtue of His eternal power over each of these. The Karrāmiyya used a special terminology, much derided by their opponents, to make this point: God, for example, is a speaker not because of the utterances (*aqwāl*) that occur within Him but by virtue of His capacity to speak, his *qāʾiliyya*. More generally, God is a creator not on the basis of the occurrences that constitute the inner process of bringing into existence but on the basis of His power over this process, and because God's power is eternal, He is appropriately regarded as eternally a creator. Negatively, the Karrāmiyya insisted that God acquires no real attributes (*ṣifāt*) through the occurrences within Him, for His true attributes must be eternal. Neither do the inner occurrences ever constitute the basis for real attributions (*waṣf*) (al-Shahrastānī, *Milal*, 1/183–8). To the extent that the inner occurrences are referred to in relation to God they are never more than mere predicates (*nuʿūt*, sing. *naʿt*) (al-Sālimī, *Tamhīd*, 50).

The Karrāmī teaching on divine attributes represents one line of defence against the criticism that their account of God's creative activity renders Him mutable and thus temporal. The thrust of this defence is that the various occurrences that constitute the creative process within God are simply activations of His eternal attribute of power. The effort is to remove all significance to the fact that they come to be within God, as indeed they must, rather than outside Him. This approach suggests a certain interiorization of God within His body, the substrate for these occurrences. Throughout His actions God remains eternal in all of His real attributes.

The Karrāmiyya also adopted another quite different line of defence that addresses the question of mutability and temporality more explicitly. This was their teaching that the various occurrences within God can never cease to exist. They are necessarily enduring (*wājibat al-baqāʾ*). The gist of the Karrāmī argument was that mutability and temporality require a succession (*taʿāqub*) of coming-to-exist followed by coming-to-an-end. Without such a succession there is no change (*taghayyur*). Because the occurrences within God never come to an end, and in fact never can come to an end, the process of creation within God is not correctly characterized as involving change or time. The thrust of this line of defence is quite counter to that based on the eternity of the true divine attributes. It does not seek to minimize the reality of the inner occurrences but to vest them with a considerable measure of God's eternity.

Underlying the complex process of creation that the Karrāmiyya posit within God is a fundamental analogy with human action. Humans act on their environment by bringing about occurrences in their bodies in the form of movement. Modern analytic philosophy of action has acknowledged this obvious truth by introducing the notion of basic actions, actions by which other actions are performed but which are not themselves performed by means of other actions. Muslim theologians, despite the very substantial disagreement among them on the ultimate metaphysics of human action, did not deny the fact of basic actions, and it was from this intimately familiar phenomenon that the Karrāmiyya took their model of God's actions. He too acts beyond Himself by acting within His body. The locus of action, both human and divine, is in the 'substrate of power' (*maḥall al-qudra*) (al-Nīsābūrī, *Ghunya*, 1/437). The pre-eminent role of power among God's eternal attributes was also mirrored in an unusual Karrāmī teaching on human power. Such mental accidents as knowledge, intention, and perception could inhere in dead bodies. The accident of power alone required the presence of life (al-Baghdādī, *Uṣūl*, 29).

While it cannot be claimed that the Karrāmiyya played a role in the history of Islamic theology remotely comparable to that of their great rivals, the Muʿtazilīs, Ashʿarites, or Māturīdīs, they did gain for themselves enduring mention in the theological literature of their own time and thereafter. Because they did not limit themselves to citing Qurʾān and *ḥadīth* for their positions but were fully committed to the give and take of theological argument, they could not be dismissed out of hand by other theologians, at least not across the board. The issues they took it upon themselves to defend against the mainstream were often of the greatest interest. They remain so today.

References

Abū l-Muʿīn al-Nasafī (*Tabṣira*). *Tabṣirat al-adilla*. Ed. C. Salamé. Damascus: Institut Français de Damas, 1990.

al-Baghdādī, ʿAbd al-Qāhir b. Ṭāhir *(Milal). Kitāb al-Milal wa-l-niḥal.* Ed. A. Nader. Beirut: Dār al-Mashriq, 1970.

al-Baghdādī, ʿAbd al-Qāhir b. Ṭāhir *(Uṣūl). Kitāb Uṣūl al-dīn.* Istanbul: Maṭbaʿat al-Dawla, 1346/1928.

Crone, P. (2012). 'Al-Jāḥiẓ on *Aṣḥāb al-Jahālāt* and the Jahmiyya'. In R. Hansberger, M. Afifi al-Akiti, and C. Burnett (eds.), *Medieval Arabic Thought: Essays in Honour of Fritz Zimmermann*. London: Warburg Institute, 27–39.

van Ess, J. (1980). *Ungenützte Texte zur Karrāmīya*. Heidelberg: Carl Winter.

Frank, R. (1965). 'The Neoplatonism of Jahm ibn Ṣafwān'. *Muséon* 78: 395–424. Reprinted in R. Frank (2005). *Philosophy, Theology and Mysticism in Medieval Islam: Texts and Studies on the Development and History of Kalām*. Ed. D. Gutas. Aldershot: Ashgate.

al-Hayṣam b. Muhammad b. al-Hayṣam (*Qiṣas*). *Qiṣaṣ al-Qurʾān al-karīm*. Ed. Muḥammad ʿAbduh Ḥatāmila and Muḥammad Jāsim al-Mashhadānī. Amman, 1427/2006.

Ibn Fūrak (*Sharḥ*). *Sharḥ al-ʿĀlim wa-l-mutaʿallim*. Ed. Aḥmad ʿAbd al-Raḥmān al-Sāyiḥ and Tawfīq ʿAlī Wahba. Cairo: Dār al-thaqāfa al-dīniyya, 1430/2009.

al-Isfarāyīnī, Abū l-Muẓaffar Shāhfūr b. Ṭāhir (*Tabṣīr*). *al-Tabṣīr fī l-dīn*. Ed. Majīd al-Khalīfa. Beirut: Dār Ibn Ḥazm, 1429/2008.

Jantzen, G. (1984). *God's World, God's Body*. Philadelphia: Westminster Press.

al-Jūraqānī, al-Ḥusayn b. Ibrāhīm (*Abāṭīl*). *al-Abāṭīl wa-l-manākīr*. Ed. ʿAbd al-Raḥmān al-Farīwāʾī. Riyad: Dar al-Ṣumayʾī, 1422/2002.

al-Juwaynī, Imām al-Ḥaramayn (*Shāmil*). *al-Shāmil fī uṣūl al-dīn*. Ed. ʿAlī Sāmī al-Nashshār, Fayṣal Budayr ʿAwn, and Suhayr Muḥammad Mukhtār. Alexandria: Munshaʾat al-Maʿārif, 1969.
al-Nasafī, Abū Muṭīʿ Makḥūl (*Radd*). *Kitāb al-Radd ʿalā l-bidaʿ*. Ed. Marie Bernand. *Annales islamologiques* 16 (1980), 39–126.
al-Nīsābūrī, Abū l-Qāsim Salmān b. Naṣir (*Ghunya*). *al-Ghunya fī l-kalām (qism al-ilāhiyyāt)*. Ed. Muṣṭafā Ḥasanayn ʿAbd al-Hādī. Cairo: Dār al-Salām, 1431/2010.
al-Sālimī, al-Muhtadī Abū Shakūr (*Tamhīd*). *al-Tamhīd*. Delhi: al-Maṭbaʿ al-Fārūqī, 1309.
al-Shahrastānī, Muḥammad b. ʿAbd al-Karīm (*Milal*). *Kitāb al-Milal wa-l-niḥal*. Ed. Muḥammad b. Fatḥ Allāh Badrān. Cairo: Maṭbaʿat al-Azhar, 1370/1951.
Sūrābādī, Abū Bakr ʿAtīq (*Tafsīr*). *Tafsīr al-tafāsīr*. Ed. Saʿīdī Sīrjānī. Tehran: Farhang-i Nashr-i Naw, 2002.
van Ess, J. (1980). *Ungenützte Texte zur Karrāmīya*. Heidelberg: Carl Winter.
Zadeh, T. (2012). *The Vernacular Qurʾan: Translation and the Rise of Persian Exegesis*. Oxford: Oxford University Press.
Zysow, A. (2011). 'Karrāmiya'. *Encyclopaedia Iranica*, xv. 590–601.

CHAPTER 16

SCRIPTURALIST AND TRADITIONALIST THEOLOGY

BINYAMIN ABRAHAMOV

I Scripturalist Theology

A central debate in religion revolves around the sources of religious ideas and practices and their authoritativeness. Do these perceptions and acts derive from ancient customs and traditions, whether written or oral, or from written sacred texts, or from the intellect? Islam is no exception to this controversy, and these three elements played an important role in early Islam until the beginning of the third/ninth century. From this era onward theologians and jurists have argued on the authoritativeness of written texts vis-à-vis the intellect (Melchert 1997: 1f.).

In the first two centuries of Islam some thinkers adhered to the authority of ancient habits and traditions and rejected new practices and ideas based on reason. In this era scripturalism also emerged to exhort a strict following of the literal meaning of the Qurʾānic text. In the middle of the third/ninth century this tendency also assumed the shape of literal interpretation of the written traditions now called *ḥadīth* (pl. *aḥādīth*—a prophetic report, understood as a norm, on spiritual and practical matters transmitted from the Prophet or from his companions (*ṣaḥāba*) by a chain of transmitters).

The following terms are used in this chapter:

1. 'Scripturalists'/'literalists'—learned individuals who adhere to the literal meaning of the Qurʾānic text (and of the traditions), regarding the Qurʾān (and the traditions) as the sole authority of law and theology and who oppose other sources, such as custom or rational reasoning, as devices which may lead to error (Crone and Zimmermann 2001: 292). However, some scripturalists do not regard reason and even syllogistic reasoning as something to be avoided.
2. 'Traditionists'—scholars who deal with traditions, whether transmitting them or by investigating their authenticity.

3. 'Traditionalists'—people who keep to the teachings of the Qur'ān, the Sunna (the prophetic norms expressed in the traditions also referred to in the following discussion as 'the Tradition') and the 'Consensus' (*ijmāʿ*), preferring these to the use of reason. This term is correctly applied only to people acting from the third/ninth century onward. They must be distinguished from people who adhered to ancient customs and habits, or to unwritten traditions (Hodgson 1977: i. 64) whom I would call 'traditionalistics', a term used only for the sake of clarity in this article.
4. 'Rationalists'—scholars who regard reason as the principal device to attain religious truths (Abrahamov 1998: ix).

In the first two centuries of Islam, the arena is filled with scripturalists, traditionalistics, traditionalists, and rationalists. The scripturalists can be placed into two subdivisions; the first is embodied in groups and the second in individuals. The first people who adhered to scripturalism were those sections among the Khārijites who 'left' (*kharaja min*) ʿAlī b. Abī Ṭālib's camp, or 'rebelled against his authority' (*kharaja ʿalā*) after the battle of Ṣiffīn (37/657). They rejected the arbitration with ʿAlī's rival Muʿāwiya and claimed that God's judgement as expressed in the Qur'ān is preferable to the judgement produced by human beings (Cook 1987: 170). The Khārijites conveyed their adherence to the Qur'ān by the slogan 'The judgement belongs to God alone' (*lā ḥukma illā li-Llāh*). It is also possible that the Khārijites espoused scripturalism not because of their opposition to the arbitration, but because of their disapproval of certain traditions transmitted from the Prophet, although these traditions referred to the Qur'ānic text and interpreted them. In contrast to the Khārijites, ʿAlī claimed that the Qur'ān needs interpretation (Hawting 1978: 460–2). An instructive example of the Khārijite understanding of the Qur'ān is shown in Q 9: 29 which reads, 'Fight those who do not believe in God and the Last Day, who do not forbid what God and His messenger forbid, who do not follow the rule of justice.' The Khārijites applied this verse to their adversaries and used it to justify their extreme behaviour toward them. There are some reports that the Azāriqa, a subsect of the *Khawārij*, adopted scripturalism in relating to several legal issues, such as rejection of stoning of the fornicators which is not mentioned in the Qur'ān and is based on a tradition instead of the punishment of lashes that is mentioned in Q 24: 2 (Lewinstein 1991: 261, 268).

Another group of theologians who embraced scripturalist inclinations are some Murji'ites, who did not incorporate prophetic traditions in their discussions and accused their adversaries of using these traditions (Cook 1981: 16–19). To some extent early Muʿtazilites can also be reckoned as scripturalists, for they rejected prophetic traditions as a source of theological notions and used, in addition to rational arguments, Qur'ānic verses as support for their theological notions. The Baṣran Muʿtazilite al-Naẓẓām (d. 221/836) attacked prophetic traditions and based his theories on reason and Qur'ānic verses. He claimed that prophetic traditions were suspect of being spurious and that they contradicted each other (Cook 1987: 168–9). Also, later Muʿtazilites like ʿAbd al-Jabbār (d. 415/1025) admonished people against using *ḥadīth* based on individual transmitters (*khabar al-āḥād*) in theological issues. However, ʿAbd al-Jabbār was prepared to accept as true those traditions handed down by many chains of transmitters (*khabar mutawātir*)—thus only these may be relied upon as being true in his view (ʿAbd al-Jabbār, *Faḍl*, 187–96).

Not only groups of early theologians were inclined toward scripturalism in theological issues, but also individual scholars, who sometimes incorporated scripturalism into theology, while being traditionalists in other religious spheres. Such is the case of the theologian and traditionist al-Ḥasan al-Baṣrī (d. 110/728), who wrote an epistle advocating free will which was addressed to the caliph ʿAbd al-Malik (d. 86/705). Even if this epistle is not al-Hasan al-Baṣrī's (Cook 1987: 117–23; Mourad 2006: 176–239), it teaches a tendency prevalent in early Islam which preferred the sacred text to the prophetic traditions. The author plainly says that 'every statement which is not supported by a proof deriving from God's Book is an error' (Ritter 1933: 68; Wansbrough 1977: 160–3). The epistle is free from prophetic traditions, and the theses in it are based on the plain meanings of the Qurʾānic text (Schwarz 1972: 15–30). The debate between traditionalistic tendencies, which defended ancient customs, scripturalist orientation, and a traditionalist direction that espoused prophetic traditions, came to a turning point with the revolution of the famous jurist al-Shāfiʿī (d. 204/820), who stated that prophetic traditions are more important than the Qurʾān. Al-Shāfiʿī developed the thesis, prevalent for generations up to our era, that there are four principal sources, or roots of the law: the Qurʾān, the Sunna (Muḥammad's ways of religious life and thought which are expressed in the literary form of *ḥadīth*), analogical reasoning (*qiyās*), and consensus (*ijmāʿ*). In al-Shāfiʿī's view the Prophet is a lawgiver and authoritative interpreter of the Qurʾān, hence his commentary on the Qurʾān is preferable to other commentaries (Coulson 1978: 53–61). As we shall see, this approach to the prophetic traditions in matters of law is also applicable to theological issues.

The third/ninth century witnessed the emergence of a school of scripturalism whose founder Dāwūd b. ʿAlī b. Khalaf al-Iṣfahānī (d. 270/884) associated himself at first with the Shāfiʿite school of law. Contrary to the scripturalist tendencies of groups and individuals mentioned above which acknowledged only the Qurʾān and rejected traditions of any source, whether oral or written, the new school, which was called the 'school of the plain meaning' (*madhhab al-ẓāhir, al-Ẓāhiriyya*) or the 'school of Dāwūd' (*madhhab Dāwūd*), also interpreted, in addition to the Qurʾān, the prophetic traditions using the plain meaning of the text (Goldziher 2007: 1, 27; van Ess 1991–7: *passim*).

Works written by Dāwūd are no longer extant. All that we know about his views has reached us through later writings, including biographical dictionaries and legal treatises of other schools, among which are most prominently the works by the Andalusī theologian and jurist Ibn Ḥazm (d. 456/1063) (Turki 2010: xi. 394; Adang 2006: 16). Dāwūd adhered to the plain meanings of the Qurʾān and the Tradition, hence his rejection of analogical reasoning (*qiyās*) in these two kinds of text is a logical outcome. Accordingly, he denied the employment of *taʿlīl*, that is, finding the cause (*ʿilla*) of the appearance of a rule or theological thesis in the religious texts. For example, drinking wine is forbidden according to the Qurʾān. Now, having found the cause of this interdiction, which is intoxication, the other schools of law prohibited drinking all kinds of alcoholic drinks, such as one produced from dates (*nabīdh*), whereas the Ẓāhirīs argued that if God wished to forbid other kinds of drinks, He would have indicated it plainly in the Qurʾān or the Tradition. Contrary to other schools of law whose representatives used personal insight (*raʾy*) in their legislation in varied degrees, Dāwūd rejected *raʾy* (Goldziher 2007: 30). Finally, because of practical pressure, Dāwūd used *qiyās* (Goldziher 2007: 35). We shall see that even Ibn Ḥazm, the greatest exponent of Ẓāhirism, was not always loyal to his own system of thought.

Dāwūd opposed the uncritical following (*taqlīd*) of individuals or schools in matters of law. One should use the roots of law oneself in order to reach a legal decision (Goldziher 2007: 30). Also, in addition to forbidding the use of *raʾy*, he believed in the power of the consensus (*ijmāʿ*) of Muḥammad's companions as a source of the Law. All the sources mentioned above, whether they were lawful or unlawful in the eyes of the Ẓāhirīs, referred to the Law. Ibn Ḥazm was the first Ẓāhirī scholar who applied them to theological issues (Goldziher 2007: 112; Adang, Fierro, and Schmidtke 2012), and his theology constitutes the climax of the Ẓāhirī religious thought.

Ibn Ḥazm was born at Cordova in 384/994 and died at Manta Līsham in 456/1064. He was well versed in Islamic religious sciences and in Islamic theology and philosophy. At first, he was affiliated with the Mālikī school of law, but then embraced Shāfiʿism and finally followed Dāwūd and his tenets, including the latter's opposition to *taqlīd* and acceptance of the companions' *ijmāʿ*. Being a subtle psychologist and moralist, he wrote a treatise on love entitled *The Ring of the Dove* (*Ṭawq al-ḥamāma*) and a book on morals entitled *Kitāb al-Akhlāq wa-l-siyar*. He was a theoretician of language, believing that words speak for themselves and that there is no need to investigate the inner meaning of words, because this procedure would lead to personal priorities and deviation from the true objective meaning. The correct meaning is established in accordance with linguistic rules, without the intervention of other criteria. Closely connected with his attitude toward language is his acceptance of logic, sometimes in the form of syllogistic reasoning (Chejne 1984: 57–72), as a device for understanding the texts of the Qurʾān and the Tradition (Arnaldez 2006: iii. 790–4; Adang 2006: 18–20).

Ibn Ḥazm's doctrine is based on the plain meaning of those Qurʾān verses which characterize the text of the Qurʾān itself. First, the Sacred Book was revealed in a clear Arabic language (Q 26: 195). Second, it explains everything (Q 16: 89). Moreover, the Qurʾān says as follows: 'Today I have perfected My religion for you' (Q 3: 5). Taking into consideration these three notions, our author does not hesitate to conclude that because the Qurʾān treats everything in a clear manner and because Islam was completed in the lifetime of the Prophet and his companions, there was no need to change anything in religion or to add anything to it. *Taqlīd* is not admitted, but following the Prophet is not *taqlīd*, but rather obedience to Muḥammad's orders (Adang 2006: 21–5). According to Ibn Ḥazm, the first three generations of Muslims were regarded by Muḥammad as the righteous, because they did not follow their personal views and inclinations. In Ibn

Ḥazm's view, deterioration in the sphere of religion began in the mid-second/eighth century, because by then people were starting to use personal insights in their judgements (Adang 2006: 32).

Ibn Ḥazm believed that the best way to deal with religious matters is by exerting personal efforts or independent endeavours (*ijtihād*) to understand what God and the Messenger intend in their communications and accordingly to reach conclusions, in both the legal and theological realms. His point of departure is the notion that God does not require of a human being that which he is not capable of carrying out (Q 2: 286). In principle every human being has the capacity to learn the sacred texts, although people differ in this capacity. Only when one is unable to find a solution to his problem on his own, is one advised to turn to someone more learned than he is, on the condition that the latter bases himself on the texts and not on the opinions of others. The tools of the learned individual are the Qurʾān, the Tradition (*ḥadīth*), lexicography, and grammar; analogical reasoning (*qiyās*) and finding causes (*taʿlīl*) of God's will are totally excluded. When a contradiction occurs between a legal decision derived from the Qurʾān and a legal decision in the same matter derived from the Tradition, the Tradition is preferred, because the Prophet explains the Qurʾān through the Tradition and because the Prophet proves the authenticity of the Qurʾān. Hence, a true tradition may cancel a Qurʾānic rule (Adang 2006: 40–5).

Having discussed the general approach of Ibn Ḥazm on the authoritativeness of the religious sources, we may now examine some of Ibn Ḥazm's theological doctrines—a thorough study of his doctrinal views is still a major desideratum. This discussion will also touch on some general principles of the Ẓāhirīs.

One much debated issue in Islamic theology is free will vis-à-vis predestination. While the Arabs in the pre-Islamic era believed in fatalism (*dahr*), a belief which appeared later in the Tradition, the Qurʾān when taken literally expresses two approaches, one of which defends predetermination and the other free will (Watt 1948: 12–31). A verse which can be interpreted to mean predestination is Q 54: 29 (*innā kull shayʾ khalaqnāhu bi-qadar*), 'We have created everything in measure' or 'We have predetermined the creation of everything'. The question is whether this verse is interpreted in a general (*ʿumūm*) or in a particular manner (*khuṣūṣ*). Loyal to their belief in free will, the Muʿtazilites understood this verse as applying to a particular case, while al-Ashʿarī claimed that a verse should be interpreted in a general way only when it has an external corroboration for this use.

Contrary to the two preceding approaches, Ibn Ḥazm held that every Qurʾānic verse should be interpreted in a general way unless some other verse cancels the generality of a verse (Goldziher 2007: 113–15). In this case, the Qurʾān teaches God's predetermination. Because, in Ibn Ḥazm's view, a sacred text should be understood in keeping with linguistic rules, he, for example, opposes the Muʿtazilite understanding of the verb *aḍalla*, which frequently occurs in the Qurʾān, as naming someone a deviator. For the Muʿtazilites, accepting the usual meaning of this verb, that is, God causes a human being to deviate from the correct path, means the negation of human free will in which they believed. One should note that aberration from the linguistic criterion can be made through using the consensus (*ijmāʿ*) or another sacred text. Also the literal meaning of a verse or a tradition may diverge into various directions (Goldziher 2007: 115–18).

Muslim theologians differed on the nature of the Qurʾān. The Muʿtazilites held that the Qurʾān was created, whereas their opponents believed that it was eternal. Some traditionalist theologians also debated the question of the physical elements of the Book, such as the act of reading or the written text—whether they were created or not. Contrary to the Ashʿarites who taught that the Qurʾān is God's one speech (*kalām wāḥid*), Ibn Ḥazm claimed on the basis of Qurʾānic verses, for example Q 18: 109, that God's speech is infinite and not restricted to the Qurʾān. In his view, the Qurʾān, God's speech, has five manifestations: 1. revelation; 2. the voices of the Book when it is recited; 3. its contents; 4. the written copy of the text; and 5. the memorized text. Each of these parts has a different value. All elements of the Qurʾān which involve acts of the human being, such as the voices when it is recited and the written text, are created, while God's knowledge which is embodied in His speech or in the Qurʾān is eternal (Ibn Ḥazm, *Fiṣal*, 3: 7–11; Goldziher 2007: 130–2).

Ibn Ḥazm opposes applying the term *ṣifāt* ('attributes') to God and in fact the very notion that the 'names' given to God in the Qurʾān are 'attributes'. There is no evidence in the Qurʾān or in the Tradition or by the consensus, he argues, that either God, or Muḥammad or his followers employed the term 'attributes'. Our author ascribes the use of this term to the Muʿtazilites whom others later followed. 'It is allowable to name God or to inform of Him only by what He named Himself or informed of Himself' (Ibn Ḥazm, *Fiṣal*, 2: 140f.). Hence, the name 'Eternal' (*qadīm*) is not legitimate, while the name the 'First' (*awwal*), which appears in the Qurʾān (Q 57: 3), is applicable (Goldziher 2007: 134–9). Apart from the argument from the absence of textual evidence for the 'attributes', Ibn Ḥazm also uses rational arguments to deny the application of 'attributes' to God. The existence of an attribute means that there exists an entity which is its ontological foundation and is different from it. Furthermore, if we regard the name 'Merciful' as an attribute, it follows that God does not cause people to suffer pain, which is not the case. All these arguments lead Ibn Ḥazm to consider God's appellations proper 'names' rather than 'attributes' (Goldziher 2007: 140–2).

Notwithstanding the use of rational arguments, Ibn Ḥazm accepts textual statements even if they contradict reason. For example, responding to the Muʿtazilite claim that if God were to predetermine a human being's sin He would be angry at His own decision after the human being commits a sin, he admits that God is wrathful and curses the devil whom He created. Likewise, good and evil are not objective values which can be disclosed by the human intellect, but rather are established by God's will. What God wills is good and what He detests is evil. There is nothing which is absolutely good or evil (Goldziher 2007: 149).

Generally Muslim theologians take three main approaches to the much debated problem of anthropomorphism (*tashbīh*): (1) Very few theologians believed in the literal meaning of the texts of the Qurʾān and the traditions and held that, for example, God's hands (Q 38: 75) are like human hands; (2) at the other extreme, the rationalists, mainly the Muʿtazilites, interpreted Qurʾānic anthropomorphic expressions in a figurative manner, thus God does not sit on His Throne (Q 20: 5) but the throne symbolizes His rule of the whole cosmos; (3) a middle approach between the two extremes is al-Ashʿarī's system, whose elements were introduced by early theologians, according to which *tashbīh* is totally rejected and anthropomorphic expressions should be accepted as they are, without trying to interpret their modality (*kayfiyya*) (Abrahamov 1995: 365–7).

Taking into consideration Ibn Ḥazm's rules of interpretation, one would expect him to have adopted the first approach, that of the *mushabbiha*, i.e. those who adhered to the literal meanings of the sacred texts. However, surprisingly enough, our author rejects anthropomorphism as well as the Muʿtazilite and Ashʿarite positions. In his interpretation of anthropomorphic expressions, he employs linguistic and also simple rational arguments. For example, the tradition 'God created Adam in His image' (Watt 1959–60) is interpreted to mean that God created a scheme according to which He created Adam. Ibn Ḥazm even uses *taqdīr* (the supposition that a part of the sentence is either missing or redundant) in order to eschew the ascription of human acts to God. Thus, 'Your Lord came' (*jāʾa rabbuka*, Q 89: 22) becomes, in Ibn Ḥazm's interpretation, 'The order of your Lord came' (*jāʾa amr rabbika*). In employing such a device and other linguistic tools, Ibn Ḥazm comes very close to the Muʿtazilites whom he criticizes for their arbitrariness in interpreting the Qurʾān and the traditions (Goldziher 2007: 151–4).

In sum, Ibn Ḥazm's system of dealing with theology accords with his system of treating Islamic law. However, Ẓāhirī theology does not serve as a device for disclosing the identity of a Ẓāhirī individual; this remained the function of the Ẓāhirī law. The Ẓāhirī school of law, as an independent school, enjoyed its Golden Era under the third ruler of the Almohad dynasty in al-Andalus and North Africa, Abū Yūsuf Yaʿqūb (r. 580/1184–595/1199). The power of the Ẓāhirīs held sway until the end of the seventh/thirteenth century and thereafter their law and theology was found only in books (Goldziher 2007: 171; Chejne 1982: 16). Some scholars after this period, such as the historian al-Maqrīzī (d. 845/1441), are considered Ẓāhirīs, although this phenomenon of individuals who are deemed Ẓāhirīs came to an end and from the tenth/sixteenth century onward their teachings ceased to carry much weight. However, some features of the school regained popularity in contemporary Islamic thought (Adang, Fierro, and Schmidtke 2012: *introduction*).

II Traditionalist Theology

As noted, the term 'traditionalism' refers to the prophetic traditions which began to spread in Islam shortly after Muḥammad's death. The first two centuries of the Islamic era witnessed the struggle of four main approaches over the sources of knowledge and their authoritativeness, these being scripturalism, ancient or local traditions, prophetic traditions, and personal or rationalist argumentation. This debate reached its climax by the time of al-Shāfiʿī, who succeeded in persuading his co-religionists to hold the superiority of the prophetic traditions over other devices as a source of legal and theological knowledge and of interpretation of the Qurʾān. This essential phase in the development of Islamic law and theology does not signal the end of the discussion, which has continued up to the present day.

Building on our definition of traditionalism at the outset of this chapter, we can now proceed by stating that the foundations of traditionalism can be known through examining the texts from the middle of the third/ninth century onward. Traditionalism is based on three positive principles: (1) adherence to the Qurʾān, the Sunna, and the consensus; (2) the religious content derived from the three devices mentioned here is homogeneous; and (3) the embracing of the scholars who are responsible for the application of these devices. A negative principle is the fierce opposition to innovations (*bidʿa*, pl. *bidaʿ*). We shall now examine these three principles.

The Shāfiʿite theologian Ismāʿīl b. Muḥammad al-Taymī (d. 535/1140) lucidly explains the role of the Qurʾān and the Sunna in a paragraph which sums up the perception of the traditionalists:

> The people of the truth make the Qurʾān and the Sunna their model (*imām*) and they search for religion through both of them. What they have attained through their intellect and mind, they subject to the examination of the Book and the Sunna. If they find it compatible with both of them, they accept it, and they thank God for showing them this and for His guidance. If they find it opposing the Qurʾān and the Sunna, they leave what they have attained and turn to both of them and blame themselves (for finding such a notion). That is because the Book and the Sunna guide the people only to the truth, while man's opinion may be true or false. (al-Taymī, *Ḥujja* 2: 224; cf. Abrahamov 1998: 1)

In addition to the function of being sources of truth, the Qurʾān and the Sunna serve as the criterion for what the human being attains through his intellect.

The Shāfiʿite theologian Hibat Allāh b. al-Ḥasan al-Lālakāʾī (d. 418/1027) supplies us with an example of using the three tools of knowledge. He begins his discussion of the question of God's predestination through relevant Qurʾānic verses which are interpreted by using the system of *al-tafsīr bi-l-maʾthūr* (interpretation through using traditions, *athar*, pl. *āthār*). Q 37: 96 reads: 'God has created you and your actions' (*Allāh khalaqakum wa-mā taʿmalūna*). According to a tradition '*mā taʿmalūna*' means *ʿamalakum* ('your action') and hence God's predetermination. This author interprets other verses to the same effect. Then he adds the consensus of Muḥammad's companions and their followers about God's predetermination. No speculative argument or comparison between verses or traditions is employed. The author adheres to the dictum, espoused by some traditionalists, that there is no analogy in the Sunna (*laysa fī l-sunna qiyās*), which means that one should not ask 'how' or 'why' regarding a theological principle. Denying the use of any rational argument when dealing with the Qurʾān and the Sunna characterizes some traditionalists, and one may call this approach 'pure traditionalism'.

Because of the debate with rationalist thinkers, the traditionalists tried to strengthen the authoritativeness of these devices of attaining knowledge. Since the Qurʾān was acknowledged by all kinds of theologians as divine speech, notwithstanding the controversy over whether it is created or uncreated/eternal, their efforts concentrated on the two other tools. Traditions are recruited to show that the position of the Sunna equals that of the Qurʾān, for Jibrīl sent down the Sunna just as he did regarding the Qurʾān. And traditions quote Muḥammad as saying that he received the unrecited texts, the Sunna, with the recited texts, the Qurʾān. Q 3: 104 relates that the Messenger teaches people 'the book and the wisdom', which is interpreted to mean the Sunna.

Efforts to defend the Sunna have not stopped, and even in the ninth/fifteenth century we encounter a work entitled *Miftāḥ al-janna fī l-iʿtiṣām bi-l-sunna* written by the famous Shāfiʿite scholar Jalāl al-Dīn al-Suyūṭī (d. 911/1505). According to al-Suyūṭī, the Qurʾān (Q 3: 164, 4: 171, 24: 62) connects the belief in Muḥammad with the belief in God, thus comparing the Qurʾān with the Prophet's traditions. Furthermore, the Sunna contains all of what one needs to know regarding religion, laws, theology, the prophets' stories, the Prophet's biography, and Qurʾān interpretation. In sum, the Sunna becomes the second revelation after the Qurʾān which means its being sacred like the Qurʾān and its being an object of learning as is the Qurʾān (Abrahamov 1998: 3f.).

The authoritativeness of the consensus is proven through using Qurʾānic verses and traditions. Q 4: 115 speaks of 'the way of the believers' (*sabīl al-muʾminīn*), which is interpreted to mean the consensus of the Muslim community. 'What the believers regard as good is good in God's eyes and what they regard as evil is evil in God's eyes' is a tradition which helps the Muslims to legitimize the consensus. The same applies to the tradition which states that 'my community does not agree on an error'. The Sunna also promises paradise to those who join the community (*jamāʿa*) and states that God protects the community so that whoever leaves the community may be liable to the devil's attack. Adherence to the *jamāʿa* leads to success of the Muslims, while its opposite, *iftirāq* ('division'), causes their perdition. Hence, the consensus is an important principle not only as a source of knowledge, but also as a device which guarantees the well-being of the Muslims (Abrahamov 1998: 4–6; Hourani 1985: 190–226).

The traditionalists believed that the theological fundamentals deriving from the three sources of knowledge, the Qurʾān, the Sunna, and the *ijmāʿ* are homogeneous, thus constituting the second foundation of traditionalism. Basing himself on Q 3: 105 'Be not as those who scattered (*tafarraqū*) and fell into variance (*iftaraqū*) after the clear signs (*bayyināt*) came to them' (trans. Arberry 1983: 59), the Shāfiʿite theologian al-Bayhaqī (d. 395/1005) expresses the idea that the Qurʾān, the Sunna, and the consensus of Muḥammad's companions affirm three fundamental principles of Islamic theology: the existence of attributes (*ṣifāt*) in God as separate spiritual entities, the believer's seeing of God in the world to come (*ruʾyat Allāh*), and Muḥammad's intercession on behalf of the sinners (*shafāʿa*). To deny these principles means to deny God's signs, the Qurʾān, the Sunna, and the consensus, set forth in the above-mentioned verse.

The principle of homogeneity was corroborated by two kinds of proofs. The first are traditions which reject dispute (*jadal*) such as 'the early scholars hated diversity in religion' or 'beware of debates in religion', and the second is based on the scholars' actual experiences. The famous traditionist and the compiler of one of the canonical collections of *ḥadīth*, Muḥammad b. Ismāʿīl al-Bukhārī (d. 256/870), relates that during forty-six years he met more than a thousand scholars who lived in different areas, all of whom accepted the tenets of Islam (Abrahamov 1998: 6). A similar notion appears in a creed written in the second half of the third/ninth century by Abū Zurʿa ʿUbayd Allāh b. ʿAbd al-Karīm (d. 264/878) and Abū Ḥātim Muḥammad b. Idrīs b. Mundhir (d. 277/890) (al-Lālakāʾī, *Sharḥ* 151–86). Probably, seeking homogeneity, the traditionalists thought that adhering to the same three sources of knowledge, the Qurʾān, the Sunna, and the consensus, would bring about the same results. However, a scrutiny of various creeds dating from the mid-ninth century reveals certain differences in dogma.

A polemical argument against the *mutakallimūn* appears in this context. Whereas the *mutakallimūn* have no homogeneous theology—they move from one idea to another and have different schools of thought—the traditionalists believe in stable teachings which cannot be shaken even by severe circumstances. Stability in ideas is a sign of certain belief and truth (Abrahamov 1998: 6f.).

Adherence to the Sunna of the Prophet logically causes the traditionalists to adopt an attitude of adoration toward the traditionists, those who are responsible for the collection and transmission of traditions. This is the third foundation of traditionalism which is gleaned from the sources. The first objects of this veneration were Muḥammad's companions (*ṣaḥāba*) who were the best, purest, and most just people chosen by God. People should not abuse them. This foundation exists in all schools of law and the writings of theologians, some of whom dedicated large portions of their books to this subject. In al-Lālakāʾī this topic occupies the seventh and eighth out of the eight parts of his book. A representative paragraph of this attitude is shown in the creed of the Mālikite jurist Ibn Abī Zayd al-Qayrawānī (d. 386/996):

> The best of generations is the generation who saw the Messenger of God and believed in him. Next are those who followed them, and next are those who followed these. The most excellent of the companions (of Muḥammad) are the rightly and the truly guided caliphs, Abū Bakr, ʿUmar, then ʿUthmān, then ʿAlī. Let not any of the companions of the Messenger be mentioned except most honourably and without reference to what was disputed among them. They, above other people, deserve to have the best construction put upon (their conduct) and to have the best views attributed to them. (Watt 1994: 72; Abrahamov 1998: 7–9)

It seems that out of the awareness of unified teachings based on three reliable sources and dealt with by pious people, an opposition to any innovation (*bidʿa*, pl. *bidaʿ*) has emerged. The traditionalists believed that just as their doctrines derive from unchanged and definite principles, so innovations derive from different, changeable principles. The opposition to innovations took the form of prohibition against disputing with the innovators, speaking with them, and listening to their innovative views. The hostility toward the innovators was so immense that they were regarded as those who cannot repent of their innovations—unlike the polytheists who can repent of their sin—and that even those who sit with them are dangerous to Islam.

The innovators were ill-treated also because they did not obey the prohibition expressed in traditions that believers should not deal with metaphysical questions such as God's attributes and essence, and predestination (*qadar*). A tradition repeated in the traditionalists' writings is 'Think of God's creation and not of Him (or not of His essence)'. Another tradition interdicts treating the question of God's predetermination: 'Do not speak of anything relating to *qadar*, for it is God's secret, so do not disclose God's secret'. The Qadarites, those who believe in free will, were regarded as heretics and unbelievers and hence deserving the death penalty. As a result, the Muslim was forbidden to pray behind them, marry them, eat animals slaughtered by them, or accept their testimonies (Abrahamov 1998: 9–11).

A different approach to the innovators, which allows disputing with them, is discerned in the traditionalists' writings. ʿUmar b. al-Khaṭṭāb, the second caliph, is the source of a tradition according to which in future time people will dispute with the traditionalists by using the ambiguous verses of the Qurʾān (Q 3: 7). The tradition recommends that the believers should use traditions in order to refute such adversaries, because traditions, being definitive, are irrefutable and hence very useful in interpreting the Qurʾān and rejecting their opponents (Abrahamov 1998: 9–11).

The adherence of the traditionalists to the Qurʾān, the Sunna, and the consensus does not mean their neglecting the use of reason. However, contrary to the rationalists who base their doctrines on reason, reason in the traditionalists' view occupies the secondary place after the basic three sources of knowledge. Rational arguments serve as proofs of what was revealed in the Qurʾān and the Sunna. If these arguments were the basis of religion, say the traditionalists, then revelation and the prophets would become superfluous. Besides, people would search for the reasonability of every religious phenomenon or precept, though there are many religious matters for which reason cannot account. People are required to believe in God's attributes, in Paradise and Hell, in the punishment in the tomb (*ʿadhāb al-qabr*) even though the meaning of these cannot be perceived by reason.

The traditionalists' attitude toward reason as a device to prove religious principles led them to differentiate between two apparently similar terms, *taqlīd* and *ittibāʿ*. While *taqlīd* means blindly following scholars and teachings without supplying proofs, *ittibāʿ* is understood as adherence to doctrines through using proofs. The Qurʾān and the Sunna do not reject bringing proofs to their teachings in order to increase the certainty and tranquility of the soul (al-Taymī, *Ḥujja*, 2: 116f.). The proofs that many traditionalists brought were not only proofs from the Qurʾān and the Sunna but also rational proofs, sometimes even *kalām* arguments. When Ibn Ḥanbal (d. 241/855), no doubt an epitome of traditionalism, refuted the Jahmites who argued that God is everywhere, he first adduced verses from the Qurʾān to show that God is in one place, on the Throne (Q 7: 54, 20: 5). Then he argued that there are places which are not appropriate for God's greatness (*ʿiẓam*), such as the human being's body, which means that it is inconceivable for God to be there. Ibn Ḥanbal used the contradiction between the Jahmite approach of God's being everywhere and one of God's most beautiful names, His being the greatest (*al-aʿẓam*) to refute their view (Ibn Ḥanbal, *Radd*, 92f.). In this context Ibn Ḥanbal uses the *kalām* argument from disjunction (*qisma* or *taqsīm*) in which the adversary is confronted with a series of questions and at the end of this procedure he is forced to admit his failure (Ibn Ḥanbal, *Radd*, 95).

Another device used by the traditionalists is *istinbāṭ*, a logical argument based on a Qurʾān verse. One of the traditionalists' dogmas is the uncreatedness of the Qurʾān. They base their doctrine on Q 36: 82 which reads: 'His command, when He desires a thing, is to say to it "be" (*kun*) and it is.' Thus, God creates by uttering the word '*kun*'. This word is a part of God's speech considered by the Muʿtazilites to be created. Hence, a created being creates another created being which brings about an endless chain of creations, which is an absurdity (al-Lālakāʾī, *Sharḥ*, i. 217–18).

Linguistic considerations also play a role in the theological discussions of the traditionalists. The Muʿtazilites divide God's attributes into two types, viz. essential attributes (*ṣifāt al-dhāt*), which always exist in God, and attributes of action (*ṣifāt al-fiʿl*), which are applied to God only when He acts. Hence the attributes 'Creator', 'Provider', 'Benefactor', and so on refer to Him only after He creates, provides, and gives support, which means that they are not eternal. However, examples from linguistics show that the notion of attributes of action is not correct, for people say 'cutting knife', a 'satiating bread', and 'quenching water' as permanent attributes of these things even before their acts are carried out. Hence, the attributes 'Creator', 'Provider', and 'Benefactor' can be predicated of God before He creates, provides, and gives support (al-Taymī, *Ḥujja*, 1: 300f.).

The traditionalists emphasize the fact that the Qurʾān contains rational proofs of God's existence, His unity, prophecy, and the world to come. ʿAbd Allah b. al-ʿArabī (d. 543/1148) states that the Qurʾān introduces the principles of rational arguments in concise manner and in allusions, and that the function of the scholar is to extend and explain these arguments in detail. In his view another function of these arguments is to show the unbelievers and the innovators that using rational proofs does not appertain only to them. Using an *a fortiori* argument, the Qurʾān proves God's revivification of the dead in the next world by saying that for God who was able to create the world it will be easier to revive the dead (Q 17: 50). In like manner, whoever can cause the earth to give birth to plants, can revive the dead (Q 35: 9). In sum, reason plays an important role in the traditionalist theology, both as a device for demonstrating their beliefs and as a tool in their debates with unbelievers and innovators. Notwithstanding their reliance on reason, the traditionalists criticized the rationalist thinkers, because for the latter rational arguments often serve as the core of their theology (Abrahamov 1998: 17f.).

Whereas pure traditionalists rejected the use of rational arguments, their moderate colleagues used such arguments to prove God's existence, His unity, and attributes, whether they are based on the Qurʾān or not. However, the traditionalists criticized the rationalists for their adherence to rational arguments in order to prove the principles of religion, a criticism which deals with both the essence of their systems and their consequences. *Taʾwīl mukhtalif al-ḥadīth* by Ibn Qutayba (d. 276/889) is an early example of a traditionalist response to a rationalist censure of the contradictory nature of the Tradition. Ibn Qutayba accuses the *mutakallimūn* of holding contradictory and differing views on the principles of religion. In fact, he levelled the same accusation that was used against the traditionalists by the rationalists. Contemporary scholars of Ibn Qutayba, such as al-Dārimī (d. 280/893), pointed to the multifaceted nature of the rational arguments referring to Jahmite sects, each of which claimed that their principles are intelligible (Abrahamov 1998: 19f.).

In summing up the traditionalist attitude toward rational arguments Ibn Taymiyya states:

> The preference of rational arguments over traditional ones is impossible and unsound. As for the preference of the traditional proofs, it is possible and sound... that is on account of the fact that being known through reason or not is not an inherent attribute (*ṣifa lāzima*) of a thing but rather a relative one (*min al-umūr al-nisbiyya al-iḍāfiyya*), for Zayd may know through his reason what Bakr does not know, and a man may know at a certain time through his reason what he will not know at another time. (Abrahamov 1992: 259; 1998: 21)

In contrast to the stableness of the Tradition, states Ibn Taymiyya, reason is an unstable device and leads people to different and even contradictory approaches. In his view, remoteness from the Tradition and adhering to rationalist approaches cause disputes among the Muslims. Thus, he supports the notion of early traditionalist theologians on the homogeneity of traditionalism.

Doubts, perplexity, and mixture of truth and falseness also characterize the rational arguments. Furthermore, the use of these arguments does not accord with the common people and may lead to declaring them unbelievers (*takfīr al-ʿāmma*), for these people cling to the religion only through believing in the Qurʾān, the Sunna, and their ancestors (Abrahamov 1998: 20–3).

The traditionalists' criticism of the rationalists, mainly the *mutakallimūn*, caused the former to develop an unfavourable attitude toward the latter. The traditionalists' disapproval took the form not only of refutation of their tenets but also of prohibition against engaging in *kalām* and even breaking off relations with and excommunication of the *mutakallimūn*. This attitude is attested beginning from the second/eighth century. When the famous Baṣran traditionist Yūnus b. ʿUbayd (d. 138/756–7) heard that his son visited the Muʿtazilite *mutakallim* ʿAmr b. ʿUbayd (d. 144/761), disobeying his father's interdiction not to visit him, he said that it is better to meet God on the Day of Judgement with grave sins such as fornication, theft, and drinking wine than to meet Him with the Muʿtazilite views of ʿAmr b. ʿUbayd and his followers (al-Dāraquṭnī, *Akhbār*, 12).

Generally the traditionalists regard the ideas of free will, the creation of the Qurʾān, and the figurative interpretations of anthropomorphic expressions in the Qurʾān and the Sunna as deriving from rationalist circles, mainly the Muʿtazilites. These scholars were accused of abandoning the Qurʾān and the Sunna and their true interpretations, the views of the religious scholars, and of being impious. They were also accused of adhering to the teachings of the philosophers and of corrupting Islam. As a result, some traditionalist scholars called on people to excommunicate them or to punish them at one extreme, while others allowed disputing with them at the other. Such attitudes do not characterize a specific school of law—extremism or moderation in treating the rationalists exist in every branch of traditionalist learning (Abrahamov 1998: 27–31).

The body of the traditionalist religious doctrines is found in their creeds, which were written beginning from the mid-ninth century, and in treatises dedicated to theological notions, such as *al-Sharīʿa*, by Abū Bakr Muḥammad b. al-Ḥusayn al-Ājurrī (d. 360/970). Both the creeds and the treatises are imbued with polemics, whether implicit or explicit, against the 'sectarians' and the rationalist thinkers (very often the two groups are identical). As a sample of traditionalist dogma, we shall introduce the creed of Abū Zurʿa ʿUbayy Allah b. ʿAbd al-Karīm al-Rāzī (d. 264/878) and Abū Ḥātim Muḥammad b. Idrīs al-Rāzī (d. 277/890) as recorded by al-Lālakāʾī (*Sharḥ*, 1: 176–9).

The creed begins with the definition of belief, which is composed of action and speech and hence can be increased or decreased. This stand contradicts the extreme Murjiʾites who claimed that belief is only knowledge of God and His Messenger and what comes from God, that is, the Qurʾān (al-Ashʿarī, *Maqālāt*, 132). The Qurʾān in this creed is God's uncreated speech in all its aspects, that is, as a written text, as recited, and as memorized by heart. This dogma is directed against the Muʿtazilites who believed that the Qurʾān was created, and also against some groups of traditionalists who believed that certain aspects of the text are created. The third dogma which also opposes the rationalist approach is the belief in God's predestination of all things whether good or evil. At the end of the third/ninth century the theory of acquisition (*kasb*) had not yet been completed; the task of its completion would be left to al-Ashʿarī. Articles four and five are devoted to the best people of the Muslim community who are first the four caliphs in their historic succession and then ten individuals from among Muḥammad's companions whom the Prophet called the 'people of Paradise'. However, all his companions should be honoured. The rejection of anthropomorphism is expressed (article 6) through the question of God's place (on His Throne) in accordance with the *bi-lā kayfa* doctrine (Abrahamov 1995). However, seeing God in the Hereafter (article 7), a question which pertains to anthropomorphism, appears in its literal meaning ('people of Paradise will see Him with their eyes'), but with the qualification that it will occur in the manner God wills, thus allowing for something other than seeing with the eyes. Articles 8–13 are devoted to the phenomena of the world to come according to the Qurʾān and the Sunna: Paradise and Hell really exist. The way to paradise, the balance which weighs one's deeds, the basin (*al-ḥawḍ*) through which the Prophet will be honoured, the Prophet's intercession for sinners, and the resurrection are all true. Against the Muʿtazilites who regarded the grave sinners as unbelievers until they repent and the Khārijites who considered the grave sinners as unbelievers and even as polytheists, articles 14 and 15 adopted the Murjiʾite approach to the grave sinners which entrusts their judgement to God and denies the notion that grave sins cancel one's belief. The Murjiʾite lenient attitude toward the impious leaders of the community is expressed in articles 16–20. These articles call on the believer to obey the rulers, be they just or unjust, and to cooperate with them in carrying out the precepts for which they are responsible such as the Holy War (*jihād*) and the pilgrimage. The question of who is a believer is so important in the eyes of the scholars who composed this creed that they stressed the fact that one cannot declare himself to be a believer in the eyes of God, because one cannot know God's will and hence cannot know his status in God's eyes (article 21).

A group of articles (22–6) refers explicitly to 'sectarians' (Qadarites, Murjiʾites, Jahmites, Khārijites, and Rafiḍites) calling them innovators, deviators, unbelievers, and apostates, but does not always call attention to their doctrines. In this context some theological issues are repeated, but stressing different aspects. For example, the question of free will and predestination arises through God's foreknowledge. The Qadarites, whether by this appellation the early group of the second/eighth century is meant or here the term is used as a pejorative name of the Muʿtazilites, believed in free will and hence denied God's foreknowledge which impairs the human being's free will. Believing in God's absolute knowledge, the traditionalists could not deny this trait of God. Denial of God's foreknowledge amounts to unbelief. The issue of the Qurʾān is so important to our two scholars that they return to it at the end of the creed with four articles; here the text refers to those who hold inappropriate views regarding the Qurʾān. Thus, those who believe in the creation of the Qurʾān are named 'unbelievers', while those who do not know whether the Qurʾān was created or not, or state that their reciting of the Qurʾān is created are deemed 'Jahmites'.

The creed ends with a statement by Abū Muḥammad ʿAbd al-Raḥmān, the son of Abū Ḥātim, who cites his father as saying that the sign of the innovators (*ahl al-bidaʿ*) is their defaming of the traditionists (*ahl al-athar*). Other groups, the heretics (*zanādiqa*), the Jahmites, the Qadarites, the Murjiʾites, and the Rāfiḍites are characterized as opposing the tenets of the traditionalists by calling the latter inappropriate names.

Notwithstanding al-Lālakāʾī's statement that the teachings of the traditionalists are homogeneous, an examination of the ten creeds (eight of them are complete creeds) introduced in his book shows some differences (Abrahamov 1998: 54–7). For example, Ibn Ḥanbal opens his creed by setting forth the foundations of the Sunna: 'In our view, the principles of the Sunna are: "Adhering to the teachings of the Messenger's companions, following them and abandoning innovations. Each innovation is an error. One should abandon disputes and debates in religion and sitting with the people of the sects"' (al-Lālakāʾī, *Sharḥ*, 1: 156). Like Sufyān b. ʿUyayna (d. 196/811), ʿAlī b. ʿAbd Allāh al-Madīnī (d. 234/848) begins his creed with the belief in God's predetermination, be it good or evil, and then follows the belief in the traditions. An extraordinary article of belief is the notion that abandoning prayer is deemed unbelief to such an extent that whoever abandons prayer it is lawful to kill him. Also, he stresses the requirement that every Muslim must have a religious leader (*imām*) (al-Lālakāʾī, *Sharḥ*, 1: 155, 165–7).

In sum, despite some divergences between the creeds, there is a significant element of homogeneity in them which results from the adherence to the three principles put forth above, that is, the Qurʾān, the Sunna, and the consensus. Cleaving to these principles appears as an article of faith in many creeds. Another feature of the creeds is the polemics with the sectarians, which occupies much of the content. This shows that traditionalism has developed, *inter alia*, as a reaction to the teachings of 'the sects', mainly through rejection of the sects' doctrines, but sometimes through acceptance of and agreement with them, such as the attitude of the Murjiʾites toward the unjust ruler. In like manner, the Khārijite and the Muʿtazilite insistence on the importance of carrying out the religious commandments and of avoiding grave sins probably contributes to the inclusion of acts in the definition of belief.

The challenge of rationalism has not only created debates between traditionalists and rationalists, but has also produced compromise between the two approaches. Two areas of compromise may be identified:

a. Reason and Tradition are two separate devices, both serving to reach knowledge of certain religious principles. Sometimes the two devices are employed to prove a religious idea but from different points of view. Thus, according to the intellect, the resurrection is possible and its true existence is proved by the Sacred Texts.
b. Rational and traditional arguments do not contradict each other for both tools derive from God. God supplies human beings with two kinds of revelation, the Qurʾān and the rational arguments, hence there can be no contradiction between the two devices. For example, the denial of anthropomorphism is based both on Qurʾānic verses (Q 42: 11, 112: 1–4) which teach that God is unlike any thing, hence human forms or acts cannot be ascribed to Him, and on reason. Had God possessed the forms of created things, He would have been like the created things and could not have been a creator (Abrahamov 1998: 49–51, 60–2).

References

ʿAbd al-Jabbār al-Hamadānī (*Faḍl*). *Faḍl al-iʿtizāl wa-ṭabaqāt al-muʿtazila*. Ed. Fuʾād Sayyid. Tūnis: al-Dār al-Tūnisiyya li-l-Nashr, 1986.

Abrahamov, B. (1992). 'Ibn Taymiyya on the Agreement of Reason with Tradition'. *Muslim World* 82: 256–72.

Abrahamov, B. (1995). 'The *bi-lā kayfa* Doctrine and its Foundations in Islamic Theology'. *Arabica* 42: 365–79.

Abrahamov, B. (1998). *Islamic Theology: Traditionalism and Rationalism*. Edinburgh: Edinburgh University Press.

Adang, C. (2006). '"This Day I Have Perfected your Religion for You": A Ẓāhirī Conception of Religious Authority'. In G. Krämer and S. Schmidtke (eds.), *Speaking for Islam: Religious Authorities in Muslim Societies*. Leiden: Brill, 15–48.

Adang, C., M. Fierro, and S. Schmidtke (eds.) (2012). *Ibn Ḥazm of Cordoba: The Life and Work of a Controversial Thinker*. Leiden: Brill.

al-Ājurrī, Abū Bakr Muḥammad b. al-Ḥusayn (*Sharīʿa*). *Al-Sharīʿa*. Ed. Muḥammad Ḥāmid al-Fiqī. Beirut: Dār al-kutub al-ʿilmiyya, 1983.

Arberry, A. J. (1983). *The Koran Interpreted*. Oxford: Oxford University Press.

Arnaldez, R. (2006). 'Ibn Ḥazm'. *The Encyclopaedia of Islam*. New edn. iii. 790–4.

al-Ashʿarī, Abū l-Ḥasan (*Maqālāt*). *Maqālāt al-islāmiyyīn wa-ikhtilāf al-muṣallīn*. Ed. H. Ritter. Wiesbaden: Steiner, 1963.
Chejne, A. G. (1982). *Ibn Hazm*. Chicago: Kazi Publications.
Chejne, A. G. (1984). 'Ibn Ḥazm of Cordova on Logic'. *Journal of the American Oriental Society* 104: 57–72.
Cook, M. (1981). *Early Muslim Dogma: A Source-Critical Study*. Cambridge: Cambridge University Press.
Cook, M. (1987). 'ʿAnan and Islam: The Origins of Karaite Scripturalism'. *Jerusalem Studies in Arabic and Islam* 9: 161–82.
Coulson, N. J. (1978). *A History of Islamic Law*. Edinburgh: Edinburgh University Press.
Crone, P., and F. Zimmermann (2001). *The Epistle of Sālim Ibn Dhakwān*. Oxford: Oxford University Press.
al-Dāraquṭnī, ʿAlī b. ʿUmar (*Akhbār*). *Akhbār ʿAmr ibn ʿUbayd*. Ed., trans., and comm. J. van Ess (*Traditionistische Polemik gegen ʿAmr b. ʿUbayd*). Beirut: Orient Institut Beirut, 1967.
van Ess, J. (1991–7). *Theologie und Gesellschaft im 2. und 3. Jahrhundert Hidschra: Eine Geschichte des religiösen Denkens im frühen Islam*. 6 vols. Berlin: de Gruyter.
Goldziher, I. (2007). *The Ẓāhirīs: Their Doctrine and their History*. Trans. Wolfgang Behn. With an introduction by C. Adang. Leiden: Brill.
Hawting, G. R. (1978). 'The Significance of the Slogan *lā ḥukma illā li-llāh* and the References to the *ḥudūd* in the Traditions about the Fitna and the Murder of ʿUthmān'. *Bulletin of the School of Oriental and African Studies* 4: 453–62.
Hodgson, M. G. S. (1977). *The Venture of Islam: Conscience and History in a World Civilization I*. Chicago: University of Chicago Press.
Hourani, G. F. (1985). *Reason and Tradition in Islamic Ethics*. Cambridge: Cambridge University Press.
Ibn Ḥanbal (*Radd*). *Al-Radd ʿalā l-zanādiqa wa-l-jahmiyya*. In *ʿAqāʾid al-salaf*. Ed. ʿAlī Sāmī al-Nashshār and ʿAmmār al-Ṭālibī. Alexandria: al-Maʿārif, 1971.
Ibn Ḥazm (1983). *Al-Fiṣal fī l-milal wa-l-ahwāʾ wa-l-niḥal*. Beirut: Dār al-Maʿrifa.
al-Lālakāʾī, Abū l-Qāsim Hibat Allāh (*Sharḥ*). *Sharḥ uṣūl iʿtiqād ahl al-sunna wa-l-jamāʿa min al-kitāb wa-l-sunna wa-ijmāʿ al-ṣaḥāba wa-l-tābiʿīn min baʿḍihim*. Ed. Aḥmad Saʿd Ḥamdān. Mecca: Dār al-Ṭība, 1981.
Lewinstein, K. (1991). 'The Azāriqa in Islamic Heresiography'. *Bulletin of the School of Oriental and African Studies* 54: 251–68.
Melchert, C. (1997). *The Formation of the Sunni Schools of Law, 9th–10th Centuries C.E.* Leiden: Brill.
Mourad, S. A. (2006). *Early Islam between Myth and History: Al-Ḥasan al-Baārī (d. 110H/728CE) and the Formation of his Legacy in Classical Islamic Scholarship*. Leiden: Brill.
Ritter, H. (1933). 'Studien zur islamischen Frömmigkeit I: Ḥasan al-Baṣrī'. *Der Islam* 21: 1–83.
Schwarz, M. (1972). 'The Letter of al-Ḥasan al-Baṣrī'. *Oriens* 20: 15–20.
al-Taymī, Ismāʿīl b. Muḥamad (*Ḥujja*). *Al-Ḥujja fī bayān al-maḥajja wa-sharḥ ʿaqīdat ahl al-sunna*. Ed. Muḥammad b. Rabīʿ. Riyadh: Dār al-Rāya li-l-nashr wa-l-tawzīʿ, 1990.
Turki, A. M. (2010). 'Ẓāhiriyya'. *Encyclopaedia of Islam*. New edn. xi. 394.
Wansbrough, J. (1977). *Qurʾānic Studies*. Oxford: Oxford University Press.
Watt, W. M. (1948). *Free Will and Predestination in Early Islam*. London: Luzac & Company.
Watt, W. M. (1959–60). 'Created in his Image'. *Glasgow University Oriental Society* 18: 38–49.
Watt, W. M. (1994). *Islamic Creeds: A Selection*. Edinburgh: Edinburgh University Press.

CHAPTER 17

ḤANAFĪ THEOLOGICAL TRADITION AND MĀTURĪDISM

ULRICH RUDOLPH

Abū Ḥanīfa (d. 150/767) is generally acknowledged as an outstanding scholar of Islamic law.[1] As such, he is widely known both to Muslims and to scholars of Islamic studies, who have always emphasized his ground-breaking role as a jurist and his long-lasting impact in this field. It seems, however, that Abū Ḥanīfa's influence cannot be restricted to the domain of law. Apparently, he had a comprehensive view of religious knowledge; his efforts to gain 'insight' (which was the original meaning of *fiqh*) were not confined to ethical and juridical aspects but also included reflections on theological questions and the various articles of belief. In formulating his views on these topics, he laid the ground for two intellectual traditions: the Ḥanafī law school and, more or less distinct from it, the Ḥanafī theological tradition. The latter may not have been very prominent in the beginning, at least in comparison to its sister in law, but later on it developed into one of the most widespread and recognized Sunnī *kalām* schools.

The history of this *kalām* school is of considerable length and is dealt with in several chapters of this volume. Chapter 32 deals with theology in the Ottoman lands, whereas Chapter 39 will argue that there has never been one unique interpretation but always different 'interpretations of Ashʿarism amd Māturīdism among Mamluks and Ottomans. Before the Mamluks and the Ottomans arose, however, the Ḥanafī theological tradition was already subject to important intellectual challenges and transformations. Their history will be discussed in the following pages, which aim to describe what can be called 'the formative period' of the tradition, i.e. its development from Abū Ḥanīfa up to the sixth/twelfth century. We will focus our attention on three stages: (1) the formation of the Ḥanafī theological tradition and its spread in North-Eastern Iran, which took place during the late second/eighth and early third/ninth centuries; (2) the intellectual transformation of this tradition

[1] I would like to thank James Weaver for his valuable comments on an earlier version of this chapter.

due to Abū Manṣūr al-Māturīdī (d. 333/944), who elaborated and completely reformulated Ḥanafī theology by defending it against the claims of various other theological movements such as the Muʿtazilites; (3) the emergence of Māturīdism as a well-established *kalām* school by the late fifth/eleventh or early sixth/twelfth century. As I will argue, this final stage was due to the activities of a group of important Transoxanian theologians including Abū l-Yusr al-Pazdawī (d. 493/1100), Abū l-Muʿīn al-Nasafī (d. 508/1114), al-Ṣaffār al-Bukhārī (d. 533/1139), and Abū Ḥafṣ al-Nasafī (d. 537/1142), and can be explained historically as a reaction to the proliferation and increasing impact of the Ashʿarite school in North-Eastern Iran at that time.

I The Formation of the Ḥanafī Theological Tradition

Fortunately, Abū Ḥanīfa's theological reflections are quite well documented. Unlike in the case of law, where we have no record whatsoever of his own writings at our disposal, two short treatises in the discipline of theology have been transmitted in his name. Both of them have the literary form of an epistle (*risāla*), and both are addressed to a certain ʿUthmān al-Battī. As we are told by several sources (e.g. Ibn Ḥajar, *Tahdhīb*, 7: 153), al-Battī was a contemporary of Abū Ḥanīfa and seems to have belonged to the circles of *ḥadīth* transmitters, who, as a rule, were critical of his activities. Despite the obvious parallels, however, the two epistles cannot be considered as documents of equivalent status, for each of them has reached us in a different condition. As a result, the research up to now has viewed them in different ways.

One of the epistles (henceforth *Risāla 1*) was published in 1949 and consensus has always deemed it an authentic document. Already Schacht had asserted its authenticity (Schacht 1964: 100 n. 4), and his judgement has been reconfirmed repeatedly (Cook 1981: 30; Madelung 1988: 19; van Ess 1991–7: i. 193). The indications thereof are impressive and can be seen as adequate proof. Among them, there are several formal arguments (the broad transmission of the text which is extant in several manuscripts, its personal perspective and language, the lack of literary stylizations), as well as the fact that the content of *Risāla 1* fits perfectly into the religious terminology and intellectual world of the middle of the second/eighth century.

The second epistle (henceforth *Risāla 2*), by contrast, raises a number of serious questions. It is preserved in a unique manuscript that has recently been discovered. Furthermore, the extant text seems to be incomplete. The opening statements as well as the closing formulas are missing, such that they cannot serve us as a linguistic criterion for evaluating its authenticity. The content of the epistle, however, does fit in with what we know about Abū Ḥanīfa or, more precisely, the early Ḥanafī tradition. Nevertheless, as long as no further evidence comes to light, it seems appropriate to conclude that *Risāla 2* takes us into the historical and chronological vicinity of Abū Ḥanīfa without insisting that it can be definitely ascribed to him (van Ess 1991–7: i. 204, 206f.; Rudolph 1997b: 40, 43).

Notwithstanding this reservation, both epistles are very instructive in terms of their arguments and their dogmatic positions. *Risāla 1* deals mainly with the topic of belief and sin, or rather the position of believers and sinners. While discussing these issues, Abū Ḥanīfa makes a number of interesting statements, which can be summarized as follows: a believer is a person who testifies (*yashhadu*) to the one God and affirms (*iqrār*) the prophethood of Muḥammad; he can become disobedient (*ʿāṣin*) and make (sinful) mistakes without losing his belief. Duties (*farāʾiḍ*) and deeds (*aʿmāl*) do not belong to faith (*īmān*); they only enlarge upon the actual act of affirming (*taṣdīq*) the Prophet's message. Therefore, belief is equal among all believers, be they angels or humans. A believer without sins is awaited by Paradise, a disbeliever who sins is awaited by Hell; the decision concerning a believing sinner is left to God. As a consequence, we should leave the judgement of ʿUthmān and ʿAlī to God, since both of them were Muslims (*ahl al-qibla*) and Companions of the Prophet (van Ess 1991–7: i. 194–8; v. 25–8; Rudolph 1997b: 38f.).

The dogmatic positions expressed in these statements are essentially Murjiʾī. This could not remain unnoticed in the intellectual climate prevailing in Iraq during the second/eighth century. As Abū Ḥanīfa himself explains in *Risāla 1*, his epistle was already a piece of self-defence and justification: ʿUthmān al-Battī had asked him about his affiliation with the Murjiʾites and had accused him of propagating their ideas by affirming (that a sinner is) a 'believer who has gone astray' (*muʾmin ḍāll; Risāla 1*: 34 ult.). Abū Ḥanīfa's reaction to this accusation is quite nuanced. He does not deny sharing the convictions of that group but he contests that 'Murjiʾa' would be its right name. According to him, the term 'Murjiʾa' is nothing but a polemical denomination. It insinuates that its adherents were dangerous innovators. In reality, however, they abide by the Qurʾān and the Sunna (*Risāla 1*: 35, 2–3) and stand for justice, their right name being consequently 'the people of justice and tradition' (*ahl al-ʿadl wa-ahl al-sunna; Risāla 1*: 37, 9–38, 4; cf. van Ess 1991–7: i. 199f.).

Besides these explanations, Abū Ḥanīfa could have argued that his own theological reflections were not confined to the alleged 'Murjiʾī' positions. This becomes clear when the second epistle to ʿUthmān al-Battī (*Risāla 2*) mentioned above comes into play. Its focus is not a specifically 'Murjiʾī' theme. It is rather a topic which was widely discussed by several Muslim groups in the second/eighth century (including, probably, the Islamic jurists). This is the question of free will and determination.

As Abū Ḥanīfa (or rather, the author of the second epistle) explains, he wants to avoid a radical answer to this question. Therefore he hastens to distance himself as much from 'the people of delegation' (*ahl al-tafwīḍ*), i.e. those who assigned humans power over the entirety of their deeds, as from 'the people of coercion' (*ahl al-ijbār*), i.e. the determinists who reserved for God all power over human actions (van Ess 1991–7: v. 34; Rudolph 1997b: 44). What he is seeking, instead, is a kind of a mediating perspective between these two positions, as he considers each of them to be extreme and one-sided. In fact, this search was not really new. As far as we know, it was shared by several other religious strands of the second/eighth century such as the Ibāḍites and the Kūfan Shīʿites (van Ess 1991–7: i. 205). The conceptualization of the idea of a 'middle way' in *Risāla 2* seems, however, to be quite original and to have some specific Ḥanafī connotations. The main arguments of the text read as follows: God has created all people and has shown all people (i.e. not only Muslims) the way to obedience. By doing so, He gave them responsibility for their deeds or, as the text puts it, 'He enjoined the argument (*ḥujja*) upon them'. Later on, He revealed the Qurʾān as a (final) proof and constituted the limbs of humans such that they function both as the means by which they act (*yaʿmalūna*), and the basis upon which they can be brought to reckoning (*yuḥāsabūna wa-yusʾalūna*). However, nothing can be done by humans and nothing can occur in this world unless God Himself wills it. If a human being intends (*nawā*) something good, then God lets it happen with His power and His divine assistance (*tawfīq*) and rewards him for it. If the person, in contrast, intends something bad, then God either forsakes him (*khadhalahu*) because of His justice (so that the sin can take place), or He keeps him from doing the bad deed due to his grace. Thus nothing can happen without God freeing the way (*takhliyya*) and having decided (*ḥukm*) on a course of action. Yet, the basis upon which a person may be blamed derives from himself, since God demands of His servants to do only those things that He has put them in a condition to do (van Ess 1991–7: i. 205; v. 34f.; Rudolph 1997b: 44f.).

Reflections about a 'middle way' between determinism and free will, as expressed in *Risāla 2*, later became a specific feature of Ḥanafī theology. In combination with the ideas about faith and sin which were exposed in *Risāla 1* they can be considered as the nucleus of the theological tradition which was linked to Abū Ḥanīfa's name. This tradition developed successfully in the decades after his death but, interestingly enough, it did not develop in Iraq where Abū Ḥanīfa had himself lived. The reason seems to be that, in this region, the Murjiʾites rapidly lost their good standing in the course of the second/eighth century (van Ess 1991–7: i. 221–33) and, despite his explanations and justifications, Abū Ḥanīfa was publicly notorious for his sympathy towards them. Yet matters were conducted completely differently in another geographical region, namely in North-Eastern Iran and in Transoxania. In that part of the Islamic world, the Murjiʾites had established themselves as a leading religious movement by the early second/eighth century, and scholars admired Abū Ḥanīfa for adhering to their ideas. In search of further advice, many of them went to Kūfa in order to study with him before returning to their homes. As a result, Abū Ḥanīfa's theological ideas spread widely in North-Eastern Iran and in Transoxania, which, by the end of the second/eighth century, became the new homeland of the Ḥanafī theological tradition and remained thus for many centuries to come (Madelung 1982; Madelung 1988: 14–20; Rudolph 1997b: 25–30).

Some of the scholars who contributed to this process are mentioned by name in our historical and biographical sources. This applies in particular to Abū Muqātil al-Samarqandī (d. 208/823) and Abū Muṭīʿ al-Balkhī (d. 199/814), who were probably the most eminent transmitters of Ḥanafī thought to the East. Both of them seem to have studied in Kūfa with Abū Ḥanīfa. At any rate, both of them wrote important treatises which were explicitly meant to spread his theological ideas. Abū Muqātil is the author of the *Kitāb al-ʿĀlim wa-l-mutaʿallim* which later on became a textual source for many Ḥanafī and Māturīdī authors (van Ess 1991–7: ii. 560–2; Rudolph 1997b: 45–52), whereas Abū Muṭīʿ wrote an equally influential book known as *al-Fiqh al-absaṭ* (van Ess 1991–7: ii. 536–9; Rudolph 1997b: 57–60).

The *Kitāb al-ʿĀlim wa-l-mutaʿallim* has the literary form of a dialogue between a master and his student. The student, nobody other than Abū Muqātil himself, is in search of knowledge and asks a series of questions which are answered extensively by his teacher, i.e. Abū Ḥanīfa. In the course of their conversation, they touch upon several themes which have already been dealt with in the first epistle to ʿUthmān al-Battī. Abū Ḥanīfa explains his definition of belief (affirmation and confession, but no deeds), the axiom of equality of belief among angels and humans, and the concept that judgement about believing sinners should be left solely to God. However, the schematization of the *Kitāb al-ʿĀlim wa-l-mutaʿallim* is more elaborate and much more differentiated than *Risāla 1*. Argumentation with those who think differently has grown stronger, especially when the opponents are from the Khārijī camp. A further novelty is that practical piety, in particular the worship of God (*ʿibāda*), takes a more prominent position. Finally, right at the beginning of the work, we find a long justification of the activity of rational theological speculation itself, the claims of which go far beyond the few methodological observations to be found in *Risāla 1* (Rudolph 1997b: 53–7; cf. van Ess 1991–7: i. 200–4).

Compared to the *Kitāb al-ʿĀlim wa-l-mutaʿallim*, the *Fiqh al-absaṭ* is formally much less coherent. In its preserved state, the text reveals various jumps in thematization and inconsistencies in structure and terminology. This truly justifies the assumption that it was reworked later, maybe even more than once, and that its original form differed from the one available today (van Ess 1986; Rudolph 1997b: 60–8). These difficulties notwithstanding, the general outline and argumentation of the *Fiqh al-absaṭ* fit very well within the corpus of texts which we have considered up to now. In almost all its parts, the treatise elaborates on topics which have already been touched upon in *Risāla 1* (viz. the *Kitāb al-ʿĀlim wa-l-mutaʿallim*) and in *Risāla 2*. These are, to recapitulate, the definition of belief, the equality of belief among angels and humans, the condition of the sinner, the recompense in the afterlife, the postponement of the judgement about believing sinners, and the assertion of a middle way between determinism and free will. Among these issues, the author pays particular attention to the last, introducing new details and arguments such as the concept of human capacity (*istiṭāʿa; Fiqh absaṭ*, 43, 5–7). Apart from that, the text presents some topics new to the Ḥanafī tradition, such as the principle of commanding right and forbidding wrong (*al-amr bi-l-maʿrūf wa-l-nahy ʿan al-munkar*) and the question of the ontological status of the divine attributes. Unfortunately, however, the discussion of the latter is part of a chapter which seems to be heavily reworked and whose authenticity is thus subject to doubt (Rudolph 1997b: 68–77; cf. van Ess 1991–7: i. 207–11).

At any rate, specific *kalām* topics such as God's essence and His attributes were not at the centre of Khurāsānian and Transoxanian Ḥanafī theology during the third/ninth century. It continued rather to focus on issues which had already been raised by Abū

Ḥanīfa in the century before. By following this course, the Eastern Ḥanafites established a strong theological tradition which finally became the most important religious movement in the region. This is confirmed by the fact that the Sāmānid governors of Khurāsān and Transoxania decided to adopt it as their official doctrine at the beginning of the fourth/tenth century, once their rule had been firmly established.

One of them ordered a Ḥanafī scholar named al-Ḥakīm al-Samarqandī (d. 342/953) to summarize the principles of faith in a kind of catechism. As a result, al-Ḥakīm offered him a text entitled *al-Radd ʿalā aṣḥāb al-ahwāʾ al-musammā Kitāb al-Sawād al-aʿẓam ʿalā madhhab al-imām Abī Ḥanīfa* (Madelung 1982: 39; Madelung 1988: 30; for details cf. the introduction to the Persian version of the *Sawād*). According to its title, the text appears to be a heresiography, and it does, in fact, contain a long list of sects which are to be refuted (van Ess 2011: i. 448–53). But in its main bulk, the *Kitāb al-Sawād al-aʿẓam* is nothing but a creed (*ʿaqīda*) which presents—with some minor modifications—all the Ḥanafī dogmas and convictions which we have already encountered in the previous texts (belief, the position of the sinner, free will and predestination, the judgement about the companions of the prophet, eschatology, promise and threat in the afterlife, the community, the Qurʾān, as well as some statements about God and His attributes). As such, it further served as an official presentation of the 'orthodox' doctrine in Sāmanīd lands, where it circulated in Arabic and, from the late fourth/tenth century onward, also in a Persian translation (Rudolph 1997b: 106–31; cf. van Ess 1991–7: ii. 564f.).

II The Transformation of Ḥanafī Theology by Abū Manṣūr al-Māturīdī (d. 333/944)

When al-Ḥakīm al-Samarqandī composed his creed, however, Ḥanafī theology was no longer a unified tradition. It was already on the verge of diversification and was developing into different interpretations and strands. This does not mean that the *Kitāb al-Sawād* was an anachronistic text; it certainly gave an adequate description of mainstream Ḥanafism, at least as it was understood in North-Eastern Iran and Transoxania. Yet, at the edges of this mainstream, new tendencies were emerging, which, in the long run, affected Ḥanafism in general, and which paved the way for new interpretations of its heritage, e.g. by Abū Manṣūr al-Māturīdī.

One of these elements was the emergence of a Ḥanafī *kalām* school in Western Iran, more precisely in Rayy. This was the result of the activities of Abū ʿAbd Allāh al-Ḥusayn al-Najjār (d. *c.*220/835). He and his students, among them another leading scholar named al-Burghūth (d. 240/855 or 241/856), developed a refined theological doctrine, which combined Ḥanafī convictions with teachings that were obviously taken from the Muʿtazilites, in particular from Ḍirār b. ʿAmr (van Ess 1991–7: iv. 147–70). This event appears to have been largely irrelevant to earlier Eastern Ḥanafites. Compared to al-Najjār's teaching, their own doctrines were more loyal to Abū Ḥanīfa's ideas, and overall, *kalām* discussions were not their main interest. In the long run, however, as *kalām* came ever more into the focus of the Transoxanian Ḥanāfites, they had to take into account what the Najjāriyya had taught (Rudolph 1997b: 180–3).

Another element of some importance in this context was the emergence of the Karrāmites. Based on the teachings of Ibn Karrām (d. 255/869), who hailed from Sīstān, they developed a new model of religious insight and practical piety which was attractive for many believers in Eastern Iran (van Ess 1991–7: iv. 609f.). Of course, some of the ideas propagated by the Karrāmites were inspired by Sufism. In theological matters, however, as well as in law, they were essentially an offspring of Ḥanafism (Madelung 1988: 40–2; Rudolph 1997b: 84–6). As such, the group became a prominent rival of traditional Ḥanafism in the region, which encouraged the latter to react against this challenge by refining its own doctrines and arguments.

A further point which should be considered here concerns the internal development of Khurāsānian and Transoxanian Ḥanafism. For it may well be that its diversification into different factions and strands had occurred earlier than is generally admitted in modern research. Unfortunately, we do not have any theological works written by Ḥanafī scholars from North-East Iran and Transoxania during the third/ninth century (Rudolph 1997b: 78–80). Up to now, we only know from later biographical sources that some of them—as, for instance, Abū Naṣr al-ʿIyāḍī (d. about 277/890), who was one of the teachers of al-Māturīdī—were interested in theological matters and may even have written on *kalām* topics (Rudolph 1997b: 145–9). Recently, however, a manuscript has been discovered in Istanbul (MS Şehid Ali Paşa 1648/II, fols 18a–168b) containing a commentary on Abū Salama al-Samarqandī's *Jumal uṣūl al-dīn* (for this book, see Section III). According to this commentary, two different Ḥanafī strands existed in third/ninth-century Samarqand: one being *kalām*-oriented and represented by scholars such as Abū Sulaymān al-Juzjānī and Abū Naṣr al-ʿIyāḍī who would have taught in a school named 'Dār al-Juzjāniyya', the other one being against *kalām* and represented by traditionalist authors such as Abū Bakr and Abū Aḥmad al-ʿIyāḍī (i.e. two sons of Abū Naṣr) and al-Ḥakīm al-Samarqandī (von Kügelgen and Muminov 2012: 282–7; Ak 2012: 436–46). This assertion is remarkable and will require additional substantiation from our sources. Nevertheless, it opens a new perspective which should be pursued by further research.

Apart from these developments, all of which were connected in one way or another with Ḥanafism, mention must be made finally of another event—the arrival or, strictly speaking, the return to North-East Iran of the famous Muʿtazilī thinker Abū l-Qāsim al-Kaʿbī (d. 319/931). This event was, of course, external to Ḥanafī history and, in a certain way, it was accidental but its impact on Transoxanian Ḥanafism can hardly be overestimated. Al-Kaʿbī originated from Balkh but he studied theology with al-Khayyāṭ (d. at the end of the third/ninth century) who introduced him to the doctrines of the Muʿtazilī School of Baghdad. Afterwards, he returned to Iran, working as a secretary first in Ṭabaristān and finally in Balkh (van Ess 2011: 328f.; cf. el-Omari 2006: 108–15). In his homeland, he became a celebrated theologian and teacher. This was even acknowledged by al-Māturīdī who explained at one point in his *Kitāb al-Tawḥīd* that the Muʿtazilites considered al-Kaʿbī 'the Imam of (all) the people of the world' (*imām ahl al-arḍ*; *Tawḥīd*, 78, 6). Of course, this was an ironic remark, but it also reveals a kind of respect. Obviously, al-Māturīdī felt challenged by the teaching of his rival. Therefore it is no surprise that his writings are impregnated with allusions to al-Kaʿbī's teachings and sometimes even appear to be an extensive and subtle defence of Ḥanafī theological thought against the latter.

In contrast to his opponent, al-Māturīdī seems never to have left his home town. As far as we are informed by later historians and biographers, he was born in Samarqand (possibly around 257/870) and died there in 333/944. Apart from that, we know next to nothing about his life and his career. This probably means that there was nothing sensational or unconventional to report (Cerić 1995: 17–23; Rudolph 1997b: 135–43). Much more information is given about his writings. They covered a wide range of topics including theology, Qurʾānic exegesis, polemics against the Muʿtazilites (*Bayān wahm al-Muʿtazila, Radd al-uṣūl al-khamsa, Radd Awāʾil al-adilla li-l-Kaʿbī, Radd Kitāb al-Kaʿbī fī waʿīd al-fussāq*) and the Imāmites (*Radd Kitāb al-Imāma li-baʿḍ al-Rawāfiḍ*), doxography or rather heresiography (*Kitāb al-Maqālāt*), law (*Maʾkhadh al-sharāʾiʿ*), and the art of disputation (*Kitāb al-Jadal, Radd Tahdhīb al-jadal li-l-Kaʿbī*) (Cerić 1995: 35–61; Rudolph 1997b: 198–201; Daccache 2008: 39–41; cf. van Ess 2011: 447f.). This alone demonstrates that al-Māturīdī was not a narrowly traditional religious author but an academic scholar trained in all disciplines belonging to higher theological education. Unfortunately, most of his writings are lost. However, two books which can be considered his *chefs d'œuvre* are fortuitously extant. These are his extensive commentary on the Qurʾān, entitled *Taʾwīlāt al-Qurʾān* or, in some other sources, *Taʾwīlāt ahl al-sunna*, and his still more important work on *kalām*, the *Kitāb al-Tawḥīd*.

The text of the *Taʾwīlāt al-Qurʾān* is preserved in more than thirty manuscripts. It thus seems probable that it was much read and appreciated by later scholars, in particular during the Ottoman period (Götz 1965). Modern scholarship has repeatedly confirmed its importance and its originality (Rahman 1982; Gilliot 2004; cf. van Ess 1991–7: v. 446, 453) but up to now, the commentary has been scarcely subject to research (cf. however Rofiq 2009). This may be due to its immense size and to the fact that—after the appearance of some fragmentary editions and unreliable printings—it has only recently become accessible in a complete critical edition (*Taʾwīlāt*).

The *Kitāb al-Tawḥīd*, in contrast, is preserved in only one manuscript (MS Cambridge Univ. Library Add 3651). The extant copy is littered with errors and furthermore seems to be incomplete (Gimaret 1980: 175–8). Nevertheless, the book has been edited twice, once in 1970 by Kholeif and again in 2003 by Topaloğlu and Aruçi (*Tawḥīd*). As a consequence, it has found the attention of scholarship and has been subject to several examinations, both in articles and in monographs (Cerić 1995; Rudolph 1997b; Daccache 2008).

According to these surveys, the *Kitāb al-Tawḥīd* must be considered as a true theological *summa*. Its structure is completely different from all the Ḥanafī writings which have been mentioned. Instead, it follows essentially the pattern of *kalām* works that had been developed by the Muʿtazilites in the early third/ninth century (Rudolph 1997b: 221–45; Daccache 2008: 49–67). It may even be that al-Māturīdī was inspired by a particular Muʿtazilī treatise, viz. the *Kitāb al-Tawḥīd* written by Muḥammad Ibn Shabīb (who died in the middle of the third/ninth century)—an author who is apparently his source when he presents doxographical and heresiographical material. However, Ibn Shabīb's book being lost, this can only be a conjecture which we are unable to prove (Rudolph 1997b: 251–3; cf. van Ess 2011: 163–5). Another striking feature of al-Māturīdī's *Tawḥīd* is the extensive space given to discussions with theological opponents. Again, this is in marked distinction to other early Ḥanafī writings including even the *Kitāb al-Sawād al-aʿẓam* of his contemporary al-Ḥakīm al-Samarqandī, which after all claimed to be a *Radd ʿalā aṣḥāb al-ahwāʾ* ('Refutation of the sectarians'). The list of opponents attacked by al-Māturīdī is indeed long. It encompasses numerous non-Islamic religions and worldviews, such as the Jews, Christians (Griffith 2011), Dualists of different types (Zoroastrians, Manicheans, Marcionites, and followers of Bardesanes), the Hellenistic philosophical legacy summed up in the word *dahriyya* (the alleged head of which was Aristotle), and further individuated groups ('Sumaniyya', 'Sophists', Sabeans). His main targets, however, were Muslim thinkers who held differing opinions. As such, al-Kaʿbī, Muḥammad Ibn Shabīb, al-Najjār, and the Ismāʿīlī thinker Muḥammad b. Aḥmad al-Nasafī (executed in Bukhara in 332/943) were of particular interest for him, but he does also mention Jahm b. Ṣafwān, Muqātil b. Sulaymān, al-Burghūth, al-Naẓẓām, Jaʿfar b. Ḥarb, al-Aṣamm, and some others by name (Rudolph 1997b: 162–97; cf. Daccache 2008: 39–43).

Before arguing with his opponents, al-Māturīdī explains the principles of his own epistemology (*Tawḥīd*, 3–21). As was common practice in early *kalām*, he presupposes the existence of three means to gain knowledge (*asbāb al-ʿilm*), namely sense perception (*ʿiyān*), revelation/tradition (*akhbār*), and rational speculation (*naẓar*). Already in this opening part of the *Tawḥīd*, however, one can detect a particular Ḥanafī note insofar as the importance of rational speculation is much more stressed than was usually done by Sunni thinkers of that period. According to al-Māturīdī, we are able to know God's existence and to recognize what is good and what is bad without access to revelation, i.e. solely by means of intellect. This conviction he shared with Abū Ḥanīfa, while it was completely alien, for instance, to al-Ashʿarī (Rudolph 1992: 78–85; Cerić 1995: 67–74; Daccache 2008: 119–121; cf. Nasir 2005).

The second issue to be discussed in the *Tawḥīd* is the (meta)physical structure of the created world (*Tawḥīd*, 25–33; cf. 62–9 and 162–3). What al-Māturīdī has to say about this topic, however, is rather short and not entirely clear. Evidently, he did not subscribe to atomism, which is astonishing as this theory was already accepted by most of his contemporaries. Instead he maintains that every corporeal being is composed of 'natures' (*ṭabāʾiʿ*), by which he probably meant the four natural qualities, viz. heat, cold, moisture, and dryness. Their specificity is apparently to repel each other. As a consequence, they would always remain separate had God not unified them and bound them into bodies. Apart from 'natures', al-Māturīdī presupposes the existence of 'accidents' (*aʿrāḍ*), which are probably meant to constitute the changing attributes (motion, rest, colour, etc.) of 'natural' bodies. But all of this is not really explained in detail in the *Tawḥīd* so that we need further evidence—perhaps from the recently edited *Taʾwīlāt*—in order to better understand his physical doctrine (cf. so far Frank 1974; Rudolph 1997b: 268–91; Dhanani 2012).

In contrast, his reflections on God and the divine attributes are extremely detailed and well structured. They constitute by far the largest section in the *Tawḥīd* and include chapters on his own positions and arguments, as well as extensive refutations of Muslim rivals and of infidels (*Tawḥīd*, 34–268). According to his presentation, God's most important characteristics are His oneness, His complete otherness, His freedom (*ikhtiyār*), power, will, knowledge, and creation or rather 'existentiation' (*takwīn*). The latter is understood as an eternal, divine attribute of action—which is again a particular feature of Ḥanafī and Māturīdī theology as opposed to all other Muslim schools (Cerić 1995: 187–93; Rudolph 1997: 311–18; Daccache 2008: 327–31). Apart from these considerations, the *Tawḥīd* contains a short but extremely interesting discussion on God's wisdom (*ḥikma*). It reveals that the conceptual framework of al-Māturīdī's theology is highly original and differs fundamentally from the theological concepts both of the Muʿtazilites and of al-Ashʿarī. As he explains, God has the absolute power and freedom to create what he wills and to 'set' (*waḍaʿa*) everything according to His rules. This includes God's freedom to define what is 'good' and 'bad' which, according to al-Māturīdī, are not objective norms. On the other hand, God is perfectly wise and just. Thus, He never acts arbitrarily but 'puts everything in its (specific, i.e. right) place' (*waḍaʿa kulla shayʾin mawḍiʿahu; Tawḥīd*, 152,1 2; 170 ult.; 181, 2; 192 ult.). As a result, the created world is a perfect order, the ontological structure and the moral norms of which are accessible to rational understanding (Rudolph 1997b: 330–4; Rudolph 2012).

God's wisdom comes also into play when al-Māturīdī discusses the next issue, namely prophethood (*Tawḥīd*, 271–340). According to him, the prophets have not just instituted religion, but have also been beneficial for the cultural development of mankind. This idea had already been exposed in detail by the late third/ninth-century Muʿtazilī 'dissident' Ibn al-Rāwandī (van Ess 1991–7: iv. 320–6), and interestingly enough al-Māturīdī does not hesitate to cite him in this context (van Ess 1991–7: vi. 462–4; Rudolph 1997b: 176–8).

The remaining parts of the *Tawḥīd* deal with human actions and their relationship to God's all-encompassing activity (*Tawḥīd*, 343–514), sin and punishment (*Tawḥīd*, 517–98), and belief (*Tawḥīd*, 601–42). All of these topics had been extensively discussed already in previous Ḥanafī texts. Therefore it is no surprise that, in these chapters, al-Māturīdī advocates mostly the same theses as the theologians before him. Still, the form of his presentation is different, and sometimes he also modifies the traditional Ḥanafī doctrines by introducing new conceptual elements into them. This applies especially to his discussion of human actions, which is particularly refined and comprises several new interpretations, for instance of human free choice (*ikhtiyār*) and of man's capacity (*istiṭā ʿa* or *qudra*) or rather man's capacities to act—one being the permanent capacity provided by man's physical constitution (*istiṭāʿat al-asbāb wal-aḥwāl*) and the other one the momentary actual 'capacity of acting' (*istiṭāʿat al-fiʿl*) (Cerić 1995: 208–23; Rudolph 1997b: 336–43; cf. Daccache 2008: 335–8).

III The Emergence of Māturīdism

In the long run, al-Māturīdī's teaching transformed Ḥanafī thought deeply, yet this transformation did not occur immediately following his lifetime but required a long process. Its trajectory may be broken up into three distinctive phases which will be sketched out here by way of conclusion. The first phase, which continued until the end of the fourth/tenth century, is mainly characterized by the fact that nothing of importance for the further development of the school took place. Of course, al-Māturīdī had followers, as did every prestigious *shaykh*. The most remarkable among them was Abū Salama al-Samarqandī, to whom we owe a kind of summary of the *Kitāb al-Tawḥīd*, namely the book entitled *Jumal uṣūl al-dīn*. The majority of the Ḥanafī scholars living in Transoxania in the second half of the fourth/tenth century, however, did not really take note of al-Māturīdī. On the contrary, they continued to follow the traditional understanding of religion which had already been earlier cultivated in the region. The best example for this is probably Abū l-Layth al-Samarqandī (d. 373/983), who published many works on theological themes. Among them are a creed (*ʿAqīda*), an extensive Qurʾān commentary (*Tafsīr*), and several popular texts such as the *Bustān al-ʿārifīn* and the *Tanbīh al-ghāfilīn*. Nowhere in these works, however, is al-Māturīdī's name mentioned. Instead, Abū l-Layth professes a creed which corresponds to the standard already found in al-Ḥakīm al-Samarqandī's *Kitāb al-Sawād al-aʿẓam*. Consequently, it was still possible in the late fourth/tenth century to be a good Ḥanafī without delving into the specific topics of *kalām*, which is probably because at that time no particular theological challenge was present in Transoxania (Rudolph 1997a: 397f.; Rudolph 1997b: 357).

This changed only at the turn of the fifth/eleventh century, whence begins the second phase of the development, which is marked by the fact that the Transoxanian Ḥanafites became aware of the Ashʿarite school. Indeed, the Ashʿarites, to a certain extent, had established themselves on their doorstep. From the end of the fourth/tenth century onward, one of their intellectual centres was Nishapur, which, with scholars such as Ibn Fūrak (d. 406/1015) and al-Isfarāyīnī (d. 418/1027), could boast of two important spokesmen. It was just a matter of time before both parties would take note of one another. If the sources do not mislead us, this happened by the middle of the fifth/eleventh century at the latest. At that time the Ashʿarite author Abū Bakr al-Fūrakī (d. 478/1085) documents 'the theologians of Transoxania' (Götz 1965: 50 n. 3). Around the same time, the Ashʿarites are mentioned in a work by a Transoxanian theologian, namely the *Tamhīd fī bayān al-tawḥīd* by Abū Shakūr al-Sālimī (*Tamhīd*, fo. 41a: 1–3). The mood between the groups was apparently hardened from the beginning. Each of them reproached the other one for maintaining wrong ideas about God's attributes of action, in particular existentiation (*takwīn*). For both parties, however, there was still a commonality which is of interest in our context: neither al-Fūrakī nor Abū Shakūr al-Sālimī referred to the *Kitāb al-Tawḥīd* or mentioned al-Māturīdī by name (Rudolph 1997a: 398f.; Rudolph 1997b: 357f.).

This is reserved for the third phase of the process, which can be placed at the end of the fifth/eleventh century. This period was particularly eventful, since the dispute with the Ashʿarites became a dominating motif in the theology of the Transoxanian Ḥanafites, and finally led them to view al-Māturīdī as their decisive authority. How this happened is reported to us by two eminent Ḥanafī authors. One of them, Abū l-Yusr al-Pazdawī (d. 493/1100), tells us that the debate on the attribute 'existentiation' (*takwīn*) became more and more intense. According to him, the Ashʿarite camp argued aggressively against the Transoxanians, but the Transoxanian position—that God is to be described eternally as Creator—was superior to their doctrine. In order to substantiate his own view, al-Pazdawī presents a further argument which is most interesting in our context, namely that Abū Manṣūr al-Māturīdī had already professed the eternity of the attribute of 'existentiation', and in so doing was following the traditional Ḥanafī position (*Uṣūl*, 70, 5ff.).

The second report is much more detailed. It is given by Abū l-Muʿīn al-Nasafī (d. 508/1114), who can be considered the most eminent Ḥanafī scholar of that period and the real founder of the Māturīdī school. As he explains, three Ashʿarite authors are responsible for presenting vehement attacks against the Transoxanian Ḥanafites. Two of them launched only a short polemic against them, but the third was striking in his persistence and impertinence. According to him, the Transoxanians were blaspheming innovators since what they said about the attribute 'existentiation' was not professed by any of the pious forebears (*al-salaf*), but rather was a recently invented heresy, which only arose after 400/1010 in North-Eastern Iran (*Tabṣira*, 1: 310, 8–316, 10). In order to refute these attacks, Abū l-Muʿīn gives a long list of arguments (*Tabṣira*, 1: 316–72; cf. Madelung 2000: 324–30). Interestingly, one of them is an extensive excursus into the history of the Eastern Ḥanafī school (*Tabṣira*, 1: 356, 6–361, 8). It starts off by saying that in the entirety of Transoxania and Khurāsān, all the leading heads of Abū Ḥanīfa's followers (*aʾimmat aṣḥāb Abī Ḥanīfa*) had held from the beginning to the same views on God's attributes as he himself held. This can be proven by a continuous chain of scholars starting with Abū Ḥanīfa and continuing through the generations on to the end of the fourth/tenth century. The most important of all these scholars, according to Abū l-Muʿīn, was al-Māturīdī. He is supposed to have been the most knowledgeable person concerning the views of Abū Ḥanīfa (*aʿraf al-nās bi-madhāhib Abī Ḥanīfa; Tabṣira*, 1: 162, 2–3) and to have advocated his doctrines in a particularly brilliant and perspicacious manner, such that had there been among the Ḥanafī theologians only Abū Manṣūr al-Māturīdī, this would have sufficed. For whoever surveyed his achievements could only come to the conclusion that God singled him out with miracles (*karāmāt*), gifts of grace (*mawāhib*), divine assistance (*tawfīq*), and guidance (*irshād, tasdīd*). This is so because in the normal course of things (*fī l-ʿādāt al-jāriya*) many scholars altogether do not possess the knowledge which was assembled in him alone (*Tabṣira*, 1: 358, 15–359, 14).

Abū l-Muʿīn, it is true, was not thoroughly hostile to the Ashʿarite school. His attitude to them depends rather on the topic under discussion. He criticizes them heavily when discussing the divine attribute of 'existentiation' (*takwīn*) but is quite respectful when he presents, for instance, their doctrine on God's justice, determinism, and free will (Madelung 2000: 320–4). Nevertheless, the rivalry between the two camps is indisputable. It appears to have led Abū l-Muʿīn to emphasize the continuity and the seniority of the Eastern Ḥanafī school and to insist on the pre-eminence of its outstanding representative, viz. Abū Manṣūr al-Māturīdī. As a matter of fact, he quotes al-Māturīdī most frequently in his own works and only rarely deviates from his teachings. The only detectable doctrinal difference seems to be that Abū l-Muʿīn did not accept al-Māturīdī's teaching about 'natures' (*ṭabāʾiʿ*) as being the components of sensible bodies; instead he subscribed to the more common atomistic model (*Tabṣira*, 1/44–60), which had already been favoured by Abū Shakūr al-Sālimī (*Tamhīd*, fols 24b–26a) and Abū l-Yusr al-Pazdawī (*Uṣūl*, 11f.). In most of the other issues, in contrast, Abū l-Muʿīn follows unconditionally al-Māturīdī's teaching, expounding it often more clearly and elegantly than he himself had done in the *Kitāb al-Tawḥīd*. This not only applies to his major work, the *Tabṣirat al-adilla*, but also to his *Tamhīd li-qawāʿid al-tawḥīd* and his *Baḥr al-kalām*, which presented the same ideas in abbreviated versions and thereby helped to gain them a wider public.

Abū l-Muʿīn's example was followed by many Transoxanian scholars. From the beginning of the fifth/eleventh century onward they produced numerous *kalām* works and creeds in order to express the convictions of the group they still called 'the followers of Abū Ḥanīfa' (*aṣḥāb Abī Ḥanīfa*), but what had in fact become the Māturīdī school. The best known of these writings is probably the creed (*ʿaqāʾid*) of Abū Ḥafṣ al-Nasafī (d. 537/1142). Although the text in itself is nothing but a compilation of phrases taken almost word by word from Abū l-Muʿīn's *Tamhīd li-qawāʿid al-tawḥīd* (Rudolph 1997b: 279 n. 88), it had tremendous success. Together with a commentary composed by Saʿd al-Dīn al-Taftāzānī (d. 792/1390) and several glosses and superglosses, it has served for many centuries as a manual for teaching Sunnī theology at the Madrasa.

Compared to that, the other writings received much less attention. Nevertheless, each of them deserves to be studied, since they do not simply repeat the same teachings, but often differ in form as well as in doctrinal points. Among them we find, for instance, the recently edited *Talkhīṣ al-adilla li-qawāʿid al-tawḥīd* by al-Ṣaffār al-Bukhārī (d. 543/1139) which combines elements taken from *kalām* texts with a long elaboration on God's names (*asmāʾ Allāh*); the *Lāmiyya fī l-tawḥīd* also entitled as *Badʾ al-amālī*, a didactic poem by ʿAlī b. ʿUthmān al-Ūshī (*fl.* around 569/1173); the *Kifāya fī l-hidāya* as well as its abridgement, the *Bidāya min al-kifāya*, two important *kalām* treatises written by Nūr al-Dīn al-Ṣābūnī al-Bukhārī (d. 580/1184); another important creed composed by Abū l-Barakāt al-Nasafī (d. 710/1310) and entitled *ʿUmdat al-ʿaqīda li-ahl al-sunna* and a *kalām* work by the same author entitled *al-Iʿtimād fī l-iʿtiqād* (Ismail 2003).

However, when Abū l-Barakāt composed these writings, al-Māturīdī's influence was no longer restricted to North-East Iran and Transoxania. His teachings had spread to the west and were widely accepted in territories along the Mediterranean Sea such as Anatolia, Syria, and Egypt, the latter two being at that time under Mamluk rule. As has been convincingly argued, this development was due to the Seljuqs and to other Turks following them on their way from Central Asia to the Mediterranean. Their spread into the central areas of the Islamic world led not only to a significant strengthening of Ḥanafism there, but at the same time to a distinct preponderance of the Transoxanian tradition within Ḥanafism (Madelung 1971: 140). The examples which can be given in this respect are numerous. In order to conclude it may suffice however to illustrate the whole phenomenon here just by one case: Ḥusām al-Dīn al-Ḥusayn (or al-Ḥasan) b. ʿAlī al-Sighnāqī, a distinguished scholar who originated from Turkestān. He studied Ḥanafī law and Māturīdī theology in Transoxania; obviously, the *Tamhīd li-qawāʿid al-tawḥīd* of Abū l-Muʿīn was one of the manuals from which he learned because he is reported to have written a commentary on it. Later on, however, he moved westward. First, he went to Baghdad, then to Damascus and finally to Aleppo where he died in 711/1311 or 714/1314. In all these places he taught what he had learned in Transoxania, contributing thereby to the spread of the teachings of al-Māturīdī and his school (Madelung 1971: 155 n. 125; for further examples see Madelung 1971: 140–55; for the topic in general cf. Bruckmayr 2009).

References

Abū Ḥanīfa (*Risāla 1*). *Risāla ilā ʿUthmān al-Battī*. Ed. Muḥammad Zāhid al-Kawtharī. In: *al-ʿĀlim wa-l-mutaʿallim*. Cairo: Maṭbaʿat al-Anwār, 1368/1949, 34–8. [German trans. in van Ess, *Theologie und Gesellschaft*, v. 24–9.]

Abū Ḥanīfa (*Risāla 2*). *Risāla ilā ʿUthmān al-Battī*. MS Teheran Majlis 8/31, p. 30. [German trans. in van Ess, *Theologie und Gesellschaft*, v. 34–5.]

Abū l-Layth al-Samarqandī (*ʿAqīda*). *ʿAqīdat al-uṣūl*. Ed. A. W. T. Juynboll. In *Bijdragen tot de Taal-Land-en Volkenkunde van Nederlandsch-Indië*. Ser. IV, vol. 5, 1881, 215–31 and 267–84.

Abū l-Layth al-Samarqandī (*Bustān* and *Tanbīh*). *Tanbīh al-ghāfilīn. [incl.:] Bustān al-ʿārifīn*. 2nd edn. [Egypt:] al-Maṭbaʿa al-Azhariyya al-Miṣriyya, 1308[/1890].

Abū l-Layth al-Samarqandī (*Tafsīr*). *Al-Tafsīr*. Ed. ʿAbd al-Raḥīm Aḥmad al-Ziqqa. 3 vols. Baghdad: Maṭbaʿat al-Irshād, 1985–6.

Abū Muqātil al-Samarqandī (*ʿĀlim*). *al-ʿĀlim wal-mutaʿallim*. Ed. Muḥammad Rawās Qalʿajī/ʿAbd al-Wahhāb al-Hindī al-Nadwī. Aleppo: Maktabat al-Hudā, 1972 (under the name of Abū Ḥanīfa).

Abū Mutīʿ al-Balkhī (*Fiqh absaṭ*). *al-Fiqh al-absaṭ*. Ed. Muḥammad Zāhid al-Kawtharī. In: *al-ʿĀlim wa-l-mutaʿallim*. Cairo: Maṭbaʿat al-Anwār, 1368/1949, 39–60.

Abū Salama al-Samarqandī (*Jumal*). *Jumal uṣūl al-dīn*. Ed. Ahmet Saim Kılavuz. Istanbul: Emek Matbaacılık, 1989 (under the title: Ebû Seleme es-Semerkandî ve Akâid Risâlesi).

Abū Shakūr al-Sālimī (*Tamhīd*). *Al-Tamhīd fī bayān al-tawḥīd*. MS Berlin 2456, fols 1–170b.

Ak, A. (2012). 'Matüridiliğin Ortaya Çıkışı'. In *Büyük Türk Bilgini İmâm Mâtürîdî ve Mâtürîdîlik*, 435–51.

Bruckmayr, P. (2009). 'The Spread and Persistence of Māturīdī kalām and Underlying Dynamics'. *Iran and the Caucasus* 13: 52–92.

Büyük Türk Bilgini İmâm Mâtürîdî ve Mâtürîdîlik: Milletlerarası tartişmalı ilmî toplantı: 22–24 Mayis 2009 İstanbul. Istanbul: IFAU 2012.

Cerić, M. (1995). *Roots of Synthetic Theology in Islam: A Study of the Theology of Abū Manṣūr al-Māturīdī (d. 333/944)*. Kuala Lumpur: International Institute of Islamic Thought and Civilization.

Cook, M. (1981). *Early Muslim Dogma: A Source-Critical Study*. Cambridge: Cambridge University Press.

Daccache, S. (2008). *Le problème de la création du monde et son contexte rationnel et historique dans la doctrine d'Abū Manṣūr al-Māturīdī (333/944)*. Beirut: Dar el-Mashreq.

Dhanani, A. (2012). 'Al-Māturīdī and al-Nasafī on Atomism and the Ṭabāʾiʿ'. *Büyük Türk Bilgini İmâm Mâtürîdî ve Mâtürîdîlik*, 65–76.

van Ess, J. (1986). 'Kritisches zum *Fiqh akbar*'. *Revue des études islamiques* 54: 327–38.

van Ess, J. (1991–7). *Theologie und Gesellschaft im 2. und 3. Jahrhundert Hidschra: Eine Geschichte des religiösen Denkens im frühen Islam*. 6 vols. Berlin: de Gruyter.

van Ess, J. (2011). *Der Eine und das Andere: Beobachtungen an islamischen häresiographischen Texten*. 2 vols. Berlin: de Gruyter.

Frank, R. M. (1974). 'Notes and Remarks on the ṭabāʾiʿ in the Teaching of al-Māturīdī'. In P. Salmon (ed.), *Mélanges d'islamologie: volume dédié à la mémoire de Armand Abel par ses collègues, ses élèves et ses amis*. Leiden: Brill, 137–49.

Gilliot. C. (2002). 'La théologie musulmane en Asie centrale et au Khorasan'. *Arabica* 49: 135–203.

Gilliot. C. (2004). 'L'embarras d'un exégète musulman face à un palimpseste: Māturīdī et la sourate de l'abondance (*al-Kawthar, sourate 108*), avec une note savante sur le commentaire coranique d'Ibn al-Naqīb (m. 698/1298)'. In R. Arnzen and J. Thielmann (eds.), *Words, Texts and Concepts Cursing the Mediterranean Sea: Studies on the Sources, Contents and Influences of Islamic Civilization and Arabic Philosophy and Science. Dedicated to Gerhard Endress on his Sixty-Fifth Birthday*. Leuven: Peeters, 33–69.

Gimaret, D. (1980). *Théories de l'acte humain en théologie musulmane*. Paris/Leuven: Vrin/Peeters.

Götz, M. (1965). 'Māturīdī und sein Kitāb Taʾwīlāt al-Qurʾān'. *Der Islam* 41: 27–70.

Griffith, S. H. (2011). 'Al-Māturīdī on the Views of the Christians: Readings in the *Kitāb al-Tawḥīd*'. In D. Bumazhov et al. (ed.), *Bibel, Byzanz und christlicher Orient: Festschrift für Stephen Gerö zum 65. Geburtstag*. Leuven: Peeters, 635–51.

al-Ḥakīm al-Samarqandī (*Sawād*). *al-Radd ʿalā aṣḥāb al-ahwāʾ al-musammā Kitāb al-Sawād al-aʿẓam ʿalā madhhab al-imām Abī Ḥanīfa*. Būlāq, 1253/1837–8 [Istanbul 1304/1886–7; Istanbul [no year]; Eng. trans. in al-ʿOmar, *The Doctrines*].

al-Ḥakīm al-Samarqandī (*Sawād/Persian*). Persian translation from the late fourth/tenth century. Ed. ʿAbd al-Ḥayy Ḥabībī. Tehran: Bunyād-i farhang-i Īrān, 1348sh/1969.

Ibn Ḥajar al-ʿAsqalānī (*Tahdhīb*). *Tahdhīb al-tahdhīb*. 12 vols. Hyderabad: Maṭbaʿat Majlis Dāʾirat al-Maʿārif al-Niẓāmiyya, 1325–7.

Ismail, A. M. (2003). *Die maturiditische Glaubenslehre des Abū l-Barakāt an-Nasafī (gest. 710/1310): Edition und Analyse seines* Kitāb al-Iʿtimād fī l-iʿtiqād. 2 vols. Frankfurt: Ph.D. dissertation.

von Kügelgen, A., and A. Muminov (2012). 'Mâturîdî Döneminde Semerkand İlahiyatçıları (4./10. Asır)'. In S. Kutlu (ed.), *İmam Mâturîdî ve Maturidilik*, 279–91.

Kutlu, S. (ed.) (2012). *İmam Mâturîdî ve Maturidilik: Tarihî Arka Plan, Hayatı, Eserleri, Fikirleri ve Maturidilik Mezhebi*. 4th edn. Ankara: Otto.

Madelung, W. (1971). 'The Spread of Māturīdism and the Turks'. *Actas do IV Congresso de Estudos Árabes e Islâmicos (Coimbra-Lisboa 1968)*. Leiden: Brill, 109–68 [repr. in W. Madelung, *Religious Schools and Sects in Medieval Islam*. London: Ashgate, 1985, no. VIII].

Madelung, W. (1982). 'The Early Murjiʾa in Khurāsān and Transoxania and the Spread of Ḥanafism'. *Der Islam* 59: 32–9.

Madelung, W. (1988). *Religious Trends in Early Islamic Iran*. Albany, NY: State University of New York Press.

Madelung, W. (2000). 'Abū l-Muʿīn al-Nasafī and Ashʿarī Theology'. In C. Hillenbrand (ed.), *Studies in Honour of Clifford Edmund Bosworth*, ii: *The Sultan's Turret*. Leiden: Brill, 318–30.

al-Māturīdī, Abū Manṣūr (*Tawḥīd*). *Kitāb al-Tawḥīd*. Ed. Bekir Topaloğlu and Muhammed Aruçi. Ankara: Türkiye Diyanet Vakfı, 2003 [1st edn. by Fathalla Kholeif. Beirut: Dar el-Machreq, 1970; repr. 1986].

al-Māturīdī, Abū Manṣūr (*Taʾwīlāt*). *Taʾwīlāt al-Qurʾān*, ed. Ahmet Vanlıoğlu et al. (under the supervision of Bekir Topaloğlu), 17 vols. and indexes. Istanbul: Mizan Yayınevi, 2005–11.

al-Nasafī, Abū l-Barakāt (*Iʿtimād*). *Al-Iʿtimād fī l-iʿtiqād*. *See* Ismail, A. M.

al-Nasafī, Abū l-Barakāt (*ʿUmda*). *ʿUmdat al-ʿaqīda li-ahl al-sunna*. Ed. William Cureton [in: *Pillar of the Creed of the Sunnites*]. London: Printed for the Society for the Publication of Oriental Texts, 1843.

al-Nasafī, Abū Ḥafṣ (*ʿAqāʾid*). *Al-ʿAqāʾid*. Ed. William Cureton [in: *Pillar of the Creed of the Sunnites*]. London: Printed for the Society for the Publication of Oriental Texts, 1843.

al-Nasafī, Abū l-Muʿīn (*Baḥr*). *Baḥr al-kalām*. Egypt: Maṭbaʿat Kurdistān, 1329/1911.

al-Nasafī, Abū l-Muʿīn (*Tabṣira*). *Tabsirat al-adilla fī uṣūl al-dīn ʿalā ṭarīqat al-imām Abī Manṣūr al-Māturīdī*. Ed. C. Salamé. 2 vols. Damascus: Institut français de Damas, 1990–3.

al-Nasafī, Abū l-Muʿīn (*Tamhīd*). *Al-Tamhīd li-qawāʿid al-tawḥīd*. Ed. Ḥabīb Allāh Ḥasan Aḥmad. Cairo: Dār al-Ṭibāʿa al-Muḥammadiyya, 1986.

Nasir, S. A. (2005). 'The Epistemology of Kalām of Abū Manṣūr al-Māturīdī'. *Al-Jāmiʿah: Journal of Islamic Studies* 43: 39–65.

al-ʿOmar, Farouq ʿOmar ʿAbdallah (1974). *The Doctrines of the Māturīdite School with Special Reference to Al-Sawād al-Aʿẓam of al-Ḥakīm al-Samarqandī*. Edinburgh: Ph.D. dissertation.

el-Omari, R. M. (2006). *The Theology of Abū l-Qāsim al-Balḫī/al-Kaʿbī (d. 319/931): A Study of its Sources and Reception*. Yale University: Ph.D. dissertation.

al-Pazdawī, Abū l-Yusr (*Uṣūl*). *Uṣūl al-dīn*. Ed. Hans Peter Linss. Cairo: Dār Iḥyāʾ al-Kutub al-ʿArabiyya, 1383/1963.

Rahman. M. M. (1982). *An Introduction to al-Maturidi's Taʾwilat Ahl Al-Sunna*. Dacca: Islamic Foundation Bangladesh.

Rofiq, A. C. (2009). 'The Methodology of al-Māturīdī's Qurʾanic Exegesis: Study of the *Taʾwīlāt ahl al-sunna*'. *Al-Jāmiʿah: Journal of Islamic Studies* 47: 317–42.

Rudolph, U. (1992). 'Ratio und Überlieferung in der Erkenntnislehre al-Ašʿarī's und al-Māturīdī's'. *Zeitschrift der Deutschen Morgenländischen Gesellschaft* 142: 72–9.

Rudolph, U. (1997a). 'Das Entstehen der Māturīdīya'. *Zeitschrift der Deutschen Morgenländischen Gesellschaft* 147: 394–404.

Rudolph, U. (1997b). *Al-Māturīdī und die sunnitische Theologie in Samarkand*. Leiden: Brill [Eng. trans. by Rodrigo Adem, *Al-Māturīdī and the Development of Sunnī Theology in Samarqand*. Leiden: Brill, 2013].

Rudolph, U. (2012). 'Al-Māturīdī's Concept of God's Wisdom'. *Büyük Türk Bilgini İmâm Mâtürîdî ve Mâtürîdîlk*, 45–53.

al-Ṣābūnī, Nūraddīn Abū Muḥammad (*Kifāya*). *Al-Kifāya min al-hidāya*. MS Yale 849, fols 55b–259.

al-Ṣābūnī, Nūraddīn Abū Muḥammad (*Bidāya*). *Al-Bidāya min al-Kifāya fī l hidāya fī uṣūl al-dīn*. Ed. Fathallah Kholeif. Alexandria: Dār al-Maʿārif, 1969.

al-Ṣaffār al-Bukhārī, Abū Isḥāq (*Talkhīṣ*). *Talkhīṣ al-adilla li-qawāʿid al-tawḥīd*. Ed. Angelika Brodersen. 2 vols. Beirut: Orient-Institut in Kommission bei 'Klaus Schwarz Verlag', Berlin, 2011.

Schacht, J. (1964). 'An Early Murci'ite Treatise: The Kitāb al-ʿĀlim wal-mutaʿallim'. *Oriens* 17: 96–117.

al-Taftāzānī, Saʿd al-Dīn (*Sharḥ*). *Sharḥ al-ʿAqāʾid al-Nasafiyya*. Ed. C. Salamé. Damascus: Wizārat al-Thaqāfa wal-Irshād al-qawmī, 1974 [Eng. trans.: E. Elger, *A Commentary on the Creed of Islam: Saʿd al-Dīn al-Taftāzānī on the Creed of Najm al-Dīn al-Nasafī*. New York: Columbia University Press, 1950].

CHAPTER 18

PHILOSOPHICAL THEOLOGY

PETER ADAMSON

MOST Muslim philosophers and theologians have held that God is the sole source for all other things. And most, though as we will see not all, would be willing to express this idea by calling God 'the first cause'. Unfortunately this phrase contains within it a certain tension. On the one hand, God is a 'cause'. He bears some relationship to the things He causes, that is, to all other things. This relationship presumably has something in common with other causal relations, such as the one between a fire and the thing it warms. Otherwise, why apply the term 'cause' to God at all? On the other hand, God is 'first'. At a bare minimum, we might understand by this that He is (uniquely) a cause that is not caused. As many proofs of God's existence assert, He prevents a causal regress from stretching to infinity. But His primacy is normally taken to involve more than that. The Qur'ān states that 'no thing is like' to God (*laysa ka-mithlihī shay'un*, Qur'ān 42: 11), and some Greek philosophical sources that found their way into Arabic also stress God's transcendence above all other things. If God's being 'first' involves His being unlike all other things, then He should not have the same sort of relation to His effects that other causes bear to their effects. Thus the tension: God is the *first* cause in the sense of being transcendent above all other things, but He is also the first *cause* of those things, and by this very fact apparently related and comparable to them.

It would be convenient if, in the face of this tension, intellectual traditions in the Islamic world divided neatly into those that emphasize God's transcendence and those that emphasize His causality—mystics on the one side, rationalists on the other. But things are not so simple. Though one might expect the philosophers to tend strongly in the rationalist direction and to focus on God as a cause rather than on His transcendence, they are in fact at great pains to preserve both ideas. They seek to do so by arguing that God's way of causing is not merely unique, but itself entails a degree of transcendence on His part. Greek philosophical works translated into Arabic provided resources for expounding this idea. Particularly important here were Aristotle and Plotinus, so we will need to glance at the legacy offered by these two authors before moving on to philosophy in the Islamic world.

First though, a brief remark about this phrase 'philosophy in the Islamic world'. The study of this topic should really take into consideration all works that offer arguments on philosophical topics, by authors of all religious affiliations who have lived in the territories under Muslim political control, whether they wrote in Arabic, Persian, or other languages. This would include not just Muslims, but also Jews and Christians who were inspired by Hellenic philosophy, and furthermore many *mutakallimūn*, Ismāʿīlīs, ṣūfīs, and jurists. Avicenna, Ibn ʿAdī, and Maimonides (respectively a Muslim, Christian, and Jew, and all deeply engaged with Aristotle) in this broad sense belong to the history of philosophy in the Islamic world, but so do Saadia Gaon, al-Ashʿarī, Judah Halevi, Ibn ʿArabī, Suhrawardī, Bar Hebraeus, Ibn Taymiyya, and so on (even if one might hesitate to call some of these figures 'philosophers').

This chapter will necessarily have a narrower scope.[1] Here I will deal with authors who were responding directly to the texts made available in the Greek–Arabic translation movement accomplished during the heyday of the ʿAbbāsid caliphate. This means roughly the thinkers who were known as the *falāsifa* (practitioners of *falsafa*) in the relevant period. It also means that I will be treating Avicenna as the culmination of 'philosophy', in that subsequent thinkers by and large respond to him rather than to Aristotle and other authors of the Greek tradition. There are exceptions here. Much later than Avicenna we find a resurgence of interest in Graeco-Arabic philosophy in the Safavid period, and philosophy in al-Andalus continued to focus on Aristotle rather than Avicenna. I will nonetheless be dealing here exclusively with the formative period of philosophy in the Eastern Islamic realms. Of course, I will need to be selective even within this rather narrow scope, and will focus on the three most obvious representatives of 'philosophy': al-Kindī, al-Fārābī, and Avicenna.

I The Greek Background

Ancient Greek philosophy unfolded within a society that embraced polytheism. The greatest figures of antique thought, Plato and Aristotle, both recognized a plurality of divinities, while also acknowledging one divinity supreme above the others. Thus in Plato's *Timaeus* a cosmic Demiurge is set over the so-called 'younger' gods as their father (40e–41a), and Aristotle famously compares the role of his unmoved mover to that of a king who presides over lesser celestial intellects (*Metaphysics*, 1076a, quoting the *Iliad*: 'the rule of many is not good; let there be one ruler'). Plotinus and other Neoplatonists likewise recognize divinities inferior to their completely unified first principle—even the heavenly bodies are called 'gods' (*theoi*, at e.g. *Enneads*, 4.3.11).[2] Nonetheless, readers of Graeco-Arabic translations would probably have thought of

[1] I survey the tradition more completely in Adamson 2015b and Adamson 2016.

[2] For references to this idea elsewhere in Plotinus and in other ancient authors see Wilberding 2006: 186–7.

the leading antique philosophers as monotheists. These translations sometimes eliminate references to 'gods', replacing them with 'angels',[3] or simply gloss over and eliminate pagan material. For instance a section of Plotinus's *Enneads* on this topic (6.7.6–7) seems to have been purposefully eliminated in the Arabic version known as the *Theology of Aristotle* (Adamson 2002: 14). This same text is one of many that replace references to the One or First Principle with allusions to the 'Creator', something that even happens in the Arabic version of Galen's paraphrase of the *Timaeus*.[4]

Thus the main task facing Muslim aficionados of Hellenic philosophy was usually not to explain away polytheistic tendencies in these texts. It was rather to show that the First Principle or highest God of these texts could be identified with the God of Islam. When it came to the two main sources, Aristotle and Plotinus, there was good news and bad news. With Aristotle the good news was that in *Physics* 8 and *Metaphysics* 12, Aristotle had emphasized the singularity and immateriality of God. He had also suggested a providential role for Him—a role further expounded by the leading Aristotelian commentator Alexander of Aphrodisias (Ruland 1976; Genequand 2001; cf. also Fazzo and Wiesener 1993). The bad news was that Aristotle seemed to make God a cause of motion, rather than of existence, and a cause of eternal motion at that. Furthermore, especially in the *Metaphysics* God seems to cause motion by serving as a final cause—the good sought by other things—rather than as an efficient cause or maker. This was already felt to be problematic in late antiquity. The Platonist commentator on Aristotle, Ammonius, produced arguments to show that Aristotle's God could be counted as an efficient cause of existence precisely insofar as He is a cause of motion, since the universe cannot exist without moving (Sorabji 2004: ii. 8c).

As for Plotinus, the good news was even better than what we saw with Aristotle, since the hallmark of his first principle is unity. The so-called 'One' (also known as the 'Good') is, in Plotinus's presentation, absolutely one in every respect and the source of unity for all other things (see e.g. *Enneads*, 6.9). This would later fit nicely with the priorities of Islamic theology during the period of the translation movement. At this time Muʿtazilite theologians, the 'upholders of unity and justice', were similarly stressing not just the uniqueness but the unity of God, to the point that they denied any distinction between God and His attributes (see e.g. Frank 1969). The Plotinian One seemed, in this respect, to be a Greek prefiguration of the Islamic teaching of divine oneness (*tawḥīd*). Now for the bad news. The One in Plotinus clearly does not exert causation in the way a Creator God would. It is far from clear that the One is a cause of existence or being. It seems much more to be a cause of oneness and goodness, with 'being' assigned to the second principle of the Plotinian hierarchy, the Intellect.[5] In the later Neoplatonist Proclus it is even more clear that the being of things derives from a cause distinct from the first

[3] E.g. Porphyry, *Isagoge*, 11.28: 'both we and the gods are rational' becomes 'we and the angels are rational', at Badawī 1952: iii. 1047.

[4] For a list of examples see the Greek–Arabic index of Kraus and Walzer 1951, under *ḫ-l-q*.

[5] On the other hand the One is the cause of Intellect and in this sense could be conceived as a cause of being or existence. See Gerson 1994: 12–14.

principle, which (if it has any causal relation to the things that come after it) is a source of unity alone.[6]

Another problem was that the Neoplatonic One, like Aristotle's God, has a necessary and eternal relationship to what comes after it. Plotinus's use of metaphors comparing higher causes to shining lights and flowing fountains has led this sort of causation to be described as 'emanationist'. In Arabic the word *fayḍ* ('emanation') is used by many philosophers, even those who deny the eternity of the universe. Worse still, the Neoplatonist picture seems to have God exerting direct causation on only one effect—the first intellect, or whatever serves the role of second principle. Divine causation is passed on to other things only indirectly. Here again we find frequent use of an Arabic term, *tawassuṭ*, to express this idea of 'mediation'. In al-Fārābī and Avicenna, the mediation doctrine is combined with the Aristotelian doctrine that God is set over numerous celestial intellects, and here these intellects are seen as deriving from God in a kind of chain reaction, each intellect giving rise to the next. As we shall see, already al-Kindī puts forward the idea that God's agency is mediated by secondary causes. In fact, if anything the idea of mediation was embraced more enthusiastically by philosophers in the Islamic world than by the Greek Neoplatonists, given that we should probably understand the One in both Plotinus and Proclus to be the direct cause of unity for all other things. (As Proclus says: the more perfect the cause, the further its reach; Proclus, *Elements of Theology*, proposition 57.)

These Greek ideas did not so much resolve the fundamental tension between causation and transcendence, as provide powerful considerations on both sides. Plotinus frequently stresses the transcendence of his first principle, instructing us that if we are to grasp the One we must 'take away everything' (*Enneads*, 5.3.17). This apophaticism is qualified in the Arabic paraphrase-translation of Plotinus, the so-called *Theology of Aristotle*, which introduces the claim that we can ascribe to God whatever we ascribe to His effect, but in a higher way (*Theology of Aristotle*, X.154 in the translation by Lewis 1950; in the Arabic edition at Badawi 1947: 156–7; see also Adamson 2002: 117). The author of the Arabic version is perhaps drawing here on Proclus, who similarly proposed that higher principles must possess the features of lower things 'in the way of a cause (*kat' aitian*)'—nothing can give what it does not have (D'Ancona 1995: 150–1; D'Ancona 1991: 128). Nonetheless, the overall effect of the Neoplatonic translations was to provide the basis for a philosophical version of the rigorous negative theology being put forward by the Muʿtazilites.

Yet there was also plenty of basis in the Greek sources for emphasizing God's causal role. We have not only the caveat just mentioned about predication 'in the way of a cause', but also the aforementioned integration of God into a hierarchical system of celestial entities, in which He is seen above all as a cause of eternal motion. Indeed, Aristotle proves the

[6] The still later Neoplatonist Damascius distinguishes the highest principle, the Ineffable, from the One, precisely on the basis that the Ineffable does *not* have any causal relation to other things and so cannot be responsible for bestowing unity. He thus prefigures the position we will see in Ibn Ḥazm's critique of al-Kindī.

very existence of an immaterial mover on the basis that eternal bodily motion requires some external cause.[7] Aristotle is also explicit that the activity by means of which God causes motion is an activity shared by some other things—indeed shared by humans—namely thinking. As he says, 'God is always in that good state in which we sometimes are' (1072b24–5). One advantage of this view is that we may hope to understand God, at least to some extent, by understanding ourselves. The disadvantage is that it may be felt to compromise God's transcendence, by violating the rule against comparing Him to what He creates. Admittedly, Aristotle's God is far better off than we are, in that His thought has the best possible object (Himself), grasped in the best possible way, without interruption. But a rigorous position on God's transcendence would ban all talk of divine intellection.

II Al-Kindī

For precisely this reason the first philosopher of the Islamic world, al-Kindī, rejects the Aristotelian conception of God as an intellect who gives rise to an eternal motion by thinking about Himself. This despite the fact that his most relevant and indeed most important work, *On First Philosophy*, is deeply indebted to Aristotle's *Metaphysics*.[8] In the third section of the surviving first part of *On First Philosophy*, al-Kindī argues that there must be a 'True One'. He contrasts this with all other things, which are only 'accidentally' or 'metaphorically' one, meaning that they are both one and many (XVII.1, XX.3–5). The same distinction features in a very brief (possibly fragmentary) piece which states that God is the True Agent whereas other things are 'metaphorically' agents, that is, both acting and acted upon (*On the True Agent*, 3). In *On First Philosophy*, al-Kindī also says that the True One is the source of unity for other things. He offers no explanation concerning the origin of multiplicity, but *On the True Agent* seems to imply that the complexity of the world is to be explained through a series of causes that mediate divine agency. In that context the intermediate causes are not identified, but it seems clear from other works (especially his *On the Proximate Agent Cause of Generation and Corruption*) that God's primary effect, which passes on His providential influence to other things, is the heavenly sphere.

Moving on to the fourth section of *On First Philosophy*, we find al-Kindī arguing that the True One's utter unity precludes the application of language. Here al-Kindī all but makes explicit the connection suggested above, between Plotinus's ineffable One and the one God of Muʿtazilite *kalām*.[9] Characteristically, he draws on Aristotelian logical

[7] Even after the advent of Avicenna's powerful and influential proof for God, Averroes still insists that the correct way to show that God exists is Aristotle's. The proof should go through physics, rather than metaphysics, since God is part of the subject matter of metaphysics and no science proves the existence of its own subject matter. See on this Bertolacci 2007.

[8] D'Ancona 1992; see also the useful notes to Ivry 1974. All works by al-Kindī cited by section number from the translations in Adamson and Pormann 2012. For discussion see further Adamson 2007a: ch. 3, which the following summarizes.

[9] Or so I have argued in Adamson 2003.

works to do so, moving methodically, not to say pedantically, through the various types of predication set out in Porphyry's *Eisagoge* or *Introduction* to the Aristotelian logical corpus (XIX.1–3). (In another work, he uses this same procedure to disprove the Christian doctrine of the Trinity; *Against the Trinity*, in Adamson and Pormann 2012.) Here al-Kindī uses weapons from the Aristotelian logical arsenal to fight on behalf of a Neoplatonic conception of the first principle. This is clear from his characterization of God as a 'True One' who imparts unity to other things by means of 'emanation' (XX.5). In fact only at the end of the surviving part is Qur'ānic language introduced to make clear that this One is indeed the same as the God of Islam (XX.7). The Neoplatonic inspiration becomes more evident still when al-Kindī argues that the True One must be distinguished from both soul and intellect, which 'one may suppose to be the first multiple' (XIX.6). Al-Kindī's refusal to equate God with an intellect is one of his two most striking divergences from Aristotle.

The other is his denial of the eternity of the universe. The second section of *On First Philosophy* is devoted to this topic. It reproduces arguments from the ancient Christian commentator and critic of Aristotle, John Philoponus (Davidson 1969). This reminds us that the reception of Hellenic philosophical material in Arabic was often influenced by, even filtered through, Christian reactions and adaptations by authors writing in both Greek and Syriac.[10] It also tells us that for al-Kindī the universe exists contingently and is subject to God's will. He makes the point concerning not only the past but also the future existence of the universe, saying that even though Aristotle was right to see the heavenly as consisting of an 'incorruptible' fifth element, it could be destroyed by the will of its Creator (*On the Nature of the Celestial Sphere*, 13). Aristotle was also, incidentally, right to see God as immaterial and unmoved, though al-Kindī of course reaches this conclusion by showing that materiality and motion would involve multiplicity (*On First Philosophy*, XIX.2, 4).

We can sum up al-Kindī's philosophical theology as follows: God is perfectly One and a cause of unity, like the first principle of Plotinus and other Neoplatonists. Yet He is also a 'Creator', who brings things to exist from non-being, acting by will rather than necessity. He is immaterial and unmoved, like Aristotle's God, but not an intellect. Above all, He cannot be described by the predicates which we apply to the things that are both one and many. A rare exception that al-Kindī seems to allow on this score (and he does not mention it as an exception) is that one can indeed describe God as a 'cause' (*ʿilla*), in that He is the source of unity. Even this was enough to convict al-Kindī of incoherence in the eyes of one later critic, the polymath Ẓāhirī jurist of al-Andalus, Ibn Ḥazm.[11] He composed a refutation of al-Kindī's *On First Philosophy*, pointing out the contradiction between saying that God is ineffable—in particular, that He is free of relations—and calling Him a 'cause' (*ʿilla*). For Ibn Ḥazm the language of causation implies a necessary connection between Creator and created, since nothing can be a cause unless there

[10] For the importance of Syriac literature see Brock 1993; Watt 2010.
[11] On whom see Adang, Fierro, and Schmidtke 2013.

is also an effect.[12] Instead, Ibn Ḥazm proposes that we should see God as 'establishing' (*waḍaʿa*) certain causes (such as the four elements) which do necessarily give rise to their effects (20 and 23). Ibn Ḥazm provides us with a very clear instance of the tension discussed at the beginning of this chapter: God's primacy is to be understood as transcendence, and this makes it impossible to call Him a cause. Unsurprisingly, Ibn Ḥazm quotes in this context the aforementioned Qurʾānic stricture that 'no thing is like' God (20 and 22).

III Al-Fārābī

Al-Kindī's philosophical theology is open to another objection, namely that in his view God would be the first cause of unity, rather than existence. In fact al-Kindī does try to accommodate the latter idea too, offering the rationale that 'the bringing-to-be of every multiplicity occurs through unity' (*On First Philosophy*, XX.5). But after the unmoved mover of Aristotle and the One of Plotinus and al-Kindī, we still await a philosophical theology that focuses on God as a cause of existence. Such a theology is fully accomplished in Avicenna, an achievement he manages in part thanks to ideas taken over from *kalām* and al-Fārābī. The radical dependency of each object on God for its existence is a typically *kalām* notion, a notion which we will see Avicenna articulate in a new way in his argument for God's existence. From al-Fārābī, meanwhile, Avicenna borrows the more Aristotelian understanding of God as an intellective first cause who gives rise to a chain of celestial intellects.

Consider the opening pages of al-Fārābī's *Principles of the Beliefs of the Inhabitants of the Virtuous City*.[13] The compressed series of arguments offered here looks back to al-Kindī and Neoplatonism, in describing God as a perfect unity and as source of unity for other things (1.5). But, as Avicenna will later do, al-Fārābī places far more emphasis on the claim that God is an uncaused cause of existence. Indeed he begins his treatment of God with the statement that God is the 'first cause (*sabab*) of existence of all other existents' (1.1). As he unfolds the implications of this claim, al-Fārābī draws above all on two Aristotelian texts, both from the *Metaphysics*: books Alpha Elatton and Lambda. His use of the latter is unsurprising since it is Aristotle's most prominent discussion of God. The briefer Alpha Elatton, whose authenticity is nowadays disputed, was also very important for readers of Aristotle in the Islamic world since it was considered the first book of the *Metaphysics*.[14]

[12] Daiber 1986. Arabic text in ʿAbbās 1983: iv. 363–405. Cited by section number from the Arabic edition.

[13] On the significance of the title see Rudolph 2008. I cite from the *Principles* in my own translation, by section number from Walzer 1985.

[14] See Bertolacci 2005 and Adamson 2010. Walzer's commentary on al-Fārābī, which is otherwise excellent on his Greek sources, fails to note the importance of Elatton for the argument of this opening chapter.

It gives al-Fārābī a useful source for the most fundamental claim in his philosophical theology, namely that God is an uncaused cause. For both al-Fārābī and Avicenna, this will turn out to be the key for resolving the tension observed above. Their proposal is that God's transcendence over created things, along with a range of other claims that they want to establish concerning God, can be inferred from His not being caused.

The most relevant part of Elatton for this idea is the second of its three chapters, in which Aristotle shows that there can be no infinite regress in any of the four kinds of cause he recognizes (efficient, formal, material, and final). Instead, as Aristotle says in the first sentence of the chapter, 'it is clear that there is some first principle, and that the causes of beings are not infinite' (994a1–2). It is far from obvious that Aristotle has theological implications in mind here, as he makes no explicit reference to God in the chapter. On the other hand, chapter one of Elatton has just concluded by speaking of 'the principles of eternal beings' and said that these are 'most true, for they are not true only sometimes, nor is there any cause of being (*aition tou einai*) for those things' (993b28–30). The opportunity to apply all of this to God was already eagerly taken by al-Kindī (see *On First Philosophy*, I.2–3), and al-Fārābī follows him in this respect. Later in the opening section of the *Principles* he will repeat the idea that the First Cause most deserves the name 'truth' (*al-ḥaqq*), which is of course also a Qurʾānic epithet for God. (The idea that God exceeds the grasp of our intellect, which he mentions at 1.11, probably also alludes to Elatton: the famous analogy of the bats blinded by sunlight, at 993a9–11.)

Following the lead of Aristotle in Elatton chapter two, then, al-Fārābī begins by explaining that this First Cause is subject to none of the four types of cause (1.1). This can be demonstrated on the basis of the Cause's being primary: if it is first, then it is without deficiency, 'uncontaminated by non-being', and 'eternal (*dāʾim*) of existence through its substance and through itself (*bi-jawharihi wa-dhātihi*); in being forever it has no need for anything else to prolong its persistence' (1.1). Although al-Fārābī does not call his First Cause the 'Necessary of Existence' (*wājib al-wujūd*) as Avicenna will do, the core of Avicenna's philosophical theology is already present here and in the following arguments of the *Principles*. For instance, al-Fārābī proceeds immediately to give an argument that will play a decisive role in Avicenna's discussion of the Necessary Existent. I have elsewhere called this the 'individuation argument' (Adamson 2013: 178). The idea is to suppose, for the sake of a *reductio ad absurdum*, that there are two things that share the status that belongs to the First Cause (1.2). In Avicenna's version of the argument, we suppose that there are two necessary existents, whereas al-Fārābī simply supposes that there are two things that are first. If this were the case, then some factor would be needed to distinguish the two. That cannot be, since this factor would be a cause for our two supposedly uncaused causes. Thus the First Cause is unique. To speak with al-Fārābī, nothing else 'has its existence'. Avicenna will make the link to Islamic doctrine even more clear by saying that the Necessary Existent has no 'peer' (*nidd*) (Avicenna, *Metaphysics*, 8.5.2; Avicenna, *Ishārāt*, 4.27). However the conclusion is expressed, the upshot is clear: the particularization argument yields a philosophical version of the key Islamic doctrine of *tawḥīd*, the oneness of God.

Al-Fārābī now goes on to establish a series of further traits for the First Cause. It must be perfect (*tāmm*), for 'the perfect is that aside from which nothing of the same kind exists' (1.2). This is not entirely clear, but he gives a helpful example: because the sun is perfect there is no other sun. He seems to be invoking a general rule, namely that if a kind (*nawʿ*) of thing has only one member, then that will be the perfect instance of this kind. Furthermore, the First Cause can have no contrary, no parts, and no material basis (1.3–4, 1.6). All of this is still demonstrated on the basis that the First Cause is uncaused. The observation that this Cause is immaterial—since it is uncaused, and matter is a cause for whatever is made of matter—turns out to be particularly significant. For al-Fārābī feels free immediately to infer that we are dealing with something that is 'actually an intellect' (*ʿaql bi-l-fiʿl*). It will also be 'intelligible in its substance' since intelligibility is hindered by matter, and this Cause has no matter (1.6). Here we have a link between the Elatton-based line of reasoning, which centres on the idea of an uncaused first principle, and the self-thinking God of *Metaphysics* book Lambda.

Nor do the parallels to Lambda end there. Al-Fārābī goes on to argue that God takes pleasure in his self-contemplation. This is based on Aristotle, who mentions divine pleasure in the *Nicomachean Ethics* (1154b26–8) and in Lambda. God performs intellection, which is the best possible activity, and in knowing Himself grasps the best possible object of intellection (1072b18–19). Since pleasure resides in perfect activity (a thesis established in the *Ethics*), we can conclude that God enjoys the highest pleasure. Al-Fārābī follows Aristotle on these points (1.14). There is however a subtle difference between the two. Aristotle seems to make God's intellection and pleasure comparable to ours. In fact the main contrast he draws between them is that God has *permanently* what we can have only fleetingly (mentioned twice: 1072b14–16 and 24–5). Al-Fārābī makes this point too, but then shows how concerned he is not to place God on a par with humans: there is no comparison or relation (*nisba*) between God's perception and ours, or of His pleasure and ours. Or, he adds tentatively, if there is a relation it is a slight one.

The extent to which such ideas penetrated into wider Arabic literary culture is indicated by a far less celebrated work from the pen of the historian and Platonist Miskawayh (d. 421/1030), a contemporary of Avicenna (d. 458/1037). He was one of a number of polymaths who embraced the kind of Islam-friendly, 'popular' Platonism pioneered by al-Kindī and also represented by such authors as al-ʿĀmirī and al-Tawḥīdī (Rowson 1990; Adamson 2007b). Miskawayh's ideas about God tend toward the Neoplatonic. He is strongly influenced by the Arabic version of Plotinus, and also draws on al-Kindī's *On First Philosophy*. Yet he also wrote a short treatise called *On Pleasure and Pains* (edited twice, in Arkoun 1961–2: 1–9 (Arabic pagination) and Badawī 1981: 98–104; on the treatise see Adamson 2015a), which outlines the Aristotelian position on pleasures as perceived perfections, and then applies this to God. He not only says that the greatest pleasure available to humans is the contemplation of God, and that God takes an even higher pleasure than we do in His self-contemplation. He even states that God *is* pleasure: 'because the most perfect of pleasures is the most perfect perfection and most perfect good, and God, the exalted, is the most perfect perfection and good, it is necessary that He is the absolute pleasure which is always pleasure in actuality' (Arkoun 1961–2: 3 (Arabic pagination); Badawī, *Dirāsāt*, 100).

IV Avicenna

Miskawayh's treatise on pleasure is not an outstandingly original or influential work. But it does show us that in the early fifth/eleventh century, using philosophy to understand God still meant deploying the arguments and ideas of Greek works in Arabic translation. After Avicenna, this was no longer the case. There are, admittedly, exceptions. For instance we have a work based on *Metaphysics* Lambda by ʿAbd al-Laṭīf al-Baghdādī (d. 629/1231) (Neuwirth 1976), and as I have mentioned above the whole Andalusian philosophical tradition, among both Jews and Muslims, would remain rooted in the texts of Aristotle.[15] For the most part though, in the Eastern heartlands philosophy will be synonymous with Avicenna. Thus al-Ghazālī could entitle a work *Incoherence of the Philosophers* even though—as Averroes pointed out with some asperity—it mounts a criticism of Avicennism rather than the ideas of Aristotle (al-Ghazālī, *The Incoherence*). With Avicenna we thus reach both the climax and the effective end (in the East) of philosophical theology as a direct engagement with Aristotle's theology, or for that matter with the *Theology of Aristotle*.[16]

Much of what Avicenna has to offer on our topic is an expansion and refinement of the arguments squeezed into the opening part of al-Fārābī's *Principles*. This is to take nothing away from Avicenna's breathtaking originality. For one thing, he should be credited with devising a seminal proof for God's existence, which provides the Farabian theology with an entirely new basis. The proof turns on the modal concepts of the contingent (*mumkin*) and necessary (*wājib*). Here is a somewhat simplified version (for more details see Marmura 1980; Davidson 1987; Mayer 2001: 18–39; McGinnis 2010: ch. 6; Lizzini 2012: ch. 2). Avicenna wishes to rule out that every existent exists contingently—there must be at least one existent that exists necessarily. Towards this end, he explains that a thing that in itself exists only contingently requires an external cause to 'preponderate' it to exist.

This does not yet show that anything exists necessarily. After all, it could be that each contingently existing thing is caused to exist by another contingently existing thing. But Avicenna points out that we can apply the same consideration to the entire aggregate of contingently existing things. (One can think of this aggregate simply as the universe, past, present, and future.) Could this aggregate be a necessary existent? Avicenna has arguments to rule this out, but of course if the aggregate were necessary he would have

[15] For the mostly indirect access to Avicenna among the Jews see Freudenthal and Zonta 2012.

[16] As mentioned above, the *Theology*, along with other Greek texts, will however experience a revival of interest in the later Savafid period. See on this Rizvi 2007.

his desired conclusion that something exists necessarily. If on the other hand the aggregate exists contingently then it will, like all other contingent items, require an external cause to make it exist. But if that cause is to be *external* to the aggregate of all contingent things, then it must be an existent that exists necessarily in itself.

Passing over the many difficulties that arise concerning the proof itself, let us consider what its conclusion implies for Avicenna's philosophical theology (in what follows I summarize the argument of Adamson 2013). A first thing to note is that the argument is not really a proof of God's existence. Rather, it proves that at least one thing exists necessarily. This demand could be satisfied by a necessary existent that no one would recognize as God (such as a Platonic Form, an abstractly existing number, or even, as just suggested, the universe itself). In fact the proof does not even rule out that there are a plurality of necessary existents. So Avicenna has much work ahead of him to show that this necessary existent is God. His strategy for doing so differs to some extent in different works. Particularly striking is the fact that the famous proof just summarized is never clearly laid out in the metaphysical section (*Ilāhiyyāt*) of his most famous philosophical *summa*, the *Healing* (*al-Shifāʾ*).[17] Certainly Avicenna speaks extensively about the necessary existent in this work, but his discussion of the divine attributes begins by deploying arguments reminiscent of *Metaphysics* Alpha Elatton. Like al-Fārābī's *Principles*, Avicenna's *Healing* demonstrates the impossibility of unlimited regresses in all four types of cause (8.1–3). Avicenna's choice here may be due to the 'Peripatetic' intentions of the *Healing*, in contrast to the more independent approach taken in other works like the *Pointers and Reminders* (*al-Ishārāt wa-l-Tanbīhāt*).[18]

The necessity of the First Cause nonetheless plays a crucial role in the arguments of the *Healing*, just as in the *Pointers*. For something that is necessary in itself exists without being caused. On this basis, Avicenna is able to give his own version of the individuation argument to prove that an uncaused existent must be 'one', in both the sense of being unique—there is only one necessary existent—and simple—the necessary existent has no parts (on this argument and later responses see Mayer 2003). Like al-Fārābī, he also draws consequences about divine ineffability or transcendence from the premiss that the necessary existent is uncaused (8.4.13–16: God has no quiddity, genus, or specific difference). This does not stop Avicenna from inferring a wide range of further divine attributes and epithets from necessary existence. For instance Avicenna, like al-Fārābī, infers from the necessary existent's lack of matter that it is an intellect (see further Adamson 2011). Such features as 'perfect' and 'good' are also derived from its lack of a cause. For some attributes Avicenna invokes the point that the First Cause is just that, a *cause*, as well as being uncaused. This is for instance the basis for calling God 'generous' (*Pointers: Metaphysics*, VI.5). So the idea of a Necessary Existent can accommodate the

[17] However Marmura 1980 argues that the proof can be assembled from a range of passages in this text.

[18] Gutas 1988: 111 remarks that in the prologue of the *Healing* Avicenna presents himself 'as a conscious reformer of the Aristotelian tradition'. See also Bertolacci 2006: 609–10.

two apparently clashing claims about God with which we began: such an Existent will be both ineffable and the cause of all other things.

It is worth reiterating that all this flows from Avicenna's proof of God as the Necessary Existent. Al-Fārābī simply began the *Principles* by asserting that God is a First Cause of existence.[19] Avicenna can instead say—indeed prove, assuming his proof works—that God is required to 'preponderate' contingent things to exist (for more on the metaphysical basis of this see Rahman 1958). To some extent these ideas seem to have percolated into Avicenna's metaphysics from the Islamic theological tradition of *kalām* (Wisnovsky 2003: ch. 13). So it was, perhaps, only to be expected that theologians would warmly welcome the Avicennan designation of God as 'the necessary of existence'. Yet intimately related aspects of Avicenna's philosophical theology were not so gladly received. For he did not claim just that God necessarily *exists*. Rather, for Avicenna *everything* about God is necessary. If God had contingent features He would require another cause to preponderate those features one way or another. He cannot for instance cause His effects contingently, or know anything contingently, since a further external cause would be needed to explain why He winds up causing or knowing these things when He could just as easily not have done so. This leads Avicenna to two highly contentious claims. First, God necessarily gives rise to the universe, in an act for which Avicenna uses the traditional term 'emanation' (Janssens 1997; Lizzini 2011). The universe is eternal and could not fail to exist—it is, as Avicenna puts it, 'necessary through another' (that is, in itself contingent but guaranteed to exist by God's necessary emanative causality). Second, since God's knowledge is necessary it can involve no change or passivity, and therefore cannot be directed towards particulars as such. God does know all things, but only 'in a universal way' and only by knowing Himself as their cause (Marmura 1962; Adamson 2005; Nusseibeh 2010).

One might suppose that only the latter of these two claims is distinctively Avicennan. After all Aristotle, Plotinus, and more recently al-Fārābī had all endorsed the eternity of the universe. But prior to Avicenna it was actually quite common for Hellenizing philosophers to reject this Aristotelian and Neoplatonic position. Among opponents of eternity we can mention for instance al-Kindī, al-Rāzī, Saadia Gaon, and Miskawayh. It is noteworthy too that in the non-Avicennan tradition of al-Andalus, we see authors drawn to the view that reason cannot decide the eternity issue.[20] Thanks to Avicenna though, in the East the eternity thesis became indelibly associated with 'the philosophers'. Al-Ghazālī accordingly gave pride of place to this debate in his *Incoherence of the Philosophers*, adapting Avicenna's pro-eternity arguments and then attempting to

[19] This is probably connected to the methodological status of the *Principles*, which as its title implies sets down the principles of correct belief rather than working towards these principles. Elsewhere, it seems that for al-Fārābī the right way to establish God as a First Cause would be the traditional Aristotelian one: we grasp Him through His effects, as a cause of eternal motion (see for instance *The Attainment of Happiness*, translation in Alfarabi, *Philosophy*, §§17, 19). Averroes will later retrench to this method, rejecting the metaphysical or modal proof of Avicenna. On this see Bertolacci 2007.

[20] Most famously held by Maimonides, but also Ibn Ṭufayl tries to defuse the issue by showing that God's existence can be proved on either assumption. Of course Averroes staunchly defends the eternity thesis because of his allegiance to Aristotle.

expose their flaws. His discussion of eternity is so prominent that the reader may easily miss the broader intent of al-Ghazālī's critique. He wants to defeat not just the eternity thesis, but all that it represents, namely the necessitarianism of Avicenna's philosophical theology. Thus he goes out of his way to emphasize the contingency of God's creative act, which is best exemplified by the choice of an arbitrary moment for the beginning of the universe (al-Ghazālī, *Incoherence*, §1.41, and further Kukkonen 2000). Avicenna's necessitarianism is targeted throughout the *Incoherence*, for instance when al-Ghazālī argues in the third discussion that Avicenna is in no position to say that God is an 'agent' (*fāʿil*).

Al-Ghazālī was only the most famous of the Ashʿarite theologians who criticized Avicenna on these grounds. Two other major figures of the Ashʿarite school, al-Shahrastānī and Fakhr al-Dīn al-Rāzī (the former of whom may have had an Ismāʿīlī affiliation), may be compared to him in that they attack distinctive features of Avicenna's philosophical theology, despite retaining the core identification of God as the necessary existent. Here a good example is Avicenna's above-mentioned thesis that God lacks knowledge of particulars as such (for al-Rāzī on this topic see Abrahamov 1992). Al-Shahrastānī's *Wrestling Match with the Philosophers* (*Kitāb al-Muṣāraʿat al-falāsifa*) challenges Avicenna to explain how God's necessary causation of the cosmos relates to His knowledge of particulars 'in a universal way' (al-Shahrastānī, *Wrestling Match*, §4). After all God knows Himself without causing Himself to exist, so His knowledge is clearly not the same as His causal act. Furthermore, He manages to *cause* particulars to exist, so why can't He *know* about them in a particular way?

Of course one could imagine Avicennan responses to these and other arguments presented by al-Shahrastānī. The same goes for the welter of dialectical considerations presented in Fakhr al-Dīn's critical commentary on Avicenna's *Pointers*. Yet such texts show Avicenna's critics attacking him on the basis of a detailed understanding of his philosophical theology. These Ashʿarite theologians realize that they need to detach the claim that God necessarily exists (which they would hardly wish to deny) from the Avicennan project of deriving all the divine attributes from the notion of necessity. They even raise doubts concerning Avicenna's use of the individuation argument to show that there is only one necessary existent (Mayer 2003 and al-Shahrastānī, *Wrestling Match*, §3), as well as the more contentious claims that God necessarily gives rise to the universe and that He is an intellect. Such disputes demonstrate Avicenna's impact just as surely as more favourable commentaries like that of Naṣīr al-Dīn al-Ṭūsī. With Avicenna's philosophical theology, a new agenda has been set. The question is no longer how the ideas of Aristotle or Plotinus relate to the teachings of Islam. It is rather whether a Muslim theologian should follow Avicenna in understanding God as a necessary, and therefore transcendent, cause.

References

ʿAbbās, I. (ed.) (1983). *Rasāʾil Ibn Ḥazm al-Andalusī*. 4 vols. Beirut: al-Muʾassasa al-ʿarabiyya li-l-dirāsāt wa-l-nashr.

Abrahamov, B. (1992). 'Fakhr al-Dīn al-Rāzī on God's Knowledge of the Particulars'. *Oriens* 33: 133–55.

Adamson, P. (2002). *The Arabic Plotinus: A Philosophical Study of the 'Theology of Aristotle'*. London: Duckworth.
Adamson, P. (2003). 'Al-Kindī and the Muʿtazila: Divine Attributes, Creation and Freedom'. *Arabic Sciences and Philosophy* 13: 45–77.
Adamson, P. (2005). 'On Knowledge of Particulars'. *Proceedings of the Aristotelian Society* 105: 273–94.
Adamson, P. (2007a). *Al-Kindī*. New York: Oxford University Press.
Adamson, P. (2007b). 'The Kindian Tradition: The Structure of Philosophy in Arabic Neoplatonism'. In C. D'Ancona (ed.), *Libraries of the Neoplatonists*. Leiden: Brill, 351–70.
Adamson, P. (2010). 'Yaḥyā Ibn ʿAdī and Averroes on *Metaphysics* Alpha Elatton'. *Documenti e studi sulla tradizione filosofica medievale* 21: 343–74.
Adamson, P. (2011). 'Avicenna and his Commentators on Self-Intellective Substances'. In D. N. Hasse and A. Bertolacci (eds.), *The Arabic, Hebrew and Latin Reception of Avicenna's Metaphysics*. Berlin: de Gruyter, 97–122.
Adamson, P. (2013). 'From the Necessary Existent to God'. In P. Adamson (ed.), *Interpreting Avicenna: Critical Essays*. Cambridge: Cambridge University Press, 170–89.
Adamson, P. (2015a). 'Miskawayh on Pleasure', *Arabic Sciences and Philosophy* 25: 199–223.
Adamson, P. (2015b). *Philosophy in the Islamic World: A Very Short Introduction*. Oxford: Oxford University Press.
Adamson, P. (2016). *A History of Philosophy Without Any Gaps: Philosophy in the Islamic World*. Oxford: Oxford University Press.
Adamson, P., and P. E. Pormann (trans.) (2012). *The Philosophical Works of al-Kindī*. Karachi: Oxford University Press.
Adang, C., M. Fierro, and S. Schmidtke (eds.) (2013). *Ibn Ḥazm of Cordoba: The Life and Works of a Controversial Thinker*. Leiden: Brill.
Arkoun, M. (1961–2). 'Deux épîtres de Miskawayh'. *Bulletin d'Études Orientales* 17: 7–74.
Avicenna (*Ishārāt*). *al-Ishārāt wa-l-tanbīhāt maʿa Sharḥ Naṣīr al-Dīn al-Ṭūsī*. Ed. S. Dunya. 4 vols. Cairo: Dār al-Maʿārif, 1957–60.
Avicenna (*Healing*). *The Metaphysics of the Healing*. Ed. and trans. M. E. Marmura. Provo, UT: Brigham Young University Press, 2005.
Badawi, A. (1947). *Aflūṭīn ʿinda ʾl-ʿArab*. Cairo: Dirāsa Islāmiyya.
Badawī, A. (1952). *Manṭiq Arisṭū*. Cairo: Maktabat al-Nahḍa al-Miṣriyya.
Badawī, A. (1981). *Dirāsāt wa-nuṣūṣ fī l-falsafa wa-l-ʿulūm ʿinda l-ʿArab*. Beirut: Dār al-madār al-islāmī.
Bertolacci, A. (2005). 'On the Arabic Translations of Aristotle's Metaphysics'. *Arabic Sciences and Philosophy* 15: 241–75.
Bertolacci, A. (2006). *The Reception of Aristotle's Metaphysics in Avicenna's Kitāb al-Shifāʾ*. Leiden: Brill.
Bertolacci, A. (2007). 'Avicenna and Averroes on the Proof of God's Existence and the Subject-Matter of Metaphysics'. *Medioevo* 32: 61–98.
Brock, S. (1993). 'The Syriac Commentary Tradition'. In C. Burnett (ed.), *Glosses and Commentaries on Aristotelian Logical Texts: The Syriac, Arabic and Medieval Latin Traditions*. London: Warburg Institute, 3–18.
Daiber, H. (1986). 'Die Kritik des Ibn Ḥazm an Kindī's Metaphysik'. *Der Islam* 63: 284–302.
D'Ancona, C. (1991). 'Per un profilo filosofico dell'autore della *Teologia di Aristotele*'. *Medioevo* 17: 82–134.

D'Ancona, C. (1992). 'Aristotele e Plotino nella dottrina di al-Kindī sul primo principio'. *Documenti e studi sulla tradizione filosofica medievale* 3/2: 363–422.
D'Ancona, C. (1995). *Recherches sur le Liber de Causis*. Paris: J. Vrin.
Davidson, H. A. (1969). 'John Philoponus as a Source of Medieval Islamic and Jewish Proofs of Creation'. *Journal of the American Oriental Society* 89: 357–91.
Davidson, H. A. (1987). *Proofs for Eternity, Creation and the Existence of God in Medieval Islamic and Jewish Philosophy*. New York: Oxford University Press.
al-Fārābī (*Philosophy*). *Philosophy of Plato and Aristotle*. Trans. M. Mahdi. Ithaca, NY: Cornell University Press, 2001.
Fazzo, S., and H. Wiesener (1993). 'Alexander of Aphrodisias in the Kindī Circle and in al-Kindī's Cosmology'. *Arabic Sciences and Philosophy* 3: 119–53.
Frank, R. M. (1969). 'The Divine Attributes According to the Teaching of Abū l-Hudhayl al-'Allaf'. *Le Muséon: revue des études orientales* 82: 1–53.
Freudenthal, G., and M. Zonta (2012). 'Avicenna among Medieval Jews: The Reception of Avicenna's Philosophical, Scientific and Medical Writings in Jewish Cultures, East and West'. *Arabic Sciences and Philosophy* 22: 217–87.
Genequand, C. (trans.) (2001). *Alexander of Aphrodisias on the Cosmos*. Leiden: Brill.
Gerson, L. P. (1994). *Plotinus*. London: Routledge.
al-Ghazālī (*Incoherence*). *The Incoherence of the Philosophers*. Ed. and trans. M. E. Marmura. Provo, UT: Brigham Young University Press, 1997.
Gutas, D. (1988). *Avicenna and the Aristotelian Tradition*. Leiden: Brill.
Ivry, A. (1974). *Al-Kindi's Metaphysics*. Albany, NY: SUNY Press.
Janssens, J. (1997). 'Creation and Emanation in Ibn Sīnā'. *Documenti e studi sulla tradizione filosofica medievale* 8: 455–77.
Kraus, P., and R. Walzer (eds.) (1951). *Plato Arabus 1: Galeni compendium Timaei Platonis*. London: Warburg Institute.
Kukkonen, T. (2000). 'Possible Worlds in the *Tahāfut al-Falāsifa*: al-Ghazālī on Creation and Contingency'. *Journal of the History of Philosophy* 38: 479–502.
Lewis, G. L. (1950). 'A Re-examination of the So-Called Theology of Aristotle'. Doctoral dissertation. University of Oxford.
Lizzini, O. (2011). *Fluxus (fayḍ): Indagine sui fondamenti della metafisica e della fisica di Avicenna*. Bari: Pagina.
Lizzini, O. (2012). *Avicenna*. Rome: Carocci.
McGinnis, J. (2010). *Avicenna*. New York: Oxford University Press.
Marmura, M. E. (1962). 'Some Aspects of Avicenna's Theory of God's Knowledge of Particulars'. *Journal of the American Oriental Society* 82: 299–312.
Marmura, M. E. (1980). 'Avicenna's Proof from Contingency for God's Existence in the *Metaphysics* of the *Shifā*''. *Medieval Studies* 42: 337–52.
Mayer, T. (2001). 'Avicenna's *Burhān al-Siddiqīn*'. *Journal of Islamic Studies* 12: 18–39.
Mayer, T. (2003). 'Faḫr ad-Dīn ar-Rāzī's Critique of Ibn Sīnā's Argument for the Unity of God in the Išārāt and Naṣīr ad-Dīn aṭ-Ṭūsī's Defence'. In D. C. Reisman (ed.), *Before and after Avicenna*. Leiden: Brill, 199–218.
Neuwirth, A. (1976). *'Abd al-Laṭīf al-Baghdādī's Bearbeitung von Buch Lambda der aristotelischen Metaphysik*. Wiesbaden: Steiner.
Nusseibeh, S. (2010). 'Avicenna: Providence and God's Knowledge of Particulars'. In Y. T. Langermann (ed.), *Avicenna and his Legacy: A Golden Age of Science and Philosophy*. Turnhout: Brepols, 275–88.

Proclus (*Elements*). *The Elements of Theology*. Ed. and trans. E. R. Dodds. Oxford: Clarendon, 1963.

Rahman, F. (1958). 'Essence and Existence in Avicenna'. *Mediaeval and Renaissance Studies* 4: 1–16.

Rizvi, S. (2007). '(Neo) Platonism Revived in the Light of the Imams: Qāḍī Saʿīd Qummī (d. AH 1107/AD 1696) and his Reception of the Theologia Aristotelis'. In P. Adamson (ed.), *Classical Arabic Philosophy: Sources and Reception*. London: Warburg Institute, 176–207.

Rowson, E. (1990). 'The Philosopher as Littérateur: al-Tawḥīdī and his Predecessors'. *Zeitschrift für Geschichte der arabisch-islamischen Wissenschaften* 6: 50–92.

Rudolph, U. (2008). 'Reflections on al-Fārābī's Mabādiʾ Ārāʾ Ahl al-Madīna al-Fāḍila'. In P. Adamson (ed.), *In the Age of al-Fārābī: Arabic Philosophy in the Fourth/Tenth Century*. London: Warburg Institute, 1–14.

Ruland, H.-J. (1976). 'Die arabische Fassungen von zwei Schriften des Alexander von Aphrodisias: Über die Vorsehung und Über das liberum arbitrium'. Doctoral dissertation. Universität Saarbrücken.

al-Shahrastānī (*Struggling*). *Struggling with the Philosopher: A Refutation of Avicenna's Metaphysics*. Ed. and trans. W. Madelung and T. Mayer. London: I. B. Taurus, 2001.

Sorabji, R. (2004). *The Philosophy of the Commentators 200–600 AD*. 3 vols. London: Duckworth.

Walzer, R. (trans.) (1985). *Al-Farabi on the Perfect State*. Oxford: Oxford University Press.

Watt, J. (2010). *Rhetoric and Philosophy from Greek into Syriac*. Farnham: Ashgate.

Wilberding, J. (2006). *Plotinus' Cosmology*. Oxford: Oxford University Press.

Wisnovsky, R. (2003). *Avicenna's Metaphysics in Context*. London: Duckworth.

CHAPTER 19

ISMĀʿĪLĪ THEOLOGY

DANIEL DE SMET

Including a chapter on Ismāʿīlī theology in this volume is all but self-evident, as one may legitimately question the existence of 'theology' as a distinct field in medieval Ismāʿīlī thought. Unlike Zaydī and Imāmī Shīʿism, which underwent the increasing influence of Muʿtazilism and developed their own forms of *Kalām*, the third major branch of Shīʿite Islam remained overtly hostile to all kinds of Muslim speculative theology, be it of Muʿtazilite, Ashʿarite, or other inspiration. Moreover, most Ismāʿīlī authors had such a radical conception of the absolute transcendence of God that 'theology'—in the sense of a 'discourse about God'—becomes for them an impossible science.

Nevertheless, Ismāʿīlī doctrine—designated by the Ismāʿīlīs themselves as 'wisdom' (*ḥikma*) or as 'the science of the realities [of things]' (*ʿilm al-ḥaqāʾiq*)—could be considered both as 'philosophical' and as 'theological', as its main concern is the understanding of revelation through a philosophical reflection based on reason (*ʿaql*) and to establish religious doctrines on a rational basis. Although Ismāʿīlī authors made extensive use of Neoplatonic and Aristotelian sources when writing about the act of creation, the 'divine names and attributes', the first created being (the Intellect), and the other entities of the intelligible world, they sometimes use terms and arguments borrowed from *Kalām*—mainly Muʿtazilism, but also Ashʿarism. But they always integrate them in their own vision of God and the world, which is very distinct from all the other traditions in Islamic thought. The main difference resides in the fact that, according to the Ismāʿīlī viewpoint, all that Muslim theologians say about 'God', the Ultimate reality, only applies to His creation, in particular the first created being—the Intellect.

I The Rejection of *Kalām*

In his *Tanbīh al-hādī wa-l-mustahdī*, which is still unpublished, the famous Ismāʿīlī thinker Ḥamīd al-Dīn al-Kirmānī (d. after 411/1020) presents the different schools of Islamic theology as 'sects' (*firaq*) whose members are labelled as 'exoterists' (*ahl al-ẓāhir*). This means that they only adhere to the outward, literal meaning (*ẓāhir*) of the Qurʾān, ignoring or rejecting its true, 'inner' (*bāṭin*) sense which is taught by the Ismāʿīlī Imams.

Of all these theological 'sects', the most erring are, according to al-Kirmānī, the Ashʿarites and other groups of *ḥashwiyya* ('people professing futilities'), a derogatory term Ismāʿīlīs use to denote Sunnism in general. Taking the text of the Qurʾān literally, these theologians apply to God all kinds of names and attributes, thus associating Him with His creatures. By ascribing to God human characteristics (such as power, knowledge, life, liberality (*jūd*), or mercy), they are all guilty of *tashbīh*. Those who accept that the attributes are entities distinct from God's essence—as the Ashʿarites are supposed to do—profess *shirk*, 'polytheism'. The worst of all these people even go so far in their exoteric reading of the Qurʾān that they represent God under the shape of a man, sitting on a throne, with two hands, two legs, two eyes, two ears, a nose, and a mouth, speaking and commanding as a monarch. Their anthropomorphism is qualified by al-Kirmānī as *tajsīm* ('incorporation')—they claim that God has a (human) body, which is a form of unbelief (*kufr*) shared by the *ghulāt*, the members of ultra-Shīʿite movements who consider their Imam as God (al-Kirmānī, *Tanbīh*, 149–53). Manifestly, nothing is more incompatible with Ismāʿīlism than Ashʿarite and other Sunnite conceptions of God.

When dealing with the Muʿtazilites, al-Kirmānī is even more severe, perhaps because some Muʿtazilite positions are closer to the Ismāʿīlī approach. Time and again, al-Kirmānī and other Ismāʿīlī authors stress in their works that religious doctrine must fit the principles of reason (*ʿaql*)—what is contrary to reason cannot be true—and has to be exposed by way of demonstration (*burhān*), following the rules of logic. As the literal meaning of the Qurʾān contains many elements contrary to reason and as the Prophets expressed their message by using a symbolic language that is not built on apodictical demonstration, the text of the revelation has to be interpreted according to reason and by applying the method of demonstration (al-Kirmānī, *Maṣābīḥ*, 5–6, 8, 32, 38–9 of the Arabic text).

According to al-Kirmānī, this is exactly what the Muʿtazilites do, but in a wrong way. Starting from the Qurʾān, they formulate their doctrines about the divine attributes, the unicity of God (*tawḥīd*) or His justice (*ʿadl*), by rational deduction (*istidlāl bi-l-ʿaql*). The result of their reasoning is however a lot of 'lies' about God, as they are unable to avoid anthropomorphism or to escape from assimilating God to His creatures. The reason for their failure is the use of reason without any teacher: 'deduction by way of reason without teacher is vain' (*al-istidlāl min ṭarīq al-ʿuqūl min ghayr muʿallim bāṭil*) (al-Kirmānī, *Tanbīh*, 148).

This teacher is, of course, the Ismāʿīlī Imam. Being the only source of knowledge, he instructs his followers—the dignitaries of the Ismāʿīlī *daʿwa* and their 'respondants' (*mustajīb*) or initiates having subscribed to the pact of fidelity (*ʿahd*) to the Imam—how to interpret the text of revelation in a coherent and rational manner.

II 'Theology': An Impossible Science

Although Ismāʿīlism lacks a uniform doctrine, but covers a wide diversity of traditions and movements that all defend their own positions, there seems to be a kind of consensus on the matter of *tawḥīd*. As understood by the Ismāʿīlīs, *tawḥīd* means that the Ultimate principle—called *al-Mubdiʿ* ('The Creator')—is 'one' in such an absolute way that He has no name nor definition, and that He cannot be perceived in any way by His creatures. Being totally different from creation, the Creator remains outside the universe, hidden behind an impenetrable veil.

The absolute unity of the *Mubdiʿ* implies that He cannot be an intellect, as an incorporeal intellect necessarily has three aspects: it is intellect (*ʿaql*), the intellector (*ʿāqil*), and the intelligible (*maʿqūl*), which supposes a form of multiplicity. Therefore, the Ismāʿīlīs side with Plotinus against Aristotle and the Muslim philosophers (*falāsifa*) who conceive the First as an Intellect. They further follow Plotinus by claiming that the Intellect is inferior to the One, but they explicitly reject the idea that the Intellect proceeds from the One by emanation. The *Mubdiʿ* created (*abdaʿa*) the Intellect and put in him, 'all at once' (*dufʿatan wāḥidatan*), the totality of the Forms or Ideas of which all the species in the sensible world are the realizations in matter.

The Ismāʿīlīs reject the possibility of an emanation from the One not only to save the Muslim belief in creation, but also in order to preserve His absolute unicity. As emanation implies 'participation' between the emanated and its source and as the emanated is different from its source, the latter has in its essence a part that is not participated and a part that is participated by the emanated, which implies a form of duality in the source. For the same reason, Ismāʿīlī authors deny the existence of any link of causality between the Creator and the created. As the effect is already in the cause, the created shares something with its Creator but not His whole essence (otherwise, it would be identical with Him), which again leads to duality in the Creator. In consequence, the Creator created the Intellect, the first created being, in such a way that He is not the cause of the Intellect. According to Ismāʿīlism, there is no causality in God, as the Intellect is the First Cause, the 'Cause of causes' (*ʿillat al-ʿilal*). The Ismāʿīlī God is not the cause of the events in the intelligible and sensible worlds. This, of course, is completely incompatible with all forms of Muslim *Kalām*.

The Intellect, the first created being, only thinks himself and, by doing so, the Soul or another Intellect (according to the system followed) proceeds from him by way of emanation (*inbiʿāth*). Although he is the most perfect being in the universe, the Intellect is unable to think the Creator, which is not an intellect and hence not intelligible. The Intellect is conscious of the fact that there is 'something' above him whose existence he attests (*ithbāt*), without being able to perceive this Ultimate Reality in any way.

If the Intellect is unable to grasp the *Mubdiʿ*, how could our human rational faculty have any notion of Him? The 'exoterists' believe that God reveals Himself in the Books of the Prophets, for instance in the Qurʾān. Taking the text literally, they speak about God and ascribe to Him various names and attributes which in fact only refer to creation. Ismāʿīlī authors have developed a philosophy of language in order to show that any speech about God is impossible. Every word and every name, belonging necessarily to human language and hence to the order of creation, refers to a meaning (*maʿnā*) which also belongs to creation. God being outside the universe, there is no 'concept' of Him nor a 'meaning' referring to His essence which could be thought by our mind and expressed by our human language. Therefore, when common Muslims speak about God and when Sunnite (Ashʿarite) theologians speculate about His names and attributes, they commit anthropomorphism by assimilating God to His creatures (*tashbīh*).

The Ismāʿīlī authors of the Fāṭimid period (such as Abū Yaʿqūb al-Sijistānī (d. after 361/971) and al-Kirmānī) were aware of the fact that some Muslim philosophers (al-Kindī, for instance) and Muʿtazilite *mutakallimūn* had developed a kind of negative theology. But, according to the Ismāʿīlīs, simply denying attributes of God does not mean that the problem of *tashbīh* is solved. For this reason, al-Kirmānī accuses the Muʿtazilites of hypocrisy: despite all their theories about the negation of attributes to the divine essence, they say that God is living, knowing, and powerful, all attributes that are only applicable to created beings (al-Kirmānī, *Rāḥat al-ʿaql*, 149).

Negative theology is not a solution to preserve the transcendence of God. Even denying the three basic divine attributes of the Muʿtazilites leads to anthropomorphism. Saying that God is 'living' means associating Him with living beings; saying that He is 'not living' means associating Him with inanimate beings, such as stones and dead bodies. The same is true for the two other attributes, as knowledge and power, along with their negations, are qualities which only belong to created beings.

In consequence, both positive and negative theologies are wrong ways to speak about God. The only possibility left is to deny in turn every negation of an attribute: God is not living and not not living; He is not knowing and not not knowing; He is not powerful and not not powerful, and so on. But such a double negative approach to God does nothing more than stating that He is totally different from His creatures and that He shares not the slightest quality with them. This is indeed the ultimate aim of *tawḥīd*: 'denudation' (*tajrīd*). Or, as al-Sijistānī puts it: 'There is no more sublime and more noble form of denudation than the way we denudate our Creator by those statements which juxtapose two negations: a negation and the negation of this negation' (al-Sijistānī, *Kitāb al-Iftikhār*, 88).

In other words, *tawḥīd* means professing the absolute unity of God by removing from Him all that implies multiplicity (including the number 'one' which refers to the Intellect and which is, as all other numbers, somehow composed) and thus asserting His absolute transcendence and remoteness from creation. At the same time, *tawḥīd* implies the recognition that any form of speech about God, every 'theo-logy' is impossible. According to al-Kirmānī: 'The veracity of those who profess *tawḥīd* is confirmed when they attest that He cannot be expressed neither by an outward speech, nor by an interior thought. How could letters refer to an entity that brings into existence all things created, emanated and produced?' (al-Kirmānī, *Rāḥat al-ʿaql*, 145).

Nevertheless, if the ultimate object of *tawḥīd* is *tajrīd* ('denudating God from all qualities which belong to creation'), it has also another purpose: escaping from both *tashbīh* and *taʿṭīl*. The Ismāʿīlīs refuse to assimilate God with His creatures (*tashbīh*) by dissociating themselves not only from the common Muslim understanding of God, but also from the way the philosophers (*falāsifa*) and the theologians—the Ashʿarites, the Muʿtazilites, but also the Zaydīs and Twelver Shīʿites—speak about God. This is the task al-Kirmānī pursues in his *Tanbīh al-hādī wa-l-mustahdī*. But what about *taʿṭīl* ('the emptying of the notion of God from every content')? Is the absolute transcendent, hidden, unknown, and inexpressible *Mubdiʿ* of the Ismāʿīlīs not a sheer abstraction, 'empty' of every content? What is the difference between *tajrīd* and *taʿṭīl*?

It is not easy to answer this question, the more that it involves the delicate problem of the referent of the name *Allāh* and of all other divine names and attributes. Ismāʿīlī religious works contain many statements about *Allāh*, including pious Islamic sentences, prayers, quotations from the Qurʾān and from the *Ḥadīth*. But are these texts referring to the *Mubdiʿ*? Of course, authors such as al-Sijistānī and al-Kirmānī admit that one can speak about God in a traditional manner for religious purposes, but this speech has to be taken in a metaphorical way (*ʿalā ṭarīq al-majāz*). Common people, philosophers, and theologians who are not aware of this inevitably indulge themselves in *tashbīh*. On the other hand, what the Qurʾān says about *Allāh* has to be interpreted in such a way that it does not hamper the absolute transcendence of the *Mubdiʿ*. But any interpretation, if applied to the *Mubdiʿ*, seems impossible, as He is hidden and unknown to us.

The only exit from this paradox is to admit that the Creator, although unknown and inaccessible in His essence, reveals Himself in His creation. In other words, what the revelation states about God does not refer to the *Mubdiʿ* but to His most perfect creatures: the Intellect and the other entities of the intelligible world. The Creator in Himself is 'denudated' (*tajrīd*), but He is not an empty concept, as by creating the Intellect He reveals the richness of His essence, although its contents remain inaccessible to us.

III The Divine Word (*kalima*), the Will (*irāda*), and the Command (*amr*)

The act of creation (*ibdāʿ*) by which the *Mubdiʿ* brings into existence the first created being—the Intellect (*al-ʿAql*), bearing also other names, such as the 'Pen' (*al-qalam*), the Preceder (*al-Sābiq*), or *Kūnī*—is in its essence as unknowable as the *Mubdiʿ* Himself. Nevertheless, many verses of the Qurʾān hint at this creation, for instance Q 2: 117: 'Creator of the heavens and the earth. When He decrees a thing, He needs only say "Be" and it is (*kun fa-yakūnu*)'. Of course, according to Ismāʿīlī doctrine, such a statement has to be understood in a symbolical and metaphorical way. God does not speak at all—how could He? He is outside the universe; even in the intelligible world, there is no air, and thus no sound nor speech—a principle taken from the Arabic Plotinus. The *Mubdiʿ* has no decree, no will, no word, no command—all these are human qualities. To apply them to God is sheer anthropomorphism. Hence, the Qurʾānic verse reflects only the way the Prophet attempted to translate into human language the unknowable and inexpressible initiative by which the *Mubdiʿ* created being: *kun fa-yakūnu*. This means that, according to Ismāʿīlism, the Qurʾān has been 'created' by the Prophet—a position highly reminiscent of Muʿtazilism. The Prophet receives from the Intellect, through the intermediary of the other entities of the intelligible world, a non-verbal 'inspiration' (*taʾyīd*), which he translates into the language of his people, using images suitable to their culture, their understanding, and their intellectual level.

Once the initiative to create was taken by the *Mubdiʿ*—metaphorically expressed by the imperative *kun* ('Be!')—created being appeared (*fa-yakūnu*). Due to the increasing influence of Neoplatonism on Ismāʿīlī doctrine during the fourth/tenth century, many authors deemed it as evidence that only one single being proceeded from the *Mubdiʿ* ('from the one only one proceeds', *ex uno non fit nisi unum*, according to a well-known *adagium*)—the first created being, the Intellect. However, during its initial phase (third/ninth century) Ismāʿīlism also underwent the influence of some gnostic doctrines, claiming that from the Ultimate principle a multiplicity of hypostases proceeded all at once, such as the Will (*irāda, bouleisis*), the Word (*kalima, logos*), the Command (*amr*), and even the letters of the alphabet (in first instance *kāf* and *nūn*, the two consonants forming the imperative *kun*).

The Ismāʿīlī authors of the fourth/tenth century had a lot of trouble to conceive the nature of these 'divine' hypostases and their relation to the *Mubdiʿ* and to the 'first created being' (*al-mubdaʿ al-awwal*, i.e. the Intellect). Some of them thought that these are intermediate entities between the *Mubdiʿ* and the Intellect, while others (such as al-Kirmānī) claimed that they are all identical with the Intellect. Whatever the position adopted, these entities are considered as created beings through which the unknowable *Mubdiʿ* reveals Himself in some way, although they appear to be totally different from the Creator. The same applies to the Intellect who is the 'revealed God', the God of the prophetic revelations.

IV Allāh and His 'Most Sublime Name': Divinity and the Intellect

From an Ismāʿīlī perspective, all Muslim speculations about the divine attributes and the ninety-nine 'most beautiful names' (*al-asmāʾ al-ḥusnā*) of God constitute anthropomorphism when applied to the *Mubdiʿ*. As most of them are mentioned in the Qurʾān, they have necessarily a 'meaning' (*maʿnā*) and they refer to an 'essence' (*huwiyya*). According to Ashʿarite theology, the names of God are derived from His attributes, which in turn refer to *maʿānī*, 'realities' existing eternally in God's essence, although being distinct from it. As these *maʿānī* coexist in the essence of God from eternity, God is composed and marked by multiplicity, which for an Ismāʿīlī implies a form of polytheism (*shirk*). The Muʿtazilites, by contrast, consider the divine names and attributes as not distinct from His essence—they are only 'words' used to express God's essence in a human language. This position is considered by the Ismāʿīlīs as anthropomorphism (*tashbīh*).

By consequence, the 'divine' names and attributes, including *Allāh*, do not refer to the *Mubdiʿ*. If they refer to something that is not the *Mubdiʿ*, the reference must be to a created being. The Ismāʿīlī author of the *Kitāb al-Shajara* (fourth/tenth century) claims that the so-called 'ninety-nine names of God' all refer to *Allāh* and to *al-ilāhiyya* ('divinity'), which apply to the Intellect. *Allāh* and *al-ilāhiyya* are the highest attributes of the Intellect from which all the other 'divine' attributes—in fact attributes of the Intellect and of the lower entities of the intelligible world—derive. Hence, *Allāh* is not the 'name' of the Intellect (it is not a name at all, but an attribute: 'the divine'), as his name—the 'most sublime name' (*al-ism al-ʿaẓam*), a concept taken from the Muslim tradition—is only known to the Prophets, the Imams, and those having reached the highest degree of initiation. This 'most sublime name' expresses a meaning (*maʿnā*) and an 'essence' (*huwiyya*) that is hidden to all creatures—both in the intelligible and the sensible worlds—and to the Intellect himself: 'no creature can grasp it by no trick (*ḥīla*) whatsoever' (*Kitāb al-Shajara*, 83).

As a consequence, what the Qurʾān and other revealed Books—such as the Bible and the Gospel—have to say about 'God' applies in the first place to the first created being (the Intellect), and then to the higher principles in the intelligible world (the Soul or some lower cosmic entities). If some privileged persons know the 'real' name of the Intellect, which allows them to enter into conjunction with him—this is the highest form of felicity, according both to the Ismāʿīlīs and the *falāsifa*—this name refers to an essence that remains forever outside the reach of created beings—the *Mubdiʿ*. Nevertheless, there exists a reference and thus a link between the Creator and the Intellect, although the nature of this link is unknown, even to the Intellect. This means that the Creator reveals Himself, in some way or another, in His creation, so that He is not an empty abstraction of the human mind. The notion of the Ismāʿīlī *Mubdiʿ* is not 'emptied' (*taʿṭīl*), as His richness is reflected in the perfection of the Intellect. But as we are ignorant of the nature of this reflection, every attempt to deduce by analogy (*qiyās*) some knowledge of the Creator from creation is necessarily in vain. It only leads to assimilating the Creator to His creation (*tashbīh*).

The Intellect is 'the Divine' (*Allāh*) and he possesses the quality of 'divinity' (*ilāhiyya*) because, in his supreme perfection, he is fully aware of his incapacity to grasp the nature of his relation to the Creator. As an intellect, he can only think his own essence, but this act of auto-intellection does not teach him anything about the *Mubdiʿ*. He had liked to know Him, but his essence as an intellect forbids such a knowledge. The incapacity (*ʿajz*) to reach the ultimate object of his desire causes sadness to the Intellect. He is 'afflicted, grieved by sorrow' (*walaha*). This sadness is 'divinity' (according to an etymology deriving *ilhāniyya* or *ulhāniyya* from the verb *walaha*).

V The Unity of the Intellect: 'One in Essence and Multiple by Annexations'

In Ismāʿīlī doctrine, the major problems of Muslim theology, although removed from the Ultimate Principle due to its radical transcendence, appear nevertheless at a lower level: that of the first created being, the Intellect.

First, there is the question of the divine names and attributes. Taken for granted that they do not apply to the Creator but to the Intellect, the Ismāʿīlīs generally adopt a position very close to Muʿtazilism. They distinguish two kinds of attributes—attributes of essence (*ṣifāt al-dhāt*) and attributes of action (*ṣifāt al-fiʿl*). According to the author of the *Kitāb al-Shajara*, the attributes of action—such as 'the one who speaks' (*al-mutakallim*), 'the one who wills' (*al-murīd*), or 'the one who creates' (*al-khāliq*)—are characterized by the fact that it is legitimate to apply their contrary to God. Thus, one may say that God has spoken to Moses but not to Pharaoh; that He wanted for his servants all that is easy but not what is difficult; that He created man, but not his actions (this last example being overtly anti-Ashʿarite). As to the attributes of essence—such as 'the one who knows' (*al-ʿālim*) or 'the one who has power' (*al-qādir*)—it is not allowed to apply their contrary to God. For instance, it is illegitimate to say that God has known Moses but that He ignored Pharaoh, or that He had power for certain actions of ʿAlī but remained powerless as to his other actions (*Kitāb al-Shajara*, 83).

As the whole context of the passage is about the Intellect, the examples chosen by the author clearly show that the God of the Qurʾān is not the *Mubdiʿ* but the first created being, which bears all the names and attributes Muslims generally apply to Allāh. Hence the question arises how these attributes relate to the essence of the Intellect.

We saw that, according to Ismāʿīlī doctrine, the *Mubdiʿ* is 'one', but in a way that transcends 'oneness' in a numerical sense—in fact, the *Mubdiʿ* is above oneness and unity as He is above being and existence. The Intellect, on the contrary, represents being, existence, oneness, and unity at the most sublime level of perfection. But, as a created being, his unicity is relative—although being one, his essence is somehow marked by multiplicity.

With arguments close to Muʿtazilite theology, the Ismāʿīlīs claim that the attributes of essence and the attributes of action all refer to the one and uncomposed essence of the Intellect. These attributes are only means by which we conceive the perfection of his essence and his action in the universe, without denoting any form of composition in his essence. Al-Kirmānī formulated this principle in the following *adagium*: the Intellect is 'one by essence and multiple by annexations' (*wāḥid bi l-dhāt kathīr bi-l-iḍāfāt*) (al-Kirmānī, *Rāḥat al-ʿaql*, 177–8). This means that the Intellect is multiple as far as our human mind perceives both the richness of his essence and of his actions in the universe.

As far as the Intellect, situated at the highest level of the created universe, represents the fullness of being, his essence includes all the Forms or Ideas (in a Platonic sense) the Creator established in it 'all at once', at the very moment He created the Intellect. But these Forms are not distinct from the essence of the Intellect: they *are* his essence (*hiya huwa*). The attributes of essence are nothing more than the way the human mind grasps the ultimate perfection of the Intellect, or rather, the way the Prophets translate this perfection in a metaphorical, human language accessible to our rational faculty. By thinking his own essence as an intellect, the Intellect causes the emanation of a second being, of lesser perfection: the Universal Soul. By the intermediary of the Soul and some lower cosmic principles emanating from the Soul, the Intellect has an action upon the universe. His multiple actions, which in no way contradict the unicity of his essence, are expressed by the Prophets and conceived by the human mind by means of the attributes of action.

According to al-Kirmānī, the Intellect has ten principal attributes: 'truth' (*al-ḥaqq*), 'existence' (*al-wujūd*), 'unicity' (*al-waḥda*), 'completion' (*al-tamām*), 'perfection' (*al-kamāl*), 'eternity' (*al-azaliyya*), 'intellect' (*al-ʿaql*), 'science' (*al-ʿilm*), 'power' (*al-qudra*), and 'action' (*al-fiʿl*). All these attributes are rooted in an ultimate attribute—'life' (*al-ḥayāt*). Without life, the Intellect could not have power, nor knowledge, nor action. 'Life' is what animates the Intellect as a self-thinking intellect generating the universe and acting upon it. This is supposedly what the Prophet had in mind when he described God as *al-ḥayy al-qayyūm* ('The Living, the Ever-existent One' (Q 2: 255, 3: 2)) (al-Kirmānī, *Rāḥat al-ʿaql*, 186–90).

VI The Intellect as the Source of Revelation

Ismāʿīlī doctrine ascribes to the Intellect numerous functions. As the most perfect of all creatures, the Intellect is the efficient cause that produces, by way of emanation, the whole universe, from the Universal Soul to the lowest beings in the sublunary world, including the celestial spheres, the stars and the planets, the three 'reigns' on earth (the minerals, the plants, and the animals), and finally mankind. Due to his perfection, the Intellect is the principle of providence (*ʿināya*), providing the harmonious structure of the world and its subsistence; by the intermediary of the celestial spheres and their perfect circular motions, he regulates in a perfect way the cycles of generation and corruption on earth.

Moreover, the Intellect acts as a final cause, as all beings, from the Universal Soul to the lowest species of animals (and according to some authors even plants and minerals), are moved 'upwards' by a desire to return to the Intellect, the ultimate source of their existence. This Neoplatonic concept of a universal 'desire' (*shawq*) is explained by the Aristotelian distinction between potentiality (*quwwa*) and act (*fiʿl*). Only the essence of the Intellect is, from the very moment of its creation, completely actualized (from the outset it had reached its 'second perfection'), whereas all other beings in the universe, as they are less perfect than the Intellect, need their essence to be actualized: they are in potentiality (their 'first perfection') and desire to acquire the actualization they are lacking. Hence they are moved towards the Intellect.

The Intellect's providential action in the world is expressed by two notions which are fundamental in Ismāʿīlī thought: *mādda* ('influx') and *taʾyīd* ('support', 'inspiration'). *Mādda* is a kind of emanation that the Intellect continually provides to all beings in order to maintain them into existence, or, in other words, to grant them the degree of actualization necessary for their subsistence. By contrast, *taʾyīd* is a support especially addressed to mankind. Despite the Neoplatonic inspiration of Ismāʿīlī doctrine, its conception of revelation and of salvation has deep roots in Aristotelian noetics, going back to Aristotle's *Treatise on the Soul* (*De Anima*) and further developed by later Greek and Muslim philosophers. According to Aristotle, the rational faculty characteristic for the human soul is at the moment of birth in a state of sheer potentiality and must be progressively actualized by an intellect that is already in act, in order to become in turn an intellect in act. Greek commentators of Aristotle have called this intellect that actualizes the human potential intellect the 'Active Intellect' and they have identified it with a divine Intellect, situated outside the human mind. Most *falāsifa* adopted this position—the rational faculty can only be actualized when it enters into conjunction with the Active Intellect; once a perfect conjunction is realized, which implies that the rational faculty gets its complete actualization, it becomes immortal and subsists eternally, enjoying ultimate felicity.

Most of the Ismāʿīlī thinkers have adopted this theory, but they integrated it into their own Shīʿite vision of prophetology and imamology. The 'support' or 'inspiration' (*taʾyīd*) proceeding from the Intellect (eventually through the intermediary of other cosmic entities) joins with the rational faculty of some elected people—the 'Messengers', i.e. the Prophets and the Imams. As soon as they enter into conjunction with *taʾyīd*, their intellect is fully actualized—they accede at once to their 'second perfection'. This means that they grasp, in a perfect manner, the totality of intelligibles accessible to the human mind. The Prophets acquire moreover the capacity to translate this knowledge into images and symbols expressed in the language of their people (the outward, exoteric meaning of Scriptures), whereas the Imams obtain the science of their hidden, esoteric meaning (*ʿilm al-bāṭin*). Only by accepting the instruction (*taʿlīm*) of the Imam, can the rational faculty of the initiate (the 'Respondant', *mustajīb*) pass from potentiality to act. The intellect of the Imam, which is always in act, plays the same role as the Active Intellect in Greek and Arabic philosophy.

When the initiate has reached the final stage of instruction, his rational faculty accedes to its 'second perfection', becoming similar to the intellect of the Imam. It survives after the death of its body and will enjoy eternal felicity in a purely spiritual Paradise, located somewhere in the intelligible world.

VII Is Ismāʿīlī Doctrine after all a Kind of 'Theology'?

As we have shown in Section II, 'theology' in the narrow sense of a science, a rational speech (*logos*) about God, the Ultimate Reality, is not only impossible for an Ismāʿīlī, but it leads necessarily to false conceptions and 'heretical' positions, such as anthropomorphism and even polytheism. Without exception, all the Muslim *mutakallimūn*—both Ashʿarites and Muʿtazilites, both Zaydīs and Twelver Shīʿites—are considered as 'exoterists' (*ahl al-ẓāhir*), either adhering naively to the literal meaning of the Qurʾān, or using in a wild manner rational arguments, without the guidance of the true Imams. Nevertheless, as the first created being the Intellect is in fact the divinity adored by the monotheistic religions, and as this divinity, being an intellect, is perfectly intelligible, a rational science, a 'theology' of the Intellect should be possible. And indeed, when treating the essence of the Intellect, his attributes and names, and his action upon the universe, Ismāʿīlī authors use sometimes the same concepts and arguments as the *mutakallimūn*, mainly of the Muʿtazilite tradition.

But the main sources of Ismāʿīlī thought do not belong to *Kalām* but rather to philosophy—the Arabic versions of Plotinus's *Enneads* and of Proclus's *Elements of Theology*, along with the writings of the *falāsifa*, in particular al-Kindī, al-Fārābī, and Ibn Sīnā. Ismāʿīlī thought is often very close to Islamic philosophy, although the Ismāʿīlīs reject *falsafa* for the same reason they condemn Muʿtazilite *Kalām*: the philosophers make an abusive use of their rational faculty, as they do not follow the instruction of the Imams. In conclusion, one can say that Ismāʿīlī thought is both theological and philosophical without being *Kalām* nor *falsafa*. It is an 'esoteric science' (*ʿilm al-bāṭin*) whose object is the 'true meaning' (*ḥaqīqa*) of revelation, taught under the sole authority of the Imam.

Bibliography

ʿAbdān (attrib.) *Kitāb Shajarat al-yaqīn*. Ed. ʿĀ. Tāmir. Beirut: Dār al-āfāq al-jadīda, 1982.

Daftary, F. (2007). *The Ismāʿīlīs: Their History and Doctrines*. 2nd edn. Cambridge: Cambridge University Press.

De Smet, D. (1989). 'Le Verbe-impératif dans le système cosmologique de l'ismaélisme'. *Revue des Sciences Philosophiques et Théologiques* 73: 397–412.

De Smet, D. (1995). *La Quiétude de l'intellect: Néoplatonisme et gnose ismaélienne dans l'œuvre de Ḥamīd ad-Dīn al-Kirmānī*. Louvain: Peeters.

De Smet, D. (2007). 'Les Bibliothèques ismaéliennes et la question du néoplatonisme ismaélien'. In C. D'Ancona (ed.), *The Libraries of the Neoplatonists: Proceedings of the Meeting of the European Science Foundation Network 'Late Antiquity and Arabic Thought. Patterns in the Constitution of European Culture' held in Strasbourg, 12–14 March 2004*. Leiden: Brill, 481–92.

De Smet, D. (2008a). 'Al-Fārābī's Influence on Ḥamīd al-Dīn al-Kirmānī's Theory of Intellect and Soul'. In P. Adamson (ed.), *In the Age of al-Fārābī: Arabic Philosophy in the Fourth/Tenth Century*. London/Torino: The Warburg Institute/Nino Aragno Editore, 131–50.

De Smet, D. (2008b). 'Miroir, savoir et émanation dans l'ismaélisme fatimide'. In D. De Smet, M. Sebti, and G. de Callataÿ (eds.), *Miroir et savoir: la transmission d'un thème platonicien, des Alexandrins à la philosophie arabo-musulmane. Actes du colloque international tenu à Leuven et Louvain-la-Neuve, les 17 et 18 novembre 2005*. Louvain: Leuven University Press, 173–87.

De Smet, D. (2011). 'Ismāʿīlī Philosophical Tradition'. In H. Lagerlund (ed.), *Encyclopedia of Medieval Philosophy: Philosophy between 500 and 1500*. Wiesbaden: Springer, i. 575–7.

De Smet, D. (2012). *La Philosophie ismaélienne: un ésotérisme chiite entre néoplatonisme et gnose*. Paris: Éditions du Cerf.

Halm, H. (1978). *Kosmologie und Heilslehre der frühen Ismāʿīlīya: Eine Studie zur islamischen Gnosis*. Wiesbaden: Steiner.

al-Kirmānī, Ḥamīd al-Dīn (*Rāḥat al-ʿaql*). *Kitāb Rāḥat al-ʿaql*. Ed. M. Ghālib. Beirut: Dār al-Andalus, 1983.

al-Kirmānī, Ḥamīd al-Dīn (*Maṣābīḥ*). *Kitāb al-Maṣābīḥ fī ithbāt al-imāma*. Ed. P. E. Walker, *Master of the Age: An Islamic Treatise on the Necessity of the Imamate. A Critical Edition of the Arabic Text and English Translation of Ḥamīd al-Dīn Aḥmad b. 'Abd Allāh al-Kirmānī's al-Maṣābīḥ fī ithbāt al-imāma*. London: I. B. Tauris, 2007.

al-Kirmānī, Ḥamīd al-Dīn. *Kitāb Tanbīh al-hādī wa-l-mustahdī*. MS London, The Institute of Ismaili Studies, 723.

al-Sijistānī, Abū Yaʿqūb (*Iftikhār*). *Kitāb al-Iftikhār*. Ed. I. K. Poonawala. Beirut: Dār al-Gharb al-Islāmī, 2000.

Walker, P. E. (1993). *Early Philosophical Shiism: The Ismaili Neoplatonism of Abū Yaʿqūb al-Sijistānī*. Cambridge: Cambridge University Press.

Walker, P. E. (1999). *Ḥamīd al-Dīn al-Kirmānī: Ismaili Thought in the Age of al-Ḥākim*. London: I. B. Tauris.

CHAPTER 20

SUFI THEOLOGICAL THOUGHT

MARTIN NGUYEN

Sufism (*taṣawwuf*) may be broadly understood as one of the major mystical traditions of Islam, though its historical manifestations are exceedingly diverse in terms of ideas, teachings, practices, and institutions. While Sufism, as a distinctive mystical movement, does not appear until the third/ninth century in Baghdad, its latter-day proponents trace its origins back to the Prophet Muḥammad and his Companions. Additionally, a number of mystical trends were developing concurrently in areas like Baṣra, Egypt, Khurāsān, and Transoxania that would also inform the formation of the Sufi tradition. The following is not intended to be a comprehensive treatment of Sufi theological thought, but is aimed at providing a survey that is nonetheless representative of the major concerns, trends, and tensions that arose within the broad Sufi tradition.

Historically speaking, Sufism emerged out of the non-homogeneous spiritual milieu of the early Islamic period (Sviri 2005). Early Muslims devoted to pursuing the spiritual life, however that was conceived, were variously referred to as pietists (*nussāk*), renunciants (*zuhhād*), and worshippers (*ʿubbād*). A pietistic attitude of renunciation, focused on religious rectitude, moral fastidiousness, asceticism, and a vigilant fear of God, was prevalent prior to the rise of Sufism and continued after it (Melchert 1996; Melchert 2011). Early Sufis sought to interiorize the spiritual life, in contrast to the outward aspects of renunciation, and to cultivate or discipline the self as a means of obtaining greater relational proximity to God. Sufi theological thought is thoroughly theocentric in this regard. A distinctive set of beliefs developed as a result of this experiential reorientation toward God and a unique technical terminology gradually emerged as these ideas were articulated and elaborated upon by successive generations of Sufi exponents.

Later Sufi authors have cast a number of spiritual personalities, who historically precede the advent of Sufism, as being influential in the formation of the Sufi thought. Among them are the female ascetic Rābiʿa al-ʿAdawiyya (d. 185/801), Dhū l-Nūn al-Miṣrī (d. 254/860) in Egypt, Abū Yazīd (Bāyazīd) al-Bisṭāmī (d. 261/874–5) in Persia, and the moralizing theologian al-Ḥārith al-Muḥāsibī (d. 243/857) in Baghdad. The last of these individuals likely had a more direct influence on the coalescing Sufi movement given that al-Junayd (d. 298/910), a pre-eminent figure of early Baghdadi Sufism, counted himself a student of al-Muḥāsibī (Picken 2011). Two other important peers in the city were Abū Saʿīd al-Kharrāz (d. 286/899) and Abū l-Ḥusayn al-Nūrī (d. 295/907–8). Other contemporaneous mystics whose ideas would prove pivotal for later Sufi thought include al-Ḥākim al-Tirmidhī (d. *c.*295–300/905–10) in Transoxania and Sahl al-Tustarī (d. 283/896) in Basra. The famous mystic Abū Manṣūr al-Ḥallāj (d. 309/922) studied with al-Tustarī before coming to Baghdad where his positions (discussed herein) would diverge from those taken by the Sufis of Baghdad.

Beginning a century later mystic writers like Abū Naṣr al-Sarrāj (d. 378/988), Abū ʿAbd al-Raḥmān al-Sulamī (d. 412/1021), Abū Saʿd al-Khargūshī (d. 406/1015 or 407/1016), Abū l-Qāsim al-Qushayrī (d. 465/1072), al-Hujwīrī (d. *c.*465/1072–3 or 469/1076–7), and ʿAbd Allāh al-Harawī al-Anṣārī (d. 481/1089) composed a blend of handbooks and biographical dictionaries in an attempt to provide a lexical lens for mystical experience and a historical genealogy to support it (Mojaddedi 2001; Ansari and Schmidtke 2011). Through these efforts earlier ascetics, mystics, and concurrently developing spiritual groups, like the Sālimiyya and Malāmatiyya movements, were selectively incorporated into the expanding conceptual universe of Sufism (Melchert 2001a; Sviri 2005; Karamustafa 2007). An enduring tradition of Sufi poetry also developed and flourished in Arabic, as with Ibn al-Fāriḍ (d. 632/1235), but especially in Persian, with poets like Abū Saʿīd Ibn Abī l-Khayr (d. 440/1049), Farīd al-Dīn ʿAṭṭār (d. 627/1230), and Jalāl al-Dīn Rūmī (d. 672/1273). It is within these expository, contemplative, biographical, pedagogical, and poetic works that Sufi beliefs were expressed and developed.

I Sufi Engagement with Scholastic Theology

Before proceeding to the major principles of Sufi theological thought, Sufism's long engagement with scholastic theology warrants consideration. The work of scholastic theology was not the exclusive domain of the theologians, the *mutakallimūn*, nor were theological discussions solely circumscribed within the disciplines of scholastic theology (*ʿilm al-kalām*) and creedal formulation (*ʿaqīda*). The theocentrism underlying much of Sufi thought naturally led to the contemplation and elaboration of beliefs connected to the Godhead and God's relationship to creation, especially the human being. Additionally, pedagogical concerns and accusations of heterodoxy motivated many mystics and spiritual adepts to partake in the theological discourse. They composed as a result doctrinal creeds, contributed to the growing discourse of apologetics and polemics, and articulated their own systems of theology. Many Sufi texts collected and addressed sayings and expositions on conventional theological topics (conventional, at least, by the standards of Muslim scholasticism). These subjects included such matters as the nature of God, the soul, cosmology, theodicy, prophecy, soteriology, and eschatology. For instance, al-Muḥāsibī's *Kitāb al-Tawahhum* is a meditation on eschatological subjects channelled through the religious imagination. An apophatic or negative theology is expressed in the two creeds ascribed to al-Ḥallāj that appear respectively in the *Kitāb al-Taʿarruf* of al-Kalābādhī (d. 380/990 or 385/995) and *al-Risāla* of al-Qushayrī.

Even when theology was not the primary subject of a composed text, theological concerns and doctrinal positions were often acknowledged, addressed, or disputed as a matter of course, even if implicitly so. Theological matters could well be taken up and discussed in devotional and mystical treatises. The Ḥanbalī Sufi ʿAbd al-Qādir al-Jīlānī (d. 561/1166) appears to be addressing more than a Sufi audience in *al-Ghunya li-ṭālib ṭarīq al-ḥaqq* since the author presents traditionalist theological opinions while restricting his usage of technical Sufi terminology. Abū l-Qāsim al-Lajāʾī (d. 599/1202–3) begins his *Quṭb al-ʿārifīn* with a lengthy theological discussion of God's nature before undertaking his treatment of the principles of Sufism. This is not surprising given the theocentrism underlying much of Sufi thought and the fact that many adepts were educated in *uṣūl al-dīn* ('fundamentals of the religion') during the course of their spiritual training. Indeed, clear lines cannot always be drawn between theology and Sufi thought. Take for instance the writings and remembrance of al-Junayd, whose Sufi thought is born from his deep concern for *tawḥīd* or declaring the oneness of God (Abdel-Kader 1986). Similarly *al-Tajrīd fī kalimat al-tawḥīd* by Aḥmad al-Ghazālī (d. 520/1126) is a mystical series of exposition that emerges from a sustained meditation on the proclamation 'there is no god but God'. A sophisticated discourse on God pervades and indeed directs the mystical vision articulated by Muḥyī al-Dīn Ibn al-ʿArabī (d. 638/1240), especially his magnum opus *Futūḥāt al-makkiyya*. A number of Sufis after him, such as his student al-Qūnawī (d. 673/1274) and al-Jāmī (d. 898/1492), extensively commented upon the Sufi theological ideas presented by Ibn al-ʿArabī in their respective works.

Additionally, many Sufis explicitly addressed specific theological questions that were of critical importance to their mystical worldviews. The motivation was partially apologetic since the opponents of Sufism challenged the perceived orthodoxy of certain Sufi beliefs. The Hanbalī scholar Ibn Taymiyya (d. 728/1328), for example, wrote rectifying, or at least clarifying, commentaries of several sermons from al-Jīlānī's *Futūḥ al-ghayb* and the theological sayings gathered in al-Qushayrī's *al-Risāla*, especially the creed of al-Ḥallāj (Michot 2007). The renunciant and preacher Ghulām Khalīl (d. 275/888), disquieted by Sufi teachings, actually instigated and led an inquisition against them in Baghdad (Melchert 2001b, 360–2). The Sufi discussions that emerged in response, then, were meant to affirm the veracity and legitimacy of these particular claims. Hence, extended and careful discussions appear in Sufi writings that seek to differentiate and clarify subtle theological distinctions like the categorical distinctiveness of *walāya* or *wilāya* ('friendship with God') from *nubuwwa* ('prophethood'), the concomitant distinction between two types of miracle, *karāma* and *muʿjiza*, the beholding of God via ascension (*miʿrāj*) or vision (*ruʾya*), and the status of experiential knowledge (*maʿrifa*). A prime example of this phenomenon is al-Kālabādhī's *Kitāb al-Taʿarruf* where the early chapters are dedicated to introducing Sufism's conformity with mainstream Sunni positions on subjects like divine attributes (*ṣifāt*), the Qurʾān, predestination (*qadar*), and faith (*īmān*). Then the text turns to doctrines more directly relevant to the Sufi worldview. Al-Hujwīrī borrows from the heresiographical tradition within scholasticism in a section of his *Kashf al-maḥjūb* that emulates the *al-milal wa-l-niḥal* genre by enumerating different Sufi sects and then raising critiques wherever deemed appropriate.

The works of the Ashʿarite Sufi al-Qushayrī provide a broad range of examples of Sufi engagement with scholasticism. Not only does his *al-Risāla* furnish an introductory Sufi creed in line with mainstream theological positions, it also provides a series of supporting sayings ascribed to prominent early mystics. Then, later in the work, al-Qushayrī discusses the topics of *karāmāt, walāya*, and *ruʾya* while invoking the positions of both Sufis and Ashʿarite theologians like Ibn Fūrak (d. 406/1015), Abū Isḥāq al-Isfarāʾīnī (d. 418/1027), and al-Bāqillānī (d. 403/1013). Moreover, al-Qushayrī composed two brief treatises, *al-Lumaʿ* and *al-Fuṣūl fī l-uṣūl*, that are clearly concerned with conveying the fundamentals of Ashʿarite theology rather than mysticism (Frank 1982; Frank 1983). Finally, al-Qushayrī himself suffered persecution for his Ashʿarism under the reign of the Saljūqs, who were newly arrived in Khurāsān (Nguyen 2012, 40–42). In the midst of his tribulation al-Qushayrī issued a *fatwā* defending the orthodoxy of Abū l-Ḥasan al-Ashʿarī (d. 324/935–6) and composed an Ashʿarite apologia entitled *Shikāyat ahl al-sunna*. Doctrinally, many Sufis found Ashʿarism appealing given the space made for key Sufi principles like post-prophetic miracles as evidenced by al-Bāqillānī's *Kitāb al-Bayān*. Similarly the Sufi Ibn Khafīf (d. 371/982), who studied with al-Ashʿarī, incorporated Sufi tenets into his theological outlook, which is apparent in his *ʿaqīda* where *karāmāt* and *maʿrifa* are included alongside more conventional points. In fact his creed concludes with a section on the tenets of *taṣawwuf*.

Ashʿarism was not the only scholastic recourse for Sufis. A few references to Muʿtazilī Sufis are found for the early third/ninth century in Baghdad (Sobieroj 1999). However, the association appears short-lived as Muʿtazilī positions developed in contradistinction to Sunni ones, particularly over the created or uncreated nature of the Qurʾān. The Muʿtazilī denial of *karāmāt* exacerbated the rift with the Sufis and anti-Muʿtazilī sentiments can be found in early Sufi texts from Central Asia to al-Andalus (Fierro 1992). The tradition of *falsafa* also found occasional, though partial, support from certain Sufis. For instance, the writings of ʿAyn al-Quḍāt al-Hamadhānī (d. 525/1131) express a partiality for some of the views of Ibn Sīnā (d. 428/1037), which he attempts to apologetically defend (Safi 2006, 178–182). A more concerted synthesis of philosophy and Sufism thought is found in the *Ishrāqī* or Illuminist thought of Shihāb al-Dīn al-Suhrawardī (d. 587/1191). There are also several figures who bring together Shīʿism and Sufism in their thought, especially through Ibn al-ʿArabī's school of mystical thought. Examples can be found in the writings of Ḥaydar Āmulī (d. after 787/1385), Ibn Abī Jumhūr al-Aḥsāʾī (d. after 904/1499), and Fayyāḍ (d. 1072/1661–2).

Not all mystics, of course, were interested in participating in or aligning with the scholastic discourse. Al-Tustarī and Abū Ṭālib al-Makkī (d. 386/996), for example, instead preferred to articulate their theological positions through reference to the Qurʾān and prophetic reports. Nor does al-Qushayrī's contemporary Abū Saʿīd Ibn Abī al-Khayr (d. 440/1049) evince any serious concern for scholastic matters in his recorded poetry or sayings. Even Abū Ḥāmid al-Ghazālī (d. 505/1111), though an Ashʿarite in theology, expressed reservations concerning *ʿilm al-kalām* in both *al-Munqidh min al-ḍalāl* and *Iljām al-ʿawāmm*. Likewise, ʿAyn al-Quḍāt al-Hamadhānī, though he was familiar with and draws upon the theological lexicon, firmly believed Sufism to be the superior salvific path. Centuries later, al-Jāmī composed a *muḥākama* work entitled *al-Durra al-fākhira* in which the views of the Sufis on eleven major theological issues are presented in contrast to those of the philosophers and theologians. The work not only argues for the superiority of the Sufi position, but it also demonstrates that in later periods the Sufi position was understood by some as an independent and coherent theological perspective. Indeed, a number of Sufis were even openly opposed to the speculative discussions of *ʿilm al-kalām*. The Ḥanbalī Sufi ʿAbd Allāh al-Anṣārī (d. 481/1089) went so far as to compose *Dhamm al-kalām*, a voluminous critique of scholastic theology. As the historical tradition demonstrates, adherence to Sufism did not necessarily imply adopting one theological position over others nor did it preclude any such partnerships.

II The Discourse on 'States' and 'Stations' of the Sufi Path

Sufi adepts envisioned the spiritual life as an interior path (*ṭarīqa*) oriented towards God with those committed to this mode of religiosity described as wayfarers on it. The literature that emerged in conjunction with this notion focused on describing a series of spiritual states (*aḥwāl*, sing. *ḥāl*) and stations (*maqāmāt*, sing. *maqām*) that a spiritual seeker could anticipate experiencing. The *aḥwāl* generally referred to passing and potentially recurring conditions that descend upon the heart in response to one's developing relationship with God. They included such notions as contraction (*qabḍ*) and expansion (*basṭ*), union (*jamʿ*) and separation (*farq*), proximity (*qurb*), certainty (*yaqīn*), and witnessing (*mushāhada*). The *maqāmāt* were largely seen as stages through which the wayfarer passes on his/her journey to God and included spiritual stations like trust (*tawakkul*), renunciation (*zuhd*), repentance (*tawba*), patient perseverance (*ṣabr*), and sincerity (*ikhlāṣ*). Despite the recurring focus on *aḥwāl* and *maqāmāt*, Sufi writers were far from systematic in their classification nor consistent with previous articulations. The notion of fear (*khawf*), for instance, might be classified as a *ḥāl* by al-Sarrāj in his *Kitāb al-Lumaʿ* and a *maqām* by al-Qushayrī in his *al-Risāla*.

Dhū l-Nūn al-Miṣrī, in some accounts, is credited as the first to describe such a system of spiritual states and stations. In addition to the texts just mentioned, others that follow a similar model of spiritual discourse include al-Kharrāz's *Kitāb al-Ṣidq*, al-Nūrī's *Maqāmāt al-qulūb*, al-Tirmidhī's *Manāzil al-ʿubbād*, al-Kālabādhī's *Kitāb al-Taʿarruf*, Abū Ṭālib al-Makkī's *Qūt al-qulūb*, al-Sulamī's *Jawāmiʿ ādāb al-ṣūfiyya*, al-Khargūshī's *Tahdhīb al-asrār*, al-Hujwīrī's *Kashf al-maḥjūb*, ʿAbd Allāh al-Anṣārī's *Ṣad maydān* and *Manāzil al-sāʾirīn*, Abū Ḥāmid al-Ghazālī's (d. 505/1111) *Iḥyā ʿulūm al-dīn*, Ibn al-ʿĀrif's (d. 536/1141) *Maḥāsin al-majālis*, Shihāb al-Dīn al-Suhrawardī's (d. 587/1191) *Risālat Maqāmāt al-Ṣūfiyya*, and Abū Ḥafs ʿUmar al-Suhrawardī's (d. 632/1234) *ʿAwārif al-maʿārif* down through to later works like al-Suyūṭī's (d. 911/1505) *Taʾyīd al-ḥaqīqa al-ʿaliyya*, Zakariyyā al-Anṣārī's (d. 926/1520) *al-Futūḥāt al-ilahiyya*, or Ibn ʿAjība's (d. 1224/1809) *Miʿrāj al-tashawwuf*. The mystic al-Niffarī (d. *c.*366/977) appears to differ with the early tradition in his preference for spiritual stayings or *mawāqif*, though later Sufis, like Ibn al-ʿĀrif, Ibn al-ʿArabī, and ʿAfīf al-Dīn al-Tilimsānī (d. 690/1291) would make some use of his ideas. Najm al-Dīn Kubrā (d. 617/1220) in *Fawāʾiḥ al-jamāl* expands the discourse by including a spiritual phenomenology of coloured lights that associated with the various conditions of the path.

III Experiential Knowledge of God and Divine Union

The concept of *maʿrifa*, 'gnosis' or 'experiential knowledge', is a key tenet of Sufism and was typically positioned as the culminating point of the spiritual path. *Maʿrifa* is typically contrasted with *ʿilm* ('acquisitive knowledge'), referring to knowledge that is acquired through learning, or *ʿaql* ('intellect'), referring to the rational faculty seated in the mind. While conventional theologians might consider *ʿilm* and *maʿrifa* synonyms for one another Sufis set the latter above and beyond the former. Sufi writers generally describe *maʿrifa* as an experiential knowledge of the Divine that is not obtained, but bestowed upon the heart of the aspirant by God. This gradual positioning of *maʿrifa* over *ʿilm* or *ʿaql* can be traced in the literature. In *Kitāb Māʾiyyat al-ʿaql* al-Muḥāsibī takes up the question of the intellect and explores its nature and relationship to God. Then, the Baghdadi Sufi al-Nūrī in *Maqāmāt al-qulūb* turns to the heart and its reception of divine favours. Later sayings attributed to al-Nūrī and others, as in al-Sarrāj's *Kitāb al-Lumaʿ* and al-Kalābādhī's *Kitāb al-Taʿarruf*, are more explicit in asserting the primacy of *maʿrifa* over *ʿaql*. Although Dhū l-Nūn al-Miṣrī leaves no text on the subject of *maʿrifa* the later collections of al-Sulamī and Abū Nuʿaym al-Iṣfahānī (d. 430/1038) ascribe to him some of the earliest discussions of it. The paramount importance of *maʿrifa* is more evident in the later manuals of al-Sarrāj, al-Kalābādhī, al-Khargūshī, al-Qushayrī, and al-Hujwīrī given the extended discussions granted it. This understanding is elaborated upon by later figures like Abū Ḥāmid al-Ghazālī, who places the way of the Sufis at the apex of his hierarchy of ways of seeking truth in *al-Munqidh min al-ḍalāl*, and ʿAyn al-Quḍāt al-Hamadhānī (d. 526/1131), who discussed Sufis accessing a realm of apprehension beyond that which is obtainable by the intellect.

A related foundational doctrine is articulated by al-Junayd in his surviving *rasāʾil* (Abdel-Kader 1976). In speaking of *tawḥīd*, al-Junayd posits four stages of it, the last two of which are reserved for those privy to *maʿrifa*. He describes these stages as a transformation of one's existence such that one's actions are no longer motivated by hope or fear, but rather are brought into harmony with the divine will. At the utmost level of *tawḥīd*, one experiences a true realization of God's oneness. Al-Junayd is here delineating a doctrine of union with God. In support of this assertion are his theories on the pre-eternal covenant, *al-mīthāq*, and the passing away or annihilation of the human self, *fanāʾ*. The term *al-mīthāq* is used to invoke the Qurʾānic verse in which God asks humanity prior to its creation 'Am I not your Lord?' to which humanity replies 'Yes, we do testify!' (Q 7: 172). According to al-Junayd the unitive experience of *tawḥīd* is in fact a return to this primordial state of existence with the Creator. As the individual progresses through the stages of *tawḥīd* and attains greater realizations of proclaiming God's oneness the individual also gains in proximity to the Divine. Al-Junayd's doctrine of *fanāʾ* asserts that the individual's sense of self passes away in the approach, which in essence is a reunion with God.

Yet, the notion that one could experience union with God pre-dates al-Junayd. Al-Sarrāj records al-Junayd's attempts to interpret the earlier words of Abū Yazīd al-Bisṭāmī on such experiences. In one place al-Bisṭāmī describes undertaking a journey to God that is resonant with the *miʿrāj* or heavenly ascension of the Prophet Muḥammad. Elsewhere, ecstatic utterances or *shaṭḥiyāt* are attributed to him that presumably result from a unitive experience of God, like the exclamation 'Glory be to me! Glory be to me! (*subḥānī! subḥānī!*)', which explicitly invokes a formula of praise typically reserved for God (Ernst 1985). Those sympathetic to al-Bisṭāmī understand such theologically scandalous proclamations as God speaking through him given that al-Bisṭāmī's sense of self had passed away before the overwhelming divine presence. Al-Junayd and al-Sarrāj followed this line of argument in their attempts to absolve al-Bisṭāmī's statements from any possible heterodox taint. Such cases were made to counter criticisms that the doctrine of *fanāʾ* implied a union with God in which the distinction between the human self and God was lost (*ittiḥād*). Rather, the type of union being argued for preserved an essential distinctiveness between the human self and God (*ittiṣāl*). Later theorists like al-Qushayrī maintained that only certain blameworthy aspects of the self passed away in *fanāʿ* and that the person still maintained some degree of distinctive individuality before the overwhelming presence of God. Al-Junayd also partnered his theory of *fanāʾ* with the concomitant theory of *baqāʾ* ('subsistence'), which held that even after the stage of passing away, there was a greater stage in which the human self continues to abide with the Divine. In essence, a greater state of mastery exemplified by self-possession was posited as existing beyond the ecstatic moment that could be prompted by *fanāʾ*.

Al-Junayd's doctrinal paradigm, however, was significantly challenged by the life and teachings of al-Ḥallāj, his younger contemporary (Massignon 1954). Al-Ḥallāj had studied with Sahl al-Tustarī and was even initiated into Baghdādī Sufism though he publicly broke with this latter tradition and developed his own repertoire of spiritual teachings and miracle working, and social and political criticisms. His popularity as a preacher and the public nature of his societal critique put him at odds with various power interests, which resulted in a series of trials where his spiritual practices and teachings were made the ostensible object of scrutiny. The actual nature of his views is substantially obfuscated by the later, often hagiographic, literature. Ascribed to al-Ḥallāj are a number of ecstatic utterances, the most famous of which is 'I am the Truth (*anā l-ḥaqq*)' (Ernst 1985). Although the attribution is likely apocryphal, it nevertheless became a hallmark of his legacy and speaks to a similar understanding of the mystical experience of divine union expressed by al-Bisṭāmī. Al-Ḥallāj in purportedly uttering the proclamation was expressing the annihilation of his self such that only God remained. Additionally al-Ḥallāj is said to have preached of an intense love of God such that he actively desired his own martyrdom. His understanding of *tawḥīd* at the level of the Divine also collapsed seemingly necessary theological distinctions, like that of belief (*īmān*) and infidelity (*kufr*). The importance of the *sharīʿa*, while never dismissed, was relativized and made to recede before the powerful experience of divine union. For his views, some Sufis criticized al-Ḥallāj for exposing to the public the highly particularized and private experiences born out of mystical union. Others sought to justify or exempt his views. More vehement critiques, especially those unconcerned with the mystical worldview, accused al-Ḥallāj of outright heterodox beliefs, either subscribing to a conception of union as *ittiḥād* or to the doctrine of divine incarnation or in-dwelling (*ḥulūl*). Whatever the case, the public profile of al-Ḥallāj's life and death ensured a divisive legacy in which later mystics were compelled to espouse positions of deliberative abstention, support, or condemnation of al-Ḥallāj.

IV Oneness of Being

Perhaps the most influential doctrine based upon the principle of *tawḥīd* and Sufi notions of experiential knowledge is the theory of *waḥdat al-wujūd* or 'oneness of being', which is ascribed to Ibn al-ʿArabī and is indeed expressed by him although the precise term does not seem to have been used by him (Chittick 2012, 71–88). According to Ibn al-ʿArabī God is the only real existent in that the attribute of existence (*wujūd*) in actuality belongs to God alone. In this respect, God as the Real and only true existent is transcendent and beyond all creation. All other entities, as things of creation, do not exist in-and-of themselves but can only be said to exist through the share of existence granted to them via God's attribute of *wujūd*. Thus, the theory of *waḥdat al-wujūd* also speaks to the simultaneous immanence of God in that all of creation, in all its multiplicity and derived existence, is in fact a manifestation of God the Real. A possible antecedent to this theory, at least the immanence aspect, may arguably be found with the Badghdadi Sufi al-Kharrāz who states that *tawḥīd* is to perceive creation as a manifestation of the Creator. For Ibn al-ʿArabī, one simultaneously affirms divine immanence and transcendence in asserting the oneness of being.

The doctrine of *waḥdat al-wujūd* was further articulated and disseminated by Ibn al-ʿArabī's students and later followers: among the most prominent are Ibn Sabʿīn (d. 669/1270), Ṣadr al-Dīn al-Qūnawī (d. 673/1274), and Saʿīd al-Dīn al-Farghānī (d. 699/1300), ʿAbd al-Ghanī al-Nābulusī (d. 1143/1731), and Ibn ʿAjība. The doctrine, however, also attracted harsh criticism from a diverse array of scholars like Ibn Taymiyya, Ibn Khaldūn (d. 784/1382), al-Taftazānī (d. 793/1390), and others (Knysh 1999). These attacks largely focused on the immanence claim within the doctrine while ignoring the assertion of transcendence critically joined to it. Modern critics of *waḥdāt al-wujūd* have largely accused Ibn al-ʿArabī and his followers of subscribing to monism (the belief that there is no distinction between God and the cosmos), pantheism (the belief that the cosmos is a manifestation of God), or panentheism (the belief that God is greater than the cosmos while also inclusive of it). The Sufi thinker Aḥmad Sirhindī (d. 1034/1624) attempted an emendation to the doctrine by positing *waḥdat al-shuhūd* such that the focus was on the subjective 'witnessing' of the spiritual adept rather than on any perceived impugnment of the existential transcendence of God. This was a means of maintaining the doctrine through a semantic and perspectival shift.

V Ascensions and Visions

The notion of divine encounter addressed by early figures like al-Bisṭāmī, al-Junayd, and al-Ḥallāj would inform the worldview of later Sufis in a number of ways. The ascension experience described by al-Bisṭāmī drew attention to the Prophet Muḥammad's heavenly ascension such that it became an important source of spiritual reflection. For instance, a discussion of the *miʿrāj* is the last session listed in al-Khargūshī's *Kitāb al-Lawāmiʿ* (Ansari and Schmidtke 2011). His contemporary al-Sulamī gathered a collection of earlier sayings on the ascension in his *Laṭāʾif al-miʿrāj*. Then, their student al-Qushayrī provided a more theological investigation of the ascension experience in *Kitāb al-Miʿrāj*, where he addresses the details and questions surrounding the *miʿrāj* of the Prophet Muḥammad as well as ascensions ascribed to other prophets. More significantly for Sufi theological thought, he also asserted the possibility of non-bodily ascensions for the spiritual elite, mentioning the case of al-Bisṭāmī specifically. Later, Ibn al-ʿArabī would return to and take up the *miʿrāj* as a means of symbolically conveying aspects of their cosmology and metaphysical thought. In fact, he records four personal ascension experiences, once in his *Kitāb al-Isrāʾ* and *Risālat al-Anwār* and twice in the *Futūḥāt al-makkiyya*. The *miʿrāj* narrative, then, became a symbolic means of communicating aspects of the unitive experience or experiential knowledge.

Related to the *mirʿāj* was the question of the direct vision of God (*ruʾyat Allāh*) since some claimed that the Prophet Muḥammad saw God at the apex of his journey. Writers like al-Kalābādhī and al-Qushayrī claimed that the vision of God was not attainable in this life. Yet other early mystics spoke of some sort of divine communion via *ruʾya*, typically understood as a 'vision' or 'dream'. Sahl al-Tustarī of Basra was reportedly prone to spiritual visions, which in turn greatly informed his mystical teachings. Similarly, Ruzbihān al-Baqlī's (d. 606/1209) *Kashf al-asrār* is entirely shaped by the author's experience of symbolically rich visions (Ernst 1996). These visions also served the initiatic purpose of affirming Ruzbihān's authority and rank within his envisioned spiritual hierarchy. A number of pivotal visions also figure into the life of Ibn al-ʿArabī that shape the course of his spiritual development. As for dreams, they played an important role in the life of al-Ḥākim al-Tirmidhī as documented in his autobiography and likewise serve to impart spiritual insights or provide initiatic indications. Notably he reports of his wife's dreams in addition to his own. Whatever the source, the dreams are implicitly granted a degree of authoritative insight in accordance with a prophetic tradition in which divinely originated dreams are said to have a share in revelation. In later Sufi collections the reports of dreams are abundant. Accounts describe encounters with the Prophet Muḥammad, past spiritual paragons, or living masters in which some teaching, affirmation, admonishment, or foresight is conveyed.

VI Mystical Love, *Maḥabba* and *ʿIshq*

In many strands of Sufi thought a language of intimacy developed in order to better convey the notions of proximity, longing, and approach in pursuit of the experiential knowledge of God. A number of proto-Sufi figures are attributed sayings in which they speak of God in intimate relational terms. Spiritual personalities like Rābiʿa al-ʿAdawiyya and Dhū l-Nūn al-Miṣrī are remembered for framing their relationship with God in terms of *uns* ('intimacy') and *maḥabba* ('love'). Al-Hujwīrī and others characterized those following al-Bisṭāmī's ecstatic example as being intoxicated with divine love, which was then contrasted with al-Junayd's belief that sobriety was the more perfect form of response. The teachings of al-Ḥallāj were also frequently couched in terms of love of God, rather than the fear of God attitude found among many of the early renunciants. Notions of mystical love persisted within the Sufi tradition and were variously expounded upon. The Ottoman Sufi Maḥmūd Hüdāʾī (d. 1038/1628–9), for example, composed the mystical treatise *Ḥabbat al-maḥabba* that is dedicated to explicating three forms of *maḥabba* as they respectively relate to God, the Prophet Muḥammad, and the Prophet's family.

This turn in language can also be framed according to the contrasting conceptions of a transcendent and immanent God. Both sides found precedent in the attributes, names, and actions used to describe God in scripture. Those more closely aligned with the scholastic or traditionalist theological discourses spoke of a largely transcendent God at a conceptual remove. The apophatic theology found in the creeds of al-Ḥallāj and al-Qushayrī evince this mode of discussing the nature of God. The relational language of intimacy, however, was not without its scriptural precedent either. The usage of a term like *maḥabba* could equally be anchored in the Qurʾān. Furthermore a genre of commentarial literature on the divine names developed, which provided Sufis with a wide lexicon with which they could articulate both the transcendence and immanence of God. Some of the Sufis who produced such commentaries were al-Qushayrī, al-Ghazālī, Ibn Barrajān (d. 536/1141), Ibn al-ʿArabī, Aḥmad Zarrūq (d. 1493), and ʿAbd al-Ghanī al-Nābulusī. Sufis also engaged with the divine names beyond the commentarial literature as found, for example, in the many works of Ibn al-ʿArabī, but especially the *Futūḥāt* (Chittick 1989).

Yet the language of intimacy used by mystics was hardly confined to the vocabulary anchored in scripture. A prominent case is demonstrated in the Sufi discussions over the appropriateness of using the term *ʿishq*, meaning passionate or sensual love, in reference to God. What survives of Ibn Khafīf's views, for instance, expresses a decisive judgement against the appropriateness of *ʿishq* while his student and biographer Abū l-Ḥasan al-Daylamī (d. early fifth/eleventh century) composed a work approving of it. Indeed al-Daylamī finds precedent for its usage with al-Bistāmī, al-Junayd, and al-Ḥallāj and even alleges that his master Ibn Khafīf eventually changed his position. Another Sufi, ʿAyn al-Quḍāt al-Hamadhānī, is remembered as *sulṭān al-ʿushshāq* given the love-oriented nature of his mystical discourse. In Aḥmad al-Ghazālī's work *Sawāniḥ al-ʿushshāq* the author refers to love as both *maḥabba* and *ʿishq* and makes it the central organizing principle to his larger system of mystical thought.

An enduring tradition of mystical poetry developed hand-in-hand with the turn to mystical love. Such poems first appeared in Arabic and Persian and then in Turkish, Urdu, and other Islamicate languages. The theme of mystical love found fertile ground in this form and erotic imagery was often invoked. For instance, divine love is the subject of the Arabic poem *al-Khamriyya* by Ibn al-Fārid (d. 632/1235) and as the title indicates the poem plays upon the motif of intoxication. Similar themes of love are also expressed in the poetry of Farīd al-Dīn ʿAṭṭār (d. 627/1230), Jalāl al-Dīn Rūmī (d. 672/1273), and Ḥāfiẓ (d. 792/1390). That some Sufis felt compelled to clarify the theocentrism underlying their rhetoric of love is shown in the history of Ibn al-ʿArabī's poem *Tarjumān al-ashwāq*, for which the author added a commentary after hearing criticisms that his poetry was in actuality not about God, but the mentioned woman.

Yet many Sufis had no issue in finding their love of God reflected in various aspects of the worldly realm. Figures like Awḥad al-Dīn al-Kirmānī (d. 635/1238) and Fakhr al-Dīn ʿIrāqī (d. 688/1289) spoke of witnessing God through the contemplation of a beautiful woman or a male youth, a practice referred to as *naẓar ʿilā aḥdāth* or *shāhid-bāzī*. While a notable theme and practice, these notions were also challenged or adapted by other Sufis, as al-Hujwīrī and Rūmī respectively did. Tales of earthly love and devotion also served as allegories for love of God in the poetic tradition. Some of the most prominent examples are the tales of Layla and Majnūn, Maḥmūd and Ayāz, the prophet Yūsuf and Zulaykha, and the namesakes of al-Jāmī's poem *Salamān wa-Absāl*. In a similar vein, a substantial portion of the poems in Rūmī's *Dīwān* explicitly invoke his memory of Shams-i Tabrīzī while simultaneously expressing his love of God (Lewis 2003).

Integral to this development in Sufi thought were the concepts *ʿishq-i majāzī* ('figurative or metaphorical love') and *ʿishq-i ḥaqīqī* ('real love'). The former immediately represents the varieties of love experienced in the world, while the latter refers to love of God. Many Sufi advocates of mystical love argued that *ʿishq-i majāzī* was a means of attaining *ʿishq-i ḥaqīqī* or even that the distinction between the two was superficial since all other forms of love are indeed manifestations of one's true love of God.

This latter line of thinking is especially resonant with the earlier discussion of *waḥdat al-wujūd* and was similarly accused of blurring the distinction between Creator and creation.

VII Friendship with God (*walāya*) and Miracles (*karāmāt*)

Walāya or *wilāya* within Sufism refers to the doctrine of 'friendship with God' in which *walī* (pl. *awliyā'*) refers to a 'friend of God'. The doctrine generally asserts that certain individuals are the recipients of divine blessings and favours on account of their high spiritual rank (Mojaddedi 2012). The discussions of *walāya* often centred on differentiating the friend of God from a messenger (*rasūl*) and/or prophet (*nabī*). Additionally, it was emphasized that *awliyā'* could continue to appear in the present despite the eventual ascendancy of the doctrinal understanding of *khātam al-nabiyyīn* ('the seal of the prophets') to mean that the Prophet Muḥammad signalled the end of prophethood (*nubuwwa*). Closely connected to this concern was the insistence of Sufis that post-prophetic miracles could still occur. As *al-Kashf wa-l-bayān* of al-Kharrāz and *Sīrat al-awliyā'* of al-Ḥākim al-Tirmidhī indicate, the debates concerning *walāya* were already under way by their time and they were specifically responding to a group of mystics who actually espoused the superiority of *walāya* over *nubuwwa*.

Al-Tirmidhī himself interpreted *khātam al-nabiyyīn* differently and took it to mean that the Prophet Muḥammad stood superior to the other prophets given that he was protected from the machinations of the lower self and Satan. He then proposed a theory of *khātam al-walāya* ('the seal of friendship of God') in which a specially designated friend of God would similarly be protected from lapses and temptations, possess an eschatological and salvific intercessory role, and receive a personal form of divine communication (*ḥadīth*) distinct from revelation (*waḥy*), which was reserved for prophets (Radtke and O'Kane 1996). For al-Kharrāz the superiority of the prophets lay in their public mission to spread God's message whereas the friends of God had no such calling. Other voices like Ibn Khafīf, al-Kalābādhī, al-Qushayrī, and al-Hujwīrī were even more categorical in asserting the superiority of prophets to friends of God. For example al-Hujwīrī states that the end of friendship with God is just the beginning of prophethood. Following a similar line of thought, ʿAyn al-Quḍāt al-Hamadhānī states that while the friends of God are in a state of knowing beyond that of reason, the prophets are accordingly in a state beyond that of the friends of God.

Not all mystics were as concerned with maintaining or arguing for a clear distinction. When al-Tustarī discusses the *awliyā'* in his *tafsīr* he grants them a high rank close to that of the prophets as well but is not at pains to stress difference. Instead, he claims that the friends of God can possibly attain a proximity to God that the prophets are naturally granted. Yet, he too does add a distinction. While both groups serve as reminders for the rest of humankind, prophets have the added duty of *tablīgh* or the active dissemination of God's message. Abū Ṭālib al-Makkī was also less concerned with arguing a difference and paired the *awliyā'* with the *anbiyā'* in a commonly shared spiritual fraternity. Rumi likewise frequently speaks of the *awliyā'* and *anbiyā'* together, but does so to emphasize a person's potential to attain high degrees of spiritual advancement and not to assert a theological distinction. What is important for these figures appears to be a continuity of mystical access rooted in prophetic experience but enduring in *walāya*.

A notion of spiritual hierarchy is also implicit in *walāya*. For al-Tirmidhī some friends of God are given higher stations than others in emulation of the different favours shown to the prophets. Many later mystics would expand and elaborate upon this hierarchical structure of *walāya*. It pervades, for instance, the mystical visions of Ruzbihān al-Baqlī in which he is continually cast as being the apex of such a spiritual order. Ibn al-ʿArabī actually comments extensively upon al-Ḥākim al-Tirmidhī's ideas of *walāya* in his *Futūḥāt* and furnishes his own arrangement of the friends of God that begins with a singular *qutb* for every age and then broadens as it descends down through the ranks of imams, *awtād, abdāl*, and so on (Chodkiewicz 1986).

Finally, typological discussions of miracles are found among several early mystic writers. Notably, the earliest Sufis refer to prophetic miracles as *āyāt* with the terminology later shifting to *muʿjizāt* likely in a move to align with the developing scholastic discourse. Whatever the terms used, Sufi writers offered an array of arguments in support of non-prophetic miracles or *karāmāt* appearing after the prophetic period as well as arguments for how the two were different. Al-Tirmidhī, for instance, not only addressed miracles during the course of his *Sīrat al-awliyā'*, but he composed a more concerted treatment called *al-Farq bayna l-āyāt wa-l-karāmāt*. In general, he dismisses the claim of opponents that argue that miracles belong to prophets alone and instead distinguishes between two types of miracles: an *āya* is an act of God's power and is what is manifest with prophets while the *karāma* is an act of God's generosity and is what is manifest with the friends of God. Al-Kharrāz makes a qualitative assertion and states that *āyāt* are superior to *karāmāt* in addition to being the exclusive domain of prophets. In *Tahdhīb al-asrār* al-Khargūshī offers a number of distinctions like the public nature of *muʿjizāt* versus the more private and hidden nature of *karāmāt*, the uniqueness of certain *muʿjizāt* to which *karāmāt* cannot compare, and the possible continued endurance of a *muʿjiza* after the life of a prophet versus *karāmāt* which cannot endure beyond the life of a *walī* (Melchert 2010). Similarly al-Qushayrī, following certain earlier Ashʿarite arguments, believed that a *muʿjiza* was accompanied by a challenge to (futilely) imitate it (*taḥaddī*) and a claim to prophethood (*daʿwa al-nubuwwa*), while a *karāma* lacked these two things and was more inwardly oriented. However the case was made, with time the possibility of *karāma* came to be a conventionally accepted doctrinal position held by a great many later mystics and religious scholars.

VIII Theological Refigurations

Certain trends within Sufi theological thought also reimagined or reinterpreted figures of religious significance in different ways according to their respective mystical outlooks. One of the earliest examples is Sahl al-Tustarī who professed through his commentary of the Qurʾān a light cosmology concerning the primordial creation of Muḥammad (Böwering 1980, 149–53). According to al-Tustarī Muḥammad was created as a pillar of light from the light of God in a moment prior to the rest of creation. As a result light symbolism permeates al-Tustarī's theology and humanity is cast as emanations of preceding prophetic lights, which in turn emanate from the light of Muḥammad (*nūr Muḥammad*). In this schema Muḥammad is elevated in rank and given primordial priority over Adam.

Later mystics like al-Ḥallāj and Najm al-Dīn Rāzī Dāya (d. 654/1256) expanded upon this central idea; for al-Ḥallāj all prophecy issues from the lamp that is Muḥammad and for Najm al-Dīn Rāzī the lights of other prophets all derive their luminosity from him. Under Ibn al-ʿArabī the primordial Muḥammad is described as the archetype of humanity as well as of creation in general. Indeed, in preceding the rest of creation Muḥammad comes to be understood as the divine impetus for creation itself. The cycle of prophecy begun *in illo tempore* culminates with the earthly manifestation of the Prophet Muḥammad. This enduring essence of Muḥammad came to be identified as the highest level of realization and was called *ḥaqīqa Muḥammadiyya* or 'the Muḥammadan Reality' (Schimmel 1985, 132–4). Related is the concept of *al-insān al-kāmil*, the Complete Human Being or Perfect Man, which was also discussed by Ibn al-ʿArabī and then elaborated upon by his followers like ʿAzīz al-Dīn Nasafī (d. before 699/1300), Quṭb al-Dīn al-Jīlī (d. 832/1428), and al-Jāmī (Chittick 2012, 143–52). Once again Muḥammad represents an ideal archetype. He is, as the complete human being, the microcosm of the macrocosm that is the rest of creation. But he is also the complete human being in that all the divine names of God are manifest in him. In this regard *al-insān al-kāmil* is a mirror for the self-disclosure of God. Invoking the meaning-laden Qur'anic term *barzakh* (Q 23: 100, 25: 53, 55: 20) the Perfect Man is cast as the intermediate locus between creation and the Divine. The goal of the spiritual aspirant then is to attain union with the clarity of realization associated with the *ḥaqīqa Muḥammadiyya* and to manifest in the world the divine names as completely as *al-insān al-kāmil*.

Another prominent example of a personality who was refigured within Sufi thought was Iblīs (Awn 1983). While typically cast as an exemplar of pride, a rebel, or as a tempter, and hence closely tied to theological conceptions of theodicy, several Sufis recast him as a tragic self-sacrificing figure or as a true devotee or even lover of God. For al-Ḥallāj, Iblīs was a true monotheist for his refusal to bow before Adam. In his poetic verses Sanāʾī develops a strong pathos for Iblīs, who is turned into a tragic character whose condemnation is destined on account of his unswerving devotion to *tawḥīd*. ʿAyn al-Quḍāt al-Hamadhānī in his Persian work *Tamhīdāt* actually heralds

Iblīs as a lover of God who guards the way to proclaiming God's oneness. Through a series of poetic reversals, Iblīs is transformed into one worthy of honour or at least sympathy since his ecstatic defiance is described as predetermined and integral to the divine plan. Indeed, Iblīs's assumption of this duty was understood by some Sufis as the example *par excellence* of self-sacrifice for the sake of the Divine. In these ways, conventional theological understandings of sacred persons were given new significations for different Sufi worldviews.

IX Socially Deviant Renunciant Movements

From the seventh/thirteenth century onwards there arose a number of renunciant movements that differed dramatically from the pietistic trend of renunciation found throughout the early Islamic period (Karamustafa 1994). Two of the most notable of such movements were the Qalandariyya, who looked to Jamāl al-Dīn Sāvī, and the Ḥaydariyya founded by Quṭb al-Dīn Ḥaydar (d. *c.*618/1221–2). While far from a homogeneous phenomenon, these movements were generally more intensive in their austerity and asceticism. Social deviance was also strikingly exhibited in their practices, appearance, and beliefs. These movements were intentionally counter-cultural and often developed in direct response to the gradual institutionalization of Sufism. Though these groups were often marginalized by other Sufis, they nevertheless represent a significant development of certain elements of Sufi thought.

Nonetheless, elements of Sufi thought were adopted and adapted by many of these socially deviant renunciant movements. Concepts like *fanāʾ* and *walāya* were given more radical interpretations. For instance, the Ḥaydarīs believed that the prophetic spirit could be beheld in the human face and so they refrained from growing beards. Otman Baba (d. 883/1478–9) believed *walāya* was the inner dimension of *nubuwwa* and elaborated a typology of friends of God reflective of his views. There were, for him, insane (*dīvānah*) and licit (*mashrūʿ*) *awliyāʾ* of which the former were superior to the latter since the licit friends of God remained bound by the *sharīʿa* while the insane ones were free of it. Indeed, aspects of antinomianism were common to these groups. If the presence of God pervaded creation, then there was no longer any need to observe the religious law. Indeed, those who followed Baraq Baba (d. 707/1307–8) in Syria were known for not observing outward religious rituals and for consuming prohibited substances. Others, like the Abdāls of Rūm and Jalīlīs in India, exhibited a different counter-cultural vein by adopting Shīʿī beliefs as a means of opposing their predominantly Sunnī environment. The Abdāls of Rūm venerated the twelve Imams and looked to ʿAlī as their model. A similar case is found with the Bektashīs whose reverence for ʿAlī sets him alongside God and the Prophet Muḥammad.

Bibliography

Abdel-Kader, A. H. (1976). *The Life, Personality and Writings of Al-Junayd*. London: E. J. W. Gibb Memorial.

Ansari, H., and S. Schmidtke (2011). 'Abū Saʿd al-Ḫargūšī and his Kitāb al-Lawāmiʿ: A Ṣūfī Guide Book for Preachers from 4th/10th century Nīšāpūr'. *Arabica* 58: 503–18.

al-Anṣārī, Zakariyyā (*Ḥaqīqa*). *Ḥaqīqat al-taṣawwuf al-Islāmī yaḥwā kitābayn al-Futūḥāt al-ilāhiyya fī nafʿ arwāḥ al-dhawāt al-insāniyya li-Zakariyyā al-Anṣārī wa-risāla fī al-kalām ʿalā nashʾat al-taṣawwuf wa-l-Ṣūfiyya wa-aʿmālihim*. Ed. Muḥammad Tawfīq al-Bakrī. Cairo: Maktabat al-Ādāb, 2nd edition, 1992.

Awn, P. (1983). *Satan's Tragedy and Redemption: Iblīs in Sufi Pyschology*. Leiden: Brill.

al-Bāqillānī, Abū Bakr (*Bayān*). *Kitāb al-Bayān ʿan al-farq bayna al-muʿjizāt wa-l-karāmat wa-l-ḥiyal wa'l-kahāna wa-l-siḥr wa-l-nāranjāt*. Ed. R. McCarthy. Beirut: Librairie Orientale, 1958.

al-Baqlī, Ruzbihān (*Unveiling*). *The Unveiling of Secrets: Diary of a Sufi Master*. Trans. C. Ernst. Chapel Hill: Parvardigar Press, 1997.

Böwering, G. (1980). *The Mystical Vision of Existence in Classical Islam: The Qurʾānic Hermeneutics of the Ṣūfī Sahl At-Tustarī (d. 283/896)*. Berlin: de Gruyter.

Chittick, W. C. (1989). *The Sufi Path of Knowledge: Ibn al-ʿArabi's Metaphysics of Imagination*. Albany, NY: SUNY Press.

Chittick, W. C. (2012). *In Search of the Lost Heart: Explorations in Islamic Thought*. Ed. M. Rustom, A. Khalil, and K. Murata. Albany, NY: SUNY Press.

Chodkiewicz, M. (1986). *Seal of the Saints: Prophethood and Sainthood in the Doctrine of Ibn ʿArabī*. Trans. L. Sherrard. Cambridge: Islamic Text Society.

Chodkiewicz, M. (1993). *An Ocean without Shore: Ibn Arabi, The Book, and the Law*. Trans. D. Speight. Albany, NY: SUNY Press.

al-Daylamī, ʿAlī b. Muḥammad (*Love*). *A Treatise on Mystical Love*. Trans. J. N. Bell and H. M. Abdul Latif Al Shafie. Edinburgh: Edinburgh University Press, 2005.

al-Daylamī, ʿAlī b. Muḥammad (*Sīra*). *Sīrat al-shaykh al-kabīr Abī ʿAbd Allāh Muḥammad b. Khafīf al-Shīrāzī*. Cairo: al-Hayʾa al-ʿāmma li-shuʾūn al-maṭābiʿ al-amīriyya, 1977.

Ernst, C. W. (1985). *Words of Ecstasy in Sufism*. Albany, NY: SUNY Press.

Ernst, C. W. (1996). *Ruzbihan Baqli: Mysticism and the Rhetoric of Sainthood in Persian Sufism*. Surrey: Curzon Press.

van Ess, J. (1961). *Die Gedankenwelt des Ḥāriṯ al-Muḥāsibī: Anhand von Übersetzungen aus seinen Schriften dargestellt und erläutert*. Bonn: Orientalisches Seminar der Universität Bonn.

Fierro, M. (1992). 'The Polemic about the Karāmāt al-awliyāʾ and the Development of Ṣūfism in al-Andalus (Fourth/Tenth–Fifth/Eleventh Centuries)'. *Bulletin of the School of Oriental and African Studies* 55: 236–49.

Frank, R. M. (1982). 'Two Short Dogmatic Works of Abū l-Qāsim Al-Qushayrī. First Part: Edition and Translation of "Lumaʿ fī l-iʿtiqād"'. *Mélanges: Institut Dominicain d'Études Orientales du Caire* 15: 53–74.

Frank, R. M. (1983). 'Two Short Dogmatic Works of Abū l-Qāsim Al-Qushayrī. Second Part: Edition and Translation of "Al-Fuṣūl fī l-Uṣūl"'. *Mélanges: Institut Dominicain d'Études Orientales du Caire* 16: 59–75.

al-Ghazālī, Abū Ḥāmid (*Deliverance*). *Deliverance from Error: An Annotated Translation of al-Munqidh min al Dalāl and Other Relevant Works of Al-Ghazālī*. Trans. R. J. McCarthy. Louisville, KY: Fons Vitae, 1999.

al-Ghazālī, Abū Ḥāmid (*Iḥyāʾ*). *Iḥyā ʿulūm al-dīn*. Ed. Muḥammad Wahbī Sulaymān and Usāma ʿUmūra. 5 vols. Damascus: Dār al-Fikr, 2006.

al-Ghazālī, Aḥmad (*Sawāniḥ*). *Sawāniḥ*. Ed. H. Ritter. Tehran: Markaz-i Nashr-i Dānishfāhī, 1368/1989.

al-Ghazālī, Aḥmad (*Tajrīd*). *Al-Tajrīd fī kalimat al-tawḥīd*. Ed. Aḥmad Mujāhid. Tehran: Intishārāt-i Dānishgāh-i Tihrān, 1384[/2005–6].

al-Hamadhānī, ʿAyn al-Quḍāt (*Apologia*). *A Sufi Martyr: The Apologia of ʿAin al-Quḍāt al-Hamadhānī*. Trans. A. J. Arberry. London: George Allen and Unwin Ltd, 1969.

al-Hamadhānī, ʿAyn al-Quḍāt (*Tamhīdāt*). *Tamhīdāt*. Ed. ʿAfīf ʿUsayrān. Tehran: Dānishgāh-i Tihrān, 1341/1962.

al-Harawī, ʿAbd Allāh (*Manāzil*). *Kitāb Manāzil al-sāʾirīn*. Beirut: Dār al-kutub al-ʿilmiyya, 1988.

Heer, N. L. (trans.) (1979). *The Precious Pearl: Al-Jāmī's Al-Durrah al-Fakhirah together with his Glosses and the Commentary of ʿAbd al-Ghafūr al-Lārī*. Albany, NY: SUNY Press.

al-Hüdāʾī, Maḥmud b. Faḍl Allāh (*Maḥabba*). *Ḥabbat al-maḥabba*. Ed. Saʿīd ʿAbd al-Fattāḥ. Cairo: Maktabat al-thaqāfa al-dīniyya, 2001.

al-Hujwīrī (*Revelation*). *Revelation of the Mystery (Kashf al-Mahjub)*. Trans. R. A. Nicholson. Accord, NY: Pir Press, 1999.

Ibn ʿAjība (*Miʿrāj*). *Miʿrāj al-tashawwuf ilā ḥaqāʾiq al-taṣawwuf*. Ed. Maḥmūd Bayrūtī. Beirut: Dār al-Bayrūtī, 2004.

Ibn ʿAjība (*Oneness*). *Two Treatises on the Oneness of Existence by the Moroccan Sufi Aḥmad Ibn ʿAjība (1747–1809)*. Trans. J.-L. Michon. Cambridge: Archetype, 2010.

Ibn al-ʿArabī, Muḥyī al-Dīn (*Collection*). *The Tarjumán al-Ashwáq: A Collection of Mystical Odes*. Trans. R. A. Nicholson. London: Theosophical Publishing House, 1978.

Ibn al-ʿArabī, Muḥyī al-Dīn (*Futūḥāt*). *Al-Futūḥāt al-Makkiyya*. Ed. Osman Yahya. 14 vols. Cairo: al-Hayʾa al-miṣriyya al-ʿāmma li-l-kitāb, 1972–92.

al-Iṣfahānī, Abū Nuʿaym (*Ḥilya*). *Ḥilyat al-awliyāʾ wa-ṭabaqāt al-aṣfiyāʾ*. 8 vols. Ed. Sāmī Anūrjāhīn. Cairo: Dār al-Ḥadīth, 2009.

De Jong, F., and B. Radtke (eds.) (1999). *Islamic Mysticism Contested: Thirteen Centuries of Controversies and Polemics*. Leiden: Brill.

al-Kalābādhī, Abū Bakr (*Taʿarruf*). *The Doctrine of the Ṣūfīs (Kitāb al-Taʿarruf li-madhhab ahl al-taṣawwuf)*. Trans. A. J. Arberry. Cambridge: University of Cambridge Press, 1935.

Karamustafa, A. (1994). *God's Unruly Friends: Dervish Groups in the Islamic Later Middle Period 1200–1550*. Salt Lake City: University of Utah Press.

Karamustafa, A. (2007). *Sufism: The Formative Period*. Berkeley: University of California Press.

al-Kargūshī, Abū Saʿd (*Tahdhīb*). *Tahdhīb al-Asrār*. Ed. Bassām Muḥammad Bārūd. Abu Dhabi: al-Majmaʿ al-Thaqafī, 1999.

al-Kharrāz, Abū Saʿīd (*Ṣidq*). *The Book of Truthfulness (Kitāb al-Ṣidq)*. Ed. A. J. Arberry. London: Oxford University Press, 1937.

Knysh, A. (1999). *Ibn ʿArabī in the Later Islamic Tradition: The Making of a Polemical Image in Medieval Islam*. Albany, NY: SUNY Press.

Knysh, A. (2000). *Islamic Mysticism: A Short History*. Leiden: Brill.

al-Lajāʾī, ʿAbd al-Raḥmān b. Yūsuf *(Quṭb). Quṭb al-ʿārifīn fī l-ʿaqāʾid wa-l-taṣawwuf*. Ed. Muḥammad al-Dībājī. Beirut: Dār al-Ṣādir, 2001.

Lewis, F. (2003). *Rumi: Past and Present, East and West: The Life, Teachings and Poetry of Jalâl al-Din Rumi*. Oxford: Oneworld.

al-Makkī, Abū Ṭālib *(Qūt). Qūt al-qulūb fī muʿāmalat al-maḥbūb wa-waṣf ṭarīq al-murīd ilā* maqām al-tawḥīd. Ed. Bāsil ʿUyūn al-Sūd. 2 vols. Beirut: Dār al-kutub al-ʿilmiyya, 1997.

Massignon, L. (1954). *Essai sur les origins du lexique technique de la mystique musulmane*. Paris: Vrin.

Massignon, L. (1975). *La Passion de Husayn Ibn Mansūr Hallāj: martyr mystique de l'Islam exécuté à Bagdad le 26 mars 952. Étude d'histoire religieuse*. 4 vols. Paris: Gallimard.

Meier, F. (1957). *Die Fawāʾiḥ al-jamāl wa-fawātiḥ al-jalāl des Nağm al-Dīn al-Kubrā*. Wiesbaden: Steiner.

Melchert, C. (1996). 'The Transition from Asceticism to Mysticism at the Middle of the Ninth Century C.E.'. *Studia Islamica* 83: 51–70.

Melchert, C. (2001a). 'Sufis and Competing Movements in Nishapur'. *Iran: Journal of Persian Studies* 39: 237–47.

Melchert, C. (2001b). 'The Ḥanābila and the Early Sufis'. *Arabica* 48: 352–67.

Melchert, C. (2010). 'Khargūshī, Tahdhīb al-asrār'. *Bulletin of the School of Oriental and African Studies* 73: 29–44.

Melchert, C. (2011). 'Exaggerated Fear in the Early Islamic Renunciant Tradition'. *Journal of the Royal Asiatic Society* 21: 283–300.

Michel, T. (1981). 'Ibn Taymiyya's Sharḥ on the Futūḥ al-ghayb of ʿAbd al-Qādir al-Jīlānī'. *Hamdard Islamicus* 4/2: 3–12.

Michot, Y. (2007). 'Ibn Taymiyya's Commentary on the Creed of al-Ḥallāj'. In A. Shihadeh (ed.), *Sufism and Theology*. Edinburgh: Edinburgh University Press, 123–36.

Mojaddedi, J. (2001). *The Biographical Tradition in Sufism: The Ṭabaqāt Genre from al-Sulamī to Jāmī*. Richmond: Curzon.

Mojaddedi, J. (2012). *Beyond Dogma: Rumi's Teachings on Friendship with God and Early Sufi Theories*. Oxford: Oxford University Press.

al-Muḥāsibī, al-Ḥārith (*Sharaf*). *Sharaf al-ʿaql wa-māhiyya*. Ed. Muṣṭafā al-Qādir ʿAṭā. Beirut: Dār al-kutub al-ʿilmiyya, 1986.

Nguyen, M. (2012). *Sufi Master and Qur'an Scholar: Abū'l-Qāsim al-Qushayrī and the Laṭāʾif al-ishārāt*. Oxford: Oxford University Press.

al-Niffarī (*Mawāqif*). *The Mawāqif and Mukhāṭabāt of Muḥammad ibn ʿAbdi ʾl-Jabbār al-Niffarī with Other Fragments*. Ed. and trans. A. J. Arberry. London: E. J. W. Gibb Memorial, 1935.

Nwyia, P. (1968). 'Textes mystiques inédits d'Abū-l-Ḥasan al-Nūrī (m. 295/907)'. *Mélanges de l'Université Saint-Joseph* 44: 117–43.

Picken, G. (2011). *Spiritual Purification in Islam: The Life and Works of al-Muḥāsibī*. London: Routledge.

al-Qushayrī, Abū l-Qāsim *(Miʿrāj). Kitāb al-Miʿrāj*. Ed. ʿAlī Ḥasan ʿAbd al- Qādir. Cairo: Dār al-Kutub al-Ḥadītha, 1964.

al-Qushayrī, Abū l-Qāsim (*Rasāʾil). al-Rasāʾil al-Qushayriyya*. Ed. Muḥammad Ḥasan. Karachi: al-Maʿhad al-markazī li-l-abḥāth al-Islāmiyya, 1964.

al-Qushayrī, Abū l-Qāsim (*Risāla). Al-Risāla al-Qushayriyya*. Ed. ʿAbd al-Ḥalīm Maḥmūd and Maḥmūd b. al-Sharīf. 2 vols. Cairo: Dār al-Kutub al-Ḥadītha, 1966.

Radtke, B. (1986). 'Theologen und Mystiker in Ḫurāsān und Transoxanien'. *Zeitschrift der Deutschen Morgenländischen Gesellschaft* 136: 536–69.
Radtke, B., and J. O'Kane. (1996). *The Concept of Sainthood in Early Islamic Mysticism*. London: Routledge Curzon.
Ritter, H. (2003). *The Ocean of the Soul: Man, the World, and God in the Stories of Farīd al-Dīn ʿAṭṭār*. Ed. B. Radtke. Trans. J. O'Kane. Leiden: Brill.
Safi, O. (2006). *The Politics of Knowledge in Premodern Islam: Negotiating Ideology and Religious Inquiry*. Chapel Hill, NC: The University of North Carolina Press.
al-Sāmarrāʾī, Q. (1967). *'Rasāʾil al-Kharrāz'*. *Majallat al-Majmaʿ al-ʿilmī al-ʿIrāqī* 15/1387: 186–213.
al-Sarrāj, Abū Naṣr (*Lumaʿ*). *Kitāb al-Lumaʿ fī al-taṣawwuf*. Ed. R. A. Nicholson. Leiden: Brill, 1914.
Schimmel, A. (1975). *Mystical Dimensions of Islam*. Chapel Hill, NC: The University of North Carolina Press.
Schimmel, A. (1985). *And Muhammad is His Messenger: The Veneration of the Prophetic in Islamic Piety*. Chapel Hill, NC: The University of North Carolina Press.
Shihadeh, A. (ed.) (2007). *Sufism and Theology*. Edinburgh: Edinburgh University Press.
Sobieroj, F. (1998). *Ibn Ḫafīf aš-Šīrāzī und seine Schrift zur Novizenerziehung (Kitāb al-Iqtiṣād)*. Beirut/Stuttgart: Steiner.
Sobieroj, F. (1999). 'The Muʿtazila and Sufism'. In F. De Jong and B. Radtke (eds.), *Islamic Mysticism Contested: Thirteen Centuries of Controversies and Polemics*. Leiden: Brill, 68–92.
al-Suhrawardī, Shihāb al-Dīn (*Maqāmāt*). *Maqāmāt al-ṣūfiyya*. Ed. E. Maalouf. Beirut: Dar El-Machreq, 1986.
al-Sulamī, Abū ʿAbd al-Raḥmān (*Majmūʿa*). Majmū*ʿa-yi āthār-i Abū ʿAbd al-Raḥman Sulamī*. Ed. N. Pourjavady and M. Soori. 3 vols. Tehran: Iranian Institute of Philosophy, 2009.
al-Sulamī, Abū ʿAbd al-Raḥmān (*Rasāʾil*). *Rasāʾil ṣūfiyya li-Abī ʿAbd al-Raḥmān al-Sulamī*. Ed. G. Böwering and B. Orfali. Beirut: Dar el-Machreq, 2009.
al-Sulamī, Abū ʿAbd al-Raḥmān (*Subtleties*). *The Subtleties of the Ascension: Early Mystical Sayings on Muhammad's Heavenly Journey*. Ed. and trans. F. S. Colby. Louisville, KY: Fons Vitae, 2006.
al-Sulamī, Abū ʿAbd al-Raḥmān (*Ṭabaqāt*). *Ṭabaqāt al-ṣūfiyya*. Leiden: Brill, 1960.
al-Suyūṭī (*Taʾyīd*). *Taʾyīd al-ḥaqīqa al-ʿaliyya wa-tashyīd al-ṭarīqa al-Shādhiliyya*. Ed. ʿAbd Allāh b. Muḥammad b. al-Ṣiddīq al-Ghumārī al-Ḥasanī. Cairo: al-Maṭbaʿa al-islāmiyya, 1934.
Sviri, S. (2005). 'The Early Mystical Schools of Baghdad and Nīshāpūr: In Search of Ibn Munāzil'. *Jerusalem Studies in Arabic and Islam* 30: 450–82.
al-Tirmidhī, al-Ḥākim (*Muṣannafāt*). *Thalāthat muṣannafāt li-l-Ḥākim al-Tirmidhī*. Ed. B. Radtke. Beirut/Stuttgart: Steiner, 1992.
al-Tustarī, Sahl b. ʿAbd Allāh (*Tafsīr*). *Tafsīr al-Tustarī*. Ed. Muḥammad Bāsil ʿUyūn al-Sūd. Beirut: Dār al-Kutub al-ʿIlmiyya, 2007.

PART II

INTELLECTUAL INTERACTIONS OF ISLAMIC THEOLOGY(IES)—FOUR CASE STUDIES

CHAPTER 21

OCCASIONALISM

ULRICH RUDOLPH

OCCASIONALISM is a theory which stresses God's absolute power by negating any kind of natural causality and attributing every causal effect in the world immediately to Him.[1] As such, it is generally held to be a distinctive, if not exclusive, feature of Sunnī *kalām* as opposed to Muʿtazilism, Shīʿism, and Islamic philosophy, let alone intellectual traditions outside Islam. A closer look, however, reveals things to be more complicated. As it turns out, not all Sunnī theologians subscribed to occasionalism, and not every occasionalist thinker was a Sunnī Muslim. The history of the theory began rather in Muʿtazilī discussions of the third/ninth century and continued in a variety of Islamic contexts. Besides this, it underwent an impressive and long-lived continuation in Europe: having been introduced there in the thirteenth century CE by means of a Latin translation of Maimonides's *Dalālat al-ḥāʾirīn*, i.e. *The Guide of the Perplexed* (the relevant passages are to be found in *Dalāla*: 139.22–142.2/Eng. trans. 200–3 and 144.1–148.6/Eng. trans. 206–12; for an analysis of this text cf. Schwarz 1991–2), it was apparently transmitted by several scholastic authors (although they did not agree with it) and experienced a tremendous revival in the seventeenth century CE, when it was adopted and elaborated anew in Cartesian philosophy, finally receiving its current name.

Of course, all of this history cannot be covered in the present chapter. The development of European occasionalism has its historical roots in Islamic occasionalism (Perler and Rudolph 2000: 245–58) but it is not the subject of this handbook. Readers who are interested in this part of the story should consult some of the relevant references, which are given below. They present all the necessary information about occasionalism in Europe, treating either its history in general (Specht 1971, 1972b, 1972–3, 1984; Radner 1993; Nadler 1996; Perler and Rudolph 2000: 127–244), or some individual thinkers who made substantial contributions, such as René Descartes (1596–1650; cf. Specht 1972a; Garber 1993; Nadler 1994), Arnold Geulinxc (1624–69; cf. de Lattre 1967), Louis de La

[1] I would like to thank James Weaver for his valuable comments on an earlier version of this chapter.

Forge (1632–66; cf. Nadler 1993b, 1998) and—most important—Nicolas Malebranche (1638–1715; cf. Nadler 1993a).

In contrast, the present chapter is confined to the Islamic tradition. Even in this context, its scope cannot but be restricted, for up to now serious research has been done only on the first stages of Islamic occasionalism, i.e. its development until the fifth/eleventh century. Consequently, the presentation will focus on this period. Section I deals with the question of how the foundations of the occasionalist theory were prepared layer by layer in the evolving Muʿtazilī discussions of the third/ninth and the early fourth/tenth centuries. In Section II, it will be argued that its completion and final formulation was due to Abū l-Ḥasan al-Ashʿarī (d. 333/935). Section III is devoted to later developments originating with some Ashʿarī theologians of the late fourth/tenth and the fifth/eleventh centuries. Its focus will be on the famous seventeenth chapter of *Tahāfut al-falāsifa*, in which Abū Ḥāmid al-Ghazālī (d. 505/1111) discusses occasionalism and the whole problematic of causality extensively, but mention will also be made of some later commentaries on the *Tahāfut* by authors of the sixth/twelfth and the ninth/fifteenth centuries.

I The Foundations of Occasionalism in the Third/Ninth and Early Fourth/Tenth Centuries

The emergence of the occasionalist theory resulted from a long series of theological discussions. These covered a wide range of arguments and aspects but most of them focused on one central topic: the question of how to describe and explain what we mean when we talk about God's 'omnipotence'. In principle, this topic was not subject to dispute among Muslims. Muslims are convinced that God *is* omnipotent because throughout the Qurʾān they can read sentences such as 'God has the power to do everything' (*Allāh ʿalā kulli shayʾin qadīr*; Qurʾān 2: 20, 2: 106, 2: 109, 2: 148, and many other verses). However, there were obviously some individuals and some groups in early Islamic times who did not share this conviction. This applies in particular to the so-called 'Dahriyya', i.e. thinkers who followed cosmological models of Hellenistic origin and, as a consequence, were suspected of teaching the eternity of the world. According to them, the world is not the result of God's acting and creating it *ex nihilo*. Rather, it has an intrinsic, autonomous, and permanent natural order which does not depend on the power and the activity of any external cause (van Ess 1991–7: iv. 451–5). As a result, the 'Dahrites' negated the existence of an omnipotent Creator. They even declared the notion of God's 'omnipotence' to be a misconception which allegedly contradicted itself and was highly problematic from a theoretical point of view. In order to demonstrate this, they raised a number of sophisticated questions, which Muslim thinkers were compelled to answer in order to defend their own theological position (van Ess 1975–6).

One of these questions is reported in a third/ninth-century text, entitled *Sirr al-khalīqa* (*Sirr*) and attributed to a certain Ps.-Apollonios (see Weisser 1980). It reads as follows: does your 'omnipotent' God have the power to create another God who is like Himself? If not, His power is apparently not unlimited. Hence it is false to call God 'omnipotent'. The argument was malicious, yet at a closer look it turned out to be problematic in itself. In order to refute it the Muslim theologians could refer (and did refer) to logical evidence by arguing the following: if we assume that God is creating something, the result of this act can never be like Himself. For God is by definition uncreated. Hence, He cannot be compared and likened to any created being (*Sirr*, 68.5–8; cf. the Germany summary by Weisser 1980: 83; for further evidence in Arabic sources cf. Perler and Rudolph 2000: 26–7).

Another question was less easy to answer. It is reported in several variations, the following being one of them: does God have the power to put the whole world into a mustard seed? (or, formulated otherwise: does God have the power to put the whole world into an egg?). If not, He must not be named 'omnipotent'. This argument appears to have been embarrassing to Muslim theologians. At any rate, they were unable to answer it unanimously and convincingly. Instead, their respective answers differed widely: some denied God's ability to put the world into a mustard seed or into an egg (cf. the reports in Ashʿarī, *Maqālāt*, 572.12–15, and Māturīdī, *Tawḥīd*, 201.4–7), while others affirmed it. However, even the second group was apparently not unanimous about the arguments on which their affirmation relied (Māturīdī, *Tawḥīd*, 201.11–12; Kulaynī, *Uṣūl*, I: 102.10ff.; Ibn Bābūya, *Tawḥīd*, 77apu.–78.3; *Sirr*, 691–5; cf. Perler and Rudolph 2000: 27–8).

The crucial point in this case seems to have been that the question did not touch on logic but on physics. To answer it therefore presupposed some knowledge of physical matters. In other words, the *mutakallimūn* needed some idea about the material constituents of the creation, their interactions, and how they were related to God's activities in the world. As a consequence, the physical structure of this world became one of the central topics in third/ninth-century Islamic theology. As far as we know, Muslim thinkers of that time discussed it frequently and with great controversy, developing thereby a variety of different theoretical models (van Ess 1967–8; Dhanani 1994; van Ess 1991–7: iii. 37–44, 67–74, 224–44, 309–69; iv. 459–77 and *passim*). Some of these models soon fell into oblivion. Others, in contrast, were extremely successful in the long run. This applies in particular to the great Muʿtazilī thinker Abū l-Hudhayl (d. 227/842), whose ideas on physics and on God's omnipotence not only created a conceptual framework for many later discussions but also seem to have been what might be called, from a later perspective, the first step towards occasionalism.

(a) Abū l-Hudhayl (d. 227/842)

As far as the physical structure of the world is concerned, Abū l-Hudhayl opted for atomism. By doing so, he basically followed another Muʿtazilī thinker named Muʿammar (van Ess 1991–7: iii. 67–74), but Abū l-Hudhayl's theory was more elaborate than Muʿammar's had been and more attractive by far. According to him, every created being consists of two kinds of components, namely atoms and accidents. The first constitute its most basic corporeal aspects, such as its materiality and its extension. The second, in contrast, are identical with the secondary physical qualities to be found in a created being, such as its colour, its roughness (or smoothness), its movement (or rest), its being living (or non-living) etc. None of these components, however, ever had an autonomous existence.

In Abū l-Hudhayl's theory, neither atoms nor accidents are considered as the primary elements of being in a cosmological sense. They do not exist separately and autonomously but only come into existence when God creates a corporeal entity *ex nihilo*, endowing it with a certain number of atoms and qualities (van Ess 1991–7: iii. 224–9; cf. Dhanani 1994: 38–43; Perler and Rudolph 2000: 30–1). As a consequence, God could have created things differently. It was His decision, and it will always be His decision, to create things with the particular configuration of atoms and accidents He wants to give them. This leads to the second point: the problem of God's omnipotence. For assuming that God can combine atoms and accidents just as He likes, this raises the question of whether His acts are subject to any limitations and rules at all.

Abū l-Hudhayl's answer to this question became famous. As we are told by several later authors, he declared it to be possible (*jawwaza*) that God let a heavy stone float in the air without the stone falling. Likewise, he declared it to be possible that the Creator bring a piece of cotton into contact with fire without the cotton being burnt (Ashʿarī, *Maqālāt*, 312.10–13). According to him, God's power can even arrange two things which seem to us to be contradictory to coincide in His creation. For example, He is able to make death coincide with action (of the dead), talking with muteness and visual perception with blindness (Ashʿarī, *Maqālāt*, 312.13–313.2; cf. ʿAbd al-Jabbār, *Mughnī*, IX: 12.13–17).

In view of these examples, one could easily imagine Abū l-Hudhayl to have developed an occasionalist position. He might have declared for instance that God makes permanent use of His absolute power by deciding at every moment for all created beings (e.g. the aforementioned stone) the configuration of atoms and accidents to be realized in them (e.g. 'falling' or 'floating'). As a matter of fact, however, Abū l-Hudhayl did not argue in this direction. His reflections on God's omnipotence are not meant to describe God as the only and all-encompassing actor in His creation but to demonstrate *hypothetically* that He *could* do everything and *could* produce any kind of effect (even the unexpected) if He only wanted to do so. Actually, God does not make permanent use of His omnipotence. Instead, He has delegated some power to His creatures and, by doing so, has enabled them to act on their own and to produce their own causal effects. This applies in particular to mankind. According to Abū l-Hudhayl, man can act on himself (*fī nafsihi*) and on others (*fī ghayrihi*). He can even produce secondary effects. This is expressed by the famous theory of generation (*tawlīd*) which means that a primary act done by some person (e.g. his shooting an arrow) can generate a secondary effect on another person (e.g. his being wounded or even his death) (Gimaret 1980: 25–6, 38–9). As for the other created beings, Abū l-Hudhayl's teaching is less clear. In any case, we do not know exactly how he explained the course of events in the surrounding environment, what is nowadays usually called 'nature'. Nevertheless, it seems likely that even in this realm he admitted some kind of 'autonomy' (in the sense that it does not permanently depend on God's acting) because he taught that, once created, the atoms and a great part of the accidents do not perish but continue to exist (van Ess 1991–7: iii. 232–3; Dhanani 1994: 44–7).

Consequently, Abū l-Hudhayl's theory cannot be qualified as occasionalism. Rather, he articulated certain reflections and certain positions which later on instigated other theologians to conceptualize the occasionalist theory. This conceptualization was not realized at once but was apparently the result of developments in which several *mutakallimūn* made important contributions. Most of the primary sources from this period being lost, it is unfortunately impossible to reconstruct all the details of this process, but we can at least identify some of the major contributing theologians by name.

(b) Abū l-Hudhayl's Successors

One of them was Ṣāliḥ b. Abī Ṣāliḥ (d. probably 245/860), who in later times became known under his nickname Ṣāliḥ Qubbah (van Ess 1991–7: iii. 422–8; Perler and Rudolph 2000: 38–41). He was certainly not the most prominent thinker in the generation of Muʿtazilites succeeding Abū l-Hudhayl and Ibrāhīm al-Naẓẓām, yet his teaching about human acts or rather about the limits of human acts reveals several interesting and original features which had a lasting impact on later Islamic theology.

Like Abū l-Hudhayl (and many other Muʿtazilites), Ṣāliḥ Qubbah was convinced that man is able to act upon himself. In contrast to the master, however, he added an important qualification to this statement. According to Ṣāliḥ, man can *only* act upon himself (*inna l-insāna lā yafʿalu illā fī nafsihi*; Ashʿarī, *Maqālāt*, 406.6; for a German translation of the whole passage see van Ess 1991–7: vi. 208 no. 9), which implies that man is neither able to act upon other persons (*fī ghayrihi*) nor to produce secondary effects, i.e. the so-called *mutawallidāt*. As a result, none of the events happening 'outside' a human being is actually done or produced by him. Whatever occurs does not occur *because of* his acts but only *when* he is acting (*ʿinda fiʿlihi*; Ashʿarī, *Maqālāt*, 406.7). There is no causal connection between our acts and what Abū l-Hudhayl thought to be their effects. According to Ṣāliḥ Qubbah, the real cause of all these effects is no one else but God.

In order to illustrate this statement, Ṣāliḥ gives a series of interesting examples. As he explains, God creates spontaneously (*ibtadaʾa*) the movement of a stone when the stone has been pushed by a human being. God creates the feeling of pain in a person that has been hit by somebody else (Ashʿarī, *Maqālāt*, 406.6–8; cf. Gimaret 1990: 402–3). He can create in us the sensation of lust instead of pain when we have been thrown into fire (Ashʿarī, *Maqālāt*, 406.13–14; this is an allusion to the Qurʾānic story about Abraham; cf. Qurʾān 21: 68–9). Moreover, he can even create knowledge in a person who has passed away (Ashʿarī, *Maqālāt*, 406.14–15 and 568.12–13; ʿAbd al-Jabbār, *Mughnī*, IX: 13.5–6).

This was apparently meant to secure the religious dogma that sinners will remember their sins when they are punished in the grave (van Ess 1991–7: iii. 427).

Many of these examples had already been mentioned by Abū l-Hudhayl, but Ṣāliḥ Qubbah's way of understanding and explaining them is completely different from the interpretation of his elder colleague. In Abū l-Hudhayl's view, such examples served as an illustration of what God the Almighty *hypothetically* could produce if He only wanted to do so (in reality, however, Abū l-Hudhayl considered most of these things to be generated by man). In the case of Ṣāliḥ Qubbah, in contrast, they illustrate what God the Almighty *actually* does (because man is not able to do it himself). In other words, whereas Abū l-Hudhayl had reflected on the notion of God's omnipotence, Ṣāliḥ Qubbah insists on God's all-encompassing efficient causality—a concept which later on was to become an element vital to the occasionalist theory.

A second theologian should be mentioned in this context: Abū ʿAlī al-Jubbāʾī (d. after 303/915), the famous head of the Basran Muʿtazila at the end of the third/ninth and the beginning of the fourth/tenth centuries (for al-Jubbāʾī's teaching in general cf. still Frank 1978, for his contribution to occasionalism cf. Perler and Rudolph 2000: 41–6). In contrast to Ṣāliḥ Qubbah, he accepted Abū l-Hudhayl's teaching about man's ability to cause secondary effects; he even completed it with a detailed analysis of the whole problematic, which led him to identify six different kinds of 'generation' (Gimaret 1980: 39–44). On the other hand, al-Jubbāʾī rejected Abū l-Hudhayl's ideas about the events occurring in the created world surrounding us (i.e. in the realm of what nowadays would be called 'nature'). In order to explain them more coherently, he formulated a new theory which became extremely influential in later times.

As mentioned above, Abū l-Hudhayl's explanation of the events taking place in the created world was not really clear (or perhaps was not prominent enough to be transmitted clearly). As far as we know, he assigned permanent existence to all of the atoms and most of the accidents, yet without offering a consistent theory of how they interact and thereby contribute to the 'natural' course of events (van Ess 1991–7: iii. 232–44). In contrast to that, al-Jubbāʾī's position on the same topic was very precise. He said, in short, that nothing which happens in the created world (with the exception of events being 'generated' by human acts) can be considered as the effect of 'natural' causes (in the sense of 'intramundane' causes). Instead, all of these events are directly caused by the Creator Himself.

Again, this statement is illustrated by a number of impressive examples. As al-Jubbāʾī tells us, it is God who creates satiety in us when we are eating (ʿAbd al-Jabbār, *Mughnī*, IX: 109.6–7; XV: 353.15). He makes our faces blush when we feel ashamed and makes them pale when we are in fear (ʿAbd al-Jabbār, *Mughnī*, IX: 61.9–10). God makes the plants sprout when they are sown and generates the child when his parents have had sexual intercourse (ʿAbd al-Jabbār, *Mughnī*, IX: 43.3; cf. VIII: 33.7). He is even the one who creates the accident 'death' (*mawt*) in a man whom somebody else has killed (*qatl*) (ʿAbd al-Jabbār, *Mughnī*, IX: 109.18–20). All of this happens regularly, not by necessity but as a consequence of God's will. For He has established the 'habit' (*kāna qad ajrā l-ʿāda*; ʿAbd al-Jabbār, *Mughnī*, XI: 43.1) to connect certain things in a regular manner. So, at each time 'when we are acting' (*ʿinda fiʿlinā*), He creates the particular event corresponding by habit to our act (cf. ʿAbd al-Jabbār, *Mughnī*, IX: 109.4–11).

Admittedly, these statements sound very much like occasionalism. To consider God as the immediate cause of all 'natural' events in the world and to explain the regularity in the physical world as a result of God's 'habit' are doctrinal elements which have a strong occasionalist flavour and actually were integrated into Islamic occasionalism later on. In sum, however, al-Jubbāʾī was not an occasionalist. For him, God's 'habit' is not the only explanation of the events occurring in the created world. Instead, he still considers man to be an actor in his own right, being able to act upon others and to generate thereby various kinds of secondary effects. Thus, causal effectiveness is not confined to the activities of the Creator: man still has to be taken into consideration when we want to explain the complex interactions between causes and effects in this world.

Apart from that, the list of doctrinal elements which seem to have contributed to the conceptualization of occasionalism would be incomplete if it were restricted to the teachings of Ṣāliḥ Qubbah and al-Jubbāʾī. There was at least one more doctrine emerging at the end of the third/ninth century which also has to be mentioned in this context. Its connection to occasionalism may be less obvious than in the cases of Ṣāliḥ Qubbah and al-Jubbāʾī because it did not focus on the problematic of causality. Nevertheless, it appears to have influenced the specific way in which occasionalism was finally conceptualized in Islamic theology and, as such, it deserves to be mentioned here.

In order to situate this doctrine, we have to refer once more to Abū l-Hudhayl. This time, however, the starting point is not what he taught about God's omnipotence and man's capacity of acting but what he taught about atomism. This teaching consisted of two parts, one of them being a theory of the physical structure of matter and the other being a theory of time. Both of them stressed the discontinuity of the created world by defining matter as a conglomerate of distinct atoms (connected to various accidents) and time as a series of distinct moments (*awqāt*), which may be called atoms of time (van Ess 1991–7: iii. 241–3 with indications to similar concepts of time in late antiquity and in early Islam). Despite this parallel, Abū l-Hudhayl did not connect the two ends of the theory: he did not describe the minimal elements of the material world (i.e. the atoms and the accidents) as only having a minimal extension in time (i.e. as existing only for one moment). Instead of drawing this conclusion, he was convinced, as mentioned above, that once created all the atoms and a great part of the accidents do not perish after one moment but continue to exist.

On this point, some of his successors, starting from the second half of the third/ninth century, did not follow his doctrine. Apparently, their critique focused on the idea that some parts of the created world should exist continuously whereas others should not. This applied in particular to Abū l-Hudhayl's assumption that the accidents can be divided into two classes, one of them enduring and the other one not (van Ess 1991–7: iii. 232–3). In order to avoid such inconsistencies, these theologians declared that every accident is, by the sheer fact of being an 'accident', transitory. The argument given for this statement is reported by al-Ashʿarī (*Maqālāt*, 358.2–5) as follows: 'No accident can endure (*tabqā*) for two moments (*waqtayni*). For what endures does so either by itself (*bi-nafsihi*) or by an(other accident called) endurance (*baqāʾ*) (occurring) in him.' The first option ('enduring by itself') is impossible because every accident has come into existence at some moment in time, which excludes its existing continuously by itself. The second option ('enduring by another accident') is impossible because, as a rule, no accident can inhere in another accident. Consequently, it has been proven that (all) accidents exist only for one moment (Perler and Rudolph 2000: 48–9).

The first thinker who is on record for this argument (Ashʿarī, *Maqālāt*, 358.5) was a Muʿtazilite named Aḥmad b. ʿAlī al-Shaṭawī (d. 297/910). He is not known to have been a great teacher, but in this case he was able to find followers. Among them there were several important figures such as Muḥammad b. ʿAbd Allāh Ibn Mumlak (early fourth/tenth century), a friend of al-Jubbāʾī and later convert to Shīʿism, and Abū l-Qāsim al-Kaʿbī al-Balkhī (d. 319/931), the famous head of the Muʿtazila of Baghdad at that time (Perler and Rudolph 2000: 49; for al-Kaʿbī's teaching in general see now el-Omari 2006). The fact that these theologians agreed on the transitoriness of accidents does not imply that their doctrines on physical matters were similar in all respects. The axiomatic statement that accidents, by definition, exist only for one moment can be combined with various ways of explaining the physical structure of the created world, and this is what actually happened in fourth/tenth-century theology. In all these cases, however, it gave rise to a similar trend: it strengthened the idea that the created world cannot exist by itself even for one moment, as one of its constitutive elements, i.e. the accidents, always tend to cease and to perish. This led, in one way or another, to the assumption that God has to act *at every moment* as creator and as cause in his creation, an assumption which seems to have contributed to the development of occasionalism.

II The Completion of Occasionalism in the Teaching of al-Ashʿarī (d. 324/935)

This is, at least, the impression one gets when reading the works of al-Ashʿarī. He certainly knew all the arguments and reflections presented so far. In many cases, his famous book *Maqālāt al-islāmiyyīn* is even the only extant source of the various theological discussions of the third/ninth century which have been mentioned hitherto. However, al-Ashʿarī's own contribution to our topic is not confined to reporting the arguments of former theologians. Rather, he adopted and connected the ideas which he learned from his teacher al-Jubbāʾī and from the other Muʿtazilites of the third/ninth and early fourth/tenth centuries, forming thereby his own view on God's omnipotence and His acting in the created world.

The result was what we nowadays call 'occasionalism'. In a systematic perspective, it can be considered as a novel theory and as an extremely original contribution to the debate on causality, which had been running in early Muslim theology for more than a century. In a historical perspective, however, al-Ashʿarī's achievement is less impressive, for what he did was mainly to draw together the conclusions from the ideas of his predecessors. This becomes evident when we look at his presentation of 'occasionalism'. It is not really a fundamental and systematic explanation of the theory but rather an enumeration of the various elements constituting it, all of which had already been formulated separately by previous thinkers. One of these elements is the idea that man is unable to generate secondary effects (*tawlīd*). This is a conviction which al-Ashʿarī shared with Ṣāliḥ Qubbah, the only difference between them being that al-Ashʿarī expressed the position in a more rigorous and consistent fashion. According to him, the simple fact that something has been created in time implies already that it is not able itself to produce causal effects. For 'things which originate in time cannot act upon something outside themselves' (Ibn Fūrak, *Mujarrad*, 283.18). There is no causal relationship or interaction between created entities but 'everything which originates in time is created spontaneously and anew by God exalted, without a reason (*sabab*) necessitating it and without an (intramundane) cause generating it' (Ibn Fūrak, *Mujarrad*, 131.7–8). Any kind of generation (*tawlīd*) by human beings is thus excluded. Everything which we tend to explain as an effect of our own acts is actually caused by God. Al-Ashʿarī illustrates this by an example which we already know from Ṣāliḥ Qubbah: 'The fact that a stone moves (*dhahāb*) is not an act of him who pushes (it) but an original creation (*ikhtirāʿ*) by God. It would be perfectly possible that one of us pushed it without the stone moving because God did not produce its movement, or that there is none who pushes it and the stone still moves because God has created movement in it' (Ibn Fūrak, *Mujarrad*, 132.23–133.2; cf. Gimaret 1990: 403–6).

What applies to man applies a fortiori to the rest of the creation according to al-Ashʿarī's teaching. Consequently, he not only denies the idea of *tawlīd* (as did Ṣāliḥ Qubbah) but also the idea of 'natures' in the sense of 'natural forces' (*ṭabīʿa* or *ṭabʿ*) acting in this world (as did al-Jubbāʾī and other Basran Muʿtazilites). God is the only and overall acting actor. This is repeatedly expressed by al-Ashʿarī, for instance in his creedal work entitled *al-Ibāna ʿan uṣūl al-diyāna*. There he states: 'We declare … that there is nothing good and nothing bad on earth which is not willed by God; that everything (without any exception) exists by God's will (*bi-mashīʾat Allāh*); that nobody is able to act before He enables him to do so … that there is no Creator except God; that the acts of man are created and determined by Him … that man cannot produce anything because he is himself originated' (al-Ashʿarī, *Ibāna*, 23, -7-ult.).

Most important in this context is that al-Ashʿarī did not accept any precondition or any objective rule for God's acting. In his opinion, the Creator's will is absolutely autonomous. He can create whatever He wants at whatever time and in whatever chronological order: 'Every accident that God creates (*faʿala*) together with, after or before another accident could (just as well) be created together with the opposite (accident) or in the opposite chronological order' (Ibn Fūrak, *Mujarrad*, 131.8–9). God is completely free.

This is again illustrated by a series of examples which have apparently been taken from former thinkers. They comprise statements such as: God can create satiety in a man who has not eaten anything, He can let a heavy stone float in the air without the stone falling, He can bring combustible things in contact with fire without the things burning etc. (Ibn Fūrak, *Mujarrad*, 134.5–6; 283.12–14).

In order to explain why most of the events in this world nevertheless occur in a regular and foreseeable way despite God's liberty to arrange them as He wills, al-Ashʿarī refers to a position which was already expressed by his master al-Jubbāʾī. As mentioned above, al-Jubbāʾī had taught that the regularity of events to be observed in the creation was due to God's habit (*ʿāda*) with the exception of events which he supposed to be generated (*tawlīd*) by man. Al-Ashʿarī takes up the concept of the *ʿāda* but he interprets it in a more radical way, thereby avoiding the kind of exceptions admitted by al-Jubbāʾī. For him, everything and every event in this world is an element of God's habit, submitted absolutely to His will. There is no causality besides this and there is, in particular, no *tawlīd*. Therefore al-Ashʿarī can say in his clear and unambiguous language: 'God has established the habit (*qad ajrā l-ʿāda*) of creating (all) things in this (regular) manner' (Ibn Fūrak, *Mujarrad*, 134.7–8). 'All of this is the free choice (*ikhtiyār*) of God who creates things according to a habit (*ʿala ʿādatin*) which He has established when originating them in time (*ajrāhā fī iḥdāthihā*)' (Ibn Fūrak, *Mujarrad*, 28315–16; cf. 33.9ff.).

In addition to these 'borrowings' from al-Jubbāʾī and other Basran Muʿtazilites, al-Ashʿarī takes up a position held at his time by al-Kaʿbī, the head of the Baghdadian branch of the Muʿtazila. This is the aforementioned idea that all the accidents in the world only exist for one moment and have to be constantly renewed. What al-Ashʿarī taught in this respect sounds very close to the explanations of al-Shaṭawī, al-Kaʿbī, and other thinkers (cf. above Section I (b)). For instance, he is reported to have said: 'The defining characteristic (*ḥukm*) of accidents is to pass away in the moment which follows the moment of their existentiation (*fī thānī ḥāli wujūdihi*)' (Ibn Fūrak, *Mujarrad*, 242.3; cf. 258.3–5 and 12 ult.f.). Or: 'A body is (only) enduring because the accident 'endurance' (*baqāʾ*) is at every moment (*ḥālan fa-ḥālan*) renewed in it' (Ibn Fūrak, *Mujarrad*, 238.18–19; cf. 230.8–9). What he meant by these sentences, however, seems to differ from the intentions of the others. For the idea of a constant renewal that is a *creatio continua* of all accidents was in the context of his teaching not just one physical doctrine among others (as was the case in the teachings of al-Shaṭawī, al-Kaʿbī, etc.); it was the cornerstone of al-Ashʿarī's occasionalism. It confirms in a radical way that everything in the created world is at every moment dependent upon God, who must constantly act therein, in order to preserve its existence and to maintain the habitual course of events.

Al-Ashʿarī's role in the history of occasionalism can thus be qualified as crucial. As far as we know from the theological discussions of the third/ninth and fourth/tenth centuries, he was not the first to conceptualize any of the individual theoretical elements constitutive of the occasionalist theory (for a general discussion of which elements are indispensable for a theory to be called 'occasionalist' cf. Perler and Rudolph 2000: 250–4). However, by adopting them all from his predecessors, by generalizing them and by connecting them to a coherent argumentative framework, he conceptualized the occasionalist theory as such. In any case, al-Ashʿarī's teaching about causality and God's omnipotence was extremely successful. What he taught about these topics spread quickly among his disciples and his successors and was to become, in the long run, one of the features characteristic of the teaching of many Sunnī *mutakallimūn*.

III Later Developments

The path to success for the occasionalist theory was paved by the Ashʿarite theologians of the fourth/tenth and fifth/eleventh centuries. As far as we know, all of them accepted their master's teaching on causality and on God's all-encompassing activities. More than that, they applied their master's method of presenting this teaching. For none of the Ashʿarite *kalām* works of the fourth/tenth or fifth/eleventh centuries contains a systematic account of the occasionalist theory. Rather, they present the topic as al-Ashʿarī himself had done it: by enumerating separately and in different contexts the various elements related to it.

This usually materialized in four statements repeated in similar words author by author: (1) There is neither causal force nor causal effectiveness in non-human created beings. In other words, there are no 'natures' in the created world (e.g. al-Bāqillānī, *Tamhīd*, 34ff./nos. 59–84; al-Baghdādī, *Uṣūl*, 68.13–69.18; al-Juwaynī, *Irshād*, 133.21ff./ French trans. 213ff.). (2) Man cannot generate any kind of effect on other creatures. In other words, there is no *tawlīd* (e.g. al-Bāqillānī, *Tamhīd*, 296ff./nos. 507–16; al-Baghdādī, *Uṣūl*, 137.10–139.8; al-Juwaynī, *Irshād*, 131.5ff./French trans. 210ff.). (3) Everything occurring in this world occurs in accordance to God's habit (*ʿādat Allāh*) (e.g. al-Bāqillānī, *Tamhīd*, 300.5ff./nos. 514–16; al-Baghdādī, *Uṣūl*, 138.13–15; al-Juwaynī, *Irshād*, 179.15ff./French trans. 272ff.), the only exception being miracles which were of course considered as God's acts but deviating from (*khilāf al-ʿāda*) or breaking with His habit (*kharq al-ʿāda*). (4) Accidents can only endure for one moment and must be constantly recreated (e.g. al-Bāqillānī, *Tamhīd*, 18.4ff./no. 29; al-Baghdādī, *Uṣūl*, 50.10–52.14).

All of this demonstrates that occasionalism was transmitted as a kind of *communis opinio* in early Ashʿarism. Apparently, there was no need to analyse the theoretical implications of the theory at a deeper level. Early Ashʿarite theologians could confine themselves to repeating the different aspects of their position by defending them against opposing positions, such as the concepts of *tawlīd* and the *ṭabāʾiʿ* still held by some Muʿtazilites.

Things changed, however, towards the end of the fifth/eleventh century. At that time, Ashʿarites started to study Avicenna's philosophy, which led them, alongside many other consequences, to a new kind of reflection on occasionalism and the problem of causality in general. In a certain way, this can already be observed in al-Juwaynī's later works (cf.

Griffel 2002: 128–33). But the process culminated, as is well known, in al-Ghazālī's teaching. His contribution to our field is thus of particular interest.

Al-Ghazālī dealt with the problem of causality in several of his writings. Sometimes, his presentation is conventional in the sense of being close to the older Ashʿarite tradition. This applies for instance to his most important *kalām* work, the *Iqtiṣād fī l-iʿtiqād*. What is said there about causality is certainly more systematic than any earlier Ashʿarite exposition of the same topic (cf. *Iqtiṣād*, 99.3–7 and 223.8–225.10) but its purpose remains restricted to the presentation of the traditional position of the *ahl al-sunna* (*Iqtiṣād*, 224.6). In other writings, al-Ghazālī's arguments have a much wider scope. This is particularly true for the famous chapter seventeen of his *Tahāfut al-falāsifa* (*Tahāfut* 1, 166–77). It is devoted to an extensive and completely innovative discussion of causality, comparing and weighing up for the first time different positions such as (1) occasionalism, (2) the idea of natural forces (*ṭabāʾiʿ*) acting autonomously in the world (which might be ascribed to some kind of 'Dahrites'), and (3) the idea of a complex interaction between effects emanating from 'the principles of temporary events' (*mabādiʾ al-ḥawādith*) and various dispositions (*istiʿdād*) existing in this world (which was the position of Avicenna and other philosophers).

The seventeenth chapter of the *Tahāfut* is probably one of the most prominent pieces of Arabic philosophical literature and has been subject over the years to varying comments and interpretations (see, besides many others, Goodman 1978, Marmura 1981, and Riker 1996; for the wider context of the discussion see Frank 1992 and 1994 as well as the critical reactions to Frank's publications, especially by Marmura 1995 and 2002). All of this has been discussed and extensively commented on in recent publications (Perler and Rudolph 2000: 68–105; Lizzini 2002; Griffel 2009: 147–73) so that there is no need to repeat all the arguments here. What should be mentioned in this context, however, are the basic assumptions which al-Ghazālī seems to have promoted in the course of his intensive and subtle discussion. They may be summarized as follows: (1) A theory about the causal structure of the universe must (a) explain the usual course of events in the world and (b) at the same time leave room for unusual and unexpected events contravening this usual course of events. In other words, it must be open to admitting miracles (*muʿjizāt*), including all those miraculous events (e.g. Abraham sitting in the fire without burning) which are mentioned in the Qurʾān (see here Qurʾān 21: 68–9 and 37: 97–8). (2) The theories of the philosophers, including Avicenna's, do not fulfil these requirements. According to them, every cause (and in particular the First Cause) is always acting *by necessity*, the world being therefore a coherent and completely intelligible system of causes and effects. What we call a 'miracle' is thus misunderstood by the philosophers. For them, it is either the necessary effect of a particular natural cause (as in the case of prophets and their imagination) or a miraculous report which has to be interpreted in a symbolic and allegorical way (as in the case of Abraham in the fire). (3) In contrast to this erroneous position, occasionalism is a valuable causal theory. By attributing every causal effect immediately to God, it is able to explain any event occurring in the created world, be it a regular event which is familiar to us (because it follows God's habit) or a miracle (which breaks with God's habit). (4) Nevertheless, occasionalism is not necessarily the only theory to fulfil the aforementioned requirements. An alternative way would be to accept secondary causation in the created world (besides God's immediate causation) but to assume at the same time that the interaction of causes, dispositions, and effects in this world is so complex that humans are not in a position to understand and to explain everything occurring in it. In this case, God would have established a marvellous and perfect structure in His creation which nevertheless leaves room for 'astonishing and miraculous things' (*gharā'ib wa-'ajā'ib*) whose explanation is beyond our comprehension (for the details see Perler and Rudolph 2000: 69, 84–93, and Griffel 2009: 150–73, who stresses particularly the point that al-Ghazālī did not argue against secondary causality but against the necessitarianism attendant upon Avicenna's position). It must be added, however, that there are still divergent interpretations of the text, the divergence concerning mainly point (4) of the summary (cf. e.g. Marmura's introduction to his translation of the *Tahāfut: Tahāfut 1*, xxiv–xxv), the other three points being more or less consensual.

In any case, al-Ghazālī's discussion of occasionalism was extremely innovative, and it would be most interesting to follow its repercussions in later Islamic philosophy and theology. Unfortunately, this is next to impossible because there is still a considerable lack of research in the field. The only glimpse at later developments which can be offered at the moment is a look at some texts which have been explicitly written as reactions or as commentaries to his *Tahāfut al-falāsifa*. These texts are (1) the *Tahāfut al-tahāfut* by Ibn Rushd (d. 595/1198) and (2) two books commissioned by the Ottoman Sultan Mehmed II (reg. 848/1444–850/1446 and 855/1451–886/1481) in order to comment on the notorious debate between al-Ghazālī and Averroes, namely 'Alā' al-Dīn al-Ṭūsī's (d. 886/1482) *Kitāb al-Dhakhīra* and Muṣliḥ al-Dīn Khājazāda's (d. 893/1488) *Tahāfut al-falāsifa* (for both of them see now van Lit 2011 and Yücedoğru and Kaya 2011; for Khājazāde's book see Karadaş 2011; Michot 2011; Shihadeh 2011; and Türker 2011). Some further writings from the Ottoman period such as Kamālpaşazāda's (d. 940/1534) *Hāshiya 'alā l-Tahāfut*, which were obviously meant to comment on Khājazāda's *Tahāfut al-falāsifa*, unfortunately cannot be taken into account because they have neither been edited nor subject to research as yet (cf. van Lit 2011: 176).

As for Ibn Rushd, his main concern was to refute the objections raised against the philosophers in the *Tahāfut al-falāsifa*. When it comes to the seventeenth discussion, he thus argues that the critique articulated by al-Ghazālī against the causal theory of the philosophers was neither sound nor valuable. Yet, more important for us is how Ibn Rushd understands and describes al-Ghazālī's own position. As he explains, it was full of inconsistencies for, in the beginning of chapter seventeen, al-Ghazālī allegedly maintained the occasionalist dogma, whereas in the latter parts of the same chapter he dismissed his conviction and made considerable concessions to the philosophers (*Tahāfut 2*, 537.9ff./van den Bergh 330–1). This may be a dialectical argument. Ibn Rushd was certainly eager to show that al-Ghazālī, having accused the philosophers of numerous inconsistencies, was himself an inconsistent thinker (cf. *Tahāfut 2*, 541.5ff./ van den Bergh 332–3, where the theologians are generally accused of being inconsistent and confused). Yet, at the same time it has to be admitted that Ibn Rushd was a keen and perspicuous observer. His comment on al-Ghazālī's alleged 'fickleness' may thus be interpreted as confirming that chapter seventeen of the *Tahāfut al-falāsifa* actually was not a monochrome plea for occasionalism but a complex and multilevel reflection on causality.

As to ʿAlāʾ al-Dīn al-Ṭūsī, his point of view was rather different. He admired al-Ghazālī as a leading authority of Sunnī Islam (*al-Dhakhīra*, 5.14–16) who had successfully attacked the philosophers and considered himself as a loyal Ashʿarite *mutakallim*. Therefore, it is no surprise that when talking about causality al-Ṭūsī heavily criticizes the philosophers (*al-Dhakhīra*, 219.13–227.3) and holds himself firmly to the classical occasionalist position (*al-Dhakhīra*, 218.18–219.13). By doing so, he does not mention al-Ghazālī by name but clearly insinuates that his master has followed the same line of argumentation. As a result, there is no room for the idea that al-Ghazālī himself could have had some inclination towards a philosophical interpretation of causality. This fits very well with the general observation confirmed in other parts of the *Dhakhīra* that al-Ṭūsī had neither particular interest in nor extensive knowledge of philosophical matters (cf. van Lit 2011: 197).

In contrast to him, his contemporary Khājazāda was well aware of the undertones to be found in chapter seventeen of the *Tahāfut*. Khājazāda was even ready to follow al-Ghazālī on his way to combine Ashʿarite convictions with theoretical aspects inspired by philosophical arguments (cf. van Lit 2011: 197 and Michot 2011: 237; Shihadeh 2011: 146 seems to be a bit more sceptical concerning the originality of Khājazāda's reflections). Part of his Ashʿarite heritage is, for instance, that he adheres explicitly to the concept of God's habit (*Tahāfut* 3, II: 73.2–4). In the same sense, he stresses the idea that God is always acting freely, His acts never being subject to any kind of necessity (*Tahāfut* 3, II: 73.4–7; cf. Karadaş 2011). On the other hand, Khājazāda has certain sympathies for philosophical positions. Such seems already to be the case when he declares that created things are composed of matter and form (*Tahāfut* 3, II: 75.17–24) and it becomes evident when he even admits created things to possess natures as well as natural forces (*Tahāfut* 3, II: 74.22–32). All of this makes it probable that he was searching for a new interpretation of the concept of *ʿāda* in the sense that, after all, 'God's habit' could be understood as the totality of stable connections (*iqtirānāt*) established in His creation. This may well have been the position which al-Ghazālī wanted to promote in chapter seventeen of his *Tahāfut* when he described a complex theory of causality which could be an acceptable alternative to occasionalism (cf. Section II above; Perler and Rudolph 2000: 108–9).

References

ʿAbd al-Jabbār b. Aḥmad al-Qāḍī (*Mughnī*). *Al-Mughnī fī abwāb al-tawḥīd wal-ʿadl*. Ed. Muḥammad Muṣṭafā al-Ḥilmī. 16 vols. Cairo: al-Muʾassasa al-Miṣriyya al-ʿĀmma li-l-Taʾlīf wa-l-Anbāʾ wa-l-Nashr, 1958–65.

(Ps.)-Apollonios of Tyana (*Sirr*). *Sirr al-khalīqa*. Ed. Ursula Weisser. Aleppo: Institute for the History of Arabic Science, 1979.

al-Ashʿarī, Abū l-Ḥasan (*Ibāna*). *Al-Ibāna ʿan uṣūl al-diyāna*. Ed. Fawqiyya Ḥusayn Maḥmūd. Cairo: Dār al-Anṣār, 1977.

al-Ashʿarī, Abū l-Ḥasan (*Maqālāt*). *Maqālāt al-Islāmiyyīn wa-khtilāf al-muṣallīn*. Ed. Hellmut Ritter. 2 vols. and indexes. Istanbul/Leipzig: Brockhaus, 1929–33.

al-Baghdādī, ʿAbd al-Qāhir b. Ṭāhir (*Uṣūl*). *Uṣūl al-dīn*. Istanbul: Maṭbaʿat al-Dawla, 1928.

al-Bāqillānī, Abū Bakr Muḥammad (*Tamhid*). *Al-Tamhīd*. Ed. R. J. McCarthy. Beirut: Al-Maktaba al-Sharqiyya, 1957.

Dhanani, A. (1994). *The Physical Theory of Kalām: Atoms, Space, and Void in Basrian Muʿtazilī Cosmology*. Leiden: Brill.

el-Omari, R. M. (2006). *The Theology of Abū l-Qāsim al-Balḫī/al-Kaʿbī (d. 319/931): A Study of its Sources and Reception*. Ph.D. dissertation, Yale University.

van Ess, J. (1967–8). 'Ḍirār b. ʿAmr und die "Cahmīya": Biographie einer vergessenen Schule'. *Der Islam* 43: 241–79 and 44: 1–70.

van Ess, J. (1975–6). 'Göttliche Allmacht im Zerrbild menschlicher Sprache'. *Mélanges de l'Université Saint-Joseph* 49: 653–88.

van Ess, J. (1991–7). *Theologie und Gesellschaft im 2. und 3. Jahrhundert Hidschra: Eine Geschichte des religiösen Denkens im frühen Islam*. 6 vols. Berlin: De Gruyter.

Frank, R. M. (1978). *Beings and their Attributes: The Teaching of the Baṣrian School of the Muʿtazila in the Classical Period*. Albany, NY: State University of New York Press.

Frank, R. M. (1992). *Creation and the Cosmic System: Al-Ghazâlî and Avicenna*. Heidelberg: Carl Winter.

Frank, R. M. (1994). *Al-Ghazālī and the Ashʿarite School*. Durham, NC: Duke University Press.

Garber, D. (1993). 'Descartes and Occasionalism'. In S. Nadler (ed.), *Causation in Early Modern Philosophy: Cartesianism, Occasionalism, and Preestablished Harmony*. University Park, PA: Pennsylvania State University Press, 9–26.

al-Ghazālī, Abū Ḥāmid (*Iḥyāʾ*). *Iḥyāʾ ʿulūm al-dīn*. 4 vols. Cairo, 1334 H.

al-Ghazālī, Abū Ḥāmid (*Iqtiṣād*). *Al-Iqtiṣād fī l-Iʿtiqād*. Ed. Ibrahim Agâh Çubukçu/Hüseyin Atay. Ankara: Nur Matbaası, 1962.

al-Ghazālī, Abū Ḥāmid (*Tahāfut 1*). *Tahāfut al-falāsifa/The Incoherence of the Philosophers*. A parallel English–Arabic text translated, introduced, and annotated by Michael E. Marmura. Provo, UT: Brigham Young University, 1997, [2]2000.

Gimaret, D. (1980). *Théories de l'acte humain en théologie musulmane*. Paris: Vrin.

Gimaret, D. (1990). *La Doctrine d'al-Ashʿarī*. Paris: Les Éditions du Cerf.

Goodman, L. E. (1978). 'Did Al-Ghazâlî Deny Causality?'. *Studia Islamica* 47: 83–120.

Griffel, F. (2009). *Al-Ghazālī's Philosophical Theology*. Oxford and New York: Oxford University Press.

Ibn Bābūya (*Tawḥīd*). *Kitāb al-Tawḥīd*. Najaf, 1386/1966.

Ibn Fūrak, Abū Bakr (*Mujarrad*). *Mujarrad maqālāt al-Ashʿarī*. Ed. Daniel Gimaret. Beirut: Dār al-Mashriq, 1987.

Ibn Rushd (*Tahāfut 2*). *Tahāfut al-tahāfut*. Ed. Maurice Bouyges. Beirut: Imprimerie catholique 1930. (Eng. trans. S. van den Bergh, *Averroes' Tahafut al-Tahafut*. 2 vols. London: Luzac, 1954.)

al-Juwaynī, Abū l-Maʿālī (*Irshād*). *Al-Irshād*. Ed. J.-D. Luciani (with a French trans.). Paris: Ernest Leroux, 1938.

Karadaş, C. (2011). 'Hocazâde'nin Tehâfüt'ünde Sebeplilik Meselesi'. In T. Yücedoğru, O. Ş. Koloğlu, U. M. Kılavuz, and K. Gömbeyaz (eds.), *Uluslararası Hocazâde Sempozyumu*

(22–24 Ekim 2010 Bursa)—Bildiriler—International Symposium on Khojazāda (22–24 October 2010 Bursa)—Proceedings. Bursa: Büyükşehir Belediyesi Yayınları, 163–73.

Khājazāda, Muṣliḥ al-Dīn Muṣṭafā b. Yūsuf (*Tahāfut 3*). *Tahāfut al-falāsifa*. 2 vols. Cairo, n.d.

al-Kulīnī (*Uṣūl*). *Uṣūl al-kāfī*. Ed. S. J. Mustafūya. 4 vols. Tehran, n.d.

de Lattre, A. (1967). *L'Occasionalisme d'Arnold Geulinxc: étude sur la constitution de la doctrine*. Paris: Éditions de Minuit.

van Lit, L. W. C. (Eric) (2011). 'The Chapters on God's Knowledge in Khojazāda's and ʿAlāʾ al-Dīn's Studies on al-Ghazālī's Tahāfut al-Falāsifa'. In T. Yücedoğru, O. Ş. Koloğlu, U. M. Kılavuz, and K. Gömbeyaz (eds.), *Uluslararası Hocazâde Sempozyumu (22–24 Ekim 2010 Bursa)—Bildiriler—International Symposium on Khojazāda (22–24 October 2010 Bursa)—Proceedings*. Bursa: Büyükşehir Belediyesi Yayınları, 175–99.

Lizzini, O. (2002). 'Occasionalismo e causalità filosofica: la discussione della causalità in al-Ġazâlî'. *Quaestio* 2: 155–83.

Maimonides, Moses (*Dalāla*). *Dalālat al-ḥāʾirīn*. Ed. Salomon Munk (with French trans.): *Le Guide des égarés*. 3 vols. Paris: Franck, 1856–66. (Eng. trans. S. Pines, *The Guide of the Perplexed*. 2 vols. Chicago: University of Chicago Press, 1963.)

Marmura, M. (1981). 'Al-Ghazālī's Second Causal Theory in the 17th Discussion of the Tahāfut'. In P. Morewedge (ed.), *Islamic Philosophy and Mysticism*. Delmar, NY: Caravan Books, 85–112.

Marmura, M. (1995). 'Ghazālian Causes and Intermediaries'. *Journal of the American Oriental Society* 115: 89–100.

Marmura, M. (2002). 'Ghazali and Asharism Revisited'. *Arabic Sciences and Philosophy* 12: 91–110.

al-Māturīdī, Abū Manṣūr (*Tawḥīd*). *Kitāb al-Tawḥīd*. Ed. Bekir Topaloğlu and Muhammed Aruçi, Ankara: Türkiye Diyanet Vakfı, 2003. (1st edn. by Fathalla Kholeif. Beirut: Dar el-Machreq, 1970 (repr. 1986).)

Michot, Y. M. (2011). 'Wisdom and its Sciences in Khojazāda's Tahāfut'. In T. Yücedoğru, O. Ş. Koloğlu, U. M. Kılavuz, and K. Gömbeyaz (eds.), *Uluslararası Hocazâde Sempozyumu (22–24 Ekim 2010 Bursa)—Bildiriler—International Symposium on Khojazāda (22–24 October 2010 Bursa)—Proceedings*. Bursa: Büyükşehir Belediyesi Yayınları, 227–38.

Nadler, S. (1993a). 'Occasionalism and General Will in Malebranche'. *Journal of the History of Philosophy* 31: 31–47.

Nadler, S. (1993b). 'The Occasionalism of Louis de la Forge'. In S. Nadler (ed.), *Causation in Early Modern Philosophy: Cartesianism, Occasionalism, and Preestablished Harmony*. University Park, PA: Pennsylvania State University Press, 57–73.

Nadler, S. (1994). 'Descartes and Occasional Causation'. *British Journal for the History of Philosophy* 2: 35–54.

Nadler, S. (1996). '"No Necessary Connection": The Medieval Roots of the Occasional Roots of Hume'. *The Monist* 79: 448–66.

Nadler, S. (1998). 'Louis de la Forge and the Development of Occasionalism: Continuous Creation and the Activity of the Soul'. *Journal of the History of Philosophy* 36: 215–31.

Perler, D., and U. Rudolph (2000). *Occasionalismus: Theorien der Kausalität im arabisch-islamischen und im europäischen Denken*. Göttingen: Vandenhoeck & Ruprecht.

Radner, D. (1993). 'Occasionalism'. In G. H. R. Parkinson (ed.), *The Renaissance and Seventeenth-Century Rationalism*. Routledge History of Philosophy, vol. 4. London/New York: Routledge, 349–83.

Riker, S. (1996). 'Al-Ghazali on Necessary Causality in The Incoherence of the Philosophers'. *The Monist* 79: 315–24.

Schwarz, M. (1991–2). 'Who were Maimonides' Mutakallimûn? Some Remarks on Guide of the Perplexed, Part 1, Chapter 73'. *Maimonidean Studies* 2: 159–209 and 3: 143–72.

Shihadeh, A. (2011). 'Khojazāda on al-Ghazālī's Criticism of the Philosophers' Proof of the Existence of God'. In T. Yücedoğru, O. Ş. Koloğlu, U. M. Kılavuz, and K. Gömbeyaz (eds.), *Uluslararası Hocazâde Sempozyumu (22–24 Ekim 2010 Bursa)—Bildiriler—International Symposium on Khojazāda (22–24 October 2010 Bursa)—Proceedings*. Bursa: Büyükşehir Belediyesi Yayınları, 141–61.

Specht, R. (1971). 'Über "occasio" und verwandte Begriffe vor Descartes'. *Archiv für Begriffsgeschichte* 15: 215–55.

Specht, R. (1972a). 'Über "occasio" und verwandte Begriffe bei Zabarella und Descartes'. *Archiv für Begriffsgeschichte* 16: 1–27.

Specht, R. (1972b). 'Die Vorstellung von der Ohnmacht der Natur'. In S. M. Stern, A. Hourani, and V. Brown (eds.), *Islamic Philosophy and the Classical Tradition*. Oxford: Cassirer, 425–36.

Specht, R. (1972–3). 'Über "occasio" und verwandte Begriffe im Cartesianismus I/II'. *Archiv für Begriffsgeschichte* 16: 198–226 and 17: 36–65.

Specht, R. (1984). 'Occasionalismus'. In J. Ritter and K. Gründer (eds.), *Historisches Wörterbuch der Philosophie*, vol. vi. Basel: Schwabe, 1090–1.

Türker, Ö. (2011). 'Tehâfüt Tartışmaları Bir Gelenek Sayılabilir mi?'. In T. Yücedoğru, O. Ş. Koloğlu, U. M. Kılavuz, and K. Gömbeyaz (eds.), *Uluslararası Hocazâde Sempozyumu (22–24 Ekim 2010 Bursa)—Bildiriler—International Symposium on Khojazāda (22–24 October 2010 Bursa)—Proceedings*. Bursa: Büyükşehir Belediyesi Yayınları, 203–10.

al-Ṭūsī, ʿAlāʾ al-Dīn (*Dhakhīra*). *Kitāb al-Dhakhīra*. Hyderabad, n.d.

Weisser, U. (1980). *Das 'Buch über das Geheimnis der Schöpfung' von Pseudo-Apollonios von Tyana*. Berlin/New York: De Gruyter.

Yücedoğru, T., and V. Kaya (2011). 'Tehâfütler—İçerik ve Yöntem Açısından Bir Karşılaştırma'. In T. Yücedoğru, O. Ş. Koloğlu, U. M. Kılavuz, and K. Gömbeyaz (eds.), *Uluslararası Hocazâde Sempozyumu (22–24 Ekim 2010 Bursa)—Bildiriler—International Symposium on Khojazāda (22–24 October 2010 Bursa)—Proceedings*. Bursa: Büyükşehir Belediyesi Yayınları, 365–80.

CHAPTER 22

ABŪ HĀSHIM AL-JUBBĀʾĪ'S (d. 321/933) THEORY OF 'STATES' (*AḤWĀL*) AND ITS ADAPTION BY ASHʿARITE THEOLOGIANS

JAN THIELE

THE notion of 'states' (*aḥwāl*, sing. *ḥāl*) was introduced into Muʿtazilite theology by Abū Hāshim al-Jubbāʾī.[1] By adopting this concept, he intended to solve a fundamental problem that had challenged theologians for several generations. The principal question which Muslim theologians posed was: How can we conceive of God as one and, at the same time, describe Him by a multitude of qualities? With the concept of *ḥāl*, Abū Hāshim provided a category alongside the nature of mere things or entities (*ashyāʾ*, sing. *shayʾ*). Because only things were believed to be either existent or non-existent, Abū Hāshim's definition of God's multiple qualities as 'states' helped him to avoid asserting the existence of other beings within God. None of Abū Hāshim's own writings are any longer extant and we therefore do not have access to his original formulation of this theory. Consequently, his teachings can only be reconstructed on the basis of later sources. In his study of Abū Hāshim's theory of attributes, Richard Frank was the first modern scholar to rely extensively on the writings of the later adherents of Abū Hāshim's school, which was named after him as Bahshamiyya. Frank's interpretation was later fundamentally questioned by Ahmed Alami. On the basis of recently explored Bahshamī primary sources, Alami's critique is, however, no longer tenable. These sources actually confirm Frank's results and, furthermore, allow scholars to refine his understanding of the theory. The concept of 'states' was at first rejected by Ashʿarite theologians. With Abū Bakr

[1] This chapter was prepared within the framework of a M4HUMAN fellowship awarded by the Gerda Henkel Foundation.

al-Bāqillānī (d. 403/1013), however, an important representative of the school eventually came to use the term within the framework of his theory of attributes. Later, Abū l-Maʿālī al-Juwaynī (d. 478/1085–6) also followed al-Bāqillānī in adopting the notion of *ḥāl*.

I The Problem of Divine Attributes

Discussions on the characteristics of beings, and in particular God's attributes, have always been of central concern to Muslim theologians. Essentially, these discussions arose from two principal assumptions about the nature of God that are, from a logical standpoint, difficult to reconcile. Appealing to divine revelation, theologians argued for a strict understanding of monotheism and negated any multiplicity in God. However, the Qurʾān does not only stress that God is one. It equally characterizes God by a plurality of properties, reflected in His 'most beautiful names' (*al-asmāʾ al-ḥusnā*). It was, therefore, necessary for theologians to explain the precise sense in which predications such as 'God knows' reflect His reality. They could then ask to what such predications like God's knowing refer. The answer to this problem was exceptionally difficult. On the one hand, to affirm that God possesses eternal knowledge could be interpreted as positing the reality of something distinct from God that, like Him, is also eternal. In the opinion of some theologians, such an affirmation would fundamentally violate the notion of monotheism. On the other hand, however, there were theologians who pointed out that to affirm that God *is* knowledge undermines divine transcendence. If neither of these two solutions were satisfactory, how then could the Qurʾānic description of a knowing God be true?

According to reports by later authors, the earliest speculation on God's attributes emerged towards the end of the second/eighth century. It appears that earlier Muslim theologians who applied rational argumentation were initially more concerned with issues other than those centred on resolving the problem of God's attributes. The Muʿtazilite Ḍirār b. ʿAmr (d. *c.*200/815) is said to have formulated a negative theology when interpreting the epithets of God found in the Qurʾān. According to his position, the statement 'God is knowing' merely means that He is not ignorant. Like any other form of negative theology, this approach attempted to do justice to God's nature on the linguistic level, since His reality was actually believed to be beyond what can be expressed through language. In the specific case of Ḍirār b. ʿAmr, the theory's aim was to preserve God's absolute transcendence by avoiding the postulation of any multiplicity within God that undermines His oneness. This negative theology was, however, unsatisfactory because it was not entirely consistent with the Qurʾānic text, which usually expresses God's characteristics by way of affirmation rather than negation (van Ess 1991: iii. 37–8).

The first theologian to analyse systematically what the Qurʾān means when it predicates something of God was the Muʿtazilite Abū l-Hudhayl (d. 227/841–2). He was not convinced by his older contemporary's negative theology and therefore maintained that such properties as 'knowing' do refer to a reality, namely the act of knowing. It is possible that Abū l-Hudhayl believed his position was supported by Qurʾānic references to actual attributes, for example 'Say: The knowledge is with God' (*qul: innamā l-ʿilm ʿinda Llāh*, Q 67: 26) or 'My Lord embraces all things in His knowledge' (*innamā ʿilmuhā ʿinda rabbī*, Q 6: 80). Abū l-Hudhayl therefore argued that it was valid to infer from statements like 'God is knowing' the presence of knowledge (*ʿilm*) by which God is knowing. Nevertheless, in interpreting such references he was always conscious that he had to avoid positing the reality of distinct knowledge or power in God at all costs, since this would violate the idea of God's absolute oneness. Abū l-Hudhayl therefore affirmed the identity between God and His knowledge, His power, and so forth (van Ess 1991: iii. 272–6, iv. 441–2).

Abū l-Hudhayl's exegetical approach was a turning point in the theological discussion on divine attributes and marked the end of the negative theology of earlier thinkers. His conclusions were, however, received with scepticism; he had not resolved the fundamental problem, which arose in relation to the principle of monotheism when a plurality of attributes in God was affirmed. In addition, Abū l-Hudhayl's theory raised new questions. His formulation suggested that asserting that God knows, creates etc. still refers to one and the same reality, namely God Himself. Assuming this is the case, why then should the act of knowing be distinguished from the act of creating if, according to Abū l-Hudhayl, each of these acts is identical with God? Consequently, should we not conclude that God in Himself is an act of knowledge and of creating and that, therefore, knowing and creating have exactly the same meaning when applied to God?

It was specifically in reaction to such problems raised by Abū l-Hudhayl's theory that his younger contemporary, al-Naẓẓām (d. between 220/835 and 230/845), completely rejected the idea that God is knowing by an act of knowledge or creating by an act of creation. To solve the problem of attributes, he sought categorically to avoid positing entitative knowledge or power when speaking about the ontological ground of God's attributes. Al-Naẓẓām's solution was to argue that God's knowing, creating, etc. refer to God Himself (*ithbāt dhātihi*), rather than to an act of knowledge or creation, since He is knowing and creating by virtue of Himself (*ʿālim/qādir bi-nafsihi*) (van Ess 1991: iii. 399f.). With al-Naẓẓām's overturning of Abū l-Hudhayl's thesis, a major step was taken in the discussion of the problem of attributes. The later Baṣran tradition of the Muʿtazila adopted the same formulation, which they took as their point of departure for further reflection on this topic. Abū ʿAlī al-Jubbāʾī (d. 303/915), the first of 'the two masters' of Baṣran Muʿtazilism, used al-Naẓẓām's label '*li-nafsihi*' whenever referring to attributes that describe objects as what they are in themselves. With his adaption of the notion, Abū ʿAlī went beyond al-Naẓẓām's original idea, since he discussed the issue of God's attributes within the broader context of the nature of both created and uncreated being. He maintained that if the affirmation 'God is eternal' (*Allāh qadīm*) refers to the reality of the described object, the same applies when we say that 'black is black' (*al-sawād sawād*): both predications express that by which an object is called by virtue of itself (*li-nafsihi*). This specific type of predication constitutes only one among several categories of attributes, including attributes that are not grounded in the described object itself but, for example, in another entity (*li-ʿilla*) that is distinct from the qualified object (Frank 1982a: 261f.).

II The Origin and Significance of Abū Hāshim's Concept of 'States'

Following al-Naẓẓām's reasoning, Abū ʿAlī al-Jubbāʾī argued against Abū l-Hudhayl that a description of God as being knowing cannot possibly refer to entitative knowledge. Abū ʿAlī agreed with al-Naẓẓām's critique of Abū al-Hudhayl's thesis that divine knowledge was identical with God. For both theologians, Abū l-Hudhayl's thesis did not satisfactorily resolve the problem of attributes. They consequently argued that the predication 'God is knowing' refers to nothing but God himself.

The logical corollary of this theory is that predications such as 'he is knowing' reflect different ontological realities when affirmed of God and human beings. The meaning of 'being knowing' was, according to Abū ʿAlī, the same whether applied to God or man—it simply negates ignorance in the subject of predication. However, that which 'being knowing' refers to is not identical when applied to God and created bodies: unlike God, a body's 'being knowing' always refers to something distinct from the knower, namely an entity of knowledge that is the ground of its being so. However, for Abū ʿAlī the descriptive term (or attribute: *ṣifa*) itself has no extralinguistic reality in either case. He simply regarded the *ṣifa* as identical with the act of description or attribution (*waṣf*). Consequently, it was impossible in the context of Abū ʿAlī's theory to explain or even talk about the qualities of beings without referring to their specific grounds. Abū ʿAlī's theory thus failed to provide a framework within which to conceive of attributes as such (Frank 1978: 15–19; Frank 1982a: 259).

Within the Baṣran Muʿtazilite tradition, Abū ʿAlī's son Abū Hāshim was the first to provide a theoretical foundation for the ontological nature of attributes, one which was consistent with his understanding of beings, and of God in particular. He built on his father's theory by introducing a new category into the conception of the reality of beings and thereby avoided the limitations set by an ontology that only conceived of either existent or non-existent categories. According to the Baṣran tradition, the world consists of things or entities (pl. *ashyāʾ/dhawāt*, sing. *shayʾ/dhāt*). These things can be the subject in a predicative sentence and can be described by specific qualities, which a fortiori implies that they become objects of knowledge. 'Things' are subdivided into God, whose existence is eternal and necessary, and created things, whose existence is only temporal and possible. The Baṣran Muʿtazilites believed the created world to be composed of atoms (pl. *jawāhir*, sing. *jawhar*), i.e. indivisible particles of which bodies are made up, and accidents (pl. *aʿrāḍ*, sing. *ʿaraḍ*), which are considered as the grounds of the changing qualities of atoms and bodies, including their annihilation, and also of location, motion, colours etc. (Dhanani 1993: 15–20, 29–33; Thiele 2013: 59–74). Following intense internal debate within the early Muʿtazilite tradition, the Baṣran school ultimately settled on a controversial position regarding the non-existence of created beings. They claimed that the non-existent is also a *shayʾ/dhāt*, that is, that existence is not required for things to become objects of knowledge and of predication (Frank 1980). According to the Baṣrans, if the non-existent is not a 'thing' then this also entails that it cannot be an object of knowledge. This position would consequently lead to the inescapable but unacceptable conclusion that God could not be eternally omniscient—since omniscience necessarily implies that God knows His creatures before He creates them. The upshot of this line of reasoning is that without antecedent knowledge of His creatures, God would be unable to create them. Some Baṣran theologians put forward the ancillary argument that if the non-existent cannot be known, man himself would then be unaware of any action he performed in the past, since after having been performed such actions of course no longer existed.

Abū Hāshim added to the three aforementioned subcategories of 'things' (God, atoms, and accidents) a new ontological category that is neither existent nor non-existent. To conceive of and express this new category he adopted the concept of 'states' (*aḥwāl*, sing. *ḥāl*) developed in the field of grammar and transferred it to the ontology of attributes. In Arabic grammar, *ḥāl* denotes the function of indefinite accusative nouns that describe the circumstances of the subject or the object in a verbal sentence. This so-called 'accusative of state' is also required for predicates of the verb *kāna/yakūnu* ('to be'). It seems that Abū Hāshim's analysis of the verb *kāna* was adopted from the grammarians of Baṣra. They distinguished between the use of *kāna*, *yakūnu* as a 'complete verb' (*fiʿl tāmm*) in the meaning of 'to exist' on the one hand, and an 'incomplete' (*nāqiṣa*) verb on the other hand. Whereas the 'complete' *kāna* together with its subject forms a self-contained sentence, the 'incomplete' *kāna* is transitive and requires an accusative object. However, some syntactical constructions with *kāna* followed by an accusative noun only appear to be transitive on the surface. In fact, the presumed complement has to be interpreted as a *ḥāl* by which the subject of the 'complete', intransitive *kāna* is characterized. In such cases, the predicate must not be understood as an equivalent to the subject, but rather expresses a manner of being or circumstance of the subject. Abū Hāshim applied this grammatical analysis to predications about things and interpreted the properties attributed to a subject as a 'state' (*ḥāl*). By adopting this line of reasoning, Abū Hāshim and his followers consistently avoided speaking of 'knowledge' (*ʿilm*), 'will' (*irāda*), etc. whenever referring to the attributes of things as such. The characteristics of beings were instead expressed by way of an accusative of state, for example by such formulations as *kawnuhu ʿāliman* ('his being knowing'), *kawnuhu murīdan* ('his being willing'), etc. (Frank 1978: 20–2; Frank 1982b: 344f.). When the Bahshamīs used the nouns 'knowledge' (*ʿilm*) or 'will' (*irāda*), they exclusively denoted accidents, that is distinctly existing grounds of a body's 'being knowing' or 'being willing'.

With his conception of attributes as 'states', Abū Hāshim assigned an ontological reality to the attributes and thereby diverged significantly from his father's position.

According to Abū ʿAlī, only the grounds of the properties of beings have any reality in the qualified subject, whereas attributes (*ṣifāt*) merely denote the act of describing a subject. In principle, the Bahshamīs also applied the notion of *ṣifa* to the act of describing itself. The extant literature reflects, however, a more flexible use of the term *ṣifa*, with theologians tending to use it as a synonym of *ḥāl*. Consequently, affirming the same ontological reality for the *ṣifa* that was posited for the *ḥāl* became widely accepted. In their terminology, the Bahshamīs described the reality of the *ḥāl* (or *ṣifa*) by the term *thubūt* (or *thabata/yathbutu*) as opposed to the existence (*wujūd*) of things or entities.

As previously outlined, only entities can be known when considered in isolation. In contrast, attributes (whether referred to as *ḥāl* or *ṣifa*) cannot be objects of knowledge. They are rather 'intelligible' (*maʿqūl* or *ʿuqila*), so that a thing is known as being in the state by which it is qualified. Stating that someone is living (*kawnuhu ḥayyan*) consequently means that I know the subject referred to as being living. It does not, however, entail that that subject *is* life, while similarly, if it is affirmed as living, this of itself does not account for why the subject is living. The conceptual distinction between the reality of the *ḥāl* and that of its ontological ground allowed for a univocal understanding of two subjects' being living, irrespective of whether or not they are alive for the same reason. This Bahshamī conception was made possible because knowledge of the ontological ground of a property was no longer regarded as a prerequisite for understanding the specific property of a subject (Frank 1978: 22–4).

III The Typologies of Attributes in Bahshamī Theology

In assigning to attributes a reality by way of a *ḥāl*—i.e. a reality that is conceived independently of the *ḥāl*'s ontological root—the identification of an attribute's specific ground was thereby deferred and left to a higher level of theological analysis. The reasoning behind this is that we become aware of an object being qualified by a property *before* we even understand anything about how it is qualified by this property. For example, we would usually become aware *that* a specific object actually exists before we understand *why* it exists. In order to ascertain the ground of the object's existence, we then have to consider further factors. Whenever an object comes into existence at a given moment in time and later ceases to exist, we have to conclude that its existence is contingent and therefore depends on an act of creation. If, however, the object in question exists eternally, it must necessarily have an eternal ground that causes it to exist. It was, therefore, only a logical further step to classify attributes according to the manner or modality (*kayfiyya*) by which they become actual (*thabata*). Richard Frank was the first to make a comprehensive attempt to reconstruct this classification on the basis of Bahshamī sources from the fourth/tenth to early fifth/eleventh centuries (Frank 1978; Frank 1982b: 345f.).

Since Abū Hāshim's own writings are no longer extant, his original typology of attributes cannot be securely established. It appears, however, quite likely that he distinguished between various types of attributes according to their causes, since this is a common feature of later accounts of the theory. This picture is also confirmed by Ashʿarite discussions of the Bahshamī theory of attributes (Gimaret 1970). Nonetheless, any attempt to reconstruct Abū Hāshim's original thought remains speculative and therefore controversial, because the extant literature composed by his later followers does not provide a unified picture of the classification of attributes.

In a more recent interpretation of Abū Hāshim's theory of *aḥwāl*, Ahmed Alami fundamentally questioned whether the manner by which attributes become actual represented a criterion for Abū Hāshim and his school's classification of attributes. Rather, Alami interprets Abū Hāshim's notion of *ḥāl* as constituting a central element of a new ontology of immanence, which is founded on three 'modes'. According to Alami, each of these 'modes' has the same meaning when applied to God and His creatures. Based on this assumption, Alami detects in Abū Hāshim's theory an 'ontology of univocity' between divine and created beings, that radically broke with the transcendentalism of earlier thinkers (Alami 2001). New Bahshamī sources have come to light since Alami's publication, including treatises that deal with the theory of attributes in a much more comprehensive fashion than the texts explored by him and Frank. In the light of these findings, both Alami's rejection of the classification of attributes according to causal criteria and his immanentist reading of the notion of *ḥāl* appear highly problematic. The texts rather confirm the overall understanding of the theory as outlined by Frank, but also allow further refinement of his analysis (Thiele 2013: 131–200).

In relation to the classification of attributes, there appears to be much common ground in the Bahshamī sources. Aside from some categories that are central to the theory, there are variations in some definitions of specific categories and also in their precise number. These variations probably emerged according to developments in different periods and regions, which were the natural result of the spread of Bahshamī teachings over a wide geographic area and continuing refinements within the school tradition over several centuries.

(1) A category of attributes that consistently figures in Bahshamī accounts, called *al-ṣifa al-dhātiyya*, *ṣifat al-dhāt*, or *al-ṣifa al-nafsiyya*, is commonly rendered in modern studies as the 'attribute of the essence'. This type of attribute describes or defines what a thing is in itself. It identifies specific objects in such expressions as 'the atom's being an atom' (*kawn al-jawhar jawharan*). In other words, qualifying something as an atom distinguishes it from other objects that are not atoms, such as, for example, God or the colour black.

Since a qualification expressed by the 'attribute of the essence' describes what an object fundamentally is, it is not grounded in or conditioned by any other entity. An atom is only described as being an atom because it is what it is. There is nothing outside this object that necessarily causes it either to be or to eventually become an atom.

Since the identity of an object finds its expression in the 'attribute of the essence', the Bahshamīs regard this attribute as the ground or basis on which something is intelligible and thereby becomes an object of knowledge (*maʿlūm*). Two different things, such as the accidents of the colours black and white, are distinguishable because they do not share their 'attribute of the essence'. Accordingly, the Bahshamīs spoke of similarity between any two things whenever their 'attribute of the essence' was interchangeable.

Unlike any other category of attributes, the 'attribute of the essence' has an eternal and necessary reality, irrespective of whether or not the qualified object actually exists. This theory allowed the Bahshamīs to account for how the actual existent can be known and also the non-existent or the possible. Furthermore, it also gave them a firm basis on which to argue that God is eternally omniscient, that is, that He also knows His creatures before they come into existence.

The 'attributes of the essence' of created things were, as a rule, derived from the terms that denote particular objects—such as the atom's being an atom (*kawn al-jawhar jawharan*) or the colour black's being black (*kawn al-sawād sawādan*). In contrast, when applied to God the 'attribute of the essence' was defined by various Bahshamī theologians in different terms. It appears that most of the earlier texts identified the 'attribute of the essence' with God's 'being eternal' (*kawnuhu qadīman*)—a position that was adopted from Abū ʿAlī al-Jubbāʾī (Gimaret 1970: 73f.; Frank 1978: 53, 68, 86 n. 57). In particular, Zaydī scholars inclined to Bahshamī teachings—including the Persian al-Ḥākim al-Jishumī (d. 494/1101) and scholars belonging to the Yemeni strand founded in the sixth/twelfth century such as al-Ḥasan al-Raṣṣāṣ (d. 584/1188)—preferred instead to speak of 'God's most characteristic attribute' (*ṣifat Allāh al-akhaṣṣ*) (Thiele 2013: 164f.). Although the sources are silent about this inconsistency in identifying God's 'attribute of the essence', a reasonable argument for the latter choice may have been that the idea of God's eternity was too closely related, if not tantamount, to His being eternally existent. As will be seen, God's attribute of existence—or more precisely 'His being eternally existent' (*kawnuhu mawjūdan fīmā lam yazal*)—was, however, considered an attribute belonging to the following category of attributes, that is one of those four attributes entailed by God's 'attribute of the essence'.

(2) The second category of attributes constitutes a fundamental pillar of Abū Hāshim's solution to the problem of attributes. By affirming the *ḥāl* as an ontological reality, Abū Hāshim introduced a new concept that had not been considered by earlier Muʿtazilites as a potential ground for the attributes of beings. He did not conceive of the reality of the *ḥāl* as an existing entity that is distinct from the qualified being but instead understood it as a manner of being. Consequently, Abū Hāshim was able to explain the foundation of specific properties, distinct from the description of things in themselves, without having to posit any other entity as the ground of the property in question. For example, the Bahshamīs reasoned that any existing atom must occupy space (*taḥayyaza*). However, affirming that an atom occupies space is not, according to the Bahshamīs, a description or definition of the atom as such. The only property an atom possesses by virtue of itself is 'its being an

> atom' (*kawnuhu jawharan*), that is, its 'attribute of the essence'. Nevertheless, simply describing something as an atom already implies that it occupies space when it is brought into existence. The Bahshamīs therefore argued that the ground for an atom occupying space must be its 'attribute of the essence', that is, a *ḥāl*, and that the *ḥāl* is effective once the atom exists. The idea that one attribute could effect another was only conceivable because according to Abū Hāshim's theory of *aḥwāl* the attribute was no longer regarded as a pure utterance, but instead was considered to be ontologically real.

The same reasoning was applied to God's eternal attributes. Since it is in the very nature of God that He is necessarily existent, capable of creating the world, omniscient, and living, the Bahshamīs regarded these properties as entailed by His 'attribute of the essence'. Unlike al-Naẓẓām or Abū ʿAlī, the Bahshamīs thereby rejected that these attributes are directly grounded in God as He is in Himself (*li-nafsihi/li-dhātihi*), since none of the four aforementioned eternal properties expresses the fullness of His being. Consequently, predicating that He is God has to be distinguished from predicating that He is eternally powerful, knowing, living, or existing. For the Bahshamīs, He is characterized by these properties *because* He is God. From a reverse perspective, the knowledge that He is God (i.e. that what He is in Himself) is inferred from the knowledge that He is eternally powerful, knowing, living, and existent.

As is the case with the four characteristics God necessarily has, attributes that are in turn effected by other attributes can have eternal reality. Unlike the 'attributes of the essence', however, they are not eternal by themselves. Rather, they are eternal because the conditions for attributes like God's being powerful, knowing, living, and existing are eternally fulfilled: God's 'attribute of the essence' unconditionally effects His being existent, which is the only prerequisite for His being living, and in turn being living is the condition for His being powerful and knowing. It has to be noted that the hierarchical order between these four attributes is a mere logical dependence and that none of them temporally follows another.

Moreover, attributes of this category that stand apart from God's eternal attributes have a temporal reality, since they are conditioned by the temporal existence of the object they qualify. An atom's occupying space is, for example, only a necessary property of an atom during the limited period of its existence.

The Bahshamīs employed the verb *iqtaḍā* ('to entail') to describe the way in which one attribute causes another attribute. The effective attribute was therefore denoted by the active participle (*al-muqtaḍī*) and the effected attribute as *al-ṣifa al-muqtaḍāt*. In Bahshamī texts, we find a narrow and a broader definition of what can be termed as belonging to the category of 'entailed attributes'. In particular, the earlier extant works restrict the *ṣifāt muqtaḍāt* to those attributes that become actual by virtue of the 'attribute of the essence' whenever a thing comes into existence—such as the atom's occupying space or God's four eternal attributes. Occasionally, these sources speak of *al-ṣifa al-muqtaḍāt ʿan ṣifat al-dhāt* (i.e. 'the attribute entailed by the "attribute of the essence"'). Later Bahshamī theologians from the late fifth/eleventh century onwards, and primarily their Yemeni representatives, tended to broaden the definition of the *ṣifāt muqtaḍāt* to any kind of attribute that is grounded in another attribute (Thiele 2013: 146f.).

In his analysis of the Bahshamī theory of attributes, Richard Frank only deals with the narrow definition of the *ṣifāt muqtaḍāt* for which he suggests the translation 'essential attributes'. In fact, the attributes entailed by the 'attribute of the essence' do not describe things as what they are in themselves, but they sometimes reveal the distinctiveness of the 'attribute of the essence' by which they are effected. The reasoning behind this was that some attributes can only be entailed by a specific 'attribute of the essence'. For example, something described as occupying space can only be identified as an atom, because no other class of being can occupy space. Therefore, the attribute of 'occupying space' (*kawnuhu mutaḥayyizan*) must necessarily be entailed by the atom's 'attribute of the essence' (*kawnuhu jawharan*), so that 'the atom's being an atom' becomes manifest through 'its occupying space' (= the *ṣifa muqtaḍāt*). Although Frank's translation of *ṣifa muqtaḍāt* by 'essential attribute' makes sense in this context, it does not sufficiently clarify the central distinction in the Bahshamī theory between *ṣifat al-dhāt* (i.e. the first category in the typology of attributes) and *ṣifa muqtaḍāt*. In some cases, the translation 'essential attribute' is even inappropriate, because it is not applicable to the broader understanding of *ṣifa muqtaḍāt* and does not render the exact sense of the Arabic term.

(3) The category of the attributes effected by an agent (*al-ṣifāt bi-l-fāʿil/al-mustaḥaqqa bi-l-fāʿil/al-ḥāṣila bi-l-fāʿil*) has to be understood in the framework of the Bahshamī theory of existence. According to this theory, not only the existent but also the non-existent is considered as a potential object of knowledge. The Bahshamīs therefore strictly distinguished between the attribute that describes a thing in itself and its attribute of existence. Consequently, predicating that an object is an atom has a different meaning than asserting that the atom exists. Whereas the former predication merely expresses that I know the object as being an atom, the latter asserts that I know the atom as being existent. Things can therefore be known irrespective of whether or not they actually exist. Existence is thus a supplemental quality, and in the case of created beings, it is only temporal and possible, as opposed to the eternal reality of the 'attribute of the essence' by virtue of which all things are knowable.

Bahshamī theologians argued that the existence of created beings cannot be grounded in the qualified being itself. Instead, their possible existence must be founded on an exterior reason that is not necessarily effective. According to the Bahshamī theory of causation, only autonomous agents (*fāʿil*) are effective in such a way that they could refrain equally from producing their effect and vice versa: agents never act necessarily, since their ability to perform an act always implies the ability to do the opposite. The Muʿtazilite school regarded God and human beings as autonomous agents, each of which has different capacities: since God is omnipotent, He is able to bring atoms and accidents into existence, while human abilities are restricted to the creation of certain accidents only.

The temporal attribute of existence is not the only attribute that was considered as belonging to the category of attributes effected by agents. The Bahshamīs also included further qualities derived from an object's coming into existence. If, for example, an act of creation is motivated by specific intentions, the created object is further qualified by additional attributes that are correlated to the agent's will. The act then occurs 'in a specific manner' (*ʿalā wajh*): depending on the intentions of the agent, speech can, for example, be uttered as a command, a statement, or a question.

(4) The Bahshamīs agreed with a predominant theory among theologians that was used to explain the changing properties of bodies. They claimed that such contingent properties are grounded in accidents that inhere in the discrete parts of bodies. According to this idea, a moving (*mutaḥarrik*) body is the substrate of accidents of motion (*ḥaraka*), a resting (*sākin*) body is inhered by accidents of rest (*sukūn*), etc. In the Bahshamī terminology, such accidents are called *ʿilla* or *maʿnā*. These terms gave their name to the category of attributes caused by an accident: they are called *ṣifāt maʿnawiyya, li-maʿnā* or *li-ʿilla*. Like attributes effected by an agent, these 'accidental' properties are grounded in an entity other than the qualified object.

Within the classical ontology of *kalām*, accidents belong to the group of created beings and have, by definition, possible existence. This explains why the attributes grounded in accidents are temporal and possible, since their reality depends on the existence of accidents: a moving body only moves as long as it is a substrate of accidents of movement; it still continues to exist when it stops moving and even could exist without ever having moved.

The Bahshamī notion of 'accidental attributes' also includes such attributes as men's being knowing, capable of action, and living. As opposed to God, these attributes do not necessarily qualify the human body: some people are unable to perform certain acts which others are able to perform, human knowledge is restricted, and humankind's life limited. Ontologically, human imperfection was interpreted as a non-presence of such accidents by virtue of which he would be knowing or able to perform certain acts; and death, too, was conceived as the absence of an accident of life.

(5) A fifth category of attributes is frequently mentioned in the writings of the prominent fourth/tenth-century theologian ʿAbd al-Jabbār (d. 415/1025) and his students, but is increasingly absent in later Bahshamī sources. This group of attributes is said to be grounded neither in the qualified object nor in another entity (*lā li-l-nafs wa-lā li-maʿnā*), and applied to the attribute of being perceiving (*kawnuhu mudrikan*). Against his father's position, Abū Hāshim maintained that perception is not an accident like the will or human knowledge. He argued that living beings are perceiving whenever an object of perception exists, unless

> they suffer from physical defects. Consequently, God is not eternally perceiving, although He possesses all necessary prerequisites: since His creation is only temporal, He cannot perceive it from pre-eternity. Abū Hāshim therefore claimed that the attribute of being perceiving is effected by the attribute of being living, provided that all conditions are fulfilled.

While Bahshamī theologians agreed that beings are perceiving by virtue of an attribute, and so neither by the perceiver himself (*li-l-nafs*) nor by another entity (*li-maʿnā*), they differed about the necessity of positing a category in its own right for the attribute of perception. Towards the second half of the fifth/eleventh century, the Ḥanafī Bahshamī scholar al-Ḥākim al-Jishumī (d. 494/1101) appears to have been one of the first to omit the fifth category. In his 'Book on the effect and the effector' (*Kitāb al-Taʾthīr wa-l-muʾaththir*), he cites the attribute of perception as an example of an attribute 'entailed' (*muqtaḍā*) by another attribute and apparently concluded it to be considered as analogous to the atom's occupying space or God's eternal attributes (Thiele 2012: 308). Nevertheless, al-Ḥākim al-Jishumī's position was inconsistent. In other theological works, he stuck to the concept of attributes that are neither grounded in the qualified object nor in another entity and associated it with the attribute of perception. It was only among later Yemeni Zaydīs inclined to Bahshamī doctrines that the quadripartite classification became the predominant doctrine. By adopting a broader understanding of the *ṣifāt muqtaḍāt* and defining them as any attribute entailed by another attribute, the fifth category of attributes eventually became obsolete: the attribute of perception then fulfils all conditions for classification as an 'entailed attribute' (Thiele 2013: 146f., 167f.).

The most comprehensive and systematic account of the theory of attributes we possess is relatively late. It was written by the sixth/twelfth-century Zaydī theologian al-Ḥasan al-Raṣṣāṣ, who belonged to the founding generation of a new Bahshamī school in Yemen. His treatise on attributes exhibits some features of later conceptual developments, e.g. a consistent reduction of the formerly five to four categories. In addition, al-Raṣṣāṣ adopts a genuine approach that provides insightful perspectives on how the classification outlined above could be used in theological reflections and argumentations.

Al-Raṣṣāṣ addresses the topic of attributes in a manner that could be characterized as an epistemological approach. Bearing in mind that in Bahshamī teaching, attributes or 'states' are not conceived as objects of knowledge, but as that by which 'things' (*ashyāʾ/dhawāt*) are known, al-Raṣṣāṣ's intention was to explore systematically what each category of attributes reveals about things. The question arose since a number of predications that were made of God were equally made of created beings. Moreover, the Bahshamīs maintained that whenever a property is predicated of various subjects, the affirmed *ḥāl* is univocal. Being able to act (*kawnuhu qādiran*) has one and the same meaning for all beings capable of autonomous actions: it entails the possibility that a subject performs an act and that an act occurs by virtue of the agent's capability. In this sense, affirming that God is able to act is tantamount to predicating the same about human beings, although God is necessarily capable of actions while human abilities are only possible ones. Necessity and possibility are, however, only modalities (*kayfiyyāt*) of the same *ḥāl* (Frank 1978: 66–72; Alami 2001: 101–39).

Nonetheless, the Bahshamīs certainly did not intend to claim that two subjects with a common attribute are necessarily alike. In order to avoid any anthropomorphic misinterpretations of their thought, they had to answer an essential theological question: how can it be true that God is knowing in the same sense as humans are, without undermining God's absolute transcendence? It was precisely this issue to which al-Raṣṣāṣ responded through his epistemological approach. For each category of attributes, he establishes a set of criteria to analyse whether a common attribute shared by two things reveals a similarity between the qualified beings or between that in which the common attribute is grounded. As explained by al-Raṣṣāṣ, attributes caused by the presence of an accident (*al-ṣifāt al-maʿnawiyya*) and attributes entailed by another attribute (*al-ṣifāt al-muqtaḍāt*) are, for example, not by themselves a sufficient indication as to the identity of the qualified being. An attribute like being living can be a possible or a necessary property. Whenever a being is contingently living, it is so by virtue of an accident that inheres in a created body, whereas the necessarily living refers to God, who is living by virtue of His 'attribute of the essence'. The fact that God and His creatures share the attribute of being living, however, neither means that they are living for the same reason, nor that they resemble each other in any way. Therefore, 'accidental attributes' and attributes grounded in other attributes are not by themselves an indication of the identity of all beings described by the same predicate.

Through an additional feature, al-Raṣṣāṣ's analysis further expands the perspective encountered in other sources: he also takes into consideration the so-called *aḥkām* (sing. *ḥukm*), i.e. 'characteristics', that are ontologically distinct from attributes or *aḥwāl*. The notion of *ḥukm* already occurs in our earliest Bahshamī sources, but the concept remains rather obscure. It appears that the Bahshamī understanding of the term *ḥukm* was only elaborated under the impact of Abū l-Ḥusayn al-Baṣrī (d. 436/1044). Abū l-Ḥusayn was a student of the eminent *qāḍī* ʿAbd al-Jabbār al-Hamadānī, but he had also been trained in medicine and philosophy. His education awakened him to new perspectives, leading him to criticize some principles of Bahshamī theology in an attempt to defend Muʿtazilite teachings against their opponents. He was, therefore, harshly attacked by his Bahshamī fellows.

Abū l-Ḥusayn's theological teaching is mainly known through the works of his later follower, Rukn al-Dīn Ibn al-Malāḥimī (d. 536/1141). It is in Ibn al-Malāḥimī's writings that we find the earliest account of a clear conceptual distinction between *ṣifa* and *ḥukm*. His definition of the two terms is subsequently quoted in Bahshamī sources from Yemen, namely in the writings of al-Raṣṣāṣ and later Zaydī scholars, who generally tend to reject Abū l-Ḥusayn al-Baṣrī's and Ibn al-Malāḥimī's teachings. According to this understanding, *ṣifāt* and *aḥkām* differ in the manner in which things are known through them. Unlike attributes, we have to consider two objects qualified by the same *ḥukm* to infer knowledge about a thing. In contrast, it suffices to consider only one subject qualified by the attribute of living to know the subject as being living. In analogy to the attributes, al-Raṣṣāṣ establishes three categories of *aḥkām*: a first category effected by an autonomous agent (*al-aḥkām al-mustaḥaqqa bi-l-fāʿil*), a second grounded in an accident (*al-aḥkām al-maʿnawiyya*), and a third category of *aḥkām* entailed by an attribute (*al-aḥkām al-muqtaḍāt*). Following the pattern of exploring the attributes, al-Raṣṣāṣ also establishes for the three categories of *aḥkām* whether they reveal a similarity of what they qualify (Thiele 2013: 131–200).

The case of al-Raṣṣāṣ brings to our attention the fact that Bahshamī theologians developed, on the basis of Abū Hāshim's concept of *ḥāl*, different perspectives on, and approaches to, the classification of attributes. The Bahshamī theory of attributes was, consequently, not transmitted as a static system, but rather underwent continuous modifications and diachronic developments.

IV The Adaption of the Concept of *Ḥāl* by Ashʿarite Theologians

The story of al-Ashʿarī (d. 324/935), the eponym of the Ashʿariyya school, is well known. He belonged to the circle of Abū ʿAlī al-Jubbāʾī's students and followed Muʿtazilite teachings until he abandoned his teacher's school at the age of about 40. Instead of adopting the pure scripturalist doctrine of the Muʿtazilites' opponents, he sought to find a compromise between rationalism and traditionalism—an approach that had already been sketched out by the third/ninth-century theologian Ibn Kullāb (d. *c.*240/854).

Al-Ashʿarī's teaching on God's attributes appears to have followed the major axioms of Ibn Kullāb's theory. Consequently, it differed significantly from the Muʿtazilite interpretation: al-Ashʿarī affirms that God's attributes are real entities (*maʿānī*), and that knowledge (*ʿilm*), life (*ḥayāt*), power (*qudra*), etc. 'subsist' (*taqūmu*) in Him. These entities are denoted by al-Ashʿarī as *ṣifāt*, and he posits that they actually exist. The notion of *ṣifa* is, in this sense, analogous to the accidents (*aʿrāḍ*) of created bodies: both are termed *maʿānī*, that is entities, whose presence necessitates a qualification of the object to which the *maʿnā* belongs.

According to al-Ashʿarī, the descriptive term has, unlike its entitative ground, no reality: for him, affirming that God is knowing (*ʿālim*) refers to His entitative knowledge (*ʿilm*), while he identified the descriptive term 'knowing' (*ʿālim*) with the act of attribution (*waṣf*), that is a pure utterance without any extralinguistic reality (in this respect, his position was nearer to that of Abū ʿAlī than that of Abū Hāshim). It has, however, to be noted that in his extant writings, al-Ashʿarī did not consistently distinguish between *ṣifa* and *waṣf*. In a predication such as 'God is knowing' (*Allāh ʿālim*), *ṣifa* can, consequently, refer to His entitative knowledge (*ʿilm*) and to the descriptive term 'knowing' (*ʿālim*) (Gimaret 1990: 235–43).

Considering the central concern of monotheism to Muslim theologians, al-Ashʿarī's conception of God's attributes inevitably raised a fundamental question: if entitative knowledge, power, life, will, etc. eternally exist in Him, how then could it be true that He is one and free from multiplicity of any kind? Al-Ashʿarī countered the problem by affirming that the *ṣifāt*, that is God's entitative attributes, are neither identical with, nor other than Him (Gimaret 1990: 276–81).

The theories of al-Ashʿarī and his contemporary Abū Hāshim al-Jubbāʾī were opposed to each other in a complex manner, in particular because the two theologians did not apply their terminology in the same way. In al-Ashʿarī's teaching, the *ṣifāt* denote entities that are not identical with God Himself, by virtue of which He is described by eternal properties. From the Muʿtazilite standpoint, positing the existence of eternal entities in God was unacceptable for the reasons previously explained. Therefore, the Muʿtazilites often faced the reproach of negating the *ṣifāt*. This objection is, however, not entirely correct, as far as Abū Hāshim and his followers are concerned: Bahshamī theologians did affirm the ontological reality of *ṣifāt*, but not in the same sense al-Ashʿarī affirmed it. For the Bahshamīs, *ṣifāt* are not conceived as entitative grounds of predications about God, but rather as a 'manner of being', a *ḥāl*. Al-Ashʿarī, in turn, rejected the idea that properties which are predicated of beings have, unlike their entitative grounds, a reality. In this respect, al-Ashʿarī agreed with his and Abū Hāshim's teacher Abū ʿAlī, for whom an affirmation that God is knowing or living is only an act of predication (*waṣf*), i.e. nothing but words.

The rejection of the concept of *ḥāl* still prevailed among the first followers of al-Ashʿarī. It was only two generations after the school's founder that a major representative of the Ashʿariyya, Abū Bakr al-Bāqillānī, adopted the concept. Al-Bāqillānī's position on the notion of *ḥāl* was, however, not consistent. In his *Kitāb al-Tamhīd*, he devotes a whole chapter to refuting Abū Hāshim's concept. Nonetheless, it is well known from the writings of later Ashʿarites that al-Bāqillānī eventually came to approve of the notion of *ḥāl* and that he maintained it in his *magnum opus*, the *Hidāyat al-mustarshidīn*. His change in opinion can be explained, as has been convincingly argued, by the chronology of al-Bāqillānī's works: the *Tamhīd* was in fact one of al-Bāqillānī's earliest works and merely represents a compilation of his masters' teachings, rather than his independent thought (Gimaret 1970: 76f.; Gimaret 1980: 94f.). Not surprisingly, al-Bāqillānī's framing of the divine attributes in the *Tamhīd* merely follows al-Ashʿarī's position. His main concern appears to have been to arrange al-Ashʿarī's teachings in a coherent line of argumentation by employing a systematized terminology (Allard 1965: 299–312). Al-Bāqillānī's approval of the concept of *ḥāl* must consequently have been a revision of his early position, possibly developed under the impact of his debates with Muʿtazilite scholars.

For long, modern scholarship had to rely on later accounts of al-Bāqillānī's adoption of the notion of *ḥāl*, such as the writings of Abū l-Maʿālī al-Juwaynī, who equally approved it. Since al-Juwaynī's teaching was significantly shaped by philosophical notions and theories, we have to be careful about identifying his position with that of al-Bāqillānī. Only the recent manuscript discoveries of substantial parts of the *Hidāya* provide a sound basis for an examination of al-Bāqillānī's original theory (Gimaret 2009; Schmidtke 2011).

As has already been observed for al-Juwaynī, al-Bāqillānī did not insist on an unconditional subscription to the theory of *aḥwāl*. Both theologians were less categorical, possibly because they were aware that the theory encountered much reservation among Ashʿarite theologians. Therefore al-Bāqillānī often presents in his *Hidāya* two alternative lines of argumentation whenever discussing questions related to attributes, and so his audience was able to follow his reasoning irrespective of whether or not they approved the notion of *ḥāl* (Gimaret 1970: 78; Thiele forthcoming).

Considering some obvious analogies with the Bahshamī concept, there is no doubt that al-Bāqillānī's notion of *ḥāl* was borrowed from his theological adversaries. Following Abū Hāshim's original reasoning, he revised his earlier understanding of the ontological reality expressed through predications about things. Against his position in the *Tamhīd*, which was in fact in accordance with that of al-Ashʿarī, al-Bāqillānī assigned in his *Hidāya* a reality to such properties that cannot be described by the dichotomy of existence and non-existence (Thiele forthcoming). The same position was also later adopted by al-Juwaynī (Gimaret 1970: 79). When al-Bāqillānī introduced the notion of *ḥāl*, he did not use it as an alternative to the concept of entitative attributes, which was in fact Abū Hāshim's primary preoccupation. Al-Bāqillānī rather combines the traditional Ashʿarite understanding of *ṣifa* with the notion of *ḥāl*. As is developed in the *Hidāya*, a *ḥāl* like God's 'being knowing' (*kawnuhu ʿāliman*) is founded in an actually existing 'knowledge' (*ʿilm*), which is termed a *ṣifa* or an entitative ground (*maʿnā*) for His being so. Al-Bāqillānī explains his reasoning by referring to al-Ashʿarī's principle that a specific predication has always the same sense or expresses the same truth (*ḥaqīqa*): if we posit a *maʿnā*, that is an entity of knowledge (*ʿilm*) as necessarily belonging to a human being described as knowing, the same holds true for God, so that He equally cannot be knowing but by virtue of a *maʿnā* (Thiele forthcoming). Similarly, al-Ashʿarī held that that which expressions like 'being knowing' (*ʿālim*) refer to must always be the same: therefore, 'being knowing' cannot refer in one case to the object of predication (*nafs*) and in another case to a distinct entity (*maʿnā*). Instead, *ʿālim* has always the same meaning (*ḥaqīqa*) in that it is equivalent to asserting an entity of knowledge that belongs to the object qualified as knowing (*lahu ʿilm*) (Frank 1982a: 270). Al-Bāqillānī's adoption of the concept of *ḥāl* did not replace the theory of his predecessors but rather expanded its conceptual framework.

Consequently, al-Bāqillānī and later al-Juwaynī had to adjust the concept of *ḥāl* to the doctrinal frame of the Ashʿarite school. A major modification of the original Bahshamī notion concerned a point of criticism al-Bāqillānī had made to substantiate his earlier rejection of the concept of *ḥāl* as a whole. In the *Tamhīd*, he argues that the Bahshamī position was, in itself, contradictory, in that it posited that (1) an agent who is capable of performing a certain act (*qādir*) must be distinguished from somebody incapable of the same act by a feature which has, by way of a *ḥāl*, an ontological reality; and (2) that, by definition, a *ḥāl* as a non-entity cannot be known. How then, al-Bāqillānī argues, can the *ḥāl* be established as a differentiating and ontologically real feature, if there is no way for it to be known? When al-Bāqillānī later approved the reality of the *ḥāl*, he took his earlier objection into consideration and argued that a *ḥāl* must necessarily be knowable (*maʿlūm*) even though it is not an entity (*dhāt*). The reasoning behind this was that if two things are qualified by the same *ḥāl*, we are able to detect their identity, and so we can distinguish it from a different *ḥāl*—as, for example, when we differentiate between 'living' and 'knowing' (Thiele forthcoming).

Even more important is, however, that al-Bāqillānī and al-Juwaynī no longer used the concept of *ḥāl* for the same purposes as the Bahshamīs did in their metaphysics. As was previously explained, the *aḥwāl* served in Bahshamī theology to reconcile God's oneness with the plurality of His properties. In this context, the *ḥāl* fulfils a crucial purpose in that it is conceived as having a non-entitative reality and thereby acts as a neither existent nor non-existent ground for entailing (*iqtaḍā*) other predications. In the Ashʿarite context, however, the original Bahshamī notion of *iqtiḍāʾ* is not taken over. Consequently, al-Juwaynī's classification of the *aḥwāl* does not include a category of attributes caused by other attributes that would be comparable to the Bahshamī category *ṣifāt muqtaḍāt*.

In fact, the Ashʿarite teaching on the non-existent and the possible rendered the Bahshamī distinction between the 'attribute of the essence' and the attributes 'entailed' by the 'attribute of the essence' of existent things obsolete. Whereas the Bahshamīs affirmed the reality of the 'attribute of the essence' of even non-existing things, the non-existent lacks, according to the Ashʿarites, any positive qualification. For them, it has no reality and is not considered a thing (*laysa bi-shayʾ*) (Frank 2000). Accordingly, predications that describe things as what they are in themselves (such as 'the atom is an atom', 'the colour black is black', etc.) and those specific qualifications that things necessarily have when they exist (such as the atom's occupying space) are both inseparably linked to existence. Sticking to the example of the atom, the traditional Ashʿarite teaching posited that atoms cannot possibly be conceived as atoms unless they actually exist. In addition, an existing atom cannot be imagined but as occupying space and vice versa. Therefore, being an atom, being an entity, being existent, and occupying space are, ontologically speaking, tantamount to each other in that each of these qualities affirms the reality of an atom. Essentially, these predications are founded in the atom itself and they are therefore only distinguished from a logical point of view.

Accordingly, al-Juwaynī only distinguishes between two classes of predicates in his classification of the *aḥwāl*: one category that is grounded in a distinctly existing entity (*muʿallal*), and another category of which this is not the case (*ghayr muʿallal*). Alternatively, al-Juwaynī also refers to these categories as those attributes affirming the reality of the qualified thing itself (*ṣifat ithbāt li-dhāt qāʾima bihā* or *ṣifa nafsiyya*, i.e. the latter 'non-grounded' attributes) and those affirming the existence of a *maʿnā*, that is an entity subsisting in the qualified being by virtue of which the *ḥāl* becomes actual (*thābit li-l-dhāt ʿan maʿnā* or *ṣifa maʿnawiyya*) (Frank 2004: 771–7).

Despite its terminological similarity, the Ashʿarite concept of the *ṣifa nafsiyya* is sharply distinguished from its homologue in the Bahshamī theory. Whereas the Bahshamīs identified a single predicate that expresses the fullness of its being for each entity, the Ashʿarites established a set of properties to frame the distinctiveness of any individual class of beings. For the reasons previously explained, they regarded the totality of these properties as defining a thing as such. It is in this particular context that the translation of *ḥāl* by 'states' has been problematized.

The inappropriateness of the translation 'state' can be exemplified by the case of the atom: the Ashʿarites explicitly denied that, ontologically speaking, the existence of atoms can be distinguished from their 'being an atom', and so they claimed with regard to all other attributes affirming the atom itself (or the 'essential attributes', i.e. the *ṣifāt nafsiyya*). Unlike the Bahshamīs, the Ashʿarites consequently did not conceive of existence and non-existence as two different conditions or circumstances under which atoms have reality. Nor did they agree with the Bahshamī theory, that atoms do not necessarily occupy space unless they actually exist. For that reason, such predications as 'the atom exists' or 'the atom occupies space' cannot be considered as changing states because they are necessarily implied by the meaning expressed by describing something as an atom. According to the Ashʿarites, predicating that the atom is an atom, that it exists and occupies space, denotes various aspects which, in their totality, describe the atom as what it is in itself. Therefore, it was recently suggested by Richard Frank to translate *ḥāl* in the Ashʿarite context as 'feature'. Beyond the *ṣifāt nafsiyya*, the problematic of translating *ḥāl* as 'state' equally applies to God's 'grounded attributes' (*ṣifāt maʿnawiyya* or *muʿallala*), since, according to classical Ashʿarite teaching, the entitative grounds (*maʿānī*) for such predications as God's 'being powerful' and His 'being knowing' are neither identical with, nor other than, Him. In other words, the necessary presence of power and knowledge in God does not, according to the Ashʿarites, entail any multiplicity in Him, although He is not power and knowledge. Consequently, God's existence is inconceivable unless power, knowledge etc. subsist in Him and so it is impossible to affirm God's reality without affirming that He is powerful, knowing etc. In this respect, God's 'grounded attributes' are similar to the *ṣifāt nafsiyya* in that they denote distinct features that a subject necessarily has (Frank 2004: 771–6).

When Ashʿarite theologians started adopting the concept of *ḥāl*, they came to use the term *ḥukm* frequently when referring to the properties of beings. By doing so, it appears that al-Bāqillānī and later supporters of the theory of *aḥwāl* strove to resolve a terminological ambiguity with regard to the term *ṣifa*. In the classical Ashʿarite vocabulary, *ṣifa* was applied to God's entitative knowledge, power, and so forth (*ʿilm*, *qudra*, etc.), that is, the so-called *maʿānī* in which some of His properties are founded. Because the Muʿtazilites negated the existence of eternal entitative attributes, they were blamed by the Ashʿarites for denying the *ṣifāt*, although this reproach was polemical if not inappropriate, in particular when it comes to the Bahshamī theory of *aḥwāl*. When Ashʿarite scholars eventually incorporated the concept of *ḥāl* in their theological system, they affirmed the ontological reality of both the entitative grounds of predications and the properties which they predicated. When applied to God, the term *ṣifa* was, however, coined in classical Ashʿarite terminology to denote the *maʿnā*, that is the entitative grounds (*ʿilm*, *qudra*...) for such predications as 'He is knowing', 'He is powerful' etc. (*kawnuhu ʿāliman, qādiran*...). It was therefore necessary to distinguish terminologically between the ground (i.e. the *ṣifa* in its traditional meaning of *maʿnā*) and the effect (i.e. the *ḥāl* or the *ṣifa muʿallala* as it termed by al-Juwaynī). Therefore, al-Bāqillānī and later Ashʿarites avoid using *ṣifa* whenever referring to ontologically real properties (i.e. the *aḥwāl*) and tend to employ the term *ḥukm* as a synonym for *ḥāl* (Frank 2004).

V Conclusion

The theory of *aḥwāl* was formulated in response to the problem of how God's oneness can be reconciled with the idea that He is qualified by a multitude of eternal qualities. The question had been debated over several generations of theologians before Abū Hāshim al-Jubbāʾī suggested a solution by borrowing from the grammarians a new ontological category: he conceived of attributes as neither existing nor non-existing 'states' (*aḥwāl*) and thereby avoided ascribing to them an entitative reality. Abū Hāshim's theory was highly successful in that it became a central pillar in the theological system of his followers for many centuries. Over the course of this time, the theory of *aḥwāl* was modified and elaborated in various aspects, so that theologians applied it with different focuses of interest, including merely epistemological approaches.

The impact of Abū Hāshim's theory was not confined to the theological tradition that was named after him as Bahshamiyya. With al-Bāqillānī, the concept of *ḥāl* was also introduced into and adapted to the framework of Ashʿarite theology. Al-Bāqillānī's adoption of the theory of *aḥwāl* was also approved by later Ashʿarites, including the outstanding *imām al-ḥaramayn* Abū l-Maʿālī al-Juwaynī and even later by less well-known scholars from the Islamic west, the Maghrib. Ashʿarite theologians used the concept of *ḥāl* in a different way from their Bahshamī opponents: in the Ashʿarite context, the *aḥwāl* were rather understood as distinguishable features of beings, which can be known although they do not exist. The adoption of the concept of *aḥwāl* is one of the many historical examples of the flexibility of the Ashʿarite school in integrating specific notions from other scholarly traditions and reinterpreting them for their own theological purposes. It is among the oddities of the history of Muslim theology that Ashʿarite scholars relied on the concept of *ḥāl* to argue for the existence of God's entitative attributes, a hypothesis the Bahshamīs originally sought to disprove by introducing the *ḥāl* into the ontology of *kalām* (Gimaret 1970: 79f.).

References

Alami, A. (2001). *L'ontologie modale: étude de la théorie des modes d'Abū Hāšim al-Ǧubbāʾī*. Paris: Vrin.

Allard, M. (1965). *Le problème des attributs divins dans la doctrine d'al-Ašʿarī et de ses premiers grands disciples*. Beirut: Imprimerie Catholique.

Dhanani, A. (1993). *The Physical Theory of Kalām: Atoms, Space, and Void in Basrian Muʿtazilī Cosmology*. Leiden: Brill.

van Ess, J. (1991). *Theologie und Gesellschaft im 2. und 3. Jahrhundert Hidschra: Eine Geschichte des religiösen Denkens im frühen Islam.* 6 vols. Berlin/New York: de Gruyter.

Frank, R. M. (1978). *Beings and their Attributes: The Teaching of the Basrian School of the Muʿtazila in the Classical Period.* Albany, NY: State University of New York Press.

Frank, R. M. (1980). '*Al-Maʿdūm wal-Mawjūd.* The Non-Existent, the Existent and the Possible in the Teaching of Abū Hāšim and his Followers'. *Mélanges de l'Institut Dominicain d'Études Orientales* 14: 185–210.

Frank, R. M. (1982a). 'Attribute, Attribution, and Being: Three Islamic Views'. In P. Morewedge (ed.), *Philosophies of Existence: Ancient and Medieval.* New York: Fordham University Press, 258–78.

Frank, R. M. (1982b). 'Ḥāl'. In E. Bosworth et al. (eds.), *The Encyclopaedia of Islam.* New edn. Supplement, Fasc. 5–6, 343–8.

Frank, R. M. (2000). 'The Non-Existent and the Possible in Classical Ashʿarite Teaching'. *Mélanges de l'Institut Dominicain d'Études Orientales* 24: 1–37.

Frank, R. M. (2004). '*Al-Aḥkām* in Classical Ašʿarite Teaching'. In R. Morelon and A. Hasnawi (eds.), *De Zénon d'Élée à Poincaré: receuil d'études en hommage à Roshdi Rashed.* Leuven: Peeters, 753–77.

Gimaret, D. (1970). 'La théorie des *aḥwâl* d'Abû Hâšim al-Ǧubbâʾî d'après des sources ašʿarites'. *Journal asiatique* 258: 47–86.

Gimaret, D. (1980). *Théories de l'acte humain en théologie musulmane.* Paris: Vrin.

Gimaret, D. (1990). *La doctrine d'al-Ashʿarī.* Paris: Cerf.

Gimaret, D. (2009). 'Un extrait de la *Hidāya* d'Abū Bakr al-Bāqillānī: le *Kitāb at-tawallud*, réfutation de la thèse muʿtazilite de la génération des actes'. *Bulletin d'études orientales* 58: 259–313.

Schmidtke, S. (2011). 'Early Ašʿarite Theology: Abū Bakr al-Bāqillānī (d. 403/1013) and his *Hidāyat al-mustaršidīn*'. *Bulletin d'études orientales* 60: 39–71.

Thiele, J. (2012). 'La Causalité selon al-Ḥākim al-Ǧišumī'. *Arabica* 59/3–4: 291–318.

Thiele, J. (2013). *Theologie in der jemenitischen Zaydiyya: Die naturphilosophischen Überlegungen des al-Ḥasan ar-Raṣṣāṣ.* Leiden: Brill.

Thiele, J. (forthcoming). 'Al-Bāqillānī's Notion of *ḥāl* or the Principle of Reciprocal Correlation'.

CHAPTER 23

THEORIES OF ETHICAL VALUE IN *KALĀM*

A New Interpretation

AYMAN SHIHADEH

THIS chapter offers a new interpretation of the debate on the nature of ethical value in the developed *kalām* tradition. In some key respects it proposes to revise the reading, conventional since G. Hourani's seminal studies published in the early 1970s, of the ethical realism propounded in Baṣran and Baghdādī Muʿtazilism (Sections II–III) and of the rival views of classical Ashʿarism (Section IV). I shall argue that the latter school did not subscribe to a simple divine command theory of ethics, but in fact grounded this theory in a fairly developed anti-realism, which became the basis for the more sophisticated consequentialist ethics advanced in neo-Ashʿarite sources (Section V). First of all, however, we need to situate the problem in its proper theological context.[1]

I The Framework: Metaethics, Applied Theological Ethics, Normative Ethics

Having proved the existence of God and investigated His essence and attributes, the typical *kalām* summa will then turn to theodicy. The Muʿtazila usually discuss the subject under the heading 'On Justice' (*fī l-ʿadl*), shorthand for one of the two most defining and pivotal theories of their school, the other being the theory of God's oneness (*tawḥīd*): whence their self-bestowed appellation, 'the Affirmers of God's Oneness and Justice' (*ahl al-tawḥīd wa-l-ʿadl*). Among the three other doctrines that, alongside these

[1] Due mainly to considerations of space, this chapter will not consider Māturīdī or Traditionalist views.

two major theories, comprise the five principles (*al-uṣūl al-khamsa*) taught by Abū l-Hudhayl (d. between 226/840 and 236/850) and the later Muʿtazilī tradition, the doctrine of the promise and the threat (*al-waʿd wa-l-waʿīd*) too turns largely on ethical problems and could easily have been incorporated in the discussion of God's justice.

In Ashʿarite sources, God's justice is normally discussed under the heading 'Deeming [acts] just or unjust [for God to perform]' (*al-taʿdīl wa-l-tajwīr*) (occasionally also used in Muʿtazilī sources), the focus from the outset being to criticize Muʿtazilī claims concerning God's justice, rather than to offer an alternative rationalist theodicy. Ashʿarites instead advocate a theological voluntarism: the view that God's will and acts are free and never subject to ethical considerations. The bulk of classical Ashʿarite discussions, hence, are dedicated to demolishing the ethical theory and theodicean teachings of the Muʿtazila, a task that they considered of paramount importance given that most heretical doctrines (*bidʿa*), we are told, are theodicean in nature (al-Rāzī, *Uṣūl al-dīn*, fo. 174b). The Muʿtazila are said to have as their predecessor no less a figure than Satan, who refused to obey God's command to prostrate himself before Adam on the grounds that he was 'better' than him: an ethical objection, it was often noted, since it implied that God was obligated to treat Satan in accordance with his status and rights (for instance, al-Ṭūfī, *Darʾ*, 67–8).

At the start of Muʿtazilī expositions of God's justice, the central doctrine is normally stated in very general (*mujmal*) terms: for instance, 'It is impossible for God to perform a bad act, or to omit an obligation' (Ibn al-Malāḥimī, *Fāʾiq*, 119). This principle (*aṣl*) is then unpacked in two main stages. First, a number of basic, *primary* doctrines (*muqaddima*) are set out to lay the foundation to the theory. Ibn al-Malāḥimī (*Fāʾiq*, 119ff.; cf. Ibn Mattawayh, *Majmūʿ*, 1: 227–64), for instance, lists the following:

i. That an act (*fiʿl*) is produced by its agent's (*fāʿil*) capacity (*qudra*) and in accordance with his volition (*irāda*). This affirms that both God and human beings are real and autonomous agents.
ii. That the ethical value of an act is objective. This central doctrine shall be the focus of the following sections in the present chapter.
iii. That God is capable of performing bad acts. So, as a voluntary agent, He can make genuine choices between good acts and bad ones.
iv. That it is nonetheless impossible, on ethical grounds, for God to perform bad, including unjust, acts, that He may perform good acts, and that He undoubtedly performs obligatory acts.

With respect to the last two doctrines, the Muʿtazila differed on whether God is capable of performing bad acts, but necessarily refrains from doing so out of His goodness, or whether He is categorically incapable of performing bad acts (on this, see Frank 1985). Though the lists of primary doctrines discussed vary slightly from source to source, they will invariably include discussions of the metaethical question of the nature of ethical value and of the goodness of God's acts.

Second, a web of specific (*mufaṣṣal*), *secondary* doctrines (*farʿ*) that set out Muʿtazilī theodicy in detail are then explicated and grounded in the primary discussions. This body of secondary doctrines, which I describe as 'applied theological ethics', explains in detail how God's acts in some of the main aspects of human-related divine activity are necessarily all good and just (see, for example, ʿAbd al-Jabbār, *Mukhtaṣar*, 232). (Needless to say, although construing these secondary doctrines as 'applied theological ethics' helps to understand their relation with metaethical and normative components of *kalām* and juristic discussions, there are significant differences with the usual branches of applied ethics, since the agent here is God, rather than man.) For instance, was it wise and good to create the world and human beings? How responsible is God for the evil committed by the human beings He creates? How exactly is God good when He creates natural causes of human suffering? How does the Creator resolve the problem of the otherwise unjustified suffering experienced by human beings in this world? How can the reward and retribution that God dispenses to human beings in the hereafter be justified? And so forth. Detailed Muʿtazilī doctrines of theodicy thus include, for example:

i. The doctrine that human acts are produced by the autonomous volition and power of their human agents, and related doctrines. If Zayd's acts were determined or produced by God, he would not be morally responsible and deserving of praise, blame, reward, or punishment for them, and it would consequently be unjust of God either to put him under ethical obligations, or to praise, blame, reward, or punish him for his acts. God moreover would be responsible for human evil.
ii. That it was good to create both the world and human beings, and to impose obligations (*taklīf*) on them, since this condition gives humans the opportunity to attain great advantages that surpass any suffering they may experience in this world.
iii. That none of the obligations imposed on humans are beyond their capacity (*mā lā yuṭāq*).
iv. That it is obligatory on God to assist and motivate human agents to fulfil the obligations imposed on them. The different forms of divine assistance (*alṭāf*, sing. *luṭf*) include the provision of prophetic teachings and the infliction of certain types of pain, which serve to warn and to remind the agent of the severe consequences of neglecting one's duties.
v. That all undeserved and uncompensated suffering that an individual experiences in this world, whether it is produced by God, another human being, or an animal, will be compensated for in the hereafter. God dispenses this compensation (*ʿiwaḍ*) in the form of either extra rewards in heaven or lighter punishment in hell.
vi. The aforementioned doctrine of the promise and the threat, which refers to the praise and reward deserved for good acts, and the blame and punishment deserved for bad acts. Despite the name given to this doctrine, the Muʿtazila maintain that the human agent's knowledge of these deserts is attained, in the first

instance, by reason independently of revelation. Revealed 'promises and threats' only confirm and reinforce this knowledge.

Unsurprisingly, almost all secondary doctrines discussed in expositions of God's justice are theocentric, in the sense that they focus first and foremost on the moral agency of God. (For discussions of some of these doctrines, see, for example, Heemskerk 2000; Abrahamov 1993; Brunschvig 1974; van Ess 1991–7: *passim*; Hoover 2007; Shihadeh 2013).

Ashʿarites reject all these doctrines on the grounds that they impose obligations on God, whose will and acts, they rejoin, are free and not restricted by ethical considerations. Concerning the grounds of God's action, they maintain that none of His acts are ethically motivated. For instance, He may compensate some for the suffering they endure in this world, but only out of choice and compassion, not out of duty. Ashʿarites go further to point out that in some cases God actually acts, and in other cases He may act, in ways that the Muʿtazila claim to be unjust and hence bad. For instance, He may forgive some unrepentant sinners, He causes at least some human evil, and He rewards and punishes humans although they do not act autonomously. This criticism of Muʿtazilī theological ethics was grounded in an alternative theory of ethical value: it was argued, as we shall see, that the expressions 'good' and 'bad', predicated of acts, do not refer to real and objective properties of which acts are possessed. No act, hence, is intrinsically bad or good, or in and of itself prohibited or obligatory, be the agent human or divine.

Further, often more anthropocentric discussions, which too are underpinned by the same considerations of the nature of ethical value, are encountered in various other contexts in theological compendia. Examples of these include:

i. The doctrine of 'enjoining good and forbidding bad' (*al-amr bi-l-maʿrūf wa-l-nahy ʿan al-munkar*), which is another of the five principles of the Muʿtazila (on which see Cook 2001).
ii. Discussions of repentance (see van Ess 1991–7: iv. 579ff.; Mensia 2004; Vasalou 2008; Pomerantz 2007).
iii. Discussions of the nature of man (*ḥaqīqat al-insān*) (see Shihadeh 2012).
iv. Discussions of the obligation both to acquire certain items of theological knowledge (*maʿrifa*) and to undertake theological reflection (*naẓar*) for that purpose (see Shihadeh 2008: 197–201).
v. The Twelver Shīʿī doctrine that it is obligatory on God to establish the imāmate (for instance, al-Ḥillī, *Kashf*, 338–40). Others consider it obligatory on people, not on God. For the Baghdādī Muʿtazila it is established by the dictates of reason (see, for instance, el-Omari 2007). The Baṣrans and the Ashʿarites consider it a religious obligation.

Apart from problems treated in theological works, metaethical discussions of moral value are often also included in works on the theory of jurisprudence (*uṣūl al-fiqh*), where they lay some of the theoretical foundations for this discipline, the main normative science in the Islamic religious tradition. Though the significance of these discussions remains sorely understudied, the following preliminary observations can be made. The theory of ethical value and obligation (*taklīf, wujūb*), first of all, serves a foundational purpose: in the juristic works of *kalām*-influenced Shāfiʿīs, for instance, it underpins the broader divine command theory of ethics that establishes revelation, at least in principle, as the sole source for legislation. The theory of ethical value also informs jurisprudence in more substantive ways, as it affects some of the key normative principles and methods of the discipline, which are guided largely by practical, and hence properly *ethical*, rather than theoretical or theological, concerns and potentially address a wide array of human acts. Two cases in point are the discussion on whether the default, pre-scriptural, or 'original state' of the act is permissibility, proscription, or neither (Reinhart 1995), and, in some sources, discussions of the juristic principle of utility (*maṣlaḥa*), which presuppose a consequentialist ethical theory (Shihadeh 2006: 63ff.).

Discussions of metaethics, normative ethics, and applied ethics, including applied theological ethics, are all brought together in a unique work devoted to the subject written by the Ashʿarite-influenced Ḥanbalī theologian Najm al-Dīn al-Ṭūfī (d. 716/1316). In *Darʾ al-qawl al-qabīḥ bi-l-taḥsīn wa-l-taqbīḥ*, al-Ṭūfī begins by discussing ethical value—this being the principal doctrine (*aṣl*)—before treating the secondary doctrines (*farʿ*) that fall under theology, the theory of jurisprudence and, most unusually, even substantive law (*furūʿ fiqhiyya*), each in a separate chapter. His main target of criticism in the chapter on substantive law is not the Muʿtazila, but the Ḥanafīs, whom he accuses of basing many of their legal rulings on considerations of utility, or convenience (*munāsaba*), without scriptural sanction, much in the same way that the Muʿtazila devise their theological ethics (*Darʾ*, 123). Paradoxically, al-Ṭūfī nowadays is notorious for a slightly later work in which he articulates the more radical view that considerations of utility may even override scriptural rulings (*Taʿyīn*, 246). The development of his thought remains unstudied.

We shall turn next to the pivotal problem of the nature of ethical value, starting off with the doctrines of the Baghdādī and Baṣran Muʿtazila, before moving on to the teachings of classical Ashʿarism and neo-Ashʿarism.

II Muʿtazilī Ethical Realism: The Baghdādī View

The ethics of divine action were discussed from as early as the first century of Islam, mainly in the controversies on the nature of faith (*īmān*) and on free will and predestination, the best extant illustration of the latter controversy arguably being al-Ḥasan al-Baṣrī's (d. 110/728) *Risāla fī l-Qadar* (on this epistle and the debate on its authenticity, see Mourad 2005; for a critical commentary on al-Ḥasan's epistle, see al-Ṭūfī, *Darʾ*, 207–59). He argues, for instance, that since God is good, He creates only good, and that human evil is hence produced not by God, but by freely choosing human agents, who are solely responsible and accountable for their acts.

As theology developed, it became vital to define the terms 'just', 'unjust', 'good', and 'bad', and to explain these characteristics of acts and occurrences within a broader and more systematic epistemological and ontological framework. Two major trends appear to have affected this development. In the closely related discipline of jurisprudence, one of the primary concerns of jurists was to assign judgements (*ḥukm*) to different types of (human) action: 'fasting is obligatory', 'drinking wine is prohibited', etc. It was only natural for some theologians to incorporate the same paradigm into their own discipline, and to begin to ground earlier, unsystematic discussions of theological ethics in more basic ethical principles, such that the same judgements are assigned to acts with a view to determining exactly which acts God may, may not, or must do. At the same time, Muʿtazilism was developing, partly under the influence of the Arabic grammatical tradition, a theological system that analysed all sorts of facts about beings and occurrences in terms of attributes (*ṣifa*). And since, as we shall see, acts (*fiʿl*) are construed as things (*shayʾ*, *dhāt*)—accidents (*ʿaraḍ*), to be precise (or, in the case of God's acts, both atoms and accidents)—their ethical characteristics too would have been eligible for consideration as attributes.

The early history of Muʿtazilī attempts to pin down the ethical attributes of acts remains quite obscure, given the limited range of extant sources. It appears that from a relatively early stage the school opted for ethical realism, at least partly in order to counter the theological voluntarism embodied in prevalent conceptions of God. The main challenge that school members had to grapple with was to develop a form of realism that was in tune with their ontology and epistemology but without falling into an extreme ethical absolutism, that is, the view that certain acts are absolutely good or bad regardless of their circumstances. This was not an easy task, given the extremely limited options that *kalām* atomism presented.

Among the most primitive attempts recorded in the sources, the form of ethical realism ascribed to the Baghdādī Muʿtazilī Abū l-Qāsim al-Kaʿbī al-Balkhī (d. 319/931) treats goodness and badness as essential (*nafsī*) attributes of certain acts (Mānkdīm, *Sharḥ*, 310; Abū Rashīd, *Masāʾil*, 354). The handful of extant Baghdādī sources shed no light on this theory; so we have to depend on second-hand accounts in rival Baṣran Muʿtazilī sources. These portray al-Kaʿbī's ethical essentialism as amounting to crude absolutism: if a given class of act is essentially bad, all instances of that act will be absolutely and invariably bad, regardless of their circumstances. The Baṣrans then proceed to confute this absolutist view simply by pointing out that in fact identical instances of the same act can be good in some situations and bad in others (Hourani 1971: 64; Reinhart 1995: 141ff.). The act of killing another human being, for instance, can be bad if the killing is undeserved, but good if performed as appropriate punishment. This Baṣran interpretation of the Baghdādī position was accepted by Hourani.

However, it would have been well-nigh impossible for al-Kaʿbī, at least as a Muslim theologian, to sustain such a radical view. I propose that the account transmitted in our later Baṣran sources must not be taken at face value, but should be treated as part genuine report and part *ad hominem* (*ex concessis*) argument (*ilzām*): although al-Kaʿbī does appear to subscribe to a form of ethical essentialism, absolutism is only an implication that, according to the Baṣrans, follows from his ethical essentialism, rather than a thesis that he himself articulated. Proceeding on the basis of this hypothesis, the question we should now ask is this: does al-Kaʿbī subscribe to any views concerning the essences of acts that would allow him to advocate ethical essentialism without having to concede an absolutism that any Muslim theologian would find absurd?

A significant clue that sheds light on some crucial details is offered in two reported views of his concerning the nature of speech (*kalām*), a form of action that consists of a series of individual sounds (*ṣawt*), or phonemes (*ḥarf*), each being a primary act produced by the speaker. First, according to al-Kaʿbī, a sentence is designated a 'statement' (*khabar*) (as opposed, say, to a command or a prohibition) on account of its essence (*innamā yakūnu khabaran li-ʿaynihi*) (Ibn Mattawayh, *Tadhkira*, 1: 211). Despite consisting of a series of discrete and consecutive sound-acts each lasting no more than a fraction of a second, the spoken sentence, 'My name is Zayd', somehow has a single and unified essence (*ʿayn*) which makes it a statement. Second, having affirmed that a statement has an essence, al-Kaʿbī goes further to maintain that statements are divided into two essentially distinct, contrary classes (*jins*): a statement is, in and of itself (so, at least in the first instance, not on account of any non-essential facts, such as the speaker's intention [*irāda*] or circumstances), either a lie (*kadhib*) or a truthful statement (*ṣidq*) (Ibn Mattawayh, *Tadhkira*, 1: 210). Hence, if both Zayd and I each state, 'My name is Zayd', his sentence will be essentially, in and of itself, a truthful statement, whereas mine will be essentially, in and of itself, a lie. How al-Kaʿbī was able to sustain these two positions is unclear and requires further investigation, which goes beyond the scope of the present study. It may be that he held that prima facie identical acts can be essentially different one from the other on the grounds that the essence of the act is, to some extent, affected by its circumstances. In any case, if an act (say, a spoken statement) can have one essence (a lie) in some instances and another essence (a truthful statement) in other instances, and since things that are essentially different differ in their essential attributes, it follows that badness can be an essential attribute of the former essence (lying) and goodness an essential attribute of the latter essence (truth-telling). The 'same' act, accordingly, can be essentially bad in some cases, and essentially good in other cases. So, despite his ethical essentialism, al-Kaʿbī, after all, does not appear to be an ethical absolutist.

Contrary to what is widely assumed, al-Kaʿbī's form of essentialism was not the only position current among the Baghdādī Muʿtazila. Certain, unidentified later school members in fact refined the theory slightly by proposing that ethically evaluable acts divided into two types: some acts are possessed of the attributes of goodness or badness in and of themselves, essentially, while other acts are possessed of either of these attributes on account of an entitative determinant (*maʿnā*), i.e. an accident, of goodness or badness that accompanies the act, but is distinct from it. The sources, however, do not explain how the latter accident is engendered. This view seems to come with the odd implication that the accident of ethical value will only qualify the body (*jism*) in which it inheres (hence, Zayd, or his tongue), rather than the act performed by the body (the lie uttered by Zayd), since no accident can qualify another accident (Abū Rashīd, *Masāʾil*, 355). Yet unlike al-Kaʿbī's theory of ethical value, this modified theory cannot be reduced by its adversaries to a naive absolutism, as it situates the ethical value of some acts outside the act itself and allows for greater flexibility depending on the act's circumstances. The act of killing, it thus appears, would not be bad in itself, but would be accompanied, in instances where it is unjustified, with the accident of badness which would inhere in the murderer's body, or, in instances where it is justified, with the accident of goodness, or perhaps with neither accident of ethical value, in which case it would be ethically neutral.

III Muʿtazilī Ethical Realism: The Baṣran View

In Baṣran Muʿtazilism too, ethical value terms refer to real and objective properties of acts, though, in contrast to the Baghdādī brand of realism, their causes are not as concrete as the essences of acts or some ethical accidents that accompany acts. The exploration that follows is based largely on the discussion of ethical value in ʿAbd al-Jabbār's (d. 415/1025) *Mughnī*, the most extensive treatment in an extant Baṣran source.

At the start of his discussion, ʿAbd al-Jabbār sets out the following taxonomy of acts according to their ethical properties (*Mughnī*, 6/1: 7–51). Some acts are ethically evaluable, i.e. they are predicated of an ethical value judgement (*ḥukm*) extraneous to the act itself. Others are ethically neutral, such as the acts of movement or speech produced during sleep. Evaluable acts divide into two main categories: bad (*qabīḥ*) acts, defined as those acts on account of the performance of which the agent will deserve blame (*dhamm*), and good (*ḥasan*) acts, defined as those for the performance of which the agent will not deserve blame. Of good acts, three judgements can be predicated. Some are simply good, yet solicit neither praise nor blame for the agent; these are permissible (*mubāḥ*) acts. Other acts carry an 'added' ethical property over and above basic goodness: those that the performance of which solicits praise but the omission of which solicits no blame are recommended (*mandūb*), while those that the performance of which solicits praise and the omission of which solicits blame are obligatory (*wājib*).

Alongside the nature of these ethical categories, the mind also grasps immediately the ethical properties of certain types of acts: for instance, that wrongdoing (*ẓulm*), subscribing to erroneous beliefs, and lies from which the liar attains no benefit and prevents no harm are all self-evidently bad, and that thanking the benefactor is self-evidently good and obligatory. From these self-evident (*ḍarūrī*) moral axioms, other principles can be arrived at by means of rational reflection: for instance, that all instances of lying are bad, regardless of their consequences.

Given that we know that an act can carry an ethical property (*ḥukm*), ʿAbd al-Jabbār further argues, that property must be dependent on an attribute (*ṣifa, ḥāl*) that is particular to (*ikhtuṣṣa bi-*), and qualifies, the act itself (*Mughnī*, 6/1: 52). Each of the four ethical properties that we predicate of acts, hence, is connected to a distinct attribute: 'bad' to badness, or the act's 'being bad' (*kawnuhu qabīḥan*), 'good' to goodness, 'recommended' to recommendedness, and 'obligatory' to obligatoriness, the last two attributes being conditional on, and additional to, the attribute of goodness (*Mughnī*, 6/1: 72–3). Ethical properties, hence, are objective and real attributes of things in the external world, and not dependent on the subjective judgements of individuals. ʿAbd al-Jabbār argues for this point in detail, as we shall see later in this section.

If a thing (and the act, as we shall see shortly, is a thing) has a non-essential attribute, then there must be a determinant (*muqtaḍī*), or a cause (*ʿilla, muʾaththir, mūjib*), knowable to the mind (*maʿqūl*), that engenders the attribute. Some acts, however, are good or bad, not because of attributes that qualify them, but since they lead to an act that is itself qualified by such an attribute (*Mughnī*, 6/1: 57–8).

The Baṣran Muʿtazila maintain that the cause of the ethical property of an act is not the act itself (that is, its essence), nor a special ethical accident, nor any of a number of other external factors to be discussed later in this section, but rather only the '*wajh*' of the occurrence of the act. Mānkdīm, for instance, writes, 'All acts without exception can occur upon a certain *wajh* and be good, and upon a different *wajh* and be bad. We do not accept that any act can per se (*bi-mujarradihi*) be either bad or good' (*Sharḥ*, 564).

This all-important concept of '*wajh*', in my view, has been inadequately interpreted ever since it was examined by Hourani (1971), with some sources describing it as vague and difficult.[2] However, I propose that the concept is in fact a rather simple one, but only once the more basic concept of 'act' has been clarified. The confusion arises partly from the fact that when the Baṣran Muʿtazila employ the expressions 'an act' (*fiʿl*) or 'to act' (*faʿala*), they do so in one of two ways: either in the strictest sense of the word (*ḥaqīqa*), or loosely (*tawassuʿan*). They often refer, for instance, to lies, wrongdoing, and ingratitude as 'acts', but they do so only in a loose sense, since none of these is an act in the strictest sense. However, it is only in the narrowest sense of the word that they use 'act' when they assert that the badness of the act is caused, not by the act itself, but by its *wajh*.

So what do the Baṣran Muʿtazila refer to, strictly speaking, by 'act', as the proper subject of ethical predication? An act, first of all, is a concrete thing (*shayʾ, dhāt*) brought into being by the agent. It consists of nothing but a simple, indivisible accident (*ʿaraḍ*), and as such is an irreducible instantiation of a class (*jins*) of accidents possessed of an essence that differentiates it from all other classes of accidents. Some acts are bodily (of the limb, *afʿāl al-jawāriḥ*), such as motion, and others are mental (of the heart, *afʿāl al-qulūb*), such as volition (*irāda*) and thinking (*naẓar*) (ʿAbd al-Jabbār, *Mughnī*, 9: 11ff.; cf. Gimaret 1980; Bernand 1982). Even mental acts, however, occur in the agent's body, as

[2] The root problem seems to be that Hourani does not clearly define '*wajh*', nor distinguish it sufficiently from either 'act' or 'an aspect of a *wajh*' (see, in particular, 1, 29ff., 62ff.; especially the discussion of lying, 76–81).

they are accidents that come to be in the atoms of the heart. Some acts, such as motion, volition, and thinking, are produced immediately (*mubtada'*) by the agent, and hence occur within his body (e.g. the motion in the archer's arm), while other acts, such as pain and knowledge, are generated (*mutawallid*) by the former, immediately produced acts, and can occur in physical objects other than the agent's body (e.g. the motion in the arrow, and the injury, pain, and death it causes).

Take speech (*kalām, qawl*), for instance (for an extensive discussion of the ontology of speech, see Ibn Mattawayh, *Tadhkira*, 1: 177ff.). The oral statement (*khabar*), 'My name is Zayd', consists of a series of primitive and irreducible sounds, or phonemes, each being an accident that lasts for a fraction of a second and as such is an individual speech act in its own right. The whole spoken sentence may be said to be 'an act' (in the singular), as opposed to a series of successive acts, only in a loose and figurative sense. (On the view that a composite object, even one that consists of coexisting things, is called 'one' or 'a thing' only figuratively, and that it lacks a unifying essence, see Shihadeh 2012; compare this to al-Kaʿbī's aforementioned view that the whole sentence can have the unified essence of a statement, a command, etc., and hence be in effect a single act.) So when the Baṣrans assert that the badness of an act of speech cannot be due to the act itself (*li-nafsihi, li-ʿaynihi*), or on account of its class (*li-jinsihi*), they mean that the oral sounds, 'z', 'y', 'd', etc., can be bad neither in themselves (otherwise, the mere utterance of 'Zayd' will be invariably bad), nor because they belong to the class of speech accidents (otherwise, anything I say will be bad).

As the act, strictly speaking, is thus nothing more than an accident, and since no accident is in and of itself ethically evaluable, no act can be essentially, and hence invariably, good or bad. The determinant that engenders the ethical attribute an act carries is rather its *configuration* (*wajh*), a concept that includes the totality of all the relevant factors, or circumstances (*qarīna*), that accompany and contextualize the act. In some cases, these circumstances include the agent's volition (*irāda*), or intention (*qaṣd*) (ʿAbd al-Jabbār, *Mughnī*, 6/1: 83). Ibn al-Malāḥimī (*Fā'iq*, 121) writes,

> Bad acts, such as wrongdoing, lying, imposing obligations beyond [the agent's] capacity, useless acts, corruption and commanding a bad act, are bad on account of configurations that accompany their occurrence. Good acts, such as seeking to benefit [oneself] and beneficence towards others, are good on account of configurations that accompany their occurrence. Obligations, such as preventing harm from oneself, thanking the benefactor, returning deposits and paying back debts, are obligatory on account of configurations that accompany their occurrence. By 'configurations that accompany their occurrence' (*wujūh taqaʿu ʿalayhā*), we mean that their occurrence is accompanied by circumstances (*qarīna*), be they the negation or affirmation [of a thing], on account of which circumstances [the act] will be described as being 'wrongdoing', 'benefit' or 'preventing harm'.

Relevant circumstances, hence, need not be existent, but can be 'negations'; for instance, the absence of a motive is a circumstance characteristic of the configuration of 'uselessness' (*ʿabath*). Act configurations are denoted either by a dedicated label (e.g. 'lying' and 'wrongdoing'), or in descriptive terms (e.g. 'imposing an obligation that is beyond the obligated person's capacity'). If an act exhibits any configuration of badness, it will be bad. To be good, however, the act must both have a configuration of goodness and exhibit no configurations of badness. For 'when configurations of goodness and badness coincide in the same act, badness will predominate' (*Mughnī*, 6/1: 70; cf. 59). Certain configurations engender the extra attribute of either recommendedness or obligatoriness in a good act.

The configuration of lying is a case in point. If I say, 'Zayd is at home', the series of speech (or sound) acts (*jumlat al-ḥurūf*) that I produce will carry the attribute of badness on account of their having the configuration of a lie, as follows. First, the arrangement of the sounds into words, and the words into a sentence, is that of a statement (*khabar*). Second, the sentence is a statement because I have the volition to articulate a statement. Third, the statement is false, either because it does not correspond to the fact being stated (*mukhbar*) (if in fact Zayd is not at home), or because the object of the statement (my imaginary friend Zayd) does not exist (Ibn Mattawayh, *Tadhkira*, 1: 207). This set of circumstances comprises the act configuration we denote 'lie', and it is only this act configuration that engenders the attribute of badness that qualifies each of the individual speech acts that constitute the statement (ʿAbd al-Jabbār, *Mughnī*, 6/1: 123). Other configurations that engender the same attribute in speech acts can be analysed in the same way to their most basic relevant circumstances: for instance, a command that imposes an obligation beyond the person's capacity ('Lift this mountain, Zayd!'), or a command to omit a duty ('Don't pay back your debts!') (*Mughnī*, 6/1: 61–2).

Likewise, the generated (*mutawallid*) act of bodily pain (*alam*) or mental distress (*ghamm*) produced in another human being cannot be bad in and of itself. Nor is the immediately produced act that generates it (for instance, the accident of movement in the knife-wielding arm). For amputating a gangrenous leg is painful and harmful in some respects, but nonetheless good since it may save the patient's life. Pain and its generating act can only be bad if they occur in one of two configurations: wrongdoing (*ẓulm*) or uselessness. ʿAbd al-Jabbār defines 'wrongdoing' as 'any [1] harm that [2] does not lead to a greater benefit [to the one harmed], [3] nor prevents a greater harm, [4] nor is deserved, [5] nor is believed to have any of these respects', where 'harm' is pain or distress or anything that leads to either (*Mughnī*, 13: 298). Whatever act occurs within these circumstances, which comprise the act configuration known as 'wrongdoing', will be bad, and its badness will be engendered by this configuration. Such an act will occur *unjustly*, that is, 'in the manner of wrongdoing' (*yaqaʿu ẓulman*), rather than *justly*, 'in a just manner' (*yaqaʿu ʿadlan*) (*Mughnī*, 6/1: 77).

Volition (*irāda*), or intention (*qaṣd*), is no exception. The badness of the act of willing a bad act (*irādat al-qabīḥ*) is not essential to the act of volition itself (as suggested by Frank 1983: 206); for all instances of volition are identical in essence. It owes its badness rather to its configuration, namely that the act of will relates (*taʿallaqa*) to a bad act (Ibn Mattawayh, *Tadhkira*, 2: 566–7; ʿAbd al-Jabbār, *Mughnī*, 6/1: 79). For this reason, the goodness or badness of the will that Zayd be harmed depends entirely on whether the harm caused is just or unjust.

So, goodness and badness are never essential to acts themselves, but are engendered by nothing other than certain act configurations. The only exception, it seems, was made by the leading Baṣran Muʿtazilī Abū ʿAlī al-Jubbāʾī (d. 303/915), who in one work maintained that a misbelief, i.e. an erroneous conviction (*jahl*, here not to be rendered as 'ignorance'), regardless of its object, is bad essentially (*yaqbuḥu li-nafsihi*, or *li-ʿaynihi*), though in other works he reportedly restricted that to misbeliefs concerning God (*al-jahl bi-llāh*) (Ibn Mattawayh, *Tadhkira*, 2: 648). ʿAbd al-Jabbār remarks that Abū ʿAlī treated badness as an essential attribute of misbelief on account of the necessary and inalienable concomitance of the former to the latter (*Mughnī*, 6/1: 78–9). No such exception is made, however, by Abū Hāshim al-Jubbāʾī (d. 321/933) and the later Baṣran tradition, who apply the same paradigm by which they analyse lies: 'erroneous conviction' and 'true conviction' (knowledge) are not primitive classes of acts, but are only distinct configurations (*wajh*) of the same class of act, namely conviction (*iʿtiqād*) (Ibn Mattawayh, *Tadhkira*, 2: 591ff., 635). Baṣrans, therefore, assert that a particular misbelief is bad 'because it is a misbelief' (*li-annahu jahl*). That is to say, an accident of conviction that inheres in the agent's heart obtains its badness because it has the configuration of 'misbelief' (*jahl*), namely that the conviction, whether its object be God or another thing, fails to correspond to 'the thing as it is'. It is argued that although, in contrast to my convictions that 'Zayd is at home' and 'The world will continue to exist tomorrow', the falsity of some misbeliefs concerning God is unconditional and absolute, this does not entail that, unlike other misbeliefs, their badness is essential.

The available Baṣran sources describe act configurations in detail, but offer no explanation as to why certain combinations of circumstances engender certain ethical attributes for certain classes of acts. Some configurations, such as wrongdoing, have consequentialist underpinnings. Yet others are deontological and make no reference to the consequences of acts. Examples include lying, subscribing to a misbelief, and ingratitude (most evidently when the benefactor is God and hence subject to neither benefit nor harm), which are all bad, and their contraries which are good, or at least neutral. The absence of an explanation for the causal nature of act configurations, however, is no accident. For, in the reasoning of classical *kalām*, such an explanation would involve the identification of a new cause (*ʿilla*), be it part of the configuration itself or extrinsic to it, for the ethical property; and this would violate the central principle that the irreducible cause for the ethical property is none other than the act's configuration.[3]

[3] It has recently been argued that the ethical theory of the Baṣran Muʿtazila has a teleological, or consequentialist, basis even where it appears deontological. For example, al-Attar (2010: 133) maintains that, according to ʿAbd al-Jabbār, the badness of lying is ultimately due to its consequences, most compellingly because he writes, 'it is right of us to praise lying, which is said to repel harm' (*Mughnī*, 6/1: 24). ʿAbd al-Jabbār's point, however, is that some people do in fact believe that lying to prevent harm is praiseworthy, and that they do so because the badness of such lying is known discursively, rather than immediately (see p. 391 above). So, '*yaṣiḥḥu min*' should be rendered as, 'it is possible that', rather than 'it is right of'.

In ʿAbd al-Jabbār's extensive discussion of ethical value, the theory of act configurations as causes of ethical properties is appended with a comprehensive elimination of all other possible causes (*Mughnī*, 6/1: 77–114). As we have already seen, the cause cannot be the essence, class, or coming-to-be (*ḥudūth*) of the act. Nor can it be the volition, or intention, of either the agent, another human being, or God (though, as mentioned, volition is an element in some act configurations). I cannot will, for instance, that a lie performed by either me or Zayd be good. And though God wills that humans perform certain acts and detests that humans perform others, His will necessarily conforms to His knowledge of the objective goodness and badness of these acts, and does not itself make them good or bad (*Mughnī*, 6/1: 86; cf. Ibn Mattawayh, *Tadhkira*, 2: 566). Nor can the cause of an act's ethical property be its agent's attributes or status, such as his being pre-eternal or created, powerful or weak, a master and lord or a servant (*Mughnī*, 6/1: 87–101, 115–21). This confirms that a bad act would be bad even if performed by God and that His acts are as ethically evaluable as ours. Nor can it be command (*amr, ījāb*) and prohibition (*nahy*), even if the commander and prohibiter is God. Otherwise, if I prohibit Zayd from charity, then charity will become bad. Divine prohibition, ʿAbd al-Jabbār writes, 'is only an indication (*dalāla*) of the badness of the thing [in question]. An indication only indicates [a fact about] the thing as it actually is (*ʿalā mā huwa bihi*), and does not itself make the act as it actually is' (*Mughnī*, 6/1: 105). By rejecting that volition, status, or command engender an act's ethical property, ʿAbd al-Jabbār counters the rival Ashʿarite theory of ethical value, to which we shall now turn.

IV The Theological Voluntarism of Classical Ashʿarism

It is widely thought that classical Ashʿarites simply taught a divine command theory of ethics: that they rejected the ethical rationalism of the Muʿtazila, and instead defined ethical value terms by reference to divine command. This, as I will attempt to demonstrate in what follows, is an oversimplification, due in large part to the dearth of adequate primary sources. As more classical Ashʿarite texts have recently come to light, it is now possible to offer a fuller account of their teachings on the subject.[4]

Classical Ashʿarites counter the theological ethics of the Muʿtazila by defending a theological voluntarism founded on two basic views:

[4] For instance, the abridgement of al-Juwaynī's *Shāmil* produced by a certain Ibn al-Amīr, and Abū l-Qāsim al-Anṣārī's *Ghunya*. As the editions of these two texts, cited here, are imperfect, citations have been checked against extant manuscript copies (respectively, MSS Istanbul, Topkapı Sarayı Müzesi Kütüphanesi, Ahmet III, 1322 and 1916).

1. An anti-realist account of ethical value, the antithesis of Muʿtazilī realism. This metaethical view comprises two main lines of reasoning:
   1A. The refutation of Muʿtazilī claims that ethical value is a real attribute of acts and consequently cognizable to the mind.
   1B. The defence of an alternative account of the reference of ethical value expressions as used in ordinary language.
2. The definition of ethical value terms by reference to divine command.

The refutation of ethical realism (1A) is carried out by means of a range of arguments targeting both its ontological and epistemological underpinnings (on this, see also Hourani 1975). They seek to illustrate, first, that ethical value terms do not refer to real and objective attributes of acts themselves, and second, that the mind therefore has no moral objects of knowledge in the external world. Only a handful of representative arguments can be considered here.

Al-Juwaynī (d. 478/1085) introduces his criticism of Muʿtazilī ethical epistemology in his medium-sized theological compendium the *Irshād* (259ff.) by referring to the distinction that his adversaries make between acts whose ethical properties are known immediately and acts whose ethical properties are known by reasoning on the basis of the former, primary principles of ethical knowledge. He declares that his strategy is to concentrate on the purportedly self-evident class of ethical claims, with a view to demonstrating that in fact they are not self-evident at all. As soon as this task is accomplished, all discursive ethical claims will collapse, and so will all the theological doctrines grounded therein.

For instance, he counters the Muʿtazilī contention that the fact that all people, even those who reject revealed religions, assert such truths as the badness of wrongdoing and the goodness of thanking the benefactor attests to their self-evidence. Such assertions, he argues, could be mere expressions of widely held beliefs (*iʿtiqād*), rather than of knowledge (*ʿilm*). Many beliefs are held with great conviction despite being based on uncritical imitation (*taqlīd*). For instance, certain communities believe that the slaughter of animals is evil: a conviction that, the Muʿtazila would concede, is a misbelief (*jahl*) and does not constitute knowledge, despite being affirmed by its exponents as firmly as the ethical judgements that the Muʿtazila claim to be self-evident truths.

Al-Juwaynī (*Irshād*, 264–5) also turns to the Muʿtazilī argument that if we postulate a sound-minded agent who, again, does not accept any revealed religions or indeed has not even been exposed to one (for instance, because he lives on a remote island), we can be certain that if in a given situation he had a choice between telling the truth and lying, neither involving any personal benefit or harm to him, he would undoubtedly choose to tell the truth, as he will be motivated by his knowledge of its goodness and of the badness of lying (on this argument, see Marmura 1994). He responds that if this hypothetical individual *believes*, with the Muʿtazila, that lying is intrinsically bad, then, indeed, he will be inclined to choose to tell the truth. If, however, this person does not adhere to this belief, we cannot be certain that he will prefer truth-telling to lying. He is more likely to choose neither.

Al-Juwaynī then advances the following argument against the ontology of Muʿtazilī ethics. An act's attribute of badness is either essential to the act itself, or not so. It cannot be essential to the act, since the same act (say, the infliction of pain on another human being) can be good in some situations (as deserved punishment), bad in others (as wrongdoing). So an act can only be bad on account of a factor external to it. This can be either divine prohibition, or an accident of badness. However, it cannot be an accident, since an accident can only qualify an atom (or, in Baṣran Muʿtazilism, sometimes a composite body) but cannot qualify another accident. Therefore, the badness of the act cannot be objective and real (*Irshād*, 266–7; al-Anṣārī, *Ghunya*, 2: 1006–7). Since, in classical Ashʿarism, there can be no other cause for attributes, al-Juwaynī here omits to consider act configurations.

However, in his more extensive work, the *Shāmil*, al-Juwaynī offers some brief objections to the Baṣran theory of act configurations as causes of ethical properties (*Ikhtiṣār*, 2: 738–9). For instance, if God produces pain in a human being with the intention that it serve as divine assistance (*luṭf*), but does not compensate him for it, then this act will be, at once, good on account of the former configuration (as divine assistance) and bad on account of the latter (as uncompensated pain). A Baṣran would simply respond that this act is good, since the absence of compensation is not the sole condition for wrongdoing, and is not by itself a configuration that could render pain bad.

What has remained hitherto unknown is that classical Ashʿarites couple this refutation of Muʿtazilī ethical realism with an *alternative* metaethical theory of the referents of the expressions 'good' and 'bad' as employed in ordinary language (*fī l-lugha*) (point 1B at the beginning of the present section). According to this theory, which developed probably out of lexicographical expositions of these and similar expressions, occurrences of prima facie moral expressions in ordinary language can be divided into two distinct classes. Both are encountered in Ibn Fūrak's account of Abū l-Ḥasan al-Ashʿarī's (d. 324/936) teachings. And both are introduced together in al-Juwaynī's *Shāmil* (*Ikhtiṣār*, 2: 732):

> 'Badness' and 'goodness' have different senses. [1] 'Badness' (*qubḥ*) may refer to the badness of form (*qubḥ al-ṣūra*) [i.e. ugliness], which is that it be lacking in proper arrangement (*intiẓām*) and proportional composition (*tanāsub al-khilqa*). [2] It may also refer to what the disposition, in the normal course of events, is repulsed by and rejects (*mā yanfiru minhu al-ṭabʿ wa-yaʾbāhu ʿādatan*), such as pain and what leads to it. The same is true of 'goodness' (*ḥusn*). The upshot is that the mind does not apprehend any 'goodness' or 'badness' [in acts themselves] such that the performance or omission of them could be grounds for reward or punishment.

The first class includes occurrences in which these expressions are employed in what we may characterize as a descriptive, but non-moral sense connected to a thing's perfection or imperfection (for instance, 'a good car'). Al-Ashʿarī seems to appeal to this sense only in interpreting a limited range of evaluative expressions, most notably 'justice' (*ʿadl*), 'injustice' (*jawr, ẓulm*), and cognate expressions, which are given non-moral definitions in terms of 'balance', 'order', and 'right measure', or the contraries thereof. He reportedly thus maintained that, in ordinary language (*ʿalā iṭlāq al-lugha*), describing an act as 'unjust' is not the same as describing it as 'bad', or 'evil' (*qabīḥ*) (Ibn Fūrak, *Mujarrad*, 96).

Most later classical Ashʿarites, however, analyse a broader array of value expressions, including the central expressions 'good' and 'bad', by reference to this sense. Abū Isḥāq al-Isfarāʾīnī (d. 418/1027) reportedly writes (al-Anṣārī, *Ghunya*, 2: 1015):

> 'Justice' is to put things in their appropriate places, and this is the literal sense of 'goodness' (*ḥaqīqat al-ḥusn*). 'Injustice' is to put things in other than their appropriate places, and this is the literal sense of 'badness'.

In the foregoing citation, al-Juwaynī likewise gives the example of the sense in which 'badness' (*qubḥ*) is said of the form (*ṣūra*) of a bodily object only to denote imbalance and disproportion in the manner of its composition. Such an aesthetic judgement is understood as a descriptive, and hence objective, statement of a fact about the way in which the object in question is formed and arranged. Nonetheless, despite its objective reference, this sense of 'bad' does not signify any ethical properties that qualify things themselves.

This descriptive sense is appealed to in interpreting several divine names, such as 'Just' and 'Wise' (*ḥakīm*), both of which are said to denote the masterly production (*iḥkām*) observed in God's creation. The thoroughly ethical Muʿtazilī expositions of these divine names are rejected.

The second lexical sense of 'good' and 'bad' is the more important one in our present context, since it is meant to explain instances in which the main value terms are employed in an undeniably moral sense, rather than in the foregoing descriptive non-moral sense. Al-Ashʿarī, as mentioned, excludes 'good' and 'bad' from the former, descriptive explanation of evaluative expressions. According to Ibn Fūrak (*Mujarrad*, 141–2),

> ... he maintained that there is only one sense for 'bad' and 'good' in the observable realm (*al-shāhid*) [i.e. the created world]: that what is bad is avoided for the imperfection and harm that it results in for one who does it, and that the good and wise act is chosen because of the benefit and perfection that it results in for one who does it. There is no ground for the act's performance or omission in the observable realm except this or its like.

In the same vein, al-Juwaynī, as we have seen, writes that 'badness' can refer to 'what the disposition, in the normal course of events, is repulsed by and rejects, such as pain and what leads to it'. 'Goodness', likewise, will refer to what the individual's disposition is attracted to and accepts. Ethical judgements, for al-Anṣārī, 'are not judgements of the mind, but judgements based on convention (*ʿurf*) and on the individual's repulsion and attraction' (*Ghunya*, 2: 1008). As such, they

> are rooted in inborn dispositions[5] that God instilled in His servants when He created (*faṭara*) them. So [people] became accustomed and habituated[6] to them, until they came to conceive of them as judgements of the mind. This [conception] is far off the mark! For the sound mind does not make a distinction between the two [i.e. good and bad acts]. Rather, these [judgements] are nothing but deep-rooted habits stemming from [considerations of] harm and benefit (*ʿādāt mustamirra ṣādira ʿan al-ḍarar wa-l-nafʿ*).

Value terms, accordingly, are subjective and refer, not to any items of knowledge of real and objective attributes in the act itself, but to emotive impulses that arise within the agent in reaction to acts and occurrences. In other words—to use the terms of classical *kalām* ontology and epistemology—if I perceive Zayd, say, utter a lie, what will occur in my heart (the central locus of cognition) is not an accident of knowledge (*ʿilm*) of an objective ethical attribute within Zayd's act, but an accident of pain or repulsion that follows from my perception of that act, as well as an instance of immediate knowledge of my pain or repulsion. (On that pleasure and pain are known immediately, see al-Baghdādī, *Uṣūl al-dīn*, 8.) The object of that item of knowledge, hence, is not external, in the act itself, but internal to me.

The innate dispositions that effect these instinctive impulses are instilled by God in man's inborn make-up, and are essentially the same as dispositions innate to animals. They can cause man to experience sympathy (*riqqa*), or 'sympathy towards other members of the same class of beings' (*riqqa jinsiyya*), that engenders pain when one perceives others drowning or on the verge of death, and can motivate (*tastaḥiththu*) one to assist (Ibn Fūrak, *Mujarrad*, 142; al-Juwaynī, *Niẓāmiyya*, 173). Al-Anṣārī, in the quoted passage, seems to hold that these dispositions give rise to mores (*ʿurf*) by a process of collective habituation, to the extent that the habitual moral customs (*ʿādāt*) might become conceived of as objective truths.

This second, subjective lexical definition of value terms allows the Ashʿarites to offer an alternative explanation for the ethical judgements that people ordinarily pass on acts without appeal to formal belief systems—evidence that the Muʿtazila cite and interpret differently in support of their ethical realism. What the Muʿtazila 'claim that one finds in oneself (*wujdān al-nafs*)', al-Anṣārī writes, 'stems in fact from nothing other than [the individual's] personal needs (*aghrāḍ*)' (*Ghunya*, 2: 1008). Al-Juwaynī thus dismisses the Muʿtazilī contention that people find beneficence and saving a person in mortal danger good because their minds, even in the absence of any religious influence, discern the intrinsic goodness of these acts, and find wrongdoing and aggression bad because their minds discern the intrinsic badness thereof. These judgements, he maintains, can

5 Reading, with the MS, *akhlāq jibilliyya*.
6 Reading, with the MS, *marinū*.

be explained by the individual agent's inborn attraction towards pleasure and repulsion from pain (*Irshād*, 265). 'The sound-minded person finds pleasure in beneficence and likes one who does it, and finds pain in offence and detests one who does it' (*Ikhtiṣār*, 2: 734).

By reference to this definition, al-Juwaynī also responds to the previously mentioned Baṣran Muʿtazilī argument that if faced with a choice between truth-telling and lying, and in the absence of self-interest in either option, the sound-minded agent will undoubtedly choose the former (*Ikhtiṣār*, 2: 734; cf. Ibn Fūrak, *Mujarrad*, 142). In *ad hominem* (*ex concessis*) manner, he invokes the Muʿtazilī notion that one who commits lying will become blameworthy and deserve punishment for it. If, for the sake of the argument, this is conceded to be the case, truth-telling and lying will be distinguished, not merely by their ethical values as the Muʿtazila claim, but also by their consequences on the agent. And it is precisely the difference between the subjective consequences the agent expects from each choice that will be his true motive to prefer truth-telling to lying. The equivalence the Muʿtazila postulate between the two choices is, thus, a false one. 'The sound-minded person', al-Juwaynī writes, 'will prefer truth-telling only to avert blame and the [retribution] of which he was threatened (*al-waʿīd*), not for the reason you [the Muʿtazila] assert', i.e. the intrinsic badness of lying.

Al-Anṣārī likewise dismisses the Muʿtazilī contention that we know intuitively that a given act is bad if done by a sound-minded agent, but not bad if done by an unsound-minded agent (*Ghunya*, 2: 1008). Not so, he responds. For we find in ourselves abhorrence and repulsion towards murder, be it committed by an adult or a prepubescent adolescent (*murāhiq*), although the Law prescribes a different ruling for each. We also loathe, and are repulsed by, the slaughter of animals and separating their young from their parents, although these acts are religiously good (either permitted or recommended).

Classical Ashʿarites employ this subjectivist, anti-realist definition of ethical value expressions only to explain cases in which they are used mundanely in ordinary language, rather than in a religious sense, the sole purpose of this definition being to account for evidence that the Muʿtazila adduce for their ethical realism. The definition, therefore, is irrelevant in the normative sphere, that is, to the religious obligation that applies to human agents (*taklīf*), as al-Juwaynī indicates in the passage cited earlier in the present section: 'The *upshot* is that the mind does not apprehend any "goodness" or "badness" [in acts themselves] such that the performance or omission of them could be grounds for reward or punishment'. Practical religious rulings, after all, cannot be founded, at least in the first instance, on considerations of subjective interest. It is, furthermore, inapplicable to the evaluation of divine action, considering that God can experience neither pleasure nor pain (al-Juwaynī, *Irshād*, 265; al-Anṣārī, *Ghunya*, 2: 1008).

The irrelevance of the lexical (*lughawī*) definitions of ethical value expressions to these two spheres of action creates space for a formal, religious (*sharʿī*) definition (one, like many other technical terms in theology, based on convention and assignment, *tawqīf*) tied exclusively to God's command and prohibition. Al-Juwaynī, for instance, writes that 'what is meant by "good" is that which revelation (*sharʿ*) specifies praise for one who does it, and what is meant by "bad" is that which revelation specifies blame for one who does it' (*Irshād*, 258). Divine command and prohibition, hence, are not simply the grounds that *make* certain acts good and others bad, as may be suggested in statements such as, 'the bad is bad on account of the relation of God's prohibition to it' (Ibn Fūrak, *Mujarrad*, 94; cf. al-Bāqillānī, *Tamhīd*, 185). They rather define the very meaning of the terms 'good' and 'bad'.

This definition of 'good' and 'bad' works at two levels. In the sphere of human action, it underpins a theory of divine command ethics by establishing that revelation is the sole legitimate source for norms that govern human action and behaviour. At the same time, it supports a broader theological voluntarism: since God's command applies only to His creatures, His own will and acts are unconstrained by any duties or prohibitions.

V The Consequentialist Ethics of Neo-Ashʿarism

A subtle, but significant, shift towards a different, consequentialist theory of ethics can be seen in the theological and juristic works of al-Juwaynī's student al-Ghazālī (d. 505/1111) (*Mustaṣfā*, 1: 178ff.; *Iqtiṣād*, 160ff.; Hourani 1976; Marmura 1969). A more developed version of this theory, which exhibits the combined influence of classical Ashʿarism and Avicenna, is expounded about a century later by Fakhr al-Dīn al-Rāzī (d. 606/1210), and through his works becomes influential on later neo-Ashʿarite sources. The following overview is based on two of al-Rāzī's later works, particularly the *Maṭālib* and the *Maʿālim*. (For the gradual progression of his views in earlier works, see Shihadeh 2006: 56ff.).

Al-Rāzī presents his theory of ethical value as being distinct from the theories propounded by both the Muʿtazila and earlier Ashʿarites (*Maṭālib*, 3: 289; *Maʿālim*, 86–7). Like the Muʿtazila, he supports an ethical rationalism at the human level: only the mind (*ʿaql*) can judge acts as good or bad (*al-taḥsīn wa-l-taqbīḥ*). However, like the Ashʿarites, he denies that ethical rationalism is applicable to God's acts.

Al-Rāzī's ethical rationalism is antithetical to the realism propounded by the Muʿtazila. To him, 'good', when predicated of acts, can only refer to benefit, what leads to benefit, or what prevents harm, whether past or expected. Similarly, 'bad' can only refer to harm, what leads to harm, or what prevents benefit. The same act or occurrence, hence, can be good to Zayd, if it results in consequences favourable to him, but bad to ʿAmr, if it results in consequences unfavourable to him. This makes moral judgement agent-relative, not in the sense that it can be measured against some objectively determinable standards of advantage and disadvantage, but in the more radical sense that it is entirely subjective, reducible to self-interest, and dependent on the agent's disposition and the emotive impulses of attraction and repulsion it engenders. Al-Rāzī explains that an individual possessed of a sensitive disposition will be inclined to compassion, since he will experience pleasure in aiding and assisting others and pain in perceiving their suffering. Not so for the individual possessed of a harsh and aggressive disposition (*Maṭālib*, 3: 350–1):

> I have seen one of the greatest kings—he was utterly ruthless and his sole pleasure was to watch massacre and pillage. The more brutal the kinds of torture he watched, the more complete would be his joy and the happier the expression on his face.

The impulses that give rise to moral judgements stem from the primary perceptions of pleasure and pain. Albeit a form of egoism, al-Rāzī's theory nonetheless does not amount to hedonism, since it allows for a hierarchy of pleasures and pains, including higher, intellectual or spiritual pleasures.

Within this subjectivist framework, al-Rāzī offers a more sophisticated explanation for non-religious ethical norms than that put forth by classical Ashʿarites (Shihadeh 2006: 73ff.). Like his predecessors, he maintains that some judgements can be explained easily as arising from the pleasure or pain that an individual possessed of a sympathetic disposition may experience instinctively when he perceives the suffering of others. If, walking in a desert, I encounter a blind man on the verge of dying of thirst, I will experience pain, and this will motivate me to relieve this person's suffering and to save his life: to me, this would be a good act, since it alleviates my pain and may bring me satisfaction and pleasure. Not all value judgements, however, can be explained by reference to emotive impulses so straightforwardly. Why, for instance, do individuals normally consider lying and wrongdoing bad, even when these acts are beneficial to them? And why do they consider other acts good, even if they cause them harm? The explanation that al-Rāzī gives is this. Even if an individual breaks an ethical norm of society, say by committing an instance of wrongdoing, it will still be in his best interest to preserve the principle that wrongdoing is bad. For if that principle ceases to be a widely accepted social norm, that wrongdoer himself will immediately find himself at risk of being wronged by others. This awareness leads individuals, and hence society as a whole, to consent to a set of norms, the conventionality of which will then be forgotten as they eventually, through habituation, become treated as a priori truths.

Al-Rāzī presents his consequentialist ethics as an alternative to Muʿtazilī ethical realism, which he criticizes at length. Earlier Ashʿarite refutations, he writes, fail since they target the notion that an act is good or bad on account of its essence, and exhibit little understanding of the theory that ethical value is connected to act configurations (*wajh*) (*Maṭālib*, 3: 338–9). So he attempts a criticism of the latter view, arguing that the Muʿtazila are correct in asserting that the ethical value of an act depends on its circumstances, though only in the relativist sense that these circumstances affect the self-oriented calculations and subjective judgement of the individual (*Maṭālib*, 3: 347ff.; Shihadeh 2006: 83ff.).

The upshot of al-Rāzī's ethical subjectivism is that it does not apply to God's acts. Since ethical value is subjective, and since God experiences neither pleasure nor pain and can receive neither benefit nor harm, He is not ethically motivated to perform, or to omit, any acts. On this point, al-Rāzī is in full agreement with his classical Ashʿarite predecessors.

In contrast to these predecessors, however, al-Rāzī's conception of ethical value makes no reference to revelation: in his later works, he characterizes it as being a rational (*ʿaqlī*), rather than religious (*sharʿī*), concept. On the basis of his theory of action, he argues that command in and of itself, even if it comes from God, cannot motivate action, and hence cannot constitute the root basis for duties. It is only on account of the individual's calculations of expected benefits or harms that it becomes imperative to obey divine commands, considering that the posthumous rewards and punishments that revelation stipulates as consequences for obedience and disobedience are, both qualitatively and quantitatively, by far the greatest possible pleasures and pains that a human being may experience. Al-Rāzī (*Maṭālib*, 3: 289–90) writes:

> 'Badness in the religious sense' (*qubḥ sharʿī*) has no meaning other than this: Religion tells [the agent], 'If you perform such-and-such an act, you will become punishable for it'. His mind then tells him, 'Ought I, or ought I not, judge the avoidance of that punishment obligatory?' If [the mind] judges it [obligatory in this way], it will be evident that 'good' and 'bad' are rational [concepts]. If, however, his mind does not judge it such, [the agent] will be dependent on religion to obligate him to avoid punishment. Yet what is true of the former [obligation] applies equally to the latter. This would lead to infinite regress, which is absurd.

Elsewhere, he writes that 'though debauchery provides a certain type of pleasure, the mind nonetheless prohibits it; and it prohibits it only on account of its conviction that it will result in greater pain and torment', that is, in the hereafter (*Maʿālim*, 87).

The outcome is not a classical-Ashʿarite divine command ethics. For al-Rāzī implements consequentialism not only as the background on which the revealed law is superimposed, but also as the chief rational normative principle in jurisprudence through which the law is refined and extended. Although God's commands are not motivated, al-Rāzī nevertheless contends that they generally serve the interest of humans. So, in discussing the problem of the religious status of advantageous acts on which revelation is silent (*maṣlaḥa mursala*), he argues that the agent ought to seek such advantages and to avoid harms, since these principles 'are known almost immediately (*bi-l-ḍarūra*) to be at the heart of the teachings of the prophets (*dīn al-anbiyāʾ*) and the objective of revealed laws (*al-maqṣūd mina l-sharāʾiʿ*)' (*Maḥṣūl*, 6: 166; Shihadeh 2006: 68ff.).[7]

Bibliography

ʿAbd al-Jabbār al-Hamadānī (*al-Mughnī*). *Al-Mughnī fī abwāb al-tawḥīd wa-l-ʿadl*. Vol. 6/1: *al-Taʿdīl wa-l-tajwīr*. Ed. M. M. Qāsim. Cairo: al-Dār al-Miṣriyya li-l-Taʾlīf wa-l-Tarjama, 1962.

ʿAbd al-Jabbār al-Hamadānī (*Mughnī*). *Al-Mughnī fī abwāb al-tawḥīd wa-l-ʿadl*. Vol. 9: *al-Tawlīd*. Ed. T. al-Ṭawīl and S. Zāyid. Cairo: al-Dār al-Miṣriyya li-l-Taʾlīf wa-l-Tarjama, 1964.

[7] I would like to thank Dr Harith bin Ramli for his comments on this chapter.

ʿAbd al-Jabbār al-Hamadānī (*Mughnī*). *Al-Mughnī fī abwāb al-tawḥīd wa-l-ʿadl*. Vol. 13: *al-Luṭf. Ed.* A.ʿA. al-ʿAfīfī. Cairo: al-Dār al-Miṣriyya li-l-Taʾlīf wa-l-Tarjama, 1963.

ʿAbd al-Jabbār al-Hamadānī (*al-Mukhtaṣar*). *Al-Mukhtaṣar fī uṣūl al-dīn*. In *Rasāʾil al-ʿadl wa-l-tawḥīd*. Ed. M. ʿImāra. Cairo: Dār al-Shurūq, 1988, 189–282.

Abrahamov, B. (1993). "ʿAbd al-Jabbār's Theory of Divine Assistance (*luṭf*)". *Jerusalem Studies in Arabic and Islam* 16: 41–58.

Abū Rashīd al-Nīsābūrī (*al-Masāʾil*). *Al-Masāʾil fī l-khilāf bayna l-baṣriyyīn wa-l-baghdādiyyīn*. Ed. M. Ziyāda and R. al-Sayyid. Tripoli: Maʿhad al-Inmāʾ al-ʿArabī, 1979.

al-Anṣārī, Abū l-Qāsim Salmān (*al-Ghunya*). *Al-Ghunya fī l-kalām*. Ed. M. Ḥ. ʿAbd al-Hādī. Cairo: Dār al-Salām, 2010.

al-Attar, M. (2010). *Islamic Ethics: Divine Command Theory in Arabo-Islamic Thought*. Abingdon/New York: Routledge.

al-Baghdādī, ʿAbd al-Qāhir (*Uṣūl al-dīn*). *Uṣūl al-dīn*. Istanbul: Madrasat al-Ilāhiyyāt bi-Dār al-Funūn al-Turkiyya, 1928.

al-Bāqillānī, Muḥammad b. al-Ṭayyib (*al-Tamhīd*). *Kitāb al-Tamhīd*. Ed. R. J. McCarthy. Beirut: Librairie Orientale, 1957.

Bernand, M. (1982). *Le Problème de la connaissance d'après le Muġnī du cadi ʿAbd al-Ǧabbār*. Algiers: Société Nationale d'Édition et de Diffusion.

Brunschvig, R. (1974). 'Muʿtazilisme et Optimum (*al-aṣlaḥ*)'. *Studia Islamica* 39: 5–23.

Cook, M. (2001). *Commanding Right and Forbidding Wrong in Islamic Thought*. Cambridge/New York: Cambridge University Press.

van Ess, Josef (1991–7). *Theologie und Gesellschaft im 2. und 3. Jahrhundert Hidschra: Eine Geschichte des religiösen Denkens im frühen Islam*. 6 vols. Berlin: de Gruyter.

Frank, R. M. (1978). *Beings and their Attributes: The Teaching of the Basrian School of the Muʿtazila in the Classical Period*. Albany, NY: SUNY Press.

Frank, R. M. (1983). 'Moral Obligation in Classical Muslim Theology'. *The Journal of Religious Ethics* 2/2: 204–23.

Frank, R. M. (1985). 'Can God do What is Wrong?' In T. Rudavsky (ed.), *Divine Omniscience and Omnipotence in Medieval Philosophy: Islamic, Jewish and Christian Perspectives*. Dordrecht: Reidel, 69–79.

al-Ghazālī, Abū Ḥāmid (*al-Iqtiṣād*). *Al-Iqtiṣād fī l-iʿtiqād*. Ed. I. A. Çubukçu and H. Atay. Ankara: Nur Matbaasi, 1962.

al-Ghazālī, Abū Ḥāmid (*al-Mustaṣfā*). *Al-Mustaṣfā min ʿilm al-uṣūl*. Ed. Ḥ. Z. Ḥāfiẓ. 4 vols. Medina: n.p., n.d.

Gimaret, D. (1974–5). 'Un problème de théologie musulmane: Dieu veut-il les actes mauvais? Thèses et arguments'. *Studia Islamica* 40: 5–73; 41: 63–92.

Gimaret, D. (1980). *Théories de l'acte humain en théologie musulman*. Paris: Librairie Philosophique J. Vrin/Leuven: Peeters.

Gimaret, D. (1990). *La Doctrine d'al-Ashʿarī*. Paris: Cerf.

Heemskerk, M. (2000). *Suffering in the Muʿtazilite Theology: ʿAbd al-Jabbār's Teaching on Pain and Divine Justice*. Leiden: Brill.

al-Ḥillī, al-Ḥasan b. Yūsuf (*Kashf*). *Kashf al-murād fī sharḥ Tajrīd al-iʿtiqād*. Beirut: Muʾassasat al-Aʿlamī li-l-Maṭbūʿāt, 1988.

Hoover, J. (2007). *Ibn Taymiyya's Theodicy of Perpetual Optimism*. Leiden: Brill.

Hourani, G. F. (1971). *Islamic Rationalism: The Ethics of ʿAbd al-Jabbār*. Oxford: Clarendon Press.

Hourani, G. F. (1975). 'Juwayni's Criticism of Muʿtazilite Ethics'. *Muslim World* 65: 161–73.

Hourani, G. F. (1976). 'Ghazālī on the Ethics of Action'. *Journal of the American Oriental Society* 96: 69–88.

Hourani, G. F. (1985). *Reason and Tradition in Islamic Ethics*. Cambridge: Cambridge University Press.

Ibn Fūrak, Muḥammad b. al-Ḥasan (*Mujarrad*). *Mujarrad maqālāt al-Shaykh Abī l-Ḥasan al-Ashʿarī*. Ed. D. Gimaret. Beirut: Dār al-Mashriq, 1987.

Ibn al-Malāḥimī, Rukn al-Dīn (*al-Fāʾiq*). *Al-Fāʾiq fī uṣūl al-dīn*. Ed. W. Madelung and M. McDermott. Tehran: Iranian Institute of Philosophy/Berlin: Freie Universität Berlin, 2007.

Ibn Mattawayh, al-Ḥasan b. Aḥmad (*al-Majmūʿ*). *Al-Majmūʿ fī l-muḥīṭ bi-l-taklīf*. Vol. 1. Ed. J. J. Houben. Beirut: Imprimerie Catholique, 1965.

Ibn Mattawayh, al-Ḥasan b. Aḥmad (*al-Tadhkira*). *Al-Tadhkira fī aḥkām al-jawāhir wa-l-aʿrāḍ*. Ed. D. Gimaret. 2 vols. Cairo: Institut Français d'Archéologie Orientale, 2009.

Jackson, S. A. (1999). 'The Alchemy of Domination? Some Ashʿarite Responses to Muʿtazilite Ethics'. *The International Journal of Middle Eastern Studies* 31: 185–201.

al-Juwaynī, Abū l-Maʿālī ʿAbd al-Malik (*al-Irshād*). *Kitāb al-Irshād*. Ed. M. Y. Mūsā and ʿA. ʿA. ʿAbd al-Ḥamīd. Cairo: Maktabat al-Khānjī, 1960.

al-Juwaynī, Abū l-Maʿālī ʿAbd al-Malik (*al-ʿAqīda*). *Al-ʿAqīda al-Niẓāmiyya*. Ed. M. al-Zubaydī. Beirut: Dār Sabīl al-Rashād and Dār al-Nafāʾis, 2003.

al-Juwaynī, Abū l-Maʿālī ʿAbd al-Malik [abridged by a certain Ibn al-Amīr] (*Ikhtiṣār*). *Al-Kāmil fī ikhtiṣār al-Shāmil*. Ed. J. ʿA. ʿAbd al-Munʿim. 2 vols. Cairo: Dār al-Salām, 2010.

Mānkdīm Shashdīw (*Sharḥ*). *Sharḥ al-uṣūl al-khamsa*. Ed. ʿA. ʿUthmān. Cairo: Maktabat Wahba, 1965.

Marmura, M. E. (1969). 'Al-Ghazālī on Ethical Premises'. *The Philosophical Forum* (New Series) 1/3: 393–403.

Marmura, M. E. (1994). 'A Medieval Islamic Argument for the Intrinsic Value of the Moral Act'. In E. Robbins and S. Sandahl (eds.), *Corolla Torontonensis: Studies in Honour of Ronald Morton Smith*. Toronto: TSAR, 113–31.

Mensia, M. A. (2004). 'Théories du repentir chez les théologiens musulmans classiques'. In A. Destro and M. Pesce (eds.), *Rituals and Ethics: Patterns of Repentance: Judaism, Christianity, Islam*. Paris: Peeters, 107–23.

Mourad, S. (2005). *Early Islam between Myth and History: Al-Ḥaṣan al-Baṣrī (d. 110H/728CE) and the Formation of his Legacy in Classical Islamic Scholarship*. Leiden: Brill.

el-Omari, R. (2007). 'Abu l-Qāsim al-Balkhī al-Kaʿbī's Doctrine of the *Imāma*'. In C. Adang et al. (eds.), *A Common Rationality: Muʿtazilism in Islam and Judaism*. Würzburg: Ergon Verlag, 39–57.

Pomerantz, M. A. (2007). 'Muʿtazilī Theory in Practice: The Repentance (*tawba*) of Government Officials in the 4th/10th Century'. In C. Adang et al. (eds.), *A Common Rationality: Muʿtazilism in Islam and Judaism*. Würzburg: Ergon Verlag, 463–93.

al-Rāzī, Fakhr al-Dīn (*Maʿālim*). *Maʿālim uṣūl al-dīn*. Ed. Ṭ. ʿA. Saʿd. Cairo: Maktabat al-Kulliyyāt al-Azhariyya, n.d.

al-Rāzī, Fakhr al-Dīn (*al-Maḥṣūl*). *Al-Maḥṣūl fī ʿilm uṣūl al-fiqh*. Ed. Ṭ. J. al-ʿAlwānī. 6 vols. Beirut: Muʾassasat al-Risāla, 1992.

al-Rāzī, Fakhr al-Dīn (*al-Maṭālib*). *Al-Maṭālib al-ʿāliya mina l-ʿilm al-ilāhī*. Ed. A. Ḥ. al-Saqqā. 8 vols. in 4. Beirut: Dār al-Kitāb al-ʿArabī, 1987.

al-Rāzī, Fakhr al-Dīn. *Uṣūl al-Dīn*. MS Beirut, American University of Beirut Library, 297:R27kA.

Reinhart, K. (1995). *Before Revelation: The Boundaries of Muslim Moral Thought*. Albany, NY: SUNY Press.

Shihadeh, A. (2006). *The Teleological Ethics of Fakhr al-Dīn al-Rāzī*. Leiden: Brill.

Shihadeh, A. (2008). 'The Existence of God'. In T. Winter (ed.), *The Cambridge Companion to Classical Islamic Theology*. Cambridge: Cambridge University Press, 197–201.

Shihadeh, A. (2012). 'Classical Ashʿarī Anthropology: Body, Life and Spirit', *The Muslim World* 102: 433–77.

Shihadeh, A. (2013). 'Favour, Divine (*Luṭf*)', *Encyclopaedia of Islam. Three.*

al-Ṭūfī, Najm al-Dīn (*Darʾ*). *Darʾ al-qawl al-qabīḥ bi-l-taḥsīn wa-l-taqbīḥ*. Ed. A. Shihadeh. Riyadh: King Faisal Centre for Research, 2005.

al-Ṭūfī, Najm al-Dīn (*al-Taʿyīn*). *Al-Taʿyīn fī sharḥ al-Arbaʿīn al-Nawawiyya*. Ed. A. ʿUthmān. Beirut: Muʾassasat al-Rayyān, 1988.

van Ess, Josef (1991–7). *Theologie und Gesellschaft im 2. und 3. Jahrhundert Hidschra: Eine Geschichte des religiösen Denkens im frühen Islam*. 6 vols. Berlin: de Gruyter.

Vasalou, S. (2003). 'Equal before the Law: The Evilness of Human and Divine Lies: ʿAbd al-Ǧabbār's Rational Ethics', *Arabic Sciences and Philosophy* 13: 243–68.

Vasalou, S. (2008). *Moral Agents and Their Deserts: The Character of Muʿtazilite Ethics*. Princeton/Oxford: Princeton University Press.

CHAPTER 24

THEOLOGY AND LOGIC

KHALED EL-ROUAYHEB

I Early Opposition to Greek Logic among Theologians (Ninth–Tenth Centuries)

In the ninth and tenth centuries CE, Islamic 'theologians' (*mutakallimūn*) and Arabic 'logicians' (*manṭiqiyyūn* or *ahl al-manṭiq*) constituted distinct and rival groups. The Muʿtazilī theologian Abū l-ʿAbbās al-Nāshiʾ (d. 293/906) is reported to have written a number of (non-extant) refutations of the logicians, and another non-extant refutation was penned by the Shīʿī theologian Ḥasan b. Mūsā al-Nawbakhtī (d. *c.*305/917) (Ibn al-Murtaḍā, *Ṭabaqāt*, 92–3; Hallaq 1993, xlii–xliii). In the year 320/932, the grammarian and Muʿtazilī theologian Abū Saʿīd al-Sīrāfī (d. 368/979) engaged in a disputation in the presence of the Abbasid Vizier Ibn al-Furāt with the leading figure amongst the Baghdad Aristotelians of his time, the Nestorian Christian Abū Bishr Mattā (d. 328/940) (for modern studies of this exchange, see Mahdi 1970; Elamrani-Jamal 1983: 61–7; Endress 1986: 194–200). When Mattā claimed that logic (*manṭiq*) serves to distinguish between correct and incorrect discourse (*kalām*), Sīrāfī countered that this was the province of Arabic grammar, and proceeded to expose Mattā's ignorance of that discipline. Whatever the Greeks had written was, Sīrāfī pressed, useless for distinguishing between correct and incorrect *Arabic* discourse. As for correct thinking, Sīrāfī scornfully rejected the suggestion that there was a need to learn this from a Greek. People had reasoned correctly before Aristotle and continued to do so after him without having any inkling of logic (Tawḥīdī, *Imtāʿ*, 1: 109–10). The prominent Muʿtazilī theologian Abū Hāshim al-Jubbāʾī (d. 321/933) is supposed to have said to the same Abū Bishr Mattā, 'Is logic (*manṭiq*) not simply derived from utterance (*nuṭq*)?' (van Ess 1970: 21), perhaps echoing Sīrāfī's complaint that the word *manṭiq* for logic is a misnomer since Mattā and his cohort knew next to nothing about the grammatical rules of speech.

The hostility of these early theologians is not difficult to understand. The early Arabic Aristotelians constituted a new school of thought that claimed to possess a standard—derived from the Greeks—with which to distinguish between adequate and inadequate proof. According to Abū Bishr Mattā's student al-Fārābī (d. 339/950), a proof is conclusive only if it can be reformulated, without any loss of meaning, as either an Aristotelian categorical syllogism or a Stoic hypothetical syllogism (*modus ponens, modus tollens*, or disjunctive syllogism) (Fārābī, *Qiyās*, 2: 37; see more generally Lameer 1994). The early theologians predictably resented and disputed such claims. They had their own developed patterns of argumentation and sense of what constitutes a satisfactory proof (van Ess 1970: 26–42; al-Nashshār 1947: 84–110). They tended to divide knowledge (*ʿilm*) into (i) 'necessary' (*iḍṭirārī*) or 'evident' (*badīhī*), and (ii) 'inferential' (*istidlālī*) or 'ratiocinative' (*naẓarī*). The process by which non-evident knowledge is derived from evident knowledge was typically called *istidlāl*. Its paradigmatic form was analogical reasoning (*qiyās*), for example: 'The heavens are created in time, since they are composite bodies like animals and plants and these are created in time'. The premiss that animals and plants are created in time is taken as known. This judgement (*ḥukm*) is then transferred to the heavens since the heavens, like animals and plants, are composite bodies. The subject of the premiss (e.g. animals and plants) was referred to as the 'root' (*aṣl*); the subject of the sought conclusion (e.g. the heavens) was referred to as the 'branch' (*farʿ*); and the common characteristic that purports to justify the transfer of the judgement (e.g. being composite bodies) was usually referred to as the *jāmiʿ*.

The early Islamic theologians were regularly involved in disputations with a myriad of opponents: theologians of rival Islamic sects and rival monotheist religions, dualists, deists who denied prophecy, and even non-theists. They could therefore hardly afford to be unreflective about their forms of argumentation. Already by the late ninth and early tenth centuries there is evidence for sophisticated reflection on the difference between acceptable and unacceptable analogies (early Islamic theologians were thus considerably more reflective about their use of analogy than the pre-Socratic philosophers discussed in Lloyd 1966: 172ff.). In a correct analogy, the common characteristic to which one appeals must be the 'cause' (*ʿilla*) of the original judgement. A condition for something being a 'cause' of a judgement is that it be sufficient (*muṭṭarid*) and on some accounts also necessary (*munʿakis*) for the judgement. In other words, the cause must be such that whenever it is present the judgement is present too (this was termed *ṭard*), and that whenever the judgement is present the proposed cause is present as well (this was termed *ʿaks*)—the latter condition was often relaxed in the case of the 'cause' of a legal judgement (Ibn Fūrak, *Mujarrad*, 304). Abū l-Ḥasan al-Ashʿarī (d. 324/935), the founder of what was to become the most influential school of theology in Islam, explicitly undertook to explain what was wrong with an analogy like the following: 'God is a body, for He is an agent (*fāʿil*) like worldly agents and these are bodies'. The proof is faulty, explained Ashʿarī, since being an agent is not a 'cause' of being a body. After all, there are bodies that are not agents and therefore the condition of necessity (*ʿaks*) is not satisfied (Ibn Fūrak, *Mujarrad*, 289).

The 'cause' played a prominent role in the early Islamic 'science of disputation' (*ʿilm al-jadal*) (on which, see van Ess 1976; Miller 1984). A disputant could challenge his opponent to 'verify the cause' (*taṣḥīḥ al-ʿilla*), i.e. justify that the adduced reason is indeed sufficient for the judgement. Alternatively, he could challenge his opponent to 'consistently apply his purported cause' (*jarayān al-ʿilla*) in the hope of deriving an absurdity or self-contradiction. For example, a *mulḥid* (a deist or naturalist who denies prophecy, creation, and resurrection) may claim that the world is not created *ex nihilo* because he has never observed things to come into existence out of nothing. A questioner could then respond by asking the *mulḥid* to 'verify the cause': why should the observation of the *mulḥid* be sufficient ground for the denial of creation *ex nihilo*? Would this be any different from someone who claims that there is no salt water because he has only experienced fresh water? Alternatively, the questioner could ask the *mulḥid* to apply the 'cause' consistently and hold that the world is not eternal since he has also not observed anything eternal. The *mulḥid* believes that the world is eternal (since he denies creation *ex nihilo*) and hence the questioner has forced him to contradict himself (Ibn Fūrak, *Mujarrad*, 296–7).

The argument just imputed to the *mulḥid* seems to be an example of a recognized type of *istidlāl* in which an analogy is made on the basis, not of an explicitly stated 'common characteristic' (*jāmiʿ*), but of the supposed absence of a relevant difference (*farq mu'aththir*) between two cases. The *mulḥid* argues to a conclusion about the world (the 'branch') on the basis of his observations concerning ordinary perceptible objects (the 'root') without specifying what the *jāmiʿ* is. Another example—more to the liking of early Islamic theologians—would be the inference from the premiss that God has the power to create living beings to the conclusion that He has the power to resurrect them after death (Ibn Fūrak, *Mujarrad*, 288; Bāqillānī, *Tamhīd*, 12). Again, no mention is made of a *jāmiʿ*, but it is assumed that the extrapolation from the original case to the conclusion is nevertheless legitimate since there is no relevant difference—or so the theologians contend—between the two cases.

There were other forms of inference recognized by early theologians that were not analogical. The Ashʿarī theologian al-Bāqillānī (d. 403/1013) mentioned appeal to Scripture (Qurʾān or *Ḥadīth*) as a legitimate form of *istidlāl* (Bāqillānī, *Tamhīd*, 13). Another recognized non-analogical form of reasoning was what was later called *sabr wa-taqsīm*: to make an exhaustive list of alternatives and then exclude all but one (Ibn Fūrak, *Mujarrad*, 288; Bāqillānī, *Tamhīd*, 11–12). Also attested in early sources is reasoning on the basis of 'the determination of language users' (*tawqīf ahl al-lugha*) (Ibn Fūrak, *Mujarrad*, 289; Bāqillānī, *Tamhīd*, 12–13). If language users have determined that the word 'fire' be used of bright, burning things, then we can infer that even fire that we have not directly perceived is also bright and burns. Conversely, language users have not determined that the word 'water' only be used of fresh water, and someone who has only experienced fresh water should therefore not infer that water that is beyond direct experience is also fresh. Rather, he should concede that it is possible that God create water that is not fresh (Ibn Fūrak, *Mujarrad*, 290).

Notwithstanding the recognition of non-analogical forms of reasoning, the analogy (*qiyās*) retained pride of place in early theologians' reflections on 'proof' (*istidlāl*) and 'disputation' (*jadal*). Appeal to Scripture was of course recognized to be ineffectual in inter-religious disputes and was for that matter rarely effective in inter-Islamic disputes. Invoking the Qur'ān and *Ḥadīth* in support of a contested point was as a rule merely countered by other Qur'ānic passages or other *Ḥadīth* that suggest otherwise, or by a challenge to the authenticity of the adduced *Ḥadīth*, or by the argument that the Scriptural passage must be reinterpreted so as to conform with other passages or with the evident truths of reason. Indeed, the whole discipline of *kalām* was based on the assumption that, for the mentioned reasons, appeals to Scripture were of limited effectiveness in combating heresy and unbelief, this of course being the assumption that particularly incensed fideist, anti-*kalām* groups such as the Ḥanbalīs. Appeals to linguistic conventions, though certainly not unknown, did not play a major role in theological argumentation or disputation. The method of *sabr wa-taqsīm* was often employed as a preliminary step to determine the *ʿilla* that would then be used in an analogy, and hence some early sources do not present it as an independent form of *istidlāl* (Nashshār 1947: 92–4). This left analogy as the paradigm form of inference. Writing in the year 355/966, the historian and theologian Muṭahhar b. Ṭāhir al-Maqdisī stated that various definitions had been given of *qiyās*: to assimilate one thing to its like on the basis of a common cause (*raddu l-shayʾi ilā naẓīrihi bi-l-ʿillati l-mushārika*), or to know the unknown on the basis of the known (*maʿrifatu l-majhūli bi-l-maʿrūf*), or everything that is known by proof and is not evident or sensed (*kullu mā ʿulima bi-l-istidlāli min ghayri badīhatin wa lā ḥāssa*). Revealingly, he then wrote that these suggestions were 'close in meaning' (*qarībatu l-maʿānī*) (Maqdisī, *Badʾ*, 1: 34). There was obviously little difference for Maqdisī between inference in general (to know the unknown on the basis of the known) and analogy (assimilating one thing to its like on the basis of a common cause).

II The Assimilation of Logic by Theologians (Eleventh–Fourteenth Centuries)

The opposition between theologians and logicians was eroded between the eleventh and fourteenth centuries. The powerful impact of the philosophy of Avicenna (d. 428/1037) quickly made itself felt in Islamic theological circles especially in Persia and central Asia. Already by the mid- and late eleventh century, prominent Eastern theologians were beginning to incorporate Avicennan terminology and arguments, and even modifying substantial doctrinal commitments in response to serious engagement with Avicennan philosophy (Wisnovsky 2004b). The first major theologian (*mutakallim*) to call for the adoption of Greek logic in theology was al-Ghazālī (d. 505/1111), but his advocacy was clearly part of a larger current of cross-fertilization between *kalām* and Avicennan philosophy that was occurring in his time. Ghazālī wrote a number of expositions of logic: *al-Qisṭās al-mustaqīm, Miḥakk al-naẓar, Miʿyār al-ʿilm*, and the introductory chapter of his summa of jurisprudence *al-Mustaṣfā*. These expositions were not especially original or advanced, but their clarity and the wide esteem enjoyed by their author undoubtedly helped promote Greek logic to theologians and jurists. Given Ghazālī's prominence as a Shāfiʿī jurist and (at least ostensibly) Ashʿarī theologian and his powerful attack in *Tahāfut al-falāsifa* on a number of theses of Avicenna's metaphysics and physics, it was difficult to dismiss his advocacy of Greek logic as nothing but uncritical imitation of the infidel philosophers.

Of particular interest in the present context is Ghazālī's wholesale acceptance of earlier logicians' criticism of analogical argumentation as inconclusive unless it could be regimented into syllogistic form. Consider the already mentioned example of a theological analogical argument: 'The heavens are created in time, since they are composite bodies like animals and plants and these are created in time.' In his *Miʿyār al-ʿilm*, Ghazālī noted that the argument is inconclusive unless being composite can be shown to be the 'cause' of the judgement that animals and plants are created in time. This was hardly a controversial observation. However, Ghazālī's next step constituted a more serious challenge: we cannot know that being composite is a sufficient 'cause' for being created in time without also knowing that anything composite is created in time (the condition that the 'cause' be *muṭṭarid* ensures this). Why not simply use this universal premiss to construct the following syllogism in the first figure?

> The heavens are composite
> Everything composite is created in time
> The heavens are created in time

The appeal to the original judgement concerning animals and plants plays no role in establishing the conclusion and might as well, Ghazālī noted, be left out of consideration entirely (Ghazālī, *Miʿyār*, 123–4). He gave another example of an analogical argument in theology that should be reduced to syllogistic form: God knows by means of possessing the attribute of knowledge, for humans know by means of possessing the attribute of knowledge. Again, the analogy is only legitimate if what is common to God and humans (in this case that they know) is a 'cause' for the judgement in the premiss (in this case that humans know by means of possessing the attribute of knowledge). But there is no way of knowing this without also knowing that 'Everything that knows does so by means of possessing the attribute of knowledge'. In this case, we can derive the wanted conclusion syllogistically from the following two premisses:

> God knows
> Everything that knows does so by means of possessing the attribute of knowledge
> God knows by means of possessing the attribute of knowledge

The mention of humans plays no role in the argument at all and may as well be dispensed with (Ghazālī, *Miʿyār*, 125).

Ghazālī's point was *not* that the translation of the initial argument into syllogistic form somehow, as if by magic, confers certainty upon the conclusion. Immediately after formulating the argument as a syllogism he went on to write:

> In this case, one would dispute your statement 'Everything that knows knows by means of possessing the attribute of knowledge', and if this is not self-evident then you must prove it through another syllogism. (Ghazālī, *Miʿyār*, 125)

Ghazālī was in other words well aware that his reformulation of the original argument into a first-figure syllogism does not suddenly make the conclusion certain, for the universal premiss is open to doubt and will be challenged by a disputant who does not wish to accept the conclusion. His point was rather that the original analogical formulation of the argument falsely suggests that the fact that humans know by means of possessing the attribute of knowledge plays a role in establishing the conclusion. It does not. The case of humans is irrelevant unless it is known that what is common to God and humans is the 'cause' of the initial judgement. In turn this cannot be known unless it is known that 'Everything that knows does so by means of possessing the attribute of knowledge', and if this universal proposition is known then there is no need for mentioning the case of humans at all.

Having thus disallowed traditional analogical arguments in theology, Ghazālī went on to argue that they nevertheless play a legitimate role in legal reasoning (Ghazālī, *Miʿyār*, 127ff.). If we know that grape wine (*khamr*) is prohibited and we have a preponderant belief that the 'cause' for the prohibition is that it is intoxicating then we are justified in concluding that date wine (*nabīdh*), which is also intoxicating, is also prohibited. Why did Ghazālī allow for analogy in legal reasoning but not in theological reasoning? He himself justified the difference by stating that preponderant belief is all that is needed in legal reasoning whereas it is insufficient in theology (Ghazālī, *Miʿyār*, 133–4). The distinction between theological and legal reasoning seems to have been related to two assumptions, neither of which were in any way peculiar to Ghazālī. First, the law serves urgent practical needs and it would defeat the purpose to set the standard of legal reasoning too high. Second, articles of faith have to be established with certainty. The very nature of religious belief was generally held to be incompatible with the believer admitting that the ground for this belief is inconclusive. Someone who claimed that the prophecy of Muḥammad, or creation *ex nihilo*, or bodily resurrection, or God's knowledge of particulars were all plausible but not certain was widely held not to have religious belief at all (Frank 1989: 43).

However, a problem remains, even granted the distinction between the standards of legal reasoning and theological reasoning. Why not use syllogistic reasoning across the board and then add the qualifier that in legal syllogisms the premisses are merely probable? On this account the above-mentioned argument is as follows:

> Date wine is an intoxicant
> <u>Every intoxicant is prohibited</u>
> Date wine is prohibited

Again, the 'root' (in this case grape wine) would be irrelevant to establishing the conclusion. One could then just add the qualification that the second, universal premiss is merely probable, but that this is good enough for legal purposes. Why did Ghazālī not adopt this position? It cannot be because he believed a syllogism's premisses must be certain. A syllogism can, by agreement of all logicians (including Ghazālī), be composed of non-certain premisses (*ẓanniyyāt*) (Ghazālī, *Miʿyār*, 102; Ghazālī, *Miḥakk*, 44–5). An answer may possibly be found in Ghazālī's discussion of the way in which jurists derive a general rule from a legal injunction that is phrased in specific terms (Ghazālī, *Miʿyār*, 156–7). In the legal analogy just mentioned, for example, the premiss that grape wine is an intoxicant and prohibited is *ex hypothesi* our only ground for asserting that 'Every intoxicant is prohibited.' This is, of course, far from a perfect induction. However, the jurist may surmise that there is no other ground for the prohibition and proceed to extrapolate from this single case. This suffices for justified belief that falls short of certainty. In such a case, the judgement concerning the 'root' does play a role in the argumentation (since there is no other ground for asserting the universal 'Every intoxicant is prohibited') and it is presumably more perspicuous to mention it explicitly. It is possible that this was Ghazālī's underlying thought for allowing analogy in legal reasoning and disallowing it in theological reasoning. However, it is not possible to be certain about this, for he did not address the question directly. By not doing so, he could easily impart the impression that syllogistic forms of reasoning are suitable for areas in which demonstrative certainty is the aim, whereas non-syllogistic forms are adequate in areas where preponderant belief is sufficient. This impression could only have been strengthened by Ghazālī's use of the term *burhān* (usually reserved for demonstration) for syllogism (usually called *qiyās* by logicians) in the logical introduction to his *Mustaṣfā* (Ghazālī, *Mustaṣfā*, 1: 116ff.). This may have been one source for the systematic conflation of syllogism and demonstration that is evident in the later attack on Greek logic by Ibn Taymiyya.

The process of adopting Greek logic continued apace after Ghazālī. The list of prominent Ashʿarī and Māturīdī theologians in the thirteenth and fourteenth centuries who also wrote works on logic is remarkable: Fakhr al-Dīn al-Rāzī (d. 606/1210), Sayf al-Dīn al-Āmidī (d. 631/1233), Nāṣir al-Dīn al-Bayḍāwī (*fl.* 674/1275), Shams al-Dīn al-Samarqandī (d. 702/1303), Ṣadr al-Sharīʿa al-Maḥbūbī (d. 747/1346), Shams al-Dīn al-Iṣfahānī (d. 749/1348), ʿAḍud al-Dīn al-Ījī (d. 756/1355), Saʿd al-Dīn al-Taftāzānī (d. 791/1390), and al-Sayyid al-Sharīf al-Jurjānī (d. 816/1413). Amongst the Shīʿīs, Ibn Abī l-Ḥadīd (d. 655/1258), Naṣīr al-Dīn al-Ṭūsī (d. 672/1274), and Ibn al-Muṭahhar al-Ḥillī (d. 726/1325) wrote works on both theology and logic.

It has often been assumed that the adoption of Greek logic led to the acceptance of metaphysical assumptions that were at odds with those of earlier theologians. For instance, a number of medieval Muslim critics of Greek logic claimed that it is committed to the extra-mental existence of universals (Rosenthal 1958: iii. 145). Some modern observers have taken this claim as obviously true, but it is nevertheless not clear what exactly the connection is supposed to be. In the widely studied logic handbook *al-Risāla al-Shamsiyya* by Najm al-Dīn al-Kātibī (d. 675/1277), the question of the extra-mental existence of universals is explicitly stated not to belong to logic (Taḥtānī, *Taḥrīr*, 43–4). Especially in later centuries, it was not uncommon for Arabic logicians to be nominalists—for example the Illuminationist philosopher Yaḥyā al-Suhrawardī (d. 587/1191), the thirteenth-century logician, dialectician, and Māturīdī theologian Shams al-Dīn al-Samarqandī, the Tīmūrid polymath Saʿd al-Dīn al-Taftāzānī, the Azharī scholar Aḥmad al-Mallawī (d. 1181/1767), and the Ottoman Turkish scholar Ismāʿīl Gelenbevī (d. 1205/1791) (Ziai and Walbridge 1999: 7–8; Walbridge 2005: 207–10; Samarqandī, *Qistās*, fo. 19b; Taftāzānī, *Sharḥ*, 21; Ṣabbān, *Ḥāshiya*, 63 main text ll. 6–7; Gelenbevī, *Burhān*, 43, 46–8 top rubric). Some of the most prominent logicians in the medieval Latin tradition, for example William of Ockham (d. 1348) and John Buridan (d. *c*.1360), were also nominalists (see Spade 1999; Klima 2008).

It has also been suggested that the acceptance of the Aristotelian scheme of genera led Ghazālī to modify earlier Ashʿarī beliefs about divine omnipotence, for such a scheme implies that there is an objective 'ontological structure' that limits God's Power (Rudolph 2005: 97). Again, the issue bears closer examination. The passage that has been adduced in support of the suggestion is from Ghazālī's *Tahāfut al-falāsifa*. Ghazālī was there addressing the objection that the Ashʿarī denial of natural causation leads to absurdities. In response, he explained that occasionalism and divine omnipotence should not be taken to mean that God may flout the law of non-contradiction, or create one person in two different places simultaneously, or create will without knowledge, or 'change genera' (*qalb al-ajnās*) such as change blackness into power or change a substance into an attribute. By 'genera' in this context Ghazālī seems to have meant the highest genera, i.e. the categories, for he countenanced change within a single category. For example, a stick might be changed into a snake, for we can conceive of an underlying matter (*mādda*) that first assumes one form (*ṣūra*) and then assumes another (Marmura 1997: 175–6). It is instructive to compare Ghazālī's discussion with a passage from *Mujarrad maqālāt al-Ashʿarī* by Ibn Fūrak (d. 406/1015) in which Ashʿarī is quoted as responding to a similar worry about occasionalism and the denial of natural causation (Ibn Fūrak, *Mujarrad*, 132–3). Ashʿarī too explained that this theological position does not imply that God may flout the law of non-contradiction. Nor does it imply that God may, for example, create an accident without a non-accident that possesses it. It is also difficult to see, given Ashʿarī's definitions of the three basic categories of created being—accident, atom, and body—how he could have countenanced that for example an accident may change into an atom or body, or vice versa (see *jism, jawhar*, and *ʿaraḍ* in the index to Ibn Fūrak, *Mujarrad*, 364, 365, 371). Though Ashʿarī stated that God could create cold and wet in fire, he immediately added that in such a case we would cease to call it 'fire' if language users had determined that the word 'fire' only be used of what is hot and bright. Ashʿarī also believed that for example knowledge (*ʿilm*) presupposes life (*ḥayāt*) and that it would be impossible to have the former without the latter (Ibn Fūrak, *Mujarrad*, 205). The upshot is that both Ashʿarī and Ghazālī recognized an objective 'ontological structure' in the world. Ghazālī's use of the Aristotelian language of genera and hylomorphism is certainly novel, but it is less clear that this amounted to a significantly different view of divine omnipotence.

The question of the metaphysical baggage, if any, that came along with the adoption of Greek logic bears much more detailed consideration than it has received so far. Any such consideration must heed the point that Aristotelian logic was not adopted wholesale but was transformed in important ways as it came to be 'naturalized' into Islamic theological and juridical circles (Spevack 2010). As noted by the famous North African historian Ibn Khaldūn (d. 808/1406), the 'later logicians' (*al-muta'akhkhirūn*) starting with Fakhr al-Dīn al-Rāzī and Afḍal al-Dīn al-Khūnajī (d. 646/1248) ceased to be concerned with all parts of the Aristotelian *Organon* and came to focus exclusively on definition and formal syllogistic (Rosenthal 1958: iii. 142–3). In the logical writings of Rāzī and Khūnajī there is indeed little or no interest in the Aristotelian categories or Aristotelian demonstration, and the same is true of the standard *madrasa* handbooks on logic from the thirteenth and fourteenth centuries (Street 2004: 279–81). Rāzī, Khūnajī, and the logicians following in their wake also accepted Avicenna's position that real definition of extra-mental quiddities is exceedingly difficult and that for most purposes nominal or stipulative definition is all that can be hoped for (Goichon 1963: 2ff.; Rāzī, *Mulakhkhaṣ*, 118; Khūnaji, *Kashf*, 60). Echoing this point, Quṭb al-Dīn al-Shīrāzī (d. 710/1311) wrote in his commentary on Suhrawardī's *Ḥikmat al-ishrāq* that the problems with Peripatetic definition raised by Suhrawardī only pertained to the definition of things 'according to reality' (*bi-ḥasab al-ḥaqīqa*). As for defining things 'according to our understanding' (*bi-ḥasab al-mafhūm*), this was straightforward: we can stipulate that we mean by 'human' a rational animal, in which case being rational and an animal is essential to being human, whereas being capable of laughing or a biped is accidental (Shīrāzī, *Sharḥ*, 60–1). Later Islamic scholars who assimilated Greek logic were not particularly interested in logical definition for the purpose of 'cutting nature at its seams'. For theologians, jurists, or grammarians the real definition of, say, 'human' was presumably of little concern. Like the prominent grammarian Ibn Hishām (d. 761/1360) they would instead have been interested in using the Aristotelian scheme of genera and differences to fix the nominal or stipulative definitions of the technical terms of their disciplines (see for example Ibn Hishām, *Qaṭr*, 27–8). The logical writings of the early Baghdad Aristotelians might perhaps be seen as intimately intertwined with an overarching commitment to an Aristotelian/Neoplatonic metaphysics and physics. It is far from obvious that this was the case with the works of Rāzī, Khūnajī, and later logicians.

III Some Protests against the 'Naturalization' of Greek Logic

The widespread adoption of Greek logic amongst theologians and jurists did not occur without resistance. In the early thirteenth century, the prominent Shāfiʿī scholar Ibn al-Ṣalāḥ al-Shahrazūrī (d. 643/1245) issued a strongly worded *fatwā* against Greek logic and the incipient trend of studying it in madrasas (Goldziher 1916/1981: 205–6; Nashshār

1947: 142). A few generations later, an all-out attack on Greek logic—considerably more detailed than any other that has come down to us—was made by the Damascene Ḥanbalī scholar Ibn Taymiyya (d. 728/1328). This attack has attracted a good deal of attention in modern times, both in the Sunni Islamic world and amongst Western scholars of Islam (classic studies include Nashshār 1947: 144–99; Heer 1988; Hallaq 1993; von Kügelgen 2005). Ibn Taymiyya's rejection of real, essential definition has been seen as anticipating the position of Locke and Hume. His insistence that traditional analogy is more useful than deductive syllogism and that even the principle of non-contradiction and the truths of mathematics are based on extrapolation from sense-experience has been seen as prefiguring the epistemological ideas of John Stuart Mill. Yet, 'nominalist empiricism' constitutes just one of many strands in Ibn Taymiyya's criticism, and arguably one that has received disproportionate attention (for a sober discussion of the parallels with British empiricism, see von Kügelgen 2005: 214–21). There are other strands that are much more akin to Lorenzo Valla's (d. 1457) humanist criticism of Aristotelian logic as contrived and useless to those with sound minds and good language skills.[1] Both Ibn Taymiyya and Valla, for example, pressed the point that informal arguments long recognized outside Aristotelian logic were more natural and effective than the stilted insistence on always casting proofs into two-premissed syllogisms (on Valla's criticism of logic, see Nauta 2009: §3).

By contrast to the keen modern interest, Ibn Taymiyya's attack seems to have been largely ignored by later logicians and advocates of the use of logic in Islamic theology and law. There appears to have been no explicit reference to it in later logical writings, let alone a refutation of it, before the modern period (for a recent refutation by an Ashʿarī scholar, see Fūda 2002). Some modern observers have suggested that this was due to the fact that logic was simply too entrenched in scholarly circles by the time Ibn Taymiyya was writing (Hallaq 1993: xlix; Sabra 1980: 749). This explanation, with its suggestion that the prescient criticism of Ibn Taymiyya went unheeded due to conservative complacency, has tended to fit well with the image of Ibn Taymiyya as a heroic figure living in a dark age of blind 'imitation' (*taqlīd*)—an image that has appealed to those nineteenth- and twentieth-century Islamic scholars who share Ibn Taymiyya's hostility to *kalām*, mysticism, scholastic jurisprudence, and religious practices such as shrine- and saint-veneration (see for example Shawkānī, *Badr*, 1: 63–72). The hold of this image might explain why there has been little or no work done on studying Ibn Taymiyya's attack in conjunction with the writings of especially thirteenth- and fourteenth-century Arabic logicians. The assumption appears to have been that Ibn Taymiyya's depictions of the logical doctrines of his day were, on the whole, accurate and can be taken at face value. However, closer attention to the works of the logicians suggests a more complicated picture. It also suggests that there may have been more than inert conservatism behind the lack of interest that logicians showed in Ibn Taymiyya's work.

[1] The parallels between Valla and Ibn Taymiyya were first pointed out to me in conversation by Tony Street.

A central part of Ibn Taymiyya's attack is devoted to refuting what he takes to be the claim of logicians that 'assent' (*taṣdīq*) can only come about through syllogism. This was not in fact standard logical doctrine (as noted in Hallaq 1993: 30 §41 n. 2). According to the Arabic logicians, assents can be 'evident' (*badīhī*), a category that was broad enough to include self-evident truths of reason but also propositions derived from sense perception (*ḥiss*), repeated experience (*tajriba*), introspection (*wijdān*), and reports that are attested in numerous, mutually independent ways (*tawātur*). Other assents are, by contrast, not evident and must be derived from those that are. The typical position of thirteenth- and fourteenth-century logicians was that non-evident propositions can be acquired in one of three ways: syllogism, induction, or analogy (Ghazālī, *Miʿyār*, 43–4; Rāzī, *Sharḥ*, 1: 271ff.; Rāzī, *Mulakhkhaṣ*, 241–2; Taḥtānī, *Taḥrīr*, 16–8; Taḥtānī, *Lawāmiʿ*, 17). Of these three kinds of 'proof' (*ḥujja* or *dalīl*), only deductive syllogism was held by logicians to establish its conclusion with certainty. Ibn Taymiyya disputed this, of course. He wrote:

> These people claim that analogy leads to probability, while their syllogism yields certainty. Elsewhere, we have shown that their doctrine is the most fallacious of doctrines and that analogy and the categorical syllogism are equivalent and that [their yielding] certainty or belief differs according to the matter. If the particular matter is certain in one of them, it will be certain in the other; and if it is probable in one of them, it will be probable in the other. (Ibn Taymiyya, *Radd*, 116; Hallaq 1993, 44 §60)[2]

Ibn Taymiyya gave the following example. If we know that 'Date wine is intoxicant' and 'Every intoxicant is forbidden' then indeed we would know that 'Date wine is forbidden', but in that case we might as well advance the analogical argument: 'Date wine is forbidden, for it is an intoxicant like grape wine and grape wine is forbidden.' The analogy only yields knowledge if being intoxicating is indeed the 'cause' of the judgement concerning the 'root', but similarly the syllogism only yields knowledge if the universal premiss 'Every intoxicant is forbidden' is true. The difference between syllogism and analogy is, Ibn Taymiyya reiterated again and again, merely one of nomenclature and form, not probative force. Ibn Taymiyya was here eliding what logicians saw (and still see) as a key distinction between syllogistic inference and analogical inference. A syllogistic inference is formally productive in a way in which analogy is not. Logicians like Avicenna, Rāzī, and Khūnajī were careful to clarify the idea that—contrary to Ibn Taymiyya's assumption—even a syllogism with false or contingent premisses conclusively entails a conclusion as long as the formal conditions of productivity are satisfied. They all addressed the objection that the conclusion of a syllogism with contingent premisses may be contingent, so how can it be said to follow *necessarily* from the premisses? They answered by distinguishing between following necessarily from certain premisses and being necessarily true. A formally productive syllogism, they explained,

[2] In this and following quotations from Ibn Taymiyya's work, I have slightly modified Hallaq's translation.

can consist of false premisses and false conclusion but it is still the case that its conclusion follows necessarily from these premisses in the sense that it cannot fail to be true if the premisses are true (Ibn Sīnā, *Shifāʾ*, 66–7; Rāzī, *Mulakhkhaṣ*, 244; Rāzī, *Sharḥ*, 1: 279; Khūnajī, *Kashf*, 235–6). The quoted lemma by Ibn Taymiyya suggests that he was not aware of this central distinction between the necessity of a conclusion and the necessity of entailment. Logicians did not claim that 'syllogism' (*qiyās*) affords certainty in the sense that its conclusion must be true, for a productive syllogism can on all accounts have false premisses and a false conclusion. Rather, their claim was that in a formally productive syllogism the conclusion follows with certainty from the premisses in the sense that it would be an outright contradiction to concede the premisses (Date wine is an intoxicant & Every intoxicant is forbidden) and refuse to concede the conclusion (Date wine is forbidden). By contrast, the premisses of an analogy (Date wine is an intoxicant like grape wine & Grape wine is forbidden) do not necessitate the conclusion (Date wine is forbidden) in this sense—consider the formally similar and invalid 'Grape juice is a liquid pressed from grapes like grape wine & Grape wine is forbidden, so Grape juice is forbidden'. It might perhaps be objected that if we explicitly state that the common characteristic in an analogy is a sufficient cause (*ʿilla*) then the conclusion does follow with certainty: for example 'Date wine is forbidden, for it is an intoxicant like grape wine & Grape wine is forbidden *because* it is an intoxicant'. But such an explicit statement of the 'cause' would make the argument deductive rather than analogical, and the 'root' of the purported analogy would, as Ghazālī had pointed out, become an idle wheel that plays no role in establishing the conclusion.

It has been asserted that Ibn Taymiyya did not dispute the formal validity of the syllogism (Hallaq 1993: xxviii; von Kügelgen 2005: 205). On this account, he cannot have confused the certain truth of the conclusion of a syllogism with the certain entailment of the conclusion by the premisses. The textual basis for this assertion is at first sight strong. Ibn Taymiyya wrote:

> We argue that in the syllogistic form the conclusion is undoubtedly certain if the matter is known. If we say: 'Every A is B', and 'Every B is C', there will be no doubt that, if the two premises are known, this combination will yield the knowledge that 'Every A is C'. There is no disputing this. The correctness of the form of the syllogism cannot be gainsaid. (Ibn Taymiyya, *Radd*, 293; Hallaq 1993: 141 §253)

However, on closer consideration there is no clear indication here or elsewhere that Ibn Taymiyya recognized the formal validity of the syllogism, at least not as 'formal validity' is understood by logicians. He agreed that the syllogistic form yields knowledge (*yufīdu l-ʿilm*) but took pains to add that this is only if the matter or premisses are 'known' (*maʿlūma*). The passage just quoted should be read in conjunction with other passages, such as the following:

> We have explained elsewhere that analogy and the categorical syllogism imply each other and that if one yields knowledge or belief, the other will yield the same if the

> matter is the same. What is important is the matter of knowledge, not the form of the proposition. In fact, if the matter is certain, there will be no difference between it [the argument] being in the form of an analogy or in the form of a syllogism... Nor will there be a difference if the argument is expressed in their terminology or in any other terminology, especially if such terminology is better than theirs, more evident to the mind, and pithier. (Ibn Taymiyya, *Radd*, 200–1; Hallaq 1993: 114–5 §190)

Ibn Taymiyya thus insisted that the probative force of syllogism and analogy depends on the matter: both yield certainty if the matter is certain, and otherwise not. There is nothing to suggest that Ibn Taymiyya recognized that the syllogistic form is inherently such as to entail a conclusion, whereas the analogical form is not. In the following passage he explicitly denied that a syllogism entails a conclusion by virtue of its form alone:

> The truth about their syllogism is that it offers nothing but the mode and the form of the proof. As for the specific proof entailing its conclusion (*ammā kawnu l-dalīlī l-muʿayyani mustalziman li-madlūlihi*), there is nothing in their syllogism that affirms or denies this. This depends rather on knowledge of the premises included in the proof. (Ibn Taymiyya, *Radd*, 252; Hallaq 1993: 136 §240–1)

When Ibn Taymiyya conceded that there is nothing wrong with the form of the syllogism, he was not conceding its 'formal validity'. His position was rather that the syllogistic 'form' may lead to knowledge of a conclusion in certain material instances, just as the analogical 'form' may lead to knowledge of a conclusion in certain material instances as well. A knowledge-yielding argument may take the 'form' of a syllogism or an analogy. Indeed, he suggested, there is no limit to the number of 'forms' that such an argument can take, most of these being more natural and less contrived than the 'form' of the categorical or hypothetical syllogism (Ibn Taymiyya, *Radd*, 296–7). The whole thrust of Ibn Taymiyya's argument is thus that syllogism and analogy are *equally* 'correct' forms of argument and that there are countless other 'correct' forms of argument. This is to ignore rather than recognize what traditional and modern logicians mean by the 'formal validity' of the syllogism.

Even if one supposes that Ibn Taymiyya did recognize that the syllogism is 'formally valid' (in a way in which analogy is *not* 'formally valid'), it is clear that he did not assign much importance to this fact. This is presumably because formal syllogistic—since it disregards the question of the truth or falsity of premisses—does not by itself expand our stock of knowledge of the extra-mental world (as suggested in Hallaq 1993: xxxix). However, that point is so uncontroversial and so readily conceded by the logicians that it is decidedly odd to use it as a reason for rejecting the discipline of logic. By the thirteenth and fourteenth centuries, Arabic logicians showed little interest in demonstration (*burhān*) and obviously did not consider it to be their task (qua logicians) to pronounce on the truth of premisses and conclusions. Rather, they claimed to have developed a general and content-neutral yardstick that can be used to distinguish between conclusive and inconclusive arguments or, as the logic manuals tended to state, 'An instrument the use of which protects against committing errors of reasoning' (Khūnajī, *Kashf*, 8–9;

Taḥtānī, *Taḥrīr*, 10ff.). One may consider the following well-known *ḥadīth* attributed to the Prophet Muḥammad: 'Every innovation is waywardness and every waywardness is in hell-fire (*kullu bidʿatin ḍalālatun wa kullu ḍalālatin fī l-nār*)'. Post-Avicennan logicians tended to believe that the subject matter of their discipline is 'second intentions' (*al-maʿqūlāt al-thāniya*)—roughly, second-order concepts such as 'genus', 'species', 'subject', and 'predicate' (Sabra 1980). The two mentioned propositions have first-order concepts as subjects ('innovation' and 'waywardness') and determining their truth would therefore not have been considered to be the province of the logician at all (but presumably the province of the *ḥadīth* scholar and jurist). The perceived task of the logician was rather to establish that the two propositions (regardless of their truth value) formally entail the conclusion 'Every innovation is in hell-fire'.[3]

Apart from such serious misunderstandings of logical doctrine, there is another striking feature of Ibn Taymiyya's polemic that may well have made the substantial number of scholars who advocated the use of logic wary and unresponsive. He rarely if ever took it upon himself to present the position of the logicians at any length. Their views were almost invariably presented, in one or two sentences, as stark claims with no indication of what the justification of these claims might be, and he almost never tried to anticipate a possible reply that they might make to his objections. The style is very different from the critical discussions of Neoplatonic/Aristotelian philosophy by for example Ghazālī and Fakhr al-Dīn al-Rāzī, or by the authors of widely studied handbooks on theology such as Ījī and Taftāzānī, or by the fifteenth-century Ottoman scholars who wrote their own refutations of the philosophers modelled on that of Ghazālī. In those works, the beliefs of the philosophers and their supporting arguments were as a rule presented carefully and dispassionately. Objections to the philosophers were then proposed and discussed. Real or anticipated rejoinders to these objections were then also taken into account. Often, objections to the philosophers proposed by previous theologians were deemed unsatisfactory and modified, and especially on points that the theologians considered non-central (for example the truth of atomism) the discussion could well end on an inconclusive note. By comparison, Ibn Taymiyya systematically presented the ideas of the logicians as peculiar and arbitrary—his reader cannot help wondering why anyone should ever have held

[3] On Hallaq's interpretation, syllogisms for Ibn Taymiyya are of no use for acquiring knowledge of the world in part because reason unaided by revelation cannot ascertain universal propositions, and at least one universal premiss is needed for syllogistic productivity (Hallaq 1993: xxx–xxxiv). The problem with this interpretation is that it contradicts Ibn Taymiyya's repeated insistence that analogy, contrary to the claim of logicians, affords certainty in some instances. This clearly presupposes that the common characteristic (*jāmiʿ*) is sufficient (*muṭṭarid*) for the judgement and this in turn implies the truth of a universal proposition. Ibn Taymiyya also repeatedly stressed that analogy and syllogism are only distinct in nomenclature and that anything that can be shown by one form of argument can be shown by the other. This implies that if analogy may yield knowledge of the world then syllogism may yield it too and, by contraposition, that if syllogism cannot yield knowledge of the world then neither can analogy. Even if one were to grant Hallaq's interpretation of Ibn Taymiyya, the sceptical point that unaided reason cannot ascertain the truth of universal premisses would first and foremost be a problem for first-order scholarly disciplines, not for formal logic.

such views. He sometimes even made outrageously false attributions: 'the logicians', for example, supposedly believe that quiddities are in the extra-mental world apart from their existence (a scarcely intelligible claim), that religious reports with multiple and independent lines of transmission (*tawātur*) do not have probative force, and that God knows by means of syllogisms (Ibn Taymiyya, *Radd*, 64, 92, 157, 474). Of course, mainstream religious scholars could sometimes adopt an equally uncharitable and vituperative tone in their polemics, especially against less cerebral opponents than the Islamic philosophers or in works meant for a more popular readership. But Ibn Taymiyya used this tone in attacking ideas that had been advocated by widely respected scholars such as Ghazālī, Fakhr al-Dīn al-Rāzī, and Sayf al-Dīn al-Āmidī. The assumption that logicians were unreceptive to Ibn Taymiyya's criticism because they were mired in conservatism and therefore unable to appreciate its power needs to be seriously reconsidered.

IV The Later Tradition of Logically Informed Theology and its Opponents (after the Fourteenth Century)

The resistance to Greek logic by figures like Ibn al-Ṣalāḥ and Ibn Taymiyya had little effect. Ibn Taymiyya's major attack on logic has apparently only survived in a single manuscript, and its abridgement by the Egyptian scholar Jalāl al-Dīn al-Suyūṭī (d. 911/1505) has survived in two (Hallaq 1993: liii–lvi). By comparison, there are thousands of extant Arabic manuscripts on logic that date from the period between the fourteenth and nineteenth centuries. The website of manuscripts established by the Turkish Ministry of Culture and Tourism (<http://www.yazmalar.gov.tr>) lists 4,179 manuscripts on logic copied between 700/1300 and 1300/1882—this being a (non-exhaustive) list of dated manuscripts extant in Turkey alone. Handbooks on logic such as *Īsāghūjī* by Abharī (d. 663/1265), *al-Risāla al-Shamsiyya* by Kātibī, *Tahdhīb al-manṭiq* by Taftāzānī, *Mukhtaṣar al-manṭiq* by Muḥammad b. Yūsuf al-Sanūsī (d. 895/1490), and *al-Sullam al-murawnaq* by ʿAbd al-Raḥmān al-Akhḍarī (d. 953/1546) elicited a plethora of commentaries and glosses in later centuries (Wisnovsky 2004a: 161–9). The sheer number and geographic spread of these indicates that studying logic was a regular part of the education of *madrasa* students in most parts of the Islamic world from the fourteenth century to the nineteenth. The study of logic was widely held to be a necessary part of the training of an Islamic theologian, and a number of later jurists accordingly opined that the study of logic is a communal duty (*farḍ kifāya*) of Muslims, precisely because it is needed in the science of *kalām* which is a communal duty. The prominent Egyptian-born, Meccan-based Shāfiʿī jurist Ibn Ḥajar al-Haytamī (d. 973/1566), whose legal works continued to be authoritative amongst Shāfiʿīs well into the twentieth century, issued a lengthy fatwa on the status of logic which espoused this view. He first mentioned that Ibn al-Ṣalāh had prohibited the discipline. He then cited the following remarks from Ghazālī's *al-Munqidh min al-ḍalāl*:

> Nothing in logic is relevant to religion by way of denial and affirmation. Logic is the study of the methods of demonstration and forming syllogisms, of the conditions for the premises of proofs, of the manner of combining the premises, of the conditions of sound definition, and the manner of ordering it... What connection has this with the essentials of religion, that it should be denied or rejected? (Montgomery Watt 1953: 35–6)

Ibn Ḥajar al-Haytamī added:

> Consider these words without bias and you will find that he—may God bless him—has clarified the way and established the proof to the effect that there is nothing in it [i.e. logic] which is reprehensible or leads to what is reprehensible, and that it is of use in the religious sciences such as the science of the principles of religion (*uṣūl al-dīn*) and of jurisprudence (*fiqh*). The jurists have established the general principle that what is of use for the religious sciences should be respected and may not be derided, and it should be studied and taught as a *farḍ kifāya*. (Ibn Ḥajar al-Haytamī, *Fatāwā*, 1: 50)

Haytamī then suggested that the prohibitions of earlier venerable jurists like Ibn al-Ṣalāḥ were due to the fact that they were thinking of 'the logic of the old philosophers' (*manṭiq al-falāsifa al-uwal*) in which logical discussions were intermixed with physical and metaphysical principles that were contrary to religion. He then added:

> As for the logic that is known now amongst prominent Sunnī scholars: it contains nothing that is reprehensible and nothing of the doctrines of the philosophizers, but is an intricate science, requiring mental exertion and consideration, which can be relied on for guarding against errors in reasoning as much as possible. God forbid that Ibn al-Ṣalāḥ or even someone of lesser stature should think ill of this. (Ibn Ḥajar al-Haytamī, *Fatāwā*, 1: 50)

Haytamī was not so charitable toward later scholars who would prohibit logic. Possibly thinking of Ibn Taymiyya (of whom he was a harsh critic) and his abridger Suyūṭī, he added:

> A group of later scholars have attacked it because they were ignorant of it—as the saying goes: 'he who is ignorant of something is against it.' It is sufficient for it to be deemed useful in religion that it is not possible to reply to the doubts raised by the philosophers or other [heretical] sects except by adherence to its principles. It ought to be motive enough for him who is ignorant of it that he will not be able to say a single word to the philosopher or anyone else who masters it. Rather, the philosopher

> or his like will deploy specious arguments and the person who is ignorant of it—even if he were one of the prominent scholars—will remain silent, not knowing how to reply. (Ibn Ḥajar al-Haytamī, *Fatāwā*, 1: 50)

Ibn Ḥajar al-Haytamī's Ottoman Turkish contemporary Meḥmed Birgevī (d. 981/1573) expressed similar sentiments in his major work *al-Ṭarīqa al-muḥammadiyya*. He endorsed the view that *kalām* should not be studied for its own sake but that it is a *farḍ kifāya* once a doubt (*shubha*) has been raised concerning the creed (Khādimī, *Barīqa*, 1: 258). He then went on to state that logic should be considered a part of *kalām*. Two later Ottoman commentators on Birgevī's work, Receb Āmidī (d. 1087/1676) and Ebū Saʿīd Khādimī (d. 1176/1762), spelled out that this meant that logic too is a *farḍ kifāya* (Khādimī, *Barīqa*, 1: 262). The prominent Imāmī Shīʿī jurist Zayn al-Dīn al-ʿĀmilī (d. 965/1558) likewise considered logic to be 'a noble instrument to verify proofs in general and to know that which leads to a desired conclusion and that which does not' (ʿĀmilī, *Munyat*, 378). It should be studied, ʿĀmilī noted, after memorizing the Qurʾān and learning Arabic grammar, and before moving on to sciences like *kalām* and jurisprudence (ʿĀmilī, *Munyat*, 386).

The authors of widely studied works on *kalām* after the thirteenth century clearly presumed knowledge of at least basic logic on the part of the reader. For example, the Timurid scholar al-Sayyid al-Sharīf al-Jurjānī, in his esteemed commentary on Ījī's widely studied summa of theology *al-Mawāqif*, explained that arguments for or against the eternity of the Qurʾān could be presented in the form of two syllogisms with conflicting conclusions (Jurjānī, *Sharḥ*, 495–6). The first of these is:

> The word of God is an attribute of God
> Every attribute of God is eternal
> The word of God is eternal

Two theological groups, the Ashʿarīs and the Ḥanbalīs, accept the conclusion of the syllogism, while two other groups, the Muʿtazilīs and the Karrāmīs, reject it. The Muʿtazilīs dispute the minor premiss (*al-ṣughrā*—i.e. 'The word of God is an attribute of God') whereas the Karrāmīs dispute the major premiss (*al-kubrā*—i.e. 'Every attribute of God is eternal'). The second syllogism is:

> The word of God is a composite of sounds and letters
> Every composite of sounds and letters is created in time
> The word of God is created in time

The conclusion of this syllogism is accepted by the Muʿtazilīs and Karrāmīs but rejected by the Ashʿarīs and Ḥanbalīs. The Ḥanbalīs dispute the major premiss of the syllogism (i.e. 'Every composite of sounds and letters is created in time'), whereas the Ashʿarīs dispute the minor premiss ('The word of God is a composite of sounds and letters').

This way of presenting the dispute seems to have become widespread in later centuries. It even appears in Imāmī Shīʿī theological works such as the commentary by Mīr Abū l-Fatḥ al-ʿArabshāhī (d. 976/1568) on Ibn al-Muṭahhar al-Ḥillī's *al-Bāb al-ḥādī ʿashar* (Mīr Abū l-Fatḥ, *Miftāḥ*, 122). It also appears with an interesting twist in the commentary by the Ottoman scholar and judge Aḥmed Beyāżīzāde (d. 1098/1687) on the Māturīdī creed *al-Fiqh al-akbar*. Beyāżīzāde modified Jurjānī's statement to include the Māturīdīs as well as the Ashʿarīs, who together constitute the Sunnīs (*Ahl al-Sunna*), whereas the Ḥanbalīs were subsumed under the derogatory term *Ḥashwīyya* and not considered Sunnīs at all (Beyāżīzāde, *Ishārāt*, 141ff.).

The explicit use of syllogistic argument forms in theology is perhaps most striking in the works of the fifteenth-century North African Ashʿarī theologian Muḥammad b. Yūsuf al-Sanūsī. This is all the more remarkable given that Sanūsī was resolutely opposed to the 'philosophers' and disapproved of the practice of theologians such as Fakhr al-Dīn al-Rāzī and Bayḍāwī who devoted considerable space to the presentation and discussion of the philosophers' heresies (Sanūsī, *Ṣughrā*, 19). Yet, this attitude did not prevent Sanūsī from writing a number of works on logic and making extensive use of syllogistic argument forms in his own theological writings. In his commentary on his own major creed entitled *ʿAqīdat ahl al-tawḥīd* (often referred to simply as *al-ʿAqīda al-kubrā*), he began his proof for the existence of God by addressing the reader and urging him to construct the following syllogistic proof (Sanūsī, *Kubrā*, 72):

> I exist after not having existed
> Everything that exists after not having existed has been brought into existence by something
> I have been brought into existence by something

Sanūsī then presented the following two syllogisms showing that this something that has brought the reader's individual self into existence is a voluntary agent and not a natural cause like a sperm (*nuṭfa*) (Sanūsī, *Kubrā*, 81):

> Your self is in one of several possible ways
> Everything that is in one of several possible ways has been brought about by a voluntary agent
> Your self has been brought about by a voluntary agent

The conclusion of this syllogism is then used as a premiss in the following syllogism in the second figure (Sanūsī, *Kubrā*, 82):

> Your self has been brought about by a voluntary agent
> No natural cause is a voluntary agent
> Your self has not been brought about by a natural cause

Of course, Sanūsī tried to show that each premiss he used in these syllogisms is either evident or can be proven by further arguments.

Sanūsī is a little-known figure today.[4] However, this obscurity is a twentieth-century phenomenon and would seem to be related to the fact that the kind of logically informed Ashʿarism that he espoused has largely been eclipsed in modern times by other religious currents (especially neo-Muʿtazilism and Salafism). The large number of commentaries and glosses on his creedal and logical works is clear evidence of his influence until the nineteenth century, especially in Islamic Africa but also beyond—there are pre-modern Turkish, Malay, and Javanese translations of his creeds (Brockelmann 1937–49: ii. 323–6 and Suppl. ii. 352–6; Wisnovsky 2004a: 168, 185–6). His theological and logical works were obviously still being studied in the Azhar in the nineteenth century, for they were repeatedly printed then in Cairo along with commentaries and glosses by prominent Azhari scholars such as Ibrāhīm al-Bājūrī (d. 1276/1860) and Muḥammad ʿIllaysh (d. 1299/1882) (see Bājūrī, *Ḥāshiyah*; ʿIllaysh, *Hidāyat*).

There were of course still opponents of logic in later centuries, but it is important to note that these opponents tended to oppose *kalām* as well. The fideist Yemeni Zaydī scholar Ibn al-Wazīr (d. 840/1436), for example, wrote a tract entitled *Tarjīḥ asālīb al-Qurʾān ʿalā asālīb al-yūnān* that is aimed primarily against the discipline of *kalām* and its basic assumption that simple appeal to Scripture is not sufficient to refute heresy and establish the creed beyond doubt. His condemnation of logic is mentioned in passing (Ibn al-Wazīr, *Tarjīḥ*, 42). The fifteenth-century Egyptian scholar al-Suyūṭī, who abridged Ibn Taymiyya's attack on logic, was also an opponent of both *kalām* and logic. His treatise *Ṣawn al-manṭiq wa-l-kalām ʿan fannay al-manṭiq wa-l-kalām* argues for the prohibition of the study of logic by analogy with the prohibition of *kalām*. The greater part of the work is devoted to amassing statements by venerable early figures in the Sunnī Islamic tradition that condemn *kalām*, and then extrapolating from this that logic too is prohibited since the 'cause' of the prohibition of *kalām* is present in logic too—the common 'cause' being that both easily lead to the raising of doubts (*ithārat al-shubah*) and to creedal innovations (*bidaʿ*) (Suyūṭī, *Ṣawn*, 19–20). The Indian-born, Cairo-based scholar Muḥammad Murtaḍā al-Zabīdī (d. 1205/1791), in his monumental commentary on Ghazālī's *Iḥyāʾ ʿulūm al-dīn*, also attacked both logic and *kalām*. Like Ibn Ḥajar al-Haytamī, Zabīdī quoted Ghazālī's statement in *al-Munqidh* to the effect that 'nothing in logic is relevant to religion by way of denial and affirmation' but he derived a radically different conclusion from it. If logic is not relevant to religion, then there is no pious reason to study it and it becomes an instance of immersion in worldliness. He wrote:

> The faith that comes from the profession of the unity of God is not based on logical demonstration, contrary to what they [i.e. the logicians and theologians] suggest, but on knowledge bringing the one who possesses it to the truth of the matter. Its sign

[4] A modern editor of the commentary of Aḥmad al-Damanhūrī (d. 1778) on al-Akhḍarī's *Sullam* misidentifies a reference by Damanhūrī to 'al-Sanūsī' and takes it to refer to the King of Libya (r. 1951–69) despite the fact that Damanhūrī is an eighteenth-century scholar and is clearly referring to a logician—see Damanhūrī *Īḍāḥ*, 32 (n. 4). There is not a single reference to Sanūsī and his widely studied works on *kalām* in Halverson 2010 which deals among other things with what the author mistakenly assumes to have been the demise of *kalām* in Sunni Islam after Ghazālī.

> is the opening of the heart to the stations of faith, and acceptance of the decree of God, and turning to the recollection (*dhikr*) of Him, and loving Him while turning away from the world of vanity... He who is preoccupied with it [i.e. logic] is preoccupied with his outward aspect and visible conditions, to the detriment of the inward condition (*bāṭin ḥālihi*), and the reason for him being in this sorry state is his love of prominence and his desire for acclaim from people... and so he wastes his days for their days, and his life for their desires, just so he can be called a scholar. (Zabīdī, *Itḥāf*, 1: 181)

Zabīdī's point was aimed at theologians (especially the North African Ashʿarī tradition of Sanūsī) as well as logicians. When Ghazālī wrote in the *Iḥyā'* that *kalām* is a *farḍ kifāya*, Zabīdī (tendentiously) specified that this kind of *kalām* is dogmatics (*ʿilm al-ʿaqā'id*) based on Scriptural and transmitted reports (*barāhīn naqliyya*) and not the kind of *kalām* that sets up rational proofs (*al-adilla al-ʿaqliyya*) (Zabīdī, *Itḥāf*, 1: 185). Of course, the former type of '*kalām*' was usually not called *kalām* at all, as suggested by the reports that Zabīdī himself adduced in this context which condemn *kalām* as such.

The Indo-Muslim scholar (and Prince of Bhopal) Ṣiddīq Ḥasan Khān al-Qannawjī (d. 1308/1890) also rejected logic and *kalām*. In his encyclopedia of the sciences *Abjad al-ʿulūm*, he endorsed and referred the reader to Ibn al-Wazīr's attack on *kalām* and Ibn Taymiyya's attack on logic (the unique extant manuscript of the latter was owned by Qannawjī himself) (Qannawjī, *Abjad*, 441, 523). Qannawjī had considerable influence on the Arabic *Salafiyya* of the late nineteenth and early twentieth centuries, as well as the *Ahl-i ḥadīth* in South Asia (Bīṭār 1961–3: ii. 738–46; Khān 1998; Commins 1990: 24–5). The increased prominence of these movements in the twentieth century has led to a resurgence of interest in the writings of Ibn Taymiyya and an increased hostility to *kalām* and logic in Sunni Islamic circles. The fact that the hostility is to both disciplines is significant, however. After the thirteenth century, at least in the core areas of the Islamic world, proponents as well as opponents of *kalām* had apparently come to see it as intimately bound up with *manṭiq*. In this respect, the relationship between the two disciplines had changed dramatically since the attacks on Greek logic by the Muʿtazilī and Shīʿī theologians of the ninth and tenth centuries.

BIBLIOGRAPHY

al-ʿĀmilī, Zayn al-Dīn (*Munyat*). *Munyat al-murīd fī adab al-mufīd wa l-mustafīd*. Ed. Riḍā al-Mukhtārī. Beirut: Dār al-Amīra, 2006.

al-Bājūrī, Ibrāhīm (*Ḥāshiya*). *Ḥāshiya ʿalā matn al-Sanūsiyya*. Būlāq: Dār al-ṭibāʿa al-ʿāmira, 1283/1866.

al-Bāqillānī, Muḥammad b. al-Ṭayyib (*Tamhīd*). *Kitāb al-Tamhīd*. Ed. J. McCarthy. Beirut: Dar El-Machreq, 1957.

Beyāżīzāde, Aḥmed (*Ishārāt*). *Ishārāt al-marām min ʿibārāt al-Imām*. Ed. Yūsuf ʿAbd al-Razzāq. Cairo: Muṣṭafā al-Bābī al-Ḥalabī, 1949.

al-Bīṭār, ʿAbd al-Razzāq (1961–3). *Ḥilyat al-bashar fī tārīkh al-qarn al-thālith ʿashar*. Ed. Muḥammad Bahjat al-Bīṭār. Damascus: Maṭbaʿat majmaʿ al-lugha al-ʿarabiyya.

Brockelmann, C. (1937–49). *Geschichte der arabischen Literatur*. Leiden: Brill.

Commins, D. (1990). *Islamic Reform: Politics and Social Change in Late Ottoman Syria*. New York/Oxford: Oxford University Press.

al-Damanhūrī, Aḥmad (*Īḍāḥ*). *Īḍāḥ al-mubham fī maʿānī al-Sullam*. Ed. ʿUmar Fārūq al-Ṭabbāʿ. Beirut: Maktabat al-Maʿārif, 1996.

Elamrani-Jamal, A. (1983). *Logique aristotélicienne et grammaire arabes: études et documents*. Paris: J. Vrin.

Endress, G. (1986). 'Grammatik und Logik, arabische Philologie und griechische Philosophie in Widerstreit'. In B. Mojsisch (ed.), *Sprachphilosophie in Antike und Mittelalter*. Amsterdam: Verlag B. R. Grüner, 165–233.

Endress, G. (1996). 'Reading Avicenna in the Madrasa. Intellectual Genealogies and Chains of Transmission of Philosophy and the Sciences in the Islamic East'. In J. E. Montgomery (ed.), *Arabic theology, Arabic philosophy: from the many to the one: essays in celebration of Richard M. Frank*. Leuven: Peeters, 371–422.

van Ess, J. (1970). 'The Logical Structure of Islamic Theology'. In G. E. von Grunebaum (ed.), *Logic in Classical Islamic Culture*. Wiesbaden: Otto Harrassowitz, 21–50.

van Ess, J. (1976). 'Disputationspraxis in der islamischen theologie: Eine vorläufige Skizze'. *Revue des études islamique* 44: 23–60.

al-Fārābī, Abū Naṣr (*Qiyās*). *Kitāb al-qiyās*. In *al-Manṭiq ʿinda l-Fārābī*. Ed. Rafic al-ʿAjam. Beirut: Dār al-Mashriq, 1985, 2: 11–64.

Frank, R. M. (1989). 'Knowledge and Taqlīd: The Foundation of Religious Belief in Classical Ashʿarism'. *Journal of the American Oriental Society* 109: 37–62.

Fūda, Saʿīd (2002). *Tadʿīm al-manṭiq*. Amman: Dār al-Rāzī.

Gelenbevī, Ismāʿīl (*Burhān*). *al-Burhān fī ʿilm al-mīzān*. Cairo: Maṭbaʿat al-Saʿāda, 1347/1928–9.

Ghazālī, Abū Ḥāmid (*Miʿyār*). *Miʿyār al-ʿilm*. Ed. Ḥ. Sharāra. Beirut: Dar al-Andalus, 1964.

Ghazālī, Abū Ḥāmid (*Miḥakk*). *Miḥakk al-naẓar*. Ed. M. al-Naʿsānī and M. al-Qabbānī. Cairo: al-Maṭbaʿa al-Adabiyya, n.d.

Ghazālī, Abū Ḥāmid (*Mustaṣfā*). *al-Mustaṣfā fī ʿilm al-usūl*. Ed. Ḥamza Ḥāfiẓ. Medina: Ḥamza b. Zuhayr Ḥāfiẓ, 1413/1993–4.

Goichon, A.-M. (1963). *Avicenne: livre des definitions*. Cairo: Institut Français d'Archéologie Orientale.

Goldziher, Ignaz (1916/1981). 'The Attitude of Orthodox Islam toward the Ancient Sciences'. In M. L. Swartz (trans. and ed.), *Studies on Islam*. New York and Oxford: Oxford University Press, 185–215.

Hallaq, W. (1990). 'Logic, formal arguments and formalization of arguments in Sunni Jurisprudence', *Arabica* 87: 315–58.

Hallaq, W. (trans.) (1993). *Ibn Taymiyyah against the Greek Logicians*. Oxford: Clarendon Press.

Halverson, J. R. (2010). *Theology and Creed in Sunni Islam: The Muslim Brotherhood, Ashʿarism, and Political Sunnism*. New York: Palgrave Macmillan.

Heer, N. (1988). 'Ibn Taymiyah's Empiricism'. In F. Kazemi and R. D. McChesney (eds.), *A Way Prepared: Essays on Islamic Culture in Honor of Richard Bayly Winder*. New York/London: New York University Press, 109–15.

Ibn Fūrak (*Mujarrad*). *Mujarrad maqālāt al-Ashʿarī*. Ed. D. Gimaret. Beirut: Dar El-Machreq, 1987.

Ibn Ḥajar al-Haytamī (*Fatāwā*). *al-Fatāwā al-kubrā al-fiqhiyya*. Cairo: al-Maṭbaʿa al-Muyammaniyya, 1308/1891.

Ibn Hishām (*Qaṭr*). *Sharḥ Qaṭr al-nadā*. Ed. Emil Badīʿ Yaʿqūb. Beirut: Dār al-Kutub al-ʿIlmiyya, 2007.

Ibn al-Murtaḍā (*Ṭabaqāt*). *Ṭabaqāt al-Muʿtazila*. Ed. S. Diwald-Wilzer. Wiesbaden: Franz Steiner Verlag, 1961.

Ibn Sīnā (*Shifāʾ*). *al-Shifāʾ: al-Qiyās*. Ed. S. Zāyid and I. Madkour. Cairo: n.p., 1964.

Ibn Taymiyya (*Radd*). *al-Radd ʿalā l-manṭiqiyyīn*. Ed. ʿAbd al-Ṣamad al-Kutubī. 2nd edn. Lahore: Maṭbaʿat-i Maʿārif, 1976.

Ibn al-Wazīr (*Tarjīḥ*). *Tarjīḥ asālīb al-Qurʾān ʿalā asālīb al-yūnān*. Cairo: Maṭbaʿat al-Maʿāhid, 1349/1930–1.

ʿIllaysh, Muḥammad (*Hidāyat*). *Hidāyat al-murīd li-ʿAqīdat ahl al-tawḥīd*. Cairo: Maṭbaʿat Muḥammad Efendī Muṣṭafā, 1306/1888.

al-Jurjānī, al-Sayyid al-Sharīf (*Sharḥ*). *Sharḥ al-Mawāqif*. Istanbul: Maṭbaʿat al-Ḥājj Muḥarram al-Būsnawī, 1286/1869.

Khādimī, Ebū Saʿīd (*Barīqa*). *Barīqa maḥmūdiyya fī sharḥ al-Ṭarīqa al-muḥammadiyya*. Cairo: Muṣṭafā al-Bābī al-Ḥalabī, 1348/1929–30.

Khān, Ẓafarul-Islām (1998). 'Nawwāb Sayyid Ṣiddīḳ Ḥasan Khān'. *Encyclopaedia of Islam*, 2nd edn. Leiden: Brill, vii. 1048.

al-Khūnajī, Afḍal al-Dīn (*Kashf*). *Kashf al-asrār ʿan ghawāmiḍ al-afkār*. Ed. K. El-Rouayheb. Tehran and Berlin: Iranian Institute of Philosophy and Institute for Islamic Studies, 2010.

Klima, G. (2008). *John Buridan*. Oxford: Oxford University Press.

Lameer, J. (1994). *Al-Fārābī and Aristotelian Syllogistics: Greek Theory and Islamic Practice*. Leiden: Brill.

Lloyd, G. E. R. (1966). *Polarity and Analogy: Two Types of Argumentation in Early Greek Thought*. Cambridge: Cambridge University Press.

Mahdi, M. (1970). 'Language and Logic in Classical Islam'. In G. E. von Grunebaum (ed.), *Logic in Classical Islamic Culture*. Wiesbaden: Otto Harrassowitz, 51–83.

Maqdisī, Muṭahhar b. Ṭāhir (*Badʾ*). *Kitāb al-Badʾ wa l-tārīkh*. Ed. C. Huart. Paris: Ernest Leroux, 1899–1919.

Marmura, M. (1975). 'Ghazali's Attitude to the Secular Sciences and Logic'. In G. Hourani (ed.), *Essays in Islamic Philosophy and Science*, Albany: State University of New York Press, 100–11.

Marmura, M. (trans.) (1997). *Ghazālī: The Incoherence of the Philosophers*. Provo, UT: Brigham Young University Press.

Miller, L. (1984). 'Islamic Disputation Theory: A Study of the Development of Dialectic in Islam from the Tenth through the Fourteenth Centuries'. Unpublished Ph. D. Dissertation, Princeton University.

Mīr Abū l-Fatḥ (*Miftāḥ*). *Miftāḥ al-Bāb*. Ed. M. Mohaghegh. Tehran: Institute of Islamic Studies, 1986.

Montgomery Watt, W. (1953). *The Faith and Practice of Ghazali*. London: George Allen & Unwin.

al-Nashshār, ʿAlī Sāmī (1947). *Manāhij al-baḥth ʿinda mufakkirī al-Islām*. Cairo: Dār al-Fikr al-ʿArabī.

Nauta, L. (2009). 'Lorenzo Valla'. In E. N. Zalta (ed.), *Stanford Encyclopedia of Philosophy* (Summer 2009 edn.), <http://plato.stanford.edu/archives/sum2009/entries/lorenzo-valla/>.

al-Qannawjī, Ṣiddīq Ḥasan Khān (*Abjad*). *Abjad al-ʿulūm*. Lahore: al-Maktaba al-Quddūsiyya, 1983.

al-Rāzī, Fakhr al-Dīn (*Mulakhkhaṣ*). *Manṭiq al-Mulakhkhaṣ*. Ed. A. F. Karamaleki and A. Asgharinezhad. Tehran: ISU Press, 2003.

al-Rāzī, Fakhr al-Dīn (*Sharḥ*). *Sharḥ al-Ishārāt*. Ed. A. Najafzāde. Tehran: Anjuman-i Āṣār va Mafākhir-i Farhangī, 2005.

Rosenthal, F. (trans.) (1958). *The Muqaddimah of Ibn Khaldun*. New York: Pantheon Books.

El-Rouayheb, Kh. (2005). 'Sunni Islamic Scholars on the Status of Logic, 1500–1800', *Islamic Law and Society* 11: 213–32.

Rudolph, U. (2005). 'Die Neubewertung der Logik durch al-Ghazālī'. In D. Perler and U. Rudolph (eds.), *Logik und Theologie: Das Organon im arabischen und im lateinischen Mittelalter*. Leiden: Brill, 73–97.

al-Ṣabbān, Muḥammad b.ʿAlī (*Ḥāshiya*). *Ḥāshiya ʿalā Sharḥ al-Mallawī*. Cairo: Muṣṭafā al-Bābī al-Ḥalabī, 1938.

Sabra, A. I. (1980). 'Avicenna on the Subject Matter of Logic'. *Journal of Philosophy* 77: 746–64.

Sabra, A. I. (1987). 'The Appropriation and Subsequent Naturalization of Greek Science in Medieval Islam: A Preliminary Statement'. *History of Science*, 25: 223–43.

Sabra, A. I. (1994). 'Science and Philosophy in Medieval Islamic Theology: The Evidence of the Fourteenth Century'. *Zeitschrift für Geschichte der Arabisch-Islamischen Wissenschaften* 9: 1–42.

al-Samarqandī, Shams al-Dīn (*Qistās*). *Sharḥ Qisṭās al-afkār*. MS. Yale University Library (Beinecke), Arabic 11.

al-Sanūsī, Muḥammad b. Yūsuf (*Kubrā*). *Sharḥ al-ʿAqīda al-kubrā*. Beirut: Dār al-Kutub al-ʿIlmiyya, 2006.

al-Sanūsī, Muḥammad b. Yūsuf (*Ṣughrā*). *Sharḥ Umm al-barāhīn*. Cairo: Maṭbaʿat al-Istiqāma, 1934.

Schöck, C. (2006). *Koranexegese, Grammatik und Logik: zum Verhältnis von arabischer und aristotelischer Urteils-, Konsequenz- und Schlusslehre*. Leiden: Brill.

al-Shawkānī, Muḥammad (*Badr*). *al-Badr al-ṭāliʿ fī maḥāsin man baʿda al-qarn al-sābiʿ*. Cairo: Maṭbaʿat al-Saʿāda, 1348/1928–9.

al-Shīrāzī, Quṭb al-Dīn (*Sharḥ*). *Sharḥ Ḥikmat al-ishrāq*. Ed. A. Nourani and M. Mohaghegh. Tehran: Institute of Islamic Studies, 2002.

Spade, P. V. (ed.) (1999). *Cambridge Companion to Ockham*. Cambridge: Cambridge University Press.

Spevack, A. (2010). 'Apples and Oranges: The Logic of the Early and Later Arabic Logicians'. *Islamic Law and Society* 17: 159–84.

Street, T. (2004). 'Arabic Logic'. In D. Gabbay and J. Woods (eds.), *Handbook of the History of Logic, i: Greek, Indian and Arabic logic*. Amsterdam: Elsevier, 523–96.

Street, T. (2008). 'Arabic and Islamic Philosophy of Language and Logic'. In E. N. Zalta (ed.), *Stanford Encyclopedia of Philosophy* (Fall 2008 Edition), <http://plato.stanford.edu/archives/fall2008/entries/arabic-islamic-language/>.

al-Suyūṭī, Jalāl al-Dīn (*Ṣawn*). *Ṣawn al-manṭiq wa al-kalām ʿan fannay al-manṭiq wa l-kalām*. Ed. ʿAlī Sāmī al-Nashshār. Cairo: Maṭbaʿat al-Saʿāda, 1947.

al-Taftāzānī, Saʿd al-Dīn (*Sharḥ*). *Sharḥ al-Shamsiyya*. Lucknow: al-Maṭbaʿ al-Yūsufī, 1899.

al-Taḥtānī, Quṭb al-Dīn al-Rāzī (*Lawāmiʿ*). *Lawāmiʿ al-asrār bi-sharḥ Maṭāliʿ al-anwār*. Istanbul: Maṭbaʿa-yi ʿĀmire, 1861.

al-Taḥtānī, Quṭb al-Dīn al-Rāzī (*Taḥrīr*). *Taḥrīr al-qawāʿid al-manṭiqiyya bi-sharḥ al-Risāla al-Shamsiyya*. Istanbul: Ahmed Efendi Matbaası, 1907.
al-Tawḥīdī, Abū Ḥayyān (*Imtāʿ*). *al-Imtāʿ wa l-muʾānasa*. Ed. A. Amīn and A. al-Zayn. Cairo: Lajnat al-taʾlīf, 1939–44.
von Kügelgen, A. (2005). 'Ibn Taymīyas Kritik an der aristotelischen Logik und sein Gegenentwurf'. In D. Perler and U. Rudolph (eds.), *Logik und Theologie: Das Organon im arabischen und im lateinischen Mittelalter*. Leiden: Brill, 167–225.
Walbridge, J. (2005). 'Suhrawardi and Illuminationism'. In P. Adamson and R. C. Taylor (eds.), *The Cambridge Companion to Arabic Philosophy*. Cambridge: Cambridge University Press, 201–23.
Wisnovsky, R. (2004a). 'The Nature and Scope of Arabic Philosophical Commentary in Post-Classical (ca.1100–1900) Islamic Intellectual History: Some Preliminary Observations'. In P. Adamson, H. Balthussen, and M. W. F. Stone (eds.), *Philosophy, Science and Exegesis in Greek, Arabic and Latin Commentaries*. London: Institute of Advanced Studies, ii. 149–91.
Wisnovsky, R. (2004b). 'One Aspect of the Avicennian Turn in Sunnī Theology'. *Arabic Sciences and Philosophy* 14: 65–100.
al-Zabīdī, Muḥammad Murtaḍā (*Itḥāf*). *Itḥāf al-sāda al-muttaqīn bi-sharḥ Iḥyāʾ ʿulūm al-dīn*. Cairo: al-Maṭbaʿa al-muyammaniyya, 1311/1893–4.
Ziai, H., and J. Walbridge (eds. and trans.) (1999). *Suhrawardī: The Philosophy of Illumination*. Provo, UT: Brigham Young Press.

PART III

ISLAMIC THEOLOGY(IES) DURING THE LATER MIDDLE AND EARLY MODERN PERIOD

CHAPTER 25

THEOLOGY ENGAGES WITH AVICENNAN PHILOSOPHY

al-Ghazālī's Tahāfut al-falāsifa *and Ibn al-Malāḥimī's* Tuḥfat al-mutakallimīn fī l-radd ʿalā l-falāsifa

FRANK GRIFFEL

DURING the fifth/eleventh century, the philosophical system of Ibn Sīnā (Avicenna, d. 428/1037) became the most potent challenge to the various theological schools of Islam that had developed in the centuries earlier. Coping with the views of Ibn Sīnā and his followers was a long process that continued for many centuries. A significant part of theological literature in Islam in its post-classical period after the fifth/eleventh century was devoted to discussing the merits and the errors of the Avicennan system. Ibn Sīnā found defenders among Muslim theologians as well as critics. Learning the system of the 'philosophers' (*falāsifa*)—a word that became to mean Ibn Sīnā and his followers—was part of almost every advanced *madrasa* education up until the thirteenth/nineteenth century. What is more, right from the beginning of the discussion about Ibn Sīnā among Muslim theologians, we see that some of his teachings have a very significant influence even among those theologians who rejected his general direction of thought and who argued against it. Ibn Sīnā's explanation of prophecy, divination, and the quicker insight of some humans compared to others, for instance, were soon adapted by Muslim theologians. In this adapted and slightly changed form they had an enormous influence on how Muslims thought about prophecy and the superior insights of Sufi saints (*awliyāʾ*) or the Shīʿite Imams (Griffel 2010).

This chapter looks at a crucial stage in the early engagement of Muslim theologians with the Avicennan system that began with al-Ghazālī (b. *c.*447/1056, d. 505/1111). Recent studies have shown that the process of engaging with Avicennism and integrating it into Islamic theology had already begun before al-Ghazālī, arguably already during Ibn Sīnā's lifetime (Wisnovsky 2004). This earliest stage, however, is not well researched and as of yet it is still unclear how much Ibn Sīnā took from Muslim theologians—mostly

Muʿtazilites such as his contemporaries al-Qāḍī ʿAbd al-Jabbār (d. 415/1025) or Abū l-Ḥusayn al-Baṣrī (d. 436/1044)—and how much Muslim theologians before al-Ghazālī took from him. The latter were mostly Ashʿarites, such as al-Ghazālī's teacher al-Juwaynī (d. 478/1085), but also Twelver Shīʿite *mutakallimūn*, such as al-Sharīf al-Murtaḍā (d. 436/1044), who discussed Ibn Sīnā's arguments.

Al-Ghazālī was the first Muslim theologian we know of who explicitly engaged with the Avicennan system. It is clear that he studied the works of Ibn Sīnā early in his life, maybe under the direction of al-Juwaynī, and that they fascinated him right from the beginning. Modern scholars have suggested that there was a period in al-Ghazālī's early career, when he was himself a follower of Ibn Sīnā. If so, his seemingly neutral report of Ibn Sīnā's teachings, *Maqāṣid al-falāsifa*, may come from that period and was later adapted as an introduction for his students that would prepare them to fully understand al-Ghazālī's refutation of Ibn Sīnā (Janssens 2003). *The Maqāṣid* is an Arabic adaptation, thoroughly reworked at times, of one of Ibn Sīnā's Persian textbooks of logic, the natural sciences, and metaphysics, *Dānishnāma-yi ʿAlāʾī*. There is, however, no clear proof that al-Ghazālī went through such an Avicennan period early in his career. Neither his biographers nor his enemies mention it, although the latter complain that al-Ghazālī studied philosophy before he had fully mastered the religious sciences. It is also possible that al-Ghazālī composed *Maqāṣid* later in his life, after his refutation of philosophy because he realized that his students needed a more thorough preparation than what he had written before. The *Maqāṣid* became a very successful textbook in its own right, particularly in its Hebrew and Latin translations (al-Ghazālī, *Metaphysics, Logica*; Lohr 1965).

The earlier view that al-Ghazālī composed his *Maqāṣid* in the time period immediately before writing his refutation—a view that is based on his own comments in his autobiography—is now largely dismissed. Al-Ghazālī's autobiography *al-Munqidh min al-ḍalāl* is a highly apologetic work, written in 500/1106 or shortly after in response to attacks from both friends and foes. Here, al-Ghazālī tries to counter the impression that he is too deeply influenced by philosophical literature. His presentation that he studied philosophy for two years while teaching at the Niẓāmiyya *madrasa* in Baghdad 484/1091–488/1095, and that he needed a third year to write his refutation is not credible (al-Ghazālī, *Deliverance*, 61). It is much more likely that al-Ghazālī's occupation with Ibn Sīnā's philosophy began much earlier in his life and that he worked on his response for years and maybe even decades. His appointment to the prominent teaching position at the Niẓāmiyya in Baghdad may be one of the fruits of his studies of philosophy rather than the beginning of it (Griffel 2009: 30–6).

One of the manuscripts of al-Ghazālī's refutation of philosophy, *Tahāfut al-falāsifa*, mentions that the book was finished in Muḥarram 488/January 1095. At this point al-Ghazālī was a highly respected teacher at the Ashʿarite Niẓāmiyya *madrasa*. He was close both to the caliph's court in Baghdad and to that of the Seljuq Sultan in Isfahan. Apart from a few shorter books in legal theory, this was al-Ghazālī's first major work that he put on the bookmarket. Together with it he published a number of books on logic and epistemology (al-Ghazālī, *Miḥakk, Miʿyār*), first aimed as preparations for studying the

Tahāfut but also because al-Ghazālī wished to establish the study of philosophical logic at Muslim *madrasas*, a project that would prove to be successful. Soon after the *Tahāfut*, he published his second major book of refutation. This was directed against the Ismāʿīlī Shīʿites and had the long title *Faḍāʾiḥ al-bāṭiniyya wa-faḍāʾil al-Mustaẓhiriyya*. The two books pursue similar goals insofar as they both aim to establish in a legal argument that the philosophers as well as the Ismāʿīlites are clandestine apostates from Islam who can be killed if they publicly teach or propagate their positions. The *Faḍāʾiḥ* is also important since it is in this book that al-Ghazālī addresses the philosophers' teachings about the authority of revelation and the political function of prophecy (al-Ghazālī, *Faḍāʾiḥ*, 153f., partly trans. in al-Ghazālī, *Deliverance*, 228), a subject left untouched in his *Tahāfut*. Comparing these two books, however, reveals that the *Tahāfut* is a much more thorough work than the *Faḍāʾiḥ*, with far wider-ranging aims. The legal condemnation of the philosophers in that book takes only a single page and it appears almost as an afterthought to a highly philosophical engagement with the teachings of Ibn Sīnā.

I The Overall Strategy of the *Tahāfut al-Falāsifa*

Scholars have pointed out that the word 'Incoherence' is not an accurate translation of the Arabic *tahāfut* and does not reflect the gravity of the accusation levelled against the philosophers (Treiger 2011: 108–15). The Arabic term describes the philosophers' jumping to unwarranted and ill-founded conclusions that do not result from their arguments. 'Precipitance' might be a more accurate translation, in the sense that the book describes the over-hasty construction of a philosophical edifice that cannot last. Al-Ghazālī clearly thought of the *Tahāfut* as a refutation (*radd*). The overall goal of the book is to show that the *falāsifa*'s claim of being able to prove their teachings through demonstrative arguments is unfounded and no more than a delusion.

Al-Ghazālī begins his *Tahāfut* with a preface and with four different introductions. Here, he clarifies what prompted the writing of the book and what it wishes to accomplish. In the preface he describes his annoyance with a group of Muslims who think they are smarter and more intelligent than the rest and who therefore believe they are not bound to perform religious duties such as praying. These people claim that they follow the teachings of the ancient philosophers like Socrates, Hippocrates, Plato, Aristotle, and their likes, whom they regard of masters of all sciences. This group of Muslims says about these ancient philosophers that,

> concurrent with the sobriety of their intellect and the abundance of their merit is their denial of revealed laws and religious confessions and their rejection of the details of the religions and faiths, and they are convinced that the [religious] laws are composed [by humans] and that they are embellished tricks. (*Tahāfut*, 2)

This 'group' (*ṭā'ifa*), however, are not the philosophers themselves, as al-Ghazālī clarifies, or at least not their heads and leaders. Later on he will mention 'the *vulgus* of the philosophers' (*jamāhīruhum*) (*Tahāfut*, 12) and he seems to have these in mind here. The 'prominent and leading philosophers' are explicitly exempt from the accusation of neglecting the religious duties, the denial of revealed religion, or teaching that religions are embellished tricks (*Tahāfut*, 2). The group al-Ghazālī complains about at the very beginning of his *Tahāfut* creates a false philosophical tradition, based on the idea that the ancient philosophers were the masters of all sciences, and they follow teachings that were never popular among the prominent philosophers. The leaders among the *falāsifa* however, are not entirely innocent when some followers misinterpret their teachings. The leaders themselves created a myth, namely that their own teachings are proven through demonstrative arguments that render them indubitable. The *falāsifa* create the impression that they have a way to truth that is superior to all other groups and even superior to revelation.

Al-Ghazālī does not dispute the possibility of demonstrative arguments that prove their conclusions beyond any doubt. On the contrary, he endorses demonstration in his own writings on logic and he urges his peers in the religious sciences to accept this method. In an important passage in the second introduction that will be often quoted by later Muslim scientists, al-Ghazālī mocks religious scholars who dismiss the astronomers' explanation of a solar eclipse as an alignment of sun, moon, and earth. This explanation is demonstratively proven, and denying it creates more harm for religion than what its enemies could ever inflict (*Tahāfut*, 6).

Al-Ghazālī knew well that the demonstrative method is taught in books that take their teachings—and often also their titles—from Aristotle's logical works, most importantly his *Posterior Analytics*. There, demonstration is described as the combination between (1) correct forms of arguments and (2) indubitable premisses that are either self-evident or that have themselves been proven in earlier demonstrations. The fourteen correct forms of arguments, the syllogisms, are again described in the philosophers' books that present the teachings of Aristotle's *Prior Analytics*. Finally, how to form correct definitions and premisses is clarified in books that are equivalent to Aristotle's *Categories* and the *Isagoge*. Al-Ghazālī accepted this so-called 'toolbox' (Greek *organon*) of reasoning and he adopted the demonstrative method for his own. He also accepted that it yields indubitable results in mathematics, geometry (like explaining a solar eclipse), and the natural sciences. When it comes to metaphysics (*ilāhiyyāt*), however, al-Ghazālī concluded that many teachings of the philosophers could not be proven demonstratively. Metaphysics is the philosophical discipline most closely aligned with theology. It deals with ontology, asking how the world is structured and what are its most basic constituents, with cosmology, looking into how the basic constituents relate to one another, and finally it deals with God, His attributes, and how He relates to His creation.

In the fourth introduction of his *Tahāfut* al-Ghazālī explains the overall goal of this book. He addresses the *falāsifa*'s claim that all or most of their teachings are supported by demonstrations and responds:

> We will make it plain that in their metaphysical sciences they have not been able to fulfil the claims laid out in the different parts of the logic and in the introduction to it, i.e. what they have set down in the *Posterior Analytics* on the conditions for the truth of the premise of a syllogism, and what they have set down in the *Prior Analytics* on the conditions of its figures, and the various things they posited in the *Isagoge* and the *Categories*. (*Tahāfut*, 9)

Philosophical metaphysics, according to al-Ghazālī, is not based on demonstrative arguments. Rather, the arguments the philosophers claim as demonstrative are faulty and do not fulfil the conditions for demonstration set out in their own books of logic. The problem lies in their premisses. These are, despite the *falāsifa*'s claims, not indubitable. They neglect to critically examine the foundations of their own thinking but accept them on the authority of their teachers and their leaders. All this amounts for al-Ghazālī to a quasi-religious attitude. The leading philosophers ask their students and followers to agree on the premisses they postulate without, in fact, being able to prove them. A science that uses formally correct arguments and employs premisses that are unproven but agreed upon by everybody who shares in that science is, according to Aristotle, not demonstrative but merely dialectical. The religious sciences, for instance, are all dialectical since they are based on premisses taken from revelation. The point al-Ghazālī makes in the above passage is that philosophical metaphysics is not superior to religious theology. Both are dialectical sciences, based on premisses that its practitioners have agreed upon. But while the philosophers' agreement is a case of blind emulation (*taqlīd*) of what has been passed down from generation to generation of philosophers, the basis of theology is divine revelation.

Showing that the *falāsifa*'s arguments in metaphysics are not demonstrative serves a number of purposes for al-Ghazālī. First, it destroys the conviction of the 'vulgar' followers of the philosophical movement that the philosophers were masters of all sciences and more intelligent than anybody else. Rather, their arguments are far from perfect and quite often wrong. Secondly, it destroys the conviction of those who follow the 'prominent and leading philosophers' that their metaphysics is superior to theology and can replace it. Rather, while the former is based on mere *taqlīd* of bygone authorities (Aristotle etc.), the latter is based on divine revelation. Thirdly, and this is not fully mentioned in the introductions but only later on in his *Tahāfut*, al-Ghazālī also wants to show that many teachings of the *falāsifa*'s that are correct are not based on demonstrative inquires but taken from earlier revelations, such as those of Moses or Jesus, or from the inspirational insight of the *awliyāʾ*, 'friends of God' or saints who already existed in the religions before Islam. This third goal is most clearly expressed in a passage from the 15th discussion of the *Tahāfut*. That discussion addresses the *falāsifa*'s teachings of the celestial souls and why they move the spheres of the heavens. Al-Ghazālī disagreed with the rational explanation of the heavenly movements only on minor points, limited to *why* things are the way they are. He does, however, object that the arrangement of the heavens is a subject where rational insight is limited. Humans know what they know about the celestial movements not from observation or mathematical calculation but from another source:

> The secrets of the heavenly kingdom are not known with the likes of these imaginings. God makes them known only to his prophets and saints by way of inspiration (*ilhām*), not by way of inferential proof. (*Tahāfut*, 152)

This point is supported elsewhere in al-Ghazālī's oeuvre, such as in his autobiography, where he draws on an older argument that other Muslim theologians such as the Ismāʿīlī Abū Ḥātim al-Rāzī (d. *c*.933) had applied against *falsafa* (al-Ghazālī, *Deliverance*, 85). How can the knowledge in astronomy be drawn from observation and calculation given that some celestial events are so rare that they occur only once in a thousand years? The mathematical pattern between such rare events can only be deduced with the help of divine inspiration. The same applies to medicine. How can experience lead to an understanding of how drugs work, given that many kill the patient if applied before humans have medical expertise. Medical knowledge comes to humans through divine inspiration not through experiments or logical deductions.

The third goal explains why al-Ghazālī 'refutes' some teachings in his *Tahāfut* that he later applied in his own works. He addresses, for instance, the philosophers' explanation of the movement of stars through spheres (15th discussion) or Ibn Sīnā's view that the celestial souls have knowledge of the future that some humans might be able to connect to (16th discussion). In some of his later works, al-Ghazālī adopts both these teachings as his own. In the *Tahāfut*, the dispute is not about the truth of these teachings but whether the philosophers are able to prove them demonstratively. Unproven teachings can still be true. Al-Ghazālī aims at forcing the philosophers to admit that these teachings cannot be deduced in philosophy but are taken from revelation or the insights of saints. He says in the 16th discussion, 'the only way for this to be known would be from revelation (*al-sharʿ*) not from reason (*al-ʿaql*)' (*Tahāfut*, 157). The rational justification in *falsafa* is a mere construction that happened after they were adopted and it does not withstand a critical investigation of the kind al-Ghazālī undertakes in his *Tahāfut*.

The fact that al-Ghazālī criticizes teachings he later adopts has led to much confusion among some of his readers. *Falāsifa* such as Ibn Rushd (Averroes, d. 595/1198) accused him of being inconsistent. Some modern scholars think that al-Ghazālī fielded a 'pseudo-refutation' (Treiger 2011: 93). A close reading of the *Tahāfut*, however, reveals that al-Ghazālī is very careful in his language and nowhere takes a position that is inconsistent with those of his later works that are unanimously believed to express his opinion. It is true that in the *Tahāfut* he is often polemical and sometimes unfair. There is, however, consistency among the works unanimously ascribed to him even if he shouted out his criticism of the philosophers and whispered when he thought they were correct.

If we follow the headings of the twenty discussions in the *Tahāfut*, then there are eight where al-Ghazālī sets out to show that the teachings discussed in that chapter are not supported by valid demonstrations and where he leaves open whether they are true or not (nos. 4, 5, 9, 11, 12, 14, 18, 19). In the remaining twelve discussions, he sets out to show that the philosophical teachings are unproven *and* wrong. Often, however, they could be easily mended if one gives up wrong premisses such as the pre-eternity of the world. In some cases he accuses them of deceptively misrepresenting (*talbīs*) their teachings in ways that make them look Islamic. In three cases (nos. 1, 13, and 20) the error of the *falāsifa* is so grave as to warrant accusations of unbelief (see Sections II and III).

Even in those discussions where he aims at refuting the truth of the philosophers' teachings, he often does not argue in favour of the position he thinks is true. 'I do not enter into objecting them except as one who demands and denies, not as one who claims and affirms', he writes in the third introduction of his book (*Tahāfut*, 7). Behind this strategy lies al-Ghazālī's conviction of the truth of revelation. This becomes manifest in his 'rule of interpretation' that he will explain in some of his later works but that also underlies the *Tahāfut* (Griffel 2009: 112–22). According to that rule, statements in the apparent meaning (*ẓāhir*) of revelation can only become subject to allegorical interpretation (*taʾwīl*) and be given an inner meaning if they are contradicted by demonstrative arguments. Without such a firm proof the authority of revelation cannot be challenged and opinions opposed to it are considered defeated. Whenever he argues that the *falāsifa* are wrong, al-Ghazālī assumes that revelation teaches something different. Were they able to prove these views demonstratively, al-Ghazālī would be willing to reconsider his opinion about the teachings of revelation. Failing that, however, the truth of the outward sense of revelation stands against the claims of the *falāsifa*, and since the latter cannot substantiate them, revelation prevails. Much of the *Incoherence* is devoted to the task of making room for the epistemological claims of revelation.

Al-Ghazālī made his refutation of philosophy easy for himself. Showing that their arguments are not demonstrative refutes the hubris and dismissive religious attitude of some followers of *falsafa* and also their view that philosophy is independent from revelation. He does not need to prove where and why these teachings are *false*. In fact, they do not need to be false but only unproven. Even in those cases where al-Ghazālī sets out to refute the truth of some of the philosophers' teachings, he does not need to show they are false. He only needs to show they are unproven and contradict the outward wording (*ẓāhir*) of revelation. The way he sets out his book, most of his goals are fulfilled once al-Ghazālī has proven that the arguments he criticizes are not demonstrative. They may even be persuasive, but as long as they do not reach the high standard of demonstration, they do not, in his opinion, establish the authority of *falsafa*. The twenty discussions of this book are, therefore, often very technical disputes about the logical status of certain explanations and proofs. Their function can only be determined once the overall goal of the book as a refutation, first of the truth of certain teachings, second of claims of originality and the provenance of some teachings, and third of the exuberant self-confidence and attitude of some people, is kept in mind.

II The Three Discussions on the World's Eternity in the *Tahāfut*

Although al-Ghazālī tries to give his readers the impression that he does not want to argue *for* any position in this book but merely destroy convictions held among his doctrinal enemies, the book overall does argue in favour of a theological position. This happens most forcefully in the first three discussions on the world's eternity. Ibn Sīnā and many philosophers before him had argued that the world has no beginning in time and will never end. Still, they maintained that the world has a Creator who is the ultimate cause of every event in this world. Philosophers like Ibn Sīnā thought of God not as someone who would create the world at one point in time out of nothing, but as the 'essential cause' of the world. An essential cause is an efficient cause of a thing or event that is sufficient to bring about its existence or occurrence. Imagine a dark room with a fireplace and no other light source. Light exists in that room if and only if there is fire in the fireplace. The fire is the essential cause of light in that room; any time there is fire there is light and vice versa. The two are temporally coextensive although one is the cause of the other. Light follows with necessity from fire. This is the relationship between God and the world. The world exists as long as God exists and God cannot exist alone without the world just as there is no fire in that room without light. God, for Ibn Sīnā, does not have a temporal priority over this world but an ontological one. He does not exist 'before' the world but He exists 'prior' in terms of rank of being, since He causes all that is other than Him. The existence of the world follows necessarily out of God's existence.

It is this idea of God as a mere cause (*ʿilla*) of the world that triggered al-Ghazālī's opposition. The problem can be highlighted using the example of the light from the fireplace. It is in the nature of fire to emit light and we cannot conceive of a fire that does not emit light. The fire has no choice but to emit light. Similarly, according to al-Ghazālī, it is in the nature of Ibn Sīnā's God to create the world. Such a God exercises no choice about whether to create or not. In fact, Ibn Sīnā's God never exercises any free choice (*ikhtiyār*), or, in the language of al-Ghazālī, there is no delay (*intiẓār*) of God's action from His essence. God becomes a creation-automaton who turns His knowledge, which may be regarded as the blueprint of creation, into the world that we live in.

None of this, however, is clearly expressed by al-Ghazālī in his *Tahāfut*. Like many works from this period, the *Tahāfut* is a book intended to be studied with a qualified teacher, who might explain these connections. From al-Ghazālī's other works, however, and also from the understanding of later scholars in his tradition, it becomes clear that this is the issue addressed in the discussion on the world's eternity. The issue also comes up in other discussions and it is clear that this is the most important objection of al-Ghazālī against the teachings of the *falāsifa*. For him, they teach a completely impersonal understanding of God that reduces Him to a mere automated cause that has no real will or knowledge, a God to whom very few people can relate as the omnipotent and omniscient master of existence.

The first three discussions on the world's eternity make up almost a third of the *Tahāfut*. Here, the character of the book as a refutation is most evident. Al-Ghazālī brings forward a great number of objections against the view that the world is or even could be eternal. The first discussion, the longest of the three, is devoted to refuting the teaching that the world is pre-eternal, i.e. that it exists from eternity in the past. Although he never reveals his sources, al-Ghazālī brings a number of arguments that we are familiar with from John Philoponus's refutation of Aristotle's and Proclus's works on the world's pre-eternity (Davidson 1987: 86–127). John Philoponus (in Arabic: Yaḥyā al-Naḥwī) was a Christian philosopher of the sixth century, who was active in Alexandria and who wrote in Greek.

In the course of the discussion, a disagreement about the nature of the modalities becomes most important. The modalities are 'necessary', 'possible', and 'impossible'. Ibn Sīnā treats the modalities as attributes of things or events. Something *is* possible for Ibn Sīnā, or it *is* necessary. The world as a whole is, for Ibn Sīnā, possible with regard to itself and necessary with regard to God, meaning it follows necessarily from God's existence. In his basic understanding of the modalities Ibn Sīnā followed Aristotle and went so far as to require a substratum (*maḥall*) for possibility and for necessity. All necessity resides in God, Ibn Sīnā teaches, who is the 'being necessary by virtue of itself' (*wājib al-wujūb bi-dhātihi*). The substratum of possibility was found in the unformed prime-matter (*hylē*) that underlies all physical creations. Since the world has always been possible, so one of Ibn Sīnā's arguments goes, the substratum of this possibility, namely prime-matter, exists from eternity in the past.

Al-Ghazālī's response to this is radical in that he objects to the whole Aristotelian understanding of the modalities. Al-Ghazālī maintains that 'possible' is not an attribute of a thing but a mere judgement of the mind:

> Anything whose existence the mind supposes, [nothing] preventing its supposing it possible, we call 'possible,' and if it is prevented we call it 'impossible.' If [the mind] is unable to suppose its nonexistence, we name it 'necessary.' For these are rational propositions that do not require an existent so as to be rendered a description thereof. (*Tahāfut*, 42)

Al-Ghazālī confronts the Aristotelian 'statistical' understanding of the modalities that have thus far reigned supreme among Aristotelian philosophers with the understanding of the modalities as developed in *kalām* literature. There, 'possible' has been understood as a synchronic alternative, i.e. something is possible if we can mentally conceive it as an alternative to what exists in actuality or what will exist. We call something impossible if we cannot mentally conceive of it as an alternative. In his *Tahāfut*, al-Ghazālī posits 'alternative worlds' to the one that exists (Kukkonen 2000). This is a powerful argumentative device and it is applied throughout the book. If we can conceive of the world as being created at one moment in time—or sooner or later than that moment—then an omnipotent God must have the ability to actualize these possibilities. This is quite plausible for us; for reasons that we cannot get into here, however, it is hard to swallow or even to comprehend for someone trained in an Aristotelian understanding of the modalities. In the history of philosophy, al-Ghazālī's *Tahāfut* was an important step in moving away from that understanding toward the modern view of possibility as a synchronic alternative.

The *falāsifa* not only argued that the world is pre-eternal, they also claimed they can prove this demonstratively, setting all doubts to rest. If al-Ghazālī is able to convince his readers that the world *can* be created in time, he has already achieved what he set out to do, namely to show that there is something wrong with the philosophers' assumed demonstrations. In this particular case, however, he goes further and provides arguments that the world is, in fact, created in time. His main argument is that every action (*fiʿl*) must have a temporary beginning, which is again an argument developed in *kalām* literature from philosophical predecessors, such as John Philoponus. In the long discussions on the eternity of the world, al-Ghazālī aims at showing philosophically—meaning without recourse to the authority of revelation—that the world must be created in time.

III Bodily Resurrection and God's Knowledge of Particulars

Elsewhere in his *Tahāfut*, al-Ghazālī is quite content to rely on the authority of revelation. In the 20th discussion, for instance, he tries to show that there can be a creation of bodies in the afterlife. His philosophical argument is again based on mental conceivability. We can conceive of an afterlife where the souls of humans exist entirely without bodies. This is the position al-Ghazālī ascribes to the philosophers and it is possible. We can also conceive, as an alternative to this, that at one time during the long afterlife, a body—any kind of body—will be created for every soul (*Tahāfut*, 219). The fact that we can conceive of such a process means it is possible. The Qurʾānic descriptions of bodily pleasures and pains that we experience after our deaths are therefore not impossible. Here, al-Ghazālī tries to force the philosophers to acknowledge the authority and the truth of revelation.

Al-Ghazālī confronts the Aristotelian tradition with a nominalist or at least conceptualist understanding of the modalities, and this is an important event in the history of Muslim theology and of philosophy as such. Equally important was his novel understanding of knowledge—novel at least for the Aristotelian tradition—introduced in the 13th discussion. Ibn Sīnā had argued that God is characterized by total unity and therefore cannot change from one state to the next. This implies that God's knowledge only contains eternal truths, which were understood to be 'universals' (*kulliyāt*). These are genera, species, or eternal concepts, such as 'humanity' or 'horseness'. Ibn Sīnā's God knows 'particulars' (*juzʾiyyāt*), i.e. individual objects and their attributes, only 'in a universal way'. What that meant was difficult to understand, but for al-Ghazālī it entails—not entirely unjustified—the denial of God's knowledge of individuals. For Ibn Sīnā, God cannot know individuals as individuals because if He did, His knowledge would change with each change that occurs in them, whereas change in God is impossible. Al-Ghazālī rejects this vigorously, pointing out that nobody will obey God's law if they think He does not know them and does not know their transgressions (*Tahāfut*, 136). In his philosophical response, he does not reject Ibn Sīnā's premiss that God does not change. His own strict monotheism prevented Him from introducing a God whose knowledge changes. Rather, he reinterpreted the relationship between the knower and the thing known, again drawing on ideas and solutions that were developed earlier in *kalām* literature. He denies the Aristotelian understanding that 'knowledge follows the object of knowledge'. He replaces the identity of knower and object of knowledge with the concept of knowledge as a 'relation' (*iḍāfa*) between the two. Knowledge of an object is like the relation of a stationary observer to a moving object. While the object's position relative to the knower changes, the knower does not change (*Tahāfut*, 138).

IV The Legal Condemnation of Three of the Philosophers' Teachings

Al-Ghazālī believed that some teachings of the *falāsifa* make people disregard the religious law (*sharīʿa*). Writing the book was triggered by the observation that some followers of the *falāsifa* rejected performing the religious rites because they deemed their ideas and their ethics above religion. The leading philosophers, said al-Ghazālī, are innocent of this. He acknowledges that they see themselves as Muslims, yet even they may have fallen into unbelief. On the last page of his *Tahāfut*, al-Ghazālī answers a legal question by way of a *fatwā*. Are any of the twenty teachings discussed in this book unbelief (*kufr*) punishable by death? Al-Ghazālī's legal concept behind this accusation is that whenever Muslims hold unbelief, they have implicitly rejected Islam and have become clandestine apostates, no matter whether they realize that or not. For al-Ghazālī the unbelief of a Muslim equals apostasy from Islam, a point that other jurists saw quite differently (Griffel 2001). He thus employs the judgement of apostasy to persecute opinions he thought could not be tolerated.

On the last page of the *Tahāfut* he singles out three such opinions: that the world is pre-eternal, that God does not know particulars, and that there is no resurrection of bodies in the afterlife. The latter two directly concern people's observance of the religious law. People will not fear the punishment of God in the afterlife if they think He does not know them or these punishments are mere metaphors and only apply to the souls and not the bodies. Making people observe the religious law is a very important motivation in al-Ghazālī's oeuvre. It is not entirely clear, however, why he also included the first point about the world's pre-eternity. The Muslim revelation nowhere explicitly teaches creation out of nothing and al-Ghazālī was most probably aware of that. In later repetitions of his condemnation this point is sometimes left out (al-Ghazālī, *Deliverance*, 138). Wherever he mentions it he stresses that all Muslims agree on the world's creation in time and he may have regarded its denial as too grave a challenge to Islam and the consensus of its scholars. All the other positions of the philosophers, including the view of God as an involuntary actor, are indeed tolerated. In the *Tahāfut* al-Ghazālī says these may be *bidʿa*, i.e. inappropriate innovations, but not cases to apply the law of apostasy. Elsewhere he says more explicitly that they should be tolerated and not harmed (al-Ghazālī, *Deliverance*, 137, 143–9).

Al-Ghazālī's *Tahāfut* is a very important work not only for the history of Islamic theology but for the tradition of Greek and Western philosophy overall. It confronts Aristotelianism with potent challenges to its self-understanding of grounding the philosophical sciences on demonstrative proofs. Many of the argumentative objections brought forward in that book come from *kalām*, and for Aristotelians such as Ibn Rushd or Maimonides (d. 601/1204, who never mentions the book but was aware of it) the *Tahāfut* remained a work of *kalām* literature. One would need to step out of Aristotelianism to fully appreciate its value. Ibn Rushd did not do that and his own refutation of al-Ghazālī's book, the *Tahāfut al-tahāfut*, remains an often limited engagement with the latter's arguments and had little influence.

For the discourse of philosophy (*falsafa*) in the Islamic East, the *Tahāfut* was a watershed. Before it *mutakallimūn* did not need to engage with *falsafa*. Some did, of course, but never as deeply as after the *Tahāfut*. Now, *mutakallimūn* and *falāsifa* openly discussed the faults and merits of arguments current in the other tradition. The *Tahāfut* brings these two discourses together. It clearly identifies the three teachings that the jurist al-Ghazālī condemned and the larger number that the theologian al-Ghazālī objected to. In doing so, it opened the way for integrating into *kalām* those philosophical positions that are not criticized.

Hardly any Islamic philosopher after al-Ghazālī mentions the book. From the mid-twelfth century on, however, all philosophers and all *mutakallimūn* show familiarity with its accusations of *taqlīd* and *talbīs* against Ibn Sīnā and his followers. They also know and react to the main points al-Ghazālī makes within the twenty discussions. One can say without exaggeration that much of what will be written in Islamic philosophy and theology between the twelfth and sixteenth centuries is a response to Ibn Sīnā's philosophical system and to al-Ghazālī's *Tahāfut*.

V Ibn al-Malāhimī and his *Tuḥfat al-mutakallimīn*

Whereas al-Ghazālī's refutation of philosophy had a prominent career right from the day it was published, the second major work of this category in Islam was unknown to most scholars until it was rediscovered recently in a unique manuscript in a library in Mashhad (Anṣārī 2001). Its author is Rukn al-Dīn Maḥmūd Ibn al-Malāḥimī, an important Muʿtazilite theologian who was active during the first half of the sixth/twelfth century in Khwarezm, the delta region where the Amu Darya (Oxus) flows into the Aral Sea, in today's Uzbekistan. Ibn al-Malāḥimī died there in 536/1141.

Khwarezm was an important centre of scholarship during the sixth/twelfth century and it was one of the few regions where Muʿtazilism was still active and alive even after it had disappeared elsewhere in the Islamic world. Together with his contemporary and colleague al-Zamakhsharī (d. 538/1144), who wrote an influential Qurʾān commentary, Ibn al-Malāḥimī was the most important Muʿtazilite thinker in the centuries after its golden period had ended. He presents himself as the torchbearer of Abū l-Ḥusayn al-Baṣrī's (d. 436/1045) theology, and he may have studied with his students or students of his students. Abū l-Ḥusayn al-Basrī was active in Baghdad and had studied theology with the Qāḍī ʿAbd al-Jabbār (d. 415/1025). A practising physician, Abū l-Ḥusayn came into contact with Greek learning. He also studied philosophy, which may well have triggered the important innovations in his thought (Madelung 2006). Many of his arguments were directed against teachings of the school of Abū Hāshim al-Jubbāʾī (d. 321/933), the so-called Bahshamiyya, of whom ʿAbd al-Jabbār was the leading proponent during Abū l-Ḥusayn al-Baṣrī's lifetime.

Next to the school founder, Ibn al-Malāḥimī became the most important representative of Abū l-Ḥusayn al-Baṣrī's Muʿtazilite theology. Ibn al-Malāḥimī wrote two important compendia of *kalām*, the very extensive and comprehensive *al-Muʿtamad fī uṣūl al-din*, and the shorter *al-Fāʾiq fī uṣūl al-dīn*, which was conceived as an abridgement of the former. Only the first quarter of the long work has come down to us (Ibn al-Malāḥimī, *Muʿtamad*). The shorter work, however, which was completed in 532/1137, is fully available (Ibn al-Malāḥimī, *Fāʾiq*). These two works were fairly widespread and major theologians such as Fakhr al-Dīn al-Rāzī (d. 606/1210) used them. Ibn al-Malāḥimī's third work of importance is *Tuḥfat al-mutakallimīn fī l-radd ʿalā l-falāsifa*, which is intended as an invalidation (*radd*) of Aristotelian, or more specifically Avicennan philosophy. The *Tuḥfa* depends heavily on the *Muʿtamad*, particularly on the section dealing with the teachings of the philosophers (Ibn al-Malāḥimī, *Muʿtamad*, 683–798). It mentions both earlier works of the author (*Tuḥfa*, 178, 185), so it was written between 532/1137 and the author's death in 536/1141.

In contrast to al-Ghazālī's book, which follows a complex strategy to refute *falsafa* of which some might say that it never does so directly, Ibn al-Malāḥimī addresses *falsafa* in a much more straightforward way. He engages in an open confrontation with the teachings of Ibn Sīnā, aiming to show where they are wrong and why (Madelung 2007: 333–5). Whereas in al-Ghazālī the main doctrinal dispute with Ibn Sīnā is about the philosophers' understanding of God as a cause of the world that does not exercise free choice, Ibn al-Malāḥimī has much more to complain about. Comparing these two books illustrates the great amount of agreement that existed between Aristotelian philosophical theories in Islam and Ashʿarite theology. It also shows how complex al-Ghazālī's strategy is and how much more confrontational many other Muslim theologians were.

In the introduction of the *Tuḥfa*, Ibn al-Malāḥimī explains what prompted his interest in writing this book. At the beginning he complains that many of his contemporaries who consider themselves experts of Islamic law (*mutafaqqiha*) began to study the works of the Muslim philosophers. Ibn al-Malāḥimī particularly singles out the Shāfiʿite school of law—al-Ghazālī's school—but sees this tendency also getting hold among the Ḥanafites, his own school of law. He sees Islam in the same position as Christianity in the first centuries of its history. According to a view widespread among Muslims, Christian theologians who had studied Greek philosophy distorted Jesus's original message:

> I have become afraid that our community might relate to Islam like the Christians relate to the [original] religion of Jesus, peace be upon him. The leaders of the Christians sympathized so much with the learning of the Greeks in philosophy that they ended up leaving the religion of Jesus… on the path of the philosophers and proposed such things as the three hypostases, the union [of Jesus with God], Jesus becoming a god after he had been human, and other such nonsense. (*Tuḥfa*, 3)

The Muslim philosophers such as al-Fārābī and Ibn Sīnā, so Ibn al-Malāḥimī says, did indeed 'leave the religion of Islam' (*kharajū dīn al-Islām*) by following the ways of the ancient philosophers (*Tuḥfa*, 3). Like al-Ghazālī, Ibn al-Malāḥimī complains about the hubris of the philosophers and their conviction that philosophy is superior to all other studies. He mocks the claim that philosophy makes people overcome their religious divisions as it makes them appreciate all religious traditions equally. Philosophy, according to Ibn al-Malāḥimī, makes people misunderstand their religious differences (*Tuḥfa*, 14). Similar to al-Ghazālī, Ibn al-Malāḥimī regards the philosophers mainly as people who lead others astray. The Muslim philosophers present their teachings as the true Islam and because many of them work in jurisprudence (*fiqh*) they are more dangerous than even the propagandists of the Ismāʿīlites. They give the impression that what they teach would bring people closer to Islam. The opposite, however, is true and they are enemies of the prophets. Their message has nothing at all in common with that of the prophets and it seems that the latter were only sent to defeat the influence of people like the philosophers, who have always led others into error (*Tuḥfa*, 8).

VI Ibn al-Malāḥimī and al-Ghazālī

Ibn al-Malāḥimī wrote more than four decades after al-Ghazālī's *Tahāfut* came out, and we can assume that he was familiar with the book. Unlike al-Ghazālī in his *Tahāfut*, Ibn al-Malāḥimī identifies many philosophers by name, Ibn Sīnā and Aristotle first of all, but also minor philosophers and even contemporaries of him such as Abū l-Barakāt al-Baghdādī (*Tuḥfa*, 14). He also mentions book titles and quotes from philosophical works, allowing us a view into what was known and used at this point. Given all this, it is astonishing that he mentions neither al-Ghazālī nor any of his works. Al-Ghazālī, however, was such an important figure at his time and he lived so close to Ibn al-Malāḥimī's centre of activity that everybody interested in philosophy and in religion would have known him.

It is certain that Ibn al-Malāḥimī knew al-Ghazālī's *Maqāṣid al-falāsifa* or—and this is less likely—a maybe anonymous adaptation of that work that would be unknown to us today. This adaptation would still be different from the one that we already know from this period, namely the so-called *Major Maḍnūn*, which has recently been published (Pourjavady 2002: 1–62). A study of this latter adaptation claims the text was written by al-Ghazālī himself and that it represents those elements from the teachings of the *falāsifa* that he was ready to accept (al-Akiti 2009). Some severe problems, however, remain, like when the author of the text claims that God, 'knows the individual things in a universal way (*bi-naw*^{ʿin} *kulliyy*^{in})' (Pourjavady 2002: 14). This is an utterly un-Ghazalian position. In any case, Ibn al-Malāḥimī did not use this *Major Maḍnūn*, but most likely the *Maqāṣid al-falāsifa* in a form that is identical or at least very similar to how we know it today. He made highly eclectic use of that book, sometimes quoting it verbatim, sometimes distilling longer passages from it into a few sentences, and sometimes even restructuring it. The *Maqāṣid al-falāsifa* is one of his most important sources for the teachings of Ibn Sīnā and his followers. In his refutation of their teachings on God's essence, God's attributes, and God's actions, Ibn al-Malāḥimī applies the basic divisions in al-Ghazālī's *Maqāṣid* and quotes it frequently.

We do not know whether Ibn al-Malāḥimī was aware that al-Ghazālī's *Maqāṣid* was meant to be a neutral report of Ibn Sīnā's teachings in logic, metaphysics, and the natural sciences. The book itself still poses many riddles. Once the short introduction and an even shorter afterword are taken off, it may well have passed as a work written by a follower of Ibn Sīnā. We know Arabic manuscripts without these sections (Shihadeh 2010). Quite often the book speaks in the third person plural ('we hold... for instance') when it presents convictions and arguments of the Avicennists. It is highly likely that Ibn al-Malāḥimī took al-Ghazālī to be one of them. His refutation targets philosophers within the ranks of the Ḥanafites and particularly the Shāfiʿites, and the latter may well be a reference to al-Ghazālī and his students and followers.

Ibn al-Malāḥimī explicitly claims to be the first *mutakallim* who ever wrote a refutation of philosophy (*Tuḥfa*, 4), a claim al-Ghazālī also had made four decades earlier. Both will have done some bibliographical research. If Ibn al-Malāḥimi knew al-Ghazālī's book, which is likely, he might not have been much impressed by its strategy and probably did not accept it as a proper refutation. There is a passage in the *Tuḥfa* which indicates that even if he knew al-Ghazālī's *Tahāfut* he was not very familiar with its content. In that passage, Ibn al-Malāḥimī talks about 'one of the philosophers', who is different from the rest insofar as he at least engages in identifying those actions that lead to reward in the afterlife and those that lead to punishment (*Tuḥfa*, 185f.). This may well be a reference to al-Ghazālī, who in his *Iḥyāʾ ʿulūm al-dīn* and elsewhere writes much about what people should do and what avoid to gain happiness in the afterlife. Ibn al-Malāḥimī continues and says that this philosopher had claimed that the resurrection of bodies in the afterlife is possible even under those premisses that the Aristotelian philosophers accept.

Al-Ghazālī does precisely this in the 20th discussion of *Tahāfut*. Ibn al-Malāḥimī, however, does not refer his readers to that book. He rather quotes this argument from a different book, where the unnamed philosopher says the same and where he develops arguments how the Day of Resurrection could come about according to the ontology of Ibn Sīnā. The quote includes al-Ghazālī's so-called 'rule of interpretation' (*Tuḥfa*, 186, l. 17) and is from a work known as *Nafḫ al-rūh wa-l-taswiya* (al-Ghazālī, *Nafḫ*, 41). This work circulates in a number of versions and appears to go back to questions al-Ghazālī answered about the nature of the human soul and the afterlife. Taking its departure from Q 15: 29 and 38: 72, the book tries to show how Ibn Sīnā's teachings on the soul explain the Qur'ān. Parts of this book (which do not contain the quoted passage) circulate as *al-Maḍnūn al-ṣaghīr* and also under the title *al-Ajwiba al-Ghazāliyya fī l-masā'il al-ukhrawiyya*. Scholars still have doubts whether this book is truly by al-Ghazālī or rather a pseudo-epigraphy, although it is significantly less problematic than the *Major Maḍnūn*. The work is quoted a few more times in Ibn al-Malāḥimī's chapter on the afterlife (Koloğlu 2010: 320–30), where it is always introduced by the words, 'that one says... ' (*Tuḥfa*, 188–93). These quotations strengthen the case for its authenticity given that the still vague description of its author fits al-Ghazālī quite well.

Ibn al-Malāḥimī most likely regarded al-Ghazālī as one of those philosophers who mixed *falsafa* with Islam. He acknowledges, however, that Shāfiʿite scholars such as al-Ghazālī at least accept moral obligations (*taklīf*) and prepare their readers for them, something that other philosophers did not do. Still, accepting Ibn Sīnā's teachings on the soul and adopting one's understanding of the afterlife accordingly, as al-Ghazālī did, was too much for Ibn al-Malāḥimī, who criticizes scholars like him for that. Ibn Taymiyya, in fact, includes the name of Ibn al-Malāḥimī in a list of more than a dozen scholars of Islam who were known critics of al-Ghazālī's leanings toward philosophy (Ibn Taymiyya, *Dar'*, 6: 240).

VII The Twenty Chapters of the *Gift to the Mutakallimūn*

At the beginning of his book, Ibn al-Malāḥimī lists the issues where the philosophers hold erroneous opinions. Many of these are also addressed by al-Ghazālī, such as the temporal origination of the world, God's attributes, particularly that of being the designer of the world, and their teachings on the afterlife. In addition Ibn al-Malāḥimī lists the philosophers' position on prophecy and on the laws that the prophets brought. Al-Ghazālī's assessment of these two points was mixed, which is why he did not include them in his *Tahāfut*. Finally Ibn al-Malāḥimī also takes issue with the philosophers' position on moral obligations (*taklīf*), a point al-Ghazālī does not bring up because the Ashʿarite view on this subject turns out to be quite compatible with that of Ibn Sīnā.

It might or might not be a coincidence that Ibn al-Malāḥimī divided his book into twenty main chapters (sing. *bāb*), the same as the number of discussions in al-Ghazālī's *Tahāfut*. Three of those main chapters have the character of introductions. In Chapter 4, Ibn al-Malāḥimī begins his refutation of philosophical teachings with the same subject that al-Ghazālī begins it with, the pre-eternity of the world. The book overall does not have such an original structure as that of al-Ghazālī. After establishing that the world was created in time, Ibn al-Malāḥimī continues with the proof of the world's temporary creation and the existence of an originator (*muḥdith*), i.e. God. From here on the discussion of subject matters in the book follows roughly that of a *kalām* compendium such as Ibn al-Malāḥimī's *Fā'iq*. After establishing God's existence the next six chapters (nos. 6–12) are devoted to God's attributes and God's actions. Ibn al-Malāḥimī begins by discussing the *falāsifa*'s argument for the world's pre-eternity out of God's everlasting creative activity, quoting among other works Proclus (d. 485 CE) as well as John Philoponus's refutation of him (*Tuḥfa*, 52–7). In his discussion of the negative as well as positive attributes of God, he sticks closely to the table of contents of al-Ghazālī's *Maqāṣid* (*Tuḥfa*, 58–137; al-Ghazālī, *Maqāṣid*, 2: 59–97). The remainder of the *Tuḥfa* deals with various philosophical teachings on prophecy, on the nature of the soul, and the afterlife and includes fundamental disagreements between Muʿtazilites and Aristotelians in matters of ontology. The final chapter refutes the claim that there are esoteric teachings (*bāṭin*) in the Qur'ān, something Ibn al-Malāḥimī associates with the philosophers as well as with Shīʿite groups such as the Ismāʿīlites, who say that only their leader (*Imām*) knows the esoteric meaning.

In his *Tahāfut*, al-Ghazālī refrains from arguing in favour of the true position—at least he presents it that way—and when he rejects the philosophical view that God has no positive attributes (*ṣifāt*) but is absolute unity, for instance, he does not explain the Ashʿarite alternative on this subject. Not so Ibn al-Malāḥimī who most often confronts the teachings of the philosophers with that of 'the Muslims', as he says, a word that here stands for Muʿtazilites. In earlier centuries, the Muʿtazilites had developed their own ontology, based on a theory of powerless atoms, as well as their own explanations of physical processes. These theories are highly incompatible with the ontological assumptions of Aristotelianism, which gives Ibn al-Malāḥimī much occasion to voice his disagreement and present the arguments for his school.

Their disagreement on human acts and moral obligation (*taklīf*) is equally deep. Ibn Sīnā had taught that human actions are causally determined by factors such as the human's volition, his or her motives, and other causes, which are themselves determined by causes that all begin in God. For Ibn Sīnā all chains of causes and effects end in God—or rather they begin there—which means God is the ultimate cause of everything. From the point of view of a Muʿtazilite, the Ashʿarites—whom Ibn al-Malāḥimī polemically calls 'compulsionists' (*mujbira*)—hold very similar opinions on human actions as the Avicennans (*Tuḥfa*, 51). Both groups believe that God is the creator of *all* events in this world and they explicitly include human actions. God would thus predetermine all human actions and He would also become the source and the creator of good *and* evil in this world, two positions that were unacceptable for any Muʿtazilite. Ibn al-Malāḥimī insists that God is only the source of good and that evil comes into this world through the agency of humans. God does not create human actions and their immediate consequences. Humans also have free will and respond in their decisions to the moral obligations God puts on them. They act either in accord with these obligations and are rewarded in the afterlife or they violate them and are punished.

Ibn Sīnā taught that human actions are determined by their causes just like all other events in this world. Free will (*ikhtiyār*) exists only insofar as humans will always choose what they think is best (*khayr*) for them. All events in this world and the next are predetermined, reward and punishment in the afterlife included. Ibn Sīnā does not have a notion of moral obligation (*taklīf*); his ethical theory resembles that of Aristotle and is teleological. Acts are valuable if they serve a certain end. That end is for Ibn Sīnā the human's happiness in this world and the next. Such happiness is attained when humans actualize their potentiality. Acts conducive to this end are good, while those detrimental to it are bad. In themselves, acts have no autonomous moral value for Ibn Sīnā.

There are very few elements in Ibn Sīnā's theory of human actions and of moral value where it clashes with that of al-Ghazālī (Griffel 2009: 215–22). None of these subjects ever comes up in his *Tahāfut*. Quite the opposite in Ibn al-Malāḥimī, who objects to virtually every element in Ibn Sīnā's theory of human actions. He also objects to the Avicennan position that all humans have a soul that will survive after death (*Tuḥfa*, 154–68). A number of discussions are devoted to the refutation of philosophical cosmology with its explanation of the movements of stars and planets through celestial spheres (*Tuḥfa*, 114–35). According to al-Ghazālī, such subjects are inconsequential for religion. In fact, he said denying explanations that are geometrically proven is harmful to it. For Ibn al-Malāḥimī, these elements of the philosophical wordview serve to establish a fully determinist position on human actions. Ibn al-Malāḥimī wishes to establish human free will and argues therefore against the existence of celestial objects that might determine human acts. This, among other things, makes his refutation a much more comprehensive attempt than that of al-Ghazālī.

The overall projects of these two books, however, are not so different after all. Both want to discredit the Avicennan philosophical system and destroy its attraction to Muslim scholars. Their ultimate goal is to attract those who were drawn to Avicennism to their own teachings. Ibn al-Malāḥimī chooses the direct way and aims at showing the falseness (*fasād*) of the philosophers' teachings wherever they disagree with Muʿtazilism. Al-Ghazālī focuses on the *falāsifa*'s two claims of their sciences' demonstrability and independence of revelation. The demonstrative method also comes up in Ibn al-Malāḥimī and he ridicules the philosophers for assuming their teachings are superior to that of the ordinary believers or to those of the *mutakallimūn* because they are based on demonstrations. He, however, does not focus on the demonstrability of the philosophers' teachings. Al-Ghazālī chose that strategy, which allowed him to refute philosophy *and* take over many of their teachings as his own.

VIII Conclusions

The two refutations of Avicennan philosophy discussed in this chapter are themselves highly philosophical works that take the views and arguments of the Muslim Aristotelians very seriously and discuss them on a highly elaborate intellectual level. Decades of studying al-Ghazālī's book have shown that his objections are often original. They contributed to and sometimes even triggered the serious argumentative challenges Neoplatonic Aristotelianism would face in the West and in Islam. Similar studies still need to be undertaken with Ibn al-Malāḥimī's *Tuḥfa*.

Both books are highly polemical at times but they also show how much their authors appreciated the complexity and the versatility of Ibn Sīnā's philosophical system. Both authors realized that this system posed a threat to the authority of the theology they had grown up with and the scholars who represented it. Their reactions to that threat, however, are quite different. Ibn al-Malāḥimī takes this challenge as an occasion to defend Muʿtazilism and present the truths of its teachings. Al-Ghazālī, on the other hand, adopts numerous teachings of Ibn Sīnā and appropriates them to the demands of Ashʿarite theology. Before doing so, however, he needed to point out those elements in Ibn Sīnā's system that are unfit to be integrated into Muslim theology. This is one of the purposes of his *Tahāfut*.

Their different strategies are partly the result of different views of what the philosophical movement was. For al-Ghazālī, it was a movement that pursued its own quasi-religion, outside of Islam. His multilayered responses to that movement all serve the purpose of taking the wind out of the sails of that parallel religious tradition and making it part of Islam. He aimed at domesticating philosophy and bringing it under the banner of Islam. For Ibn al-Malāḥimī, who writes four decades after al-Ghazālī began this project, the philosophical movement had become a part of Islam. He responded to the philosophical movement the way one would respond to any other competing theological group in Islam, namely by writing a straightforward refutation of their teachings.

One final difference is the legal aspect of both books. Al-Ghazālī combines his theological and philosophical refutations with a legal condemnation. His willingness to adopt so much from Ibn Sīnā coincided with a forcefully intolerant, one can even say violent attitude toward those elements he regarded as dangerous. Ibn al-Malāḥimī's refutation lacks that kind of intolerance. As a Ḥanafite he did not have the legal tools at hand that allowed him to excommunicate certain teachings of the philosophers the way al-Ghazālī did (Griffel 2001). Also, as a Muʿtazilite he did not think that unbelief (*kufr*) should or could be punished by state authorities or leading members of the Muslim community (Griffel 2009: 104). Even if Ibn al-Malāḥimī held that the Muslim philosophers had 'left the religion of Islam' he did not plead for their persecution. His work as a Muʿtazilite theologian was to reveal what he regarded as the falseness of their teachings in order to diminish their appeal.

References

al-Akiti, A. (2009). 'The Good, the Bad, and the Ugly of Falsafa: Al-Ghazālī's Maḍnūn, Tahāfut, and Maqāṣid, with Particular Attention to their Falsafī Treatments of God's Knowledge of Temporal Events'. In Y. T. Langermann (ed.), *Avicenna and his Legacy: A Golden Age of Science and Philosophy*. Turnhout: Brepols, 51–100.

Anṣārī, Ḥ. (2001). 'Kitāb-i tāza yāb dar naqḍ-i falsafa: Paydā shudan-i Kitāb-i Tuḥfat al-mutakallimīn-i Malāḥimī'. *Nashr-i dānish* 18/3: 31f.

Davidson, H. (1987). *Proofs for the Eternity, Creation and the Existence of God*. Oxford: Oxford University Press.

al-Ghazālī (*Deliverance*). *Deliverance from Error: Five Key Texts Including his Spiritual Autobiography al-Munqidh min al-Dalal*. Trans. R. McCarthy. Louisville, KY: Fons Vitae, 2000.

al-Ghazālī (*Faḍā'iḥ*). *Faḍā'iḥ al-Bāṭiniyya wa-faḍā'il al-Mustaẓhiriyya*. Ed. ʿA. Badawī. Cairo: al-Dār al-Qawmiyya, 1964.

al-Ghazālī (*Logica*). *Logica et philosophia Algazelis Arabis*. Frankfurt: Minerva, 1969 [1st edn. 1506].

al-Ghazālī (*Maqāṣid*). *Maqāṣid al-falāsifa*. Ed. M. Ṣ. al-Kurdī. 3 parts. Cairo: al-Maṭbāʿa al-Mahmūdiyya al-Tijāriyya, 1936.

al-Ghazālī (*Metaphysics*). *Algazel's Metaphysics: A Medieval Translation*. Ed. J. T. Muckle. Toronto: St Michael's College, 1933.

al-Ghazālī (*Miḥakk*). *Miḥakk al-naẓar fī l-manṭiq*. Ed. M. B. al-Naʿsānī and M. al-Qabbānī. Cairo: al-Maṭbaʿa al-Adabiyya, 1925.

al-Ghazālī (*Miʿyār*). *Miʿyār al-ʿilm fī fann al-manṭiq*. Ed. M. Ṣ. al-Kurdī. Cairo: al-Maṭbāʿa al-ʿArabiyya, 1927.

al-Ghazālī (*Nafḥ*). *Nafḥ al-rūḥ wa-l-taswiya*. Ed. M. Ḥ. al-Saqqā. Cairo: Maktabat al-Madīna al-Munawwara, 1979.

al-Ghazālī (*Tahāfut*). *The Incoherence of the Philosophers/Tahâfut al-falâsifa, a Parallel English-Arabic Text*. Ed. and trans. M. E. Marmura. Provo, UT: Brigham Young University Press, 2nd edn., 2000.

Griffel, F. (2001). 'Toleration and Exclusion: al-Shāfiʿī and al-Ghazālī on the Treatment of Apostates'. *Bulletin of the School of Oriental and African Studies* 64: 339–54.

Griffel, F. (2009). *Al-Ghazālī's Philosophical Theology*. New York: Oxford University Press.

Griffel, F. (2010). 'Muslim Philosophers' Rationalist Explanation of Muḥammad's Prophecy'. In J. E. Brockopp (ed.), *The Cambridge Companion to Muhammad*. New York: Cambridge University Press, 158–79.

Ibn al-Malāḥimī, Rukn al-Dīn Maḥmūd b. Muḥammad (*Fā'iq*). *Kitāb al-Fā'iq fī uṣūl al-dīn*. Ed. W. Madelung and M. McDermott. Tehran/Berlin: Iranian Institute for Philosophy/Institute of Islamic Studies, 2007.

Ibn al-Malāḥimī, Rukn al-Dīn Maḥmūd b. Muḥammad (*Muʿtamad*). *Kitāb al-Muʿtamad fī uṣūl al-dīn*. Ed. W. Madelung. Tehran/Berlin: Mīrāth-i Maktūb/Research Unit Intellectual History of the Islamicate World, 2nd edn., 2012.

Ibn al-Malāḥimī, Rukn al-Dīn Maḥmūd b. Muḥammad (*Tuḥfa*). *Tuḥfat al-mutakallimīn fī l-radd ʿalā l-falāsifa*. Ed. H. Ansari and W. Madelung, Tehran/Berlin: Iranian Institute of Philosophy/Institute of Islamic Studies, 2008.

Ibn Rushd (*Tahāfut al-tahāfut*). *Averroes' Tahafut al-Tahafut (The Incoherence of the Incoherence)*. Trans. S. van den Bergh. 2 vols. Cambridge: E. J. W. Gibb Memorial Trust, 1954.

Ibn Taymiyya (*Dar'*). *Dar' ta'āruḍ al-'aql wa-l-naql*. Ed. M. R. Sālim. 11 vols. Beirut: Dār al-Kunūz al-Adabiyya, 1980.

Janssens, J. (2003). 'Al-Ghazzālī and his Use of Avicennian Texts'. In M. Maróth (ed.), *Problems in Arabic Philosophy*. Piliscaba: Avicenna Institute of Middle East Studies, 37–49.

Koloğlu, O. Ş. (2010). *Mutezile'nin Felsefe Eleştirisi: Harezmli Mutezilî İbnü'l-Melâhimî'nin Felsefeye Reddiyesi*. Bursa: Emin Yayinlari.

Kukkonen, T. (2000). 'Possible Worlds in the Tahâfut al-Falâsifa: Al-Ghazâlî on Creation and Contingency'. *Journal of the History of Philosophy* 38: 479–502.

Lohr, C. H. (1965). 'Logica Algazelis: Introduction and Critical Text'. *Traditio* 21: 223–90.

Madelung, W. (2006). 'Abū l-Ḥusayn al-Baṣrī's Proof for the Existence of God'. In J. E. Montgomery (ed.), *Arabic Theology, Arabic Philosophy: From the Many to the One*. Leuven: Peeters, 273–80.

Madelung, W. (2007). 'Ibn al-Malāḥimī's Refutation of the Philosophers'. In C. Adang, S. Schmidtke, and D. Sklare (eds.), *A Common Rationality: Mu'tazilism in Islam and Judaism*. Würzburg: Ergon, 331–6.

Pourjavady, N. (ed.) (2002). *Majmū'ah-yi falsafī-yi Marāghah/A Philosophical Anthology from Maragha*. Tehran: Markaz-i Nashr-i Dānishgāh.

Shihadeh, A. (2010). 'New Light on the Reception of al-Ghazālī's *Doctrines of the Philosophers (Maqāṣid al-Falāsifa)*'. In P. Adamson (ed.), *In the Age of Averroes: Arabic Philosophy in the Sixth/Twelfth Century*. London/Turin: Warburg Institute/Nino Aragno Editore, 77–92.

Treiger, A. (2011). *Inspired Knowledge in Islamic Thought: Al-Ghazālī's Theory of Mystical Cognition and its Avicennian Foundation*. London: Routledge.

Wisnovsky, R. (2004). 'One Aspect of the Avicennian Turn in Sunnī Theology'. *Arabic Sciences and Philosophy* 14: 65–100.

CHAPTER 26

TWELVER SHĪʿĪ THEOLOGY

REZA POURJAVADY AND SABINE SCHMIDTKE

I Ilkhanid and Post-Ilkhanid Eras

Naṣīr al-Dīn al-Ṭūsī (d. 672/1274) is usually credited with having 'modernized' Twelver Shīʿī theology by introducing Avicennan notions into the *kalām* discussions, a development that had started among the Ashʿarites with Abū Ḥāmid al-Ghazālī (d. 505/1111) and, more importantly, Fakhr al-Dīn al-Rāzī (d. 609/1210).* Al-Ṭūsī grew up as an Imami and his principal teacher in *kalām* was Muʿīn al-Dīn Abū l-Ḥasan Sālim b. Badrān al-Māzinī al-Miṣrī (alive in 629/1231–2), a student of the prominent Twelver Shīʿī theologian Abū l-Makārim ʿIzz al-Dīn Ḥamza b. ʿAlī b. Zuhra al-Ḥusaynī al-Ḥalabī (b. Ramaḍān 511/1117, d. 585/1189–90), author of *Ghunyat al-nuzūʿ ilā ʿilmay al-uṣūl wa-l-furūʿ*, one of the most comprehensive (extant) summae of Imami theology, law, and legal theory of the sixth/twelfth century. It was this work which al-Ṭūsī had studied with Ibn Badrān for which the latter granted him an *ijāza* on 18 Jumādā II 619/30 July 1222 (Mudarris Raḍawī 1991: 161–7). Despite his training in *kalām*, al-Ṭūsī devoted most of his scholarly life to Avicennan philosophy, astronomy, and mathematics. Moreover, during the decades between 630/1233 and the fall of the Ismāʿīlī fortress in Alamut in 654/1256 while he had joined the ranks of the Ismāʿīlīs al-Ṭūsī had composed numerous important works on Ismāʿīlī thought. At the time of the Ilkhanid conquest of Iraq in 656/1258 he gained the ear of the conqueror Hülagü, whom he managed to convince to spare the Shīʿī sanctuaries from destruction. In 657/1259, the Ilkhan entrusted al-Ṭūsī with the reconstruction and leadership of the Marāgha observatory, which subsequently developed into an important intellectual centre for astronomers, philosophers, as well as theologians, Shīʿīs, and non-Shīʿīs. Naṣīr al-Dīn al-Ṭūsī remained at Marāgha until a few months before his death in 672/1274 when he returned to Baghdad (Daiber and Ragep 2000; see also the contributions to Pourjavady and Vesel 2000).

It was following his rupture with the Ismāʿīlīs around the year 654/1256 that al-Ṭūsī composed several doctrinal tracts, viz. his *Risālat al-Imāma*, a treatise supporting the

* Part I has been written by S. Schmidtke, Part II by R. Pourjavady.

Twelver Shīʿī notion of the imamate, as well as two concise *kalām* treatises, *Qawāʿid al-ʿaqāʾid* and *Tajrīd al-iʿtiqād*.[1] These two tracts soon became very popular and proved influential for the later development of Twelver Shīʿism, as is suggested by the numerous commentaries written upon them (Ṣadrāʾī 2003; editor's introduction to al-Ḥimmaṣī al-Rāzī, *Kashf*, iv–vi).[2] In them al-Ṭūsī combined theological discussions with philosophical terminology, methodology, and style and accepted a number of Avicennan concepts that were compatible with Imami theological doctrine—the amalgamation of *kalām* theology as it had been formulated by Abū l-Ḥusayn al-Baṣrī (d. 436/1044), the founder of the last innovative school of Muʿtazilism, and Peripatetic philosophy became the rule for Imami theologians from the seventh/thirteenth century onwards. The writings of Fakhr al-Dīn al-Rāzī constituted a major source for al-Ṭūsī. Fakhr al-Dīn had significantly revised Ashʿarite doctrinal thought in the light of Abū l-Ḥusayn al-Baṣrī's teachings and Avicennan philosophy. The antagonism between Naṣīr al-Dīn al-Ṭūsī's Muʿtazilite worldview in his doctrinal works and Fakhr al-Dīn al-Rāzī's Ashʿarite positions notwithstanding, it was primarily through the latter's works that Naṣīr al-Dīn as well as later Twelver Shīʿīs received Abū l-Ḥusayn's doctrines.[3]

The most immediate impact of Naṣīr al-Dīn's doctrinal thought was on the scholarly circles of al-Ḥilla—one of the leading intellectual centres of Twelver Shīʿism (Ṭāliʿī 2013: 19–78) with a distinctly positive attitude towards *kalām* since the time of Sadīd al-Dīn Maḥmūd b. ʿAlī b. al-Ḥasan al-Ḥimmaṣī al-Rāzī, who had completed his comprehensive theological *summa, al-Munqidh min al-taqlīd*, on 9 Jumādā I 581/8 August 1185 in this city. Al-Ḥimmaṣī had introduced the theologians of al-Ḥilla during his sojourn here to the teachings of Abū l-Ḥusayn al-Baṣrī. Among the prominent scholars who were active in this city shortly before and during the time of al-Ṭūsī were Sadīd al-Dīn Sālim b. Maḥfūẓ al-Ṣūrāwī al-Ḥillī (d. *c.*630/1232), his student Najm al-Dīn Abū l-Qāsim Jaʿfar b. al-Ḥasan b. Saʿīd ('al-Muḥaqqiq al-Ḥillī') (d. 676/1277) (on him see Chapter 11), Muḥammad b. ʿAlī b. Muḥammad Ibn Juhaym (d. 680/1282), and Sadīd al-Dīn Yūsuf b. al-Muṭahhar al-Ḥillī. It was also during this period that

[1] The section on the imamate in the *Qawāʿid* includes a detailed exposition of Ismāʿīlī doctrines (in addition to extensive discussions of the positions of the *ghulāt*, the Kaysāniyya, the Imāmiyya, the Zaydiyya, and the Sunnites on this issue). This has been interpreted as an indication that even after the fall of Alamut and his departure from the Ismāʿīlīs, al-Ṭūsī continued to sympathize with Ismāʿīlī doctrines (Landolt 2000: 14). In view of the doxographic character of the section this seems hardly justified.

[2] As is well known, the *Tajrīd* was also widely received and commented upon by Sunni scholars, the most renowned being the commentary by ʿAlā al-Dīn ʿAlī al-Qūshjī (d. 879/1474), the point of departure of numerous supercommentaries and glosses by later Sunnī as well as Shīʿī thinkers. See Ṣadrāʾī 2003: 59ff. For a commentary on the *Qawāʿid* by the Sunnī scholar Rukn al-Dīn al-Astarābādī, see Ansari 2011: 787–5.

[3] There is no evidence that al-Ṭūsī or any later Imami theologian had access to any of the theological writings of Abū l-Ḥusayn al-Baṣrī. However, al-Ṭūsī as well as the ʿAllāma al-Ḥillī were familiar with some of the writings of Rukn al-Dīn Ibn al-Malāḥimī (d. 536/1141), a later prominent follower of Abū l-Ḥusayn, as well as with the *Kitāb al-Kāmil* by Ibn al-Malāḥimī's student Abū l-Maʿālī Ṣāʿid b. Aḥmad al-Uṣūlī (on him, see Chapter 9).

the Banū l-ʿAwd emerged in al-Ḥilla, a family of several generations of theologians (Schmidtke 2009a).

Sadīd al-Dīn Yūsuf's son, Ḥasan b. Yūsuf ('al-ʿAllāma al-Ḥillī', d. 726/1325), was one of the most prolific students of Naṣīr al-Dīn al-Ṭūsī. He composed commentaries on several works of al-Ṭūsī, most notably on the latter's *Tajrīd*, entitled *Kashf al-murād fī sharḥ Tajrīd al-iʿtiqād* (completed in 696/1297). The numerous extant manuscripts of the work as well as the supercommentaries and glosses that were later written on it testify to its lasting popularity (Schmidtke 1991: 90 no. 85; al-Ṭabāṭabāʾī 1995: 163–6 no. 75; Ṣadrāʾī 2003: 35–41 no. 19). Al-Ḥillī also commented upon al-Ṭūsī's other credal writing, *Qawāʿid al-ʿaqāʾid* (Schmidtke 1991: 51, 90 no. 84; al-Ṭabāṭabāʾī 1995: 162f. no. 74), and he composed numerous independent works on theology which also proved immensely influential. His probably most popular independent tract in the field of dogmatics was his concise *al-Bāb al-ḥādī ʿashar fīmā yajibu ʿalā ʿāmmat al-mukallafīn min maʿrifat uṣūl al-dīn* which he added as the eleventh chapter to his *Minhāj al-ṣalāḥ fī ikhtiṣār al-miṣbāḥ* (completed in 723/1323). As the title indicates, it was written for a general readership rather than for students of theology. As was the case with al-Ṭūsī's *Tajrīd*, it was repeatedly commented upon by later theologians. Together with its most famous commentary by al-Miqdād al-Suyūrī (d. 826/1423), it has been published repeatedly and translations of the two works in Persian and English are currently available (Schmidtke 1991: 55, 80f. no. 36; Ṭabāṭabāʾī 1995: 65–71 no. 25). Among al-Ḥillī's larger theological works mention should be made of his *Manāhij al-yaqīn* (completed in 680/1281), a work that was well known among later Imami theologians (Schmidtke 1991: 47, 94 no. 107; Ṭabāṭabāʾī 1995: 191–3 no. 99), and the *Kitāb Nihāyat al-marām fī ʿilm al-kalām*, his last work in this discipline as it seems, which is only partly preserved and was possibly never completed (Schmidtke 1991: 50f., 96 no. 117; Ṭabāṭabāʾī 1995, 208f. no. 112).

In the domain of *kalām*, al-Ḥillī was less of an original thinker but rather an accomplished propagator of al-Ṭūsī's new type of *kalām*. In addition to being a prolific writer, al-Ḥillī was surrounded by a large number of pupils who studied with him either in al-Ḥilla, at the court of the Ilkhanid ruler Uljaytū (r. 703/1304–716/1316), or in the *madrasa sayyāra* that had been founded by Uljaytū to accompany him (Schmidtke 1991: 35–40). It was still prior to Uljaytū's conversion to Shīʿism in 709/1310 that al-Ḥillī and his son Fakhr al-Muḥaqqiqīn Muḥammad (b. 682/1283; d. 771/1369) were summoned to court where they stayed for several years during which al-Ḥillī composed numerous works at the request of the Ilkhan, among them works on theological questions (Schmidtke 1991: 23–32). Fakhr al-Muḥaqqiqīn later became a renowned scholar in his own right with several titles in *kalām* and particularly jurisprudence to his credit, among them numerous commentaries on works by his father. After the death of the ʿAllāma, he took over numerous former students of his father. Among his pupils were scholars such as Niẓām al-Dīn ʿAlī b. ʿAbd al-Ḥamīd al-Nīlī (d. after 791/1389), the renowned Shams al-Dīn Muḥammad b. Makkī, ('al-Shahīd al-awwal', 734/

1333–786/1384) (al-Mukhtārī 2005: 64–7),[4] and al-Murtaḍā Abū l-Saʿīd al-Ḥasan b. ʿAbd Allāh b. Muḥammad b. ʿAlī b. al-Aʿraj al-Ḥusaynī (Schmidtke 1991: 35).

Among the students of the Shahīd al-awwal were Fakhr al-Dīn Aḥmad b. ʿAbd Allāh b. Saʿīd *al-shahīr bi*-Ibn al-Mutawwaj al-Baḥrānī (d. between 802/1399–1400 and 836/1432–3) (Anwār 1991) as well as another prominent theologian who hailed from al-Ḥilla, viz. al-Miqdād b. ʿAbd Allāh al-Suyūrī al-Ḥillī al-Asadī ('al-Fāḍil al-Miqdād', d. 826/1422–3). Al-Miqdād is mostly renowned for his commentaries on some of the theological works of the ʿAllāma al-Ḥillī: *al-Nāfiʿ yawm al-ḥashr*, a commentary on the *Bāb al-ḥādī ʿashar* (MTK 5/350f. no. 11959); and *Irshād al-ṭālibīn*, a commentary on *Nahj al-mustarshidīn fī uṣūl al-dīn* (MTK 1/229 no. 784).[5] Among his independent *kalām* works, mention should be made of his *al-Lawāmiʿ al-ilāhiyya fī l-mabāḥith al-kalāmiyya*, his most comprehensive book in this discipline (MTK 4/572f. no. 10203).

The scholars of al-Ḥilla were in close contact with those of Bahrayn, another vibrant intellectual centre of Twelver Shīʿism throughout the seventh/thirteenth century and beyond (al-Oraibi 1992; 2001). A leading figure of the sixth/twelfth century was Nāṣir al-Dīn Rāshid al-Baḥrānī (d. 605/1208), followed by Kamāl al-Dīn Aḥmad b. ʿAlī Ibn Saʿāda al-Baḥrānī (d. *c.*640/1242). Both Rāshid and Ibn Saʿāda had already studied in al-Ḥilla. Ibn Saʿāda's pupil Jamāl al-Dīn ʿAlī b. Sulaymān al-Baḥrānī (d. *c.*670/1271) corresponded with Naṣīr al-Dīn al-Ṭūsī—he sent him a tract composed by his teacher Ibn Saʿāda containing twenty-four questions on the divine attribute of knowledge, titled *Risālat al-ʿIlm* or *Masʾalat al-ʿilm*, asking al-Ṭūsī to comment upon the text, a request with which al-Ṭūsī complied. ʿAlī b. Sulaymān in turn is the author of a doctrinal work, entitled *Miṣbāḥ al-ʿirfān wa-miftāḥ al-bayān* (Ansari 2011: 779–85). The preserved writings of both Ibn Saʿāda and even more so ʿAlī b. Sulaymān indicate that philosophy, mysticism, and *kalām* were firmly rooted in Bahrayn during their time (Madelung 1989; Taghavi 2013). ʿAlī b. Sulaymān's pupils were his son Ḥusayn and Maytham b. Maytham al-Baḥrānī (b. 636/1238; d. after 681/1282) (Yūsuf 2007). Maytham al-Baḥrānī is usually said to have studied with al-Ṭūsī while he is also reported to have been the latter's teacher in jurisprudence. In the field of *kalām*, al-Baḥrānī composed the *Kitāb Qawāʿid al-marām*, a work that enjoyed lasting popularity and that shows similar characteristics as was the case with al-Ṭūsī's and al-Ḥillī's doctrinal works (MTK 4/469 no. 9760). By contrast, al-Baḥrānī's voluminous commentary on the *Nahj al-balāgha*, titled *Miṣbāḥ al-sālikīn* or *Sharḥ Nahj al-balāgha*, gives evidence of his intimate familiarity with the mystical tradition.

The interpretations and adaptations of Ibn al-ʿArabī's notions through the commentary on *Nahj al-balāgha* of ʿAlī b. Sulaymān al-Baḥrānī and, later on, the writings of

[4] Although al-Shahīd al-awwal was primarily a legal scholar, he also composed a few doctrinal tracts; see *Arbaʿ rasāʾil kalāmiyya*. These were commented upon by Zayn al-Dīn ʿAlī b. Muḥammad b. Yūnus al-ʿĀmilī al-Nabāṭī al-Bayāḍī (d. 788/1472–3), author of *ʿUṣrat al-manjūd fī ʿilm al-kalām*.

[5] al-Miqdād is also usually credited with *al-Iʿtimād*, a commentary on al-Ḥillī's *Risāla fī wājib al-iʿtiqād ʿalā jamīʿ al-ʿibād* (e.g. MTK 1/400f. no. 1670), while this is in fact a work by Shams al-Dīn Muḥammad b. Ṣadaqa, a student of Naṣīr al-Dīn al-Kashshī. See Ansari 2015: 88–96.

Bahā᾿ al-Dīn Ḥaydar b. ʿAlī al-Āmulī (d. after 787/1385) proved authoritative and significantly influenced Twelver Shīʿī doctrinal thought of the seventh/thirteenth century and beyond (Agha-Tehrani 1996). This specifically concerned Ibn al-ʿArabī's doctrine of the two seals of sainthood which were reinterpreted to fit Twelver Shīʿī imamology (cf. al-Oraibi 1992: 216). Besides traditional Muʿtazilite *kalām*, Peripatetic philosophy, and Akbarian thought, Shihāb al-Dīn al-Suhrawardī's (d. 587/1191) philosophy of illumination soon developed into one of the dominant schools of Islamic philosophy and had a long-lasting impact on Imami theology and philosophy from the seventh/thirteenth century onwards. Most of the later Twelver Shīʿite thinkers saw Illuminationist teachings through the eyes of Shams al-Dīn Muḥammad b. Maḥmūd al-Shahrazūrī (alive in 687/1288), the author of the popular philosophical encyclopedia *al-Shajara al-ilāhiyya fī ʿulūm al-ḥaqāʾiq al-rabbāniyya* (completed in 680/1281) (Pourjavady and Schmidtke 2006). Ibn Abī Jumhūr al-Aḥsāʾī (b. *c.*838/1434–5, d. after 906/1501) was the first Imami scholar to amalgamate in his magnum opus Muʿtazilite and Ashʿarite *kalām*, Peripatetic and Illuminationist philosophy, as well as philosophical mysticism, thus creating an unprecedented synthesis of these strands (Schmidtke 2000; 2009b; 2013). Ibn Abī Jumhūr hailed from al-Ḥasā᾿ where he began his formation with the leading scholars of Bahrayn. Later on he studied with a variety of scholars in Najaf, Jabal ʿĀmil, and Kāshān. During an advanced stage of his career, he sojourned repeatedly and for extended periods in Mashhad, a city that had apparently become as a second home to him.

Taking into consideration his entire œuvre in the field of *kalām* (al-Ghufrānī 2013), Ibn Abī Jumhūr developed from a conventional theologian whose doctrinal views were characterized by Muʿtazilite positions into a thinker who predominantly maintained philosophical and mystical notions. One trait, however, that characterizes his entire œuvre in this field throughout his life is his concern to mediate between opposing views of different strands of thought, be it within the field of *kalām* (Muʿtazilism versus Ashʿarism) or beyond (doctrinal thought versus philosophical notions). This is best exemplified in Ibn Abī Jumhūr's magnum opus, entitled *Kitāb Mujlī mirʾāt al-munjī fī l-kalām wa-l-ḥikmatayn wa-l-taṣawwuf* (completed in 895/1490). The work was an autocommentary on the *Kitāb al-Nūr al-munjī min al-ẓalām* (finished in 893/1488), which in turn was a commentary on the author's very concise *Kitāb Maslak* (or: *Masālik*) *al-afhām fī ʿilm al-kalām*. As the title of the basic work indicates, it was essentially a work on theology. In his *al-Nūr al-munjī*, the author comments on the text of the *Maslak* in a comprehensive manner, often expanding on the mystical and philosophical (mostly Illuminationist) dimensions of the issues under consideration. On the level of the *Mujlī*, he usually restricts himself to elaborating on specific Illuminationist or mystical notions mentioned in the two other works. Throughout the *Mujlī*, Ibn Abī Jumhūr freely combined traditional Muʿtazilite theology with notions of Peripatetic and Illuminationist philosophy and of philosophical mysticism. On this basis he also sought to mediate between the doctrines of the Muʿtazilites and the Ashʿarites.

Philosophical notions characterize Ibn Abī Jumhūr's views in his *Mujlī* in his discussion about the divine attribute of power, viz. whether God is a necessary cause or a freely choosing agent, whether He has created the world *ex nihilo* or whether creation is co-eternal with God, its first cause, and whether God can create an endless multiplicity without intermediary or whether from God, who is one in every respect, only one immediate effect can result while creation in its entirety occurs as a hierarchic emanation—Ibn Abī Jumhūr invariably opts for the philosophical view rather than that of the theologians and argues that the views of the philosophers and the theologians are essentially identical. Moreover, Ibn Abī Jumhūr endorses in his *Mujlī* the philosophical understanding of the Divine when equating the divine attribute of will with the philosophical notion of divine providence. The notion of divine providence also determines his concept of the 'why' of God's acting. He negates the Muʿtazilite doctrine according to which God acts on the basis of specific, concrete motives. God rather acts on the basis of the essential primary intention, i.e. His knowledge of Himself and of the perfect order. In all these issues in which Ibn Abī Jumhūr adopts the philosophical points of view, his elaborations in the *Mujlī* rely on Shahrazūrī's *Shajara*. Ibn Abī Jumhūr also follows Shahrazūrī when adopting the latter's doctrines of transmigration of incomplete souls following their deaths into bodies of animals for the purpose of purification. However, unlike Shahrazūrī, Ibn Abī Jumhūr maintains at the same time the theological doctrine of bodily resurrection. Like Shahrazūrī, Ibn Abī Jumhūr believes that imperfect human souls are transferred at death into animal bodies, corresponding to their moral traits. According to their progress in purification they ascend into bodies of more noble animals until they are sufficiently purified to escape to the lower ranks of paradise. Souls that remain unsuccessful in attaining purification are eventually also transferred to animal bodies within the World of Images. Ibn Abī Jumhūr only disagrees with Shahrazūrī insofar as he adheres at the same time to the Islamic belief that God will restore the flesh and bones of the dead for the Judgement following His annihilation of the physical structure and order of the world. In order to harmonize this belief with the notion of metempsychosis, he adopts some elements of one of the anonymous views related by Shahrazūrī in the *Shajara* in his account of metempsychosis, whose adherents combined their notion of metempsychosis with their belief in the resurrection of the material world. As has been stated for the proponents of this doctrine, Ibn Abī Jumhūr distinguishes between the 'minor resurrection' (*al-qiyāma al-ṣughrā*), which consists in the disembodiment of the particular soul, and the 'major resurrection' (*al-qiyāma al-kubrā*), that is, the eventual restoration of the material world that follows its prior annihilation.

Ibn Abī Jumhūr also adopts in his *Mujlī* key notions that he had gleaned from philosophical mysticism. The doctrine of the unity of being (*waḥdat al-wujūd*) proved essential for his understanding of divine unicity (*tawḥīd*). Ibn Abī Jumhūr distinguishes three levels of *tawḥīd*: 'existential unity' (*tawḥīd wujūdī*) at the top level, followed by 'unity of the divine attributes' (*tawḥīd ṣifātī*) at the next lower level. The lowest rank corresponds to the orthodox Islamic definition of monotheism (*tawḥīd islāmī*), i.e. the denial of polytheism as expressed in Qurʾān 47: 19. The mystical notion of the unity of existence also marks Ibn Abī Jumhūr's conceptionalization of the divine attributes. He argues that divine attributes vanish at the highest level of *tawḥīd wujūdī* whereas at the lower level of *tawḥīd ṣifātī* they can be observed as manifestations of the divine essence. As such, neither mentally nor externally could they be taken to be something additional to God's essence. Mystical notions further influenced Ibn Abī Jumhūr's views regarding the issue of man's freedom to act. Ibn Abī Jumhūr argues for a middle position between determinism and free will on the basis of the notion of unity of existence. Considered from the level of the revealed law, the actions of man are attributable to him. From the more elevated point of view, the level of being, which allows a deeper insight into the true existential unity, all multiplicity vanishes and the observer grasps that all is included in divine providence. The true understanding of the intermediary position between determinism and free will implies both levels of consideration simultaneously. Another topic with respect to which Ibn Abī Jumhūr was influenced by the mystical tradition is the realm of prophecy and imamate. He argues for the necessity of the prophetic mission and the instalment of the Imam with the mystical notion of the necessary existence of the Perfect Man (*insān kāmil*). As manifestations of the divine completeness both the prophet and the Imam serve as intermediary between the absolute, transcendent Divine and man. In addition, Ibn Abī Jumhūr adopts the Akbarian notions of apostleship (*risāla*), prophethood (*nubuwwa*), and sainthood (*walāya*). In agreement with Twelver Shīʿī notions, however, he identifies sainthood with the imamate. Moreover, as was the case with Maytham al-Baḥrānī and Ḥaydar Āmulī, Ibn Abī Jumhūr rejects Ibn al-ʿArabī's identification of Jesus with the seal of absolute sainthood and replaces him with the Imam ʿAlī and the hidden Imam (Schmidtke 2000; forthcoming).

II Safavid Era

In 907/1501, the founder of the Safavid dynasty, Shah Ismāʿīl I (r. 907/1501–930/1524), announced Twelver Shīʿism as the religion of the newly established Safavid state. Following this announcement, writing Twelver Shīʿī theological work was welcomed by the Safavid court. The first known Twelver Shīʿī doctrinal book written during the reign of the Safavids is a commentary on al-Ṭūsī's *Tajrīd al-iʿtiqād* by Najm al-Dīn Maḥmūd al-Nayrīzī (d. after 933/1526). Completed sometime before 916/1510, this commentary, titled *Taḥrīr Tajrīd al-ʿaqāʾid*, is dedicated to Shah Ismāʿīl I. At the time of al-Nayrīzī, al-Ṭūsī's *Tajrīd* had commonly been read along with two Ashʿarite commentaries by Shams al-Dīn al-Iṣfahānī (d. 749/1348) (often studied together with al-Sayyid al-Sharīf al-Jurjānī's (d. 816/1414) supergloss) and by ʿAlāʾ al-Dīn ʿAlī al-Qūshjī (d. 879/1474) (Ṣadrāʾī Khūyī 2003: 42–95). The latter explicitly criticized al-Ṭūsī for his Twelver Shīʿī positions, particularly in the chapter on the imamate. Al-Nayrīzī's primary intention was thus to correct what he calls 'misinterpretations' and 'sophistries' of these previous commentaries when writing his own commentary on the *Tajrīd*. Throughout his *Taḥrīr*, al-Nayrīzī identifies with the views of the Imamiyya, which, so he admits, often correspond with those of the Muʿtazilites, for example that human actions are based on free choice (*ikhtiyār*) and that it is through reason that man is able to grasp the ethical value of his actions. Concurring with the Muʿtazilites he also rejects the Ashʿarite and Māturidite notion that the divine attributes exist externally. He maintained, however, that the Muʿtazilites had adopted in all those issues the views of the Shīʿī Imams (Pourjavady 2011: 65–7).

Other Iranian scholars of the time also commented on the *Tajrīd*. However, unlike al-Nayrīzī, they all wrote glosses on al-Qūshjī's commentary. This was the case with Ghiyāth al-Dīn al-Dashtakī (d. 949/1542), Shams al-Dīn al-Khafrī (d. 942/1535–6), Ḥusayn al-Ilāhī al-Ardabīlī (d. 950/1543), Jamāl al-Dīn Maḥmūd al-Shīrāzī (d. 962/1554–5), and Fakhr al-Dīn al-Sammākī al-Astarābādī (d. 984/1576–7) (Ṣadrāʾī Khūyī 2003: 136f.). Their glosses were primarily concerned with the first two chapters of the *Tajrīd*, in which philosophical preliminaries (*al-umūr al-ʿāmma*) as well as substances and accidents (*al-jawāhir wa-l-aʿrāḍ*) are discussed. Al-Khafrī and al-Sammākī al-Astarābādī also wrote separate commentaries on the third chapter, on metaphysics (*al-ilāhiyyāt bi-l-maʿnā al-akhaṣṣ*), as did Aḥmad b. Muḥammad al-Muqaddas al-Ardabīlī (d. 993/1585–6) (Ṣadrāʾī Khūyī 2003: 144–8). However, none of these scholars seems to have commented on the *Tajrīd*'s chapter on the imamate, which would have compelled them to affirm—or deny—their allegiance with Twelver Shīʿism. They rather confined themselves to uncontroversial topics. This general attitude only changed in the eleventh/seventeenth century. Sayyid Aḥmad al-ʿAlawī al-ʿĀmilī (d. between 1054/1644 and 1060/1650) commented on the *Tajrīd* with a work titled *Riyāḍ al-quds*, completed in 1011/1602–3 (MTK 3/487 no. 7161). ʿAbd al-Razzāq al-Lāhījī (d. 1072/1661–2) also wrote a new commentary on the *Tajrīd*, entitled *Shawāriq al-ilhām fī sharḥ Tajrīd al-kalām* (MTK 4/126f. no. 8141). In the twelfth/eighteenth century, Sayyid Muḥammad Ashraf al-ʿAlawī al-ʿĀmilī (d. 1145/1732) wrote a Persian commentary on the *Tajrīd*, titled *ʿAlāqat al-Tajrīd* (MTK 4/274 no. 8823). All three authors commented on the text of the *Tajrīd* in its entirety, including the chapter on the imamate, from a Twelver Shīʿī perspective. It is also noteworthy that during the eleventh/seventeenth and twelfth/eighteenth centuries al-Khafrī's gloss on the chapter on metaphysics (*ilāhiyyāt*) of al-Qūshjī's commentary was extremely popular—more than thirty superglosses were written on this gloss during this period (Ṣadrāʾī Khūyī 2003: 102–29).

Beside the *Tajrīd*, the ʿAllāma al-Ḥillī's *al-Bāb al-ḥādī ʿashar* was also repeatedly commented upon during the Safavid era (Firouzi 2011). Following the earlier commentaries on this text by al-Miqdād al-Suyūrī and Ibn Abī Jumhūr al-Aḥsāʾī (see Section I), commentaries on the *Bāb al-ḥādī ʿashar* were composed during the first decades of the Safavid era by Iranian migrant scholars to India such as Shāh Ṭāhir al-Dakanī (d. between 952/1545 and 956/1549) and Muḥammad b. Aḥmad al-Khʷājagī al-Shīrāzī (*fl.* 953/1546) (MTK 4/36 no. 7688; see also Chapter 34). Among the scholars who flourished in Iran, Mīr Abū l-Fatḥ b. Makhdūm al-Ḥusaynī al-ʿArabshāhī (d. *c.*976/1568) seems to have been the first to comment on al-Hillī's *al-Bāb al-hādī ʿashar*. His commentary, titled *Miftāḥ al-bāb*, was dedicated to Safavid Shāh Ṭahmāsb (r. 930/1524–984/1576) (MTK 5/215f. no. 11299; al-Ḥillī, al-Suyūrī, and al-ʿArabshāhī, *Bāb* 206). In it, the commentator championed Sufi explanations for various doctrinal matters (Rizvi 2007a: 94).

Another popular *genre* during the Safavid period were independent tracts discussing God's existence and His attributes, typically entitled *Risāla fī ithbāt al-wājib wa-ṣifātih* (MTK 1/142–59). Proofs for God's existence, His unicity (*tawḥīd*), His attributes, as well as their relation to His essence were the subjects characteristically dealt with in these works. The earliest contributor to this *genre* was the Sunni-Ashʿarite philosopher of Shiraz, Jalāl al-Dīn al-Dawānī (d. 908/1502), who composed two distinct epistles devoted to the proofs for the existence of God and His attributes (Pourjavady 2011: 12, 13f.; MTK 1/151–3, nos. 427 and 428). These treatises became the subject of many commentaries and glosses, including those by Imami scholars of the Safavid era, many of whom criticized Dawānī's positions. In addition, Dawānī's tracts served as an influential model to scholars of later generations for their own contributions to this *genre*. Shams al-Dīn al-Khafrī (MTK 1/150f. no. 425), Najm al-Dīn al-Nayrīzī, Abū l-Ḥasan ʿAlī b. Aḥmad al-Qāʾinī al-Kāshānī (d. 966/1558–9) (MTK 1/146 no. 396), Afḍal al-Dīn Muḥammad al-Turka al-Iṣfahānī (d. 991/1583–4) (MTK 1/153f. no. 429), and Aḥmad b. Muqaddas al-Ardabīlī (MTK 1/143f. no. 387) were among those who wrote on this topic.

Although one might imagine that Twelver Shīʿī credal works would have played a significant role in spreading the new denomination in the process of religious conversion of Iran, it is striking that there were hardly any creeds composed during the early Safavid period. Within the Safavid realm, the earliest known Imami creed was written by Shaykh al-Islām of Iṣfahān, Bahāʾ al-Dīn al-ʿĀmilī (d. 1030/1621), either shortly before or during the reign of Shah ʿAbbās I (r. 996/1588–1038/1629). This Arabic creed, titled *Iʿtiqādāt al-Imāmiyya* (or simply *al-Iʿtiqādāt*), as its author states, was primarily written for non-Twelver Shīʿīs, lest they confuse the views of the Twelvers with those of other Shīʿī denominations who maintained 'corrupted' dogmas (MTK 1/390f. no. 1623). In structure and contents, al-ʿĀmilī's creed is based on a short creed by Fakhr al-Muḥaqqiqīn (ʿĀmilī, *Iʿtiqādāt*, 189–94). Rather than being exclusively concerned with theological questions, the treatise also discusses at length how to observe religious duties and to avoid wrongdoing. This creed was later also translated into Persian and commented upon by several scholars including Adham al-Khalkhālī (d. *c.*1052/1642), and Sulṭān Ḥusayn al-Astarābādī (d. after 1077/1666) (ʿĀmilī, *Iʿtiqādāt*, 202–66).

Following al-ʿĀmilī, numerous scholars composed creedal works, often amalgamating theological and philosophical notions and argumentative strategies. A number of authors also composed more comprehensive doctrinal books. Rafīʿ al-Dīn Muḥammad b. Ḥaydar al-Ḥusaynī al-Ṭabāṭabāʾī al-Nāʾīnī (d. 1099/1687–8), for example, composed in 1047/1637 *Shajara-yi ilāhiyya* and dedicated it to Shāh Ṣafī (r. 1038/1628–1052/1642) (MTK 4/14 no. 7576), and in 1070/1660 he wrote another more concise creed based on the *Shajara*, titled *Thamara-yi Shajara-yi ilāhiyya* (MTK 2/400 no. 4349). ʿAbd al-Razzāq al-Lāhījī was the author of a philosophical creed, *Gawhar-i murād* which he completed in 1053/1643 and dedicated to Shah ʿAbbās II (r. 1052/1077–1642/1666) (MTK 4/551f. no. 10117). Later al-Lāhījī penned a credal work, again in Persian, *Sarmāya-yi īmān*, which he also dedicated to Shah ʿAbbās II in 1058/1648 (ʿAṭāyī Naẓarī 2011a: 9–16; MTK 3/530f. no. 7343). Shortly after al-Lāhījī, in 1063/1653, Mullā Muḥsin al-Fayḍ al-Kāshānī (d. 1090/1679) composed his *ʿAyn al-yaqīn fī uṣūl al-dīn* (MTK 4/319f. no. 9051), written in a style that echoes that of al-Lāhījī's works. Muḥammad Bāqir al-Sabzawārī's (d. 1090/1679–80) *al-ʿAqāʾid al-jāmiʿa* and Jamāl al-Dīn Muḥammad b. Ḥusayn al-Khʷānsārī's (d. 1122/1710–1) *Risāla dar uṣūl-i dīn* are other works in the same *genre* composed during the reign of Shah ʿAbbās II and dedicated to him (Āghā Buzurg 1983–6: ii. 186, xv. 282; MTK 4/248 no. 8684; 1/335 no. 1324). Towards the end of the Safavid period, Ḥasan b. ʿAbd al-Razzāq al-Lāhījī (d. 1121/1709) and Muḥammad b. ʿAbd al-Fattāḥ al-Tunkābunī (d. 1124/1712–3) also composed credal works—al-Lāhījī wrote *Shamʿ al-yaqīn dar uṣūl-i dīn* in 1092/1681 (MTK 4/112 no. 8065) and al-Tunkābunī authored *Ḍiyāʾ al-qulūb* in 1102/1691 (MTK 4/184 no. 8400).

In the late Safavid period another type of creed became popular which was intended to excommunicate holders and performers of certain beliefs or practices from the Twelver Shīʿī community. An anti-Sufi theologian of the time, Muḥammad Hādī al-Sabzawārī ('Mīr Lawḥī', d. after 1083/1672), wrote *Uṣūl al-ʿaqāʾid wa-jāmiʿ al-fawāʾid* in 1081/1671 in Persian (MTK 1/363 no. 1483). Muḥammad Shafīʿ Astarābādī (d. 1117/1705) composed a treatise titled *Uṣūl-i dīn* (also: *Āb-i ḥayāt*) which he dedicated to Shah Sulaymān (r. 1076/1666–1105/1694) (MTK 1/63 no. 2). Ismāʿīl Khātūnābādī, a teacher at the *madrasa* associated with the Jāmiʿ-i ʿAbbāsī, also dedicated his *Risāla-yi iʿtiqādiyya* to the Shah. The work contains an introduction followed by three chapters: on various kinds of existents (*dar aqsām-i mawjūdāt*), on the objections of philosophers and others to the principles of religions (*dar mukhālafāt-i uṣūl-i madhāhib-i arbāb-i kamālāt wa-sāʾir ṭabaqāt*), and on the requirements of salvation for those who seek to attain the highest stages (*dar sarmāya-yi najāt-i ṭālibīn-i wuṣūl bi rafīʿ darajāt*). Apart from doctrinal matters, the work contains some discussions of actions which are forbidden, according to the author, such as listening to music (*ghinā*) (Khātūnābādī, *Risāla*, 266f.). Muḥammad Bāqir al-Majlisī also composed *Ḥaqq al-yaqīn fī uṣūl al-dīn* in 1109/1698 which he dedicated to Shah Sulṭān Ḥusayn (r. 1105/1694–1135/1722) (MTK 3/123f. no. 5313).

During the early Safavid era, the Imami theologians were primarily concerned to defend the positions of their predecessors against the criticism of the Ashʿarites. Being fully aware of the overall agreement between their own doctrinal views and those of the Muʿtazilites, they argued that the latter had in fact adopted the views of Shīʿī Imams—a topos that had already been voiced during the early years of the occultation (*ghayba*) period. This is evident, for instance, in Nayrīzī's above-mentioned commentary on the *Tajrīd* (Pourjavady 2011: 66). Similarly, Mīr Abū al-Fatḥ al-Ḥusaynī al-ʿArabshāhī states explicitly that Imami doctrines are mostly identical with those of Muʿtazilites and, to a certain extent, with those of the philosophers (*al-ḥukamāʾ*). He also distinguishes between 'earlier' and 'later' Imami doctrines and usually sided with the 'later' doctrines by which he presumably means those formulated since Naṣīr al-Dīn al-Ṭūsī. On resurrection, for instance, he states that both the 'verifiers' among the early Muʿtazilites (*al-muḥaqqiqūn min qudamāʾ al-Muʿtazila*) as well as later Imamis (*mutaʾakhkhiriyyat al-Imāmiyya*) believed in bodily and spiritual resurrection, while early Imamis, like other theologians, believed in bodily resurrection only (al-Ḥillī, al-Suyūri, and al-ʿArabshāhī, *Bāb*, 206).

From the second half of the tenth/sixteenth century onwards, Imami scholars of Iran gradually became familiar with the four major *ḥadīth* collections of the Twelver Shīʿīs, viz. *al-Kāfī* by Muḥammad b. Yaʿqūb al-Kulaynī (d. 328/939 or 329/940), *Man lā yaḥḍuruhu al-faqīh* by Muḥammad Ibn Bābawayh al-Qummī ('al-Ṣadūq', d. 381/991), and *Tahdhīb al-aḥkām* and *al-Istibṣār* by Muḥammad b. Ḥasan al-Ṭūsī (d. 460/1067). Mīr Abū al-Fatḥ al-Ḥusaynī al-ʿArabshāhī, who seems to have gained access to some of these *ḥadīth* collections, maintains that one should comply with the traditions to the extent they are plausible (al-Ḥillī, al-Suyūri, and al-ʿArabshāhī, *Bāb*, 208, 214). One of the results of the increasing availability of these *ḥadīth* collections was a growing awareness of the numerous critical remarks of the Imams about *kalām* practices, culminating in occasional outright prohibition to engage in *kalām*. To circumvent this, Imami theologians sought to interpret these statements to allow at least for some types of theological discussions. Some argued that the only *kalām* discourse exempted from the Imams' prohibition would be one derived by means of traditions (*akhbār*) from the Imams. As a result, the supporters of this position relied increasingly on the traditions in their discussions of *kalām*. This was, for instance, the view of Muḥammad Amīn al-Astarābādī (d. 1036/1461), the founder of the Akhbārī strand. He argues that according to the *akhbār* from the infallible Imams it is forbidden to rely upon the intellect. Likewise, it is forbidden to study the science of *kalām* and to teach it unless one is referring to the *kalām* derived from their [the Imams'] words (Gleave 2007: 104). In his writings, Astarābādī distinguishes between an early discourse in Imami *kalām* and legal theory and a later one. Whereas earlier theological doctrines and principles of legal theory were exclusively derived from the sayings of the infallible Imams, later scholars recognized intellectual reasoning as one of the methods to attain certainty in these fields (Astarābādī, *Dānishnāma*, 3a–4a). The shift, to him, occurred gradually in the fourth/tenth century when Muḥammad b. Aḥmad al-Iskāfī (*fl.* 340/951) and Ibn Abī ʿAqīl al-ʿUmānī (d. *c.*340/951) applied intellectual reasoning to their treatment of theology and legal theory on grounds of *taqiyya* ('dissimulation'). Later on, al-Shaykh al-Mufīd who was unaware that their recourse to reason was grounded on *taqiyya* promoted intellectual reasoning in his treatment of *kalām* and legal theory (Astarābādī, *Dānishnāma*, 3a–4a).

The *Kāfī* of al-Kulaynī developed into an important platform for theological discussions during this period, as is suggested by the numerous glosses that were now written on the text (Pourjavady and Schmidtke 2015: 255ff.). A pre-eminent scholar of Isfahan in the early eleventh/seventeenth century, Muḥammad Bāqir Astarābādī, known as Mīr Dāmād (d. 1040/1632), seems to have been the first to write glosses on the *Kāfī*. Following him, numerous scholars of the eleventh/seventeenth century, including Muḥammad Amīn al-Astarābādī, Ṣadr al-Dīn al-Shīrāzī ('Mullā Ṣadrā', d. 1045/1635–6), Sayyid Aḥmad al-ʿAlawī, Rafīʿ al-Dīn al-Nāʾīnī, Khalīl al-Qazwīnī (d. 1089/1678), Muḥammad b. Ṣāliḥ b. Aḥmad al-Māzandarānī (1086/1675–6), and finally Muḥammad Bāqir al-Majlisī (d. 1110/1699, who titled his work *Mirʾāt al-ʿuqūl*) wrote commentaries and glosses on this work, in the course of which they regularly discussed doctrinal issues (Rizvi 2007b: 47–50). The *Kitāb al-Tawḥīd* by Ibn Bābawayh also served as a model for the scholars of the Safavid era for writing traditional theology. This text, which was evidently not easily accessible in Iran during the first half of the tenth/sixteenth century, became one of the prominent theological works during the following century. In her inventory of manuscripts of Ibn Bābawayh's works, M. Tafaḍḍulī has identified ninety-two copies of this work in the libraries of Iran. The earliest extant copy of the *Tawḥīd* was completed in 953/1546–7. Over the following decades the work was rarely copied. The demand seems to have increased in the early eleventh/seventeenth century and then culminated in the second half of that century—over fifty copies of this work were produced between 1048/1638 and 1098/1687. During the same period, several commentaries were written on this text (Pourjavady and Schmidtke 2015: 255ff.). The Shaykh al-Islām of Isfahan, Muḥammad Bāqir al-Sabzawārī, seems to have been the first scholar who wrote a Persian commentary on this text (Āghā Buzurg 1983–6: xiii. 153f.). Following him at least two more commentaries were composed in Arabic on this work: *Anīs al-waḥīd fī sharḥ al-Tawḥīd* by Sayyid Niʿmat Allāh Jazāʾirī (d. 1112/1701), completed in 1099/1687–8 (MTK 1/502 no. 2213), and a commentary by Qāḍī Saʿīd al-Qummī (d. 1107/1696), completed in 1107/1696 (MTK 4/44f. no. 7729). Some of the doctrinal works by other early Imami theologians, such as *Awāʾil al-maqālāt* by al-Shaykh al-Mufīd and *al-Fuṣūl al-mukhtāra* by al-Sharīf al-Murtaḍā (d. 436/1044), also became popular during this period, and of most of them, including the latter two, no copy prior to the eleventh/seventeenth century is known to be extant (al-Ṭabāṭabāʾī 1992, 59f., 107f.).

It did not take long until this intellectual shift manifested itself in a distinct style of theological writing. Al-Fayḍ al-Kāshānī's *ʿIlm al-yaqīn*, completed in 1042/1632–3, seems to have been one of the early examples of refashioning old style Twelver Shīʿī creed. Al-Fayḍ presents in this work theology through the lights of the relevant sayings of the Imams, referring mainly to *al-Kāfī* and *al-Tawḥīd*. The author is also innovative in the way he structured this work—the book contains four chapters: Chapter One on God, Chapter Two on the Angels, Chapter Three on the Holy books and prophets, and Chapter Four on the Hereafter. The author composed a summary of his *ʿIlm al-yaqīn*, titled *Anwār al-ḥikma* (MTK 1/521 no. 2304).

The Safavid scholars' predilection towards early Twelver Shīʿī *kalām* not only manifested itself in style and argumentation but also in doctrine. An evidence for this is their view on *badāʾ*, literally God's ability to change His mind. Because of its roots in the transmitted sayings of the Imams, for many Imami theologians this distinctively Shīʿī notion needed to be accommodated in theology in some way. Al-Ṣadūq, al-Mufīd, and al-Murtaḍā had treated it as merely signifying abrogation (*naskh*), otherwise a universally acknowledged Islamic principle that is rooted in the Qurʾān. Al-Sharīf al-Murtaḍā also considered the reports supporting *badāʾ* to be single traditions (*āḥād*), and thus not yielding certain evidence. Naṣīr al-Dīn al-Ṭusī rejected *badāʾ* altogether, similarly arguing that the notion is based on an isolated tradition (*khabar wāḥid*) and as such not trustworthy (Sajjadi 2013: 45–7). In view of the numerous sayings of the Imams in which the idea of *badāʾ* is espoused the scholars of the Safavid era again endorsed this notion. Again, Mīr Dāmād seems to have been the first Ṣafavid scholar to discuss this doctrine. In his *Nibrās al-ḍiyāʾ wa-taswāʾ al-sawāʾ*, a monograph on this very topic (MTK 5/355 no. 11975), Mīr Dāmād responds to the counter-arguments of al-Ṭusī (Rizvi 2006:

173f.). Muḥammad Amīn Astarābādī, Muḥammad Ḥasan Shīrwānī (d. 1098/1688), Muḥammad Bāqir al-Majlisī (d. 1110/1698), and Muḥammad Shafīʿ Gīlānī (*fl.* 1090/1679) also wrote monographs on this subject (MTK 2/30 no. 2622). Many other thinkers, including Mullā Ṣadrā, Rafīʿ al-Dīn al-Nāʾīnī, and al-Fayḍ al-Kāshānī, also contributed to this discussion in their writings (Subḥānī 1996–7: 451–5; Sajjadi 2013: 47–9). In the late Safavid period the idea of the occultation (*ghayba*) and return (*rajʿa*) also received the scholars' renewed attention. According to Twelver Shīʿī thought *rajʿa* denotes the return of a group of Muslims to this world following the appearance of the Mahdī and prior to the resurrection. A copy of a treatise attributed to al-Faḍl b. Shādhān al-Nishābūrī (d. 260/874) titled *Risāla fī ithbāt al-rajʿa* was available to Mīr Lawḥī who used it when writing his *Kifāyat al-muhtadī fī maʿrifat al-Mahdī* (MTK 4/517 no. 9958). Muḥammad b. Ḥasan al-Ḥurr al-ʿĀmilī (d. 1104/1692) seems to have used the same source when writing his *al-Īqāḍ min al-hajʿa bi-l-burhān ʿalā l-rajʿa* (MTK 1/553f. no. 2452; Ansari 2011: 726f). Al-Majlisī also devoted a short treatise to the issue (MTK 2/27f. no. 2613).

As discussed in Section I of this chapter, the majority of Twelver Shīʿī theologians since the seventh/thirteenth century integrated philosophical notions and demonstrations into their theological discussions. During the Safavid era and particularly during the eleventh/seventeenth century, philosophy played a more central role in some theological writings. Some theologians largely identified philosophy with theology to the extent that they no longer recognized *kalām* to constitute a distinct discipline. The works of ʿAbd al-Razzāq al-Lāhījī belong to the category of books that equally belong to philosophy and to *kalām*. Al-Lāhījī held that 'true philosophy' (*al-falsafa al-ḥaqqa*) constitutes a common truth that is equally expressed both by the infallible Imams and the true philosophers. Thus, most of the principles of the Imamis, as they are derived from the Imams' reports, fully correspond to the principles of the outstanding Muslim philosophers and their predecessors among the Greek philosophers (ʿAṭāyī Naẓarī 2011b: 74). This also explains, al-Lāhījī states, the similarities between Muʿtazilite and Twelver Shīʿī theology—it is not that one group adopted the doctrines of the other, but rather the fact that both employed philosophy in their methodology.

Al-Lāhījī admits that the early Shīʿī *mutakallimūn* had a different approach to theology and that their task was to derive doctrinal positions from the Imams' traditions. But it seems that to him this is a by now accomplished task. The task at hand now, so he suggests, is to scrutinize the nature of these doctrines through inference—inference for him being syllogistic reasoning—and thus achieve the same level of certainty as can possibly be gained on the basis of the sayings of the infallible Imams (ʿAṭāyī Naẓarī 2011a: 77–9). Although metaphysics and *kalām* share both subject and methodology, al-Lāhījī recognizes a distinction between them. Unlike *kalām*, metaphysics does not need to defend religion. In case of a conflict between demonstrative reasoning and a tradition, the tradition should possibly be rejected as a false one or the conflict should be resolved through interpretation. Resolving such a conflict, however, is the task of *kalām* and not metaphysics (ʿAṭāyī Naẓarī 2011a: 19f.). Another prominent scholar engaged in philosophical theology during this period, al-Fayḍ al-Kāshānī, held that ordinary students should not engage in rational theology. Accordingly, he refrained from popularizing some of his theological works for general readers.

Despite the efforts of scholars such as al-Lāhījī and al-Fayḍ al-Kāshānī in justifying philosophical theology, the opponents of philosophy undertook tireless efforts to establish themselves as the official representatives of Twelver Shīʿism. They not only referred to traditions according to which the Imams condemned engagement in rational investigation, they also held that a number of philosophical ideas were incompatible with doctrinal principles. Among them was Muḥyī al-Dīn Ibn ʿArabī's doctrine of unity of existence that had been appropriated by some philosophers of this period, most notably Mullā Ṣadrā and his student al-Fayḍ al-Kāshānī. The latter two also allowed for the possibility of resurrection in the form of imaginal bodies instead of bodily resurrection, which again aroused the opposition of tradition-oriented scholars. Mīr Dāmād's notion of 'perpetual origination' of the world (*ḥudūth dahrī*), in which the creation of the world as an act of a volitional deity was combined with the philosophical concept that God eternally necessitates the world, was likewise considered to be in conflict with religion. These ideas were also criticized among the philosophers of the time. ʿAbd al-Razzāq al-Lāhījī and Ḥusayn al-Khʷānsārī (d. 1098/1687), for example, criticized Mullā Ṣadrā's ontology and Jamāl al-Dīn al-Khʷānsārī rejected Mīr Dāmād's doctrine and proposed instead al-Ghazālī's notion of an estimative time prior to the creation of the world (Ghazālī, *Incoherence*, 30–8). But even these critiques from within the philosophical circles did not appease the radical opponents, who did not tolerate any rational reasoning in theological matters. In his *Iʿtiqādāt*, Muḥammad Bāqir al-Majlisī declares anyone who shares the belief in eternal intellects or prime matter or rejects the temporal origination of the world and bodily resurrection to be an infidel (*takfīr*).

References

ʿAbbās, D. (1995). *Bahāʾal-Dīn al-ʿĀmilī: Adīban wa-faqīhan wa-ʿāliman*. Beirut: Dār al-Ḥawār.

Āghā Buzurg al-Ṭihrānī (1983–6). *al-Dharīʿa ilā taṣānīf al-shīʿa*. 25 vols. Beirut: Dār al-Aḍwāʾ, 1403–6.

Agha-Tehrani, M. (1996). *Sayyid Haydar Amuli (719–787/1319–1385): An Overview of his Doctrines*. MA dissertation, University of Toronto.

ʿĀmilī, Bahāʾ al-Dīn Muḥammad (*Iʿtiqādāt*). *Iʿtiqādāt-i shaykh-i Bahāyī: matn-i ʿArabī-i Risālat al-iʿtiqādāt-i Shaykh-i Bahāʾ al-Dīn Muḥammad ʿĀmilī bi hamrāh-i si tarjuma u sharḥ-i fārsī-yi ān*. Ed. Jūyā Jahānbakhsh. Tehran: Asāṭīr, 1387/2008.

Ansari, H. (2012). *Barrisīhā-yi Tārīkhī dar ḥawza-yi Islām u tashayyuʿ*. Tehran: Kitābkhāna, Mūza va markaz-i Asnād-i Majlis-i Shūrā-yi Islāmī, 1390.

Ansari, H. (2015). *Az ganjīna-hā-yi nusakh-i khattī: Muʿarrifī-i dast-niwishta-hā-yī arzishmand az kitābkhāna-hā-yi buzurg-i jahān dar ḥawza-yi ʿulūm-i islāmī*. Vol. i. Isfahan: Daftar-i tablīghāti islāmī, Shoʿba-yi ustān-i Iṣfahān, 1394.

al-Anṣārī, Murtaḍā (*Fawāʾid*). *Fawāʾid al-uṣūl*. Ed. ʿAbd Allāh Nūrānī. Qum: Muʾassasat al-Nashr al-Islāmiyya, 1408/1987–8.

Anwār, M. J. (1991). 'Ibn Mutawwaj'. *Dāʾirat al-maʿārif-i buzurg-i islāmī*, Tehran, iv. 569f.

Arbaʿ rasāʾil kalāmiyya. al-Maqāla al-taklīfiyya wa-l-Bāqiyyāt al-ṣāliḥāt li-l-Shahīd al-awwal. al-Risāla al-yūnisiyya wa-l-Kalimāt al-nāfiʿāt li-l-ʿAllāma al-Bayāḍī. Qum: Markaz al-abḥāth wa-l-dirāsāt al-islāmiyya. Qism iḥyāʾ al-turāth al-islāmī, 1380/2001.

Astarābādī, Muḥammad Amīn (*Dānishnāma*). *Dānishnāma-yi shāhī*. MS Qum, Marʿashī 10144/1, ff. 1b–73b.

ʿAṭāyī Naẓarī, Ḥ. (2011a). 'Nukātī dar bāb-i Fayyāḍ-i Lāhījī u andishahā-yi kalāmī-i u'. *Āyīna-yi Pazhūhish* 22/2 (1390): 7–26.

ʿAṭāyī Naẓarī, Ḥ. (2011b). 'Naqsh-i Fayyāḍ-i Lāhījī dar falsafī shodan-i kalām-i Shīʿa'. *Andīsha-yi nuwīn-i dīnī* 7 (Autumn 1390): 65–92.

al-Baḥrānī, Maytham b. Maytham (*Sharḥ*). *Sharḥ Nahj al-balāgha*. 3 vols. Tehran: Muʾassasat al-Naṣr, 1378/1958.

al-Bayāḍī, ʿAlī b. Muḥammad b. Yūnus (*ʿUṣra*). *ʿUṣrat al-manjūd fī ʿilm al-kalām*. Ed. Ḥusayn al-Tunkābunī. Qum: Muʾassasat al-Imām al-Ṣādiq, 1428/2007.

Daiber, H., and J. Ragep (2000). 'al-Ṭūsī, Naṣīr al-Dīn'. *The Encyclopaedia of Islam*. New edn. Leiden: Brill, 10/746–52.

Firouzi, J. (2011). 'Al-Bāb al-Ḥādī ʿashar'. *Encyclopaedia Islamica*. Leiden: Brill, iii. 1002–4.

al-Ghazālī, Abū Ḥāmid Muḥammad (*Incoherence*). *The Incoherence of the Philosophers*. Translated, introduced, and annotated by M. E. Marmura. Provo, UT: Brigham Young University Press, 2000.

al-Ghufrānī, ʿAbd Allāh (2013). *Fihris muṣannafāt al-Shaykh Muḥammad b. ʿAlī b. Abī Jumhūr al-Aḥsāʾī: Kashshāf biblīyūghrāfī li-muṣannafāt Ibn Abī Jumhūr al-makhṭūṭa wa-l-maṭbūʿa wa-ijāzātihi fī l-riwāya wa-ṭuruqihi fī l-ḥadīth*. Beirut: Dār al-Maḥajja al-Bayḍāʾ li-l-tibāʿa wa-l-nashr wa-l-tawzīʿ, 1434.

Gleave, R. (2007). *Scripturalist Islam: The History and Doctrines of the Akhbārī Shīʿī School*. Leiden: Brill.

al-Ḥillī, Jamāl al-Dīn al-Ḥasan b. Yūsuf, al-Miqdād al-Suyūrī, and Abū l-Fatḥ al-Ḥusaynī al-ʿArabshāhī (*Bāb*). *al-Bāb al-ḥādī ʿashar li-l-ʿAllāma al-Ḥillī maʿa sharḥayhi al-Nāfiʿ yawm al-ḥashr li-Miqdād ʿAbd Allāh al-Suyūrī wa-Miftāḥ al-Bāb li-Abī l-Fatḥ b. Makhdūm al-Ḥusaynī*. Ed. Mahdī Muḥaqqiq. Tehran: McGill University, Institute of Islamic Studies, Tehran Branch, 1986.

al-Ḥimmaṣī al-Rāzī, Maḥmūd b. ʿAlī b. Maḥmūd (*Kashf*). *Kashf al-maʿāqid fī sharḥ Qawāʿid al-ʿaqāʾid. Facsimile Edition of MS Wetzstein 1527 (State Library Berlin)*. Introduction and Indexes by S. Schmidtke. Tehran: Iranian Institute of Philosophy.

Ibn Abī Jumhūr al-Aḥsāʾī (*Mujlī*). *Mujlī mirʾāt al-munjī fī l-kalām wa-l-ḥikmatayn wa-l-taṣawwuf*. Ed. R. Yaḥyā Pūr Fārmad. 5 vols. Beirut: Dār al-Maḥajja al-Bayḍāʾ li-l-tibāʿa wa-l-nashr wa-l-tawzīʿ, 2012.

Khātūnābādī, Ismāʿīl (*Risāla*). 'Risāla-yi Iʿtiqādiyya'. Ed. Faṭima Fanā. In ʿAlī Awjabī (ed.), *Ganjīna-yi bahāristān: Ḥikmat 2*. Tehran: Kitābkhāna, Mūzih va Markaz-i Asnād-i Majlis-i Shūrā-yi Islāmī, 1387/2006, 219–73.

Landolt, H. (2000). 'Khwāja Naṣīr al-Dīn al-Ṭūsī (597/1201–672/1274), Ismāʿīlism, and Ishrāqī Philosophy'. In N. Pourjavady and Ž. Vesel (eds.), *Naṣīr al-Dīn Ṭūsī: Philosophe et savant du xiiie siècle. Actes du colloque tenu à l'Université de Téhéran (6–9 mars 1997)*. Tehran: Presses universitaires d'Iran/Institut français de recherche en Iran, 13–30.

Madelung, W. (1989). 'Baḥrānī, Jamāl-al-Dīn'. *Encyclopaedia Iranica*. London: Routledge & Kegan Paul, iv. 529.

MTK = *Muʿjam al-turāth al-kalāmī*, taʾlīf al-Lajna al-ʿilmiyya fī Muʾassasat al-Imām al-Ṣādiq, taqdīm wa-ishrāf Jaʿfar al-Subḥānī. Qum: Muʾassasat al-Imām al-Ṣādiq, 1424[/2003–4].

Mudarris Raḍawī, M. T. (1991). *Aḥwāl u āthār-i Khwāja Naṣīr al-Dīn Ṭūsī*. Tehran: Muʾassasa-yi muṭālaʿāt u taḥqīqāt-i farhangī, 1370[/1991].

al-Mukhtārī, R. (2005). *Al-Shahīd al-awwal: Ḥayātuhu wa-āthāruhu*. Qum: Markaz al-nashr li-maktab al-iʿlām al-islāmī, 1426/1384.

al-Oraibi, A. (1992). *Shiʿi Renaissance: A Case Study of the Theosophical School of Bahrain in the 7th/13th Century*. Ph.D. dissertation, McGill University, Montreal.

al-Oraibi, A. (2001). 'Rationalism in the School of Bahrain: A Historical Perspective'. In L. Clarke (ed.), *Shīʿite Heritage: Essays on Classical and Modern Traditions*. Binghampton, NY: Global Publications, 331–43.

Pourjavady, N., and Ž. Vesel (eds.) (2000). *Naṣīr al-Dīn Ṭūsī: Philosophe et savant du xiiie siècle. Actes du colloque tenu à l'Université de Téhéran (6–9 mars 1997)*. Tehran: Presses universitaires d'Iran/Institut français de recherche en Iran.

Pourjavady, R. (2011). *Philosophy in Early Safavid Iran: Najm al-Dīn Maḥmūd al-Nayrīzī and his Writings*. Leiden: Brill.

Pourjavady, R., and S. Schmidtke (2006). 'Some Notes on a New Edition of a Medieval Philosophical Text in Turkey: Shams al-Dīn al-Shahrazūrī's *Rasāʾil al-Shajara al-ilahiyya*'. *Die Welt des Islams* 46: 76–85.

Pourjavady, R., and S. Schmidtke (2015). 'An Eastern Renaissance? Greek Philosophy under the Safavids (16th–18th centuries ad)'. In D. Gutas, S. Schmidtke, and A. Treiger (eds.), *New Horizons in Graeco-Arabic Studies. = Intellectual History of the Islamicate World*, 3: 248–90.

Qummī, Mīrzā (*Risāla*). *Riṣāla dar uṣūl-i dīn*. Tehran: lithograph edn., 1308/1890–1.

Rizvi, S. (2006). 'Between Time and Eternity: Mīr Dāmād on God's Creative Agency'. *Journal of Islamic Studies* 17: 158–76.

Rizvi, S. (2007a). 'A Sufi Theology Fit for a Shīʿī King: The Gawhar-i murād of ʿAbd al-Razzāq Lāhījī'. In A. Shihadeh (ed.), *Sufism and Theology*. Edinburgh: Edinburgh University Press, 83–98.

Rizvi, S. (2007b). *Mullā Ṣadrā Shīrāzī: His Life and Works and the Sources for Safavid Philosophy*. Oxford: Oxford University Press on behalf of the University of Manchester.

Ṣadrāʾī Khūyī, ʿA. (2003). *Kitābshināsī-yi Tajrīd al-iʿtiqād*. Qum: Kitābkhāna-yi buzurg-i Ḥaḍrat Āyat Allāh al-ʿuẓmā Marʿashī Najafī, 1382/1424.

Sajjadi, S. J. (2013). 'Badāʾ'. *Encyclopaedia Islamica*. Leiden: Brill, iv. 433–49.

Schmidtke, S. (1991). *The Theology of al-ʿAllāma al-Ḥillī (d. 726/1325)*. Berlin: Klaus Schwarz.

Schmidtke, S. (2000). *Theologie, Philosophie und Mystik im zwölferschiitischen Islam des 9./15. Jahrhunderts: Die Gedankenwelten des Ibn Abī Ǧumhūr al-Aḥsāʾī (um 838/1434–35—nach 906/1501)*. Leiden: Brill.

Schmidtke, S. (2009a). 'The Doctrinal Views of the Banu l-ʿAwd (Early 8th/14th Century): An Analysis of ms Arab. f. 64 (Bodleian Library, Oxford)'. In M. A. Amir-Moezzi, M. Bar-Asher, and S. Hopkins (eds.), *Le Shiʿisme imamite quarante ans après: hommage à Etan Kohlberg*. Turnhout: Brepols, 357–82.

Schmidtke, S. (2009b). 'New Sources for the Life and Work of Ibn Abī Jumhūr al-Aḥsāʾī'. *Studia Iranica* 38: 49–68.

Schmidtke, S. (2013). 'Ibn Abī Jumhūr al-Aḥsāʾī and his *Sharḥ al-Bāb al-ḥādī ʿashar*'. In M. A. Amir-Moezzi (ed.), *Islam: identité et altérité: Hommage à Guy Monnot, O.P.* Turnhout: Brepols, 369–84.

Schmidtke, S. (forthcoming). 'Ibn Abī Jumhūr al-Aḥsāʾī and his *Kitāb Mujlī Mirʾāt al-munjī*'. In Kh. el-Rouayheb and S. Schmidtke (eds.), *Oxford Handbook of Islamic Philosophy*. New York: Oxford University Press.

Subḥānī, J. (1996–7). 'Badā''. In *Dānishnāma-yi jahān-i Islām*. Vol. ii. Tehran, 1375, 451–5.

al-Ṭabāṭabā'ī, al-Sayyid ʿAbd al-ʿAzīz (1992). 'Al-Shaykh al-Mufīd wa-ʿaṭā'uhu al-fikrī al-khālid'. *Turāthunā* 8/1–2 (1413): 10–143.

al-Ṭabāṭabā'ī, al-Sayyid ʿAbd al-ʿAzīz (1995). *Maktabat al-ʿAllāma al-Ḥillī*. Qum: Mu'assasat Āl al-Bayt (ʿalayhum al-salām) li-iḥyā' al-turāth.

Tafaḍḍulī, M. (2002). *Kitābshināsī-i nuskhaha-yi khaṭṭī-i Āthār-i shaykh-i Ṣadūq dar Īrān*. Tehran: Vizārat-i farhan u irshād-i Islāmī, 1381.

Taghavi, A. S. (2013). 'Al-Baḥrānī, Abū al-Ḥasan Jamāl al-Dīn'. *Encyclopaedia Islamica*. Leiden: Brill, iv. 187–8.

Ṭāliʿī, ʿAbd al-Ḥusayn (2013). *Faqīh-i Ḥillī: Murūrī bar zandagī wa āthār-i ʿAllāma-yi Ḥillī*. Tehran: Hamshahrī, 1392.

Yūsuf, ʿA. A. (2007). *Al-ʿAllāma al-Shaykh Maytham al-Baḥrānī: Rajul al-ʿilm wa-l-akhlāq wa-l-siyāsa*. Beirut: Dār al-Rasūl al-Akram.

CHAPTER 27

ZAYDĪ THEOLOGY IN YEMEN

HASSAN ANSARI, SABINE SCHMIDTKE, AND JAN THIELE

For most of its history, Zaydī theology was heavily influenced by Muʿtazilite doctrines.[1] Yemen is the only region with a significant Zaydī community until the present day. It is therefore in the country's historical libraries that thousands of Muʿtazilite manuscripts have survived. These collections include both texts that were lost in majoritarian Sunni lands as well as many other theological works written by members of the Zaydī community themselves. This chapter provides a survey of theological trends and movements from the beginnings of the Zaydī imamate in Yemen over its political unification with the Caspian Zaydiyya down to theologians from the ninth/fifteenth century. Theologians in Yemen were inclined towards various sub-schools of Muʿtazilism from as early as the beginnings of the country's imamate; its impact became even more important when intellectual exchanges with their Caspian co-religionists (a tradition discussed in Chapter 10) increased during the sixth/twelfth century. Yet there was always a lively theological trend that was sceptical about or even completely rejected the adoption of Muʿtazilism and stressed the independent nature of Zaydī doctrines.

I Zaydī Theology before and after the Unification of the Yemeni and the Caspian Imamates

Since the foundation of the Zaydī imamate in the northern mountainous highlands of Yemen by Imam al-Hādī ilā l-Ḥaqq (d. 298/911), the Zaydīs of Yemen developed

[1] When preparing this chapter, Jan Thiele received funding from the Gerda Henkel Foundation's M4HUMAN programme. Hassan Ansari wishes to thank the Institute for Advanced Study at Princeton, NJ, which hosted him as a member during the preparation of this chapter.

a canon of doctrinal writings of the Imams which remained authoritative over the coming centuries. First and foremost among these was a collection (*majmūʿ*) of epistles by Imam al-Qāsim b. Ibrāhīm al-Rassī (d. 246/860) which is preserved in numerous collective manuscripts, among them an early copy that may possibly be dated to the fourth/tenth century (Madelung 1965: 96 n. 1). While al-Qāsim advocated in his authentic writings human free will and the absolute otherness of God from His creation he was clearly not influenced by Muʿtazilism but rather informed by *kalām* debates among his Christian contemporaries whom he encountered while residing in Egypt—W. Madelung has shown the striking structural resemblances between al-Qāsim and Theodore Abū Qurra (Madelung 1965, 1989, 1991a).[2] However, later on a number of epistles were ascribed to al-Qāsim which were clearly written at a stage when the Zaydīs were already under the influence of Muʿtazilite thought. These are included in the majority of collective manuscripts of al-Qāsim's epistles that circulated in Yemen. The literary and doctrinal legacy of al-Qāsim as it was perceived by the Yemeni Zaydīs was therefore somewhat different from the authentic al-Qāsim.[3] The collection of writings of his son Muḥammad (d. 284/897–8) also became part of the canon (Muḥammad b. al-Qāsim, *Majmūʿ*). As was the case with his father, al-Qāsim, Muḥammad's thought shows affinities with cognate Muʿtazilite doctrines but he can certainly not be described to have endorsed Muʿtazilite thought.[4] Al-Qāsim's grandson, Yaḥyā b. al-Ḥusayn, the later Imam al-Hādī ilā l-ḥaqq (d. 298/911) and founder of the Zaydī imamate in Yemen, is reported to have studied during his sojourn in Northern Iran with Abū l-Qāsim al-Kaʿbī al-Balkhī (d. 319/931) (Jundārī, *Tarājim*, 41; Zaryāb 1994: 151)—if true, he was in fact the first Zaydī Imam to study with a representative of the Muʿtazila. As a result, his doctrinal thought was deeply influenced by the theological views of the Muʿtazilite school of Baghdad, although al-Hādī refrained from expressly stating his agreement with their doctrines or even identifying himself with the Muʿtazila (Madelung 1965: 164–7; ʿAbd al-Raḥmān 2003a). His literary legacy was likewise transmitted among the Zaydīs of Yemen in a

[2] As a result, al-Qāsim's doctrinal views differed from those of the prominent representatives of the early Kūfan Zaydiyya, esp. Aḥmad b. ʿĪsā b. Zayd (d. 247/861), his companion Muḥammad b. Manṣūr al-Murādī (alive in 252/866), and the latter's younger contemporary al-Ḥasan b. Yaḥyā b. al-Ḥusayn b. Zayd; for example, the earlier Zaydīs were proponents of divine determinism. See Madelung 1965: 80–5; Madelung 1989; Ansari 2011.

[3] W. Madelung has distinguished in detail the authentic from the unauthentic works of al-Qāsim (Madelung 1965: 97ff.). B. Abrahamov, by contrast, considers most of the works that were classified by Madelung as inauthentic as authentic and concludes that the latter endorsed at a later stage of his life Muʿtazilite thinking (Abrahamov 1987, 1990, 1996). For a critical discussion of his conclusions see Madelung 1989; 1991b—at some stage the Zaydīs of Yemen, following the Kufan tradition, also added a collection allegedly containing the doctrinal writings of Imam Zayd b. ʿAlī b. al-Ḥusayn (b. 75/694–5; d. 122/740) (Zayd b. ʿAlī, *Majmūʿ*). These are evidently not authentic and rather originate partly with the early Kūfan Zaydiyya and partly with the Yemeni Zaydiyya who claimed that Zayd b. ʿAlī's theological thought agreed with the views of the Muʿtazila (Madelung 2002).

[4] A thorough investigation of his writings, as well as the writings of the Zaydī Imams of Yemen of the fourth/tenth to sixth/twelfth century, is still a major desideratum. Moreover, the authenticity of the writings included in the respective *majāmīʿ* collections still needs to be established.

popular *majmūʿ* of epistles (al-Hādī ilā l-ḥaqq, *Majmūʿa fākhira; Majmūʿ*). Among the Yemeni Zaydīs of later centuries, the teachings of al-Hādī and his grandfather al-Qāsim were largely identified with each other. Canonical status was also accorded to the writings of al-Hādī's sons Muḥammad al-Murtaḍā li-Dīn Allāh (d. 310/922) (al-Murtaḍā li-Dīn Allāh, *Majmūʿ*) and Imam Aḥmad al-Nāṣir li-Dīn Allāh (301/913–322/934) (Madelung 1965: 169–74, 191–3; Madelung 1985; 1990).

With Imam al-Manṣūr bi-llāh al-Qāsim b. ʿAlī b. ʿAbd Allāh al-ʿIyānī (b. between 310/922 and 340/951, d. 393/1003) (Madelung 1965: 194–8; al-Wajīh 1999: 773–5 no. 833), a great-grandson of al-Qāsim b. Ibrāhīm's son Muḥammad, the doctrinal development of the Zaydiyya entered a new phase. Unlike earlier Imams, al-Qāsim al-ʿIyānī addresses in his writings philosophical notions and issues belonging to the so-called subtleties of *kalām* (al-Qāsim al-ʿIyānī, *Majmūʿ*), and the same applies to his son, al-Mahdī li-Dīn Allāh al-Ḥusayn (d. 404/1013), who wrote a book on the nature of beings, *Kitāb al-Ṭabāʾiʿ* (al-Ḥusayn b. al-Qāsim al-ʿIyānī, *Majmūʿ*; on him, see Madelung 1965: 198–200; al-Wajīh 1999: 384–8 no. 385). Other than this, both Imams remained by and large faithful to the doctrines of al-Hādī ilā l-ḥaqq. The works of both Imams were referred to by the adherents of a theological doctrine that evolved among the Zaydīs of Yemen during the fifth/eleventh century who otherwise took the teachings of the early Imams as their starting point.[5]

A major role in formulating and systematizing this new tradition was played by Muṭarrif b. Shihāb b. ʿĀmir b. ʿAbbād al-Shihābī (d. after 459/1067). It was after him that this strand was retrospectively labelled as the 'Muṭarrifiyya'. Muṭarrif b. Shihāb also founded the first *hijra* ('abode of emigration'), in the village of Sanāʿ, south of Ṣanʿāʾ (Madelung 1991a). *Hijra*s were a characteristic institution of the Muṭarrifī community that considerably helped them to spread and establish their teaching over wide parts of the country. While the adherents of this doctrine claimed to cling fervently to the theological teachings of al-Hādī and the latter's sons Muḥammad and Aḥmad, they actually developed a cosmology and natural philosophy of their own. Most renowned among their doctrines was their view that God had created the world out of three or four elements, viz. water, air, winds, and fire. Changes in the world result, as they claim, from the interaction of these constituents of the physical world—in other words from a natural causality—rather than God's directly acting upon it (Madelung 1965: 202f.; 1975; 1991a; Ansari 2006).

[5] Again, the authenticity of the various epistles still needs to be verified in detail. Since none of their writings has been studied in any detail, it cannot be ruled out at present that some epistles were later on ascribed to one of the Imams by later adherents of the Muṭarrifiyya. After al-Ḥusayn was killed in Ṣafar 404/September 1013, his followers believed in his imminent return as the Mahdī—the adherents of this belief later became known as the Ḥusayniyya. As a result, his successors refrained from using the title of Imam for themselves but rather called themselves amīrs—viz. his oldest brother Jaʿfar b. al-Qāsim al-ʿIyānī (d. 450/1059) as well as his sons al-Sharīf al-Fāḍil al-Qāsim (d. 468/1075) and Dhū l-Sharafayn Muḥammad (d. 477/1084) (al-Rabaʿī, *Sīra*; Madelung 1977). The followers of the Ḥusayniyya also developed their own peculiar doctrinal views which were later criticized by the Zaydīs. Cf., for example, al-Rabaʿī, *Sīra*, 345–65.

During the reign of Imam Abū Ṭālib *al-akhīr* Yaḥyā b. Aḥmad b. al-Ḥusayn b. al-Muʾayyad bi-llāh Aḥmad b. al-Ḥusayn al-Hārūnī (d. 520/1126) (al-Wajīh 1999: 1088f. no. 1163) the Yemeni and the Caspian Zaydīs were eventually unified for the first time in history under a common political and religious leadership. After many years of quasi-isolation, the change of the politico-religious framework exposed the Yemeni Zaydīs to new theological influences. In order to strengthen the authority of the Imam in both communities, the intellectual gap between them was supposed to be bridged by a harmonization of their respective scholarly traditions. Unlike their Yemeni co-religionists, the Zaydīs of Rayy and Northern Iran had embraced Bahshamite theology as early as the fourth/tenth century (see Chapter 10). The Bahshamiyya was a branch of Basran Muʿtazilism named after Abū Hāshim al-Jubbāʾī (d. 321/933), a towering figure of Muslim theology, who had, in many respects, redefined the doctrinal foundations of the school. Bahshamite theology experienced a flowering in Rayy and in the Caspian region under the reign of the Būyids, who made the city of Rayy the centre of the Bahshamiyya's chief theologians. This also affected the Zaydīs' intelligence in the region: many scholars were attracted by the study circles of such eminent thinkers as ʿAbd al-Jabbār al-Hamadānī (d. 415/1025) or al-Ḥasan b. Aḥmad Ibn Mattawayh.

Some information about the doctrinal developments among their Iranian co-religionists may have reached Yemen as early as during the time of the Imam al-Nāṣir li-Dīn Allāh Abū l-Fatḥ al-Nāṣir b. al-Ḥusayn al-Daylamī, who hailed from the Caspian region and arrived in al-Bawn in Yemen in 430/1039, that is one year after claiming the Zaydī imamate in 429/1038 (Madelung 1965: 203, 205; Madelung 1980; Mohaqqeq 2008). Abū l-Fatḥ engaged in combats with the local descendants of al-Hādī and with Jaʿfar b. al-Qāsim al-ʿIyānī, the leader of the Ḥusayniyya. He also waged war on the Ismāʿīlī al-Ṣulayḥī who killed Abū l-Fatḥ in 444/1052–3. Reportedly, Abū l-Fatḥ wrote a refutation of the local Zaydī doctrines, *al-Risāla al-mubhija fī l-radd ʿalā l-firqa al-ḍālla al-mutalajlija* (lost[6]) which may have been the first refutation of what was later to be called 'Muṭarrifiyya', suggesting that it was already at this time that the political conflict had doctrinal dimensions as well.

The attempts to introduce the Caspian intellectual tradition into Yemen and to establish it among local scholars gradually increased under Imam al-Mutawakkil ʿalā llāh Aḥmad b. Sulaymān (r. 532–66/1137–70) (for his biography, see al-Thaqafī, *Sīra*). During his reign, the dissemination of Bahshamite *kalām* by travelling scholars significantly grew and Yemeni students in theology undertook extended visits to the Caspian region. Al-Mutawakkil himself studied with several of these scholars, the most illustrious theologian of whom was Zayd b. al-Ḥasan b. ʿAlī al-Bayhaqī (d. *c.*545/1150–1). Al-Bayhaqī had studied with the Muʿtazilite theologian Abū Saʿd al-Muḥassin b. Muḥammad b. Kirāma (or: Karrāma) al-Bayhaqī al-Barawqanī ('al-Ḥākim al-Jishumī', d. 494/1101; on him, see Chapter 9, Section III) and might

[6] According to Mohaqqeq 2008: 758, a copy of the tract is preserved in a manuscript of the State Library Berlin, 'Ahlwardt, no. 4950'. This information, which is wrong, is based on a misunderstanding of Ahlwardt 1887–99: iv. 331.

consequently have contributed to the transmission of al-Jishumī's writings and their high popularity in Yemen. During his first years in Yemen, al-Bayhaqī taught at the heavily symbolic al-Hādī Mosque in Ṣaʿda, which houses the tombs of the founder of the Yemeni imamate and of several of his successors. He then relocated his teaching activities southwards and settled in the Muṭarrifiyya's oldest *hijra* Sanāʿ—a choice that was certainly well considered (Madelung 1965: 210–12; Schwarb 2011: 268–70). Al-Bayhaqī succeeded in convincing a number of students of the superiority of Bahshamite doctrines over Muṭarrifī theology. Credibility for the imported doctrinal notions was provided by the authority they received through the Imams of Northern Iran, the Buṭḥānī brothers al-Muʾayyad bi-llāh Aḥmad b. al-Ḥusayn al-Hārūnī (d. 411/1020) and al-Nāṭiq bi-l-Ḥaqq Abū Ṭālib Yaḥyā b. al-Ḥusayn (d. 424/1033) who both espoused Bahshamite *kalām* and whose writings became available in Yemen during this period. This development ushered in an unprecedented 'muʿtazilization' of the Zaydīs of Yemen. The impact of Muʿtazilite *kalām* is already visible in the doctrinal works of Imam al-Mutawakkil ʿalā llāh, e.g. in his comprehensive *Ḥaqāʾiq al-maʿrifa fī ʿilm al-kalām* (al-Mutawakkil ʿalā llāh, *Ḥaqāʾiq*). In its structure, the book resembles the *majāmīʿ* of the earlier Imams; yet in doctrine, al-Mutawakkil endorses as a rule the positions of the Muʿtazila, siding at times with the Bahshamiyya and at times with the School of Baghdad (Ansari 2012: 195–211; for similar observations for his works on legal theory, see Ansari and Schmidtke 2013a: 101 n. 37).

Among al-Bayhaqī's successors was Jaʿfar b. Aḥmad b. ʿAbd al-Salām al-Buhlūlī (d. 573/1177–8), who would play an important role in the future intellectual development of Yemen's theological landscape. Jaʿfar b. Aḥmad came from an influential Ismāʿīlī family of judges. Before he attended al-Bayhaqī's lectures, he had followed Muṭarrifī teachings. The fact that he eventually migrated to the opposing camp and approved al-Mutawakkil's imamate was officially acknowledged: in 545/1150–1 he was appointed judge (*qāḍī*) of Ṣanʿāʾ, and still in the same year he was selected to accompany his teacher on his travels in order to seek further instruction outside Yemen. Shortly after their departure, al-Bayhaqī died still on Yemeni soil, and so Jaʿfar b. Aḥmad continued his travel alone. He spent about eight years at several centres of learning in Iraq and Northern Iran. When he eventually sojourned in Rayy, he studied with Aḥmad b. Abī l-Ḥasan al-Kanī (d. *c.*570/1165–6), al-Bayhaqī's former student, and he is known to have likewise been taught by Muḥammad b. Aḥmad al-Farrazādhī, one of the members of the renowned Farrazādhī family in this town. Jaʿfar b. Aḥmad also spent some time in Kufa and in Mecca, where he studied with the eminent Zaydī scholar Abū l-Ḥasan ʿUlayy b. ʿĪsā b. Ḥamza b. Wahhās al-Sulaymānī (d. 556/1161–2) (on him, see Lane 2006: 26–9, 48–53, 251).

Upon his return to Yemen, Jaʿfar b. Aḥmad brought along many Muʿtazilite works—many of which were later on copied for the library of Imam al-Manṣūr bi-llāh ʿAbd Allāh b. Ḥamza (on him see Section II)—and he settled again in Hijrat Sanāʿ and established his *madrasa* next to the village's Muṭarrifī *madrasa*. His teachings laid the basis for the emergence of a new generation of scholars. This new theological movement was given the label of *'al-mukhtariʿa'*. The description was derived from the notion of *ikhtirāʿ*, a term that refers to the idea that God spontaneously creates accidents (*aʿrāḍ*, sing. *ʿaraḍ*). Following the Bahshamite theory, Jaʿfar b. Aḥmad and his followers believed accidents to be the grounds of such changing qualities of bodies as motion and rest, colours, or their annihilation. For them, God's omnipotence necessarily implies that He is able to create *ex nihilo* such accidents. This position consequently contradicted the Muṭarrifī doctrine that events and changes in the created world are the result of a natural causality inherent to bodies.

In public disputations and in his writings Jaʿfar b. Aḥmad not only attacked his Muṭarrifī detractors but also the Sunnis of Yemen. A number of polemical tracts from his pen have survived in manuscript form. In addition, he was the author of a doctrinal summa, titled *Kitāb Mishkāt al-miṣbāḥ wa-ḥayāt al-arwāḥ* (Sobieroj 2007: 285f. no. 133) and of some shorter theological manuals, in which he embraces Bahshamite doctrines. However, his subscription to their teaching explicitly excluded their theory of imamate. Jaʿfar therefore wrote a refutation of Ibn Mattawayh's chapter on the imamate contained in *al-Majmūʿ fī l-Muḥīṭ bi-l-taklīf*. Jaʿfar b. Aḥmad survived Imam al-Mutawakkil and experienced the beginning of the vacancy of the Zaydī imamate—a period that lasted about twenty-seven years. Jaʿfar died in 573/1177–8 and was buried in Hijrat Sanāʿ (Madelung 1965: 212–16; Zayd 1997; al-Wajīh 1999: 278–82 no. 257; Schwarb 2011: 270–3).

It was one of Jaʿfar b. Aḥmad's students, al-Ḥasan b. Muḥammad b. al-Ḥasan al-Raṣṣāṣ (b. 546/1152, d. 584/1188), who then gave a lasting intellectual impetus to the Yemeni appropriation of Bahshamite theology. Still during his teacher's lifetime, al-Raṣṣāṣ started writing his first works on theology and legal theory. Following his teacher's death, he succeeded Qāḍī Jaʿfar as the new head of the school and continued the latter's teaching activities in Hijrat Sanāʿ. Al-Raṣṣāṣ further wrote extensively on theological topics, putting much emphasis on the so-called subtle questions (*daqāʾiq* or *laṭāʾif*). He also was most probably motivated by his desire to disprove the teachings of the Muṭarrifiyya. Although al-Raṣṣāṣ rarely mentions his detractors and their doctrines explicitly, this scenario is quite likely: it was precisely the subtle questions related to natural philosophy over which both schools were deeply divided. The deeper reason behind their fierce opposition was that the conceptual construct of God and His relation to the created world was built upon these very questions. Therefore, the denial of such fundamental assumptions pulled the rug out from under the whole theological system. It is therefore not surprising that both schools quarrelled so harshly about rather detailed issues whilst agreeing at the same time on such central principles as that of free will or the denial of anthropomorphism.

Al-Raṣṣāṣ's doctrines in theology and natural philosophy fully stand in the tradition of Bahshamite teaching and, at the same time, set some new tones. With regard to the basic concepts of ontology, his ideas and thoughts about 'things' or 'entities' (*ashyāʾ*, *dhawāt*) follow the axioms of earlier representatives of the school. He adopts their definition of 'things' as that which can become objects of knowledge and of predication. The generic term of 'things' encompasses God, atoms (*jawāhir*)—i.e. indivisible particles of which created bodies are made up—and accidents (*aʿrāḍ*). In this context, it is of some historical importance that al-Raṣṣāṣ refuted a passage from Rukn al-Dīn Maḥmūd Ibn al-Malāḥimī's (d. 536/1141) *Tuḥfat al-mutakallimīn fī l-radd ʿalā l-falāsifa*. In his treatise, al-Raṣṣāṣ argues against Ibn al-Malāḥimī that predications about the very nature of things (such as 'the atom is an atom') are not identical with describing them as existing. Al-Raṣṣāṣ's defence of the classical Bahshamite distinction between existence and that which things are in themselves is one of the oldest testimonies to the Yemenite reception of the school founded by Abū l-Ḥusayn al-Baṣrī (d. 436/1044) (Ansari 2007).

Al-Raṣṣāṣ does not add anything substantial to the Bahshamite theories of atoms and accidents. These topics had already been comprehensively covered in fundamental works by theologians of the fifth/eleventh century. Among these works are al-Ḥasan b. Aḥmad Ibn Mattawayh's extensive *Kitāb al-Tadhkira fī aḥkām al-jawāhir wa-l-aʿrāḍ*. Al-Raṣṣāṣ was familiar with this text and used it as a reference in several of his works.

Later generations of Zaydī theologians attached great importance to al-Raṣṣāṣ's treatise on 'effectors' (*Kitāb al-Muʾaththirāt*) (Thiele 2011). This concise text has survived in a number of important manuscripts, dating up to the middle of the eleventh/seventeenth century. Al-Raṣṣāṣ wrote this work in an attempt to formulate a comprehensive theory of causation. He possibly relied on al-Ḥākim al-Jishumī's earlier, in some respects inconsistent thoughts about this matter (Ansari 2012: 313–28; Thiele 2012). In the framework of Bahshamite teaching, al-Raṣṣāṣ develops a taxonomy of what is labelled 'effectors' (*muʾaththirāt*) and 'analogous phenomena' (*mā yajrī majrā l-muʾaththir*). He furthermore seeks to theoretically explain why some of these 'effectors' are necessarily and others contingently effective.

Another work, entitled *Kayfiyyat kashf al-aḥkām wa-l-ṣifāt ʿan khaṣāʾiṣ al-muqtaḍiyāt wa-l-muʾaththirāt*, offers rare insight into the historical development of the Bahshamite teaching on attributes. In this text, al-Raṣṣāṣ elaborates his approach to the so-called 'theory of states', that is the theory introduced by Abū Hāshim al-Jubbāʾī (see Chapter 22). In addition to exploring the *ṣifāt*, i.e. that which is usually translated from the Arabic as 'attributes', al-Raṣṣāṣ opens his analysis to broader considerations on the concept of *aḥkām*—a term which might be rendered as 'characteristics', but actually denotes an ontological category distinct from the 'attributes'. Earlier Bahshamite theologians already made a conceptual distinction between *ṣifa* and *ḥukm*. However, their understanding of the latter remains, to some extent, vague. It was only with Abū l-Ḥusayn al-Baṣrī's revision of the Muʿtazilite theory of attributes that the term *ḥukm* was eventually used in a more formal sense (Schmidtke 1991: 174–7). It seems that al-Raṣṣāṣ's usage of the term was shaped from this angle, since he adopts a definition of *ḥukm* that is only known from the writings of Ibn al-Malāḥimī. According to this understanding, the distinction between *ṣifāt* (or *aḥwāl* which is used as a synonym) and *aḥkām* is an epistemological one: in order to gain knowledge about things, we have to consider *two* objects qualified by the same *ḥukm*, whereas a *ṣifa* can only specify *one* object.

The *Kayfiyya* is divided into chapters devoted to four categories of *ṣifāt* and three categories of *aḥkām*. This classification is made in an introductory chapter according to the manner or modality (*kayfiyya*) by which properties of things become actual (*thabata*). As is expressed in the title of the book, one of the author's main interests consists in the question of what each category of properties reveals about the very nature of its object of qualification. This particular approach can be seen as a corollary of the Bahshamite theory that things are known by virtue of their properties. The purpose of al-Raṣṣāṣ's raising this question consequently derived from a central theological problem: if we describe God and His creatures by univocal properties, how then can His absolute transcendence be preserved (Thiele 2013a: 131–200)?

Al-Raṣṣāṣ wrote a number of additional works on *laṭīf al-kalām* that have as yet not been found in manuscript form and appear to be lost. Only some self-quotations provide selective insight into their content and reveal that he discussed the nature of attributes, accidents, and of 'things' (*dhawāt*) in general (Thiele 2010: 549; Thiele 2013a: 37–9).

Prompted by their opponents' focus on doctrinal issues, the Muṭarrifīs in turn countered the attack: they claimed that they were faithful followers of the teachings of the early Imams and argued that it was in fact the adoption of Basran Muʿtazilism that constituted a deviation from the truth and as such an illegitimate innovation. Moreover, with the new arrival of Muʿtazilite works, the Muṭarrifīs apparently used increasingly the doctrines of the Baghdādī Muʿtazilites to refine their own *kalām* in their intellectual conflict against their opponents. These could be gleaned from the *Maqālāt* of Abū l-Qāsim al-Balkhī al-Kaʿbī (d. 319/931) as well as the *K. al-Masāʾil fī l-khilāf bayn al-Baṣriyyīn wa-l-Baghdādiyyīn* of Abū Rashīd al-Nīsābūrī, a systematic comparison between the doctrines of the adherents of the two Muʿtazilite schools (Ansari and Schmidtke 2010). The influence of the Baghdādī doctrines among the representatives of the Muṭarrifiyya during this period is evident, for example, in the *K. al-Burhān al-rāʾiq* by the Muṭarrifī theologian Sulaymān b. Muḥammad b. Aḥmad al-Muḥallī who flourished during the second half of the sixth/twelfth century (Madelung 1975). As such the conflict took on the dynamics of the old opposition between the Baghdādīs and the Basrans. However, whereas the conflict between the two Muʿtazilite systems remained a purely theological one, the confrontation between the different Zaydī groups of Yemen eventually led to an open war between the two. There are some indications that the Muṭarrifī theologians also made use of the doctrines of Abū l-Ḥusayn al-Baṣrī and his followers, who in many ways had departed from the theology of the Bahshamites. The few Muṭarrifī theological texts that were written during the sixth/twelfth century testify to the development of the Muṭarrifī doctrine at the time (ʿAbd al-ʿĀṭī 2002; Ansari 2001).

II The Continuity of Bahshamite Theology from the Seventh/ Thirteenth Century Onwards

When al-Raṣṣāṣ died in 584/1188 the religious and political leadership of the Zaydī community was still vacant. It was only in 593/1197 that al-Raṣṣāṣ's former student ʿAbd Allāh b. Ḥamza (d. 614/1217) rose as Imam al-Manṣūr bi-llāh. It was under his reign that the Bahshamite strand irrevocably overcame its ideological detractors: the Imam, who himself left a number of important theological works, led a merciless war against the Muṭarrifiyya. Their persecution and the destruction of their *hijra*s under his reign eventually led to the extinction of the sect.[7] Numerous of ʿAbd Allāh b. Ḥamza's doctrinal writings are refutations of the Muṭarrifiyya (as well as justifications of the Imam's merciless persecution of their followers, for which he faced severe criticism). Other than that he composed *Sharḥ al-Risāla al-nāṣiḥa bi-l-adilla al-wāḍiḥa*, a detailed theological compendium (with particular focus on the concept of the imamate) in which he endorses Bahshamite theological notions. In its overall structure, however, the book resembles that of the writings of the earlier Imams rather than theological summae by professional theologians (e.g. by his teacher al-Raṣṣāṣ) and it is replete with quotations from the writings of the Zaydī Imams, a characteristic that also ensured the work's lasting popularity among the Zaydī community. Al-Manṣūr's *Kitāb al-Shāfī* is a refutation directed against the Ashʿarites of Yemen, focusing specifically on the notion of the imamate. Moreover, it is noteworthy that al-Manṣūr is one of the first Zaydī authors of Yemen to cite Sunnī traditions supporting the cause of ʿAlī b. Abī Ṭālib and the *ahl al-bayt* in his battle against the Shāfiʿīs in Yemen who were polemicizing against Shīʿism (Ansari and Schmidtke 2013a; Ansari and Schmidtke 2013b). Doctrinal issues are also discussed in his *al-ʿIqd al-thamīn*, a book that is directed against the Imāmiyya (Jarrar 2012), as well as in his numerous responsa (see al-Wajīh 1999: 578–86, no. 592; al-Manṣūr bi-llāh, *Majmūʿ*).

At the turn and during the first decades of the seventh/thirteenth century, a number of other theologians who had studied with al-Raṣṣāṣ gained some scholarly prominence. Among them was Muḥyī l-Dīn Muḥammad b. Aḥmad b. al-Walīd al-Qurashī al-Anf (d. 623/1226), author of *al-Jawāb al-ḥāsim bi-ḥall shubah al-Mughnī*, a critical response to ʿAbd al-Jabbār al-Hamadānī's account of the imamate in his voluminous *Kitāb al-Mughnī fī abwāb al-tawḥīd wa-l-ʿadl*. Apart from being a scholar in his own right, Muḥammad Ibn al-Walīd also belonged to the staff of professional scribes who were instrumental in the establishment of al-Manṣūr bi-llāh's library in his residential

[7] The principal historical source for al-Manṣūr's fight against the Muṭarrifiyya is the *sīra* of the Imam by his chief secretary Abū Firās b. Diʿtham. Vols. ii and iii have been published as Ibn Diʿtham, *Sīra*. Another copy of vol. ii that was not consulted by the editor is preserved as MS Vatican ar. 1061; cf. Levi Della Vida 1935: i. 131. H. Ansari has identified copies of vols. i and iv of the *sīra* that previously had been presumed lost; see Ansari 2013.

town Ẓafār. The foundation of this library can be regarded as the culmination of the endeavour to transmit as many books as possible from Northern Iran to Yemen. Many of the texts copied for al-Manṣūr bi-llāh's library have survived as unique manuscripts (Ansari and Schmidtke 2010).

Another of al-Raṣṣāṣ's students, Sulaymān b. ʿAbd Allāh al-Khurāshī (d. after 610/1214), wrote a commentary on his teacher's *al-Taḥṣīl fī l-tawḥīd wa-l-taʿdīl*, a short theological compendium. The third volume of this commentary has been preserved in manuscript form and shows al-Khurāshī's remarkably close familiarity with the works of Ibn al-Malāḥimī (al-Khurāshī, *Taḥṣīl*; Ansari and Thiele 2015). Al-Khurāshī's text is only the first in the chronology of several commentaries on the *Kitāb al-Taḥṣīl* that were written within a period of thirty years after al-Raṣṣāṣ's death. Consequently, it appears that the *Kitāb al-Taḥṣīl* was a popular work among this generation of theologians. The commentaries on al-Raṣṣāṣ's theological manual include one in several volumes by Ḥusayn b. Musallam al-Tihāmī, who studied with al-Raṣṣāṣ's own student Abū l-Qāsim b. Shabīb al-Tihāmī. Ḥusayn b. Musallam al-Tihāmī's text appears to be partially preserved and is related in its structure and content to the third and shortest commentary on the *Kitāb al-Taḥṣīl* by al-Raṣṣāṣ's son Shams al-Dīn Aḥmad b. al-Ḥasan al-Raṣṣāṣ (d. 621/1224) (Thiele in press).

Aḥmad al-Raṣṣāṣ's historically most influential work was a brief introduction to the fundamentals of Bahshamite doctrines. This text, entitled *Miṣbāḥ al-ʿulūm fī maʿrifat al-ḥayy al-qayyūm* (also known as *al-Thalāthūn mas'ala*), was widely read among the Zaydīs of Yemen and still serves as a textbook in contemporary circles of religious learning. In addition, *Miṣbāḥ al-ʿulūm* was subject to several commentaries, one of them being *al-Īḍāḥ li-fawā'id al-Miṣbāḥ* by his student Ḥumayd b. Aḥmad al-Muḥallī *al-shahīd* (killed in 652/1254) (Ansari and Schmidtke 2011: 196 no. 50). Ḥumayd al-Muḥallī had studied with ʿAbd Allāh b. Ḥamza, Ibn al-Walīd, and Zayd b. Aḥmad al-Bayhaqī, who coming from Iran arrived in Yemen in 610/1213–14, and he is primarily known as the author of the biographical work *al-Ḥadā'iq al-wardiyya*. That he was also a well-versed theologian is shown by his comprehensive works on *kalām*, viz. his *ʿUyūn al-mustarshidīn fī uṣūl al-dīn*, a theological summa in four parts in which the author comments upon a credal work by al-Manṣūr bi-llāh (al-Wajīh 1999: 408), and his *al-Kawākib al-durriyya fī tafṣīl al-nafaḥāt al-miskiyya* (Ansari and Schmidtke 2011: 197f. no. 60). The latter work is not a conventional *summa* but rather encompasses all major aspects of the subtleties of theology. The first part of the work discusses logical and epistemological questions. The second and longest chapter then deals with the definition of 'things' or 'entities' (*dhawāt*), followed by a comprehensive exposition of the basic constituents of the world, namely atoms (*jawāhir*) and accidents (*aʿrāḍ*). The last part finally addresses the topic of 'attributes' (*ṣifāt*) and 'characteristics' (*aḥkām*). Ḥumayd's work highlights how centrally theologians of this time were concerned with the field of *laṭīf al-kalām*.

Ḥumayd al-Muḥallī resided in Mislit, located in Banū Qays, where he taught along with other prominent scholars of his time. The village's *madrasa* had built up a considerable reputation as a centre of learning, and so the later Imam al-Mahdī li-Dīn Allāh

Abū Ṭayr Aḥmad b. al-Ḥusayn b. Aḥmad b. al-Qāsim (d. 656/1285) studied there theology and legal theory, as is reported in his biography (*sīra*) which contains a detailed chapter on his formation (Ansari and Schmidtke 2011). A further centre of theological teaching was the *madrasa al-manṣūriyya* in Ḥūth, Aḥmad's next station. Although the detailed report about Aḥmad's studies is only a snapshot of the Zaydīs' educational culture during the first half of the seventh/thirteenth century, they allow us to catch a glimpse of the time's intellectual milieu and the texts that were considered as fundamental in the scholarly instruction in the science of *kalām*. Alongside the writings by such leading (Sunnī-Muʿtazilite) authorities as Abū Rashīd al-Nīsābūrī, Ibn Mattawayh, or Ibn al-Malāḥimī, many Yemeni-Bahshamite authors are prominently represented in the curriculum: the textbooks include several writings by al-Ḥasan al-Raṣṣāṣ, Ḥusayn b. Musallam al-Tihāmī's commentary on al-Raṣṣāṣ's *al-Taḥṣīl* or Ḥumayd al-Muḥallī's *al-Kawākib al-durriyya* (Ansari and Schmidtke 2011). Another influential theologian during this period was al-Ḥusayn b. Badr al-Dīn Muḥammad (d. 662/1263–4), author of *Yanābiʿ al-naṣīḥa fī uṣūl al-dīn*, a theological summa with Bahshamite tendencies which again resembles in structure and its reliance on the Qurʾān and *ḥadīth* the doctrinal works of al-Manṣūr bi-llāh. Al-Ḥusayn also wrote a concise credal work, titled *al-ʿIqd al-thamīn fī maʿrifat rabb al-ʿālamīn*, which enjoyed immense popularity over the centuries. From his pen we also have numerous refutations directed against the Muṭarrifiyya (al-Wajīh 1999: 390–3 no. 388). Similar tendencies can be found in *Qawāʿid ʿaqāʾid Āl Muḥammad* by Muḥammad b. al-Ḥasan al-Daylamī (d. 711/1311–12) who wrote at about the same time.

Over the course of several centuries, we can identify several important scholarly families that brought forth a number of prominent theologians: alongside the descendants of al-Ḥasan al-Raṣṣāṣ, a number of members of Ḥumayd al-Muḥallī's family were reputed theologians and authors. One of them was the *shahīd*'s grandson al-Qāsim b. Aḥmad al-Muḥallī, who lived in the first half of the eighth/fourteenth century. The dictation of his critical remarks on, and corrections to, al-Ḥasan al-Raṣṣāṣ's *Kayfiyya*, that is the latter's treatise on the Bahshamite theory of attributes, is recorded in manuscript form (Thiele 2013b). Al-Qāsim's main work in theology is, however, *al-Ghurar wa-l-ḥujūl*, an important supercommentary on Mānkdīm Shashdīw's (d. *c.*425/1034) *Taʿlīq Sharḥ al-Uṣūl al-khamsa*. This text is a rich source on earlier Zaydī and non-Zaydī theologians and is in several respects fairly independent from the *Taʿlīq*. Al-Qāsim al-Muḥallī takes greater interest in the topics of the preliminaries and the section on God's unity (*tawḥīd*): both parts comprise more than half of the whole text and consequently occupy a significantly larger portion than in Mānkdīm's work. In specific questions, al-Qāsim was apparently influenced by the teachings of al-Ḥasan al-Raṣṣāṣ: he applies the same taxonomy to the 'effectors' (*muʾaththirāt*) and also follows al-Raṣṣāṣ's conceptual distinction between 'attributes' (*ṣifāt*) and 'characteristics' (*aḥkām*) (Gimaret 1979: 63–5; al-Wajīh 1999: 765f.; Thiele 2013a: 75, 134).

Less than a century later, we see the rise of what might be called an encyclopedic attempt to canonize the teachings in theology and jurisprudence. Imam al-Mahdī li-Dīn

Allāh Aḥmad b. Yaḥyā al-Murtaḍā (d. 840/1436–7) wrote several works that became standard texts in Zaydī curricula and, in addition, attracted much attention from later commentators. His major work is *al-Baḥr al-zakhkhār al-jāmiʿ li-madhāhib ʿulamāʾ al-anṣār*, a multi-volume encyclopedia of *fiqh*. The first introductory part of the work contains several textual units devoted to doctrine, viz. *Kitāb al-Qalāʾid fī taṣḥīḥ al-ʿaqāʾid; Kitāb Riyāḍat al-afhām fī ʿilm al-kalām* and *Miʿyār al-ʿuqūl fī ʿilm al-uṣul*. These were later supplemented by Ibn al-Murtaḍā's own commentaries (al-Kamālī 1991: 105ff.; al-Wajīh 1999: 206–13 no. 199; van Ess 2011: ii. 986–95; Zysow 2012). Ibn al-Murtaḍā's doctrinal works are largely based on al-Ḥākim al-Jishumī's *Kitāb ʿUyūn al-masāʾil* and his autocommentary, *Sharḥ al-ʿUyūn*, respectively. With regard to some subtle questions, Ibn al-Murtaḍā modifies al-Jishumī's positions according to the revisions suggested by al-Ḥasan al-Raṣṣāṣ (Thiele 2011: 82f.; Schwarb 2015).

One of the most prolific theologians of the following generation was ʿAlī b. Muḥammad b. Aḥmad al-Bukurī (d. 882/1478) (al-Wajīh 1999: 709–10 no. 760; Schwarb 2015: *passim*). He authored a very popular commentary on al-Ḥasan al-Raṣṣāṣ's treatise on causation, which was read down to the eleventh/seventeenth century (Thiele 2011: 10f.). Numerous copies of the text with extensive glosses provide us with further details on the ongoing theological tradition of Bahshamite teaching in Yemen. They also reveal some details on treatises that were transmitted and read by scholars in theology: from these bits of texts, we can distil a list of quoted works by such theologians as al-Ḥasan al-Raṣṣāṣ (namely his *Kayfiyya*), Ḥumayd al-Muḥallī (*al-Kawākib al-durriyya*), al-Qāsim b. Aḥmad al-Muḥallī (*al-Ghurar wa-l-ḥujūl*), Ibn al-Murtaḍā (*al-Baḥr al-zakhkhār*), and, as the most important non-Zaydī authority, Ibn Mattawayh with many references to his *Tadhkira*.

III Counter-reactions

While the theological trend of al-Ḥasan al-Raṣṣāṣ and his adherents continued to set the tone during the seventh/thirteenth century, growing opposition emerged among the Zaydīs of Yemen against Muʿtazilism in general and the theological views of the Bahshamiyya in particular. The most outspoken opponent of Muʿtazilite *kalām* was Nūr al-Dīn Abū ʿAbd Allāh Ḥumaydān b. al-Qāsim b. Yaḥyā b. Ḥumaydān (d. mid-seventh/thirteenth century), who sought to weaken its influence on Zaydī theology and to emphasize the latter's independence. For this purpose, he took recourse to the *majāmīʿ* literature of the earlier Imams (Madelung 1965: 218ff.; ʿAbd al-Raḥmān 2003b; Ansari 2012: 179–94; see also Section I). Moreover, the Zaydīs of Yemen were also introduced during this period to the teachings of Abū l-Ḥusayn al-Baṣrī, a former student of ʿAbd al-Jabbār. Abū l-Ḥusayn, who had also been trained in medicine and philosophy, had criticized the principles of the Bahshamiyya in an attempt to correct some of their concepts and arguments in order to defend Muʿtazilite notions more effectively against objections of their opponents. While there is no indication that Jaʿfar b. Aḥmad had known any of Abū l-Ḥusayn's works, his student Sulaymān b. Nāṣir al-Suḥāmī (d. after 600/1203–4), who had also studied with Imam al-Mutawakkil ʿalā llāh, wrote a *Mukhtaṣar al-Muʿtamad*, a summary of Abū l-Ḥusayn al-Baṣrī's *Kitāb al-Muʿtamad fī uṣūl al-fiqh* on legal theory.[8] The numerous manuscript copies of Yemeni provenance of Abū l-Ḥusayn's *Muʿtamad* also indicate that it was widely read among Zaydī scholars (Ansari and Schmidtke 2013a). This is not the case with Abū l-Ḥusayn's theological works. Al-Ḥasan al-Raṣṣāṣ's student and follower of al-Manṣūr bi-llāh, Abū l-Qāsim b. al-Ḥusayn b. Shabīb at-Tihāmī (d. after 600/1203–4) is reported to have defended some specific views of Abū l-Ḥusayn al-Baṣrī against the Bahshamiyya (Madelung 1965: 222). There is no indication that Abū l-Ḥusayn's most comprehensive *kalām* work, *Taṣaffuḥ al-adilla*, ever reached Yemen. Yet, although no manuscript has surfaced so far of Abū l-Ḥusayn's other important work, *Kitāb Ghurar al-adilla*, there is some indication that this text may have been accessible to Zaydī scholars in Yemen and Mecca. Ibn al-Walīd reports that al-Ḥasan al-Raṣṣāṣ wrote a refutation (*radd*) of the '*Kitāb al-Madkhal ilā Ghurar al-adilla li-l-Shaykh Abī l-Ḥusayn al-Baṣrī naqḍan shāfiyan kāfiyan*' which is not known to be extant. Since al-Raṣṣāṣ was apparently concerned with the section on the imamate in particular, it is likely that '*Kitāb al-Madkhal ilā Ghurar al-adilla*' was the title under which Abū l-Ḥusayn's *Kitāb al-Ghurar* (or perhaps only a section) was known among the Zaydīs of Yemen (Ansari 2010: 50). Moreover, the seventh/thirteenth-century Yemeni author ʿAbd Allāh b. Zayd al-ʿAnsī quotes from the *Ghurar* in his *al-Maḥajja* (Schmidtke 2013), and the above-mentioned Muḥammad b. al-Ḥasan al-Daylamī explicitly refers to the *Madkhal al-Ghurar* on numerous occasions throughout his *Qawāʿid ʿaqāʾid Āl Muḥammad*.

The principal sources through which the Zaydīs of Yemen became acquainted with Abū l-Ḥusayn's doctrines were the writings of Rukn al-Dīn Maḥmūd b. Muḥammad al-Malāḥimī al-Khʷārazmī (d. 536/1141), and the *Kitāb al-Kāmil fī uṣūl al-dīn* by one Abū l-Maʿālī Ṣāʿid b. Aḥmad al-ʿUjālī al-Uṣūlī—possibly a student of Ibn al-Malāḥimī. The latter was a contemporary and associate of Jār Allāh al-Zamakhsharī (d. 538/1144) and the chief representative of Abū l-Ḥusayn's thought a century after his death (Ansari and Schmidtke forthcoming b). Several partial copies of his *al-Muʿtamad fī uṣūl al-dīn* are preserved in the libraries of Yemen, and the Maktabat al-awqāf of the Great Mosque in Ṣanʿāʾ also holds three copies of his *Kitāb al-Fāʾiq fī uṣūl al-dīn*, an abridged version of his *Muʿtamad*, among them one copy that is dated 630/1232–3. There is documentary evidence that Aḥmad b. Muḥammad b. al-Ḥasan al-Raṣṣāṣ *al-Ḥafīd* taught Ibn al-Malāḥimī's *Muʿtamad*, and his grandfather's student Sulaymān b. ʿAbd Allāh al-Khurāshī regularly refers to and quotes from Ibn al-Malāḥimī's *al-Fāʾiq* and his

[8] Al-Suḥāmī also wrote *Shams sharīʿat al-islām fī fiqh ahl al-bayt ʿalayhim al-salām*, containing two brief introductory sections on *uṣūl al-dīn* and *uṣūl al-fiqh*, while the majority of the work is devoted to *fiqh*. A manuscript of vol. i of this work, transcribed by ʿAbd Allāh b. Ḥamza b. Muḥammad b. Ṣabra al-Aslamī and dated Jumādā II 682/August–September 1283, is preserved in the library of Muḥammad b. Ḥasan b. Qāsim al-Ḥūthī. cf. al-Wajīh 1999: 470f.

al-Muʿtamad in his *al-Tafṣīl li-jumal al-Taḥṣīl* (Ansari and Thiele 2015). Al-Khurāshī's contemporary Ibn al-Walīd wrote (in Ramaḍān 608/February–March 1212) a refutation of the section on the imamate in Ibn al-Malāḥimī's *al-Fāʾiq*, entitled *al-Jawāb al-nāṭiq al-ṣādiq bi-ḥall shubah kitāb al-Fāʾiq* (Ansari 2009). Ibn al-Malāḥimī's *Tuḥfat al-mutakallimīn fī l-radd ʿalā l-falāsifa* was likewise known to Yemeni scholars of the sixth/twelfth century. Al-Ḥasan al-Raṣṣāṣ wrote a refutation of the criticism that had been launched by Ibn al-Malāḥimī against the philosophers' view that the existence (*wujūd*) of created beings is supplemental to their essence (*māhiyya*), *al-Barāhīn al-ẓāhira al-jaliyya ʿalā anna l-wujūd zāʾid ʿalā l-māhiyya*, quoting extensively from Ibn al-Malāḥimī's *Tuḥfa* (Ansari 2007). The collection of the Maktabat al-awqāf of the Great Mosque in Ṣanʿāʾ contains a manuscript of the *Kitāb al-Kāmil* by the above-mentioned Ṣāʿid b. Aḥmad. This work systematically compares the teachings of the Bahshamiyya with those of Abū l-Ḥusayn al-Baṣrī. The manuscript suggests that the *Kitāb al-Kāmil* was one of the earliest sources for the Zaydīs of Yemen for Abū l-Ḥusayn al-Baṣrī's doctrinal views. The colophon states that it was collated with a *Vorlage* transcribed from a copy of Sadīd al-Dīn ʿAmr b. Jamīl [Jumayl], a teacher of the Imam al-Manṣūr bi-llāh.[9] Muḥammad b. Ibrāhīm Ibn al-Wazīr (d. 840/1436) also quotes extensively from the *Kitāb al-Kāmil*, although indirectly via the *Kitāb al-Mujtabā fī uṣūl al-dīn* of the Khʷārazmian Ḥanafī scholar Najm al-Dīn Mukhtār b. Maḥmūd al-Zāhidī al-Ghazmīnī (d. 658/1260) (Ansari and Schmidtke forthcoming b).

A leading figure of seventh/thirteenth-century Zaydī scholarship in Yemen was the *mutakallim* and legal scholar Ḥusām al-Dīn Abū Muḥammad ʿAbd Allāh b. Zayd b. Aḥmad b. Abī l-Khayr al-ʿAnsī (b. 593/1196–7, d. Shaʿbān 667/April 1268), a prolific author in a variety of fields. According to the later biographical tradition, he has 105 titles to his credit (Ansari and Schmidtke forthcoming a). To judge from the number of extant manuscripts, his most popular work was *al-Irshād ilā najāt al-ʿibād*, a work with Ṣūfī tendencies, which al-ʿAnsī completed in Rabīʿ II 632/January 1235. His magnum opus was the *Kitāb al-Maḥajja al-bayḍāʾ fī uṣūl al-dīn*, a comprehensive theological summa he completed on 14 Rabīʿ II 641/1 October 1243. The *Kitāb al-Maḥajja* consists of eight parts (*aqsām*, sing. *qism*), a division that is characteristic for most of al-ʿAnsī's theological works: (i) divine unicity (*tawḥīd*); (ii) justice (*ʿadl*); (iii) prophecy (*nubuwwa*); (iv) revealed legislation (*sharāʾiʿ*); (v) imamate; (vi) commanding what is good and prohibiting what is reprehensible (*al-amr bi-l-maʿrūf wa-l-nahy ʿan al-munkar*); (vii) promise and threat (*al-waʿd wa-l-waʿīd*); (viii) attributes and characteristics (*al-asmāʾ wa-l-aḥkām*).

[9] The work has been partly edited on the basis of a second copy of the text, MS Leiden OR 487, by E. Elshahed (al-Shahīd) (Elshahed 1983). Cf. the critical review by W. Madelung in *Bulletin of the School of Oriental and African Studies* 48 (1985) 128–9. Al-Shahīd has meanwhile published a full edition of the text ('Najrānī', *Kāmil*), again on the basis of the Leiden manuscript only. As is the case with Elshahed 1983, his introduction and edition is marred with glaring errors and misidentifications, including the author's *nisba* 'al-Najrānī'. (See Ansari and Schmidtke forthcoming b).

Al-ʿAnsī was a severe critic of al-Ḥasan al-Raṣṣāṣ and his followers in both doctrinal and political questions. As had been the case with Sayyid Ḥumaydān, al-ʿAnsī attempted to strengthen the influence of the doctrines of the earlier Imams, particularly those of al-Hādī, while reducing at the same time the influence of the Bahshamiyya. However, al-ʿAnsī did not share Ḥumaydān's critical attitude towards Muʿtazilite *kalām* in general. Al-ʿAnsī was familiar with a wide spectrum of Muʿtazilite *kalām* literature: in addition to the theological writings of the earlier Imams al-Qāsim and al-Hādī, al-ʿAnsī was well acquainted with the theological literature of the Bahshamiyya and more specifically with texts written by students and companions of ʿAbd al-Jabbār. He explicitly refers to the *Kitāb al-Muḥīṭ* of ʿAbd al-Jabbār—no doubt referring to the paraphrastic commentary on the work by al-Ḥasan b. Aḥmad Ibn Mattawayh, *al-Majmūʿ fī l-Muḥīṭ bi-l-taklīf*—and he regularly mentions the views of Abū Rashīd al-Nīsābūrī, Ibn Mattawayh, and al-Nāṭiq bi-l-Ḥaqq. Moreover, al-ʿAnsī was also familiar with the theological writings of Ibn al-Malāḥimī. Throughout the *Maḥajja*, the views of Abū l-Ḥusayn and Ibn al-Malāḥimī are regularly cited and discussed, and it seems that al-ʿAnsī gleaned the relevant information primarily from Ibn al-Malāḥimī's *K. al-Muʿtamad*. As mentioned above, al-ʿAnsī also quotes repeatedly from Abū l-Ḥusayn al-Baṣrī's *K. Ghurar al-adilla* throughout the *Maḥajja* although it remains unclear whether or not he had the work at his disposal or was quoting from an intermediate source (Schmidtke 2013). In many respects, al-ʿAnsī preferred the views of Abū l-Ḥusayn and Ibn al-Malāḥimī which, in his view, were often closer to the doctrines of the earlier Zaydī Imams than those of the Bahshamiyya and which he largely identified with those of the School of Baghdad. His approach towards their doctrinal thought is nevertheless critical, and al-ʿAnsī follows their views only as long as they fit his overall agenda of formulating a theology that remains faithful to the teachings of the Imams (Ansari and Schmidtke forthcoming a: chapter 3).

At a later stage of his life, al-ʿAnsī composed the *Kitāb al-Tamyīz*, a refutation of the Muṭarrifiyya which consists of three parts—a first introduction divided into the same eight fields of theology as the *Maḥajja*: divine unicity, justice, prophecy and revealed laws, imamate, commanding what is good and prohibiting what is reprehensible, promise and threat, attributes, and characteristics. For each domain, al-ʿAnsī first presents the beliefs of the '*ahl al-islām*', followed by those of the Muṭarrifiyya which he then refutes. A second introduction, by far the most extensive portion of the text, contains a detailed refutation of the Muṭarrifiyya arranged in eighty questions (*maʿārif*, sing. *maʿrifa*). The work is concluded by a *khātima* in which the author explains his own theological positions. This third section of the text constitutes a theological *summa* in its own right and has the same structure of eight parts (*aqsām*, sing. *qism*) as the *Maḥajja*. The work represents an important cornerstone in the development of his thought: while the theological doctrine in the *khātima* of this work fully corresponds to what he maintained in his *Maḥajja*, he now refrains from pointing out his agreement with either the Baghdādīs and/or Abū l-Ḥusayn and Ibn al-Malāḥimī (these two are only mentioned at one single occasion throughout the entire *khātima*). Instead, he strongly and repeatedly insists on his agreement with the theological views of the Imams al-Qāsim and al-Hādī, while his opposition to the Basran and, more specifically, Bahshamite doctrine remains outspoken in this work (Ansari and Schmidtke forthcoming a: chapters 3 and 5 no. 28, for an edition of the text, see chapter 6 Text 6).

Al-ʿAnsī's doctrinal outlook also manifested itself in a conflict with the Banū Raṣṣāṣ, particularly Aḥmad b. Muḥammad al-Raṣṣāṣ *al-Ḥafīd* who, like his ancestors, was a staunch supporter of the Bahshamiyya. Apart from occasional critical remarks against al-Ḥasan al-Raṣṣāṣ throughout the *Maḥajja*, the later biographical tradition reports that al-ʿAnsī's conflict with the *Ḥafīd* focused on the issue of whether or not the grave offender (*fāsiq*) holds an intermediary position (*al-manzila bayn al-manzilatayn*) between the believer and the unbeliever—while Aḥmad al-Raṣṣāṣ supported the Muʿtazilite doctrine of the intermediary position, it was completely rejected by al-ʿAnsī. While the relevant part of his *Maḥajja* (the issue would have been addressed within Part Eight on *al-asmāʾ wa-l-aḥkām*) is not preserved, al-ʿAnsī discusses the issue in his brief tract *Māʾ al-yaqīn*. Here, he states that the grave offender (*al-fāsiq*) is an unbeliever by ingratitude (*kāfir al-niʿma*) (MS Glaser 123/3, ff. 235a–b; edition in Ansari and Schmidtke forthcoming a: chapter 6 Text 3). Consequently, al-ʿAnsī opted for the traditional Zaydī doctrinal notion that had been favoured by al-Qāsim b. Ibrāhīm (Madelung 1965: 60ff., 121ff., 164ff.). According to Aḥmad b. Ṣāliḥ b. Muḥammad b. Abī l-Rijāl (d. 1092/1690), the author of the bibliographical encyclopedia *Maṭlaʿ al-budūr* (Ibn Abī l-Rijāl, *Maṭlaʿ*, i. 421; iii. 364 no. 957), the conflict gradually escalated. Al-ʿAnsī corresponded on the issue with ʿAlī b. Yaḥyā al-Fuḍaylī and subsequently wrote a tract against the doctrine of the intermediate position. Aḥmad al-Raṣṣāṣ then intervened and composed a refutation of this tract, entitled *Manāhij al-inṣāf al-ʿāṣima ʿan shabb nār al-khilāf* to which he later added a *Muqaddimat al-manāhij*. None of these writings has been preserved (Ansari and Schmidtke forthcoming a: chapter 3).

Over the following generations, the tendency to prefer the doctrines of Abū l-Ḥusayn al-Baṣrī and Ibn al-Malāḥimī to those of the Bahshamiyya continued and even increased among the Zaydīs of Yemen, and the conflict between the two groups seems to have become harsher. For example, al-ʿAnsī's student Yaḥyā b. Manṣūr b. al-ʿAfīf is specifically reported to have adopted the entire theological system of Abū l-Ḥusayn al-Baṣrī (al-Shahārī, *Ṭabaqāt*, iii. 1263–4 no. 800). Moreover, Yaḥyā disputed and corresponded with some '*ʿulamāʾ al-ẓāhir*' who followed the doctrines of Abū Hāshim with the specific aim to defend the views of the family of the Prophet (*ahl al-bayt*) and of Abū l-Ḥusayn (Ibn Abī l-Rijāl, *Maṭlaʿ*, iv. 515). ʿAlī b. al-Murtaḍā b. al-Mufaḍḍal (b. 704/1304–5, d. 784/1382–3) was another renowned adherent of the doctrines of Abū l-Ḥusayn al-Baṣrī who wrote a *qaṣīda* in support of the latter. According to the later biographical tradition, he also corresponded and disputed with a number of scholars maintaining the views of Abū l-Ḥusayn and Ibn al-Malāḥimī whereas his opponents are described as Bahshamites, as was the case with Aḥmad b. Ṣalāḥ b. al-Hādī b. Ibrāhīm b. Tāj al-Dīn (Ibn Abī l-Rijāl, *Maṭlaʿ*, iii. 351). ʿAlī also disputed and subsequently corresponded with the jurist Ibrāhīm al-ʿArārī (d. *c.*794/1391–2) (Ibn Abī l-Rijāl, *Maṭlaʿ*, iii. 351; i. 159 no. 36; cf. also al-Wajīh 1999: 722f. no. 778). The latter so staunchly supported the Bahshamiyya that he is reported to have stated that Abū ʿAlī al-Jubbāʾī and his son Abū Hāshim are preferable to the Imams al-Qāsim and al-Hādī (Ibn Abī l-Rijāl, *Maṭlaʿ*, iii. 351). Word about this conflict spread and other scholars got involved, writing refutations of Ibrāhīm al-ʿArārī's unacceptable statement (Ibn Abī l-Rijāl, *Maṭlaʿ*, iii. 352)—namely Imam al-Mahdī ʿAlī b. Muḥammad b. ʿAlī b. Manṣūr b. al-Mufaḍḍal (b. 705/1305–6, d. 773/1371–2) (*al-Namraqa al-wusṭā fī l-radd ʿalā munkir āl al-muṣṭafā*), Imam al-Wāthiq bi-llāh (d. 802/1400) (*al-Naṣr al-ʿazīz ʿalā ṣāḥib al-tajwīz*), and ʿAlī b. al-Murtaḍā's sister, Ṣafiyat bt. al-Murtaḍā (*al-Jawāb al-wajīz ʿalā ṣāḥib al-tajwīz*), all supporting the doctrinal views of Abū l-Ḥusayn al-Baṣrī. The evolution of the conflict between the two strands supports the assumption that the positive appreciation of the doctrinal views of Abū l-Ḥusayn as against those of the School of Basra and, more specifically, the Bahshamiyya was founded mostly on their identification as being closer to, or perhaps even identical with, the traditional theology of the earlier Zaydī Imams (Ansari and Schmidtke forthcoming a: chapter 4).

In this context, the case of Imam al-Muʾayyad bi-llāh Yaḥyā b. Ḥamza al-Naqawī al-Mūsawī (b. 669/1270, d. 749/1348–9) rather seems to be an exception: in his encyclopedic *Kitāb al-Shāmil fī uṣūl al-dīn* (or: *bi-ḥaqāʾiq al-adilla al-ʿaqliyya wa-uṣūl al-masāʾil al-dīniyya*), written in 711–12/1311–12, he adopted virtually the entire doctrinal system of Abū l-Ḥusayn al-Baṣrī. Moreover, he was the first to study in depth Sunnī-Ashʿarite works. Throughout his *Shāmil*, he regularly refers to Abū Ḥāmid al-Ghazālī (d. 505/1111) and Fakhr al-Dīn al-Rāzī (d. 606/1209)—for the latter, he explicitly cites from his *Nihāyat al-ʿuqūl fī dirāyat al-uṣūl*—whose positions he refutes. The popularity of his writings is indicated by the numerous extant manuscript copies as well as the fact that most of his theological works have been published (Schmidtke forthcoming).

Both traditions, the Bahshamite strand as well as the more conservative strand whose representatives sought to cling closely to the teachings of the Imams, continued over the centuries up until the modern period (Schwarb 2012).

References

ʿAbd al-ʿĀṭī, ʿAbd al-Ghanī M. (2002). *al-Ṣirāʿ al-fikrī fī l-Yaman bayna l-Zaydiyya wa-l-Muṭarrifiyya: Dirāsa wa-nuṣūṣ*. al-Haram [Giza]: ʿAyn li-l-dirāsāt wa-l-buḥūth al-insāniyya wa-l-ijtimāʿiyya.

ʿAbd al-Raḥmān, M. (2003a). *al-Imām Yaḥyā b. al-Ḥusayn al-Rassī wa-ārāʾuhu al-kalāmiyya wa-l-falsafiyya*. Alexandria: Dār al-Wafāʾ li-dunyā l-ṭibāʿa wa-l-nashr.

ʿAbd al-Raḥmān, M. (2003b). *al-Imām Ḥumaydān b. Ḥumaydān wa-ārāʾuhu al-kalāmiyya wa-l-falsafiyya*. Alexandria: Dār al-Wafāʾ li-dunyā l-ṭibāʿa wa-l-nashr.

Abrahamov, B. (1987). 'al-Ḳāsim ibn Ibrāhīm's Theory of the Imamate'. *Arabica* 34: 80–105.

Abrahamov, B. (1990). *Al-Ḳāsim Ibn Ibrāhīm on the Proof of God's Existence:* Kitāb al-Dalīl al-Kabīr. Leiden: Brill.

Abrahamov, B. (1996). *Anthropomorphism and Interpretation of the Qurʾān in the Theology of al-Qāsim ibn Ibrāhīm*. Leiden: Brill.

Ahlwardt, W. (1887–99). *Verzeichnis der arabischen Handschriften der Königlichen Bibliothek zu Berlin*. 10 vols. Berlin: A. W. Schade [repr. Hildesheim: Olms, 1980–1].

Ansari, H. (2001). 'Yād-dāsht-i dar bāra-yi Muṭarrifiyya wa raddī-hā-yi qāḍī Jaʿfar b. ʿAbd al-Salām'. *Kitāb-i māh-i dīn* 49–50 (1380): 112–26.

Ansari, H. (2006). 'Falsafa-yi ṭabīʿī-yi muʿtaziliyān-i muṭarrifī'. *Kitāb-i māh-i dīn* 102–3 (1385): 4–17.

Ansari, H. (2007). '*Al-Barāhīn al-ẓāhira al-jaliyya ʿalā anna l-wujūd zāʾid ʿalā l-māhiyya* by Ḥusām al-Dīn Abū Muḥammad al-Ḥasan b. Muḥammad al-Raṣṣāṣ'. In C. Adang, S. Schmidtke, and D. Sklare (eds.), *A Common Rationality: Muʿtazilism in Islam and Judaism*. Würzburg: Ergon, 337–48.

Ansari, H. (2009). 'Risāla-yi dar radd-i bar Maḥmūd b. al-Malāḥimī.' <http://ansari.kateban.com/entry1573.html> (accessed 12 May 2015).

Ansari, H. (2010). 'Maḥmūd al-Malāḥimī l-Muʿtazilī fī Yaman wa-taʿrīf bi-risāla fī l-radd ʿalayhi ḥawla ziyādat al-wujūd ʿalā l-māhiyya'. *al-Masār* 11/2: 48–58.

Ansari, H. (2011). 'Aḥmad b. ʿĪsā b. Zayd'. *Encyclopaedia Islamica*. Leiden: Brill, iii. 249–52.

Ansari, H. (2012). *Barrasī-hā-yi tārīkhī dar ḥawza-yi islām wa ṭashayyuʿ: Majmūʿa-yi nawad maqāla wa yaddāsht*. Tehran: Kitābkhāna, mūze wa markaz-i asnād-i majlis-i shūrā-yi islāmī, 1390.

Ansari, H. (2013). 'Dū jild-i tāze yābe sīra-yi Manṣūr bi-llāh'. <http://ansari.kateban.com/entry2096.html> (accessed 13 May 2015).

Ansari, H., and S. Schmidtke (2010). 'Muʿtazilism after ʿAbd al-Jabbār: Abū Rashīd al-Nīsābūrī's *Kitāb Masāʾil al-khilāf fī l-uṣūl*'. *Studia Iranica* 39: 225–77.

Ansari, H., and S. Schmidtke (2011). 'The Literary-Religious Tradition among 7th/13th Century Yemeni Zaydīs: The Formation of the Imām al-Mahdī li-Dīn Allāh Aḥmad b. al-Ḥusayn b. al-Qāsim (d. 656/1258)'. *Journal of Islamic Manuscripts* 2: 165–222.

Ansari, H., and S. Schmidtke (2013a). 'The Muʿtazilī and Zaydī Reception of Abū l-Ḥusayn al-Baṣrī's *Kitāb al-Muʿtamad fī uṣūl al-fiqh*: A Bibliographical Note'. *Islamic Law and Society* 20: 90–109.

Ansari, H., and S. Schmidtke (2013b). 'Between Aleppo and Ṣaʿda: The Zaydī Reception of the Imāmī Scholar Ibn al-Biṭrīq al-Ḥillī'. *Journal of Islamic Manuscripts* 4: 160–200.

Ansari, H., and S. Schmidtke (forthcoming a). *Zaydī Muʿtazilism in 7th/13th Century Yemen: The Theological Thought of ʿAbd Allāh b. Zayd al-ʿAnsī (d. 667/1268)*.

Ansari, H., and S. Schmidtke (forthcoming b). *The Transmission of Abū l-Ḥusayn al-Baṣrī's (d. 436/1044) Thought and Writings*.

Ansari, H., and J. Thiele (2015). 'MS Berlin, State Library, Glaser 51: A Unique Manuscript from the Early 7th/13th-Century Bahšamite Milieu in Yemen'. In D. Hollenberg, C. Rauch, and S. Schmidtke (eds.), *The Yemeni Manuscript Tradition*. Leiden: Brill, 66–81.

Elshahed, E. (1983). *Das Problem der transzendenten sinnlichen Wahrnehmung in der spätmuʿtazilitischen Erkenntnistheorie nach der Darstellung des Taqiaddin an-Nağrānī*. Berlin: Klaus Schwarz.

van Ess, J. (2011). *Der Eine und das Andere: Beobachtungen an islamischen häresiographischen Texten*. 2 vols. Berlin: de Gruyter.

Gimaret, D. (1979). 'Les *Uṣūl al-ḫamsa* du Qāḍī ʿAbd al-Ǧabbār et leurs commentaires'. *Annales Islamologiques* 15: 47–96.

al-Hādī ilā l-ḥaqq, Yaḥyā b. al-Ḥusayn (*Majmūʿ*). *Majmūʿ rasāʾil al-Imām al-Hādī ilā l-Ḥaqq ...: al-Rasāʾil al-uṣūliyya*. Ed. ʿAbd Allāh b. Muḥammad al-Shādhilī. Amman: Muʾassasat al-Imām Zayd b. ʿAlī al-thaqāfiyya, 2001.

al-Hādī ilā l-ḥaqq, Yaḥyā b. al-Ḥusayn (*Majmūʿa fākhira*). *Al-Majmūʿa al-fākhira: Kitāb fīhi majmūʿ min kutub al-Imām al-Hādī* ... Ed. ʿAlī Aḥmad Muḥammad al-Rāziḥī. Sanaa: Dār al-ḥikma al-yamaniyya, 1420/2000.

al-Ḥusayn b. Badr al-Dīn Muḥammad. *Yanābīʿ al-naṣīḥa fī l-ʿaqāʾid al-ṣaḥīḥa*. Ed. al-Murtaḍā b. Zayd al-Maḥaṭwarī al-Ḥasanī. Sanaa: Maktabat Badr, 1422/2001.

al-Ḥusayn b. al-Qāsim al-ʿIyānī (*Majmūʿ*). *Min majmūʿ kutub wa-rasāʾil al-Imām al-ʿIyānī*. Sanaa: Markaz al-turāth wa-l-buḥūth al-yamanī, 2006.

Ibn Abī l-Rijāl Aḥmad b. Ṣāliḥ (*Maṭlaʿ*). *Maṭlaʿ al-budūr wa-majmaʿ al-buḥūr fī tarājim rijāl al-zaydiyya* 1–4. Ed. Majd al-Dīn b. Muḥammad b. Manṣūr al-Muʾayyidī. Ṣaʿda: Markaz ahl al-bayt li-l-dirāsāt al-islāmiyya, 2004.

Ibn Diʿtham, Abū Firās (*Sīra*). *al-Sīra al-sharīfa al-Manṣūriyya: Sīrat al-Imām ʿAbd Allāh b. Ḥamza, 593–614*. Ed. ʿAbd al-Ghanī Maḥmūd ʿAbd al-ʿĀṭī. Beirut: Dār al-fikr al-muʿāṣir, 1414/1993.

Jarrar, M. (2012). 'Al-Manṣūr bi-Llāh's Controversy with Twelver Šīʿites Concerning the Occultation of the Imam in his *Kitāb al-ʿIqd al-ṯamīn*'. *Arabica* 59: 319–31.

Jundārī, A. (*Tarājim*). 'Tarājim al-rijāl al-madhkūra fī Sharḥ al-Azhār'. Published in the introduction to ʿAbd Allāh b. Abī l-Qāsim Ibn Miftāḥ, *al-Muntazaʿ al-mukhtār min al-Ghayth al-midrār al-maʿrūf bi-Sharḥ al-Aẓhār*. Sanaa, 1341/1922–3.

al-Kamālī, M. M. al-Ḥājj Ḥ. (1991). *al-Imām al-Mahdī Aḥmad b. Yaḥyā al-Murtaḍā wa-atharuhu fī l-fikr al-islāmī siyāsiyan wa-ʿaqāʾidiyyan*. Sanaa: Dār al-ḥikma al-yamaniyya, 1411.

al-Khurāshī, Sulaymān b. ʿAbd Allāh (*Tafṣīl*). *Kitāb al-Tafṣīl li-ǧumal al-Taḥṣīl*. Facsimile edn. of MS Berlin, Glaser no. 51. With Introductions and Indexes by H. Ansari and J. Thiele. Tehran: Mīrāth-i maktūb, 2013.

Lane, A. J. (2006). *A Traditional Muʿtazilite Qurʾān Commentary: The Kashshāf of Jār Allāh al-Zamakhsharī (d. 538/1144)*. Leiden: Brill.

Levi Della Vida, G. (1935). *Elenco dei manoscritti arabi islamici della Biblioteca vaticana: Vaticani, Barberiniani, Borgiani, Rossiani*. Vatican: Biblioteca apostolica vaticana.

Madelung, W. (1965). *Der Imam al-Qāsim ibn Ibrāhīm und die Glaubenslehre der Zaiditen*. Berlin: de Gruyter.

Madelung, W. (1975). 'A Muṭarrifī Manuscript'. In *Proceedings of the VIth Congress of Arabic and Islamic Studies*. Stockholm: Almqvist & Wiksell, 75–83.

Madelung, W. (1977). 'The Sīrat al-Amīrayn al-Ajallayn al-Sharīfayn al-Fāḍilayn al-Qāsim wa-Muḥammad ibnay Jaʿfar ibn al-Imām al-Qāsim b. ʿAlī al-ʿIyānī as a Historical Source'. In *Studies in the History of Arabia, I: Sources for the History of Arabia, part 2. Proceedings of the First International Symposium on Studies in the History of Arabia*. Riyad, April 1977. Riyad: University of Riyadh Press, 69–87.

Madelung, W. (1980). 'Abū l-Fatḥ al-Daylamī'. *The Encyclopaedia of Islam*. New edn. Leiden: Brill, Supplement, 22.

Madelung, W. (ed.) (1985). *Streitschrift des Zaiditenimams Aḥmad an-Nāṣir wider die ibaditische Prädestinationslehre*. Wiesbaden: Steiner.

Madelung, W. (1989). 'Imam al-Qāsim ibn Ibrāhīm and Muʿtazilism'. In U. Ehrensvärd and C. Toll (eds.), *On Both Sides of al-Mandab: Ethiopian, South-Arabic and Islamic Studies Presented to Oscar Löfgren*. Stockholm: Svenska Forskningsinstitutet i Istanbul, 39–47.

Madelung, W. (ed.) (1990). *The* Sīra *of Imām Aḥmad b. Yaḥyā Al-Nāṣir li-Dīn Allāh from Musallam al-Laḥjī's* Kitāb Akhbār Al-Zaydiyya bi l-Yaman. Exeter: Ithaca Press.

Madelung, W. (1991a). 'The Origins of the Yemenite Hijra'. In *Arabicus felix luminosus britannicus: Essays in Honour of A. F. L. Beeston on his Eightieth Birthday*. Reading: Ithaca Press, 25–44.

Madelung, W. (1991b). 'Al-Qāsim ibn Ibrāhīm and Christian Theology'. *Aram* 3: 35–44.

Madelung, W. (2002). 'Zayd b. ʿAlī b. al-Ḥusayn'. *The Encyclopaedia of Islam*. New edn. Leiden: Brill, 11/473f.

al-Manṣūr bi-llāh ʿAbd Allāh b. Ḥamza (*Sharḥ*). *Sharḥ al-Risāla al-nāṣiḥa bi-l-adilla al-wāḍiḥa*. Ed. Ibrāhīm Yaḥyā al-Darsī al-Ḥamzī and Hādī b. Ḥasan b. Hādī al-Ḥamzī. Ṣaʿda: Markaz ahl al-bayt (ʿ) li-l-dirāsāt al-islāmiyya, 1423/2002.

al-Manṣūr bi-llāh ʿAbd Allāh b. Ḥamza (*ʿIqd*). *al-ʿIqd al-thamīn fī aḥkām al-aʾimma al-hādīn*. Ed. ʿAbd al-Salām b. ʿAbbās al-Wajīh. McLean, VA: Muʾassasat al-Imām Zayd b. ʿAlī al-thaqāfiyya, 1421/2001.

al-Manṣūr bi-llāh ʿAbd Allāh b. Ḥamza (*Majmūʿ*). *Majmūʿ rasāʾil al-Imām al-Manṣūr bi-llāh ʿAbd Allāh b. Ḥamza*. Ed. ʿAbd al-Salām b. ʿAbbās al-Wajīh. 2 vols. McLean, VA: Muʾassasat al-Imām Zayd b. ʿAlī al-thaqāfiyya, 1422/2002.

Mohaqqeq, S. (2008). 'Abū l-Fatḥ al-Daylamī'. *Encyclopaedia Islamica*. Leiden: Brill, i. 756–8.

Muḥammad b. al-Qāsim al-Rassī (*Majmūʿ*). *Majmūʿ kutub wa-rasāʾil al-Imām Muḥammad b. al-Qāsim al-Rassī*. Ed. ʿAbd al-Karīm Aḥmad Jadbān. Ṣaʿda: Maktabat al-turāth al-islāmī, 1423/2002.

al-Murtaḍā li-Dīn Allāh Muḥammad b. Yaḥyā al-Hādī (*Majmūʿ*). *Majmūʿ kutub wa-rasāʾil al-Imām al-Murtaḍā Muḥammad b. Yaḥyā al-Hādī*. 2 vols. Ṣaʿda: Maktabat al-turāth al-islāmī, 1423/2002.

al-Mutawakkil ʿalā llāh, Aḥmad b. Sulaymān (*Ḥaqāʾiq*). *Ḥaqāʾiq al-maʿrifa fī ʿilm al-kalām*. Ed. Ḥasan b. Yaḥyā al-Yūsufī. Sanaa: Muʾassasat al-Imām Zayd b. ʿAlī al-thaqāfiyya, 1424/2003.

'al-Najrānī, Taqī al-Dīn' (*Kāmil*). *Al-Kāmil fī l-istiqṣāʾ fīmā balaghanā min kalām al-qudamāʾ*. Ed. al-Sayyid al-Shahīd. Cairo: Wizārat al-awqāf, 1999.

al-Qāsim al-ʿIyānī (*Majmūʿ*). *Majmūʿ kutub wa-rasāʾil al-Imām al-Qāsim al-ʿIyānī*. Ṣaʿda: Maktabat al-turāth al-islāmī, 2002.

al-Rabaʿī, Mufarriḥ b. Aḥmad (*Sīra*). *Sīrat al-amīrayn al-jalīlayn al-sharīfayn al-fāḍilayn al-Qāsim wa-Muḥammad ibnay Jaʿfar b, al-Imām al-Qāsim b. ʿAlī al-ʿIyānī: Naṣṣ tārīkhī Yamanī min al-qarn al-khāmis al-Hijrī*. Ed. R. al-Sayyid and ʿAbd al-Ghanī M. ʿAbd al-ʿĀṭī. Beirut: Dār al-muntakhab al-ʿarabī, 1413/1993.

Schmidtke, S. (1991). *The Theology of al-ʿAllāma al-Ḥillī (d. 726/1325)*. Berlin: Klaus Schwarz.

Schmidtke, S. (2013). 'Biblical Predictions of the Prophet Muḥammad Among the Zaydīs of Yemen (6th/12th and 7th/13th Centuries)'. *Orientalia Christiana Analecta* 293: 221–40.

Schmidtke, S. (forthcoming). 'Imām al-Muʾayyad bi-llāh Yaḥya b. Ḥamza (b. 669/1270, d. 749/1348–9) and his *K. al-Shāmil li-ḥaqāʾiq al-adilla al-ʿaqliyya wa-uṣūl al-masāʾil al-dīniyya*'.

Schwarb, G. (2011). 'Muʿtazilism in the Age of Averroes'. In P. Adamson (ed.), *In the Age of Averroes: Arabic Philosophy in the Sixth/Twelfth Century*. London: The Warburg Institute, 251–82.

Schwarb, G. (2012). 'Muʿtazilism in a 20th Century Zaydī Qurʾān Commentary'. *Arabica* 59: 371–402.

Schwarb, G. (2015). 'MS Munich, Bavarian State Library, Cod. arab. 1294: A Guide to Zaydī Kalām-Studies During the Ṭāhirid and Early Qāsimī Periods (Mid-15th–Early 18th Centuries)'. In D. Hollenberg, C. Rauch, and S. Schmidtke (eds.), *The Yemeni Manuscript Tradition*. Leiden: Brill, 155–202.

al-Shahārī, Ibrāhīm b. al-Qāsim (*Ṭabaqāt*). *Ṭabaqāt al-zaydiyya al-kubrā (al-qism al-thālith) wa-yusammā Bulūgh al-murād ilā maʿrifat al-isnād*. Ed. ʿAbd al-Salām b. ʿAbbās al-Wajīh. 3 vols. McLean, VA: Muʾassasat al-Imām Zayd b. ʿAlī al-thaqāfiyya, 1421/2001.

Sobieroj, F. (2007). *Arabische Handschriften der bayerischen Staatsbibliothek zu München unter Einschluss einiger türkischer und persischer Handschriften*. Vol. i. Stuttgart: Steiner.

al-Thaqafī, Sulaymān b. Yaḥyā (*Sīra*). *Sirat al-Imām Aḥmad b. Sulaymān 532–566 H*. Ed. ʿAbd al-Ghanī Maḥmūd ʿAbd al-ʿĀṭī. Giza: ʿAyn li-l-dirāsāt wa-l-buḥūth al-insāniyya wa-l-ijtimāʿiyya, 2002.

Thiele, J. (2010). 'Propagating Muʿtazilism in the VIth/XIIth Century Zaydiyya: The Role of al-Ḥasan al-Raṣṣāṣ'. *Arabica* 57: 536–58.

Thiele, J. (2011). *Kausalität in der muʿtazilitischen Kosmologie: Das Kitāb al-Muʾaṯṯirāt wa-miftāḥ al-muškilāt des Zayditen al-Ḥasan ar-Raṣṣāṣ (st. 584/1188)*. Leiden: Brill.

Thiele, J. (2012). 'La Causalité selon al-Ḥākim al-Ǧišumī'. *Arabica* 59: 291–318.

Thiele, J. (2013a). *Theologie in der jemenitischen Zaydiyya: Die naturphilosophischen Überlegungen des al-Ḥasan ar-Raṣṣāṣ*. Leiden: Brill.

Thiele, J. (2013b). 'A propos de l'attribution du ms Ambrosiana ar. F 122, fol. 35b: un fragment d'un texte zaydite du Yémen'. *Chroniques du manuscrit au Yémen* 16: 16–24.

Thiele, J. (in press). 'Theological Compendia in Late 6th/12th and Early 7th/13th Century Zaydism: al-Ḥassan al-Raṣṣāṣ's K. al-Taḥṣīl and its Commentaries'. In L. Mühlethaler, S. Schmidtke, and G. Schwarb (eds.), *Theological Rationalism in the Medieval World of Islam: New Texts and Perspectives*. Leuven: Peeters.

al-Wajīh, ʿAbd al-Salām b. ʿAbbās (1999). *Aʿlām al-muʾallifīn al-Zaydiyya*. McLean, VA: Muʾassasat al-Imām Zayd b. ʿAlī al-thaqāfiyya.

Zaryāb, ʿA. (1994). 'Abū l-Qāsim Balkhī'. *Dāʾirat al-maʿārif-i buzurg-i islāmī* 6: 150–7.

Zayd, ʿA. M. (1997). *Tayyārāt Muʿtazilat al-Yaman fī l-Qarn al-Sādis al-Hijrī*. Sanaa: al-Markaz al-faransī li-l-dirāsāt al-yamaniyya.

Zayd b. ʿAlī b. al-Ḥusayn (*Majmūʿ*). *Majmūʿ kutub wa-rasāʾil al-Imām al-aʿẓam Amīr al-muʾminīn Zayd b. ʿAlī b. al-Ḥusayn b. ʿAlī b. Abī Ṭālib*. Ed. Ibrāhīm Yaḥyā al-Darsī al-Ḥamzī. Ṣaʿda: Markaz Ahl al-bayt li-l-dirāsāt al-islāmiyya, 1422/2001.

Zysow, A. (2012). '*Kalām* Works by Ibn al-Murtaḍā'. Unpublished paper delivered at the occasion of the International Workshop 'The Yemeni Manuscript Digitization Initiative (YMDI)'. Staatsbibliothek zu Berlin, 9–10 May 2012.

CHAPTER 28

HANDBOOKS IN THE TRADITION OF LATER EASTERN ASHʿARISM

HEIDRUN EICHNER

DEALING with the later Ashʿarite tradition in the Eastern parts of the Islamic world we speak of texts which from the later Middle Ages until most recent times represent a most substantial constituent of the theological identity of Sunni Islam. On closer analysis, however, notwithstanding the importance of Ashʿarism for Sunni belief systems, we realize that only few aspects of the later development of this school are known precisely. A certain tendency towards essentialism can be detected in the portrayal of Ashʿarism as representing a standard in Sunni theological thought. Classical manuals on Ashʿarite theology are widespread and easily accessible. Many of them have been continuously and intensively used in Muslim theological instruction until today. Nevertheless, details of the historical development of Ashʿarite doctrine are clearly understudied, and this holds true in particular for the later period. Research interests are frequently dominated by the paradox that the more easily accessible the texts are, the less they are studied. Thus, later Ashʿarism is frequently perceived as a theological system codified in comprehensive handbooks (e.g. Nāṣir al-Dīn al-Bayḍāwī's (d. 685/1286, 691/1292, or 692/1293) *Ṭawāliʿ al-anwār* and ʿAḍud al-Dīn al-Ījī's (d. 756/1355) *Kitāb al-Mawāqif*), which were commented and glossed upon over and over, and individual authors' intellectual profiles are supposed to disappear behind a hypostasized system of Ashʿarite theology.[1]

This feature of an ahistorical perception of later Ashʿarism is present in modern studies, but it goes back to tendencies in our source material as well. A static perception of the school seems very much driven by its own interest to present the school as the

[1] We possess only few detailed studies which trace the development of specific doctrines with Ashʿarite authors. A comprehensive monograph to be mentioned in this context is most notably Gimaret 1980.

only defender and proponent of Sunni Islam, a perspective particularly successfully propagated by al-Ījī's *Mawāqif*. In al-Ījī's systematical presentation of a coherent body of Ashʿarite teachings, Ashʿarism is set into contrast with doxographical reports on a variety of views of early Muʿtazilī theologians, and 'the philosophers' are introduced as the most important major group of opponents. The views of al-Ījī's opponents are presented in a doxographical mode—both the Muʿtazila and 'the philosophers' seem to stand at a clearly defined and well-preserved distance to the Ashʿarite body of thought.

Contextualizing the *Mawāqif* within the textual tradition of other theological manuals of the time, the situation changes radically. It appears that the impression of a monolithic Ashʿarite group identity conveyed by the presentation in the *Mawāqif* is the product rather of a skilful auctorial strategy. Al-Ījī reacts by this to two very dynamic challenges to his claim of the hegemony of time-dispatched Ashʿarism which were driving the contemporary theological discourse of his time. On the one hand, there are Māturīdites as a competing group aiming at representing Sunni mainstream, and on the other hand stands the intense entanglement of any type of *kalām* reasoning (including that of Ashʿarites) contemporary to al-Ījī with the system of Avicennan philosophy (Eichner forthcoming).

Thus, a comparative analysis of theological manuals suggests that there are forceful dynamics operative in the elaboration of Ashʿarite school teachings of 'classical' Ashʿarite textbooks. These, however, are virtually unknown until today, and even more so are the dynamics guiding the authors of glosses and commentaries. In order to overcome this situation, a careful re-examination of the texts is needed, guided by a methodological approach which aims at freeing the texts from ahistorical harmonistic approaches, propagated already by some early foundational texts themselves. This ahistorical attitude is transported by the commentary literature as well, and it dominates the standard reception of Ashʿarite theology. An innovative approach for present day research must not project back later interpretations on earlier texts or aim at elaborating a unified essence of Ashʿarite theological teachings. Rather it should aim at detecting the complexity and plurality of layers in the refinement and transformations of doctrines as well as terminology. In addition to a more nuanced understanding of doctrinal developments, better knowledge of group identities involved in the exchange of arguments is required.

I The Interaction with Māturīdite Teachings

The interaction of Ashʿarite scholars with Māturīdite teachings during the Ilkhanid period has passed completely unnoticed thus far. An important document of Māturīdism of that period is Shams al Dīn al-Samarqandī's (d. 702/1303) *al-Ṣaḥīfa al-ilāhiyya*, together with the author's own commentary, the *Kitāb al-Maʿārif fī sharḥ al-Ṣaḥāʾif*.[2] Comparing the *Ṣaḥīfa* to al-Ījī's *Mawāqif* it can be discerned that the interaction with Māturīdism is an important catalyst for al-Ījī, and it motivates him to present Ashʿarism as a coherent body of thought. In many instances, the much more pronounced articulation of an Ashʿarite group identity in al-Ījī's *Mawāqif* as compared to al-Bayḍāwī's *Ṭawāliʿ*, written some decades earlier, is prompted by al-Ījī's encounter with al-Samarqandī's presentation of Māturīdite teachings. In the *Ṣaḥāʾif*, al-Samarqandī typically portrays his own views as representing Sunni mainstream, nowhere referring explicitly to his own position as that of the school. Only rarely does he choose Ashʿarites as targets of his criticism. Al-Samarqandī rather stresses frequently the unanimity of various scholars; divergences are described in the *Ṣaḥāʾif* as ultimately going back only to expressions. We can observe repeatedly that exactly in contexts where the *Ṣaḥāʾif* propagates a harmonistic perspective on a theological problem, al-Ījī's *Mawāqif* gives a quite sharp and unambiguous account of the Ashʿarite doctrine—without, however, ever explicitly singling out the Māturīdite position as laid out in the *Ṣaḥāʾif* as a target of its own criticism.

In general, a better understanding of the interaction between Ashʿarism and Māturīdism is an important desideratum for understanding the constitution of Sunni mainstream theology. Close (but not exclusive) correlations exist between an Ashʿarite affiliation and the Shāfiʿī school (in the West, the Mālikī school is more prominent), and between a Māturīdite affiliation and the Ḥanafī school. While the legal *madhhab* is a basic marker of identity for individuals in a Muslim community, theological doctrinal affiliations are far less conspicuous. The violent clashes between Ḥanafītes and Shāfiʿītes during the Seljuq period have attracted some attention to the theological implications of this as well (Madelung 1971). As could be shown, the retrospective view of Ottoman sources where Ashʿarism and Māturīdism appear as two theological schools distinguished by a well-defined series of points of disagreement is to be revised. During the earliest phase both schools have a somewhat comparable intellectual profile, the Māturīdites being confined primarily to Transoxania. There is a correlation between the regional distribution and the adherence to a legal *madhhab*, the Ḥanafiyya being the dominant *madhhab* in Transoxania (Rudolph 1997). Direct interaction between the two groups both claiming to represent the Sunna typically occurs in periods with significant geographical mobility. Just as is the case in the clashes of the Seljuq period, the spread of al-Samarqandī's works by Eastern scholars moving West during the Ilkhanid period is one more instantiation of this pattern. This phenomenon has passed unnoticed so far, and it pre-dates by more than one generation the much better accounted move of al-Ījī's student al-Taftāzānī (d. 793/1390) to the Tīmurid court and hence the introduction of Ashʿarite teachings in a Māturīdite environment. With the *Sharḥ al-Maqāṣid* of al-Ījī's student Saʿd al-Dīn al-Taftāzānī, Sunni *kalām* enters yet another stage: al-Taftāzānī refers to Ashʿarite (al-Ījī), Māturīdite (al-Samarqandī), and Imāmī Shīʿī (Naṣīr al-Dīn al-Ṭūsī) *kalām* authors and he includes comprehensive discussions of the teachings of the philosophers.

[2] Shams al Dīn al-Samarqandī is mostly known as an author writing on *ādāb al-baḥth*, cf. Miller 1995. On the importance of al-Samarqandī's theological work *al-Ṣaḥīfa al-ilāhīya* see Eichner 2009: 379–424.

II Philosophy

Recently, an increased interest in more detailed research into the later Ashʿarite tradition has been motivated not so much by its theological importance but rather by its interaction with the philosophical tradition. An emphasis on the significance of the post-Avicennan period forms an important part of a new research agenda in the investigation of Arabic Islamic philosophy. Aiming at overcoming the prevalence of decline paradigms in the investigation of later phases of Islamic intellectual history, this research agenda emphasizes not only the very existence of a huge number of texts that affiliate themselves to the philosophical tradition (Gutas 2002), but also tries to understand the mechanisms by which elements of Avicenna's philosophical system and its derivatives have entered various Islamic religious disciplines such as *ʿilm al-kalām* and *uṣūl al-fiqh*, but also *tafsīr* or *taṣawwuf*. In theological texts of the period under consideration, an increasing familiarity with concepts, arguments, and contexts from the philosophical tradition can be detected. The entanglement of philosophical elements and the tradition of *kalām* shows certain features that may lead us to see parallels between this phenomenon and 'scholasticism' as we know it in the Latin West—and a rediscovery of this important part of Sunni intellectual heritage and a re-appreciation of its originality is one of the major challenges to current research in the field.

This new research agenda stands in sharp contrast with what may be labelled the 'Ghazālī-myth', i.e. the claim that after the attacks of al-Ghazālī's (d. 505/1111) *Tahāfut al-falāsifa* philosophy was virtually banned from Sunni Islam.[3] This very 'Ghazālī-myth' may be countered by inversing its central argument: one may argue instead that—by singling out *three* teachings of the philosophers as unbelief (*kufr*)—the *Tahāfut* has rather *facilitated* the integration of philosophy into Islam. As long as he is abstaining from these three problematic teachings of the philosophers a Muslim can safely engage in the study of philosophy (Rudolph 2008: 58–60). Another point worth noticing is that the intellectual pedigree of *mutakallimūn* active in the integration of philosophical teachings into Ashʿarite *kalām* goes back not to al-Ghazālī but rather to a fellow student with the Imām al-Ḥaramayn al-Juwaynī (d. 478/1085), viz. Abū l-Qāsim al-Anṣārī (d. 512/1117). Al-Shahrastānī (d. 548/1153) explicitly mentions al-Anṣārī as his teacher and his *Nihāyat al-iqdām* seem to be engaged in a critical dialogue with al-Anṣārī's *al-Ghunya fī l-kalām*. Fakhr al-Dīn al-Rāzī (d. 606/1209) also traces his lineage through his father to Abū l-Qāsim al-Anṣārī.[4] Subsequently, the dominance of Fakhr al-Dīn al-Rāzī's various writings over the later reception is an important channel through which elements of Avicennan philosophy have entered this tradition, and by adopting

[3] Note that this already is being reported as a 'myth' in the earliest historical sketch devoted specifically to Arabic-Islamic philosophy; cf. de Boer 1901: 151.

[4] On the importance of al-Anṣārī for al-Rāzī's father Ḍiyāʾ al-Dīn al-Makkī cf. the introduction to Ḍiyāʾ al-Dīn, *Nihāyat al-marām*, esp. x–xii.

templates of al-Rāzī's works, the very structure of typical *kalām summae* is determined by conventions originally stemming from philosophy.

The readiness to accept these conventions from a reportedly rather hostile discipline requires an explanation. The integration of philosophical elements in the Islamic religious sciences is evidently closely connected to a growing awareness and self-reflectiveness as to how a discipline is constituted. Apparently, this development takes its beginning from the context of the *uṣūl al-fiqh* where there is at stake the problem of how a *mujtahid* qualified by mastering the *uṣūl al-fiqh* is to be defined. Starting with al-Juwaynī's *Kitāb al-Burhān* and then most notably al-Ghazālī's *Kitāb al-Mustaṣfā*, Aristotle's/Avicenna's theory of how a science is constituted and how it relates to other sciences is discussed (Eichner 2009: 201–30). Here, Ashʿarite *kalām* faces the situation that many of the problems typically discussed in *kalām* are motivated by earlier phases of the history of *kalām*—and this means *kalām* among Muʿtazilī thinkers. Literary conventions defining how a comprehensive exposition of *kalām* is to be designed are marked by the influence of Muʿtazilī positions, most notably a discussion of the 'five principles' (*al-uṣūl al-khamsa*). This situation may be one reason why by the late seventh/thirteenth century representatives of (non-Muʿtazilī) *kalām*-traditions were so easily ready to adopt a template heavily influenced by philosophy—shaping a theological *summa* under the influence of a coherent system developed in the context of Avicennan philosophy becomes an attractive alternative to taking over a template from 'heretical' Muʿtazilī theologians.

In order to convey an impression of the shape of the body of doctrines of later Ashʿarite thought, I shall outline in the following the structure of several important *kalām* works, distinguishing between two periods. First I sketch some works by al-Shahrastānī and Fakhr al-Dīn al-Rāzī—rather random samples that attest to a stage in the development of Ashʿarite *kalām* where the details of its contents and structure was much in flow, and some or all of the Muʿtazilī 'five principles' are used as basic parts of the structure. Then, I shall introduce a second type of *kalām* manual which—being a hybrid of two works by Fakhr al-Dīn al-Rāzī—was used from the 680s/1280s onwards.

III Al-Shahrastānī

Al-Shahrastānī seems to be the earliest Ashʿarite author among the generations of students of the Imām al-Ḥaramayn who has authored an exposition explicitly devoted to *kalām*, viz. *Nihāyat al-iqdām fī ʿilm al-kalām*. While al-Shahrastānī's overall intellectual profile—in particular his relation to Ismāʿīlism—remains somewhat enigmatic (Madelung and Mayer 2001; Mayer 2009), we can discern how his concern with *kalām* and philosophy stands in a coherent continuum. Al-Shahrastānī's *Kitāb al-Muṣāraʿa* (best known by its refutation *Maṣāriʿ al-muṣāriʿ*, by Naṣīr al-Dīn al-Ṭūsī) is devoted to a refutation of the teachings of Avicenna who is described as the 'outstanding man in the philosophical sciences, the most learned of all times in philosophy' (*Muṣāraʿa* 3, 4–5). The *Muṣāraʿa* deals with seven issues from the context of 'divine science' (*ʿilm ilāhī*), and al-Shahrastānī points out that this is just a selection from more than seventy issues in the fields of logic, physics, and metaphysics where he could refute Avicenna (*Muṣāraʿa* 5, 1–2). Al-Shahrastānī's *Kitāb al-Milal wa-l-niḥal* (together with *al-Farq bayn al-firaq* by ʿAbd al-Qāhir al-Baghdādī, d. 429/1037) is one of our most important classical sources for doxographical information. Other than the *Farq*, it supplements its account of the seventy-three Islamic sects by outlines of non-Islamic groups as well—among these, Greek philosophers figure prominently. When at the beginning of the *Nihāya* (*qāʿida* 1) al-Shahrastānī deals with the origination of the world, he points out in a very comprehensive perspective that the proponents of the truth in all religious communities (*milal*) agree on the origination of the world and that it was created by a Creator not accompanied by anything else. The 'pillars of wisdom and the ancient philosophers' also agree with this (here he singles out important names among the Presocratics, Socrates, and Plato). Aristotle and the later Islamic philosophers have a somewhat specific conception regarding the origination of the world (they hold that God is necessary of existence, *wājib al-wujūd*) (*Nihāya* 5, 1–6, 14). For further information on doctrinal divergences of the various groups he refers the reader to his earlier *Milal* (*Nihāya* 5, 10).

The arrangement of the twenty *qāʿida*s of the *Nihāya* loosely follows the traditional order of earlier *kalām* works. Other than later theological *summae*, the *Nihāya* very often points out at the beginning of a chapter what the 'teachings of the proponents of truth' (*madhhab ahl al-ḥaqq*) are. Opinions and positions which do not agree with this are then introduced and discussed. This includes paraphrases from Avicennan writings. Thus, as compared to later Ashʿarite *summae* that will be discussed in Sections IV and V the style of the *Nihāya* is marked by two characteristics: (1) its emphasis on the correct teachings stands much closer to a tradition of creeds than later texts and (2) the presentation of divergent teachings follows a 'doxographical' approach, i.e. who has held this opinion is more important than systematic aspects, how the divergent teachings may be classified. While the influence of al-Anṣārī's *Ghunya* can be frequently identified in the way arguments are framed, the *Nihāya* includes extensive paraphrases of Avicennan works.

The *Nihāya* is divided into twenty 'principles' (*qawāʿid*, sing. *qāʿida*), followed by some appendices. The following topics are discussed: origination of the world, God as the creator (*qāʿida* 1–2); God's unity (*qāʿida* 3–5); ontology and ontological basis of physical reality (the concept of *aḥwāl*, existence and non-existence, matter and form) (*qāʿida* 6–7); divine attributes (*qāʿida* 8–15); vision of God (*qāʿida* 16); rational motivation for ethical qualifications (*qāʿida* 17–18); prophecy and revelation (*qāʿida* 19–20). The imamate, miracles of saints (*karāmāt*), abrogation, and atomism are issues discussed towards the end of the work—due to the bad shape of our editions it is not clear whether these sections form part of the original text or were appended later.

IV Fakhr al-Din al-Rāzī

In most writings by Fakhr al-Dīn al-Rāzī we can discern him striving to develop a coherent structure, a feature that may have triggered the overwhelming influence of his writings on the later tradition. With the exception of al-Rāzī's ethical works (Shihadeh 2006), attempts at a comprehensive reassessment of his doctrines and their development are still lacking.

Fakhr al-Dīn al-Rāzī is also well known as an author writing on Avicennan philosophy—often with a critical undertone. His commentary on Ibn Sīnā's *al-Ishārāt wa-l-tanbīhāt* (partly inspired by the critical remarks of Sharaf al-Dīn al-Masʿūdī[5]) has most decisively shaped the later reception of this work—even the reception of al-Rāzī opponents such as Naṣīr al-Dīn al-Ṭūsī.[6] A complex example for the problem of the conception of theology are al-Rāzī's *al-Maṭālib al-ʿāliya*. This book is heavily marked by Neoplatonic elements and contains extensive quotations from the writings of Abū Bakr Zakarīyāʾ al-Rāzī (d. 311/923). The *Maṭālib* are devoted to the 'divine science' (*al-ʿilm al-ilāhī*), a name which following Avicenna is typically used to designate Aristotelian metaphysics. Al-Rāzī, however, equates *al-ʿilm al-ilāhī* of the *Maṭālib* with 'theology' (*ūthūlūjīyā*) and further explains that the science under consideration deals with the 'divine self'. This same description referring to the 'divine self', however, he also applies to the sciences contained in his *Nihāyat al-ʿuqūl* and in his *Ishāra fī ʿilm al-kalām*, i.e. *kalām* (Eichner 2009: 275–80).

Al-Rāzī's engagement in the study of philosophy has left its traces in nearly all of his theological writings as well. A most salient feature—much more so than in the writings of al-Ghazālī—is that the analytical frameworks which he applies to the context of philosophy and of *kalām* are more or less identical. This new framework and its terminology render neither of the two contexts in a fully adequate way. However, in this very feature of impreciseness and its tendency towards a systematic simplification, we may discern a precondition for the overwhelming success which al-Rāzī's works have had for the amalgamation of the two disciplines.

Among al-Rāzī's *kalām* writings, the *Nihāyat al-ʿuqūl* is less concerned with developing a tight overall structure than other comparably elaborate works. Like al-Shahrastānī's *Nihāyat al-iqdām* it consists of twenty units (*aṣl*) which can loosely be grouped according to their contents. The first *aṣl* is devoted to preliminaries which include some discussion regarding how the present science is constituted and methodological considerations regarding its epistemological foundations. The second *aṣl* is devoted to epistemological foundations. Origination of bodies and the Creator (*aṣl* 3–4); divine attributes, including vision and what is impossible for God (*aṣl* 5–12); divine names and actions (*aṣl* 13–14); proof of God's existence (*aṣl* 15); prophecy (*aṣl* 16), the afterlife (*aṣl* 17–18), judgement (*aṣl* 19); the imamate (*aṣl* 20).[7]

Other writings of al-Rāzī that we may classify as belonging to a systematic theological tradition properly speaking (such as the *Maʿālim fī uṣūl al-dīn, Muḥaṣṣal afkār*

[5] Ed. A. Shihadeh (Shihadeh 2006).

[6] Cf. the forthcoming study on the commentary tradition on Avicenna's *Ishārāt* by Adam Gacek, Reza Pourjavady, and Robert Wisnovsky.

[7] Ed. Saʿīd ʿAbd al-Laṭīf Fawda, 4 vols, Beirut: Dār al-Dhakhāʾir, 1436/2015. This survey is based on Mss. Yeni Cami 758 (*Mukhtaṣar Nihāyat al-ʿuqūl* by Burhān al-Dīn al-Nasafī) and Yeni Cami 759.

al-mutaqaddimīn wa-l-mutʾakhkhirīn, al-Ishāra) share a simpler and more unified structure. For the later reception, the *Muḥaṣṣal* is of particular importance. It consists of four parts: Part One is devoted to preliminaries (*muqaddamāt*, dealing mostly with epistemological issues). Part Two lays out a division of objects of knowledge (i.e. a classificiation of existents, *mawjūdāt*, as subspecies of objects of knowledge, *maʿlūmāt*). Part Three (entitled *ilāhiyyāt*) consists of units devoted to the divine self (*dhāt*), the attributes (*ṣifāt*), actions (*afʿāl*), and names (*asmāʾ*). Part Four is entitled *samʿiyyāt*, 'issues based on transmission', and consists of units devoted to prophecy, the hereafter, names and stipulations, and the imamate.[8]

Some basic features of al-Rāzī's theological teachings properly speaking may be gained from the following survey (based on Chapter Three of his *Maʿālim*): bodies are originated, contrary to the view of the philosophers (*masʾala* 1); establishing knowledge of the Creator (*al-ṣāniʿ*) can proceed by two ways, either based on contingency (*imkān*) or based on [temporal] origination (*ḥudūth*) (*masʾala* 2); 'the One Who knows' cannot be a body (3); He cannot be a substance/atom (*jawhar*, being defined here as that which occupies space and cannot be divided, *mutaḥayyiz ghayr munqasim*) (*masʾala* 4); He cannot be in a place (*makān*) (*masʾala* 5); inherence (*ḥulūl*) is impossible for Him (*masʾala* 6); temporally originated beings cannot subsist in the 'divine self', contrary to the view of the Karrāmites (*masʾala* 7); God cannot enter conjunction (*ittiḥād*) with something (*masʾala* 8); pain is impossible for God (*masʾala* 9); Avicenna's view that God's true essence is existence only is false (*masʾala* 10); something may be distinct from something else by its specific essence, not by something else (*masʾala* 11).

In Chapters Four and Five on the attributes, al-Rāzī is quite explicit about his opponents. In the first of the two chapters on attributes, 'power' and 'knowledge' are singled out as particularly important. Here again I provide a survey of the contents, based on the introductory statements: God exerts an influence on the existence of the world (*muʾaththir fī wujūd al-ʿālam*). Either He does so based on possibility (*ṣiḥḥa*), so that He is acting and wilfully choosing (*fāʿil mukhtār*) or He does so by way of necessity, then He is necessitating by His essence. The latter is false (*masʾala* 1); the Creator is knowing (*masʾala* 2); the philosophers deny that He knows the particulars (*masʾala* 3). He knows all objects of knowledge (*kull al-maʿlūmat*) (*masʾala* 4), and He has power over all possible things (*kull al-mumkināt*) (*masʾala* 5). The entirety of possible things (*jamīʿ al-mumkināt*) fall under His power (*masʾala* 6). The Creator of the world is living (*masʾala* 7) and is in possession of will (*masʾala* 8). Seeing and hearing are distinct from knowing (*masʾala* 9); all prophets agree that God is speaking (*mutakallim*) (*masʾala* 10). It is established that He is knowing and has knowledge (*masʾala* 11). The specific relations which are called power and knowledge are not self-subsistent (*ghayr qāʾima bi-anfusihā*) (*masʾala* 12). The Muʿtazilites claim that God is willing by a will which is temporally originated (*masʾala* 13). Some jurisprudents from Transoxania maintain that

8 The subdivision of the text is obscured in parts of the manuscript transmission and in the various prints of the text. An early manuscript is Ms. Ayasofya 2351 (dated 616/1219–20).

there is an attribute, *takhlīq* ('active creation'), which is distinct from 'power' (*mas'ala* 14). Speech (*kalām*) is an attribute distinct from the letters and sounds (*mas'ala* 15); God's speech is pre-eternal (*qadīm*) (*mas'ala* 16). The Ḥanbalites hold that God's speech is the letters and sounds (*mas'ala* 17) while most people who adhere to the Sunna say that God's speech is one (*mas'ala* 18). Contrary to al-Ashʿarī, God is remaining because of His self (*bāqī li-dhātihi*) (*mas'ala* 19). Finally, the lack of a proof for something does not entail the non-existence of what is aimed at by the proof (*lā yalzimu ʿadam al-dalīl ʿalā l-shayʾ ʿadam al-madlūl*) (*mas'ala* 20).

The second chapter on the attributes has a somewhat different character. It begins with a relatively long discussion of the possibility of the vision of God, a fact on which 'all those who adhere to the Sunna' (*ahl al-sunna*) agree. This is followed by a series of brief arguments for specific issues regarding the very nature of God: human beings have no knowledge of God to the utmost degree (*ḥaqīqatuhu al-makhṣūṣa ghayr maʿlūma*) (*mas'ala* 2); God is one (*mas'ala* 3); there are several classes of polytheists with false conceptions regarding the true nature of the Divine (*mas'ala* 4). In the *Maʿālim*, al-Rāzī adds a separate chapter on the old debate between the Ashʿarites and the Muʿtazilites regarding predestination and free will (Chapter Six). Here, al-Rāzī heavily relies on the medico-philosophical concept of a balanced constitution of the body in order to distance his own analysis from that of al-Ashʿarī. Additional chapters concern prophecy (Chapter Seven), the human soul (Chapter Eight) and its afterlife (Chapter Nine), and the imamate (Chapter Ten).

(a) Al-Rāzī's *al-Mulakhkhaṣ fī al-Ḥikma*: A Philosophical Compendium as Template of Later *Kalām Summae*

Some of al-Rāzī's theological writings have gained very broad circulation and have left their traces in the further course of reception. However, in our present context, the overwhelming importance of a currently little known book of his needs to be pointed out, viz. his *al-Mulakhkhaṣ fī l-ḥikma*.[9] As its title indicates this book was written as an exposition of (mostly Avicennan) philosophy. Its overall structure is identical to the nowadays much more widespread *al-Mabāḥith al-mashriqiyya* of which it is most probably a revised abridgement. In the course of the thirteenth century, the reception of the *Mulakhkhaṣ* dominates the reception of Avicennan philosophy not only in the philosophical tradition but also among theologians. For the *kalām* tradition, from the 680s/1280s onwards, the *Mulakhkhaṣ* provides a new template for the systematic exposition of its teachings. Elements of another theological work by al-Rāzī, the *Muḥaṣṣal*, are likewise integrated into the structure of

[9] On the structure of the *Mulakhkhaṣ* cf. Eichner 2009: 31–61; on its interaction with the 'traditional' pattern of the philosophical tradition cf. Eichner 2009: 97–132; on precursors in the philosophical tradition cf. Eichner 2009: 3–10.

the *Mulakhkhaṣ*. Thus, a new template for the exposition of *kalām* writings is being established which will be adopted by many important theological handbooks, such as the *Tajrīd* by Naṣīr al-Dīn al-Ṭūsī, the *Ṭawāliʿ al-anwār* by Nāṣir al-Dīn al-Bayḍāwī, the *Ṣaḥāʾif* by al-Samarqandī, the *Mawāqif* by al-Ījī, and the *Maqāṣid* by al-Ījī's student al-Taftāzānī. Most notably during the Ilkhanid period, theological *summae* following this template are being produced. Many of them have become classics having been commented and glossed upon over and over in subsequent centuries. In the Ilkhanid period, the template is familiar to Imāmī Muʿtazilīs, Māturīdites, and Ashʿarites alike, and it provides the context in which arguments and teachings from the stock of the philosophical tradition are integrated in a theological context. This constitutes a considerable shift in the very constitution of *ʿilm al-kalām*. The 'disappearance' of philosophy in the Sunni world can better be described as an integration of Sunni *kalām* into the framework of Avicennan philosophy and a subsequent amalgamation of the two traditions. The framework of 'Avicennan philosophy' in the thirteenth century does not refer primarily to Avicenna's oeuvre but to its contemporary interpretation, as it is documented by the writings of Fakhr al-Dīn al-Rāzī, Athīr al-Dīn al-Abharī (d. 663/1264), al-Kātibī al-Qazwīnī (d. 675/1276), or Sirāj al-Dīn al-Urmawī (d. 693/1294).

The most striking feature of the structure of the *Mulakhkhaṣ* is the dissolution of the philosophical disciplines as constituted by the Aristotelian books and reinterpreted by Avicenna. In hindsight, the hypothesis that this dissolution evinces the impact of *kalām* traditions might, at first glance, seem plausible. However, a closer analysis of the earliest phases of the philosophical tradition after Avicenna shows that this stands in a continuous development within the philosophical tradition properly speaking which aims at restructuring the presentation and conception of philosophical teachings. Just as Avicenna himself had done, his early followers al-Lawkarī (d. 517/1123–4) and Bahmanyār b. al-Marzubān (d. 458/1066) continue to rearrange the structure of expositions of the system of Avicenna's philosophy, and in particular Bahmanyār's *Kitāb al-Taḥṣīl* preludes important features of the approach of the *Mulakhkhaṣ*.

This new structure of the *Mulakhkhaṣ*, after a section on logic, consists of a section on 'common things' (*al-umūr al-ʿāmma*), i.e. things common to contingent (*mumkin*) and necessary (*wājib*) entities, a section on contingent beings, and a section on the necessary being, i.e. God. The section on 'common things' is further divided into chapters on existence, essence, unity and multiplicity, necessary and contingent, temporally originated and pre-eternal. The section on contingent beings is first divided into accidents and substances (*jawāhir wa-aʿrāḍ*), the section on accidents is further divided into 'quality', 'quantity', and 'remaining categories', the section on substances is divided into 'body', 'soul', and 'intellect'. The terms *jawāhir* and *aʿrāḍ* are used based on the philosophers' conception and do not primarily refer to the *mutakallimūn*'s 'atoms' and their 'accidents'. These basic divisions are further subdivided by several layers of increasingly subtle subdivisions.

V The Later Development

The massive transformation of the theological tradition in basically all theological schools relevant in the area within a very short time asks for an explanation. The texts we possess tell us nothing about their authors' motivation. In the preface to his *Tajrīd* al-Ṭūsī simply tells us that he thinks the structure is appropriate, and in the preface to the *Ṭawāliʿ* al-Bayḍāwī only points out that his exposition is based on rational reasoning and strikes the right balance between succinctness and clear explanation. Al-Samarqandī's preface is somewhat more explicit. He tells us: 'For some time I have been erring in the darkness of the views of the ancients, and I have been a fanatic for the dark night of the would-be philosophers until the morning of truth opened on me and the love of truthfulness became evident; and I was led on the path of guidance' (*Ṣaḥīfa*, 60, 3–6). He complains that most books are just filled by useless adornment and lack the gems of philosophical questions and rational investigation. These he has adduced in the book, together with new aspects (*abḥāth badīʿa*) and doubts. He adds that he has 'filled the book with texts from the Torah and the Gospel as a proof for the prophethood of the best and as a hint to the falsity of their convictions which ought to be refuted'. Al-Ījī's introduction repeats many elements familiar from the *Ṭawāliʿ* (most notably he emphasizes the importance of rationality for the human species as a whole). However, he makes no explicit statement regarding his attitude towards 'philosophy' properly speaking. In a passage of the dedication which plays with the title of his work al-Ījī states: 'In them (i.e., standplaces, *mawāqif*) religion is strengthened by the sword and lances, and it climbs up to standplaces where it is led to victory by argument and demonstration'. While al-Samarqandī refers to inter-religious interaction as the context for which his arguments are designed, al-Ījī emphasizes the importance of rational arguments as a weapon for religion.

In order to provide some access to this group of texts which very much determines the perception of Ashʿarism as a systematic belief system, I base my account on al-Bayḍāwī's *Ṭawāliʿ*. I shall also discuss divergences in al-Ījī's *Mawāqif* and complement this by references to al-Samarqandī's *Ṣaḥāʾif* in order to contextualize this and give a sharper profile.[10]

(a) Epistemology, the (Physical) World and its Ontological Foundations

The majority of the *Ṭawāliʿ* is not devoted to religious teachings in a narrower sense (labelled as *ilāhiyyāt* and *fī l-nubuwwa* in the terminology of our sources). The work

[10] For an English translation of al-Bayḍāwī's *Ṭawāliʿ* see Calverley and Pollock 2002; for partial translations of al-Ījī's *Mawāqif* see van Ess 1966 (German) and Sabra 2006 (English).

opens with an introduction describing issues which concern *naẓar* ('the use of reason', 'deliberation'). This includes the formation of concepts, definitions, a classification of arguments, and how the use of reason can lead to certain knowledge. While al-Samarqandī's *Ṣaḥāʾif* has no such section, al-Ījī's *Mawāqif* includes this as first *mawqif*. Al-Ījī combines this with a complex discussion of how *ʿilm al-kalām* is constituted as a science—a discussion in which al-Ījī elaborates on elements present also in al-Samarqandī's *Ṣaḥāʾif*.

The first book 'On contingent beings' of the *Ṭawāliʿ* includes a chapter on 'universal things' (*al-umūr al-kulliyya*) which deals with existence (*wujūd*), essence (*māhīya*), necessity and contingency (*wujūb wa-imkān*), pre-eternity and temporal origination (*qidam wa-ḥudūth*), unity and plurality, and causation (*al-ʿilla wa-l-maʿlūl*). This unit (under the title 'common things') is a characteristic structural feature of al-Rāzī's *Mulakhkhaṣ*, and later on it becomes a prominent and distinctive feature of theological *summae* as discussed here. In our texts, the Avicennan distinction between essence and existence is projected back on al-Ashʿarī himself. It is coordinated with the discussion regarding the classical debate between the Muʿtazilites and Ashʿarites concerning whether or not a non-existent is 'a thing' (*hal al-maʿdūm shayʾ*). Al-Bayḍāwī and the later tradition derive from these projections the statement that al-Ashʿarī denies that existence is being shared (*mushārakat al-wujūd*). By this, al-Ashʿarī is presented as excluded from a general agreement to which also al-Bayḍāwī himself adheres (*Ṭawāliʿ*, 78, 4–9). Contrary to al-Bayḍāwī, al-Ījī votes for the position of al-Ashʿarī (*Mawāqif*, 46, 18–47, 21). In the discussion of pre-eternity, al-Bayḍāwī points out that this defies the conception of God as acting based on choice and free will (*taʾthīr al-mukhtār*) (*Ṭawāliʿ*, 91, 8–15). The inclusion of causation among 'common things' is characteristic of the later theological *summae*—al-Rāzī's *Mulakhkhaṣ* had dealt with it in the section on 'accidents'. Al-Bayḍāwī avoids any in-depth discussion of divergences in the theologians' and the philosophers' conception of causation (*Ṭawāliʿ*, 98–9) while al-Ījī dwells on this extensively (*Mawāqif*, 85–95).

The next major section of the first book 'On contingent beings' of the *Ṭawāliʿ* is devoted to 'accidents'. Here, al-Bayḍāwī's decision to follow the structure of the *Mulakhkhaṣ* sets him in a sharp contrast with basic features of 'traditional' *kalām* ontology: the further subdivision of the section on *aʿrāḍ* and on *jawāhir* shows in an unambiguous way that the terms *ʿaraḍ* and *jawhar* are not conceived as following the ontological framework of atomism (as it is typically associated with *kalām*) but rather rely on Aristotelian concepts. The discussion of 'accidents' is based on the nine accidental Aristotelian categories—not on accidents which the *mutakallimūn* typically discuss, such as 'life', 'colour', etc. Likewise, *jawhar* does not refer to an atom (*al-jawhar al-fard, al-juzʾ alladhī lā yatajazzaʾ*) according to the *mutakallimūn*'s discourse but rather means 'substance' in an Aristotelian sense, and the discussion is further subdivided into 'intellect' (separate substances), 'soul' (immaterial substances), and 'body' (material substances). In contrast to al-Bayḍāwī, the Māturīdite al-Samarqandī is clearly aware of the implicit antagonism between the two ontological frameworks. While drawing on the same stock of topics, the section on accidents of his *Ṣaḥāʾif* is organized in an innovative way according to whether or not the issues discussed are objects of perception (*idrāk*)—this possibly being a reflection of earlier *kalām* classifications of accidents/ divine attributes according to whether or not they presuppose 'life'.

Al-Ījī opens the third *mawqif* with an introduction that is devoted to the division of attributes (*ṣifāt*). Here, he refers to the distinction between *ṣifāt nafsiyya* and *ṣifāt maʿnawiyya* among the (divine) attributes. After this he begins his discussion of 'accidents' with the definition of *ʿaraḍ*, and then refers to the philosophers and the *mutakallimūn*'s division of accidents. Here we can easily discern al-Ījī's strategy: discussions on the very conception and nature of atoms and their accidents are a prominent feature in early (and hence: (proto) Muʿtazilī) *kalām*. In earlier Ashʿarite *kalām* works, however, the discussion of the conception of accidents (as accidents of atoms) was no longer complex or diverse—it had lost much of its importance and played no major role in the actual structure of works. However, the discussion of divine attributes continued to play a central role and was important also as a marker of identity as opposed to Muʿtazilī *kalām*, having a certain well-established order. By dwelling on the *mutakallimūn*'s division of *ṣifāt*, and by then equating *ṣifa* with the notion of *ʿaraḍ*, al-Ījī fills to a certain extent the conceptual vacuum in which the discussion of accidents is placed on the *mutakallimūn*'s side. Notwithstanding this, in the actual discussion of accidents in *mawqif* 3, al-Ījī follows al-Bayḍāwī in adopting the philosophers' division according to the Aristotelian categories. Unlike al-Bayḍāwī, al-Ījī frequently inserts subchapters that explicitly point to the philosophers' and the *mutakallimūn*'s disagreement on conceptual issues, and al-Ījī—like elsewhere in the *Mawāqif*—sides with what he describes as the Ashʿarite position. In al-Bayḍāwī's discussion, basic ontological divergences between the *mutakallimūn*'s and the philosophers' conceptions are pointed out in the discussion of the category 'where' (*al-ayn*). Al-Bayḍāwī tells us that the *mutakallimūn* call this category *kawn*, 'being', which they define as 'the being of an atom in one place during two or more instants' (*ḥuṣūl al-jawhar fī ānayn fa-ṣāʿidan fī makān wāḥid*) (*Ṭawāliʿ*, 127, 10–11). This he contrasts with the philosophers' definition of motion as 'first entelechy of something potential insofar as it is potential' (*Ṭawāliʿ*, 127, 12).

In Section Three of the first book, 'On contingent beings', al-Bayḍāwī deals with *jawāhir*, 'substances'. Here, he adduces the divergent definitions of the philosophers and the *mutakallimūn*. The philosophers distinguish between different types of *jawhar* ('substance'), viz. matter, form, the composite out of these two (i.e. body), and separate substances. The latter (separate) substances are soul (if associated to body) and intellect (if not associated). The *mutakallimūn*'s definition of *jawhar* is 'anything which occupies space' (*mutaḥayyiz*). If it accepts division, it is body, if not, it is an atom (*al-jawhar al-fard*) (*Ṭawāliʿ*, 133, 1–6). In the section on 'body', conceptual divergences between the *mutakallimūn* and the philosophers (atomism vs. hylomorphism) stand in the background of the discussion, but in contrast to al-Ījī, al-Bayḍāwī does not spell them out. Al-Ījī inserts many excursuses on basic concepts of *kalām* atomism.

In the introduction to the section on 'separate substances', al-Bayḍāwī occasionally remarks that most *mutakallimūn* deny their existence and therefore assume that angels, demons, and Satan are subtle bodies (*jism laṭīf*) (*Ṭawāliʿ*, 147, 4). Then he goes on to discuss extensively the philosophers' conception of 'separate substance' while alluding frequently to religious concepts. Al-Bayḍāwī tells us that the philosophers identify 'intellect' with the greatest angels and the first thing created—referring to the *ḥadīth* 'The first thing God has created is intellect' (*Ṭawāliʿ*, 147). Al-Bayḍāwī goes on to explain the Avicennan conception of emanation of the universe from the one (*al-wāḥid*) as a self-reflective process of an intellect's considering its necessity vs. its contingency (*Ṭawāliʿ*, 148, 1–15). After a brief discussion of the celestial souls al-Bayḍāwī turns to the human rational soul. He reports that the philosophers and al-Ghazālī agree that it is a 'separate substance', and he adduces rational (*ʿaqlī*) and scriptural (*naqlī*) arguments (*Ṭawāliʿ*, 150, 7–155, 3). Then he discusses the origination of souls, and whether or not they continue to exist infinitely.

Compared to al-Bayḍāwī, al-Ījī's *Mawāqif* inverses the order of the discussion. Al-Ījī first discusses the human rational soul, and in this section he reports the philosophers' arguments without pointing to any disagreement between them and the *mutakallimūn* regarding the nature of 'separate substances'. Instead, at the beginning of the section on 'intellect', he stresses that the *mutakallimūn* do not accept the very concept of 'separate intellects', and throughout the following section on 'intellect' he makes it explicit that these are arguments as brought forward by the philosophers (*Mawāqif*, 262–5).

(b) The Divine

Al-Bayḍāwī's section (*bāb*) on the divine 'self' (*dhāt*) is brief and consists of three thematic units. The first is devoted to 'the knowledge of it' and contains the Avicennan proof of God's existence. The second deals with issues relating to divine transcendence (*tanzīhāt*) and amounts to an enumeration of various aspects of negative theology: God's true essence does not resemble anything else, God has no body and no directions, He does not enter conjunction and does not inhere in anything; entities that originate in time cannot inhere in God. In the last unit, on divine unity (*tawḥīd*), al-Bayḍāwī distinguishes between the philosophers' proof (based on the fact that the necessity of God's existence is identical to His essence/self) and the *mutakallimūn*'s approach (if we were to assume two divine beings they would have equal share in power over contingent beings—this would imply 'preponderance without a preponderator', *tarjīḥ bi-lā murajjiḥ*).

In the section (*bāb*) on the attributes, the first chapter (*faṣl*) deals with those attributes on which divine action is based, i.e. power (*qudra*), knowledge (*ʿilm*), life (*ḥayāt*), and will (*irāda*). The beginning of the discussion of *qudra* is dominated by the conception of necessity and contingency. Next follows some doxographical information on 'the dualists' and Muʿtazilites, such as al-Naẓẓām, al-Balkhī, and the two al-Jubbāʾīs. Other attributes (discussed in the second chapter) are hearing (*samʿ*), seeing (*baṣar*), speech (*kalām*), permanence (*baqāʾ*), 'attributes which al-Ashʿarī affirms' (sitting on the throne (*istiwāʾ*), the hand, the eye, the face), i.e. attributes which others explain by exegetical efforts (*taʾwīl*), and *takwīn*, 'bringing to existence', which the Ḥanafīs define as an independent attribute distinct from *qudra*. This is concluded by a discussion of the vision of God (*ruʾya*).

Al-Ījī chooses a somewhat different classification. He refers to 'existential attributes' (*ṣifāt wujūdiyya*), while 'vision of God' and the question whether human beings can have knowledge of the true essence of God are labelled under the header 'what is possible' regarding the divine. After a discussion of 'powerful', 'living', 'willing', 'hearing and seeing', and 'speaking' (note that al-Ījī consistently uses adjectives in order to refer to the attributes) he enumerates attributes 'on which there is disagreement' between the theological schools (*Mawāqif*, 297–311).

In al-Bayḍāwī's exposition, the section (*bāb*) on divine action is, again, quite brief. Prominently discussed is the problem of whether the power (*qudra*) to act is to be ascribed to God or to human beings. Al-Bayḍāwī mentions several Ashʿarite theologians (e.g. 'the Shaykh [al-Ashʿarī] says that the actions of the servants all take place by the power of God which is created by Him'; *Ṭawāliʿ*, 197, 4), the philosophers, and the Muʿtazila. The Ashʿarite notion of acquisition (*kasb*) is referred to only in the concluding remarks: 'You must know that our companions ... harmonize the two [extreme positions, i.e. "power belongs to God" and "power belongs to human beings"] and say: actions take place by the power of God and by acquisition of the servant. This means that if a servant intends something (*ṣammama al-ʿazm*) God creates action in him. But this, too, is a problem. Because this issue is so problematic, the [pious] ancestors (*al-salaf*) reproached those who discuss this issue (*al-munāẓirīn fīhi*)' (*Ṭawāliʿ*, 200, 12–201, 1). Al-Bayḍāwī further mentions the problem of whether God actually wills good and evil things in the world when bringing them to existence and the problem of whether good and evil are defined by God (the Ashʿarite position) or are good and evil 'in themselves' (the Muʿtazilī position). Further topics include the proposition that nothing constitutes an obligation for God; that God's actions are not caused by external motivation; and the Muʿtazilite notion of why human beings are in fact exposed to moral obligation (*taklīf*).

In the section on divine action in al-Ījī's *Mawāqif* quite substantial transformations as compared to the *Ṭawāliʿ* occur. Only at the beginning, the section on 'the acts of the servants based on choice (*al-afʿāl al-ikhtiyāriyya*) take place only by the power of God' (*marṣad* 1) follows the exposition of the *Ṭawāliʿ* while adding some more detailed information on the historical background of the positions of the Ashʿarites and the Muʿtazilites (including the discussion of *taklīf*). The following section (*marṣad* 2) is devoted to a detailed discussion and refutation of the Muʿtazilī doctrine of 'generated actions' (*tawlīd*) (a topic completely absent from the *Ṭawāliʿ*), supplemented by a series of Qurʾānic quotation to refute the Muʿtazilites (*marṣad* 3). The basic issues of the following sections can be traced to the *Ṭawāliʿ*. These are followed by a discussion of the problem of *taklīf mā lā yuṭāq*, i.e. whether there can be obligation to perform acts beyond one's capacity (*marṣad* 7). *Mawqif* 5 on *Ilāhīyāt* ends with a section on 'divine names' (*marṣad* 7). This has again no parallel in the *Ṭawāliʿ*.

The massive transformations in the last two sections of the *mawqif* on the 'divine actions and divine names' (*Ilāhiyyāt*) in al-Ījī's *Mawāqif* as compared to the *Ṭawāliʿ* can be explained by the rise to prominence of the antagonism and competition with Māturīdite teachings—the section on 'divine names' in its entirety is directed against a corresponding section (*ṣaḥīfa* 13) in al-Samarqandī's *Ṣaḥīfa*. While the latter presents his theory of divine names and their relation to the divine attributes as representing a harmonistic synthesis of the teachings of the *ahl al-sunna wa-l-jamāʿa*, insisting that apparent disagreements with the teachings of the Ashʿarites are just a matter of expression (*lafẓ*), al-Ījī affirms a distinct profile of the Ashʿarite position. He points out that this is not just a quarrel about expressions—the issue at stake is rather whether the names refer to the 'divine self as such' (*al-dhāt min ḥaythu hiya hiya*) or whether they refer to 'something accidental' (*amr ʿāriḍ*). As al-Ījī points out, al-Ashʿarī's position would be that some names like 'Allāh' refer to the self while others 'such as *khāliq* and *rāziq* point to the relation to something else which undoubtedly is not identical to Him (*ghayrahu*), while others point to something which is neither identical to Him nor not identical to Him (*lā huwa wa-lā ghayrahū*), such as *ʿalīm* and *qadīr*. These point to a really existing attribute (*ṣifa ḥaqīqiyya*)' (*Mawāqif*, 333, 7–10). In other words, al-Ījī insists that the debate between contemporary Ashʿarites and Maturidites regarding the relation between names and attributes links immediately to the historical debate regarding the nature of divine attributes between the Muʿtazilites and the Ashʿarites. Although al-Ījī nowhere refers to al-Samarqandī explicitly, the latter's *Ṣaḥāʾif* can help to understand al-Ījī's motivation and the contemporary positions against which his exposition is directed. For example, al-Ījī concludes his exposition of divine names with a complete enumeration of ninety-nine names to be applied to God (*Mawāqif*, 333, 19–236, 10). He states at the beginning: 'The application of names to God is based on position (*tawqīf*), i.e. their application rests on permission (*idhn*). This is so out of caution (*iḥtiyāṭ*) and in order to avoid false ideas because there lies a great danger' (*Mawāqif*, 333, 19–20). In the context of al-Ījī's exposition itself, this very explicit remark seems not to be motivated. However, comparing it to the *Ṣaḥīfa* we can discern its motivation—al-Samarqandī states that the Baṣran Muʿtazilites had held that the divine names were based on terminological convention (*iṣṭilāḥ*) or analogical reasoning (*qiyās*) while the *ahl al-sunna wa-l-jamāʿa* base the application of names on what is contained in the Qurʾān, the Sunna, and consensus (*ijmāʿ*).

While further features remain to be substantiated by more detailed analysis, al-Ījī's strong interest in the historical background of theological doctrines and earlier Muʿtazilite teachings regarding the theory of attributes and divine actions is not to be explained simply in terms of a 'theologization' of al-Bayḍāwī's very abstract and brief sketch. Notwithstanding the fact that al-Ījī's inclusion of additional information on earlier theological doctrines shares elements with the commentary tradition, explicit auctorial interests and strategies lead his selection of material.

(c) Prophecy

The third book of the *Ṭawāliʿ* is devoted to 'prophecy and what has to do with it'. It consists of three major chapters (*bāb*), i.e. prophecy (*nubuwwa*), afterlife (*al-ḥashr wa-l-jazāʾ*), and imamate (*imāma*).

The need of human beings for prophets is emphasized at the outset of the text (*mabḥath* 1), based on an argument ultimately going back to al-Fārābī and Ibn Sīnā: human beings cannot exist independently without society but have to rely in their daily living (*maʿāsh*) on the cooperation (*muʿāwana*) of fellow human beings. Only in this way can the human species be preserved. The just balance (*ʿadl*) necessary for this can be maintained only by revealed regulations (*sharʿ*) by a lawgiver (*shāriʿ*) which are specified by evident signs (*āyāt ẓāhira*) and miracles (*muʿjizāt*) 'which call for obedience to him, summon to respond to him, confirm what he says, threaten the sinner with punishment and promise reward to those who obey' (*Ṭawāliʿ*, 209, 8–10). Next, the feasibility of miracles is discussed (*mabḥath* 2). Physical explanations are given for long abstinence from food and veridical dreams including predictions regarding the future. The prophecy of Muḥammad (*mabḥath* 3) is addressed in much detail and is discussed in the framework of earlier Ashʿarite arguments and terminology: 'He has claimed prophethood, as it is generally agreed (*bi-l-ijmāʿ*), he has shown the miracle (*aẓhara bi-l-muʿjiza*), viz. the Qurʾān, he has provoked [potential adversaries] (*taḥaddā*) and was not defeated by an opponent (*lam yuʿāraḍ*), and he has given information regarding what is hidden (*akhbara ʿan al-mughībāt*)' (*Ṭawāliʿ*, 211, 5–7). After some examples for Muḥammad's and the Qurʾān's ability to predict the future, al-Bayḍāwī refers to the tradition of *dalāʾil al-nubuwwa*. Al-Bayḍāwī also points out (*mabḥath* 4) that according to the majority (*jumhūr*) prophets are protected from unbelief/ungratefulness and disobedience after the revelation (*ʿiṣma ʿan al-kufr wa-l-maʿāṣī baʿd al-waḥy*). He states that prophets stand higher than angels (*mabḥath* 5), and then briefly discusses miracles other than the miracles of the prophets (*karāmāt*) (*mabḥath* 6).

Compared to *Ṭawāliʿ*, al-Ījī's exposition is more comprehensive, and it insists on differentiating between the theologians' tradition and the philosophers' theories. The *Mawāqif* begins with a discussion of the very conception of a prophet (*nabī*) (*maqṣad* 1). Al-Ījī refers to how this word is used in ordinary language, and then provides the best definition: 'The one to whom God has said: I have sent you' (*Mawāqif*, 337, 8). The philosophers, we hear, refer to three characteristics (*khāṣṣiyyāt*) of a prophet: (1) he must have knowledge of what is hidden; (2) he performs unusual actions (*afʿāl khārija ʿan al-ʿāda*); (3) he sees the angels 'in a form' (*muṣawwara*). In all three we can recognize elements of how al-Bayḍāwī had rendered Ashʿarite positions. Al-Ījī then closely investigates the phenomenon of 'miracle' (*muʿjiza*) (*maqṣad* 2), defined as 'something by which it is intended to make evident the truthfulness of someone who claims to be the messenger of God' (*Mawāqif*, 339, 5–6). He discusses seven conditions, how miracles occur, and how they point to something. Again, al-Ījī repeatedly identifies elements which we encounter in al-Bayḍāwī's exposition as stemming from the philosophers. When al-Ījī discusses the possibility (*imkān*) of the sending of prophets (*maqṣad* 3) he distances himself from the philosophers' position that prophecy is a necessity according to rational insight (*wājib ʿaqlan*, cf. *Ṭawāliʿ*, where al-Bayḍāwi argues that there exists a need (*iḥtiyāj*) for prophets in order for humans to survive as a species) as well as from the Muʿtazilite view that sending prophets is an obligation for God (*yajibu ʿalā Llāh*) (*Mawāqif*, 342, 11–14). Al-Ījī argues that although there are several possibilities to prove Muḥammad's prophethood (*maqṣad* 4), the one to be relied on (*al-ʿumda*) can be summarized as follows: 'He has claimed prophecy and has performed a miracle. The first has been confirmed in an uninterrupted chain dating back to the eyewitness, and his miracle is the Qurʾān' (*Mawāqif*, 349, 7–8). This brief summary is followed by a comprehensive discussion of the miraculous features of the Qurʾān, most notably Qurʾānic rhetoric (*Mawāqif*, 349–55), and this is complemented by other miracles (*Mawāqif*, 355–8). In his discussion of the prophets' protection from sin, al-Ījī dwells more extensively on the veracity of the prophetic message, and the *Mawāqif* discusses the various theological views on 'sin' and the status of sinners in more detail than is the case in the *Ṭawāliʿ*. Al-Ījī further differentiates the discussion of impeccability (*ʿiṣma*) by elaborating on its 'true nature' (*ḥaqīqa*) and the *ʿiṣma* of angels (*maqṣad* 6 and 7). The following discussion of the superiority of prophets over angels and the possibility of *karāmāt* resembles that in the *Ṭawāliʿ*.

(d) Afterlife

The discussion of the afterlife begins in the *Ṭawāliʿ* with the problem whether what has been annihilated may return to existence (*iʿādat al-maʿdūm*)—which, according to the philosophers, would not be possible. Al-Bayḍāwī refutes the ontological assumption that no judgement can be passed regarding the non-existent. After this, he turns to bodily resurrection. For this he quotes from the Qurʾān. Then (*mabḥath* 3) he argues that paradise and hell are located in this world, and he points out that they were created. In the discussion of reward in the hereafter (*mabḥath* 4) he turns against the position of the Baṣran Muʿtazila, stressing that divine action is not directed by a purpose (*gharaḍ*). 'Our companions say that reward (*thawāb*) is a favour (*faḍl*) by God, and that punishment (*ʿiqāb*) is justice (*ʿadl*) by Him. Actions (*ʿamal*) are a pointer (*dalīl*) [indicating how a person is to be judged]' (*Ṭawāliʿ*, 228, 6–7). Further topics are the intercession of the prophet (*shafāʿa*) for grave sinners, the punishment in the grave (*ʿadhāb al-qabr*) and further contents of 'tradition' (*samʿiyyāt*). Finally, positions on 'belief' (*īmān*) as qualifying name in the revelation (*ism sharʿī*) are discussed.

The relevant discussion in the *Mawāqif* by and large resembles that of the *Ṭawāliʿ*. Occasionally, more detailed information is given on relevant Muʿtazilite doctrines. Al-Ījī devotes a brief section to *iḥbāṭ* ('mutual cancellation of reward for obedience and punishment for offences'), and (following al-Samarqandī's *Ṣaḥīfa*) deals in more detail with eschatological concepts stemming from tradition. Like al-Bayḍāwī, al-Ījī argues that these things are possible, and that since there exist reliable accounts about them, their existence is to be assumed.

(e) Imamate

This section in the *Ṭawāliʿ* opens with a discussion of the necessity (*wujūb*) of the imamate (*mabḥath* 1): Twelver Shīʿīs and Ismāʿīlīs say that it is incumbent upon God, the Muʿtazila and the Zaydiyya maintain that it is necessary according to intellect, while the Ashʿarites hold that it is necessary because of transmitted information (*samʿan*)

(*Ṭawāliʿ*, 235, 5–6). Al-Bayḍāwī then enumerates the attributes (*ṣifāt*) of the imām: (1) he is a *mujtahid* in the field of *uṣūl al-dīn*; (2) he possesses an opinion and the ability to perform political decisions (*tadbīr … al-umūr al-siyāsīya*); (3) he is brave; (4) he is 'just' (*ʿadl*); (5) he possesses intellect; (6) he is of age; (7) he is male; (8) he is free; (9) he stems from Quraysh. Other than the Ismāʿīlīs and the Twelver-Shīʿīs, the Ashʿarites do not stipulate protection from mistakes and sin (*ʿiṣma*). Al-Bayḍāwī enumerates (*mabḥath* 3) various views on how the Imām is designated (*naṣṣ*). The last two sections discuss the legitimacy of the first four caliphs, most notably the imamate of Abū Bakr (*mabḥath* 4) and the excellence of the companions of the prophet (*faḍl al-ṣaḥāba, mabḥath* 5). Al-Ījī's discussion of the imamate very much resembles that of the *Ṭawāliʿ*.

At the end of his *Mawāqif*, al-Ījī adds two elements that link his *kalām summa* to other traditions of theological expositions: he adds an appendix (*tadhyīl*) on the seventy-three sects of the Islamic *umma* (which he emumerates), and concludes his book by a creed:

> The sect which is saved … are the Ashʿarites and the ancient ones among the newer ones (*al-salaf min al-muḥdathīn*) and among the *ahl al-sunna wa-l-jamāʿa*. Their teachings are free from all these innovations. They agree on the origination of the world, the existence of the Creator (*bāriʾ*), that no one else is a creator (*khāliq*), that He is pre-eternal, attributed with knowledge, power and the other attributes of majesty. Nothing resembles Him, He has no opposite and nothing corresponds to Him. He does not inhere in anything, in His self nothing originated subsists. He is not in a place nor in a direction. Motion and change in location do not apply to Him, nor does ignorance, lie or any other attribute of imperfection. He is seen by the believers in the thereafter. What God wills is the case, what He does not will, is not. He is independent and does not need anything, nothing is an obligation for Him. If He rewards [someone] He does so by His favour, and if He punishes He does so by His justice. His action is not determined by a purpose, no one except Him sets up rules. Whatsoever He does or sets up as a rule can not be attributed with oppression and injustice. He has no parts, no definition and no limits. Additions and diminutions pertain to his creation. The return [to God after death] is truly the case, and likewise recompensation and billing, 'the street', 'the scales', the createdness of Paradise and Hell. The sending of messengers with miracles from Adam to Muḥammad is truly the case. Those who submitted to the ruler agreed upon (*bayʿat al-riḍwān*) and those who were at Badr are among the inhabitants of Paradise. An imām must be installed upon those who are bound by legal commands, and the true imām after the prophet was Abū Bakr, then ʿUmar, then ʿUthmān, then ʿAlī. This enumeration does not indicate a preference in excellence. We do not mark anyone among the *ahl al-qibla* as unbeliever unless based on something which denies a poweful and knowing creator, or based on *shirk* or denial of prophecy, or based on something which the mission of Muḥammad claims by necessity, or based on something on which there is agreement such as permitting what is prohibited. As to anything else: the one who claims this may be the source of blameful innovation (*mubtadiʿ*) but not an unbeliever (*kāfir*). The jurisprudents and their practice do not concern us in this science here.

References

al-Anṣārī, Abū l-Qāsim (*Ghunya*). *K. al-Ghunya fī l-kalām*. Ed. Muṣṭafā Ḥasanayn ʿAbd al-Hādī. Cairo: Dār al-Salām, 2010.

al-Bayḍāwī, ʿAbd Allāh (*Ṭawāliʿ*). *Ṭawāliʿ al-anwār min maṭāliʿ al-anẓār*. Ed. ʿAbbās Sulaymān. Beirut: Dār al-Jīl, 1991.

de Boer, T. (1901). *Geschichte der Philosophie im Islam*. Stuttgart: Frommann.

Calverley, E. E., and J. W. Pollock (2002). *Nature, Man and God in Medieval Islam: 'Abd Allah Baydawi's text, Tawaliʿ al-anwar min mataliʿ al-anzar, along with Mahmud Isfahani's Commentary, Matali' al-anzar, Sharh Tawali' al-anwar*. 2 vols. Leiden: Brill.

Ḍiyāʾ al-Dīn al-Makkī (*Nihāya*). *Nihāyat al-marām fī dirāyat al-kalām*. Ed. A. Shihadeh. Tehran: Mīrāth-i maktūb, 2013.

Eichner, H. (2009). *The Post-Avicennian Philosophical Tradition and Islamic Orthodoxy: Philosophical and Theological Summae in Context*. Halle: unpublished Habilitation.

Eichner, H. (forthcoming). 'Tracing Changing Identities through Static Doxographical Information'. In Muehlethaler, S. Schmidtke, and G. Schwarb (eds.), *Theological Rationalism in Medieval Islam: New Sources and Perspectives*. Leuven: Peeters [forthcoming].

van Ess, J. (1966). *Die Erkenntnislehre des 'Aḍudaddīn al-Īcī: Übersetzung und Kommentar des ersten Buches seiner Mawāqif*. Wiesbaden: Harrassowitz.

Fakhr al-Dīn al-Rāzī (*Ma'ālim*). *Critical Remarks by Najm al-Dīn al-Kātibī on the Kitāb al-Ma'ālim by Fakhr al-Dīn al-Rāzī, Together with the Commentaries by 'Izz al-Dawla Ibn Kammūna*. Ed. R. Pourjavady and S. Schmidtke. Tehran: Iranian Institute of Philosophy & Institute of Islamic Studies, Freie Universität, Berlin, 1386/2007.

Fakhr al-Dīn al-Rāzī (*Manṭiq al-Mulakhkhaṣ*). *Manṭiq al-Mulakhkhaṣ*. Ed. Aḥad Farāmarz Qarāmalikī. Tehran: Dānishgāh-i Imām al-Ṣādiq, 2002.

Gimaret, D. (1980). *Théories de l'acte humain en théologie musulmane*. Paris: Vrin.

Gutas, D. (2002). 'The Heritage of Avicenna: The Golden Age of Arabic Philosophy, 1000—ca. 1350'. In J. Janssens and D. de Smet (eds.), *Avicenna and His Heritage: Acts of the International Colloquium*. Leuven: Peeters, 81–97.

al-Ījī, 'Aḍud al-Dīn (*Mawāqif*). *Kitāb al-Mawāqif*. Cairo: Maktabat al-Mutanabbī, n.d.

Madelung, W. (1971). 'The Spread of Māturīdism and the Turks'. In *Actas di IV Congresso de Estudos Árabes e Islâmicos, Coimbra-Lisboa 1968*. Leiden: Brill, 109–68. [Reprinted in W. Madelung. *Religious Schools and Sects in Medieval Islam*. Aldershot: Ashgate, 1985, II.]

Madelung, W., and T. Mayer (2001). *Struggling with the Philosopher: A Refutation of Avicenna's Metaphysics*. London: Tauris.

Mayer, T. (2009). *Keys to the Arcana: Shahrastānī's Esoteric Commentary on the Qur'an*. Oxford: Oxford University Press.

Miller, L. (1995). 'al-Samarkandī, Shams al-Dīn'. *The Encyclopaedia of Islam*. New Edition. Leiden: Brill. viii. 1038f.

Rudolph, U. (1997). *al-Māturīdī und die sunnitische Theologie in Samarkand*. Leiden: Brill.

Rudolph, U. (2008). *Islamische Philosophie: Von den Anfängen bis zur Gegenwart*. Munich: Beck.

Sabra, A. I. (2006). '*Kalām* Atomism as an Alternative Philosophy to Hellenizing *Falsafa*'. In J. Montgomery (ed.), *Arabic Theology, Arabic Philosophy: from the Many to the One*. Leuven: Peeters, 199–272.

al-Samarqandī, Shams al-Dīn (*Ṣaḥāʾif*). *al-Ṣaḥāʾif al-ilāhiyya*. Ed. Aḥmad ʿAbd al-Raḥmān al-Sharīf. Kuwait: Maktabat al-Falāḥ, 1985.

al-Shahrastānī (*Nihāya*). *Nihāyat al-iqdām fī ʿilm al-kalām*. Ed. A. Guillaume. Oxford: Oxford University Press, 1934.

Shihadeh, A. (2005). 'From al-Ghazālī to al-Rāzī: 6th/12th Century Developments in Muslim Philosophical Theology'. *Arabic Sciences and Philosophy* 15: 141–79.

Shihadeh, A. (2006). *The Teleological Ethics of Fakhr al-Dīn al-Rāzī*. Leiden: Brill.

Shihadeh, A. (2016). *Doubts on Avicenna: A Study and Edition on Sharaf al-Dīn al-Maʿūdī's Commentary on the Ishārāt*. Leiden: Brill.

CHAPTER 29

LATER ASHʿARISM IN THE ISLAMIC WEST

DELFINA SERRANO RUANO*

THE title of this chapter involves a certain chronological inconsistency in that it is not the sequel of a former chapter on early Ashʿarism in the pre-modern Islamic West.[1] Rather, the subject is reviewed from its beginnings in tenth century CE Ifrīqiyā, to the fifteenth century CE, including a span in the general history of Ashʿarism (1100–1250 CE) that, as pointed out by K. Karimullah (2007: 8–9), is in great need of attention.

The study of Western Ashʿarism has been subsidiary to the interest raised by inter-religious polemics, mysticism, and Averroes's *Tahāfut al-tahāfut*. Apart from these questions, specific historical periods and geographical settings have been focused on, with a general preference for Ifrīqiyā and al-Andalus on the one hand, and Almohad doctrine on the other. Ashʿarism has received renewed attention after scholars like D. Urvoy started to exploit bio-bibliographical literature to reconstruct the intellectual history of al-Andalus. Despite being fragmentary, all these efforts have set a sufficiently safe ground on which to undertake the filling of the remaining gaps in our present knowledge about the spreading and development of Ashʿarism in the pre-modern Islamic West.

The adoption of Ashʿarism in North Africa and al-Andalus follows a chronological and geographical sequence that parallels these regions' entering the orbit of Islamic religious sciences. Ashʿarism arrived in Ifrīqiyā and parts of central Maghrib by the middle of the tenth century CE (Idris 1962: ii. 700–2). Initially, Ifrīqiyā played a springboard role for *kalām* to be propagated in al-Andalus through Andalusī scholars who stopped in Qayrawān on their way to and from Mecca and the Eastern centres of Islamic learning,

* To my beloved mother, Julia Ruano García

1 This chapter has benefited from the wise remarks of the anonymous reader of the first draft, especially as far as late North African Ashʿarite theologians are concerned. In this latter regard I would also like to thank Justin Stearns for providing me with a series of useful bibliographical references.

e.g. al-Aṣīlī and Abū ʿAlī al-Ghassānī (Idris 1962: ii. 702). Eventually, Ashʿarism spread in the Far Maghrib thanks to the joint influence of Ifrīqī and Andalusī theologians.

I Ifrīqiyā: Reception and Dissemination of Ashʿarism

In Ifrīqiyā, the array of theological, legal, and political interrelations was particularly complex compared to al-Andalus and the Far Maghrib where Ashʿarism, more often than not, was connected with Mālikism. Be that as it may, the methods of Ashʿarite *kalām* provided North African Mālikīs with dialectical skills that were instrumental in keeping Ḥanafīs, Shāfiʿīs, and Ibāḍīs at bay.[2] Indeed 1049 CE, the year the Zirid ruler al-Muʿizz b. Bādīs released himself from Fāṭimid authority to pay formal allegiance to the ʿAbbāsids in Baghdad and adopt Sunni Islam, marked a turning point for Ifrīqī Mālikīs, who emerged then as the leading religious scholars. A series of polemics held by local Mālikīs concerning the connection between intention and the outer expression of faith through words and deeds, God's relation to His creatures, the interpretation of certain Qurʾānic descriptions of God, and other issues of the like (Idris 1962: ii. 697, 700–4, 716f., 724) suggest that, subsequently, Ashʿarism evolved from an instrument to make Mālikīs' way in a politically adverse context into a factor of internal differentiation.

Ashʿarite doctrines had been introduced to Ifrīqiyā by scholars who studied with some of the eponymous master's immediate followers. Among the former was Ibn Mujāhid al-Baṣrī (d. 370/980–1), while al-Qābisī (d. 403/1012) and his disciple Abū ʿImrān al-Fāsī (d. 430/1038) figure prominently among the main agents of their dissemination (Idris 1953: 133–6; 1962: ii. 701–3, 722f.). The first wrote an epistle (*risāla*) on al-Ashʿarī with the aim of establishing his authority above that of other Muslim theologians on the grounds that al-Ashʿarī 'resorted to *kalām* with the sole intention to clarify the meaning of traditions, to fix them and to remove any doubtful element from them' whereby he had contributed to 'rendering truth victorious' (Idris 1962: ii. 703). Abū ʿImrān al-Fāsī (d. 430/1038)—better known for his symbolic role in the formation of the Almoravid movement—studied directly under Ibn Mujāhid's disciple, Abū Bakr al-Bāqillānī, (d. 403/1013) who became the chief Ashʿarite authority for North African scholars (Idris 1953: 131f.; 1962: ii. 726f.; Urvoy 1983: 214). This latter process is illustrated by the debate held between Ibn Abī Zayd al-Qayrāwanī and a number of Sufis, jurists, and traditionists from Qayrawān (d. 386/996) concerning saints' capacity to perform miracles. Ibn Abī Zayd's nuanced position and objections were interpreted in the sense that he was opposed to the *karāmāt al-awliyāʾ*, being branded a Muʿtazilī. The view of al-Bāqillānī was sought by the parties to settle the dispute and this—namely the view that saints

[2] The Ḥanafis had in their majority converted to Shīʿism during the Fāṭimid period and many Shāfiʿis were themselves adherents of Ashʿarism.

can perform extraordinary acts (*karāmāt*) yet that these must be distinguished from *muʿjizāt*, i.e. the kind of miracles that only prophets can perform—became the most authoritative opinion on the issue (Idris 1962: ii. 695; Fierro 1992; Rahman 2009: 291–322, discussing Fierro in 312–19). Another relevant aspect of the debate lies in its having involved jurists, Sufis, traditionists, and *mutakallimūn*, which points to a crossroads of interests that will acquire new significance in al-Qushayrī's and, overall, al-Ghazālī's endeavour to give doctrinal grounding to the idea of a complete compatibility among *fiqh*, *kalām* (in its Ashʿarite version), and Sufism.

Nevertheless, al-Bāqillānī's embodiment of orthodox theology for Western Mālikīs required a certain effort to stress his Mālikī affiliation, as can be documented in sources from the Almoravid period (Ibn Rushd, *Fatāwā*, ii. 1060–1; Qāḍī ʿIyāḍ, *Tartīb*, 47–70). Conversely, Ibn Abī Zayd al-Qayrawānī's adherence to Ashʿarism was subject to controversy. Idris considers him a follower of the school (Idris 1953: 128–30, 139; 1962: ii. 700–2) contrary to Hintati (Hintati 1992: 310) and, more recently, to Rahman who holds that al-Qayrawānī was 'a conservative scholar who is best classified as a moderate traditionalist' (Rahman 2009: 321). Be that as it may, by the first quarter of the twelfth century CE, the question had still not received a conclusive answer (Ibn Rushd, *Fatāwā*, ii. 1060f.). Moreover, al-Qayrawānī's position concerning the Qurʾānic reference to God's sitting on the throne was held as blatant anthropomorphism by no more and no less than Abū Bakr Ibn al-ʿArabī (Ibn al-ʿArabī, *ʿAwāṣim*, 214f.; Serrano 2005a: 831–3).

II Al-Andalus: Assimilation and Granting of Quasi-official Status

In al-Andalus, the assimilation of Ashʿarite doctrine and methodology—and not just the transmission of works written by Ashʿarite theologians like Ibn Mujāhid or al-Bāqillānī—was operated through scholars who studied in the East, with Abū l-Walīd Sulaymān b. Khalaf al-Bājī (d. 474/1081) deserving special mention (Urvoy 1972: 102f., 105f.). This process is part of a broader trend of intellectual borrowing which, by the end of the fourth/tenth and the beginning of the fifth/eleventh century, had already brought Neoplatonism, logic, and dialectics. According to Urvoy, *kalām* shared with Sufism and philosophy a space for intellectual speculation disconnected from the other religious sciences. Gradually, it started to spread as an extension of *ḥadīth*, Qurʾān, *adab*, or Arabic language and ended by developing a strong link with *fiqh* through legal methodology (*uṣūl al-fiqh*) (Urvoy 1990: 165) so that, normally, an expert in Ashʿarite *kalām* was also an expert in *uṣūl al-fiqh* but not necessarily the other way round. The association between Ashʿarite *kalām* and Mālikī *uṣūl al-fiqh* remained constant for the next two centuries (Urvoy 1990: 165).

By the end of the fifth/eleventh century, the spread of *kalām* was stimulated by the need to gain argumentative capacities against Christian polemicists who had grown more defiant since the balance of military forces had started to shift in favour of their co-religionists (Fierro 1994: 399, 405, 446f., 455, 466–86). Yet, the most active anti-Christian polemicist at that time, Ibn Ḥazm (d. 456/1064), was not a follower of al-Ashʿarī but a staunch opponent of his doctrines, which he attacked even more vehemently than anthropomorphism and Muʿtazilism, a fact attesting to the Ashʿarites' rising influence in fifth/eleventh-century al-Andalus. Within the general contention on the role of reason and its limits, Ibn Ḥazm targeted the Ashʿarites' method of non-literal interpretation of the sacred texts. In his view, these latter admit to be examined and explained on the grounds of rational, sensitive, and linguistic intuition (Arnáldez 1981: 168) but non-literal interpretation is permitted only when proof thereof can be identified in a parallel textual source of authority (e.g. pre-Islamic poetry). However, this line of argumentation did not prove satisfactory to clarify the meaning of the anthropomorphic expressions that are found in the Qurʾān and Prophetic tradition, and he had to admit that they must be understood in a spiritual metaphorical sense. Ibn Ḥazm further criticized the Ashʿarites for considering the Qurʾān to be different from God's word and His attributes to be distinct from His essence but consonant with His oneness. They were also accused by him of upholding the reality of divine attributes that are not mentioned in the sacred texts but derived through analogical reasoning from other mentioned attributes (*ishtiqāq*)[3] (Goldziher 1884: 137–60; Arnáldez 1971; Urvoy 1972: 129–32).

The question of the sources, oral or written, from which our scholar got acquainted with Ashʿarism has been recently addressed by S. Schmidtke, according to whom, Ibn Ḥazm's textual basis was narrow, having mainly consisted of a theological *summa* entitled *Kitāb al-Simnānī* from which he would have drawn most of al-Bāqillānī's and Ibn Fūrak's doctrines he discusses in his *Fiṣal*. Among his oral sources stand out his countryman and opponent Abū l-Walīd al-Bājī, and other Andalusī and non-Andalusī scholars who provided him with relevant information (Schmidtke 2013: 382–9). Also and according to his own testimony, he refuted an apology of Ashʿarism written by someone from Qayrawān (Idris 1962: ii. 702; Fórneas 1978: 5; 1977–9; Ibn al-Abbār, *Takmila*, ed. Codera, i: 126, no. 443; Asín Palacios 1927–32: i. 199, 200; Urvoy 1972: 98 n. 22; Achekar 1998: 12 n. 54; Schmidtke 2013: 388–9 and n. 68).

Abū l-Walīd al-Bājī studied under Abū Jaʿfar Muḥammad b. Aḥmad al-Simnānī (d. 444/1052), a companion of al-Bāqillānī whom he met in Mosul, and his mastery of *kalām* and *uṣūl al-fiqh* was central for Ashʿarism to take root in al-Andalus. In fact, most of the experts in the fundamentals of religion and law of the Almoravid period—during which Western Ashʿarism reached maturity—were either his disciples or disciples of these latter. Al-Bājī wrote a series of tracts on *kalām*, legal methodology, and dialectics (Fierro n.d.: 121) and, like Ibn Ḥazm, engaged in anti-Christian polemics as documented in the so-called 'Letters of the Monk of France' (Fierro 1994: 471–9). Apart from playing a crucial role in the introduction of Ashʿarism in al-Andalus, al-Bājī was also the most serious opponent of Ibn Ḥazm's legal literalism, although Urvoy believes that al-Bājī was the target of most of Ibn Ḥazm's anti-Ashʿarite invectives as well (Urvoy 1972: 129). Their debate

[3] E.g. to uphold the reality of the attribute of will (*irāda*) or of being wilful (*murīd*) from those Qurʾānic verses in which God is described to want or not to want something.

was allegedly won by al-Bājī (Turki 1973) thanks, precisely, to the religious knowledge he acquired during his journey to the East and to the mastering of dialectics (ʿIyāḍ, *Tartīb*, 8: 122). Conversely, al-Bājī's capacity to make Mālikism prevail over Ẓāhirism gave him the right to stand as an Ashʿarite *mutakallim* in a milieu still quite unfavourable to rational theological speculation (Ibn ʿAbd al-Barr, *Jāmiʿ*, 2: 94–9 esp. 95) since it evidenced the utility of dialectics, a discipline that used to be studied in connection to legal methodology and *kalām*. The need to overcome the challenge represented by Ẓāhirism and the role played by a Mālikī Ashʿarite like al-Bājī in facing it efficiently seems thus to be the origin of the close interrelation between Mālikī hermeneutics and Ashʿarism in al-Andalus.

The Almoravid movement contributed in quite a significant manner to the further spreading and development of Ashʿarim in al-Andalus and North Africa (Dandash 1991; Hintati 1992) which, for the first time in history, became part of a single political unity. Rather than having merely tolerated *kalām* and its practitioners, the Almoravids appear to have implemented a conscious policy of promotion, likely inspired by Abū ʿImrān al-Fāsī (Idris 1953: 135; Hintati 1992: 302). Be that as it may, the credit of introducing rational theology (*ʿilm al-iʿtiqādāt*) into the Far Maghrib—present-day Morocco—is given to the teachings of Abū Bakr Muḥammad b. al-Ḥasan al-Murādī al-Ḥaḍramī (d. 489/1095) (Maqqarī, *Azhār*, 3: 161; Dandash 1988b: 143; Achekar 1998: 13f.), while the subsequent consolidation of Ashʿarism in the area, with the emergence of Fez as a pole of *kalām* studies under the leadership of Abū ʿAmr ʿUthmān b. ʿAbd Allāh al-Salāluqī/Salālujī (d. *c*.580/1184), is attributed to the action of the Andalusī Abū l-Ḥasan ʿAlī b. Muḥammad b. Khulayd al-Lakhmī al-Ishbīlī (d. 567/1171) (Serrano 2003: 503, 513, 514).

The Almoravids' support of Ashʿarism translated into a series of initiatives, first of which was public acknowledgement of the school doctrine. The selected procedure bears a remarkable resemblance with that previously adopted in Zīrid Ifrīqiyā: instead of instructing his subjects to adhere to the doctrines of al-Ashʿarī via an official decree, the *amīr* or one of his representatives addressed Ibn Rushd al-Jadd (d. 520/1126), the most prestigious *ʿālim* of the moment. Legal advice was requested from him concerning the status of Ashʿarite theologians *vis-à-vis* those who refused to accept them as sound religious authorities. The tone of the question (*istiftāʾ*) anticipated the answer (*fatwā*), namely that the followers of al-Ashʿarī are right (*ʿalā l-ḥaqīqa*) because they are familiar with the principles (*uṣūl*) of religious beliefs and with the categories of necessary, possible, and impossible with respect to God. For this reason, their authority must be given precedence over that of the experts in the branches (*al-furūʿ*, i.e. rituals and applied law) since these latter cannot be known without knowing the principles. Indeed, knowledge of the fundamentals of Islamic faith and law (*uṣūl al-dīn wa-l-fiqh*) is essential to understand the textual and rational arguments on which rely sound belief, to clarify ambiguities, to solve uncertainties, and last but not least to refute heretic and deviant opinions. Those who refuse to acknowledge their authority are stupid and ignorant. Those who insult them and level unfounded accusations against them are evil doers (*fāsiq*). They must be invited to retract, but if they refuse they must be punished until they repent (Ibn Rushd, *Fatāwā*, 2: 802–5, 943–5 and 1060f.; Dandash 1988a: 363; Urvoy 1998: 27–9; Achekar 1998: 15–16; Serrano 2003: 467–75; cfr. Lagardère 1994).

The result was a sublimation of the study of the fundamentals of both religion and law and, consequently, an improvement in the position of its practitioners with the rulers. In fact, scholars combining Mālikī *fiqh* and Ashʿarite *kalām* performed relevant public functions like *qāḍī*ship and issued legal opinions on question of high political voltage. The figures of Ibn Rushd al-Jadd, ʿIyāḍ b. Mūsā, and Abū Bakr Ibn al-ʿArabī stand out here.

From a substantial point of view, the Almoravids' promotion of Ashʿarism focused on the eradication of both anthropomorphism—declared the most evil consequence of theological literalism—and its antithesis, i.e. esoteric interpretation of the sacred texts, Ashʿarism propounded thus as the ideal middle term between the two extremes. Refutations of both anthropomorphism and Bāṭinism were written by Ibn al-Sīd al-Baṭalyawsī (d. 521/1127), and Abū Bakr Ibn al-ʿArabī (Serrano 2002; 2005a; forthcoming). Unlike Ibn al-ʿArabī, however, al-Baṭalyawsī seems to have operated rather independently from the Almoravids and the Mālikī establishment (Serrano 2002). Abū Bakr Ibn al-ʿArabī, for his part, represents the summit of Ashʿarism in al-Andalus. He studied directly under al-Ghazālī (Griffel 2009: 62–71) and brought his books to his homeland, contributing to the assimilation of the great master's thought by his many disciples (Urvoy 1983: 144, 196, 198–201; Lucini 1995) which, in turn, was instrumental for the consolidation of *kalām*, Neoplatonism, and logic in the region (Urvoy 1974: 168). Abū Bakr Ibn al-ʿArabī can thus be credited with completing al-Bājī's endeavour.

The steps taken by the Almoravids and their scholars to purge the common believer's mind of corporealism and of the interpretive excesses of the esotericists also gave rise to a series of new professions of faith of which the *ʿaqīda* of Qāḍī ʿIyāḍ became the most popular (Wensinck 1932: 227–9, 274). To judge by the testimony of Abū Bakr Ibn al-ʿArabī, these *ʿaqīdas*' main target was not Ḥanbalism, Muʿtazilism, or Bāṭinism. The threat they were meant to prevent lay rather within Mālikīs' own ranks in which theological literalism had allegedly wreaked havoc, as was manifest in the opening chapters of Ibn Abī Zayd al-Qayrawānī's *Risāla*, now judged to lean too much towards anthropomorphism to keep on being regarded as the Mālikī profession of faith par excellence (Serrano 2005a: 831–3).

Kalām thus experienced a remarkable progress in this period, along with philosophy and mysticism, due to the adoption of Aristotelian logic and much of Neoplatonic metaphysics (Urvoy 1974: 167–70) which al-Ghazālī had borrowed from Ibn Sīnā and other thinkers to fight them on their own turf (Watt 1960). Qāḍī ʿIyāḍ's aforementioned profession of faith provides an illustrative example in that regard, with the introduction of the logical categories of obligatory (*wājib*) and impossible (*mustaḥīl*) (Wensinck 1932: 227–9). However, the few known philosophers or supporters of philosophy of the Almoravid period (e.g. Ibn al-Sīd al-Baṭalyawsī and Ibn Bājja) did not enjoy the advantageous position reached by the Mālikī *mutakallimūn*. Mālik b. Wuhayb (b. Seville 453/1061, d. Marrakech 525/1130) is an exception to this, but the influence he managed to exert with ʿAlī b. Yūsuf b. Tāshufīn was at the cost of downplaying, if not hiding, his interest in the profane sciences (*ʿulūm al-awāʾil*) (Serrano and Forcada 2007).

As regards the circulation of al-Ghazālī's works and the spread of Sufism, the existence of a superior category of believers (*al-muttaqīn*) who had the capacity to perform miracles (*karāmāt*) did not pose major concerns for Almoravid Ashʿarites (Burzulī, *Fatāwā*, 6: 224f.), notwithstanding that the issue went on being subject to debate (Fierro 1992: 239–42). Yet controversies around the relationship between the certainty of God's existence that leads to the perfection of faith on the one hand, and deeds, on the other (i.e. whether bad deeds and sins have the capacity to corrupt faith to the point of rendering one an unbeliever), seems to have had far more serious consequences, e.g. public condemnation of al-Ghazālī's books. Ibn Rushd al-Jadd tried to settle the matter by stating that 1) it is certainty of God's existence that leads faith to perfection. Certainty of God's existence can be reached without intellectual knowledge though the faith of he who combines true belief in God with intellectual knowledge about Him is better than that of he who lacks that knowledge. Ibn Rushd refuses to give preponderance to either performing rituals and good deeds, or acquiring knowledge: it all depends on the particular believer's circumstances and the aim sought with these activities (Ibn Rushd, *Muqaddamāt*, 1: 51, 54–57, esp. 56–57). Meanwhile, al-Ghazālī was thought to promote the idea that the source of certainty is not the intellect but divine illumination and that the spiritual purification necessary to receive illumination is reached through deeds—especially supererogatory acts of worship—rather than through intellectual effort (Serrano 2006: 150f.). Given that the position a Muslim occupies in the rank of religious authority is determined by his level of knowledge about God, the idea that deeds prevail over intellectual knowledge gave an argument to its proponents, i.e. 'extreme Sufis' according to Abū Bakr Ibn al-ʿArabī and Qāḍī ʿIyāḍ, to claim superiority with respect to traditional scholars. Further, those who, according to some *fuqahāʾ*, held in favour of making deeds prevail over intellectual knowledge claimed that prophecy could be reached through spiritual purification as well. This amounted to saying that prophecy can be reached through performing supererogatory acts of worship and to questioning Muḥammad's superiority and exclusive status as seal of the prophets (Serrano 2006: 150f.; 2009: 414, 428).

Actual political circumstances in al-Andalus and the Maghrib led the aforementioned scholars and others to suspect of mystics who, availing themselves of the *Iḥyāʾ*, defined themselves as Sufis or claimed to be saints (*awliyāʾ Allāh*), a 'hadith oriented "Sunni underground", largely maintained by Sufis' (Cornell 1987: 72, 82) assembling a significant part of discontent with the Almoravids. Apprehensions created a climate that cost imprisonment, death, or both to a group of mystics including Ibn al-ʿArīf, Ibn Barrajān, and Abū Bakr al-Mayūrqī (Fierro 1999: 184–94) but none of these men appears to have aimed at getting rid of Almoravid authority. When the real threat materialized in both the revolt of Ibn Qasī, the leader (*imām*) of a Sufi movement (the *murīdūn*) that took control of the Gharb al-Andalus, and Ibn Tūmart's preaching of the need to 'enjoin good and forbid evil', Almoravids were too weakened to face them in any effective manner. ʿAlī b. Yūsuf had ignored his ministers' advice to imprison or execute Ibn Tūmart, and made do with banishing him from Marrakech. By the time the emir changed his mind, it was too late. In the shelter of the High Atlas Mountains Ibn Tūmart's ideas evolved into a serious political challenge whose leader claimed to be the infallible *mahdī* (*al-mahdī al-maʿṣūm*) possessing 'supreme knowledge about God' (*maʿrifa bi-Llāh*) (Baydhaq, *Akhbār*, 27–8). ʿAlī b. Yūsuf's attempt to curb Almohads' ideological pressure by presenting himself as a saint as well (Peña and Vega 2006; Fierro 2007: 104–9) was to no avail and by the second half of the twelfth century CE most of the former Almoravid empire had fallen into the hands of Ibn Tūmart's follower and new leader of his movement, ʿAbd al-Muʾmin.

It would be thus tempting to qualify Western Muslim scholars' antipathy towards the *Iḥyāʾ* as a conflict between pro-Almoravid *fuqahāʾ-mutakallimūn* on the one side, and pro-Ghazālian Sufi-traditionists on the other. Yet well-known *uṣūlī*s like the Qāḍī Ibn Ward (d. 540/1146) held contrary to the burning of al-Ghazālī's books ordered by ʿAlī b. Yūsuf and his son Tāshufīn, and endorsed a *fatwā* establishing that he who ordered the burning of the *Iḥyāʾ* in particular should be punished instead (Ibn al-Abbār, *Takmila*, ed. Harrās, 2: 182 n. 455; Idris 1962: ii. 732; Serrano 2006, 137f.; Cherif in Ibn Ward, *Ajwiba*, 26–8 of the introduction). For his part, another contradictor of al-Ghazālī of the Almoravid period, namely Abū ʿAbd Allāh Muḥammad b. Khalaf b. Mūsā al-Anṣārī of Elvira, who was a Mālikī jurist, a traditionist, and an Ashʿarite *mutakallim* with mystic leanings (Urvoy 1993), does not appear to have been concerned by the political implications of the doctrines he tried to refute. Be that as it may, the opposition of the Mālikī-Ashʿarite establishment to al-Ghazālī's *Iḥyāʾ* is a fact Ibn Tūmart and his followers knew well how to use to their advantage (Akasoy 2012: 33–5).

III Almohad Ashʿarism

According to D. Urvoy, during the Almohad period, *kalām* lost its former association with Qurʾān sciences to become tied, almost exclusively, to the study of legal methodology and Arabic language. This latter development, Urvoy explains, resulted from the increasing need to engage in anti-Christian polemics which used to turn around terminology (Urvoy 1990: 165). Yet it might also respond to internal dynamics, given Islamic legal hermeneutics' strong reliance upon the mastery of Arabic language.

There is broad consensus among modern students of Ibn Tūmart—e.g. A. Bel, R. Basset, H. R. Idris, W. M. Watt, and D. Urvoy—in considering him an Ashʿarite thinker, as did some pre-modern Muslim historians like Ibn Abī Zarʿ and al-Subkī (Urvoy 1974: 19). In fact, he studied under Ashʿarite theologians like Abū Bakr al-Shāshī and Mubārak Ibn ʿAbd al-Jabbār during his stay in the East (Cornell 1987: 74). According to Ibn Khaldūn, however, he occupied a middle position between Ashʿarism and Shīʿism while for Ibn Taymiyya, both philosophy and Ismāʿīlism had merged in his doctrines (Laoust 1960; Urvoy 1974: 19).

Ibn Tūmart's theological system[4] has attracted the attention of a number of scholars who have tried to tackle its complexities and internal contradictions[5] from different points of view (Cressier, Fierro, and Molina 2005). According to D. Urvoy, despite being made up of disparate elements (stemming from Ibn Tūmart's native Berber-Maṣmūda and Khārijī-Ibāḍī milieu, his scholarly journeys to al-Andalus and to the East, and his personal intellectual constitution), Almohad theology consists of a radical but innovative and internally coherent system of remarkable density, revealing a great mind. Its apparent inconsistencies can be explained in the three-dimensional character—i.e. religious ideology, social reform, and government—of a movement which, however extreme it may have been at times, was not exceptional in resorting to violence in order to prevail (Urvoy 1974: 20, 30). V. Cornell stresses that Ibn Tūmart's writings and statements are linked by a 'moral imperative to action on the part of each individual believer' in which (a) action must be preceded by understanding and knowing the fundamental principles of Islamic faith and law (i.e. Qurʾān, recurrent *ḥadīth*, and the consensus of the Companions), and (b) understanding and knowing are mandatory for all those endowed with full mental capacity (*ʿuqalāʾ*), be they experts or lay Muslims (Cornell 1987; Urvoy 1974: 27, 30; 2003). These ideas are embodied in the call to implement the principle of enjoining good and forbidding evil. Disobedience, but also equivocation and omission of that duty, amount to infidelity (*kufr*) (Cornell 1987). According to F. Griffel, Ibn Tūmart's teachings were influenced by al-Juwaynī and al-Ghazālī especially as far as divine creation and predetermination are concerned. Reception of these doctrines did not necessarily imply personal contact but must have rather resulted from theological ideas that were taught at the Niẓāmiyya during the time our scholar studied there (Griffel 2009: 77–81).

Another fact to be taken into account in order to tackle Almohad ideology is the progressive assimilation of different ideas and tendencies experienced by Ibn Tūmart and his successors and the need to accommodate different audiences and contexts (e.g. illiterate and learned Muslims, Andalusīs and Maghribīs, Arabophones and Berberophones, etc.) (Urvoy 1974: 12–14; 2005; Fierro 2003), e.g. the second *Murshida* reflects an eventual surrender to the realization that the masses—notwithstanding their possessing full legal capacity and responsibility on the grounds of that capacity (*taklīf*)—are unable to grasp the subtleties of Almohad theology; consequently, their obligation must be restricted to the sole memorizing of a simpler and adapted version of the Almohad credo (Urvoy 1974: 31).

Be that as it may, Almohad theology cannot be approached as an endeavour to 'fill the gap of Almoravids' alleged disdain of dogmatics' (Urvoy 1974: 22) any longer. Rather, our present knowledge about the activity of Ashʿarite scholars during the Almoravid

[4] Laid down in a book known as *Aʿazz mā yuṭlab*, attributed to Ibn Tūmart. It contains several tracts plus the *Murshida*, which includes two 'spiritual guides', and a profession of faith (*ʿaqīda*). These latter texts make up the quintessence of Almohad theology.

[5] E.g. support of al-Ghazālī as both a Sufi thinker and an Ashʿarite theologian and concomitantly support of the philosophers; God's attributes are rejected in the *Murshida* while their reality is asserted in the *ʿAqīda*; obligation for every capable Muslim under moral obligation (*mukallaf*) to exercise reason in order to try and understand the arguments underlying the tenets of Islamic faith but imposition of the fixed form of Muslim creed put forward by Ibn Tūmart.

period invites a reconsideration of Almohad theology—all its originality and consistency with a pre-established programme of spiritual, social, and political reform notwithstanding—mainly as an attempt to stand out with respect to its most immediate precedent. Yet, discrediting Almoravid Ashʿarism and devising a plausible alternative without abandoning the legitimacy frame of Ashʿarism must have represented a big challenge even for the most gifted mind. Going radical and good doses of manipulation were thus required for the endeavour to succeed. Almoravid religious policy was thus submitted to a sophisticated process of manipulation from which Almoravids emerged as obscurantist rulers who reviled *kalām* and its practitioners to the point of threatening them with punishment.

Certainly, the radical character of some of his ideas (or, rather, of their implementation), e.g. the suppression of the *dhimma* status with the ensuing obligation for Christian and Jewish subjects to choose between conversion to Islam or death (Bennison and Gallego 2010),[6] or the declaration of infidelity (*takfīr*) for all those who did not adhere to the Almohad creed, render Ibn Tūmart's consideration as an Ashʿarite thinker very problematic. However, a *fatwā* addressed to Ibn Rushd al-Jadd (Ibn Rushd, *Fatāwā*, 2: 966–72) attests to a group of self-defined Ashʿarites who held that faith is not perfect without knowledge of the science of the fundamentals of religion and law (*ʿilm al-uṣūl*). Their remark that knowledge of the fundamentals is mandatory for both the expert and the lay believer invites us to identify that group with Ibn Tūmart and/or his followers. Ibn Rushd sharply denied that those ideas be in conformity with Ashʿarite doctrine,[7] and he appears to be right as far as 'mainstream' Ashʿarism is concerned (Frank 2008b: 16–17),[8] yet they cannot be said to be completely alien to the school doctrine as a whole (Burzulī, *Fatāwā*, 6: 213; Frank 2008a). Further, the *muftī* established a clear-cut distinction between experts and laymen: study and investigation of the arguments that underlie the fundamentals of the Islamic faith are incumbent only upon experts while laymen should be dissuaded from theological speculation and from reading books on *kalām* with the threat of punishment. With this latter qualification he added a rider to the enthusiastic praise of hermeneutics he had expressed elsewhere (see Ibn Rushd, *Fatāwā*, 2: 802–5, 943–5 and 1060f. and above). These and other similar remarks (Ibn Rushd, *Bayān*, 16: 369f.; Muḥammad b. ʿIyāḍ, *Taʿrīf*, 4) were likely taken out of context and used

[6] During the Almoravid period, legal discourse concerning non-Muslims had become more wary of intercommunal mingling and its corollary, religious syncretism. Also, deportations of Andalusī Christians to the Maghrib took place on the grounds of the support they allegedly lent to Christian raiders into Muslim territory. However, this measure was branded as the official response to those Christians' alleged breach of the *dhimma* pact, not as an overall abolition of Christians' and Jews' right to live in the Almoravid empire.

[7] In his *Muqaddamāt* 1: 43 he qualifies the obligation to acquire religious knowledge as *farḍ kifāya*, similar to *jihād*. Subsequently (*Muqaddamāt*, 1: 57f.) he states, drawing on Abū l-Walīd al-Bājī, that knowledge is not a precondition for the validity of faith and that it is correct to reach certainty about God by means of *taqlīd*.

[8] Though it is qualified as minority opinion by al-Sanūsī in his *ʿAqīda al-ṣughrā*. Cf. Kenny 1970: ch. 3 ('The Theology of al-Sanūsī'). Significantly, al-Sanūsī is the author of a commentary on Ibn Tūmart's *Murshida*.

by Almohad propagandists to present Almoravids as the enemies of *kalām* and rational interpretation of the sacred law (Marrākushī, *Muʿjib*, 122–4). Once established, this characterization was mixed up with Almoravids' rejection of al-Ghazālī (Urvoy 1993: 114f; Serrano 2003: 465–8), on the one hand, and related to their reluctance to impose on lay believers a non-literalist profession of faith, on the other—they had just tried to promote it, rather. The final conclusion was that Almoravid rulers were guilty of anthropomorphism for having contributed, by sin of omission, to the spreading of abominable beliefs in their dominions.

To a certain extent, Almohad doctrine presented itself as a continuation of al-Ghazālī's endeavour to revive religious sciences and enhance the theological position of sound knowledge as the foremost source of faith and fulfilment of the sacred law. No doubt, cultivation of a relationship with al-Ghazālī—woven around the story of an alleged encounter between him and Ibn Tūmart during the latter's stay in the East—stemmed from sincere admiration. Yet al-Ghazālī's burgeoning prestige set against Almoravids' ban of his books provided the Almohads with another opportunity to stress their departure from 'Almoravid Ashʿarism'. Al-Ghazālī was then rehabilitated as an expert in legal methodology (Serrano 2003: 482), a step illustrated by Averroes's epitome of the *Mustaṣfā* (*Mukhtaṣar al-Mustaṣfā*). Also and notwithstanding that, as noted by V. Cornell, Ibn Tūmart's concept of knowledge is not metaphysical but anchored in specific fundamental principles to be applied to the derivation of legal rules, the rise of the Almohads brought about widespread acceptance of the science of Sufism as laid down by al-Ghazālī (Ferhat 2005: 1076). In fact, Almohad caliphs tried to co-opt the mystics either to enhance their cause or to neutralize their influence (Ferhat 2005: 1075). Local biographical dictionaries covering that period also testify to convergence between Sufism and Ashʿarism (Serrano 2011), a process responding to a general trend that has been tracked down elsewhere much earlier (Shihadeh 2007: 281) and which, in the Islamic West, would eventually crystallize in the figure of Abū ʿAbd Allāh Muḥammad b. Yūsuf b. ʿUmar b. Shuʿayb al-Sanūsī (d. Tlemcen 895/1490). He combined a classical training in Qurʾān, *ḥadīth*, Arabic language, *fiqh*, arithmetic, and theology (*uṣūl al-dīn*) with a strong inclination to asceticism which, together with his capacity to interpret dreams, earned him a reputation in the mystical sciences. His many disciples and the composition of a series of creeds (*ʿaqāʾid*)[9] covering different levels of theological insight no doubt contributed to the widespread and continuous influence of his thought that reached as far as West Africa, as shown by the curriculum of a scholar like Aḥmad Bābā al-Timbuktī (Bencheneb 1997; Ḥajjī 1977–8: i. 143). Other possible forms of combination brought about by Almohad rule include Ẓāhirism and Ashʿarism, as can be inferred from the case of Abū Muḥammad ʿAbd Allāh b. Sulaymān b. Ḥawṭ Allāh (b. 548/1153, d. 612/1215) (Urvoy 1972: 128).

Support of Sufism paralleled that accorded to philosophy and its practitioners in that neither of the two appeared in the programmatic design of Almohad doctrine.

[9] I.e. the *Sharḥ al-kubrā*, *Sharḥ al-wusṭā*, *Sharḥ al-ṣughrā*, and *Sharḥ ṣughrā al-ṣughrā* which were all studied together with al-Sanūsī's own commentary.

According to V. Cornell, Ibn Tūmart was a systematizer rather than a theorist and his interests focused on 'the search of a science of legal rather than philosophical certainty' (Cornell 1987: 92). S. Stroumsa, for her part, has argued against the idea of a total affinity between Andalusī philosophers and the Almohad regime (Stroumsa 2005). Yet Ibn Tūmart's attachment to the teachings of al-Ghazālī—the scholar who had tried to adapt Avicennan Aristotelism to Sunnī theological discourse—as well as his concern for the nature of knowledge, his asking how one acquires certain knowledge, and his overall quest to provide a rational basis to faith, created a scenario in which *falsafa* could coexist with *kalām* and attain an unprecedented level of development, notwithstanding al-Ghazālī's branding the philosophers as infidels in his *Tahāfut al-falāsifa* for holding three doctrines that, in his view, go against the consensus of the Muslim community[10] (Cornell 1987: 92; Urvoy 2003: 742f.; Stroumsa 2005: 1143). The reasons for the persecution of philosophers orchestrated during the reign of the third Almohad caliph Abū Yūsuf Yaʿqūb al-Manṣūr, counting Averroes among its victims, have not been fully elucidated. They do not seem to have been triggered by Averroes's counter-refutation of al-Ghazālī,[11] but the day he decided to target Ibn Tūmart's prohibition to entertain a corporeal representation of God he got into real trouble, for he was obliged to retract (Geoffroy 2005: 872–82), perhaps not to fuel further weariness with aspects of Almohad doctrine (e.g. the doctrine of the impeccability of the *mahdī*), considered to have been instrumental for the political consolidation of the Almohad revolution but too alien to local religious idiosyncrasy to prevail for long (Geoffroy 2005: 870, 881; Fierro 2008: 79). 'It is dangerous', Averroes stated, 'to impose upon a simple mind a belief that, its truth notwithstanding, he is unable to grasp. In the absence of a truth that can only be accessed through philosophy, the descriptions of God in anthropomorphic terms contained in the Qurʾān provide the believer with an image of the truth on which he can rely to get a representation of God that is appropriate to his mental capacities' (Geoffroy 2005: 864–6). Whether this was connected with his falling into disgrace and his banishment to Lucena, a city that, until the Almohad conquest of al-Andalus, had been densely populated by Jews, cannot be ascertained here and now (Serrano 2010: 225f.). However, if mention of philosophy as the exclusive path to reach accurate knowledge about God is overlooked, Averroes's argument is in striking tune with his grandfather's abovementioned dismissal of the obligation for the ordinary Muslim to engage in the study of *uṣūl al-dīn wa-l-fiqh*. In this light, the claim of crypto-Judaism implicit in Averroes' banishment to Lucena (Serrano 2010) seems a warning not to be too insolent and self-confident in his outstanding intellectual capacities addressed to his person but also to the memory of his ancestors—an insinuation that 'wrong' ideas may be engendered by a 'wrong' genealogy, providing a posteriori justification to the persecutions of the

[10] Namely that the world has no beginning and is not created in time, that God's knowledge includes universals but does not extend to particulars, and that the souls do not return to bodies after death. See Griffel 2009: 5.

[11] Carried out in three of his works, viz. *al-Kashf fī manāhij al-adilla*, *Faṣl al-maqāl*, and *Tahāfut al-Tahāfut*.

Jews ordered by Almohad authorities and to the suspicions about the sincerity of those forced to convert.

IV Post-Almohad Developments

R. Brunschvig's classic essay on Ifrīqiyā and the central Maghrib during the Ḥafṣid period refers only cursorily to Ashʿarism to state that the study of *kalām* was limited to a very tiny elite and that the relevant syllabus in local *madrasas* included al-Juwaynī's *Irshād*, al-Ghazālī's *Mustaṣfā*, and the works of Fakhr al-Dīn al-Rāzī (Brunschvig 1940–7: ii. 365). As to Morocco, the most popular manuals for the teaching of Islamic theology under the Saʿdīs were the four professions of faith by al-Sanūsī, along with a series of commentaries of Ibn Tūmart's and al-Ḥāḥī's respective *ʿaqīdas*, the *Kifāyat al-murīd* by al-Zawāwī, and the *Muḥaṣṣal al-maqāṣid* by Aḥmad b. Zakarī al-Tilimsānī (d. 898/1493) (Ḥajjī 1977–8: i. 143). Apart from providing a useful starting point to undertake the study of Ashʿarism in sixteenth- and seventeenth-century Morocco (Ḥajjī 1977–8, *passim*), Ḥajjī's study documents continuity of the debate about the status of the lay believer's faith and other issues (Ḥajjī 1977–8: i. 282–90). Concerning al-Andalus, *kalām* became restricted according to D. Urvoy to apologetics and eschatology (Urvoy 1983: 188).

This period has been qualified resorting to Ibn Khaldūn's (d. 808/1406) assessment of the evolution of discursive theology up to his time (Ibn Khaldūn, *Muqaddima*, 3: 17–23, 25–59). Concerning Ashʿarism, Ibn Khaldūn identifies al-Juwaynī's *Irshād* as the best handbook for the school's doctrine. Further, he states that the Ashʿarite theologians' adoption of logic brought about a new argumentative technique which came to be known as 'method of the modern ones (*ṭarīqat al-mutaʾakhkhirīn*)' having in al-Ghazālī and Fakhr al-Dīn al-Rāzī (d. 606/1209) its most important representatives. Al-Juwaynī, for his part, is considered to have acted as a hinge between the method elaborated by al-Bāqillānī and that of the 'modern ones'. The implementation of the new methodology to the rules formulated by al-Ashʿarī and the first generations of his followers, especially al-Bāqillānī, led to the replacement of a significant part of their teachings by doctrines stemming from philosophical discussions about physics and metaphysics. Ibn Khaldūn states that logic enabled the Ashʿarites to jump from debating with the Muʿtazilites and the anthropomorphists to refuting the quintessence of rational thinkers, i.e. the philosophers. However, plunging into this latter discipline in order to oppose its practitioners in an effective manner led to confusion between *kalām* and philosophy, due to the false assumption on the part of the *mutakallimūn* that both disciplines shared the same object. Certainly, Ibn Khaldūn acknowledges that logic can be studied independently from philosophy and that its use as a mere pattern or rule to demonstrate the accuracy of a certain argument made it possible to overcome the simplicity of the early Ashʿarites and the shortcomings of their argumentative technique. Yet he laments the syncretism in which fell the 'modern ones', for which reason he rejects them, showing rather his preference for al-Bāqillānī and al-Juwaynī. More than being a question of principle, Ibn Khaldūn's opposition to the mixing of philosophy and *kalām* might have been motivated by his well-known rivalry with Ibn ʿArafa (Tunis, d. 803/1401) who, in his *Mukhtaṣar al-Shāmil* on *kalām*, does not appear to reject the methods of the 'modern ones'.[12] Rather he holds in favour of learning *uṣūl al-dīn* and, on the grounds of Qurʾān 2: 13, declares it to be a religious duty to go beyond mere faith and reflect rationally (*naẓar*) upon one's beliefs. In the earnest defence of *uṣūl al-dīn* as an academic discipline essential to the training of a religious scholar, Ibn ʿArafa is followed by his disciple, al-Burzulī (d. 841/1438). Significantly, the latter resorts to the authority of Ibn Rushd al-Jadd to provide additional underpinning to his position (Ghrab 1992–6: i. 402–4).

It would be tempting to consider Ibn Khaldūn's stance as representative of his place and time, and to adhere to S. Ghrab's thesis in the sense of a prevalence of the traditionalist trend after the alleged failure of Ibn ʿArafa's rationalism (Ghrab 1992–6: i. 403–6). Yet it might be more effective to approach the relationship between traditionalist and rationalist Ashʿarīs in the pre-modern Islamic West by focusing on ideas like the balance of material and symbolic powers or the capacity to exert a qualitative and enduring influence, rather than on binary and quantitative characterizations in terms of victory and defeat or popularity and marginality. Certainly, the career of scholars like the Moroccan Aḥmad Zarrūq (d. 899/1493) with his combination of Sufism and *kalām* and his preference for pre-Ghazālian Ashʿarism (Karimullah 2007: 10) appears to add credit to Ibn Khaldūn's stance. However, Zarrūq's most important master, al-Sanūsī (Karimullah 2007: 18f., 85, 87, 101, 108f.), had favoured the more intellectualist approach of the 'modern ones' and their resort to the Avicennan proof of God's existence, implicit in al-Sanūsī's use of the triad 'necessary-possible-impossible' (Wensinck 1932: 274; Karimullah 2007: 84–6, 110f.). Further, as has been mentioned above, Fakhr al-Dīn al-Rāzī's works were imported to teach *kalām* in Ḥafṣid Ifrīqiyā. The list of *uṣūl al-dīn* works studied by Ibn ʿArafa bears testimony to that (Ghrab 1992–6: i. 260–2, 266–7)

The assumption that Andalusī Ashʿarism remained within the boundaries of the early development of the school might be deceptive as well. Certainly, al-Ghazālī's works on *kalām* are absent from the sources relevant to study of the transmission of Islamic religious sciences during the Nasrid period, which does not prevent that his teachings on *uṣūl al-dīn wa-l-fiqh* be actually assimilated by local scholars as al-Shāṭibī's theory of the objectives of the *sharīʿa* would reflect (Griffel 2009: 81). Yet works of al-Juwaynī,[13] al-ʿĀmidī, and Fakhr al-Dīn al-Rāzī are mentioned on a constant basis in bio-bibliographical literature from the Nasrid period as well as those of Abū l-Qāsim and Abū Isḥāq al-Isfarāʾīnī, contrary to those of two 'traditional' Ashʿarites—to follow Ibn

[12] As suggested by one of the anonymous readers of a former draft of this chapter.

[13] According to D. Urvoy, he was the most favoured Ashʿarite theologian in al-Andalus, which does not mean that his teachings met no opposition there. Maghribīs, for their part, are said to have preferred al-Bāqillānī (see Urvoy 1983: 188). On the popularity of al-Juwaynī's *Irshād* in al-Andalus and the Maghrib also see Schmidtke 2013: 388 n. 68.

Khaldūn's characterization—like al-Bāqillānī and Ibn Fūrak.[14] Moreover, the list of disciplines taught at the Granadan *madrasa* included philosophy and other rational sciences (Viguera 2000: 165). Further, Maghribī scholars are reported to have reintroduced the study of logic into Egypt by the beginning of the twelfth/eighteenth century (Griffel 2009: 81). Ibn Khaldūn's apprehensions aside, integration between Islamic religious sciences (e.g. *kalām* and Sufism, Sufism and philosophy, philosophy and *kalām*) was the natural outcome of these sciences' converging objectives or methods (Winter 2008: 13; Taylor 2010; Mayer 2008) and their limitations to respond individually to the religious concerns of the believers (Frank 2008b: 35–7). Be that as it may, one important conclusion to be drawn from Ibn Khaldūn's sketch of the history of Islamic rational theology on the one hand and from al-Sanūsī's legacy on the other is that integration of Sufism and Ashʿarism and the rise of an 'orthodox Sufi theology' did not end with the old dichotomy between good deeds and intellectual effort as fundamental causes of true knowledge about God (*maʿrifa bi-Llāh*). However, it seems clear that those Ashʿarite Sufis who favoured good deeds over intellectual knowledge in defining the path to sanctity and nearness to God, had to accept the existence of a net distinction between 'perfect faith, a degree reached through combining faith and good deeds and which prevents the believer from sinning and from falling into the slightest error', and infallibility (*ʿiṣma*), the latter being the sole prerogative of the Prophets (Lory 1997; Serrano 2008: 260–7).

References

Achekar, M. S. (1998). 'Otra visión sobre la vida intelectual en época almorávide'. *Miscelánea de Estudios Árabes y Hebráicos*, sección Árabe e Islam 47: 1–26.

Akasoy, A. (2012). 'Al-Ghazālī, Ramon Llull and Religionswissenschaft'. *Muslim World* 102: 33–59.

Aʿrāb, S. (1987). *Maʿa l-qāḍī Abī Bakr b. al-ʿArabī*. Beirut: Dār al-Gharb al-Islāmī.

Arnáldez, R. (1971). 'Ibn Ḥazm'. *Encyclopaedia of Islam*. New edn. iii. 790–9.

Arnáldez, R. (1981). *Grammaire et théologie chez Ibn Hazm de Cordoue: essai sur la structure et les conditions de la pensée musulmane*. Paris: J. Vrin.

Asín Palacios, M. (1927–32). *Abenházam de Córdoba y su historia crítica de las ideas religiosas*. 5 vols. Madrid: Revista de Archivos.

al-Baydhaq, Abū Bakr b. ʿAlī (*Akhbār*). *Akhbār al-mahdī Ibn Tūmart wa-bidāyat dawlat al-Muwaḥḥidīn*. Ed. ʿAbd al-Wahhāb b. Manṣūr. Rabat: Dār al-Manṣūr li-l-ṭabāʿa wa-l-wirāqa, 1971.

Bencheneb, H. (1997). 'Al-Sanūsī'. *The Encyclopaedia of Islam*. New edn. ix. 20–2.

Bennison, A. K., and M. A. Gallego (eds.) (2010). *Religious Minorities under the Almohads = Special Issue of Journal of Medieval Iberian Studies* 2/2 (June 2010), 143–292.

[14] I draw this conclusion from materials concerning *kalām* collected by the team of the HATA file (History of the Authors and Transmitters of al-Andalus), a project under the direction of Maribel Fierro whom I thank for granting me permission to consult the file several times between 2000 and 2002. For more information on the HATA file and its value to reconstructing the intellectual history of al-Andalus see Fierro 1998.

Brunschvig, R. (1940–7). *La Berbérie orientale sous les Hafsides: des origines à la fin du XVe siècle*. 2 vols. Paris: Adrien-Maisonneuve.

al-Burzulī (*Fatāwā*). *Fatāwā al-Burzulī*. Ed. Muḥammad al-Ḥabīb al-Ḥīla. 7 vols. Beirut: Dār al-Gharb al-Islāmī, 2002.

Cornell, V. (1987). 'Understanding is the Mother of Ability: Responsibility and Action in the Doctrine of Ibn Tūmart'. *Studia Islamica* 66: 71–103.

Cressier, P., M. Fierro, and L. Molina (eds.) (2005). *Los Almohades: problemas y perspectivas*. 2 vols. Madrid: CSIC.

Dandash, ʿI. (1988a). *al-Andalus fī nihāyat al-murābiṭīn wa-mustahall al-muwaḥḥidīn: ʿAṣr al-ṭawāʾif al-thānī*. Beirut: Dār al-Gharb al-Islāmī.

Dandash, ʿI. (1988b). *Dawr al-murābiṭīn fī nashr al-Islām fī Gharb Ifrīqiyā 430–515h.-1038–1211 m. = The Contribution of the Almoravids to the Diffussion of Islam in West Africa*. Beirut: Dār al-Gharb al-Islāmī.

Dandash, ʿI. (1991). 'Mawqif al-murābiṭīn min ʿilm al-kalām wa-l-falsafa'. In ʿI. Dandash, *Adwāʾ jadīda ʿalā l-Murābiṭīn*. Beirut: Dār al-Gharb al-Islāmī, 83–99.

Ferhat, H. (2005). 'L'Organisation des soufis et ses limites à l'époque almohade'. In P. Cressier et al. (eds.), *Los almohades: problemas y perspectivas*, ii, 1075–90.

Fierro, M. (1992). 'The Polemic about the "karamāt al-awliyāʾ" and the Development of Sufism in al-Andalus (Fourth–Tenth, Fifth–Eleventh Centuries)'. *Bulletin of the School of Oriental and African Studies* 54: 236–49.

Fierro, M. (1994). 'La Religión'. In M. J. Viguera (ed.), *Los reinos de Taifas: Al-Andalus en el siglo XI*. Madrid: Espasa Calpe, 397–496.

Fierro, M. (1998). 'Manuscritos en al-Andalus: el proyecto H.A.T.A (Historia de los Autores y Transmisores Andalusíes)'. *Al-Qanṭara* 19: 473–501.

Fierro, M. (1999). 'Opposition to Sufism in al-Andalus'. In F. De Jong and B. Radtke (eds.), *Islamic Mysticism Contested: Thirteen Centuries of Controversies and Polemics*. Leiden: Brill, 174–206.

Fierro, M. (n.d.). 'Al-Bāŷī, Abū l-Walīd'. In J. Lirola Delgado and J. M. Puerta Vílchez (eds.), *Enciclopedia de al-Andalus: diccionario de autores y obras Andalusíes*. Granada: Fundación El Legado Andalusí, i. 118–23.

Fierro, M. (2003). 'Las genealogías de ʿAbd al-Muʾmin, primer califa almohade'. *Al-Qanṭara* 24: 77–107.

Fierro, M. (2007). 'Entre el Magreb y al-Andalus: la autoridad política y religiosa en época almorávide'. In F. Sabaté (ed.), *Balaguer, 1105. Cruïlla de civilitzacions. Reunió Científica. X Curs d'Estiu Comtat d'Urgell celebrat a Balaguer els dies 13, 14 i 15 de juliol de 2005 sota la direcció de Flocel Sabaté i Maribel Pedrol*, I. Lérida: Pagès editors, 99–120.

Fierro, M. (2008). 'The Almohads (524–668/1130–1269) and the Ḥafṣids (627–932/1229–1526)'. In M. Fierro (ed.), *The Western Islamic World Eleventh to Eighteenth Centuries. The New Cambridge History of Islam*, vol. ii, part 1. Cambridge: Cambridge University Press, 66–105.

Fórneas, J. M. (1977–9). '*Al-Tamhīd* de al-Bāqillānī y su transmisión en al-Andalus'. *Miscelánea de Estudios Árabes y Hebráicos* 27–8: 433–40.

Fórneas, J. M. (1978). 'De la transmisión de algunas obras de tendencia ašʿarí en al-Andalus'. *Awrāq* 1: 4–11.

Frank, R. M. (2008a). 'Knowledge and *taqlīd*: The Foundations of Religious Belief in Classical Ashʿarism'. In R. M. Frank, *Classical Islamic Theology: The Ashʿarites. Texts and Studies on the Development and History of Kalām*. Vol. iii, ed. D. Gutas. Aldershot: Ashgate, Part VII.

Frank, R. M. (2008b). 'The Science of kalām'. In R. M. Frank, *Classical Islamic Theology: The Ashʿarites. Texts and Studies on the Development and History of Kalām*. Vol. iii, ed. D. Gutas. Aldershot: Ashgate, Part II.

Geoffroy, M. (2005). 'À propos de l'almohadisme d'Averroès: l'anthropomorphisme (tağsīm) dans la seconde version du *Kitāb al-Kašf ʿan manāhiğ al-adilla*'. In P. Cressier et al. (eds.), *Los almohades: problemas y perspectivas*, ii. 853–94.
Ghrab, S. (1982). 'Ḥawla iḥrāq al-murābiṭīn Iḥyāʾ al-Ghazālī'. *Actas del IV Coloquio Hispano-Tunecino (Palma de Mallorca, 1979)*. Madrid, 133–63.
Ghrab, S. (1992–6). *Ibn ʿArafa et le mālikisme en Ifriqiya au VIII*ᵉ*/XIV*ᵉ *siècles*. 2 vols. Tunis: Université de Tunis I, Faculté des Lettres de la Manouba.
Goldziher, I. (1884). *Die Zâhiriten: Ihr Lehrsystem und ihre Geschichte. Beitrag zur Geschichte der muhammedanischen Theologie*. Leipzig: Otto Schulze.
Griffel, F. (2009). *Al-Ghazālī's Philosophical Theology*. Oxford: Oxford University Press.
Ḥajjī, M. (1977–8). *al-Ḥaraka al-fikriyya bi-l-Maghrib fī ʿahd al-saʿdiyīn*. 2 vols. Rabat: Manshūrāt Dār al-Maghrib li-l-taʾlīf wa-l-tarjama wa-l-nashr.
Hintati, N. (1992). 'Taṭawwur mawqif ʿulamāʾ al-mālikiyya bi-Ifrīqiyā min al-khawḍ fī l-masāʾil al-kalāmiyya wa-tabannīhim li-l-ʿaqīda al-ashʿariyya'. *IBLA: Revue de l'Institut des Belles Lettres Arabes* 55: 297–322.
Ibn al-Abbār (*Takmila*). *Kitāb al-Takmila li-Kitāb al-Ṣila*. Ed. F. Codera. 2 vols. Madrid: Rojas, 1886; ed. ʿAbd al-Salām Harrās, 4 vols., Casablanca: Dār al-Maʿrifa.
Ibn ʿAbd al-Barr (*Jāmiʿ*). *Jāmiʿ bayān al-ʿilm wa-faḍlihi wa-mā yanbaghī fī riwāyātihi wa-ḥamlihi*. Cairo: al-Maṭbaʿa al-munīriyya, 1978.
Ibn al-ʿArabī, Abū Bakr (*ʿAwāṣim*). *K. al-ʿAwāṣim min al-qawāṣim*. Ed. ʿA. Ṭālibī. Doha: Dār al-thaqāfa, 1992.
Ibn Khaldūn (*Muqaddima*). *Muqaddima*. Ed. M. Quatremère. Paris: Typographie de Firmin Didot, 1858.
Ibn Rushd al-Jadd (*Bayān*). *al-Bayān wa-l-taḥṣīl*. Ed. M. Ḥajjī. 22 vols. Beirut: Dār al-Gharb al-Islāmī, 2nd edn., 1991.
Ibn Rushd al-Jadd (*Fatāwā*). *Fatāwā Ibn Rushd al-Jadd*. Ed. Muḥammad al-Ṭalīlī. 3 vols. Beirut: Dār al-Gharb al-Islāmī, 1987.
Ibn Rushd al-Jadd (*Muqaddamāt*). *al-Muqaddamāt al-mumahhadāt*. Ed. Muḥammad Ḥajjī. 3 vols. Beirut: Dār al-Gharb al-Islāmī, 1988.
Ibn Ward, Abū l-Qāsim Aḥmad (*Ajwiba*). *Ajwibat Ibn Ward al-Andalusī, naṣṣ jadīd min fiqh al-nawāzil bi-l-gharb al-islāmī*. Ed. M. Cherif. Rabat: Top Press, 2008.
Idris, H. R. (1953). 'Essai sur la diffusion de l'Ašʿarisme en Ifrīqiyā'. *Cahiers de Tunisie* 1/2: 126–40.
Idris, H. R. (1962). *La Berbérie orientale sous les zirides: X*ᵉ*–XII*ᵉ *siècles*. 2 vols. Paris: Adrien-Maisonneuve.
ʿIyāḍ b. Mūsā (*Iʿlām*). *al-Iʿlām bi-ḥudūd qawāʿid al-islām*. Ed. Muḥammad b. Tāwīt al-Ṭanjī. Muḥammadiyya: Wizārat al-Awqāf wa-l-Shuʾūn al-Islāmiyya, 1983.
ʿIyāḍ b. Mūsā (*Tartīb*). *Tartīb al-madārik wa-taqrīb al-masālik li-maʿrifat aʿlam madhhab Mālik*. 8 vols. Rabat: Wizārat al-Awqāf wa-l-Shuʾūn al-Islāmiyya, 1965–83.
Karimullah, K. (2007). *Aḥmad Zarrūq and the Ashʿarite School*. MA dissertation, Institute of Islamic Studies, McGill University.
Kenny, J. E. (1970). *Muslim Theology as Presented by Muhammad b. Yūsuf al-Sanūsī Especially in his* al-ʿAqīda al-Wusṭā. Ph.D. dissertation, University of Edinburgh.
Lagardère, V. (1994). 'Une théologie dogmatique de la frontière en al-Andalus aux XIᵉ et XIIᵉ siècles: l'ašʿarisme'. *Anaquel de Estudios Árabes* 5: 71–98.
Laoust, H. (1960). 'Une fetwā d'Ibn Taimīya sur Ibn Tūmart'. *Bulletin de l'Institut Français d'Archéologie Orientale du Caire* 59: 157–84.
Lory, P. (1997). 'Al-Shādhilī'. *Enclyclopaedia of Islam*. New edn. ix. 179–82.

Lucini, M. M. (1995). 'Discípulos de Abū Bakr Ibn al-ʿArabī en al-Ḏayl wa-l-Takmila de al-Marrākušī'. In M. Marín and H. de Felipe (eds.), *Estudios Onomástico-Biográficos de al-Andalus*, vii. Madrid: CSIC, 191–201.

al-Maqqarī al-Tilimsānī, Aḥmad b. Muḥammad (*Azhār*). *Azhār al-Riyāḍ fī Akhbār ʿIyāḍ*, vol. iii. Rabat: Ṣundūq Iḥyāʾ al-Turāth al-Islāmī al-Mushtarak bayna al-Mamlaka al-Maghribiyya wa-l-Imārāt al-ʿArabiyya al-Muttaḥida, 1978.

al-Marrākushī, ʿAbd al-Wāḥid (*Muʿjib*). *al-Muʿjib*. Ed. R. P. Dozy. Amsterdam: Oriental Press, 1968.

Marín, M. (1994). 'La actividad intelectual'. In M. J. Viguera (dir.), *Los reinos de Taifas: Al-Andalus en el siglo XI*. Madrid: Espasa Calpe, 497–561.

Mayer, T. (2008). 'Theology and Sufism'. In T. Winter (ed.), *The Cambridge Companion to Classical Islamic Theology*. Cambridge: Cambridge University Press, 258–87.

Muḥammad b. ʿIyāḍ (*Taʿrīf*). *al-Taʿrīf bi-l-qāḍī ʿIyāḍ*. Ed. M. Bencherifa. Muḥammadiyya: Wizārat al-Awqāf wa-l-Shuʾūn al-Islāmiyya, 2nd edn., 1982.

Norris, H. T. (1993). 'Al-Murābiṭūn'. *Encyclopaedia of Islam*. New edn. vii. 583–9.

Peña, S., and M. Vega (2006). 'Rebuilding the Contexts of the Andalusi Epigraphic Legacy: "The Friend of God" in the Almoravid Numismatic Discourse'. *TRANS: Revista de Traductología* 10: 73–83.

Rahman, S. (2009). *The Legal and Theological Thought of Ibn Abī Zayd al-Qayrawānī*. Ph.D. dissertation, Yale University.

Schmidtke, S. (2003). 'Ibn Ḥazm's sources on Ash`arism and Mu`tazilism'. In C. Adang, M. Fierro, and S. Schmidtke (eds.), *Ibn Ḥazm of Cordoba. The Life and Works of a Controversial Thinker*. Leiden: Brill, 375–401.

Serrano Ruano, D. (2002). 'Ibn al-Sīd al-Baṭalyawsī (444/1052–521/1127): de los reinos de taifas a la época almorávide a través de la biografía de un ulema polifacético'. *Al-Qanṭara* 23: 53–92.

Serrano Ruano, D. (2003). 'Los almorávides y la teología ašʿarí: ¿Contestación o legitimación de una disciplina marginal?' In C. de la Puente (ed.), *Identidades marginales: Estudios Onomástico Biográficos de al-Andalus*, xiii. Madrid: CSIC, 461–516.

Serrano Ruano, D. (2005a). '¿Por qué llamaron los almohades antropomorfistas a los almorávides?' In M. Fierro, P. Cressier, and L. Molina (eds.), *Los almohades: problemas y perspectivas*. Madrid: CSIC/Casa de Velázquez, ii. 815–52.

Serrano Ruano, D. (2005b). 'Ibn al-Sīd al-Baṭalyawsī y su obra sobre la discrepancia entre los musulmanes'. In A. Sidarus and B. Soravia (eds.), *Literatura e cultura no Gharb al-Andalus*. Lisbon: IICT/Hugin, 221–44.

Serrano Ruano, D. (2006). 'Why did the Scholars of al-Andalus Distrust al-Ghazālī? Ibn Rushd al-Jadd's fatwā on *awliyāʾ Allāh*'. *Der Islam* 83: 137–56.

Serrano Ruano, D. (2008). 'La teólogía dialéctica (*kalām*) en el Occidente islámico a través de la *Muqaddima* y de la biografía de Ibn Jaldūn'. In J. L. Garrot Garrot and J. Martos Quesada (eds.), *Miradas Españolas sobre Ibn Jaldún*. Madrid: Ibersaf Editores, 249–68.

Serrano Ruano, D. (2009). "ʿIyāḍ b. Mūsā'. In J. Lirola Delgado (ed.), *Biblioteca de al-Andalus*. Almería: Fundación Ibn Tufayl de Estudios Árabes, vi: 404–34 no. 1479.

Serrano Ruano, D. (2010). 'Explicit Cruelty, Implicit Compassion: Judaism, Forced Conversions and the Genealogy of the Banū Rushd'. *Journal of Medieval Iberian Studies* 2: 217–33.

Serrano Ruano, D. (2011). 'Mutakallimes y sufíes del Occidente islámico: variaciones narrativas sobre la confluencia de dos formas emergentes del saber islámico (Ibn al-Abbār, Ibn ʿAbd al-Malik al-Marrākušī e Ibn al-Zubayr)'. In J. P. Monferrer and M. J. Viguera (eds.),

Legendaria Medievalia en honor de Concepción Castillo Castillo. Cordoba: Biblioteca Viva de al-Andalus-Ediciones El Almendro, 81–97.

Serrano Ruano, D. (forthcoming). 'A Matter of Faith, a Matter of Reason: Two Andalusian Refutations against Anthropomorphism'. In M. A. Gallego (ed.), *Rationalism and Sacred Text, 10th–12th Centuries*. Leiden: Brill.

Serrano Ruano, D., and M. Forcada (2007). 'Mālik b. Wuhayb'. In J. Lirola Delgado (ed.), *Biblioteca de al-Andalus: De Ibn Saʿāda a Ibn Wuhayb*. Almería: Fundación Ibn Tufayl de Estudios Árabes, v. 603–8.

Shihadeh, A. (ed.) (2007). *Sufism and Theology*. Edinburgh: Edinburgh University Press.

Stroumsa, S. (2005). 'Philosophes Almohades? Averroès, Maïmonide et l'idéologie Almohade'. In Cressier et al. (eds.), *Los Almohades: problemas y perspectivas*, ii. 1137–62.

Taylor, R. (2010). 'Philosophy'. *New Cambridge History of Islam*, vol. iv, ed. Robert Irwin, part IV: *Learning, Arts and Culture*. Cambridge: Cambridge University Press, 532–63.

Turki, A. M. (1973). *Polémiques entre Ibn Hazm e Bagi sur les principes de la loi musulmane: essai sur le littéralisme zahirite et la finalité malikite*. Algiers: Études et documents.

Urvoy, D. (1972). 'La Vie intellectuelle et spirituelle dans les baléares musulmanes'. *Al-Andalus* 37: 87–132.

Urvoy, D. (1974). 'La Pensée d'Ibn Tūmart'. *Bulletin d'Études Orientales* 27: 19–44.

Urvoy, D. (1983). *El mundo de los ulemas andaluces del siglo V/XI al VII/XIII: estudio sociológico*. Madrid: Ediciones Pegaso.

Urvoy, D. (1990). *Pensers d'al-Andalus: la vie intellectuelle à Cordoue et à Séville au temps des empires berbères (fin XIe siècle–début XIIIe siècle)*. Toulouse: Presses Universitaires du Mirail.

Urvoy, D. (1993). 'Le Manuscrit Ar. 1483 de l'Escurial et la polemique contre Ġazālī dans al-Andalus'. *Arabica* 40: 114–19.

Urvoy, D. (1998). *Averroès: les ambitions d'un intellectuel musulman*. Paris: Flammarion.

Urvoy, D. (2005). 'Les Professions de foi d'Ibn Tūmart: problèmes textuels et doctrinaux'. In Cressier et al. (eds.), *Los almohades: problemas y perspectivas*, ii. 739–52.

Viguera, M. J. (2000). 'La Religión y el derecho'. In M. J. Viguera (ed.), *El reino nazarí de Granada (1232–1492): sociedad, vida y cultura*. Madrid: Espasa Calpe.

Watt, W. M. (1960). 'Ashʿariyya'. *Encyclopaedia of Islam*. New edn. i. 696.

Wensinck, A. J. (1932). *The Muslim Creed: Its Genesis and Historical Development*. Cambridge: Cambridge University Press.

Winter, T. (2008). 'Introduction'. In T. Winter (ed.), *The Cambridge Companion to Classical Islamic Theology*. Cambridge: Cambridge University Press, 1–16.

CHAPTER 30

EGYPT AND THE LATER ASHʿARITE SCHOOL

AARON SPEVACK

EGYPTIAN Ashʿarism, especially between the sixteenth and nineteenth centuries CE, is an insufficiently studied phenomenon in Islamic intellectual history. It is a period in which the works of post-twelfth-century Persian and north-west African (Maghribī) scholars were studied, and new texts by Egyptian scholars entered into the standard Ashʿarite curriculum. In tracing the contours of late Egyptian Ashʿarism, oft-neglected due to arguably erroneous assumptions of decline and stagnation, a number of important characteristics come to light that challenge the standard narrative of decline.

The following paragraphs offer a preliminary sketch of the development and contours of late Ashʿarism in Egypt, discussing some key players in the discourse as well as some prominent features of Egyptian Ashʿarite thought. By no means exhaustive in its scope, this chapter emphasizes the following three concepts which are important indicators of the continued vibrancy and diversity in Egyptian Ashʿarite thought, especially between the seventeenth and nineteenth centuries. They are the continued study, development, and nuanced discussion of the rational sciences (philosophy, logic, dialectical theology, etc.), the prominent influence of post-thirteenth-century Persian and Maghribī *muḥaqqiqūn* ('scholarly verifiers'), and the dense and often dismissed sea of *ḥawāshī* ('glosses' and 'commentaries') on a variety of texts wherein evidence of continued discussions of philosophy, Sufi metaphysics, comparative theology, and various interpretive methodologies can be found. Addressing the historical development, key figures, and a sample of some important key features indicates that Egyptian Ashʿarism during this period reflects a vital synthesis of Maghribī, Persian, and local influences with which Egyptian scholars critically engaged, indicating a continued vibrancy and diversity of thought.

I Ashʿarism in Egypt

I offer as a convenient though not absolute historical framework for the discussion of Ashʿarism in Egypt, the following general timeframes:

1. Pre-Ghazālī (al-Ashʿarī and his immediate successors through al-Juwaynī)
2. The era of al-Ghazālī and Ṣalāḥ al-Dīn al-Ayyūbī (5th/11th and 6th/12th centuries)
3. Persian influence (7th/13th to 10th/16th centuries)
4. Maghribī influence (10th/16th and 11th/17th centuries)
5. Persian, Maghribī, and Egyptian synthesis (approx. 11th/17th to 13th/19th centuries)

These eras are approximate and not entirely neat; for example, the Maghribī scholars themselves were reading, processing, and developing the texts of Persian Ashʿarites, and some sixteenth-century scholars may have been exposed to both. However, the beginning of each approximate era also corresponds to major historical and intellectual developments that impacted the contours of Ashʿarite thought.

(a) Pre-Ghazālī to the Era of al-Ghazālī and Ṣalāḥ al-Dīn al-Ayyūbī

Egyptian centres of learning, especially al-Azhar University in Cairo, have a long and rich history with the Ashʿarite school. Along with other important centres of Ashʿarite learning, from North Africa to Persia to the Levant, al-Azhar and other Egyptian *madrasas* have played a central role in the development and spread of the Ashʿarite school, especially from the sixth/twelfth century until the present day.

Although adherents to the Ashʿarite school existed in Egypt during the pre-Ghazālī era of Fatimid rule (969–1171 CE), their presence and dominance was cemented with the founding of the Ayyūbid dynasty by Ṣalāḥ al-Dīn al-Ayyūbī (d. 589/1193) (Leiser 1981). Despite its establishment by Shīʿī Fāṭimids in 359/970, al-Azhar University has been a bulwark of Ashʿarite thought since Ṣalāḥ al-Dīn took control of Egypt and its institutions in 1171. Ṣalāḥ al-Dīn was an active proponent of the Ashʿarite school; he established several institutions in Egypt devoted to the teaching and spread of Ashʿarite thought, and made the Ashʿarite school the official creed of all institutions under his domain, regardless of one's *madhhab* affiliations. In particular, he established the Ṣalāḥiyya *madrasa*, whose 'surviving inscription states that it had been constructed for Ashʿarī jurists' (Leiser 1981: 167).

If we are to accept Ibn Khaldūn's account of the development of *kalām* as found in his *al-Muqaddima* (Ibn Khaldūn, *Muqaddima*, 1: 52), the Ashʿarite school during the reign of Ṣalāḥ al-Dīn would have reflected the developments ushered in by al-Ghazālī and others, namely the refutation of some of the early Ashʿarite *kalām* proofs and replacing them with stronger and more logically consistent proofs. Alternatively, perhaps a synthesis of the old (pre-Ghazālī) and new (Ghazālī) ways of Ashʿarite theology existed in Egypt as the transition took place, though it would be necessary to carefully study the works of Egyptian Ashʿarites from this period to determine how, when, and to what degree these changes occurred.

(b) The Persian Influence: Seventh/Thirteenth to Tenth/Sixteenth Centuries

In the thirteenth and fourteenth centuries CE, the works of Persian scholars such as Fakhr al-Dīn al-Rāzī (d. 606/1210), Saʿd al-Dīn al-Taftazānī (d. 792/1390), ʿAbd Allah b. ʿUmar al-Bayḍāwī (d. 685/1286), Afḍal al-Dīn al-Khūnājī (d. 646/1249), Athīr al-Dīn al-Abharī (d. 663/1264), Najm al-Dīn al-Qazwīnī (al-Kātibī) (d. 675/1276) and others, had ushered in yet another stage in the development of Ashʿarite thought and soon impacted Egyptian theologians. As discussed later, the works of these aforementioned scholars and their peers received significant attention in Egypt, as is evidenced by the numerous commentaries Egyptian scholars produced.

Ibn Khallikān (d. 681/1282), author of the famed biographical dictionary *Wafayāt al-aʿyān wa-anbāʾ abnāʾ al-zamān*, lived in Egypt for a number of years, assisted the chief judge Badr al-Dīn al-Sakhāwi, and taught at al-Azhar. He had studied under Kamāl al-Dīn b. Yūnus (d. 639/1242), known to be a master of Fakhr al-Dīn al-Rāzī's theories and methods of logic and theology (Tuʿmī, *Nūr*, 16; cf. Spevack 2010: 174). Ibn Khallikān reports that his teacher Kamāl al-Dīn b. Yūnus was the only one in Mosul who properly understood the technical terminology of al-Rāzi's books when they first arrived there (Spevack 2010: 165), so it is likely that Egyptian scholars of the Ashʿarite school would also have a steep learning curve in determining the new technical terminology in al-Rāzi's books of logic and *kalām*. Perhaps Ibn Khallikān played a role in introducing al-Rāzi's theories and technical terminology to Egyptian scholars in his day.

By Jalāl al-Dīn al-Suyūṭī's day (d. 911/1505), it appears that both methods, that of the pre-thirteenth century Ashʿarite scholars as well as the methods of those Persian scholars writing in the thirteenth century and beyond, were present in Egypt, the latter increasing in popularity and impact. Al-Suyūṭī resisted this process, declaring the study of logic forbidden (*ḥarām*), and boasted of his having learned jurisprudence, grammar, and rhetoric from sources free of the Persian and philosophical influences (el-Rouayheb 2006: 268).

Despite his disdain for the rational sciences, al-Suyūṭī nonetheless recognized Fakhr al-Dīn al-Rāzī and other scholars of the rational sciences (including his own teachers) as his intellectual forefathers and superiors (al-Suyūṭī, *Sharḥ*, 2: 917–18). Among al-Suyūṭī's primary teachers was Muḥyi al-Dīn al-Kāfiyajī (d. 879/1474) who wrote a commentary on al-Taftāzānī's *Tahdhīb al-manṭiq wa-l-kalām* (Ḥibshī 2004: i. 686). Discussed in Section II, al-Taftāzānī's works have had a profound impact on Egyptian Ashʿarism, as indicated by the numerous commentaries they have received.

II The Sixteenth-Century Persian Effervescence

Soon after al-Suyūṭī's time, a number of proponents of Persian-influenced Ashʿarism rose to prominence in Egypt, occupying key judgeships and teaching appointments. These include, but are not limited to, Zakariyyā al-Anṣārī (d. 926/1520), Ibn Ḥajar al-Haytamī (d. 974/1566–7), and Shams al-Dīn Muḥammad b. Aḥmad al-Ramlī (d. 1004/1596). Though known primarily for their indelible and profound impact on the recension and application of the Shāfiʿī school of law, these scholars and their contemporaries helped further fortify the contours of late Egyptian Ashʿarism (Spevack 2014, 76–82). They considered Ashʿarism, along with the Māturīdī school, the only valid standard bearers of Sunnī Islam, with harsh condemnations of Ibn Taymiyya and other proponents of similar strains of *atharī* theology[1] (Ibn Ḥajar, *Fatāwā*, 143–4). Their Ashʿarism was married to the logic of later logicians (*muta'akhkhirūn*) such as al-Khūnajī, al-Rāzī, al-Abharī, and others, indicating that opposition to syllogistic logic in Ashʿarite theology grew more and more rare.

This is particularly important because the opinions of Ibn Ḥajar and al-Ramlī, when in agreement, became the standard relied-upon position (*muʿtamad*) of the Shāfiʿī school, further connecting the Shāfiʿī school with Ashʿarism, but in its later Persian-influenced and pro-logic form.

Zakariyyā al-Anṣārī, a prominent contemporary of Ibn Ḥajar and al-Ramlī whose legal opinions were still referenced in nineteenth-century Shāfiʿī legal texts, wrote a number of commentaries on legal, philosophical, and theological texts. On the study of syllogistic logic, he wrote *al-Muṭṭalaʿ*, being a commentary on al-Abharī's (663/1264) *al-Īsāghūjī* (Ḥibshī 2004: i. 353). Regarding the science of rhetoric, he wrote *Fatḥ al-wahhāb* (Ḥibsī 2004: 1/60), being a commentary on Shams al-Dīn Muḥammad b. Ashraf al-Ḥusaynī al-Samarqandī's (*fl.* c.690/1291) *Risāla fī ādāb al-baḥth*. As so many Egyptian Ashʿarites before and after him would, he also wrote a gloss on al-Taftazānī's commentary on the *ʿAqā'id* of al-Nasafī (Ḥibshī 2004: ii. 1183).

Egyptian scholars of the following generations (seventeenth to nineteenth centuries) were also actively engaged with the works of the Persian logicians and theologians. In

[1] The term *atharī* refers to those theologians, often though not always followers of the Ḥanbalī school of law, who in theory reject using rational proofs in theology, opting instead to reference only the Qur'ān and *ḥadīth* for their theological positions. The term *atharī* implies knowledge which has been transmitted from primary texts, being derived from various usages including 'remnant' and 'narration'.

addition to the previously mentioned fifteenth- and sixteenth-century commentaries of al-Anṣārī and al-Kāfiyajī, the works of al-Taftazānī received commentaries by a number of scholars, including but not limited to:

- Ibrāhīm al-Laqānī (d. 1041/1631) [gloss on al-Taftāzānī's commentary on *ʿAqā'id al-Nasafī*] (Ḥibshī 2004: ii. 1190)
- Ibrāhīm al-Bājūrī [unfinished gloss of more than 200 leafs on al-Taftāzānī's commentary on *ʿAqā'id al-Nasafī*] (Cuno and Spevack 2009; Spevack forthcoming)
- Shams al-Dīn Muḥammad al-Inbābī (d. 1895) [critical assessment (*taqrīr*) of al-Taftazānī's commentary on *Talkhīṣ al-Miftāḥ li-l-Qazwīnī*] (Ḥibshī 2004: i. 637)
- Muḥammad b. Aḥmad b. ʿĀrifa al-Dasūqī (d. 1230/1815) [gloss on Qārā Dāwūd's commentary on al-Taftāzānī's *Tahdhīb al-manṭiq wa-l-kalām* (Ḥibshī 2004: i. 690), gloss on al-Taftāzānī's *sharḥ* on *Talkhīṣ al-Miftāḥ li-l-Qazwīnī* (Ḥibshī 2004; i. 636), and *al-Tajrīd al-Shāfī*, being a gloss on ʿUbayd Allāh b. Faḍl Allāh al-Khabīṣī Fakhr al-Dīn's (d. *c.*1050/1640) commentary on the same work (Ḥibshī 2004: i. 694)]
- Ḥasan b. Muḥammad al-ʿĀṭār (d. 1250/1834–5) [gloss on ʿUbayd Allāh al-Khabīṣī's commentary on al-Taftāzānī's *Tahdhīb al-manṭiq wa-l-kalām*]

Another prominent Persian scholar whose works continued to be studied and commented upon by later Egyptian scholars is ʿAḍud al-Dīn ʿAbd al-Raḥmān b. Aḥmad al-Ījī (d. 756/1355). Al-Ījī was a prominent theologian of his time, a contemporary of al-Abharī, and the teacher of al-Taftāzānī. Among his many works is *al-Risāla al-waḍʿiyya al-ʿAḍudiyya* which received al-Dasūqī's glosses on the respective commentaries of Abū l-Qāsim al-Laythī al-Samarqandī (d. *c.*888/1483) (Ḥibshī 2004: ii. 982) and ʿIṣām al-Dīn Ibrāhīm b. Muḥammad b. ʿArabshāh al-Isfarā'īnī (d. 944/1537) (Ḥibshī 2004: ii. 983). The Azharī scholar Aḥmad al-Dardīr al-Mālikī (d. 1201/1786) also wrote a commentary on al-Ījī's *Ādāb al-baḥth*.

This sample, along with the expressed familiarity with other Persian scholars found in the various works of later Egyptian Ashʿarites, indicates a continued interest in the works of al-Taftazānī, al-Ījī, al-Abharī, al-Khūnājī, al-Rāzī, and others throughout the seventeenth to nineteenth centuries. The stream of Persian-influenced Ashʿarite theology had by the seventeenth to nineteenth centuries merged, via the works of Egyptian scholars, with that of the Maghribī Ashʿarite scholars who had themselves been studying and commenting upon the works of Persian scholars, as discussed in what follows.

(a) The Maghribī Influence: Sixteenth to Seventeenth Centuries

Around the same time that al-Suyūṭī was lamenting the influence of Persian scholars, Muḥammad b. Yūsuf al-Sanūsī (d. 895/1490) of Tlemcen wrote his seminal works on Ashʿarite theology which would impact the Ashʿarite world, including Egypt, down to the present day. Al-Sanūsī was a scholar of *fiqh*, *ḥadīth*, and Qurʾānic recitation, though he is primarily remembered for his works on logic and *kalām* which spread to Egypt, Nigeria, Mali, Malaysia, and beyond (Bencheneb 2007). Less than a half century after al-Sanūsī's death, an Egyptian scholar by the name of Nūr al-Dīn ʿAlī b. Muḥammad b. Muḥammad b. Khalaf al-Minūfī al-Shādhilī (Ḥibshī 2004: i. 276)[2] wrote a commentary on al-Sanūsī's *Umm al-barāhīn*. While this is a very early example of al-Sanūsī's works reaching an Egyptian scholar, it was close to a century later that his work would have an even greater number of proponents among Egyptian Ashʿarites (Ḥibshī 2004: i. 271–91 *passim*).

In the early seventeenth century, an influx of north-west African scholars impacted the Egyptian theological milieu. Fleeing the political turmoil of Morocco, a number of scholars from the region introduced popular works on logic and theology to Egyptian scholars, including those of al-Sanūsī (el-Rouayheb 2007). The first to hold the position of Shaykh al-Azhar, Shaykh Muḥammad al-Kharāshī (d. 1101/1690), lived during this period and lists among his works *al-Farāʾid al-saniya fī ḥall alfāẓ al-Sanūsiyya* and *al-Anwār al-Qudsiyya fī al-Farāʾid al-Kharāshiyya* being commentaries on al-Sanūsī's theological texts (Tuʿmī, *Nūr*, 108). Aḥmad b. ʿAbd Allāh al-Ghadāmiṣī al-Miṣrī is another Egyptian scholar from the same time period who wrote a commentary on al-Sanūsī's *Umm al-Barāhīn* (completed 1064/1654) (Ḥibshī 2004: i. 280).

Later professors and rectors of al-Azhar would also study and write commentaries on al-Sanūsī's works. Al-Dasūqī wrote a gloss on al-Sanūsī's autocommentary on his *Umm al-barāhīn* (Ḥibshī 2004: i. 287) and Muḥammad al-Amīr al-Kabīr (d. 1232/1817) wrote a commentary on ʿAlī b. Aḥmad b. ʿAlī al-Fāsī al-Saqqāṭ's (d. 1183/1769) versification of al-Sanūsī's *Umm al-Barāhīn* (Ḥibshī 2004: i. 291). Shaykh al-Azhar ʿAbd Allāh al-Sharqāwī (d. 1812) wrote a gloss (*ḥāshīya*) on al-Hudhudī's commentary on al-Sanūsī's *al-ʿAqīda al-ṣughrā* as well (Ḥibshī 2004: i. 274). Al-Sharqāwī's contemporary, Shaykh Muḥammad al-Faḍālī (d. 1821) also wrote works on Ashʿarite theology, quoting frequently from al-Sanūsī.

Shaykh al-Azhar Ibrāhīm al-Bājūrī (d. 1860),[3] a student of al-Sharqāwī, al-Faḍālī, and al-Kabīr, wrote a commentary on al-Sanūsī's logic text called *Ḥāshīya ʿalā mukhtaṣar al-Sanūsī fī l-manṭiq*, as well as a commentary on al-Sanūsī's theology primer called *Ḥāshīya ʿalā matn al-Sanūsiyya fī ʿilm al-tawḥīd*. His exposure to al-Sanūsī was likely most substantial via his main teacher al-Faḍālī, upon whose theological works he also commented, as well as al-Amīr al-Kabīr from whom he also narrates *ḥadīth* and received *ijāzas* in various sciences. Furthermore, al-Bājūrī bases his short epistle on Islamic creed, entitled *Risālat al-Bājūrī*, on al-Sanūsī's work (al-Shirbīnī and Muḥammad al-Nashshār, 1900), and intersperses references to al-Sanūsī in his *Tuḥfat al-murīd*, being a commentary on the didactic poem *Jawharat al-tawḥīd* by Ibrāhīm al-Laqānī (d. 1041/1631). A contemporary of al-Bājūrī's and highly influential Mālikī scholar in his day,

[2] He might be identical with ʿAlī b. Nāṣir al-Dīn b. Muḥammad al-Miṣrī al-Fāḍilī (d. 939/1532), mentioned in *Geschichte der Arabischen Litteratur*, 2:1902.

[3] For more on al-Bājūrī, see Cuno and Spevack; Spevack forthcoming.

Muḥammad ʿIllaysh (d. 1299/1882) wrote a commentary on al-Sanūsī's *ʿUmdat ahl al-tawfīq wa-l-tasdīd*, being an autocommentary on his *ʿAqīdat ahl al-tawḥīd wa-l-tasdīd al-mukhrija min ẓulumāt al-jahl wa-rabqat al-taqlīd* (also known as *al-ʿAqīda al-kubrā*) (Ḥibshī 2004: i. 288).

It may not be an exaggeration to say that al-Sanūsī's direct impact on the logical and theological training of Egyptian students, from at least the seventeenth century onwards, was more pronounced than that of earlier scholars such as al-Ghazālī (despite the indebtedness of the former to the latter).

Another important Maghribī scholar of logic and Ashʿarite theology is ʿAbd al-Raḥmān b. Muḥammad b. ʿĀmir b. al-Walī al-Ṣaḥīḥ al-Sayyid al-Ṣaghīr al-Akhḍarī. He wrote a commentary on al-Sanūsī's primer (Ḥibshī 2004: i. 276), though he is widely known in the realm of *fiqh* for his primer on law in the Mālikī *madhhab*, commonly called *Matn al-Akhḍarī*. His versification of al-Abharī's *Īsāghūjī*, entitled *al-Sullam al-munawwaraq* is also very well known, having received numerous commentaries. Scholars of al-Azhar who commented on *al-Sullam* include al-Bājūrī, his teacher al-Quwaysnī (d. 1255/1839), al-Damanhūrī, as well as Aḥmad b. ʿAbd al-Fattāḥ b. Yūsuf al-Mallawī (d. 1181/1767) who wrote a major and minor commentary (Spevack 2014, 134–7). Al-Mallawī's commentary serves as an important source for al-Bājūrī's commentary as well.

Aḥmad b. ʿAbd Allāh (Muḥammad) al-Jazāʾirī (d. 898/1493), though less well known than the two previously mentioned scholars, authored a creedal poem entitled *al-Manẓūma al-lāmiyya al-Jazāʾiriyya fī l-tawḥīd* (Ḥibshī 2004: iii. 1000). This text received a commentary by al-Jazāʾirī's contemporary al-Sanūsī, and later would receive a commentary by the Egyptian theologian ʿAbd al-Salām al-Laqānī (d. 1078/1667) (Ḥibshī 2004: iii. 1001). An important aspect of al-Laqānī's period is that we begin to see scholars writing on both Maghribī and Persian texts, indicating, perhaps, a synthesis of both traditions, as discussed in the next subsection.

(b) The Persian-Maghribī-Egyptian Synthesis: Seventeenth to Nineteenth Centuries

Ibrāhīm al-Laqānī is one of the most important Egyptian scholars of the eleventh/seventeenth century. He was a scholar of Mālikī law, *ḥadīth*, Sufism, and *kalām*. As mentioned previously, he was steeped in the Persian influences of al-Taftazānī, but his main contribution to Ashʿarite theology was his didactic poem *Jawharat al-tawḥīd*, which has received many commentaries, including his own self-commentaries, as discussed in this section. His son, ʿAbd al-Salām al-Laqānī, mentioned previously, wrote commentaries on his father's works, including a commentary on *Jawharat al-tawḥīd* and a gloss on his father's autocommentary on the same poem. Between the father and son, we see both familiarity with the Persian and Maghribī traditions, as well as the popularization of an Egyptian-born text, namely *Jawharat al-tawḥīd* (cf. Bājūrī, *Tuḥfat al-murīd*).

Henceforth, it becomes increasingly common to see scholars commenting on some combination of the Maghribī, Persian, and Egyptian texts (i.e. *Jawharat al-tawḥīd* and its commentaries), as well as referencing prominent scholars from each region in their commentaries. For example, in *Tuḥfat al-murīd*, a commentary on al-Laqānī's *Jawharat al-tawḥīd*, al-Bājūrī discusses the problem of defining the attribute of existence and its relation to an entity (*dhāt*). The issue at hand regards whether the attribute of existence is synonymous with the existent thing—an opinion held by some theologians—or whether they are different, yet inextricable from each other, as other theologians believed. In discussing the various opinions, al-Bājūrī mentions the opinions of Fakhr al-Dīn al-Rāzī, al-Taftazānī, al-Laqānī, and Muḥammad al-Ṣaghīr (d. 1155/1742), that is to say, he cites Persian, Maghribī, and Egyptian scholars. Fakhr al-Dīn al-Rāzī is cited by al-Bājūrī as arguing that the thing being described (*mawṣūf*) and the attribute (*ṣifa*) describing it (i.e. existence) are not one and the same, while al-Taftazānī is cited as claiming that the attribute cannot exist independently of the thing it is describing (Bājūrī, *Tuḥfat al-murīd*, 105–6). The Egyptian scholar al-Laqānī himself (via his self-commentary) as cited by al-Bājūrī confirms al-Taftazānī's view, and the Maghribī scholar Muḥammad al-Ṣaghīr is mentioned, reminding the reader that it is sufficient to affirm that God exists, without getting into the aforementioned issue, which he considers to be from the obscure and debated matters of *kalām*. A near verbatim discussion is included in al-Bājūrī's commentary on al-Sanūsī's *Umm al-barāhīn* as well (*Ḥāshiyat al-Bājūrī-a*, 14).

In addition to cross-referencing between Persian, Maghribī, and Egyptian works, al-Bājūrī's corpus of works contains commentaries on works by authors from all three categories. Along with his commentaries on the works of Egyptian scholars such as al-Laqānī and al-Faḍālī, al-Bājūrī also wrote commentaries on al-Akhḍarī's *al-Sullam*, al-Sanūsī's *Umm al-Barāhīn* and *Mukhtasar al-Sanūsī fi al-mantiq*, al-Samarqandī's *Matn al-Samarqandiyya* on the science of rhetoric, and al-Taftazānī's commentary on al-Nasafī's *ʿAqāʾid* (Cuno and Spevack 2009; Spevack 2014, 18–25).

Other Egyptian scholars who drew from the Persian and Maghribī wells of Ashʿarism include al-Dasūqī, al-Dardīr, and others. Al-Dardīr has a commentary on al-Ījī's *Adab al Baḥth*, a commentary based on al-Sanūsī's autocommentary on his *Umm al-Barāhīn*, and an autocommentary on his own introductory poem on Ashʿarite theology called *al-Kharīdat al-bahīya fī l-ʿaqāʾid al-tawḥīdiyya*. Al-Dasūqī commented on al-Sanūsī's autocommentary on *Umm al-barāhīn*, as well as al-Taftazānī's and al-Ījī's works, as mentioned previously. It is clear that by the eighteenth and nineteenth centuries, the Persian-Maghribī-Egyptian synthesis had become the norm amongst Egypt's Ashʿarites, much like the works of the post-sixth/twelfth-century Persian scholars had become the predominant approach of Ashʿarites in tenth/sixteenth-century Egypt, as mentioned previously of the age of al-Anṣārī, Ibn Ḥajar, and al-Ramlī.

III Key Features of Late Egyptian Ashʿarite thought

Three key features of late Egyptian Ashʿarite thought which help to underscore the diversity and vibrancy of the period are discussed here. Each requires extensive discussion. However, the broad strokes discussed here further evidence the vibrant synthesis of post-seventh/thirteenth-century Persian, Maghribī, and local Egyptian influences that imbue the late Egyptian Ashʿarite milieu.

The *first* feature is the prominence of the study of logic and *kalām*. Despite possible ebbs and flows in interest in logic between the fifteenth and nineteenth centuries, as well as the diversity of approaches and depth of study, it was nonetheless a mainstay of the theological and legal education of the Egyptian scholar. The subject of logic from the thirteenth to nineteenth centuries contained subtle developments in content and arrangement of subject matter, to the extent that it was deemed sufficiently distinct from the logic of earlier logicians, such that it received a different ruling (*ḥukm*) by the jurists. That is to say, the logic of earlier logicians was a matter of juristic debate; some scholars considered it *ḥarām*—including Ibn Yūnus's contemporaries al-Nawawī (d. 676/1277) and Ibn al-Ṣalāḥ (d. 643/1245)—while others considered it a required subject of study, such as al-Ghazālī. Furthermore, the popular opinion—though, according to al-Bājūrī, not necessarily the majority opinion—was that the study of the logic of the earlier scholars was permissible for one who was firmly established in his knowledge, faith, and practice. According to al-Bājūrī, his teacher al-Quwaysnī, and others, this disagreement was over the logic of earlier logicians, whose books were not free from the heretical metaphysical beliefs of the philosophers. As for the works of the Persian and Maghribī scholars mentioned previously, their study was considered communally obligatory (*farḍ kifāya*) without disagreement, with the notable exception of al-Bayḍāwī's works which al-Damanhūrī considered to belong to the previous category (the logic of the earlier logicians) (Spevack 2010: 173).

As logic was deemed the handmaiden of *kalām*, so to speak, and as the latter (*kalām*) was communally obligatory, therefore the former (logic) too must be communally obligatory, as *kalām* depended on logic. This is the reasoning al-Bājūrī offers. Inherent in this position is the belief that the term *kalām* refers primarily to the *kalām* that employs the methods and terminology of logic, and that logic, unless otherwise specified, is the logic of the later Persian and Maghribī scholars. Despite the developments in *kalām* and logic, a historical survey of the prominent scholars who studied and wrote on these topics, the prominence of those who deemed them communally obligatory, and the interconnectedness of logic and *kalām* to the study of law (via *uṣūl al-fiqh*), indicates that Ashʿarite *kalām*—with significant Māturīdī representation—has been a central part of an Egyptian scholar's education from at least the time of Ṣalāḥ al-Dīn al-Ayyūbī, through the late nineteenth century.

The *second* key feature in late Egyptian Ashʿarite thought is the prominent influence of the Persian and Maghribī *muḥaqqiqūn* ('scholarly verifiers'), who explained and at times challenged inherited theological positions, often offering their own opinion. Their emphasis on *taḥqīq*, which has been defined as 'giving the evidential grounds ... for a scientific proposition' (el-Rouayheb 2006: 265), implies that there was not a sense that post-thirteenth-century logicians and theologians saw themselves as bound by past scholarship, capable of merely transmitting and explaining. Rather, they were comfortably challenging others' opinions, and offering proofs for their chosen opinions. This is clearly evident in the diverse perspectives on many issues mentioned in *kalām* and logic texts, wherein two contemporaneous scholars might write commentaries on the same work and offer differing or contradictory explanations.

Scholars of the eighteenth and nineteenth centuries, such as al-Bājūrī, al-Damanhūrī, al-Dasūqī, al-Dardīr, al-Sharqāwī, al-Laqānī, Aḥmad b. Muḥammad al-Ṣāwī (d. 1241/1825), and others, were well versed in the texts of the Persian and Maghribī *muḥaqqiqūn* and were no doubt emboldened by them, as is evidenced in the diversity of opinion found amongst themselves and their comfort in expressing their differing opinions. Indeed, some of these scholars, including al-Bājūrī, were given the title of *al-muḥaqqiq* (i.e. the scholarly verifier who does *taḥqīq*).

The *third* key feature, connected to the previous feature, is the prominence of the commentary as the literary genre of choice for scholars. While some have seen the commentary tradition as evidence of decline, as original monographs became increasingly rare, it is arguable that, despite the limitations of the medium, the commentaries are the repositories of evidence of continued vibrancy and originality.

Though often dense, presumptive of the readers' familiarity with other texts and topics, and requiring significant training and contextualization, the commentaries of later scholars can be mined for evidence of the continued vibrancy championed by the *muḥaqiqqūn*. In the works of al-Bājūrī and al-Faḍālī, we see them disagreeing with al-Sanūsī's position that one who does not know the *kalām* proofs for God's existence and necessary attributes is therefore a disbeliever. They argue, rather, that such a person is potentially sinful as their faith is not safe from wavering, yet still counted as a Muslim. We also see in later Ashʿarites' insistence on the communally obligatory nature of logic and *kalām*, its widespread teaching in various learning institutions, and their insistence that everyone should know the proofs in general (*ijmālī*) rather than specific (*tafṣīlī*) terms, a clear disagreement with al-Ghazālī's position in *Iljām al-ʿawwām ʿan ʿilm al-kalām*, which advocates for a far more restricted study of and exposure to *kalām*.

Another example pertains to a discussion of the phrase 'God is existent in every place', often stated by the common folk. Al-Ṣāwī, in his commentary on al-Laqānī's *Jawharat al-tawḥīd*, considers the expression acceptable when interpreted as 'He is with every existent thing, that is, he is not absent from anything' (Ṣāwī, *Ḥāshīya*, 146). Al-Bājūrī, on the other hand, in his own commentary on al-Laqānī's text considers the statement impermissible, as it can give the mistaken impression of indwelling and incarnation.

Al-Bājūrī freely disagrees with al-Laqānī in several matters, including whether or not the 'necessary attributes' of the Prophets, as mentioned by al-Laqānī, al-Sanūsī, and others, are rationally necessary (*wājib ʿaqlī*) or necessary due to their mention in primary texts (*wājib sharʿī*). He also differs with al-Laqānī and other Ashʿarites on the matter of the superiority of angels to humans. Al-Laqānī holds that all angels are superior to all humans, other than the prophets, whereas al-Bājūrī and al-Ṣāwī adopt the Māturīdī opinion that some non-prophets are better than some angels, as in the case of Abū Bakr, ʿUmar, ʿUthman, and ʿAlī who are deemed superior to the generality of angels other than Gabriel, Isrāfil, Mikāʾīl, and ʿIzrāʾīl (Spevack 2014, 27).

One sees a diversity of opinions in the study of logic with regards to subtle matters such as whether affirmation (*taṣdīq*) is a composite of conceptions and a judgement, or merely a judgement (Quṭb al-Dīn al-Rāzī, *Taḥrīr*, 7–11), whether or not a categorical syllogism requires an entire middle term (el-Rouayheb 2010: 41), whether or not universals exist in the extra-mental world (Spevack 2010: 175), whether a definition entails the apprehension of the thing defined or the apprehension of its distinction from everything else (Spevack 2010: 175), and numerous other nuanced matters. These discussions can be found in the works of al-Jurjānī, Fakhr al-Dīn al-Rāzī, Quṭb al-Dīn al-Rāzī, al-Kātibī, al-Taftazānī, and others, and were contemplated by the later Egyptian scholars who inherited the discussions from their Persian and Maghribī forefathers.

The texts and subjects that later Egyptian Ashʿarites were treating in their discussions of logic and theology indicate a dynamic, nuanced, vibrant, and diverse enterprise, carried out by scholars unencumbered by the absolute reliance on *taqlīd* ('following the opinions of others without knowing their proofs') so often predicated of them by late nineteenth-century reformists and Orientalists. Late Egyptian Ashʿarite thought by the seventeenth century was, therefore, a vibrant synthesis of Persian, Maghribī, and Egyptian perspectives, rooted in the developments of the later logicians and theologians, guided by the independent ethos of the 'scholarly verifiers' (*muḥaqqiqūn*), and woven into the dense and highly technical language and format of the commentary genre.

References

al-Bājūrī, Ibrāhīm (*Ḥāshīya*). *Hādhihi ḥāshiyat al-ʿallāma al-Shaykh Ibrāhīm al-Bājūrī ʿalā risālat al-ustādh al-Shaykh Muḥammad al-Faḍālī fī Lā ilāha illa-Llāh*. Cairo: Maṭbaʿat ʿUthmān ʿAbd al-Rāziq, 1301/1884.

al-Bājūrī, Ibrāhīm (*Hāshīyat al-Bājūrī-a*). *Ḥāshīyat al-Bājūrī*. Lithographed copy. [Cairo: n.p.], 1279[/1863]. (A commentary on al-Sanūsī's *Umm al-barāhīn*.)

al-Bājūrī, Ibrāhīm (*Hāshīyat al-Bājūrī-b*). *Ḥāshīyat al-Bājūrī ʿalā l-Sullam fī ʿilm al-manṭiq*. Cairo: Maktabat wa-Maṭbaʿat Muḥammad ʿAlī Ṣabīḥ wa-awlādihi, 1966. (A commentary on al-Akhḍarī.)

al-Bājūrī, Ibrāhīm (*Ḥāshīyat al-Bājūrī-c*). *Ḥāshīyat Ibrāhīm al-Bājūrī al-musammāt bi-Taḥqīq al-maqām ʿalā Kifāyat al-ʿawāmm fī ʿilm al-kalām li-Muḥammad al-Faḍālī*. Būlāq: al-Maṭbaʿa al-Azhariyya, 1329/1906.

al-Bājūrī, Ibrāhīm (*Tuḥfa*). *Tuḥfat al-murīd ʿalā jawharat al-tawḥīd*. Ed. ʿAlī Muḥammad Jumʿa. Cairo: Dār al-Salām, 2006.

Bencheneb, H. (2007). ʻal-Sanūsī, Abū ʿAbd Allāh Muḥammad b. Yūsuf b. ʿUmar b. Shuʿaybʼ. *The Encyclopaedia of Islam*. New edn. ix. 20–2.

Cuno, K. M., and A. Spevack (2009). ʻal-Bājurī, Ibrāhīm b. Muḥammadʼ. *The Encyclopaedia of Islam*, fasc. 2009–2, 130–2.

al-Fuḍālī, M. (1960). ʻThe Sufficiency of the Commonality in the Science of Scholastic Theologyʼ. In D. B. MacDonald (ed.), *Development of Muslim Theology, Jurisprudence, and Constitutional Theory*. Lahore: Premier Book House.

al-Ḥibshī, ʿAbd Allāh M. (2004). *Jāmiʿ al-shurūḥ wa-l-ḥawāshī: Muʿjam shāmil li-asmāʾ al-kutub al-mashrūḥa fī l-turāth al-islāmī wa-bayān shurūḥihā*. 3 vols. Abu Dhabi: Abu Dhabi Authority for Culture and Heritage Cultural Foundation, 1425.

Ibn Ḥajar al-Haytamī (*Fatāwā*). *al-Fatāwā al-ḥadīthiyya*. Egypt: Muṣṭafā l-Bābī l-Ḥalabī, 1970.

Ibn Khaldūn (*Muqaddima*). *The Muqaddimah: An Introduction to History*. Trans. F. Rosenthal. 3 vols. New York: Pantheon Books, 1958.

Ibn Khallikān (*Wafayāt*). *Wafayāt al-aʿyān wa-anbāʾ abnāʾ al-zamān*. Beirut: Dār Ṣādir, 1994.

al-Ījī, ʿAḍud al-Dīn (*Sharḥ*). *Sharḥ Mukhtaṣar al-Muntahā al-uṣūlī*. Beirut: Dār al-kutub al-ʿilmiyya, 2004.

al-Ījī, ʿAḍud al-Dīn (*Mawāqif*). *al-Mawāqif fī ʿilm al-kalām*. Lebanon: ʿĀlam al-Kutub, n.d.

Leiser, G. (1981). ʻHanbalism in Egypt before the Mamluksʼ. *Studia Islamica* 54: 155–8.

Quṭb al-Dīn al-Rāzī (*Taḥrīr*). *Taḥrīr al-Qawāʿid al-manṭiqiyya*. Surabaya: Sharikah Pīrāmīd li-ṭabāʿa wa-l-nashr wa-l-tawzīʿ, n.d.

al-Quwaysnī, Ḥasan b. Darwīsh (*Sharḥ*). *Sharḥ Naẓm al-sullam al-munawraq fī l-manṭiq li-ʿAbd al-Raḥmān al-Akhḍarī*. Casablanca: Dār al-Rashād al-Ḥadītha, 2006.

El-Rouayheb, Kh. (2006). ʻOpening the Gate of Verification: The Forgotten Arab-Islamic Florescence of the Seventeenth Centuryʼ. *International Journal of Middle East Studies* 38: 263–81.

El-Rouayheb, Kh. (2007). ʻOpening the Gates of Verification: Intellectual Trends in the Arabic-Islamic Worldʼ. *International Institute for Asian Studies (IIAS) Newsletter*, no. 43 (Spring 2007).

El-Rouayheb, Kh. (2010). *Relational Syllogisms and the History of Arabic Logic*, 900–1900. Leiden: Brill.

al-Ṣāwī, Aḥmad b. Muḥammad (*Ḥāshīya*). *Kitāb Sharḥ al-Ṣāwī ʿalā Jawharat al-tawḥīd*. Beirut: Dār Ibn Kathīr, 1997.

al-Shirbīnī, Muḥammad al-Nashshār (*Ḥāshīya*). *Ḥāshīyat al-Tuḥfa al-saniyya ʿalā l-risāla al-Bājūriyya wa-bi-hāmishihā Minḥat al-barāyā bi-mā fī l-basmala min al-mazāyā*. Egypt: Maṭbaʿat Muḥammad Muṣṭafā, 1318 [/1900].

Spevack, A. (2010). ʻApples and Oranges: The Logic of the Early and Later Logiciansʼ. *Islamic Law and Society* 17: 159–84.

Spevack, A. (2014). *The Archetypal Sunni Scholar: Law, Theology, and Sufism in the Synthesis of al-Bājūrī*. Albany, NY: SUNY Press.

al-Suyūṭī, Jalāl al-Dīn (*Sharḥ*). *Sharḥ Maqamāt*. Vol. 2. Ed. Maḥmūd al-Durūbī. Beirut: Muʾassasat al-Risāla, 1989.

al-Taftāzānī, Saʿd al-Dīn (*Commentary*). *A Commentary on the Creed of Islam: Saʿd al-Dīn al-Taftāzānī on the Creed of Najm al-Dīn al-Nasafī*. Trans. E. E. Elder. New York: Columbia University Press, 1950.

Ṭuʿmī, Muḥyī l-Dīn (*Nūr*). *Al-Nūr al-abhar fī ṭabaqāt shuyūkh al-Jāmiʿ al-Azhar*. Beirut: Dār al-Jīl, 1991.

Wisnovsky, Robert. 'Post-classical (1100CE–1900CE) Islamic Philosophy: A Handlist (by Author) of Major Extant Arabic Works and Commentaries.' [Online: <http://islamsci.mcgill.ca/RASI/docs/pipdi.htm#dd7>]

CHAPTER 31

EXCURSUS III

The Coptic and Syriac Receptions of Neo-Ashʿarite Theology

GREGOR SCHWARB

I Introduction

THE large-scale adoption of works by contemporaneous non-Christian authors from various disciplines of knowledge, their integration into the established body of authoritative texts and the composition of encyclopedic *summae* offering a new synthesis of philosophico-theological and philosophico-scientific knowledge are three salient features of the so-called 'Syriac Renaissance' of the twelfth and thirteenth centuries and of the 'Renaissance of Copto-Arabic literature' of the thirteenth and fourteenth centuries (Teule 2010; Sidarus 2010a).* For Syriac and Coptic Christianity these 'Renaissances' marked periods of profound literary and cultural flowering which took place on the eve and in the course of politically turbulent times with far-reaching geo-political changes in the Islamic world: the emergence of the Mongol Il-Khanate in Persia and Iraq, the disintegration of Ayyūbid and the transition to Mamluk rule in Egypt, Syria, the Ḥijāz, and parts of south-eastern Anatolia, the presence of the Crusader armies occupying strategic points along the Eastern Mediterranean coast and the following collapse of the Crusader States (Teule 2012a, b).

The factors contributing to the 'Golden Age' of Syriac and Copto-Arabic literature were manifold (Sidarus 2010a: 328–32; Swanson 2010: 83–4):

- The Ayyūbid rule was a period of relative political stability and thus provided favourable conditions to a florescence of the socio-cultural life among Muslims and non-Muslims. The educational policy of the Ayyūbids furthered the expansion of a

* I would like to thank A.Y. Sidarus for his valuable comments on an earlier version of this article.

network of teaching institutions and libraries and the circulation of texts. Over the course of the sixth/twelfth and seventh/thirteenth centuries the rational sciences became an integral part of the traditional educational curriculum of the Sunnī *madāris*.

- Of particular significance to the Renaissance of Copto-Arabic literature was the unification of Egypt, Bilād al-Shām, and Yemen under one single political power. This territorial continuity helped to strengthen the long-standing historical relations between Copts and Syrian Orthodox Christians and facilitated the exchange of ideas, texts, and artefacts between the two regions (Fiey 1973; Den Heijer 2004). The Coptic community in Damascus was steadily growing and gathering strength and until the middle of the thirteenth century had assumed sufficient political power to defy the authority of the Coptic patriarch in Cairo (*MTQ* 5: 152–4). As we shall see, almost all protagonists of the Renaissance of Copto-Arabic literature during the thirteenth century resided for shorter or longer intervals in Damascus and maintained close relations with the Coptic community there.
- Within the Coptic church, the language shift from Coptic to Arabic, which was a precondition of the Copto-Arabic Renaissance, was only completed during the twelfth century (Rubenson 1996; Zaborowski 2008; Swanson 2010: 61–81; Sidarus 2013b). Towards the middle decades of the twelfth century there existed a sufficient number of Coptic monks and lay scholars who had received an appropriate formation to access an ample corpus of religious and scientific literature in Arabic and to engage in intensive literary activity. This aptitude was coupled with a widening breadth of interest and an increased willingness to draw on sources from outside the Coptic tradition.
- The driving force behind the Copto-Arabic Renaissance was a class of highly educated Coptic notables who had the means and the capacity to lavish patronage on Coptic scholars and artists (Sidarus 2013a). During the Fāṭimid and Ayyūbid eras several Coptic families became an integral part of the governmental bureaucracy and staffed the *dawāwīn* of the Ayyūbid regime over several generations. Most scholars associated with the Copto-Arabic 'Renaissance' belonged to or were closely associated with these families of State officials. Similarly, the foremost scholars of the Syriac Renaissance benefited from the patronage of local rulers and church institutions (Eddé 1995).

The main exponents of the Syriac and Copto-Arabic Renaissances were scholars of profound erudition who exhibited conspicuous intellectual openness to various linguistic and religious traditions. Besides the scholastic and ecclesiastic literature of Eastern Christian communities, the Church Fathers, and Graeco-Arabic philosophy, they also studied works by contemporaneous Jewish and Muslim men of letters (Schwarb 2007, 2014a). Many of them had extensive private libraries and developed the passionate skill of bibliophiles to track down manuscripts of rare and neglected texts. A vivid and characteristic description of this inquisitive scholarly attitude is given by al-Muʾtaman Ibn al-ʿAssāl in the preface of his *Majmūʿ fī uṣūl al-dīn* (1: 20f., §16):

> Whenever I found someone who owned a book [relevant to a certain subject matter], I would buy it from him in order to study it thoroughly and to examine it carefully; if someone was not willing to sell it, I would borrow it to make a copy of it (or: to have it copied) and then summarise its main goals and commit them to memory. I collected these books from all religious and confessional denominations as well as from any party/group having knowledge and cognisance of it (*min kulli niḥlatin wa-ṭāʾifatin wa-min kulli jamāʿatin ʿālimatin bihi wa-ʿārifatin*); I persisted in studying [these books] with the perseverance of a rational animal that looks for reasoning and reflection.

The Coptic and Syriac Renaissances affected virtually all disciplines of scientific-literary production, including philosophy, logic, sciences, theology, jurisprudence, literary theory and criticism, historio- and chronography, grammar and lexicography. In the domain of religious thought the process of 'appropriation' of new non-Christian sources was mainly a reaction to preceding developments in Islamic *kalām* and *falsafa* following the spectacular ascendancy of Avicennian thought and its amalgamation with Ashʿarite *kalām* and the ensuing emergence of a new type of philosophical theology (Endress 2006; Eichner 2009).

It is needless to recall that Christian scholars were well acquainted with various intellectual trends of late antiquity as well as with early Islamic theology well before the thirteenth century. The works of Greek and Syrian Church Fathers, which were part and parcel of the curriculum in Christian schools and monasteries during the first centuries of Islam, are imbued with terms and concepts derived from Greek and Hellenistic philosophy, logic, medicine, and rhetoric (Becker 2006). The foremost Christian *mutakallimūn* writing in Arabic from the ninth to eleventh centuries, among them Theodore Abū Qurra (d. *c.*830; *GCAL* 2: 7–26; *CMRBH* 1: 439–91; Coquin 1993: 61f.), ʿAmmār al-Baṣrī (d. *c.*845; *GCAL* 2: 210f.; *CMRBH* 1: 604–10; Coquin 1993: 70), Ḥabīb b. Khidma Abū Rāʾiṭa (d. *c.*855; *GCAL* 2: 222–6; *CMRBH* 1: 567–81; *CC* 70f.), Moses bar Kepha (d. 903; *GCAL* 2: 229–33; *CMRBH* 2: 98–101; Coquin 1993: 71), Qusṭā b. Lūqā (d. 912; *GCAL* 2: 30–2; *CMRBH* 2: 147–53; Coquin 1993: 62), Yaḥyā Ibn ʿAdī (d. 974; *GCAL* 2: 233–49; *CMRBH* 2: 390–438; Coquin 1993: 71f.), Sāwīrus Ibn al-Muqaffaʿ (d. *c.*1000; *GCAL* 2: 300–18; *CMRBH* 2: 491–509; Coquin 1993: 75), Elias of Nisibis (d. 1043; *GCAL* 2: 177–84; *CMRBH* 2: 727–41; Coquin 1993: 68), Abū l-Faraj ʿAbd Allāh Ibn al-Ṭayyib (d. 1043; *GCAL* 2: 160–76; *CMRBH* 2: 667–97; Coquin 1993: 68), had first-hand knowledge of contemporaneous trends in *falsafa* and *kalām* and in many cases established personal ties with Muslim *mutakallimūn* and *falāsifa*.

For the exponents of the Syriac and Copto-Arabic Renaissances of the thirteenth century these earlier authors of Christian-Arabic literature were central points of reference and figure prominently in their writings. Indeed, some of their writings were effectively 'rediscovered' during this period (Sidarus 2010a: 331). Now, however, these earlier authors were read in conjunction with the more recent proponents and detractors of Avicennian thought. From the vantage point of many Christian scholars of the twelfth and thirteenth centuries these new intellectual trends were strongly reminiscent of their own Hellenic and Hellenistic heritage of theological discourse; to some extent they even conveyed the impression of returning to a familiar, though completely overhauled and refurbished home. This sentiment was aptly captured by Barhebraeus in his *Chronography* (*Chronography*, 1: 91f.; vol. 2, fo. 98a–b):

> And there rose among them (*scil.* the Muslims) philosophers, mathematicians, and physicians who surpassed the ancient [sages] by the precision of their knowledge. The only foundations on which they set up their buildings were Greek houses; the buildings of wisdom which they erected were great by reason of their highly polished diction, and their greatly skilled investigations. Thus it has happened that we, from whom they (*scil.* the Muslims) have acquired wisdom through translators, all of whom were Syrians, find ourselves compelled to ask for wisdom from them.

It was precisely this supposedly Christian complexion of the new philosophizing tendency in Islamic theology and the traditional affinity of Christian theology with the legacy of ancient and late ancient philosophical doctrines that prompted some Muslim *mutakallimūn* of the late eleventh and twelfth centuries to oppose it, because they feared that it would lead to a creeping Christianization of Islamic religious doctrine and

> pervert Islam into something like what Christianity became in relation to the religion of Jesus. The leading proponents [of the Christian doctrine] were inclined towards the Greeks in philosophy, to the point that they modelled the religion of Jesus upon (the docrines of) the philosophers. (Rukn al-Dīn Ibn al-Malāḥimī, *Tuḥfa*, 4)

II The Christian Reception of Fakhr al-Dīn al-Rāzī in Ayyūbid Syria and Egypt

The reception of an Avicennizing Islamic theology among Syriac and Coptic Christians was mediated first and foremost through the works of Fakhr al-Dīn al-Rāzī (d. 606/1210). For scholars of all religious denominations they became templates for a new philosophico-theological discourse and structural and conceptual models on which they would form their own philosophico-theological compositions (Schwarb 2014b: 144–8). In this respect 'the son of the orator from Rayy' (*Ibn Khaṭīb al-Rayy*), as he would be called by his contemporaries, clearly outweighed the role played by the works of earlier representatives of a 'philosophizing' Ashʿarite theology, including Abū Ḥāmid al-Ghazzālī (d. 505/1111).

Already during his lifetime Rāzī was perceived as an outstanding mediator who brilliantly succeeded in creating a synthesis of two purportedly incompatible systems of thought, Avicennian philosophy and the science of *kalām*. Over the course of the thirteenth century he emerged as 'the pre-eminent figure among modern scholars and the master of the intellectual vanguard' (*afḍal al-muta'akhkhirīn wa-Sayyid al-ḥukamā' al-muḥdathīn*; Ibn Abī Uṣaybiʿa, *ʿUyūn*, 2: 23) of all religious denominations. His writings would now figure prominently in many private and public libraries of Muslims and non-Muslims. For though several *mutakallimūn* before Rāzī had pointed to the benefit of logic and select *philosophoumena* for solving aporias inherent in the *Kalām* system, it was his extensive critical exposition of Avicennian thought that served as an ultimate catalyst for the introduction of Peripatetic logic, *falsafa*, and sciences into the curriculum of the *madrasa*; it made theologians and jurists read, refute, defend, or refine the works of Ibn Sīnā and his epigons and showed how they could be assimilated with the fundamentals of their creed and theological doctrine (Endress 2006; Schwarb 2014c).

The fostering of a Shāfiʿite-Ashʿarite alliance under the Ayyūbids was another decisive factor for the spread of Ashʿarite *kalām* and the diffusion of Rāzī's works in Syria, Egypt, and Yemen. Two of our principal sources for the intellectual life during the Ayyūbid era, Barhebraeus's *Tārīkh mukhtaṣar al-duwal* (254.14–17) and Ibn Abī Uṣaybiʿa's *ʿUyūn al-anbā'* (2: 29.31–2), point to multiple Ayyūbid connections with Fakhr al-Dīn al-Rāzī and his intellectual legacy. Rāzī's *Ta'sīs al-taqdīs* (= *Asās al-taqdīs*), a treatise on the rationalist interpretation (*ta'wīl*) of the Qur'ān, was commissioned by al-Malik al-ʿĀdil (r. 596/1200–615/1218), the brother of Ṣalāḥ al-Dīn, and accordingly opens with a dedication to the Ayyūbid ruler (Rāzī, *Asās*, 339). Some of Rāzī's students became prominent scholars in the entourage of Ayyūbid rulers. Shams al-Dīn ʿAbd al-Ḥamīd b. ʿĪsā al-Khusrawshāhī (d. 652/1254), who according to Ibn Abī Uṣaybiʿa counts among Rāzī's most eminent disciples (*min ajalli talāmidhatihi*), instructed al-Malik al-Nāṣir Dāwūd (d. 624/1227), the Ayyūbid sultan of Kerak and later Damascus, in the rational sciences (*al-ʿulūm al-ḥikmiyya*) and played a major role in promoting Ibn Sīnā's and Rāzī's writings among Shāfiʿī jurists in the Ayyūbid domain (*ʿUyūn*, 2: 173.1–174.7; Ibn Wāṣil, *Mufarrij*, 4: 206). Significantly, al-Khusrawshāhī's promotion of Rāzī's work came at the expense of his arch-rival, Sayf al-Dīn al-Āmidī (d. 631/1233), who had been a favourite of al-Nāṣir's father, al-Malik al-Muʿaẓẓam ʿĪsā (r. 597/1201–615/1218 resp. –624/1227) and prior to Khusrawshāhī's arrival was regarded as the principal teacher of logic, natural philosophy, and philosophical theology in Damascus. Al-Āmidī, who had studied Avicennian philosophy with Jewish and Christian teachers in the Karkh quarter of Baghdad, was a renowned critique of Fakhr al-Dīn whom, in Khusrawshāhī's view, 'he was unable to match'.

Another influential student of Fakhr al-Dīn al-Rāzī who promoted his teacher's work in Egypt was Afḍal al-Dīn Abū ʿAbd Allāh Muḥammad b. Nāmawār al-Khūnajī (d. 646/1249) (Ibn Abī Uṣaybiʿa, *ʿUyūn*, 2: 120f.; *GAL* I^2: 607; *GAL* S 1: 838). In Ayyūbid

Yemen, too, the reception of Ashʿarite *kalām* in general and the works of Fakhr al-Dīn in particular gained currency over the seventh/thirteenth century not only among the Shāfiʿites of Lower Yemen, but also among Rāzī's Zaydī detractors in the highlands of northern Yemen. Shams al-Dīn al-Baylaqānī, who taught logic and Ashʿarite *uṣūl* at the Manṣūriyya *madrasa* in ʿAden, was a direct student of Fakhr al-Dīn.

In Iraq, it was Kamāl al-Dīn ibn Yūnus's (d. 639/1242) teaching of Avicennian philosophy and Rāzī's works which was of paramount importance to Syrian Christians. After his studies at the Niẓāmiyya *madrasa* in Baghdad Ibn Yūnus spent his life teaching at a succession of colleges in Mosul. To his students belonged not only many leading figures of thirteenth-century intellectual history, such as Athīr al-Dīn al-Mufaḍḍal b. ʿUmar al-Abharī (d. 660–3/1263–5) and Naṣīr al-Dīn al-Ṭūsī (d. 672/1274), but also several Jews and Christians to whom he apparently taught not only the works of al-Fārābī, Ibn Sīnā, Abū l-Barakāt al-Baghdādī and Fakhr al-Dīn al-Rāzī, but also the philosophical exegesis of Torah and Gospels (Ibn Khallikān, *Wafayāt*, 5: 312.19–313; Barhebraeus, *Tārīkh*, 273.4–17; Takahashi 2002b: 148 n. 3).

In what follows I will allege a few examples for the reception of Fakhr al-Dīn al-Rāzī during the Renaissance of Syriac and Copto-Arabic literature. It is but a first step towards a more comprehensive source analysis of this literature (Schwarb forthcoming), but sufficient to demonstrate the significance of Christian religious thought to an adequate understanding of parallel developments in Islamic theology during the post-classical period.

(a) Awlād al-ʿAssāl

The protagonists of the 'Renaissance' of the Copto-Arabic literature were four (half-) brothers of a prestigious Coptic family from Old-Cairo (Wadīʿ 1997a; Sidarus 2013a). For several generations it provided secretaries and high-level officials in the administration (*Dīwān al-Daraj, al-Inshāʾ, al-Juyūsh*) of the Ayyūbid state and played an active role in the civic, cultural, and ecclesiastical life of the Coptic community, leading the faction of New Cairo against the conservative demeanour of the clerical establishment in Fusṭāṭ-Miṣr (Wadiʿ 1985). The exact order of the half-siblings remains a matter of dispute, but the available data would suggest that al-Asʿad Abū l-Faraj and Ṣafī l-Dawla Abū l-Faḍāʾil were sons from their father's first marriage and thus born in the late 1180s and 1190s, while al-Amjad Ibn al-ʿAssāl (d. *c.*1260) and Muʾtaman al-Dawla Abū Isḥāq Ibrāhīm were born into the second marriage (for alternative views see Wadīʿ 1985: 31–79; 1997a: 81–89.124; Samir 1985: 9–22). Three of the four brothers became scholars of great renown, while the fourth (al-Amjad) occupied senior positions in the Ayyūbid administration and became an important patron of his brothers and their entourage and the Coptic community as a whole. For most exponents of the Copto-Arabic Renaissance the libraries of the ʿAssāl brothers in Cairo and Damascus became important resources of knowledge. The library of al-Asʿad (*al-Khizāna al-Asʿadiyya*), for instance, was also used by Abū Shākir Ibn al-Rāhib and Abū l-Barakāt Ibn Kabar (Wadīʿ 1997a: 91f. nn. 41–3).

Al-Amjad owned at least two precious libraries, one in his multi-storey house in Ḥārat Zuwayla (New Cairo), the other in his Damascus residence. Both libraries renownedly contained many rare manuscripts, in particular works by East- and West-Syrian and Melkite authors (Wadīʿ 1997a: 66 n. 73). Numerous manuscripts in al-Amjad's library were copied by Gabriel, a monk of Syrian origin, who for over fifteen years had served as his private scribe. He was also the private tutor of al-Amjad's son, Fakhr al-Dawla, and assisted the scholarly projects of his patron's brothers. In the 1250s and 60s Gabriel was the candidate of the ʿAssāl brothers and the notables of New Cairo for the Patriarchate, but it was not until 1268 that he was consecrated as Patriarch Gabriel III (Sidarus 1975: 23; Samir 1985: 624–8; Swanson 2010: 97–100; Wadīʿ 1997a: 66 n. 73).

(b) Al-Asʿad Abū l-Faraj Hibat Allāh Ibn al-ʿAssāl (d. before 1259)

Al-Asʿad socialized with the highest echelons of the Ayyūbid government and is likely to have occupied an official position within the state administration. This would help to explain his frequent travels to Syria and Yemen which afforded him with opportunities to purchase manuscripts (Wadīʿ 1997a: 89–96). Al-Asʿad is best known for his translation of the four Gospels from Coptic into Arabic, which he completed in Damascus in 650/1252–3 (ed. Moawad 2014). His aforementioned library (*al-Khizāna al-Asʿadiyya*) contained many manuscripts written in his hand (Sidarus 1975: 172; 2010b: 143f.; Wadīʿ 1997a: 91f.). At the behest of his brother al-Amjad he composed in 628/1231 a *Maqāla fī l-nafs*, an abridgement of which was later incorporated into the sixtieth chapter of *Majmūʿ uṣūl al-dīn* by his half-brother al-Muʾtaman (see Section II.d). The treatise offers a typology and doxographical summary of philosophical and theological views on the subject of the soul. Among al-Asʿad's sources figure Ibn Sīnā, Fakhr al-Dīn al-Rāzī, and Maimonides (Wadīʿ 1997a: 93f.; Schwarb 2007:14–15; 2014a: 118–23).

(c) Ṣafī l-Dawla Abū l-Faḍāʾil Mājid Ibn al-ʿAssāl (d. *c.*1260)

Al-Ṣafī was the most prolific and prominent figure of the Awlād al-ʿAssāl (*GCAL* 2: 388–403; *CMRBH* 4: 538–51 with further references; Samir 1985; 1987; Wadīʿ 1985, 1987, 1997a: 97–116). Most, if not all of al-Ṣafī's theological, philosophical, and polemical works as well as his *Nomocanon* (*al-Majmūʿ al-Ṣafawī; Majmūʿ al-qawānīn*), the influential legal compilation of the Coptic church, were written in the late 1230s and 1240s during the Patriarchate of Cyril (Kīrillus) III (Dāʾūd b. Yuḥannā al-Fayyūmī) Ibn Laqlaq (1235–43; *CMRBH* 4: 320–4; Swanson 2010: 83–95; Werthmuller 2010) and the ensuing seven-year vacancy (1243–50; Swanson 2010: 88–95). Al-Ṣafī was an arduous copyist; several works by earlier Christian and Muslim authors have only survived on account of his excerpts and summaries (*GCAL* 2: 240f., 247; Wadī' 1997a: 108–15; Samir 1987: 174f.). To many of these excerpts he would later add glosses and explanatory notes (*al-Ḥawāshī al-Ṣafawiyya*) which became an important source for his later works and are frequently quoted in the *Majmū'* of his younger half-brother al-Mu'taman (see Section II.d). Like his brothers he was a passionate collector of rare manuscripts. In the 1230s he resided over a longer period in Damascus to collect source material for his *Nomocanon* which displays definite influence from Islamic law in terminology, structure, and conceptualization. His manuscript collection included several autograph copies of Yaḥyā b. 'Adī's writings as well as Ibn 'Adī's copy (dated 311/923) of al-Nāshi' al-Akbar's (d. 293/906) *K. al-Awsaṭ fī l-Maqālāt* (ed. van Ess 1971: 76–87; Thomas 2008: 35–77; *CMRBH* 2: 85–8; Wadī' 1997a: 120f., §§ 52–3). Ibn 'Adī, whom al-Ṣafī used to call 'Shaykhunā' (e.g. *Ṣaḥā'iḥ*, 5, 20), occupies a very special position in his writings. It is worth recalling here that Ibn 'Adī was an eminent detractor of Abū l-Ḥasan al-Ash'arī's thought and as such was also well known to and quoted by Fakhr al-Dīn al-Rāzī (*CMRBH* 2: 390–438; Endress 1977: 57f., 73–81, 89f.; Platti 2004; Wisnovsky 2012: 321–4). The ubiquitous presence of Rāzī in al-Ṣafī's writings can be illustrated with the following two examples:

al-Ṣaḥā'iḥ fī jawāb al-naṣā'iḥ (= *al-Ṣaḥā'iḥ fī l-radd 'alā l-naṣā'iḥ*, *CMRBH* 4: 542–4; Graf 1910: 64–70; Wadī' 1997a: 104f.) was written in refutation of *K. al-Radd 'alā l-Naṣārā* by Abū l-Ḥasan 'Alī b. Sahl Rabbān al-Ṭabarī (*c.*780–*c.*860), the famous East-Syrian physician who late in his life converted to Islam (*CMRBH* 1: 669–74). The treatise comprises fifteen chapters. The first introductory chapter mentions the main sources of the *Ṣaḥā'iḥ*, including Ibn Sīnā and Fakhr al-Dīn al-Rāzī, chapters two and three advance ten methodological and doctrinal principles; the remaining twelve chapters comprise the refutation proper which follows the order of al-Ṭabarī's *Radd* (Wadī' 1997a: 104; Samir 1983). In the eighth methodological principle (ed. 20) al-Ṣafī refers to Rāzī as 'one of the most perspicacious of modern savants' (*min aṣdaq al-muta'akhkhirīn 'ilm*^{an}), while Plato is accorded the honour of being 'one of the most exquisite philosophers of antiquity' (*min afḍal al-mutaqaddimīn falsafat*^{an}). In chapter 3 (ed. 30) al-Ṣafī quotes a short passage from Rāzī's refutation of the Christian doctrine (*al-faṣl al-thāmin fī l-radd 'alā l-Naṣārā*) in *K. Nihāyat al-'uqūl wa dirāyat al-uṣūl* (*hākadhā qāla Ibn al-Khaṭīb fī Kitāb Nihāyat al-'uqūl*), introducing Rāzī as 'one who writes on philosophical topics as well as on the fundamentals and branches of their religious doctrine' (*wa-huwa muṣannif fī l-falsafa (wa-)uṣūl dīnihim wa-furū'ihi*). In response to Rāzī's critique of the trinity doctrine he writes:

> Just as it is possible to say of a person that he is perceiving, thinking and speaking without that this turns him into three separate beings and just as philosophers like Ibn al-Khaṭīb say of God that He is being, knowing and omnipotent, the Christians cannot be blamed for describing the divine as being Father, Son and Holy Spirit. There is a difference in wording (*lafẓ*), but not in meaning (*ma'nā*).

Nahj al-sabīl fī takhjīl muḥarrifī l-injīl (= *al-Radd ʿalā l-Jaʿfarī*; *CMRBH* 4: 548f.; Wadīʿ 1997a: 104f.) comprises a summary and refutation of *K. Takhjīl muḥarrifī l-Injīl* (= *Takhjīl man ḥarrafa l-Tawrah wa-l-Injīl*) by Taqī al-Dīn Abū l-Baqāʾ Ṣāliḥ b. al-Ḥusayn al-Jaʿfarī (d. 668/1270) which draws on ʿAlī b. Rabbān's aforementioned *K. al-Radd* as well as on other early Muslim literature on Christianity and had a significant impact on later Muslim authors writing on Christianity (*CMRBH* 4: 480–5). The *Nahj* was written at the behest of the patriarch Cyril III and consists of a preface (*muqaddima*) and five *qawāʿid* which correspond to five arguments against the Christian doctrine adduced in the *Takhjīl* that had only been touched upon in the *Ṣaḥāʾiḥ*. Within the refutation of the third *qāʿida* al-Ṣafī quotes at length from his otherwise lost refutation of the aforementioned chapter against Christianity (*al-Faṣl al-thāmin fī l-radd ʿalā l-Naṣārā*) in Rāzī's *Nihāyat al-ʿuqūl* (*Jawāb al-radd ʿalaynā fī kitāb Nihāyat al-ʿuqūl, wa-hādhihi nuskhatuhu: […]*) (*Nahj*, 34–6). The citation comprises two short lemmata from the *Nihāya* (ed. Fūda i:554) followed by the corresponding replies. In reply to Rāzī's claim that there was no difference between Christ and other prophets with regard to miracles, al-Ṣafī first refers to his refutation of al-Nāshiʾ al-Akbar (*Jawāb al-Nāshiʾ al-Akbar* = *Jawāb ʿAbd Allāh al-Nāshiʾ fī l-Maqālāt* = *al-Radd ʿalā K. al-Maqālāt lil-Nāshiʾ* = *Ijābat al-Nāshiʾ*) and then to his summary of Rāzī's *K. al-Arbaʿīn* (*Mukhtaṣar K. al-Arbaʿīn*). A summary and refutation of the ninth *masʾala* of *K. al-Arbaʿīn* (*al-masʾala al-tāsiʿa fī annahu taʿālā yastaḥīlu an taḥulla dhātuhu fī shayʾin wa-yastaḥīlu an taḥulla ṣifatun min ṣifātihi fī shayʾin*) is found in an appendix of some manuscripts of the *Ṣaḥāʾiḥ* (Mss. Vat., BAV, Ar. 38, fos. 118v–125v; Florence, Biblioteca Medicea Laurenziana, Or. 299, fos. 131r–141r; *CMRBH* 4: 547; Wadīʿ 1997a: 105 with n. 82, p. 186, § 21) and quoted in full in chapter 40 of al-Muʾtaman's *Majmūʿ* (*al-shakk al-wārid (/al-shukūk al-wārida) min al-imām Fakhr al-Dīn Ibn al-Khaṭīb (raḥimahu llāh) ʿalā l-ittiḥād wa-jawāb al-shaykh (/al-akh al-fāḍil) al-Ṣafī (raḥimahu llāh) fī l-masʾala al-tāsiʿa min Kitāb al-Arbaʿīn*). Al-Ṣafī's reply is divided into eight paragraphs which aim at establishing Christ's divinity and the necessity of God's incarnation in Christ on rational and scriptural grounds.

(d) Muʾtaman al-Dawla Abū Isḥāq Ibrāhīm Ibn al-ʿAssāl (d. after 1270)

The honorific title 'Muʾtaman al-Dawla' suggests that the younger half-brother of al-Asʿad and al-Ṣafī occupied some official position in the Ayyūbid administration (*GCAL* 2: 407–14; *CMRBH* 4: 530–7; Wadīʿ 1998, no. 51; 1997a: 125–76, 184–9). During the patriarchate of Cyril III Ibn Laqlaq (1235–43) he apparently acted as the patriarch's secretary (Wadiʿ 1997a: 65, 101, 104). For longer periods of time he resided in Damascus (Wadiʿ 1997a: 131). He was also in Damascus in 658/1260, the year which marks the end of the Ayyūbid control over the city, when his library was looted in the course of anti-Christian riots (Wadiʿ 1997a: 138–45). In that year he wrote *K. al-Tabṣira al-mukhtaṣara* (= *Maqāla mukhtaṣara fī uṣūl al-dīn*), an apologetical enchiridion defending the fundamental Christian doctrines for use of his co-religionists in Damascus (*CMRBH* 4: 532f.;

Wadiʿ 1997a: 170–3). In the preface to this treatise (*Tabṣira*, 101–4) he refers to his plan to dedicate a more comprehensive work to these subjects. This plan was implemented in his *opus magnum*, entitled *K. Majmūʿ uṣūl al-dīn wa-masmūʿ maḥṣūl al-yaqīn*, a comprehensive theological *summa* in five parts and seventy chapters, which he completed between 1265 and 1275 (Wadīʿ 1997a: 177–89; Sidarus 2008: 350). The work draws on a plethora of Christian and non-Christian sources (Wadiʿ 1997a: 184–9; 1990–1). While many of them are explicitly mentioned and acknowledged, the book also contains numerous unmarked quotations and paraphrases. '*al-Imām al-ʿālim Fakhr al-Dīn Ibn al-Khaṭīb*' is by far the most cited non-Christian author in the *Majmūʿ* (Wadīʿ 1997a: 188, § 27). The following conspectus lists but the most important quotations from Rāzī's works:

Chapter 2 offers an introduction to the basics of logic which is mainly based on Najm al-Dīn al-Kātibī's *al-Risāla al-Shamsiyya*, but also includes quotations from Rāzī's *K. al-Maʿālim* (e.g. 1: 47f., §§ 4f.; 1: 68–70, §§ 122–9).

Chapter 3 on God's essence and divine attributes largely consists of extracts from *K. al-Arbaʿīn* (e.g. 1: 71–5, §§ 4–22) and Abū l-Barakāt al-Baghdādī's *K. al-Muʿtabar* (1: 80–94, §§ 48–104).

In Chapter 4 on the createdness of the world al-Muʾtaman quotes *K. (al-Masāʾil) al-Khamsīn* (1: 109–111, §§ 67–79); *K. al-Arbaʿīn* (1: 102–4, §§ 36–42; 1: 104–7, §§ 44–59; 1: 107f., §§ 60–3).

Chapter 5 on intellect and soul, form and matter, and human agency (*fī l-ʿaql wa-l-nafs wa-l-jism wa-l-ṣūra wa-l-hayūlā wa-afʿāl al-insān*) contains a lengthy quotation from *K. al-Maʿālim fī uṣūl al-dīn* VIII:9 (1:121, §§ 32–37) and two long passages from *K. al-Arbaʿīn* (1: 116–20, §§ 11–29; 1: 124f., §§ 52–7). Rāzī's deterministic concept of human agency is rejected, whereas the rival Muʿtazilī doctrine is said to be identical with the correctly understood Christian position (Schwarb 2014c). A century later the same passage (i.e. *masʾala* no. 22 of *K. al-Arbaʿīn*) was incorporated into a chapter (*fī l-qaḍāʾ wa-l-qadar*) of *K. al-Ḥāwī al-mustafād min badīhat al-ijtihād* by al-Makīn Jirjis Ibn al-ʿAmīd (the younger). In the *Majmūʿ* the quotation is followed by a cross-reference (1: 125, § 58) to chapter 56 (2: 330–69; *Bāb al-qaḍāʾ wa-l-qadar*).

Chapter 6 deals with issues of abrogation and quotes among others *K. al-Arbaʿīn* (1: 127, § 3) and *K. al-Maʿālim fī uṣūl al-fiqh* (1: 140–4, §§ 70–88).

Chapter 7 adduces arguments based on reason and Scripture to establish the authenticity of the Christian tradition and quotes Rāzī's definition of *al-khabar al-mutawātir* from *K. al-Arbaʿīn* (1: 151f., §§ 16–18) and *K. al-Maʿālim fī uṣūl al-fiqh* (1:161f., §§ 59–66).

Chapter 17 cites the ninth *masaʾla* of *K. al-Masāʾil al-khamsīn* (1: 354, § 8) and *K. al-Mabāḥith al-mashriqiyya* (1: 354f., §§ 9f.) which he ranks among Rāzī's most splendid works (*min ajalli kutubihi*).

Chapter 18 includes a short quotation from *Nihāyat al-ʿuqūl* (1: 377, § 15).

Chapter 40 cites al-Ṣafī's aforementioned summary and refutation of Rāzī's *K. al-Arbaʿīn* (2: 142–50, §§ 3–33).

Two long sections in Chapter 51 on angelology are quotations from *K. al-Arbaʿīn* (2: 248–57, §§ 37–64, 73–99).

Chapter 54 on repentance incorporates a quotation from *K. al-Maʿālim* (2: 319f., §§ 77–81).

K. al-Arbaʿīn is again a central source for matters of eschatology. In chapter 62 (2: 423–6, §§ 4–14), for instance, he quotes *mas'ala* 30 (*fī l-maʿād*).

(e) Al-Rashīd Abū 'l-Khayr Ibn al-Ṭayyib (d. after 1270)

Al-Rashīd was a contemporary and confidant of al-Muʾtaman in Damascus where he acted as priest and physician and as secretary of a certain al-Tiflīsī (*GCAL* 2: 344–8; *CMRBH* 4: 431–7; Khouzam 1941; Schwarb 2007: 24–39; 2014a: 127–41; Wadīʿ 1997b; Zanetti 2003).

The exact use of Fakhr al-Dīn al-Rāzī's works in the *Tiryāq al-ʿuqūl fī ʿilm al-uṣūl al-musammā bi-Kashf al-asrār al-khafiyya min asbāb al-Masīḥiyya* (*GCAL* 2: 345; Khouzam 1941) and in *Khulāṣat al-īmān al-masīḥī* still awaits close analysis (Schwarb 2014b: 146; Schwarb forthcoming). Previous research has focused on citations from *K. al-Maʿālim* and Maimonides's *Guide* found in the annex to several manuscripts of the *Tiryāq*. In a postface to the *Khulāṣa* Abū l-Khayr writes that 'this entire book has only been written in response to those Muslims and Jews who inquired after the Christians' creed about God' and then adds that in order to explain to Jews and Muslims the underlying rationale of the doctrines of incarnation and trinity

> it seemed natural to me to quote against the followers of both religious communities statements by their most important authorities to confront (or: defeat) them with it, ... so that by virtue of the statements of the most important authority of their nation they will realise that the Christian religion tallies with the divine intentions in spiritual matters and rational methods.

While Maimonides was rated as 'the most important authority' of the Jews, his Muslim equivalent was Fakhr al-Dīn al-Rāzī. Both authors are extensively quoted in both the *Tiryāq* and the *Khulāṣa* which essentially depend on their works, though allegedly only for the sake of his pedagogical objectives. At times, his critique of Rāzī and Maimonides is but a fig-leaf for forthright anti-Muslim and anti-Jewish polemic.

Rāzī is also the main source of al-Rashīd's *Risālat al-Bayān al-aẓhar fī l-radd ʿalā man yaqūl bi-l-qaḍāʾ wa-l-qadar* (= *Risāla fī l-maʿād*) (ed. Khouzam, 1938). Al-Muʾtaman Ibn al-ʿAssāl inserted a summary of this treatise in chapter 56 of his *Majmūʿ* (*al-qawl fī l-qaḍāʾ wa-l-qadar, Majmūʿ*, 2: 338–47, §§ 36–72). Both al-Rashīd and al-Muʾtaman fail to acknowledge that the treatise is nothing but a summary and critique of the first *mas'ala* of the third part (*al-Kalām fī l-afʿāl*) of Rāzī's *K. al-Muḥaṣṣal* supplemented with scriptural prooftexts that are meant to bolster his position (Schwarb 2014b: 150–64). In this *mas'ala* Rāzī discusses human agency and factors affecting the freedom and autonomy of human actions, scathingly criticizing the Muʿtazilī position. In many respects al-Rashīd's critique of Fakhr al-Dīn amounts to a defence of the Muʿtazilī position.

(f) Nushūʾ al-Khilāfa Abū Shākir ibn al-Sanāʾ Abī l-Karam Buṭrus al-Rāhib Ibn al-Muhadhdhab (*c.* 1210–95)

Ibn al-Rāhib belonged to the Banū l-Muhadhdhab, another prominent and powerful Cairene Coptic family of notables, clergies, and officials of the Ayyūbid administration (*CMRBH* 4: 471–9; Sidarus 1975, 2013a). His father, al-Shaykh al-Sanāʾ [Abū l-Majd Buṭrus b. al-Muhadhdhab] al-Rāhib, was twice in charge of the State finances and enjoyed a high standing among Muslim notables. For several decades he was a key manipulator of ecclesiastical politics within the Coptic community and during a nineteen-year vacancy of the Patriarchate (1216–35) he de facto acted as interim patriarch and played an active role in the conflict surrounding the election of patriarch Cyril III ibn Laqlaq (1235–43; Swanson 2010: 83–95; Werthmuller 2010). Abū Shākir started his ecclesiastical career as deacon of the *Muʿallaqa* church in Old Cairo around the middle of the century. At about the same time he occupied a high position in one of the Ayyūbid *dawāwīn* and for a period acted as official representative (*raʾīs*) of the Christian communities vis-à-vis the Ayyūbid government. He was a close associate of the ʿAssāl brothers whom he sided with against his father in the quarrels for the Patriarchate. The period of his literary activity was limited to the years between 1257 and 1271.

Fakhr al-Dīn al-Rāzī is again a key source of Ibn al-Rāhib's theological works, including *K. al-Shifāʾ fī kashf mā statara min lāhūt sayyidinā l-masīḥ wa-khtafā*, a comprehensive christological-exegetical work, written in 1267–8, *Maqāla fī ḥadath al-ʿālam wa-qidam al-Ṣāniʿ* (Sidarus 2011a, b), and most importanly *K. al-Burhān fī l-qawānīn al-mukmala wa-l-farāʾiḍ al-muhmala*, an extensive philosophico-theological compilation in fifty *masāʾil* (Sidarus 1975, 2006, 2009, 2010b) which draws on a large variety of Muslim sources (Sidarus 2010b: 151–6, §§ 21–6), including al-Fārābī (*ʿUyūn al-masāʾil*), Ibn Sīnā (*ʿUyūn al-ḥikma*), al-Ghazālī (*Maqāṣid al-falāsifa, Iḥyāʾ ʿulūm al-dīn*), al-Khūnajī (*Mūjiz*), al-Kishshī (*Muqaddima fī l-ḥikma wa-l-manṭiq*).

A long section of thirteen *masāʾil* on the divine attributes (*mas.* 28–40; Ms. Vat., BAV, ar. 104, ff. 119ᵛ–183ʳ) consists of a patchwork of rearranged and partly rephrased excerpts from Rāzī's *K. al-Arbaʿīn fī uṣūl al-dīn* supplemented with Ibn al-Rāhib's own comments and insights (*al-jawāb/al-tafsīr li-muṣannifihi*). These chapters amount to a comprehensive attempt at construing Christian trinitarianism in terms of the *kalāmic* doctrine of God's unicity (*tawḥīd dhātihi wa-tathlīth ṣifātihi*) and evincing the compatibility of the two doctrines. In the majority of cases Ibn al-Rāhib gives the precise reference to the passage cited from *K. al-Arbaʿīn*, indicating the number of the *masʾala* and at times also the number of the subsection (*faṣl/nawʿ*) (Sidarus 1975: 104–7, 134f.). Occasionally, these citations from *K. al-Arbaʿīn* include second-hand quotations from works by other Muslim *mutakallimūn*, as for instance in *masʾala* 33 (*fī kawnihi taʿālā ḥayyᵃⁿ*, Ms. Vat., BAV, ar. 104, f. 157ᵛ) where Ibn al-Rāhib quotes from *masʾala* 14 of *K. al-Arbaʿīn* (*Arbaʿīn*, 1: 218) which in turn 'cites' the famous Muʿtazilī scholar Abū l-Ḥusayn al-Baṣrī (d. 436/

1044) (Sidarus 1975: 135, n. 50; misidentified as an East-Syrian Christian scholar in *GCAL* 2: 177; *BDIC* 1976: 202f.; *CMRBH* 2: 665–6).

Apart from *K. al-Arbaʿīn*, which is the main source of several other chapters in *K. al-Burhān*, Ibn al-Rāhib also cites Rāzī's *al-Āyāt al-bayyināt* (*fī ʿilm al-manṭiq*) (Sidarus 2010b: 154–6). A large number of Muslim authors are also quoted in Ibn al-Rāhib's *K. al-Tawārīkh* (Sidarus 2013).

(g) Shams al-Riʾāsa Abū l-Barakāt Ibn Kabar (d. 1324)

Abū l-Barakāt likewise belonged to a renowned and wealthy family of Coptic notables and state officials (*GCAL* 1: 389 and 2: 438–45; *CMRBH* 4: 762–6; Saleh 1982). On several occasions he occupied the position of personal secretary of the Emir Rukn al-Dīn Baybars al-Manṣūrī (d. 1325). Presumably as a consequence of an anti-*dhimmī* edict issued by al-Malik al-Ashraf in 1293 he had to abandon his public functions and applied himself to the study of Coptic philology and religious sciences. In 1300 he was ordained priest at the *Muʿallaqa* Church, assuming the priestly name 'Barṣawmā'. His influential *K. Miṣbāḥ al-ẓulma fī īḍāḥ al-khidma* (ed. Samir, Cairo 1971), a monumental and systematic ecclesiastical compilation, was most probably written during the last three decades of his life. Only the first four (out of twenty-four) sections (*abwāb*) of the *Miṣbāḥ* are dedicated to the Christian doctrine and sacred history. They are partly based on works by al-Ṣafī and al-Muʾtaman Ibn al-ʿAssāl and al-Rashīd Abū l-Khayr Ibn al-Ṭayyib and contain several indirect quotations from Rāzī's writings. Such secondary quotations may also be found in *K. al-Jawhara al-nafīsa fī ʿulūm al-kanīsa*, a significant exposition of Coptic ecclesiology in 115 chapters, written towards the end of the same century by Yūḥannā b. Abī Zakariyyā Ibn Sabbāʿ (*CMRBH* 4: 918–23). The *Jawhara* frequently quotes from Ibn al-Rāhib's *K. al-Burhān*.

(h) al-Makīn Jirjis Ibn al-ʿAmīd (the younger)

He is a grand-nephew of the namesake, but better-known historian of the thirteenth century, al-Makīn Jirjis Ibn al-ʿAmīd (the elder) (1206–92; *CMRBH* 4: 566–71), with whom he has often been confused. The Banū l-ʿAmīd were a wealthy Coptic family of merchants of Syrian origin (Sidarus 2013a). By the late thirteenth and early fourteenth centuries the social context of the Coptic aristocracy had changed insofar as many of its members had by then coverted to Islam to preserve their social privileges (El-Leithy 2005; Little 1990; Wadīʿ 1997a: 89f. n. 35). To these 'Muslim Copts' belonged Jirjis's brother, al-Asʿad Ibrāhīm, who served as a *kātib* in the Mamlūk *Dīwān al-Juyūsh*. Jirjis himself was a physician and Coptic priest (*GCAL* 2: 450–3; Coquin 1993: 86; *CMRBH* 5; Sidarus in press; Wadīʿ 1999: 5–24). His main work, *K. al-Ḥāwī al-mustafād min badīhat al-ijtihād = Mukhtaṣar al-bayān fī taḥqīq al-īmān* (Cairo, 1999–2001) has been characterized as a loosely structured 'philosophico-theological reflection on a great spectrum of religious questions, highly speculative and dialectic, at times apologetic, at others polemic, then again merely exegetical or hermeneutic' (Sidarus 2008: 348).

On a few occasions the *Ḥāwī* quotes from Rāzī's works (Swanson 2014). A lengthy unmarked quotation from the 22nd *mas'ala* (*fī khalq al-afʿāl*) of *K. al-Arbaʿīn* (*Arbaʿīn*, 1: 319–21), which—as we have seen—had already been quoted in chapter 5 of al-Muʾtaman Ibn al-ʿAssāl's *Majmūʿ* (1: 124f., §§ 52–7), is incorporated in the lengthy chapter on *al-qaḍāʾ wa-l-qadar* (*Ḥāwī*, 1: 168–85). In this passage (*Ḥāwī*, 1: 180–2) Rāzī refers to Abū l-Ḥasan al-Ashʿarī and some major exponents of the early Ashʿariyya, such as al-Bāqillānī and Abū Isḥāq al-Isfarāʾīnī (misread by the editor as 'al-Istiqrāʾī'), and, once again, to the Muʿtazilī Abū l-Ḥusayn al-Baṣrī. The reception history of this chapter can be traced up to the twentieth century when the Coptic hegumen Daniel Dāʾūd (d. 1961) inserted a long quotation of it in his *K. al-ʿUqūd al-luʾluʾiyya fī sharḥ ʿaqāʾid wa-afḍaliyyat al-masīḥiyya*. The *Ḥāwī* also contains a long marked quotation from Rāzī's *K. al-Maʿālim* (*nubayyinu baʿḍa mā dhakara Fakhr al-Dīn Ibn al-Khaṭīb*) in the section on the soul (*taḥqīq wujūd al-nafs al-ʿāqila min jihat al-taḥqīq al-naẓarī*, *Ḥāwī*, 2: 15–19).

III The 'Syriac Renaissance'

Similar to the Copto-Arabic Renaissance, the slightly earlier upsurge of literary activity in Syriac during the twelfth and thirteenth centuries, which affected East and West Syrians alike, was characterized by the growing influence of the surounding Islamic and Arabic literature and culture (Teule 2010: 23–8). The protagonists of the Syriac Renaissance, such as Patriarch Michael I (d. 1199), Dionysius Bar Ṣalībī, Jacob Bar Shakkō, Ishoʿyahb Bar Malkon, Barhebraeus, and ʿAbdishoʿ of Nisibis were driven by the endeavour to create a new type of scientific literature in Syriac and to forge the older Syriac materials with the more recent philosophical and scientific works written in Arabic.

(a) Jacob Bar Shakkō (Yaʿqūb b. Sakkā)

The work of Jacob (Severus) Bar Shakkō (d. 1241) had long been overshadowed by the fame of his younger contemporary, Gregory Barhebraeus (see Section III.b). Bar Shakkō lived in the monastery of Mar Mattay near Mosul. In Mosul he was one of several non-Muslim students of Kamāl al-Dīn Mūsā b. Yūnus who was renowned for his teaching of Avicennian philosophy and the works of Fakhr al-Dīn al-Rāzī (see Section II). According to Barhebraeus, Bar Shakkō had an extensive private library which after his death was transferred to the public treasury/library of the governor of Mosul (*CMRBH* 4: 240–4).

The two most important of his extant works clearly display his thorough acquaintance with a wide range of philosophical and scientific literature by Muslim authors: the *Book of Treasures* (*Ktābā d-sīmāṯā*), a theological compendium with apologetic outlook, contains several sections which are shaped on the model of parallel discussions in Muslim works (Teule 2007), while the *Book of Dialogues* displays his close familiarity with the scientific literature of his time, including Rāzī's *K. al-Mabāḥith al-mashriqiyya*, Abū l-Barakāt al-Baghdādī's *K. al-Muʿtabar*, and presumably the writings of al-Abharī (Takahashi 2006).

(b) Barhebraeus

Barhebraeus (ar. Jamāl al-Dīn Abū l-Faraj Ghrīghūriyūs b. Tāj al-Dīn Hārūn al-Malaṭī al-ʿIbrī, syr. Bar ʿEbrāyā, 1226–86; *CMRBH* 4: 588–609; Takahashi 2005) is the scholar who more than anybody else epitomizes the Syriac Renaissance and the familiarity of Syriac authors with Arabic and Muslim culture. He was exposed to Muslim philosophical and scientific literature early on when he studied logic and medicine in Tripoli. In 1264 he was appointed maphrian (representative of the patriarch for the eastern territories) of the Syrian Orthodox Church. While his official maphrianate residence was the monastery of Mar Mattay near Mosul where Bar Shakkō had lived, he travelled extensively and frequently stayed in Marāgha, Tabrīz, Baghdad, and Takrīt. In Marāgha he established personal ties with Muslim scholars in the ambit of Naṣīr al-Dīn al-Ṭūsī and possibly with Ṭūsī himself.

In the fields of philosophy and exact sciences Barhebraeus was largely influenced by Ibn Sīnā (Takahashi 2003), al-Ghazālī (Takahashi 2002b), Abū l-Barakāt al-Baghdādī (Takahashi 2002b), Fakhr al-Dīn al-Rāzī, and Naṣīr al-Dīn al-Ṭūsī. He translated long sections and entire works of Muslim scientific, philosophical, and spiritual works into Syriac (Takahashi 2005: 27ff., 96ff.). His *Candelabrum Sanctuarii* (*Mnāraṯ quḏshē*) is full of passages translated from Ibn Sīnā and Fakhr al-Dīn al-Rāzī (Takahashi 2002a, b). His *Cream of Wisdom* (*Butyrum sapientiae*) is manifestly based upon Ibn Sīnā's *Shifāʾ* and contains numerous references to Ibn Sīnā, Rāzī, and Ṭūsī. Of Rāzī he says (*Chronography*, 1: 366) that

> by him and by the great number of books which he composed the Arabs throughout the world have been enlightened and they are to this day. For I would compare this man [*scil.* Rāzī] to Origen, through whose books the doctors of the Church have become rich and illustrious, and they have turned round and called him a 'heretic'. Thus it is also with the Arabs, who call this man an 'infidel', and an adherent to Aristotelian doctrine.

(c) Dionysius Bar Ṣalībī, Ishoʿayb Bar Malkon, and ʿAbdishoʿ of Nisibis

For many other prominent representatives of the Syriac Renaissance, such as Dionysius Bar Ṣalībī (d. 1171; *CMRBH* 3: 665–70), Ishoʿayb Bar Malkon (d. 1246; *CMRBH* 4: 331–8), or ʿAbdishoʿ of Nisibis (ʿAbdishoʿ Bar Brikhā, ʿAbdishoʿ Ṣūbāwī, d. 1318; *CMRBH* 4: 750–61), a detailed source analysis of their extant writings is still pending.

References

Abū Shākir Ibn al-Rāhib (*Burhān*). *Kitāb al-Burhān* ('Livre de la Démonstration'): *Prolégomènes philosophiques et christologiques (QQ. 1–8)*. Ed. and trans. A. Sidarus. Rome: Biblioteca Apostolica Vaticana, 2013.

Barhebraeus (*Chronography*). *The Chronography of Gregory Abû'l Faraj, the Son of Aaron, the Hebrew Physician, Commonly Known as Bar Hebraeus: Being the First Part of his Political History of the World*. Trans. from the Syriac by Ernest A. Wallis Budge. London: Oxford University Press, 1932.

Barhebraeus (*Chronography*). Ms. Oxford, Bodleian, Hunt. no. 52.

Barhebraeus (*Tārīkh*). *Tārīkh mukhtaṣar al-duwal*. Ed. A. Ṣāliḥānī. Beirut: al-Maṭbaʿa al-Kāthūlīkiyya, 1958.

BDIC = *Bibliographie du dialogue islamo-chrétien*, in *Islamochristiana* 1 (1975)–15 (1989).

Becker, A. H. (2006). *Fear of God and the Beginning of Wisdom: The School of Nisibis and Christian Scholastic Culture in Late Antique Mesopotamia*. Philadelphia: University of Philadelphia Press.

CMRBH = D. Thomas et al. (eds.), *Christian-Muslim Relations: A Bibliographical History*. Leiden: Brill, 2009–.

Coquin R.-G. (1993). 'Langue et littérature arabes chrétiennes'. In M. Albert et al. (eds.), *Christianismes orientaux: Introduction à l'étude des langues et des littératures*. Paris: Les Éditions du Cerf, 35–106.

Davis, S. J. (2008). *Coptic Christology in Practice: Incarnation and Divine Participation in Late Antique and Medieval Egypt*. Oxford/New York: Oxford University Press.

Den Heijer, J. (2004). 'Les Patriarches coptes d'origine syrienne'. In R. Ebied and H. Teule (eds.), *Studies on the Christian Arabic Heritage in Honour of Father Prof. Dr. Samir Khalil Samir S.I. at the Occasion of his Sixty-Fifth Birthday*. Leuven: Peeters, 45–63.

Eddé, A.-M. (1995). 'Les Médecins dans la société syrienne du VIIe/XIIIe siècle'. *Annales Islamologiques* 29: 91–109.

Eichner, H. (2009). *The Post-Avicennian Philosophical Tradition and Islamic Orthodoxy: Philosophical and Theological Summae in Context*. Habilitationsschrift, University of Halle.

El-Leithy, T. (2005). *Coptic Culture and Conversion in Medieval Cairo, 1293–1524* A.D. 2 vols. Ph.D. dissertation, Princeton University.

Endress, G. (1977). *The Works of Yaḥyā ibn ʿAdī: An Analytical Inventory*. Wiesbaden: Reichert.

Endress, G. (2006). 'Reading Avicenna in the *Madrasa*: Intellectual Genealogies and Chains of Transmission of Philosophy and the Sciences in the Islamic East'. In J. E. Montgomery (ed.), *Arabic Theology, Arabic Philosophy. From the Many to the One: Essays in Celebration of Richard M. Frank*. Leuven: Peeters, 371–422.

van Ess, J. (1971). *Frühe muʿtazilitische Häresiographie*. Beirut: Deutsches Orient-Institut.

Fiey, J.-M. (1973). 'Coptes et Syriaques: contacts et échanges'. *Studia Orientalia Christiana Collectanea* 15: 297–365.

GCAL = G. Graf, *Geschichte der christlichen arabischen Literatur*. 5 vols. Città del Vaticano: Biblioteca Apostolica Vaticana, 1944–53.

Graf, G. (1910). *Die Philosophie und Gotteslehre des Jaḥjâ Ibn ʿAdî und späterer Autoren: Skizzen nach meist ungedruckten Quellen*. Münster: Aschendorff.

Griffel, F. (2007). 'On Fakhr al-Dīn al-Rāzī's Life and the Patronage He Received'. *Journal of Islamic Studies* 18: 313–44.

Historical Dictionary of the Coptic Church. Ed. G. Gabra, with contributions by B. A. Pearson, M. N. Swanson, and Y. N. Youssef. Lanham, MD: Scarecrow Press, 2008.

Ibn Abī Uṣaybiʿa (*ʿUyūn*). *ʿUyūn al-anbāʾ*. Ed. A. Müller. Königsberg: Selbstverlag, 1884.

Ibn Khallikān (*Wafayāt*). *Wafayāt al-aʿyān*. Ed. I. ʿAbbās. Beirut: Dār al-Thaqāfa, 1968–72.

Ibn Wāṣil (*Mufarrij*). *Mufarrij al-kurūb fī akhbār Banī Ayyūb*. Ed. Jamāl al-Dīn al-Shayyāl et al. Cairo: Maṭbaʿat Jāmiʿat Fuʾād I. and Maṭbaʿat Dār al-Kutub, 1953–[1975].

Khouzam, M. (1938). 'Abū l-Khayr Ibn al-Ṭayyib: Radduhu ʿalā l-qāʾilīn bi-l-qaḍāʾ wa-l-qadar'. *al-Ṣalāḥ* 9: 66–78, 131–7, 323–30.

Khouzam, M. (1941). *L'Illumination des intelligences dans la science des fondements: synthèse de l'enseignement de la théologie Copto-Arabe sur la révélation Chrétienne aux XIIIe et XIVe siècles d'après les écrits d'Abu-l-Khair ibn at-Tayyib and Abu'l-Barakat ibn Kabar*. Rome: Tip. Poliglotta 'Cuore di Maria'.

Little, D. P. (1990). 'Coptic Converts to Islam during the Baḥrī Mamluk Period'. In M. Gervers and R. J. Bikhazi (eds.), *Conversion and Continuity: Indigenous Christian Communities in Islamic Lands, Eighth to Eighteenth Centuries*. Toronto: Pontifical Institute of Mediaeval Studies, 263–88.

al-Makīn Jirjis Ibn al-ʿAmīd (the younger) (*Ḥāwī*). *K. al-Ḥāwī al-mustafād min badīhat al-ijtihād = Mukhtaṣar al-bayān fī taḥqīq al-īmān*. Ed. 'Rāhib min Dayr al-Muḥarraq'. 4 vols. (*ʿal-Mawsūʿa al-lāhūtiyya al-shahīra bi-ʾl-Ḥāwī*'). Cairo: Dayr al-Sayyida al-ʿadhrāʾ al-muḥarraq, 1999–2001.

MTQ = *Mawsūʿa min Turāth al-Qibṭ*. Ed. M. Asʿad. Cairo: Maktabat al-Rajāʾ, 2004.

Muʾtaman al-Dawla Abū Isḥāq Ibrāhīm Ibn al-ʿAssāl (*Majmūʿ*). *Majmūʿ uṣūl al-dīn wa-masmūʿ maḥṣūl al-yaqīn*. Ed. A. Wadīʿ. 2 vols. Cairo/Jerusalem: The Franciscan Centre of Christian Oriental Studies, 1998–9.

Muʾtaman al-Dawla Abū Isḥāq Ibrāhīm Ibn al-ʿAssāl (*Tabṣira*). *K. al-Tabṣira al-mukhtaṣara* (= *Maqāla mukhtaṣara fī uṣūl al-dīn*). Ed. K. Samir (forthcoming; see Wadiʿ 1997a: 173).

Platti, E. (2004). 'Yaḥyā ibn ʿAdī. Réflexions à propos de questions du kalām musulman'. In R. Ebied and H. Teule (eds.), *Studies on the Christian Arabic Heritage in Honour of Father Prof. Fr. Samir Khalil Samir S.I. at the occasion of his sixty-fifth birthday*. Leuven: Peeters, 177–97.

al-Rāzī, Fakhr al-Dīn (*Arbaʿīn*). *K. al-Arbaʿīn*. Cairo: n.p., 1986.

al-Rāzī, Fakhr al-Dīn (*Asās*). *Taʾsīs al-taqdīs* (= *Asās al-taqdīs*). Ed. A. E. al-Saqq. Cairo: Maktabat Kulliyyat al-Azhariyya, 1406/1986.

Rubenson, S. (1996). 'Translating the Tradition: Some Remarks on the Arabization of the Patristic Heritage in Egypt'. *Medieval Encounters* 2: 4–14.

Rukn al-Dīn Maḥmūd b. Muḥammad al-Malāḥimī al-Khwārazmī (*Tuḥfa*). *Tuḥfat al-mutakallimīn fī l-radd ʿalā l-falāsifa*. Ed. H. Ansari and W. Madelung. Tehran: Iranian Institute of Philosophy, 2008.

Ṣafī l-Dawla Abū l-Faḍāʾil Mājid Ibn al-ʿAssāl (*Nahj*). *Nahj al-sabīl fī takhjīl muḥarrifī l-injīl*. Ed. Marqus Jurjis. Cairo: Maṭbaʿat ʿAyn Shams, 1927.

Ṣafī l-Dawla Abū l-Faḍāʾil Mājid Ibn al-ʿAssāl (*Ṣaḥāʾiḥ*). *al-Ṣaḥāʾiḥ fī jawāb al-naṣāʾiḥ*. Ed. Marqus Jurjis. Cairo: Maṭbaʿat ʿAyn Shams, 1927 (a critical edition of chapters 1–3 is included in A. Wadīʿ's unpublished MA thesis *I Primi tre capitoli del libro* aṣ-Ṣaḥāʾiḥ fī ǧawāb an-Naṣāʾiḥ *d'aṣ-Ṣafī Ibn al-ʿAssāl; edizione critica preceduta da uno studio sulla vita, opere e influsso dell'Autore*. Rome: Pontifical Oriental Institute, 1983).

Saleh, A. H. (1982). 'Ibn Kabar'. *The Encyclopaedia of Islam.* New Edition. Supplement. Fascicules 5–6. Leiden: Brill, 388f.

Samir, K. (1983). 'La Réponse d'al-Ṣafī Ibn Al-ʿAssāl à la réfutation des chrétiens de ʿAlī al-Ṭabarī'. *Parole de l'Orient* 11: 281–328.

Samir, K. (1985). *Brefs Chapitres sur la trinité et l'incarnation*. Turnhout: Brepols.

Samir, K. (1987). 'Auteurs arabes chrétiens du XIIIe siécle'. (*BDIC*, septième partie.) *Islamochristiana* 13: 173–80.

Schwarb, G. (2007). 'Die Rezeption Maimonides' in der christlich-arabischen Literatur'. *Judaica: Beiträge zum Verstehen des Judentums* 63: 1–45.

Schwarb, G. (2014a). 'The Reception of Maimonides in Christian-Arabic Literature'. In Y. Tobi (ed.), *Ben ʿEver la-ʿArav: Contacts between Arabic Literature and Jewish Literature in the Middle Ages and Modern Times, Volume Seven: Maimonides and His World. Proceedings of the Twelfth Conference of the Society for Judaeo-Arabic Studies.* Haifa: The University of Haifa, 109–75.

Schwarb, G. (2014b). 'The 13th Century Copto-Arabic Reception of Fakhr al-Dīn al-Rāzī: Al-Rashīd Abū l-Khayr Ibn al-Ṭayyib's *Risālat al-Bayān al-aẓhar fī l-radd ʿalā man yaqūlu bi-l-qaḍāʾ wa-l-qadar'. Intellectual History of the Islamicate World* 2 i–ii, 143–69.

Schwarb, G. (2014c). 'The Reception of Ibn Sīnā and Avicennian Philosophy in Christian-Arabic Literature'. In A. Shihadeh and S. Rizvi (eds.), *Colloquium: Avicenna and Avicennisms.* London: The Neal A. Maxwell Institute for Religious Scholarship and the Brigham Young University London Centre (http://meti.mi.byu.edu/home/meti-info/2014-avicenna/ [accessed January 2016]).

Schwarb, G. (forthcoming). *Reaching beyond Religious Borders: The Reception of Maimonides (d. 601/1204) and Fakhr al-Dīn al-Rāzī (d. 606/1210) in Christian-Arabic Literature.*

Shams al-Riʾāsa Abū l-Barakāt Ibn Kabar (*Miṣbāḥ*). *Miṣbāḥ al-ẓulma fī īḍāḥ al-khidma*, vol. 1, ed. K. Samir. Cairo: Maktabat al-Kārūz, 1971.

Sidarus, A. Y. (1975). *Ibn ar-Rāhibs Leben und Werk: Ein koptisch-arabischer Enzyklopädist des 7./13. Jahrhunderts.* Freiburg i.Br.: Klaus Schwarz.

Sidarus, A. Y. (2006). 'Une justification du "monophysisme" due à un médecin-philosophe copte du XIIe/XIIIe siècle'. In A. Boud'hors et al. (eds.), *Études coptes IX: Onzième Journée d'études (Strasbourg, juin 2003).* Paris: De Boccard, 355–66.

Sidarus, A. Y. (2008). 'Encyclopédisme et savoir religieux à l'âge d'or de la littérature copte arabe (XIIIe–XIVe siècle)'. *Orientalia Christiana Periodica* 74: 347–61.

Sidarus, A. Y. (2009). 'Un débat sur l'existence de Dieu sous l'égide prétendue d'Alexandre le Grand: extrait d'une somme théologique copto-arabe du XIIIe siècle (Abū Shākir Ibn al-Rāhib, *Kitāb al-Burhān*)'. *Arabic Sciences and Philosophy* 19: 247–83.

Sidarus, A. Y. (2010a). 'La Renaissance Copte arabe du Moyen Âge'. In H. Teule et al. (eds.), *The Syriac Renaissance.* Leuven: Peeters, 311–40.

Sidarus, A. Y. (2010b). 'Les Sources d'une somme philosophico-théologique copte arabe (*Kitāb al-Burhān* d'Abū Šakir Ibn al-Rāhib, XIIIe siècle)'. *Miscellanea Bibliothecae Apostolicae Vaticanae* 17: 127–64.

Sidarus, A. Y. (2011a). 'À propos de deux textes sur la creation-contingence du monde transmis dans un recueil médiéval copto-arabe (Yaḥyā al-Naḥwī et Abū Šākir Ibn al-Rāhib)'. *Zeitschrift für die Geschichte der Arabisch-Islamischen Wissenschaften* 19: 121–34.

Sidarus, A. Y. (2011b). 'Notes sur la littérature médiévale chrétienne d'expression arabe'. *Mélanges de Sciences Religieuses*, 68 iii: 17–30.

Sidarus, A. Y. (2013a). 'Families of Coptic Dignitaries (*buyūtāt*) under the Ayyūbids and the Golden Age of Coptic Arabic Literature (13th Cent.)'. *Journal of Coptic Studies* 15: 189–208.

Sidarus, A. Y. (2013b). 'From Coptic to Arabic in the Christian Literature of Egypt'. *Coptica* 12: 35–56.

Sidarus, A. Y. (2014). 'Copto-Arabic Universal Chronography. Between Antiquity, Judaism, Christianity and Islam: The *K. al-Tawārīkh* of N. al-Khilāfa Abū Shākir Ibn al-Rāhib (655 Heg. / 973 Mart. / 1257 Chr. / 1569 Alex. / 6750 AM)'. *Collectanea Christiana Orientalia* 11: 221–50.

Swanson, M. N. (2010). *The Coptic Papacy in Islamic Egypt (641–1517)*. Cairo: The American University in Cairo Press.

Swanson, M. N. (2014). 'Christian Engagement with Islamic *kalām* in Late 14th-Century Egypt: The Case of *al-Ḥāwī* by al-Makīn Jirjis Ibn al-ʿAmīd "the Younger"'. *Intellectual History of the Islamicate World* 2 i–ii, 214–26.

Takahashi, H. (2002a). 'The Graeco-Syriac and Arabic Sources of Barhebraeus' Mineralogy and Meteorology in *Candelabrum of the Sanctuary*, Base II'. *Islamic Studies* (Islamabad) 41: 215–69.

Takahashi, H. (2002b). 'Barhebraeus und seine islamischen Quellen: *Têḡrāṯ têḡrāṯā* (*Tractatus tractatuum*) und Ġazālīs *Maqāṣid al-falāsifa*'. In M. Tamcke (ed.), *Syriaca. Zur Geschichte, Theologie, Liturgie und Gegenwartslage der syrischen Kirchen. 2. Deutsches Syrologen-Symposium (Juli 2000, Wittenberg)*. Münster/Hamburg/London: LIT Verlag, 147–75.

Takahashi, H. (2003). 'The Reception of Ibn Sīnā in Syriac: The Case of Gregory Barhebraeus'. In D. C. Reisman (ed.), *Before and after Avicenna: Proceedings of the First Conference of the Avicenna Study Group*. Leiden: Brill, 249–81.

Takahashi, H. (2005). *Barhebraeus: A Bio-Bibliography*. Piscataway, NJ: Gorgias Press.

Takahashi, H. (2006). 'Fakhr al-Dīn al-Rāzī, Qazwīnī and Bar Shakko'. *The Harp* 19: 365–79.

Takahashi, H. (2014). 'Reception of Islamic Theology among Syriac Christians in the Thirteenth Century: The Use of Fakhr al-Dīn al-Rāzī in Barhebraeus' *Candelabrum of the Sanctuary*'. *Intellectual History of the Islamicate World* 2 i–ii, 170–92.

Teule, H. G. B. (2007). 'Jacob Bar Shakkō, the Book of Treaures and the Syrian Renaissance'. In J. P. Monferrer-Salá (ed.), *Eastern Crossroads: Essays on Medieval Christian Legacy*. Piscataway, NJ: Gorgias Press, 143–54.

Teule, H. G. B. (2010). 'The Syriac Renaissance'. In H. G. B. Teule et al. (eds.), *The Syriac Renaissance*. Leuven: Peeters, 1–30.

Teule, H. G. B. (2012a). 'Christian-Muslim Religious Interaction 1200–1350: A Historical and Contextual Introduction'. In *CMRBH* 4: 1–16.

Teule, H. G. B. (2012b). 'Ishoʿyahb bar Malkon'. In *CMRBH* 4: 331–8.

Teule, H. G. B. (forthcoming). 'Barhebraeus and Islam'. In H. Ibrahim et al. (eds.), *Barhebraeus Symposium July 2010 Aleppo*.

Thomas, D. (2008). *Christian Doctrines in Islamic Theology*. Leiden: Brill.

Wadiʿ, A. (1985). 'Bibliografia commentata sugli Aulād al-ʿAssāl, Tre fratelli scrittori del sec. XIII'. *SOC Collectanea* 18: 31–79.

Wadiʿ, A. (1987). 'Vita e opere del pensatore copto al-Ṣafī Ibn al-ʿAssāl (sec. XIII)'. *SOC Collectanea* 20: 119–61.

Wadiʿ, A. (1990-1). 'Les Sources du *Majmūʿ uṣūl al-dīn* d'al-Muʾtaman Ibn al-ʿAssāl'. *Parole de l'Orient* 16: 227–38.

Wadiʿ, A. (1997a). *Dirāsa ʿan al-Muʾtaman b. al-ʿAssāl wa-kitābihi* 'Majmūʿ uṣūl al-dīn' *wa-taḥqīqihi*. Cairo and Jerusalem: Franciscan Press.

Wadiʿ, A. (1997b). 'Al-Rašīd Ibn Al-Ṭayyib et son *Tiryāq*'. *SOC Collectanea* 28: 271–84.

Wadiʿ, A. (1998). 'Introduzione alla Letteratura arabo-cristiana dei Copti (*Muqaddima fī l-adab al-ʿarabī al-masīḥī lil-Aqbāṭ*)'. *SOC Collectanea* 29/30: 441–92.

Wadiʿ, A. (1999). 'Al-Makīn Jirjis Ibn al-ʿAmīd wa-Tārīkhuhu'. In A. Wadiʿ (ed.), *Actes de la septième rencontre des amis du patrimoine arabe-chrétien (Aʿmāl al-nadwa al-sābiʿa lil-turāth al-ʿarabī al-masīḥī): al-Fajjāla, Le Caire, 25–26 février 1999*. Cairo: Franciscan Centre of Christian Oriental Studies, 5–24.

Werthmuller, K. J. (2010). *Coptic Identity and Ayyubid Politics in Egypt, 1218–1250*. Cairo: The American University in Cairo Press.

Wisnovsky, R. (2012). 'New Philosophical Texts of Yaḥyā Ibn ʿAdī: A Supplement to Endress' *Analytical Inventory*'. In F. Opwis and D. Reisman (eds.), *Islamic Philosophy, Science, Culture, and Religion: Studies in Honor of Dimitri Gutas*. Leiden: Brill, 307–26.

Yūḥannā b. Abī Zakariyyā Ibn Sabbāʿ (*Jawhara*). *al-Jawhara al-nafīsa fī ʿulūm al-kanīsa*. Ed. V. M. Mastrīḥ. Cairo: al-Markaz al-Faransiskānī li-l-Dirāsāt al-Sharqī al-Masīḥī, 1966; ed. and trans. J. Perier, *La Perle précieuse traitant des sciences ecclésiastiques (chapitres I–LVI) par Jean, Fils d'Abou-Zakariyâ, surnommé Ibn Sabâʿ*. Paris: Firmin-Didot, 1922. An edition of the remaining part is being prepared by S. K. Samir.

Zaborowski, J. R. (2008). 'From Coptic to Arabic in Medieval Egypt'. *Medieval Encounters* 14: 15–40.

Zanetti, U. (2003). 'Abū 'l Ḫayr Ibn al-Ṭayyib sur les icônes et la croix'. *Parole de l'Orient* 28: 667–701.

CHAPTER 32

THEOLOGY IN THE OTTOMAN LANDS

M. SAIT ÖZERVARLI

OTTOMAN Islamic theology was not a new phenomenon in the main Ottoman lands but rather a continuation of an existing religious culture established by the Anatolian Saljūqs (*Salājiqa-i Rūm*) since the sixth/twelfth century. Its scholarly investigation is still in its infancy. Modern studies on Ottoman theology date back to the early twentieth century when Mehmed Şerafeddin Yaltkaya (1879–1947) published a study on Turkish theologians (Yaltkaya 1932). Another late-period Ottoman scholar, Bursali Mehmed Tahir (1861–1926), includes about 550 theological book titles in his renowned bio-bibliographical work of Ottoman authors, *Osmanlı Müellifleri*. Moreover, the prominent historian İsmail Hakki Uzunçarşılı (1889–1977) regularly provides information on theological works in his *Osmanlı devletinin ilmiye teşkilâtı* as a part of his survey of the Ottoman educational system (Uzunçarşılı 1965), while Mustafa S. Yazıcıoğlu has more recently published in French on the place of *kalām* in Ottoman *madrasas* (Yazıcıoğlu 1990). There are also some recent Turkish monographs devoted to the thought of individual Ottoman thinkers (Sarıkavak 1998; Öçal 2000), but the existing literature falls short of providing a critical analysis of Ottoman Islamic theology in its historical context.

Rather than investigating Ottoman intellectual history from a predominantly modern point of view, as a dark age of pre-modernity, it should be examined in its historical context, as a continuation of and an expansion on Islamic culture and civilization. Moreover, attention will also be paid in the following sections to the Byzantine influence and to the contacts Ottoman thinkers entertained with representatives of other religious cultures throughout the centuries.

As will be shown in this chapter, the Ottomans engaged in a lively intellectual activity, especially during the fifteenth century during the reigns of Mehmed II (reigned 1444–6, 1451–81) and Bayezid II (reigned 1481–1512). This not only concerned the religious disciplines but also philosophy and science which led scholars of theology to criticize some earlier opinions and to integrate ideas developed by a variety of earlier schools, a pursuit that was continued during the sixteenth century during the reigns of Selim I (reigned 1512–20) and Süleyman I (reigned 1520–66). Thus, although authors of Ottoman *kalām* works followed the tradition of post-Ghazālian scholars in methodology and content, they added new approaches in argumentation, classification, and interpretation of the questions they dealt with. At the same time, however, the engagement of Ottoman scholarship in discursive theology did not remain uncontested. As was the case during most periods of Islamic history, a conservative minority among Ottoman scholars opposed any engagement in *kalām*, as well as the personalities and movements engaged in it. At the same time, *mutakallimūn* and their opponents tended to respect each other, partly because the rational sciences did play a prominent role in the Ottoman *madrasa* education.

Although officially being adherents of the Māturīdiyya, one of the two main Sunnī schools of rational theology, Ottoman theologians were significantly attracted and influenced by the thirteenth- and fourteenth-century representatives of the other major Sunnī school of theology, the Ashʿariyya. Their works allowed Ottoman theologians in fact to formulate a new synthesis between the two Sunnī schools. Moreoever, it was through the works of the later Ashʿarites that Ottoman scholars explored issues that were controversially discussed among Muslim theologians and philosophers. Whenever their views disagreed, however, with those of the Ḥanafiyya and the Māturīdiyya, the Ottomans opted for the traditional Ḥanafī/Māturīdī positions rather than for the opposing views of the Ashʿarites.

Scholars of the post-Ghazālian period beginning with Fakhr al-Din al-Rāzī (d. 606/1209) mixed notions of Sunnī theology with philosophy and they included in their works extensive discussions on physical and metaphysical issues as they originated with philosophy. As a result, theology now became a combination of Ashʿarite thought with Avicennan interpretation of Aristotelian philosophy, absorbing earlier Muslim philosophical tradition within its theological framework. Islamic theology was now less polemical and more comprehensive in scope, thematically as well as methodologically (Shihadeh 2005; Eichner 2009).

This broader approach towards theological as well as philosophical conceptions and discussions, that is characteristic for Fakhr al-Dīn al-Rāzī's synthesis of Ashʿarite *kalām* and philosophy, entered in an even more sophisticated period of interpretation by the fourteenth century. The theological writings of Shams al-Dīn al-Iṣfahānī (d. 749/1348), ʿAḍud al-Din al-Ījī (d. 756/1355), and his students Saʿd al-Dīn al-Taftāzānī (d. 793/1390) and Sayyid Sharīf al-Jurjānī (d. 816/1414)—mostly commentaries on earlier works—expanded on the views of al-Rāzī by comparing them to earlier Ashʿarite and Muʿtazilite notions, analysing their differences from or similarities to those of earlier Muslim philosophers, and finally arguing for their own positions. Ottoman theologians wrote countless commentaries on the writings of those four fourteenth-century Ashʿarite theologians, who hailed from Central Asia and Iran, and the significance of their works for the development of Ottoman theology can hardly be overestimated.

I Transmission of Islamic Theology from Anatolian Saljūqs to the Ottomans

The Ottomans erected their culture upon the heritage of the Anatolian Saljūqs, with notable Byzantinian and East European influences. Anatolia especially during the thirteenth century attracted scholars from the Arab and Persian regions seeking refuge to teach and work under better conditions (Robinson 1997). It was particularly in the aftermath of the Mongol invasion of Iran and Iraq and their threat towards Mamluk Syria and Egypt that well-known scholars, such as the mystic thinker Jalāl al-Dīn al-Rūmī (d. 672/1273), found safe havens in Anatolian towns, or *bilād al-Rūm* as they were then called. Ṣadr al-Dīn al-Qūnawī (d. 673/1274), Sirāj al-Dīn al-Urmawī (d. 682/1283), and Quṭb al-Dīn al-Shirāzī (d. 710/1311) were other influential scholars who taught in pre-Ottoman Anatolian *madrasas*. The most renowned scholar who came to Anatolia was philosopher and logician Athīr al-Dīn al-Abharī (d. 663/1265), some of whose writings were repeatedly commented upon by later Ottoman scholars. The Twelver Shīʿī Nāsir al-Dīn al-Ṭūsī (d. 672/1274) was also influential in Ottoman scholarship through his *Tajrīd al-ʿaqāʾid*, a work that was popular among Shīʿīs and Sunnīs alike.

There are three important developments that shaped the evolution of classical Ottoman scholarship: the establishment of the first Ottoman teaching institution (*medrese/madrasa*) by Orhan Gazi (reigned 1324–59) in Nicea (1331), the foundation of the Fatih Mosque and Complex (Fatih Camii ve Kulliyesi) with eight *madrasas* by Mehmed II in Constantinople (1471), and the foundation of the Suleymaniye, named after Suleyman the Magnificent (1557). These three institutions generated a body of elite theologians and jurists that shaped the intellectual life of the Empire's classical age. Although informal teachings began earlier in various towns under the supervision of personalities like Şeyh Edebali and Tursun Fakih, the advisers of the eponymous founder of the Ottoman dynasty Osman I (d. after 1326), a more organized religious and scientific type of scholarship began in Nicea. The *madrasa* included in the Orhaniye Complex in Nicea was headed by Dāwūd al-Qayṣarī (Davud Kayseri) (d. 751/1350), who had studied post-Ghazalian theology with his first teacher al-Urmawī in Kayseri and who was well acquainted with Ibn al-ʿArabī's philosophical mysticism with its notion of unity of existence (*waḥdat al-wujūd*) through his studies in Iran with ʿAbd al-Razzāq al-Kāshānī (d. 730/1329). Davud also wrote a commentary on al-Jurjānī's *Sharḥ al-Mawāqif* and dealt with various philosophical issues in separate treatises, such as the concept of time in his *Nihāyat al-bayān wa-dirāyat al-zamān* criticizing the views of Aristotle and the independent philosopher Abū l-Barakāt al-Baghdādī (d. after 560/1164–5). The district of Kayseri, where Davud came from, was home to the earliest *madrasas* in Anatolia and along with Konya it constituted one of the two important Saljūq cities of learning.

The number of Ottoman *madrasas* increased during the reigns of Bayezid I, Mehmed I, and Murad II, the most noteworthy examples of which are the Sultaniye, Yeşil, and Muradiye *madrasas* in Bursa, as well as the Darülhadis and Üç Şerefeli *madrasas* in Edirne. Among the scholars of the fourteenth century, Shams al-Dīn Muḥammad Fenārī (d. 834/1431), a typical representative of the Ottoman scholarly tradition, was the most important. Fenārī began his studies in Bursa and then moved to the Iznik *madrasa*. Later he went to Aksaray, a town in the region of Karaman, where Jamāl al-Dīn al-Aksarayī (d. 789/1388), a descendant of Fakhr al-Dīn al-Rāzī, taught in the Zincirli *madrasa*. It is noteworthy that Aksarayī followed the ancient Greek practice in his *madrasa* by dividing his students into three levels: the first group consisted of young students whom he taught on the way from his place to the *madrasa* (*mashshā'iyyūn*, 'Peripatetics'); the second were the more advanced students whom he taught under the pillars of the *madrasa* (*riwāqiyyūn*, 'Stoics'); the third were the mature students whom he taught in the interior of the *madrasa*. Fenārī is reported to have studied among the *riwāqiyyūn*. *Madrasas* in the small Anatolian towns such as these helped to transfer Saljūq Islamic thought to the Ottoman capital. Moreover, they served as a meeting place for Ottoman students with scholars and teachers who hailed from Central Asia. From Karaman, Fenārī went to Egypt where he studied with Akmal al-Dīn al-Bābartī (d. 785/1384) who introduced him to the Ḥanafite/Māturidite tradition. While in Egypt, Molla Fenārī also met al-Jurjānī, another student of al-Bābartī at the time. This direct encounter between Fenārī and al-Jurjānī is remarkable, especially in view of the large number of commentaries that were later composed by Ottoman scholars on al-Jurjānī's works. Following his return from Egypt at the end of the eighth/fourteenth century, Fenārī was appointed as a teacher at the Manāstir *medrese* in Bursa and served as the judge (*kadı*) of Bursa. Later Fenārī was appointed as Grand Mufti (*şeyhülislam*) of the Ottoman lands, the highest position of Ottoman religious authority, which was established during the 1420s by Murad II.

Fenārī's writings include a commentary on Ṣadr al-Dīn al-Qūnawī's *Miṣbāḥ al-uns*. In it, Fenārī mixes mysticism with Avicennan notions and post-Ghazalian theology, and he discussed nature and other topics that were not typically included in theological works of earlier periods. Fenārī also commented upon al-Ījī's *Jawāhir al-kalām*, a summary of *al-Mawāqif*, as well as on al-Jurjānī's *Sharḥ al-Mawāqif*. He also wrote a short treatise, *'Awīsat al-afkār* (MS Süleymaniye Library, Kasidecizade, no. 675/6), in the course of which he discussed issues such as causality, which was extensively debated among theologians and philosophers. He also criticized some Muʿtazilite views that were controversial such as God's transcendence (*tanzīh*), His obligation to act in man's best interest (*aṣlaḥ*), or the reality of the non-existent (*ma'dūm*). Being a prolific scholar who covered a wide range of disciplines, including theology, philosophy, and mysticism, Fenārī came to serve as a model for later Ottoman scholars during the fifteenth and sixteenth centuries.

Ottoman theologians were also influenced by Byzantinian thinkers and entertained intellectual exchanges with Christian and Jewish theologians. The Ottoman conquerors are commonly acknowledged for not having purged Constantinople from its Byzantinian and Greek heritage following their conquest of the city on 29 May 1453 and for having forged close relations with their non-Muslim subjects. Mehmed II (reigned 1451–81) re-established the Patriarchate and asked the Christian Greek community in Constantinople to elect a church leader. The Church Fathers named Georgios Kourtesios Scholarios (d. before October 1474), known as Gennadius II, as the new Patriarch. The Sultan visited Gennadius II at the monastery of Pammakaritos, discussed with him at length on Christianity, and requested him to write a clear book on the Christian faith. Gennadius Scholarius subsequently composed his famous *Confession of Faith*, which was later translated into Arabic and Ottoman Turkish (Todt 2013).

Patriarch Maxim III (served 1476–82) was also requested to prepare an exegesis of the Creed, which was subsequently also translated into Arabic and read by the Sultan (Patrinelis 1971). More interestingly, the Greek theologian and philosopher George of Trebizond had the ambition to reconcile Islam and Christianity and to create a kind of 'Ottoman Christianity'. Apart from other writings that he had dedicated to the Sultan, he composed a book titled *On the Truth of the Christian Faith to the Emir when He Stormed Constantinople*, and presented it to the Sultan, suggesting its translation and comparison with the principles of the Qurʾān (Monfasani 1984).

The relation with non-Muslim theologians during the fifteenth century was not restricted to the Greeks. Accompanied by Ottoman scholars, the Sultan held frequent meetings and discussions with representatives of other religious communities and he supported their publishing initiatives in their respective languages on issues of faith. For example, a leading member of the fifteenth-century Jewish community in Istanbul, Mordechai ben Eliezer Comtino (1402–82), a renowned Rabbanite philosopher, philologist, mathematician, and astronomer, wrote a Hebrew commentary on Maimonides's *Dalālat al-ḥāʾirīn* (*Guide of the Perplexed*), completed in 1480, a copy of which is extant in Topkapi Palace Library (Ms. no. GI 53), and he is known to have entertained contacts with contemporary Ottoman Muslim theologians (Ayalon 2010). It is also noteworthy that the Grand Vizier Mahmud Pasha officially ordered Latin commentaries of Avicenna for the Jewish physician Jacopo da Gaeta from Ragusa in 1465 (Raby 1983). Interest in Greek and Western thought also created a sympathy and admiration among some Byzantine humanists of the fifteenth century, such as Georgius Gemistos Plethon (1355–1452), Georgios Amirutzes (1400–70), Georgios of Trebzinod (1394–1473), and Michael Critobolus of Imbros (*c.*1410–70) (Badenas 2001). The Ottomans' interest in both Eastern and Western traditions was therefore evident and it comprised virtually all disciplines of learning, such as theology and philosophy as well as geography and history. These relations and interactions encouraged Ottoman theologians to learn more about other religions and to refer to Greek and Judaeo-Christian sources in their own writings.

II Growth of Ottoman Theological Thought

Having Fenārī and the intellectual environment of his time as their model, a group of well-trained Ottoman scholars and judges emerged during the reign of Mehmed II, most of whom were based in Bursa, Edirne, and Istanbul, the three most highly regarded centres of learning. Fenārī's successor, the Grand Mufti Mehmed b. Armağan, known as Yegan, was the teacher and father-in-law of Hızır Bey (Khiḍr Beg) of Sivriḥiṣār (d. 863/1458), who in turn led a circle of theologians in Bursa at the Sultaniye Medresesi. Although they continued in the tradition of their encyclopaedically trained predecessors, Hızır Bey and his three students Dervīş Hayālī (d. 875/1470), Hocazade (d. 893/1488), and Kesteli (d. 901/1495) should also be considered among the first representatives of a new type of Ottoman philosophical theology.

The Ottoman capital in particular had attracted scholars from other Muslim lands from an early period, especially during the reign of Mehmed II. Mehmed had invited prominent scholars in order to establish a scholarly community in Constantinople and to revive Islamic thought. Being a man imbued with intellectual ambitions similar to those of the early ʿAbbāsid caliph al-Maʾmūn, he invited renowned scholars such as Alaaddin-i Tusi (ʿAlāʾ al-Dīn Ṭūsī) (d. 877/1472 or 887/1482) and Ali Kuşçu (Qūshjī) (d. 879/1474) and ordered others to compose new books or to translate works from 'classical languages'. Mehmed was interested in comparing the methodological differences among theologians, philosophers, and Sufis in their quest for truth and certainty, and he specifically invited ʿAbd al-Raḥmān al-Jāmī (d. 998/1492) to compare their methodologies in a systematic manner. Jāmī completed a short version of the book, *al-Durra al-fākhira* (*The Precious Pearl*), which arrived in Istanbul only after the death of the Sultan (Heer 1979). It is worthwhile mentioning that Jāmī, who lived and wrote in Herat, specifically referred to Fenārī in this work comparing his views to those of others.

The majority of Ottoman scholars were occupied with commenting upon the works of al-Taftazānī and al-Jurjānī, a trend that continued over many generations. During the time of Bayezid II, interest in classical learning and theological debates continued unabated, with Ottoman scholars enjoying the privilege to freely criticize earlier Muslim thinkers as well as contemporary ones. Muslihuddin Kesteli (Muṣliḥ al-Dīn al-Qastalānī) (d. 901/1496), for example, in his *Risāla fī Ishkālāt Sharḥ al-Mawāqif* critically discussed al-Jurjānī's views on a number of philosophical issues, such as the possibility of necessary knowledge or the relations between essence and attributes etc. (Ms. Süleymaniye, Laleli, no. 3030). Kesteli's views, in turn, were debated and rejected by Hızır Bey's son Sinan Paşa (d. 891/1486) in another treatise (Ms. Köprülü, Asım Bey, no. 721). Other Ottoman theologians experienced less academic freedom. Molla Lutfi (d. 900/1494), for example, a critical and outspoken scholar, was sentenced to death and executed for his provocative lectures.

The interest of Ottoman scholars in philosophy and philosophical theology led them to revive the long forgotten tradition of the debate on the relation between theology and philosophy, which al-Ghazālī had initiated with his *Tahāfut al-falāsifa*. Two prominent scholars of ninth/fifteenth-century Istanbul, Hocazade (Khūjazāda) and Alaaddin-i Tusi, were commissioned to discuss the controversies between al-Ghazālī and the philosophers and to present their findings in writing. Both scholars accepted the invitation and completed their respective commentaries on al-Ghazālī's *Tahāfut* within six months. A scholarly committee examined and evaluated the two books. Numerous scholars of later generations composed super-commentaries on the two works. The *Tahāfut* debate fascinated Ottoman scholars of the time—the systematic comparison between the views of theologians and philosophers helped them to shape their own views (Özervarlı 2015). Public debates, as well as verbal and written contests on this topic, were popular among Ottoman scholarly circles of the period. These discussions prompted Ottoman theologians to formulate new syntheses and interpretations on these issues. As a result of their endeavour to compare and combine theology and philosophy they were exposed to new questions, contradictions, and ambiguities that prompted further explorations. Ottoman scholars continued to compare the views of theologians and philosophers up until the early twelfth/eighteenth century, when Mestcizade Abdullah b. Osman (Mastjizāda ʿAbd Allāh b. ʿUthmān) (d. 1148/1735) composed his *al-Masālik fī l-khilāfiyyāt bayn al-mutakallimīn wa-l-ḥukamāʾ* (ed. Seyid Bahçivan 2007).

The focus of Ottoman theologians who engaged in this kind of comparision was on philosophical questions rather than purely theological issues, as is indicated by their topical choices in short treatises devoted to specific subjects or partial commentaries on earlier works. In addition to this, they also composed systematic commentaries on earlier writings, a genre that comprised commentaries, super-commentaries, annotations, or epitomes of earlier works. Whereas modern scholars often dismissed the commentary literature as merely repetitive and devoid of any originality, many of them are in fact innovative in outlook and original in thought. As has been shown for the Greek commentary tradition of late antiquity (Sorabji 1990: 24–7), commentaries by Ottoman scholars should also be regarded as a continuous and original expansion of an earlier intellectual tradition that often yielded new insights. A Turkish translation of al-Taftāzānī's *Sharḥ al-ʿAqāʾid* by Sırri Giridi (Sirrī Pāsha Girīdī) (d. 1303/1895), for example, which includes selections from significant Ottoman super-glosses (*ḥāshiya*) on the text, such as Hayālī, Ramazan Efendi, ʿIsam, and Siyalkuti, gives evidence of the distinctive character of each one of them (Taftāzānī 1292 [1875]). Independent treatises by Ottoman scholars focused on a large variety of topics, such as existence/non-existence, necessity/contingency, reason/revelation, spirit/soul, faith/practice, etc. Another prominent topic that gave rise to a genre of its own during the Ottoman period was concerned with *ithbāt al-wājib*, the characteristic philosophical term for proving the existence of God.

In addition to the Eastern intellectuals who have been mentioned before, it was primarily Avicenna's oeuvre that indirectly influenced the thought of Ottoman scholars. It was mostly through Fakhr al-Dīn al-Rāzī's and Nāsir al-Dīn al-Ṭūsī's commentaries on Avicenna's *al-Ishārāt wa-l-tanbīhāt* that Central Asian thinkers of the fourteenth century and Ottoman intellectuals of the fifteenth century received views of Avicenna. Another purely philosophical work that was popular among Ottoman scholars was the *Hidāyat al-ḥikma* by Athīr al-Dīn al-Abharī (d. 663/1264). Many Ottoman as well as Imami scholars commented on the work, which contained detailed expositions of the Peripatetic understanding of logic, physics, and metaphysics.

A strong link with mystical traditions was another characteristic of Ottoman thought and theology. Despite their reservations about Sufi practices, scholars such as Davud-i Kayseri, Fenārī, and Kemalpaşazade (d. 940/1534) were significantly influenced by Sufi thought and highly regarded Ibn al-ʿArabī and his mystical philosophy (Zildzic 2012). In his *fatwā* on Ibn al-ʿArabī, Kemalpaşazade praises him as a perfect applicant of Islamic teachings and a virtuous guide, urging those who do not understand his teachings to remain silent rather than to voice disapproval (Winter 2007).

Vested with the authority as Grand Mufti of Suleyman the Magnificent, Kemalpaşazade made a substantial contribution to Ottoman theology by synthesizing various strands of thought. A student of philosophically minded scholars like Molla Lutfi (d. 900/1494) and Müeyyedzade (d. 922/1516), he was well trained in a large variety of Islamic disciplines. His oeuvre consists of more than 200 titles, in Arabic, Persian, Turkish, in a variety of fields, among them theology, Ottoman history, literature, and law. He was instrumental to adapting Ḥanafite law to the historical conditions of the Ottoman period. In addition, he was also one of the leading theorists behind the formulation of Ottoman orthodox beliefs and the Sunnī campaign against Shīʿism as a part of political rivalry with the Safavids, and he actively opposed any heterodox tendencies (Eberhard 1970; Al-Tikriti, 2005).

Most of Kemalpaşazade's commentaries and treatises were devoted to issues of philosophical theology, including questions of existence, causality, reason, faith, soul, predestination, human actions, heresy, etc. (Öçal 2000). Among pre-Ottoman and contemporary sources he frequently referred to Fakhr al-Dīn al-Razī, Naṣīr al-Dīn al-Ṭūsī, Najm al-Dīn al-Kātibī, Quṭb al-Dīn al-Rāzī, Saʿd al-Dīn al-Taftāzānī, Sayyid Sharīf al-Jurjānī, Jalāl al-Dīn al-Dawānī, Hocazade, and others. In view of his authority and his wide-ranging oeuvre, he is often labelled an 'Ottoman philosopher' or 'Anatolian Avicenna' in the historical-biographical sources.

For Kemalpaşazade, all existents—with the exception of the Necessary Existent—are 'contingent' (*mumkin*), their existence depending on something other than themselves. Apart from discussing the subject in his commentaries, he devoted at least four treatises to the issue of contingency, which he accepted as an inseparable quality of the essence of possible existents, which need a cause for coming into existence. In his discussion of ontology, Kemalpaşazade cited the views of earlier philosophers and theologians. Unlike most theologians he accepts the notion of mental existence (*al-wujūd al-dhihnī*) alongside real existence. Although his works were significantly influenced by al-Jurjānī's view on this issue, Kemalpaşazade found the latter's comments and replies to earlier Ashʿarite objections insufficient—al-Jurjānī maintained that the essence was not identical with either existence or non-existence and could thus not be denied. In a separate treatise on the issue, Kemalpaşazade argued for the distinction between existence and essence by employing a different argument. He claimed that during the process of integration of the essence to existence, the essence was qualified as neither existent nor non-existent; thus, they cannot be identical. He then discussed the possibility of an intermediary level between existence and non-existence, such as humanity in regard to human.

To prove the existence of God, Kemalpaşazade employed both cosmological and teleological proofs in his writings. As for *takfīr*, Kemalpaşazade refrained from accusing Muslim philosophers and mystics of unbelief despite his disapproval of heresy. He pointed out that the revealed books lack indeed clear statements about the createdness of the world and he stressed that knowledge about theological issues that is based on single traditions only cannot be regarded as completely certain, so that one should be cautious to condemn an opposing theological position as apostasy.

Kemalpaşazade's discussions of other theological questions, such as divine wisdom or man's freedom, show him to have a more flexible approach than that of the Ashʿarites. He distinguished between creating something that had evil aspects and willingly performing evil actions. Divine wisdom, he argued, required justice for all beings and entailed the use of every means provided it serves a good purpose, such as the use of poison as a remedy for certain diseases. If things were treated wisely and put in their proper place, this will ensure that all existent beings function well. Things or actions are not bad or evil per se, but only become so by means of a will attached to them through acquisition. Since Kemalpaşazade considered knowledge to be dependent on what is known; pre-eternal divine knowledge does not constitute an obstacle in his eyes for man's freedom to act. Thus, the general goodness within this system could not be undermined because of some particular or specific bad acquisitions.

The authority of Kemalpaşazade ensured the continuity of an open scholarly-minded atmosphere throughout the sixteenth century. Nevʿi Efendi Yaḥyā b. Pīr ʿAlī (d. 1007/1599), for example, unlike most contemporary thinkers, was known for his anti-atomism. In his *Natāʾij al-funūn*, a book written in Turkish on the classification of knowledge, he defended the divisibility of atoms (Nevʿi 1995). Although some Ottoman scholars opposed the study of theology for its dialectical and polemical character, it continued to be one of the major disciplines of central and regional Ottoman scholarship during the seventeenth and eighteenth centuries. Among the main representatives mention should be made of Beyazizade Ahmed (Bayadī zāda Aḥmad) (d. 1098/1687), Kara Halil Tirevi (Qara Khalīl Tīrawī) (d. 1123/1711), Abdülkadir Arif (ʿAbd al-Qādir ʿĀrif) (d. 1125/1713), Yanyalı Esad (Yanyavī Asʿad) (d. 1143/1730), ʿAbd al-Ghanī al-Nābulusī (d. 1143/1731), Mehmed Saçaklızade Marʿaşi (Muḥammad Sachaqlī zāda Marʿashī) (d. 1145/1732), Akkirmani Mehmed (Aq Kirmānī Muḥammad) (d. 1174/1760), Ebu Said Hadimi (Abū Saʿīd al-Khādimī) (d. 1176/1762), and İsmail Gelenbevi (Ismāʿīl al-Galanbawī) (d. 1205/1791).

Yanyalı Esad's contribution to Ottoman theology is particularly noteworthy. His theological works, especially those devoted to God's existence, are considered to be among the best in this field. Mention should be made of his *Hāshiya ʿalā Ithbāt al-wājib*, a commentary on earlier works on the proof for God's existence, primarily Jalāl al-Dīn al-Dawānī's treatise on the topic, as well as of his *Risāla al-Lāhūtiyya*. In this treatise, the author elaborated in a highly original manner on divine unity and the proofs for the existence of God.

Among the students of Yanyalı Esad were a number of non-Muslims, among them the Moldovian Prince Dimitrie Cantemir (1673–1723), John Mavrocordatos (1689–1719), and Chrysanthos Notaras (*c.*1663–1731), the Patriarch of Jerusalem (1707–31). Cantemir declared in his book, *The History of the Growth and Decay of the Ottoman Empire*, that he owes his Turkish and Islamic knowledge to Esad. There is also evidence for a continuing correspondence between Esad and his non-Muslim students when they left Istanbul to take up various positions. Esad's interest in different cultures is supported by a note on the cover of a manuscript copy of one of his books, *al-Taʿlīm al-thālith* (Ms. Istanbul University Library, Arabic Manuscripts, no. 4024, fo. 1a) testifying to his knowledge of other religions, from which even Christian and Jewish scholars had benefited greatly. It should be noted that the non-Muslim circle of students at the Academy of the Orthodox Patriarchate in Istanbul (known as the 'Great School') in the early eighteenth century were interested in Islamic thought and Arabic and Turkish languages. Esad Efendi also collaborated with non-Muslim scholars on other projects, such as translating commentaries on Aristotle into Arabic (Özervarlı 2011).

As I pointed out at the beginning of the chapter, although most of the Ottoman theologians especially in its early period were Ḥanafites, they did not confine themselves to Māturīdī doctrines, the dominant Sunnī theological school among the Ḥanafites. Ottoman theologians were rather deeply influenced by the writings of Ashʿarite thinkers from Central Asia and Iran, whose writings were well represented in the Ottoman lands and served as the primary texts on which Ottoman scholars wrote commentaries. The most popular of these were al-Jurjānī's *Sharḥ al-Mawāqif*, al-Taftazānī's *Sharḥ al-ʿAqāʾid*, al-Iṣfahānī's *Sharḥ al-Ṭawāliʿ* and *Sharḥ al-Tajrīd*, as well as Dawānī's *Sharḥ al-ʿAdūdiyya*. Some of these fourteenth-century Ashʿarite theologians were familiar with Māturīdī doctrines—they had debates with Māturīdīs, had commented on their writings, and were at times influenced by their ideas. This applies in particular to al-Taftāzānī whose *Sharḥ* is concerned with the *K. ʿAqāʾid* by the Māturīdī theologian ʿUmar al-Nasafī (d. 537/1142) and in the course of which its author endorsed some of al-Nasafī's theological views. Shams al-Dīn al-Iṣfahānī also commented on al-Nasafī's *ʿAqāʾid*. The named Ashʿarite authors and their writings appealed far more to the Ottomans than the writings of the later Māturīdī thinkers—in contrast to the Ashʿarites, the Māturīdī authors were engaged in the disputes between theology and philosophy rather than interactions. Influenced by hermeneutic and linguistic approaches of these Ashʿarites, Ottoman scholars strove to form an eclectic thought between Maturidism and Ashʿarism. In books devoted to the differences between Ashʿarism and Maturidism, the Ottoman authors emphasized that there was not much difference between the two schools, and that the existing differences were not doctrinal but rather verbal. In a number of key issues, however, the Ottoman theologians remained faithful to the doctrinal heritage of the Māturīdiyya, such as man's freedom to act or the issue of ethical subjectivism versus objectivism. The opposing Ashʿarite views were unacceptable in their eyes, whose adherents they characterized as semi-predestinists.

III Renewal of Islamic Theology in the Modern Ottoman Period

The renewal of theology as an attempt to reconcile religion with modernity began in the late Ottoman Empire as well as in other parts of the Muslim world. In the nineteenth century the classical theological curriculum lost its appeal and dynamism, since the new books were less sophisticated than those written in earlier centuries, and they failed to address the changed conditions of modernity. Nineteenth-century scholars were, however, aware of the traditional importance of theology for Islamic intellectual history, its close relationship with philosophy, and its adaptivity to new methodologies and ideas. This prompted them to recover—or rediscover—theology as the suitable discipline for their attempts to revitalize Islamic religious thought in order to meet the challenges of modern philosophy and science (Özervarlı 1999a and 2008).

Ottoman defenders of modernizing theological texts, such as Abdüllatif Harputi (ʿAbd al-Laṭīf al-Kharpūtī) (1842–1914) and Şeyhülislam Musa Kazım (Shaykh al-Islām Mūsā Kāzim) (1858–1920), argued that the use of modern scientific and philosophical methodologies was necessary in order to strengthen faith in Islam and to bring its disciplines up to date. In his *Tarih-i İlm-i Kelam* and *Tanqīḥ al-kalām* Harputi pointed out that Muslim theologians of earlier periods embarked on the study of philosophy whenever they felt this to be necessary. Theologians of today should do likewise and study philosophy through modern writings and select what was needed from them. According to Harputi, the theologians' methodology had constantly developed throughout Islamic history, and was now poised to enter a new stage with the introduction of modern scientific methods. Harputi was particularly interested in modern astronomy, which, he believed, would challenge the traditional religious idea of the universe, and he wrote a separate treatise on the harmony of new astronomical data with the Qurʾān and other revealed texts.

Similarly, Musa Kazım (1858–1920), one of the last Grand Muftis of the Ottoman era, wrote in his *Külliyat* an emphatic article on the need to reform Islamic theological texts, in which he accused scholars of blind rejection of Western ideas and of failing to meet the needs of the day. He considers reviewing the theological books in accordance with the needs of present times as the most pressing task of contemporary scholars. In order to achieve this goal, Kazım argues, theologians should know the views of the opponents to be able to present counter-arguments. When earlier scholars engaged in translating philosophical works into Arabic they deemed it necessary to reform theology and add new topics accordingly. Today there is a similar need to revive the efforts of scholars and to revitalize the discipline (Reinhart 2001; Kazım, 2002).

In a series of articles that appeared in the journal *Sebilürreşad* as well as in his major book *New Islamic Theology* (*Yeni İlm-i Kelam*) (published 1922–3), İzmirli İsmail Hakkı (Ismāʿīl Ḥaqqī) (1868–1946) joined the modernization efforts of his contemporaries more effectively and focused on the importance of rational thinking and the contribution of Islamic theology in particular. Historian of Turkish philosophy Hilmi Ziya Ülken emphasized that Hakkı successfully presented in his *Yeni İlm-i Kelam* medieval theological questions from a modern point of view. As evidence for the necessity for change in both the method and content, İsmail Hakkı listed examples of comparable turning points in the history of Islamic theology: in the twelfth century, Fakhr al-Dīn Rāzī's theology replaced al-Bāqillānī's because of the inadequacy of al-Bāqillānī's system vis-à-vis the new methodology in al-Rāzī's age. Therefore, al-Rāzī's theology, too, was to be replaced with a new formulation when it no longer met the needs of the age. Since Aristotelian philosophy, on which al-Rāzī depended, had collapsed in recent centuries, and a new, modern philosophy had emerged, Hakkı argued, al-Rāzī's theology was no longer adequate. Therefore, the scholars of modern Islamic theology should examine modern philosophy and select new ideas, arguments, and methods from various thinkers, provided that they fit the system of theological thought, while rejecting the materialistic ideas that were inappropriate to Islam.

Moreover, scholars of new theology, Hakkı suggested, should also stop using outdated scholastic methods that were no longer understood by the new generation; instead, they should employ the logic and method of modern thinkers such as Descartes. Similarly, instead of focusing on ancient schools such as Peripatetics and Stoics, much more attention should be paid to modern schools of thought such as Neo-Materialism, Positivism, Spiritualism, and others. In this way, Muslim theology would conform to contemporary philosophical subjects and develop according to contemporary needs. Underlying this approach was Hakkı's belief that the methods and presuppositions of theology were changeable from age to age, although its essentials and principles remained the same. Hakkı's methodology in fact led him to prefer rational interpretations in some theological issues. For instance, although he accepted the existence of miracles, he did not give great weight to these supernatural factors in his evaluation of Muḥammad's prophethood. For evidence of the truth of the Prophet's mission, he rather opted for a rationalist approach, referring to the civilizing effects of Islam on tribal Arab communities and later Muslim societies. Likewise, he wrote an essay questioning eternal punishment in the hereafter, using both rationalist and religious evidence (Özervarlı 2007a).

Despite promoting the use of philosophical discussions, İsmail Hakkı did not deem it appropriate to include purely natural sciences and astronomy in his proposed new theology. According to Hakkı, an intensive use of scientific theories and terminology would require such frequent renovation of theological texts that it risked surpassing its philosophical content. Moreover, science in the Middle Ages was contained within philosophy, and therefore, when earlier Muslim theologians imported and synthesized philosophical questions in their texts they inevitably had to deal with scientific questions of their time. But since science had gained its independence from philosophy and developed through experimental methods in modern times, contemporary theologians should not delve into scientific questions. It might only indirectly refer to some recent conclusions of science about particular questions when needed. İsmail Hakkı also considered it inappropriate to interpret Qurʾānic verses as scientific statements about the physical universe, since the Qur'ān was revealed to strengthen the faith of believers, but not to provide scientific information.

The main purpose of Hakkı's writing a new theology was to respond to the challenges of modern materialist thought. In this context, unlike previous attempts, he put his criticisms in a larger theological framework as was the case in his effort to reconstruct a modern theological theory in accordance with the requirements and developments of the new age. In his *Yeni İlm-i Kelam*, he stressed that in modern times materialism re-emerged partly with the ideas of Hobbes in England, and of Gassendi in France by the seventeenth century. The neo-materialists, Hakkı explained, regarded 'the knowledge about God' as 'the enemy of knowledge', while they saw no beginning for matter and motion. He criticized materialists for holding on to a mechanistic approach to natural laws despite contrary recent developments in physics and astronomy. Materialists, he argued, based their principles of nature on a strict determinism instead of teleological voluntarism, while explaining human psychological realities through mental functions of the body, thereby completely denying all spiritual dimensions of life.

Hakkı also discussed Comtean positivism, though to a lesser extent, which was the other influential movement among radical Ottoman thinkers, such as Ahmed Rıza (1859–1930). The positivists did not consider any source of knowledge other than physical senses, Hakkı explains, and therefore denied the ability of the human rational faculty to discover any absolute or transcendental notion. Contrary to the positivists, he questioned the unique role of the senses, emphasizing that human knowledge cannot be limited to the sensible world. He also disagreed with the rejection of unknown realities as well as the underestimation of the capacity of reasoning, arguing that ignoring questions related to the beginning and the end of existence would be a total loss for human knowledge. Hakkı, in fact, found Comte's division of the history of science into three periods quite remarkable, but he did not agree with him about the closeness of the age of religion and metaphysics. It should be remembered that social and biological theories of nineteenth-century European materialism and positivism had a broad impact on many Ottoman thinkers through numerous translations. What was peculiar about Hakkı was also underlying the task of modern Islamic theology to deal with the views of these schools and respond to them in a systematic philosophical way (Özervarlı 2007a). Other central Ottoman figures, such as Elmalılı Hamdi (1878–1942) and Said Nursi (1877–1960), followed this path of revitalization in Islamic theology and religious thought (Özervarlı 2006 and 2010).

Another different approach was presented by Mehmed Şerafeddin Yaltkaya (1879–1947), who aimed to establish a synthesis between theology and modern social sciences rather than philosophy. He called his project *Ictima-i Ilm-i Kelām*, or 'Islamic Social Theology'. Under the influence of Ziya Gökalp (1876–1924), who closely followed Durkheim's theory of religion, Şerafeddin argued that religious beliefs are activated by society and that the idea of sacredness, whether found in symbols or actions, derives from their social aspect. Therefore, in his view, there is a close link between the type of social assembly of society and the formation of traditional or religious beliefs. Mehmed

Şerafeddin also discussed the argumentation method and the employment of rational proof for the existence of God in classical *kalām*. Unlike classical Muslim theologians (*mutakallimūn*), Şerafeddin prefers to emphasize religious experience and the human inner capacity to believe in God rather than rational proofs (Özervarlı 1999b). This social approach to religion and theology was found to be too modernistic compared to the roots of historical theology by other modern theologians, such as İzmirli İsmail Hakkı (Özervarlı 2007b).

At the same time, scholars in other regions of the Ottoman world raised analogous points for reform in theological methods. In the Arab provinces, for instance, there was a vigorous movement and activity in discussing new approaches to theology. Egypt was semi-independent in the nineteenth century under Khedives and needs to be treated separately in the North African region for this purpose, but especially in Baghdad and Damascus, scholars like Maḥmūd Shukrī al-Alūsī (1857–1924) and Jamāl al-Dīn al-Qāsimī (1866–1914) revived a Salafī rationalism under the influence of Muhammad Abduh (1849–1905) of Egypt, whose *Risālat al-tawhīd* was considered one of the examples of modern *kalām*. Al-Alūsī in his polemical writings against the conservative scholar Yūsuf al-Nabhānī (1849–1932) emphasized the necessity of reasoning (*ijtihād*) and defended a theology based on the Qurʾān in the path of Ibn Taymiyya.

Jamāl al-Dīn al-Qāsimī, however, employed a more reformist structure compared to the classical theological texts. In the introduction to his *Dalāʾil al-tawḥīd* he presented his methodological basis in order to demonstrate the rational character of Islamic beliefs, describing reason as the mother of knowledge. Al-Qāsimī then adduced twenty-five proofs for the existence of God in the first chapter, and named human nature (*al-fitra*) as the first proof. Al-Qāsimī explained that despite its being necessary, the inner nature of the human being was a decisive argument, due to its openness to be relied upon, and its being unaffected by doubts and sceptical views. Referring to classical Muslim theologians and quoting numerous Qurʾānic verses, he emphasized the human being's need to believe, to trust, and to pray. Like other animal beings, humans swayed between hope and fear, he emphasized, and therefore needed a trustworthy being, especially when they were in desperate situations.

IV Opposition towards Philosophical Theology among the Ottomans

Throughout the history of the Ottoman Empire there was also criticism of and opposition to theology or philosophical thought, although such voices never gained the upper hand. In his encyclopedic work *Miftāh al-saʿāda*, Taşköprizade (d. 968/1561) discussed in the chapter on *ʿilm al-kalām* how some of the religious scholars of his time, relying on statements by earlier *ʿulamāʾ* directed against philosophical theology, dismissed those engaged with this discipline, and thus caused confusion and doubts in the minds of students about its merits. Taşköprizade argued that the opposition against theological philosophy in early Islam was restricted to opposition against the Muʿtazila and should not be generalized. Bemoaning how some circles banished theologians and disregarded them as *ʿulamāʾ*, Taşköprizade expressed the patent illogicality of recognizing those who work on the status of human actions as scholars, while ruling out those who mused over divine actions and attributes.

Katib Çelebi also recounts the resistance of some later scholars to the teaching of theology in the *madrasa* education. According to his report, during the reigns of Mehmed II, the scholars who integrated philosophy among the religious sciences were more popular, so that philosophical *kalām* books, such as *Ḥāshiyat al-Tajrīd* and *Sharḥ al-Mawāqif*, were part of the regular curriculum, but that later on they were replaced with legal works, as they were considered too philosophical (Katib Çelebi, *Balance*, 26). Moreover, even in popular poetry, reflections indicating the inferiority of theology and philosophy could be traced. The following lines from a traditional Ottoman scholar against rational disciplines can be an example: 'Are theology and philosophy worth a coin? | Would a clever critic bow (submit) to them'? (Katib Çelebi, *Balance*, 136; with a different translation). However, these remarks by Katib Çelebi, as well as similar comments by Gelibolulu Mustafa Ali (1541–1600), reflect a general sentiment rather than being based on precise information about the curriculum.

Opposition to theology and philosophy by some *fuqahāʾ* was not specific to the Ottoman period. Rather, similar phenomena can be encountered throughout Islamic history. That some Ottoman scholars of law were influenced by the reports of earlier authorities against philosophical/theological disciplines and became even more sceptical about its legitimacy amid an enthusiastic integration of theology with philosophy in their time, is therefore not surprising. Despite these objections the opponents never gained a strong footing during Ottoman history. A strict version of radicalism emerged, however, during the sixteenth and seventeenth centuries among the Kadızadelis, a group inspired by the views of Mehmed Birgevi (d. 981/1573). Birgevi, though in principle not opposed to the teaching of theology and logic, was fighting against certain popular religious practices and extreme Sufi interpretations. He was also not in favour of discussing metaphysical questions among *madrasa* scholars. Kadızade Mehmed (d. 1044/1635), a student of Birgevi, elevated the level of criticism with a group of preachers who finally led a social upheaval against what they called innovations (*bidʿa*) against religion, including tobacco, coffee, and music, demanding the elimination of mathematics, philosophy, and other intellectual sciences from the *madrasa* curricula. Contrary to the earlier Ottoman policy of flexibility, Murad IV accepted some of their demands in order to inveigle popular support. When they intended to attack all Sufi tekkes in Istanbul in 1656, Grand Vizier Köprülü Mehmed Paşa, with the support of *ʿulamāʾ*, suppressed the turmoil and had the Kadızadelis exiled (İnalcık 1973: 183–4). However, the seventeenth century could not be labelled as the age of fanaticism as it produced efforts of rational thought especially in logic (El-Rouayheb, 2006 and 2008). Apart from this exceptional case, a few traditional scholars, such as Davud-i Karsi (d. 1756), also expressed their disapproval of philosophical approaches, as well as esoteric views of mysticism.

The demands voiced by a minority group of Kadızadelis to end the teaching of rational theology, philosophy, and science underlines the important role those disciplines played in the *madrasa* curricula. This is corroborated by other Ottoman sources bearing direct evidence on the teaching of rational disciplines in the *madrasas*. The anonymous author of *Kevakib-i Seb'a* (Ms. Paris, Bibliotheque nationale, Supplement turcs, Ms. no. 196), a book on the classification of knowledge written in 1741 at the request of French ambassador Marquis de Villeneuve, suggested that people of foreign countries, especially Christians who lived far from Muslim lands, did not have access to Arabic sources and therefore thought Muslim scholars to be ignorant. On the contrary, he argued that Muslims did research in all fields and wrote about them. By writing this book, he stated, he aimed to remove the doubts and stereotypes of foreigners, by virtue of providing correct information about the disciplines that were taught in *madrasas*. In theology, according to the author, after some elementary texts, al-Jurjānī's *Sharḥ al-Mawāqif* and al-Taftazānī's *Sharḥ al-Maqāṣid* were the focus of the teaching. Although essentially works on theology, the author maintained that they covered all branches of knowledge including philosophy, astronomy, geometry, and mathematics.

In the modern period, too, there was some opposition against theology and its assumed implications for Ottoman society. İsmail Hakkı's above discussed attempt to rewrite Islamic theology, for example, attracted criticism from among some of his contemporaries who objected to the use of modern philosophy in Islamic discourse. An interview by *Sebilürreşad* with Hakkı exploring his project of *Yeni İlm-i Kelam* evoked strong criticism from Hüseyin Kazım Kadri (Ḥusayin Kāzim Qadrī) (1870–1934), a scholarly-minded politician with Salafi tendencies in matters of faith, who usually used the pen name Şeyh Muhsin-i Fani el-Zahiri. Hakkı responded to Kadri's critique, and the two men exchanged a series of essays in the journal *Sebilürreşad* (Özervarlı 2007a).

In his critique of Hakkı, Kadri expressed his disappointment at Hakkı's attempts to revitalize theology in accordance with contemporary thought. Although he accepted the need for Muslim scholars to write new books and contribute to the Islamic intellectual tradition, he believed that such endeavours should be restricted to commenting and translating the Qur'ān, and this by a group of Muslim experts who would in no way be exposed to any Western influence. Kadri mentioned that he had already at an earlier stage asked Şeyhülislam Musa Kazım to give up a similar attempt to modernize Islamic theology, although Musa Kazım's call for reformed *kalām* education was less harmful in Kadri's opinion than Hakkı's *Yeni İlm-i Kelam*, possibly because Musa Kazım's reform remained only a proposal, while Hakkı's was more specific.

The new Islamic theology, in Kadri's opinion, would reintroduce useless disputes that had been abandoned for centuries in the darkness of the history. The invention of classical theology, as well as the translation of philosophical books from Greek into Arabic, was a mistake of the 'Abbāsid caliphs of the ninth century, whose methods of governing introduced many negative trends into Islam. Muslim philosophers referred to Plato as 'the divine Plato' (*Eflatun-i ilahi*), Aristotle as 'the first teacher' (*muallim-i evvel*), and Galen as 'guide' (*İmam*)—terms that ought to be reserved for Islamic figures in Kadri's view. Even the term '*kalām*' (derived from the Arabic word for 'speech') was patterned after the Greek word '*logos*', which had nothing to do with Islam. For the new theology to introduce the modern European thought of Locke, Malebranche, Kant, Descartes, and Comte, as well as probabilism, positivism, materialism, dogmatism, and so on, was just as pointless, according to Kadri, as the early Muslim theologians' introduction of ancient Greek thought. He urged Muslim scholars to concentrate on legal and Qurʾānic studies, rather than theology or philosophy. What society needs, especially the young generation, in Kadri's opinion, is a contemporary catechism (*ilmihal*), and not theology. Kadri emphasized that great Muslim scholars of the past—Abū Ḥanīfa, al-Shāfiʿī, Aḥmad b. Ḥanbal, Ibn Taymiyya, and Ibn Qayyim al-Jawziyya—had also criticized discursive theology.

As is obvious from his writings, Kadri was not only against the revival attempts of Hakkı, but was also an opponent of philosophical theology per se, both in the past and the present. In an earlier work he gave many examples of how debates over Islamic theology involved disputes that had caused confusion and disorder in Muslim society. The best solution for contemporary problems, Kadri thought, was to return to the early original understanding of Islam by removing the alien cultural influences on Muslim societies that had built up over the centuries. Apart from his opposition to the revival of Muslim theology, Kadri was also against any sort of contact with Western philosophy. He strongly emphasized the materialistic aspects of modern thought and the need for strengthening the spiritual values of Islam against the possible challenges of Western ideas in the nineteenth century. According to Kadri, Islamic faith does not need in any way to be strengthened with Western philosophical ideas. However, although Kadri opposed the ideological bases of Western modernity like most of his contemporary conservative thinkers, he supported administrative reforms and technological developments for necessary transformations in his society.

V Conclusion

In this chapter it has been demonstrated that Islamic theology and its integration to philosophy in the late medieval period was vibrant in the Ottoman lands as was the case among Iranian and Imami thinkers of the time. Ottoman theology was observed as an active and productive follower of its Muslim Anatolian background in combining rational and mystical schools. From the beginning it renewed itself through the reworking on the pre-Ottoman texts and the transmitting of the tradition to their society. Ottoman scholarly environment also provided a base for interactions with other cultures of thought, by virtue of transcribing books, translating valuable sources, and commentating on some selected works. Generally speaking, this activity more or less continued undeterred till the end of the Empire.

Commentary writing was widespread among Ottoman theologians, which should be regarded as a sign of continuation and expansion of Ottoman intellectual history, and in some cases as a way to express different ideas in a safe and unthreatening format.

They were not primarily interested in building new theological systems or theories, but rather in understanding, expanding, and detailing ideas, which cannot simply evoke the absence of thought. However, Ottoman texts were not always commentaries, but also independent treatises on various topics were written during this period.

The exploration of the topics, discussions that took place in the Ottoman theological sources, and terminology that is used, demonstrates the continuity between the pre-Ottoman and Ottoman periods. Ottoman theologians, like their fourteenth-century predecessors, were well acquainted with theological doctrines and familiar with the techniques of logical and philosophical argumentation. The Ottoman period was not a period of innovations and great thinkers in terms of theological methodology, but certainly of intellectual activity through interpretations, evaluations, and discussions concerning rational and metaphysical questions. Ottoman theologians such as Kemalpaşazade and others continued to work on new combinations of *kalām* and *falsafa*, focusing on some meticulous discussions about existence, possibility, eternality, faith, reason, revelation, and so on. As they expressed their thoughts mostly through commentaries on selective texts or short treatises on very specific subjects, they aimed to augment and deepen the tradition of post-Ghazālian philosophical theology. This verifies how deeply post-Ghazālian scholars transferred the philosophical tradition into theology. Ottoman theologians contributed to this process by exploring mostly the philosophical subjects, asking new questions that were not contemplated by their predecessors, or providing additional interpretations in order to illuminate the issues. In the modern period, however, the same efforts were spent to revitalize Islamic theology according to the need of the age, and to answer questions raised by modern philosophy.

References

Al-Tikriti, N. (2005). 'Kalam in the Service of State: Apostasy and Defining of Ottoman Islamic Identity'. In H. Karateke and M. Rainkowski (eds.), *Legitimizing the Order: The Ottoman Rhetoric of State Power*, Leiden: Brill, 131–49.

Ayalon, Y. (2010). 'Comtino, Rabbi Mordecai ben Eliezer'. In N. Stilman (ed.), *Encyclopaedia of the Jews of the Islamic World*. Leiden: Brill, <http://referenceworks.brillonline.com/entries/encyclopedia-of-jews-in-the-islamic-world/comtino-rabbi-mordecai-ben-eliezer-SIM_0005670>.

Badenas, P. (2001). 'The Byzantine Intellectual Elite at the Court of Mehmed II: Adaptation and Identity'. In Ali Çaksu (ed.), *Proceedings of the International Congress on Learning and Education in the Ottoman Empire*. Istanbul: IRCICA.

Brusalı, Muḥammad Ṭāhir ibn Rifʿat (1914–28). *Osmanlı müellifleri*. 3 vols. İstanbul: Matbaa-ʾi Amire, 1333–42.

Eberhard, E. (1970). *Osmanische Polemik gegen die Safawiden im 16. Jahrhundert nach arabischen Handschriften*. Freiburg i. Br: Klaus Schwarz.

Eichner, H. (2009). *The Post-Avicennian Philosophical Tradition and Islamic Orthodoxy: Philosophical and Theological summae in Context*. Habilitation, Martin-Luther-Universität Halle-Wittenberg.

Heer, N. (1979). *The Precious Pearl: al-Jāmī's al-Durrah al-fākhirah, together with his glosses and the commentary of 'Abd al-Ghafūr al-Lārī.* Translated with an introduction, notes, and glossary. Albany, NY: SUNY Press.

İnalcık, H. (1973). *The Ottoman Empire: The Classical Age 1300–1600*. London: Weidenfeld and Nicolson.

Katib Çelebi. *The Balance of Truth*. Trans. G. L. Lewis. London: George Allen and Unwin, 1957.

Kazım, M. (2002). 'The Principles of Consultation and Liberty in Islam and Reform and Review of Religious Writings'. In C. Kurzman (ed.), *Modernist Islam, 1840–1940: A Source Book*. New York: Oxford University Press, 173–80.

Mestcizade Abdullah b. Osman (Mastji zāda Abdullah b. Uthmān) (2007). *al-Masālik fī l-khilāfiyyāt bayn al-mutakallimīn wa-l-ḥukamā*. Ed. Seyid Bahçivan (Sayyid Bağchevān). Beirut: Dār Sāder.

Monfasani, J. (ed.) (1984). *Collectanea Trapezuntiana: Texts, Documents, and Bibliographies of George of Trebizond*. Binghamton, NY: Renaissance Society of America.

Nev'i Efendi, Yahya b. Pir Ali (1995). *Netayic el-Fünûn—İlimlerin Özü*. Transliterated into modern Turkish by Ömer Tolgay. Istanbul: İnsan Yayınları.

Öçal, Ş. (2000). *Kemal Paşazâde'nin Felsefi ve Kelami Görüşleri*. Ankara: Kültür Bakanlığı Yayınları.

Özervarlı, M. S. (1999a). 'Attempts to Revitalize Kalam in the Late 19th and Early 20th Centuries'. *The Muslim World* 89: 90–105.

Özervarlı, M. S. (1999b). 'Son Dönem Osmanlı Düşüncesinde Arayışlar: Mehmed Şerafeddin'in 'İctimai İlm-i Kelam'ı. *Islam Arastirmalari Dergisi = Turkish Journal of Islamic Studies* 3: 157–70.

Özervarlı, M. S. (2006). 'Modification or Renewal? Elmalili Hamdi's Alternative Modernization Project in Late Ottoman Thought'. In L. Somigli and D. Pietropaolo (eds.), *Modernism and Modernity in the Mediterranean World*. New York: Legas, 43–60.

Özervarlı, M. S. (2007a). 'Alternative Approaches to Modernization in the Late Ottoman Period: İzmirli İsmail Hakkı's Religious Thought against Materialist Scientism'. *International Journal of Middle East Studies* 39: 77–102.

Özervarlı, M. S. (2007b). 'Transferring Traditional Islamic Disciplines into Modern Social Sciences in Late Ottoman Thought: The Attempts of Ziya Gokalp and Mehmed Serafeddin'. *The Muslim World* 97: 317–30.

Özervarlı, M. S. (2008). *Kelâmda Yenilik Arayışları: 19. Yüzyıl Sonu—20. Yüzyıl Başı*. Istanbul: ISAM Yayınları.

Özervarlı, M. S. (2010). 'The Reconstruction of Islamic Social Thought in the Modern Period: Nursi's Approach to Religious Discourse in a Changing Society'. *Asian Journal of Social Sciences* 38: 532–53.

Özervarlı, M. S. (2011). 'Yanyalı Esad Efendi's Works on Philosophical Texts as a Part of Ottoman Translation Movement in the Early Eighteenth Century'. In B. Schmidt-Haberkamp (ed.), *Europa und die Türkei im 18. Jahrhundert / Europe and Turkey in the 18th Century*. Göttingen: Vandenhoeck & Ruprecht, 457–72.

Özervarlı, M. S. (2015). 'Arbitrating between al-Ghazzali and the Philosophers: The Tahafut Commentaries in the Ottoman Intellectual Context'. In G. Tamer (ed.), *Islam and Rationality: The Impact of al-Ghazzali. Papers Colllected on His 900th Anniversary*. Vol. 1, Leiden: Brill, 375–97.

Patrinelis, C. G. (1971). 'Mehmed II The Conqueror and His Presumed Knowledge of Greek and Latin'. *Viator: Medieval and Renaissance Studies* 2: 349–54.

Raby, J. (1983). 'Mehmed the Conqueror's Greek Scriptorium'. *Dumbarton Oaks Papers* 37: 15–31.

Reinhart, K. (2001). 'Musa Kazım: From Ilm to Polemics'. *Archivum Ottomanicum* 19: 281–306.

Robinson, F. (1997). 'Ottoman-Safavids-Mughals: Shared Knowledge and Connective Systems'. *Journal of Islamic Studies* 8: 151–84.

El-Rouayheb, K. (2008). 'The Myth of "The Triumph of Fanaticism" in the Seventeenth-Century Ottoman Empire'. *Die Welt des Islams* 48: 196–221.

El-Rouayheb, K. (2006). 'Opening the Gate of Verification: The Forgotten Arab-Islamic Florescence of the 17th Century'. *International Journal of Middle East Studies* 38: 263–81.

Sarıkavak, K. (1998). *XVIII. Yüzyılda Bir Osmanlı Düşünürü: Yanyalı Esad Efendi (Bir Rönesans Denemesi)*. Ankara: Kültür Bakanlığı Yayınları.

Shihadeh, A. (2005). 'From al-Ghazali to al-Razi: 6th/12th Century Developments in Muslim Philosophical Theology'. *Arabic Sciences and Philosophy* 15: 141–79.

Sorabji, R. (ed.) (1990). *Aristotle Transformed: The Ancient Commentators and Their Influence*. London: Duckworth.

Taftāzānī, Saʿd al-Dīn Umar (1292[/1875]). *Sharḥ al-ʿAqāʾid*. Translated into Ottoman Turkish with its commentaries by Sırri Giridi. Ruscuk: Vilayet-i Celile-i Tuna.

Todt, Kl.-P. (2013). 'Gennadius II Scholarius'. In D. Thomas and A. Mallett (eds.), *Christian-Muslim Relations: A Bibliographical History*. Vol. v (1350–1500). Leiden: Brill, 501–18.

Uzunçarşılı, İ. H. (1965). *Osmanlı devletinin ilmiye teşkilâtı*. Ankara: Türk Tarih Kurumu Basımevi.

Winter, T. (2007). 'Ibn Kemal (d. 940/1534) on Ibn ʿArabi's Hagiology'. In A. Shihadeh (ed.), *Sufism and Theology*. Edinburgh: Edinburgh University Press, 137–57.

Yaltkaya, M. Şerafeddin (1932). 'Türk Kelamcıları'. *Darülfünun İlâhiyat Fakültesi Mecmuası* 23: 1–19.

Yazıcıoğlu, M. S. (1990). *Le Kalam et son role dans la société turco-ottomane aux XV. et XVI. Siècles*. Ankara: Éditions de ministère de la culture.

Zildzic, A. (2012). *Friend and Foe: The Early Ottoman Reception of Ibn ʿArabi*. Doctoral Dissertation, University of Berkeley.

CHAPTER 33

THEOLOGY IN CENTRAL ASIA

NATHAN SPANNAUS

THE historical development of theology in Central Asia is marked—as it is virtually everywhere in the Islamic world—by the 'philosophizing' of Sunni *kalām*, wherein methods and concepts from Hellenized Arabic *falsafa* came to exert a tremendous influence on the subsequent theological tradition. This shift in *kalām* discourse has recently been located in the works of the renowned polymath Ibn Sīnā (Avicenna, d. 428/1037) and accordingly labelled the 'Avicennian Turn' (Wisnovsky 2005).

One of the most important developments in Islamic intellectual history, the Avicennian Turn represents a profound transformation in theological reasoning. Metaphysical and ontological questions came to predominate at the expense of issues of morality and free will that had been central during the formative period of *kalām*. Though the Avicennian Turn spread across the entirety of the Muslim world relatively quickly, its developments owed much to the Central Asian scholarly *milieu*. Ibn Sīnā himself was born near Bukhara, and he spent much of his early life in the city (then the capital of the Samanid dynasty), where he studied—among other things—Ḥanafism, the school (*madhhab*) of Islamic law to which the vast majority of Central Asian *'ulamā'* adhered.[1] In addition, R. Wisnovsky points out that a conceptual framework for adopting the philosophical concerns of the Avicennian Turn was already present in Abū Manṣūr al-Māturīdī's (d. 333/944) *Kitāb al-Tawḥīd* (Wisnovsky 2005: 66). Al-Māturīdī was one of the leading figures of the Ḥanafī *'ulamā'* of Samarqand, who developed a theological school that would come to bear his name—Maturidism (Rudolph 1996).

Aspects of the Avicennian Turn soon began appearing in Māturīdite texts, such as Abū l-Yusr Bazdawī's (d. 493/1099) *Kitāb Uṣūl al-dīn* (e.g. Bazdawī, *Uṣūl*, 27f.) and Abū Mu'īn Nasafī's (d. 508/1114) *Tabṣirat al-adilla* (Nasafī, *Tabṣira*, 105–8). But the fullest expression of the new discourse initiated by the Avicennian Turn can be found in Sa'd

[1] D. Gutas has claimed that Ibn Sīnā was in fact a Ḥanafī, though others, using different evidence, have claimed that he was an Ismā'īlī; Gutas 1988. cf. Nasr 1993: 183.

al-Dīn al-Taftāzānī's (d. 792/1390) commentary (*sharḥ*) on the creedal work of Najm al-Dīn ʿUmar Nasafī (d. 537/1142), the *ʿAqāʾid nasafiyya*.[2]

The philosophizing of *kalām* that took place in this period resulted in a shift in the primary concerns of *mutakallimūn*, a shift which is evident in the differences between al-Nasafī's *ʿAqāʾid* and Taftāzānī's *Sharḥ*. While the former is a straightforward assertion of established principles of Sunni belief, including that of the uncreated Qurʾān and the Māturīdite conception of faith, by al-Taftāzānī's time these issues either had ceased to be points of contention or had been subsumed within other theological questions. Al-Taftāzānī's commentary, accordingly, places its focus on more abstract questions of ontology, reflecting Avicenna's influence. Issues of faith and works that predominated the early theological tradition are of decidedly secondary importance.

As a result of this shift, most of the works of the early Māturīdite masters fell into obsolescence. The *ʿAqāʾid nasafiyya* survived as the subject of al-Taftāzānī's commentary, but the works of Abū Layth al-Samarqandī (*fl.* fourth/tenth century), Abū Muʿīn al-Nasafī, and al-Māturīdī himself ceased to be widely studied or commented upon. Instead, the theological tradition was elucidated and transmitted via new books that reflected the shift in discourse. Only Abū Shakūr al-Sālimī's (*fl.* fourth/tenth century) *Tamhīd fī bayān al-tawḥīd* remained current; it served as an important marker of orthodoxy into the nineteenth century.[3] This may be due to the fact there are a number of philosophical elements present in the work that presage the Avicennian Turn, though much more study is needed on this text.[4]

As noted, the *kalām* discourse that emerged from the Avicennian Turn focused on metaphysical and ontological matters, and the most central debates in post-Avicennian *kalām* in Central Asia revolved around questions of the nature of being and existence (*wujūd*) and the relationship between an entity or essence (*dhāt*) and its existence and attributes (*ṣifāt*, sing. *ṣifa*), in particular God and His attributes. Most important is the Avicennian notion of God as being necessary of existence in Himself (*wājib al-wujūd bi-l-dhāt*), which became the widely accepted understanding of God's existence. This stance is based on the concept of the three modalities of existence, found in Aristotle, that posits that all existents are necessary (*wājib*), possible (*mumkin*), or impossible (*mumtaniʿ*) of existence,[5] an ontological schema that was quickly incorporated into

[2] Taftāzānī's commentary has been published in numerous editions, as well as in an English translation; Elder 1950.

[3] Cf. Marjānī, *Mustafād*, 2: 172–3.

[4] In the proof of God's oneness (*waḥdāniyya*), Sālimī writes that 'we have affirmed the Maker (*athbatnā al-ṣāniʿ*) because of the necessity of the existence of the Maker (*li-ḍarūrat wujūd al-ṣāniʿ*) and [the necessity of] the creation of the world, and this necessity is increased by the affirmation of one maker (*bi-ithbāt ṣāniʿ*ⁱⁿ *wāḥid*ⁱⁿ);' Sālimī, *Tamhīd*, 36. Compare this with the discussion of the necessity of existence (*wujūb al-wujūd*), which was predicated of God by Avicenna.

[5] One of the central aspects of the Avicennian Turn is the adaptation of these modalities to earlier Islamic discourse of entities' eternality or createdness, wherein a thing that was previously considered eternal (in the sense of uncaused, or having no beginning) came to be seen instead as necessary (in the sense that it must exist), and, likewise, a thing that is caused (in the sense of having a beginning and therefore not being eternal) came to be seen as possible (in the sense that it might or might not exist at a given point); see Wisnovsky 2005; 2004a.

mainstream Sunni *kalām*. These issues, which remained prevalent up until the modern period, are addressed in works such as al-Taftāzānī's commentary on al-Nasafī.

I The Continued Importance of Theology

Al-Taftāzānī's works, in particular the *Sharḥ al-ʿAqāʾid al-nasafiyya*, came to dominate Central Asian theological discourse up to the twentieth century. His *Sharḥ* is often considered the epitome of *kalām*, and a number of histories of theology in Central Asia stop at this point, believing the ostensible apotheosis of *kalām*'s development in the region to be the *end* of *kalām*'s development in the region (e.g. Gilliot 2002). This view was certainly fostered by the sustained prevalence of al-Taftāzānī's work, which obscured the continued evolution of *kalām* beyond the positions contained in it (Elder 1950: xx).

Furthermore, it was common in secondary scholarship to consider Central Asia in later periods a cultural and intellectual backwater, cut off from the rest of the Sunni world by Shīʿī Iran and ruled by (nominally Muslim) Turkic nomads.[6] As a result, very little scholarly attention was paid to any developments in the region falling between the end of the Timurid era (roughly 1500) and the Russian invasions of the 1860s.

All of this has started to change in recent decades, as the fall of the Soviet Union has made research on the region far more accessible. At the same time, scholars of Islamic theology have begun to devote new attention to Māturīdism.[7] This research is in its early stages, however, and considerable work remains in order to produce a detailed and nuanced picture of the development of theology in Central Asia over the roughly five centuries following al-Taftāzānī's death. Thanks to recent studies, much of what we do know is limited to concerns adjacent to theology—Sufism, Islamic scholarly institutions, socio-political trends, economic developments—rather than the history of theology itself.[8] Nevertheless, we are not in total darkness on the subject.

First, we may dispense with the notion that Islamic scholarship in Central Asia had stagnated in this era, and that theological study had become repetitive and derivative (cf. Shorish 1986). This era saw the theological tradition continue unabated, but there were new developments as well, such that the *kalām* debates of the post-classical period should not be seen as mere rehashing of earlier trends. There were substantive connections with other regions, too—namely India, the Ottoman Empire, and even Iran—that allowed for the exchange of ideas across frontiers.

[6] E.g. Spuler 1970. For a discussion of the trope of Eurasian nomads' lack of religiosity, see DeWeese 1994.

[7] The Māturīdī school was little studied among Western Islamicists prior to the 1970s; cf. Rudolph 1996: 1ff.

[8] In addition to the works cited here, see e.g. the collections edited by Dudoignon 1996; Muminov 2007; DeWeese 2001; and von Kügelgen 1996–2002.

Our most reliable knowledge relevant to theology falls within the realm of bibliography. The vast majority of theological texts from this era remain unpublished, and their contents unstudied. Thanks to the cataloguing of regional manuscript collections, however, it is possible to determine which texts and which scholars held the most importance for the study of theology.[9] By looking at the frequency with which texts were copied and commented upon, we can discern the parameters of the theological tradition in the region.[10] The study of commentaries (*shurūḥ*, sing. *sharḥ*) and glosses (*ḥawāshī*, sing. *ḥāshīya*) is particularly important for this era. They were the primary textual vehicles for the transmission of scholarship in the post-classical period; at the very least, they give us an idea of the contours of theological discourse over time.[11] Thanks to bibliographic sources, we know that commentaries on theological texts continued to be written into the twentieth century.

A major circumstantial component in the perseverance of theology was institutional support for religious scholarship. Central Asia at this time was ruled primarily by Turkic military dynasties of Chingissid descent (succeeded in the eighteenth century by non-Chingissid lineages), and it was common for members of the political and military elite to promote scholarly activity.[12] Following the collapse of Timurid rule at the turn of the sixteenth century, their capital Samarqand was surpassed in political and economic importance by Bukhara, which became the pre-eminent urban centre in the region. Religious scholarship flourished in the city as a result; many of its *madrasas* date from the post-Timurid period, when the city became a destination for students from all over the Persianate world. As the capital of the leading dynasties, the *ʿulamāʾ* in Bukhara received significant support from political elites. For instance, one of Bukhara's most important *madrasas* was founded by Qul Bābā Kūkaltāsh (*fl.* tenth/sixteenth century), who was both a prominent military leader (*amīr*) and closely involved in the civil

[9] The two most important collections for Central Asia are located in St Petersburg, at the Institute of Oriental Manuscripts, and Tashkent, at the Abu Rayhan Biruni Institute of Oriental Studies. The St Petersburg collection has been extensively catalogued; Khalidov et al. 1986; Akimushkin et al. 1998; Dmitrieva et al. 2002. The Tashkent collection, however, has only been partially catalogued, and somewhat haphazardly so; Semenov 1952–87. New subject-specific catalogues have been compiled in recent years, but unfortunately theology has not yet been addressed; cf. Karimova 2010. Other important collections include the regional museums of Nukus and Qarshi, Uzbekistan (respectively); Muminov et al. 2007; Szuppe et al. 2004; see also Muminov et al. 1999b. In addition, there are two catalogues for the manuscript collection of Kazan University, Russia that have recently been published (the first of which suffers from poor arrangement and frequent errors); Fātiḥnizhād et al. 2003; Arslanova 2005.

[10] This is similar to the approach used by P. Bruckmayr in his study of Māturīdism's influence and spread, an article that also shows the drawbacks of this approach, as it allows for very little detail regarding the ideas contained in these works; Bruckmayr 2009.

[11] It is the very use of the commentary that has led to the idea of stagnation, but this is far from true. Commentaries were a major source of original and inventive scholarship within the bounds of the scholarly tradition. On the importance of commentaries in the post-classical period, see Zaman 2002; Wisnovsky 2004b.

[12] For a discussion of the ruling dynasties of the era and their manner of governance, see McChesney 1992.

administration of the Bukharan khanate (McChesney 1992; Liechti 2008: 31–3). The decentralized nature of Chingissid rule, however, allowed for substantial patronage opportunities elsewhere, and Balkh, Herat, and Khorezm, as well as Samarqand, also served as scholarly centres.[13] Figures like Kūkaltāsh—including members of the ruling dynasties—established *madrasas*, patronized scholars, and endowed libraries and teaching positions. Rulers too would sponsor public debates on theological topics and encourage leading scholars to participate.

Such support for religious scholarship served to provide these dynasties—whose authority was based on military conquest and whose rule involved near-constant warfare—with sorely needed religious legitimacy. These rulers sought to justify their position via the *ʿulamāʾ*, who acted as intermediaries between the population and the ruling elite, especially in urban centres. Presenting themselves as the upholders of Sunni orthodoxy—vis-à-vis Shīʿī Iran in particular—these dynasties patronized theological scholars whose views could be considered staunchly anti-Muʿtazilī and anti-Shīʿī (and therefore pro-Sunni).

There was considerable room to manoeuvre within this understanding of Sunnism, however, and such support for orthodoxy was not an obstacle to active theological reasoning. Importantly, the general conception of Sunni orthodoxy was not exclusively aligned with Māturīdism, and there was not insignificant exchange with Ashʿarism. Al-Taftāzānī himself merges Ashʿarism and Māturīdism in the *Sharh al-ʿAqāʾid al-nasafiyya*, and the works and teachings of a number of Ashʿarite scholars were incorporated into the ostensibly Māturīdite Central Asian *kalām* tradition.

II Shirazi Influence

Most noteworthy is the influence of the so-called school of Shiraz, a collection of predominantly Ashʿarite scholars who shared a marked philosophical bent.[14] This school, whose primary founder was ʿAḍud al-Dīn al-Ījī (d. 756/1356), incorporated a wide array of different philosophical perspectives, including Muḥyī l-Dīn Ibn ʿArabī's (d. 638/1240) metaphysics, Shihāb al-Dīn al-Suhrawardī's (d. 587/1191) Illuminationist philosophy, and Avicennian ideas—often by way of the Shīʿī philosopher Naṣīr al-Dīn al-Ṭūsī (d. 672/1274)—along with post-Avicennian Sunni *kalām*. Al-Ījī's major theological work, the *Mawāqif fī ʿilm al-kalām*, was famously commented upon by Sayyid Sharīf al-Jurjānī (d. 816/1413), a scholar who travelled extensively and whose thought reflected this scope of diverse influences. This commentary was in fact composed in Samarqand, the Timurid capital, where al-Jurjānī had been brought following Timur's conquest of Shiraz in 1387 (van Ess 2011). Al-Taftāzānī, who had been a student of al-Ījī, was already

[13] There is evidence that the intellectual environment in one city could differ substantially from that of another, even when ruled by the same dynasty.

[14] For a detailed history of the school, see Pourjavady 2011.

established at Timur's court, and the two formed an occasionally contentious scholarly rivalry, fostered by frequent public disputations held at Timur's behest.[15]

Al-Jurjānī's *Sharḥ al-Mawāqif fī ʿilm al-kalām* became widely studied in Central Asian theological circles, along with a commentary on another of al-Ījī's works, the *Sharḥ al-ʿAqāʾid al-ʿaḍudiyya* by Jalāl al-Dīn Dawānī (d. 908/1502).[16] Dawānī, who studied under a number of al-Jurjānī's students, became very influential in Central Asian *kalām*, and many of his works were widely studied and commented upon in places like Bukhara and Herat.[17]

Dawānī's influence in Central Asia may be attributed in part to scholarly connections. A chain of transmission (*silsila*) from the early nineteenth century links some of the most prominent *ʿulamāʾ* in Bukhara to Dawānī.[18] One of his students, Jamāl al-Dīn Astarābādī (d. 931/1526), settled for a time in Herat (Pourjavady 2011: 15), and one of Astarābādī's students, Mīrzājān Ḥabīb Allāh (d. 994/1586), a native of Shiraz, in turn later settled permanently in Bukhara (Brockelmann 1937–42: ii. 594). Mīrzājān taught Yūsuf Qarabāghī (d. 1034/1624), who became one of the major figures of the Bukharan *ʿulamāʾ*. The *silsila* continues on to Muḥammad Hādī Bukhārī (*fl.* twelfth/eighteenth century) and his son, ʿAṭāʾ Allāh Bukhārī (d. after 1223/1808), both of whom served as *shaykh al-Islām* under the Manghit dynasty (1753–1920).[19] In addition, ʿInāyat Allāh Bukhārī (d. after 1223/1808), who served as chief *qāḍī* (*qāḍī-yi kalān*) in Bukhara, also traced his scholarly lineage to Qarabāghī, linking him back to Dawānī as well.

These scholars continued the ideas of the school of Shiraz through their commentaries and supercommentaries. Indeed, with the exception of Muḥammad Hādī Bukhārī, all of the scholars listed above are known to have composed supercommentaries on Dawānī's *Sharḥ al-ʿAqāʾid al-ʿaḍudiyya*.[20] The degree to which the school of Shiraz became integrated into the Central Asian *kalām* tradition is shown by the ubiquity of

15 It is said that Taftāzānī's defeat to Jurjānī in a debate led to the former's death; Madelung 2000.

16 Dawānī's commentary has been published many times along with other commentaries and supercommentaries on Ījī's *Mawāqif*. To my knowledge, the only edition of the work by itself is found (strangely) in a collection of the writings of the modernist scholar al-Afghānī (al-Afghānī, *Āthār*, 37–147).

17 Most commonly studied beyond the *Sharḥ al-ʿAqāʾid al-ʿaḍudiyya* were two of his shorter works, the *Risālat ithbāt al-wājib al-qadīma* and the *Risālat al-zawrāʾ*, both recently published in al-Dawānī, *Sabʿ rasāʾil*.

18 The *silsila* ends with two scholars from the Volga-Ural region of the Russian Empire, reflecting the substantial scholarly links between this region and Central Asia. The full *silsila*, which is contained in a biographical dictionary of Volga-Ural *ʿulamāʾ*, reads: ʿAbd al-Wahhāb b. ʿAbd al-Rashīd Īshquwwat (d. 1248/1833) < Sayf al-Dīn b. Abī Bakr Shinkārī (d. 1240/1824) < ʿAṭāʾ Allāh b. Hādī Bukhārī < his father, Hādī Bukhārī < 'Mawlā Fayḍī' (unknown) < 'Mawlānā Sharīf' (unknown) < Qarabāghī < Mīrzājān < Astarābādī < Dawānī; Fakhr al-Dīn, *Āthār*, 6: 291.

19 M. Kemper notes that they were descended from a line of prominent theological scholars dating back to the sixteenth century; Kemper 1998: 51.

20 Unfortunately, none of these works has been published. The supercommentaries of Mīrzājān and Qarabāghī exist in numerous copies, as does that of ʿInāyat Allāh, which is a third-level commentary on Qarabāghī's supercommentary. ʿAṭāʾ Allāh's partial supercommentary is preserved in the Institute of Oriental Manuscripts, St Petersburg; Ms. B4038, fos. 128b–137b.

this work, which was surpassed in importance only by al-Taftāzānī's *ʿAqāʾid nasafiyya*. The fact that Dawānī's *sharḥ* has a marked Sunni perspective—it is staunchly pro-Ashʿarite—may have hastened its adoption among Central Asian *mutakallimūn*, but Dawānī's oeuvre as a whole evinces a wide array of influences—reflective of the Shirazi milieu—and less-orthodox works, like his commentary on Suhrawardī, the *Shawākil al-ḥūr fī sharḥ hayākil al-nūr*, were also studied in Central Asian *madrasas*.[21]

There were substantive contacts between the school of Shiraz and Central Asian *ʿulamāʾ*, and the mélange of ideas circulating in Shiraz was also present—if to a lesser extent—in Samarqand. There is, for instance, the case of ʿAlī b. Muḥammad Qūshjī (d. 879/1474), a philosopher-astronomer from Samarqand who was active at the Timurid court under Ulugh Beg, after whose death in 853/1449 he quit the city, eventually settling in Istanbul. Qūshjī (sometimes 'Qūshchī') wrote a commentary on Naṣīr al-Dīn al-Ṭūsī's *Tajrīd al-iʿtiqādāt*, upon which there are several supercommentaries by Dawānī and other contemporary Shirazi scholars (Pourjavady 2011: 10–12, 18, 21). Qūshjī's commentary reflects the pro-Sunni environment of Timurid Samarqand, and he argues against the explicitly Shīʿī elements of al-Ṭūsī's creed while adopting the latter's Avicennian philosophical approach (Rahman 1985). Similarly, the Persian mystical poet ʿAbd al-Raḥman Jāmī (d. 898/1492), who spent much of his life between Herat and Samarqand, engaged with philosophical matters—particularly regarding the nature of existence—from a self-consciously Sufi perspective.

III The Role of Sufism

This perspective is reflective of a long-standing and important trend in Central Asia's unique scholarly tradition—the role of Sufism. Sufism was an essential aspect of Central Asian society and was intimately linked with not only the religious, but also the social and political life of the region. Accordingly, there was a substantial history of theology from the region that was deeply informed by Sufism. This is evident in one of the most important works written from a Sufi perspective, the *Kitāb al-Taʿarruf li-madhhab ahl al-taṣawwuf* by Abū Bakr Kalābādhī (d. 385/995). A Ḥanafī from Bukhara, Kalābādhī in this text addresses theological questions in a way that, according to A. J. Arberry, combines aspects of Māturīdism with mystical thought.[22] The *Taʿarruf*—a detailed explication of Sufi beliefs—was very influential among Sufi thinkers, including luminaries such as al-Suhrawardī and Ṣadr al-Dīn al-Qūnawī (d. 673/1274), Ibn ʿArabī's student and

[21] There is a supercommentary on Dawānī's *sharḥ* attributed to Qarabāghī (not listed in Brockelmann); Yūsuf Qarabāghī, *Shawāʾil al-ṭūr ḥāshīyat Shawākil al-ḥūr sharḥ Hayākil al-nūr*. Ms. Kazanskii Gosudarstvennyi Universitet (Kazan, Russia), no. A-606; cf. Brockelmann 1943–9: i. 438.

[22] Arberry here likens Kalābādhī's effort to present a combination of Sufism and Māturīdism with Ghazālī's combination of Sufism and Ashʿarism in his celebrated *Iḥyāʾ ʿulūm al-dīn*; Arberry 1977: xv.

foremost interpreter, and it remained current in Central Asia for centuries and was frequently studied and commented upon.[23]

Ibn ʿArabī himself loomed large over Central Asian Sufism. His *wujūdī* metaphysics was incredibly influential, inspiring a significant number of theological works. His ontological ideas were quickly adopted into pre-existing trends of Sufi thought among followers of the Kubravi order, which was well established in Central Asia in the thirteenth and fourteenth centuries (Morris 1986: 745–51),[24] and his philosophy became central to the theological and metaphysical beliefs of the Naqshbandiyya, the order that would quickly rise to prominence under Timurid patronage in the fifteenth century.[25]

Several early masters of the Naqshbandiyya were proponents of Ibn ʿArabī's thought, most notably Jāmī. According to J. Morris, Jāmī was one of the foremost members of what can be called Ibn ʿArabī's 'school', a group of scholars linked to Ibn ʿArabī through al-Qūnawī who further interpreted and developed Ibn ʿArabī's philosophy (Morris 1987: 110–14). These scholars engaged primarily with Ibn ʿArabī's theological and metaphysical views, often to the exclusion of more characteristically 'Sufi' aspects, such as mystical practice, through the study of his celebrated philosophical work, the *Fuṣūṣ al-ḥikam* (Morris 1986: 751–3).[26]

The fundamental principle of Ibn ʿArabī's metaphysics is the notion that existence comes from and is God; as the Necessary Being in Himself, it is only He who can be said to exist, in contrast to all other things, which are merely possible of existence.[27] This principle is conventionally labelled *waḥdat al-wujūd* ('unity of existence'), even though this phrase never occurs in his works. In fact, Morris writes, it was members of Ibn ʿArabī's 'school', particularly in Central Asia, who developed this term. Morris notes that these scholars, rather than merely explaining Ibn ʿArabī's ideas, took them in directions he did not necessarily intend, specifically by reformulating 'Ibn ʿArabī's thought in primarily ontological, rather than theological, terms, drawing largely on Ibn Sīnā's vocabulary' (Morris 1986: 755 n. 65).

These scholars used these ideas as a starting point for their own philosophical ventures, while linking these ideas with other strands of Islamic thought. This is apparent in Jāmī's writings, where he devotes considerable attention to questions of existence.[28] In his *al-Durra al-fākhira*, he explicitly compares the positions of—respectively—the philosophers (*ḥukamāʾ*), the Muʿtazila (which includes the Ashʿarites, interestingly), Sunni

[23] This work was also popular in the western Islamic world; Arberry 1977: xiif.

[24] Morris's works on scholars' engagement with Ibn ʿArabī is essential reading for the study of the subsequent developments of his ideas in later periods, if for no other reason than for the extensive citations to secondary literature.

[25] For an account of the order's founding and background, see Algar 1990.

[26] Jāmī in fact composed two commentaries on the *Fuṣūṣ*, including his very prominent *Naqd al-nuṣūṣ fī sharḥ naqsh al-Fuṣūṣ*, which exists in multiple editions.

[27] A very useful overview of Ibn ʿArabī's philosophy by William Chittick can be found in the *Stanford Encyclopedia of Philosophy*.

[28] See his *Lawāyiḥ*, which features an extensive discussion of ontological issues in Persian verse form, which was translated into French by Y. Richard.

mutakallimūn, and *wujūdī* Sufis; in doing so, he utilizes a common philosophical idiom, wherein the views of each of these groups is expressed in the same language and terminology, namely that of post-Avicennian *kalām*.[29]

By employing a single philosophical idiom to express these disparate strands of thought, Jāmī was attempting to integrate them into a single philosophical discourse. Indeed, such attempts formed a major aspect of post-classical theology in Central Asia. If the Avicennian Turn can be characterized as a merging of *kalām* and philosophy, this era—up through the nineteenth century—saw the incorporation of *wujūdī* metaphysics into the same discursive and philosophical parameters. This project was undertaken not only by Sufi thinkers like Jāmī, but by Sunni *mutakallimūn* like Dawānī, as well (cf. Pourjavady 2011: 89).

Not all Central Asian scholars shared this affinity for Ibn ʿArabī, however. Most notably, al-Taftāzānī wrote a refutation of his metaphysics, based on the premises of Sunni *kalām*. He argued that Ibn ʿArabī's understanding of existence, in particular the relationship between God and the objective (*khārij*) world, was inherently flawed and logically untenable (Knysh 1999: 147–58). Many of these criticisms were later taken up by ʿAlī Qārī Harawī (d. 1014/1605), a traditionist scholar from Herat who settled in Mecca, in his own refutation of Ibn ʿArabī.[30] But neither of these refutations was particularly influential and did little to diminish the importance of *wujūdī* metaphysics in Central Asian theology.[31]

Efforts like al-Taftāzānī's were hindered by the level of political influence that Sufi orders possessed, in particular the Naqshbandiyya. Naqshbandi *shaykh*s had perpetually close ties with ruling dynasties in the region—Jāmī himself initiated a Timurid vizier, the celebrated Chagatay poet ʿAlī Shīr Navāʾī (b. 844/1441, d. 906/1501), into the order (Losensky 2008)—and, as a result of their support for *wujūdī* metaphysics, these ideas became accepted under the Sunni orthodoxy of the region.

The importance of *wujūdī* metaphysics, as well as the emphasis on orthodoxy, only increased with the establishment of the Mujaddidi order in the mid-seventeenth century. Founded as an offshoot of the Naqshbandiyya in Mughal India, the Mujaddidiyya quickly became one of the most dominant orders in Central Asia.[32] Part of its rapid rise to prominence can be attributed to respect for traditional scholars espoused by its founder, Aḥmad Sirhindī (d. 1034/1624), and the order attracted a great many adherents

[29] The *Durra al-fākhira* has been translated into English, along with a commentary on the work, by N. Herr (1979).

[30] Both Taftāzānī and ʿAlī Qārī's refutations were published in Istanbul in 1877; Taftāzānī, *Majmūʿa*.

[31] According to Knysh, it was also not a very persuasive critique and only engaged with Ibn ʿArabī's ideas on a 'superficial' level; Knysh 1999: 161f.

[32] There is some disagreement as to how dominant it was in the region. Arthur Buehler believes that the Mujaddidiyya were clearly the most important order, while Bakhtiyar Babajanov states that there is insufficient documentary evidence from this period. He also notes that there was broad acceptance for different Sufi affiliations under the Manghit dynasty, members of which were closely linked with the Mujaddidiyya; Buehler 1996: 208, 228; Babadžanov 1996: 385–6; Babadžanov 2003: 68; also von Kügelgen 1998: 132f.

among the *ʿulamāʾ*. Sirhindī himself preached that adherence to the *sharīʿa*, as encompassed in Ḥanafī *fiqh* and Māturidī *kalām*, was of supreme importance, over and above any mystical practice (Ter Haar 1992: 47–52).

Despite this regard for the *ʿulamāʾ*, Sirhindī himself was not a conventional scholar, and many of his theological ideas—contained primarily in his collected letters, the *Maktūbāt*[33]—reflect above all a Sufi perspective.[34] Specifically, Sirhindī's views are based on *wujūdī* metaphysics—which he terms *tawḥīd-i wujūdī*[35]—though they differ from Ibn ʿArabī's.[36] For Sirhindī, only God exists in reality. There is, however, a secondary level of existence at which everything other than God (lit. *mā siwāʾ Allāh*) can be said to exist. Sirhindī describes the relationship between the two levels of existence as the same as the relationship between a thing and its shadow; accordingly, he calls the second type 'shadow existence' (*wujūd-i ẓillī*).[37] At the level of shadow, entities receive their existence from God—who is, indeed, existence Himself.[38]

IV The Importance of Ontology

Sirhindī's metaphysics fit well into the existing theological debates in Central Asia. As noted, ontological questions came to dominate theological discourse after the Avicennian Turn, and Mujaddidi ideas were incorporated into Central Asian *kalām* in ways similar to Ibn ʿArabī's ideas before them. Muḥammad Maʿṣūm (d. 1079/1668), Sirhindī's son, attempted to combine his father's metaphysics with Sunni *kalām*,[39] as Dawānī and Jāmī had done with Ibn ʿArabī.

That Sirhindī shared the *wujūdī* framework certainly helped this process. Post-classical Persianate philosophy has been described as concerned with *refining*, rather than *refuting*, existing philosophical systems (Ziai 2005: 406), and we can see such efforts at refinement by Central Asian theologians at work.[40] Scholars sought to bring

[33] See A. Buehler's incredibly helpful index to the Persian text; Buehler 2001. The *Maktūbāt* have unfortunately not been fully translated into English. Piecemeal translations can be found in Ansari 1986: 171–316.

[34] Sirhindī himself studied Kalābādhī as a student; Ansari, 'Wahdat al-Shuhud', p. 285.

[35] e.g. Sirhindī, *Maktūbāt*, 1:272, p. 8.

[36] The degree to which Ibn ʿArabī and Sirhindī disagree is often overstated in scholarship, a fact that can be attributed to later polemics between followers of each; see esp. Ansari 1998.

[37] Cf. Sirhindī, *Maktūbāt*, 2:98, p. 112.

[38] At the level of shadow, there is little difference between Ibn ʿArabī's understanding of how things come into being and Sirhindī's. For both, there is the process of individuation (*taʿayyun*) through which entities become existents (*mawjūdāt*). However, for Sirhindī this is not real existence; therefore, existents do not share in God's existence as they do for Ibn ʿArabī.

[39] Cf. *Maktūbāt-i Khwāja Muḥammad Maʿṣūm*.

[40] See, for instance, Yūsuf Qarabāghī's combination of Illuminationist epistemology with Ashʿarite-influenced *kalām* in his supercommentary on Dawānī's *Sharḥ al-ʿAqāʾid al-ʿaḍudiyya*, extant in numerous copies. The Hathi Digital Trust has made a digital copy available online: <http://catalog.hathitrust.org/Record/006834427>. Although Sirhindī's metaphysics have often been described as

these disparate strands of thought, including conventional Sunni *kalām* and the diversity of the Shirazi school, into a single discourse. As a result, these different ideas were expressed in shared terms, allowing for the active engagement with the broad scope of them. Though these ideas were by no means accepted by everyone—quite the opposite, in fact—as far as we can tell very vibrant debates about these ideas continued into the nineteenth century in *madrasa*s, public disputations, and commentaries.

The nature of these debates was strongly philosophical, and the distinction between one position and another was often highly nuanced and subtle. As a result, such debates have usually been presented in secondary literature as petty squabbling, reflecting nothing new of substance or interest (e.g. Dinorshoev 2003: 747f.). In fact, the scholarship of this period represents a distinct stage in the evolution of Islamic theology. We may find the concept of 'scaffolding' relevant here. Proposed by S. Jackson in regard to Islamic law, 'scaffolding' is the notion that once bigger, more structural questions had been settled, scholars had little need to revisit them. Instead, they could direct their efforts at more minute—though no less important—matters, leading to more sophisticated and often more advanced forms of reasoning (Jackson 1996).[41]

This very subtle theological reasoning is apparent particularly in the debates going on in Central Asia regarding ontology. These debates focused primarily on the relationship between God's existence and the existence of everything else, reflected in the notion that God is the only necessary existent (*wājib*) while all other entities are in themselves only possible of existence (*mumkin al-wujūd*) or impossible (*mumtaniʿ*). This distinction led to a conflation of necessity and existence (expressed in the idea that only God exists), which in turn led to the position, discussed by scholars such as Qarabāghī, that everything other than God is in itself impossible of existence, but is only made possible by a cause (and thus by God, if indirectly) (Qarabāghī, *Sharḥ*, 12 a–b [pp. 25–6]).[42]

The conflation of necessity and existence resulted in the latter becoming God's primary meta-attribute, which in turn had a significant impact on debates regarding the divine attributes.[43] One of the major questions in the Islamic theological tradition, the issue of the divine attributes revolved around their relationship to the divine essence, and it was complicated considerably by this emphasis on ontology. The conventional Sunni position on the attributes was that they are neither identical to the divine essence nor other than it, expressed in the formula *lā huwa wa-lā ghayruh* (lit. 'not it and not

refuting Ibn ʿArabī's, this is not how Sirhindī himself saw it; rather, he explicitly considers himself to be correcting certain mistakes in Ibn ʿArabī's thought; ter Haar 1992: 125f.

[41] This 'scaffolding' was in essence the framework of *taqlīd*, which involved not the blind adherence to earlier scholars' views, but rather the reliance upon them and their views as authoritative. However, more research is needed to discern specifically how *taqlīd* functioned in the theological context.

[42] This idea is initially found in Ibn ʿArabī; Ibn ʿArabī, *Inshāʾ*, p. 10–1.

[43] A meta-attribute in this sense is something that can be predicated of both God and the divine attributes themselves; in this case, it can be said that God exists/has the attribute of existence, while the divine attributes too exist/have the attribute of existence. Such a predication is of course ambiguous and formed one of the bases for the controversy regarding the attributes' status; see Wisnovsky 2004a: 72–5.

other than it'). As such, the attributes posed a distinct problem for the position that only God exists while everything else does not—namely, do the attributes exist along with God, or do they not, and if so, how?

Scholars put forward a number of different answers to these questions, and debates on the divine attributes played an important role in theological reasoning in Central Asia in the post-classical period. The precise contours of these debates remain obscure, but it is clear that al-Taftāzānī's view, taken from conventional Sunni *kalām*—that the attributes exist eternally, but are only possible of existence—represented the standard position. But this did not preclude scholars from attempting to answer these questions, which remained very much unsettled.

Debates regarding the attributes continued in Central Asia, as well as among the Muslim communities of the Russian Empire. Due to the work of M. Kemper, we know far more about the latter, in particular scholars from the Volga-Ural region of the Russian Empire, particularly in the eighteenth and nineteenth centuries. This region was closely linked with Central Asia, with which it formed a single cultural space, and *ʿulamāʾ* played a significant role in linking the two regions. A great many Volga-Ural *ʿulamāʾ* studied in Bukhara and Samarqand, while scholars from Central Asia travelled to, and settled in, the Russian Empire.

Both groups were engaged in the same theological discourse, revolving around metaphysics and the divine attributes. One of the first scholars to bring these debates to the Russian Empire was Īshniyāz b. Shīrniyāz (d. 1205/1791), a native of Khorezm who settled in the steppe trading centre of Orenburg.[44] Īshniyāz took the position, found in al-Taftāzānī, that the attributes are in themselves only possible of existence, but he also argued, *pace* al-Taftāzānī, that God's existence is superadded to His essence (*z āʾida ʿalā al-dhāt*).[45] Another scholar, Fatḥ Allāh Ūriwī (d. 1259/1843), a Mujaddidi from a village near Kazan, Russia, put forward the notion of *waḥda ʿadadiyya* (lit. 'numerical oneness') for the attributes. Though the work in which Ūriwī describes this idea is unfortunately lost, it seems that it may have been based on Sirhindī's stance on the attributes—i.e. that the attributes are identical with God at the level of real existence (as only God exists in reality), while at the level of shadow existence the eight divine attributes[46] exist separate from God. *Waḥda ʿadadiyya* may be an attempt to combine these two levels, by allowing for a multiplicity of attributes to exist simultaneously with the singular divine essence.[47] Indeed, Ūriwī writes elsewhere that God is one in the sense of having no partner, so it would be possible for multiple attributes to inhere within the essence without violating God's fundamental oneness (*tawḥīd*).[48]

44 Īshniyāz was a major figure in the Mujaddidiyya, which spread to Russia in the mid-eighteenth century; Marjānī, *Mustafād*, 2: 216; Fakhr al-Dīn, *Āthār*, 2: 59–60; also Kemper 1998: 220.

45 On this metaphysical question, see Wisnovsky 2011.

46 Knowledge (*ʿilm*), power (*qudra*), life (*ḥayāt*), hearing (*samʿ*), sight (*baṣar*), will (*irāda*), speech (*kalām*), and creating (*takwīn*). The last, *takwīn*, was considered an essential attribute by Māturīdīs but not by Ashʿarites, though Central Asian theological works often acknowledge this disagreement, speaking of the 'eight or seven attributes'; e.g. Marjānī, *Mustafād*, 2: 172.

47 A similar idea is found in Jāmī, though not regarding the attributes specifically; Jāmī, *Durra*, 4–5.

48 Ūriwī, [Untitled], 1b; see also Ūriwī, *Risāla*, 39a–40b.

The most widely known Volga-Ural scholar involved in these debates was Abū Naṣr Qūrṣāwī (d. 1227/1812), who put forward a new understanding of the attributes' existence based on the ontological premisses of Sunni *kalām*.[49] In a commentary on the *ʿAqāʾid nasafiyya* that bypasses al-Taftāzānī's *sharḥ*, Qūrṣāwī argues—*contra* al-Taftāzānī—that the attributes are not possible of existence in any sense, but rather are necessary by virtue of being 'not other than' the divine essence. He also rejects the notion of the multiple attributes (and, explicitly, *waḥda ʿadadiyya*) on the grounds that the existence of multiple, distinct entities within the essence violates *tawḥīd*.

As noted, al-Taftāzānī's position represented the baseline of orthodoxy in Central Asia, and Qūrṣāwī, who spent several years studying in Bukhara at the very turn of the nineteenth century, found himself at the centre of sustained controversy as a result of his views. The criticism levelled against him by scholars such as ʿAṭāʾ Allāh Bukhārī and ʿInāyat Allāh Bukhārī (mentioned in Section II) was that holding the attributes to be necessary of existence was tantamount to denying their existence as real entities distinct from the divine essence. This, Qūrṣāwī's opponents claimed, was equivalent to the conventional Muʿtazilite position that the attributes have no existence of their own, but are identical to God (*ʿayn al-dhāt*). Such a position would take Qūrṣāwī beyond the bounds of Sunnism, and this is precisely what was charged against him. In 1223/1808 he was condemned to death for heresy by the Bukharan *ʿulamāʾ* on the order of the Manghit *amīr* Ḥaydar (r. 1799–1826) (on this incident, see Kemper 1998: 228–34; Spannaus forthcoming). Though he was spared execution, his books were burned and for the next several decades it was forbidden in Bukhara to discuss him or his ideas. Returning to Russia, he continued his outspoken criticisms of al-Taftāzānī, and the controversy surrounding him—including scholars like Ūriwī, who openly condemned Qūrṣāwī—persisted long after his death.

One of the scholars involved in this controversy in the second half of the nineteenth century was Shihāb al-Dīn Marjānī (d. 1306/1889), who is widely regarded as the most important scholar of the Muslim communities of the Russian Empire. Marjānī was an active proponent of Qūrṣāwī's views, having first become acquainted with them as a student in Samarqand (he also studied in Bukhara), and he refined and restated some of the philosophical premisses underlying them, particularly in his own commentary on the *ʿAqāʾid nasafiyya* (Marjānī, *al-Ḥikma al-bāligha*), as well as his supercommentary on Dawānī's *Sharḥ al-ʿAqāʾid al-ʿaḍudiyya*[50] (Spannaus 2015).

V Modernity

Qūrṣāwī and Marjānī are both viewed as the direct predecessors of Jadidism, the Muslim modernist movement that developed in the Russian Empire at the turn of the twentieth

[49] Qūrṣāwī was deeply influenced by the works of Nasafī, Sālimī, and Kalābādhī, respectively. On his thought, see Kemper 1998; Spannaus 2015; forthcoming.

[50] This work was published in Istanbul in 1316/1898 along with other supercommentaries on Dawānī and is widely available; Kalanbawī, *Ḥāshiyat*.

century.[51] Concerned with what they saw as the backwardness of Muslim society, Jadidist intellectuals sought to remake their society initially through the reform of Islamic education, and later through a broad project of social and cultural modernization.

With its goal of modernizing Islam and adapting Muslim society to the twentieth century, Jadidism represented a general rejection of the Islamic scholarly tradition, and theology in particular was singled out for intense criticism, reflecting the Jadidist belief that knowledge of *kalām* was at best irrelevant, and at worst harmful to society. For Jadidists, it was the 'conservative' *ʿulamāʾ*, those most responsible for Muslims' backwardness, who immersed themselves in the useless study of theology, while they taught themselves practical subjects such as mathematics and world geography.

Though it did not attract huge numbers of Muslims to its cause, Jadidism's importance in urban settings was undeniable. In Bukhara, Tashkent, and Samarqand, to say nothing of the Muslim urban centres of Russia proper, significant sections of the *ʿulamāʾ* and merchant classes were drawn to the movement. They founded schools, newspapers, and printing presses that had no use for theological writings (Khalid 1998; Kanlidere 1997). After the Russian Revolution of 1905, many Jadidists associated themselves with left-wing Russian political parties, and during the Revolution of 1917 and ensuing Russian Civil War (1917–22), many Jadidist factions were allied with the communists (often out of necessity).

The Bolshevik Revolution was the death knell for the Islamic scholarly tradition in the Russian Empire-*cum*-Soviet Union. The *ʿulamāʾ*, regardless of their individual political inclinations, were treated as a 'reactionary' feudal class and faced widespread repressive measures (Mohammatshin 2004). These only intensified with the rise of officially anti-religious policies in the 1930s. Religious institutions and forms of religiosity of all kinds were repressed, in particular theology, which was viewed as a means for the masses' oppression at the hands of the parasitic *ʿulamāʾ* (e.g. Klimovich 1936: 24). By the end of the decade, virtually all of the *ʿulamāʾ*, as well as the left-wing Muslim intelligentsia, had been wiped out. Allen Frank describes the demise of Islamic learning in the Soviet Union:

> Not only were thousands of mosques closed, but all Islamic education was banned, all madrasas were closed, tens of thousands of Islamic books and manuscripts

[51] There is considerable uncertainty regarding the origins of Jadidism (first raised by Adeeb Khalid). The conventional narrative posits that it was initiated by Qūrṣāwī, whose reformism was then taken up by Marjānī and some of his contemporaries, before reaching full flower a generation later. This narrative ignores the significant discrepancies between Jadidism and the work of these two scholars, in particular their theological writings. Any connection, particularly with Qūrṣāwī, is quite tenuous. His condemnation in Bukhara served as an important example for Jadidists' own struggles towards reform. More substantively, Marjānī was linked with the reformist faction of the Bukharan *ʿulamāʾ*, out of which Bukharan Jadidism sprang. However, this reformist faction counted among its earlier members some of the same scholars who had condemned Qūrṣāwī, including ʿInāyat Allāh Bukhārī; Khalid 1998: 100; Dudoignon 2004: 67, 83; Spannaus forthcoming.

> were burned. Most decisively, perhaps thirty thousand members of the *ʿulamāʾ* were executed or exiled to labor camps in Siberia. By the late 1930s this dynamic Islamic culture had for all intents and purposes ceased to exist... (Frank 2001: 6)[52]

The study of theology, already denigrated by Muslim modernists,[53] became a subject for ideological academic research that was inclined to present *kalām* in Central Asia as something that had ceased developing centuries before. In truth, an active, vibrant tradition of theology enriched by numerous outside influences had remained in Central Asia up to the twentieth century. It had continued to evolve up to this time, incorporating many of the metaphysical and philosophical aspects of post-Avicennian *kalām* and, rather than merely repeating previous debates, brought forward a new ontological perspective as part of the discourse of Sunni theology. Though more study is needed into the precise contours of that discourse and the scholars integral in its elaboration, that it continued as an important part of post-classical Islamic scholarship in Central Asia is beyond doubt.

References

al-Afghānī, al-Sayyid Jamāl al-Dīn (*Āthār*). *al-Āthār al-kāmila*. Vol. 5. Ed. S. Kh. Shāhī. Cairo: Maktabat al-shurūq al-dawliyya, 1423/2002.

Akimushkin, O. F., et al. (eds.) (1998). *Persidskie i tadzhikskie rukopisi Instituta vostokovedeniia Rossiiskoi akademii nauk: kratkii katalog*. New York: Norman Ross.

Algar, H. (1990). 'A Brief History of the Naqshbandi Order'. In M. Gaborieau et al. (eds.), *Naqshbandis: Cheminements situation actuelle d'un ordre mystique musulman*. Istanbul: Éditions ISIS, 3–44.

Ansari, A. H. (1986). *Sufism and Shariʿah: A Study of Shaykh Ahmad Sirhindi's Effort to Reform Sufism*. Leicester: Islamic Foundation.

Ansari, A. H. (1998). 'Shaykh Ahmad Sirhindi's Doctrine of "Wahdat al-Shuhud"'. *Islamic Studies* 37: 281–313.

Arberry, A. J. (1977). *The Doctrine of the Sufis*. Cambridge: Cambridge University Press.

Arslanova, A. A. (ed.) (2005). *Opisanie rukopisei na persidskom iazyke Nauchnoi biblioteki im. N.I. Lobachevskogo Kazanskogo gosudarstvennogo universiteta*. Kazan: Gosudarstvennyi universitet.

ʿAynī, Ṣadr al-Dīn (2002). *Tārīkh-i inqilāb-i fikrī dar Bukhārā*. Tehran: Sorush, 1381.

Babadžanov, B. (1996). 'On the History of the Naqsbandiya Mugaddidiya in Central Mawara'annahr in the Late 18th and Early 19th Centuries'. In M. Kemper et al. (eds.), *Muslim Culture in Russia and Central Asia from the 18th to the Early 20th Centuries*. Vol. i. Berlin: Klaus Schwarz, 385–414.

Babadžanov, B. (2003). 'About a Scroll of Documents Justifying Yasavi Rituals'. In N. Kondo (ed.), *Persian Documents: Social History of Iran and Turan in the Fifteenth to Nineteenth Centuries*. London: Routledge Curzon, 53–72.

[52] The Mīr-i ʿArab in Bukhara was the only *madrasa* in Central Asia allowed to continue as a religious school, and only after 1948; cf. Khalid 2007: 110.

[53] ʿAynī, *Tārīkh-i inqilāb*; Fiṭrat, *Munāẓarah*.

al-Bazdawī, Abū l-Yusr Muḥammad (*Uṣūl al-dīn*). *Uṣūl al-dīn*. Ed. H. P. Linss et al. Cairo: al-Maktaba al-azhariyya li-l-turāth, 1424/2003.

Brockelmann, C. (1937–42). *Geschichte der arabischen Litteratur*. Erster–Dritter Supplementband. Leiden: Brill.

Brockelmann, C. (1943–9). *Geschichte der arabischen Litteratur*. Zweite den Supplementbänden angepassten Auflage. Leiden: Brill.

Bruckmayr, P. (2009). 'The Spread and Persistence of Maturidi Kalam and Underlying Dynamics'. *Iran and the Caucasus* 13: 59–92.

Buehler, A. (1996). 'The Naqshbandiyya in Timurid India: The Central Asian Legacy'. *Journal of Islamic Studies* 7: 208–28.

Buehler, A. (2001). *Fahāris-i taḥlīlī-i hashtgāna-yi Maktūbāt-i Aḥmad Sirhindī*. Lahore: Iqbal Academy Pakistan.

Chittick, W. (2008). 'Ibn Arabi'. In E. N. Zalta (ed.), *The Stanford Encyclopedia of Philosophy (Fall 2008 Edition)*. <http://plato.stanford.edu/archives/fall2008/entries/ibn-arabi/>

al-Dawānī, Jalāl al-Dīn (*Shawākil*). *Shawākil-al-ḥūr fī sharḥ hayākil-al-nūr: A Commentary on Hayakil-al-nur by Shihabuddin Abul Futuh Yahya ibn Habash ibn Amirak al-Suhrawardi*. Ed. M. Abdul Haq et al. Madras: Government Oriental Manuscripts Library, 1953.

al-Dawānī, Jalāl al-Dīn (*Rasā'il*). *Sab'rasā'il*. Ed. A. Tūysirkānī. Tehran: Mīrāth-i maktūb, 1381/2002.

DeWeese, D. (1994). *Islamization and Native Religion in the Golden Horde: Baba Tukles and Conversion to Islam in Historical and Epic Tradition*. University Park, PA: Pennsylvania State University Press.

DeWeese, D. (ed.) (2001). *Studies on Central Asian History*. Bloomington, IN: Indiana University Press.

Dinorshoev, M. (2003). 'Philosophy, Logic and Cosmology'. In *History of Civilizations of Central Asia, v: Development in Contrast: From the Sixteenth to the Mid-Nineteenth Century*. Paris: UNESCO, 747–58.

Dmitrieva, L. V., et al. (eds.) (2002). *Katalog tiurkskikh rukopisei Instituta vostokovedeniia Rossiiskoi akademii nauk*. Moscow: Izd-vo Vostochnaia literatura.

Dudoignon, S. (ed.) (1996). *Le Réformisme musulman en Asie centrale: du 'premier renouveau' à la soviétisation, 1788–1937* [Special issue]. *Cahiers du monde russe* 37.

Dudoignon, S. (2004). 'Faction Struggles among the Bukharan Ulama during the Colonial, the Revolutionary and the Early Soviet Periods (1868–1929): A Paradigm for History Writing?' In S. Tsugitaka (ed.), *Muslim Societies: Historical and Comparative Aspects*. New York: Routledge Curzon, 62–96.

Elder, E. E. (1950). *A Commentary on the Creed of Islam: Sa'd al-Din al-Taftazani on the Creed of Najm al-Din al-Nasafi*. New York: Columbia University Press.

van Ess, J. (2011). 'Jorjāni, Zayn-al-Din Abu'l-Ḥasan 'Ali'. *Encyclopedia Iranica*, xv. 21–9.

Fakhr al-Dīn, Riḍā' al-Dīn (*Āthār*). *Āthār*. 15 parts in 2 vols. Part 1: Kazan: Tipo-litografiia imperatorskogo universiteta, 1900. Parts 2–15: Orenburg: Tipografiia G. I. Karimova, 1901–8.

Fātiḥnizhād, 'Ināyat Allāh et al. (eds.) (2003). Fihrist-i nuskha-*hā-yi khaṭṭī-yi Kitābkhāna-yi Dānishgāh-i Qāzān, Jumhūrī-yi Tātārstān, Fidrāsiyūn-i Rūsiya*. Qom: Kitābkhāna-yi buzurg va ganjīna-yi makhṭūṭāt-i islāmī-i Ḥaḍrat Āyat Allāh al-'uẓmā Mar'ashī Najafī, 1382.

Fiṭrat, ['Abd al-Ra'ūf] (*Munāẓara*). *Munāẓara: Mudarris-i bukhārā-yī bāyik nafar-i farangī dar Hindustān darbārah-i makātib-i jadīda*. Istanbul: Maṭba'a-i islāmiyya-i 'Ḥikmat', 1327[/1909].

Frank, A. J. (2001). *Muslim Religious Institutions in Imperial Russia: The Islamic World of Novouzensk District and the Kazakh Inner Horde, 1780–1910*. Leiden: Brill.

Gilliot, C. (2002). 'La Théologie musulmane en Asie centrale et au Khorasan'. *Arabica* 49: 135–203.

Gutas, D. (1988). 'Avicenna's Madhhab with an Appendix on the Question of His Date of Birth'. *Quaderni di Studi Arabi* 5–6: 323–36.

ter Haar, J. G. J. (1992). *Follower and Heir of the Prophet: Shaykh Ahmad Sirhindi (1564–1624) as Mystic*. Leiden: Het Oosters Instituut.

Ibn ʿArabī, Muḥyī l-Dīn (*Inshāʾ*). *Inshāʾ al-Dawāʾir*. In H. S. Nyberg (ed.), *Kleinere Schriften des Ibn al-ʿArabī*. Leiden: Brill, 1919.

al-Ījī, ʿAḍud al-Dīn (*Mawāqif*). *Al-Mawāqif fī ʿilm al-kalām*. Cairo: Maktabat al-mutanabbī, [1983].

Jackson, S. A. (1996). 'Taqlid, Legal Scaffolding and the Scope of Legal Injunctions in Post-Formative Theory: Mutlaq and ʿAmm in the Jurisprudence of Shihab al-Din al-Qarafi'. *Islamic Law and Society* 3: 165–92.

al-Jāmī, ʿAbd al-Raḥmān b. Aḥmad (*Naqd*). *Naqd al-nuṣūṣ fī sharḥ naqsh al-Fuṣūṣ*. Ed. W. Chittick. Tehran: Anjuman-i shāhanshāhī-yi falsafa-yi Īrān, 1977.

al-Jāmī, ʿAbd al-Raḥmān b. Aḥmad (*Lawāʾiḥ*). *Lawaʾih: A Treatise on Sufism*. Ed. and trans. E. H. Whinefield and Mirza Muhammad Kazvini. London: Theosophical Publishing House, 1978.

al-Jāmī, ʿAbd al-Raḥmān b. Aḥmad (*Pearl*). *The Precious Pearl: Al-Jami's Al-Durrah Al-Fakhira together with his Glosses and the Commentary of ʿAbd al-Ghafur al-Lari*. Trans. N. Herr. Albany, NY: State University of New York Press, 1979.

al-Jāmī, ʿAbd al-Raḥmān b. Aḥmad (*Durra*). *al-Durra al-fākhira fī taḥqīq madhhab al-ṣūfiyya wa-l-mutakallimīn wa-l-ḥukamāʾ al-mutaqaddimīn*. Ed. N. Herr et al. Tehran: Dānishgāh-i MakGīl, 1358[/1980].

al-Jāmī, ʿAbd al-Raḥmān b. Aḥmad (*Jaillissements*). *Les Jaillissements de lumière*. Ed. and trans. Y. Richard. Paris: Les Deux Océans, 1982.

Kalābādhī, Abū Bakr Muḥammad b. Ishāq (*Taʿarruf*). *Kitāb al-Taʿarruf li-madhhab ahl al-taṣawwuf*. Ed. A. J. Arberry. Cairo: Maktabat al-Khānjī, 1934.

Kalanbawī, Ismāʿīl b. Muṣṭafā (*Ḥāshiya*). *Ḥāshiyat al-Kalanbawī ʿalā Sharḥ al-Dawānī*. Dersaadat [Istanbul]: Maṭbaʿa ʿUthmāniyya, 1316[/1898].

Kanlidere, A. (1997). *Reform within Islam: The Tajdid and Jadid Movement among the Kazan Tatars (1809–1917): Conciliation or Conflict?* Istanbul: Eren.

Karimova, S. (2010). 'The Study of Islamic Manuscripts in Uzbekistan: Results and Tasks'. *Asian Research Trends* 5 (NS): 35–57.

Kemper, M. (1998). *Sufis und Gelehrte in Tatarien und Baschkirien, 1789–1889: Der islamische Diskurs unter russischer Herrschaft*. Berlin: Klaus Schwarz.

Khalid, A. (1998). *The Politics of Muslim Cultural Reform: Jadidism in Central Asia*. Berkeley and Los Angeles: University of California Press.

Khalid, A. (2007). *Islam after Communism: Religion and Politics in Central Asia*. Berkeley and Los Angeles: University of California Press.

Khalidov, A. B., et al. (eds.) (1986). *Arabskie rukopisi Instituta vostokovedeniia: kratkii katalog*. Moscow: Izd-vo Nauka.

Klimovich, L. (1936). *Islam v tsarskoi Rossii: Ocherki*. Moscow: Gosudarstvennoe antireligioznoe izd-vo.

Knysh, A. (1999). *Ibn ʿArabi in the Later Islamic Tradition: The Making of a Polemical Image in Medieval Islam*. Albany, NY: State University of New York Press.

von Kügelgen, A. (1998). 'Die Entfaltung der Naqšbandiya Muǧaddidiya im mittleren Transoxanien vom 18. bis zum Beginn des 19. Jahrhunderts: Ein Stück Detektivarbeit'. In von Kügelgen et al. (eds.), *Muslim Culture in Russia and Central Asia from the 18th to the Early 20th Centuries*. Vol. ii: *Inter-Regional and Inter-Ethnic Relations*. Berlin: Klaus Schwarz, 101–51.

von Kügelgen, A., et al. (eds.) (1996–2002). *Muslim Culture in Russia and Central Asia from the 18th to the Early 20th Centuries*. 4 vols. Berlin: Klaus Schwarz.

Liechti, S. (2008). *Books, Book Endowments, and Communities of Knowledge in the Bukharan Khanate*. Ph.D. dissertation, New York University.

Losensky, P. (2008). 'Jami: i. Life and Works'. *Encyclopedia Iranica*, xiv. 469–75.

McChesney, R. (1992). 'Central Asia: vi. In the 16th to 18th Centuries'. In *Encyclopedia Iranica*, v. 176–93.

Madelung, W. (2000). 'al-Taftāzānī'. *Encyclopedia of Islam*. New edn. x. 88–9.

Maktūbāt-i Khwāja Muḥammad Maʿṣūm. Karachi: Asrār Muḥammad Khān, 1977.

Marjānī, Shihāb al-Dīn (*Ḥikma*). *Kitāb al-Ḥikma al-bāligha al-jāniyya fī sharḥ al-ʿaqāʾid al-ḥanafiyya*. Kazan: Maṭbaʿa Wiyācheslāf, 1888.

Marjānī, Shihāb al-Dīn (*Mustafād*). *Mustafād al-akhbār fī aḥwāl Qazān wa-Bulghār*. 2 vols. Vol. i: Kazan: tipografiia B. L. Dombrovskago, 1897. Vol. ii: Kazan: tipografiia Universitetskago, 1900. [Repr. as Şehabeddin Mercani. *Müstefad'ül-ahbar fi ahval-i Kazan ve Bulgar*. 2 vols. Ankara: Ankara Üniversitesi basımevı, 1997].

Mohammatshin, R. (2004). 'The Tatar Intelligentsia and the Clergy, 1917–1937'. In S. A. Dudoignon (ed.), *Devout Societies vs. Impious States? Transmitting Islamic Learning in Russia, Central Asia and China, through the Twentieth Century*. Berlin: Klaus Schwarz, 29–38.

Morris, J. (1986). 'Ibn ʿArabi and his Interpreters. Part II: Influences and Interpretations'. *Journal of the American Oriental Society* 106: 733–56.

Morris, J. (1987). 'Ibn ʿArabi and his Interpreters. Part II (Conclusion): Influences and Interpretations'. *Journal of the American Oriental Society* 107: 101–19.

Muminov, A., et al. (eds.) (1999a). *Patrimonie manuscrit et vie intellectuelle de l'Asie centrale islamique* [Special issue]. *Cahiers d'Asie centrale* 7.

Muminov, A., et al. (1999b). 'Fonds nationaux et collections privées de manuscripts en écriture arabe de l'Ouzbékistan'. *Cahiers d'Asie centrale* 7: 17–38.

Muminov, A., et al. (eds.) (2007). *Manuscrits en écriture arabe du Musée regional de Nukus (République autonome du Karakalpakstan, Ouzbékistan): Fonds arabe, persan, turki et karakalpak*. Rome: Instituto per l'oriente C. A. Nallino.

al-Nasafī, Abū Muʿīn (*Tabṣira*). *Tabṣirat al-adilla fī uṣūl al-dīn*. Ed. Ḥ. Ātāy. Ankara: Nashriyyāt riʾāsat al-shuʾūn al-dīniyya li-l-Jumhūriyya al-turkiyya, 1993.

Nasr, S. H. (1993). *An Introduction to Islamic Cosmological Doctrines: Conceptions of Nature and Methods Used for its Study by the Ikhwan al-Safaʾ, al-Biruni and ibn Sina*. Albany, NY: State University of New York Press.

Pourjavady, R. (2011). *Philosophy in Early Safavid Iran: Najm al-Din Mahmud al-Nayrizi and his Writings*. Leiden: Brill.

Qarabāghī, Yūsuf (*Ḥāshiya*). *Ḥāshiyat Yūsuf Qarabāghī ʿalā Sharḥ ʿaqāʾid Mullā Jalāl*. MS University of Michigan, Isl. MS no. 1027. <http://catalog.hathitrust.org/Record/006834427>

Qūrṣāwī, Abū l-Naṣr ʿAbd al-Naṣīr (*Sharḥ qadīm*). *Sharḥ al-ʿAqāʾid al-nasafiyya al-qadīm*. MS Kazanskii Gosudarstvennyi Universitet A-1347, fos. 17a–18b.

Qūrṣāwī, Abū l-Naṣr ʿAbd al-Naṣīr (*Sharḥ jadīd*). *Sharḥ jadīd li-l-ʿAqāʾid al-nasafiyya*. MS St Petersburg, Institut vostochnykh rukopisei A1241, fos. 92b–147a.

al-Qūshjī, ʿAlī b. Muḥammad (*Sharḥ*). *Sharḥ al-Qūshjī ʿalā Tajrīd al-ʿaqāʾid li-l-Ṭūsī*. Alexandria: Dār al-Wafāʾ li-dunyā al-ṭibāʿa wa-l-nashr, [2002].

Rahman, F. (1985). "Ali Qušji: i. Life and Theological Works'. *Encyclopedia Iranica*, i. 876–7.
Rudolph, U. (1996). *Al-Maturidi und die sunnitische Theologie in Samarkand*. Leiden: Brill.
al-Sālimī, Abū Shakūr (*Tamhīd*). *Tamhīd Abī Shakūr al-Sālimī*. Delhi: al-Maṭba' al-fārūqī, 1309[/1892].
Semenov, A. A. (ed.) (1952–87). *Sobranie vostochnykh rukopisei Akademii nauk Uzbekskoi SSR*. 11 vols. Tashkent: Izd-vo Akademiia nauk UzSSR.
Shorish, M. M. (1986). 'Traditional Islamic Education in Central Asia prior to 1917'. In C. Lemercier-Quelquejay et al. (eds.), *Passé Turco-Tatar, présent Soviétique: études offertes à Alexandre Bennigsen*. Paris: Éditions Peeters, 317–44.
Sirhindī, Aḥmad (*Maktūbāt*). *Maktūbāt-i Imām-i Rabbānī ḥaḍrat mujaddid-i alf-i thānī*. Ed. Nūr Aḥmad Amritsarī. Karachi: H. M. Sa'īd Kampanī, 1392[1972].
Spannaus, N. (2015). 'Šihab al-Din al-Marǧani on the Divine Attributes: a Study in Kalam in the 19th Century'. *Arabica* 62: 74–98.
Spannaus, N. (forthcoming). *Preserving Islamic Tradition: Abu Nasr Qursawi and the Beginnings of Modern Reformism*. New York: Oxford University Press.
Spuler, B. (1970). 'Central Asia from the Sixteenth Century to the Russian Conquests'. In P. M. Holt et al. (eds.), *Cambridge History of Islam, ia: The Central Islamic Lands from Pre-Islamic times to the First World War*. Cambridge: Cambridge University Press, 468–94.
Szuppe, M., et al. (eds.) (2004). *Catalogue des manuscripts orientaux du musée regional de Qarshi, Ouzbékistan*. Rome: Instituto per l'Oriente C. A. Nallino.
al-Taftāzānī, Mas'ūd b. 'Umar (*Majmū'a*). *Majmū'at rasā'il fī waḥdat al-wujūd*. Istanbul: n.p., 1294[/1877].
al-Ūriwī, Fatḥ Allāh b. al-Ḥusayn. [Untitled work.] MS Kazanskii Gosudarstvennyi Universitet, T-3571, fos. 1a–3a.
al-Ūriwī, Fatḥ Allāh b. al-Ḥusayn. (*Risāla*). *Risāla fī ṣifāt al-bārī*. MS St Petersburg, Institut vostochnykh rukopisei C234, fos. 35b–43a.
Wisnovsky, R. (2004a). 'One Aspect of the Avicennian Turn in Sunni Theology'. *Arabic Sciences and Philosophy* 14: 65–100.
Wisnovsky, R. (2004b). 'The Nature and Scope of Arabic Philosophical Commentary in Post-Classical (ca. 1100–1900) Islamic Intellectual History: Some Preliminary Observations'. In P. Adamson et al. (eds.), *Philosophy, Science and Exegesis in Greek, Arabic and Latin Commentaries*. London: Institute of Advanced Studies, ii. 149–91.
Wisnovsky, R. (2005). 'Avicenna and the Avicennian Tradition'. In P. Adamson et al. (eds.), *The Cambridge Companion to Arabic Philosophy*. Cambridge: Cambridge University Press, 92–136.
Wisnovsky, R. (2011). 'Essence and Existence in the Eleventh- and Twelfth-Century Islamic East (Mašriq): A Sketch'. In A. Bertolacci and D. Hasse (eds.), *The Arabic, Hebrew and Latin Reception of Avicenna's Metaphysics*. Berlin: de Gruyter, 27–50.
Zaman, M. Q. (2002). *The Ulama in Contemporary Islam: Custodians of Change*. Princeton: Princeton University Press.
Ziai, H. (2005). 'Recent Trends in Arabic and Persian Philosophy'. In P. Adamson et al. (eds.), *The Cambridge Companion to Arabic Philosophy*. Cambridge: Cambridge University Press, 405–25.

CHAPTER 34

THEOLOGY IN THE INDIAN SUBCONTINENT

ASAD Q. AHMED AND REZA POURJAVADY

THIS is a first exploratory attempt to sketch a map of Muslim theology in India for the pre-modern and early modern periods.* The vast majority of texts in this discipline have remained unpublished and practically no substantive work on their contents has appeared to date. Thus, at this stage of research, it appears suitable that the tradition be gauged in a preliminary fashion from three related angles: socio-intellectual networks of relevant scholars; a tally of the most significant texts; and brief references to prominent debates and to the contribution of certain outstanding personalities. Taken together, it is hoped that the information to follow will open up some vistas for future research.

I From the Emergence to the End of the Seventeenth Century

(a) Iranian Theologians in India

Interest in the professional study of *kalām* was revived in India in the second half of the eighth/fifteenth century. The courts of the rulers of Sind, Gujarat, and especially the Bahmani Sultanate (748/1347–933/1527) in the Deccan seem to have played a significant role in developing an academic environment and patronizing the rational sciences. Jalāl al-Dīn al-Dawānī (d. 908/1502), the well-known theologian/philosopher of the time, enjoyed the patronage of an Indian ruler, namely Sultan Maḥmūd I of Gujarat (r. 863/1458–917/1511). Moreover, at least two of Dawānī's students, Mīr Shams al-Dīn Muḥammad al-Jurjānī (who was the great-grandson of al-Sharīf al-Jurjānī) and a

* Part I was written by R. Pourjavady, Part II by A. Q. Ahmed.

certain Mīr Muʿīn al-Dīn, headed to India and eventually were present at Niẓām al-Dīn Shāh Sindī's (r. 866/1461–914/1508) court (Barzigar 2001: 2561).

The rise of the Safavid Shah Ismāʿīl (r. 907/1501–930/1524) and his declaration of Twelver Shīʿism as the state religion of Iran had a direct impact on the development of the theological discourse in India. Following Shah Ismāʿīl (or at least inspired by him), three rulers of the Deccan region declared Twelver Shīʿism to be the official religion of their respective states: (1) Yūsuf ʿĀdil Shāh (r. 908/1502–916/1510), founder of the ʿĀdil Shāhī dynasty, which ruled the Sultanate of Bijapur; (2) Sultan Qulī Quṭb Shāh (r. 924/1518–950/1543), founder of the Quṭb Shāhī dynasty in Golkonda (in modern-day Andhra Pradesh); and (3) Burhān Niẓām Shah (r. 914/1508–961/1554), the ruler of the Ahmadnagar state.

While the first two seem to have converted to Twelver Shīʿism before they took power and hence adopted Twelver Shīʿism from the first day of their rule, Burhān Niẓām Shah converted to Twelver Shīʿism as late as 944/1537, and it was only after this conversion that he proclaimed Twelver Shīʿism to be the official religion of his kingdom. A migrant Iranian Shīʿī preacher and scholar, Shāh Ṭāhir Dakanī (d. between 952/1545 and 956/1549), seems to have played a significant role in this conversion (Ivanow 1938: 58–61; Poonawala 1997: 200). Shāh Ṭāhir had escaped by sea to India in 926/1520 after being accused of being Ismāʿīlī. First he went to the court of Ismāʿīl ʿĀdil Shah (r. 916/1510–944/1538) in Bijapur and then in 928/1522 went on to Ahmadnagar, where he remained until his death. Following the conversion of Burhān Niẓām Shah, Shāh Ṭāhir made an effort to promote Twelver Shīʿism. He invited several Iranian Shīʿī scholars to the Sultanate (Dhābiṭ 1998: 98). Moreover, he wrote at least one Twelver Shīʿī theological work consisting of a commentary on al-ʿAllāma al-Ḥillī's (d. 726/1325) *al-Bāb al-ḥādī ʿashar* (Poonawala 1977: 274). Ivanow suggests that Shāh Ṭāhir's accusation of being Ismāʿīlī was correct and that he was observing *taqiyya* while preaching 'a moderate and Sufic-like form, in the guise of Ithnā-ʿasharism' (Ivanow 1938: 77). His argument for this is mainly based on the writings of Shāh Ṭāhir's followers. But the latter's own works, if extant, have yet to be examined.

Apart from Shāh Ṭāhir, there was at least one other Twelver Shīʿī theologian at the court of Burhān Niẓām Shah, namely Muḥammad b. Aḥmad al-Khʷājagī, known as al-Shaykh al-Shīrāzī (*fl.* 953/1546). Khʷājagī is best known for his Twelver Shīʿī creed, *al-Niẓāmiyya fī madhhab al-Imāmiyya*, composed at the request of Burhān Niẓām Shah. Another Twelver Shīʿī creed of Khʷājagī, entitled *al-Maḥajja al-bayḍāʾ fī madhhab āl al-ʿabā*, was dedicated to the head of the ʿĀdil Shāhī dynasty of the time, who was presumably Ibrāhim ʿĀdil Shah I (r. 1534–58 CE). Moreover, he seems to have resided for some time in Golkonda (ruled by the Quṭb Shāhī dynasty), where he composed an Arabic commentary on Naṣīr al-Dīn al-Ṭūsī's (d. 672/1274) Twelver Shīʿī creed *al-Fuṣūl*, entitled *Tuḥfat al-fuḥūl fī sharḥ al-Fuṣūl* (completed in 953/1547), a Persian commentary on the same text completed in the same year, and possibly his commentary on the ʿAllāma Ḥillī's *al-Bāb al-ḥādī ʿashar*, completed shortly before the two aforementioned works, in 952/1545. Khʷājagī also commented upon the works of Jalāl al-Dīn al-Dawānī, Ṣadr al-Dīn al-Dashtakī (d. 903/1498), and Nūr al-Dīn al-Jāmī (d. 898/1492) on the proof of God's existence and His attributes (Khʷājagī, *Niẓāmiyya*, 94f.).

Another effect of the new Safavid religious policy was the migration of Sunnī scholars to neighbouring lands, including India. The hostility towards Sunnī scholars, which had started during the rise to power of the Safavid Shah Ismāʿīl, had become even more ruthless at the time of his successor, Shah Ṭahmāsb (r. 930/1524–984/1576). One of the Sunnī theologians who moved to India in the early decades of the Safavid era was Muṣliḥ al-Dīn al-Lārī (d. 979/1572). Muṣliḥ al-Dīn, who studied theology (as well as other rational and traditional sciences) in Shīrāz with a number of outstanding scholars such as Kamāl al-Dīn Ḥusayn al-Lārī (d. after 918/1512), Shams al-Dīn al-Khafrī (d. 942/1535–6), and Ghiyāth al-Dīn Manṣūr al-Dashtakī (d. 949/1542), moved to India most likely during the early years of Shah Ṭahmāsb's reign. The specific reason for his migration is unknown, but in his world history, entitled *Mirʾāt al-adwār wa-mirqāt al-akhbār*, he cites Shah Ṭahmāsb's hostility towards Sunnī scholars as the main reason behind the migration of scholars from Iran to other lands (Nawshāhī 1997: 109). At first, Lārī spent some time at the court of Shah Ḥasan Arghūn (r. 930/1524–963/1556) in the province of Sind (Nawshāhī 1997: 91). Then he was able to acquaint himself at the court of the Bābirīd, Sultan Humāyūn (r. 937/1531–963/1556). Subsequently he was appointed by the Sultan as the *ṣadr* ('administrator'). Following Humāyūn's death on 11 Rabīʿ II 963/22 February 1556, Lārī left India for the Ottoman territory. Lārī wrote the following works on rational theology: (i) Glosses on al-Sharīf al-Jurjānī's (d. 816/1414) commentary on ʿAḍud al-Dīn al-Ījī's (d. 756/1355) *al-Mawāqif*; (ii) glosses on Jalāl al-Dīn al-Dawānī's first set of glosses on ʿAlāʾ al-Dīn al-Qūshjī's (d. 782/1474) commentary on Naṣīr al-Dīn al-Ṭūsī's *Tajrīd al-iʿtiqād*; (iii) *Risāla fī bayān qudrat Allāh*; and (iv) *Risāla fī taḥqīq al-mabdaʾ wa-l-maʿād*. However, it is unclear which of the above works were composed during his stay in India; nor is it known whether or not he was also engaged in teaching theology while he resided in India.

The first migrant scholar who can safely be assumed to have been involved with teaching theology in India is Fatḥ Allāh al-Shīrāzī (d. 998/1590). Born into a scholarly family in Shīrāz, Fatḥ Allāh studied theology and philosophy with Ghiyāth al-Dīn Manṣūr al-Dashtakī and Jamāl al-Dīn Maḥmūd al-Shīrāzī. Later he was invited to India by Mīrzā Jānī, the ruler of Thatta. He also spent some time in the service of ʿAlī ʿĀdil Shah (r. 965/1558–987/1580) in Bijapur as his *wakīl* ('administrator'). For a while he also resided in Ahmadnegar, where he became acquainted with Sultan Murtaḍā Niẓām Shah II (r. 972/1565–996/1588). In response to the theological questions of the latter he composed in Persian *al-Asʾila al-sulṭāniyya*. In 990/1582, he was summoned to the imperial court of Mughal Emperor Akbar (r. 963/1556–1014/1605), where he was conferred the title of *ʿAḍud al-dawla*. He remained at the Emperor's service until his death in Kashmir in 998/1590 (Qasemi 1999: 421). Fatḥ Allāh al-Shīrāzī was considered by later historiographers as having been the main conduit for the serious study of philosophy and theology in India. It is common, therefore, for intellectual historians of Islamic thought in India to trace a lineage from Fatḥ Allāh al-Shīrāzī to the scholars of Farangī Maḥal in the eighteenth century CE. Among his theological works, his gloss on Jalāl al-Dīn al-Dawānī's earlier gloss on ʿAlāʾ al-Dīn al-Qūshjī's commentary on Naṣīr al-Dīn al-Ṭūsī's *Tajrīd al-iʿtiqād* is noteworthy. This work was probably among the texts he was actively teaching.

Although it is almost certain that Fatḥ Allāh al-Shīrāzī was a Shīʿī scholar, later generations of Sunnī scholars in India have shown no hesitation in linking their chain of transmission of theology to him. Perhaps this is because he was not so explicit about his Shīʿī beliefs in writing. His Iranian disciple, Muḥammad b. Maḥmūd Dihdār (d. 1016/1607), seems by comparison not to have attracted many Sunnī students. Dihdār, who was likewise associated with the court of Sultan ʿAlī ʿĀdil Shah in Bijapur, moved after the latter's death to Ahmadnegar where he enjoyed the patronage of Sultan Murtaḍā Niẓām Shah II. But subsequently, unlike his teacher, who went to the court of Mughal Emperor Akbar, he moved to Burhanpur, and eventually to Surat. Dihdār wrote several short treatises on *kalām* including a *Risāla fī maʿrifat al-imām*, the title of which makes it clear that he was explicit about his Shīʿī beliefs. Dihdār's other theological works include *Risāla fī l-kalām, Risāla fī l-tawḥīd* dedicated to Murtaḍā Niẓām Shah II (r. 972/1564–996/1588), *Risāla dar tawḥīd-i istidlālī, Risāla fī l-nubuwwa*, and *Risāla fī ithbāt al-wājib taʿālā fī ṭarīq al-mutakallimīn wa-l-ḥukamāʾ wa-l-ṣūfiyya, Kawākib al-thawāqib* (Dihdār Shīrāzī, *Rasāʾil*, 11–25; Mīr 1989: ii. 801–4).

In 982/1575, the Mughal Emperor Akbar, who had a keen interest in religious discussion, ordered the construction of an elegant building close to his palace in Fatehpur Sikri for holding religious debates. These debates were mainly on Islamic religious issues, although they gradually came to include inter-religious discussions with Zoroastrians and Christians. Questions regarding certain *ḥadīth*s or the interpretation of Qurʾānic verses were among the more commonly addressed. But sometimes theological issues, such as God's unity (*tawḥīd*), the eternity of the world and its Creator, the nature of God–human relation, the human soul, and questions relating to the resurrection were debated (Rizvi 1975: 119). The discussion at first involved only the Sunnī scholars who tended to rely on the theological works of al-Ghazālī (d. 505/1111) as their main source. However, it was not long before the Shīʿī scholars began to be invited, and this led to the raking up of several controversial issues. Mullā ʿAbd Allāh Sulṭānpūrī, known as Makhdūm al-Mulk (d. 1006/1597), was one of the key disputants in these debates. Makhdūm al-Mulk was an anti-Shīʿī scholar, who wrote *Minhāj al-dīn wa-miʿrāj al-muslimīn* in criticism of Twelver Shīʿism and ordered several Shīʿī works to be burned. A certain Mullā Muḥammad Yazdī was the most vocal and frank among the Shīʿī disputants. As the two sides showed no compromise in their attitudes, the debates became rather bewildering for audiences, including the Emperor (Rizvi 1975: 125).

At the turn of the eleventh/seventeenth century, the Shīʿī–Sunnī conflict in India came to a head. The Sunnī authoritative scholar of the time, Shaykh Mujaddid Aḥmad Sirhindī (d. 1034/1624), regarded Shīʿism as the worst form of heresy and devoted his full energy to prevent the expansion of Shīʿī doctrines. He wrote an anti-Shīʿī polemical pamphlet, entitled *Radd-i Rawāfiḍ* (Ziauddin 2005: 135).

On the Shīʿī side, one of the most vociferous scholars was Qāḍī Nūr Allāh al-Shūshtarī (d. 1019/1610). After receiving his early education in his home town, Shūshtar, Nūr Allāh moved to Mashhad in 974/1566–7 to continue his education. Following the invasion of Mashhad by Uzbek forces, on 1 Shawwāl 992/6 October 1584, he migrated to Lahore, where he attracted the notice of Akbar (963–1014/1556–1605) and was appointed by the latter as the chief *qāḍī* of Lahore. As a scholar, Shūshtarī devoted his efforts mainly to promoting the Shīʿī faith. His *Majālis al-muʾminīn*, completed in 990/1582, contains biographies of famous Shīʿīs from the beginning of Islam to the rise of the Safavid dynasty. On theology he wrote a Twelver Shīʿī creed, entitled *al-ʿAqāʾid al-imāmiyya*, a treatise on infallibility (*ʿiṣma*), a treatise on God's knowledge, as well as supercommentaries on theological textbooks, such as a gloss on Saʿd al-Dīn al-Taftāzānī's commentary on ʿUmar al-Nasafī's (d. 537/1142) *al-ʿAqāʾid*, glosses on Jalāl al-Dīn al-Dawānī's first and second glosses on ʿAlāʾ al-Dīn al-Qūshjī's commentary on Naṣīr al-Dīn al-Ṭūsī's *Tajrīd al-iʿtiqād*, and a gloss on Shams al-Dīn al-Iṣfahānī's commentary on Naṣīr al-Dīn al-Ṭūsī's *Tajrīd al-iʿtiqād*.

His most controversial work was *Maṣāʾib al-nawāṣib*, a refutation of *Nawāqiḍ-al-rawāfiḍ*, an anti-Shīʿī work by Mīr Makhdūm al-Shīrāzī (d. 998/1589). Mīr Makhdūm completed this work in 988/1580 while he resided in the Ottoman Empire. As Shūshtarī mentions, this work had become popular in India soon after its completion when about a hundred copies of it were taken to India by those who went on a pilgrimage to Mecca. Less than ten years after the completion of the *Nawāqiḍ*, in 995/1587, Shūshtarī completed the draft of his response and soon after its fair copy, which he dedicated to Safavid Shāh ʿAbbās. In his correspondence with Shūshtarī, Mīr Yūsuf ʿAlī al-Astarābādī blames him for not observing the Shīʿī principle of religious dissimulation (*taqiyya*) when writing this work. Shūshtarī responds that India with its just king (*padishah-i ʿādil*) is not a place for religious dissimulation and even if it were, he is exempted, for if he were killed because of his assistance to the true religion, it would strengthen the religion even more (Astarābādī/Shūshtarī, *Asʾila*, 137–8). Shūshtarī composed two other polemical works of the same type: *Ṣawārim al-muhriqa*, a refutation of Ibn Ḥajar al-ʿAsqalānī's (d. 852/1449) *Ṣawāʿiq al-muḥriqa*, and *Iḥqāq al-ḥaqq wa-izhāq al-bāṭil*, completed in 1014/1605–6, which is a response to Amīn al-Dīn Faḍl Allāh b. Rūzbahān al-Khunjī's (d. 927/1520–1) *Ibṭāl nahj al-bāṭil wa-ihmāl kashf al-ʿātil*, which itself is a refutation of the ʿAllāma al-Ḥillī's *Nahj al-ḥaqq wa-kashf al-ṣidq*. On 26 Rabīʿ I 1019/17 June 1610, at the order of the Emperor Jahāngīr (1014/1605–1037/1628), he was flogged to death at the entrance of the city of Agra (Afandī, *Riyāḍ*, 5: 260–74).

During the eleventh/seventeenth century, the Quṭb Shāhī rulers continued patronizing the Twelver Shīʿite theological works. Zayn al-Dīn ʿAlī b. ʿAbd Allāh al-Badakhshī (fl. 1023/1614) dedicated his Persian commentary on the third chapter of *Tajrid al-iʿtiqād* (on Metaphysics) to Muḥammad Quṭb Shāh (r. 1020/1612–1035/1626). This commentary, titled *Tuḥfa-yi shāhī*, was completed in 1023/1614 (Ṣadrāyī Khūyī 2003: 183). Muḥammad Amīn al-Astarābādī's theological work (d. 1036/1626–7), *Dānishnāma-yi shāhī* was also sent as a gift to Muḥammad Quṭb Shāh (Gleave 2007: 35). While residing in Isfahan, Sayyid Aḥmad al-ʿAlawī al-ʿĀmilī (d. between 1054/1644 and 1060/1650) also dedicated his commentary on Naṣīr al-Dīn al-Ṭūsī's *Tajrīd al-iʿtiqād* to Muḥammad's son, ʿAbd Allāh Quṭb Shāh (r. 1035/1626–1082/1672). This commentary, titled *Ḥaẓīrat al-uns min arkān kitāb Riyāḍ al-quds*, was completed in 1037/1628 (Ṣadrāyī Khūyī 2003: 133). At the same time efforts were made by several Iranian Shīʿī theologians to convert

Indian Sunnī scholars to Twelver Shīʿism. One of the most outstanding examples was ʿAbd al-Wahhāb al-Daybulī al-Shīrāzī (d. after 1073/1662). Daybulī was originally a Sunnī scholar. According to his autobiographical note, he debated in 1042/1632–3 with a certain ʿAbd al-ʿAlī al-Shīrāzī on the issue of the *imāma*, which persuaded him of the truth of Twelver Shīʿism. He then had several debates with his former Sunnī colleagues. In his work entitled *Ibṣār al-mustabṣarīn* (Persian), he recorded some of these debates. The last of them took place in Shāh-Jahān-Ābād (Old Delhi) in 1073/1663–4 (Subḥānī 2004: iv. 124).

Another scholar who was active in the same direction was Niẓām al-Dīn Aḥmad al-Jīlānī (d. after 1066/1656). Niẓām al-Dīn, who had studied in Isfahan with Mīr Dāmād (d. 1040/1631–2) and Bahāʾ al-Dīn al-ʿĀmilī (d. 1030/1621), moved in 1040/1631–2 to India and resided in Hyderabad, where he enjoyed the patronage of the prominent Mughal general, Shāh Mahabat Khan (d. 1044/1634) and the ruler of the Quṭb Shāhī dynasty, ʿAbd Allāh Quṭb Shāh (r. 1034/1625–1082/1672). He was appointed as the representative of ʿAbd Allāh Quṭb Shāh in Iran in 1050/1640–1 and then as his representative in Delhi in 1066/1655–6. He had a debate with the Indian scholars on Shīʿī–Sunnī differences, which he recorded in a treatise. He also wrote the following works in theology: *Risāla fī l-jabr wa-l-tafwīḍ; Risāla fī ithbāt al-wājib; Risāla fī bayān al-qaḍāʾ wa-l-qadar*; and *Risāla fī kayfiyyat al-iʿtiqād fī madhhab al-ḥaqq* (Subḥānī 2004: iv. 390–1; Āghā Buzurg 1983–6: v. 21).

Similar efforts were made by Mirzā ʿAlī Riḍā al-Tajallī al-Ardakānī al-Shīrāzī (d. 1085/1674). Tajallī studied in Isfahan with Ḥusayn al-Khwānsārī (d. 1098/1686). Some time during the 1060s/1650s or shortly before, Tajallī went to India and spent a few years under the patronage of Mughal Emperor Aurangzeb (r. 1067/1658–1118/1707). It was during his residence in India that he wrote a Twelver Shīʿī creed in Persian, entitled *Safīnat al-najāt*, completed on 17 Rabīʿ II 1067/9 September 1634, in the course of which he dealt in detail with the imamate. His other theological works include *Manẓūmat al-qaḍāʾ wa-l-qadar* and *Ṣiḥḥat al-naẓar fī taḥqīq al-firqa al-nājiyya al-ithnā ʿashariyya* (Subḥānī 2004: iv. 144f.).

(b) Sunnī Scholastic Theology in India: Early Development

The teaching of Sunnī theology in a systematic way seems to have been naturalized in the Indian Subcontinent in the early decades of the eleventh/seventeenth century. This development apparently first took root in the city of Lahore and, after a few decades, it spread to other major cities. At this stage, the theological training was most commonly Ashʿarite and Māturīdī, as together with al-Sayyid al-Sharīf al-Jurjānī's commentary on ʿAḍud al-Dīn al-Ījī's *al-Mawāqif*, Jalāl al-Dīn al-Dawānī's commentary on Ījī's *al-ʿAqāʾid*, and Saʿd al-Dīn al-Taftāzānī's commentary on ʿUmar al-Nasafī's *al-ʿAqāʾid* were the most popular theological textbooks. Naṣīr al-Dīn al-Ṭūsī's *Tajrīd al-iʿtiqād* was generally avoided during this formative period. Nūr Allāh al-Shūshtarī who was present in Lahore in the early eleventh/seventeenth century states that the Indian scholars regarded this text 'ominous' (Astarābādī/Shūshtarī, *As'ila*, 138). In the few instances that *Tajrīd al-iʿtiqād* was taught, the teaching was based on its Ashʿarite commentary by Shams al-Dīn al-Iṣfahānī.

Bio-bibliographical works credit two Iranian scholars as the main sources for the transmission of scholastic theology into the Indian Subcontinent: Mīrzā-Jān Ḥabīb Allāh al-Bāghnawī (d. 995/1587) and Fatḥ Allāh al-Shīrāzī. Both having come from Shīrāz, these scholars familiarized with the latest trends of Islamic theology developed in Shīrāz in the late ninth/fifteenth and early tenth/sixteenth centuries by the two outstanding theologians of the city, namely Jalāl al-Dīn al-Dawānī and Ṣadr al-Dīn al-Dashtakī. However, whereas Bāghnawī was closer to the views of Dawānī, Fatḥ Allāh al-Shīrāzī favoured the ideas of Dashtakī.

Bāghnawī was an Ashʿarite theologian from Shīrāz and had studied in his hometown with Jamāl al-Dīn Maḥmūd al-Shīrāzī (d. 962/1554–5) and Naṣr al-Bayān al-Kāzirūnī (*fl.* 950/1543). He taught in the same city for decades, but later in life he moved to Bukhara. It seems that while in Bukhara, where he must have stayed less than seven years, Bāghnawī was able to teach some courses in theology. Among the texts on which he lectured were most probably his own works, namely his gloss on Jalāl al-Dīn al-Dawānī's commentary on ʿAḍud al-Dīn al-Ījī's *Risāla fī l-ʿAqāʾid*, and his gloss on al-Sayyid al-Sharīf al-Jurjānī's commentary on al-Ījī's *al-Mawāqif*.

One of Bāghnawī's most outstanding students was Yūsuf Muḥammad Jān al-Kawsaj al-Qarabāghī (d. 1035/1625–6), who remained in Bukhara following his teacher's death. It is unclear, however, whether Qarabāghī only benefited from Baghnawī during his last years in Bukhara or whether he knew his teacher before and even moved with him to Bukhara. In any case, following Baghnawī's death, Qarabāghī taught theology in Bukhara for about forty years. The only theological contributions that we have from him are concerned with al-Dawānī's commentary on al-Ījī's *Risāla fī al-ʿAqāʾid*. In 1000/1591–2 he completed his first set of glosses on this commentary, called *Khānqāhiyya*. Thirty-three years later, and following the critical remarks that he received from his colleague Ḥusayn al-Khalkhālī (*fl.* 1024/1615–16), he wrote a final set of glosses, which he called *Tatimmat al-ḥawāshī fī izālat al-ghawāshī*.

This intellectual legacy is significant because the teachings of Qarabāghī and Bāghnawī were transmitted to India by Muḥammad Fāḍil Badakhshī (d. 1051/1641–2). Muḥammad Fāḍil studied in Bukhara with Qarabāghī for a while, reading various theological works with the latter. He then moved to Lahore where he served as judge of the Mughal army for the emperors Jahāngīr and Shāh-Jahān (r. 1037/1628–1068/1658). At the same time he was teaching in Lahore (Ḥasanī, *Nuzha* (1955), vol. 5, p. 384).

One well-known student of Badakhshī was Mīr Muḥammad Zāhid b. Muḥammad Aslam al-Harawī (d. 1101/1689–90). Harawī, like his teacher, was appointed as judge of the Mughal army first in Lahore, and then in Agra. Later in life he was granted the administrative leadership (*ṣidārat*) of Kabul. Theology and logic were the two fields he was most interested in. In theology his main contribution was his gloss on al-Sayyid al-Sharīf al-Jurjānī's commentary on al-Ījī's *Mawāqif*. It seems that he usually taught his students al-Jurjānī's commentary alongside his own gloss. The latter gloss was to become one of the major textbooks on theology in the later period. He also wrote a gloss on Shams al-Dīn al-Iṣfahānī's (d. 749/1348) commentary on the *Tajrīd al-iʿtiqād* (Rāhī 1978: 234–7; Rāzī/Shīrāzī/Harawī, *Risālatān*, pp. 24–30). It is via Harawī's works that this branch of the Shīrāzī legacy passed on to India, where the scholarly networks tracing themselves to Fatḥ Allāh Shīrāzī were in fact much more prominent and significant (see Section II, a).

As mentioned, the other chain of transmission of theology goes back to Fatḥ Allāh al-Shīrāzī. ʿAbd al-Salām al-Lāhūrī, who studied with Shīrāzī, seems to have played the major role in transmitting the theological teachings of the latter. After completing his education, ʿAbd al-Salām moved back to his home town of Lahore, where he taught until his death in 1037/1530–1. It is said that he had a long career as a teacher that lasted about fifty years. Yet, while it is known that he was teaching theology, we do not know exactly which texts he was teaching. Moreover, as a matter of fact he never contributed any of his own writings to the field (Ḥasanī, *Nuzha* (1955), vol. 5, pp. 223–4).

One of the students of ʿAbd al-Salām al-Lāhūrī was ʿAbd al-Salām al-Kirmānī al-Dīwī (d. 1039/1629–30). Born in Dīwā, a village close to Lucknow, al-Dīwī seems to have moved to Lahore in his early youth where he resided until his death. After completing his education, he worked as chief mufti of the Mughal army and, at the same time, gave lessons in various fields, including theology. He wrote a gloss on Khayālī's (d. 875/1470–1) gloss on Saʿd al-Dīn al-Taftāzānī's commentary on al-Nasafī's *al-ʿAqāʾid* as well as a gloss on the commentary that Shams al-Dīn al-Samarqandī (*fl. c.*690/1291) wrote on his own *Kitāb al-Ṣaḥāʾif* (Ḥasanī, *Nuzha* (1955), vol. 5, pp. 222–3; Robinson 1997: 159). The latter work seems to be particularly significant. Apart from the numerous superglosses that have been written on it, it is important to note that Samarqandī was a Māturīdī, and it is possible that Dīwī might have advocated Māturīdī doctrines in his commentary.

The most advanced student of Dīwī was ʿAbd al-Ḥakīm al-Siyālkūtī (d. 1067/1656–7). Siyālkūtī started his education in Sialkot and continued it in Lahore, where apart from al-Dīwī, he benefited from Kamāl al-Dīn al-Kashmīrī (d. 1017/1608–9), about whom little is known. Later in his life, while serving as counsellor to the Mughal emperor Shāh-Jahān, Siyālkūtī found himself teaching in Shāh-Jahān-Ābād (Old Delhi). A prolific writer, Siyālkūtī penned the following works on theology: (1) *al-Durra al-thamīna fī ithbāt al-wājib (or Khāqāniyya)*, a treatise on the proof of existence of God (completed on 12 Rabīʿ II 1057/16 May 1647); (2) *Nujūm al-hidāya*, a treatise on God's knowledge in which he condemns the philosophers (*falāsifa*) as unbelievers for their rejection of God's knowledge of particulars; (3) a gloss on al-Jurjānī's commentary on al-Ījī's *al-Mawāqif* (written for his son ʿAbd Allāh Labīb); (4) a gloss on al-Dawānī's commentary on al-Ījī's *al-ʿAqāʾid*; and (5) a gloss on Shams al-Dīn al-Khayālī's gloss on al-Taftāzānī's commentary on al-Nasafī's *al-ʿAqāʾid* (Rāhī 1978: 138–45, Dirāyatī 2010: xi. 592).

Another significant link in this chain of transmission was Quṭb al-Dīn al-Anṣārī al-Sihālawī (or al-Sihālī) (d. 1103/1691–2). Quṭb al-Dīn studied with a certain Dānīyāl al-Chawrasī who was in turn a student of ʿAbd al-Salām al-Kirmānī al-Dīwī. He wrote glosses on several theological works: (1) a gloss on al-Jurjānī's commentary on al-Ijī's *al-Mawāqif*; (2) a gloss on al-Dawānī's commentary on al-Ījī's *Risāla fī l-ʿAqāʾid*; and (3) a gloss on al-Taftāzānī's commentary on al-Nasafī's *al-ʿAqāʾid* (Bilgrāmī, *Ṣubḥa*, 194–6; Thubūt 1994: 114).

II The Eighteenth and Nineteenth Centuries

(a) Intellectual Networks and Texts

The history of Islamic theology in India during the twelfth/eighteenth and thirteenth/nineteenth centuries can be said to be tied generally with two scholarly traditions and their offshoots. The first, that of the Farangī Maḥall, emerged in the late eleventh/seventeenth century and, passing through the Khayrābādīs, was partially absorbed into the Barīlavī (Barelwi) movement by the late thirteenth/nineteenth century. The second tradition, that of Shāh Walī Allāh, emerged in the twelfth/eighteenth century and greatly influenced major doctrines of the later Diyōbandī (Deobandi) movement of the thirteenth/nineteenth century.

Farangī Maḥallī scholars trace their intellectual lineage to scholars of Shīrāz, who have already been mentioned in Section I. It is reported that, until the appearance of the Farangī Maḥallī tradition, the *Sharḥ al-Saḥāʾif* of the aforementioned ʿAbd al-Salām al-Dīwī (d. 1039/1629–30), was the main theology text under study (Gīlānī, *Pāk*, 187–9), though, as observed in Section I, other texts of the Dawānī/Jurjānī/Taftāzānī commentary and gloss cycles were surely also studied. ʿAbd al-Salām was the teacher of Shaykh Dāniyāl al-Chawrasī, also already mentioned, who, in turn, trained the fountainhead of the Farangī Maḥallīs, Mullā Quṭb al-Dīn Sihālavī (d. 1103/1691–2) (see Ahmed 2013a, where detailed master–disciple stemmata are provided). It appears from a survey of bio-bibliographical sources (Ḥasanī, *Nuzha* (1992); Khan 1996; Khayrābādī, *Tarājim*) that, from this point on, the following texts of theology received focused attention in teaching circles and garnered a multitude of commentaries and glosses (logic, however, remained the main topic of scholarly attention and output for the next two centuries): al-Dawānī's *Qadīma* (his earliest gloss on Qūshjī's commentary on the *Tajrīd* of Naṣīr al-Dīn al-Ṭūsī), Dawānī's *Sharḥ al-ʿAqāʾid al-ʿaḍudiyya*, al-Jurjānī's *Sharḥ al-Mawāqif*, Taftāzānī's *Sharḥ al-ʿAqāʾid al-nasafiyya*, Harawī's (1101/1689) *Ḥāshiya* on Jurjānī's *Sharḥ al-Mawāqif*, Taftāzānī's *al-Maqāṣid*, Khayālī's (875/1470) *Ḥāshiya* on Taftāzānī's *Sharḥ al-ʿAqāʾid al-nasafiyya*, and the *ʿAqāʾid nasafiyya* itself.

Beyond this, a number of works not traditionally classed as theological attracted attention for their theological content. Thus, Qāḍī Mubārak's (d. 1162/1748) commentary on the *Sullam al-ʿulūm* of Muḥibb Allāh al-Bihārī (d. 1119/1707–8), a work on logic, ought to be mentioned here; a large number of glossators on this work focused on the early sections that deal with the possibility of the definition and conceptualization of God (Ahmed 2013b). Similarly, Harawī's commentary on Quṭb al-Dīn al-Taḥtānī's (766/1364) *al-Risāla fī l-taṣawwur wa-l-taṣdīq* and a gloss on this commentary of Harawī by Ghulām Yaḥyā b. Najm al-Dīn al-Bihārī (d. 1180/1766) came to be of great interest for discussions of the nature of God's knowledge. These two topics were also presented in a number of independent treatises, as were subjects central to the philosophy of Mīr Dāmād (d. 1040 or 1041/1631 or 1632) and Mullā Ṣadrā (d. 1050/1640), such as the modulation of essences, cosmogony (especially atemporal origination (*ḥudūth dahrī*), simple and compound causation (*jaʿl murakkab wa-basīṭ*), and dependent/relative existence (*al-wujūd al-rābiṭī*). By the late thirteenth/nineteenth century, it appears that inter-religious debates and the contact with Western scientific notions resulted in some treatises against the transmigration of souls (e.g. Saʿādat Ḥusayn b. Raḥmat ʿAlī Bihārī (d. 1360/1941), cf. Khan 1996: 63–4) and the Copernican system. The latter was generally argued against both on the basis of the arbitrariness and contradictoriness of various foundational premisses and Scriptural proof texts (e.g. by ʿAbd Allāh b. Amīn al-Dīn Maydānīpūrī (d. 1303/1885), ʿAbd al-Waṣīʿ b. Yūsuf ʿAlī Amīthavī, ʿAbd al-Raḥīm b. Maṣāḥib ʿAlī Gūrakhpūrī, and Aḥmad Riḍā Khān Barīlavī (d. 1339/1921); cf. Khan 1996: 46, 73–5). In the early thirteenth/nineteenth century, perhaps the most significant theological issue and one that became emblematic of sectarian identity in India appears to be the possibility of God's lying and the related possibility of another prophet equal to Muḥammad. Some details about this topic will be presented in the course of this chapter.

Recent research has established that theology in Muslim lands after Avicenna had come to depend rather heavily on some fundamental aspects of his synthesis for the articulation and systematization of its own concerns. This development is something that was already apparent to pre-modern Muslim scholars, who generally classed theology under the rubric of 'rationalist sciences' (*maʿqūlāt*). And this classification was eminently suitable, particularly in the context of India, where most scholars writing on theological topics were trained heavily in the books of the *falāsifa*. For all purposes then, it would be rather difficult to draw a clean line between theology and philosophy for this region and period and we have, therefore, adopted the term 'rationalist theology' to refer to the theological corpus of Indian scholars. It also appears that the influence of *falsafa* and the deep commitment to systematization blunted the lines of sectarian division within theology. Though the thesis requires a greater investment in details, at this stage, it may also be argued that both Sunnīs and Shīʿīs were generally trained in the same pedagogical networks, engaged the same theological subjects, commented and glossed the same texts, and displayed an eclecticism in their theological outlook that cannot be easily and holistically classified as Ashʿarite, Māturīdī, or Muʿtazilī. There are certainly some exceptions, as will be noted, but they generally concern religio-political debates about the imamate or topics that lie at the centre of sectarian polemics.

The information gleaned from the bio-bibliographical sources suggests that, starting with the mid-eleventh/seventeenth century and into the late thirteenth/nineteenth, the centres of rationalist theology were found mainly in the north. The main cities of concentrated activity were Sandīla, Sihāla, Lucknow, Delhi, and Rampur, with an important presence of scholars also in Allāhābād, Kolkatta, Banaras, Jawnpūr, Gūpāmaw, Khayrābād, and, after the mid-thirteenth/nineteenth century, also in Aligarh. In addition, in the thirteenth/nineteenth century, Hyderabad in the Deccan, Tonk in Rajasthan, and Madras in the south also hosted leading theologians. The contribution of each of these areas and their associated scholars has yet to be studied.

As noted above, the twelfth/eighteenth- and thirteenth/nineteenth-century scholarly networks that proliferated the study of systematic rationalist theology in the north had their roots in the Farangī Maḥall. Mullā Niẓām al-Dīn (d. 1153/1740), who set down the celebrated Niẓāmī curricular lists (Ahmed 2016a), was taught by his father, the aforementioned Quṭb al-Dīn Sihālavī, in Sihāla, and also by the well-regarded Amān Allāh Banārasī (d. 1132/1720) in Lucknow, where Farangī Maḥall was established with the help of a royal gift from Awrangzīb. Al-Banārasī, himself a student of Quṭb al-Dīn Sihālavī, was the author of glosses on al-Dawānī's *Qadīma*, al-Dawānī's *Sharḥ al-ʿAqāʾid*, and al-Jurjānī's *Mawāqif* (Khan 1996: 20). Niẓām al-Dīn wrote a gloss on al-Dawānī's *Sharḥ al-ʿAqāʾid* and his *Qadīma* (Khan 1996: 30). In Sandīla, a celebrated Shīʿī logician and student of Niẓām al-Dīn, Ḥamd Allāh b. Shukr Allāh (d. 1160/1747), had established a *Madrasa-yi manṣūriyya*, where a number of leading theologians were trained. Among these was Ghulām Yaḥyā b. Najm al-Dīn al-Bihārī, whose gloss on Harawī's commentary on the *Risāla quṭbiyya* has already been mentioned as a text on logic that became important in scholarly circles for its theological concerns. Ghulām Yaḥyā is also known to have written a treatise called *Kalimat al-ḥaqq*, in which he refuted Shāh Walī Allāh's (d. 1175/1762) position on the subject of the oneness of existence (*waḥdat al-wujūd*) and the oneness of appearance (*waḥdat al-shuhūd*), a central topic of theological dispute in the Subcontinent, starting from the mid-eleventh/seventeenth century. Ghulām Yaḥyā's refutation was challenged later by Walī Allāh's son Rafīʿ al-Dīn (Ḥasanī, *Nuzha* (1992), 6: 224; Khan 1996: 23).

In the mid-twelfth/eighteenth century, just as the social and intellectual strengths of the Farangī Maḥall were coming to mature, another circle of scholars began to emerge from it. These scholars eventually came to be known as the Khayrābādiyya and they traced their intellectual lineage to Muḥammad Aʿlam Sandīlavī (d. 1197/1783), a student of Niẓam al-Dīn Sihālavī and author of a treatise on the modulation of essences (Khan 1996: 25). Muhammad Aʿlam's nephew ʿAbd al-Wājid Khayrābādī (d. 1216/1803), who had studied with the former and with Ṣifat Allāh b. Madīnat Allāh Khayrābādī (d. 1157/1744), trained the first scholar of the Khayrābādī circle to gain wide renown, Faḍl-i Imām Khayrābādī (d. 1243/1828) (Ḥasanī, *Nuzha* (1992), 6: 122–3, 345; Ahmed 2016b). And it is mainly in the Khayrābādī circles that the commentary of Ṣifat Allāh's student, Qāḍī Mubārak Gūpāmawī (d. 1162/1749), on the *Sullam al-ʿulūm* of Muḥibb Allāh b. ʿAbd al-Shukūr al-Bihārī (d. 1119/1707), came to be in vogue. Among the Khayrābādīs, a number of glosses on this commentary focused mainly on the question of the possibility of the conceptualization and definition of God. Much of the other material in this logic work generally did not receive as much sustained scholarly attention from the Khayrābādīs.

Thus by the middle of the twelfth/eighteenth century, two branches of the Shīrāzī scholars of rationalist theology were beginning to bifurcate in northern India. The contributions of neither have been assessed so far in modern scholarship. Thus at this stage of research, in addition to the works generally noted here, we supply the names and relevant titles of works of the most significant scholars in the hopes that this will pave the way for detailed study in the future.

In the twelfth/eighteenth century, Mullā Ḥasan b. Ghulām Muṣṭafā b. Muḥammad Asʿad Farangī Maḥallī (d. 1199/1794), a student of Niẓām al-Dīn Sihālavī, was both a leading scholar of rationalist sciences and a teacher of a number of prominent scholars of the next century. His commentary on the *Sullam al-ʿulūm* devotes some space to the question of the knowability of God; in addition, he also wrote glosses on Harawī's commentary on parts of the *Mawāqif* of Ījī (Ḥasanī, *Nuzha* (1992), 6: 304). His student, Mullā Mubīn b. Muḥibb Allāh b. Aḥmad b. Muḥammad Saʿīd Farangī Maḥallī (d. 1225/1810) also wrote a commentary on the *Sullam al-ʿulūm* and glosses on all three aforementioned works of Harawī (Ḥasanī, *Nuzha* (1992), 7: 442). Commentaries of both authors on the *Sullam* were absorbed into the curriculum. Similarly, Ẓuhūr Allāh b. Muḥammad Walī Farangī Maḥallī also wrote commentaries on all three works of Harawī. All of these scholars were descended from the fountainhead of the tradition, Quṭb al-Dīn Sihālavī. Baḥr al-ʿUlūm ʿAbd al-ʿAlī b. Niẓam al-Dīn Sihālavī (d. 1225/1810) was perhaps the most prolific and celebrated Farangī Maḥallī author of the century (Ahmed 2016c). In addition to penning multiple glosses on the Harawī texts noted above, he also wrote treatises on *waḥdat al-wujūd* and God's knowledge of particulars (Ḥasanī, *Nuzha* (1992), 7: 313ff.). His *al-ʿUjāla al-nāfiʿa*, a detailed work on metaphysics, also tackles a number of problems of theology (Rizvi 2011: 18 n. 43). Baḥr al-ʿUlūm left behind a strong legacy of students.

The Farangī Maḥallī contributions continued in the thirteenth/nineteenth century with scholars such as ʿAbd al-Ḥayy b. ʿAbd al-Ḥalīm Farangī Maḥallī (d. 1304/1886), who wrote a gloss on Ghulām Yaḥyā's gloss on Harawī's commentary on Quṭb al-Dīn al-Taḥtānī's *Risāla fī l-taṣawwur wa-l-taṣdīq* and a number of glosses directly on Harawī's aforementioned commentaries and a commentary on al-Ījī's *Mawāqif* (Khan 1996: 69). But by the middle of the century, the Khayrābādīs were beginning to emerge as more prominent and prolific authors in the field of theology. Among this circle of scholars, the greatest contributions to theology were made by Faḍl-i Ḥaqq b. Faḍl-i Imām Khayrābādī (d. 1277/1861), who dealt with various theological subjects ranging from *waḥdat al-wujūd* and the possibility of God's lying to the nature of God's knowledge, in the following works: *al-Rawḍ al-majūd fī ḥaqīqat al-wujūd*, *Ḥāshiyat al-Ufuq al-mubīn*, *Ḥāshiya [ʿalā] Mubārak ʿalā Sullam al-ʿulūm*, *Risāla fī taḥqīq al-ʿilm wa-l-maʿlūm*, *Risāla fī tashkīk al-māhiyāt*, and *Risāla fī imtināʿ al-naẓīr*. Other leading theologians, whose works explored a number of these same issues, included Faḍl-i Rasūl Badāyūnī (d. 1289/1872) (*Ḥāshiyat Mīr Zāhid Harawī ʿalā al-Risāla al-quṭbiyya*, *al-Muʿtaqad al-muntaqad*) (Khan 1996: 51), ʿAbd al-Ḥaqq b. Faḍl-i Ḥaqq Khayrābādī (d. 1318/1900) (*Ḥāshiyat Ghulām Yaḥyā ʿalā al-Harawī ʿalā l-Risāla al-quṭbiyya*, *Ḥāshiyat Harawī ʿala Sharḥ al-Jurjānī ʿalā l-Mawāqif*, *Ḥāshiya ʿalā Ḥamd Allāh ʿalā Sullam al-ʿulūm*, *Ḥāshiya ʿalā Mubārak ʿalā Sullam al-ʿulūm*) (Ḥasanī, *Nuzha* (1992), 8: 238–40), and Faḍl-i Ḥaqq

b. ʿAbd al-Ḥaqq Rāmpūrī (d. 1358/1939) (*Ḥāshiya ʿalā Ḥāshiyat al-Harawī ʿalā l-Jurjānī ʿalā l-Mawāqif, Ḥāshiya ʿalā Ḥamd Allāh ʿalā Sullam al-ʿulūm, Afḍal al-taḥqīqāt fī masʾalat al-ṣifāt, al-Wujūd al-rābiṭī*) (Ḥasanī, *Nuzha* (1992), 8: 383–4).

(b) Shīʿī Theologians

The Quṭb Shāhī rule, mentioned in the previous section (a), ended in south India with the Mughal victory over Hyderabad in 1098/1687; and the ʿĀdil Shāhīs had lost their sovereignty to the Mughals the previous year. This effectively marked the end of formal Twelver Shīʿī rule in southern India. In the north, Shīʿism had a considerable presence in Kashmir, with minorities in Multan. After the fall of Hyderabad to the Mughals, sizable Shīʿī populations settled in Delhi, Bengal, or Awadh, the latter being a Shīʿī princely state from 1134/1722 to 1272/1856. From sources explored thus far, it appears that it is in these northern regions that Shīʿī theologians thrived most in the twelfth/eighteenth and thirteenth/nineteenth centuries. Yet, it must surely be conceded that further explorations of the intellectual history of Bijapur and Golkonda may yield a rich harvest (Cole 1988: 22ff.).

In the twelfth/eighteenth century, a number of Shīʿī scholars were drawn to rationalist theology. These included Shaykh Muḥammad ʿAlī 'Ḥazīn' Gīlānī (d. 1180/1766), who belonged to the Uṣūlī school, promoted *ijtihād*, and wrote commentaries on the theological positions of mystical thinkers. Tafaḍḍul Ḥusayn Khān Kashmīrī (d. 1215/1800), who had studied with 'Ḥazīn' Gīlānī and Mullā Ḥasan Farangī Maḥallī, noted above, was primarily a scholar of mathematical sciences and had also translated books in European mathematics and physics; but he is also said to have participated in heated debates on logic and *kalām* (Rizvi 1986: ii. 227ff.). Muḥammad ʿAskarī al-Jawnpūrī (d. 1190/1776), the author of *Tajallī-yi nūr*, was another prominent theologian, known for presenting rationalist theological discussions with vocabulary borrowed from Sufi texts. Most prominent and prolific of these scholars was Sayyid Dildār ʿAlī b. Muḥammad Muʿīn al-Naṣīrābādī (d. 1235/1820), a student of Tafaḍḍul Ḥusayn (above), ʿAbd al-ʿAlī Farangī Maḥallī (above), Mullā Ḥasan (above), and Ghulām Ḥusayn Dakanī Ilāhābādī. The last scholar was of Shīʿī persuasion and himself a student of the Aʿlam Sandīlavī and author of a treatise on compound and simple causation (*jaʿl muʾallaf wa-basīṭ*). Dildār ʿAlī is one of the most influential Shīʿī scholars of pre-modern north India and is in large part responsible for the conscious reformulation of Shīʿī identity in India via theological refutations of polemical Sunnī works (such as Shāh ʿAbd al-ʿAzīz's *Tuḥfa-yi ithnā ʿashariyya*), the establishment of insular ritual spaces and rites, and the production of theological dispensations. Unfortunately, practically no sustained study of his theological contributions—which include *ʿImād al-islām* (his theological *magnum opus*, where he refutes Ashʿarism), *al-Shihāb al-thāqib* (against the doctrine of *waḥdat al-wujūd*), and *Risāla fī ithbāt al-jumʿa wa-l-jamāʿa* (on reinstating the Friday communal prayers in the absence of the Imām)—has been carried out. Dildār ʿAlī's efforts at refuting the

Tuḥfa were carried forward in the next generations as Shīʿa identity was being cultivated ever more intensely in the changing political environment of the British Raj. Thus the magisterial *ʿAqabāt al-anwār* by Ḥāmid Ḥusayn (d. 1305/1888) and continued by Sayyid Nāṣir Ḥusayn (d. 1361/1942) deserves mention here. The multi-volume work deals with topics ranging from the imamate and prophethood to metaphysics and resurrection (Jones 2012: 53f., 244f.). Bio-bibliographical works also list a number of his descendants as rationalist scholars; for a study of Dildār ʿAlī's legacy, their works will also need to be consulted (Ḥasanī, *Nuzha* (1992), 6: 342, 7: 125–6, 186–8, 388; Cole 1988: 50ff.).

(c) Two Reformist Theologians: Shāh Walī Allāh and Shiblī Nuʿmānī

The preceding section (b) dealt mainly with works prevalent in the *madrasa* system. Most of them are in the form of commentaries and glosses, which have yet to be studied piecemeal and which constitute part of a complex system of internal dialectic within the Islamic scholarly tradition; a sense of their contribution to Islamic theology is still lacking. There are strong indications that the genre was exceptionally vibrant and it is hoped that future scholarship will be able to determine its contours in detail (Ahmed 2013b).

This section focuses on two representative scholars—Quṭb al-Dīn Aḥmad Abū al-Fayyāḍ (Shāh Walī Allāh) (d. 1176/1762) and Shiblī b. Ḥabīb Allāh Nuʿmanī (d. 1318/1914)—whose contributions to the development of Islamic theology in India are somewhat better known.

Shāh Walī Allāh, who is also a central figure for the revival of the study of *ḥadīth* and the influence of non-Ḥanafī (especially Mālikī) *fiqh* in South Asia, grounds his theology in the concept of *maṣāliḥ*, the beneficial purposes for which divine law was decreed. Thus he argues that prayer is legislated so that man may converse privately with God, alms are prescribed so that attachments to base things may be wiped out, the *lex talionis* exists as a deterrent to killing, and so on. Underlying this principle of *maṣāliḥ* is thus the idea of a certain optimal form of human existence, one to which man draws near by intentionally following divine laws; these divine laws have inner meanings, some of which have been explained by the forebears and some of which still remain obscure. Whatever the depth of one's knowledge of such laws may be, they must be followed by one in the same way as a sick man follows the instructions of a physician.

It is on the foundation of this principle of *maṣāliḥ* that the edifice of Shāh Walī Allāh's theology stands. His *magnum opus*, *Ḥujjat Allāh al-bāligha*, opens with a detailed analysis of this concept, which then naturally flows into a discourse on various theological matters. Thus, in the first chapter, Shāh Walī Allāh outlines three types of creation by God: creation *ex nihilo* (*ibdāʿ*), fashioning of something out of something else (*khalq*), and the management of the world by intervention, so as to make it conform to the system approved by His wisdom (*tadbīr*). This last form of creation pertains to His redirecting one of two alternative potentialities to actuality, in order that the beneficial purpose of creation may be obtained. Thus, for example, he notes that the Dajjāl has the instruments to kill mankind a second time, but God does not give him this power and so curtails his effect via *tadbīr*. It is in this fashion that, though properties are specific to each species and their effects in themselves are good, God redirects potentialities in view of the greater benefit (*maṣlaḥa*) of creation. This is a kind of occasionalism, driven by a positive teleology.

Other aspects of his theology include a belief in the World of Images (*ʿālam al-mithāl*), as presented by Abū l-Faḍl al-Suyūṭī (d. 911/1505), a hierarchical order of angels, who have causal capacity in relation to humans and who are joined by those humans whose ranks are closest to them, God's habitual act and commands, in view of the receptive potentiality of His creatures (along with other factors, such as the prayers of the highest angels and the states of existence in the World of Images), and a firm and purified monotheism. The idea of *maṣlaḥa* remains central to the elaboration of these and other theological points, which deserve a concentrated study. It is worth noting that Shāh Walī Allāh's theological discourse is heavily interspersed with scriptural quotations, something that stands in sharp contrast to the commentary/gloss texts noted above. However, the influence of various strands of *falsafa* and *kalām* doctrines remains not far below the surface of his reformist theology (Walī Allāh, *Ḥujjat Allāh*; Ahmad 1969: 8–9; Ansari 1991). The *Nachleben* of this theology in the works of scholars in Shāh Walī Allāh's direct intellectual and kinship lineage needs to be studied. These include such theologians as Shāh ʿAbd al-ʿAzīz b. Shāh Walī Allāh (d. 1239/1824), who sought to synthesize the doctrines of *waḥdat al-wujūd* and *waḥdat al-shuhūd* and wrote a creedal work (*Mīzān al-ʿaqāʾid*), Shāh Rafīʿ al-Dīn b. Shāh Walī Allāh (d. 1233/1818), Qāḍī Thanāʾ Allāh Pānīpatī (d. 1225/1810), and Muftī Ilāhī Bakhsh (d. 1246/1831) (Ghazi 2002: 164ff., 238ff.; Hāshimī 2008; Inayatullah 1986). All these scholars had close associations with the Madrasa-yi Raḥīmiyya, which was established by Shāh Walī Allāh's father. In the generations to follow, the impact of the tradition seems to have spread to all parts of India, culminating ultimately in 1867 in the Dār al-ʿUlūm Deoband. The contours of the theological contributions of this long-standing tradition have yet to be brought to light.

Shiblī Nuʿmānī, who is known primarily as a historian, literary critic, and litterateur, composed one of the few works of 'new theology' (*kalām-i jadīd*) in the Subcontinent. His work on this subject is divided into two parts: the first (*ʿIlm al-kalām*) deals with a history of *kalām* and the second (*al-Kalām*) concerns itself with proposing its reorientation. The latter is a reworking and deployment of a number of theological points of Fakhr al-Dīn al-Rāzī (d. 605/1209), al-Ghazālī (d. 505/1111), and Shāh Walī Allāh, in view of the needs and concerns of his age.

By his own admission, the guiding principle of the work is to reveal (in clear language) to the general public the truths about creedal matters, which, according to Nuʿmānī, had been deliberately obfuscated by earlier theologians. The aim of the latter was to preserve the religion from the onslaught of innovations, not to burden their co-religionists with details that might instead confuse them and lead them astray. In addition and as an equally important endeavour, Nuʿmānī sought to present a theology that would (1) guard the religion against attacks from newer concerns of theological discourse—ethics and politics—that had been made salient by European influence and (2) to give scriptural proofs of creedal matters where previous rational proofs failed. And finally, (3) he wished to present theology as a discipline steeped in matters entirely distinct from what he calls European science. The subject matter of the former cannot be presented by empirically verifiable methods, whereas, for the latter, these are the only suitable starting points. This work, which deserves careful study, engages matters such as the dichotomy between rationality and religion, proofs of God's existence and the creation of the world, prophecy and miracles, the essence and attributes of God, and, ultimately, ethics and politics (Nuʿmānī, *al-Kalām*; Haywood 1997).

(d) A Theological Dispute and the Emergence of Institutionalized Sects

In this section, we briefly wish to bring to attention two related theological disputes in thirteenth/nineteenth-century India that appear to have had a major impact on the emergence of sectarian identities. Their role in the self-articulation of Muslim groups in India is still rather massive and they require a full and diachronic study.

In the 1230s/1820s, a *fatwā* of *takfīr* was issued by the celebrated rationalist scholar Faḍl-i Ḥaqq Khayrābādī, generally, against anyone who believed that it was not impossible in itself for God to lie and, particularly, against Shāh Ismāʿīl, the grandson of Shāh Walī Allāh. This *fatwā* was the product of a series of exchanges between Shāh Ismāʿīl and his supporters, on the one hand, and theologians of the rationalist bent, on the other; these exchanges had themselves been sparked ultimately by a theological dispensation of Shāh Ismāʿīl, the *Taqwiyat al-īmān*. In this latter work, which, in many ways, is inspired by the reformist programme of Muḥammad b. ʿAbd al-Wahhāb (d. 1206/1792), the author had claimed that God's omnipotence is such that, if He so wished, he could bring into existence another Muḥammad equal in status to the historical prophet. This statement, perhaps meant to be a mere exaggerated expression of God's omnipotence, led to an impasse for rationalist theologians, one that, via a convoluted compound syllogism preserved in some treatises, pitted the Qurʾānic promise of Muḥammad's finality against the eternity of divine Will. And this in turn meant that Shāh Ismāʿīl, who had granted the eternity of divine Will, had endorsed that it was not impossible per se for God to lie or for another Muḥammad to be created by Him.

The details of the debate, which lasted throughout the nineteenth century (and which has become emblematic of sectarian identity in South Asia), are fascinating. They are equally driven by political, social, and academic motives; and their impact on society is conditioned by changing systems of patronage and the use of print. And they revive classical and post-classical theological arguments, deploy technical subjects in the field of logic, such as the Liar Paradox, and reorient and reinterpret certain conceded deontological positions of the Ashʿarite school (among other things). In the course of the century, the two sides—one arguing for the impossibility per se and the other for the possibility of God's lying and of another Muḥammad—ultimately contributed to the crystallization of the Deobandi and Barelwi movements of South Asia. The former absorbed many aspects of the argument and the tradition represented by Shāh Ismāʿīl (including various elements of the theology of his grandfather, Shāh Walī Allāh) and the latter, with leanings towards Sufi thought and practice, absorbed parts of the rationalist tradition, represented by the Khayrābādīs. This thesis needs to be tested carefully and the details of the aforementioned debate and similar other points of sectarian contention about Shāh Ismāʿīl's work require attention for understanding the history and trajectory of theology in thirteenth/nineteenth-century India (Khayrābādī, *Imtināʿ*; Aḥmad, *Ṣimṣām*).

References

al-Afandī al-Iṣbahānī, Mīrzā ʿAbd Allāh (*Riyāḍ*). *Riyāḍ al-ʿulamāʾ*. 8 vols. Qum: s.n., 1401/1981.

Āghā Buzurg al-Ṭihrānī (1983–6). *al-Dharīʿa ilā taṣānīf al-shīʿa* 1–25. Beirut: Dār al-Aḍwāʾ, 1403–6.

Ahmad, A. (1969). *An Intellectual History of Islam in India*. Edinburgh: Edinburgh University Press.

Ahmed, A. Q. (2013a). 'Logic in the Khayrābādī school of India. A preliminary exploration'. In M. Cook et al. (eds.), *Law and Tradition in Classical Islamic Thought. Studies in Honor of Professor Hossein Modarressi*. New York: Palgrave.

Ahmed, A. Q. (2013b). 'Post-classical philosophical commentaries/glosses. Innovation in the margins'. *Oriens* 41/3–4: 317–48.

Ahmed, A. Q. (2016a). 'Dars-i Niẓāmī'. *Encyclopaedia of Islam, THREE*.

Ahmed, A. Q. (2016b). 'Faḍl-i Imām Khayrābādī'. *Encyclopaedia of Islam, THREE*.

Ahmed, A. Q. (2016c). 'Baḥr al-ʿUlūm, ʿAbd al-ʿĀlī'. *Encyclopaedia of Islam, THREE*.

Aḥmad, Barakāt (n.d.). *al-Ṣimṣām al-qāḍib li-raʾs al-muftarī ʿalā Llāh al-kādhib*. Lithograph edition. Karachi: Barakat Academy.

Ansari, A. S. Bazmee (1991). 'al-Dihlawī, Shāh Walī Allāh', *Encyclopedia of Islam*. New edn. ii. 254–5.

Astarābādī, Yūsuf ʿAlī and Nūr Allāh Shūshtarī (*Asʾila*). *Asʾila-yi Yūsufiyya: Jidāl andishagī-i tafakkur-i shīʿa-yi Uṣūlī bā akhbārī | Mukatibāt-i Mīr Yūsuf ʿAlī Astarābādī va Shahīd Qāḍī Nūr al-Allāh Shūshtarī*. Ed. Rasūl Jaʿfarīyān. Tehran: Kitābkhāna, Mūzih va Markaz-i Asnād-i Majlis-i Shūrā-yi Islāmī, 1388/2009.

Barzigar Kashtlī, Ḥ. (2001). 'Niẓām al-Dīn Shāh Sindī'. In *Dānishnāma-yi adab-i Fārsī [4] Adab-i Fārsī dar shibha qārrah (Hind, Pākistān, Banglādish)*. Ed. Ḥ. Anūshah. Tehran 1380, iii. 2561–3.

Bilgrāmī, Ghulām ʿAlī Āzād (*Subḥa*). *Subḥat al-marjān fī āthār Hindūstān*. Ed. Muḥammad Faḍl al-Rahmān al-Nadwī al-Sīwānī. 2 vols. Aligarh: Jāmiʿat ʿAlīgarh al-Islāmiyya, 1976–80.

Cole, J. R. I. (1988). *Roots of North Indian Shīʿism in Iran and Iraq: Religion and State in Awadh, 1722–1859*. Berkeley and Los Angeles: University of California Press.

Dhābīṭ, Ḥaydar Riḍā (1998). 'Adyān u makātib: tashayyuʿ dar shibha qārra-yi hind'. *Andīsha-yi ḥawza* 12 (Spring 1377): 82–102.

Dihdār Shīrāzī, Muḥammad b. Maḥmūd (*Rasāʾil*). *Rasāʾil-i Dihdār*. Ed. Muḥammad Ḥusayn Akbarī Sāwī. Tehran: Mīrāth-i maktūb, 1375/1996.

Dirāyatī, Muṣṭafā (2010). *Fihrist-i dastnivishthā-yi Īrān (dinā)*. 12 vols. Tehran: Kitābkhāna, Mūzih va Markaz-i Asnād-i Majlis-i Shūrā-yi Islāmī, 1389.

Ghazi, M. A. (2002). *Islamic Renaissance in South Asia, 1707–1867*. Islamabad: Islamic Research Institute.

Gīlānī, Sayyid Manāẓir Aḥsan (n.d.). *Pāk o Hind mein musulmānūn kā niẓām-i taʿlīm o tarbiyat*. Lahore: Maktaba-yi Raḥīmiyya.

Gleave, R. (2007). *Scripturalist Islam, The History and Doctrines of the Akhbārī Shīʿī School*. Leiden: Brill.

al-Ḥasanī/Lakhnawī, ʿAbd al-Ḥayy b. Fakhr al-Dīn (1931–1970). *Nuzhat al-khawāṭir wa-bahjat al-masāmiʿ fī l-nawāẓir*. Ḥaydarābād al-Dakkan: Maṭbaʿat Dāʾirat al-Maʿārif al-ʿUthmān-iyya.

al-Ḥasanī/Lakhnawī, ʿAbd al-Ḥayy b. Fakhr al-Dīn (1992). *Nuzhat al-khawāṭir wa-bahjat al-masāmiʿ fī l-nawāẓir.* Multān: n.p.

Hāshimī, Muḥammad Ṭufayl (2008). 'Qāḍī Thanāʾ Allāh Pānīpatī'. In M. K. Masʿūd, *Aththāriwīn ṣadī ʿīsawīn mein barr-i ṣaghīr mein islāmī fikhr kī rahnumā*. Islamabad: International Islamic University, 301–22.

Haywood, J. A. (1997). 'Shiblī Nuʿmānī'. *Encyclopedia of Islam*. New edn. ix. 433–4.

Inayatullah, S. (1986). "*Abd al-ʿAzīz Dihlawī*'. *Encyclopedia of Islam*. New edn. i. 59.

Iskandar Bey Munshī (*Tārīkh*). *Tārikh-i ʿĀlam-ārā-yi ʿAbbāsī*. 2 vols. Ed. Īrāj Afshār. Tehran: n.p., 1334/1955.

Ivanow, W. (1938). 'A Forgotten Branch of the Ismailis'. *Journal of the Royal Asiatic Society* 1: 57–79.

Jones, J. (2012). *Shiʿa Islam in Colonial India: Religion, Community and Sectarianism*. New York: Cambridge University Press.

Khan, ʿAbd al-Salām (1996). *Barr-i ṣaghīr kī ʿulamāʾ-yi maʿqūlāt awr un kī taṣnīfāt*. Patna: Khuda Bakhsh Oriental Public Library.

Khayrābādī, Faḍl-i Ḥaqq (*Imtināʿ*). *Imtināʿ al-naẓīr* (retrieved from <http://www.alahazratnetwork.org> [May 2010]).

Khayrābādī, Faḍl-i Imām (*Tarājim*). *Tarājim al-fuḍalāʾ: Being a Chapter of the Amad Namah*. Ed. Intiẓāmallāh Shihābī and A. S. B. Anṣārī. Karachi: Pakistan Historical Society, 1956.

Khwājagī Shīrāzī, Muḥammad b. Aḥmad (*Niẓāmiyya*). *Al-Niẓāmiyya fī madhhab al-Imāmiyya. Matn-i kalāmī-i fārsī-yi qarn-i dahum H.Q.* Tehran: Daftar-i nashr-i Mīrāth-i maktūb, 1376/1997.

Mīr, Muḥammad Taqī (1989). *Buzurgān-i nāmī-i Pārs*. Shīrāz: Markaz-i Nashr-i Dānishgāh-i Shīrāz, 1368.

Nawshāhī, ʿĀ. (ed.) (1997). 'Muṣliḥ al-Dīn Muḥammad Lārī, Mirʾāt al-adwār wa mirqāt al-akhbār. Faṣl-ī dar sharḥ-i ḥāl-i buzurgān Khurāsān u Māwarāʾ al-nahr u Fārs [athar-e Muṣliḥ al-Dīn al-Lārī]'. *Maʿārif* 13 iii (Isfand 1375): 91–113.

Nuʿmānī, Sh. (1979). *ʿIlm al-kalām awr al-Kalām*. Karachi: Nafīs Akādimī.

Poonawala, I. (1977). *Biobibliography of Ismāʿīlī literature*. Malibu: Undena.

Poonawala, I. (1997). 'Shāh Ṭāhir'. *Encyclopaedia of Islam*. New edn. ix. 200–1.

Qasemi, Sharif Husain (1999). 'Fath Allah Shīrāzī'. *Encyclopaedia Iranica*. ix. 421 [online version updated in 2012: <http://www.iranicaonline.org/articles/fath-allah-sirazi>]

Quṭb al-Dīn al-Rāzī, Ṣadr al-Dīn al-Shīrāzī, and al-Ḥusaynī al-Harawī (1996). *Risālatān fī l-taṣawwur wa-l-taṣdīq wa-yalīhimā Sharḥ al-risāla al-maʿmūla fī l-taṣawwur wa-l-taṣdīq*. Ed. Mahdī Sharīʿatī. Qum: Muʾassasa-yi Ismāʿīliyān, 1416.

Rāhī, A. (1978). *Tadhkira-yi muṣannifīn-i dars-i Niẓāmī*. Lahore: Maktaba-yi Raḥmāniyya.

Rizvi, S. A. A. (1975). *Religious and Intellectual History of the Muslims in Akbar's Reign with Special Reference to Abu'l Fazl (1556–1605)*. New Delhi: Munshiram Manoharlal Publishers Pvt. Limited.

Rizvi, S. A. A. (1986). *A Socio-Intellectual History of Isnā 'Asharī Shī'īs in India* (*sic*). 2 vols. Canberra: Ma'rifat Publishing House (*sic*).

Rizvi, S. H. (2011). 'Mīr Dāmād in India: Islamic Philosophical Traditions and the Problem of Creation'. *Journal of the American Oriental Society* 131: 9–25.

Robinson, F. (1997). 'Ottomans-Safavids-Muhghals: Shared Knowledge and Connective Systems'. *Journal of Islamic Studies* 8: 151–84.

Ṣadrā'ī Khūyī, ʿA. (2003). *Kitābshināsī-yi Tajrīd al-iʿtiqād*. Qum: Kitābkhāna-yi buzurg-i Ḥaḍrat Āyat Allāh al-ʿuẓmā Marʿashī Najafī, 1382/1424.

Subhānī, Jaʿfar et al. (2004). *Muʿjam ṭabaqāt al-mutakallimīn*. 5 vols. Qum: Mu'assasa-yi Imām Ṣādiq, 1383.

Thubūt, A. (1994). 'Hawza-yi farangī maḥal wa kitāb Sharḥ al-Hidāya'. *Kayhān-i andīsha* 58 (Bahman-Isfand 1373): 114–20.

Walī Allāh, Shāh (*Conclusive Argument*). *The Conclusive Argument from God: Shāh Walī Allāh of Delhi's* Ḥujjat Allāh al-Bāligha. Trans. M. K. Hermansen. Leiden: Brill, 1996.

Ziauddin, M. (2005). *Role of Persian at the Mughal Court: A Historical Study. During 1526 A. D. to 1707 A. D.* Doctoral dissertation, University of Balochistan, Quetta, Pakistan.

CHAPTER 35

ḤANBALĪ THEOLOGY

JON HOOVER

THE modern study of Ḥanbalī theology was initially plagued by the problem of viewing Ḥanbalism through the eyes of its Ashʿarite opponents. I. Goldziher (d. 1921) and D. B. Macdonald (d. 1943) labelled the Ḥanbalīs 'reactionary' and bemoaned the harm that they had done to the cause of a conciliatory Ashʿarite orthodoxy. The work of H. Laoust (d. 1983) and G. Makdisi (d. 2002) turned the tide of scholarship toward closer examination of Ḥanbalī texts on their own terms and deeper understanding of Ḥanbalism in its historical context. Makdisi in particular argued that Ḥanbalism had a disproportionate impact on the development of Islamic theology because it was the only Sunnī law school to maintain a consistently traditionalist theological voice. For Makdisi, the Ḥanbalīs were the 'spearhead' of a wider traditionalist movement in medieval Islam against the rationalism of Muʿtazilī and Ashʿarite *Kalām* (Makdisi 1962–3; 1981). Aspects of Makdisi's narrative require modification, especially as some leading Ḥanbalīs of the fifth/eleventh and sixth/twelfth centuries were more rationalist than earlier thought, but the main thrust of his argument still stands. It may be added that Ḥanbalī theology has also had a disproportionate impact on modern Islamic theology. The Wahhābī movement in Arabia and contemporary Salafism have appropriated and spread the theology of the eighth/fourteenth-century scholar Ibn Taymiyya far beyond the confines of the modern Ḥanbalī school of law. This chapter begins with the formation and early development of Ḥanbalism in order to clarify Makdisi's claim, and it continues by surveying key Ḥanbalī figures from Aḥmad b. Ḥanbal in the third/ninth century to Ibn ʿAbd al-Wahhāb in the twelfth/eighteenth and giving extended attention to the unique theology of Ibn Taymiyya.

I The Formation of Ḥanbalism

The Ḥanbalī law school originated in the ʿAbbāsid capital Baghdad in the late ninth and early tenth centuries CE as the most rigorous heir of the traditionalist movement that had emerged nearly two centuries earlier. The traditionalists nurtured the collection and study of *Ḥadīth*, and they sought to ground Islamic belief and practice solely in the Qurʾān and *ḥadīth* reports from the Prophet Muḥammad, his Companions, and their Successors. Opposite the traditionalists were the more dominant proponents of *raʾy* ('common sense' or 'rational discretion'). Advocates of *raʾy* relied to some degree on Qurʾān and *Ḥadīth*, but they also located religious authority in existing Muslim practice, general notions of upright conduct from the past, and the considered opinion of prominent scholars of the day. Traditionalists and proponents of *raʾy* came into conflict by the late second/eighth century, and, in response to traditionalist pressure, the advocates of *raʾy* began adjusting their jurisprudence toward traditionalist positions and grounding it in the precedents of an eponymous founder and *ḥadīth* reports from the Prophet to a far greater extent. The Ḥanafī law school emerged through the course of the third/ninth and fourth/tenth centuries by vesting authority in a body of jurisprudence ascribed to its eponym Abū Ḥanīfa (d. 150/767) and in turn linking these rulings to Prophetic *ḥadīth*. The notion that law should be based on *ḥadīth* from the Prophet, but not *ḥadīth* from the Prophet's Companions and Successors, was argued by al-Shāfiʿī (d. 204/820), the eponym of the Shāfiʿī law school, and he worked to interpret the Qurʾān and the *Ḥadīth* so that it correlated with received legal practice. Al-Shāfiʿī's position may be called 'semi-rationalist' because he made more room for reasoning by analogy (*qiyās*) than did the pure traditionalists. He also favoured a ruling derived by analogy from a Prophetic *ḥadīth* over a report from a Companion or Successor, and, in this, al-Shāfiʿī was at odds with Aḥmad b. Ḥanbal (d. 241/855) (Melchert 1997; Hallaq 2009: 36–71).

Aḥmad was the most prominent traditionalist of the third/ninth century and the eponym of the Ḥanbalī school. He gave priority to *ḥadīth* from the Companions and Successors over analogy, and he also sought to prevent people from recording his opinions because, in his view, Islamic doctrine and law should be based in the revealed sources, not a later scholar like himself. Such a rigorist methodology proved untenable in the long run, and, in a shift away from pure traditionalism, Abū Bakr al-Khallāl (d. 311/923) gathered Aḥmad's views into a vast collection to form the textual foundation for the Ḥanbalī school. A little later, Abū Qāsim al-Khiraqī (d. 334/945–6) produced the first handbook of Ḥanbalī jurisprudence, and Ibn Ḥāmid (d. 403/1013) worked to reconcile conflicting views within these preceding Ḥanbalī sources (Melchert 1997; al-Sarhan 2011: 96–107). In the realm of legal theory (*uṣūl al-fiqh*), Abū Yaʿlā (d. 458/1065) carried forward al-Shāfiʿī's project of correlating the law to the Qurʾān and the *Ḥadīth* with unprecedented thoroughness and consistency. By pressing the claim that the law corresponded to the literal (*ẓāhir*) sense of revelation, he elided the historical and hermeneutical process by which the law came into existence. The point was to rationalize the equation of revelation with prescribed belief and practice as inherently obvious (Vishanoff 2011). For most Ḥanbalīs, affiliating with the school meant following the rulings attributed to Aḥmad b. Ḥanbal loyally, much as Shāfiʿīs followed the rulings of al-Shāfiʿī and Ḥanafīs the rulings of Abū Ḥanifa. However, being Ḥanbalī could also mean engaging in creative jurisprudence (*ijtihād*) according to Aḥmad's traditionalist method without necessarily following his rulings. This is the sense in which Ibn Taymiyya considered himself Ḥanbalī. As a creative jurist (*mujtahid*), Ibn Taymiyya did not hesitate to criticize Aḥmad's rulings, but he nonetheless claimed loyalty to the Ḥanbalī school and Aḥmad's juristic method (al-Matroudi 2006).

The classical Sunnī law schools were committed first and foremost to the study of their respective jurisprudential systems, and by the fifth/eleventh century Sunnī orthodoxy consisted most fundamentally in belonging to a school of law. Other religious groupings such as Sufis and Muʿtazilī *Kalām* theologians had to take their places within this structure in order to protect themselves from traditionalist persecution. The Muʿtazilī theologians found refuge in both the Ḥanafī and Shāfiʿī schools, but, with time, Muʿtazilism died out among Sunnīs and continued on only among Shīʿīs. Shāfiʿism appears to have been semi-rationalist in both jurisprudence and theological doctrine in the late third/ninth century before confining itself to jurisprudence in the course of the fourth/tenth. Shāfiʿīs of semi-rationalist persuasion in theology eventually took up Ashʿarite *Kalām*. Other Shāfiʿīs were traditionalist in theology and took their theological lights from the Ḥanbalīs. This is apparent in biographical dictionary entries describing such scholars as 'Shāfiʿī in law, Ḥanbalī in principles of religion' (*shāfiʿiyyat al-fiqh, ḥanbaliyyat al-uṣūl*). As Makdisi observed, the Ḥanbalīs were the most consistently traditionalist in both law and theology. Traditionalists within the Shāfiʿī and Ḥanafī law schools also opposed *Kalām*. However, they did not voice their criticism as openly in order to safeguard the unity of their respective schools. As we will see, some Ḥanbalī scholars drew on *Kalām* and later the philosophy of Ibn Sīnā in their theologies, but, on the whole, the Ḥanbalīs were the most vociferous in propagating traditionalist theological doctrines (Melchert 1997; Makdisi 1962–3; 1981).

II Early Ḥanbalī Theological Doctrine

A number of texts used to depict the doctrinal views of Aḥmad b. Ḥanbal in past research are evidently not his. It has been shown recently that the six creeds attributed to him in the biographical dictionary *Ṭabaqāt al-ḥanābila* of Ibn Abī Yaʿlā (d. 526/1133) (see Laoust 1957 for locations; three are translated into English in Watt 1994: 29–40) go back to diverse traditionalist sources in the third/ninth and fourth/tenth centuries rather than Aḥmad himself. The creeds were apparently linked to him at a later date, probably to consolidate his position as the seminal authority for Ḥanbalī doctrine. Another work, *al-Radd ʿalā l-Jahmiyya wa-l-Zanādiqa* ('Refutation of the Jahmīs and the Irreligious'), may go back to Aḥmad in earlier forms. However, the final edition (trans. in Seale 1964: 96–125) includes substantial rational argument against non-traditionalist doctrines, and it was probably written in the fifth/eleventh century to rally Aḥmad to the side of Ḥanbalīs seeking to justify rational argument in theology (al-Sarhan 2011: 29–54).

These sources aside, a few things may still be known about Aḥmad's doctrine. Prior to Aḥmad, some traditionalists had been apprehensive to include ʿAlī as the fourth of the Rightly Guided Caliphs (*al-khulafāʾ al-rāshidūn*) after Abū Bakr, ʿUmar, and ʿUthmān. Aḥmad, however, tipped the balance in favour of this four-caliph thesis, which then became the bedrock of emerging Sunnī orthodoxy. The four-caliph doctrine conciliated a number of conflicts in the early Islamic era that continued to divide Muslims in later centuries, but it firmly excluded the Shīʿīs, who claimed that ʿAlī was the first caliph rather than the fourth (al-Sarhan 2011: 111–21).

It is also likely that Aḥmad, like other traditionalists of his day, had no qualms about speaking of God in creaturely or corporeal terms, so long as there were Qurʾān or *Ḥadīth* texts in support. He affirmed for example that the *ḥadīth* 'God created Adam in his form (*ṣūra*)' meant that God created Adam in God's form, which implied that God himself had a form or shape like that of Adam. To *Kalām* theologians this constituted the grave error of assimilating God to creatures (*tashbīh*, also called 'anthropomorphism' in much scholarship). Taking their cue from 'There is nothing like [God], and He is all-Hearing and all-Seeing' (Q 42: 11), later Ḥanbalīs such as al-Barbahārī (d. 329/941) sought to avoid the charge of assimiliationism by denying any likeness between God's attributes and those of creatures while yet affirming that God indeed had the attributes mentioned in revelation. This 'noninterventionist' (Swartz 2002) or 'noncognitive' (Shihadeh 2006) approach refused to inquire into the modality (*kayf*) of God's attributes—a position known as *balkafa* or *bi-lā kayf* ('without how')—or to interpret the meaning of the attributes in any way. The texts should be passed over without comment (*imrār*). Some scholars have identified this kind of non-interventionism in Aḥmad b. Ḥanbal as well (e.g. Abrahamov 1995: 366–7). However, there is no evidence that Aḥmad affirmed the *balkafa* doctrine explicitly (Williams 2002; see also Melchert 2011).

Questions of *tashbīh* and the status of *Kalām* theology were at the centre of the Inquisition (*miḥna*) initiated by the ʿAbbāsid caliph al-Maʾmūn in 218/833 and famously resisted by Aḥmad b. Ḥanbal. It has been often said that al-Maʾmūn imposed the created Qurʾān on judges and leading religious scholars to support Muʿtazilī *Kalām*. However, the Muʿtazilīs were not the only or even the main beneficiaries of the Inquisition. The doctrine of the created Qurʾān was also known among followers of Abū Ḥanīfa going back to the master himself, and the Inquisition sought primarily to support the Ḥanafīs, as well as other rationalist and semi-rationalist currents, against an increasingly assertive traditionalism. In the face of al-Maʾmūn's Inquisition, Aḥmad b. Ḥanbal would affirm only that the Qurʾān was the word of God. No Qurʾānic verse or *ḥadīth* report stated explicitly that the Qurʾān was created (*makhlūq*), and Aḥmad discounted on principle the *Kalām* reasoning supplied for the doctrine. Aḥmad was subjected to imprisonment and flogging under al-Maʾmūn's successor al-Muʿtaṣim, but the later caliph al-Mutawakkil brought the Inquisition to a gradual halt from 233/847 to 237/852. In a letter to al-Mutawakkil, Aḥmad did go a bit beyond the witness of the texts to affirm that the Qurʾān was also 'uncreated' (*ghayr makhlūq*), and he added that anyone who refused to affirm this was an unbeliever. The failure of the Inquisition marked a major setback for *Kalām* theology and the caliphate's gambit for religious authority. Aḥmad emerged from the Inquisition the hero of the traditionalist cause (Melchert 2006: 8–18; Hinds 1960–2004: vii. 2–6; Madelung 1974; Patton 1897).

Aḥmad was known for his complete disinterest in political affairs. He lived a quiet life, and he interacted with the ruling authorities as little as possible during and after the Inquisition. However, later Ḥanbalīs were much more active, and Ḥanbalī preachers and crowds constituted a powerful social force in Baghdad from the fourth/tenth century onward. The most famous figure in the first half of the fourth/tenth century was the fiery preacher al-Barbahārī, author of a comprehensive creedal statement *Sharḥ al-sunna* (in Ibn Abī Yaʿlā 1952: ii. 18–45). He was implicated in Ḥanbalī attacks on Shāfiʿī jurists and purveyors of vice and innovation (*bidʿa*), and he often went into hiding to escape the authorities. Al-Barbahārī may have been involved in riots that began in 317/929 over interpretation of the divine address to the Prophet Muḥammad 'Perhaps your Lord will raise you up to a praiseworthy station' (Q 17: 79). Al-Barbahārī understood this to mean that God would seat Muḥammad on the Throne beside Himself whereas semi-rationalists of the time—including followers of the renowned Qurʾān commentator al-Ṭabarī (d. 310/923)—preferred to interpret this metaphorically as Muḥammad's right to intercede for grave sinners (Melchert 2012). With the Būyid takeover of Baghdad in 334/945, Ḥanbalī animosities turned against the Shīʿīs as well, and Ḥanbalīs engaged in numerous attacks on Shīʿīs, *Kalām* theologians, and others well into the seventh/thirteenth century. M. Cook attributes this Ḥanbalī social power to their great numbers and a weakened state. Additionally, with the rise of the Būyids and then later the Saljuq conquest of Baghdad in 447/1055, the Ḥanbalīs and the ʿAbbāsid caliphs found common cause in undermining those foreign rulers (Sabarī 1981: 101–20; Cook 2000: 115–28).

A key fourth/tenth-century author on Ḥanbalī theological doctrine beyond al-Barbahārī was Ibn Baṭṭa (d. 387/997). Ibn Baṭṭa composed *al-Ibāna al-kubrā*, a large collection of traditions on belief, the Qurʾān, God's predetermination, and other doctrinal matters. He also wrote *al-Ibāna al-ṣughrā*, a shorter creedal text that is also amply supplied with supporting traditions (ed. and trans. in Laoust 1958). A brief survey of this treatise will serve to summarize the key points of early Ḥanbalī doctrine.

Ibn Baṭṭa begins *al-Ibāna al-ṣughrā* with a long exhortation to adhere to the community (*jamāʿa*) and the Sunna of the Prophet and to avoid division and innovation. Then, he mentions belief (*īmān*), which is affirming what God says, commands, and prohibits and putting this into practice. Unlike the Murjiʾīs for whom belief depends on confession alone, belief can increase or decrease according to one's deeds. 'If God wills' should be added when affirming that one is a believer, not out of doubt over one's religious status as a believer, but because the future is unknown. Ibn Baṭṭa affirms that the Qurʾān is the Word of God, and he deems it uncreated no matter where it is found, even written on the chalkboards of children. Not one letter is created, and whoever deems otherwise is an unbeliever worthy of death. God's attributes mentioned in revealed texts must be affirmed. Among other things, God is living, speaking, powerful, wise, and knowing. He gives life and death, and He speaks and laughs. Believers will also see God on the Day of Resurrection. Ibn Baṭṭa does not mention *balkafa* with this list of attributes, but he does invoke it later when affirming God's descent each night to the lowest heaven. This, he says, should be affirmed without asking how (*kayf*) or why (*lima*). In opposition to the Qadarī and Muʿtazilī doctrine that humans create their own acts, Ibn Baṭṭa affirms God's determination (*qadar*) of all things, both good and evil, according to the timing of God's will and foreknowledge. He goes on to affirm numerous elements of eschatology: the punishment in the tomb, the weighing of deeds in the scales at the Resurrection, intercession for believers, and so on. The latter part of the treatise extols the virtues of the prophets and the Prophet Muḥammad's Companions—especially Abū Bakr, ʿUmar, ʿUthmān, and ʿAlī, in that order to oppose the Shīʿīs—and treats several matters of practice. Overall, *al-Ibāna al-ṣughrā* provides very little explanation or rational argument. It is largely a series of affirmations supported with Qurʾānic verses and *ḥadīth* reports.

III Ḥanbalī Theology from the Eleventh Century to the Thirteenth

Research on Ḥanbalī theology in the fifth/eleventh to seventh/thirteenth centuries remains spotty, but it is readily apparent that this period marks a new departure as some of the leading Ḥanbalī scholars of the time adopted *Kalām* views and argumentation. The earlier Ḥanbalī Abū l-Ḥusayn b. al-Munādī (d. 335/947) had advocated metaphorical interpretation (*taʾwīl*) of God's attributes, and the lost *Sharḥ Uṣūl al-dīn* of Ibn Ḥāmid may have been a *Kalām*-style work (Swartz 2002: 61, 94). But it is from Ibn Ḥāmid's student Abū Yaʿlā Ibn al-Farrāʾ (d. 458/1066), the most prominent Ḥanbalī of his time, that we have our first extant Ḥanbalī *Kalām* manual, *al-Muʿtamad fī uṣūl al-dīn*, a summary of a larger lost work by the same title. Typical of *Kalām* manuals, *al-Muʿtamad* first outlines the foundations of knowledge and explains that the initial human obligation is reasoning (*naẓar*) to knowledge of God. The book then outlines the basics of *Kalām* atomism, proves the existence of God from the origination of the world, and treats, among other things, God's attributes, God's creation of the world and human acts, prophecy, eschatology, belief, and the Imāmate. Abū Yaʿlā adopts Ashʿarite positions on a number of issues in *al-Muʿtamad*. For example, he bases the obligation to *naẓar* on revelation as do the Ashʿarites, not reason as held by the Muʿtazilīs, and he employs the Ashʿarite notion of acquisition (*kasb*) to give humans responsibility for the acts that God creates in them (Gimaret 1977: 161–5). Abū Yaʿlā also wrote two other theological works that are extant: *Ibṭāl al-taʾwīlāt li-akhbār al-ṣifāt* and *Kitāb al-Īmān*. The *Kitāb al-Īmān*, also known as *Masāʾil al-īmān*, is a detailed treatment of belief and the status of believers and bad sinners. *Ibṭāl al-taʾwīlāt* is a lengthy work on the interpretation of God's corporeal qualities.

Abū Yaʿlā's approach to God's corporeal qualifications seeks to mediate between *Kalām* rationalism and Ḥanbalī traditionalism. In *al-Muʿtamad*, he joins the *Kalām* theologians in arguing that God cannot have a body (*jism*). This means that God's corporeal qualifications such as eyes, hands, face, and laughter cannot mean that God has body parts. Yet, Abū Yaʿlā also rejects metaphorical interpretation (*taʾwīl*) of these qualifications, and he maintains that they are simply attributes of God, some essential (*dhātī*) and others added (*zāʾid*) to God's essence (Abū Yaʿlā 1974: 51–60). He also condemns *taʾwīl* in *Ibṭāl al-taʾwīlāt*. For example, he affirms that God laughs such that His molars and uvula will be seen, as stated in the *Ḥadīth*. This should be taken literally (*ʿalā ẓāhir*), Abū Yaʿlā explains, but without interpreting it further to imply that God opens his mouth or that He has body parts such as molars or an uvula, and without interpreting it metaphorically to mean God's grace and generosity. God's laughing is an attribute (*ṣifa*), but its meaning (*maʿnā*) is not understood (Holtzman 2010: 186–7). Despite Abū Yaʿlā's attempt to avoid corporealism (*tajsīm*) on the one hand and *taʾwīl* on the other, he and his teacher Ibn Ḥāmid later came under sharp attack from fellow Ḥanbalī scholar Ibn al-Jawzī for crass literalism and corporealism.

Abū Yaʿlā's foremost student was Ibn ʿAqīl (d. 513/1119), a precocious reader of Muʿtazilī *Kalām* alongside his Ḥanbalī legal studies. With the death of his patron in 460/1067–8, Ibn ʿAqīl suffered under the intrigues of rival Ḥanbalī jurist Sharīf Abū Jaʿfar (d. 470/1077) and was eventually forced to retract his Muʿtazilī writings in 1072, as well as his sympathies for the Sufi martyr al-Ḥallāj (d. 309/922). G. Makdisi ties Ibn ʿAqīl's retraction to the ʿAbbāsid Caliph al-Qādir's (d. 422/1031) earlier promulgation of a traditionalist Ḥanbalī creed as official doctrine of the caliphate and interprets it as the culmination of traditionalist ascendancy in Baghdad: '[The retraction] represents the triumph of the Traditionalist movement supported by the caliphate, against Rationalist Muʿtazilism, on the decline, and a militant Rationalist Ashʿarism, on the ascendant' thanks to support from the Saljuqs (Makdisi 1997: 14; also Makdisi 1963). As Makdisi indicates, the traditionalist battle with *Kalām* was not done, and Ashʿarism continued to rival Ḥanbalism for centuries to come. Ibn ʿAqīl's major work on theology *al-Irshād fī uṣūl al-dīn* is not extant. Otherwise, it appears that Ibn ʿAqīl, post-retraction, was moderately rationalist within a traditional Ḥanbalī doctrinal framework and advocated a limited use of *taʾwīl* (Makdisi 1997).

Mention of Ibn ʿAqīl's interest in al-Ḥallāj raises the question of Ḥanbalī–Sufi relations, especially as Ḥanbalīs have often been seen to be opponents of Sufism. This reputation derives from the later Ḥanbalī polemic of Ibn al-Jawzī and Ibn Taymiyya against innovated practices and doctrines linked to Sufism, although not against its ideal of a spiritual path to God. Ḥanbalīs and Sufis share common origins in traditionalist currents of renunciant piety, and, like other traditionalists, early Sufis studied *Ḥadīth* and rejected *Kalām*. As the legal schools formed from the late third/ninth century onward, Sufis affiliated largely with semi-rationalist schools such as the Shāfiʿī and the Mālikī. However, Sufi relations with the traditionalist Ḥanbalīṣ were generally good. Traditionalist Sufi writers such as Abū Nuʿaym al-Iṣfahānī (d. 430/1038) included Aḥmad b. Ḥanbal among the pious saints (*awliyāʾ*) of past generations, and some notable Sufis were Ḥanbalīs including Ibn ʿAṭāʾ (d. 309/921–2 or 311/923–4), who was killed for defending al-Ḥallāj, ʿAbd Allāh al-Anṣārī (d. 481/1089), and the eponym of the Qādiriyya Sufi order ʿAbd al-Qādir al-Jilānī (d. 561/1166). Al-Anṣārī and ʿAbd al-Qādir al-Jilānī are both of significance for Ḥanbalī theology. Al-Anṣārī battled against Ashʿarite *Kalām* theologians in Khorasan, and out of this came his large work *Dhamm al-kalām*. ʿAbd al-Qādir, for his part, provides a full and well-organized statement of traditionalist Ḥanbalī doctrine in his large spiritual work *al-Ghunya* (trans. ʿAbd al-Qādir al-Jīlānī 1995: i. 171–279) (Karamustafa 2007; Makdisi 1979; 1997).

The most sophisticated Ḥanbalī theological voice after Ibn ʿAqīl was Ibn al-Zāghūnī (d. 527/1132), author of *al-Īḍāḥ fī uṣūl al-dīn*. *Al-Īdāḥ* is a well-organized theological manual similar in length and structure to Abū Yaʿlā's *Muʿtamad*, and it treats God's corporeal qualifications in much the same way. To take God's eyes, for example, Ibn al-Zāghūnī denies that God's eye consists of a fleshly eyeball—God's eye is not an originated body. Yet, he also disallows interpreting God's eye metaphorically along *Kalām* lines as God's 'protection'. Rather, God's eye is an attribute to be taken literally without assimilationism or modality (Ibn al-Zāghūnī 2003: 291–4). With this, Ibn al-Zāghūnī sought to find his way between corporealism and *ta'wīl*, but it failed to please his foremost student Ibn al-Jawzī.

Ibn al-Jawzī (d. 597/1201) was the leading Ḥanbalī scholar and preacher of his day. He initially opposed the Ashʿarites and Muʿtazilīs, partly because they were aligned with the Saljuq sultans, but, as Saljuq power waned and the ʿAbbāsid caliphate revived, he took a more relaxed attitude toward *Kalām* and eventually drew on *Kalām* argumentation to produce his fullest theological work, *Kitāb Akhbār al-ṣifāt*, in the late 1180s or early 1190s. This book contains a stinging condemnation of assimilationism and corporealism within the Ḥanbalī school, and it probably contributed to his banishment to Wāsiṭ in 590/1194 (Swartz 2002: 33–45). Ibn al-Jawzī also wrote a similar but shorter work called the *Dafʿ shubah al-tashbīh* (trans. ʿAlī 2006), also known as *al-Bāz al-ashhab*.

The targets of Ibn al-Jawzī's *Kitāb Akhbār al-ṣifāt* are three of the most prominent Ḥanbalīs of the preceding two centuries—Ibn Ḥāmid, Abū Yaʿlā, and Ibn al-Zāghūnī—whom he accuses of interpreting God's corporeal qualifications literally and disallowing metaphorical interpretation. In a strongly rationalist tone, Ibn al-Jawzī explains that reason apart from revelation knows God's existence, God's unity, God's necessary attributes, the originated quality of the world, and prophecy. Reason also knows that God is not a body; otherwise He would be subject to temporality. Thus God cannot be said to have corporeal attributes in any literal sense.

Then, in *Kitāb Akhbār al-ṣifāt*, Ibn al-Jawzī sets forth two approaches to God's corporeal qualifications: non-interventionism for the masses and metaphorical interpretation (*ta'wīl*) for the scholars. The error of the *Kalām* theologians is to subject the public to their dialectic because it only sows doubt and spreads heresy. Rather, God has spoken to the masses in language that they can understand and readily accept, and, in public, God's corporeal qualifications such as His hands and eyes should be read in the texts and passed over as they are without comment (*imrār*). Taking aim at Abū Yaʿlā, Ibn Jawzī declares that nothing further should be said about what kind of attributes these qualifications might be (e.g. essential (*dhātī*) or additional (*zā'id*) to the essence) or about their literal meaning. However, among the scholars, Ibn al-Jawzī explains, God's corporeal qualifications should be reinterpreted metaphorically to accord with the demands of reason, that is, to deny that God has a body. The bulk of *Kitāb Akhbār al-ṣifāt* is then discussion and reinterpretation of Qurʾān and *Ḥadīth* texts portraying God in corporeal terms. Ibn Jawzī's elitism—that *taʾwīl* is only for the scholars—may have been driven by a desire for scholarly respectability. Ibn al-Jawzī displays considerable embarrassment at Ḥanbalī assimilationism in his book, and his objective in writing appears to be salvaging the reputation of the Ḥanbalī school in the eyes of the wider community of Sunnī scholars. Ibn al-Jawzī claims the highly regarded Aḥmad b. Ḥanbal for the non-interventionism that he advocates for the masses, and he rejects later Ḥanbalī attempts at literality as deviant corporealism (Swartz 2002: 46–64, 77–138).

Ibn al-Jawzī's polemic did not escape Ḥanbalī criticism. Abū l-Faḍl al-Althī (d. 634/1236) wrote a diatribe that may have helped get the senior Ḥanbalī scholar exiled to Wāsiṭ. Al-Althī takes Ibn al-Jawzī to task for his elitist advocacy of *taʾwīl* and calls him to repentance. There is, however, no evidence that Ibn al-Jawzī ever recanted (Swartz 2002: 282–97). Later on, sometime after 603/1206, the Syrian Ḥanbalī jurist Ibn Qudāma (d. 620/1223) wrote his *Taḥrīm al-naẓar fī kutub ahl al-kalām* in which he discusses the retraction of Ibn ʿAqīl at length. No mention is made here of Ibn al-Jawzī, but it seems likely that Ibn Qudāma had him and his admirers in mind (Swartz 2002: 42, 62).

Ibn Qudāma's *Taḥrīm al-naẓar* provides a lengthy refutation of *taʾwīl*, and it repeatedly sets out the traditionalist Ḥanbalī position on God's attributes. Citing the authority of Aḥmad b. Ḥanbal, Ibn Qudāma explains that corporeal depictions of God in the Qurʾān and the *Ḥadīth* must be accepted as true without saying anything more or less. God is described as He has described Himself, and the texts are passed over as they are without comment (*imrār*) and without inquiring into modality (*kayf*) or meaning (*maʿnā*). Ibn Qudāma also claims that whatever God's attributes might mean is of no practical import, and believing in them in ignorance is the correct path. If one wants to inquire into something, Ibn Qudāma argues, one should inquire into jurisprudence, not the attributes of God (Makdisi 1962).

Ḥanbalism weakened in Baghdad after Ibn al-Jawzī, and the Mongol destruction of the city in 1258 dealt the Ḥanbalīs a further setback. Damascus took over as the intellectual centre of Ḥanbalism with Ibn Qudāma being one of its great early figures. Damascus was dominated by Shāfiʿīs, and Ḥanbalīs could not exercise the same social and political power that they had enjoyed in Baghdad. Nonetheless, the Damascene Ḥanbalīs thrived and eventually produced the most creative theologian in the Ḥanbalī tradition and one of the greatest minds in medieval Islam: Ibn Taymiyya.

IV Ibn Taymiyya

Ibn Taymiyya (d. 728/1328) is at times portrayed as anti-rationalist due to his polemic against the main claimants to reason in his day: Ashʿarite and Muʿtazilī *Kalām* theology, Aristotelian logic, and the Aristotelian-Neoplatonist *falsafa* of Ibn Sina. However, it has been made clear that Ibn Taymiyya did not reject reason as such but argued for its congruence with revelation (Michot 1994; 2003). It has also become apparent that his criticism of *Kalām* and *falsafa* was not simply a matter of haphazard polemics. It was instead rooted in a fundamentally different construal of God as perpetually creative and temporally dynamic (Hoover 2004; 2010a). Drawing on both *Kalām* and *falsafa* and giving distinctive authority to the Qurʾān, the Sunna, and the Salaf (the early Muslims), Ibn Taymiyya introduced a new current of theology unprecedented in the Ḥanbalī school and not found elsewhere in medieval Islam (el Omari 2010; Hoover 2007; Özervarli 2010).

The theological world in which Ibn Taymiyya worked was permeated with philosophized Ashʿarite *Kalām*, especially that of Fakhr al-Dīn al-Rāzī (d. 606/1209). Ibn Taymiyya read al-Rāzī with his students, and he wrote extensively against al-Rāzī's ideas. His major works *Bayān talbīs al-jahmiyya* and *Darʾ taʿāruḍ al-ʿaql wa-l-naql* both respond directly to al-Rāzī's thought. The former work refutes al-Rāzī's book *Asās al-taqdīs* on the metaphorical interpretation of God's corporeal attributes. The latter work *Darʾ taʿāruḍ* confutes the 'Rule of Metaphorical Interpretation' (*qānūn al-taʾwīl*) espoused by al-Ghazālī and al-Rāzī, which gives reason precedence over the literal meaning of revelation when the two contradict. Although Muʿtazilī *Kalām* had died out in Sunnī Islam by the eighth/fourteenth century, it lived on in Imāmī Shīʿī theology, and Ibn Taymiyya's large refutation of Shīʿism *Minhāj al-sunna al-nabawiyya* directly rebuts Muʿtazilī notions of divine justice.

In addition to the tomes just mentioned, Ibn Taymiyya wrote several other large works, including major refutations of Christianity and Aristotelian logic, and important treatises on Sufism, political theory, and prophecy. While a few of Ibn Taymiyya's works may be dated with precision, many cannot, and change or development in his thinking is often difficult to establish. However, his thought is remarkably consistent and coherent, and it is thus with some confidence that we may speak of a characteristic Taymiyyan theology that retained its essential contours throughout the course of his scholarly life. Except where indicated otherwise, the following overview of Ibn Taymiyya's theology is based on my own writings (Hoover 2004; 2007; 2010a; see also Laoust 1939; Bell 1979).

As Ibn Taymiyya saw it, the fundamental problem of his time was that God was no longer worshipped and spoken of correctly. A great many Muslims had strayed from true theological doctrine and proper religious practice and fallen into the errors of philosophers and *Kalām* theologians, as well as Shīʿis, Sufis, Christians, and others. The solution was to return Islam to its sources, the Qurʾān, the *Ḥadīth*, and the doctrine and practice of the Salaf, the first two or three generations following the Prophet Muḥammad, before the religion was corrupted by error and sectarian division. In Ibn Taymiyya's view, the accumulated judgements and the consensus of later scholars were subject to error, and they had to be measured against the doctrine of the Salaf.

At the core of Ibn Taymiyya's polemic against *Kalām* and *falsafa* is the subordination of metaphysics to ethics and the theoretical to the practical. *Kalām* and *falsafa* reverse the order. Both disciplines reason from the nature of reality to the existence of God, God's unity, and God's attributes and eventually to prophecy and the practical obligations that follow on from that. For Ibn Taymiyya, this approach fails to place worship of God at the fore. Taking his cue from the order of invocations in 'You alone we worship; You alone we ask for help' (Q 1: 5), Ibn Taymiyya argues that God's exclusive worthiness of worship, praise, and love is prior to God's exclusive creation of the world and provision of help for His servants. God is the sole creator of the world, but for Ibn Taymiyya this metaphysical monotheism follows on from the more foundational reality of God's pre-eminent worthiness of obedience and praise. Humans should love and worship God alone because of who God is in Himself and not simply because He alone creates and sustains. Here is how Ibn Taymiyya distinguishes *Kalām* from his own method, which he takes to be that of the Qurʾān:

> The distinction between the Qurʾānic and the *kalām* theological methods is that God commands worship of Him, a worship which is the perfection of the soul, its prosperity, and its ultimate goal. He did not limit it to mere affirmation of Him, as is the purpose of the *kalām* method. The Qurʾān relates knowledge of Him and service to Him. It thus combines the two human faculties of knowledge and practice; or sensation and motion; or perceptive volition and operation; or verbal and practical. As God says, 'Worship your Lord'. Worship necessarily entails knowledge of Him, having penitence and humility before Him, and need of Him. This is the goal. The *kalām* method secures only the benefit of affirmation and admission of God's existence. (Quoted in Özervarli 2010: 89)

Ibn Taymiyya also speaks of the priority of worship and ethics over metaphysics in theological terms that later became widespread among Wahhābīs and modern Salafīs. He distinguishes two *tawḥīd*s, or two ways of confessing God's unity. Ibn Taymiyya's first *tawḥīd* is that of God's divinity (*ulūhiyya*). *Al-tawḥīd al-ulūhiyya* signifies God's sole worthiness to be a god, that is, God's sole right to be an object of worship (*ʿibāda*). *Al-tawḥīd al-ulūhiyya* is exclusive worship of God that refuses to give devotion and love to anything or anyone else. Then flowing out from this is the second *tawḥīd*, the *tawḥīd* of God's lordship (*rubūbiyya*). God's lordship refers to His creative power, and *al-tawḥīd al-rubūbiyya* means confessing that God is the only source of created beings. For Ibn Taymiyya *al-tawḥīd al-ulūhiyya* is logically prior to *al-tawḥīd al-rubūbiyya*: God in Himself in His pre-eminent worthiness of love and worship comes first.

Ibn Taymiyya's practical turn effectively transforms theology into an aspect of Muslim jurisprudence. He rejects the commonplace medieval distinction between the principles (*uṣūl*) of religion and the branches (*furūʿ*), in which the principles treat theological doctrines like God's existence and attributes from a theoretical perspective and the branches discuss religious obligations such as prayer and fasting from a practical, legal vantage point. Rather, for Ibn Taymiyya, the principles treat those matters of greatest importance in both theological doctrine and religious practice, and the branches deal with lesser matters of detail. Moreover, theological beliefs and religious practices are both practical matters concerned with correct worship of God, and theology is primarily about getting the language of praise and worship right, not establishing the existence of God.

Nevertheless, Ibn Taymiyya still holds a place for reason and its capacity to prove the existence of God, and his view of what reason can know is very optimistic. He asserts that the very fact of creaturely existence is sufficient to prove the existence of the Creator just as it is known that every effect necessarily requires a cause. Ibn Taymiyya speaks as well of the human natural constitution (*fiṭra*) which likewise knows that anything originated needs an originator. Additionally, Ibn Taymiyya asserts, reason and the natural constitution know that it is God alone who should be worshipped and that the fullest human benefit is found in exclusive love of God. Speaking in Aristotelian terms, Ibn Taymiyya frames the natural constitution as an innate potency toward the religion of Islam at birth that is actualized as the human being develops; the role of prophecy and revelation is then to perfect the natural constitution and help it overcome corruption.

For Ibn Taymiyya, reason and the natural constitution on the one hand and revelation on the other do not contradict. They both come from the same source, and they provide much the same information and argument. Rational minds and natural constitutions can know the existence of God and the proper human end apart from revelation, but when they encounter revelation they immediately recognize it as true and congruent with what they already know. Ibn Taymiyya observes that *Kalām* theologians and philosophers confine revelation to information that cannot be attained by reason, and he counters that revelation includes not merely information but also rational argument. Revelation contains the correct proofs of reason, and reason recognizes the truth of revelation. In making the claim that revelation and reason agree, Ibn Taymiyya is trying to take the rational high ground away from *falsafa* and *Kalām*, which he believes are based on faulty foundations and lead to misguided conclusions.

A case in point is the *Kalām* proof for God's existence. The *Kalām* proof in simplified form assumes that the world is made up of indivisible atoms and the accidents that subsist in them. Accidents are temporally originating (*ḥādith*), and—this is key—anything in which something temporally originating subsists—the atom—must also be temporally originating. Seeing that all atoms are temporally originating, and in view of the *Kalām* conviction that an infinite regress of temporally originating events is impossible, the world as a whole must have been originated in time. Having proved that the world had a beginning, the *Kalām* argument concludes that it required a Maker who was not originated but eternal.

Ibn Taymiyya often dismisses this proof and its talk of atoms and accidents as unnecessarily complex. Yet, apart from a bit of complexity, it can be difficult to see why he would find it so problematic. However, the proof is based on two postulates that are incompatible with Ibn Taymiyya's theological vision: the impossibility of an infinite regress and the notion that something in which temporally originating events subsist is itself temporally originating. As will become apparent, Ibn Taymiyya has no objection to an infinite regress. His own view of God as perpetually creative from eternity entails an infinite regress of created things. Additionally, his temporally dynamic view of God implies that originating events subsist in God's very essence. Ibn Taymiyya cannot accept the *Kalām* postulate that originating events render their host substrate temporally originating because he himself posits temporality in the essence of God. In his view, the *Kalām* postulates are faulty and lead to irrational conclusions while his own formulations accord with both revelation and reason.

Concerning God's attributes and names, which he discusses at times under the rubric *al-tawḥīd fī l-ṣifāt* ('the uniqueness of God's attributes'), Ibn Taymiyya's position is that of traditionalist non-interventionism or non-cognitivism, but with a crucial difference that I will signal later on. Ibn Taymiyya's non-cognitivism is straightforward: God should be qualified with the names and attributes with which He is qualified in revelation without, on the one hand, inquiring into their modality (*takyīf*) and assimilating (*tashbīh*) or likening (*tamthīl*) them to the attributes and names of creatures, or, on the other hand, stripping them away (*taʿṭīl*) from God with metaphorical interpretation. God is affirmed as all-Hearing, all-Seeing, but there is nevertheless nothing like Him (Q 42: 11). This applies equally to all qualifications given in the Qurʾān and the *Ḥadīth*, from God's 'willing' to God's 'laughter' and God's 'sitting' on the Throne. Ibn Taymiyya rejects the *Kalām* practice of reinterpretation (*taʾwīl*) and dismisses the distinction between the literal (*ẓāhir*) and the metaphorical (*majāz*) upon which it is based. To take one of Ibn Taymiyya's examples, Ashʿarite *Kalām* theologians reinterpret God's 'love' metaphorically as God's 'will' on the grounds that speaking of God's love literally would assimilate Him to creaturely qualities; God cannot be ascribed with creaturely passions like love. Ibn Taymiyya retorts that this reinterpretation in fact involves both likening and stripping away. First, the *Kalām* theologians imagine the love ascribed to God to be like human love in a literal sense and thereby conclude that 'love' may not be ascribed to God. Then, to free God of the untoward passions of human love, they strip God of His love by calling it instead 'will'. The only reasonable course, according to Ibn Taymiyya, is to affirm all of God's names and attributes equally and without modality. The only similarity between the names and attributes of God and the names and attributes of creatures are the very names.

The non-interventionism of a Ḥanbalī like Ibn Qudāma stopped at this point and forbade further inquiry into the meanings of God's attributes because they were of no practical consequence. God's names and attributes must be passed over without inquiring into their meaning (*imrār*). Ibn Taymiyya, on the contrary, believes that the meanings do matter, and this propels him on to a wide-ranging project of theological hermeneutics. He discards the *Kalām* device of *taʾwīl* and places in its stead a project of linguistic inquiry (*tafsīr*) that seeks to interpret God's attributes and names in ways that he deems praiseworthy. While humans may know nothing about God's names and attributes except the names, these names still evoke meaning in the human mind, and this meaning impacts human response to God for good or ill, depending on the character of the portrayal. For Ibn Taymiyya it is thus imperative to give sense to God's names and attributes that will evoke love and praise for God and ward off scepticism and disdain. This is the aim of Ibn Taymiyya's whole theological endeavour, and his foremost difficulty with rival theological visions is that they fail to give God sufficient praise.

An instructive example of how this works is Ibn Taymiyya's contrast of his own notion of God's justice (*ʿadl*) with that of the Ashʿarites and the Muʿtazilīs. In the voluntarism of the Ashʿarites, God's justice consists in whatever God wills, without consideration of cause or wise purpose. God is just to punish humans for the bad deeds that He creates in them, and he would even be just to punish prophets without cause. Ibn Taymiyya rejects such a God as capricious and unworthy of praise. The Muʿtazilīs, for their part, argue against the Ashʿarites that it would in fact be unjust of God to punish bad deeds that He creates. Thus, God gives humans freedom to create their own deeds, and He deals out retribution in complete fairness: reward for good deeds and punishment for bad deeds. Ibn Taymiyya rejects the Muʿtazilī understanding of God's justice because it posits a plurality of creators in the universe—both God and humans—and because it makes God look foolish. God in his foreknowledge knows that humans will commit evil deeds with the creative power that He gives them, and yet He stupidly gives it to them anyway. This, Ibn Taymiyya remarks, is like one person giving another a sword to fight unbelievers when he already knows that the other person will use it to kill a prophet. In sum, Ibn Taymiyya castigates both the Muʿtazilīs and the Ashʿarites for depicting God in an unworthy manner. While God cannot be subjected to human moral standards because He is wholly unlike creatures, He must nonetheless be spoken of with the highest praise. For Ibn Taymiyya, this means that God's justice consists in 'putting things in their places' in accord with His wise purpose (*ḥikma*), and, in one of his late texts, he affirms with Ibn Sīnā and al-Ghazālī that God has created the best possible world.

Ibn Taymiyya also sets forth a mechanism for deriving God's names and attributes rationally. While he disallows use of the juristic analogy (*qiyās*) and the categorical syllogism in theology because they bring God and creatures into direct comparison, he does permit their use in an *a fortiori* argument (*qiyās al-awlā*). In accord with the Qurʾānic assertion that God is ascribed with the 'highest similitude' (*al-mathal al-aʿlā*) (Q 16: 60), Ibn Taymiyya claims that God is all the worthier (*awlā*) of perfections found in creatures than are the creatures themselves because He is their cause and source. Thus, using *a fortiori* reasoning, God is all the worthier of being ascribed with perfections found in creatures such as power, life, sight, and speech. Similarly, God is all the worthier of being disassociated from anything considered imperfect in creatures, and the pinnacle of perfection in God is for His attributes to be unlike those of creatures entirely. Ibn Taymiyya sums it up thus: '[God] is qualified by every attribute of perfection such that no one bears any likeness to Him in it' (quoted in Hoover 2007: 65). On this basis Ibn Taymiyya ascribes to God a wide range of attributes that he deems perfections in humans including laughter, joy, and movement. These attributes are of course attested in revealed texts, but Ibn Taymiyya maintains that they are apparent from reason as well. Moreover, God must be ascribed with such attributes of perfection. Otherwise, He will be regarded as imperfect and unworthy of worship.

Ibn Taymiyya's view of what constitutes God's essential perfection—perpetual, temporal, and purposeful activity—sets him apart from practically the entire preceding Islamic tradition. Elements of his formulation are found in Karrāmī theology, Fakhr al-Dīn al-Rāzī, and the philosopher Abū l-Barakāt al-Baghdādī (d. 560/1165), but Ibn Taymiyya surpasses all of these in developing a consistently dynamic understanding of God. According to Ibn Taymiyya, God has been acting, creating, and speaking by His will and power for wise purposes from eternity (*min al-azal*). God's acts subsist in His very essence, and they occur in temporal succession. He writes, 'The Lord must inevitably be qualified by acts subsisting in Him one after another' (quoted in Hoover 2007: 96). Ibn Taymiyya rarely uses the term temporally originating events (*ḥawādith*) to qualify God's acts, preferring to speak instead of God's voluntary acts and with other language closer to the revealed texts. However, he does indicate that the sense is that of temporality, and he takes it upon himself to refute the *Kalām* arguments against originating events subsisting in God's essence.

In maintaining that God has been creating from eternity, Ibn Taymiyya carves out a middle position between the *falsafa* of Ibn Sīnā on the one hand and *Kalām* on the other. Ibn Taymiyya agrees with the *falsafa* tradition that God's perfection entails eternal productivity. To posit a starting point in God's creative action, as does *Kalām*, implies that God was imperfect prior to beginning to create and subject to change when He switched from not creating to creating. Moreover, an efficient cause or preponderator (*murajjiḥ*) was needed to tip the balance in favour of God beginning His creative activity. Resisting this argument, Ashʿarite *Kalām* held that it was in the very nature of God's eternal will to preponderate or cause creation to begin at a certain point; no additional cause need be posited. Ibn Taymiyya rejects this. Nothing can arise without a prior cause. Ibn Sīnā concluded from these considerations that God's eternal productivity entailed the emanation of an eternal world. Ibn Taymiyya affirms similarly that God's perpetual creativity entails that there have always been created things of one sort or another. However, he has no patience for Ibn Sīnā's emanation scheme and its hierarchy of eternal celestial spheres. In agreement now with the *Kalām* tradition, he denies that any created thing can be eternal. Rather, created things by definition come into existence in time after they were not. To make sense of his position, Ibn Taymiyya distinguishes between the genus (*jins*) of created things on the one hand and individual created things on the other. The genus is eternal—there have always been created things of one sort or another—but each individual created thing originates in time. Additionally, God does not create new things out of nothing but out of prior created things, and this present world that God created in six days (Q 11: 7) was preceded by and created out of prior worlds. Ibn Taymiyya's view of creation is remarkably close to that of the philosopher Ibn Rushd, but it is not clear whether there was direct influence.

Regarding God's speech, Ibn Taymiyya rejects the Ashʿarite doctrine of the eternal Qurʾān, but he does not follow the Muʿtazilīs in calling the Qurʾān created. Instead, he holds that God has been speaking from eternity by His will and power and that God's acts of speaking subsist in God's essence. As with created things, the genus of God's speaking is eternal while His individual speech acts are not. However, it is not said that God's speech acts are created. This is because they subsist in God's essence, not outside of God. Thus, God's individual speech acts are neither created nor eternal, and, likewise, God's speech in the Qurʾān is 'uncreated' (*ghayr makhlūq*) but not eternal. As is apparent, the term 'uncreated' does not mean timeless eternity for Ibn Taymiyya. Rather, it distinguishes God's acts from created things in the world. On the verbal level, Ibn Taymiyya is faithful to the traditional Ḥanbalī doctrine of the Qurʾān's uncreatedness, and he claims that his position is that of Aḥmad b. Ḥanbal. But his introduction of temporal sequence into the speech acts of God may be novel in Ḥanbalism. By way of contrast, the earlier Ḥanbalī Ibn Qudāma, in a debate with an Ashʿarite, denied succession in the speech of God because God does not speak with the physical organs with which humans speak (Daiber 1994: 258, 261).

In Ibn Taymiyya's theology of God's perpetual creativity, as in Ibn Sīnā's emanation scheme, creation is in some sense necessary alongside God, and this poses the question of God's independence and self-sufficiency. *Kalām* theology makes clear that God is fully God without the world by positing a beginning to the world's creation, and Ashʿarites such as al-Rāzī and Sayf al-Dīn al-Āmidī (d. 631/1233) deny that God creates for purposes or causes in order to render God's creation of the world entirely gratuitous. In this Ashʿarite voluntarism, God has no need of the world, and the world is strictly the product of God's sheer will. Ibn Taymiyya does not interpret God's independence or sufficiency apart from the world in this voluntarist sense. Instead, he explains that God's sufficiency consists in needing no help in creating the world, and he follows Ibn Sīnā in giving priority to God's self-intellection and self-love and making that the ground for the rest of existence. We see this for example in Ibn Taymiyya's statement: 'What God loves of worship of Him and obedience to Him follows from love for Himself, and love of that is the cause of [His] love for His believing servants. His love for believers follows from love for Himself' (quoted in Hoover 2007: 99). Here, God's self-love is the ground for all other love. God does not need human love, and, likewise, God does not need the creation. Nevertheless, human love and the whole of creation follow necessarily from God's love for Himself and from His perfection.

The necessity with which God's acts flow from God's perfection would appear to obviate the reality of God's choice. Ibn Taymiyya responds, however, that it is possible for something predetermined to occur through God's will and power. God's will and power are the means by which the concomitants of God's perfection are brought into existence. Ibn Taymiyya writes, 'It is not impossible that something, which is necessary of occurrence because the decree that it must inevitably be has preceded it, occur by… His power and His will, even if it is among the necessary concomitants of His essence like His life and His knowledge' (adapted from Hoover 2010a: 66).

A similar question arises at the level of human acts. If God predetermines and creates all human acts, how are humans to be held accountable for their deeds? Following in the steps of Fakhr al-Dīn al-Rāzī, Ibn Taymiyya affirms that the human act is real and that humans undertake their acts by means of their own will and power. Nonetheless, it is God who creates the human will and power, and it is by means of these that He necessitates human acts. Nothing occurs independently of God's will and creation. Ibn Taymiyya denies any contradiction in this formulation, and when pressed on the point, he sometimes switches from the perspective of God's creation to the human perspective of responsibility to evade the inference that humans cannot be held accountable for deeds that God creates. Faced with a similar paradox between God's command to do good deeds and God's creation of bad deeds, Ibn Taymiyya appeals to God's wise purpose in the creation of all things and suggests ways of mitigating the difficulty. He submits, for example, that a king might command his subject to do something that will benefit that subject. Yet, the king might also refrain from helping his subject obey his command lest the subject be empowered to rise up against him. Ibn Taymiyya acknowledges that such examples fail to find an exact parallel in God. Rather, he argues, if we can imagine that creatures act for wise purposes in the fashion of this king, then God is all the more worthy of being ascribed with wise purposes in his acts as well. Ibn Taymiyya's primary theological aim is to find ways to speak well of God, and drawing attention to contradictions in God's acts would defeat his purpose.

V Ḥanbalī Theology from the Fourteenth Century to the Eighteenth

The early eighth/fourteenth century was an especially fertile period for Ḥanbalī theology, and two figures beyond Ibn Taymiyya are worthy of note. The first, Najm al-Dīn al-Ṭūfī (d. 716/1316), was something of an eccentric among Ḥanbalīs. Arriving in Damascus from Baghdad in 704/1304–5, he was briefly a student of Ibn Taymiyya before moving on to Cairo the next year. He wrote a commentary on parts of the Bible and a refutation of Christianity, and he was accused of Shīʿī sympathies in later life. He is well known among modern Muslim legal theorists for his bold appeal to benefit (*maṣlaḥa*) over revealed texts in law formulation, although it seems that this had little impact in his own time. He also wrote a non-extant defence of logic and *Kalām: Dafʿ al-malām ʿan ahl al-manṭiq wa-l-kalām*. His last work, *al-Ishārāt al-ilāhiyya*, is a commentary on Qurʾānic verses relating to principles of jurisprudence and theology (Heinrichs 1960–2004).

Al-Ṭūfī's eccentricity is readily evident in his *Darʾ al-qawl al-qabīḥ bi-l-taḥsīn wa-l-taqbīḥ*. He refutes the Muʿtazilī views that reason discerns the ethical value of acts and that humans create their own acts independently of God's control, and he argues that God determines and creates all acts. Yet, he notes that the Qurʾānic evidence supporting God's determination of human acts is not unequivocal. Some verses also indicate human responsibility and choice, which implies that the Qurʾān is contradictory. What al-Ṭūfī does with this observation may be unique among Muslim theologians. He suggests that contradiction in the Qurʾān is in fact a proof for the prophethood of Muḥammad. Everyone agrees that Muḥammad was eminently intelligent and that intelligent authors will necessarily work to remove all contradictions from their writings. Seeing that the Qurʾān contains contradiction, it is evidently not from Muḥammad and so must be from God. It might be objected that Muḥammad introduced contradiction into the Qurʾān as a ruse, but al-Ṭūfī insists that intelligent authors would never judge introducing contradiction intentionally to be in their interest (Shihadeh 2006).

The second major eighth/fourteenth-century figure beyond Ibn Taymiyya is his foremost student Ibn Qayyim al-Jawziyya (d. 751/1350). While remaining faithful to the basic contours of his teacher's theology, he wrote more systematically and with greater literary flair, which goes some way toward accounting for the popularity of his books in Salafi circles today. A hallmark of his literary production is a distinctively therapeutic concern for healing the ailments of mind, body, and soul impeding praise and worship of God, and many of Ibn al-Qayyim's books focus on theological issues to remove intellectual obstacles to correct belief as he understands it. One of his earlier works, *al-Kāfiyya al-shāfiyya*, is a long anti-Ashʿarite theological poem that received many commentaries and became popular enough to garner a refutation in 1348 from the Ashʿarī-Shāfiʿī chief judge of Damascus Taqī al-Dīn al-Subkī. Another early work *Miftāḥ dār al-saʿāda* explains, among other things, God's wise purposes in the creation of the diverse phenomena of this world (Holtzman 2009: 209–10, 216–17; Bori and Holtzman 2010: 25–6).

Two of Ibn al-Qayyim's later books, written after 1345, are among the fullest treatments of their respective theological topics in the Islamic tradition. *Shifāʾ al-ʿalīl* fleshes out the contours of Ibn Taymiyya's theodicy at great length. The first half elaborates God's determination and creation of all things, and it explains that, while God creates human acts, humans are the agents of their acts and therefore responsible for their deeds. The second half of the book argues that God creates all things for wise purposes in a causal sense. Evils are in fact good in view of God's wise purposes in creating them, and pure evil does not exist. Ibn al-Qayyim then outlines, in detail far exceeding anything found in Ibn Taymiyya, the wise purposes that God has in creating everything from poisons to disobedience, and even Iblīs (Perho 2001; Hoover 2010b).

The second work, Ibn al-Qayyim's *al-Ṣawāʿiq al-mursala*, is a massive refutation of the presuppositions underlying *Kalām* metaphorical reinterpretation. Only the first half of the work is extant, and resort must be made to the abridgement *Mukhtaṣar al-ṣawāʿiq al-mursala* of Shams al-Dīn b. al-Mawṣilī (d. 774/1372) to gain a sense of the whole. Writing along Taymiyyan lines, Ibn al-Qayyim denies that reason and revelation ever contradict in the interpretation of God's attributes. He attacks the *Kalām* notion of metaphor (*majāz*) at great length and defends the reliability of traditions providing information about God's attributes (Qadhi 2010).

Ḥanbalī theology in the centuries following Ibn Qayyim al-Jawziyya has not been studied carefully (for surveys, see Laoust 1939: 493–540; Laoust 1960–2004), but it appears that Ibn Taymiyya's thought was not highly influential within the school, at least not until the Taymiyyan-inspired revivalism of the nineteenth century in Iraq, Syria, and Egypt. Even in his own day, Ibn Taymiyya's circle of students was small (Bori 2010), and Ḥanbalīs have never embraced his theology as school doctrine. However, Ibn Taymiyya's ideas did find their best-known pre-modern advocate in Ibn ʿAbd al-Wahhāb (d. 1206/1792), a Ḥanbalī scholar in central Arabia.

Taking his cue from Ibn Taymiyya, Ibn ʿAbd al-Wahhāb drew a distinction between *tawḥīd al-rubūbiyya*, the affirmation that God is the sole creator of the world, and *tawḥīd al-ulūhiyya* or *tawḥīd al-ʿibāda*, the exclusive devotion of worship and service to God according to the divine law. Ibn ʿAbd al-Wahhāb likewise gave priority to the ethical/legal *tawḥīd al-ulūhiyya* over the mere confession of God as Creator in *tawḥīd al-rubūbiyya*, and he narrowed the scope of *tawḥīd al-ulūhiyya* to exclude a wide range of popular practices such as saint veneration, tomb visitation, and magic. Ibn

ʿAbd al-Wahhāb was adamant that these practices had to be condemned as idol worship (*shirk*) and eradicated, and he aligned with the central Arabian emir Muḥammad b. Suʿūd in 1744 to put his theological vision into practice. This first Wahhābī-Suʿūdī state lasted through 1819. A second Wahhābī-Suʿūdī state emerged in the nineteenth century. The third Wahhābī-Suʿūdī state, the modern state of Saudi Arabia, began in 1902, and the country has been instrumental in spreading the ideas of Ibn Taymiyya and Ibn ʿAbd al-Wahhāb far beyond its borders, especially in the last half century (Peskes 1960–2004; Peskes 1999).

Bibliography

ʿAbd al-Qādir al-Jīlānī (1995). *Sufficient Provision for Seekers of the Path of Truth (Al-Ghunya li-Ṭālibī Ṭarīq al-Ḥaqq)*. Trans. M. Holland. 5 vols. Houston: Al-Baz Publishing.

ʿAbd al-Qādir al-Jīlānī (1999). *Al-Ghunya li-ṭālibī ṭarīq al-ḥaqq*. Ed. ʿIṣām Fāris al-Harastānī. 2 vols. Beirut: Dār al-jīl.

Abrahamov, B. (1995). 'The bi-lā kayfa Doctrine and its Foundations in Islamic Theology'. *Arabica* 42: 365–79.

Abū Yaʿlā Ibn al-Farrāʾ (1974). *Kitāb al-muʿtamad fī uṣūl al-dīn*. Ed. Wadi Z. Haddad. Beirut: Dar el-machreq.

Abū Yaʿlā Ibn al-Farrāʾ (1989–90a). *Ibṭāl al-taʾwīlāt li-akhbār al-ṣifāt*. Ed. Abū ʿAbd Allāh Muḥammad b. Ḥamad al-Ḥammūd al-Najdī. Kuwait: Maktabat Dār al-Imām al-Dhahabī.

Abū Yaʿlā Ibn al-Farrāʾ (1989–90b). *Masāʾil al-īmān*. Ed. Saʿūd b. ʿAbd al-ʿAzīz Khalaf. Riyadh: Dār al-ʿāṣima.

Aḥmad b. Ḥanbal (attrib.) (1973). *Al-Radd ʿalā al-zanādiqa wa-l-jahmiyya*. Cairo: al-Maṭbaʿa al-salafiyya wa-maktabatuhā.

ʿAlī, ʿAbdullāh bin Ḥamīd (trans.) (2006). *ʿAbd al-Raḥmān Ibn al-Jawzī: The Attributes of God*. Bristol, UK: Amal Press.

al-Anṣārī al-Harawī, ʿAbd Allāh (1998). *Dhamm al-kalām wa-ahlih*. Ed. Abū Jābir ʿAbd Allāh b. Muḥammad b. ʿUthmān al-Anṣārī. 5 vols. Medina: Maktabat al-Ghurabāʾ al-Athariyya.

Bell, J. N. (1979). *Love Theory in Later Ḥanbalite Islam*. Albany, NY: SUNY Press.

Bori, C. (2010). 'Ibn Taymiyya wa-Jamāʿtuhu: Authority, Conflict and Consensus in Ibn Taymiyya's Circle'. In Y. Rapoport and S. Ahmed (eds.), *Ibn Taymiyya and His Times*. Karachi: Oxford University Press, 23–52.

Bori, C., and L. Holtzman (2010). 'A Scholar in the Shadow'. In Bori and Holtzman (eds.), *A Scholar in the Shadow: Essays in the Legal and Theological Thought of Ibn Qayyim al-Ǧawziyyah*. *Oriente Moderno* monograph series, 90/1: 13–44.

Cook, M. (2000). *Commanding Right and Forbidding Wrong in Islamic Thought*. Cambridge: Cambridge University Press.

Daiber, H. (1994). 'The Quran as a "Shibboleth" of Varying Conceptions of the Godhead: A 12th Century Ḥanbalite-Ashʿarite Discussion and its Theological Sequel in the Protocol of Ibn Qudāma Al-Maqdisī'. *Israel Oriental Studies* 14: 249–95.

Gimaret, D. (1977). 'Théories de l'acte humain dans l'école ḥanbalite'. *Bulletin d'études orientales* 29: 156–278.

Hallaq, W. B. (2009). *Sharīʿa: Theory, Practice, Transformations*. Cambridge: Cambridge University Press.

Heinrichs, W. (1960–2004). 'Al-Ṭūfī'. In *Encyclopaedia of Islam*. New edn., x. 588–9.

Hinds, M. (1960–2004). 'Miḥna'. In *Encyclopaedia of Islam*. New edn., vii. 2–6.

Holtzman, L. (2009). 'Ibn Qayyim al-Jawziyyah'. In D. Stewart and J. Lowry (eds.), *Essays in Arabic Literary Biography 1350–1850*. Wiesbaden: Harrassowitz, 202–23.

Holtzman, L. (2010). '"Does God Really Laugh?" Appropriate and Inappropriate Descriptions of God in Islamic Traditionalist Theology'. In A. Classen (ed.), *Laughter in the Middle Ages and Early Modern Times*. Berlin: de Gruyter, 165–200.

Hoover, J. (2004). 'Perpetual Creativity in the Perfection of God: Ibn Taymiyya's Hadith Commentary on God's Creation of This World'. *Journal of Islamic Studies* 15: 287–329.

Hoover, J. (2007). *Ibn Taymiyya's Theodicy of Perpetual Optimism*. Leiden: Brill.

Hoover, J. (2010a). 'God Acts by His Will and Power: Ibn Taymiyya's Theology of a Personal God in his Treatise on the Voluntary Attributes'. In Y. Rapoport and S. Ahmed (eds.), *Ibn Taymiyya and His Times*. Karachi: Oxford University Press, 55–77.

Hoover, J. (2010b). 'God's Wise Purposes in Creating Iblīs: Ibn Qayyim al-Ǧawziyyah's Theodicy of God's Names and Attributes'. In C. Bori and L. Holtzman (eds.), *A Scholar in the Shadow: Essays in the Legal and Theological Thought of Ibn Qayyim al-Ǧawziyyah. Oriente Moderno* monograph series, 90/1: 113–34.

Ibn Abī Yaʿlā, Abū l-Ḥusayn Muḥammad (1952). *Ṭabaqāt al-ḥanābila*. Ed. Muḥammad Ḥāmid al-Fiqī. 2 vols. Cairo: Maṭbaʿat al-sunna al-muḥammadiyya.

Ibn Baṭṭa (1958). *La Profession de foi d'Ibn Baṭṭa* [*al-Ibāna al-ṣughrā*]. Ed. and trans. H. Laoust. Damascus: Institut français de Damas.

Ibn al-Jawzī (1991). *Dafʿ shubah al-tashbīh bi-akaff al-tanzīh*. Ed. Ḥasan al-Saqqāf. Amman: Dār al-Imām al-Nawawī.

Ibn al-Jawzī (2002). *A Medieval Critique of Anthropomorphism: Ibn al-Jawzī's Kitāb Akhbār aṣ-Ṣifāt. A Critical Edition of the Arabic Text with Translation, Introduction and Notes*. Ed. and trans. M. Swartz. Leiden: Brill.

Ibn al-Jawzī (2006). *The Attributes of God (Dafʿ Shubah Al-Tashbīh Bi-Akaff Al-Tanzīh)*. Trans. ʿAbdullāh bin Ḥamīd 'Alī. Bristol, UK: Amal Press.

Ibn Qayyim al-Jawziyya (1987–8). *Kitāb al-ṣawāʿiq al-mursala ʿalā al-Jahmiyya wa-l-muʿaṭṭila*. Ed. ʿAlī b. Muḥammad al-Dakhīl Allāh. 4 vols. Riyadh: Dār al-ʿĀṣima.

Ibn Qayyim al-Jawziyya (2004). *Mukhtaṣar al-ṣawāʿiq al-mursala ʿalā al-Jahmiyya wa al-muʿaṭṭila*. Abridgement Muḥammad b. al-Mawṣilī. Ed. Al-Ḥasan b. ʿAbd al-Raḥmān al-ʿAlawī. Riyadh: Maktabat aḍwāʾ al-salaf.

Ibn Qayyim al-Jawziyya (2007). *Al-Kāfiyya al-shāfiyya fī l-intiṣār li-l-firqa al-nājiyya*. Ed. Muḥammad b. ʿAbd al-Raḥmān al-ʿArīfī et al. 4 vols. Mecca: Dār ʿĀlam al-fawāʾid.

Ibn Qayyim al-Jawziyya (2008). *Shifāʾ al-ʿalīl fī masāʾil al-qaḍāʾ wa-l-qadar wa-l-ḥikma wa-l-taʿlīl*. Ed. Aḥmad b. Ṣāliḥ b. ʿAlī al-Ṣamʿānī and ʿAlī b. Muḥammad b. ʿAbd Allāh al-ʿAjlān. 3 vols. Riyadh: Dār al-ṣamīʿī.

Ibn Qayyim al-Jawziyya (2010–11). *Miftāḥ dār al-saʿāda*. Ed. ʿAbd al-Raḥmān b. Ḥasan b. Qāʾid. 3 vols. Mecca: Dār ʿĀlam al-fawāʾid.

Ibn Qudāma (1962). *Ibn Qudāma's Censure of Speculative Theology* [*Taḥrīm al-naẓar*]. Ed. and trans. G. Makdisi. London: Luzac.

Ibn Taymiyya (1979–83). *Darʾ taʿāruḍ al-ʿaql wa al-naql*. Ed. Muḥammad Rashād Sālim. 11 vols. Riyadh: Jāmiʿat al-Imām Muḥammad b. Saʿūd al-Islāmiyya.

Ibn Taymiyya (1986). *Minhāj al-sunna al-nabawiyya fī naqḍ kalām al-Shīʿa al-Qadariyya*. Ed. Muḥammad Rashād Sālim. 9 vols. Riyadh: Jāmiʿat al-Imām Muḥammad b. Suʿūd al-Islāmiyya.

Ibn Taymiyya (2005–6) *Bayān talbīs al-jahmiyya fī ta'sīs bida'ihim al-kalāmiyya*. Ed. Yaḥyā b. Muḥammad al-Hunaydī. 10 vols. Medina: Majmaʿ al-Malik Fahd.

Ibn al-Zāghūnī (2003). *Al-Īḍāḥ fī uṣūl al-dīn*. Ed. ʿIṣām al-Sayyid Maḥmūd. Riyadh: Markaz al-Malik al-Fayṣal.

Karamustafa, A. T. (2007). *Sufism: The Formative Period*. Edinburgh: Edinburgh University Press.

Laoust, H. (1939). *Essai sur les doctrines sociales et politiques de Taḳī-d-Dīn Aḥmad b. Taimīya, canoniste ḥanbalite né à Ḥarrān en 661/1262, mort à Damas en 728/1328*. Cairo: Imprimerie de l'Institut Français d'Archéologie Orientale.

Laoust, H. (1957). 'Les Premières Professions de foi Hanbalites'. *Mélanges Louis Massignon* 3: 7–35.

Laoust, H. (1958). *La Profession de foi d'Ibn Baṭṭa*. Damascus: Institut Français de Damas.

Laoust, H. (1960–2004). 'Ḥanābila'. In *Encyclopaedia of Islam*. New edn., iii. 158–162.

Madelung, W. (1974). 'The Origins of the Controversy Concerning the Creation of the Koran'. In J. M. Barral (ed.), *Orientalia hispanica*. Leiden: Brill, i/1. 504–25 [Repr. in W. Madelung, *Religious Schools and Sects in Medieval Islam*. London: Variorum Reprints, 1985, Part V].

Makdisi, G. (1962). *Ibn Qudāma's Censure of Speculative Theology*. London: Luzac.

Makdisi, G. (1962–3). 'Ashʿarī and the Ashʿarites in Islamic Religious History'. *Studia Islamica* 17: 37–80 and 18: 19–39 [Repr. in G. Makdisi, *Religion, Law and Learning in Classical Islam*. Hampshire, UK: Variorum, 1991, Part I].

Makdisi, G. (1963). *Ibn ʿAqīl et la resurgence de l'Islam traditionaliste au xie siècle*. Damascus: Institut Français de Damas.

Makdisi, G. (1973). 'The Sunnī Revival'. In D. S. Richards (ed.), *Islamic Civilisation, 950–1150*. Oxford: Cassirer, 155–68.

Makdisi, G. (1979). 'The Hanbali School and Sufism'. *Boletín de la Asociación Española de Orientalistas* 15: 115–26 [Repr. in G. Makdisi, *Religion, Law and Learning in Classical Islam*. Hampshire, UK: Variorum, 1991, Part V].

Makdisi, G. (1981). 'Ḥanbalite Islam'. In M. L. Swartz (ed.), *Studies on Islam*. New York: Oxford University Press, 216–64.

Makdisi, G. (1997). *Ibn ʿAqil: Religion and Culture in Classical Islam*. Edinburgh: Edinburgh University Press.

al-Matroudi, A. H. I. (2006). *The Ḥanbalī School of Law and Ibn Taymiyya*. London: Routledge.

Melchert, C. (1997). *The Formation of the Sunni Schools of Law, 9th–10th Centuries C.E.* Leiden: Brill.

Melchert, C. (2006). *Ahmad Ibn Hanbal*. Oxford: Oneworld Publications.

Melchert, C. (2011). '"God Created Adam in His Image"'. *Journal of Qur'anic Studies* 13: 113–24.

Melchert, C. (2012). 'al-Barbahārī'. *Encyclopaedia of Islam. edn III*. Edited by: Gudrun Krämer, Denis Matringe, John Nawas, Everett Rowson. Brill Online, 2013. University of Nottingham. 15 August 2013 <http://referenceworks.brillonline.com/entries/encyclopaedia-of-islam-3/al-barbahari-COM_22944>

Michot, J. R. (1994). *Ibn Taymiyya: Lettre à Abû l-Fidâ'*. Louvain-la-Neuve: Institut Orientaliste de l'Université Catholique de Louvain.

Michot, Y. J. (2003). 'A Mamlūk Theologian's Commentary on Avicenna's *Risāla Aḍḥawiyya*: Being a Translation of a Part of the *Dar' Al-Taʿāruḍ* of Ibn Taymiyya, with Introduction, Annotation, and Appendices'. *Journal of Islamic Studies* 14: 149–203 (Part I) and 14: 309–63 (Part II).

el-Omari, R. (2010). 'Ibn Taymiyya's "Theology of the Sunna" and his Polemics with the Ashʿarites'. In Y. Rapoport and S. Ahmed (eds.), *Ibn Taymiyya and His Times*. Karachi: Oxford University Press, 101–19.

Özervarli, M. S. (2010). 'The Qur'ānic Rational Theology of Ibn Taymiyya and his Criticism of the Mutakallimūn'. In Y. Rapoport and S. Ahmed (eds.), *Ibn Taymiyya and His Times*. Karachi: Oxford University Press, 78–100.

Patton, W. M. (1897). *Aḥmed Ibn Ḥanbal and the Miḥna*. Leiden: Brill.

Perho, I. (2001). 'Man Chooses his Destiny: Ibn Qayyim Al-Jawziyya's View on Predestination'. *Islam and Christian-Muslim Relations* 12: 61–70.

Peskes, E. (1960–2004). 'Wahhābiyya'. In *Encyclopaedia of Islam*. New edn., xi. 39–45.

Peskes, E. (1999). 'The Wahhābiyya and Sufism in the Eighteenth Century'. In F. de Jong and B. Radtke (eds.), *Islamic Mysticism Contested: Thirteen Centuries of Controversies and Polemics*. Leiden: Brill, 145–61.

Qadhi, Y. (2010). '"The Unleashed Thunderbolts" of Ibn Qayyim al-Ǧawziyyah: An Introductory Essay'. In C. Bori and L. Holtzman (eds.), *A Scholar in the Shadow: Essays in the Legal and Theological Thought of Ibn Qayyim al-Ǧawziyyah. Oriente Moderno* monograph series, 90/1: 135–49.

Sabari, S. (1981). *Mouvements populaires à Bagdad à l'époque 'abbaside, ixe–xie siècles*. Paris: Maisonneuve.

al-Sarhan, S. S. (2011). 'Early Muslim Traditionalism: A Critical Study of the Works and Political Theology of Aḥmad Ibn Ḥanbal'. Doctoral dissertation, University of Exeter.

Seale, M. S. (1964). *Muslim Theology: A Study of Origins with Reference to the Church Fathers*. London: Luzac.

Shihadeh, A. (2006). 'Three Apologetic Stances in al-Ṭūfī: Theological Cognitivism, Noncognitivism, and a Proof of Prophecy from Scriptural Contradiction'. *Journal of Qur'anic Studies* 8: 1–23.

Swartz, M. (2002). *A Medieval Critique of Anthropomorphism: Ibn al-Jawzī's Kitāb Akhbār aṣ-Ṣifāt. A Critical Edition of the Arabic Text with Translation, Introduction and Notes*. Leiden: Brill.

Ṭūfī, Najm al-Dīn (2002). *Al-Ishārāt al-ilāhiyya ilā l-mabāḥith al-uṣūliyya*. Ed. Abū ʿĀṣim Ḥasan b. ʿAbbās b. Quṭb. 3 vols. Cairo: al-Fārūq al-ḥadītha.

Ṭūfī, Najm al-Dīn (2005). *Darʾ al-qawl al-qabīḥ bi-l-taḥsīn wa al-taqbīḥ*. Ed. Ayman Shihāda. Riyadh: Markaz al-Malik Fayṣal.

Vishanoff, D. R. (2011). *The Formation of Islamic Hermeneutics: How Sunni Legal Theorists Imagined a Revealed Law*. New Haven: American Oriental Society.

Watt, W. M. (1994). *Islamic Creeds*. Edinburgh: Edinburgh University Press.

Williams, W. (2002). 'Aspects of the Creed of Imam Ahmad Ibn Hanbal: A Study of Anthropomorphism in Early Islamic Discourse'. *International Journal of Middle East Studies* 34: 441–63.

PART IV

POLITICAL AND SOCIAL HISTORY AND ITS IMPACT ON THEOLOGY—FOUR CASE STUDIES

CHAPTER 36

AL-MAʾMŪN (R. 198/813–218/833) AND THE *MIḤNA*

NIMROD HURVITZ

I Introduction

The *miḥna* was a series of interrogations that were inaugurated by the ʿAbbāsid caliph al-Maʾmūn (d. 218/833) during the last months of his life. They were executed by his governors, who asked Muslim scholars one question: Was the Qurʾān created? Most of the scholars cooperated with the authorities and replied that the Qurʾān was indeed created. However, a few refused to comply, were incarcerated, and a handful of them died in jail. After fifteen years of coercion and resistance the caliph al-Mutawakkil (d. 247/861) put an end to the interrogations in 233/848.

The interrogators questioned dozens of elderly and politically loyal scholars who were held in great esteem by the general public. This public humiliation transformed the *miḥna* into a collective trauma that captured the imagination of later generations and was retold in numerous chronicles and biographical dictionaries. Western scholars have also given this event a great deal of attention, and have gone on to ask why the interrogations focused on the createdness of the Qurʾān, why they erupted in the early third/ninth century, and why al-Maʾmūn initiated such a policy. Yet despite the interest that the *miḥna* has aroused in classical and contemporary times, many students of the event consider the reasons of its introduction to be 'a mystery' (Nawas 1994: 623).

Modern historians have approached the *miḥna* from two angles. The first depicts it as al-Maʾmūn's intervention in the theological controversies that divided the scholars into several sectarian and political factions.[1] According to this approach, the *miḥna*

[1] For a critical survey of works that espouse this approach see Nawas 1994: 616–19. Two interesting studies that mention in passing that the *miḥna* was a conflict between the *muḥaddithūn* and the *mutakallimūn* are Goldziher 1963: 85, and Hodgson 1974: i. 389. Hodgson also observes that before the *miḥna* the *muḥaddithūn* persecuted the *mutakallimūn*. This is a crucial point and is one of the arguments of this chapter.

was a measure taken to reshape Islamic theology. The second approach focuses on al-Maʾmūn's efforts to buttress caliphal authority.[2] Adherents of this approach place al-Maʾmūn's religious convictions with his political interests, and argue that he initiated the *miḥna* in order to strengthen the caliphs' spiritual authority and be 'a supreme head with authority that was unquestioned, unlimited and shared with no one else' (Nawas 1994: 624).

According to the latter group of historians, the *miḥna* was a new phase in a decades-old struggle over spiritual authority between the caliphs and the scholars. They note that in the years preceding the *miḥna* the caliphs saw their spiritual authority diminish, while the scholars' position as spiritual heirs to the Prophet only grew. Against this background they claim that the *miḥna* was introduced by al-Maʾmūn to 'enforce the role of the caliph as guide in spiritual matters . . . ' (Crone and Hinds 1986: 97). In other words, they argue that the *miḥna* was initiated to reverse the dynamic of the caliphs' declining spiritual authority and to re-establish his religious stature.

The main source of information about al-Maʾmūn's motives to introduce the *miḥna* are five letters that he wrote to his governor in Baghdad, found in the chronicles of the renowned historian Abū Jaʿfar al-Ṭabarī (d. 310/923). In the opening sentence of the first letter al-Maʾmūn contends that 'the imams (*aʾimma*) of the Muslims and their caliphs' are responsible for implementing and guarding the faith (al-Ṭabarī, *Tārīkh*, 1112; trans. 199). This remark can be understood in two ways. The first is that the *aʾimma* and the caliphs are identical, in which case it is reasonable to assume that the letter depicts the caliphs as standing apart and above the rest of society. The second is that *aʾimma* refers to outstanding scholars, such as teachers in scholarly circles and intellectual leaders in general. In this case the terms 'caliphs' and *aʾimma* describe two different groups (rulers and scholars), and the caliphs do not possess a unique spiritual standing, but are instead partners with the *aʾimma*. This would imply that the *miḥna* is not about a confrontation between the caliphs and the scholars. As the letter stands, it is not possible to determine the exact meaning of the term *aʾimma*.

A similarly obscure line comes up in the third letter, in which is written, 'His representatives [or: caliphs, *khulafāʾ*] on earth and from those entrusted by Him with authority over His servants' (al-Ṭabarī, *Tārīkh*, 1117; trans. 205). If we understand 'those entrusted by Him' as a reference to a group of individuals who are not the caliphs, then this sentence also, like the opening sentence of the first letter, means that the caliphs were part of a wider group of spiritual leaders who guided and guarded the Islamic community from straying from the true path. Thus in both letters al-Maʾmūn would be depicting the caliphs as part of an elite, and not as solitary leaders on a higher plane than all the believers.

It has been reliably demonstrated by M. Qasim Zaman that it is more accurate to speak of 'collaboration between the caliphs and the ʿulamāʾ [scholars], not a separation or divorce between them' (Zaman 1997: 12), which undermines the historical

[2] For a survey of these works see Hurvitz 2002: 16–19.

background to the claim that the *miḥna* was an effort to enhance the caliph's spiritual authority. Indeed, when we read sources such as chronicles, biographies, and epistles that mention the *miḥna*, we do not come across depictions of the caliphs as sole possessors of spiritual authority, nor general descriptions of tension between caliphs and scholars. Whatever al-Maʾmūn may have meant in his above descriptions of caliphal spiritual authority, his letters do not read as an unequivocal demand for a monopoly over spiritual authority.

How, then, should we understand al-Maʾmūn's remarks? I propose that they were intended as admission into a debate club that most caliphs rarely entered. It was not common for caliphs to participate in theological debates, and it was certainly out of the ordinary for them to clash with the Sunnī, or proto-Sunnī, scholarly elite. Al-Maʾmūn justified his exceptional step with several statements about the legitimacy of a caliph's spiritual competence. Al-Maʾmūn's claim to possess spiritual authority was a means that enabled him to participate in one of the defining controversies of early Islam—the significance of theological speculations. However, it was not an end in itself. Therefore, when historians argue that the main motivation for instigating the *miḥna* was to uphold the caliph's spiritual authority, they are confusing means and ends.

The main goal of the *miḥna* was to alter the politics of faith by placing the theological enterprise at the centre of the Islamic intellectual and religious arena, and to transform theological speculations into tenets of faith. This went hand in hand with strengthening the status of the *mutakallimūn* (theologians) and persecuting the *muḥaddithūn* (traditionists), because the latter opposed the theological enterprise and used their influence to marginalize the *mutakallimūn*. The *miḥna* was the moment when al-Maʾmūn jumped into the fray of religious politics—in siding with the *mutakallimūn* and attacking the *muḥaddithūn*, he attempted to reverse the course of Islamic intellectual and doctrinal history.

II The Authority of Theological Speculation

The controversy over the createdness of the Qurʾān consisted of two interrelated debates. The first was about the Qurʾān itself—was it, or was it not, created? The second was about theology: can humans elaborate authoritative answers to theological questions, such as the question of the createdness of the Qurʾān, by means of rational speculation? When we examine the exchange between the two currents it becomes clear that al-Maʾmūn and the *mutakallimūn* focused on the first question, while their opponents, Aḥmad b. Ḥanbal (d. 241/855) (the Traditionist leader who led the resistance during the *miḥna* interrogations) and the *muḥaddithūn*, focused on the second. Thus whereas al-Maʾmūn and his accomplices sought the most convincing theological proof that the Qurʾān was created, Ibn Ḥanbal and his allies asserted that it does not matter what the theologians argue since reason-based solutions to questions pertaining to God cannot serve as tenets of faith.

The bedrock of al-Maʾmūn's position was his interpretation of the Qurʾānic verse 43: 3, 'Indeed, we have made it (*jaʿalnāhu*) an Arabic Qurʾān'. In his letter al-Maʾmūn presented the verse in the following manner: 'Yet God has said in the clear and unambiguous parts of His Book . . . "Indeed, we have made it (*jaʿalnāhu*) an Arabic Qurʾān"' (al-Ṭabarī, *Tārīkh*, 1113; trans. 201). It is noteworthy that al-Maʾmūn described this verse as 'clear and unambiguous', because this is the point that his rivals challenged.

The crux of al-Maʾmūn's argument is the word *jaʿalnāhu* ('we made it') in the verse. According to al-Maʾmūn, the verb *jaʿala* ('to make') indicates that there is a creator, God, Who is the active agent that created all entities. At the same time there is a created entity, in this case the Qurʾān. Al-Maʾmūn understands *jaʿala* to mean 'He created [something out of nothing]', in which case it can be argued that the Qurʾān was created by God. However, al-Maʾmūn's opponents retorted that the verse was in fact not clear; it was ambiguous (*mutashābih*). Its ambiguity derived from the fact that *jaʿala* had two meanings. In *al-Radd ʿalā al-Zanādiqa wa-l-Jahamiyya*, a tract that Ibn Ḥanbal wrote after the *miḥna*, he comments:

> When referring to creatures, *jaʿala* has two different meanings in the Qurʾān: it can mean naming, *tasmiya*, or doing . . . Now when Allah says, 'We have made it an Arabic Qurʾān', He means He made it Arabic in the sense of an action performed by God, not in the sense of creation'. (Ibn Ḥanbal, *al-Radd*, 22, 24; trans. 99, 101)

In other words, one of the two meanings of *jaʿala*,[3] according to Ibn Ḥanbal, is to attribute a certain characteristic to something that already exists. In Q 43: 3, 'We have made it an Arabic Qurʾān', the act of making pertains to the Arabic—*jaʿala* refers to the act by which God gave the existing Qurʾān the quality of being in the Arabic language.

This semantic disagreement reveals another controversy: the status of ambiguous verses (*mutashābihāt*) in the Qurʾān. In *al-Radd* Ibn Ḥanbal states that the *mutakallimūn*'s claim that *mafʿūl* ('made') is synonymous with *makhlūq* ('created') is based on an ambiguous verse. From Ibn Ḥanbal's point of view, it is impossible to know the exact meaning of a verse that has several meanings, and therefore it cannot attain the degree of certainty that is required by theological doctrine. In fact, Ibn Ḥanbal accuses his opponents of having a propensity to rely on ambiguous verses (Ibn Ḥanbal, *al-Radd*, 6; trans. 96–7).

Ibn Ḥanbal's answers during his interrogation illustrate the importance that he ascribed to clear-cut Qurʾān statements that do not require sophisticated interpretation: 'You have presented an interpretation (*taʾwīl*) and you are most knowledgeable, [however] what you have interpreted (*taʾawwalta*) does not warrant jailing and binding' (Ṣāliḥ, *Sīra*, 56). In this reply Ibn Ḥanbal does not disagree with a specific interpretation. What is more, he is humble and is willing to concede that Ibn Abī Duʾād (d. 240/854), a judge and adviser

[3] For the two meanings of the term *jaʿala*, see Lane 1984: ii. 430, 'He made a thing of, or from, a thing', and a second meaning, 'brought into being, or existence'.

to al-Maʾmūn and instrumental in convincing al-Maʾmūn to initiate the *miḥna*, is 'most knowledgeable' in the matter that is being discussed. However, Ibn Abī Duʾād is mistaken in the assumption that an interpretation (*taʾwīl*) can attain the status of a tenet of faith. According to Ibn Ḥanbal, an interpretation, even one that seems impeccable, is a personal opinion of a human being, and is therefore fallible. Because of its fallibility it cannot serve as dogma. And if such an opinion is not dogma, then it 'does not warrant jailing or binding'.

Ibn Ḥanbal's insistence that only clear and unequivocal verses from the holy texts can serve as the basis of dogma comes up several times in his interrogation: 'Give me anything from the Book of Allah or the *sunna* of his Messenger' (Ṣāliḥ, *Sīra*, 56, 59; Hurvitz 2002: 135), he said, meaning nothing else qualifies as theological doctrine.

Therefore to some extent the *mutakallimūn* and *muḥaddithūn* spoke past each other. For al-Maʾmūn and the *mutakallimūn* the *miḥna* was about presenting the most compelling analysis and position regarding the Qurʾān's createdness; for Ibn Ḥanbal and the *muḥaddithūn* it was about the irrelevance of such analysis to the doctrine of faith. The *muḥaddithūn*'s lack of interest in theological investigations is exemplified by their laconic remarks before the *miḥna*, when they referred to the Qurʾān simply as the speech of God. Only after the interrogations, and as a reaction to them, did they add that it was uncreated (Madelung 1974: 520–1).

This disagreement regarding the ability of the human mind to arrive at authoritative conclusions regarding the divine, which surfaces throughout Ibn Ḥanbal's interrogation, is very similar to the controversy between the scholastics and their opponents, that would come to haunt Christendom from the eleventh century, aptly described by G. Leff as the 'conflicting claims of faith and reason' (Leff 1958: 91). Like the *mutakallimūn*, the scholastics believed that it was vital to study and speculate about questions of theology, and that the conclusions arrived at by such speculation constituted tenets of faith. By contrast the opponents of scholasticism—along with the *muḥaddithūn*—believed that the human intellect was inherently limited, its thoughts and conclusions transient, and as a result, even the most convincing act of reasoning could not attain the status of eternal doctrine. The words of the cardinal and church reformer Peter Damian (d. 1072), 'That which is from the argument of the dialecticians cannot easily be adapted to the mysteries of divine power' (Leff 1958: 96), reflect the Ḥanbalī position that there is no analogical reasoning (*qiyās*), i.e. exercise of human rational faculties, in matters of faith (*dīn*) (Ibn Abī Yaʿlā, *Ṭabaqāt*, 1: 31), and therefore, doctrine can be based solely on unequivocal sacred text.

III The Clash between the *Muḥaddithūn* and *Mutakallimūn*

Despite the virulent, anti-*muḥaddithūn* rhetoric in his letters, al-Maʾmūn does not for the most part address his opponents as a group with a distinctive name. However, he does make one reference about their collective self-view: 'They consider themselves adherents of the *sunna* ...' (al-Ṭabarī, *Tārīkh*, 1114; trans. 201). This is an accurate description of those who held the corpus of Prophetic reports in reverence, i.e. the *muḥaddithūn*. This characterization of the *miḥna*'s victims was noted by J. Nawas, who studied the backgrounds of the individuals whom al-Maʾmūn threatened in his letters and concluded that the *miḥna* was aimed at '*muḥaddithūn* of distinction' (Nawas 1996: 705).

Al-Maʾmūn's assault on the self-styled 'adherents of the *sunna*' was the first time that a caliph confronted the growing ranks of *muḥaddithūn* with such brutality. Although it was commonplace in medieval societies for rulers and courtiers to look down upon the rest of society, the kind of diatribe that al-Maʾmūn bestowed on his adversaries is exceptional. Consider his remarks about the masses and their leadership:

> The Commander of the Faithful has realized that the broad mass and the overwhelming concentration of the base elements of the ordinary people and the lower strata of the commonality are those who, in all the regions and far horizons of the world, *have no farsightedness, or vision, or faculty of reasoning by means of evidential proofs* as God approves along the right way which he provide, or *faculty of seeking illumination* by means of the light of knowledge and God's decisive proofs. [These persons are] a people *sunk in ignorance and in blindness* about God, ... a people who *fall short of being able to grasp the reality of God* ... This is because of the *feebleness of their judgment, the deficiency of their intellects and their lack of facility in reflecting upon things and calling them to mind.* (al-Ṭabarī, *Tārīkh*, 1112–13, trans. 200–1, emphasis added)

This is not an ordinary ideological critique. Such *ad hominem* accusations as '[lacking] faculty of reasoning', 'sunk in ignorance', '[suffering from] feebleness of their judgment', and '[being incapable of] reflecting upon things' reveal considerable anger and disdain. But it was not his rivals' intellectual inadequacy that triggered al-Maʾmūn's contempt and ridicule; rather it was their refusal to recognize their own limitations and behave in accordance with them. Al-Maʾmūn was livid because the self-styled 'adherents of the *sunna*' would not admit that they were uninformed about theology and incompetent to discuss it. It seems that he could not bear the thought that such 'feeble-minded' subjects spoke back and had the audacity to cast doubts about the theological project as a whole. From his vantage point, to have subjects who were ignorant about theological matters was to be expected; to be confronted by them, and to have to argue with them over the legitimacy of theology, however, was outrageous.

Al-Maʾmūn's condescending attitude towards his subjects was shared by members of his entourage, such as al-Kindī (d. 256/873), the 'philosopher of the Arabs' and a protégé of the caliphs al-Maʾmūn and al-Muʿtaṣim (d. 227/842), who wrote:

> [We must] be on guard against the evil of the interpretation of many in our own time who have made a name for themselves with speculation, people who are estranged from the truth. They crown themselves undeservedly with the crowns of truth, because of the narrowness of their understanding of the ways of truth [...] (Adamson 2007: 23)

Like al-Maʾmūn, al-Kindī was keenly aware of a fractious intellectual and religious dichotomy between, in his view, those who knew the truth and those who 'undeservedly' claimed to know it. This latter group caused al-Kindī and al-Maʾmūn great concern and references to its popularity appear in al-Maʾmūn's letters. When he discusses how these intellectual lightweights were able to convince the public that they deserved the position of spiritual leadership, al-Maʾmūn describes them as follows: 'those are the people who dispute about vain and useless things and then invite others to adopt their views' (al-Ṭabarī, *Tārīkh*, 1114; trans. 201). He further laments that they succeeded in mobilizing the masses and acquired 'for themselves glory in their [the masses'] eyes and securing for themselves leadership and a reputation for probity amongst them' (al-Ṭabarī, *Tārīkh*, 1114; trans. 202). To al-Maʾmūn's chagrin the intellectually inept *muḥaddithūn* were savvy political leaders who were able to win the public's respect and transform it into tangible social achievements.

At this point al-Maʾmūn's accusations reach a fevered pitch. The *muḥaddithūn* were not satisfied with their undeserved position of intellectual and spiritual leadership, but aimed to destroy the *mutakallimūn* and to block them from positions of influence. They 'assert that all others are people of false beliefs, infidelity and schism' (al-Ṭabarī, *Tārīkh*, 1114; trans. 202); they serve as 'the tongue of Iblis [Satan], who speaks through his companions and strikes terror into the hearts of his adversaries ' (al-Ṭabarī, *Tārīkh*, 1115; trans. 203).

Al-Maʾmūn's depiction of the *mutakallimūn* is corroborated by al-Jāḥiẓ (d. 255/869), a *mutakallim* who was a protégé of Ibn Abī Duʾād, the influential judge and adviser to al-Maʾmūn.[4] In a tract dedicated to Ibn Abī Duʾād and his son, al-Jāḥiẓ writes about the power of the masses and their propensity to use force in order to scare, or as al-Maʾmūn would have it, to terrorize the *mutakallimūn*. 'You know', writes al-Jāḥiẓ, '. . . of the intimidation of the *mutakallimūn* scholars (*ikhāfat ʿulamāʾ al-mutakallimūn*)' (al-Jāḥiẓ, *al-Tashbīh*, 285). The *mutakallimūn* had good reason to fear the masses, who relied 'on power, strength, numbers and good fortune, on the allegiance of the ruffians and the dregs of the populace' (al-Jāḥiẓ, *al-Tashbīh*, 288). In other remarks made by al-Jāḥiẓ we learn that before the *miḥna* these masses actively opposed theological inquiry (*kalām*) and refused to converse with the *mutakallimūn* (al-Jāḥiẓ, *al-Tashbīh*, 288).

These allegations made by al-Maʾmūn and al-Jāḥiẓ are echoed in numerous anecdotes that appear in biographical literature and bring into relief the intimidation and systematic campaign that the *muḥaddithūn* waged against the *mutakallimūn*. The effectiveness of this campaign is illustrated by a survey of biographical dictionaries that indicates that up until the end of the second/eighth century there was a significant group of sectarians and *mutakallimūn* among the transmitters of *ḥadīth*, but their numbers decreased significantly in the first decades of the third/ninth century (Melchert 1992: 287, 294). This decline suggests that *mutakallimūn* transmitters of *ḥadīth* were placed under pressure

[4] For a survey and samples of al-Jāḥiẓ's writings, see Pellat 1969. For a detailed interpretation of al-Jāḥiẓ's writings on the *miḥna*, see Hurvitz 2001: 97–102. For a comprehensive account of Ibn Abī Duʾād, see van Ess 1991–7: iii. 481–502. See also Patton 1897: 55–6.

and as a consequence were marginalized and excluded from the leading scholarly circles.

The key to understanding al-Maʾmūn's *miḥna* policy, which was in effect an attack on the *muḥaddithūn*, are his and al-Jāḥiẓ's descriptions of the intimidation and terror that the *mutakallimūn* suffered at the hands of the *muḥaddithūn*, before the *miḥna* was initiated. The *muḥaddithūn* created an atmosphere in which the *mutakallimūn* were maligned and ostracized. Because of this they lost their standing in intellectual circles and could no longer transmit Prophetic traditions nor contribute to the shaping of theological doctrine. Al-Maʾmūn's main motive in introducing the *miḥna* was to replace the *mutakallimūn* in what he considered to be their appropriate socio-intellectual position: the intellectual and spiritual leadership of the Islamic community.

IV The *Miḥna* in Context

In an apologetic remark about the *miḥna*, which places the onus of its initiative upon al-Maʾmūn's advisers, Tāj al-Dīn al-Subkī (d. 771/1370) describes the worldview that al-Maʾmūn and his advisers shared:

> It was in the days of al-Maʾmūn's reign [that the *miḥna*] was initiated. He, ʿAbd Allāh al-Maʾmūn b. Hārūn al-Rashīd was one [of the milieu] that was interested in philosophy and the ancient sciences (*al-ʿulūm al-awāʾil*) and he excelled in them. He gathered a group of such scholars, and they led him to the doctrine of the createdness of the Qurʾān. (al-Subkī, *Ṭabaqāt*, 2: 56)

The men who convinced al-Maʾmūn to initiate the interrogations, writes al-Subkī, shared a religious view, a vision that was embraced by many *mutakallimūn* and was characterized by a number of features. First, they were interested in corpora of knowledge (astrology, astronomy, medicine, etc.) that were composed before the rise of Islam, in distant, polytheistic civilizations such as Greece, Persia, and India. As al-Kindī wrote, 'Even if it [the truth] should come from far-flung nations and foreign peoples' it should be embraced (Adamson 2007: 23). Second, this scientific knowledge was studied and elaborated by inquiry, interpretation, and critical discussions among scholars—all of which are based on rational faculties. As a consequence the members of this milieu placed a high premium on the use of human reason to comprehend and explain the physical and meta-physical worlds. Third, they were admirers of debates, primarily about theological and legal issues (al-Masʿūdī, *Murūj*, 3: 350, 4: 13, 22–3, 74–5). The adherents of this vision can be labelled as comprising the '*mutakallimūn* milieu'.

The political influence of the *mutakallimūn* milieu in al-Maʾmūn's court is corroborated by al-Subkī, who ascribes to them the ability to manoeuvre the caliph into initiating the *miḥna*. Yet it should be noted that the *mutakallimūn*'s presence in the caliphal court did not begin with the *miḥna* and neither did it disappear after it. Their ties to the court appear to have been strong from the very outset of the ʿAbbāsid regime, lasting hundreds of years after the *miḥna*, when the empire was disassembled into dynastic regimes. Many of the rulers and elite class (*khāṣṣa*) of these dynasties served as patrons to the study of science, philosophy, and theology (Brentjes 2011).

Caliphal and dynastic courts offered the *mutakallimūn* a supportive environment in which to thrive. From the early decades of the ʿAbbāsid empire, theology, the ancient sciences (particularly medicine and astrology), and occasionally philosophy became integral components of court culture. Rulers and the elite populace purchased foreign manuscripts that dealt with the ancient sciences, saw to their translation into Arabic, and created what Gutas has coined a 'culture of translation' (Gutas 1998: 26). They also held sessions in which theology was debated and science discussed. Lastly, knowledge of theology or the sciences became a ticket of admission to the caliphal court, and in some instances members of the *mutakallimūn* milieu attained positions of influence there. A pertinent example is that of the judge Ibn Abī Duʾād, who was an admirer of theology (*kalām*) and a patron of *mutakallimūn*, and is described by many sources as the chief architect of the *miḥna*. The ʿAbbāsid court and courtly culture supported the development of theological inquiry, and more importantly, they enabled the *mutakallimūn* to reach positions of power.

Yet the court also sponsored the *muḥaddithūn*, who advanced a worldview that was often opposed to the embrace of such knowledge. These critics of the *mutakallimūn* and their worldview harboured deep suspicions toward the branches of 'foreign science', in some cases labelling them the 'repudiated sciences' (*ʿulūm mahjūra*) (Goldziher 1981: 187). Some considered the study of the ancient sciences a waste of time, others were convinced that such knowledge led believers astray. In general, they were ambivalent towards human reason. They employed rational faculties when they addressed legal questions, yet many were adamantly opposed to their same use in addressing theological issues. Lastly, they abhorred debates about theology.

Most ʿAbbāsid rulers were either genuinely respectful of the *muḥaddithūn* or they were prudent politicians who chose to stay on good terms with them, maintaining a stance of political neutrality with regard to the tensions between the *muḥaddithūn* and *mutakallimūn*. Although most caliphs did not take sides in the scholarly controversies, the *muḥaddithūn* were able to delegitimize the *mutakallimūn* and their theological project, and during the first decades of the third/ninth century seemed to be winning the struggle over Islamic religiosity. This was unacceptable to al-Maʾmūn and his entourage, who retaliated by discarding the traditional caliphal neutrality and initiating state-sponsored interrogations of the *muḥaddithūn*.

When we fit the *miḥna* into the sequence of ʿAbbāsid religio-cultural politics, it is possible to identify three stages. During the first stage (from Manṣūr to al-Maʾmūn), the ʿAbbāsid court was highly supportive of the *mutakallimūn* milieu and their intellectual endeavours. At the same time it sponsored the *muḥaddithūn*, who became very influential among religious scholars and were able to marginalize the *mutakallimūn* and minimize their influence on Islamic legal and theological doctrines. During this period the caliphs did not interfere in the struggle between the two trends. In the second stage, the fifteen years of the *miḥna* (218/833–233/848), the caliphs shed their policy of neutrality, sided with the *mutakallimūn*, and persecuted the *muḥaddithūn*. The third stage began after the *miḥna* came to a halt. The caliphs renewed their tolerance toward the *muḥaddithūn*, but continued to support the *mutakallimūn*, who remained highly influential within the caliphal court, both in terms of religio-cultural activities and in the administrative roles that they played in running the empire. Their influence on the court would continue for centuries after the *miḥna*.

V Conclusion

When al-Maʾmūn initiated the *miḥna*, Islam was a little over 200 years old and Muslim intellectuals were still formulating its beliefs. Their disagreements over Islamic doctrine led to several currents of thought that struggled among themselves, as each sought to acquire positions of social and political power from which they would define Islam's system of beliefs. One of the issues that divided them was the extent to which human reasoning ought to influence the theological tenets of Islam. This controversy was played out by two powerful parties—on the one side were conservative *muḥaddithūn* who opposed theological inquiry, and on the other side were free-thinking *mutakallimūn* who encouraged it. When al-Maʾmūn decided to take a stand in this controversy, it erupted into the exceptionally violent event known as the *miḥna*. It is worth noting that this type of controversy emerged in all three monotheistic faiths, Judaism, Christianity, and Islam, particularly when they came across Greek science and logic.

The *miḥna* enables historians to study the nature and dynamics of the power struggles among scholars, out of which emerged Islamic doctrine. It enables them to examine how scholarly power was constructed, what means of persuasion the scholars devised, and how they applied them to different socio-cultural strata. Furthermore, it highlights the alliances between scholars and political leaders, and—as the *miḥna* testifies to—the limits of such an alliance, as well as the difficulties that political leaders faced when they themselves tried to influence Islamic beliefs.

Bibliography

Adamson, P. (2007). *Al-Kindī*. Oxford: Oxford University Press.

Brentjes, S. (2011). 'Ayyubid Princes and their Scholarly Clients from the Ancient Sciences'. In A. Fuess and J.-P. Hartung (eds.), *Court Cultures in the Muslim World, Seventh to Nineteenth Centuries*. London: Routledge, 326–56.

Crone, P., and M. Hinds (1986). *God's Caliph, Religious Authority in the First Centuries of Islam*. Cambridge: Cambridge University Press.

van Ess, J. (1991–7). *Theologie und Gesellschaft im 2. und 3. Jahrhundert Hidschra: Eine Geschichte des religiösen Denkens im frühen Islam*. 6 vols. Berlin: de Gruyter.

Goldziher, I. (1981). 'The Attitude of Orthodox Islam toward the "Ancient Sciences"'. In M. L. Swartz (ed.), *Studies on Islam*. New York: Oxford University Press.

Gutas, D. (1998). *Greek Thought, Arabic Culture: The Graeco-Arabic Translation Movement in Baghdad and Early ʿAbbāsid Society (2nd–4th/8th–10th centuries)*. London: Routledge.

Hodgson, M. G. S. (1974). *The Venture of Islam: Conscience and History in a World Civilization*. 3 vols. Chicago: University of Chicago Press.

Hurvitz, N. (2001). 'The Miḥna as Self-Defense'. *Studia Islamica* 92: 93–111.

Hurvitz, N. (2002). *The Formation of Ḥanbalism: Piety into Power*. London: Routledge Curzon.

Ibn Abī Yaʿlā (*Ṭabaqāt*). *Ṭabaqāt al-Ḥanābila*. 2 vols. Cairo: Maṭbaʿat al-Sunna al-Muḥammadiyya.

Ibn Ḥanbal (*al-Radd*). *al-Radd ʿalā l-Zanādiqa wa-l-Jahamiyya*. Cairo: al-Maṭbaʿa al-Salafiyya wa-Maktabatuhā, 1393/1973 [trans. M. S. Seale, *Muslim Theology: A Study of Origins with Reference to the Church Fathers*. London: Luzac, 1964].

al-Jāḥiẓ, Abū ʿUthmān (*al-Tashbīh*). *Risāla fī nafy al-Tashbīh*. In A. M. Hārūn (ed.), *Rasāʾil al-Jāḥiẓ*. 4 vols. Beirut: Maktabat al-Khānjī, 1964–79, i. 283–308.

Lane, E. W. (1984). *An Arabic–English Lexicon*. 2 vols. Cambridge: The Islamic Text Society.

Leff, G. (1958). *Medieval Thought: From Saint Augustine to Ockham*. Harmondsworth: Penguin Books.

Madelung, W. (1974). 'The Origins of the Controversy Concerning the Creation of the Koran'. In J. M. Barral, *Orientalia hispanica sive studia F. M. Pareja octogenario dicata*. Leiden: Brill, 504–25.

al-Masʿūdī (*Murūj*). *Murūj al-dhahab wa-maʿādin al-jawhar*. Beirut: Dar al-Qalama, 1989.

Melchert, C. (1992). 'Sectaries in the Six Books: Evidence for their Exclusion from the Sunni Community'. *The Muslim World* 82: 287–95.

Nawas, J. A. (1994). 'A Reexamination of Three Current Explanations for al-Maʾmūn's Introduction of the Miḥna'. *International Journal of Middle East Studies* 26: 615–29.

Nawas, J. A. (1996). 'The Miḥna of 218 A.H./833 A.D. Revisited: An Empirical Study'. *Journal of the American Oriental Society* 116: 698–708.

Patton, W. M. (1897). *Aḥmed ibn Ḥanbal and the Miḥna: A Biography of the Imâm Including an Account of the Moḥammedan Inquisition Called the Miḥna, 218–234 A. H.* Leiden: Brill.

Pellat, C. (1969). *The Life and Works of Jaḥiz. Translations of selected texts*. Berkeley: University of California Press.

Ṣāliḥ b. Aḥmad b. Ḥanbal (*Sīra*). *Sīrat al-imām Aḥmad ibn Ḥanbal*. Alexandria: Muʾassasat Shabāb al-Jāmiʿa, 1981.

al-Subkī, Tāj al-Dīn (*Ṭabaqāt*). *Ṭabaqāt al-Shāfiʿiyya al-kubrā*. 10 vols. Cairo: Īsā al-Bābī al-Ḥalabī, 1964–76.

al-Ṭabarī, Abū Jaʿfar Muḥammad (*Tārīkh*). *Tārīkh al-rusul wa-l-mulūk*. Leiden, 1879–1901 [trans. C. E. Bosworth, *The History of al-Ṭabarī The reunification of the 'Abbāsid Caliphate = The history of al-Tabarī/Tārīkh al-rusul waʾl-mulūk*, vol. xxxii. New York: SUNY Press, 1987].

Zaman, M. Q. (1997). *Religion and Politics under the Early 'Abbāsids: The Emergence of the Proto-Sunnī Elite*. Leiden: Brill.

CHAPTER 37

THE *MIḤNA* OF IBN ʿAQĪL (D. 513/1119) AND THE *FITNAT* IBN AL-QUSHAYRĪ (D. 514/1120)

LIVNAT HOLTZMAN

THE *miḥna* of Ibn ʿAqīl (d. 513/1119) and the *fitnat* Ibn al-Qushayrī (d. 514/1120) are two events that took place in eleventh-century Baghdad and mark the victory of traditionalist Islam over rationalist Islam. Ibn ʿAqīl's *miḥna* was a series of events, starting with an open persecution of Ibn ʿAqīl by his fellow-Ḥanbalīs in 458/1066, continuing with his exile, and ending with his public retraction in 465/1072. The *fitnat* Ibn al-Qushayrī, i.e. the riots connected to Ibn al-Qushayrī, is a name given by Ḥanbalī authors to a series of protests and violent acts that occurred between Shawwāl 469/April–May 1077 and the middle of Ṣafar 470/September 1077. While the *fitnat* Ibn al-Qushayrī was an open clash between the Ḥanbalīs and the Ashʿarīs, the *miḥna* of Ibn ʿAqīl—which is described in Western research as the victory of traditionalist Islam over Muʿtazilism—was actually an internal Ḥanbalī affair.

The setting of the events is eleventh-century Baghdad: a vibrant city, with commercial, political, religious, and cultural activities that were concentrated mainly in the east side. In that period of time, the city of Baghdad underwent major changes, which are known in Western research as 'the Sunni Revival'. The most important political event of the period was the occupation of Baghdad by Toghril Beg in 447/1061, which marked the end of the Shīʿī dynasty of the Buwayhids and the rise of the Sunnī dynasty of the Seljūqs. The religious and cultural life in the city flourished with the establishment of Sunnī *madrasas* (like the *Niẓāmiyya*, see Section II) and Ṣūfī *ribāṭs*, and Baghdad was justifiably considered the cultural cosmopolitan capital of the Islamic world.

In the beginning of the Seljūq period, the city was characterized by the vigorous intellectual activities of scholars from the entire spectrum of Islamic thought: traditionalists, semi-traditionalists, and rationalists. The indisputable rulers of religious life, however, were the traditionalists, mostly identified with the Ḥanbalīs (although the traditionalists came from all four Sunnī schools). Modern researchers (Henri Laoust, Nimrod Hurvitz, Michael Cook, to name just a few), following Ira Lapidus's theories, label the Ḥanbalī *madhhab* as a social cadre and a politico-religious movement with profound influence over *al-ʿāmma* ('the masses'). The simplicity of the traditionalistic Ḥanbalī message and the accessibility of Ḥanbalī teachings, mainly delivered in public sermons and open study sessions, enabled the zealous Ḥanbalī activists to recruit the masses for their political purposes. In early researches, the Ḥanbalīs were described as an ignorant mob. However, like any other social group in Baghdad, the Ḥanbalīs had their elite *ʿulamāʾ* and rich merchants, who resided in the elegant quarter of Bāb al-Marātib and were interrelated by social and familial ties (Laoust 1959: 95–105; Sabari 1981: 101–26; Cook 2000: 114–28; Hurvitz 2003: 985–1008; Ephrat 2000: 87–8; van Renterghem 2008: 231–58).

Ḥanbalīs made for themselves the name of troublemakers in the Buwayhid period, due to the incitement of their leaders, al-Barbahārī (d. 329/941) and Ibn Baṭṭa (d. 387/997). In the Seljūq period, however, the Ḥanbalīs established close relationships with the caliph, thus becoming a part of the establishment and having the opportunity to make their mark on the religious life in Baghdad. Under the leadership of the *sharīf* Abū Jaʿfar al-Hāshimī (d. 470/1077–8), a shrewd politician and notable leader from the Hāshimī family, the Ḥanbalīs acted on two fronts: the first was the enforcement of the strictest religious rules on everyday life (such as banning music and destroying wine which they confiscated from taverns); the second was their struggle against all forms of heresy, particularly against Muʿtazilī and Ashʿarī doctrines. While *al-ʿāmma* backed the Ḥanbalīs by joining the Ḥanbalī 'spontaneous' rioting, the anti-rationalist tendency penetrated the intellectual circles. The eleventh century was not the 'right time' to be a rationalist, either a Muʿtazilī or an Ashʿarī. The debate between the traditionalists and the rationalists ceased and gave way to riots, which were directly and indirectly incited by the *sharīf* Abū Jaʿfar.

Much supported and favoured by the masses, the *sharīf* Abū Jaʿfar was a Ḥanbalī role model, being a pious scholar, a humble ascetic, and a fierce activist. He was held in high esteem by the caliphs: al-Qāʾim bi-Amr Allāh, who ruled for forty-four years (from 422/1031 to 467/1074), requested that Abū Jaʿfar prepare his body for burial; Abū Jaʿfar was the first among notables to give the caliph al-Muqtadī, who ruled for nineteen years (from 467/1075 to 487/1094), his pledge of allegiance (*bayʿa*). These intimate relationships with the caliphs enabled Abū Jaʿfar to execute his programmatic vision of a society subjugated to Ḥanbalī codes. In his relentless campaign against the Muʿtazilīs and Ashʿarīs, Abū Jaʿfar almost single-handedly subdued rationalist Islam.

The activities of the Ḥanbalīs against the rationalists were backed by the authorities not only because of Abū Jaʿfar's relationships with the caliphs, but also because traditionalism became the official doctrine of the caliphate. In the beginning of the eleventh century, the *Qādirī Creed*, issued in the name of the caliph al-Qādir bi-Allāh (d. 422/1031), re-established the fundamentals of the traditionalistic dogma. The *Creed*, which refuted the Muʿtazilī as well as the Ashʿarī doctrines, was consensually approved by the leading traditionalists and read in several public occasions during the reign of al-Qādir's son, the caliph al-Qāʾim bi-Amr Allāh. As a belated response to the *miḥna* of al-Maʾmūn (d. 218/833), the *Qādirī Creed* gave way to the caliph accusing scholars of Muʿtazilism, while forcing them to retract from their rationalist beliefs and embrace the traditionalist faith. In Jumādā I 460/March 1068, the *sharīf* Abū Jaʿfar led a group of scholars and notables of various religious trends, who paraded to the caliphal palace, demanding that the *Qādirī Creed* be reread and reaffirmed publicly. The pretext for this demonstration was the renewal of the Muʿtazilī Abū ʿAlī Ibn al-Walīd's (d. 478/1086) teaching sessions. Two public readings of the *Qādirī Creed* were organized with the blessing and active support of the caliphal prime minister. Afterwards, the *Creed* was read in the mosques, in which it was presented as the authentic expression of the genuine Islamic doctrine (Makdisi 1963: 337–40; van Renterghem 2010: 212–13).

The first scholar who investigated the events presented in this article was Ignaz Goldziher. Already in his 1908 article on the history of Ḥanbalism, Goldziher revealed the complex relationships between the caliphal court, the leaders of Ḥanbalism, and the proponents of Muʿtazilism and Ashʿarism. In addition, Goldziher succinctly mentioned the *miḥna* of Ibn ʿAqīl and the *fitna* connected to Ibn al-Qushayrī. Goldziher's description of the events was, however, partial and inaccurate, because of the limited sources that were at his disposal, and also because of his antagonism to Ḥanbalism. Adam Mez relied on Goldziher's description in his *Die Renaissance des Islams* (published posthumously in 1922) and added a translation of the *Qādirī Creed* (Mez 1937: 206–9). The entire picture was revealed some fifty years later in the works of George Makdisi. Makdisi, who dedicated his scholarly activities to exploring every possible aspect of life in eleventh-century Baghdad, published an article in 1957 in which he recognized Goldziher's pioneering work on Ḥanbalism, but at the same time severely criticized the latter's conclusions. Makdisi targeted what he perceived as Goldziher's misconception of Ḥanbalism in general, and eleventh-century Ḥanbalism in particular, in an article published in 1981. In our reading of the following events, we are indebted to George Makdisi. He both meticulously read the scholarly works of Ibn ʿAqīl (some of which he discovered and published in critical editions), and he embedded the theological discussion in its accurate historical context, relying on numerous accounts, one of which was Ibn ʿAqīl's personal journal.

Makdisi's reading of the existing sources is so thorough and systematic, that unless new sources are revealed, his works will remain unsurpassed and unchallenged. This is particularly true in the case of Ibn ʿAqīl's *miḥna*, the minutiae of which Makdisi meticulously investigated. The case of the *fitnat* Ibn al-Qushayrī is different, because Makdisi did not concentrate—or perhaps, did not have the opportunity to concentrate—on the different contexts of this particular event. The present chapter describes Ibn ʿAqīl's *miḥna* and the *fitnat* Ibn al-Qushayrī and is divided accordingly into two sections. The first section summarizes Ibn ʿAqīl's *miḥna*, while heavily relying on Makdisi, and also provides a limited-scale reading in the primary sources. The second section offers new insights on the *fitnat* Ibn al-Qushayrī based on a close reading of the primary sources.

I The *Miḥna* of Ibn ʿAqīl

Abū l-Wafāʾ ʿAlī b. ʿAqīl was a prolific Ḥanbalī jurist and theologian in Baghdad, who also documented the events in Baghdad, including his own personal biography. His evidence on the events in the first-person singular was preserved in the writings of Ibn al-Jawzī (d. 597/1200), Ibn Rajab (d. 795/1392), and others (Makdisi 1997: 46–51). Makdisi dedicated two monographs to Ibn ʿAqīl (Makdisi 1963; 1997), several articles, and an encyclopedic entry. The 1963 monograph is a reconstruction of the historical narrative from chronicles and biographical dictionaries, while the 1997 monograph focuses on Ibn ʿAqīl's theological and ethical thought. The first part of the 1997 monograph, which deals with Ibn ʿAqīl's biography, supplements the 1963 monograph, while using the data of an article, published in two parts in 1956 and 1957, and another article in French, published in 1957 (here: Makdisi, 1957b).

Ibn ʿAqīl came from a Ḥanafī family with Muʿtazilī tendencies, who resided in Bāb al-Ṭāq, an elegant Baghdadian quarter that was populated by respectable Ḥanafī merchants, who were mostly Muʿtazilīs as well. Bāb al-Ṭāq was a major market area, vibrant with commercial and industrial activities (Lassner 1970: 173; Makdisi 1959: 188–90). As a youngster, Ibn ʿAqīl was privileged to receive his education from the most illustrious scholars in their fields. Among Ibn ʿAqīl's many teachers, the names of the *qāḍī* Abū Yaʿlā (d. 458/1066) and the *shaykh* Abū Isḥāq al-Shīrāzī (d. 478/1085–6) stand out: Abū Yaʿlā, the illustrious Ḥanbalī scholar, taught Ibn ʿAqīl Ḥanbalī *fiqh*, while the Shāfiʿī Abū Isḥāq taught him the art of theological debating (*munāẓara*). Ibn ʿAqīl was educated by several rationalists, the most prominent of whom was the Muʿtazilī Abū ʿAlī Ibn al-Walīd (Makdisi 1997: 20). The latter secretly taught Ibn ʿAqīl Muʿtazilī *kalām*. In addition, Ibn ʿAqīl was interested in the writings of the Ṣūfī mystic al-Ḥallāj (d. 309/922). Makdisi's remark that 'Ibn ʿAqil was a product of that period, a microcosm of the world of Islam in Baghdad' (Makdisi 1997: xv) should be taken with a grain of salt—Ibn ʿAqīl indeed enjoyed the benefits of the intellectual versatility in Baghdad, but he was probably unique in this position.

Ibn ʿAqīl converted from the Ḥanafī school of law, to which he belonged by birth, to Ḥanbalism at the encouragement of the Ḥanbalī mécénat Abū Manṣūr Ibn Yūsuf (d. 460/1067–8). Ibn Yūsuf, who was also named 'the most honorable *shaykh*' (*al-shaykh al-ajall*), was a rich merchant who was held in high esteem by the caliph. Ibn ʿAqīl suffered from constant harassments by the Ḥanbalīs: 'My fellow-Ḥanbalīs wanted me to dissociate myself with a group of *ʿulamāʾ*. This might have deprived me of beneficial knowledge'. From this remark, it may be assumed that Ibn ʿAqīl refused to dissociate himself from Muʿtazilī scholars. The Ḥanbalīs, who insisted on Ibn ʿAqīl's compliance with their demands, accused Ibn ʿAqīl of deviating from the Ḥanbalī dogma: 'It appeared sometimes that he sort of deviated from the Sunna, giving figurative interpretation to the divine attributes' (Ibn ʿAqīl's biography in Ibn Rajab's *Dhayl Ṭabaqāt al-Ḥanābila*, 1: 322).

Ibn ʿAqīl's troubles began when, with the encouragement of his benefactor, he was appointed as a lecturer in the Great Mosque at the Basra Gate named after al-Manṣūr. This position was previously occupied by his mentor Abū Yaʿlā, until the latter's death in Ramaḍān 458/August 1066. As Ibn ʿAqīl himself described: 'I was extremely lucky when Abū Manṣūr Ibn Yūsuf approached me, and gave preference to my *fatāwā* over the *fatāwā* of those who were much older and senior than me. He gave me the teaching position of the Barāmika forum (*ḥalqat al-Barāmika*), when my mentor died in the year 458, and took care of my every needs.' (The passage appears in the biographical entry on Ibn ʿAqīl biography in Ibn Rajab's *Dhayl*, 1: 320; for a slightly different translation, see Makdisi 1997: 24; for al-Barmakī family, after whom the *ḥalqat al-Barāmika* was named, see Makdisi 1997: 27.)

Ibn ʿAqīl's exceptional appointment as successor to Abū Yaʿlā did not pass without opposition. The *sharīf* Abū Jaʿfar, who was also a devoted disciple of Abū Yaʿlā, embarked upon an open campaign against Ibn ʿAqīl. Abū Jaʿfar's resentment towards Ibn ʿAqīl was established during the eleven years (from 447/1055 to 458/1066) in which the young Ibn ʿAqīl was tutored by Abū Yaʿlā. According to Ibn ʿAqīl, 'Although I was very young, I enjoyed the good graces of being close to him (i.e. to Abū Yaʿlā), more than any of his disciples' (Ibn Rajab, *Dhayl*, 1: 320; Makdisi 1997: 27). Nevertheless, Abū Jaʿfar, who was granted the honour of purifying Abū Yaʿlā's body before burial, saw himself more entitled to Abū Yaʿlā's inheritance than Ibn ʿAqīl (Ephrat 2000: 89). Abū Jaʿfar's resentment towards Ibn ʿAqīl was therefore both personal and rooted in the *sharīf*'s zealous worldview.

In Muḥarram 460/November–December 1067, Abū Manṣūr died. Having lost the protection of his benefactor, Ibn ʿAqīl escaped from Abū Jaʿfar and the Ḥanbalīs, and lived in exile in the quarter of Bāb al-Marātib until Muḥarram 465/September 1072, where he sought asylum with the sons-in-law of Abū Manṣūr, and especially with Abū l-Qāsim ʿAbd Allāh b. Riḍwān. The Bāb al-Marātib quarter was populated by two rival parties: the Ḥanbalīs and the Hāshimīs. The case of Ibn ʿAqīl was one topic of conflict between the two groups—the *sharīf* led the majority of the Ḥanbalīs, while a small group of Ḥanbalī youth remained loyal to Ibn ʿAqīl. The *sharīf* had a rival in the *naqīb al-nuqabāʾ* Abū l-Fawāris, the head of the Hāshimī clan in the quarter, who was one of Ibn ʿAqīl's supporters. In his efforts to isolate and destroy Ibn ʿAqīl, the *sharīf* made several political manoeuvres, while exploiting his influence on the caliph, in order to diminish the power of Ibn ʿAqīl's benefactors, viz. the *naqīb al-nuqabāʾ* Abū l-Fawāris and Abū Manṣūr's son-in-law Abū l-Qāsim. With the help of the caliph, the *sharīf* brought Ibn ʿAqīl's case to its happy conclusion by first cornering Ibn ʿAqīl and then by forcing him to sign the retraction (Makdisi 1997: 28–41; van Renterghem 2010: 207–8).

The *sharīf*'s stratagems are described in detail in a precious source, viz. Ibn al-Bannāʾ's diary. Abū ʿAlī Ibn al-Bannāʾ al-Ḥanbalī (d. 471/1079) documented the events of the years 460–1/1068–9 in his diary, giving us a glimpse of politics in the quarter of Bāb al-Marātib. Ibn al-Bannāʾ, a Ḥanbalī jurisconsult, was both an eyewitness to the events—which unfortunately he described in fragments—and an active participant—he was a close associate of the *sharīf* Abū Jaʿfar, and according to his own avowal, he issued or planned to issue a *fatwā* on Ibn al-ʿAqīl's heresy (*zandaqa*), in which he demanded Ibn ʿAqīl's immediate execution (Makdisi 1956: ii. 43; Makdisi 1997: 34–5).

Since Ibn al-Bannāʾ recorded many types of everyday events in the neighbourhood, it is difficult to trace the Ibn ʿAqīl case in his narrative.[1] A much more remote source, both in time and place, is the account provided by the Damascene Ḥanbalī jurisconsult and theologian, who was also a devout Ṣūfī, Ibn Qudāma al-Maqdisī (d. 620/1223). Ibn Qudāma wrote his account of Ibn ʿAqīl's *miḥna* based on information he received from a traditionalist Damascene scholar, who in turn received his information from a *qāḍī*, who claimed to have witnessed Ibn ʿAqīl's retraction. Ibn Qudāma's distance from the events allows him to summarize them in a much more coherent way than they are conveyed in Ibn al-Bannāʾs diary (see Makdisi's introduction to Ibn Qudāma's *Taḥrīm Naẓar*, ix–xxvi; Makdisi 1957a: 94–6; Makdisi 1963: 504–7; Makdisi 1997: 6). Ibn Rajab's (d. 795/1393) biography of Ibn ʿAqīl is even more coherent than Ibn Qudāma's account.

The later sources, i.e. Ibn Qudāma and Ibn Rajab, connect Ibn ʿAqīl's *miḥna* to doctrinal issues. Abū Jaʿfar's personal animosity towards Ibn ʿAqīl is not mentioned in these sources. Ibn Qudāma, for instance, heard from his source that the Ḥanbalīs, among them Abū Jaʿfar, demanded Ibn ʿAqīl's execution (literally: *ahdarū damahu*, 'they called to spill his blood') before giving him an opportunity to repent. Ibn Qudāma remarks that this matter always puzzled him: 'I had no idea what forced them to do that in his case and what drove them to such an extreme reaction.' However, having learned the details of the case, and especially after reading a no-longer extant work by Ibn ʿAqīl entitled *Naṣīḥa* ('Advice'), Ibn Qudāma was forced to admit that the Ḥanbalīs were correct in this case: 'That was until I read this disgrace (*faḍīḥa*, a pun on *naṣīḥa*). Then I learned that because of the *Naṣīḥa* and similar writings he was proscribed' (Ibn Qudāma, *Taḥrīm naẓar*, 1–2). According to Ibn Rajab, several writings of Ibn ʿAqīl were examined by his rivals in 461/1068–9. In these writings, 'a certain amount of glorification for the Muʿtazila' was found, in addition to sympathetic expressions regarding al-Ḥallāj. The matter was brought to the *sharīf* Abū Jaʿfar's attention and his associates'. They found the matter intolerable, and demanded Ibn ʿAqīl's execution. But even Ibn Rajab concludes: 'And so his case continued to be in commotion until 465/1072' (Ibn Rajab, *Dhayl*, 1: 322).

We do not know how many *fatāwā* were issued in Ibn ʿAqīl's case and by whom; furthermore, it is unknown whether the *sharīf* himself demanded Ibn ʿAqīl's retraction or whether this demand was explained by the content of the *Qādirī Creed*. In fact, since the sources are almost silent about the whereabouts of Ibn ʿAqīl and his rivals in the period between 461/1068–9 and 465/1072, we have only a fragmentary picture of the events. We know that Ibn ʿAqīl wrote several works on Muʿtazilism, of which he

[1] On the diary of Ibn al-Bannāʾ, see Makdisi 1956: 1; Makdisi 1997: 28. Based on the diary, van Renterghem offers a description of the social, economic, and political life in the quarter.

retracted. In the course of his flight from the *sharīf*, Ibn ʿAqīl entrusted these works to a friend, who gave him shelter. Ibn ʿAqīl, who was severely ill at the time, asked his friend to burn the works after his death. The friend read the works, and mainly because of words of veneration for al-Ḥallāj, he betrayed Ibn ʿAqīl's trust and gave the works to the *sharīf* Abū Jaʿfar. This is how the persecution started (Makdisi 1997: 42, based on Ibn al-Jawzī's *Muntaẓam*, 16: 113). We also learn that Ibn ʿAqīl was indeed declared a heretic. An entry in Ibn al-Bannāʾ's diary records a dream of a Baghdadian, who saw 'a great fire stimulated to burn fiercely, and a person feeding it with straws of the *ḥalfāʾ* plant; and that it was Ibn ʿAqīl keeping the fire going for his companions and causing it to blaze fiercely for them' (Makdisi 1997: 31). Dreams of trustworthy people were regarded as acceptable evidence and almost as real as actual events. The dream, then, symbolizes Ibn ʿAqīl's public image as a dangerous person, causing innocent believers to deviate from Islam.

Abū Jaʿfar's triumph was completed when Ibn ʿAqīl signed a public retraction (*tawba*). The events leading up to the retraction are obscure. We can only assume that vigorous negotiations between the *sharīf*'s party and Ibn ʿAqīl's dwindling number of supporters from the Hāshimīs and Ḥanbalīs led to the retraction. In addition, because the text of the retraction was signed by witnesses in the caliphal chancery of the state, it is obvious that the retraction was preceded by activities of notables who acted on behalf of the caliph.

In the description of the retraction, Makdisi heavily relied on Ibn Qudāma's version while ignoring Ibn al-Jawzī's version. There are slight differences between the two versions: the first difference concerns the date of the retraction. According to Ibn Qudāma, the retraction occurred on 8 Muḥarram 465/24 September 1072, as against 11 Muḥarram/27 September according to Ibn al-Jawzī. Since Ibn Qudāma relies on the evidence of an eyewitness to the event, it is most likely that the date he provides is accurate. The event took place in the *sharīf* Abū Jaʿfar's mosque in the quarter of Nahr al-Muʿallā, on the east side of Baghdad. 'Many people were gathered there that day', Ibn Qudāma quoted his source (Ibn Qudāma, *Taḥrīm naẓar*, 4).

Although Ibn Qudāma does not provide a factual timeline of the events, his text is interesting because he conveys the juridical as well as the spiritual meaning of *tawba*—not in the sense of retraction, but in the sense of repentance. It is true, says Ibn Qudāma, that Ibn ʿAqīl uttered dreadful words of heresy, and had he not repented, he would have been considered one of the heretics (*zanādiqa*) and straying innovators *(al-mubtadiʿa al-māriqa*). However, since he genuinely regretted his deeds and repented (*tāba wa-anāba*) the accusation of innovation and straying should be removed. 'Perhaps his good conduct wipes off his bad conduct, and his repentance obliterates his innovation', sums up Ibn Qudāma (*Taḥrīm naẓar*, 1–2).

Ibn Qudāma's polemical text (Makdisi gives preference to this text) provides an amusing explanation to Ibn ʿAqīl's *tawba*: 'Ibn ʿAqīl feared for his life. One day, while he was sailing on a boat, he heard a young man saying: "I wish I had met this *zindīq*, Ibn ʿAqīl, so I could come closer to God by killing him and spilling his blood." The terrified Ibn ʿAqīl immediately left the boat, went to the *sharīf* Abū Jaʿfar, repented and retracted' (Ibn

Qudāma, *Taḥrīm naẓar*, 2) Although it is the only available explanation to what led Ibn ʿAqīl to repent, the unflattering way in which it depicts Ibn ʿAqīl does not allow us to take it as historical evidence. However, it indeed illustrates the constant state of persecution in which Ibn ʿAqīl found himself.

In his *tawba*, the 33-year-old Ibn ʿAqīl, a known and prominent scholar, declared that he repented for having written about the doctrines of the heretical innovators (*madhāhib al-mubtadiʿa*) and the Muʿtazila, and he also apologized for having social connections with Muʿtazilīs: 'I am not permitted henceforth to write those things, nor to say them, nor to believe in them.' Following this statement, several issues emerged. First, Ibn ʿAqīl repented on his insistence, based on the teachings of the Muʿtazilī Ibn al-Walīd, that the night was nothingness and not a cluster of black bodies;[2] second, he repented on his admiration of the mystic al-Ḥallāj; third, he prayed to God that He would forgive him for associating with Muʿtazilīs and other innovators. Those three issues do not appear in Ibn Qudāma's version of Ibn ʿAqīl's *tawba*, and Makdisi assumes that they were omitted because Ibn Qudāma was a Ṣūfī who venerated al-Ḥallāj. The appeal to God is followed by a long paragraph in which Ibn ʿAqīl justifies the *sharīf* Abū Jaʿfar and his people for persecuting him, and concludes: 'I am certain that I was wrong, that I was not right.' Makdisi claims that the document of retraction was a standard text, with blank spaces filled in by the accused. Standard or not, reading the text was probably a very humiliating event for Ibn ʿAqīl (the text in full appears in Ibn al-Jawzī's *Muntaẓam* and several other chronicles, and was translated by Makdisi 1997: 4). The retraction was signed by Ibn ʿAqīl and several witnesses, whose names are recorded in Ibn Qudāma's *Taḥrīm naẓar*.

Based on the ages of Ibn ʿAqīl's students, Makdisi assumes that Ibn ʿAqīl had to suspend his teaching activities until the death of the *sharīf* Abū Jaʿfar from poisoning in the year 470/1077. Ibn ʿAqīl taught his students *ḥadīth* and Ḥanbalī *fiqh*, thus completing his transformation to a devoted Ḥanbalī traditionalist. The majority of his Ḥanbalī successors rehabilitated Ibn ʿAqīl and meticulously studied his works, most of which are non-extant (Makdisi 1997: 44–51).

Although from a Ḥanbalī perspective, the persecution of the rationalist Ibn ʿAqīl was justified, the series of events is labelled in the Ḥanbalī sources as *miḥna*, a term laden with theological meanings and historical connotations. In Ḥanbalī sources, *miḥna* expresses the martyrological self-perception of Ḥanbalīs throughout the ages. No doubt, Ibn ʿAqīl's persecution was named *miḥna* simply because he retracted from

[2] The view that Ibn ʿAqīl expresses here from the mouth of his teacher disagrees, as it seems, with the doctrinal Muʿtazilī view of the Bahshamīs. Ibn Mattawayh expresses the opposite view when he claims that when 'black particles' (*ajzāʾ sūd*) enter the thinness (*riqqa*), then that thinness is called darkness (*ẓulma*) (*Tadhkira*, 1: 64). That the night is 'nothingness' is the view of Ibn al-ʿArabī (Chittick 1989: 13). In his commentary on Q 30: 29, Fakhr al-Dīn al-Rāzī explains why darkness and night cannot be considered as 'lack of light' (*ʿadam al-nūr*): 'because in the eternity there is no day, light or life, and it is impossible to say that all there is in eternity is night, darkness and death' (Fakhr al-Dīn al-Rāzī, *Tafsīr*, 13[part 25]: 160).

his former rationalist convictions, became a devoted traditionalist, and was therefore entitled to be acknowledged as Ḥanbalī martyr.

II The *Fitnat* Ibn al-Qushayrī

While the Ḥanbalī historiographers Ibn al-Jawzī and Ibn Rajab name the 1077 riots in Baghdad as *fitnat Ibn al-Qushayrī*, the Shāfiʿī-Ashʿarī historian Tāj al-Dīn al-Subkī (d. 769/1368) names the riots *fitnat al-Ḥanābila* (the same name was given to the riots of the Ḥanbalīs in Baghdad in 317/923 under the leadership of al-Barbahārī). Both names demonstrate the biased approach of the sources to the events. While the Shāfiʿīs-Ashʿarīs consider the Ḥanbalīs—their leadership and laymen alike—as the inciters who ignited the bloody events, the Ḥanbalīs point to Ibn al-Qushayrī as a provocateur who started the riots.

The accounts of al-Subkī and Ibn ʿAsākir (d. 571/1176) are the two main sources which present the Shāfiʿī-Ashʿarī version of the events. Al-Subkī laconically states that the *fitna* was ignited 'because the lecturer Abū l-Naṣr came to the rescue of the Ashʿarī school, and he was very vociferous in spreading his strong disapproval of his rivals. He publicly humiliated the *mujassima* in an incident that this book later explains'. Unfortunately, he does not explain what happened during the *fitna* (Subkī, *Ṭabaqāt*, 7: 162). Nevertheless, precious information is provided by Ibn ʿAsākir. He cites a compilation of letters (*maḥḍar*) that somehow made its way to Ibn ʿAsākir's family. The *maḥḍar*, which was signed by Abū Isḥāq al-Shīrāzī (d. 478/1085–6) and a group of Shāfiʿī scholars and sent to Niẓām al-Mulk, reveals the course of events from a Shāfiʿī-Ashʿarī point of view. The *maḥḍar* was first presented by Makdisi (Makdisi 1963: 368–71) although it was never thoroughly investigated. In the opening of the *maḥḍar*, the scholars denounce the riots in Baghdad, caused by 'a group of ignorant anthropomorphists (*ḥashwiyya)*, riffraff and hooligans, who are labeled as Ḥanbalīs'. The *maḥḍar* mainly concentrates on the behaviour of the Ḥanbalīs who are perceived here as one entity, scholars and mob alike, without differentiating between the two classes.

The two main Ḥanbalī sources (Ibn al-Jawzī's *al-Muntaẓam* and Ibn Rajab's *al-Dhayl ʿalā ṭabaqāt al-Ḥanābila*) that recount the tale of the *fitnat Ibn al-Qushayrī* are much more elaborate and rich in detail than is the case with the Shāfiʿī sources (Ibn ʿAqīl also dedicated a few lines about the event in his *Kitāb al-Funūn*; Makdisi 1997: 206). They provide details on Ḥanbalī activists, actual events in the streets, but also on intense negotiations between the caliphal court, the ruling circle around Niẓām al-Mulk, and the leaders of the feuding parties. In addition, both Ibn al-Jawzī and Ibn Rajab mention the exact places in which the riots occurred. Although the exact location of these places is today unknown or at best disputable, it is certain that they were all in East Baghdad, in the quarters surrounding the caliphal palace. *Al-Niẓāmiyya* itself, from which the fire started, was situated near the palace and the Tuesday Market.

Abū l-Naṣr ʿAbd al-Raḥīm b. ʿAbd al-Karīm b. Hawāzin, known as Ibn al-Qushayrī, was born in Nishapur before 434/1043. He was the fourth son of Abū l-Qāsim ʿAbd al-Karīm b. Hawāzin al-Qushayrī (b. 376/986, d. 465/1072), an Ashʿarī theologian and a Ṣūfī scholar. Al-Qushayrī the father, who is noted for his *Risāla fī ʿilm al-taṣawwuf*, a prominent manual of Ṣūfi terminology, and *Laṭāʾif al-ishārāt*, a Ṣūfī *tafsīr*, married into the family of the renowned Ṣūfī Abū ʿAlī al-Daqqāq (d. 405/1015).[3] Most of all, al-Qushayrī the father was a prominent Shāfiʿī-Ashʿarī scholar, who had studied with the notable Ashʿarī scholars, Ibn Fūrak (d. 406/1015) and Abū Isḥāq al-Isfarāyīnī (d. 418/1027), and he was a close friend of ʿAbd Allāh al-Juwaynī (d. 438/1047), the father of ʿAbd al-Malik al-Juwaynī, 'Imām al-Ḥaramayn' (d. 478/1085), who in turn was al-Ghazālī's teacher.

As a prominent leader of the Shāfiʿī-Ashʿarī faction in Nishapur, al-Qushayrī the father played a crucial role in the heated struggles between the Shāfiʿīs and the Ḥanafīs that occurred in 436/1044, but more so in the great 445/1053 *fitna* in Nishapur. The *fitna* is connected to the initiative of ʿAmīd al-Mulk Abū Naṣr Manṣūr al-Kundurī (d. 456/1064), the vizier of Ṭughril Beg, to persecute the Ashʿarīs for several personal and political reasons (Allard 1965: 343–51; Halm 1971: 208–14; Madelung 1971: 126–34; Bulliet 1973: 80–5; Bulliet 1994: 122–4). Al-Kundurī, a former unprivileged and even rejected member of the Shāfiʿī-Ashʿarī faction in Nishapur, became—at an early stage in his climb on the social ladder—a fully-fledged Muʿtazilī. As part of his political involvement, al-Qushayrī the father authored two creeds in firm defence of the Ashʿarī creed from its many enemies—the Muʿtazilīs, the Karrāmīs, and the Ḥanafīs—whom he named 'devious people' (*ahl al-zaygh*). Al-Qushayrī the father was arrested, released as a result of a heroic rescue orchestrated by his colleagues, and fled Nishapur (Nguyen 2012: 40–5; Allard 1965: 343–51; Halm 1971: 208–14; Madelung 1971: 126–34; Bulliet 1973: 80–5; Bulliet 1994: 122–4).

Growing up in the turbulent atmosphere of Nishapur and later in exile in Ṭūs, the young Ibn al-Qushayrī absorbed the intense political and doctrinal atmosphere. His father nurtured in him the sense of the intellectual superiority of the Ashʿarīs. The surviving dicta of the contemporary Nishapurian scholars reveal that although they practised Shāfiʿī traditionalism (through the transmission of *ḥadīth* and the teaching of *fiqh*), they were also eager to defend the rational methods of *kalām*. These methods, developed by Abū Bakr al-Bāqillānī (d. 403/1013) and taught by Ibn Fūrak and al-Isfarāyīnī, the great luminaries of their times, were the backbone of the Ashʿarīs' self-esteem, in addition to these scholars' thorough knowledge of *ḥadīth*. This combination of rationalism and traditionalism enabled the Ashʿarīs of Nishapur to see themselves as propagating the perfect solution to Islamic factionalism. They held a strong belief in the rationalistic *kalām* as the most appropriate tool to defend the teachings of the Prophet and the *salaf*. At the same time, they acknowledged the complexity of that tool, destined merely for

[3] The most extensive portrayal of al-Qushayrī family is Chiabotti 2013b, which came to my attention only after the completion of the present chapter. I thank the author for kindly sending me the penultimate version of his article.

the educated elite. In short, the Ashʿarīs—at least in Nishapur—saw themselves as a persecuted yet privileged intellectual elite (Madelung 1988: 28–9; Makdisi 1962–3: (17) 80; (18): 37–8).

Although the young Ibn al-Qushayrī grew up in the turbulent atmosphere of Nishapur and in exile in Ṭūs, he received the best possible education. He studied under his father and several scholars in Khurāsān, Iraq, and the Ḥijāz. Among his teachers, the name of Abū Bakr al-Bayhaqī (d. 458/1066), the Shāfiʿī jurist and Ashʿarī theologian, is the most conspicuous. Ibn al-Qushayrī's knowledge encompassed conventional fields such as the knowledge of the Arabic language, theology, and *tafsīr*, 'that he picked up from his father'. He is also described as an incredibly competent author of prose and poetry and a scholar well read in the Greek sciences (*al-ʿulūm al-daqīqa*) and arithmetic. Indeed, 'his father provided him the best education', as is stated in his biography (al-Subkī, *Ṭabaqāt*, 7: 160–1; the prominent source for Ibn al-Qushayrī's biography is al-Subkī, *Ṭabaqāt*, 7: 159–66; Ibn al-Qushayrī's education and spirituality are discussed in Chiabotti 2013a: 55–7).

When al-Qushayrī died in 465/1072, Ibn al-Qushayrī became the most devoted disciple of the Imām al-Ḥaramayn al-Juwaynī. Al-Juwaynī, who was exiled from Nishapur during the great 445/1053 *fitna* years, arrived in the city at the invitation of the celebrated Niẓām al-Mulk (assassinated in 485/1092), who requested the renowned scholar to head the Nishapur branch of *al-Madrasa al-Niẓāmiyya*. Niẓām al-Mulk, who came to Nishapur as chief adviser of the governor, Alp Arslān (who later became a sultan), in 450/1058, established the *Niẓāmiyya* in Nishapur probably in order to strengthen the dependency of the educated elite on the government and to empower the Shāfiʿīs-Ashʿarīs who were persecuted by his rival, al-Kundurī. Although the *Niẓāmiyya* was a traditionalist institution in which the teaching of *kalām* was banned (Makdisi 1961: 31–44; Makdisi 1966: 82; Makdisi 1981: 231), the academy was a haven for the Shāfiʿīs-Ashʿarites of Nishapur (Bulliet 1972: 72–4; Bulliet 1973: 84–5; Ephrat 2000: 78–81).

After four years of studying with al-Juwaynī, Ibn al-Qushayrī arrived in Baghdad. There are two different versions of the circumstances of Ibn al-Qushayrī's arrival in the city. The Shāfiʿī-Ashʿarī sources insist that Ibn al-Qushayrī's academic career in Baghdad started by chance as a response to the demand of the people. According to these sources, while in Nishapur, Ibn al-Qushayrī felt that he was ready to make the pilgrimage to Mecca. On his way, he stopped in Baghdad. His theatrical sermons excited the scholars and students in the *Niẓāmiyya*. His audience demanded more sermons, and that is how the *majlis* was set for him in the *Niẓāmiyya* (see the insightful footnote of Iḥsān ʿAbbās in the introduction to Abū Isḥāq al-Shīrāzī's *Ṭabaqāt al-Fuqahāʾ*, 9). The Ḥanbalī sources, on the other hand, insist that Ibn al-Qushayrī's arrival in Baghdad was planned and engineered by Niẓām al-Mulk himself (Ibn al-Jawzī, *al-Muntaẓām*, 16: 181). The difference in these versions relating the beginning of Ibn al-Qushayrī's career in Baghdad can be explained by the difference between the Ashʿarī and the Ḥanbalī narrative: the Ḥanbalīs present Ibn al-Qushayrī as an outsider, forced on the people by a corrupt governmental official (Niẓām al-Mulk). The Ashʿarīs, on the other hand, depict him as a bright scholar, whose appearance in Baghdad was spontaneous.

Among the participants in Ibn al-Qushayrī's lectures was Abū Isḥāq al-Shīrāzī (formerly Ibn ʿAqīl's teacher), the most prominent Shāfiʿī *faqīh* in Iraq at the time and a supporter of Ashʿarī doctrine. Niẓām al-Mulk established the *Niẓāmiyya* in South-East Baghdad (near the caliphal palace and the quarter of the Tuesday Market; Lassner 1970: 173) in his honour in 459/1066, and he was the sole professor in the academy (al-Subkī, *Ṭabaqāt*, 4: 215–56). Most importantly, al-Shirāzī would become Ibn al-Qushayrī's patron and benefactor in Baghdad.

Ibn al-Qushayrī's classes in the *Niẓāmiyya* consisted of missionary sermons (*waʿẓ*) exhorting his listeners to piety and repentance, and mystical sessions (*majlis tadhkīr*). Ibn al-Qushayrī used the entire arsenal of rhetorical devices, and his listeners were unanimous in their opinion that they never met such a brilliant scholar: 'When he performed his prayer, people were listening to his words, and you would hear no muttering in the audience. His speech was abundant with gems of wisdom. Upon listening to his sermon, the sinner would repent ... How many grave sinners repented in his *majlis* and became obedient believers! How many heretics became believers in the Hour of Judgment while listening to his sermon! ... the toughest most rebellious heart would melt to his words ...' (al-Subkī, *Ṭabaqāt*, 7: 159f.). As this passage by al-Subkī conveys, Ibn al-Qushayrī's audience comprised Muslims and members of other faiths. Indeed, almost every session of his was concluded with the conversion of a group of Jews and Christians to Islam.

Given the highly emotional and electrified atmosphere in which these repentance sessions were conducted, it is unlikely that they included the Ashʿarī *kalām*. However, Ibn al-Qushayrī indeed focused on the polemics between Ashʿarism and traditionalism (al-Subkī, *Ṭabaqāt*, 7: 160f.; Ibn ʿAsākir, *Tabyīn*, 315). According to Ibn al-Jawzī, when Ibn al-Qushayrī commenced teaching in the *Niẓāmiyya*, 'he denounced the Ḥanbalīs and accused them of extreme anthropomorphism (*tajsīm*)' (Ibn al-Jawzī, *al-Muntaẓām*, 16: 181). This was the same accusation that was levelled at the Karrāmiyya at the time of al-Qushayrī's *fitna*. Makdisi claims that the accusation of *tajsīm* was irrelevant in the case of the Ḥanbalīs, as they never interpreted anthropomorphic *ḥadīth* material (Makdisi 1963: 353). However, Ibn al-Qushayrī did not accuse the Ḥanbalīs of literally interpreting the texts, but of quoting fabricated *ḥadīth* material, in which inappropriate physical traits—that God has molars, uvula, and fingertips, that He looks like a beardless young man wearing golden sandals—were attributed to God. Indeed, later Ḥanbalī sources denounced the use of such *ḥadīth*s (Holtzman 2010; Holtzman 2011).

While Ibn al-Qushayrī's prestige in the Shāfiʿī-Ashʿarī circles in Baghdad was unshakeable (in his next pilgrimage to Mecca he accompanied the leader of the convoy), the Ḥanbalīs were greatly agitated by his sermons and accusations. Their leader, the *sharīf* Abū Jaʿfar, lived and taught at that time in al-Ruṣāfa, in East Baghdad. Abū Isḥāq al-Shīrāzī, as the representative of the Sḥāfiʿīs-Ashʿarīs, went to see Abū Jaʿfar several times in order to ask for his help in calming the atmosphere in the street. However, the *sharīf* Abū Jaʿfar never meant to calm the street, but he secretly prepared his followers for bloody attacks while he hid in a mosque situated in front of Bāb al-Nūbī, near the palace of the caliph (Ibn al-Jawzī, *Muntaẓam*, 16: 181).

The *fitna* broke out when Ibn al-Qushayrī returned from his second pilgrimage to Mecca. In Shawwāl 469/April–May 1077, a Jew converted in Ibn al-Qushayrī's public session, and then was led in the streets on a horse to celebrate his conversion in a big parade organized by Ibn al-Qushayrī's students. The whole charade was meant to intensify the buzz (*li-yuqawwiya l-ghawghā*ʾ) around Ibn al-Qushayrī's missionary activity, as Ibn al-Jawzī describes the scene in words that hit the mark. The common people, mostly Ḥanbalīs, did not swallow the bait. The word in the streets was that those acts of conversion were false: 'This is Islam of bribery and not Islam of piety!' (*hādhā islām al-rushā lā islām al-tuqā*). The parade participants, who were Ibn al-Qushayrī's students, decided to attack the *sharīf* Abū Jaʿfar, who was in the Bāb al-Nūbī mosque. However, the Ḥanbalīs were well prepared: when the supporters of Ibn al-Qushayrī arrived at the Bāb al-Nūbī mosque, the Ḥanbalīs surprised them by throwing bricks at them. This act signalled the opening salvo of the riots—a porter of the Bāb al-Nūbī mosque was killed by a brick, thrown by the Ḥanbalīs. The Ḥanbalīs also killed a tailor from the Tuesday Market, near the *Niẓāmiyya*. The followers of Ibn al-Qushayrī took shelter in the *Niẓāmiyya*. From inside the locked academy, the symbol of Ashʿarism, they called for the help of the Fāṭimī caliph, al-Mustanṣir. This act of defiance was meant to show that they held the ʿAbbāsid caliph al-Muqtadī, who was inclined to Ḥanbalism, responsible for the acts of the Ḥanbalī mob. The number of people killed and injured in the riots is unspecified (Ibn al-Jawzī, *Muntaẓam*, 16: 181–2). At that time, the vizier Niẓām al-Mulk was in Khurāsān (Ibn al-Jawzī, *Muntaẓam*, 16: 181).

Abū Isḥāq al-Shīrāzī, who was deeply aggravated by these events, organized his fellow *ʿulamāʾ* to write the petition or letters of complaint to Niẓām al-Mulk. He prepared himself for a journey to Khurāsān, to complain to Niẓām al-Mulk personally. The caliph, who was in an inferior position in comparison to the Sultan and Niẓām al-Mulk, was afraid that Abū Isḥāq would speak ill of him. The caliph therefore took immediate action—he hurried to persuade Abū Isḥāq not to go to Khurāsān. The news, however, reached Niẓām al-Mulk anyhow. Niẓām al-Mulk sent a letter to the caliphal vizier Fakhr al-Dawla, in which he expressed his anger at the behaviour of the Ḥanbalīs. 'I suggest that talk of this kind about the *madrasa* that I built will be stopped immediately!'—Niẓām al-Mulk firmly wrote to the vizier (Ibn al-Jawzī, *Mutaẓam*, 16: 182).

The caliph, then, ordered his vizier, Fakhr al-Dawla, to find a way to terminate the riots. A meeting of reconciliation between the feuding parties was convened. The date of the meeting was not specified; however, it probably took place in Shawwāl 469. The participants were the *sharīf* Abū Jaʿfar, Abū Isḥāq al-Shīrāzī, Ibn al-Qushayrī, and other notables of the Shāfiʿī-Ashʿarī milieu. The *sharīf* Abū Jaʿfar acted as the offended party who should be appeased. His position was embraced by the caliph's vizier, and the participants were required to approach him and ask for his forgiveness. Abū Isḥāq al-Shīrāzī, who was first to approach Abū Jaʿfar, kissed the *sharīf*s head, a gesture meant to show his complete humiliation. The *sharīf* Abū Jaʿfar however emphasized that he was a rival not to be taken lightly, as he mocked his rivals (among them Ibn al-Qushayrī) and refused to accept their apologies. In an address to the vizier, the *sharīf* referred to the *Qādirī Creed*: 'The leader, in whom the Muslims take refuge, and his ancestors, al-Qāʾim and al-Qādir, issued two doctrinal documents of professions of faith. Those documents were read aloud in their *diwān*. The people of Khurāsān and the pilgrims took those documents with them to the furthest places. We have the same faith as they had.' The vizier reported to the caliph about the reconciliation and then informed the convened party that everyone was allowed to go home, except the *sharīf* Abū Jaʿfar, who was 'invited' to stay in the palace: 'A special room, next to the servants was prepared for him, so he can dwell on religious affairs as much as he pleases. He is most welcome.' These were the caliph's orders. The *sharīf* Abū Jaʿfar, then, stayed in the custody of the caliph. At first, a constant stream of visitors arrived at the palace. This did not please the caliph, so he sent a message to the *sharīf* Abū Jaʿfar to reduce the number of visitors. His insulted reply was: 'I need no visitors whatsoever.' After a while he was taken ill and died. Abū Jaʿfar reportedly was poisoned by the Ashʿarīs (Ibn al-Jawzī, *Muntaẓam*, 16: 182f., 195f.; Ibn Rajab, *Dhayl*, 1: 39–43).

The affair of Ibn al-Qushayrī required a resolution. Ibn al-Jawzī provides an account of what happened immediately afterwards in the brief biographical entry of Ibn al-Qushayrī (Ibn al-Jawzī, *Muntaẓam*, 17: 190), and in his report on the events of the year 470/1078 (*Muntaẓam*, 16: 190f.), but without any dates. It is clear, however, that immediately after the *sharīf* Abū Jaʿfar was held in custody—against his will—in the palace, the caliph sent a firm letter to Niẓām al-Mulk, in which 'he was asked to order Ibn al-Qushayrī to leave Baghdad in order to put out the blazes of the *fitna*'. Niẓām al-Mulk therefore called for Ibn al-Qushayrī to come to Khurāsān. When the latter arrived in Iṣfahān, Niẓām al-Mulk treated him with the utmost respect and ordered him to return to Nishapur. Ephrat believes that Niẓām al-Mulk's aim was always to restore peace in the streets, and to reduce riots over creeds. Her view, which contradicts Laoust's (Laoust 1973: 175–85), actually provides the best explanation for Niẓām al-Mulk's disclaimer of any association with his protégé. The goal was to calm the street, and that could be achieved only by taking the bully's side, the Ḥanbalīs, and terminating Ashʿarī preaching (Ephrat 2000: 130). According to Ibn al-Jawzī, after the *fitna*, the preachers (*wuʿʿāẓ*) were forbidden to reconvene. Four years after the *fitna*, in Jumādā II 473/November–December 1080, they were permitted to practise their profession, 'however, they were ordered not to insert in their preaching any hint of theological concepts and theological trends' (Ibn al-Jawzī, *Muntaẓam*, 16: 211).

The Ḥanbalī mob continued in its unrestrained behaviour. There are several references in the biographical sources (mainly Ibn al-Jawzī) of people who were affected by the *fitna*. For example, a certain Abū l-Wafāʾ 'the Preacher' (*al-Wāʿiẓ*, d. 484/1091), was expelled from Baghdad by the Ḥanbalīs after his Ashʿarī inclinations were revealed in the *fitna*, probably through sermons he delivered (Ibn al-Jawzī, *Muntaẓam*, 16: 297).

These people were of no importance, unlike the scholars who wrote the complaint letters to Niẓām al-Mulk, and therefore it was easy to harass them.

The Ashʿarī preachers of the *Niẓāmiyya*, for their part, continued to cause trouble. In Shawwāl 470/April 1078, a preacher from the *Niẓāmiyya* by the name of al-Iskandarīnī, went to the Tuesday Market and made a public speech in which he declared *takfīr* on the Ḥanbalīs. He was stoned with bricks and made his narrow escape to the Market near the *Niẓāmiyya*, therein a group of Shāfiʿīs, most probably, attempted to rescue him, and went to the Tuesday Market. The rescue operation soon erupted into a wild campaign of looting. The people of the Tuesday Market went to a counter-campaign of looting in the Market of the *Niẓāmiyya*. Since Niẓām al-Mulk's son lived there, the situation called for military intervention and at least ten people were killed. Again, as in the case of the *fitnat* Ibn al-Qushayrī, the historical sources provide details on the delicate balance between the caliph and his ministers on the one hand, and the Sultan and Niẓām al-Mulk on the other. Another case in point was the case of the Ashʿarī preacher, al-Bakrī al-Maghribī in 475/1083. Ibn ʿAqīl, quoted by Ibn al-Jawzī, connects al-Bakrī with Ibn al-Qushayrī, as he claims that both men were nominated by Niẓām al-Mulk to teach in the *Niẓāmiyya*. However, while Ibn al-Qushayrī was a respectable man and undoubtedly a fine scholar, al-Bakrī was immoral and certainly not a scholar. He also attacked the Ḥanbalīs in his sermons (Makdisi 1963: 366–75; Ephrat 2000: 86–9; ʿAbbās 1970: 12–13; *al-Muntaẓam*, 17: 190).

The *fitna* had several repercussions. First and foremost, it damaged the Ashʿarī cause. The Ḥanbalīs saw Abū Isḥāq as the brain behind the events, and Ibn al-Qushayrī as his puppet who executed his plans. Niẓām al-Mulk was forced to clarify his purpose in establishing the *Niẓāmiyya*: 'We believe that supporting [the learning] of traditions is far better than causing riots. I built this *madrasa* only to secure the living of devout scholars (*ahl al-ʿilm wa-l-maṣlaḥa*), and not to spread controversies and dissensions' (Ibn al-Jawzī, *al-Muntaẓām*, 16: 190f.). In other words, it is best that the *Niẓāmiyya* academy concentrates on dictating *ḥadīth*s rather than on teaching *kalām*.

As for Ibn al-Qushayrī, his return to Khurāsān marked the end of his brilliant academic career. Although Niẓām al-Mulk treated Ibn al-Qushayrī with the utmost respect and lavished expensive gifts on him when the two met in Khurāsān, the message was clear—Ibn al-Qushayrī was never to return to Baghdad. 'The people of Baghdad craved for him and his lectures for a very long time'—this is how Ibn ʿAsākir and al-Subkī sum up the events—'Some of them did not break their fast years after he was gone; some never participated in a *majlis tadhkīr* again.' Ibn al-Qushayrī's life from that point on was melancholic and dull, and he never pursued politics again. He mainly dictated *ḥadīth*s in daily learning sessions, which he never missed. 'At his old age, he spoke of nothing but the Qurʾān.' Al-Subkī describes Ibn al-Qushayrī's conduct when he returned to Nishapur in terms of Ṣūfī piety and asceticism ('he preferred seclusion'); however, we are allowed to describe the obvious transformation that Ibn al-Qushayrī went through as a psychological crisis and probably self-remorse for destroying his brilliant career with his own hands. The former bright scholar who composed beautiful and melancholic love poems (fragments of which are quoted by al-Subkī), who excited and dazzled his audiences with his rhetoric, who was the centre of attention in the most sophisticated city of his time, taught himself a lesson in humility during his daily classes in Qurʾān and *ḥadīth*, in which he dictated texts like the average Ḥanbalī scholars he once so disregarded. This transformation was not the bright future that was once foretold for him by his many admirers. The highlight of his career occurred when al-Juwaynī quoted him in one of his books. Al-Subkī indicates that Ibn al-Qushayrī, who lived until an old age, was highly respected by the people of Nishapur for his piety and seclusion. He earned this respect by assimilating in the background, and by not drawing any attention to himself. Al-Subkī, however, does not say that Ibn al-Qushayrī retracted his Ashʿarī convictions (al-Subkī 7: 162). This silence raises questions about the authenticity of Ibn al-Qushayrī as a devout and humble *ḥadīth* teacher. Was it a role he took willingly upon himself, or was he forced to disappear from the public eye even in Nishapur? This we will never know. In his biography, Ibn al-Qushayrī symbolizes the defeat of the rationalistic *kalām* to the traditional branches of knowledge, or in other words, he is the forerunner of the submission of the Shāfiʿīs to strict traditionalism.

III Conclusion

The *miḥna* of Ibn ʿAqīl and the *fitnat* Ibn al-Qushayrī mark the two most important stages in 'the Sunni Revival'—the victory of traditionalist Islam over Muʿtazilism, followed by the victory of traditionalist Islam over Ashʿarism. However, behind the titles of 'traditionalism' versus 'rationalism' stands one fierce fighter against heresy in all its forms—rationalism included—viz. the *sharīf* Abū Jaʿfar. The Ḥanbalī sources, abundant with details on his personality and conduct, point to his political ambitions and wounded ego as the real motives for his persecuting Ibn ʿAqīl. The *fitnat* Ibn al-Qushayrī was a different matter altogether. In this case the *sharīf* saw how the Ashʿarīs nurtured a charismatic young leader of their own who gained the support of widening circles of followers. The Ḥanbalī hegemony in the streets was put at stake, and this the *sharīf* could not tolerate.

There is hardly any symmetry between the two case studies that were presented in this chapter. While we luckily have access to both Ḥanbalī and Ashʿarī-Shāfiʿī sources that give us two sides of the *fitnat* Ibn al-Qushayrī story, in the case of Ibn ʿAqīl we have only the Ḥanbalī side of the story. The Muʿtazilīs, whose role in the case of Ibn ʿAqīl was marginal, did not leave any account on the events. After Ibn ʿAqīl's retraction, they went underground and did not play any significant role in the Baghdadian politics any more. The Ashʿarīs, who received a severe blow in the *fitnat* Ibn al-Qushayrī, were more enduring—they had their haven in Khurāsān, and their intellectual activity as traditionalists as well as rationalists enabled them to survive the events. They simply had to tone down their sermons and not confront the Ḥanbalīs.

The riots connected to Ibn al-Qushayrī's name are described in contemporary sources as a symbol of the clash between rationalism (represented here by the

Ashʿarī preacher from Nishapur) and traditionalism (portrayed by the Ḥanbalīs of Baghdad). However, the *fitnat* Ibn al-Qushayrī stands for much more than the superficial labels of traditionalism versus rationalism. This *fitna* features several protagonists with a diversity of motives—from the ʿAbbāsid Caliph to the street hooligans in Baghdad. *Fitnat* Ibn al-Qushayrī was a consequence of many factors: political, social, and doctrinal. These factors, succinctly surveyed here, should be further elaborated elsewhere.

References

ʿAbbās, I. (1970). 'Introduction to Abū Isḥāq al-Shīrāzī, Ṭabaqāt al-Fuqahāʾ'. Beirut: Dār al-Rāʾid al-ʿArabī, 5–28.

ʿAbd al-Ghāfir (*Siyāk*). Ed. R. N. Frye. *The Histories of Nishapur: Facsimile Edition of mss. By Abū al-Ḥasan ʿAbd al-Ghāfir al-Fārisī and Abū ʿAbd Allāh Muḥammad al-Ḥākim an-Naisābūrī*. Cambridge, MA: Harvard University Press, 1965.

Allard, M. (1965). *Le Problème des attributs divins dans la doctrine d'al-Ašʿarī et des ses premiers grands disciples*. Beirut: Éditions de l'imprimerie catholique.

Bulliet, R. W. (1972). *The Patricians of Nishapur: A Study in Medieval Islamic Social History*. Cambridge, MA: Harvard University Press.

Bulliet, R. W. (1973). 'The Political-Religious History of Nishapur in the Eleventh Century'. In D. S. Richards (ed.), *Islamic Civilisation 950–1150: A Colloquium Published under the Auspices of the Near Eastern History Group Oxford*. Oxford: Bruno Cassiers, 71–91.

Bulliet, R. W. (1979). 'Conversion to Islam and the Emergence of a Muslim Society in Iran'. In N. Levtzion (ed.), *Conversion to Islam*. New York: Holmes and Meier, 30–51.

Bulliet, R. W. (1994). *Islam: The View from the Edge*. New York: Columbia University Press.

Chiabotti, F. (2013a). 'The Spiritual and Physical Progeny of ʿAbd al-Karīm al-Qushayrī: A Preliminary Study in Abū Naṣr al-Qushayrī's (d. 514/1120) Kitāb al-Shawāhid wa-l-amthāl'. *Journal of Sufi Studies* 2: 46–77.

Chiabotti, F. (2013b). 'ʿAbd al-Karīm al-Qushayrī (d. 465/1072): Family Ties and Transmission in Nishapur's Sufi Milieu during the Tenth and Eleventh Centuries'. In C. Mayeur-Jaouen and A. Papas (eds.), *Family Portraits with Saints: Hagiography, Sanctity, and Family in the Muslim World*. Freiburg im Breisgau: Klaus Schwarz Verlag, 255–307.

Chittick, W. (1989). *The Sufi Path of Knowledge*. Albany, NY: SUNY Press.

Cook, M. (2000). *Commanding Right and Forbidding Wrong in Islamic Thought*. Cambridge: Cambridge University Press.

Ephrat, D. (2000). *A Learned Society in a Period of Transition*. Albany, NY: SUNY Press.

Fakhr al-Dīn al-Rāzī (*Tafsīr*). *Tafsīr al-Fakhr al-Rāzī al-mushtahar bi-l-Tafsīr al-kabīr wa-Mafātīḥ al-ghayb*. Beirut: Dār l-Fikr, 1995.

Goldziher, I. (1908). 'Zur Geschichte der ḥanbalitischen Bewegungen'. *Zeitschrift der Deutschen Morgenländischen Gesellschaft* 62: 1–28.

Halm, H. (1971). 'Der Wesir Al-Kundurī und die Fitna von Nīšāpūr'. *Welt des Orients* 6: 205–33.

Holtzman, L. (2010). 'Does God Really Laugh? Appropriate and Inappropriate Descriptions of God in Islamic Traditionalist Theology'. In A. Classen (ed.), *Laughter in the Middle Ages and Early Modern Times*. Berlin: de Gruyter, 165–200.

Holtzman, L. (2011). 'Anthropmorphism'. In *Encyclopaedia of Islam*. THREE. Leiden: Brill, fasc. 2011–4: 46–55.

Hurvitz, N. (2003). 'From Scholarly Circles to Mass Movements: The Formation of Legal Communities in Islamic Societies'. *American Historical Review* 108.4: 985–1008.
Ibn Abī Yaʿlā (*Ṭabaqāt*). *Ṭabaqāt al-Ḥanābila*. Ed. ʿAbd al-Raḥmān b. Sulaymān al-ʿUthaymin. Riyadh: Maktabat al-Amāna al-ʿĀma bi-Murūr Miʾa Sana, 1419/1999.
Ibn ʿAsākir (*Tabyīn*). *Tabyīn Kidhb al-muftarī fīmā nusiba ilā l-Imām Abī l-Ḥasan al-Ashʿarī*. Damascus: Maktabat al-tawfīq, 1347/1928.
Ibn al-Jawzī (*Muntaẓam*). *Al-Muntaẓam fī tārīkh al-mulūk wa-l-umam*. Ed. Muḥammad ʿAbd al-Qādir ʿAṭā and Muṣṭafā ʿAbd al-Qādir ʿAṭā. Beirut: Dār al-kutub al-ʿilmiyya, 1992.
Ibn Mattawayh (*Tadhkira*). *Al-Tadhkira fī aḥkām al-jawāhir wa-l-aʿrāḍ*. 2 vols. Ed. Daniel Gimaret. Cairo: Institut Français d'Archéologie Orientale, 2009.
Ibn Qudāma (*Taḥrīm Naẓar*). Ed. G. Makdisi, *Censure of Speculative Theology: An Edition of Ibn Qudāma's Taḥrīm an-nazar fī kutub al-kalām*. London: Luzac, 1962.
Ibn Rajab (*Dhayl*). ʿAbd al-Raḥmān b. Aḥmad b. Rajab, *al-Dhayl ʿalā ṭabaqāt al-Ḥanābila*. Ed. ʿAbd al-Raḥmān b. Sulaymān al-ʿUthaymin. Riyadh: Maktabat al-ʿUbaykān, 1425/2004.
Laoust, H. (1959). 'Le Hanbalisme sous le califat de Bagdad (241/855–656/1258)'. *Revue des Études Islamiques* 1: 67–128.
Laoust, H. (1971). 'Ḥanābila'. In C. E. Bosworth (ed.), *Encyclopaedia of Islam*. New edn. Leiden: Brill, iii. 158–62.
Laoust, H. (1973). 'Les Agitations religieuses à Baghdād aux IVe et Ve siecles de l'Hegire'. In D. S. Richards (ed.), *Islamic Civilisation 950–1150: A Colloquium Published under the Auspices of the Near Eastern History Group Oxford*. Oxford: Bruno Cassiers, 169–85.
Lapidus, I. M. (1988). *A History of Islamic Societies*. Cambridge: Cambridge University Press.
Lassner, J. (1970). *The Topography of Baghdad in the Early Middle Ages*. Detroit: Wayne State University Press.
Madelung, W. (1971). 'The Spread of Māturīdism and the Turks'. *Actas do IV Congresso de Estudos Árabes e Islâmicos, Coimbra-Lisba 1968*. Leiden: Brill, 109–168a. [Reprinted in W. Madelung, *Religious Schools and Sects in Medieval Islam*. London: Variorum Reprints, 1985, no. 2.]
Madelung, W. (1988). *Religious Trends in Early Islamic Iran*. Albany, NY: SUNY Press.
Makdisi, G. (1956). 'Autograph Diary of an Eleventh-Century Historian of Baghdad. Parts I and II'. *Bulletin of the School of Oriental and African Studies* 18: 9–31, 239–60. [Reprinted in G. Makdisi. *History and Politics in Eleventh Century Baghdad*. Aldershot: Variorum, 1990, no. 2.]
Makdisi, G. (1957a). 'Autograph Diary of an Eleventh-Century Historian of Baghdad. Parts III, IV, and V'. *Bulletin of the School of Oriental and African Studies* 19: 13–48, 281–303, 426–43. [Reprinted in G. Makdisi, *History and Politics in Eleventh Century Baghdad*, Aldershot: Variorum, 1990, no. 2.]
Makdisi, G. (1957b). 'Nouveaux détails sur l'affaire d'Ibn ʿAqīl'. *Mélanges Louis Massignon*. Paris/Damascus: Institut français de Damas, 91–126. [Reprinted in G. Makdisi, *History and Politics in Eleventh Century Baghdad*. Aldershot: Variorum, 1990, no. 3.]
Makdisi, G. (1959). 'The Topography of Eleventh Century Baġdād: Materials and Notes, I and II'. *Arabica* 6: 178–97; 281–306. [Reprinted in G. Makdisi, *History and Politics in Eleventh Century Baghdad*. Aldershot: Variorum, 1990, no. 4.]
Makdisi, G. (1961). 'Muslim Institutions of Learning in Eleventh-Century Baghdad'. *Bulletin of the School of Oriental and African Studies* 28: 1–56. [Reprinted in G. Makdisi, *Religion, Law and Learning in Classical Islam*. Aldershot: Variorum, 1991, no. 8.]
Makdisi, G. (1962–3). 'Ashʿarī and the Ashʿarites in Islamic Religious History'. *Studia Islamica* 17: 37–80; 18: 19–39.

Makdisi, G. (1963). *Ibn ʿAqīl et la résurgence de l'Islam traditionaliste au XIe siècle (Ve siècle de l'Hégire)*. Damascus: Institut Français de Damas.

Makdisi, G. (1966). 'Remarks on Traditionalism in Islamic Religious History'. In Carl Leiden (ed.), *The Conflict of Traditionalism and Modernism in the Muslim Middle East, from papers delivered March 29–31, 1965*. Austin, TX: University of Texas, 77–87.

Makdisi, G. (1971). 'Ibn ʿAḳīl, Abu 'l-Wafā' ʿAlī b. ʿAḳīl b. Muḥammad b. ʿAḳīl b. Aḥmad al-Baghdādī al-Ẓafarī'. In C. E. Bosworth (ed.), *Encyclopaedia of Islam*. New edn. Leiden: Brill, iii. 699f.

Makdisi, G. (1973). 'The Sunnī Revival'. In D. S. Richards (ed.), *Islamic Civilisation 950–1150: A Colloquium Published under the Auspices of the Near Eastern History Group Oxford*. Oxford: Bruno Cassiers, 155–68.

Makdisi, G. (1981). 'Hanbalite Islam'. In Merlin Swartz (ed.), *Studies on Islam*. New York: Oxford University Press, 216–74.

Makdisi, G. (1997). *Ibn ʿAqil: Religion and Culture in Classical Islam*. Edinburgh: Edinburgh University Press.

Makdisi, G. (2004). 'Abū Manṣūr b. Yūsuf'. In *Encyclopaedia of Islam*. New edn. Leiden: Brill. Supplement 29f.

Mez, A. (1937). *The Renaissance of Islam*. London: Luzac.

Nguyen, M. (2012). *Sufi Master and a Qur'an Scholar: Abū'l-Qāsim al-Qushayrī and the Laṭā'if al-Ishārāt*. London: Oxford University Press in association with The Institute of Ismaili Studies.

van Renterghem, V. (2008). 'Le Sentiment d'appartenance collective chez les élites bagdadiennes des ve–vie/xie–xiie siècles'. *Annales Islamologiques* 42: 231–58.

van Renterghem, V. (2010). 'Structure et fonctionnement du réseau hanbalite bagdadien dans les premiers temps de la domination seldjoukide (milieu du ve/xie siècle)'. In Damien Coulon, Christophe Picard, and Dominique Valérian (eds.), *Espaces et réseau en Méditerranée*, ii: *La Formation des réseaux*. Paris: Éditions Bouchene, 207–32.

Sabari, S. (1981). *Mouvements populaires à Bagdad à l'époque ʿAbbasside, IXe–XIe siècles*. Paris: Librairie d'Amérique et d'Orient Adrien Maisonneuve.

al-Subkī (*Ṭabaqāt*). Tāj al-Dīn Abū Naṣr ʿAbd al-Wahhāb b. ʿAlī ʿAbd al-Kāfī al-Subkī, *Ṭabaqāt al-shāfiʿiyya al-kubrā*. Ed. Muḥmūd Muḥammad al-Ṭināḥī and ʿAbd al-Fattāḥ Muḥammad al-Ḥilw. Cairo: Dār Iḥyāʾ al-kutub al-ʿarabiyya, [1992].

CHAPTER 38

THE RELIGIOUS POLICY OF THE ALMOHADS

MARIBEL FIERRO

I The Mahdī Ibn Tūmart and his Profession of Faith

In the year 560/1164–5 while in Marrakech, the capital of the Almohad Empire, the preacher Abū l-Ḥasan b. al-Ishbīlī commented on the *ʿaqīdat al-tawḥīd* and other works by Ibn Tūmart, who was 'the impeccable leader and acknowledged rightly guided one' (*al-imām al-maʿṣūm al-mahdī al-maʿlūm*) and 'heir of the station of prophecy and infallibility' (*wārith maqām al-nubuwwa wa-l-ʿiṣma*) (Fierro 2012: III, XIII).[1] Ibn Tūmart, a Maṣmūda Berber from Igilliz in the Sūs region (southern Morocco), had been the inspirer and founder of the movement of the Unitarians, those who believed in the unconditional unity of God (*tawḥīd*), from which derives their name: *al-muwaḥḥidūn* (Almohads). Abū l-Ḥasan b. al-Ishbīlī explained the meaning of Ibn Tūmart's works to the *ṭalabat al-ḥaḍar* or 'learned men of the Presence', those who were attached to the Almohad caliph and accompanied him wherever he went. Al-Ishbīlī was also known for his versification of the Almohad profession of faith (Ibn Ṣāḥib al-ṣalāt, *al-Mann bi-l-imāma*, 60/160–1[2]).

The *ṭalaba*—those who studied and therefore were learned—constituted the Almohad religious and political elites, recruited among the most promising young men of the empire in order to serve the Almohad political and religious cause in different capacities (Fricaud 1997). Their recruitment had started under ʿAbd al-Muʾmin (r. 527/1133–558/1163), a Zanāta Berber and follower of Ibn Tūmart who had eventually emerged as his successor after his death in 524/1130 and who, through his military conquests,

[1] This chapter has been written within the ARG-ERC Project 229703 KOHEPOCU.
[2] The double pagination refers to the Arabic text and its translation.

was the de facto builder of the Almohad empire, stretching from Tunisia to al-Andalus. ʿAbd al-Muʾmin, a skilful and resourceful military leader, achieved for the first time the political union of the Islamic West (including today's Morocco, Algeria, Tunisia, part of Libya, and al-Andalus) and established the caliphal Muʾminid dynasty. He and his successors presented their rule as the embodiment of God's disposition (*al-amr al-ʿazīz*), as we shall see.

It is through ʿAbd al-Muʾmin that the bulk of Ibn Tūmart's works have reached us, as indicated by the title of MS Paris, Bibliothèque Nationale, Arabe 1451: *sifr fīhi jamīʿ taʿālīq al-imām al-maʿṣūm al-mahdī al-maʿlūm . . . mimmā amlāhu sayyidunā al-imām al-khalīfa amīr al-muʾminīn Abū Muḥammad ʿAbd al-Muʾmin b. ʿAlī*, 'the volume that contains all the notes by the infallible *imām* and acknowledged *mahdī* . . . according to how our lord the imam, the caliph, the Prince of the Believers ʿAbd al-Muʾmin dictated it'. The notes had allegedly been taken from Ibn Tūmart's oral teachings in the *ribāṭ* of the Berber Hargha—the Mahdī's tribe—in the Sūs valley starting in the year 515/1121–2. The codex itself was copied in the year 579/1178. A second manuscript of this collection of texts, copied in 595/1198–9, was later found in the library of the Great Mosque in Taza, Morocco (Luciani 1903; Ṭālibī 1985; Abū l-ʿAzm 1997; Griffel 2005: 765–70).

The scarce number of extant manuscripts of Ibn Tūmart's teachings reflects the eventual disappearance of the Almohad Empire and its religious and political project, as well as the process of 'de-Almohadisation' that ensued (Fricaud 1997: 332). While the Almohads had considered those who did not adhere to their movement to be unbelievers, the Almohads themselves were suspected of heresy because of their Mahdist foundation, their claim to be entitled to impose the true belief, and their formulation of that belief (Laoust 1960).

But as long as their rule lasted—from the times of ʿAbd al-Muʾmin until Marrakech surrendered to the Marinids in 668/1269—Ibn Tūmart's profession of faith and his other writings circulated widely in the territories of the Almohad empire. This diffusion is attested by the fact that Ibn Tūmart's *ʿaqīda* was very soon translated into Latin by Mark of Toledo (D'Alverny and Vajda 1951–2). An *aljamiado* translation—Romance written in Arabic characters—also exists (Wiegers 1994: 40–5, 157–61). These translations are based on the reduced version of Ibn Tūmart's profession of faith. There is a long version, known as *ʿaqīda* or *ʿaqīdat al-tawḥīd*, and two abbreviated versions both known as *murshida* (Massé 1928; Urvoy 2005).

The Almohad *ʿaqīda* insists on God's unity, eternity, incommensurability, and omnipotence. It states that God exists in an absolute manner (*ʿalā l-iṭlāq*), that He is known by the necessity of reason, that He is the Creator of humankind, and that He as Creator of everything cannot be compared to His creation. This implies that believers should avoid any comparison as well as any modality (*tashbīh, takyīf*) by being aware of the difficulties posed by the *mutashābihāt* verses of the Qurʾān such as 20: 5 where God is said to be 'established' (*istawā*) on His Throne (Ibn Tūmart, *Aʿazz*, 1903: 233; cf. Frank 1994: 40–1). Only by doing so can doubts and the fall into anthropomorphism be avoided. The names of God are those that He Himself has revealed. The profession of faith ends by stating that God will be 'seen' on the Day of Judgement but not in a manner that would imply *tashbīh* or *takyīf*, and that the Prophetic mission is confirmed by miracles (*muʿjizāt*) such as splitting the sea, resurrecting the dead, or splitting the moon, the Qurʾān being one of the miracles of the Prophet Muḥammad. It is unclear if these last two sections were always part of the text. The Almohad movement was a revolution that underwent different stages, and in this process doctrines and events were subject to changes and alterations with a chronology and extension that is often difficult to assess.

In any case, the Almohad professions of faith are concerned with and concentrate on God and His unity. The treatment of prophecy, ritual, divine law, and eschatology normally found in Islamic creeds is absent, except for the above-mentioned reference to the vision of God in the afterlife and Muḥammad's miracles. As regards the *murshida*s, they are abbreviated versions of the *ʿaqīda* that again focus exclusively on God's unity and omnipotence. They are supposed to have been written in order to facilitate the learning of Almohad *tawḥīd* by the common people.

These professions of faith are preserved in Arabic. There were Berber renditions, usually understood as having been translated from an Arabic original, although this chain of events is impossible to ascertain. Previous studies on Ibn Tūmart's creedal formulations have pointed out the difficulty of confirming his authorship with the available sources (Cornell 1987). While certain correspondences with previous professions of faith have been indicated, and scholars such as R. Brunschvig (1955; 1970), D. Urvoy (1974; 1993), M. Fletcher (1991), V. Cornell, T. Nagel (1997, 2002), and F. Griffel have considerably advanced our understanding of Ibn Tūmart's intellectual and religious context, no comprehensive study has yet been carried out on the sources of the writings attributed to him. The insistence on the fact that God is known by the necessity of reason, found in the *ʿaqīda*, may be behind the characterization of the Almohad movement as a *madhhab fikr* ('doctrine of rational understanding') found in the earliest non-Almohad source (Gabrieli 1956), and may have helped the development of philosophical enquiry, a striking feature of the religious policies of the early Almohad caliphs (Stroumsa 2005). Suffice it to note that both Ibn Ṭufayl and Averroes lived and wrote under the Almohads in whose administration they worked.

II Why the Insistence on Anti-anthropomorphism in Ibn Tūmart's Doctrine?

As indicated, the main feature of Ibn Tūmart's doctrine as it appears in writings attributed to him is its uncompromising rejection of anthropomorphism. Averroes (d. 595/1198)—who served the Almohads in different capacities and who was a member of the *ṭalaba*, as proved by the title of his lost work in which he explained how he entered Almohad service (*Maqāla fī kayfiyyat dukhūlihi fī l-amr al-ʿazīz wa-taʿallumihi fīhi wa-mā fuḍḍila min ʿilm al-Mahdī*)—tried to tone down the policy of imposing this radical anti-anthropomorphic streak on the multitudes in his theological treatise *al-Kashf ʿan manāhij al-adilla*, perhaps also in his otherwise lost commentary on Ibn Tūmart's creed (Urvoy 2005). In *al-Kashf ʿan manāhij al-adilla*, written 575–6/1179–80, Averroes's presentation of the *kalām* theses are in conformity with Ibn Tūmart's *ʿaqīda* while also proposing an anti-Ghazālian theology, in the sense of being more philosophically oriented (Urvoy 1978; 1993). In spite of this conformity, Averroes was obliged to rewrite his original version of the *Kashf* and forced to introduce explicit references to Ibn Tūmart and his anti-anthropomorphic doctrine. Ibn Tūmart's teachings had been directed against the *mujassima*—those who gave a literal reading of the anthropomorphic passages of the Qurʾān and therefore committed *tashbīh*, assimilation of the Creator to His creatures—because Ibn Tūmart preached the rational need for the knowledge of a Creator radically different from His creatures. Averroes, in the first version of his *Kashf*, had not agreed with this, as he saw in such anthropomorphic passages symbols intended for the majority of people, those who were incapable of reaching rational knowledge, and who were amenable only to rhetorical arguments. Averroes was concerned that doing otherwise was to risk having those people believe in nothing (Geoffroy 1999; 2005).

For this pedagogically driven position, Averroes found religious support in the fact that neither in the Qurʾān nor in the *sunna* was there any explicit statement regarding God having or not having a body. By pointing out this fact, Averroes was in his own way following the pedagogical programme supported by his teacher Ibn Ṭufayl (d. 581/1185) in his *Ḥayy b. Yaqẓān* (and laid down by al-Fārābī), a philosophical tale written under the second Almohad caliph Abū Yaʿqūb Yūsuf (r. 558/1163–580/1184) which, among other aims, alerted to the limits of the Almohad intellectual revolution. The tale deals with a child who grows up on an island without any contact with other human beings, and by the mere observance of nature and the reasoning of his intellect reaches both a philosophical and mystical understanding of God. Later on, Ḥayy encounters a man, Absāl, who had grown up on another island where the inhabitants were followers of the teachings of a Prophet. Absāl was interested in the allegorical interpretation of those teachings and had been drawn to retirement and meditation, this being the reason he arrived on Ḥayy's island. After meeting Ḥayy, Absāl taught him to speak his language and could then learn from Ḥayy how he had achieved knowledge of that truth that he, Absāl, was striving to reach. Ḥayy and Absāl then decided to move to Absāl's island in order to teach that truth to its inhabitants. They were ruled by Sālamān, a former friend of Absāl, who was also a scrupulous believer, but who was mostly interested in the literal meaning of the Prophet's teachings and in living with other human beings. Soon, Ḥayy and Absāl realized that they could not change Sālamān's people, and even that it was not desirable to change them; they therefore decided to return to their isolation. Having renounced the task of educating the rest of the people in the path they had discovered, they went back to their island (Conrad 1996).

Thus, for Ibn Ṭufayl certain types of knowledge were beyond the scope of understanding of most people and therefore had to be restricted to the elite, leaving the majority of the population to their old beliefs. But when Averroes insisted on the same point in the first version of the *Kashf*, he was obliged to retract and address the fact that Ibn Tūmart had in fact condemned as unbelievers those who stated that God had a body. Although there is no firm evidence, the opposition to Averroes's views most probably came from the old Almohad elites, the tribal Berber lords (*shuyūkh*) and their descendants, the legitimacy of whose participation in Almohad rule was wholly dependent on Ibn Tūmart's infallible knowledge. Also, they often resented the new intellectual elites created by the Muʾminids, and Averroes was one of them. Under pressure from these elites, Averroes explained that Ibn Tūmart had formulated his condemnation of 'anthropomorphism' on the strength of his special character, for which Averroes used the term *khāṣṣa* (found in the *Kitāb Ibn Tūmart*), while avoiding any mention of Ibn Tūmart being the *mahdī*. This *khāṣṣa* was linked to Ibn Tūmart's own era: he had been forced to condemn those who had an anthropomorphist understanding of God because of the disputes existing in his day regarding this issue, and in order to eliminate the prevailing doctrinal and legal divergences with knowledge that completed and illuminated the text of the Revelation. Ibn Tūmart had thus tried to put an end to the ambiguity found in the sources of Revelation; an ambiguity that, according to Averroes, it would be better to maintain for the people's benefit (Geoffroy 2005).

Modern scholars have stressed the political implications of Ibn Tūmart's uncompromising anti-anthropomorphism, since it allowed him and his successor ʿAbd al-Muʾmin to eliminate their adversaries by resorting to the accusation of infidelity (*takfīr*) (Urvoy 1990; Serrano 2005). Theology thus helped in the establishment of a 'totalist' regime, in which true belief resided with the Prince of Believers and the religious and intellectual elites that were entirely dependent on him. The Mahdī, his successor ʿAbd al-Muʾmin—the *khalīfat al-mahdī ilā sabīl al-muwaḥḥidīn*, i.e. 'the vicar of the Rightly guided one along the path of the Unitarians'—and the successors of the Mahdī's successor were entitled to impose this true belief on the rest of the population, an unusual configuration in Sunnī polities, as it is closer to a Shīʿī understanding of the imamate. The Muʾminid caliphs (i.e., ʿAbd al-Muʾmin and his descendants) presented their rule on earth as equal to God's order (*al-amr, al-amr al-ʿazīz, amr Allāh*) (Vega, Peña, and Feria 2002; Fricaud 2002); they adopted Arabic genealogies, and were mentioned in the coins they minted only as *amīr al-muʾminīn ibn amīr al-muʾminīn* and so on, thus indicating that the line of succession was that of an essential, sacred quality, not that of specific individuals (Marín 2005). The Almohads in fact seem to have attempted to forge a middle way between Sunnīs and Shīʿīs. While they never proclaimed themselves to be Shīʿīs, their caliphate presents many similarities with the previous Fatimid model (Fierro 2012: IV). On the other hand, the Almohads made political, ceremonial, and religious use of an alleged Cordoban relic, some pages from an ʿUthmānic code that could never have found a place in a Shīʿī polity (Bennison 2007; Buresi 2010). This tension between Sunnism and Shīʿism—to which I have referred elsewhere as the 'Sunniticization of Shīʿism'—is reflected in the fact that in Ibn Tūmart's *Kitāb* only the first two caliphs, Abū Bakr and ʿUmar, are mentioned, which may also suggest a Khārijite influence.

III The Forced Conversion of the Non-Almohads

One of the most striking and puzzling decisions taken in the early stages of the Almohad revolution was the abolishment of the *dhimma* status, when Jews and Christians living under Almohad rule had to convert or be expelled. Christians emigrated to the kingdoms of the Iberian Peninsula, while Jews either converted to Islam (many of them only feigned conversion), or emigrated from Almohad lands, many choosing other countries within Islamdom; both options—conversion or emigration—also existed in the case of Maimonides (Kraemer 2008: 116–24; Stroumsa 2009). The forced conversion would have happened after the conquest of Marrakech in the year 541/1147, when ʿAbd al-Muʾmin told the Jews and Christians who lived in the territory under his rule that their ancestors had denied the mission of the Prophet, but that now they (the Almohads) would no longer allow them to continue in their infidelity. As the Almohads had no need of the tax (*jizya*) they paid, *dhimmīs* now had to choose between conversion, leaving the land, or being killed. This policy meant the abolition of the so-called *dhimma* 'pact', an abolition that is not discussed or justified in detail in any of the extant texts dealing with the Almohads. In order to understand the religious, legal, and political context that could have determined such an unprecedented policy, five elements must be taken into account (Fierro 2011):

a) Eschatology, i.e. the conviction that the appearance of the Mahdī or Messiah (in the Almohad case, Ibn Tūmart, the founder of the movement) would bring about the disappearance of religions other than Islam.
b) Ismāʿīlī/Fāṭimid influence, in particular the policies of the Fāṭimid caliph al-Ḥākim (r. 386/996–411/1021), who ordered the destruction of non-Muslim temples, imposed dress restrictions and forced conversion, this being the closest precedent to ʿAbd al-Muʾmin's initiative.
c) Influence of the belief that all human beings possess an innate nature (*fiṭra*) that corresponds to Islam, whereas being a Jew or a Christian depends on the family into which one has been born. As stated by Ibn Ḥazm (d. 456/1064)—an influential author among the Almohads—only re-conversion to Islam allows the return to one's *fiṭra*. The Almohad movement was a revolutionary and purifying movement, obsessed with the need to put an end to the differences of opinion both within Islam and among the different monotheistic religions. Within this framework, the Almohads must have believed that they were in charge of the mission to bring back to true belief not only the Muslims—hence the imposition of their profession of faith to all those Muslims living under their rule—but also those born as Jews and Christians. Religious pluralism had to disappear, because Truth can only be One.

d) The idea that the territory ruled by the Almohads was a new Ḥijāz, as a development of the identification of Ibn Tūmart—the founder of the movement—with the Prophet Muḥammad. In the same way that Muḥammad forbade the presence of any religion other than Islam in the territory of the Arabian Peninsula—and more specifically in the Ḥijāz where the sacred towns of Mecca and Medina were located—the Almohads seem to have thought that the same prohibition applied to the territory where the doctrines of their founder the Mahdī now reigned supreme.
e) The Almohads could have also been influenced by the legal doctrine of the jurist al-Ṭabarī (d. 310/923), according to whom once demography was favourable to the Muslims, they would no longer be in need of non-Muslims, and could therefore abolish the *dhimma* 'pact'. ʿAbd al-Muʾmin's statement that the Almohads were not in need of the *jizya* of the *dhimmīs* makes sense in this context—i.e. the new rulers did not establish any pact with the conquered people (including those who called themselves Muslims, but who were not really such as they had indulged in anthropomorphism) because, having brought the true Revelation to all, everyone had to conform to it.

Thus, with the abolition of the *dhimma*, the Almohad caliphs found themselves as reigning over a polity where Islam—the true Islam condensed in their profession of faith that everyone had to learn—was the only religion. But they also soon found themselves having to face the concern of how to be sure that those who had been forced to convert were really true believers.

During the reign of the third Almohad caliph Abū Yūsuf Yaʿqūb al-Manṣūr (r. 580/1184–595/1198), 'Jews' were obliged to dress in a distinctive, humiliating, and ridiculous way. Note, however, that they were no longer Jews from a legal point of view, but 'new Muslims', i.e. those who had chosen not to emigrate and therefore had been forced to convert to Islam. The Jewish convert Ibn ʿAqnīn recorded in his *Ṭibb al-nufūs* the sufferings and discrimination to which they were subject, being forbidden to own slaves, to take part in some legal acts, to marry 'old Muslims', and so on. The following statement of his is very telling: 'The more it appears that we obey them as to everything they tell us, and incline after their Law, the more they oppress and enslave us.'

What moved the caliph Abū Yūsuf Yaʿqūb to mark the converted Jews externally was his doubts about their sincerity. Had he been sure about their faith, he would have let them intermarry with old Muslims and mix with them in all normal affairs of life. Had he been sure of their infidelity, he would have killed the men and enslaved their children, giving their properties as booty to the Muslims. The problem was precisely that he did not know the true nature or status of those Jews who externally showed their adhesion to Islam, praying in the mosques, with their children reading the Qurʾān, and following the Almohads' religion and *sunna*, with only God knowing what they really believed. The distinctive marks imposed on them were thus not intended to show those converted Jews to be *dhimmīs*, but functioned as an alarm signal proclaiming: beware, here there are believers whose belief is uncertain. During the caliphate of al-Nāṣir (r. 595/1199–610/1213), and thanks to the payments they made, these converted Jews managed to exchange that ridiculous clothing for yellow garments and turbans, so that they could still be distinguished from the old Muslims.

As regards non-Almohad Muslims, historical sources provide abundant information about the fact that the Almohads considered the mosques they encountered in the conquered territories to be polluted and therefore in need of purification (*ṭahāra*), implying that they considered non-Almohad Muslims as not being true Muslims, so that their places of worship needed to be cleansed from their impurity. Once purification was performed, and the *qibla* reoriented, non-Almohad Muslim sacred places seem to have become acceptable to the Unitarians. Did they also extend their concerns about purity to the persons of the non-Almohad Muslims? Was personal purification part of the process of becoming an Almohad? Our knowledge of Almohad doctrinal views on purity—here again we have a Shīʿī-like rather than a Sunnī concern—is still too scanty to be able to give answers to these questions at the present stage.

Al-Manṣūr's anxiety regarding the true character of the belief held by Jews forced to convert led him to discriminate between Muslims by externally marking those of Jewish descent; in other words, his doubts about belief seem to have been limited to those converts whose origins lay in a specific ethnic group. This could be interpreted as a first step towards what in Christian Spain led to the infamous statutes of pure blood (*limpieza de sangre*). No similar anxiety seems to have been felt regarding those old Muslims who 'converted' to Almohadism.

Anti-Shuʿūbī literature flourished during the Almohad period, as it was precisely at that time that most of the refutations against Ibn García's Shuʿūbī *Epistle* were written. This might come as a surprise, given the strong Berber character of the Almohad movement. We have here another of the paradoxes of Almohadism. Based on a hierarchy of Berber tribes and of precedence according to the moment in which groups and individuals had adhered to the Mahdī's message, the conquered people—including the Muslims—were considered to be the slaves (*ʿabīd*) of the first Almohad leaders (the Council of Ten or *jamāʿa*). The Zanāta Berber ʿAbd al-Muʾmin, the first Almohad caliph, was a member of this Council. Once he took power he adopted an Arab (Qaysī) genealogy that allowed him both to support his claim to the caliphate and to set himself above the rest of the members of the Council, all of them Berbers. At the same time, those under the rule of the Muʾminid caliphs who adhered to Ibn Tūmart's *tawḥīd* became one of them—i.e. the Almohads—and were saved, i.e. salvation did not depend on ethnicity.

One of the fundamental texts written by a member of the Almohad court, Ibn Ṭufayl's *Ḥayy b. Yaqẓān*, deals—among many other issues—with that of ancestry and egalitarianism. Ibn Ṭufayl records two possibilities regarding Ḥayy ibn Yaqẓān's origins: he was either born by spontaneous generation or he was a child of royal descent abandoned by his mother. Ibn Ṭufayl probably had no choice but to include the possibility of royal origins, even if he was more inclined towards the other theory. In other words, as a member of the Almohad learned elites, the *ṭalaba*, who were supposed to derive their knowledge from the Muʾminid caliph as the inheritor of the Mahdī's charisma, Ibn Ṭufayl could not but include the possibility of royal descent. The content of Ibn Ṭufayl's work points to his belief in the equality by birth between human beings, their differences being based not on lineage, but in their different rational and spiritual capacities.

IV Law, Theology, Philosophy, and Sufism under the Almohads[3]

The Almohads seem to have felt satisfied with certain external reassurances regarding their subjects' adherence to true belief: imposition of the Almohad profession of faith stressing God's unity, and acceptance of and conformity with the changes introduced in ritual (change in the direction of the *qibla*, new call to prayer, the raising of one's hands during prayer at moments previously not taken into account, avoidance of the pilgrimage to Mecca, while promoting the visiting of Ibn Tūmart's grave in Tinmall). In the legal sphere, there were attempts to impose an anti-*madhhab* orientation, sometimes presented as giving prominence to Ibn Ḥazm's Ẓāhirism (Adang 2000). Difference of opinion (*ikhtilāf*) in matters related to the revealed law was rejected: in a religious and political system that had started with an 'impeccable leader and acknowledged rightly guided one' the idea that every qualified interpreter of the law was right (*taṣwīb*) could not be accepted. Legal *ikhtilāf* had nonetheless to be accounted for. Serving the Almohads as *qāḍī*, Averroes wrote his *Bidāyat al-mujtahid wa-nihāyat al-muqtaṣid* ('The beginning for him who is striving towards a personal judgement and the end for him who contents himself with received knowledge'), a work that is striking not only for the absence of a clear-cut inclination for one school of law or another, but also for its clarity of exposition, its freedom of thought, and its concern with logic and rationality—a work that could also have opened the way for an Almohad legal codification (Fierro 2012: XII). But the resistance offered by the Malikis to Almohad innovations meant in practice that the Almohads soon started to move towards a reformed Malikism, thus offering their subjects an easier transition to the new order, but also profoundly changing—or betraying—the original revolution.

In the early stages of their movement, emphasis was put not so much on the fact that the Almohad Truth was a revival of the Prophet Muḥammad's message, but that it was identical with God's order or disposition (*amr Allāh*). The original name of the movement was 'the *muʾminūn*', and *muʾminūn* are the 'believers' in general, regardless of time and place. The Almohad Truth was the universal religion of mankind to which every human being had to adhere not in the distant future, but in the here and now, with the three monotheistic religions being but manifestations of that same Truth. This idea was most clearly expressed by Sufis who were born under the Almohads such as

[3] Cf. Ferhat 1993; Garden 2005; Rubio 1987.

Muḥyī l-Dīn Ibn al-ʿArabī (d. 438/1240), al-Ḥarrālī (d. 637/1240), and Ibn Hūd (b. 633/1235, d. 699/1300). This Almohad conviction had to do with their Messiah or Mahdī, an infallible imam who was the rightly guided one and the one who could lead others to the right path; but also with the emphasis that a certain trend within Almohadism put upon reason and on the ability of man to perfect himself and reach a true understanding of God. This last possibility could be carried out either through philosophical Sufism, as Ibn Ṭufayl argued in his *Ḥayy ibn Yaqẓān*, or simply through philosophy, as Ibn Rushd, another Almohad scholar, devoted his life to proving.

The Almohads accused the previous rulers, the Almoravids, of having persecuted those scholars who occupy themselves with theology (*kalām*), an accusation that has been proved to be unfounded (Urvoy 1990: 165; Dandash 1991; Serrano 2003). Theology flourished under the Almohads to the extent that the Almohad defeat during the campaign of Huete against the Christians is explained as having been caused by the caliph Abū Yaʿqūb Yūsuf being more interested in a theological discussion than in fighting (Ibn Ṣāḥib al-ṣalāt, *al-Mann bi-l-imāma*: 211; Huici 1956–7: i. 259). Ibn Tūmart was said to have been an Ashʿarite with Muʿtazilī leanings, as in his alleged denial of the divine attributes (al-Marrākushī, *Muʿjib*, 135/146–7; cf. Fletcher 1991), an eclecticism that has also been attributed to Ibn Ṭufayl (Conrad 1996: 27) and to Ibn al-ʿArabī (Addas 1989: 133–4). Among the Almohads there seems to have existed a predilection for rationalism (Griffel 2005) that separated them from the less philosophically oriented Ashʿarite doctrines. These doctrines eventually became predominant, as shown by Ibn ʿAṭiyya's (d. 541/1147) *Fahrasa* and al-Lablī's (d. 671/1272) *Fihrist* (Fórneas 1978; Roldán Castro 1995; al-Idrīsī 2005; Schmidtke 2013). This predominance was due to the profound impact that the teachings of Abū Bakr b. al-ʿArabī—a student of al-Ghazālī, critical of his philosophical and Sufi leanings—had on the generation of his pupils (Ṭālibī n.d.; Lucini 1995). When the caliph al-Maʾmūn (r. 624/1227–629/1232) proclaimed that the only acceptable *mahdī* was Jesus who was to come at the end of time, thus renouncing the Almohad doctrine, he also prohibited theology, a discipline that was always suspect of entailing more dangers than benefits.

Al-Maʾmūn also prohibited philosophy. Attacks against the philosophers had started earlier, under al-Manṣūr, in the year 593/1197, when the famous episode of Averroes's 'disgrace' took place, although the philosopher and judge was later reinstated in his former position (Fricaud 2005). Averroes had been accused of giving priority to nature (*ṭabīʿa*) over the revealed law (*sharīʿa*), an issue that had already informed his polemic against al-Ghazālī (Puig 1992; Griffel 2002). In the year 586/1190, Ibn al-ʿArabī met a philosopher in al-Andalus who denied that prophets could perform miracles (*karāmāt*). The encounter took place in winter, in front of a fire. The philosopher explained that the common people believed that Abraham was thrown into the fire without being affected by it, whereas fire by its nature burns all matter susceptible of combustion—the fire mentioned in the Qurʾān in the story of Abraham had to be understood as the symbolic expression of Nimrod's anger. Among those present there was a Sufi endowed with *karāmāt* who, pointing to the fire in the room, asked if that fire was one of those that burnt matter. The philosopher answered 'yes' and threw him some of the coals, only to witness with astonishment that the Sufi was unaffected (Addas 1989: 135f.). The ability of saints to perform miracles had been a hotly debated issue in al-Andalus, as its acceptance threatened the Prophet's uniqueness and in consequence the authority of the scholars in charge of interpreting Revelation through their knowledge (Fierro 1992). The rivalry between scholars and Sufis intensified when the latter started to gain followers during the first half of the sixth/twelfth century: suffice it to mention the names of Ibn Barrajān (d. 536/1141), Ibn al-ʿArīf (d. 536/1141), Ibn Ḥirzihim (d. 559/1165), Abū Madyan (d. 594/1197), and Abū l-ʿAbbās al-Sabtī (d. 601/1205), apart from those already mentioned. On his part, Ibn Qasī (d. 546/1151), a thinker closer to Ismailism than to Sufism (Ebstein 2015), with his army of novices (*murīdūn*) had risen in rebellion against the Almoravids to take power in what is now southern Portugal. Saints and Sufis were prominent figures especially in the Maghrib, where it was not until a later stage that the process of Islamicization gave rise to a cohesive and uninterrupted scholarly tradition as had developed in al-Andalus. Berber prophets and saints provided both religious and political authority (Brett 1999; García Arenal 2006), and because of the political implications of sainthood, saints and Sufis were sometimes persecuted or their activities resented. While saints found a niche in the tribal milieu of North Africa, most Andalusi Sufis took the road to the East, as did Ibn al-ʿArabī, with lasting effects for Islamdom.

References

Adang, C. (2000). 'Ẓāhiris of Almohad Times'. In M. Fierro and M. L. Ávila (eds.), *Estudios Onomástico-Biográficos de al-Andalus. X. Biografías almohades*, ii. Madrid/Granada: CSIC, 413–79.

Addas, C. (1989). *Ibn ʿArabī ou La quête du Soufre Rouge*. Paris: Éditions Gallimard.

D'Alverny, M.-Th., and G. Vajda (1951–2). 'Marc de Tolède, traducteur d'Ibn Tumart'. *Al-Andalus* 16: 99–140, 259–307; 17: 1–56.

Bennison, A. (2007). 'The Almohads and the Qurʾān of Uthmān: The Legacy of the Umayyads of Cordoba in Twelfth Century Maghrib'. *Al-Masaq* 19/2: 131–54.

Brett, M. (1999). 'The Lamp of the Almohads: Illumination as a Political Idea in Twelfth Century Morocco'. In M. Brett, *Ibn Khaldun and the Medieval Maghrib*. Ashgate: article VI.

Brunschvig, R. (1955). 'Sur la doctrine du Mahdi Ibn Tūmart'. *Arabica* 2: 137–49.

Brunschvig, R. (1970). 'Encore sur la doctrine du Mahdī Ibn Tūmart'. *Folia Orientalia* 12: 33–40.

Buresi, P. (2010). 'D'une péninsule à l'autre: Cordoue, ʿUṯmān (644–656) et les Arabes à l'époque almohade (XIIe–XIIe siècle)'. *Al-Qanṭara* 31: 7–29.

Conrad, L. L. (ed.) (1996). *The world of Ibn Tufayl. Interdisciplinary Perspectives on Hayy ibn Yaqzan*. Leiden: Brill.

Cornell, V. J. (1987). 'Understanding is the Mother of Ability: Responsibility and Action in the Doctrine of Ibn Tumart'. *Studia Islamica* 66: 71–103.

Dandash, ʿIṣmat ʿAbd al-Laṭīf (1991). 'Mawqif al-murābiṭīn min ʿilm al-kalām wa-l-falsafa'. In *Adwāʾjadīda ʿalā l-murābiṭīn*. Beirut: Dār al-Gharb al-islāmī, 83–99.

Ebstein, M. (2015). 'Was Ibn Qasi a Sufi?'. *Studia Islamica* 11: 196–232.
Ferhat, H. (1993). *Le Maghreb aux XIIème et XIIIème siècles: les siècles de la foi.* Casablanca: Wallada.
Fierro, M. (1992). 'The Polemic about the *karāmāt al-awliyāʾ* and the Development of Ṣūfism in al-Andalus (4th/10th–5th/11th centuries)'. *Bulletin of the School of Oriental and African Studies* 55: 236–49.
Fierro, M. (2011). 'A Muslim Land without Jews or Christians: Almohad Policies Regarding the "Protected People"'. In M. Tischler and A. Fidora (eds.), *Christlicher Norden, Muslimischer Süden: Ansprüche und Wirklichkeiten von Christen, Juden und Muslimen auf der Iberischen Halbinsel im Hoch- und Spätmittelalter*. Münster: Aschendorff, 231–47.
Fierro, M. (2012). *The Almohad Revolution: Politics and Religion in the Islamic West during the Twelfth–Thirteenth Centuries*. London: Ashgate Variorum.
Fletcher, M. (1991). 'The Almohad *Tawḥīd*: Theology which Relies on Logic'. *Numen* 38: 110–27.
Fórneas, J. M. (1978). 'De la transmisión de algunas obras de tendencia *ašʿarí* en al-Andalus.' *Awraq* 1: 4–11.
Frank, R. M. (1994). *Al-Ghazālī and the Ashʿarite School*. Durham, NC: Duke University Press.
Fricaud, É. (1997). 'Les *ṭalaba* dans la société almohade (le temps d'Averroés)'. *Al-Qanṭara* 18: 331–88.
Fricaud, É. (2002). 'Origine de l'utilisation privilégiée du terme *amr* chez les Muʾminides almohades'. *Al-Qanṭara* 23: 93–122.
Fricaud, É. (2005). 'Le Problème de la disgrace d'Averroès'. In A. Bazzana et al. (eds.), *Averroès et l'averroïsme (XIIe–XVe siècle): un itinéraire historique du Haut Atlas à Paris et Padoue*. Lyon: Presses Universitaires de Lyon, 155–89.
Gabrieli, F. (1956). 'Le origini del movimento almohade in una fonte storica d'Oriente'. *Arabica* 3: 1–7.
Garden, K. (2005). *Al-Ghazālī's Contested Revival: Iḥyāʾ ʿulūm al-dīn and its Critics in Khorasan and the Maghrib*. Doctoral dissertation, University of Chicago.
Geoffroy, M. (1999). 'L'Almohadisme théologique d'Averroès (Ibn Rushd)'. *Archives d'Histoire Doctrinale et Littéraire du Moyen Âge* 66: 9–47.
Geoffroy, M. (2005). 'À propos de l'almohadisme d'Averroès: l'anthropomorphisme (*tağsīm*) dans la seconde *version du Kitāb al-kašf ʿan manāhiğ al-adilla*'. In P. Cressier et al. (eds.), *Los almohades: problemas y perspectivas*. Madrid: CSIC/Casa de Velázquez, ii. 853–94.
Griffel, F. (2002). 'The Relationship between Averroes and al-Ghazālī as it Presents itself in Averroes' Early Writings, Especially in his Commentary on al-Ghazālī's *al-Muṣṭasfā*'. In J. Inglis (ed.), *Medieval Philosophy and the Classical Tradition in Islam, Judaism and Christianity*. Richmond: Curzon Press, 51–63.
Griffel, F. (2005). 'Ibn Tūmart's Rational Proof for God's Existence and his Unity, and his Connection to the Niẓāmiyya Madrasa in Bagdad'. In P. Cressier et al., *Los almohades: problemas y perspectivas*. Madrid: CSIC/Casa de Velázquez, ii. 753–813.
Huici Miranda, A. (1956–7). *Historia política del imperio almohade*. 2 vols. Tetouan [repr. Granada: Universidad de Granada, 2000].
Ibn Ṣāḥib al-ṣalāt (*Mann*). *al-Mann bi-l-imāma*. Ed. ʿAbd al-Hādī al-Tāzī. Beirut 1964 [2nd edn. Beirut 1979; 3rd edn. Beirut: Dār al-Gharb al-islāmī, 1987; Spanish trans. A. Huici Miranda. Valencia: Anubar, 1969].
Ibn Ṭufayl (*Ḥayy*). *Ḥayy b. Yaqẓān*. Ed. A. N. Nader. Beirut: Dār al-Mashriq, 1993 [English trans. by L. E. Goodman, *Ibn Tufayl's Hayy Ibn Yaqzan: A Philosophical Tale*. Updated edn. Chicago: University of Chicago, 2009].

Ibn Tūmart (*A'azz*). *A'azz mā yuṭlab = Le livre de Mohammed Ibn Toumert, Mahdi des Almohades*. Ed. D. Luciani. Algiers: P. Fontana, 1903 [ed. ʿAmmār Ṭālibī. Algiers 1985; ed. ʿAbd al-Ghānī Abū l-ʿAzm. Rabat: Mu'assasat al-Ghani li-l-nashr, 1997].

al-Idrīsī, ʿAlī (ed.) (2005). *al-Ittijāhāt al-kalāmiyya fī l-gharb al-islāmī*. Rabat: Kulliyyat al-adab wa-l-ʿulūm al-insāniyya.

Kraemer, J. L. (2008). *Maimonides: The Life and World of One of Civilization's Great Minds*. New York: Doubleday.

Laoust, H. (1960). 'Une fetwa d'Ibn Taimiya sur Ibn Tumart'. *Bulletin de l'Institut Français d'Archéologie Orientale* 59: 157–84.

Lucini, M. M. (1995). 'Discípulos de Abū Bakr Ibn al-'Arabī en *al-Ḏayl wa-l-Takmila* de al-Marrākušī'. In Marín and H. de Felipe (eds.), *Estudios onomástico-biográficos de al-Andalus. VII*. Madrid: CSIC, 191–202.

Marín, M. (2005). 'El califa almohade, una presencia activa y benéfica'. In P. Cressier et al. (eds.), *Los almohades: problemas y perspectivas*. Madrid: CSIC/Casa de Velázquez, ii. 451–76.

al-Marrākushī (*Muʿjib*). *Kitāb al-Muʿjib fī talkhīṣ akhbār al-Maghrib*. Ed. R. Dozy. Leiden: Brill, 2nd edn. 1881 [French trans. E. Fagnan, *Histoire des Almohades*. Algiers, 1893; Spanish trans. A. Huici Miranda. Tetouan, 1955].

Massé, H. (1928). 'La Profession de foi (*ʿaqīda*) et les guides spirituels (*morchida*) du Mahdi Ibn Toumert'. In *Mémorial Henri Basset: nouvelles études nord-africaines et orientales*. Paris: P. Geuthner, ii. 105–21.

Nagel, T. (1997). 'La destrucción de la ciencia de la *šarīʿa* por Muḥammad b. Tūmart'. *Al-Qanṭara* 18: 295–304.

Nagel, T. (2002). *Im Offenkundigen das Verborgene: Die Heilszusage des sunnitischen Islams*. Göttingen: Vandenhoeck and Ruprecht.

Puig, J. (1992). 'Ibn Rushd versus al-Ghazālī: Reconsideration of a Polemic'. *Muslim World* 82: 113–31.

Roldán Castro, F. (1995). 'El *Fihrist* de Aḥmad b. Yūsuf al-Fihrī al-Lablī (s. XIII)'. In *Homenaje al profesor José María Fórneas Besteiro*. 2 vols. Granada: Universidad de Granada, i. 615–26.

Rubio, L. (1987). *El 'ocasionalismo' de los teólogos especulativos del Islam: su posible influencia en Guilermo de Ockam y en los 'ocasionalistas' de la Edad Moderna*. El Escorial: Ediciones Escurialenses.

Schmidtke, S. (2013). 'Ibn Ḥazm's Sources on Ashʿarism and Muʿtazilism'. In C. Adang, M. Fierro, and S. Schmidtke (eds.), *Ibn Ḥazm of Cordoba: The Life and Works of a Controversial Thinker*. Leiden: Brill, 375–401.

Serrano, D. (2003). 'Los almorávides y la teología ašʿarí: ¿contestación o legitimación de una disciplina marginal?' In C. de la Puente (ed.), *Estudios onomástico-biográficos de al-Andalus. XIII. Identidades marginales*. Madrid: CSIC, 461–516.

Serrano, D. (2005). '¿Por qué llamaron los almohades antropomorfistas a los almorávides'. In P. Cressier et al. (eds.), *Los almohades: problemas y perspectivas*. Madrid: CSIC/Casa de Velázquez, ii. 451–76.

Stroumsa, S. (2005). 'Philosophes almohades? Averroès, Maimonide et l'idéologie almohade'. In P. Cressier et al. (eds.), *Los almohades: problemas y perspectivas*. Madrid: CSIC/Casa de Velázquez, ii. 1137–62.

Stroumsa, S. (2009). *Maimonides in his World: Portrait of a Mediterranean Thinker*. Princeton: Princeton University Press.

Ṭālibī, ʿA. (n.d.). *Ārāʾ Abī Bakr b. al-ʿArabī al-kalāmiyya*. 2 vols. Algiers: al-Sharika al-waṭaniyya.

Urvoy, D. (1974). 'La Pensée d'Ibn Tūmart'. *Bulletin d'Études Orientales* 27: 19–44.

Urvoy, D. (1978). 'La Pensée almohade dans l'œuvre d'Averroès'. In J. Jolivet (ed.), *Multiple Averroès: Actes du Colloque Internationale organisé à l'occasion du 850e anniversaire de la naissance d'Averroès, Paris 20–23 septembre 1976*. Paris: Belles Lettres, 45–56.

Urvoy, D. (1990). *Pensers d'al-Andalus: la vie intellectuelle à Cordoue et Sevilla au temps des Empires Berberes (fin XIe siècle–début XIIIe siècle)*. Toulouse: Éditions du CNRS/Presses Universitaires du Mirail.

Urvoy, D. (1993). 'Les Divergences théologiques entre Ibn Tūmart et Gazālī'. In *Mélanges offerts à Mohamed Talbi à l'occasion de son 70e anniversaire*. Manouba: Publications de la Faculté des Lettres de la Manouba, ii. 203–12.

Urvoy, D. (2005). 'Les Professions de foi d'Ibn Tūmart: problèmes textuels et doctrinaux'. In P. Cressier et al. (eds.), *Los almohades: problemas y perspectivas*. Madrid: CSIC/Casa de Velázquez, ii. 739–52.

Vega Martín, M., S. Peña Martín, and M. C. Feria García (2002). *El mensaje de las monedas almohades: numismática, traducción y pensamiento*. Cuenca: Ediciones de la Universidad de Castilla-La Mancha.

Wiegers, G. (1994). *Islamic Literature in Spanish and Aljamiado*. Leiden: Brill.

CHAPTER 39

INTERPRETATIONS OF ASHʿARISM AND MĀTURĪDISM IN MAMLUK AND OTTOMAN TIMES

LUTZ BERGER

I Schools, the Court, and the Courts: The Social Setting of Theology in Mamluk and Ottoman Times

During the first centuries of Islam religious experts held their teaching sessions in mosques or at private houses. After the fifth/eleventh century teaching increasingly took place in specially founded schools (*madrasas*) whose endowments provided for necessary books, incomes for teachers, and scholarships for students. The founders were mostly rulers or high officials (sometimes their wives), but the institutions nonetheless kept their private character. In these schools theology did play a role, but was normally a minor field of study in comparison with *ḥadīth* (prophetical tradition) and law.

Schools were usually intended for one *madhhab* (school of Islamic law) only, but sometimes the endowment deed provided for two or even all four Sunnī schools of law generally recognized by that time to be taught. After the downfall of the Fāṭimids, Sunnism no longer had serious rivals in the Arab parts of the Islamic world (if we leave the special case of the Almohads in the Maghreb aside). Within Sunnism, the Ayyūbīd rulers of Egypt and Syria favoured the Shāfiʿī school of law but at the same time showed great tolerance towards the Mālikīs who were dominant in Upper Egypt. The same held true with respect to their treatment of the Ḥanafīs and Ḥanbalīs who were not without influence in the Syrian parts of the Ayyūbīd domains. The Mamlūks made the equal treatment of all four Sunnī schools a central part of their religious policy (on the scholarly milieu of the age see Berkey 1992; Chamberlain 1994). After the Ottoman conquest of the eastern Arab world in the early tenth/sixteenth century, *madrasa*s continued as before, but the control over teaching posts was no longer in the hands of locals, but had been taken over by the central administration in Istanbul. Even scholars only looking for a job on the spot were therefore forced to curry favour with the powerful in the Istanbul learned hierarchy and the Sultan's palace (Berger 2007: 78ff.). Pride of place was given to the Ḥanafīs as the school of the Sultan, but the other three schools were respected as well. This held true especially in the Arab parts of the Empire, where the Shāfiʿīs or (in Upper Egypt) the Mālikīs made up the majority of the population. The civilian elite of the Arab provinces showed a certain tendency to convert to Ḥanafism to further their careers in the Ottoman religious hierarchy, but this was a slow and gradual process, that was in no way marked by the use of force. The minor points of conflict existing between local scholars and the Ottoman state in the period had nothing to do with questions of theology (Rafeq 1999; for a partly different view, cf. Berger 2007: 55ff.).

In Anatolia and Rumelia, the heartlands of the Ottoman Empire, the connection between the learned hierarchy and the politically powerful was even closer. In the first decades of the Ottomans in the late seventh/thirteenth and eighth/fourteenth centuries the Islamic character of the state and even more of its population was not as marked as later memory would have it. Pre-Islamic Central Asian and local (Christian) Anatolian religious notions and practices were widespread among the heterogeneous populations over which the Ottomans ruled, even among those who were formally seen as Muslims (Kafadar 1995). For the Ottoman rulers to establish scriptural Islam as officially sponsored religion was part of the transition from tribal society to statehood. Thus, from the eighth/fourteenth century the foundation of *madrasas* accompanied the expansion of the Ottoman state. In departure from Islamic tradition these *madrasas* now became a direct part of the bureaucratic apparatus of the Empire. Students who aspired to become high ranking judges were not free to study with whom they liked, as had been the practice before. They had to study at certain Sultanic *madrasas* at the centre of the Empire, mostly in Istanbul, and had to follow a clearly prescribed curriculum. This was a fundamental change in the Islamic tradition of learning but not necessarily a reason for a decline in *kalām* studies. In the curriculum prescribed for the Ottoman learned elites it retained an honourable place, although it was not reckoned as important as e.g. *ḥadīth* studies that were deemed the crown of religious knowledge. Teaching posts at the *ḥadīth* school of Sultan Süleyman were at the top of the list, both as regards standing and as regards pay (Yazıcıoğlu 1990: 41ff.; on the social history of the Ottoman scholarly class, cf. Zilfi 1988, now to be corrected by Klein).

Theological knowledge also had a place outside schools. Already under the ʿAbbāsid caliphs listening to debating theologians was part of courtly entertainment. This practice was continued in later times when al-Jurjānī (d. 816/1413; he combined Muʿtazilī and Ashʿarite notions and had spent part of his life in Cairo) and al-Taftazānī (d. 792/1390, a Māturīdī strongly influenced by Ashʿarism) used to hold debates to entertain Timur Lenk at Samarkand (van Ess 2009; Madelung 2000). Ottoman Sultans also enjoyed theological discussions at their courts, at least during the ninth/fifteenth century. Especially Fatih Sultan Mehmet is famous in this respect. He had scholars debate on the merits of al-Ghazālī's and Ibn Rushd's views of philosophy (Köse 1998). Such debates were not always held just for the entertainment of the Sultan. They sometimes served to repress theological opinions that rulers or scholars deemed dangerous. Under Süleyman the Lawgiver (the Magnificent), Molla Kabız was accused of apostasy as he believed Jesus Christ was of a higher rank than the Prophet of Islam. It was to the great anger of the Sultan that the judges, in a session held in his presence, were not able to disprove the heretic's opinions. In a second session, the chief mufti Kemalpaşazade was called to the rescue and was able to confound the Molla thanks to his superior knowledge and understanding of the basic texts of Islam. The Sultan had Molla Kabız executed (on this and other cases of heresy among Ottoman scholars see Ocak 1998: 230ff.).

Sultans and local governors needed the services of theologically well-trained scholars when they had to deal with people of potentially dangerous opinions. Equally the scholars themselves needed the arm of the state to forcefully suppress opinions that they deemed beyond the pale (Berger 2007: 288ff.). But does this interdependence mean that the rulers' interests and politics in a more general sense had any significant impact on the debates of theologians within the mainstream paradigms of Sunnī Islam?

II · Ashʿarism and Māturīdism: A Political Compromise?

Sunnī *kalām* in the Mamluk and Ottoman periods was dominated by two schools: the Middle Eastern school of al-Ashʿarī, in the East originally connected with the Shāfiʿī school of law, that had during the fifth/eleventh century become the most dynamic and generally dominant school of *kalām* in the countries from Khorasan to Morocco and, on the other hand, the school of al-Māturīdī, which had originally been the Central Asian variant of Ḥanafī theological thought, but then moved westwards with the migration of the Turks from Central Asia (Madelung 1971). In Mamluk and Ottoman times both schools not only coexisted peacefully but had become very much entangled.

The relative peacefulness in sectarian relations among the supporters of al-Ashʿarī and al-Māturīdī in the Mamluk and Ottoman Empires (and also in Iran since the Mongol period) was a relatively new phenomenon. Although the idea of peaceful coexistence among scholars of different persuasions had always been part of the Sunnī identity, sometimes this was rather paid lip-service to than put into practice. The spread of Māturīdism was an important element in the infighting within pre-Mongol Khorasanian cities. When Māturīdism newly arrived in the lands to the south and west of Transoxania together with the Seljuq Turkish rulers during the fifth/eleventh century, it was here, and in confrontation with the local Ashʿarites, that the theological school of al-Māturīdī became conscious of its own identity (Rudolph 1997). The situation was not eased by the fact that Ashʿarites, who looked disparagingly at the Central Asian intruders, were on their part relatively new on the Khorasanian scene. They had only just, and with some difficulty, established themselves in Khorasan during the previous decades against Muʿtazilī-minded Ḥanafīs. Now Seljuq rulers built mosques for and offered jobs to their own Central Asian Māturīdī-Ḥanafī scholars and from time to time tried to purge the territories under their control from Ashʿarites/Shāfiʿīs. Radicals would even throw the *takfīr* at their Ashʿarite rivals (Madelung 1971: 126).

The cities of the Arab lands to the west of Iraq never knew the level of sectarian infighting that upset the cities of Khorasan in the pre-Mongol age. Why this should have been so, is still not entirely clear. Maybe other markers of identity than association with a certain school of law and/or theology were more important here (Cahen 1959; Chamberlain 1994; Talmon-Heller 2005). In regions, at any rate, where one school had come to dominate the scene, as was the case in Egypt (Shāfiʿī in the North, Mālikī in the South) and the Mālikī Maghreb, there was less chance that sectarian differences would lead to conflict. In comparison Syria was a more problematic terrain. Nonetheless, the immigration of Central Asian scholars in the wake of the Seljuqs does not seem to have caused violent unrest there. This holds true in spite of the fact that with the Seljuqs Ḥanafism not only gained new supporters in the countries to the west of Iraq, but also changed in character. The old local Ḥanafīs had been either of a traditional anti-rationalist or Muʿtazilī persuasion. The influx of the Turks and Central Asian scholars made the school of al-Māturīdī a feature of the Syrian landscape besides the local Ḥanafī theological tradition that nevertheless survived well into Mamluk times (Bruckmayr 2009: 62). At the same time, eastern Ḥanafī scholars from Transoxania continued to move into Syria to teach at *madrasas* that the Zengid and Ayyubid rulers had founded there throughout the seventh/thirteenth century without this apparently leading to major problems (Madelung 1971). After the seventh/thirteenth century a general openness for theological thought of different sectarian origins within the Sunnī spectrum was the norm all over the Middle East. The Seljuqs had a political interest to support scholars of their own geographical background against the local luminaries that might potentially be foci of local political opposition, but the Zengids, Ayyūbīds, and later Mamlūks, tried to present themselves as champions of a united Islam against the crusaders and Mongols (Hillenbrand 1999: 89–256). They therefore followed a more integrative policy. In the East, the Timurid rulers supported talent wherever they could find it without regard for local origin or affiliation, which made their courts a source of patronage not only for artists, but also for theologians of different persuasions. Here, this attitude is, as it seems, not to be attributed to a closing of ranks against external enemies, but rather was an outflow of Mongol ideas of world-rulership and tolerance.

After the conflictual first encounter of Ashʿarites and Māturīdīs, political factors therefore definitely did not stand in the way of theological latitudinarianism among Sunnīs. Nonetheless, the change of relations of both schools should not be explained just as solely the consequence of the broadmindedness of rulers. It also had its sources in the thinking of the theologians themselves. Already in Seljuq times, theologians of a more conciliatory tendency tried to tone down conflicts between the supporters of al-Ashʿarī and al-Māturīdī. Abū l-Yusr al-Pazdawī (d. 493/1100), a leading Māturīdite scholar, thought that although al-Ashʿarī was only second best in comparison with al-Māturīdī, his books were still useful and he and his supporters had to be counted among the *ahl al-sunna* in contrast to the *mujassima* (i.e. those who would put forward an anthropomorphic picture of God, for him the Ḥanbalīs and Karrāmites; van Ess 2011: 780). This alliance of the adherents of rationalizing *kalām* of different persuasions against what was held to be the anthropomorphism of the Ḥanbalīs remained very much alive throughout the centuries (see Section III). As regards the relations between the supporters of al-Ashʿarī and al-Māturīdī, the future did not belong to the hotspurs, but to al-Pazdawī's moderate line. In post-Mongol Iran theologians of different persuasions like al-Taftazānī and al-Jurjānī moved freely between different schools of theological thought and did not restrict themselves to the ideas and books of just one school (van Ess 2009; Madelung 2000; Robinson 1997). The theology of both schools as a consequence became very much intertwined.

A paradigmatic example for the integration of Ashʿarite and Māturīdī theology in the Mamluk Empire is the Egyptian Ashʿarite scholar Tāj al-Dīn al-Subkī's (d. 771/1370) *Nūniyya* poem (Badeen 2008: 14ff.). Here, al-Subkī tried to show that among the thirteen differences of opinion between al-Ashʿarī and al-Māturīdī he identified, seven were of a purely linguistic nature, while the six remaining differences concerned points that in no way justified *takfīr*. Al-Subkī's position was later taken up by Kemalpaşazade who, as a high-ranking member of the Ottoman religious hierarchy and therefore by definition a Māturīdī, in a way gave it official sanction (Badeen 2008: 19ff.). Other Ottoman authors were of the same opinion. But there was even more: Ottoman Ashʿarite and Māturīdī theologians not only agreed to respectfully disagree. Although Ottoman theologians (and their Turkish successors to the present day) would define themselves as followers of al-Māturīdī, their theological thought was heavily influenced by Ashʿarite authors whose writings became one of the bases of theological education within the Ottoman Empire since the ninth/fifteenth century (Ahmed and Filipovic 2004). Alone among the scholars of Mamluk and Ottoman times al-Bayāḍī (d. 1078/1687) stresses the importance of the differences between the schools (Bruckmayr 2009: 70), but his work does not seem to have got him into trouble nor to have spawned a major debate on a topic that for most Sunnī theologians (until our own day) seemed to have been solved.

This does not mean that Mamluk and Ottoman theologians did not have conflicts over minor differences that are typical of learned communities. Authors defined the conflicting points between al-Ashʿarī and al-Māturīdī differently and were at variance with one another concerning certain details. Al-Subkī informs us that the followers of al-Ashʿarī among themselves debate on whether the significant and the signified (*al-ism wa-l-musammā*) are one and the same (Badeen 2008: 18). Famous eleventh/seventeenth-century Ashʿarite scholars like al-Ḥasan al-Yūsī and Ibrāhīm al-Kurānī were at variance on the question of human agency (El-Rouayheb 2005: 17). Debates there were, then, but these, as the foregoing examples show, did not necessarily occur along the fault-lines of existing theological schools and, what is more, remained individual opinions, i.e. did not become identity markers that might relevantly separate religious groups. This being the case, it is no wonder that rulers, after the turbulent beginnings of the Ashʿarite–Māturīdī encounter, refrained from interfering in the business of theologians of both schools (if separate schools indeed they were in this age).

III Ashʿarites, Māturīdīs, and Traditionalists: Social Origins of Religious Conflict?

Thus, the differences between Ashʿarites and Māturīdīs in Mamluk and Ottoman times were of interest only to small circles of the intellectual elite who, as we have seen, furthermore had no interest any more in making them matters of principle. In the religious field, it was other topics than these that in the Mamluk and Ottoman Empires had political and social repercussions: uncompromising *ḥadīth*-orientation that for its enemies smacked of anthropomorphism; the Sufism that is associated with Ibn al-ʿArabī, messianic Sufi groups like the Ḥurūfīs, and more obvious Sufi practices in general; finally, in the Ottoman Empire the question whether *Sharīʿa* or Sultanic practice (*kanun*) should guide the reform of the state.

Of all these questions that were upsetting the religious scene in Mamluk and Ottoman times, only the first could be easily made to fit the patterns of *ʿilm al-kalām*. The others are phenomena of a later age, and their discussion was not part of the conventionalized themes and topics of *kalām* tracts. Already al-Pazdawī had argued against the *mujassima*, real or supposed anthropomorphists, as major enemies of *kalām*, as we have seen. The same holds true for al-Subkī, the author of the famous poem. While reducing the differences between al-Ashʿarī and al-Māturīdī to such a degree as to make them irrelevant, he positioned himself as a staunch enemy of a traditionalism that refused the methods and ideas of Ashʿarite *kalām*, no matter whether its proponents were Shāfiʿīs or Ḥanbalīs. Why should this have been so in an age that put a prime on integrative positions within Sunnism? Radical traditionalism would refuse large parts of the cultural heritage that, like Greek logic, had come to be common sense for the educated classes of Islamic societies and thereby put itself beyond the pale for many. By their violent criticism of iconic figures and usual practices of the Sunnī mainstream the traditionalists invited the enmity of mainstream scholars. These normally avoided the confrontative behaviour of the radical traditionalists. Al-Subkī is a good example of this stance. Even while criticizing the teachings of the *mujassima*, the anthropomorphists, as the radical traditionalists were called, al-Subkī was eager not to disparage Aḥmad b. Ḥanbal (d. 241/855), the figurehead of the movement, himself. As eponym of the generally recognized

Sunnī schools of law and Sunnī protomartyr who had suffered under the *miḥna* of the caliph al-Maʾmūn he was beyond criticism. Al-Subkī had no such qualms when it came to Aḥmad b. Ḥanbal's followers in his own age. In the focus of al-Subkī's criticism we find among other theologians Ibn Taymiyya (d. 728/1328). The radicalism with which the latter refused commonly held assumptions of contemporary Sunnī Muslims (not only with respect to what is called popular religion but also as regards the logical foundation of religious thinking in Aristotelianism) and, even more, his uncompromising insistence on his own solutions made him a nuisance in a scholarly milieu where a culture of tolerance and pluralism held pride of place (Makdisi 1962: 57–79, Badeen 2008: 13, 17; Little 1975).

The cleavage between a strictly *ḥadīth*-minded Islam and the ideas of those who strove to integrate the rationalist elements of Islam's heritage into their worldview continued even after Mamluk times. As in the age of Ibn Taymiyya, the enemies of the scholarly consensus had a tendency to be outsiders in the scholarly community. This holds true for the *ḥadīth*-minded Kadizade-movement in eleventh/seventeenth-century Istanbul that was known for its polemics and sometimes violent action not only against certain forms of Sufism but also against everything else its adherents thought had not existed in the age of the Prophet, amongst other things Aristotelian logic (El-Rouayheb 2008). Both their enmity against common practices of Sufism and their refusal of the logical foundations of mainstream theology since al-Ghazālī's time were things they had in common with Ibn Taymiyya. Although the adherents of the Kadizade-movement at times had supporters in high places and among leading scholars, they more often than not represented people in the middle and lower ranks of the learned hierarchy. Their movement was more or less restricted to Turkish-speaking milieus in the Ottoman Empire (Peters 1987; Berger 2007: 303ff.), but its success during the eleventh/seventeenth century showed that the ideas of Ibn Taymiyya were neither dead, nor restricted to adherents of the Ḥanbalī school. The supporters of the Kadizade-movement were not Ḥanbalīs but Ḥanafīs in law.

Things were coming to a head again in the twelfth/eighteenth century. The Wahhābī challenge to traditional forms of Islamic practice was part of a more general trend of the age, reaching out beyond the Ḥanbalī milieu to other schools like Mālikism. The Moroccan Sultan Muḥammad, very much interested in *ḥadīth*-studies, in the year 1786 repeated the act of his Almoravid predecessors and had the works of al-Ghazālī condemned. Included in this anathema were other great names of traditional Sunnī Islam like the Mālikī scholar Qāḍī ʿIyāḍ (d. 544/1149) and al-Subkī. The Sultan's decree did not gain him many sympathizers in the scholarly milieus of the Ottoman Empire. Al-Zabīdī (d. 1205/1791), one of the leading scholars in the Egypt of his age, felt obliged to answer with a tract written for the purpose (Reichmuth 2009: 78).

It thus seems that traditionalist critics of the scholarly consensus of the times normally came from the margins of the Mamluk and Ottoman *intelligentsia* either in social or in geographical terms. But things were slightly more complicated: Birgivi, the tenth/sixteenth-century scholar who inspired the movement, while certainly of a decisively anti-establishment vein (he had conflicts with Sheykhülislam Ebu Suud over the permissibility of cash-*awqāf* that were even used to finance learned institutions; cf. Mandaville 1979: 303), was himself a proponent of Māturīdī *kalām* and no enemy of the rational sciences (El-Rouayheb 2008). The Wahhābīs, for all their shocking radicalism, were viewed with a sympathetic eye by none other than al-Zabīdī's pupil ʿAbd al-Raḥmān al-Jabartī (d. 1240/1825) who was very much part of the scholarly elite of his time and place. Anyway, the points of conflict between scholars of Ashʿarite and Māturīdī persuasions and traditionalists were normally questions centring on certain aspects of Sufism, not on *kalām* (if we leave aside the repudiation of Aristotelian logic that, as was said before, since at least al-Ghazālī's age had become an integrative part of *kalām* studies).

IV Did *Kalām* Have a Social Function?

Ashʿarite-Māturīdī thought in Mamluk and Ottoman times continued to function on the level that had been attained in the preceding period. This holds true especially for logical studies. As El-Rouayheb has shown recently, there was no decline in the study of logic in Egypt in Ottoman times. Logic was very much alive all through the ages interesting us here (El-Rouayheb 2005; 2008). But for the rest as well, the methods used and the questions asked were more or less the same as those theology had already discussed in the pre-Mamluk period. The answers were not always identical with the solutions of any particular scholar of classical *kalām*, but a recombination of such within relatively strict boundaries.

Classical Islamic theology was born not least as an answer to political and social problems of the early Islamic community. The politico-religious problems of Mamluk and Ottoman times, by contrast, could only to a small degree be addressed by the classical canon of *kalām*. Of course, the prevailing attitude of accepting all kinds of Sunnī theological thinking eased the integration of Arab and Central Asian/Turkish scholars within the scholarly communities of the Middle East. But this might as well have been brought about by simply forgetting about *kalām* as a science. The compromise-solutions *mutakallimūn* like al-Subkī produced to certain questions that caused conflict (and indeed his polemics against the *mujassima*) would never have been necessary had there been no *mutakallimūn* around to ask such questions.

Why then did Mamluk and Ottoman *kalām* conserve the paradigm of classical theology to a large degree? The preservation of *kalām* as a science in the way described shows that it did serve a social need. The Aristotelian logic that was part of the education of theologians (and jurists) helped Ottoman scholars to confound their heretical (and at times Christian; on this Berger 2007: 202ff.) rivals, to the satisfaction of rulers and fellow scholars. But in the last resort, even this seems to be a wrong track. To keep the Christians in their place was more a question of military might than of theological argument. And as regards heresy within Islam, theologians of the age were not really interested in keeping abreast with the latest developments in the field. In the same way that they remained true to the paradigms of classical *kalām*, they held fast to the heresiographical patterns of an earlier age. They did not produce new lists of false teachings to add to the classical heresiographical catalogues, but stuck to what the classics in the field had to say (van Ess 2011: 1151ff.). The messianic movements that were so active and prominent in the period did not enter the scholarly worldview insofar as it was taught in the *madrasas*. Be this as it may, there must have been something else to the continuing study of theology in Mamluk and Ottoman *madrasas* than its obviously limited usefulness in understanding a changing world.

The repetition of classical questions and answers with (mostly) the consciousness that there were only minor variations to what others had said before on the topic provided the scholarly community with a sense of stability as regards the fundamentals of the faith. As *kalām* was not a field of heated debate any more, the recognized and tolerated existence of differences of opinion on points that were of secondary importance for contemporaries was no problem for social peace. In a way a similar thing held true for the classical canon of heresies that scholars could, if they were interested, learn about in the *madrasas*. It may have reassured people to classify new heresies as cases already known and therefore a solved problem.

Another point seems to have been even more important: proof of theological knowledge was part and parcel of the academic credentials of scholars and therefore their social standing. To know about the central topoi of *kalām* was something even beginners were expected to have learned from texts like the creed the eleventh/seventeenth-century Egyptian scholar al-Laqānī composed in the form of a poem, easy to memorize. For the more aspiring, to have a thoroughgoing knowledge of *kalām* and its methods and questions was obviously still an important asset. This knowledge could be proved by producing texts within the scholarly tradition of *kalām*, texts that although they stuck to the classical paradigm of the science, were not always devoid of new and intelligent ideas in detail. The importance of knowledge of *kalām* for a person hoping to be part of the elite of the learned classes is obvious in the contacts of al-Zabīdī, the leading Egyptian scholar of the late twelfth/eighteenth century whom we have already met. Among the people in his environment more are noted for their interest in questions of *kalām* (53) than in Qurʾānic studies (41) (Reichmuth 2009: 200ff.).

The science of *kalām* thus had a crucial function in the social world of Mamluk and Ottoman notables, but this function was independent of the social or political relevance of the topics discussed by the scholars. Thereby Mamluk and Ottoman *kalām* could safely remain within the boundaries of a paradigm stemming from a different epoch without losing its usefulness.

Bibliography

Ahmed, S., and N. Filipovic (2004). 'The Sultan's Syllabus: A Curriculum for the Ottoman Imperial medreses Prescribed in a fermān of Qānūnī I Süleymān, Dated 973 (1565)'. *Studia Islamica* 98/99: 183–218.

Badeen, E. (2008). *Sunnitische Theologie in osmanischer Zeit*. Würzburg: Ergon.
Berger, L. (2007). *Gesellschaft und Individuum in Damaskus 1550–1791*. Würzburg: Ergon.
Berkey, J. (1992). *The Transmission of Knowledge in Medieval Cairo: A Social History of Islamic Education*. Princeton: Princeton University Press.
Bruckmayr, P. (2009). 'The Spread and Persistence of Maturidi [sic] Kalām and Underlying Dynamics'. *Iran and the Caucasus* 13: 59–92.
Cahen, C. (1959). *Mouvements populaires et autonomisme urbain dans l'Asie musulmane du moyen âge*. Leiden: Brill.
Chamberlain, M. (1994). *Knowledge and Social Practice in Medieval Damascus, 1190–1350*. Cambridge: Cambridge University Press.
van Ess, J. (2009). 'Jorjānī, Zayn-al-Dīn Abu'l-Ḥasan ʿAlī'. <http://www.iranicaonline.org/articles/jorjani-zayn-al-din-abul-hasan-ali>.
van Ess, J. (2011). *Der Eine und das Andere: Beobachtungen an islamischen häresiographischen Texten*. Berlin: de Gruyter.
Hillenbrand, C. (1999). *The Crusades: Islamic Perspectives*. Edinburgh: Edinburgh University Press.
Kafadar, C. (1995). *Between Two Worlds: The Construction of the Ottoman State*. Berkeley: University of California Press.
Klein, D. (2007). *Die osmanischen Ulema des 17. Jahrhunderts: Eine geschlossene Gesellschaft?* Berlin: Klaus Schwarz.
Köse, S. (1998). 'Hocazâde Muslihuddin Efendi'. *Türkiye Diyanet Vakfı İslam Ansiklopedisi*. Istanbul: Türkiye Diyanet Vakfı İslam Araştırmaları Merkezi, 18: 207–9.
Little, D. (1975). 'Did Ibn Taymiyya have a Screw Loose?' *Studia Islamica* 41: 93–111.
Madelung, W. (1971). 'The Spread of Maturidism and the Turks'. *Actas do IV Congresso de Estudos Arabes e Islamicos 1968*. Leiden: Brill, 109–68.
Madelung, W. (2000). 'Taftazani'. *Encyclopaedia of Islam*. New edn. Leiden: Brill, x. 88f.
Makdisi, G. (1962). 'Ashʿari and the Ashʿarites in Islamic Religious History'. *Studia Islamica* 17: 37–80.
Mandaville, J. E. (1979). 'The Cash Waqf Controversy in the Ottoman Empire'. *International Journal of Middle East Studies* 10: 289–308.
Ocak, A. Y. (1998). *Osmanlı Toplumunda Zındıklar ve Mülhidler (15.–17. Yüzyıllar)*. Istanbul: Tarih Vakfı Yurt Yaınları.
Peters, R. (1987). 'The Battered Dervishes of Bab Zuwayla: A Religious Riot in Eighteenth-Century Cairo'. In N. Levtzion and J. O. Voll (eds.), *Eighteenth-Century Renewal and Reform in Islam*. Syracuse: Syracuse University Press, 93–115.
Rafeq, A.-K. (1999). 'Relations between the Syrian ʿulamāʾ and the Ottoman State in the Eighteenth Century'. *Oriente Moderno* 79: 67–95.
Reichmuth, S. (2009). *The World of Murtaḍā al-Zabidi (1732–1791): Life, Networks and Writings*. Cambridge: Gibb Memorial Trust.
Robinson, F. (1997). 'Ottomans Safavids Mughals: Shared Knowledge and Connective Systems'. *Journal of Islamic Studies* 8: 151–84.
El-Rouayheb, K. (2005). 'Was There a Revival of Logical Studies in Eighteenth-Century Egypt?' *Die Welt des Islams* 45: 1–19.
El-Rouayheb, K. (2008). 'The Myth of "The Triumph of Fanaticism" in the Seventeenth-Century Ottoman Empire'. *Die Welt des Islams* 48: 196–221.
Rudolph, U. (1997). *Al-Maturidi und die sunnitische Theologie in Samarkand*. Leiden: Brill.

Talmon-Heller, D. (2005). 'Fidelity, Cohesion, and Continuity within Madhhabs in Zangid and Ayyubid Syria'. In P. Bearman et al. (ed.), *The Islamic School of Law: Evolution, Devolution, and Progress*. Cambridge, MA: Harvard University Press, 94–116.

Yazıcıoğlu, M. S. (1990). *Le Kalâm et son rôle dans la société turco-ottomane aux XVe et XVIe siècles*. Ankara: Kültür Bakanlığı Yayınları.

Zilfi, M. (1988). *The Politics of Piety: The Ottoman Ulema 1600–1800*. Chicago: Bibliotheca Islamica.

PART V

ISLAMIC THEOLOGICAL THOUGHT FROM THE END OF THE EARLY MODERN PERIOD TO THE MODERN PERIOD

CHAPTER 40

MAIN TRENDS OF ISLAMIC THEOLOGICAL THOUGHT FROM THE LATE NINETEENTH CENTURY TO PRESENT TIMES

ROTRAUD WIELANDT

I Preliminary Clarifications

Theology in the present context is not equivalent to religious thought in general, so that it would, for instance, include theories of state and society or trends of political ideology advocated on the grounds of supposed requirements of religion. Therefore debates in such fields will be left out of consideration here. Theology is about doctrines of faith and the normative texts and methodological principles they are based on.

What Muslim scholars understand nowadays by theology when using this term or its Turkish equivalent *ilahiyat*, is not confined to *kalām* in its traditional sense. Hence the following overview will be based on a broader concept of theology: theology is defined here as the systematic rational reflection on and discussion of the tenets of the Islamic faith, as well as their foundations and the methods by which their knowledge is attained. In addition, the term 'theology' will deliberately not be restricted to the ideas of persons holding a degree of a faculty of theology or belonging to the ranks of professional religious scholars. This approach takes account of the fact that since the second half of the nineteenth century quite a few substantial contributions to Islamic theological thought were made by intellectuals mainly trained in fields outside theology.

II Innovation: Its Origins and Limits

From the late nineteenth century, a number of Muslim thinkers became fully aware of the new challenges arising for Islamic theology from the dominance of European colonial powers, as well as from Western-type modern civilization with its science, technical achievements, and political and social values. But were the responses of Islamic theology to these challenges equally new? And if so, did this result from the adoption of modern Western patterns of thought or from endogenous developments? With regard to these questions a complex picture emerges.

(a) The Question of Indigenous Roots of Islamic Modernism

One of the main trends in reacting to the impact of modern Europe—a trend that manifested itself not only in theology, but also, and even more, in legal thought and in educational projects—has been commonly called 'Islamic modernism' (since Goldziher 1920: 310–70, whose terminology was followed by Adams 1933 and Gibb 1947: 39–84). In its early phase, which lasted in some regions until the interwar period, this trend was characterized by the following features: a strong emphasis on the rationality of Islam; criticism of popular beliefs and religious practices rated as superstitious; rejection of blind acceptance (*taqlīd*, lit. 'imitation') of opinions held by prominent scholars of previous generations, and advocacy of seeking solutions by independent reasoning (*ijtihād*); appreciation of new knowledge and cultural progress; the zest to demonstrate that Islamic faith is fully compatible with modern science and most of the other values of modern Western civilization, or that Islam is even the driving force behind scientific progress; a turn towards an anthropocentric worldview, and an activist ethos in which developing one's own potentialities, educational and social reform, and shaping a prosperous future here on earth rank high.

Many modernists justified these positions as being nothing but the necessary return to the pure Islam of the righteous forefathers (*al-salaf al-ṣāliḥ*), i.e. Islam as it had originally been understood before its corruption by harmful misinterpretations and external influences. This is why the early modernists were partly called *salafiyya*, adherents of the ancestors, a term later applied to various other groups, too. On the other hand, the attention Islamic modernism has attracted among Western scholars was for a long time primarily due to the assumed novelty of its aspirations and to the fact that this novelty was one-sidedly attributed to the modernists' readiness to borrow contemporary Western ideas.

Meanwhile, a more differentiated assessment of the origins of modernist thought has come into reach. Since the 1970s, several authors have suggested a hitherto neglected degree of continuity between the views of some well-known reformers, revivalist movements, or newly founded Sufi orders of the eighteenth and early nineteenth century on the one hand and the ideas of late nineteenth-century modernists on the other hand. In fact, if R. Schulze's views concerning an Islamic Enlightenment (see Schulze 1990, Schulze 1994, and Schulze 1996) stood up to critical scrutiny (see, for instance, the critique of Hagen and Seidensticker 1998), and if the so-called Neo-Sufi movements were really marked by all the characteristics ascribed to them (O'Fahey and Radtke 1993: 57), it would be plausible that the roots of Islamic modernism are to be found mainly in Islamic tradition itself. Yet the kind of rationalism characterizing some eighteenth- and early nineteenth-century reformers is not simply identical with that of the later modernists, which was largely inspired by the ideas of European Enlightenment; the ideal of illuminated rationality cherished by eighteenth- and early nineteenth-century Sufis has little to do with autonomy of reason; these Sufis' efforts of introspection and self-conditioning are not tantamount to subjectivism, and their quest for uniting with Muḥammad's spirit cannot be regarded as indicating a propensity for more this-worldliness (O'Fahey and Radtke 1993; Radtke 1994), as has been claimed.

It is impossible to reduce what makes Islamic modernism modern to views of eighteenth- and early nineteenth-century Muslim predecessors. However, one cannot reduce it to Western influences either: Islamic intellectual history has its own traditions of highly developed rationality, especially in the fields of *kalām* and philosophy, but also in Islamic theosophical mysticism (cf. Radtke 2002: 369). These indigenous traditions of rationality provided Muslim thinkers with a stock of analytical categories and an intellectual training suitable for interacting with the stimuli coming from the modern West. They could serve as a bridge to innovative theological thought even where they did not yet engender a palpably modern theology in themselves.

An early example of this can be found in the thought of Amir ʿAbd al-Qādir al-Jazāʾirī (1808–83) who contributed much to the emergence of the reformist Syrian *salafiyya* during his exile in Damascus. Two of his works, *al-Miqrāḍ al-ḥādd li-qaṭʿ lisān man yantaqiṣu dīn al-islām bi-l-bāṭil wa-l-ilḥād* (1848) and *Dhikrā l-ʿāqil wa-tanbīh al-ghāfil* (1855) (Commins 1988: 121–4; Weismann 2001b: 157–62; cf. also, with restrictions, Neufend 2012), attest to a high esteem of reason (ʿAbd al-Qādir, *Miqrāḍ*, 9–10). ʿAbd al-Qādir rejects *taqlīd* (ʿAbd al-Qādir, *Dhikrā*, 31–3; cf. Commins 1988: 123) as well as the idea that relevant knowledge cannot be increased beyond what was already known by the ancestors. 'The results of thinking', he stresses, 'do not stop at any boundary, and the procedures of individual intellects are limitless', because 'the spiritual world is as wide as the overflowing sea, and divine emanation never breaks off or comes to an end' (ʿAbd al-Qādir, *Dhikrā*, 129; cf. Weismann 2001b: 161). Here it becomes clear that his open-mindedness for new scientific developments was based on the theosophy of Ibn al-ʿArabī (d. 638/1240), of whom he was an adherent and knowledgeable interpreter (Weismann 2001b: 162–92).

Yet ʿAbd al-Qādir was far from attributing to reason a role comparable to that which it had gained in the ambit of European Enlightenment. In his view, as for the moral principles and the details of religious belief and practice on whose observance happiness in this world and the hereafter depends, reason cannot but rely on the superior knowledge of the prophets. ʿAbd al-Qādir deemed it best to keep modern scientific rationality completely out of Islamic religious scholarship. Nevertheless, his appreciation of reason and his dynamic concept of knowledge had an important share in shaping the innovative theological approach of Jamāl al-Dīn al-Qāsimī, a representative of the second generation of the Syrian *salafiyya*.

A similar bridging function can be observed in the case of Jamāl al-Dīn al-Afghānī (1838–97): he did not develop substantially new theological ideas. However, his student Muḥammad ʿAbduh (1849–1905) profited from his profound familiarity with the rational traditions of *kalām*, Islamic philosophy, and theosophical Sufism; this facilitated ʿAbduh's access to some elements of Enlightenment rationality.

The innovation in theological treatises written since the late nineteenth century results from their authors' efforts to reason out fundamental doctrines of Islam in the framework of their current cultural horizon. Of this horizon Western modernity had become part, but at the same time it still comprised many possible sources of inspiration contained in Islamic tradition itself.

(b) The Lasting Predominance of Traditional Approaches in Academic Theology

Despite the emergence of a modernist trend, the institutional basis and social impact of innovative Islamic theology have remained quite limited over the past 150 years. In most Islamic countries academic theology does not yet differ substantially from what religious scholars used to produce in this field several hundred years ago. Islamic theology looks for the most part by no means 'modern' so far. When theologians try to refute the views of adversaries, the latter are often the representatives of schools of thought that reached their heyday in times long past. Thus, for example, most textbooks of *kalām* published in Arab countries for the use of university students still discuss and rebut Muʿtazilī positions at great length, whereas specifically contemporary challenges to Islamic dogma such as the problem of how to interpret the Qurʾānic concept of creation in view of the findings of modern science, or the question of the possible relevance of recent developments in philosophical anthropology, hermeneutics, or epistemology for the way of dealing with theological problems, are virtually absent.

The scarcity of innovation in professional academic theology can partly be explained by the fact that modernists advocating *ijtihād* in questions of Islamic law or welcoming recent achievements in natural sciences and technology were not necessarily ready to accept or even promote new ideas in theological matters, too. Besides, some modernists were simply not interested in *kalām* or were explicitly hostile to it.

The dichotomy of the educational systems in Islamic countries during the nineteenth and early twentieth centuries favoured the so far strongly traditional character of academic theology. In order to train experts in the secular sciences needed for building modern states that would be able to defend themselves against European powers, or to regain independence from them, separate Western-type secular institutions of education were set up in the Ottoman Empire, Egypt, Tunisia, and elsewhere besides the traditional religious ones. As a result of this bifurcation of the educational system, prospective religious scholars were for a long time generally much less exposed to intellectual challenges coming from the modern West than young people studying in the new secular institutions. At the same time, the members of the new intellectual elite emerging from the secular schools became competitors of the *ʿulamāʾ*, ousting them from important spheres of public life, such as the judiciary and the educational sector. This increased the tendency among the *ʿulamāʾ* to claim the superiority of their own traditional knowledge and to underrate the relevance of dealing with new questions and ideas.

The reception of new theological approaches was also hampered by the fact that prominent pioneers of modernist thought were reputed to cooperate with the colonial powers and thus often suspected of undermining Islam for the benefit of the 'infidels'. Sir Sayyid Ahmad Khan (on him see below Section III a) accepted British rule and advocated the spread of contemporary British culture in India. Muḥammad ʿAbduh was on friendly terms with the British authorities in Egypt after his return from exile in 1888. In view of the increasing national consciousness among Egyptian intellectuals, this, together with the resistance of his conservative colleagues, led to his marginalization in the last years of his life. Following his death, his works were simply ignored in Egyptian publications for more than two decades (Haddad 1998: 26, 30f., 33, 38). Moreover, all early modernist attempts to develop new theological concepts were perceived as reactions to European supremacy and thus as imposed from outside. This impeded their reception.

(c) The Exceptional Case of Contemporary Turkish University Theology

Part of contemporary Turkish university theology has moved on from the prevailing traditionalism. This was facilitated by the far-reaching break-off of the traditional theological studies in Turkey since the early days of the Kemalist era, a development that prompted the emergence of a new type of religious learning.

The *medreses*, Turkey's time-honoured schools of Islamic law and theology, were closed down in 1924. As a substitute for the most renowned one among them, the Süleymaniye Medresesi, a Faculty of Divinity (İlâhiyat Fakültesi) was opened at the University of Istanbul (at that time still called Darülfünun). It was meant to be in the vanguard of promoting a new type of religious education based on modern scientific thought and geared to the needs of the secular Republic. However, it could not function sustainably due to the lack of sufficiently prepared students, after teaching Arabic had been abolished in secondary schools since 1929. In 1933 it was replaced by an Institute of Islamic Studies attached to the Department of Oriental Studies of the Faculty of Letters of the same university (Jäschke 1951 and 1953: 121f.; Lewis 1968: 414f.). The institute did not survive more than three years and with it academic theology lost its last institutional shelter in Turkey.

In 1949 a new Faculty of Divinity was founded at the University of Ankara, followed by more than twenty similar faculties that were established all over Turkey in subsequent years. The new foundation explicitly aimed at creating a new type of theology working towards an enlightened Islam and engaging in dialogue with modern science rather than reviving the *medrese* tradition (Koştaş 1999: 150f.; Körner 2005: 48–57).

When the new İlâhiyat Fakültesi opened, there were not many employable representatives of the ancient elite of religious scholars left. The educational background of its founding faculty was accordingly diverse. Some had studied *uṣūl al-dīn* or Islamic law abroad (in Iraq, Bosnia), or had earned degrees in philosophy, history, or various Oriental languages, some had obtained doctoral degrees in Islamic Studies or Comparative Religion in Central or Western Europe. Promising junior scholars were often sent to foreign universities in Europe, North America, or the Near East for further qualification. The resulting different perspectives and methodological outlooks proved to be a fertile ground for raising theologians able and willing to tread new paths. As a result, Turkey has witnessed the growth of a type of theological reasoning which has a sound grasp of developments in contemporary humanities, although more traditional orientations still subsist concurrently there.

III Pioneers of Modernism

(a) Sayyid Ahmad Khan

The first Muslim thinker to promote many of the above-mentioned modernist ideas was the Indian Sir Sayyid Ahmad Khan (1817–98), the founder of the Muhammadan Anglo Oriental College in Aligarh and the educational movement named after its location (for him see esp. Ahmad 1967: 31–56, Troll 1978b, Malik 1980, Chaghatai 2005). Brought up in Delhi, he was not a religious scholar formally trained at a *madrasa*, but acquired his education by private tuition and self-study. His young years brought him into contact with three different reformist traditions: his parents had close connections to the Mujaddidī branch of the Naqshbandiyya; he studied the writings of Shāh Walī Allāh of Delhi (1703–62) and came in touch with his descendants who still carried on his teachings at that time, and he was also impressed by the ideas of the Mujāhidūn movement of Sayyid Aḥmad Barelwī (1796–1831) with its focus on the principle of *tawḥīd* (monotheism) and the rejection of superstitious innovations (*bidaʿ*) (Troll 1978b: 30–6). He later described his own development as that of an originally traditional Muslim who after some time adopted a Wahhābī-like position and finally became a Muʿtazilite (Troll 1978b: 37).

By relating himself to the Muʿtazila, Sayyid Ahmad Khan mainly hinted at his strong confidence in the capacity of reason, a result of his increasing familiarity with the cultural background of the representatives of British colonial rule, in whose judiciary he had served before the Mutiny Uprising of 1856/7. He admired the modern scientific civilization on which Britain's supremacy and prosperity rested, and he deemed it his mission to help young Indian Muslims to an education enabling them to participate in this civilization.

Notwithstanding, Islam always remained the true religion for him. In his days, the superiority of Christianity was intensively being propagated in Northern India by the Anglican Church Mission Society (CMS). Its members, among them the German protestant pastor Carl Gottlieb Pfander (1803–65), engaged in fierce debates with local Muslim scholars (Troll 1976: 212f.; Troll 1978b: 64–9). Sayyid Ahmad Khan looked for an indisputable criterion on which the decision on the competing claims to truth raised by the different religions could be based. He found it in the degree of rationality of a given religion and its congruence with nature (*Khuṭubāt-i Aḥmadiyya*, trans. in Troll 1978b: Appendix 246). At the same time, he was looking for a new interpretation of Islam enabling English-trained, science-minded young Indian Muslims to remain proud of their religion (see esp. *Lecture on Islam* 1884, trans. in Troll 1978b: Appendix 314).

Sayyid Ahmad Khan tried to demonstrate that and why the statements of the Qurʾān and the findings of modern science are in perfect harmony. In his *Tabyīn al-kalām* he explained that nature—God's Work—and the Qurʾān—God's Word—cannot contradict each other. This argument was most probably borrowed from John H. Pratt (1809–71), then Anglican archdeacon of Calcutta, who had used the same formula with respect to the Bible (Troll 1976: 222 with n. 23; Troll 1978b: 155). In Sayyid Ahmad Khan's view, the findings of modern natural sciences constitute inalterable certainties. Consequently, they are the touchstone for what has to be regarded as truth. Whenever Qurʾānic statements seem not to match them, these cannot be taken literally but must be reinterpreted, for example metaphorically. Sayyid Ahmad Khan's assumption of a necessary harmony between the revealed Word of God and scientific knowledge is underpinned by the idea that both are related by the same God-given order of the material and spiritual world. For him, this order is equivalent to 'the law of nature', part of which can be detected in God's creation by scientific research, while another part has been revealed in the Qurʾān.

His understanding of 'nature' and the 'law of nature' is not without ambiguities. Mostly he seems to have meant by 'nature' the entirety of what exists apart from God (Troll 1976: 226; Troll 1977/1978a: 262; Troll 1978b: 175–7), while his notion of the 'law of nature' included both regularities on the level of facts of the material world and normative precepts designed to direct human behaviour (*Khuṭubāt-i Aḥmadiyya*, trans. in Troll 1978b: Appendix 246). Although such precepts are obviously not always followed, he postulated the universal and inevitable effectiveness of the natural law: everything in the universe is determined by the principle of causality. All single causal links follow laws; the sum total of the laws regulating the causal connections constitutes the law of nature.

On this basis, Sayyid Ahmad Khan denied the existence of supernatural phenomena and of miracles breaking the natural course of things. In his *Tafsīr al-Qurʾān* (published 1880–5), he took great pains to demonstrate that miraculous events narrated in the holy text can be explained by natural causes. In cases of unusual occurrences for which such an explanation was not immediately at hand, he supposed that the underlying causes and laws are still unknown, but might be discovered later.

But was not the angel Gabriel through whom the Prophet Muhammad received revelation a supernatural apparition? Sayyid Ahmad Khan solved this problem by developing a new concept of revelation (commentary on Qurʾān 2: 23 in *Tafsīr al-Qurʾān*, vol. 1, trans. in Troll 1978b: Appendix 279–83; 'on revelation and inspiration' [1880], trans. in Troll 1978b: 290–1; *Khudā kā kalām* [1897], trans. in Troll 1978b: 248–51; cf. also Troll 1976: 228–36; Troll 1978b: 183–8): revelation does not entail a supernatural being approaching the prophet with a message from God. Prophecy is rather a natural mental ability enabling the prophet to receive directly what God is willing to reveal to him; or, as Sayyid Ahmad Khan once put it in Sufic terms, the prophet's heart mirrors God's self-manifestations (*tajalliyāt*) (*Tafsīr al-Qurʾān*, vol. 1, trans. in Troll 1978b: Appendix 282). Gabriel, explicitly mentioned in the Qurʾān as the bringer of revelation (Qurʾān 2: 97), is nothing but a word designating this natural ability of the prophetic mind. This kind of faculty is not confined to prophets, but only in the case of the prophets does it attain its maximum. Thus they brim over with their revealed knowledge and promulgate it in a metaphorical language bestowed on them directly by God. In this understanding of prophecy Sayyid Ahmad Khan is closer to Islamic philosophers like al-Fārābī and Ibn Sīnā than to the tradition of *kalām* (Troll 1978b: 191–3).

Sayyid Ahmad Khan admits that the Qurʾān's inimitability (*iʿjāz*) in terms of language and style will not convince non-Muslims and doubters of its divine origin and of the superiority of Islam (Troll 1978b: 189–90). The decisive argument in favour of Islam lies in the fact that the teachings of the Qurʾān match with human nature (*fiṭra*) in a uniquely perfect way (Abdul Khaliq 1980b). This can, he claims, be substantiated by rational proofs.

The markedly rationalist tendency permeating Sayyid Ahmad Khan's thought is neither primarily inspired by the Muʿtazila, nor can it be sufficiently explained by the influence of Islamic philosophers. Its conspicuous features—his trust in scientific reason, his insistence on the universal validity of the laws of nature, and his inclination towards discarding all interpretations not fitting into their framework—can, together with the emphasis he placed on education, be explained by the impact of the European Enlightenment and its nineteenth-century positivist offshoots that had reached India through British presence. Among the sources that possibly inspired him was the British utilitarian philosopher John Stuart Mill (1806–73), who had worked for the British East India Company in the years 1823–58 (Reetz 1987/8: 213–18).

Sayyid Ahmad Khan shares the deistic tendency of well-known thinkers of the Enlightenment: he believes that God, whose existence as *prima causa* can be proven in his view, does not interfere in the events of this world after creation, having predetermined everything, including the appearance and the messages of prophets throughout history, by causal links from the beginning (Troll 1978b: 199–202 and 192; Abdul Khaliq 1980a).

He repeatedly states the unity of God's attributes with His essence—a specifically Muʿtazilī notion (e.g. *Tabyīn al-kalām*, extract trans. in Troll 1978b: Appendix 236–7; 'Iʿtiqādī bi-llāh', published in *al-Akhlāq*, 1873, trans. Troll 1978b: Appendix 269; Lecture on Islam, given in Lahore 1884, trans. Troll 1978b: Appendix 320). In accordance with the Muʿtazilites he rejects ethical voluntarism, arguing that the basic norms for evaluating human actions can be known by reason and exist objectively and permanently, not only due to revealed commands that can be altered by God at will ('Iʿtiqādī bi-llāh', trans. in Troll 1978b: Appendix 274; 'Fifteen Principles Submitted to the *ʿulamāʾ* of Saharanpur', 1873/1874, trans. Troll 1978b: Appendix 277).

However, his position concerning free will or predestination is clearly not Muʿtazilite: he holds that all human actions correspond to the will of God, their *prima causa*, being determined by causal links from the beginning of creation of which they form part. At the same time he declares that man is, within the limits set by immutable nature, free to choose his actions (Troll 1978b: 203f.). Neither the determinist component of this concept nor the idea of immutable nature limiting human freedom agree with Muʿtazilī doctrine; for most of the Muʿtazilites, something like 'nature' did not even exist (van Ess 1997: 457f.). Nor does Sayyid Ahmad Khan employ the 'orthodox' theory of *kasb* (as affirmed by Baljon 1949: 86 n. 6). He avoids an in-depth analysis of the problem of how to understand the synergy of divine determination and human freedom.

(b) Muḥammad ʿAbduh

1 *al-Afghānī's place in ʿAbduh's intellectual biography*

When Jamāl al-Dīn al-Afghānī (1838/9–1897) settled in Cairo in 1871, Muḥammad ʿAbduh (*c.*1849–1905) (see esp. Adams 1933, Amīn 1944, Haddad 1994, Kügelgen 2007), the son of a peasant in a village of the Nile Delta, was already a student at al-Azhar. Yet he had largely retreated from the courses there, disappointed by the teaching methods, and was now pursuing the Sufi path into which he had been initiated by one of his uncles. Soon after al-Afghānī's arrival, ʿAbduh began to attend his private lectures in *kalām*, philosophy, and Sufism (ʿAbduh, *Aʿmāl*, 2: 332 and 349; Riḍā, *Tārīkh*, 1: 24). According to ʿAbduh's reports, al-Afghānī revealed unprecedented dimensions of knowledge to him (cf. preface to ʿAbduh, *al-Wāridāt*, in al-Afghānī, *Āthār*, 2–3: 49–50; cf. also al-Afghānī, *Aʿmāl*, 2: 333; for al–Afghānī's teaching activities in Cairo and their impact on Azharī students esp. Kudsi-Zadeh 1971: 6–10).

His lectures focused on those parts of Islamic tradition which had been of particular importance in his own education. Contrary to his assertions, he was of Iranian origin and had been educated as an Imāmī, first at a *madrasa* in Qazwin and then, after a short stay in Tehran, in the Iraqian shrine cities, mainly in Najaf (Keddie 1972: 15–19; Davison 1988: 110). In this way he had also acquired 'a considerable knowledge of the philosophers, particularly the Persian ones, including Avicenna, Naṣīr al-Dīn Ṭūsī and others, and of Sufism', as was testified by those who knew him in his student days

(Keddie 1972: 17–18). He was also well acquainted with Shaykhism, whose theosophical speculation combines elements of rationalist philosophy and mysticism and makes use of Avicennian concepts as well as of the ideas of Mullā Ṣadrā (1572–1640) and his school (Keddie 1972: 19–20). This line of philosophical tradition had always remained alive in Iran. Its mystical component particularly appealed to ʿAbduh after he had affiliated to Sufism. At the same time, its strong emphasis on the use of reason facilitated access to the rationality of Enlightenment and the modern sciences based on it. Al-Afghānī and ʿAbduh were in contact with ideas of the Enlightenment already in the second half of the 1870s, after both of them had been admitted to a Cairene Masonic lodge (cf. ʿAbduh's testimony in *al-Manār*, 8, 1905: 402).

ʿAbduh remained closely attached to al-Afghānī until the latter's expulsion from Egypt in 1879. He spent most of his own exile since the end of 1882 in Beirut, but in 1884 he temporarily joined al-Afghānī in Paris where both published the well-known Pan-Islamist journal *al-ʿUrwa al-wuthqā* for eight months. Otherwise, he kept in touch with al-Afghānī by correspondence. They were estranged from each other only when ʿAbduh returned to Egypt in 1888, gradually coming to an arrangement with the British overlords there.

2 *The problem of the textual basis for studying ʿAbduh's theology*

The textual basis for studying ʿAbduh's theology has been the subject of intensive debate since the 1970s due to diverging opinions on the authenticity of two works published under his name: *Risālat al-Wāridāt fī sirr al-tajalliyāt* (1st edn. printed posthumously 1908 in vol. 2 of Riḍā's *Tārīkh* under the misleading title *Risālat al-Wāridāt fī naẓariyyāt al-mutakallimīn wa-l-ṣūfiyya fī l-falsafa al-ilāhiyya*), a mystical treatise expounding a cosmology and prophetology based on the concept of *waḥdat al-wujūd* and illuminationist philosophy, and *al-Taʿlīqāt ʿalā sharḥ al-Dawānī li-l-ʿaqāʾid al-ʿaḍudiyya* (completed in 1876; first published in 1904), a series of glosses on selected passages of Jalāl al-Dīn al-Dawānī's (d. 908/1502) commentary on a brief creed by ʿAḍud al-Dīn al-Ījī (d. 756/1356).

Muḥammad ʿAmāra argued that the two works were not authored by ʿAbduh but by al-Afghānī, with the exception of twenty-two footnotes in *al-Taʿlīqāt* signed with ʿAbduh's name. According to ʿAmāra's assumption, al-Afghānī had dictated the *Risālat al-Wāridāt* to ʿAbduh, while the *Taʿlīqāt* consisted of lectures given by al-Afghānī, written down and edited by ʿAbduh (al-Afghānī, *Aʿmāl*, 2nd edn., 1: 155–66; ʿAbduh, *Aʿmāl*, 1: 206–8). Among ʿAmāra's numerous arguments for this hypothesis is his observation that many passages of *al-Taʿlīqāt* show the stylistic features of oral presentation and that ʿAbduh had listed al-Dawānī's *ʿAqāʾid* among the works he had studied with al-Afghānī (Riḍā, *Tārīkh*, 1: 26), probably referring to the commentary on which the glosses are based. ʿAmāra therefore omitted the two texts when preparing his edition of Abduh's works, and he included the *Taʿlīqāt* in his incomplete second edition of al-Afghānī's writings.

Mohamed Haddad contradicted ʿAmāra, expressing the view that both works had in fact been authored by ʿAbduh (Haddad 1994: 82–5, 88–94; Haddad 2000: 62f.); he even maintained that *al-Taʿlīqāt* was 'the most important one of ʿAbduh's theological writings' (Haddad 1994: 86). However in 1996/7, ʿAmāra's judgement found a new supporter in the Iranian scholar Sayyid Hādī Khusraw Shāhī, who had discovered new evidence of al-Afghānī's authorship. Among al-Afghānī's personal papers preserved in the Majlis Archives in Tehran he had discovered a manuscript of the *Risālat al-Wāridāt*, bearing a note by Ibrāhīm al-Laqqānī, al-Afghānī's second-closest Egyptian disciple after ʿAbduh (ʿAnḥūrī, *Siḥr*, 181–5; Riḍā, *Tārīkh*, 274; Kudsi-Zadeh 1980: 53), in which he said that he finished copying the treatise in early 1291/1874 and was sending it 'to its author' with his greetings (al-Afghānī, *Āṯār*, 2: preface, 11 and fig. 2). Moreover, ʿAbduh states in his preface to the *Risāla* that it contains a detailed exposition of general concepts (*kulliyyāt*) which al-Afghānī had taught his disciples in 1290 AH (ʿAbduh, *Wāridāt*, 2). On this basis, Shāhī concluded that the content of the treatise originated with al-Afghānī, its main author, while ʿAbduh's task was only that of wording and redacting it (al-Afghānī, *Āthār*, 2, preface, 1212), which means that he has to be considered as its secondary co-author. Shāhī accordingly published the *Risālat al-Wāridāt* in a volume of al-Afghānī's writings entitled *Rasāʾil al-falsafa wa-l-ʿirfān* (Tehran 1417/1996–7) and again in his own edition of al-Afghānī's Arabic works. As for the *Taʿlīqāt*, he regarded them, in accordance with ʿAmāra, as lectures of al-Afghānī written down and edited by ʿAbduh; he also included them in this edition, again mentioning ʿAbduh as their secondary co-author.

A closer examination of the various arguments yields the following picture: Shāhī's assumption that ʿAbduh's contribution to these works was confined to the above-mentioned role cannot be rejected out of hand, although in the prefaces to both of them ʿAbduh introduces himself as the author: al-Afghānī, who was almost as fluent in Arabic as in his native Persian according to witnesses (Keddie 1966: 519), was known for his preference to dictate his thoughts to his disciples rather than to write them down himself when he wanted to have them published, while his students did not always publish what he had dictated to them as a work by al-Afghānī (ʿAnḥūrī, *Siḥr*, 185; Keddie 1972: 97; ʿAmāra in al-Afghānī, *Aʿmāl*, 2nd edn., 1: 164). The Syrian poet and journalist Salīm ʿAnḥūrī (1856–1933), who joined al-Afghānī's circle in Cairo in 1878 and was in close contact with him and his disciples for several months, characterized ʿAbduh and al-Laqqānī as al-Afghānī's 'two scribes' (*kātibāhu*) who always volunteered to pen down what he asked them to write (*Siḥr*, 180, 181, 183, 185).

Not all arguments adduced by ʿAmāra in support of al-Afghānī's authorship are convincing. Haddad's criticism (Haddad 1994: 82–5, 88–94) seems justified with respect to some of them. However, several of them, which Haddad failed to mention, are hardly refutable. This applies especially to *al-Taʿlīqāt*. In several passages of this work terms in foreign languages, in particular Persian ones, are used for explanatory purposes (examples listed by ʿAmāra in al-Afghānī, *Aʿmāl*, 2nd edn., 1: 163f.). In contrast to al-Afghānī, ʿAbduh did not know Persian.[1] Moreover, the author frequently

[1] This is true despite the fact that he is commonly said to have translated al-Afghānī's originally Persian *Ḥaqīqat-i madhhab-i nayčirī wa-bayān-i ḥāl-i nayčiriyyān*, published in Arabic under the title *al-Radd ʿalā l-dahriyyīn*. It was in reality al-Afghānī's servant Abū Turāb (ʿĀrif Efendi) who translated this work into Arabic for ʿAbduh, within his capabilities. ʿAbduh's contribution was confined to transforming the result into an appropriate Arabic style (also confirmed by Haddad 1994: 121–2). Abū Turāb not only 'knew Persian' (as stated by Sedgwick 2010: 39), but *was* Persian (see e.g. Keddie 1966: 518; Keddie 1972: 34, 45) and knew Arabic.

criticizes various prominent *mutakallimūn* and Muslim philosophers, Sunnīs as well as Shīʿīs, sometimes even Sunni theology as a whole, quite often in derogatory words (instances listed by ʿAmāra in al-Afghānī, *Aʿmāl*, 2nd edn., 159–61). As ʿAmāra rightly remarked, this fits with al-Afghānī's well-known self-esteem, but it is unlikely that such pronouncements could have come from ʿAbduh, at the time a young student in his twenties (*Aʿmāl*, 161–3).

The two last-mentioned arguments are given further weight by al-Afghānī's Iranian-Shīʿī origin, a fact strenuously denied by ʿAmāra (e.g. ʿAmāra 1988: 19–44) for purely ideological reasons (Matthee 1989). The intellectual horizon reflected in the *Risālat al-Wāridāt* and *al-Taʿlīqāt* corresponds much more to this background than to that which can reasonably be supposed in the case of the young Sunni Egyptian student ʿAbduh even after several years of rapturous listening to al-Afghānī. The *Risālat al-Wāridat* and *al-Taʿlīqāt* show a strong influence of Avicennian and Illuminationist philosophy. The author of these works refers to Ibn Sīnā on the basis of the latter's Shīʿī commentators, draws on Mullā Ṣadrā in his pantheistic ideas, and quotes a considerable number of Iranian authors. These observations (already noted by Haddad 1994: 195f. with n. 28, 277) suggest al-Afghānī's authorship rather than ʿAbduh's. The same applies to the author's recourse to the Muʿtazilī position of the createdness of the Qurʾān and his differentiation between two separate levels of access to truth, one for the broad public and another one for the intellectual elite, interpreted by Haddad as forming part of ʿAbduh's innovative theological approach (Haddad 1994: 309–14, 235f.). These features are characteristic for a religious scholar like al-Afghānī who was well versed in Imāmī theology and in philosophy.

According to *al-Taʿlīqāt*, the tenets of faith on which all Muslims must agree are limited to the belief in God, prophecy, and the hereafter, whereas everything else can be interpreted in different ways by *ijtihād*; the book shows the general tendency to minimize the dogmatic differences between Sunnīs and Shīʿīs as well as the divergences of the various schools of theology and law. These features need not be attributed to ʿAbduh's original thought either, as done by Haddad (1994: 176–8). Their most obvious explanation is al-Afghānī's aim of uniting the Muslims in the struggle against the European colonial powers—his Panislamist ambitions have been ascertained already for his Egyptian years (Cole 2000: 33).

ʿAbduh's contribution to the ideas expressed in both works has so far not been proven, except for the footnotes of *al-Taʿlīqāt*. In this book even the wording must be largely al-Afghānī's for the reasons mentioned above. In the *Risālat al-Wāridāt* there are no identifiable traces of al-Afghānī's language. As for its content, even Oliver Scharbrodt, who followed Haddad in regarding ʿAbduh as its author, characterized it as 'the mystical and philosophical lessons which he learned from al-Afghānī and articulated in this treatise' (Scharbrodt 2007: 112). This being correct, the views expressed in the *Risālat al-Wāridāt* cannot be attributed to ʿAbduh's original thought either. Therefore, the presentation of ʿAbduh's theological efforts will focus here on the writings traditionally regarded as containing his theology, mainly his *Risālat al-Tawḥīd*.

It is Haddad's merit to have discovered the full extent of the manipulations by which Muḥammad Rashīd Riḍā tried to adjust the public perception of ʿAbduh's views to his own ideal of orthodox *salafiyya* (Haddad 1994: 79–82, 99f., 130–40; Haddad 1997; Haddad 1998: 24–30). Henceforth information provided by Riḍā concerning ʿAbduh's theology cannot be relied on any more.

3 *ʿAbduh's theological thought*

Among ʿAbduh's theological writings, the *Risālat al-Tawḥīd* (1897) has been most widely received in the Sunnī world. The book originated in lectures on *ʿilm al-tawḥīd* given by ʿAbduh in a secondary school, the Madrasa Sulṭāniyya, in Beirut during his exile in 1886. Approximately ten years later he wished to publish these lectures as a textbook, but did not own a manuscript himself. Fortunately his brother had been among his students in Beirut. ʿAbduh used the latter's transcript of his original lectures and published them following a thorough revision (preface, ʿAbduh, *Aʿmāl*, 3: 353f.).

ʿAbduh had decided to dictate a text of his own on this subject to the pupils because of his impression that the treatises of *kalām* traditionally used for teaching purposes were too difficult to understand for his young audience and related to times that were no more theirs (ʿAbduh, *Aʿmāl*, 3: 353). It was his intention to give a simplified and modernized outline of *kalām*.

Simplicity is in fact one of the main characteristics of the *Risālat al-Tawḥīd*. References to former authorities or schools of thought are limited to a minimum. Detailed discussions of controversial points are not provided. ʿAbduh had consciously avoided dogmatic differences to the extent possible, so that only 'mature men' would be able to notice them (ʿAbduh, *Aʿmāl*, 3: 353). The overall structure of the treatise and many lines of argumentation still display a scholastic approach. Two sections, however, are written from a contemporary perspective: an introductory overview of the history of *kalām*, and a concluding statement in the course of which ʿAbduh develops a distinctly modern theology of history.

The historical sketch advocates a middle course between the diverging schools of thought. It repeatedly classifies opposing positions as resulting from exaggeration (*ghulūw*) or extremism (*taṭarruf*) and stresses the harmfulness of dissent, attributing it largely to the noxious influence of non-Muslims. This presentation is in line with al-Afghānī's programme of propagating Panislamic unity.

Right from the beginning, ʿAbduh makes it clear that, in his view, properly understood Islamic theology is a harmonious combination of rational reflection and respect for the revealed texts handed down by the forefathers (*salaf*), keeping equally aloof from the extremes of traditionalist literalism and overestimation of the capabilities of reason; according to him the first Muslim scholars neglected neither the revealed texts (*naql*) nor reason (*ʿaql*) and speculation (*naẓar al-fikr*) (ʿAbduh, *Aʿmāl*, 3: 359).

He blames the 'followers of Wāṣil', i.e. the Muʿtazila, for not having sufficiently differentiated between rational axioms and mere phantasms springing from the impact of Greek thought (ʿAbduh, *Aʿmāl*, 3: 361). He characterizes the controversy over the createdness or eternity of the Qurʾān as a dispute between extremists of rational speculation and the Ḥanbalites who exaggerated the binding force of the literal sense of revelation (ʿAbduh, *Aʿmāl*, 3: 362). He praises al-Ashʿarī for having adopted a middle course between the extremes and lauds scholars such as al-Bāqillānī and al-Juwaynī for having enforced al-Ashʿarī's teachings as the Sunnī standard (ʿAbduh, *Aʿmāl*, 3: 362f.). He blames, however, the subsequent Ashʿarites for having asserted that Muslims are obliged to believe in all conclusions drawn from these premisses and forbidden to believe in anything not rationally proven, an error which was only corrected later by al-Ghazālī and Fakhr al-Dīn al-Rāzī (ʿAbduh, *Aʿmāl*, 3: 363).

ʿAbduh evaluates the emergence of Islamic philosophy positively, but criticizes the philosophers for having initially indulged in blind imitation (*taqlīd*) of the Greeks and having later interfered in discussions on theological problems. As he states, the defenders of the Islamic creed reacted to this intrusion by rejecting philosophy, but at the same time increasingly integrated philosophical patterns of reasoning into their own theological thought. The resulting amalgamation of philosophy and *kalām* led to the latter's deadlock and to the propensity of the *mutakallimūn* for *taqlīd* (ʿAbduh, *Aʿmāl*, 3: 363–5). Afterwards the rule of ignorant political leaders fostered intellectual chaos among Muslims. The decadence of *kalām* was increased by religious scholars who claimed the right to declare others as mistaken or even infidel at will. In this way *kalām* degenerated into an instrument of creating divisions among Muslims. Finally the idea of 'some earlier religious communities'—ʿAbduh is certainly thinking of Christianity here—that religion and science are hostile to each other was taken over (ʿAbduh, *Aʿmāl*, 3: 365).

ʿAbduh describes the sequence of revelations from Judaism to Christianity to Islam as a process of divine education given to humankind in analogy to the development of individuals (ʿAbduh, *Aʿmāl*, 3: 448–53): at the origins of Judaism, humanity was still in its infancy and hence preoccupied with the fulfilment of its physical needs and desires. Therefore the Pentateuch revealed to Moses had to include strict legal rules disciplining carnal impulses. When the prophet Jesus was sent, humankind had entered into the stage of adolescence in which people are very sensitive and emotional; hence the gospel worked towards the moral betterment of humans by appealing to their emotions, particularly love, as ʿAbduh explains with a slight misunderstanding of this Christian concept. At Muḥammad's time humanity had reached the state of maturity. Accordingly, the Qurʾān called upon humans to use reason; and since they had in fact developed the ability of doing so and thus ensuring their further progress, there is no need for revelation after the Qurʾān.

ʿAbduh praises (ʿAbduh, *Aʿmāl*, 3: 443–6, 450f., 453–6, 458–70) the achievements of Islamic civilization as automatic effects of Islam as such: Muḥammad's prophetical message liberated reason from the shackles of superstition as well as from oppression by rulers or priests. It awoke the spirit of independent thinking, with the result that sciences progressed and justice flourished wherever Islam spread. ʿAbduh's ensuing attempt to explain why in his own days Muslims were generally backward compared to non-Muslim Europeans in terms of science and social development contradicts this characterization of Islam as a self-acting formula of success: he attributes the present grievances to the fact that Muslims have become unfaithful to the true meaning of their religion (ʿAbduh, *Aʿmāl*, 3: 465–9).

In its structure this theology of history is akin to Comte's Law of the Three Stages, except that ʿAbduh did not follow Comte in asserting that religion in general, which would have meant also Islam, will be overcome in the age of scientific reason. At the same time it resembles the theories of history developed by Turgot and Condorcet, the two French Enlightenment philosophers by whose ideas Comte's law was largely inspired. On the basis of the information available so far, it is not possible to decide if the pertinent passages of the *Risāla* already formed part of the original lectures given before he learned French, or if they were added during the reworking process for the publication in 1897. In the latter case ʿAbduh may have read either Comte or publications about him or his Enlightenment predecessors. Otherwise he must have indirectly gained knowledge of their theories.

The idea that Islam is more conducive to scientific rationality and social progress than any other religion was also forcefully elaborated by ʿAbduh in his debate with the Syrian orthodox writer Faraḥ Anṭūn (1874–1922) (Kügelgen 1994: 77–95; Reid 1975: 80–90). His relevant articles published in *al-Manār* were reprinted, with the exception of the first one, by Riḍā under the title *al-Islām wa-l-naṣrāniyya maʿa l-ʿilm wa-l-madaniyya* (Cairo 1902; ʿAbduh, *Aʿmāl*, 3: 257–350). ʿAbduh tried to demonstrate that Islam is in perfect harmony with reason and science, whereas Christianity is basically irrational, and power-hungry Christian clergymen were suppressing free thought and science throughout history until the separation of religion and state in Western countries. In his arguments ʿAbduh drew extensively on and often literally quoted two books by John William Draper (1811–81), which he must have read in French translation (Hasselblatt 1968: 184–6, 192–5). Draper, a British-born American chemist, physicist, and philosopher, was strongly influenced by Comte's thought (Fleming 1950: 58 with n. 9 on p. 163).

ʿAbduh's emphasis on the rationality of Islam manifests itself, for example, in his constant advocacy of *ijtihād* instead of *taqlīd* and his criticism of popular superstitions (see e.g. the article 'al-Khurāfāt' published in *al-Waqāʾiʿ al-miṣriyya* in 1882, reprinted in *Aʿmāl*, 2: 159–61). It is also palpable in his exegesis of the Qurʾān, where he interprets statements of the holy book seemingly not agreeing with the modern scientific worldview. Thus, for instance, he holds that the microbes recently discovered by microscopy, these tiny little creatures not visible to the naked eye, can be rightly identified as a species of the *jinn*, to whom the theologians *(mutakallimūn)* have also attributed invisibility and a small and flimsy constitution *(Tafsīr al-Manār*, 3: 96; Adams 1933: 138; cf. his explanation of Qurʾān 105: 3–5 in *Tafsīr juzʾ ʿammā*, 157f., and Jomier 1954: 153).

ʿAbduh takes the immutable 'custom of God' (*sunnat Allāh*) mentioned in the Qurʾān (Q 33: 62; Q 35: 43; cf. Q 17: 77) as designating God-given regularities of the processes going on in the universe, thus coming close to the idea of natural laws. He also uses the term *sunnat Allāh* for intelligible laws of social and political history. His belief in the scientific verifiability of such laws sprang from his knowledge of the ideas of the English philosopher and sociologist Herbert Spencer (1820–1903), whom he once visited (ʿAbduh, *Aʿmāl*, 3: 492–4). Spencer is commonly known as an influential promoter of Social Darwinism; his theory of social evolution, essentially developed already before he knew Darwin, attracted ʿAbduh due to its suitability for fostering the activist social ethics needed by Muslims in their fight for resurgence.

ʿAbduh stresses that Islam is the first and only religion requiring belief exclusively on the basis of rational proofs and giving the judgement of reason precedence over the literal meaning of revealed texts in cases of doubt. However his trust in reason is limited where dogmatic issues are concerned: he declares that those who have once reasonably decided for believing in God and in His messenger Muḥammad are not entitled any more to object to single Qurʾānic statements with rational arguments. Contrary to Sayyid Ahmad Khan, he is thus not willing to make the findings of scientific reason the yardstick of what God can have intended in the Qurʾān. Also in several other points he is less rationalist than Sayyid Ahmad (Troll 1978b: 226–8), for instance insofar as he sees no reason to deny that miracles can actually happen. Moreover, in the question of how to understand Qurʾānic statements apparently conflicting with scientific reason ʿAbduh repeatedly pronounces for leaving their exact meaning to God.

Despite such limits to his rationalism ʿAbduh's confidence in reason can be regarded as comparable to that of Muʿtazilī theologians. However, the practice of classifying him as a Neo-Muʿtazilī (see e.g. Caspar 1957: 157–72; Khalid 1969: 320–1; Martin, Woodward, and Atmaja 1997: 129–35) has rightly been objected to (Hildebrandt 2002), not only because he took sides with the Ashʿarites in his above-mentioned account of the history of Islamic theology. ʿAbduh's supposed Neo-Muʿtazilism has, among other things, been alleged with reference to a short passage in the first edition of the *Risāla* in which he had referred to the Qurʾān as created. This passage was also contained in the French translation by B. Michel and M. Abdel Razik (32–4), but eliminated on ʿAbduh's demand in the second edition carried out by Muḥammad Rashīd Riḍā and in its reprints. It is included again in ʿAmāra's editions (ʿAbduh, *Aʿmāl*, 3: 377f. and a separate print of the *Risāla* published by Dār al-shurūq, 48f).

Riḍā explained that ʿAbduh ordered him to take this passage out of the second edition because he wished to correct himself, after the Azhari Shaykh Muḥammad Maḥmūd al-Shinqīṭī had drawn his attention to the incompatibility of the idea of the createdness of the Qurʾān with the creed of the *salaf* (reprint al-Jābī, 107 n.). Although al-Shinqīṭī's criticism of the passage really happened, Riḍā's explanation is dubious because of its tendency to trim ʿAbduh as an assiduous follower of the Islam of the forefathers, as Riḍā conceived of it. According to Haddad's alternative interpretation, when the second edition of the treatise was prepared, ʿAbduh still adhered to the Muʿtazilī idea of the createdness of the Qurʾān expressed in *al-Taʿlīqāt*, but was at that time trying to win the support of the *ʿulamāʾ* of al-Azhar for reforming this institution. Al-Shinqīṭī's criticism of the passage made him aware of the risk that the resistance of conservative *ʿulamāʾ*

against his reform project might increase if he were reputed to be lacking in orthodoxy. Hence he eliminated the passage (Haddad 1994: 98–101).

However, a close reading of the passage shows that ʿAbduh, contrary to Haddad's judgement, did not profess the Muʿtazilī dogma of the createdness of the Qurʾān: he did not characterize the Qurʾān as created in its quality as God's speech (*kalām Allāh*), which would be the Muʿtazilī position. Instead he stated, in somewhat squirming words circumscribing the Ashʿarī view, that the heavenly original (*maṣdar*) of God's word is pre-existent, but the recited Qurʾān (*al-Qurʾān al-maqrūʾ*), i.e. its audible sound produced by the voices of those reciting it, is created (Hildebrandt 2002: 252–5; similarly ʿAmāra in ʿAbduh, *Risāla*, print Dār al-Shurūq, 49 n. 3).

This observation offers a key to a more probable explanation: ʿAbduh apparently tried to promote a compromise formula between the position of the Muʿtazilīs and their opponents, in conformity with the general tendency of the *Risāla* to advocate a middle course suitable for uniting all Muslims. Consistent with this assumption are some details of his argumentation: he emphasizes that Aḥmad b. Ḥanbal was certainly too intelligent to believe that the recited Qurʾān is eternal, as he used to recite it every day with his own voice; he even claims that what prevented scholars such as Aḥmad b. Ḥanbal from subscribing to the dogma of the createdness of the Qurʾān was nothing but modesty and excessive deference to some colleagues (ʿAbduh, *Aʿmāl*, 3: 378; print Dār al-Shurūq, 49). This depiction of the problem is, of course, misleading, but it reveals ʿAbduh's lively desire to convince the readers that his compromise formula can in principle be accepted even by the staunchest representatives of the traditionalist camp. Al-Shinqīṭī's criticism must have made him aware that the compromise formula did not work, because it was too easily misunderstood as an affirmation of the Muʿtazilī position. So he decided to have it deleted, maybe out of the tactical consideration mentioned by Haddad.

ʿAbduh's manner of dealing with the question of free action or predestination cannot be classified as Muʿtazilī either: in the *Risāla* he uses the concept of man's 'acquisition' (*kasb*) of his actions, in order to explain why these are attributable to him in the Last Judgement without interference with God's justice. The concept of *kasb* is common to the schools of al-Ashʿarī and al-Māturīdī. ʿAbduh interprets the way in which *kasb* takes place by introducing the concept of man's ability to choose his own actions (*ikhtiyār*) and rejecting the idea of his being forced to commit certain actions (*qahr*) (ʿAbduh, *Aʿmāl*, 3: 387–9). The length in which ʿAbduh dwells on the criteria of *ikhtiyār* (ʿAbduh, *Aʿmāl*, 3: 390–3) can easily be traced back to the tradition of Islamic philosophical ethics. But the concept of *ikhtiyār* as such was already established in Sunni theological theory of action, in combination with that of *kasb*, by al-Māturīdī whom ʿAbduh follows here (Rudolph 1997: 231, 240f.). In accordance with al-Māturīdī ʿAbduh also affirms that it is equally obligatory to believe in man's ability to choose his actions and in the fact that everything, man's actions included, originates from the will of the Creator, although God does not command evil actions and His will is not forcing (ʿAbduh, *Aʿmāl*, 3: 388; see also ʿAbduh's interpretation of *sūra* 104 in *al-Manār* 6, 1903, 189f., partly translated in Adams 1933: 154; cf. Rudolph 1997: 232). Like Sayyid Ahmad Khan, ʿAbduh leaves it at juxtaposing man's action and the universal effectiveness of God's will. Instead of trying to explain precisely how these two levels are interrelated, he only decries the historical discussions about this problem as mere sophistries of exaggerators which did not lead to anything but divisions of the community (ʿAbduh, *Aʿmāl*, 3: 387).

ʿAbduh shares the Muʿtazilī view that the existence of God and the basic standards of good and evil can be known by reason (ʿAbduh, *Aʿmāl*, 3: 393, 394). But this view was also held by Islamic philosophers (Hildebrandt 2002: 246). In conclusion, there is not much left of ʿAbduh's alleged Neo-Muʿtazilism.

IV Modernist Theological Thought of the Early Twentieth Century

(a) Main Topics

Two of the prevalent topics of modernist theology in the early twentieth century, the rationality of Islam and its compatibility with modern science, had already been in the focus of Sayyid Ahmad Khan's and ʿAbduh's interest. An additional preoccupation came to the fore now: the struggle against the materialist and atheist worldview perceived as pushing forward from the West.

This danger had for the first time been brought to the attention of Muslim readers by al-Afghānī's treatise *Ḥaqīqat-i madhhab-i nayčirī wa-bayān-i ḥāl-i nayčiriyyān* (1881), which became mainly known in its Arabic translation *al-Radd ʿalā l-dahriyyīn* published by ʿAbduh in 1886. As has been convincingly argued (Keddie 1968), it was in reality a politically motivated polemic directed against Sayyid Ahmad Khan and his adherents, whose influence on Indian Muslims the author wanted to counteract because of their acceptance of the British colonial rule. In 1865 Sayyid Ahmad Khan had, probably after getting indirect access to rather vague information about Darwin's theory, in fact put forward an evolutionist concept according to which first inanimate matter, then plants, then animals, and finally mankind had gradually emerged from one and the same source of existence—and this at a time when Darwin himself had not yet included the human species in the chain of evolution (Riexinger 2009: 218f.). Sayyid Ahmad Khan had not adopted a materialist or atheist understanding of the world when appropriating this concept. Nonetheless al-Afghānī, who himself showed agnostic inclinations at that time, formulated his attack on him and his adherents demagogically in the guise of a fiery defence of the Islamic religion against the allegedly materialist and atheist followers of Darwin, apparently without knowing precisely what Darwin had said.

The discussion on Darwinism (cf., for example, Ziadat 1986; Elshakry 2011) was raised to a much higher level by the Lebanese Shaykh Ḥusayn al-Jisr (1845–1909) in *al-Risāla al-Ḥamīdiyya* (1888). He taught for most of his life in his native city Ṭrāblus, but was temporarily director of the Madrasa Waṭaniyya in Beirut just in the year 1887 when

ʿAbduh gave his lectures there. Although both remained in friendly contact afterwards, there is no clear indication of an influence of ʿAbduh on al-Jisr (Ebert 1991: 85).

Most probably he drafted his book titled *al-Risāla al-Ḥamīdiyya* in reaction to Shiblī Shumayyil (Ebert 1991: 142), an originally Catholic Lebanese physician and writer who emigrated to Egypt. He was the first prominent Arab author professing Darwinism, materialism, and atheism. In 1884 Shumayyil had published an Arabic translation of Ludwig Büchner's *Sechs Vorlesungen über die Darwin'sche Theorie von der Verwandlung der Arten* (1868), a decidedly materialist interpretation of Darwin's theory. Al-Jisr's book contains, after a detailed exposition of Islamic faith and ritual and of some recently contested provisions of Islamic law, an attempt to refute materialism and atheism together with the theory of evolution (analysed in Ebert 1991: 138–46).

Having familiarized himself carefully with the relevant scientific findings and opinions, al-Jisr not only uses traditional theological arguments, but also tries to demonstrate that the materialist theory of evolution is contradictory in itself in certain points. In addition, he stresses that so far the views of Darwin's adherents are not more than a theory of which it is not yet clear whether it will ever become a final certainty (al-Jisr, *Risāla*, 253)—a motive often recurring in later discussions on the compatibility of Qurʾānic statements and the results of modern science. However al-Jisr also deliberates on the question of what to do with the details of the Qurʾānic account of creation, if Darwin's theory should once turn out to be true. He thinks that in this case it would be allowed to give the pertinent Qurʾānic passages a new interpretation, on condition that the essential content of the Qurʾānic account, the statement that God is the Creator of everything in heaven and on earth, remains accepted (al-Jisr, *Risāla*, 245, 253). This opinion shows that al-Jisr did not exclude the possibility of a non-atheist understanding of Darwin's theory agreeing with the essentials of Islamic faith.

At the beginning of the twentieth century the zeal for confronting atheism and materialism was additionally spurred by a book of the Egyptian author Muḥammad Farīd Wajdī (1875–1954), *al-Islām fī ʿaṣr al-ʿilm* (published in Cairo in 1320/1902–3 and 1322/1904–5), which was widely read by Muslim intellectuals, also outside the Arab countries. Wajdī pointedly questioned whether the progress of science and civilization is inescapably synonymous with materialism and loss of religion as suggested by the dominant West (see e.g. Wajdī, *ʿAṣr*, 1: 97–102), and tried to demonstrate that Islam and science alike provide ways out of this dilemma.

(b) Syria

The Damascene scholar Jamāl al-Dīn al-Qāsimī (1866–1914) (Commins 1990: 65–88 and index; Abāẓa 1997; Dabdūb 2007) was among those who now engaged in the task of combating materialism and atheism. He belonged to the circle of the Syrian *salafiyya*, a movement of its own in the late nineteenth and early twentieth century (cf. also Escovitz 1986). It was carried by a group of *ʿulamāʾ* who, or whose fathers or teachers, had affiliated to the circle of Amīr ʿAbd al-Qādir al-Jazāʾirī and were mainly inspired by his ideas (Commins 1990: 26–9, 32; Weismann 2001a). Their endeavour to revive Islam was strengthened by two additional factors: the rediscovery of Ibn Taymiyya's works (Commins 1990: 25f., 88) and the acquaintance with al-Afghānī's and even more ʿAbduh's thought (Commins 1990: 30–3, 40, 47). Several *ʿulamāʾ* of this group corresponded with ʿAbduh from the 1880s, and two of them, ʿAbd al-Razzāq Bīṭār (1837–1917) and al-Qāsimī, met ʿAbduh personally (Commins 1990: 61f.; for the relations between Syrian and Egyptian *salafiyya* of the time, cf. Ezzerelli 2006; Commins 2006).

Al-Qāsimī's major theological work, *Dalāʾil al-tawḥīd* (1st edn. 1908), begins with some preliminary explanations mainly elaborating on the importance of rational cognition in religious issues. Then it provides a detailed exposition of not less than twenty-five different arguments for the existence of God (al-Qāsimī, *Dalāʾil*, 22–73), all of them being conclusive evidence in the author's view. Besides well-known arguments taken from the traditions of *kalām* and philosophy, al-Qāsimī also adduces recent scientific discoveries yielding, in his opinion, additional proofs of the existence of the Creator. He also uses the argument that the unanimous belief in God held by many different peoples of various religions throughout history and all over the world provides a prima facie evidence of God's existence. His argumentations against materialism (al-Qāsimī, *Dalāʾil*, 91–126) are equally diverse. In addition to a long series of philosophical and quasi-scientific reasons for the inappropriateness of a purely materialist and hence also atheist worldview, he adduces the pragmatic argument of the social necessity of religion as a means of creating solidarity and leading people to compliance with the indispensable moral standards of civilized and peaceful life (al-Qāsimī, *Dalāʾil*, 131–3; see also 112, 125).

Al-Qāsimī emphasizes (al-Qāsimī, *Dalāʾil*, 15f.) that in cases of apparent contradiction between the findings of reason (*ʿaql*) and the revealed texts being handed down (*naql*), revelation has to be interpreted by reason, and reason is to be considered as superordinate to the transmitted text, since already the mere assessment of whether a given text is revealed or not can only be made by means of reason (al-Qāsimī, *Dalāʾil*, 128–30). Correctly understood revelation is consistent with reason, although reason does not always grasp the wisdom of revealed precepts immediately (al-Qāsimī, *Dalāʾil*, 126f.).

Like ʿAbduh—and probably also referring to him without naming him—al-Qāsimī declares that humankind has grown out of the stage of childhood and reached maturity with the advent of Islam, one of the main advantages of this religion being that it addresses reason (al-Qāsimī, *Dalāʾil*, 76).[2] Like ʿAbduh, he stresses the perfect harmony of Islam and science (al-Qāsimī, *Dalāʾil*, 130). He even expresses his conviction that new findings of the natural sciences can only strengthen the belief in God, as they sharpen the perception of His signs (*āyāt*) in Creation (al-Qāsimī, *Dalāʾil*, 134).

[2] Elsewhere he reported at length how ʿAbduh had, in a discussion with a Christian opponent, pointed out that Islam is the religion of reason, apparently alluding to his controversy with Faraḥ Anṭūn (al-Qāsimī, *Taʿāruḍ*, 621f.).

Yet at the same time, he accentuates the limited reach and reliability of scientific knowledge: natural sciences can only grasp the outward appearance of things, never their essence; science is particularly unable to explore the origin of the universe (al-Qāsimī, *Dalāʾil*, 84f.); supposed discoveries of scientists have often to be corrected later (al-Qāsimī, *Dalāʾil*, 126). With respect to knowledge of God, al-Qāsimī's trust in reason is as limited as ʿAbduh's: apparently anthropomorphic qualities attributed to God in the Qurʾān are too sublime for being interpreted metaphorically by reason, although they must not be taken literally either (al-Qāsimī, *Taʿāruḍ*, 623; Commins 1990: 68).

Despite these limits al-Qāsimī constantly pleads for the use of one's own reason by *ijtihād*, when the proper understanding of Islamic doctrine and law is at issue. Besides, unity of the believers is a key requirement in his view. Therefore he rejects *taqlīd* not least on the grounds that it rigidifies people's adherence to a single one of the different schools of law or theology, dividing the Islamic community, whereas *ijtihād* opens a space for attempting to overcome the differences between them. Al-Qāsimī does not see the threat to Muslim unity in controversial positions as such, but in the rampant inclination of *ʿulamāʾ* to label all holders of dissenting opinions as hopelessly astray, instead of making allowance for the fact that they also are truth seekers, and keeping in mind what all Muslims agree on (al-Qāsimī, *Taʿāruḍ*, 617; Commins 1990: 69).

(c) Centre of the Ottoman Empire

In the centre of the Ottoman Empire, one of the schools of thought competing after the Young Turk Revolution of 1908 (details in Berkes 1964: 337–66) was that of the Islamists (İslamcılar) gathered around the journal *Sırât-ı Müstakîm* (founded in 1908, called *Sebilürreşâd* since 1912). Apart from their initially common opposition to secularization, their orientations varied considerably: among them were rigid traditionalists, but also moderate conservatives and resolute modernists. The modernists were doubtless acquainted with ʿAbduh's ideas: some of his articles and extracts from his books were published in *Sırât-ı Müstakîm / Sebilürreşâd* (Debus 1991: 109f.; Gen 2006: 77, 80, 82 n. 10 and 83 n. 20). However their main source of inspiration was Young Ottoman thought (Gen 2006: 80f.; Özervarlı 2007: 82).

Their marked interest in refuting atheism and materialism is to be understood against a particular historical background: already since the 1850s, Ottoman intellectuals aspiring to modernization were increasingly fascinated by Western natural sciences. As these sciences, which were largely based on a materialist worldview at that time, were synonymous with progress for them, not a few of them became materialists and free-thinkers. Popular Western classics of nineteenth-century scientific materialism, such as Büchner's *Kraft und Stoff* (1855), were avidly read, the German and English ones initially in French translation (Hanioğlu 1995: 11–13, 16; Özervarlı 2007: 80; Berkes 1964: 181, 292f.).

The Young Turks used an Islamic rhetoric in their official pronouncements, appealing to religious sentiments in order to move the Muslim population of the Empire where they wanted it. However the philosophical basis of their *Weltanschauung* was positivism (Hanioğlu 1995: 200–5, 211, 215). Materialist and positivist intellectuals openly dismissing religion as outdated and backward were known as their supporters. Since they used to justify their positions by philosophical arguments borrowed from Western thinkers, Islamist modernists felt called upon to combat their views with the same weapons.

One of them, Filibeli Ahmed Hilmi (1865–1914) (on him Eliaçık 2002: ii. 483–507), even shared the ideological convictions of the Young Turks in many respects, but parted with them in his relationship to religion (see e.g. Ülken 1966: ii. 459–75; Kara 1986: i. 1–44). He was not a formally educated religious scholar, but well read in European philosophy. During an exile in the desert region of Fezzan in Libya, where he had been banished because of oppositional activities against Abdülhamid II's absolutism, he had a conversion experience that made him a Sufi adhering to the idea of *waḥdat al-wujūd*. Having returned to Istanbul after the Young Turk revolution, he did his best to make his voice heard as a progressive writer who nevertheless rejected materialism and defended Islam against the accusation of incompatibility with modern science (for his intellectual biography cf. esp. Bein 2007).

His book *Allâh'ı İnkâr Mümkün müdür?* (1909) is completely devoted to the refutation of materialism and atheism. The author's approach is entirely philosophic, but the work gains theological relevance where he tries to produce a synthesis of the results of his philosophical argumentations and his Sufi beliefs. Filibeli offers an extensive critical review of materialist theories developed in the history of philosophy from antiquity to present times, followed by a presentation of the ideas of antique, Western, and Islamic thinkers who affirmed the existence of an immaterial reality, in particular man's mind or soul. Finally, he expounds the pertinent concepts of the Sufis, ending with the doctrines of Ibn al-ʿArabī to which he adheres.

A typically modern feature in his way of proceeding is that he consciously takes philosophical reflection on man, not on God as his starting point. As he states, the only thing man can never doubt of is his own self (*nafs*), his 'I' which he experiences as one and identical over time in all his thinking, feeling, and acting (Filibeli, *İnkâr*, 41). Filibeli proves to be well informed about the pertinent views of al-Ghazālī and Descartes. But he prefers to subscribe to the position of the Scottish Enlightenment philosopher Thomas Reid (1710–98), who maintained that rational thought can only be founded on a number of principles of common sense, such as the assumptions that there is an external world independent of the thinking subject and that the consciousness of the human self of being one and identical over time has a real basis which everybody legitimately calls 'my mind' (Filibeli, *İnkâr*, 135f.). As Filibeli argues, this consciousness of one's own oneness cannot be derived from the multitude of substances, forces, and processes constituting man's bodily existence. It can only be due to man's natural relation to the absolute Self. The oneness and identity of the human self must be constituted by the one God who breathed His own spirit (*rūḥ*) into Adam and gives every human individual its living soul (Filibeli, *İnkâr*, 79). Equally, the assumption that all human knowledge forms one entirety, structured by a coherent system of intelligible laws, causal chains, and similarities, an assumption without which science and civilization would not be possible, can only be justified by the existence of one God, the ultimate cause of everything (Filibeli, *İnkâr*, 1–2).

The author integrates these views into his mystical concept of *waḥdat al-wujūd* by equating the unifying cause behind the human self, as well as behind human knowledge and all its objects, with the *prima causa*, the Creator from whom everything in the universe emanates. But he anticipates an objection to this reasoning: does not just the idea of *waḥdat al-wujūd* contradict man's consciousness of his persisting personal identity, because it means that man is ultimately divine and therefore does not have a separate existence or should not perpetuate it? Filibeli rebuts this objection by emphasizing that believing in *waḥdat al-wujūd* is not equivalent to denying man's personal identity, but only to denying that it exists independently from God (Filibeli, *İnkâr*, 176f.).

Filibeli wants to keep up with recent philosophy as much as possible without abandoning his faith. Thus he states that Comte's Law of the Three Stages is valid as a historical description of the sequence in which religion, metaphysics, and positive sciences appeared in the development of human civilization, but not valid insofar as it claims that every later stage supersedes the previous one. Even the most advanced philosophers or scientists feel in the depths of their hearts that they cannot exist without any veneration of a Supreme Being. In reality religion, metaphysics, and science necessarily complement each other in forming mature personalities; their coexistence does not hamper the progress of civilization as long as everybody respects their diverging areas of competence, so that, for example, religious scholars do not intrude into the profession of scientists and vice versa (Filibeli, *İnkâr*, 33–40; *Üss*, 6–15).

The most prolific theological writer among the late Ottoman and early Republican Turkish modernists was İzmirli İsmail Hakkı (1869–1946; see esp. İzmirli, Celâleddin 1946 [the author is his son], Hizmetli 1996, Çetinkaya 2000, Birinci 2001, Özervarlı 1998: 49–51 and 79–125 *passim*, Eliaçık 2003: iii, 107–30, Özervarlı 2007). He had been educated at a Higher Teachers' Training College, but also finished a traditional *medrese* education. In addition, he was initiated in the Shādhiliyya order. For most of his professional career he taught at the Süleymaniye Medresesi and the Darülfünun (later University of Istanbul), from which he retired as Professor of Islamic Philosophy in 1935. His lectures there actually covered a broader range of Islamic subjects, not least *kalām*.

In this field İzmirli mentioned, besides many classical Islamic works, ʿAbduh's *Risālat al-Tawḥīd* and al-Qāsimī's *Dalāʾil al-tawḥīd* among his references[3] (*Kelâm*, 1: 302 and 2: 239). Being able to read French, he also acquainted himself with the history and recent developments of Western philosophy. However, he mostly confined himself to dictionaries, encyclopedias, handbooks, and introductory overviews, except for the major works of a few philosophers such as Descartes and Comte and Gustave Le Bon's *L'Évolution de la matière* (1906) which he consulted in the original (*Kelâm*, 1: 302 and 2: 240; Özervarlı 2007: 85).

[3] The latter book erroneously as *Barāhīn al-tawḥīd*.

His most widely received theological work is *Yeni ilm-i kelâm* (2 vols., 1920/1–1922/3). Although it remained incomplete—the author had announced two more volumes which were never published (Baloğlu 1996b: 273)—its existing parts give a sufficiently concrete impression of the author's approach. Its main relevance lies in the proposal of a new type of philosophical theology to which we will come back later. What interests us here are the views on some specific theological questions contained in it and in other writings from the author's pen.

İzmirli also strives to refute materialism and concomitant atheism. One of his main arguments against materialism is the assertion that in modern science the concept of matter is increasingly being abandoned in favour of that of energy (*Kelâm*, 1: 283f.). He presents many different proofs of God's existence, not only those already known in the Islamic tradition (*Kelâm*, 2: 5–30), but also additional ones gathered from modern European philosophy (*Kelâm*, 2: 30–41). Among these he rates Kant's concept of God as a regulative idea of practical reason. Though he principally endorses it, he judges its probative value for God's existence to be deficient, because it does not spring from a cogent logical conclusion, but is, in his view, rather an expression of Kant's faith or of the general need for justice (*Kelâm*, 2: 39–41). His assessment of Comte's Law of the Three Stages (*Kelâm*, 2: 80–3) corresponds to that of Filibeli.

İzmirli agrees with ʿAbduh that Islam liberated human reason from the shackles of blind submission to former authorities (*taqlīd*). According to him a conflict between the content of revelation and the findings of reason is impossible: revelation can contain supra-rational knowledge, but nothing contrary to reason (*Kelâm*, 1: 52). On the other hand, reason needs to be complemented by revelation, because alone it is not sufficiently capable to grasp the most essential truths (see his detailed comparison of the 'way of revelation' and the 'way of philosophy' in *Kelâm*, 1: 46–56). He presupposes a foregone harmony between revelation and the knowledge attainable by natural science, but opposes the so-called scientific exegesis of the Qurʾān which tries to find the latest discoveries of natural science in its text: the Qurʾān is not a book of science; it is inappropriate to look in its immutable verses for scientific theories changing every now and then (*Kelâm*, 1: 16f.).

In an account of his scholarly methods and principles he presents himself as a thinker deeply committed to critical reasoning, declaring that he accepts only the prophet Muḥammad as an infallible authority, whereas he never follows any doctrinal position of any previous scholar whosoever without rational proofs and previous impartial review of all pertinent arguments (*Mustasvife*, 6–8; simplified version in Kara 1987: ii. 95–7). His actual way of proceeding does not always conform to this ideal: sometimes he adopts an eclectic and inconsistent position between tradition and rationality (already noted by Özervarlı 1996: 125). He maintains that the universe is governed by inalterable natural laws set by God's wisdom from eternity, but does not hesitate to affirm the occurrence of miracles breaking these laws, because it is not against reason to assume that God changes these laws occasionally for specific purposes. He also accepts miracles as evidence of the authenticity of a prophetic message (*Kelâm*, 2: 46; 1: 241–4), but elsewhere he declares them to be dispensable because the prophet Muḥammad was, due to his unique moral perfection, himself the greatest miracle (*al-Jawāb*, 43–5).

A courageous contribution to theological thought was İzmirli's revision of the traditional Islamic opinion about the eternal destiny of sinners and infidels: as mercy and wisdom were the dominant qualities in his image of God, he concluded that pain and tortures imposed on the wicked ones in hell can only be a means of education by which God wants to purify their souls, so that they finally qualify for enjoying His mercy and goodness in paradise. Consequently he denied the eternity of hell punishments (*Nar; Kelâm*, 2: 197–200; cf. also Kaya 2009).

(d) A Kazan Tatar Modernist

Approximately ten years before İzmirli the Kazan Tatar Musa Carullah Bigiyef (1875–1949) had already done the same. Bigiyef (for his life and thought, cf. Taymas 1958, Görmez 2002, Akbulut 2002, Eliaçık 2003, vol. iii: 131–50, Akman 2007, Gavarof 2009), who is otherwise mainly known for having played a leading role at the All Russian Muslim Conferences from 1905 to 1917 and for his commitment to Muslim womens' liberation, had received parts of an education as a religious scholar in Bukhara and in Cairo, where he was disillusioned with the general quality of the courses at al-Azhar, but established good contact with Muḥammad ʿAbduh. Later he published a book entitled *Islâm Filsûfları* about him, the plural 'philosophers' being due to its annex containing a biography of al-Afghānī (Zarcone 1996: 56).

Like the Tatar Jadidists in general (see Kanlıdere 1997: 34–6, 68), Bigiyef was a staunch opponent of *kalām*, on which traditional *medrese* studies focused in Kazan as well as in Bukhara in his young years (Kanlıdere 1997: 80, 82f.). He accused the *mutakallimūn* of having kept the minds of Muslims busy with useless discussions about irrelevant questions for centuries and thus having caused the decline of sciences in the Islamic world (Görmez 1994: 82–7; Kanlıdere 2005: 201–3). Like other Tatar intellectuals he saw in Shihāb al-Dīn Marjanī (1818–89) the most influential reformist *ʿālim* of Kazan in the second half of the nineteenth century (Kanlıdere 1997: 42–50), some sort of a Muslim Luther whose programme of returning to the pure origins of Islam, in particular the Qurʾān, the *ḥadīth*, and the 'books of the *salaf*' (among whom Marjanī counted also al-Ghazālī, Ibn Sīnā, and Ibn al-ʿArabī), had to be followed (Kanlıdere 1997: 58–60, 44f.). Oriented in this way, Bigiyef dared to discard traditional majority positions, basing his own views on his personal interpretation of the fundamental normative texts of Islam and on a few selected classical authors, in particular mystics.

While teaching a course on History of Religions at a *medrese* in Orenburg, he developed a particular interest in the destiny of non-Muslims in the hereafter. Mainly under the impact of Ibn al-ʿArabī and Mawlānā Jalāl al-Dīn Rūmī he came to the conclusion that God's mercy encompasses all humankind and that hence also adherents of other religions than Islam will finally be admitted to paradise, even if they have to serve hell sentences before. He justified this opinion in a series of articles published in the journal

Şura (Orenburg) in 1909; they were reprinted as a book under the title *Rahmet-i İlâhiye Burhanları* two years later.

Bigiyef rejects the Muʿtazilī view that God would not be just, if He did not really impose the eternal punishment threatened in the Qurʾān on infidels and sinners. According to him this argument misses the difference between breaking one's word and forgiving, between lying and waiving an announced sanction (Bigiyef, *Rahmet*, 35). His arguments in favour of God's all-encompassing mercy are mainly based on—partly somewhat forced—interpretations of Qurʾānic verses and two *ḥadīth* texts stressing the greatness of God's mercy (for views of other Muslim thinkers on this issue see Troll 1983).

Bigiyef's thesis encountered massive criticism from the conservative part of the Tatar *ʿulamāʾ*, but also beyond their circle: his book, which was written in an idiosyncratic late Ottoman Turkish, prompted the Ottoman Şeyhülislam Mustafa Sabri (about him, cf. Karabela 2003) to publish a detailed refutation (published in 1918–19). Its title, *Yeni Islâm Müctehidlerinin Kıymet-i İlmiyesi*, already shows that he took this opportunity to attest to the modernists in general that they were devoid of scholarly competence. But Bigiyef also received support: Riḍā al-Dīn b. Fakhr al-Dīn (Rızaeddin Fahreddin) (1855/8–1936), one of the leaders of Kazan Tatar Jadidism and editor of the journal *Şura* (more about him and *Şura* in Dudoignon 2006: 98–104; Kanlıdere 1997: 50–2), wrote a treatise entitled *Rahmet-i İlâhiye Meselesi* (Orenburg 1910) to defend Bigiyef's thesis, rightly pointing out that, among others, already Ibn Qayyim al-Jawziyya had held the same opinion (Kanlıdere 2005: 60; Maraş 2002: 91 n. 15, 95).

A strong motive behind Bigiyef's and İzmirli's decision to affirm God's all-encompassing mercy was their wish to share the universalist and humanist tendency of the Enlightenment. Their acquaintance with the ideas of mystics such as Ibn al-ʿArabī enabled them to see that this tendency had also a basis in their own religious tradition. In the recent past, under the impact of globalization and international migration flows confronting people increasingly with the challenge of religious plurality, the interest in the destiny of 'infidels', in particular Jews and Christians, has gained new momentum. Among present-day Turkish theologians, Süleyman Ateş (born 1933) took again the view that because of God's mercy all sinners will be allowed to enter paradise, after being purified by punishments in hell for a time only known to God himself. By doing so Ateş triggered a fierce debate which is still going on in his country (details in Takim 2007: 223–44 and 297–309). Bigiyef's, İzmirli's, and Ateş's universalist position is still that of a small minority (for a more cautious concession to the 'infidels' made by the Indonesian Qurʾān commentator Muḥammad Quraysh Shihāb [born 1944] see Pink 2011: 251, 284).

(e) India

In India, Shiblī Nuʿmānī (1857–1914) carried on some of Sayyid Ahmad Khān's modernist ideas, but also differed from him in important respects. He was not formally educated as *ʿālim*. His vast knowledge in the different branches of religious learning resulted primarily from autodidactic efforts and contacts with scholars on a pilgrimage to Mecca. From 1882 until Sayyid Ahmad Khan's death in 1898 he taught Arabic and Persian at the Muhammadan Anglo Oriental College in Aligarh. In 1892/3 he travelled extensively in the Middle East, visiting, among other places, Istanbul, Damascus, and also Cairo, where he met ʿAbduh.

Shiblī's theology (cf. also Murad 1996, Özervarlı 1998: 79–123 *passim*, Troll 1982a, Troll 1982b) is mainly contained in two books with similar titles: *ʿIlm al-kalām* (1st edn. 1903), a history of *kalām* including the author's judgements on the described developments and positions, and *al-Kalām* (1st edn. 1904), a systematic exposition of the author's own theology in view of what he perceived as contemporary needs. The basic tendency of Shiblī's thought is rationalist. This led him, for instance, to discard the bulk of Ashʿarism because of doctrines which, in his opinion, no reasonable person can subscribe to, such as the non-existence of inner-worldly causal connections (Murad 1996: 20), and to take sides with the Muʿtazilīs and the philosophers, or at least with those Ashʿarites who were less irrational in his opinion, such as al-Ghazālī and Fakhr al-Dīn al-Rāzī (Troll 1982a: 21f.). He notes the unique rationality of Islam, in which faith has to be based on reason, in contrast to all other religions (Shiblī, *Kalām*, 24).

However, his rationalism is less far-reaching and less consistent than Sayyid Ahmad Khan's. He underscores the full compatibility of Islam with science, but does not see a need to interpret the statements of the Qurʾān in such a manner as to avoid contradictions between them and the evident results of modern natural sciences. According to him there cannot be any conflict between the Qurʾān and science, because the respective objects of religion and science belong to two separate areas, and the kinds of knowledge attained by them are based on two different types of cognition (see e.g. Shiblī, *Kalām*, 5f.). On the other hand, it does not escape him that contemporary philosophy of nature and the findings of modern science on which it is based are a serious challenge to the traditional worldview of revealed religions (Murad 1996: 8f.).

Against the Ashʿarites Shiblī affirms a coherent chain of causes and effects operating in the universe (Shiblī, *Kalām*, 69; Troll 1982b: 93). But contrary to Sayyid Ahmad Khan he does not trust reason to make definitive statements about the regularities governing the cause-and-effect relationships: human knowledge of natural laws is very incomplete, scientific theories are often preliminary (Shiblī, *Kalām*, 102; Troll 1982a: 21). He also does not want to exclude the possibility of miracles breaking natural laws (Shiblī, *Kalām*, 73f., Eng. trans. Troll 1982b: 99; Troll 1982a: 24, 28). He only rejects the idea that miracles can convince anyone of the authenticity of a prophet's mission. In his view the decision to believe in the message of a prophet is not taken on the basis of proofs, but by means of a spiritual sensitivity or 'taste' (*dhawq*) making people feel whether a given message is of divine origin or not (Shiblī, *Kalām*, 90f., Eng. trans. Troll 1982b: 113f.; Troll 1982a: 27).

Like Sayyid Ahmad Khan Shiblī considers prophecy as the highest possible degree of an inborn human talent, which he calls 'strength of sanctity' (*quwwat-i qudsiyya*) (Shiblī, *Kalām*, 90). In his view the essential content of revelation is not accessible to reason, but only to some sort of a supra-rational faculty of cognition (Shiblī, *Kalām*, 84–90, Eng. trans. Troll 1982b: 108–13; Troll 1982a: 26f.).

(f) An Example of Iranian Shiʿi Modernist Theology

Modernist tendencies were not limited to Sunni scholars: in Iran, Ayatollah Muḥammad Ḥasan (Rizā Qulī) Sharīʿat Sangalajī (1890 or 1892–1944) called for *ijtihād* instead of *taqlīd*, advocated a strictly rational approach to Islam, and prompted his fellow-believers to return to the pure origins of their religion by combating superstitions that had distorted its strict monotheism over time. What brought him into fierce conflict with his conservative colleagues was his assessment that also some beliefs traditionally regarded as belonging to the core of Imamī Shīʿism are superstitious and must be done away with. For instance, he rated the idea that the Twelfth Imam will return before resurrection in order to establish justice on earth as an illegitimate addition to Islam (Richard 1988: 166). He condemned the belief that the prophet and the imams are closer to God than ordinary people and can hence be asked for intercession (*shafāʿa*). He also rejected the popular idea that al-Ḥusayn's suffering and death were an expiatory self-sacrifice, denouncing it as un-Islamic (Sharīʿat Sangalajī, *Tawḥīd*, 63f., 140; Richard 1988: 167; for Shīʿ ī modernism in Iran and elsewhere, cf. Nasr 1993).

V Iqbal's Theology for Modern Man

The theology of the Indian philosopher and poet Muhammad Iqbal (1877–1938) is contained in his famous *Six Lectures on the Reconstruction of Religious Thought in Islam* (1st edn. 1930, enlarged 2nd edn. 1934). It goes beyond the limits of the modernizing attempts described so far, not only due to Iqbal's personal genius and to his unconventional way of tackling the question of the relation between Islam and modernity, but also because of the peculiarities of the author's educational career and the ambitious objective of his approach.

He studied Philosophy, English Literature, and Arabic at the Government College Lahore. In the years 1905–7 he continued his education at Trinity College in Cambridge, taking courses in Philosophy and Law. His main teachers there were the philosopher John McTaggart (1866–1925) and the philosopher and psychologist James Ward (1848–1925) (Schimmel 1963: 37). In summer 1907 Iqbal moved to Germany where he improved his German language skills and submitted his doctoral thesis *The Development of Metaphysics in Persia: A Contribution to the History of Muslim Philosophy* to the University of Munich towards the end of the same year. In contrast to the two English philosophers, his German supervisor Fritz Hommel (1854–1936), a professor of Semitic Languages, could not contribute substantially to the development of Iqbal's philosophical thought.

Iqbal's *Reconstruction* aims very high: what it targets is not only to prove that Islam perfectly harmonizes with modern scientific rationality or to disprove certain contemporary materialist philosophies denying that the belief in God and hence also Islam is still legitimate within a modern worldview. Iqbal intends more: he aspires to establish an entirely new religious epistemology and a new interpretation of human existence as a whole through which any Muslim misled by Western modernity, nay modern man in general, can overcome the aberrations of a type of thought keeping him imprisoned in dualistic conceptions or atheist loneliness. The means by which Iqbal wants to achieve this purpose consists in enabling man to retrieve the submerged access to personal religious experience and to discover that the prophetic message of Islam is the most adequate basis for transforming this experience into a creative force of continuous self-perfection as well as perfection of the world.

The argumentations of the seven chapters (in the enlarged version of 1934) of Iqbal's *Reconstruction* do not make easy reading because of their philosophic purport and the frequency of their references to several dozens of different Western and Muslim thinkers. They can hardly be summarized more concisely than has been done by Damian Howard (Howard 2011: 58f.), on which the following account is closely based.

Iqbal begins by stating that human thought means participating in an absolute thought which is the ground of the universe, and that the full meaning of the universe can only be grasped by religion. He identifies mystical experience as the content of religious knowledge and the most appropriate way to it. Then he propounds the following ideas: in prayer, which ideally is a mystical experience par excellence, man (a finite ego) can relate to God (the Ultimate or Absolute Ego) and thus participate in the actual creative unfolding of the universe. The universe consists of a huge number of finite egos to which God has given space at His own expense. The highest species of these egos, man, has come about by a process of evolution initiated by God, the Ultimate Ego. God has, out of His own free will, limited His power to determining everything in the universe through causal chains, in order to give freedom and immortality to man, because He wanted to make him participate in the creative perfection of the universe, an infinite, always open process. Therefore man is also called upon to strive infinitely for his self-perfection. With prophecy the mystic dimension returns to the world after being repressed or forgotten by men. Muḥammad brought about a civilization exploring the universe, making use of the power of inductive reason and fostering the sciences, so that it is now possible to discover man's place in the evolution of the universe. Only *ijtihād*, not *taqlīd*, is adequate to the task of free participation in the world's perfection assigned to man by God. The final end of the universe and Islam alike is the self-realization of the human ego that is able to share God's eternity.

As noted by Howard (Howard 2011: 60–4), Iqbal's *Reconstruction* owes more to the philosophy of Henri Bergson than his explicit references to him—after all some twenty—might suggest. One should add that this applies a fortiori to the philosophy of Iqbal's two Cambridge professors: John McTaggart is mentioned only four times in one and the same context of Iqbal's critique of his idea of the unreality of time (Iqbal, *Reconstruction*, 45f.); James Ward is not mentioned at all. Nevertheless it is not exaggerated to say that most of the key concepts of *Reconstruction* have been borrowed either from McTaggart or from James Ward without marking this fact.[4] A complete list of these borrowings and an analysis of the manner in which Iqbal integrated them in his theology would go beyond the scope of this chapter. Suffice it to delineate a few pivotal ideas of the two philosophers. Their comparison with the content of *Reconstruction* summarized above will immediately show their strong impact on Iqbal.

McTaggart was an idealist metaphysician following in the footsteps of Hegel, but also critical of him in several respects. Although he did not believe in God in any conventional sense, he was a declared mystic. In his opinion mysticism was essentially characterized by the recognition of a unity of the universe greater than that recognized by ordinary experience or science and by the view that one can be conscious of this unity in a way different from discursive thought (McDaniel 2013: section 4, paragraphs 6–7). The concept of the human self related to other selves was basic for his understanding of reality as a whole (McDaniel 2013: section 5, paragraph 2). He defended the belief in the immortality of this self (McDaniel 2013: section 4, paragraph 10).

James Ward championed, to quote H. D. Lewis (Lewis 1985: 297), a 'theistic idealism in which there was a strong panpsychic element but where the point of most significance was the distinct existence of particular beings, or monads, as Leibniz would have them, and also, in sharp contradiction to Leibniz, interaction between them'. As Lewis remarked (Lewis 1985: 297), this is 'an important departure from the traditional idealist pattern where everything is ultimately an appearance or element of the one being of God or the absolute', since it makes it easier to assume individual human freedom and responsibility—which Iqbal emphasized later. In addition, Ward developed an evolutionist natural theology. He assumed that a universe composed of interacting monads cannot move 'towards a state of increasing harmony and cohesion'—as our own universe was doing in his opinion—without 'the leadership of a supreme agent' (Basile 2009/2013: section 5, paragraph 1). Ward also believed that 'novelties could only be generated by the interplay of genuinely free agents'; therefore he conceived of God 'as limiting himself in the exercise of his power so as to let the monads free' (Basile 2009/2013: section 5, paragraph 3). 'Unless creators are created', he said, 'nothing is really created' (quoted from Ward's *The Realm of Ends or Pluralism and Theism*, Gifford Lectures 1907–10, in Basile 2009/2013: section 5, paragraph 1).

It is obvious how many essential features of Iqbal's *Reconstruction* are taken from these ideas. Consequently the originality of the philosophical component of Iqbal's new theology has to be regarded as rather limited. His own achievement lies mainly in the synthesis of the philosophical ideas of his teachers on the one hand and statements of the Qurʾān as well as of selected authorities of the Islamic tradition, e.g.

[4] After reading G. L. Dickinson's memoir book *J. McT. E. McTaggard* (Cambridge: University Press, 1931), i.e. after publishing his *Reconstruction*, Iqbal published an article entitled *McTaggard's Philosophy* (in *Indian Arts and Letters*, i (1932), 25–51, reprinted in *Statements and Speeches of Iqbal*, ed. A. R. Tariq (Lahore: Shaykh Ghulam Ali & Sons, 1973), 140–51), in which his indebtedness to McTaggart becomes more visible.

al-Ghazālī and Ibn al-ʿArabī, on the other hand. The result of this synthesis is doubtless very attractive and inspiring for many contemporary Muslims because of its aptness to support specifically modern values such as esteem of human dignity, freedom, activity, self-optimization, and creative participation in building a better future. However, not a few Muslims have also criticized it, in particular because of the pantheistic tendency not agreeing with God's transcendence presupposed in the Qurʾān, and since the author's exegesis of the Qurʾān sometimes seems to be arbitrary and dictated by his preconceived interests (cf. e.g. Raschid 1981; Fazli 2005; and the authors referred to in Masud 2007: 19).

VI New Hermeneutical and Epistemological Approaches to the Qurʾānic Revelation

(a) Pioneers of a New Hermeneutics

Towards the end of the twentieth century an increasing number of theological thinkers—still a small minority, but a highly qualified one—came to the conclusion that they had to face the consequences of modernity for Islamic faith on a much more general level than that targeted by the modernists and also that chosen by Iqbal in his selective amalgamation of modern Western philosophy and Islam's mystical heritage, namely the level of a basic reflection on the hermeneutical and epistemological implications of the belief in Qurʾānic revelation under cultural and social conditions strongly differing from those of the prophet's original audience. There were two main factors paving the way to this development: the emergence of an Egyptian school of Qurʾānic exegesis relying on methods of literary criticism; and the reception of modern European philosophical hermeneutics and epistemology by Muslim theological thinkers.

The Egyptian school of literary criticism in Qurʾānic exegesis (Wielandt 2002: 131–5) was founded on the theory of Qurʾān interpretation developed by Amīn al-Khūlī (d. 1967), a professor of Arabic Language and Literature at the Egyptian University (later University of Cairo) in several publications since the 1940s. According to his theory the Qurʾān, the most important literary work in Arabic, has to be understood, as any work of literary art, against the background of the language and stylistic conventions, but also the cultural and social conditions of those to whom it was originally addressed. Hence its exegesis has to proceed in two steps: first the language and the forms of literary expression, but also the religious, cultural, and social circumstances of the ancient Arabs who were the prophet's first audience have to be studied, together with the chronology of the enunciation of the Qurʾānic text and the occasions of its revelation (*asbāb al-nuzūl*). On this basis one has to establish the exact meaning of the Qurʾānic text as it was understood by its first listeners.

Naṣr Ḥāmid Abū Zayd (1943–2010), Professor of Arabic Language and Literature at the University of Cairo, generalized the starting point of al-Khūlī's methodology in his book *Mafhūm al-naṣṣ* (1990) by treating the Qurʾān not only as a work of literary art, but as a text (*naṣṣ*) that must be understood according to the scientific principles applying to the understanding of any text. He derived these principles from a theory of communication widely accepted in linguistics and literary text theory since the 1960s. It purports that the information contained in a message can be understood only if the sender transmits it in a code known to the recipient. According to Abū Zayd this is valid also for the process of revelation, in which a divine message is transmitted to humans: God, the 'author' of the Qurʾān, must necessarily have used a code understandable to the prophet and to the initial addressees of his message. He must have adapted the revealed text to their language and literary conventions, but also to the content of their consciousness which was largely determined by their cultural tradition and their social situation. Present-day exegetes have first to familiarize themselves with this code tied to the specific historical situation of the prophet and his Arab contemporaries, in order to be able to identify the elements belonging to it in the Qurʾānic text and to distinguish them from the immutable message of the revelation. Then they have to translate this eternal message into a code understandable to their own contemporaries, i.e. into the language and the concepts corresponding to the cultural social and situation of today.

Mohammed Arkoun (1928–2010), a scholar of Algerian origin who taught in Lyon and later Paris for many years, had already proposed a similar methodology of exegesis due to a different theoretical approach (see esp. *Lectures du Coran*, 1982). According to him, the *fait coranique*, i.e. that to which all attempts at understanding the Qurʾān have to refer, is the originally oral prophetic speech which Muḥammad and his audience believed to be God's revelation. This speech, attested in the written text of the ʿUthmānic recension of the Qurʾān, was performed in a language and in textual genres tied to a specific historical situation, and in the mythical and symbolic modes of expression of that time. The whole exegetical tradition is a process of attempts at appropriating this *fait coranique*. The ʿUthmānic text as such is open to a potentially infinite range of ever new interpretations. Contemporary scholars must use the instruments of historical semiotics and sociolinguistics in order to distinguish particular traditional interpretations of the Qurʾānic text from the normative meaning which this text might have for present-day readers.[5]

[5] The theological relevance of the ideas of the Syrian engineer and writer Muḥammad Shaḥrūr (b. 1938) about Qurʾānic exegesis has been grossly overestimated by some authors: Shahrūr's approach consists of a combination of untenable linguistic assumptions, partly misunderstood modern philosophy, and *tafsīr ʿilmī*, whereas it lacks any state-of-the-art hermeneutical reflection. This approach and the stupendous success of the book in which it was exposed for the first time (*al-Kitāb wa-l-qurʾān, qirāʾa muʿāṣirā*, 1st edn. (Damascus: al-Ahālī li-l-ṭibāʿa wa-l-nashr wa-l-tawzīʿ, 1990); 10th edn. (2011)) among Arab readers without education in Islamic theology, philosophy, or Arabic language are primarily apt to illustrate the ardent desire of the author and his public for exegetical justification of their own notions of what is modern.

The Pakistani scholar Fazlur Rahman (1919–88), who had earned his Ph.D. in Oxford, was director of the Central Institute for Islamic Research in Lahore in the years 1962–8, but emigrated to the United States under the pressure of conservative and traditionalist circles. From 1969 until his death he was professor of Islamic Thought at the University of Chicago. There he developed his hermeneutics aimed at facilitating a modernized understanding of Qurʾānic legal provisions (see esp. Rahman 1982: 1–22). In doing so, he took his cue from the Italian historian of jurisprudence Emilio Betti, whose theory of interpretation he had got to know indirectly by an English translation of Hans-Georg Gadamer's *Wahrheit und Methode* (Rahman 1982: 8; Körner 2005: 113f. with n. 256–8). According to Betti, understanding a text means reconstructing what the author had in mind when he wrote it. By applying this concept to the Qurʾān, Fazlur Rahman arrived at the conclusion that the intention of its divine author in revealing it had been to create a society guided by ethical principles. From this Fazlur Rahman inferred that it is not the concrete legal norms of the Qurʾān that are valid for all times, but the general ethical goals God wanted to achieve by imposing them. In the prophet's time and environment, the Qurʾānic legal provisions were the appropriate means for achieving these goals. Modern exegetes interpreting a particular Qurʾānic legal norm have first to study the historical situation of the original addressees of the revelation, then to distil the general ethical principle out of the situational provision by which God imparted it to the prophet's contemporaries, and finally to transform this ethical principle into a new provision apt to enforce God's intention under the circumstances of today (see esp. Rahman, *Islam and Modernity*, 5–7).

(b) The Hermeneutical Turn in Part of Turkish University Theology

Since 1981 most of Fazlur Rahman's books were successively published in Turkish translations, not least thanks to two Turkish junior researchers who had been his students in Chicago (Aktay 2005: 84f. n. 14). In the late 1980s a group of young Turkish theologians at the Ilâhiyat Fakültesi of the University of Ankara began to study them intensively. They took particular interest in Fazlur Rahman's hermeneutics, because it facilitates a historical understanding of the Qurʾān in the sense of reading it within the original context for which it was formulated and then recontextualizing its message in view of the situation of modern believers, without abandoning the belief that it is God's verbal revelation.

Fazlur Rahman thus became the major source of inspiration for a number of Turkish scholars, known as the 'School of Ankara'. They developed various approaches to an exegesis of the Qurʾān taking equally account of its historicity and of the necessity of translating its normative content into the situation of contemporary Muslims (for a thorough study and critical discussion of these approaches see Körner 2005). Among the most prominent representatives of this group are Mehmet Paçacı (b. 1959) and Ömer Özsoy (b. 1963).

Paçacı refined Fazlur Rahman's hermeneutical model by stating that the modern interpreter, before carrying out the first methodical step envisaged by Rahman, has to become aware of the presuppositions of his own understanding, because not only the text of the Qurʾān, but he too is tied to a specific historical context (see esp. Paçacı, *Kur'an ve Ben Nekadar Tarihseliz?*, 2001). With this principle Paçacı refers to the hermeneutics of the German philosopher Hans-Georg Gadamer, whose *Wahrheit und Methode* he had read in English translation. Ömer Özsoy equally draws on Fazlur Rahman, but also refers to Amīn al-Khūlī. He characterizes the Qurʾān as God's written speech on which the reactions of the original addressees were not without influence. In his view their way of dealing with it is exemplary and normative. Only by exploring their understanding and their ways of acting is it possible to penetrate to an unambiguous meaning of the often ambiguous Qurʾānic text and thus grasp its 'objective meaning'. However, Özsoy rates it as anachronistic to expect plain answers for today's questions from the literal sense of the Qurʾān: Muslims are now living in circumstances differing substantially from those of the original milieu of the divine speech. For this reason the 'objective meaning' of the Qurʾān has now to be interpreted in the light of the requirements of the present situation. This interpretation remains always 'subjective' according to Özsoy, since the results of the interpreter's analysis of his own situation are, due to his own historicity, not certain, in contrast to what he can find out about the meaning of the Qurʾān for its first addressees (Özsoy 2004a).

Since the 1990s, the ideas of Naṣr Ḥāmid Abū Zayd and the Cairene philosopher Ḥasan Ḥanafī (b. 1935) have also met with some response in Turkish university theology (Aktay 2005: 72–5), thus strengthening the new hermeneutical trend there. According to Ḥanafī one cannot know God Himself. Only human concepts of God and of His will can be known. Therefore theology must be turned into anthropology. And as these concepts have always been formed according to people's changeable political, social, and economic needs, one has to keep in mind that the *sharīʿa* as well as *kalām* are historically contextual; at the same time today's *mutakallimūn* are called upon to reformulate them in view of present needs (see e.g. Ḥanafī 1997).

The 'historicist' (*tarihselci*) hermeneutics in Qurʾānic exegesis has already been the subject of an extensive public debate in Turkey (Özsoy 2004b: 8–14; cf. also Aktay 2005). On the academic level it began in 1994 with a nationwide theological symposium in Bursa devoted entirely to this topic, and it is still going on.

(c) Iranian Ventures into Modern Hermeneutics and Epistemology

During the last few decades several Iranian theological thinkers developed new hermeneutical and epistemological approaches (cf. also Marcotte 2008). They traced each other's publications and were at times engaged in public discussions with each other. The two most original and productive ones among them, Shabistarī and Surūsh, are also familiar with Abū Zayd's theory of Qurʾānic exegesis (Amirpur 2003: 34). Nevertheless, each of them analysed the problems of a contemporary understanding of the Qurʾānic revelation in his own way and proposed his own solutions for them.

Particularly profound and systematic are the pertinent reflections of Muḥammad Mujtahid Shabistarī (b. 1936) (on him, cf. Richard 2009),[6] an upper-level Shīʿī religious scholar educated at Qom. In addition, he holds a doctoral degree in Philosophy from the University of Tehran. In the years 1970–8 he officiated as director of the (Shīʿī) Islamic Centre of Hamburg. During his stay in Germany he mastered the German language and acquainted himself with recent developments in Christian theology. He also acquired a deep familiarity with modern Western, in particular German, philosophy, studying, for instance, Kant's epistemology and Gadamer's hermeneutics. Returned to Iran, he was elected into the parliament for the first term after the Islamic Revolution in 1979, but later took a critical stance against the regime and withdrew from politics. In the years 1985–2006 he was professor at the University of Tehran, where he taught Islamic Philosophy and Theology and also lectured on non-Islamic religions.

In his writings he proves to be a universally erudite scholar who refuses to think in the simplistic terms of spiritualist East and materialist West. He is convinced that some fundamental developments of modern European intellectual history, such as the evidence provided by Kant that it is no longer possible to continue traditional metaphysics under the auspices of modern science, are valid and inescapable also for Muslims. In his view all inhabitants of this world are now living in one and the same modernity, whether they are aware of this fact or not. Muslims would thus be well advised to tackle the problem of how one can speak of the belief in revelation under the specific conditions of modernity (Shabistarī 2000a: 58f., 87).

His hermeneutics (cf. Vahdat 2000, Part I; Marcotte 2008) starts from the premiss that humans can neither know God in Himself nor the meaning of the divine revelation in itself. Combining this assessment with Gadamer's insights, he emphasizes that understanding is always shaped by the presuppositions of the human subject that tries to understand. As he states, this is also valid for all efforts to understand the meaning of the revealed text of the Qurʾān: any interpretation is shaped by the presuppositions of the interpreter, i.e. his modes of reasoning, his previous understandings (*pīshfahmhā*), his actual questions, interests, and expectations (Shabistarī 1996: 14–32). Therefore the idea of Sunni traditionalists and Ashʿarites that *naql* (the revealed text as it is transmitted) and *ʿaql* ((sc. the use of) reason) are alternatives between which they can choose, and that they are on the safe side if they opt for *naql*, is an illusion: the presuppositions of the *ʿaql* are at work in any reference to the *naql* (Shabistarī 2000b: 86f.).

As these presuppositions are influenced by the specific situation and the cultural horizon of the understanding subject in its historicity, no single human interpretation of what is said in the revealed book can ever claim to have grasped the eternal truth. Hence it is illegitimate

[6] Shabistarī's articles have been collected at http://mohammadmojtahedshabestari.com/articles.php.

to impose a particular interpretation of Qurʾānic norms or doctrines on others by political force. The coexistence of a plurality of divergent interpretations on equal terms must be accepted and protected, which is only possible in an open society and a secular state.

In conformity with Gadamer's concept of the hermeneutical circle, Shabistarī views man's efforts to understand revelation as a permanent process: on the one hand his interpretation of the holy text never reaches a final result, but always evolves under the impact of his changing presuppositions; on the other hand his presuppositions can also be corrected by the encounter with the text.

In an article entitled 'Qirāʾat-i nabavī az jahān', printed in the journal *Madraseh* in summer 2007 and later enlarged by a long series of postscripts (Shabistarī 2009: XXXVI n. 17[7]), Shabistarī expanded his approach by a new understanding of revelation. He now ascribed the Qurʾān to Muḥammad's (rather than God's) authorship and thus opened the way to its unrestricted historical contextualization, but also offered a tentative answer to the theological question of how the role of the transcendent God in the genesis of a sacred book authored by a human being in this world can be conceived of. On the basis of considerations of philosophy of language he concluded that the prophet would not have been able to make his audience understand his message, if he had only served as loudspeaker or sound carrier for the transmission of a ready-made text which was not his own. As he now judged, form and content of the Qurʾān must have originated with Muḥammad, because nothing can be textualized in a human language without originating from a human speaker. Yet the prophet experienced God as his teacher and mover who empowered him to say what he said. This divine empowerment to prophetic speech is what the Qurʾān calls *waḥy*, revelation. Its exact nature is not known, but it is clear that it cannot have been a verbal communication between God and Muḥammad, because it took place in a sphere where the conditions for a dialogue in human language are not met. However, one can see its result: the prophet's speech differs from that of ordinary people in its specific perspective on the world. The Qurʾān contains Muḥammad's prophetic reading of the world from the monotheistic point of view.

ʿAbd al-Karīm Surūsh (b. 1945) also arrived at the conclusion that Muḥammad is the author of the Qurʾān. Unlike Shabistarī, he was not educated as a religious scholar. After graduating in Pharmacology at the University of Tehran, he spent more than five years in England, where he studied Chemistry and Philosophy of Science. While doing so he came into contact with Karl Popper's Critical Rationalism. Having returned to Iran after the dawn of the Islamic Revolution in 1979, Surūsh was initially a staunch supporter of the new political system. However, he withdrew from politics in 1984 and devoted himself entirely to writing and teaching, lecturing on mysticism and philosophy, mainly at the University of Tehran. In 1996 he began to criticize the Shīʿī clergy publicly and from then on turned into one of the country's most prominent dissidents. Having been threatened and even physically attacked due to this volte-face, he

[7] The text and most of the postscripts are available at <http://resasade.com/wpcontent/uploads/2012/10/Shabestari1.pdf>, accessed 31/03/2014.

accepted several invitations for longer stays abroad and finally went into continuous exile in 2000. Since then he has carried on research at renowned scientific institutions in Berlin and Leiden and has been teaching as visiting scholar at various universities of the United States.

The core of Surūsh's contribution to theological thought is a specific epistemology which he later complemented with a new theory of revelation (cf. esp. Cooper 2000; Dahlén 2001). His epistemology was developed in the late 1980s and can be mainly found in his book *Qabḍ va-basṭ-i tiʾūrīk-i sharīʿat* (Surūsh 1990/1; concisely summarized by himself in Surūsh 1999b: 2f.; Eng. trans. in Surūsh 2009: 120). Its starting point is the distinction between religion and religious knowledge. By religion he means revealed truth. As Surūsh states, religion is eternal, but religious knowledge is changeable, as any other kind of knowledge, due to factors external to its object, for instance the individual intellectual abilities and qualifications of the believers, their language, the social and cultural circumstances in which they live, and the general state of the development of sciences in their time and milieu. Under the impact of these extra-religious factors religious knowledge can contract or expand, i.e. shrink because ideas or rules are abandoned or grow through addition and elaboration of concepts or provisions, according to the assumptions, expectations, and questions of the believers. Religion as such or, as he also says, the normative text is 'silent' (see e.g. Surūsh 1998: 245; Surūsh 1999b: 120). It takes effect only by means of human interpretation, which is always conjectural and fallible and inevitably produces a plurality of equally legitimate results (cf. the title of his book *Sirāṭhā-yi mustaqīm, Straight Paths,* boldly alluding to Qurʾān 1: 6) due to the varying extra-religious factors on which it depends. No particular interpretation can claim final authority over another one.

This epistemology obviously contradicts Khomeini's theory of *vilāyat-i faqīh*, the basis of the present political system of Iran, and is also not easily compatible with the Shīʿī belief in the infallibility of the imams. But it does not yet contest the eternal validity of the Qurʾān in its entirety. This step was taken by Surūsh in his book *Basṭ-i tajrube-yi nabawī* (Surūsh 1999a; Surūsh 2009) where he abandoned the concept of verbal revelation (for his theology of revelation see Madaninejad 2011: 60–104; Amirpur 2011: 422–37). Instead of the Qurʾān, the prophet's experience of revelation now became the benchmark of Islamic faith for him. As he now assumed, the Qurʾān is the prophet's interpretation of the experience of revelation. Surūsh conceives of this experience as a kind of mystical union in which Muḥammad immersed himself in God's will. After Muḥammad had learned to stand this experience, he could even induce it himself as circumstances required. The Qurʾān then answered his and his listeners' questions and responded to their situational needs in a form understandable to them.

All Qurʾānic verses referring to specific incidents, but also the Arabic language of the Qurʾān and the fact that it breathes Arab culture, are accidental. They do not form part of the everlasting religion God wants people to adhere to. As for present-day Muslims, according to Surūsh, their religiosity should ideally be that of a critical scholar and a mystic at the same time: on the one hand they have to separate the eternal in the Qurʾān and in Islam from the accidentals; on the other hand they should expand the prophetic experience by joining it, which means seeking mystical union with God themselves.

In an interview given to the Dutch online magazine *ZemZem* in 2007 (text in Surūsh 2009: 272–5), Surūsh's dissociation from the traditional belief in the literal revelation of the Qurʾān is made even more explicit: he now declares that revelation is a kind of inspiration comparable to that of a poet. Like a poem, the Qurʾān was not only created by inspiration, but also by the inspired person, the prophet Muḥammad. In any revelation the revealed content as such is formless, it is the prophet who shapes it. In this process 'the language he knows, the styles he masters and the images and knowledge he possesses', but also his personality and even his moods, play an important role. In view of this 'purely human side of revelation', the Qurʾān can also contain errors, for instance in what it says about historical events, other religious traditions, or practical earthly matters (Surūsh 2009: 273). Yet Surūsh still affirms the infallibility of the Qurʾanic statements about God's attributes, life after death, and rules of worship (Surūsh 2009: 273)—without naming the criteria for his decision not to attribute these components of the Qurʾān also to the prophet's knowledge.

VII Beginnings and Development of the Interest in a New *Kalām*

(a) Early Concepts of a New *Kalām*

Sayyid Ahmad Khan had already pointed out the need for a specifically modern *ʿilm al-kalām*. In his opinion, the task of this new theology was 'to make an all-out effort to harmonize the tenets of contemporary natural science and philosophy with the doctrines of Islam, or to prove the futility of the tenets of contemporary natural science and philosophy' (*Lecture on Islam*, 1884, trans. in Troll 1978b: Appendix 313). As he did not believe that the tenets of contemporary natural sciences and the underlying philosophy can be refuted by theological arguments, he saw the main function of a modern *ʿilm al-kalām* in developing an interpretation of the doctrines of Islam compatible with them. Muḥammad ʿAbduh had noted a lack of present-day relevance in the treatises of *kalām* traditionally used for teaching purposes, but without reflecting systematically on possible new themes or methods to be taken up by Muslim theologians. In his *Risālat al-Tawḥīd* (1892), he had restricted himself to trying to remedy this deficiency by presenting Islam as the religion most suitable for the age of reason and modern sciences.

The Indian scholar Shiblī Nuʿmānī has often been credited with having made the call for a new *kalām* a programmatic slogan. In his book *al-Kalām* (1904), whose first print carried the subtitle '*yaʿnī ʿilm-i kalām-i jadīd*', he urged a reform of Islamic theology in accordance with what he regarded as contemporary needs. This book was published under the title *ʿIlm-i kalām-i jadīd* in a Persian translation in 1950–1 (Nuʿmānī, *al-Kalām*); it contributed to the diffusion of the idea of a new *kalām*, particularly among Shīʿī scholars. However, Shiblī advocated a kind of new *kalām* of limited innovatory value: since in his opinion the basic theological problems were still the same as they had been many centuries ago, he thought it would sufficiently meet the needs of the present age to discard mainstream Ashʿarism and to return to the rational arguments and positions of the Muʿtazilīs or the Islamic philosophers. In view of this concept of renewing *kalām* by reverting to the rationalist trends of the Islamic past Shiblī's attitude has been characterized as 'medievalized modernism' (Murad 1996: 34; for an analysis of the problems of Shiblī's approach, see Murad 1996: 13–34).

Several late Ottoman and early Republican Turkish contemporaries of Shiblī were much more conscious of the novelty of the challenges to be faced by *kalām* in the twentieth century and rated the extent of theological innovation required by them as much greater. In 1909 the Şeyhülislam Musa Kazım gave a notable lecture in which he dwelled on the necessity of adjusting the textbooks used for teaching *kalām* to contemporary requirements. As he pointed out, the *mutakallimūn* of former times had defended the Islamic creed against the objections of Aristotelian and Illuminationist philosophers. These opponents disappeared a long time ago; thus the traditional treatises of *kalām* defending Islam against them have lost their usefulness. Instead, new books on *kalām* are needed which defend the Islamic faith against its adversaries of today, namely the adherents of materialism, naturalism, and atheism (Kütüb 290f.). In order to become able to rebut their objections effectively, contemporary *mutakallimūn* first have to make themselves thoroughly acquainted with the pertinent contemporary philosophical trends, while they may neglect some of the much-discussed subjects of the theological discourse of former times. Confronted with contemporary atheism, for instance, it is useless to discuss God's attributes at length, since to people not even believing in God's existence the question of how to understand His attributes is of no relevance (Kütüb 292).

At about the same time Abdüllatif Harputi (1842–1916), who taught Kelâm at the Darülfünun in Istanbul, also stressed the need for a new kind of *kalām* apt to refute the specifically modern false doctrines challenging the Islamic faith, in particular sensualism, materialism, and atheism which were now spreading among Muslims under the impact of Western philosophical ideas (cf. also Karaman 2004). In the preface of his *Tanqīḥ al-kalām fī ʿaqāʾid ahl al-islām* (first published in 1909), written in Arabic with extensive explanatory annotation in Ottoman Turkish, he reported to have decided to write this work because he had found the traditional treatises of *kalām* unusable for contemporary teaching purposes: the authors of these works have rebutted the errors and pernicious innovations (*bidaʿ*) of their times; nowadays it is mandatory to rebut those of the present, since 'writing *kalām* works must be done in accordance with place and time' (*Tanqīḥ*, 4f.; quotation p. 4). In a book on the history of *kalām* he pointed out that after a first phase of development in which *kalām* was mainly concerned with refuting the errors resulting from the early schisms in Islam, and a second one in which *kalām* mainly dealt with errors that had come about under the impact of Greek philosophy, it is now time for a third phase of *kalām* in which its representatives strive to defend the

Islamic creed against the dangers emanating from contemporary philosophies. In order to be able to do so they must study these philosophies in depth, as the *mutakallimūn* of the second phase had done with Greek philosophy (*Tanqīḥ*, 124–6).

Harputi failed to implement this programme. The theology deployed in his *Tanqīḥ* is for the most part still very traditional (cf. also Yar 1998: 258–60).[8] He admitted that he was not able to master the task he had assigned to the *mutakallimūn* of his time, because he did not know any Western language and hence could not get a sufficient grasp of contemporary philosophy; so he expressed his hope for better-equipped colleagues (*Tarih*, 126).

İzmirli Ismail Hakkı, who like Harputi saw the main challenge for present-day *kalām* in having to grapple with modern philosophies of Western origin, met this challenge to a greater extent (cf. above Section IV c). He also reflected on the legitimacy, the methodological requirements and the consequences of such a new approach in a more differentiated way (see also Baloğlu 1996a). His pertinent deliberations can mainly be found in the prefaces of his books *Muḥaṣṣal al-kalām wa-l-ḥikma* (1917/18) and *Yeni ilm-i kelâm* (1920/1–1922/3), in an interview on his project of a new *kalām* given to *Sebilürreşâd* in May 1923, and in an article and its continuation, both entitled 'Yeni ilm-i kelâm hakkında' and published in the same journal in August 1923.

Like Harputi, İzmirli divides the previous development of *kalām* into two phases, that of the earlier *mutakallimūn* and that of the later ones. The second phase began, according to him, in the sixth Islamic century under the influence of philosophically well-versed Ashʿarites such as al-Ghazālī. The earlier *mutakallimūn* debated on the views of different *firaq*, in particular the Muʿtazila and the Jahmiyya, whereas the later ones dealt with Greek philosophy and the views of Muslim philosophers influenced by it. By expounding the difference between this later type of theology and the earlier one İzmirli demonstrates that it is nothing new, but normal for *mutakallimūn* to change their perspectives and methods when necessary (*Muḥaṣṣal*, 10f.; *Kelâm*, 7f.), because 'the principles and means of the science of *kalām* may change according to the needs of the age' (*Kelâm*, 7); 'the science of *kalām* varies in its functions, as the adversaries, the obstinate opponents and those who seek guidance vary' (*Kelâm*, 10; cf. *Muḥaṣṣal*, 11; 'Kelâm Hakkında', 2: 38). The kind of philosophy underlying the thought of the second phase of *kalām* petered out three centuries ago (*Kelâm*, 90; *Muḥaṣṣal*, 12; Interview 59). A new kind of philosophy, that of the modern West, has established itself. It is therefore now preferable to deal with the views of English, French, and German philosophers instead of ancient Greek ones (*Kelâm*, 90). Nowadays *kalām* cannot defend Islam any more on the basis of Aristotle's logic and scholastic patterns of argumentation; it should use instead the logic of the founders of modern empiricism and rationalism and should follow the same methods and rules that are now generally valid in all sciences (*Muḥaṣṣal*, 13, 14; Interview 59).

[8] Putting aside an article ('*Astronomi*') printed in the appendix of this work in which he states that the Qurʾānic picture of the universe does not necessarily contradict that of post-Copernican astronomy, since the relevant Qurʾānic texts are not to be read as descriptions of astronomic facts, but as pointers on the greatness and power of the Creator.

All the different branches of modern philosophy as well as History of Religions must be included in its reflections (*Muḥaṣṣal*, 17). Moreover, due to the differentiation of scientific disciplines in modern times *kalām* cannot contradict the results of empirical sciences any more, but has to accept them as facts and to argue on their basis (*Muḥaṣṣal*, 16).

Contrary to Harputi, who supposed a fundamental antagonism between religion and philosophy and hence saw in Western philosophy nothing but an object of refutation (see e.g. *Tarih*, 127, 124, 126), İzmirli assumed that some views of modern Western philosophers contradict the tenets of Islam, while others do not or even confirm the Islamic positions in specific points, so that they provide useful arguments for convincing contemporary Muslim sceptics impressed by Western philosophy. According to him the task of the new *kalām* consists in sorting out which philosophical views are incompatible with Islam and which ones are compatible with it or might even support it. Views of Western philosophers must not be refuted or accepted except on the basis of proofs (*Muḥaṣṣal*, 13). He attached great importance to the point that the new *kelâm* he had in mind would not lead to changing any essentials of the Islamic faith (Interview 59), but only to reasoning Islamic doctrines in such a way as to keep them acceptable for educated Muslims, especially 'the Muslim youth whose brains are nowadays saturated with philosophical theories' (İzmirli, Kelâm Hakkında: 2, 40).

After İzmirli's writings on *yeni ilm-i kelâm* and Iqbal's proposal of a reconstruction of religious thought, there was relatively little talk about a desirable new philosophical theology for approximately half a century. Ayatollah Murtażā Muṭahharī (1920–79), who taught at the University of Tehran from 1956 to 1978, is reputed to have again advocated a new *kalām* (ʿAbbās and Qāʾimī Niyā 2011; Khosrowpanāh 2000/1: 24; Madaninejad 2011: 25), on the grounds that 'in our age doubts have arisen that formerly did not exist, and formerly unknown corroborating arguments have appeared, due to the peculiarities of scientific progress, whereas many of the old doubts are irrelevant in our time and many corroborating arguments have lost their value' (quoted in ʿAbbās and Qāʾimī Niyā 2011: 89).

(b) Wahiduddin Khan's So-called Qurʾānic *Kalām*

In a lecture given in 1976, the Indian Sunnī scholar Wahiduddin Khan (b. 1925), the founder of the Islamic Centre at New Delhi, also pleaded for what he called a new *kalām* (cf. also Altıntaş 2003). However, what he meant by this term neither corresponds to the definition of theology lying at the bottom of this chapter nor to any notion of *kalām* common to a significant number of contemporary Muslim experts: he advocated a new theology not based on philosophy at all, but solely on the results of modern natural science, psychology, and archaeology. In his opinion the representatives of classical *kalām* made the mistake of trying to explain the immutable Islamic creed by means of rational arguments taken from philosophy, that is to say from changeable patterns of human thought. A new *kalām* arguing on the basis of modern philosophy would be equally mistaken, because it would again rely on merely human rational insights that can become obsolete in the future.

According to Wahiduddin Khan today a kind of *kalām* is necessary and possible that solves the problem of theological views becoming obsolete, and this once and for all. The conceptions that can form part of a permanently valid Islamic theology are to be found in the Qur'ān. God has arranged the order of the universe and explained it in the Qur'ān, although in an abbreviated manner only, because the prophet's contemporaries were not yet able to understand more. Thanks to scientific progress this order has now become known in detail; at the same time, it is now clear that the results of the sciences prove the truth of what has been said in the Qur'ān. Hence the pertinent Qur'ānic statements have to be recorded and complemented with the findings of modern sciences specifying and confirming them (*Kalām*, 78–81). Wahiduddin Khan calls this method of elaborating on the Qur'ānic text 'Qur'ānic *kalām*' (*Kalām*, 77).

He had already presented an example of its application in his book *al-Islām yataḥaddā* (first published in Urdu in 1966, widely known in its Arabic translation published in 1974), where he addressed a broad range of modern topics that would indeed deserve to be seriously dealt with in contemporary *kalām*. However, his approach ignores that, just like philosophy, all kinds of modern sciences are based on human patterns of thought and that, hence, knowledge attained by them cannot in its entirety be rated as eternally valid either. What he practises is essentially confined to a slightly modified variety of the so-called *tafsīr ʿilmī*, i.e. the apologetic technique of reading the presumedly latest scientific discoveries and theories into the Qur'ānic text. Its main weakness is the lack of a reflected hermeneutics.

(c) Recent Pleas for a New Philosophy-based *Kalām*

Since the 1990s a new philosophy-based *kalām* has again increasingly been called for by Sunni as well as Shīʿī scholars (a first, rudimentary overview of the development of the notion of a new *kalām* by a Shīʿī author is provided by Badawi 2002). 'The new *kalām*' (*al-kalām al-jadīd, yeni kelâm, kalām-i jadīd*) has now become an established term for a goal with which an entire group of thinkers of different backgrounds identifies. In Egypt it is promoted, among others, by Ḥasan Ḥanafī. In Turkey and Iran 'New *kalām*' has also become the established term for a school of thought.

Contemporary Turkish university theologians often classify ʿAbduh, Shiblī Nuʿmānī, Harputi, and İzmirli İsmail Hakkı as major forerunners of this school called 'Yeni Kelâm' and often deal with their thought under this heading in courses as well as in textbooks (e.g. Topaloğlu 1993: 35–42; Karadaş 2010: 119–25). Some contemporary Turkish scholars specializing in Kelâm do not refer to these founding fathers, but have nevertheless factually developed a new philosophy-founded theology of their own, among them Hüseyin Atay (b. 1930), the first holder of the Chair of Kelâm at the Faculty of Theology in Ankara, as well as İlhami Güler (b. 1959) and Şaban Ali Düzgün (b. 1968), both professors at the same faculty, to name but a few.

In Iran, the programme of a new *kalām* has been advocated and pursued, among others, by Muḥammad Mujtahid Shabistarī and ʿAbd al-Karīm Surūsh in the recent past. A decided proponent of a new *kalām* on the Shīʿī side is also ʿAbd al-Jabbār al-Rifāʿī (b.

1954), professor of Islamic Philosophy at the University of Baghdad and editor of the journal *Qaḍāyā islāmiyya muʿāṣira*.

The third annual congress of the Egyptian Philosophical Society held in Cairo in June 1991 in cooperation with al-Azhar was devoted to the subject 'Towards a new science of *kalām*' (report of Ḥasan Ḥanafī on his own contribution to it in a long footnote in Ḥanafī 1997: 69–71; report shedding light also on divergent positions of other participants in al-Rifāʿī 2002a: 253f.). In April 2004 the first one of a series of international congresses on 'The Methods of Islamic Sciences between Renewal (*tajdīd*) and Imitation (*taqlīd*)' organized by the Kulliyyat Dār al-ʿulūm of the University of Cairo also focused on a new *kalām* (text of the final memorandum containing the recommendations of the participants in al-Julaynid 2004: 827f.). In his opening speech to this conference Muḥammad al-Sayyid al-Julaynid deplored that lectures on *kalām* in present-day Muslim academic institutions resemble 'a museum of cultural history' through which the students are given a guided tour, instead of being taught how to reflect on solutions for the problems of our time (al-Julaynid 2004: 27).

(d) Types of Proposed New Approaches

Among the theologians demanding a new *kalām* the notions of what its novelty should consist of vary considerably (cf. also Evkuran 2004). In view of the following typological outline it should be kept in mind that supporters of the idea of a new *kalām* often do not only hold one of these notions, but combine several of them.

1 *A new purpose?*

A first point about which there are different opinions is the function a new *kalām* should fulfil. Many of its proponents still think that the primary purpose of *kalām* is apologetics and that *kalām* should be made fit for serving this purpose more effectively in the future (see e.g. al-Julaynid 2004: 37, 68f. and the final recommendations of the conference al-Julaynid 2004: 827f.), because it has to defend Islam against ever more malicious adversaries. But not a few thinkers now plead for overcoming this primarily defensive attitude. They conceive of the new *kalām* mainly as a discipline needed by Muslims for their own sake in order to develop a rationally tenable understanding of their religion under the conditions of modernity, and of modernity in the light of their religion.

2 *New topics*

Some authors understand by the new *kalām* primarily a philosophy-based theology dealing with new, typically modern topics (for detailed reflections of a Turkish theologian on the topics that should be treated nowadays in *kalām*, see Topaloğlu 2004). Often-mentioned issues to be addressed are the relation between Islamic creed and modern natural sciences, a much-discussed subject since Sayyid Ahmad Khan and ʿAbduh, and also materialism and atheism, topics that had been in the focus of the modernists' attention already at the beginning of the twentieth century. Since the 1960s some Turkish theologians have actually resumed the refutation of atheism along the lines of early twentieth-century modernism, occasionally on the basis of a slightly updated philosophical knowledge (see e.g. the list of titles in Topaloğlu 1993: 41f. and Coşkun 2011).

Darwin's theory of evolution had been a seriously discussed topic already in the late nineteenth century. Since the 1970s creationism was propagated as an alternative to Darwinism, particularly in Turkey where religiously conservative and Islamist politicians supported it, but occasionally also elsewhere (Riexinger 2009a: 103–12; cf. also Riexinger 2009b and 2011). Yet neither Darwinism nor creationism has so far received much attention among those promoting a new *kalām*.

Much greater is the innovative potential of concepts of a new *kalām* not only allowing for new topics, but based on the assessment that *kalām* needs a new focus of interest and new methods.

3 *New focuses*

Several scholars press for a shift from the traditionally theocentric *kalām* to an anthropocentric one (see e.g. Ḥanafī 1997: 72, and above, Section VI b), or at least for a *kalām* giving the anthropological dimension of theology more weight compared to the questions related to God's unity and attributes. In view of the importance of man as a subject of theological thought Şerafeddin Gölcük (b. 1940), professor of Kelâm at Selçuk Üniversitesi in Konya, suggested that the term *ʿilm al-tawḥīd* should no longer be used as a synonym for *ʿilm al-kalām* (Gölcük 1992: 333f.).

Another demand made by quite a few thinkers is that *kalām* must become more this-worldly and political, so as to work out systematically the emancipatory potential of the ideas of individual freedom and responsibility as well as social justice contained, as they believe, in the Qurʾān and in the teachings of certain ancient schools of theological thought, particularly the Muʿtazila. According to them *kalām* should thus become an instrument of criticizing oppression, exploitation, poverty, and other concrete grievances and lay the theological foundations for a better order of state and society. One of the main protagonists of such a political *kalām* is Ḥasan Ḥanafī. His above-mentioned idea that today's *mutakallimūn* are called upon to reformulate the traditional Islamic concepts of God and true faith in view of present political, social, and economic needs is not unproblematic because it aims, beyond the mere interpretive recontextualization of Qurʾānic doctrines and provisions in view of modern circumstances, at a consciously manipulative use of the religious convictions of believers for political purposes, which he regards as legitimate.

Other authors not following Ḥanafī in this point nevertheless share his objective of developing an Islamic Theology of Liberation, primarily on a Qurʾanic basis (see e.g. Esack 1997; Güler 2002, 2004, 2011). The beginnings of a feminist exegesis of the Qurʾān, whose most prominent representative is at present Amina Wadud (b. 1952), an American convert to Islam and professor of Religious Studies at Virginia Commonwealth University in Richmond, constitute a special facet of the attempts to initiate such an emancipatory theology (e.g. Wadud 1999 and 2006).

The three Iranian thinkers, Muḥammad Mujtahid Shabistarī, ʿAbd al-Karīm Surūsh, and Muḥsin Kadīvar (b. 1959) (for Kadīvar, see Vahdat 2000, Part II),[9] have already presented a special type of political *kalām*: in different ways they all tried to demonstrate by theological arguments that it is imperative for Islam's sake to strive for a democracy not allowing clergymen or any other brand of self-appointed defenders of true religion to monopolize the interpretation of God's will and to subject everybody to their own opinions about it by dictatorial means, because in their opinion only such a political order ensures the freedom of belief required by the limits of any human comprehension of divine truth and by the plurality of individual views concerning it (for this political aspect of their theology see esp. Sadri 2001).

In the case of Shabistarī, the plea for a secular democracy also results from the relevance of freedom in his understanding of man's relation to God: as he stresses, belief in revelation is a matter of free personal choice. God himself does not want it otherwise. This can already be deduced from the mere fact that he communicated His will to man by revelation, instead of forcing him immediately to execute it, which He could have easily done. The decision for or against belief must also be free for another reason: God wants believers to give testimony (*shahādat*) of their faith; a valid testimony is, by its very nature, only conceivable as a free act of the witness (Shabistarī 2000/1: 21). In his view the freedom of the addressees of revelation includes the right to criticize religion and to adhere to a religion other than Islam or to no religion at all. Without such a choice there would not be real freedom. State and society must be ordered in such a way as to give space to all this (Shabistarī 1996/7: 184, 187). According to Shabistarī the new *kalām* should also tackle the task of developing a well-reflected Islamic foundation for recognizing universal human rights; he has already begun to work on this topic (e.g. Shabistarī 2002/3: 230–311).[10]

4 *New methods*

A view expressed by several Sunni thinkers is that the new *kalām* should be pursued in a more rational way compared to the traditional one. Thus, for instance, Ḥanafī pleads for a *kalām* in which activity of reason (*ʿaql*) is regarded as the basis of *naql* (the tradition of the revealed texts), not vice versa (Ḥanafī 1997: 71). This demand for more rationality corresponds to the general orientation of Sunni modernists since Sayyid Ahmad Khan.

For some Sunni thinkers the quest for a more rational *kalām* is equivalent to a conscious return to the Muʿtazila and the rejection of the Ashʿariyya, as already seen in the case of Shiblī Nuʿmānī. However, it is an exception that contemporary Sunni

[9] Kadīvar, a high-ranking religious scholar who has been visiting professor at Duke University in North Carolina since 2009 and is factually living in exile there, maintains the traditional concept of the verbal revelation of the Qurʾān, but regards Qurʾānic legal precepts concerning human interaction (*muʿāmalāt*) as not binding any more if they appear to contradict justice and reason under present-day conditions (Kadīvar 2002/11).

[10] Surūsh is also a vigorous supporter of human rights, but does not consider their foundation a matter of *kalām*; see Amirpur 2011: 415f.

theologians want to revive the Muʿtazilī doctrines without restriction, as was in fact the aim of the Indonesian scholar Harun Nasution (1919–98), the former rector of IAIN Jakarta (Muzani 1994: 113–20; Martin, Woodward, and Atmaja 1997: 158–96; Saleh 2001: 197–218; for a general overview of modern trends in Indonesia's Islamic theology, cf. Saleh 2001). He regarded the Muʿtazila as that part of the Islamic tradition which is still relevant to the modernizing Muslim community, having identified it as 'our rational and liberal theology' (interview 1993, quoted in Muzani 1994: 115). Unlike him, most authors take recourse to Muʿtazilī notions only selectively and to a rather limited extent. Therefore labels such as 'renewal of Muʿtazilism' (Caspar 1957; Gardet 1972), 'Neo-Muʿtazilism' (Khalid 1969), or 'New-Muʿtazilite Theology' (Demichelis 2010, ignoring Hildebrandt 2002 and 2007) are misleading with respect to their thought. This applies not only to the ideas of Sayyid Ahmad Khan, Muḥammad ʿAbduh, and Shiblī Nuʿmānī, as shown above, but also, for instance, to the authors of the Egyptian school of literary exegesis of the Qurʾān and to Naṣr Ḥāmid Abū Zayd (cf. Hildebrandt 2007: 353–417).

This much is true: contemporary Sunnīs increasingly tend not to be solicitous any more about strictly conforming to the standards of Ashʿarism or Māturīdism when giving their opinions on specific questions already debated in traditional *kalām*. Some officially Sunni thinkers even largely appropriate certain Muʿtazilī views. A case in point is İlhami Güler, professor of Kelâm at the University of Ankara, with his book *Allah'ın Ahlâkîliği Sorunu* (*The Question of God's Morality*) (2000): he opts for the Muʿtazilī notion of God's justice and of His commitment to what is intelligibly good, without embracing Muʿtazilism unrestrictedly (cf. Güler 2000: 143).

Not a few scholars are of the opinion that *kalām* should be carried on in a more Qurʾānic way. What they have in mind is not Wahiduddin Khan's 'Qurʾānic *kalām*', but a *kalām* focused on the systematic interpretation of the essentials of the Qurʾānic message in view of the questions of present-day believers. Such a theology has already been advocated and practised in Turkey, with slightly varying accentuations, by Hüseyin Atay, Bekir Topaloğlu, Şerafeddin Gölcük (Karadaş 2009: 142–8), and some others. It often comes close to what is called 'thematic interpretation' (*tafsīr mawḍūʿī*) in contemporary Arabic exegesis of the Qurʾān, but differs from it in making the purport of the Qurʾān accessible by means of philosophical categories and methods.

Other methodological demands for a new *kalām* formulated by various Muslim scholars are that it should establish closer links to a broad range of modern sciences, not least the humanities, so as to take into consideration, for instance, the insights of contemporary Psychology of Religion and Comparative Religion, and that it should adjust itself to the current level of philosophical thought.

Nowadays the principal demand made on future theologians in this field is, as a rule, not a thorough acquaintance with recent developments of natural philosophy, but rather the familiarity with and appreciation of the insights gained by philosophical hermeneutics and epistemology since the second half of the twentieth century. For Shabistarī an up-to-date Islamic hermeneutics is one of the central pillars of the new *kalām* he aspires to (Shabistarī 1996; Shabistarī 2000: 86f., 116; Shabistarī in al-Rifāʿī 2002a: 78–80[11]). At the same time he emphasizes the necessity of giving the reflection on spiritual experience a more prominent place in *kalām* (Shabistarī in al-Rifāʿī 2002a: 105f.). The importance attached by him and also by Surūsh to religious experience in a new Islamic theology is in line with Iqbal, whom both of them quote occasionally.

VIII Postscript

The foregoing overview has shown that in the last 150 years and especially in the last few decades of the development of Islamic theological thought there was no lack of promising and courageous new approaches. Whether there is a chance that they are one day taken up and developed further by a wider circle of academic theologians will not least depend on the political and social development in the many countries of Muslim majority still deprived of democracy and freedom of expression. So far the symbiotic alliance of dictatorial regimes and conservative religious scholars prevailing in a large part of the Islamic world is not favourable to such a progression.

References

Abāẓa, Nizār (1997). *Jamāl al-Dīn al-Qāsimī, aḥadu ʿulamāʾ al-iṣlāḥ al-ḥadīth fī l-Shām*. Damascus: Dār al-qalam, 1418/1997.

ʿAbbāsī, Walīyullāh, and ʿAlīriżā Qāʾimī Niyā (2011). 'Ustād-i shahīd-i Muṭahharī, muʾassis-i kalām-i jadīd'. *Maʿrifat-i kalāmī* 1/4 (1389): 85–112.

ʿAbd al-Qādir al-Jazāʾirī (*Dhikrā*). *Dhikrā l-ʿāqil wa-tanbīh al-ġāfil*. 1st edn. n.p., 1855. Ed. Mamdūḥ Ḥaqqī, Cairo: Maktabat al-Khānjī, 1976 (quoted here).

ʿAbd al-Qādir al-Jazāʾirī (*Miqrāḍ*). *al-Miqrāḍ al-ḥādd li-qaṭʿi lisāni muntaqiṣi dīni l-islām bi-l-bāṭil wa-l-ilḥād*. Rev. Muḥammad b. ʿAbd Allāh al-Khālidī al-Maghribī. Beirut: Dār Maktabat al-Ḥayāt n.d., *c*.1973.

ʿAbduh, Muḥammad (*Aʿmāl*). *al-Aʿmāl al-kāmila li-l-imām Muḥammad ʿAbduh*. Ed. Muḥammad ʿAmāra. 6 vols. Beirut: al-Muʾassasa al-ʿarabiyya li-l-dirāsāt wa-l-nashr, 1972–4.

ʿAbduh, Muḥammad (*Risāla*). *Risālat al-tawḥīd*. 1st edn. Cairo: al-Maṭbaʿa al-khayriyya, 1897; 2nd edn. Muḥammad Rashīd Riḍā, 1326/1908–9, rev. reprint, introd. Bassām ʿAbd al-Wahhāb al-Jābī. Beirut and Limassol: Dār Ibn Ḥazm, 1421/2001; ed. Muḥammad ʿAmāra, Cairo: Dār al-shurūq, 1414/1994; French trans. and commentary B. Michel and M. Abdel Razik [Mohammed Abdou]. Rissalat al Tawhid. *Exposé de la religion musulmane*. Paris:

[11] But cf. in al-Rifāʿī 2002a: 130–4 and 258, the statements of the al-Azhar professor ʿAbd al-Muʿṭī Bayyūmī and Muḥammad ʿAmāra, who declare modern hermeneutics and epistemology as exclusively Western, unnecessary, and harmful to a new *kalām*, apparently without exact knowledge of what these are.

Geuthner, 1965; English trans. I. Musaʾad and K. Cragg, *The Theology of Unity*. London: Allen Unwin, 1966.

ʿAbduh, Muḥammad (*Tārīkh*, vol. 2). Collection of articles and other short writings, ed. Muḥammad Rashīd Riḍā as vol. 2 of his *Tārīkh al-ustādh al-imām al-shaykh Muḥammad ʿAbduh*. 2nd edn. Cairo: Maktabat al-Manār, 1344/1925.

ʿAbduh, Muḥammad (*Wāridāt*). *Risālat al-wāridāt fī naẓariyyāt al-mutakallimīn wa-l-ṣūfiyya wa-l-falsafa al-ilāhiyya*. 2nd edn. Cairo: Maktabat al-Manār, 1344/1925 (title of this edn. manipulated by Muḥammad Rashīd Riḍā. Original title: *Risālat al-wāridāt fī sirr al-tajalliyāt*).

(ʿAbduh, Muḥammad). *Al-Shaykh Muḥammad ʿAbduh bayn al-falāsifa wa-l-kalāmiyyīn*, allegedly Abduh's *Taʿlīqāt* (marginal notes) on Jamāl al-Dīn al-Dawānī's commentary on al-Ījī's treatise known as *al-ʿAqāʾid al-ʿaḍudiyya*. Ed. and introd. S. Dunyā. Cairo: Dār iḥyāʾ al-kutub al-ʿarabiyya, 1958. Also attributed to ʿAbduh in Haddad 1994 and 1997. [This book has been identified by Muḥammad ʿAmāra and Sayyid Hādī Khusraw Shāhī as containing a series of lectures given by Jamāl al-Dīn al-Afghānī, rev. and ed. with some additional notes by Muḥammad ʿAbduh (see 'al-Afghānī, Jamal al-Dīn'). However, Sulaymān Dunyā's introduction (3–64) retains its importance.]

ʿAbduh, Muḥammad, and Muḥammad Rashīd Riḍā (*Tafsīr al-Manār*). *Tafsīr al-Manār*. Vol. 3. Cairo: Maṭbaʿat al-Manār, 1367/1947–8.

Abdul Khaliq (1980a). 'Sayyid Ahmad Khan's Concept of God', *Iqbal Review* 21: 27–46. (Reprinted in M. I. Chaghatai (ed.), *Herald of Nineteenth Century Muslim Thought: Sir Sayyid Ahmad Khan*. Lahore: Sang-e-Meel Publications, 2005, 245–60.)

Abdul Khaliq (1980b). 'Sayyid Ahmad Khan's Concept of Islam as the Natural Religion'. *Journal of Research* (Lahore) 15/2: 19–38. (Reprinted in M. I. Chaghatai (ed.), *Herald of Nineteenth Century Muslim Thought: Sir Sayyid Ahmad Khan*. Lahore: Sang-e-Meel Publications, 2005, 205–19.)

Adams, C. (1933). *Islam and Modernism in Egypt: A Study of the Reform Movement Inaugurated by Muhammad ʿAbduh*. London: Oxford University Press.

al-Afghānī, Jamāl al-Din (*Aʿmāl*). *Al-Aʿmāl al-kāmila*. Ed. Muḥammad ʿAmāra. 2nd edn. Part 1: *Allāh wa-l-ʿālam wa-l-insān*. Beirut: al-Muʾassasa al-ʿarabiyya li-l-dirāsāt wa-l-nashr, 1979.

al-Afghānī, Jamāl al-Dīn (and Muḥammad ʿAbduh). (*Āthār*). *al-Āthār al-kāmila*. Ed. Sayyid Hādī Khusraw Shāhī. Vol. 2: *Rasāʾil al-falsafa wa-l-ʿirfān*. Cairo: Maktabat al-shurūq al-duwaliyya, 1423/2002, and vol. 7: *al-Taʿlīqāt ʿalā sharḥ al-ʿaqāʾid al-ʿaḍudiyya* (title inside the book *al-Taʿlīqāt ʿalā sharḥ al-Dawānī li-l-ʿaqāʾid al-ʿaḍudiyya*). Cairo: Maktabat al-shurūq al-duwaliyya, 1423/2002.

Ahmad, A. (1967). *Islamic Modernism in India and Pakistan 1857–1964*. London: Oxford University Press.

Akbulut, Ahmet (2002). 'Akıl-Vahiy İlişkisi Görüşü'. In *Ölümünün 50. Yıldönümünde Musa Carullah Bigiyef (1875–1949): I. Uluslararası Musa Carullah Bigiyef Sempozyumu 6–7 Kasım 1999 Ankara* (no editor mentioned). Ankara: Türkiye Diyanet Vakfı, 37–46.

Akman, Mustafa (2007). *Musa Carullah Bigiyef'i Okumaya Giriş*. Istanbul: Çıra Yayınları.

Aktay, Yasin (2005). 'The Historicist Dispute in Turkish-Islamic Theology'. In Sinasi Gunduz (*sic*) and Cafer S. Yaran (eds.), *Change and Essence: Dialectical Relations between Change and Continuity in the Turkish Intellectual Tradition*. Washington, DC: Council for Research in Values and Philosophy, 65–85.

Altıntaş, Ramazan (2003). 'Yeni Bir Kelâm: "Vahidüddin Hân Örneği"'. *Cumhuriyet Üniversitesi İlahiyat Fakültesi Dergisi* (Sivas) 7: 101–28.

Amīn, ʿUthmān (1944). *Rāʾid al-fikr al-miṣrī al-imām Muḥammad ʿAbduh*. 1st edn. Cairo: Īsā al-Bābī al-Ḥalabī, 1944, reprints: Cairo: Maktabat al-nahḍa al-miṣriyya, 1955; Cairo: Maktabat al-anjlū al-miṣriyya, 1965; new edn. by ʿĀṭif al-ʿIrāqī, Cairo: al-Majlis al-aʿlā li-l-thaqāfa, 1996. Trans. *Muhammad Abduh: essai sur ses idées philosophiques et religieuses*. Cairo: Impr. Misr, 1944.

Amirpur. K. (2003). *Die Entpolitisierung des Islam: ʿAbdolkarīm Sorūšs Denken und Wirkung in der Islamischen Republik Iran*. Würzburg: Ergon.

Amirpur, K. (2011). 'The Expansion of the Prophetic Experience: ʿAbdolkarīm Sorūš's New Approach to Qurʾānic Revelation'. *Welt des Islams* NS 51: 409–37.

ʿAnḥūrī, Salīm (*Siḥr*). *Siḥr Hārūt*. Damascus: al-Maṭbaʿa al-ḥanafiyya, 1302/1895.

Aydın, Ömer (2002). 'Filibeli Ahmed Hilmi'nin Din Anlayışı'. *İstanbul İlahiyat Fakültesi Dergisi* 4: 2001 (published in 2002): 69–85.

Badawī, Ibrāhīm (2002). *ʿIlm al-kalām al-jadīd, našʾatuhū wa-taṭawwuruhū*. Beirut: Dār al-ʿilm.

Baljon, J. M. S. (1949). *The Reforms and Religious Ideas of Sir Sayyid Aḥmad Khân*. Leiden: Brill.

Baloğlu, Adnan Bülent (1996a). 'İzmirli İsmail Hakkı'nın "Yeni İlm-i Kelam" Anlayışı'. In Mehmet Şeker and Adnan Bülent Baloğlu (eds.), *İzmirli İsmail Hakkı (Sempoziyum: 24–25 Kasım 1995)*. Ankara: Türkiye Diyanet Vakfı, 93–107.

Baloğlu, Adnan Bülent (1996b). 'Sebilürreşâd Dergisinde "Yeni İlm-i Kelâm" Tartışmaları'. In Mehmet Şeker and Adnan Bülent Baloğlu (eds.), *İzmirli İsmail Hakkı (Sempoziyum: 24–25 Kasım 1995)*. Ankara: Türkiye Diyanet Vakfı, 265–312.

Basile, P. (2013). 'James Ward'. In E. N. Zalta (ed.), *The Stanford Encyclopedia of Philosophy* (Fall 2013 edition), <http://plato.stanford.edu/archives/fall2013/entries/james-ward/> (accessed 15 January 2014).

Bein, A. (2007). 'A "Young Turk" Islamic Intellectual: Filibeli Ahmed Hilmi and the Diverse Intellectual Legacies of the Late Ottoman Empire'. *International Journal of Middle East Studies* 39: 607–25.

Berkes, N. (1964). *The Development of Secularism in Turkey*. Montreal: McGill University Press.

Bigiyef (= Bigi), Musa Carullah (*Rahmet*). Rahmet-i *İlâhiye'nin Burhanları*. Orenburg: Vakit matbaası, 1911 (used here); simplified edn. in Roman letters by Ömer H. Özalp under the title *İlâhî Adalet*, also including Şeyhülislam Mustafa Sabri's reply *Yeni İslâm Müctehidlerinin Kıymet-i İlmiyesi*. Istanbul: Pınar Yayınları, 1996.

Birinci, Ali (2001). 'İsmail Hakkı İzmirli (1869–1946): Bir İlim Adamının Hikâyesi'. In Kemal Çiçek (ed.), *Pax Ottomana: Studies in Memoriam Prof. Dr. Nejat Göyünç*. Haarlem and Ankara: SOTA, 687–733.

Caspar, R. (1957). 'Un aspect de la pensée musulmane moderne: le renouveau du moʿtazilisme'. *Mélanges de l'Institut Dominicain d'Études Orientales du Caire* 4: 141–202.

Çetinkaya, Bayram Ali (2000). *İzmirli İsmail Hakkı. Hayatı, Eserleri, Görüşleri*. Istanbul: İnsan Yayınları.

Chaghatai, M. I. (ed.) (2005). *Herald of Nineteenth Century Muslim Thought: Sir Sayyid Ahmad Khan*. Lahore: Sang-e-Meel Publications.

Commins, D. D. (1988). 'ʿAbd al-Qādir al-Jazāʾirī and Islamic Reform'. *Muslim World* 78: 121–31.

Commins, D. D. (1990). *Islamic Reform: Politics and Social Change in Late Ottoman Syria*. Oxford: Oxford University Press.

Commins, D. D. (2006). 'Al-Manār and Popular Religion in Syria, 1898–1920'. In S. A. Dudoignon, K. Hisao, and K. Yasushi (eds.), *Intellectuals in the Modern Islamic World: Transmission, Transformation, Communication*. London and New York: Routledge, 40–54.

Cooper, J. (2000). 'The Limits of the Sacred: The Epistemology of ʿAbd al-Karim Soroush'. In J. Cooper, R. L. Nettler, and M. Mahmoud (eds.), *Islam and Modernity: Muslim Intellectuals Respond*. London and New York: I. B. Tauris, 38–56.
Coşkun, İbrahim (2011). *Ateizm ve İslam: Kelamî Açıdan Modern Çağ Ateizmin Eleştirisi*. Ankara: Ankara Okulu Yayınları.
Dabdūb, ʿAlī Maḥmūd ʿAlī (2007). *al-Qāsimī wa-ārāʾuhū l-iʿtiqādiyya*. Cairo: Dār al-muḥdithīn li-l-baḥth al-ʿilmī wa-l-tarjama wa-l-nashr.
Dahlén, A. (2001). *Deciphering the Meaning of Revealed Law: The Surūshian Paradigm in Shi'i Epistemology*. Uppsala: Uppsala University Library.
Davison, R. H. (1988). 'Jamal al-Din Afghani: A Note on his Nationality and on his Burial'. *Middle Eastern Studies* 24: 110–12.
Debus, E. (1991). *Sebilürreşâd: Eine vergleichende Untersuchung zur islamischen Opposition der vor- und nachkemalistischen Ära*. Frankfurt a.M.: Lang.
Demichelis, M. (2010). 'New-Muʿtazilite Theology in the Contemporary Age: The Relation between Reason, History and Tradition'. *Oriente Moderno* 90: 411–26.
Dudoignon, S. A. (2006). 'Echoes to al-Manār among the Muslims of the Russian Empire'. In S. A. Dudoignon, K. Hisao, and K. Yasushi (eds.), *Intellectuals in the Modern Islamic World: Transmission, Transformation, Communication*. London and New York: Routledge, 85–116.
Ebert, J. (1991). *Religion und Reform in der arabischen Provinz: Ḥusayn al-Ǧisr aṭ-Ṭarâbulusî (1845–1909). Ein Gelehrter zwischen Tradition und Reform*. Frankfurt a.M.: Lang.
Eliaçık, R. İhsan (2002 and 2003). *Islâm'ın Yenilikçileri. Islâm Düşünce Tarihinde Yenilik Arayışları: Kişiler, Fikirler, Akımlar*. 2nd edn. vols. ii and iii. Istanbul: Med-Cezir Yayınları.
Elshakry, M. (2011). 'Muslim Hermeneutics and Arabic Views of Evolution'. *Zygon* 46: 330–44.
Esack, Farid (1997). *Qur'an, Liberation and Pluralism: An Islamic Perspective of Interreligious Solidarity against Oppression*. Oxford: Oneworld.
Escovitz, J. H. (1986). '"He was the Muḥammad ʿAbduh of Syria": A Study of Ṭāhir al-Jazāʾirī and his Influence'. *International Journal of Middle East Studies* 18: 293–310.
van Ess, J. (1997). *Theologie und Gesellschaft im 2. und 3. Jahrhundert Hidschra. Eine Geschichte des religiösen Denkens im frühen Islam*. Vol. iv. Berlin: De Gruyter.
Evkuran, Mehmet (2004). '"Kelâm İlminin Yeniden İnşâsı" Sözünün Anlamı ve İçeriği Üzerine'. In Fırat Üniversitesi İlahiyat Fakültesi (ed.), *'Kelam Ilminin Yeniden İnşasında Geleneğin Yeri' Sempozyumu, 13–15 Eylül 2004*. Elazığ: Fırat Üniversitesi İlahiyat Fakültesi, 181–98.
Ezzerelli, K. (2006). 'Muḥammad ʿAbduh et les réformistes syro-libanais: influence, image, postérité'. In M. Al-Charif and S. Mervin (eds.), *Modernités islamiques. Actes du colloque organizé à Alep à l'occasion du centenaire de la disparition de l'imam Muḥammad ʿAbduh, 9–10 novembre 2005*. Damascus: Institut Français du Proche-Orient.
Fazli, A. (2005). 'Iqbal's View of Omniscience and Human Freedom'. *Muslim World* 95: 125–45.
Filibeli Ahmed Hilmi (*İnkâr*). *Allah'ı İnkâr Mümkün müdür? Yahut Huzûr-i Fende Mesalik-i Küfr*. 1st edn. Istanbul: Hikmet Matbaa-yı İslâmiyesi, 1327/1909–10 (used here), simplified edn. in Roman letters under the title *Allah'ı İnkâr Mümkün mü?* by Necip Taylan, 4th edn. Istanbul: Çağrı Yayınları, 2001.
Filibeli Ahmed Hilmi (*Üss*). *Üss-i İslâm: Hakâik-i islâmiyeye müstenid yeni ilm-i akâid*. Istanbul: Hikmet, 1332/1913–14 (used here), simplified edn. in Roman letters by Adnan Bülent Baloğlu and Halife Keskin. Ankara: Türkiye Diyanet Vakfı, 2004.
Fleming, D. (1950). *John William Draper and the Religion of Science*. Philadelphia: University of Pennsylvania Press.

Gafarov, Raim (2009). *Musa Cârullah Bigiyev'in Kader Hakkındaki Görüşü*. Bursa: Yüksek Lisans Tezi.

Gardet, L. (1972). 'Signification du "Renouveau Muʿtazilite" dans la pensée musulmane contemporaine'. In S. M. Stern, A. Hourani, and V. Brown (eds.), *Islamic Philosophy and the Classical Tradition*. Columbia, NY: University of South Carolina Press, 63–75.

Gen, K. (2006). 'The Influence of al-Manār on Islamists in Turkey'. In S. A. Dudoignon, K. Hisao, and K. Yasushi (eds.), *Intellectuals in the Modern Islamic World: Transmission, Transformation, Communication*. London and New York: Routledge, 74–84.

Gibb, H. A. R. (1947). *Modern Trends in Islam, 1895–1961*. Chicago: University of Chicago Press.

Goldziher, I. (1920). *Die Richtungen der islamischen Koranauslegung*. Leiden: Brill.

Gölcük, Şerafeddin (1992). *Kelâm Tarihi*. Konya: Kitap Dünyası Yayınları (7th edn., 2012 used here).

Görmez, Mehmet (1994). *Musa Carullah Bigiyef*. Ankara: Türkiye Diyanet Vakfı.

Görmez, Mehmet (2002). 'İslam Tecdid Geleneği ve Musa Carullah Bigiyef'. In *Ölümünün 50. Yıldönümünde Musa Carullah Bigiyef (1875–1949): I. Uluslararası Musa Carullah Bigiyef Sempozyumu 6–7 Kasım 1999 Ankara*. Ankara: Türkiye Diyanet Vakfı, 123–8.

Güler, İlhami (2000). *Allah'ın Ahlâkîliği Sorunu: Ehl-i Sünnet'in Allah Tasavvuruna Ahlâkî Açıdan Eleştirel Bir Yaklaşım*. Ankara: Ankara Okulu Yayınları.

Güler, İlhami (2002). *Politik Teoloji Yazıları*. Ankara: Kitâbiyât.

Güler, İlhami (2004). *Özgürcülükçü Teoloji Yazıları*. Ankara: Ankara Okulu Yayınları.

Güler, İlhami (2011). *Direniş Teolojisi*. Ankara: Ankara Okulu Yayınları.

Haddad, M. (1994). *Essai de critique de la raison théologique: l'exemple de M. ʿAbduh*. Diss., Université de Paris III.

Haddad, M. (1997). 'Les Œuvres de ʿAbduh, histoire d'une manipulation'. *IBLA* (*Revue de l'Institut des Belles Lettres Arabes*, Tunis) 60/180: 197–222.

Haddad, M. (1998). "Abduh et ses lecteurs', *Arabica* 45: 22–49.

Haddad, M. (2000). 'Relire Muhammad Abduh (A propos de l'article "M. Abduh" dans l'*Encyclopédie de l'Islam*)'. *IBLA* (*Revue de l'Institut des Belles Lettres Arabes*, Tunis) 63/185: 61–84.

Hagen, G., and T. Seidensticker (1998). 'Reinhard Schulzes Hypothese einer islamischen Aufklärung: Kritik einer historiographischen Kritik'. *Zeitschrift der Deutschen Morgenländischen Gesellschaft* 148: 83–110.

Ḥanafī, Ḥasan (1997). 'Tārīkhiyyat ʿilm al-kalām'. In Ḥ. Ḥanafī, *Humūm al-fikr wa-l-waṭan*, vol. i: *al-Turāth wa-l-ʿaṣr wa-l-ḥadātha*. Cairo: Dār al-maʿrifa al-jāmiʿiyya, 69–89.

Hanioğlu, M. Ş. (1995). *The Young Turks in Opposition*. New York: Oxford University Press.

Harputi, Abdullatif (al-Kharbūtī, ʿAbd al-Laṭīf) (*Astronomi*). Untitled article, printed as appendix to *Tanqīḥ al-kalām fī ʿaqāʾidi ahl al-islām*. Istanbul: Necm-i istikbal matbaası, 1327/1909–10, 440–56; simplified edn. by Bekir Topaloğlu in Roman letters under the title 'Astronomi ve Din'. *Diyanet İşleri Başkanlığı Dergisi* 13/6 (1974): 343–61.

Harputi, Abdullatif (al-Kharbūtī, ʿAbd al-Laṭīf) (*Tanqīḥ*). *Tanqīḥ al-kalām fī ʿaqāʾidi ahl al-islām*. Istanbul: Necm-i istikbal matbaası, 1327/1909–10 (used here); Turkish trans. of the Arabic original by İbrahim Özdemir and Fikret Karahan (Abdullatif el-Harputî, *Tenkîhu'l kelâm fî Akâidi ehli'l İslâm [Kelâmî Perspektiften İslâm İnanç Esasları]*). Elazığ: Türkiye Diyanet Vakfı, 2000.

Harputi, Abdullatif (al-Kharbūtī, ʿAbd al-Laṭīf) (*Tekmile*). *Tekmile-i Tenkîh-i Kelâm* (continuation of the above-mentioned book, written in Ottoman Turkish). Istanbul: Necm-i istikbal matbaası, 1330/1912–13.

Harputi, Abdullatif (*Tarih*). *Tarih-i İlm-i Kelâm*. Istanbul, 1332/1913–14 (non vidi; recorded in several Turkish bibliographies without indication of publisher); simplified by Muammer Esen and printed in Roman letters under the title *Kelâm Tarihi*. Ankara: Ankara Okulu Yayınları, 2005 (used here).

Hasselblatt, G. (1968). *Herkunft und Auswirkungen der Apologetik Muhammad ʿAbduh's (1849–1905), untersucht an seiner Schrift: Islam und Christentum im Verhältnis zu Wissenschaft und Zivilisation*. Ph.D. thesis, Göttingen.

Hildebrandt, T. (2002). 'Waren Ǧamāl ad-Dīn al-Afġānī und Muḥammad ʿAbduh Neo-Muʿtaziliten?' *Welt des Islams* NS 42: 207–62.

Hildebrandt, T. (2007). *Neo-Muʿtazilismus? Intention und Kontext im modernen arabischen Umgang mit dem rationalistischen Erbe des Islam*. Leiden: Brill.

Hizmetli, Sabri (1996). *İsmail Hakkı İzmirli*. Ankara: T. C. Kültür Bakanlığı.

Howard, D. A. (2011). *Being Human in Islam: The Impact of the Evolutionary Worldview*. New York: Routledge.

Iqbal, Muhammad (*Reconstruction*). *Six Lextures on the Reconstruction of Religious Thought in Islam*. 1st edn. Lahore: Sang-e Meel Publications, 1930; 2nd, enlarged edn. (with added chapter 7 'Is Religion Possible?') London: Oxford University Press, 1934; ed. Saeed Sheikh with introd. by Javed Majeed, Stanford, CA, 2013 (used here).

İzmirli, Celâleddin (1946). *İzmirli İsmail Hakkı: Hayatı, eserleri, dînî ve felsefî ilimlerdeki mevkii, jübilesi ve vefatı*. Istanbul: Hilmi Kitabevi.

İzmirli İsmail Hakkı (*Interview*). Interview on his project of a new *kalām*, *Sebilürreşad* 21/528–9, 30 Ramaḍān 1341/16 May 1339 RH, 59 (used here); reprint in Roman letters in Baloğlu 1996b: 270–3.

İzmirli İsmail Hakkı (*al-Jawāb*). *Al-Jawāb al-sadīd fi bayān dīn al-tawḥīd*. Ankara: Ali Şükri Matbaası, 1339 RH/1341.

İzmirli İsmail Hakkı (*Kelâm*). *Yeni ʿilm-i kelâm*. vol. 1. Istanbul, 1339 RH/1341, vol. 2. Istanbul, 1340 RH/1343 [From 1840 to 1926 all official documents of the Ottoman Empire and the Republic of Turkey, respectively, also books published by state-owned publishing houses, regularly carried a dual date. The lower figure, marked with the abbreviation RH, indicates the year according to the Rumi Calendar (Ottoman Solar Hijri Calendar) introduced for all official uses after the Tanzimat.]; reprint of both vols. in Roman letters, but without lists of references, ed. Sabri Hizmetli, Ankara: Umran, 1981 and again Ankara: Ankara Okulu Yayınları, 2013.

İzmirli İsmail Hakkı ('Kelâm hakkında'). 'Yeni ilm-i kelâm hakkında'. *Sebilürreşad*, 22/549–50, 26 Dhū l-ḥijja 1341/9 August 1339 RH, 30–2 and 22/551–2, 3 Muḥarram 1342/16 August 1339 RH, 38–40 (used here); reprint in Roman letters in Baloğlu 1996b: 286–99.

İzmirli İsmail Hakkı (*Muḥaṣṣal*). *Muḥaṣṣalu l-kalām wa-l-ḥikma*. Istanbul: Evkaf-ı Islamiye Matbaası, 1336/1917–18.

İzmirli İsmail Hakkı (*Mustasvife*). *Mustasvife Sözleri mi? Tasavvufun Zaferleri mi* (here without interrogation mark)—*Hakkın Zaferleri*. Istanbul: Evkaf-ı Islamiye Matbaası, 1341/1922–3.

İzmirli İsmail Hakkı (*Nar*). *Narın Ebediyet ve Devamı Hakkında Tedkikatlar*. Istanbul: Darülfünun Matbaası, 1341; reprinted in Roman letters in Kaya 2009: 535–52.

Jäschke, G. (1951 and 1953). 'Der Islam in der neuen Türkei: Eine rechtsgeschichtliche Untersuchung'. *Die Welt des Islams* ns 1: 1–174; 'Berichtigungen und Nachträge'. *Die Welt des Islams* ns 2: 278–85.

al-Jisr, Ḥusayn (*Risāla*). *al-Risāla al-ḥamīdiyya fī ḥaqīqat al-diyāna al-islāmiyya wa-ḥaqīqat al-sharīʿa al-muḥammadiyya*. 1st edn. Beirut: private print with the permission of the Majlis al-maʿārif of the Vilayet Beirut, sponsored by Ḥasan Efendi al-Qarq, 1306/1888.

Ed. Khālid Ziyāda. Ṭrāblus, n.d. (*c.*1985); reprint Cairo: Maktabat Madbūli, 2011 (used here).

Jomier, J. (1954). *Le Commentaire coranique du Manâr: tendances modernes de l'exégèse coranique en Égypte*. Paris: G.-P. Maisonneuve.

al-Julaynid, Muḥammad al-Sayyid (ed.) (*c.*2004). *Manāhij al-ʿulūm al-islāmiyya bayna l-tajdīd wa-l-taqlīd, al-ḥalqa al-ūlā: ʿIlm al-kalām, 20–21 ibrīl 2004*. Cairo: Jāmiʿat al-Qāhira, qism al-falsafa al-islāmiyya.

Kadīvar, Muḥsin (2002/11). 'Az Islām-i tārīkhī bih Islām-i maʿnavī'. 1st print in *Sunnat va-sikūlārism. Guftārhāyī az ʿAbdulkarīm Surūsh, Muḥammad Mujtahid Shabistarī, Muḥsin Kadīvar va-Muṣṭafā Malikyān*. Tehran: Ṣirāṭ, 1381/2002; reprint in his *Ḥaqq al-nās: Islām va-ḥuqūq-i bashar*, Tehran: Intishārāt-i kavīr, 1386/2008, 15–34 (used here); rev. English version under the title 'From Traditional Islam to Islam as an End in Itself'. *Die Welt des Islams* NS 51 (2011): 459–84.

Kanlıdere, Ahmet (1997). *Reform within Islam: The Tajdid and Jadid Movement among the Kazan Tatars (1809–1917). Conciliation or Conflict?* Istanbul: Eren Yayıncılık.

Kanlıdere, Ahmet (2005). *Kadimle Cedit Arasında Musa Carullah: Hayatı, Eserleri, Fikirleri*. Istanbul: Dergâh Yayınları.

Kara, İsmail (ed.) (1987). *Türkiye'de Islâmcılık Düşüncesi: Metinler / Kişiler*. Vol. ii. Istanbul: Risâle yayınları.

Karabela, M. K. (2003). *One of the Last Ottoman Şeyhülislâms, Mustafa Sabri Efendi (1869–1954): His Life, Works and Intellectual Contributions*. MA thesis, Montreal.

Karadaş, Cağfer (2009). 'Günümüz Türkiye'sinde (*sic*) Kelam İlmi'. *Türk Bilimsel Derlemeler Dergisi* 2: 129–51.

Karadaş, Cağfer (ed.) (2010). *Kelâma Giriş*. Eskişehir: Anadolu Üniversitesi.

Karaman, Fikret (2004). 'Yeni Kelam Düşüncesinin İnşası ve Abdullatif Harputi'nin Rölü'. In Fırat Üniversitesi İlahiyat Fakültesi (ed.), *'Kelam Ilminin Yeniden İnşasında Geleneğin Yeri' Sempozyumu, 13–15 Eylül 2004*. Elazığ: Fırat Üniversitesi İlahiyat Fakültesi.

Kaya, V. (2009). 'İzmirli İsmail Hakkı'nın Cehennem Sonluluğu Hakkında Risalesi'. *Uludağ Üniversitesi İlâhiyat Fakültesi Dergisi* 18: 529–57.

Keddie, N. R. (1966). 'Sayyid Jamāl al-Dīn al-Afghani's First Twenty-Seven Years: The Darkest Period'. *Middle East Journal* 20: 517–33.

Keddie, N. R. (1968). 'Islamic Philosophy and Islamic Modernism: The Case of Sayyid Jamāl al-Dīn al-Afghānī'. *Iran* 6: 53–6.

Keddie, N. R. (1972). *Sayyid Jamāl ad-Dīn 'al-Afghānī': A Political Biography*. Berkeley: University of California Press.

Khalid, D. (1969). 'Some Aspects of Neo-Muʿtazilism'. *Islamic Studies* 8: 319–47.

Khān, Waḥīduddīn (*al-Islām*). *al-Islām yataḥaddā. Madkhal ʿilmī ilā l-īmān*. Arabic trans. of the Urdu original (ʿIlm-i jadīd kā caylanj, 1st edn. Lucknow: Majlis-i taḥqīqāt wa-nashriyyāt-i islām, Nadvat al-ʿulamāʾ, 1965) by Ẓafaru l-islām Khān, rev. and ed. ʿAbd al-Ṣabūr Shāhīn, Beirut: Dār al-buḥūth al-ʿilmiyya, 1970; reprint New Delhi: Goodword Books, 2005 (used here).

Khān, Waḥīduddīn (*'Kalām'*). 'Naḥwa ʿilm kalām jadīd'. In Waḥīduddīn Khān, *al-Islām wa-l-ʿaṣr al-ḥadīth*. 1st edn. Beirut: Dār al-nafāʾis, 1402/1983; 4th edn. 1413/1992 (used here), 76–83.

Khosrowpanāh, ʿAbd al-Ḥusayn (2000/1). *Kalām-i jadīd*. 1st edn. Qum, 1379, online-edn. on the author's homepage <http://khosropanah.ir/fa/ke-/125-1388-04-11-07-40-30.html> (accessed 25 February 2014).

Körner, F. (2005). *Revisionist Koran Hermeneutics in Contemporary Turkish University Theology: Rethinking Islam.* Würzburg: Ergon.

Koştaş, Münir (1999). 'Ankara Üniversitesi İlâhiyat Fakültesi (Dünü Bugünü)'. *Ankara Üniversitesi Ilâhiyat Fakültesi Dergisi* 39/2 (= Özel Sayı, Cumhuriyetin 75. Yıldönümüne Armağan): 141–84.

Kudsi-Zadeh, A. A. (1971). 'Islamic Reform in Egypt: Some Observations on the Role of al-Afghānī'. *Muslim World* 61: 1–12.

Kudsi-Zadeh, A. A. (1980). 'The Emergence of Political Journalism in Egypt'. *Muslim World* 70: 47–55.

von Kügelgen, A. (2007). "'Abduh, Muḥammad', *Encyclopaedia of Islam. THREE*, Leiden: Brill, fasc. 2007–3, 25–32.

von Kügelgen, A. (1994). *Averroes und die arabische Moderne: Ansätze zu einer Neubegründung des Rationalismus im Islam.* Leiden: Brill.

Lewis, B. (1968). *The Emergence of Modern Turkey.* London: Oxford University Press.

McDaniel, K. (2013). 'John M. E. McTaggart'. In E. N. Zalta (ed.), *The Stanford Encyclopedia of Philosophy* (Winter 2013 Edition), <http://plato.stanford.edu/search/searcher.py?query=McTaggart> (accessed 15 January 2014).

Madaninejad, B. (2011). *New Theology in the Islamic Republic of Iran: A Comparative Study between Abdolkarim Soroush and Mohsen Kadivar.* Ph.D. dissertation, Austin, TX.

Malik, Hafeez (1980). *Sir Sayyid Ahmad Khan and Muslim Modernization in India and Pakistan.* New York: Columbia University Press.

Maraş, İbrahim (2002). 'Tasavvuf Anlayışı ve Rahmet-i İlâhiyenin Umumiliği Meselesi'. In *Ölümünün 50. Yıldönümünde Musa Carullah Bigiyef (1875–1949): I. Uluslararası Musa Carullah Bigiyef Sempozyumu 6–7 Kasım 1999 Ankara.* Ankara: Türkiye Diyanet Vakfı, 87–96.

Marcotte, R. D. (2008). 'Hermeneutics and the Renewal of Islamic Interpretations'. *Journal of the Henry Martyn Institute* 27: 98–109.

Martin, R. C., M. R. Woodward, and D. S. Atmaja (1997). *Defenders of Reason in Islam: Mu'tazilism from Medieval School to Modern Symbol.* Oxford: Oneworld.

Masud, M. Kh. (2007). 'Iqbāl's Approach to Islamic Theology of Modernity'. *Al-Hikmat* 27: 1–36.

Matthee, R. (1989). 'Jamal al-Din al-Afghani and the Egyptian National Debate'. *International Journal of Middle East Studies* 21: 151–69.

McDaniel, K. (2013). 'John M. E. McTaggart'. In E. N. Zalta (ed.), *The Stanford Encyclopedia of Philosophy* (Winter 2013 Edition), <http://plato.stanford.edu/search/searcher.py?query=McTaggart> (accessed 15 January 2014).

Murad, M. A. (1996). *Intellectual Modernism of Shiblī Nu'mānī.* New Delhi: Kitab Bhavan.

Musa Kâzım (Şeyhülislam) (*'Kütüb'*). 'Kütüb-i Kelâmiyenin Ihtiyacat-ı Asra Göre Islâhı ve Te'lifi' (first part of a tripartite lecture given in 1909 [The date of the lecture is indicated as '20 Ağustos 1325' according to the Rumi Calendar ('Kütüb' 289); this corresponds to 3 September 1909.]). In Musa Kâzım, *Külliyât. Dinî, ictimâ'î makaleler.* Istanbul: Evkaf-ı İslamiye Matbaası, 1336/1917–18, 289–93 (used here); in the simplified edn. of the *Külliyât* in Roman letters by Ferhat Koca, Ankara: Ankara Okulu Yayınları, 2002, 351–5 under the title 'Kelâm Kitaplarının Asrın İhtiyâçlarına Göre Islâhı ve Yazılması'; simplified version by İlyas Çelebi under the same title also in İlyas Çelebi and Ziya Yılmazer (eds.), *Osmanlı'dan Cumhuriyet'e Islâm Düşüncesinde Arayışlar.* Istanbul: Rağbet Yayınları, 1999, 47–52.

Muzani, S. (1994). 'Muʿtazilah Theology and the Modernization of the Indonesian Muslim Community: Intellectual Portrait of Harun Nasution'. *Studia Islamika* 1: 91–131.

Nasr, S. V. R. (1993). 'Religious Modernism in the Arab World, India and Iran: The Perils and Prospects of a Discourse'. *Muslim World* 83: 20–47.

Neufend, M. (2012). *Das Moderne in der islamischen Tradition: Eine Studie zu Amīr ʿAbd al-Qādir al-Ǧazāʾirīs Verteidigung der islamischen Vernunft im 19. Jahrhundert.* Würzburg: Ergon.

Nuʿmānī, Shiblī (*ʿIlm*). *ʿIlm al-kalām*. Agra: Matbaʿ–i mufīd–i ʿāmm, 1903; Pers. trans. by Muḥammad Taqī Fakhr Dāʿī Gīlānī under the title *Tārīkh-i ʿilm-i kalām*, Tehran: Čāp–i Rangīn, 1328 SH/1949; Arab. trans. (less reliable) by Jalāl al-Saʿīd al-Ḥifnāwī, rev. al-Sibāʿī Muḥammad al-Sibāʿī, in one vol. together with *al-Kalām* under the title *ʿIlm al-kalām al-jadīd*. Cairo: al-Markaz al–qawmī li–l–tarjama, 2012, 13–173.

Nuʿmānī, Shiblī (*al-Kalām*). *al-Kalām: yaʿnī ʿilm-i kalām-i jadīd.* Kanpur: Maṭbaʿ–i intiẓāmī (?), 1904; Pers. trans. Muḥammad Taqī Fakhr Dāʿī Gīlānī under the title *ʿIlm-i kalām-i jadīd*, Tehran: Čāp–i Sīnā, 1329 SH/1950 (used here); Arab. trans. (with ʿIlm al-kalām under the title *ʿIlm al-kalām al-jadīd* (see previous title), 175–359; English trans. of the part on prophethood and miracles in Troll 1982b: 90–115.

O'Fahey, R. S., and B. Radtke (1993). 'Neo-Sufism Reconsidered'. *Der Islam* 70: 52–87.

Özervarlı, M. S. (1996). 'İzmirli İsmail Hakkı'nın Kelâm Problemleriyle Ilgili Görüşleri'. In Mehmet Şeker and Adnan Bülent Baloğlu (eds.), *İzmirli İsmail Hakkı (Sempoziyum: 24–25 Kasım 1995)*. Ankara: Türkiye Diyanet Vakfı, 109–25.

Özervarlı, M. S. (1998). *Kelâmda Yenilik Arayışları (XIX. Yüzyıl sonu—XX. yüzyıl başı).* Istanbul: İSAM (Türkiye Diyanet Vakfı İslâm Araştırmaları Merkezi).

Özervarlı, M. S. (2007). 'Alternative Approaches to Modernization in the Late Ottoman Period: İzmirli İsmail Hakkı's Religious Thought against Materialist Scientism'. *International Journal of Middle East Studies* 39: 77–102.

Özsoy, Ö. (2004a). *Kur'an ve Tarihsellik Yazıları*. Ankara: Kitâbiyât.

Özsoy, Ö. (2004b). 'Koranhermeneutik als Diskussionthema in der Türkei'. Unpublished paper presented at the 29. *Deutscher Orientalistentag 'Barrieren—Passagen'*, Halle (20–4 September 2004), online <www.akademie-rs.de/fileadmin/user/pdf.../Artikel__zsoy_7-05.pdf> (accessed 29 March 2014).

Paya, A. (2006). 'Recent Developments in Shiʿi Thought: A Brief Introduction to the Views of Three Contemporary Shiʿite Thinkers'. In M. A. M. Khan (ed.), *Islamic Democratic Discourse: Theory, Debates and Philosophical Perspectives*. Lanham, MD: Lexington Books, 123–45.

Pink, J. (2011). *Sunnitischer Tafsīr in der modernen islamischen Welt: Akademische Traditionen, Popularisierung und nationalstaatliches Interesse.* Leiden: Brill.

al-Qāsimī, Jamāl al-Dīn (*Dalāʾil*). *Dalāʾil al-tawḥīd*. 1st edn. Damascus: Maṭbaʿat al–Fayḥāʾ, 1326/1908, reprint Beirut: Dār al–kutub al–ʿilmiyya, 1405/1984 (used here).

al-Qāsimī, Jamāl al-Dīn (*Taʿāruḍ*). 'Taʿāruḍ al-ʿaql wa-n-naql'. *al-Manār* 13/8 (1286/1910): 616–32.

Radtke, B. (1994). 'Erleuchtung und Aufklärung: Islamische Mystik und europäischer Rationalismus'. *Welt des Islams*, ns 34: 48–66.

Radtke, B. (2002). 'Sufik und Rationalität: Einige zusammenfassende Bemerkungen'. In R. Brunner, M. Gronke, J. P. Laut, and U. Rebstock (eds.), *Islamstudien ohne Ende: Festschrift für Werner Ende zum 65. Geburtstag*. Würzburg: Ergon, 265–9.

Rahman, Fazlur (1982). *Islam and Modernity: Transformation of an Intellectual Tradition.* Chicago and London: Chicago University Press.

Raschid, M. S. (1981). *Iqbal's Concept of God.* Boston: Kegan Paul.
Reetz, D. (1987/8). 'Enlightenment and Islam: Sayyid Ahmad Khan's Plea to Indian Muslims for Reason'. *Indian Historical Review* 14/i–ii: 206–18.
Richard, Y. (1988). 'Shariʾat Sangalaji: A Reformist Theologian of the Rida Shah Period'. In S. A. Arjomand (ed.), *Authority and Political Culture in Shiʿism.* Albany, NY: SUNY Press, 159–77.
Richard, Y. (2009). 'Un théologien chiite de notre temps, Mojtahed Šabestarī'. In M. A. Amir-Moezzi, M. M. Bar-Asher, and S. Hopkins (eds.), *Le Shi'isme imamite quarante ans après: hommage à Etan Kohlberg.* Turnhout: Brepols, 363–71.
Riḍā, Muḥammad Rashīd (*Tārīkh*, vol. 1). *Tārīkh al-ustādh al-imām al-shaykh Muḥammad ʿAbduh.* vol. 1, 2nd edn. Cairo: Dār al-Manār, 1350/1931 (2nd reprint of this edn. Cairo: Dār al-faḍīla, 1427/2006); vol. 2 see ʿAbduh (*Tārīkh*, vol. 2).
Riexinger, M. (2009a). 'Der islamische Kreationismus'. In O. Kraus (ed.), *Evolutionstheorie und Kreationismus—ein Gegensatz.* Stuttgart: Steiner, 97–118.
Riexinger, M. (2009b). 'Responses of South Asian Muslims to the Theory of Evolution'. *Welt des Islams* NS 49: 212–47.
Riexinger, M. (2011). 'Islamic Opposition to the Darwinian Theory of Evolution'. In O. Hammer and J. R. Lewis (eds.), *Handbook of Religion and the Authority of Science.* Leiden: Brill, 484–509.
al-Rifāʿī, ʿAbd al-Jabbār (ed.) (2002a). *al-Ijtihād al-kalāmī, manāhij wa-ruʾā mutanawwiʿa fī l-kalām al-jadīd.* Beirut: Dār al-Hādī, 1423.
al-Rifāʿī, ʿAbd al-Jabbār (ed.) (2002b). *ʿIlm al-kalām al-jadīd wa-falsafat al-dīn.* 1st edn. Beirut: Dār al–Hādī, 1423/2002; 2nd edn. 1429/2008 (used here).
Sadri, M. (2001). 'Sacral Defense of Secularism: The Political Theologies of Soroush, Shabestari, and Kadivar'. *International Journal of Politics, Culture, and Society* 15: 257–70.
Saleh, F. (2001). *Modern Trends in Islamic Theological Discourse in Twentieth Century Indonesia: A Critical Survey.* Leiden: Brill.
Scharbrodt, O. (2007). 'The Salafiyya and Sufism: Muḥammad ʿAbduh and his Risālat al-wāridāt (Treatise on Mystical Inspirations)'. *Bulletin of the School of Oriental and African Studies* 70: 89–115.
Schimmel, A. (1963). *Gabriel's Wing: A Study into the Religious Ideas of Sir Muhammad Iqbal.* Leiden: Brill.
Schulze, R. (1990). 'Das islamische achtzehnte Jahrhundert: Versuch einer historiographischen Kritik'. *Welt des Islams* ns 30: 140–59.
Schulze, R. (1994). '"Nur der Moderne kommt voran!" Kulturkritik in der ägyptischen und syrischen Poesie der 1. Hälfte des 18. Jahrhunderts'. In C. Wunsch (ed.), *XXV. Deutscher Orientalistentag vom 8. bis 13. 4. 1991 in München: Vorträge im Auftrag der Deutschen Morgenländischen Gesellschaft.* Stuttgart: Steiner, 155–66.
Schulze, R. (1996). 'Was ist die islamische Aufklärung?' *Welt des Islams* ns 36: 276–325.
Sedgwick, M. J. (2010). *Muhammad Abduh.* Oxford: Oneworld.
Shabistarī, Muḥammad Mujtahid (1996–7). *Hirminūtīk, kitāb va-sunnat.* Tehran: Ṭarḥ–i naw, 1375.
Shabistarī, Muḥammad Mujtahid (2000). *Madkhal ilā ʿilm al-kalām al-jadīd.* Beirut: Dār al–Hādī, 1421.
Shabistarī, Muḥammad Mujtahid (2000–1). *Īmān va-Āzādī.* Tehran: Ṭarḥ–i naw, 1379.
Shabistarī, Muḥammad Mujtahid (2002–3). *Naqdī bar qirāʾat-i rasmī-yi dīn.* Tehran: Ṭarḥ–i naw, 1381.

Sharīʿat Sangalajī, Muḥammad Ḥasan (*Tawḥīd*). Tawḥīd-i *ʿibādat—yiktāparastī*. 3rd edn. n.p., publisher not indicated, 1327 [/1948–9].

Surūsh, ʿAbdulkarīm (1990/1). *Qabḍ va-basṭ-i tiʾūrīk-i sharīʿat: Naẓarīye-yi takāmul-i maʿrifat-i dīnī*. Tehran: Ṣirāṭ, 1369 [1990–1].

(Surūsh, ʿAbd al-Karīm) Soroush, Abdul-Karim (1998). 'The Evolution and Devolution of Religious Knowledge'. In C. Kurzman, *Liberal Islam: A Sourcebook*. New York: Oxford University Press, 244–51.

Surūsh, ʿAbd al-Karīm (1999a). *Basṭ-i tajrube-yi nabawī*. 1st edn. Tehran: Ṣirāṭ, 1378 [1999–2000]; 2nd edn. same year (used here).

Surūsh, ʿAbd al-Karīm (1999b). *Sirāṭhā-yi mustaqīm*. Tehran: Ṣirāṭ, 1378 [1999–2000].

(Surūsh, ʿAbd al-Karīm) Soroush, Abdulkarim (2009). *The Expansion of Prophetic Experience [=Basṭ-i tajrube-yi nabawī]*. Trans. N. Mobasser, ed. and introd. F. Jahanbakhsh. Leiden: Brill.

Takim, A. (2007). *Koranexegese im 20. Jahrhundert: Islamische Tradition und neue Ansätze in Süleyman Ateş's 'Zeitgenössischem Korankommentar'*. Istanbul: Yeni Ufuklar.

Taymas, Abdullah Battal (1958). *Kazanlı Türk meşhurlarından, vol. ii: Musa Carullah Bigi*. Istanbul: Sıralar Matbaası.

Topaloğlu, B. (1993). *Kelâm İlmi: Giriş*. Istanbul: Damla Yayınevi.

Topaloğlu, B. (2004). *Kelâm Araştırmaları Üzerine Düşünceler*. Istanbul.

Troll, C. W. (1976). 'Sayyid Ahmad Khan (1817–1898) et le renouveau de la théologie musulmane (ʿilm al-kalām) au 19ème siècle'. *IBLA (Revue de l'Institut des Belles Lettres Arabes*, Tunis) 138: 205–41.

Troll, C. W. (1977/1978a). 'Sir Sayyid Ahmad Khān, 1817–1898, and his Theological Critics: The Accusations of ʿAlī Bakhsh Khān and Sir Sayyid's Rejoinder'. *Islamic Culture* 51: 262–72 and 52: 1–18.

Troll, C. W. (1978b). *Sayyid Ahmad Khan: A Reinterpretation of Muslim Theology*. New Delhi: Vikas Publishing House.

Troll, C. W. (1982a). 'Reason and Revelation in the Theology of Mawlana Shibli Nu'mani (1857–1914)'. *Islam and the Modern Age* (New Delhi) 13: 19–32.

Troll, C. W. (1982b). 'The Fundamental Nature of Prophethood and Miracle: A Chapter from Shibli Nu'mani's al-Kalām, Introduced, Translated and Annotated'. In C. W. Troll (ed.), *Islam in India: Studies and Commentaries*. Vol. i. New Delhi: Vikas.

Troll, C. W. (1983). 'The Salvation of Non-Muslims: Views of Some Eminent Muslim Religious Thinkers'. *Islam and the Modern Age* (New Delhi) 14: 104–14.

Ülken, Hilmi Ziya (1966). *Türkiyede Çağdaş Düşünce Tarihi*. 2 vols. Konya: Selçuk Yayınları.

Vahdat, F. (2000). 'Post-revolutionary Discourses of Mohammad Mojtahed Shabestari and Mohsen Kadivar: Reconciling the Terms of Mediated Subjectivity'. *Critique: Journal for Critical Middle Eastern Studies*, Part I: 'Mojtahed Shabestari' 16: 31–54, Part II: 'Mohsen Kadivar' 17: 135–57 [part I republished in nearly identical form as 'Post-revolutionary Islamic modernity in Iran: the intersubjective hermeneutics of Mohamad Mojtahed Shabestari'. In S. Taji-Farouki (ed.), *Modern Muslim Intellectuals and the Qurʾān*. Oxford: Oxford University Press, 2007, 193–224].

Wadud, A. (1999). *Qur'an and Woman: Rereading the Sacred Text from a Woman's Perspective*. 2nd edn. New York: Oxford University Press.

Wadud, A. (2006). *Inside the Gender Jihad: Women's Reform in Islam*. Oxford and New York: Oneworld.

Wajdī, Muḥammad Farīd (*ʿAṣr*). *al-Islām fī ʿaṣr al-ʿilm*. 2 parts, 1st edn. Cairo: Maṭbaʿat al-taraqqī and Maṭbaʿat al-shaʿb, 1320/1902–3 and 1322/1904–5; reprint Beirut: Dār al-kitāb al-ʿarabī, 2 vols. in one volume, 3rd edn., n.d. (used here).
Weismann, I. (2001a). 'Between Ṣūfī Reformism and Modernist Rationalism: A Reappraisal of the Origins of the Salafiyya from the Damascene Angle'. *Welt des Islams* ns 41: 206–37.
Weismann, I. (2001b). *Taste of Modernity: Sufism, Salafiyya, and Arabism in Late Ottoman Damascus*. Leiden: Brill.
Wielandt, R. (2002). 'Exegesis of the Qurʾan: Early Modern and Contemporary'. In J. D. McAuliffe et al. (eds.), *Encyclopaedia of the Qurʾan*. Vol. ii. Leiden: Brill, 124–42.
Yar, Erkan (1998). 'Abdullatif Harputi ve Yeni Kelam İlmi'. *Fırat Üniversitesi İlahiyat Fakültesi Dergisi* 3: 241–62.
Zarcone, T. (1996). 'Philosophie et théologie chez les djadids: la question du raisonnement indépendant (Iǧtihād)'. *Cahiers du monde russe* 37: 1–2, 53–63 (= S. Dudoignon and F. Georgeon (eds.), *Le Réformisme musulman en Asie centrale: Du 'Premier renouveau' à la soviétisation*).
Ziadat, A. A. (1986). *Western Science in the Arab World: The Impact of Darwinism, 1860–1930*. Basingstoke: Macmillan.

CHAPTER 41

STRIVING FOR A NEW EXEGESIS OF THE QUR᾿ĀN

JOHANNA PINK

A survey of new hermeneutical approaches to the Qur᾿ān is only conceivable as a qualitative endeavour. Neither is Qur᾿ānic exegesis in the modern period characterized, in its entirety, by the quest for a novel understanding of the Qur᾿ān, nor is this quest strictly confined to the period starting from the mid-nineteenth century. It is difficult, or even impossible, to draw clear demarcation lines between traditional and modern approaches, for several reasons.

For one thing, the 'traditional' genre of the Qur᾿ānic commentary (*tafsīr)* has been supplemented by novel exegetical formats in the past century or more, but is still of great relevance. *Tafsīr* has been aptly described as a genealogical tradition (Saleh 2004: 14), where much of an exegete's work consists of providing a survey and—sometimes—assessment of previous interpretations. This tradition continues until this day, but the pool of interpretations that is available to a contemporary exegete includes modernist besides pre-modern ones; and that is true even for entirely conservative commentaries on the Qur᾿ān (Pink 2011: 289–90). Thus, deciding whether a work of Qur᾿ānic exegesis is relevant for an evaluation of modern approaches to the Qur᾿ān, in a qualitative sense, is not an easy task.

Relying on genre boundaries is not helpful in identifying such approaches either. While Qur᾿ānic commentaries do play an important role, most ground-breaking hermeneutical theories have been put forward outside the narrow confines of this genre, and the genre itself has undergone some development including, for instance, thematic commentaries or works that discuss the *sūra*s in the order of their revelation. In addition, much of the ubiquitous literature on Islam and modernity, women and Islam, the *sharīʿa* in modern times, and so forth is based on modernist Qur᾿ān hermeneutics and should therefore not be entirely disregarded.

Finally, allocating the quest for a new exegesis of the Qur᾿ān to a specific period of time poses some problems. In most studies on Qur᾿ānic exegesis, this quest is considered to be a phenomenon that started in the late nineteenth century. This assessment is based on the assumption that reformist readings of the Qur'ān originated in reaction to the challenge of Western ideas and Western political and cultural hegemony. The reform movements that existed in different regions of the Islamic world in the eighteenth and early nineteenth centuries, although the subject of a broad debate in Islamic studies during the past decades, have hardly been taken into account with respect to the exegesis of the Qur'ān and, if so, have usually been dismissed as traditional and conservative.

While these movements were local in nature and differed with respect to their aims and ideas, they were united in their critique of the state of Islamic scholarship, and law in particular; they generally advocated a rejection of the schools of law (*madhāhib*) and of much of the Islamic intellectual heritage and a return to 'true religion', based on the Qur'ān and the Sunna, to the exclusion of later 'innovations' (*bidaʿ*). These notions are obviously of great relevance to the interpretation of the Qur'ān, all the more so as Muslims to this day continue to adhere to them. However, the late nineteenth-century reformers who appropriated these ideas did so with their own agenda in mind, which differed vastly from that of the earlier reformers (Dallal 2010).

In order to escape the conundrum of trying to determine the beginnings of reform, renewal, or modernization, it might thus be useful, with respect to eighteenth- and nineteenth-century reformist Qur'ānic exegesis, to distinguish between two broad trends that might have overlapped at times, both of which have certainly contributed to later reform efforts: a revivalist trend that emerged from indigenous developments, characterized by the quest for a return to the religious sources and to liberate them from the authority of later scholars, and a modernist trend that emerged in response to Western influence and tried to read the religious sources in a way that was compatible with the new paradigms that now seemed to govern the world.

I Islamic Revivalism as a Root of Reform

Islamic revivalist movements or thinkers emerged at different times in various parts of the Islamic world between the beginning of the eighteenth and the early nineteenth centuries. While they were part of very specific regional settings and traditions, the ideas they propagated displayed some remarkable common features, which is also true for their Qur'ān hermeneutics. At the core of these hermeneutics is the reliance on the obvious meaning (*ẓāhir al-maʿnā*) of the Qur'ān and the prophetic Sunna to the exclusion of the authority of earlier scholars. Although there were precursors for this kind of exegetical thinking in the pre-modern period, this had been little more than a radical trend at the margins of the *tafsīr* tradition until the eighteenth century (Saleh 2010). Works like Ibn Taymiyya's *Muqaddima fī Uṣūl al-Tafsīr*, Ibn Kathīr's *Tafsīr al-Qur'ān al-ʿaẓīm*, and al-Suyūṭī's *ḥadīth*-based Qur'ān commentary *al-Durr al-Manthūr* received increased attention by eighteenth- and nineteenth-century revivalists. Al-Suyūṭī's work was probably the most influential among these three at the time. The revival of Ibn Taymiyya and his disciples was mainly the work of Muḥammad b. ʿAbd al-Wahhāb (1703–92), which was arguably the latter's main, and most lasting, contribution to exegetical thought; in contrast to other revivalist scholars, he did not produce works that specifically dealt with the exegesis of the Qurʾān if one does not count his treatise on the virtues (*faḍāʾil*) of the Qurʾān.

The most important works in the field of Qurʾānic exegesis from this revivalist period were those by Shāh Walī Allāh al-Dihlawī (1703–62) and Muḥammad al-Shawkānī (1760–1835).

Shāh Walī Allāh, the famous Indian scholar, lived in a time in which the Moghul sultanate was under attack from many competing factions, among them Hindu rulers. These concerned him far more than the British activity on the Subcontinent, in spite of later attempts to portray him as a protagonist of anti-Imperialism (Jalbani 1967; cf. Baljon 1977) or the first Indian scholar to tentatively 'incorporate newly imported Western ideas' (Baljon 1961: 3). Rather, he expressed the need for a restatement of the Islamic religious sciences (*iqāmat ʿulūm al-dīn*) through the harmonization of differences between schools of thought.

Like many other reformers, he emphasized the need for independent reasoning (*ijithād*), if performed by qualified scholars, a category in which he included himself; but he was less radical in his attitude towards the *madhāhib* than other reformers (Hermansen 1996: xxxi–xxxiii). He also maintained his involvement with Sufism, which is apparent in his interpretation of the Qurʾān. Thus, the tradition of scholarship that he was raised in formed an important part of his work, even where he endeavoured to break with it; the same can probably be said of all reformers of this age.

Shāh Walī Allāh laid down his concepts of Qurʾānic exegesis in the Persian work *al-Fawz al-kabīr fī uṣūl al-tafsīr*, the fifth, last, and most important chapter of which he translated into Arabic under the independent title *Fatḥ al-khabīr bi-mā lā budda min ḥifẓiḥī fī ʿilm al-tafsīr*; furthermore, he produced an annotated translation of the Qurʾān into Persian under the title *Fatḥ al-Raḥmān bi-tarjamat al-Qurʾān* that is still in great demand.

He placed great emphasis on understanding the Qurʾān, first and foremost, through the Qurʾān itself, by taking into account the inner-Qurʾānic context of a verse as well as related passages of text. Thus, he heavily downplayed the importance of having studied the works of prior exegetes; in fact, Shāh Walī Allāh maintained that students of the Qurʾān, after having acquired sufficient knowledge of Arabic, should directly work with the text itself instead of reading commentaries on it. The Qurʾān, he argued, is perfectly understandable to any serious student with knowledge of Arabic, just like it was understandable to its first recipients; to the learned scholar, even those parts that are usually considered unclear (*mutashābih*), like the opening letters of the *sūras*, are comprehensible. The Qurʾān should not be understood as a scripture that was meant for its first recipients; rather, it should be read in accordance with the requirements of each age. Therefore, Shāh Walī Allāh considered *asbāb al-nuzūl* material as well as earlier interpretations, including those of the Prophet's companions, to be of relatively little relevance.

Likewise, fields of scholarship other than Qurʾānic exegesis should not interfere with the interpretation of the Qurʾān; this includes Arabic grammar, which needs to be mastered only to the level that the first listeners of the Qurʾān had reached, but not as an independent scholarly discipline. The only other discipline that has to be taken into account is *ḥadīth*. In seeking an explanation for Qurʾānic verses, Shāh Walī Allāh argued, one should not follow a particular school, be it of exegesis, grammar, or theology, but prefer the interpretation that is closest to the literal meaning (*ẓāhir al-maʿnā*) of the Qurʾān and the Sunna and that best fits the inner-Qurʾānic context.

Concerning this inner-Qurʾānic context, Shāh Walī Allāh divided the Qurʾānic content into five subject areas which the Qurʾān does not separate from each other, but between which it frequently changes, in a system that fulfils educational and literary, rather than academic, purposes. As such, the structure of the Qurʾān is perfectly meaningful and should not be neglected in exegesis. These ideas have been taken up by later proponents of *naẓm al-Qurʾān* as well as the literary exegesis of the Qurʾān.

Shāh Walī Allāh's concern with the integrity and perfection of the Qurʾānic text has a certain apologetic angle. Among other things, this is reflected in his scepticism towards the doctrine of abrogation (*naskh*). Based on al-Suyūṭī's method, but employing it much more radically, he tried to eliminate as many instances of abrogation as possible by harmonizing apparent differences between legal verses instead. Thus, he reduced the number of—according to him—real abrogations to five, as compared to al-Suyūṭī's nineteen (Baljon 1977; Jalbani 1967: 5–28).

The extensive Qurʾānic commentary *Fatḥ al-qadīr* (completed in 1814) of Muḥammad al-Shawkānī shows some remarkable similarities to the ideas Shāh Walī Allāh expounded several decades earlier with respect to its hermeneutics, although it is unlikely that there has been any direct influence.

Like Walī Allāh, al-Shawkānī considered the literal meaning of the Qurʾān, combined with the Sunna, to be the only authoritative sources of exegesis, although he deemed the level of linguistic expertise necessary for properly analysing the Qurʾānic text to be rather higher than his Indian predecessor had done. His interpretations display a firm belief in the perfection of the text. In order to resolve exegetical controversies, he favoured inclusive interpretations that combined several possible meanings. Furthermore, he saw no place for the import of controversies from other fields like theology, philosophy, or law into the exegesis of the Qurʾān unless mandated by the text of the Scripture itself. While *ḥadīth* was an important source of exegesis to him, he treated the occasions of revelation as rather irrelevant and often doubtful in their authenticity. The same is true for the exegetical accounts about the prophet's companions, which, he argued, are often conflicting and thus constitute no conclusive evidence (Pink 2014).

Of course, there are numerous differences between Walī Allāh's and al-Shawkānī's approaches. Al-Shawkānī's claim to *ijtihād* was much more radical than Walī Allāh's, and he entirely rejected the *madhāhib*. He did not share Walī Allāh's positive attitude towards Sufism, and his tolerance for polyvalent interpretations was rather higher than Walī Allāh's. Al-Shawkānī was convinced that the reduction of ambiguity towards a monovalent interpretation, unless mandated by the clear wording of the Qurʾān or the Sunna, would amount to arbitrariness, and that the Qurʾān is in some instances even so unclear (*mutashābih*) as to be uninterpretable.

Despite these differences, the approaches of Shāh Walī Allāh and al-Shawkānī towards the Qurʾān both exemplify tendencies that were, in their times, novel in many ways and are highly relevant for Muslim exegetical activity to this day. First and foremost among them is the attempt to re-establish the authority of God over the authority of men; this attempt was carried out through hermeneutics that rely primarily on the Qurʾān and the Sunna and are highly sceptical towards other sources of knowledge. Both men shared an understanding of scholarship that is considerably narrower than was customary in former times. It is limited to the interpretation of the religious sources and closely related fields of knowledge. Both scholars were highly concerned with the integrity and perfection of the Qurʾānic text, a trend that is exacerbated in modern apologetic discourses on *iʿjāz al-Qurʾān* and in the widespread rejection of abrogation (Brown 1998). Finally, their critical attitude towards the occasions of revelation, even those that are generally agreed upon, is well worth noting, for it shows serious concern with transferring the criteria of *ḥadīth* criticism to Qurʾānic exegesis and with placing the text in the centre of exegesis, while marginalizing *asbāb al-nuzūl* traditions that are often conflicting, the authenticity of which is unclear, and which do not always contribute to a better understanding of the text. Al-Shawkānī's work even reveals a slight tendency towards historical contextualization; he rejected certain occasions of revelation for being incompatible with the context of the verse they supposedly referred to, an argument that later reformist exegetes often built upon (Pink 2014).

The revivalist trend of the eighteenth and early nineteenth centuries foreshadowed and laid the hermeneutical groundwork for later reformist exegetical endeavours. The influence of early revivalists extended far beyond the regions of their origin. One work that provides ample evidence of this fact is the Indian Ṣiddīq Ḥasan Khān's (1832–90) Qurʾān commentary *Fatḥ al-bayān fī maqāṣid al-Qurʾān*. It borrows extensively from al-Shawkānī's *tafsīr* and, being written in Arabic, was widely circulated in the Arab and Ottoman world. The Syrian exegete Jamāl al-Dīn al-Qāsimī (1866–1914), in turn, frequently quotes *Fatḥ al-bayān*, thus drawing on al-Shawkānī without being aware of this. Al-Qāsimī's *Maḥāsin al-taʾwīl* is used as a reference by exegetes to this day. Al-Shawkānī was considered an authority by reformers like Muḥammad ʿAbduh and Rashīd Riḍā (Dallal 2000), just as Shāh Walī Allāh influenced generations of Muslim reformers within and beyond the Indian Subcontinent.

While the later reception of their hermeneutics makes the early revivalist exegetes extremely relevant for the understanding of modern *tafsīr*, their concerns were very different from those of later reformers, and often misconstrued by them (Dallal 2000, 2010). In *tafsīr* works like al-Shawkānī's and Walī Allāh's, neither a modernizing agenda nor an attempt to counter the threat of Western superiority is detectable, and the social changes that were brought about by the emergence of secular education and mass media were not yet in effect in their times.

II Early Modern Exegesis of the Qur'ān

The last decades of the nineteenth century mark a rupture in the intellectual history of the Islamic world; like all areas of religious thought, the Qur'ānic sciences were strongly affected. Although scholars continued to write commentaries on the Qur'ān that were traditional in style and mostly also in content, a modernist trend emerged in this period that constituted a radical departure from the tradition of Qur'ānic exegesis on several levels, including style, format, content, and target audience. This early modern period was characterized by attempts to make Islam compatible with Western science and Western values. Besides, many intellectuals hoped that religious reform would enable the Islamic world to overcome its perceived backwardness and to shake off Western imperialism. Perhaps equally importantly, this period, which lasted roughly until the 1950s with regional divergences, witnessed the emergence of an educated elite that did not consist of religious scholars and was nonetheless active in the interpretation of religious sources.

The first important proponent of early modern Qur'ānic exegesis was Sir Sayyid Aḥmad Khān (1817–98) from India, among whose writings were a seven-volume commentary on the Qur'ān (*Tafsīr al-Qur'ān*, published 1880–1904) and a small tract on Qur'ān hermeneutics (*Taḥrīr fī usūl al-tafsīr*, 1892). He was influenced by a Sufi upbringing and by the teachings of Shāh Walī Allāh al-Dihlawī. A distinctly novel and remarkable trait in his treatment of the Qur'ān, however, is the way in which he tries to prove its conformity with Western science. Since Sayyid Aḥmad Khān strongly believed that only the acquisition of modern sciences could cure the Muslim world of its backwardness, he made it his mission to counter the popular belief that there was an inherent contradiction between these sciences and the religion of Islam. According to him, the main pillar of this religion was the Qur'ān, as historical criticism had shown the bulk of transmitted *ḥadīth*s to be unreliable.

Thus, he argued that the conformity between the Copernican worldview and the cosmological statements in the Qur'ān can be established if one bears in mind the following principles of exegesis. The interpretations of earlier exegetes, who were either not concerned with natural sciences at all or based their views on Greek natural philosophy, are not authoritative. The Qur'ān has to be understood as uneducated seventh-century Arabs would have understood it and, thus, its cosmological statements are not to be interpreted in a technical scientific sense. Figurative meanings are part of the Qur'ān; just as words in any human language are inadequate to express God's essence, the same may be the case with cosmological truths. In general, Sayyid Aḥmad Khān stressed the need to return to the idiom and world of imagination of the Arabs at the time of the prophet. Thus, when the Qurʾān describes heaven as a roof that can split open, this is not meant to describe an astronomical fact, but simply conforms to the ancient Arabs' perception of the world. As they used metaphors in their speech, it is natural that the Qurʾān, although being perfect and inimitable, resorts to the same structures. In this context, Sayyid Aḥmad Khān pointed to the need to distinguish between the aim of a Qurʾānic statement and the speech used to express this aim. A reference to a natural phenomenon that occurs in an eschatological context might speak about nature, but intend to convey a message about Judgement Day, instead of establishing scientific facts.

Sayyid Aḥmad Khān took care to distinguish his conception of metaphorical exegesis from arbitrary *taʾwīl*. It is not arbitrary, he argued, because it is based on God's power and wisdom and the logic inherent in his creation. If the literal meaning of a Qurʾānic statement contradicts rational observations and scientific facts, then it cannot apply, for this would mean that God made statements that belie the laws of his own creation. Truth cannot contradict truth; the truth of what is accessible to reason and the truth of scripture have to be compatible with each other. As religion has been revealed to man, it cannot be beyond the grasp of man's intellect, even if it may take centuries to discover certain truths (Troll 1978: 144–70).

One point of criticism that has been raised about Sayyid Aḥmad Khān's exegetical approach is the lack of precision in the terms 'reason' and 'nature' (Troll 1978: 174–6). This is most probably due to the apologetic agenda that underlay his exegetical activities. Much of his rejection of miracles and 'superstitions' constituted a direct response to Orientalist critics, and much of his desire to prove the compatibility of the Qurʾān with reason and science, both of which were in his times considered positive forces intimately connected with Western modernity and indispensable for progress, had its origin in Orientalist portrayals of Islam as backward and irrational.

While Sayyid Aḥmad Khān was extremely influential on the Indian Subcontinent, the exegetical endeavour carried out by Muḥammad Rashīd Riḍā (1865–1935), based on lectures by Muḥammad ʿAbduh (1849–1905) and generally known as *Tafsīr al-Manār* (originally *Tafsīr al-Qurʾān al-ḥakīm*), was arguably the most widely circulated early modern exegetical work in the Islamic world. Its influence was not limited to the Arab world, but extended to Central Asia, Indonesia, and even China (Dudoignon et al. 2006: ch. 1–7) and is still very noticeable in contemporary *tafsīr* production (Pink 2011: 289f.).

The respective input of ʿAbduh and Riḍā is clearly discernible in this work. The bulk of *Tafsīr al-Manār* was actually written by Riḍā, who was more conservative in some ways, much less vague, and more prone to using the Qurʾān in order to convey a specific socio-political agenda (Jomier 1954). Like earlier revivalists, ʿAbduh and Riḍā were in favour of following the 'literal meaning' of the Qurʾān and of refraining from speculative interpretations of ambiguous verses. Following ideas that had been put forward by Ibn Taymiyya, but not received much attention before ʿAbduh's times, they rejected most of the narrative traditions based on biblical or other Judaeo-Christian sources, labelling them *isrāʾīliyyāt* (Tottoli 1999). They, too, thought that the Qurʾān had to be understood in accordance with the way the prophet's contemporaries must have understood it. ʿAbduh, in particular, was convinced that there is no contradiction between the contents of revelation and the results of human reasoning, including the discourse of modern science.

Science, however, was much less central to ʿAbduh and Riḍā than it was to Sayyid Aḥmad Khān, although they shared the desire to enable Muslims to participate in the blessings of Western-style progress. For ʿAbduh and Riḍā, the unity of the *umma* was a much more important concern, as expressed in the principle of *tawḥīd*; and this they hoped to achieve through the abolition of *madhāhib* and other dividing factors and through the emulation of the model of an idealized community of early Muslim believers (*salaf*). Education was the way to enable Muslims to follow this model; lack of education was considered one of the chief reasons for backwardness, poverty, and moral decay. The goal of Muslim unity is also expressed in the strong interest that Riḍā, especially, showed in the situation of Muslims across the Islamic world and the transregional exchange with other scholars, which is often embedded in the topical excurses that are liberally scattered throughout *Tafsīr al-Manār*.

These excurses exemplify a significant change in form and style, not only in content, as compared to earlier exegetical works; and indeed the novelty of *Tafsīr al-Manār* is not limited to its topical agenda. The mass medial form in which it was originally published, as part of the journal *al-Manār*, lies at the root of its narrative style, the lengthy excurses, exhortations, and attempts to provide the readers with guidance. Rashīd Riḍā had not been educated as a traditional Islamic scholar, and it shows in his unconventional approach to *tafsīr*, in the selective use of pre-modern sources, and the incorporation of Western writings from various disciplines. Many of his exegetical glosses explicitly refer to contemporary events, reflecting his desire to make the Qurʾān relevant for the concrete concerns of the *umma* of his day.

Another important feature of *Tafsīr al-Manār* that proved to be of lasting relevance for modern exegetical theory was the attempt to open each *sūra* with an introduction that treats it as a unity and as a coherent text with an inner logic, rather than an assemblage of verses revealed on different occasions (Mir 1993; Yasushi 2006: 19f.).

More conservative forms of revivalism continued to flourish besides the modernist projects outlined so far; for instance, al-Qāsimī's above-mentioned extensive Qurʾān commentary *Maḥāsin al-taʾwīl* is influenced by scripturalist ideas and places great emphasis on *ḥadīth*. Its form is more traditional than that of *Tafsīr al-Manār*, although it does occasionally address present-day issues. More frequent, however, are legal discussions with a strong inclination towards Ḥanbalism. The methodology of this commentary owes much to Ibn Taymiyya and Ibn Kathīr, which is evident from its focus on *ḥadīth*, the rejection of *isrāʾīliyyāt*, and a polemical attitude against the so-called *ahl al-raʾy*, i.e. supposedly arbitrary rationalists. While Muḥammad ʿAbduh and several Indian modernists are cited, the preoccupation with the West is not as noticeable in this work as in others of the same period, which is probably due to the fact that the commentary was completed while Damascus was still under Ottoman rule. Still, like other modernists al-Qāsimī considers the return to the two fundamental sources of Islam, the Qurʾān and *ḥadīth*, the main tool to reinstate the Muslim *umma* to its former strength.

The wide range of sources used by al-Qāsimī exemplifies the translocal nature of discourses that emerged at this time.

Besides endeavours to interpret the Qur᾽ān in its entirety from a reformist perspective, the early modern period brought forth numerous efforts with a topical focus that deal with issues such as the relationship between Islam and science or gender relations and base their views on a modernist exegetical approach. For example, the Egyptian jurist Qāsim Amīn (1863–1908), who was a disciple of Muḥammad ʿAbduh and published his book *The Liberation of Women* (*Taḥrīr al-mar᾽a*) in 1899, explicitly based many of his arguments on the Qur᾽ān. Like most modernists of his times, he was concerned with the advancement of his nation, which, he thought, could only be reached if Egyptian women—and his focus, here, was really on aristocratic women—received an education and became part of social life by ceasing to wear the veil. Realizing that many Egyptians considered the inferior status of women to be religiously determined, he used Qur᾽ānic exegesis in order to counter this view. The revelation of God, he held, had been sent in order to elevate women's status, not to oppress them. Far from being illicit innovations (*bidaʿ*) inspired by a desire to emulate the West, his propositions, he claimed, were intended to restore the status of women in Islam to what the Qur᾽ān had originally meant it to be, purified from the erroneous customs that were the result of a history of despotism. This can be translated into an attempt to separate the Qur᾽ānic message from later interpretations that were shaped by social circumstances and customs, but came to be considered as sacred and inviolable to the same degree as the scripture itself. Another modernist feature of Amīn's approach is his use of Qur᾽ānic exegesis for the purpose of social welfare. The Qur᾽ān, he argued, is not solely devoted to transcendental issues, but is to a large part concerned with worldly actions; thus, there is no justification for depriving half of mankind of being an active part of society. To substantiate this argument, Qāsim Amīn specifically pointed to the Qur᾽ānic obligation of giving alms and acting charitably, which Egyptian women, he argues, are not given the chance to do because of their exclusion from society, although this could be extremely beneficial. Qāsim Amīn explicitly embraced modernist exegetical principles that were imported from legal discourse, like *ijtihād, maṣlaḥa, taysīr*, and *maqāṣid al-sharīʿa*, and he frequently referred to reformers like Muḥammad ʿAbduh or Nawāb Ṣiddīq Ḥasan Khān in order to support his arguments. Thus, his book and many others of its kind, while not being explicit and sustained works of exegesis, showed many features of modernist exegetical discourse: a preoccupation with law and social ethics, the employment of principles derived from law that allow for a flexible adaptation of Qur᾽ānic prescriptions to the requirements of the modern age, and the interpretation of the Qur᾽ān in the light of its 'general aims'. This last feature of modernist exegesis, however, exposes its proponents to allegations of arbitrariness, for unless there is a clear hermeneutical procedure to define the general aims of the Qur᾽ān, it can easily be used in order to arrive at preconceived conclusions which are, in Qāsim Amīn's case, clearly based on a Western model of society.

The novel ideas introduced to Qur᾽ānic exegesis in the early modern period would have been inconceivable without the social and economical changes that occurred in this time. The spread of the printing press throughout the Middle East allowed for entirely new forms of translocal discourses and for reaching new audiences beyond the ranks of religious scholars. The emergence of secular education opened avenues for Muslims with a non-religious education to contribute to the field and for scholars to study abroad. These developments brought about far-reaching changes to the genre in style as well as in content.

Although exegetes of this period differ with respect to their hermeneutics and their positions on social and political issues, their works can be generally characterized by a high level of concern with Western-style progress and by an unprecedentedly strong apologetic tendency. Furthermore, they are virtually unanimous in their interest in social advancement, in the sense of providing a broader education to more Muslims, fighting poverty, and enhancing the efficiency of the economy and the state apparatus. It is this last aspect that has been the most influential in the later reception of early modern exegesis and is present even in some of the most conservative recent Qur'an commentaries (Pink 2011: 281, 289f.).

III Modern Varieties of the *Iʿjāz* Doctrine

Among the significant exegetical trends that emerged in the early modern period is the attempt to connect the Qur'ān with modern sciences. This particular branch of exegesis, in spite of having been frowned upon by many professional religious scholars and other Muslim intellectuals, continues to enjoy great popularity to this day, and not only among modernists. The *tafsīr ʿilmī* ('scientific exegesis') goes beyond such attempts to prove the compatibility of the Qur'ān with findings of rational science as Muḥammad ʿAbduh and Sayyid Aḥmad Khān had made. Rather, its aim is to demonstrate that modern scientific findings which could not have possibly been known to the Arabs at the time of the prophet are already contained in the Qur'ān. While there had already been pre-modern exegetes who thought that the Qur'ān contained all sciences and who had consequently tried to identify scientific findings of some kind in the Qur'ānic text, their approach lacked the apologetic quality of the *tafsīr ʿilmī*, which was entirely preoccupied with *Western* science.

Probably the most prominent protagonist in this field was the Egyptian Ṭanṭāwī Jawharī (1862–1940), the author of a rather unusual work entitled *al-Jawāhir fī tafsīr al-Qur'ān al-karīm*. His main aim was a didactic one; he wanted to convince Muslims of the importance of studying sciences in order to achieve progress and political independence. In order to realize this goal, he selected Qur'ānic passages that, in his opinion, referred to specific scientific topics which he then explained at length, complete with tables and pictures.

Usually, however, the *tafsīr ʿilmī* is not so much meant to acquaint the Muslim public with modern sciences, but rather to prove the Qurʾān's miraculous and inimitable nature (*iʿjāz ʿilmī*). As such, many works of this genre are targeted at 'lukewarm' Muslims or unbelievers, especially those who are incapable of reading the Qurʾān in Arabic and of appreciating the inimitability of its style. *Tafsīr ʿilmī* is often pursued by Muslims with a technical or scientific education, but some standard *tafsīr* works written by religious scholars also contain references to *tafsīr ʿilmī* (Wielandt 2002).

An especially vast discourse on scientific miracles in the Qurʾān takes place on the internet, with an ever-growing array of scientific findings allegedly contained in the Qurʾān. These are frequently complemented by other types of Qurʾānic 'miracles'. Among them are predictions of historical events that took place after the time of the prophet or allusions to archaeological discoveries that seventh-century Arabs could not have known about.

Another widespread phenomenon concerns computer-based efforts to identify numerical structure in the Qurʾān that could not have been devised by humans. One of the main protagonists of this trend was the Egyptian-born American Rashād Khalīfa (1935–90) with his book *The Computer Speaks: God's Message to the World* (1981) and other writings in Arabic and English in which he identifies within the Qurʾān numerical structures based on the number nineteen. Again, this is not an entirely new phenomenon, but the apologetic impetus and the vigour and breadth with which this type of exegesis is pursued are unheard of before the twentieth century.

The pre-modern *iʿjāz* doctrine, which mainly presupposed the inimitability of the Qurʾān's language and rhetoric, has not ceased to exist, but has increasingly been marginalized by the types of *iʿjāz* discourse described above. These have the benefit of appealing to the increasing number of literate Muslims who are neither religious scholars nor able to read Arabic.

The *tafsīr ʿilmī* has been vehemently criticized by a number of Muslim authors and exegetes for various reasons. These include proofs of factual errors, like in ʿĀʾisha ʿAbd al-Raḥmān 'Bint al-Shāṭiʾ''s detailed criticism of Rashād Khalīfa's and Muṣṭafā Maḥmūd's numerological arguments (Bint al-Shāṭiʾ 1986: 189–309). From a linguistic point of view, authors like Amīn al-Khūlī have pointed out that the *tafsīr ʿilmī* attributes modern meanings, like 'atom', to the Qurʾānic vocabulary, which is ahistorical and lexicographically unsound. Critics of the *tafsīr ʿilmī* furthermore reject the assumption that the Qurʾan was meant to convey a message that could not be understood by its first audience. Besides, proponents of the *tafsīr ʿilmī* are accused of reading words and phrases out of context; they do not take into account their function in the text, nor do they consider the circumstances they were revealed in. An example would be the reading of eschatological descriptions in the Qurʾān as a statement of astronomical facts. On a theological level, many Muslim authors consider the reliance on 'scientific exegesis' dangerous because it poses the risk that the Qurʾān is 'proven wrong' by scientific findings, or that scientific findings previously identified in the Qurʾān are corrected by later scientists, thus needlessly shedding doubt on the truthfulness and perfection of the Qurʾān. The

Qur'ān, so the critics of the *tafsīr ʿilmī* maintain, is not a book designed to teach science or history, but it is meant to provide religious and moral guidance. It is the veracity of its teachings about God and the soundness of its moral framework that should prove its divine origin, not the alleged miracles, scientific or otherwise, contained in it (Wielandt 2002).

Distinct from these modern varieties of the *iʿjāz* doctrine, but related to them, is the increasing tendency to view the Qur'ān as a coherent text with a perfect structure (*naẓm*), a hypothesis whose first prominent proponent was the Indian scholar Ḥāmid al-Dīn al-Farāḥī (1862–1930), who was heavily influenced by Shāh Walī Allāh's ideas. In his wake, Qur'ān commentaries like Amīn Aḥsan al-Iṣlāḥī's (1904–97) *Tadabbur-i Qur'ān*, Sayyid Quṭb's (1906–66) *Fī Ẓilāl al-Qur'ān*, and Saʿīd Ḥawwā's (1935–89) *al-Asās fī al-Tafsīr* make a great effort to prove that the canonical order of the Qur'ān is not accidental, but conforms to a divine plan that involves highlighting and expounding central topics in an extremely complex manner (Mir 1986). Ḥawwā in particular is adamant in pointing out that this feature of the Qur'ān is part of its *iʿjāz*. It is no coincidence that all the Qur'ān commentators mentioned here can be located in the Islamist spectrum; their desire to provide a holistic, coherent, and perfectionist vision of the Qur'ān conforms with their picture of an idealized Islamic social order.

IV Colonial State, Nation State, Islamic State

From the middle of the twentieth century onwards, Qur'ānic exegesis, like other fields of religious and intellectual activity, was increasingly influenced by structures of modern statehood. Before describing exegetical developments in this time, some of those structural aspects that were of high relevance for intellectual life need to be outlined.

The abolition of the caliphate in 1924 put an abrupt end to the illusion of a united *umma* with a religiously legitimized ruler and left the field to colonial states and emerging nation states. This had a huge impact on the religious field. By and by, religious institutions such as *awqāf* and *madāris* were placed under state control or dissolved. Religious learning was fast replaced with state schools and universities that often offered relatively little religious education, and what religious education they offered was uniform and state controlled, at least in theory. A striking example is Turkey, where traditional institutions of Islamic education were completely dissolved and later replaced by faculties of divinity (*ilahiyat*) that were extremely influential in the formation of reformist exegetical approaches (Körner 2005: 48–64). In Indonesia, the government established Islamic institutes with a modernized curriculum that likewise brought forth a large number of modernist scholars (Pink 2011: 58–60).

Moreover, the availability of secular education resulted in the emergence of a literate class that had little religious training, but took an active part in religious discourses—a phenomenon that became especially relevant for the exegesis of the Qurʾān (Taji-Farouki 2004: 12–16). At the same time, as a result of the secularization of schools and judiciary systems, religious scholars lost most of their previous avenues of income. The nationalization of *awqāf* made them dependent on the state for a livelihood, which greatly affected their standing. Of course, these developments did not occur simultaneously in the various states of the Islamic world, nor did all of them occur in each and any given state; but no country could entirely escape the logic of modern statehood.

The same is true for the Islamic movements that developed partly in response to the colonial state or to governments influenced by colonial powers. While criticizing 'Western' forms of statehood, they were unable to create counter-ideologies that were free from the logic of modern statehood, which is evident in their obsession with the creation of an Islamic state governed by Islamic law. These ideas, although referring to an idealized past, were novel and had little basis in the Islamic intellectual heritage; therefore, their proponents had to derive them directly from the sources of Islam, first and foremost the Qurʾān.

Some individual nation states played a particular role in spreading and subsidizing specific exegetical approaches. This is especially true for Saudi Arabia, which from the 1920s onwards invested in printing activities and contributed massively to the popularization of what the Saudi scholars considered to be legitimate, i.e. *ḥadīth*-based hermeneutics and exegesis, for example Ibn Kathīr's and al-Baghawī's Qurʾān commentaries and Ibn Taymiyya's *al-Muqaddima fī uṣūl al-tafsīr*. The Wahhābī promotion of Ibn Taymiyya's and Ibn Kathīr's works—especially by publishing them in print in the early twentieth century—was instrumental in making these two authors popular in the contemporary period and had a strong impact on modern exegetical activities (Saleh 2010). After 1957, when the first Saudi university was established, scholars and students from all over the Islamic world were engaged in the perpetuation of exegetical discourses in line with Wahhābī thought, which came to be labelled as *salafī*. This resulted in new exegetical works like Abū Bakr al-Jazāʾirī's *Aysar al-tafāsīr* (1987), a Qurʾān commentary that purported to offer a purified, *salafī* version of *Tafsīr al-Jalālayn*.

The traditional counter-model to this was represented by the Egyptian Azhar. This institution was engaged in publishing those Qurʾān commentaries that formed the core of the pre-modern *madrasa* curriculum—al-Rāzī, al-Zamakhsharī, al-Bayḍāwī, and the supercommentaries on those—and in producing *tafsīr* works that continued this scholarly tradition (Saleh 2010). Besides, the Azhar has a great influence on exegetes in those parts of the Islamic world where it is customary for Muslim scholars to study in Egypt, such as Indonesia.

Iran also deserves mention as a country that has produced a number of radical reformist hermeneutical approaches in past decades. These have precursors in the pre-revolutionary period, most notably ʿAlī Sharīʿatī (1933–77), but under the impression of the Islamic Republic the reform discourse has moved from a revolutionary agenda to an emphasis on human rights and individual responsibility, as opposed to the establishment of Islamic legal and political structures (Vahdat 2004).

A further structural aspect that has been of ever-increasing importance in the Muslim exegesis of the Qur᾽ān in recent decades is the growing influence of diasporic Muslims. This category comprises Muslims who migrated from the Islamic world to the West, temporarily or permanently, as well as an increasing number of second- and third-generation Muslims and converts. Without the contributions of scholars like Fazlur Rahman, Abdullah Saeed, or Amina Wadud, any picture of modern Qur᾽ānic exegesis would be incomplete.

Finally, just like the introduction of the printing press a century earlier, the emergence of new media like radio, TV, and the internet brought about significant changes in exegetical discourses. Not only are the audiences of such discourses ever-expanding; more and more lay Muslims are actively taking part in exegetical debates, and many pertinent contributions to the interpretation of the Qur᾽ān have been made by intellectuals with little or no religious education, often even by engineers or scientists. The internet offers unprecedented possibilities to spread new exegetical approaches and to engage in discussions about them (Görke 2010). Forms of oral exegesis, which have always existed but have neither been available beyond the local level nor preserved for later generations in pre-modern times, are now accessible to broad audiences. For instance, the Egyptian Muḥammad al-Shaʿrāwī's (1911–98) exegetical TV shows are available as transcripts, audio files, and printed volumes and thus have retained their popularity even after the preacher's death (Pink 2011: 95–8). Performances like these are characterized by an improvised and associative way of dealing with segments from the Qur᾽ān; through their distribution in print, they have sometimes even gained a certain level of scholarly acceptance.

V Language, History, and Major Themes of the Qur᾽ān: In Search of New Hermeneutics

While early modern Qur᾽ān interpretation offered new perspectives on the Qur᾽ān, it failed to provide an explicit, consistently applied hermeneutical model to achieve its goal of reading the Qur᾽ān in the light of the requirements of the age. Thus, its proponents were easily exposed to charges of arbitrariness, of using the Qur᾽ān in order to prove their preconceived notions, or to appease Western critics.

However, from the 1940s onwards, exegetes and intellectuals made sustained attempts to create a more coherent and refined hermeneutical basis for a modernist exegesis; they sought a hermeneutical model that went beyond the revivalist dogma of going by the literal meaning of the Qur᾽ān and *ḥadīth* alone. Many modernists were not comfortable with relying on *ḥadīth* as a source of exegesis at all, as this easily led to interpretations that presupposed the lifestyle and social conditions of Muḥammad's contemporaries as relevant and indisputable factors for the contemporary application of the Qurʾān. They were equally uncomfortable with apologetic and sometimes far-fetched attempts to prove every single statement in the Qurʾān as 'true' in a literal, material sense. A further underlying motivation for some modernists to propose new hermeneutical models might have been the fact that the dogma of going back to the literal meaning of the Qurʾān and *ḥadīth*, as exemplified in al-Shawkānī's Qurʾān commentary, frequently led to the necessity of accepting a multiplicity of meanings as equally true. This was a standard feature of pre-modern Qurʾānic exegesis, but one that many modern exegetes had difficulties with, for throughout the nineteenth and twentieth centuries the Muslim exegesis of the Qurʾān had increasingly turned its focus towards deriving practical guidance from the text (Pink 2011: 301–6; Körner 2005: 204f.). Guidance is dependent on a clear and unambiguous reading of the text. However, in order to achieve the *right* kind of guidance, one that is deemed to be in line with the spirit of the age, exegetes need a hermeneutical framework that allows them to prioritize certain parts of the text over others. Earlier modernists had often used methods derived from Islamic law to this end in a rather arbitrary fashion. From the middle of the twentieth century onwards, however, proponents of a holistic hermeneutical vision emerged.

Already in 1933, the Egyptian writer Ṭāhā Ḥusayn (1889–1973) proposed that the Qurʾān should be studied as a work of literary art, independent of its divine origin. While he did not expect religious scholars to pick up on this proposal, he thought it legitimate and fruitful for scholars in other disciplines, especially literary studies, to do so. Probably the first, and most famous, person to go along with this proposal was Amīn al-Khūlī (d. 1967), a professor of Arabic language and literature at the Egyptian University (now University of Cairo). He considered the Qurʾān the greatest and most important literary work in Arabic language, a work that can be analysed with the methods of literary studies. This involves taking into account the historical circumstances of its genesis, especially the language, style, and cultural horizon of its first audience. It also requires a thorough study of the chronology of the Qurʾānic revelation. Based on this information, the scholar's task is to identify the meaning of the text as it was understood by its first listeners, for al-Khūlī assumed that God would have phrased his speech so as to enable these first listeners to understand his message. He would also have used stylistic patterns and figures of speech that were familiar to them. Thus, al-Khūlī concludes, the Qurʾān should be studied, unit by unit, as a literary structure that uses certain formal features to bring across a specific meaning. On a methodological level, he deemed it important to take a comprehensive look at all Qurʾānic passages dealing with a specific topic and to study their interrelation. This kind of analysis, he maintained, could be performed regardless of any element of faith. Religious scholars perceived this last claim as a clear provocation.

Another provocative aspect of al-Khūlī's ideas was his assumption that, like any literary text, the Qurʾān was designed to appeal to the listeners' emotions, which was a more effective means of reaching its audience than a mere statement of rationally comprehensible facts would have been. Thus, if the Qurʾān makes reference to the movement of the stars, it does not aim at teaching its listeners about astronomy, but rather appeals to their imagination, creating a psychological effect that fosters a deep understanding of the divine message. For this reason, al-Khūlī was opposed both to the *tafsīr ʿilmī* and to narrow-minded literal readings.

It was this aspect of al-Khūlī's teachings that was transferred into an actual work of exegesis by his student Muḥammad Aḥmad Khalaf Allāh (1916–97), rousing the ire of religious scholars and leading to the rejection of the latter's doctoral thesis and to his suspension from his teaching position. He argued that in order to fulfil their function of impressing the Qurʾān's message on its listeners, the prophetic narratives in the Qurʾān had to be adapted to the listeners' linguistic usage, narrative traditions, and emotions. Thus, God chose narratives that were familiar to the ancient Arabs and that they believed to be true. Whether they were historical or not—and Khalaf Allāh tended to think they were not—is irrelevant; their perfection is derived from the flawless way in which they are adapted to their listeners' mindset. Khalaf Allāh never doubted the divine origin of the Qurʾānic text, but his assertion that the stories in the Qurʾān did not, or not entirely, correspond to historical facts was perceived as an attack on the infallibility of the Qurʾān, and thus of God.

ʿĀʾisha ʿAbd al-Raḥmān 'Bint al-Shāṭiʾ' (*c.*1913–98), a student and later the wife of al-Khūlī, successfully avoided rousing a comparable degree of hostility in her exegetical works that were based on her husband's theories. She achieved this by selecting dogmatically uncontroversial parts of the Qurʾān for her analyses, as opposed to writing a complete commentary on the Qurʾān, and by concentrating on their stylistic features. While she does pay attention to the function that specific topics in the Qurʾān had for the prophet and his community at specific times, she is careful not to overemphasize this to the point where it would cast doubt on the face value of the Qurʾānic statements. As such, her work concentrates on contributing to the study of literary structures in the Qurʾān (Wielandt 2002: 131–4).

The protagonists of the literary study of the Qurʾān provided a key hermeneutical principle that has been of great importance to reformist exegesis in recent decades and applied in various ways for different aims: the historicization of the Qurʾānic text. This principle is based on the assumption that the Qurʾān is not merely a divine, transcendent message that is equally comprehensible and applicable for all humans at all times, but that it can only be understood and properly interpreted against the background of the specific historical circumstances of its first audience. It has arguably been far more influential than the purely literary analyses of the Qurʾān performed by Bint al-Shāṭiʾ and others because it had more to offer to the majority of modernist exegetes who were primarily interested in law and ethics.

Attempts to understand the Qurʾān in its historical context most obviously include such Qurʾan commentaries that interpret the *sūra*s in the order of their revelation, such as the Palestinian nationalist Muḥammad ʿIzza Darwaza's (1888–1984) *al-Tafsīr al-ḥadīth: al-Suwar murattaba ḥasab al-Nuzūl* (1962). Darwaza was convinced that the Qurʾān was crucial to the revitalization of the Arab and Islamic world and that a new approach to Qurʾānic exegesis was necessary to reach the Arab youth who had been alienated by the tradition of *tafsīr*. He believed that the genesis of the Qur'ānic message was closely connected to the Prophet's life and that reading the *sūras* in their chronological order helps understand the evolution of its principles. This approach was new at the time. Thus, not being an *ʿālim* himself, Darwaza thought it prudent to ask religious scholars for *fatwās* that expressed approval of his method (Poonawala 1993). A similar project was undertaken by the Moroccan philosopher Muḥammad ʿĀbid al-Jābiri (1936–2010) in his Qur'ān commentary *Fahm al-Qur'ān al-ḥakīm* (2008–9). Neither of the two authors discussed the difficulty of establishing a convincing inner chronology of the Qur'ān, nor did they take into account the possibility of *sūras* containing sections or verses from different periods of Muḥammad's life. While showing a strong concern with the historicity of the Qur'ān, they did not use their method in order to develop a hermeneutical theory that would expressly allow them to identify content that was relevant for the prophet's lifetime specifically and might not be applicable today.

This, however, was the exact aim of many Muslim hermeneutical theorists from the second half of the twentieth century onwards. From among these, Fazlur Rahman (1919–88) is probably the one who is most influential and widely quoted among contemporary Muslim modernists, especially in Turkey and Indonesia and among diasporic Muslims in the West. Born in Pakistan, Fazlur Rahman completed his university education in Oxford and took up teaching posts in Britain, Canada, and finally, after a period in Pakistan that ended with fierce opposition and death threats against him, in Chicago, where he was to spend the remaining twenty years of his life and academic career. In contrast to many other reformist hermeneutical models, the theories he put forward in his *Islam and Modernity: Transformation of an Intellectual Tradition* (1982) do not focus on the Qur'ān to the exclusion of the prophetic Sunna, but take both sources into account. He was critical of former reformist thinkers for their lack of a coherent hermeneutical outlook and for their ad hoc methods. A coherent view of the Qur'ān's message is only possible, according to him, if the interpretation of the Qur'ān is based on a cohesive concept of Islamic metaphysics. Against the backdrop of this metaphysical worldview, the Qur'ān has to be read as a unity, not in the atomistic way in which it is usually treated.

Fazlur Rahman considered the Qur'ān to be primarily a work of ethics and thus aimed at developing a theory of Qur'ānic ethics. The way in which the early Muslim community applied these ethics, he believed, could be instructive, but not in the sense of providing a model that needs to be imitated until this day; rather, it serves as an example for the way in which the Qur'ānic message can be adapted to the requirements of a specific society. This adaptation of the Qur'ān to specific historical circumstances is an ongoing endeavour with no fixed, immutable solutions. The revelation of the Qur'ānic text itself was deeply embedded in a concrete historical situation and reflected the circumstances and mental condition of Muḥammad and his first audience. Many of the Qur'ān's contents, like the frequent references to war and rules for fighting, were contingent and related to the specific historical situation they originated in, while on a different level the Qur'ān describes an ethical ideal that believers should strive to implement, but that might not be fully achievable at any given historical moment.

Fazlur Rahman thus argued in favour of applying historical-critical methods in order to distinguish the contingent from the ideal in the Qurʾān. An example for this are gender issues like polygamy or divorce, which the Qurʾān disapproves of on an ethical level, but permits under strict conditions out of consideration for the historical needs of the community it was revealed to, according to Rahman. Rather than trying to apply contingent Qurʾānic regulations in modern times, Muslims should focus on identifying the universal moral values contained in the Qurʾān and on developing a comprehensive theory of social ethics. In doing so, the prophetic Sunna should be taken into account. It was organically interwoven with the Qurʾānic message and cannot be separated from it. However, the bulk of the prophetic Sunna consists of examples for the translation of the Qurʾān's moral message into actions fitting a concrete historical context; these are not meant to be replicated in later times. What is required today, according to Rahman, is the extraction of general ethical values from the concrete regulations contained in the Qurʾān and, to a lesser extent, in the Sunna, and in a second step the derivation of concrete rules from these ethical values in accordance with our contemporary situation (Saeed 2004).

Naṣr Ḥāmid Abū Zayd arrived at comparable conclusions, albeit with different theoretical underpinnings that were strongly inspired by concepts from literary studies. Abū Zayd referred mainly to models of communication that describe a text as a message transmitted by a sender to a recipient in a code that is known to the latter. Consequently, the Qurʾān as a text is not comprehensible without knowledge of this code, which does not belong to the transcendent sphere of the divine, but is a human means of communication. The code, which is closely tied to a specific historical community and its language, has to be translated into a code that is comprehensible in our time if the message is to retain its meaning. Any attempt at reading and interpreting the Qurʾān is the result of such a translational, and therefore human, activity; it is not possible to gain direct access to the pure, ahistorical, divine meaning without taking into account human language and history. Abū Zayd suffered severe legal and social repercussions for these theories as they offended religious scholars who felt their claim to a correct interpretation of the Qurʾān threatened (Wielandt 2002: 135–7).

A far less erudite, but very clear-cut approach to the historicity of the Qurʾān was offered by Maḥmūd Muḥammad Ṭāhā (1909–85), a Sudanese reformer with a secular education and a background in Sufism. His book *al-Risāla al-thāniya min al-Islām* aimed at harmonizing the Qurʾān with principles of human rights, gender equality, and democracy by distinguishing between the Meccan and the Medinan message of the Qurʾān. According to Ṭāhā, the Meccan message contains the eternal values of Islam. However, as seventh-century Arab society was not ready to understand and apply those values, God provided the Medinan message, which consists of clear rules that went back behind the Meccan Qurʾān's standards, but were comprehensible for its first recipients and were designed to prepare society for the full acceptance of the Meccan Qurʾān's universal values at a later stage. This stage, Ṭāhā held, has arrived in the twentieth century, so that legal prescriptions and other Qurʾānic statements from the Medinan phase—the 'first message of Islam'—are obsolete and the 'second message' of the Meccan Qurʾān can be implemented.

Ṭāhā was declared an apostate for his views in several *fatwās* by high-ranking scholars and executed for apostasy in 1985 (Oevermann 1993). His ideas are further developed and propagated by his disciple Abdullahi Ahmad an-Naʿim who is based in the US.

A pertinent theoretical problem in Ṭāhā's model is the lack of clear criteria for the distinction between Meccan and Medinan verses in the Qurʾān. In Ṭāhā's book, this distinction is made rather arbitrarily, depending on whether or not a verse contains ideas that have been pre-defined as Meccan or Medinan, which amounts to circular reasoning. Similar issues of circular reasoning are bound to occur in most of those reformist hermeneutical models that differentiate between eternal values and outdated legal prescriptions in the Qurʾān with the main aim of isolating those segments of the text that are deemed to be at odds with contemporary ethical standards.

While the above-mentioned approaches tend to consider the historical-critical reading of the Qurʾān as a way to arrive at an underlying, eternal truth, however minimal its contents might be, Muḥammad Shaḥrūr proposes a radically subjective way of historicizing the Qurʾān's message. In his *al-Kitāb wa-l-Qurʾān: Qirāʾa muʿāṣira* (1990), he argues that any interpretation of the Qurʾān, including the one undertaken by its first audience, is of limited relevance and dependent on the historical circumstances of the interpreter. Thus, it is impossible to uncover what the Qurʾān *really* means; it is only possible to find out what it might mean for the exegete and his time. Human understanding of the divine message is an ever-developing process that can never be finished because human society never reaches a terminal stage from which it cannot further develop. Thus, no interpretation is better or more correct than another one, but there are interpretations that are more suitable for a particular society than others. The referral to earlier exegetical authorities is pointless, as they have nothing to offer to today's society. Even the Prophet Muḥammad, Shaḥrūr held, was nothing more than an exegete providing an interpretation of the Qurʾān appropriate for his own society, and thus not a model to be emulated by later Muslims (Syamsuddin 2009: 55–61). These claims have, of course, been subject to fierce criticism from a wide range of religious scholars and intellectuals.

It is noteworthy that none of the proponents of a historicization of the Qurʾān mentioned here has received a traditional religious education, and some of them did not even have a background in the humanities. Furthermore, none of them produced a Qurʾān commentary or a work of practical exegesis; their focus was entirely on hermeneutics.

While the *historicity* of the Qurʾān is an important issue in modern Muslim exegesis of the Qurʾān, there has been virtually no discussion of the *history* of the text. Issues related to the textual integrity of the Qurʾān, its authenticity, and the process of canonization have not been approached even by the most daring of reformist scholars. As yet, there is no revisionist narrative of the genesis of the Qurʾān in Muslim circles. The Qurʾān in its present textual form, mostly in the form of the Cairene Qurʾān, is accepted as the authentic word of God, and even variant *qirāʾāt* are rarely taken into account.

Moving away from the historicization of both the Qurʾān and its interpretation, a further important approach that had already been proposed by Amīn al-Khūlī and was pursued by many later exegetes was the interpretation of the Qurʾān based on themes, rather than in its canonical or chronological order. If performed carefully, such an analysis allows for a thorough discussion of problems related to central theological or ethical issues, including apparent contradictions in the text; it may, however, also be a way to avoid the discussion of problematic verses, as those can be ignored much more easily in a thematic commentary than in a complete work of *tafsīr*.

Several authors have endeavoured to present a 'thematic commentary' (*tafsīr mawḍūʿī*) on the Qurʾān, although their ideas of what constitutes such a thematic commentary differ. The Egyptian scholars Maḥmūd Shaltūt (1893–1963) and Muḥammad al-Ghazālī (1917–1996), for example, have offered 'thematic commentaries' that deal with the Qurʾān—or at least parts of it—*sūra* by *sūra* and give an overview of the main themes of each *sūra*, but do not depart completely from the canonical structure of the Qurʾān in order to explore selected topics comprehensively. This approach has held a great appeal for many exegetes in modern times. Many recent Qurʾān commentaries, even if conventionally structured, treat *sūra*s like unities, contain introductions to the main themes of each *sūra* and sometimes undertake elaborate discussions of the perfect logic behind the seemingly haphazard make-up of individual *sūra*s (Mir 1993).

A more far-reaching approach is pursued by Fazlur Rahman's *Major Themes of the Qur'an* (1980) that, instead of analysing the Qurʾān segment by segment, tries to present a holistic view of the Qurʾān's position on central, selected issues: God, man as an individual, man in society, nature, prophethood and revelation, eschatology, Satan and evil, and the emergence of the Muslim community. As these themes are discussed in less than 150 pages in total, the book can only provide a rather cursory look at individual verses and does not discuss specific exegetical problems in detail.

A much more extensive attempt at a thematic approach to the Qurʾān with a focus on social and ethical issues has been offered by the Indonesian scholar Muhammad Quraish Shihab (b. 1944) in his *Wawasan al-Qur'an* (1996) which discusses thirty-three themes, including theological topics, practical issues like food, and aspects of religious ritual, on nearly 600 pages. He seems to be unaware of Fazlur Rahman's work, but is strongly inspired by the Egyptian scholar ʿAbd al-Ḥayy al-Farmāwī's (b. 1942) *al-Bidāya fī l-Tafsīr al-mawḍūʿī* (1977), who proposed a model for developing a thematic *tafsīr* in seven steps. However, Shihab is critical of some aspects of al-Farmāwī's theoretical approach. For instance, he suggests that the identification and discussion of relevant themes should be driven and informed by the circumstances and needs of the exegete's society, not only by the text itself. He also considers it important to pay close attention to semantic detail and to the *asbāb al-nuzūl*, despite the focus on a comprehensive thematic approach. In contrast to al-Farāḥī and the latter's disciple al-Iṣlāḥī, Shihab rejects the notion that a thematic *tafsīr* can arrive at the true, unambiguous, and indisputable meaning of a verse. It can provide a coherent vision on the Qurʾānic outlook on a particular topic, but will not offer insight into the analytical intricacies related to the exegesis of individual verses and is thus only one of several productive ways of interpreting the Qurʾān; Quraish Shihab himself has published an extensive *tafsīr musalsal.* A thematic approach, he argues, complements and refines other approaches. It is particularly effective in making the Qurʾān relevant for modern society, as it enables the exegete to derive guidance from the Qurʾānic text instead of dissecting the text in a detached academic manner—an approach that has been labelled 'purposive exegesis' (Amin and Kusmana 2005).

VI Purposive Exegesis

Related to the thematic exegesis of the Qurʾān, and even more clearly purposive than the above-mentioned exegetical endeavours, are those branches of Qurʾānic exegesis that are specifically concerned with one particular issue, the most prominent of which is the status of women. Some of the proponents of revisionist readings of gender roles in the Qurʾān endorse the term 'feminist exegesis' while others consider it problematic for invoking a Western tradition of feminism that, in their opinion, does not represent their own concerns as Muslim women. The issue that these—often female—exegetes struggle with is the patriarchal view of gender roles that is a part of both the legal prescriptions in the Qurʾān and the pre-modern *tafsīr* tradition and is apparent even in many modernist commentaries on the Qurʾān. Many of these have not proceeded beyond the ideas that Qāsim Amīn had promoted at the end of the nineteenth century, meaning that they essentially endorse the ideal of the European bourgeois family. They often support this ideal with pseudo-scientific biologist arguments (Klausing 2014).

Many of the exegetes who, for the sake of brevity, will be called 'feminist' here live in the diaspora; some are converts to Islam. However, related trends are observable in many parts of the Muslim world, both on an academic and a grassroots level, for instance in the form of Islamic women's rights initiatives. These efforts have two features in common: they focus on one issue, the gender issue, and they interpret the Qurʾān with the predetermined goal of reading it as a source of gender equality. Conversely, they argue that the complete exegetical tradition has, often unconsciously, worked the opposite way by reading preconceived patriarchical notions into the Qurʾān. The self-declared goal of these exegetes is to disentangle the Qurʾān from this patriarchical legacy.

Thus, the Pakistani-born American Asma Barlas (b. 1950) in her *'Believing Women' in Islam: Unreading Patriarchical Interpretations of the Qur'an* (2002) asserted that patriarchical meanings have merely been ascribed to the Qurʾān in order to justify existing social structures and that the Qurʾān can be read in such a way as to support the complete equality of the sexes. The African American convert Amina Wadud (b. 1952) in her *Qur'an and Woman: Rereading the Sacred Text from a Woman's Perspective* (1992) argued that sex or gender are not even meaningful categories in the Qur'ān and that the Qur'ān does not entail any concept of gender differentiation. This is especially evidenced in the accounts of creation that make no reference to man's superiority over woman or to the inherent sinfulness of women.

Based on these assumptions, both exegetes moved on to analyse specific Qur'ānic prescriptions on issues like divorce, polygamy, the husband's marital rights, and inheritance. The methods they used for this are eclectic and clearly subordinate to the goal of coming to the conclusion that the verses in question do not grant women a status different from or subordinate to that of men. They include semantic analysis, for instance in order to show that the term *ḍaraba* in Q 4: 34—a verse conventionally read as giving men the permission to use corporal punishment on their wives—means something other than 'to strike' or 'to beat'. In other cases, the grammatical or syntactic structure of verses was reinterpreted. Teleological arguments also play an important role: by providing certain rights to women which they had not possessed in pre-Islamic society, God showed human society the direction into which it was supposed to move—towards the elevation of women's status and, eventually, gender equality.

A certain discontent with these attempts at reinterpreting Qur'ānic prescriptions, which are not always convincing and sometimes seem forced, is apparent in Amina Wadud's *Inside the Gender Jihad: Women's Reform in Islam* (2006), in which she discussed Q 4: 34 and specifically the problem of a man's right to physically punish his wife. Pointing to previous exegetes' efforts to set limits to the severity of a husband's actions or to reinterpret the wording of the verse or its intention, she came to the conclusion that today the time has come to simply reject the notion of any form of physical punishment in an intermarital relationship; 'where how the text says what it says is just plain inadequate or unacceptable, however much interpretation is enacted upon it' (Wadud 2006: 192). In this later work, Wadud was also critical of her own earlier assumption that it was in her power to uncover the true, un-patriarchal meaning of the Qur'ān, as opposed to a subjective reading among others. As yet, her decision to 'say "no"' to parts of the Qur'ān constitutes an extremely radical approach that few Muslim exegetes would dare follow.

A different example of an intellectual who proposed a thematically oriented new way of reading the Qur'ān is the South African Farid Esack (b. 1959) with his book *Qur'an, Liberation and Pluralism: An Islamic Perspective of Interreligious Solidarity against Oppression* that is deeply influenced by the author's experience with fighting apartheid. He aimed at reading the Qur'ān as a text whose primary goal is the liberation of men from oppression, as exemplified in Muḥammad's struggle against Meccan society. It is based on the notions of human dignity, equality, and liberty and thus can be interpreted in such a way as to be the basis for a fight against injustice and oppression, whether the allies in such a fight be Muslim, Christian, or otherwise.

All these readings of the Qur'ān—no matter what method they apply or how erudite they are—have in common that the results of exegesis are preconceived. The same is true for most of those works of modernist exegesis that do not have a narrow thematic focus, even when they are based on elaborate hermeneutical deliberations: the focus is usually on social ethics, and the clear purpose is to read the Qurʾān in such a way that it is congruent with contemporary ideas of human rights and democracy. This is, for example, evident in the brand of exegesis proposed by the so-called 'Ankara school' in Turkey:

> The revisionists' vision is still restricted to one type of question: ethics ... Hermeneutics has then a merely mechanical function: we know what is there in the Koran, ethics; and we know what must come out, modern ethics. The only question left is, how do we get it out? Hermeneutics has become a tin-opener ... the hermeneutical approach is in danger of producing nothing but apologetics. Apologists 'use' their texts. They dare not have their own questions re-shaped. (Körner 2005: 204f.)

A way out of this conundrum has been proposed by the Iranian philosopher ʿAbd al-Karīm Surūsh (Soroush). His argument rests on the assumption that all interpretations of religion are based on presuppositions and on the expectations that people have of a particular religion. If they expect this religion to provide them with a complete social system (the 'maximal expectations' paradigm), then this is what they will seek from religion, possibly finding indications in the religious sources that enable them to do so; however, that does not mean that this necessarily captures the real content or intentions of the religious text. In Soroush's opinion, the main impetus of the Qurʾān is to teach about the existence of God and the hereafter, i.e. a 'minimal expectations' paradigm; its position on worldly issues like social ethics and law is of minor relevance and is changeable and adaptable to modern circumstances. Moreover, Soroush's expectations hypothesis is based on the assumption that religion alone is not sufficient to solve existential problems, as an individual's expectations are shaped by extra-religious circumstances and are decisive in determining whether any given religion is found to be relevant. Thus, human reason and the use of disciplines like philosophy, history, and science are indispensable for arriving at a convincing concept of religious doctrine and scriptural interpretation (cf. Soroush 1998). In his refusal to use the Qurʾān as a source of law and ethics, which he seeks to derive from other sources like universal human rights standards instead, Soroush differs greatly from the bulk of reformist exegetes, doubtless under the impression of his experiences with the Islamic Republic.

VII Going back to the Qurʾan and the Early *umma*

The counter-model to those approaches that aim at reading the Qurʾān in the light of the requirements of modern society is represented by Islamist intellectuals who build upon the reformist traditions of scripturalism and revivalism. They advocate a return to the original sources, the Qur'ān and the Sunna, and want to let them speak directly to today's believers, acknowledging no need for any translational activity. The immediate relevance of the Qur'ān for contemporary Muslims is to be limited neither by previous interpretations nor by attempts to bring the Qur'ān in line with modern ideas; adversely, the goal is to bring contemporary society in line with Qur'ānic ideals.

The most prominent works of this genre, Sayyid Quṭb's *Fī Ẓilāl al-Qur'ān* (1951–65) and Abū al-Aʿlā al-Mawdūdī's (1903–79) *Tafhīm al-Qur'ān* (1942–72), which have inspired many others, are explicitly not labelled as works of *tafsīr*. They are rather meant to be reflections on the Qur'ān's meaning, and as such often pay more attention to the spiritual and emotional aspect of the Qur'ānic message than most pre-modern and modernist exegetes have done. They are also careful to establish the inner-Qur'ānic as well as the historical context of verses instead of interpreting them in the more common disjunct, atomistic manner. Their approach to the Qur'ān is clearly shaped by an ideological perspective that views the Qur'ān as the manifest of an ideal early Islamic community which today's Muslims should strive to emulate. Thus, the Qur'ān's message is construed as coherent, holistic, and concerned with providing a model for an ideal human society that is fully governed by Islam. Contradictions, ambiguities, or the historical evolution of the Qur'ān's position towards social issues have no place in this approach. In its attempt to prove the 'true Islamic society's' superiority above Western models, it is often coloured by apologetic tendencies.

VIII Conflicts and Critique

There has been a large amount of serious, non-polemical critique of almost each and every one of the exegetical approaches presented here, from both Muslim and non-Muslim authors. In addition to this, however, many proponents of new hermeneutical approaches to the Qur'ān, especially in the Arab world and South Asia, have been confronted with considerable hostility, in some cases even prosecution or violence. Their scepticism towards established interpretations of the Qur'ān has been construed as an attack on the sanctity of the scripture itself. Religious scholars have also—and probably rightly so—understood the plea for flexibility and plurality in the interpretation of the Qur'ān as an attack on their monopoly over religious legitimacy, an all the more sensitive issue since religious scholars have lost so much ground in important sectors of society, such as education and jurisdiction, since the nineteenth century. Moreover, many governments are wary of opening the field of Qur'ānic exegesis to a plurality of legitimate perspectives conforming to a multitude of social ideals, as they tend to appeal to Islam as a unifying ideology and have often formed an alliance with the religious establishment for this purpose. Therefore, they are highly interested in upholding the fictitious concept of a unified and indisputable religious truth. Islamists essentially follow the same fictitious concept, albeit with different content, and are thus equally wary of modernist relativist ideas (Wielandt 1996). The fact that many modernist intellectuals heavily rely on notions from Western philosophy, semiotics, or literary studies serves as an additional counter-argument against new hermeneutical theories or simply prevents traditionally educated religious scholars from understanding them, as is perhaps especially evident in academics such as Mohammed Arkoun (1928–2010).

Considering these difficulties, the Kuwait-born scholar Khaled Abou El Fadl (b. 1963), a professor of law at an American university and a reformist intellectual himself, urged Muslim intellectuals to employ great caution when importing Western discourses into the field of Qur'ānic exegesis and implicitly or explicitly dismissing Muslim intellectual traditions, as this considerably decreases their chances of finding acceptance among those to whom revisionist exegetical endeavours are usually addressed, i.e. other Muslims. Rather, they should take the 'Muslim experience' as a starting point for their hermeneutics and proceed from there (Abou El Fadl 2001: 99–100). Indeed, some of the Muslim reformers mentioned in this chapter seem to be in high acclaim within Western academia and in the realm of interfaith dialogue, while their impact in the Islamic world is relatively low. This, however, depends strongly on the region they are active in and the languages in which they publish their works; evidence points to the fact that reformist hermeneutics are far more widely accepted in Turkey and Indonesia, for example, than they are in the Arab world or Pakistan. It might also be asked whether 'the Muslim experience' that Abou El Fadl recommends as a starting point for reformist exegetical endeavours is a meaningful concept, when more and more Muslims are part of Western societies. Moreover, even the experiences of Muslims in Muslim majority countries are immensely diverse and undergoing tremendous changes.

While debates about the boundaries of the legitimate interpretation of the Qur'ān are ongoing, contemporary Qur'ānic exegesis is a highly fragmented field; a further pluralization seems inevitable. During the past 150 years, the Qur'ān has become more and more central to Muslim attempts at the reconstruction of religion, with *ḥadīth* taking a back seat. There is a growing tendency to look at the Qur'ān for ethical, practical, and legal guidance and to read it as a coherent text with a unified vision. However, the ultimate goal of this guidance and the contents of this vision are more contested than ever.

Bibliography

Abou El Fadl, K. (2001). *Speaking in God's Name: Islamic Law, Authority and Women*. Oxford: Oneworld.

Amin, M., and Kusmana (2005). 'Purposive Exegesis: A Study of Quraish Shihab's Thematic Interpretation of the Qur'an'. In A. Saeed (ed.), *Approaches to the Qur'an in Contemporary Indonesia*. Oxford: Oxford University Press, 67–84.

Amīn, Q. (1899). *Taḥrīr al-Mar'a*. Cairo: al-Taraqqī.

Baljon, J. M. S. (1961). *Modern Muslim Koran Interpretation (1880–1960)*. Leiden: Brill.

Baljon, J. M. S. (1977). 'A Comparison between the Qur'ānic Views of 'Ubayd Allāh Sindhī and Shāh Walī Allāh'. *Islamic Studies* 16: 179–88.

Barlas, A. (2002). *'Believing Women' in Islam: Unreading Patriarchical Interpretations of the Qur'ān*. Austin: University of Texas Press.

Bint al-Shāṭi', A. [ʿA.] (1962–9). *Al-Tafsīr al-Bayānī li-l-Qur'ān al-karīm*. Cairo: Dār al-maʿārif.

Bint al-Shāṭi', A. [ʿA.] (1986). *Qirā'a fī Wathā'iq al-Bahā'iyya*. Cairo: Markaz al-Ahrām.

Brown, D. (1998). 'The Triumph of Scripturalism: The Doctrine of naskh and its Modern Critics'. In E. H. Waugh and F. M. Denny (eds.), *The Shaping of an American Islamic Discourse: A Memorial to Fazlur Rahman*. Atlanta: Scholars Press, 49–66.

Campanini, M. (2011). *The Qur'an: Modern Muslim Interpretations*. London: Routledge.

Dallal, A. (2000). 'Appropriating the Past: Twentieth-Century Reconstruction of Pre-Modern Islamic Thought'. *Islamic Law and Society* 7: 325–58.

Dallal, A. (2010). 'The Origins and Early Development of Islamic Reform'. In R. W. Hefner (ed.), *The New Cambridge History of Islam*, vi: *Muslims and Modernity: Culture and Society since 1800*. Cambridge: Cambridge University Press, 107–47.

Darwaza, M. (1962). *Al-Tafsīr al-Ḥadīth. Al-Suwar Murattaba ḥasab al-Nuzūl*. Cairo: Dār Iḥyā' al-kutub al-ʿarabiyya.

Dudoignon, S. A., K. Hisao, and K. Yasushi (eds.) (2006). *Intellectuals in the Modern Islamic World: Transmission, Transformation, Communication*. London: Routledge.

Esack, F. (1977). *Qur'an, Liberation and Pluralism: An Islamic Perspective of Interreligious Solidarity against Oppression*. Oxford: Oneworld.

al-Ghazālī, M. (1992–5). *Naḥwa Tafsīr Mawḍūʿī li-Suwar al-Qur'ān al-Karīm*. Cairo: Dār al-Shurūq.

Görke, A. (2010). 'Die Spaltung des Mondes in der modernen Koranexegese und im Internet'. *Die Welt des Islams* 50: 60–116.

Ḥasan [Khān], Ṣ. (1992). *Fatḥ al-Bayān fī Maqāṣid al-Qur'ān*. Beirut: al-Maktaba al-ʿAṣriyya.

Ḥawwā, S. (1985). *Al-Asās fī al-Tafsīr*. Cairo: Dār al-Salām.

Hermansen, M. (1996). *The Conclusive Argument from God: Shāh Walī Allāh of Delhi's* Ḥujjat Allāh al-bāligha. Leiden: Brill.

al-Jābirī, M. (2006). *Madkhal ilā al-Qur'ān al-karīm*. Beirut: Markaz dirāsāt al-waḥda al-ʿarabiyya.

al-Jābirī, M. (2008–9). *Fahm al-Qur'ān al-ḥakīm: Al-Tafsīr al-wāḍiḥ ḥasab tartīb al-nuzūl*. Beirut: Markaz dirāsāt al-waḥda al-ʿarabiyya.

Jalbani, G. N. (1967). *Teachings of Shāh Walīyullāh of Delhi*. Lahore: Ashraf.

al-Jazā'irī, A. (1994). *Aysar al-Tafāsīr li-Kalām al-ʿAlī al-Kabīr*. Medina: Maktabat al-ʿulūm wa-l-ḥikam.

Jomier, J. (1954). *Le Commentaire coranique du Manar*. Paris: Maisonneuve.

Khalifa, R. (1981). *The Computer Speaks: God's Message to the World*. Tucson, AZ: Renaissance Productions.

Khalīfa, R. (1983). *Muʿjizat al-Qur'ān al-Karīm*. Beirut: Dār al-ʿilm li-l-malāyīn.

Klausing, K. (2014). 'Two Twentieth-Century Exegetes between Traditional Scholarship and Modern Thought: Gender Concepts in the *tafsīr*s of Muḥammad Ḥusayn Ṭabāṭabā'ī and al-Ṭāhir b. ʿĀshūr'. In J. Pink and A. Görke (eds.), *Tafsir and Islamic Intellectual History: Exploring the Boundaries of a Genre*. Oxford: Oxford University Press, 419–40.

Körner, F. (2005). *Revisionist Koran Hermeneutics in Contemporary Turkish University Theology: Rethinking Islam*. Würzburg: Ergon.

al-Mawdūdī, A. (1988–2010). *Towards Understanding the Qur'ān: English Version of Tafhīm al-Qur'ān*. Leicester: Islamic Foundation.

Mir, M. (1986). *Coherence in the Qur'ān: A Study of Iṣlāḥī's Concept of naẓm in Tadabbur-i Qur'ān*. Indianapolis: American Trust.

Mir, M. (1993). 'The Sūra as a Unity: A Twentieth Century Development in Qurʾān Exegesis'. In G. R. Hawting and A. A. Shareef (eds.), *Approaches to the Qurʾān*. London: Routledge, 211–24.
Oevermann, A. (1993). *Die Republikanischen Brüder im Sudan: Eine islamische Reformbewegung im zwanzigsten Jahrhundert*. Frankfurt: Lang.
Ohlander, E. (2009). 'Modern Qur'anic Hermeneutics'. *Religion Compass* 3/4: 620–36.
Pink, J. (2011). *Sunnitischer Tafsīr in der modernen islamischen Welt: Akademische Traditionen, Popularisierung und nationalstaatliche Interessen*. Leiden: Brill.
Pink, J. (2014). 'Where Does Modernity Begin? Muḥammad al-Shawkānī and the Tradition of *tafsīr*'. In J. Pink and A. Görke (eds.), *Tafsir and Islamic Intellectual History: Exploring the Boundaries of a Genre*. Oxford: Oxford University Press, 323–60.
Poonawala, I. K. (1993). 'Muḥammad ʿIzzat Darwaza's Principles of Modern Exegesis: A Contribution toward Quranic Hermeneutics'. In G. R. Hawting and A. A. Shareef (eds.), *Approaches to the Qurʾān*. London: Routledge, 225–46.
al-Qāsimī, J. (1957). *Maḥāsin al-Taʾwīl*. Cairo: Dār Iḥyāʾ al-kutub al-ʿarabiyya.
Quṭb, S. (1982). *Fī Ẓilāl al-Qurʾān*. Cairo: Dār al-Shurūq.
Rahman, F. (1980). *Major Themes of the Qurʾān*. Minneapolis: Bibliotheka Islamica.
Rahman, F. (1982). *Islam and Modernity: Transformation of an Intellectual Tradition*. Chicago: Chicago University Press.
Riḍā, M. R., and M. ʿAbduh (1947). *Tafsīr al-Qurʾān al-Ḥakīm [Tafsīr al-Manār]*. Cairo: Dār al-Manār.
Saeed, A. (2004). 'Fazlur Rahman: A Framework for Interpreting the Ethico-Legal Content of the Qurʾan'. In Taji-Farouki 2004, 37–66.
Saleh, W. (2004). *The Formation of the Classical* Tafsīr *Tradition: The Qurʾān Commentary of al-Thaʿlabī*. Leiden: Brill.
Saleh, W. (2010). 'Preliminary Remarks on the Historiography of *Tafsīr* in Arabic: A History of the Book Approach'. *Journal of Qurʾanic Studies* 12: 6–40.
Shaḥrūr, M. (1992). *Al-Kitāb wa-l-Qurʾān: Qirāʾa muʿāṣira*. Cairo: Sīnā.
Shaltūt, M. ([1960]). *Tafsīr al-Qurʾān al-karīm: Al-Ajzāʾ al-ʿashara al-ūlā*. Cairo: Dār al-qalam, 1379.
al-Shawkānī, M. (1994). *Fatḥ al-qadīr al-jāmiʿ bayn fannay al-riwāya wa-l-dirāya min ʿilm al-tafsīr*. Al-Manṣūra: Dār al-Wafāʾ.
Shihab, M. Q. (1996). *Wawasan al-Qur'an: Tafsir Maudhu'i atas Pelbagai Persoalan Umat*. Bandung: Mizan.
Soroush [Surūsh], A. [ʿA.] (1991). *Qabḍ wa basṭ-i tiʾurīk-i sharīʿat: Naẓariyya-yi takāmul-i maʿrifat-i dīnī*. Tehran: Ṣirāṭ.
Soroush [Surūsh], A. [ʿA.] (1998). 'Text in Context'. In C. Kurzman (ed.), *Liberal Islam: A Sourcebook*. Oxford: Oxford University Press, 244–51.
Syamsuddin, S. (2009). *Die Koranhermeneutik Muḥammad Šaḥrūrs und ihre Beurteilung aus der Sicht muslimischer Autoren: Eine kritische Untersuchung*. Würzburg: Ergon.
Taha, M. M. (1987). *The Second Message of Islam*. Syracuse: Syracuse University Press.
Taji-Farouki, S. (2004). *Modern Muslim Intellectuals and the Qur'an*. Oxford: Oxford University Press.
Tottoli, R. (1999). 'Origin and Use of the Term *Isrāʾīliyyāt* in Muslim Literature'. *Arabica* 46: 193–210.
Troll, C. (1978). *Sayyid Aḥmad Khān: A Reinterpretation of Muslim Theology*. New Delhi: Vikas.

Vahdat, F. (2004). 'Post-revolutionary Islamic Modernity in Iran: The Intersubjective Hermeneutics of Mohamad Mojtahed Shabestari'. In Taji-Farouki 2004, 193–224.

Wadud, Amina (2006). *Inside the Gender Jihad: Women's Reform in Islam*. Oxford: Oneworld.

Wadud-Muhsin, Amina (1992). *Qur'an and Woman: Rereading the Sacred Text from a Woman's Perspective*. Oxford: Oxford University Press.

Wielandt, R. (1996). 'Wurzeln der Schwierigkeit innerislamischen Gesprächs über neue hermeneutische Zugänge zum Korantext'. In S. Wild (ed.), *The Qur'ān as Text*. Leiden: Brill, 257–82.

Wielandt, R. (2002). 'Exegesis of the Qur'ān: Early Modern and Contemporary'. In J. D. McAuliffe (ed.), *Encyclopedia of the Qur'ān*. Leiden: Brill, ii. 124–42.

Yasushi, K. (2006). 'Al-Manār Revisited: The "Lighthouse" of the Islamic Revival'. In Dudoignon et al. 2006, 3–39.

Index